SURVIVING THROUGH THE DAYS

SURVIVING THROUGH THE DAYS

Translations of Native California Stories and Songs

A CALIFORNIA INDIAN READER

EDITED BY

Herbert W. Luthin

University of California Press

BERKELEY / LOS

University of California Press
Berkeley and Los Angeles, California

University of California Press, Ltd.
London, England

Library of Congress Cataloging-in-Publication Data

Surviving through the days : translations of Native California
  stories and songs : a California Indian reader / Herbert W.
  Luthin, editor.
      p.   cm.
    Includes bibliographical references and index.
    ISBN 0-520-22269-5 (alk. paper) —ISBN 0-520-22270-9
  (pbk. : alk. paper)
      1. Indians of North America—California—Folklore.
  2. Indians of North America—California—Music.
  3. Indian mythology—California.
  I. Luthin, Herbert W., 1954–
  E78.C15.S94   2002
  398'.089'97—dc21   00-031630
  MN   CIP

Manufactured in the United States of America
12 11 10 09 08 07 06 05 04 03 02
10 9 8 7 6 5 4 3 2 1

The paper used in this publication meets the minimum
requirements of ANSI / NISO Z39 0.48-1992(R 1997)
(Permanence of Paper).♾

For Kay—
      my own true Shady Grove . . .

Tásmomaytal nevétiqankwa,
táásutal chulúpiqankwa.
'áá, temét nóó nevétqankwa,
temét nóó chulúpiqankwa.

I suppose I've survived the first little month,
I suppose I've survived the first big month.
Oh, I am surviving through the days,
I am surviving through the days.

"Chalááwaat Song"
Luiseño, Villiana Calac Hyde

CONTENTS

LIST OF ILLUSTRATIONS   xiii

LIST OF TABLES   xv

ACKNOWLEDGMENTS   xvii

PRONUNCIATION GUIDE   xix

Song from the myth "Kukumat Became Sick"
    Quechan   3

General Introduction   5

Making Texts, Reading Translations   21

PART I. SELECTIONS

"Creation Songs," *Cupeño*   57

1. Kwaw Labors to Form a World
    Atsugewi, 1996   59

NORTHWESTERN CALIFORNIA

Doctor dance song, *Yurok*   65

2. Test-ch'as (The Tidal Wave)
    Tolowa, 1985   67

3. "The Young Man from Serper" and Other Stories
    Yurok, 1951, 1985–1988   77

4. Coyote and Old Woman Bullhead
    Karuk, circa 1930   90

5. The Devil Who Died Laughing
   Karuk, 1950   98

6. "The Boy Who Grew Up at Taʼkʼimiłding"
   and Other Stories
   Hupa, 1963–1964   104

7. The Bear Girl
   Chimariko, 1921   115

NORTH-CENTRAL CALIFORNIA

Spell said by a girl desirous of getting a husband
   Northern Yana   125

8. How My Father Found the Deer
   Achumawi, 1970   127

9. Naponoha (Cocoon Man)
   Atsugewi, 1931   139

10. A Story of Lizard
    Yahi, 1915   152

11. A Selection of Wintu Songs
    Wintu, 1929–1931   178

12. Loon Woman: He-who-is-made-beautiful,
    She-who-becomes-loon
    Wintu, 1929   192

13. Four Songs from Grace McKibbin
    Wintu, circa 1982   219

14. How I Became a Dreamer
    Nomlaki, 1935   235

15. Mad Bat
    Maidu, circa 1902   248

16. Creation
    Eastern Pomo, 1930   260

17. The Trials of Young Hawk
    Southern Pomo, 1940   311

18. The Woman Who Loved a Snake
    Cache Creek Pomo, 1988   324

19. The Dead People's Home
    Lake Miwok, 1980   334

SOUTH-CENTRAL CALIFORNIA

Excerpt from "The Čiq'neq'š Myth"
Ventureño Chumash   345

20. Two Stories from the Central Valley
    "Visit to the Land of the Dead"
    Chawchila Yokuts, 1931
    "Condor Steals Falcon's Wife"
    Yowlumni Yokuts, 1930   347

21. The Contest between Men and Women
    Tübatulabal, circa 1932   363

22. The Dog Girl
    Ineseño Chumash, 1913   382

SOUTHERN CALIFORNIA

Excerpt from an account of "The Soul"
Quechan   399

23. The Creation
    Serrano, 1963   401

24. A Harvest of Songs from Villiana Calac Hyde
    Luiseño, 1988–1992   411

25. From "The Life of Hawk Feather"
    The Bear Episodes
    Cupeño, 1962, 1920   421

26. In the Desert with Hipahipa
    Mojave, 1902   436

27. An Account of Origins
    Quechan (Yuma), 1908   461

**PART II. ESSAYS ON NATIVE
CALIFORNIA LANGUAGES
AND ORAL LITERATURES**

"When I Have Donned My Crest of Stars"
Kiliwa   493

A Brief History of Collection   495

"Women's Brush Dance Song," *Luiseño*   511

Notes on Native California Oral Literatures   513

Funeral speech, *Quechan*   543

Notes on Native California Languages   545

MAPS   573

BIBLIOGRAPHY   579

ACKNOWLEDGMENTS OF PERMISSIONS   605

INDEX   609

ILLUSTRATIONS

FIGURES

1. Florence Shaughnessy   79
2. Sally Noble   117
3. Ishi   155
4. Narrative structure of Ishi's "A Story of Lizard"   158
5. Grace McKibbin   220
6. Dancer believed to be Charles Watham   237
7. William Ralganal Benson, circa 1936   262
8. Mabel McKay, 1971   325
9. Ross Ellis with his son   350
10. María Solares   385
11. Jack Jones   439
12. Sam Batwi, Alfred L. Kroeber, and Ishi   503

MAPS

1. Locator   573
2. California linguistic diversity   574
3. California language families and stocks   575
4. California linguistic prehistory   576
5. Current status of California languages   577

TABLES

1. Selections: Genre   15
2. Selections: Recording method   16
3. Selections: Date of performance   17
4. Selections: Language of narration   18
5. Language families: California
   languages and genetic affiliations   547

ACKNOWLEDGMENTS

I've been at work on this project, off and on, for more than seven years—a long enough stretch of time that I fear those who lent a hand back at the beginning will no longer remember the occasion. Yet I benefited greatly back then from formative talks with Kay Fineran, Victor Golla, Leanne Hinton, Margaret Langdon, Malcolm Margolin, Judith Rock, Bill Shipley, and Brian Swann. They helped give me a sense of what this volume could become and what it might include.

On a wide range of more specific queries and problems, I am indebted to Linda Agren, Therese Babineau, Tom Blackburn, Parris Butler, Catherine Callaghan, Edmund Carpenter, Jim Collins, Beverly Crum, Scott DeLancey, Jeffrey Ehrenreich, John Johnson, Richard Keeling, Kathryn Klar, Arnold Krupat, Julian Lang, Sally McLendon, Marian Olivas, Nancy Richardson, Alice Shepherd, Mary Stieber, and Suzanne Wash. The community of California scholars and friends, to which most of these people belong, is a giving one—so much like a family that it's easy to forget: no one *had* to "take me in" when I came calling for assistance; but these people did, often time and again.

By far my biggest debt of gratitude goes to Brian Swann, who had the idea for this book in the first place. When I started, I was alarmingly naive and new to the business of editing anthologies. Each step of the way, Brian showed me the ropes. Without his patient guidance, sound advice, and moral support across the years, this book would never have come to be.

Three anonymous reviewers for the University of California Press gave me valuable input on the manuscript—feedback that I trust I have put to good use. I am grateful for their scrutiny, and hope that, by acting on most of their suggestions, I have given them some measure of job satisfaction.

At the University of California Press, I'd like to give thanks to two people who proved themselves true friends of this book: to Stan Holwitz, for his encouragement and unfailing good judgment while I was trying to pull the manuscript together for final submission and review; and to Rachel Berchten, project editor for the book, for being so perceptive and careful and patient through the giant process of nudging all the mountains and molehills into place: more than anyone else, she helped this sprawling manuscript become a book. Finally, my thanks to Carolyn Hill, who copyedited the manuscript brilliantly, improving it in a thousand ways, with a keen eye for infelicity and bilge.

Closer to home, I would like to thank Judy Bowser and the other reference librarians at Clarion University for not locking me out of their offices when they saw me coming, even after the first hundred interlibrary loan requests; my department secretary, Carole Pasquarette, for putting up with a lot of weird text entry and scanning projects; my dean's office for photocopying support; and the College of Arts and Sciences for one-quarter release time in the fall semester of 1994 "to finish the book." Two small grants from the Clarion University Foundation in 1994 and 1995 enabled me to travel to conferences and do research at the Bancroft Library and Hearst Museum on the University of California, Berkeley, campus.

Finally, I'd like to thank my wife, Kay, for being—always, somehow—there. Without her . . . well, it's unsayable.

PRONUNCIATION GUIDE

Because this is a book of translations, not bilingual texts, pronunciation is not as pressing an issue as it might have been. Nevertheless, stray words and names and places crop up in these pages, and readers who like to meet a challenge head-on, or don't want to have to mumble and squint, may appreciate a brief, generalized guide to pronouncing tribal and linguistic orthographies. I say "generalized" because, in a land of such profound linguistic diversity as Native California, there is no such thing as a shared orthography common to all languages. The rough outlines of the various systems are fairly consistent—most are based on the phonetic alphabet, after all. But because most contemporary orthographies are phonemic (meaning that it takes a degree of "insider knowledge" to interpret the symbols with certainty), the phonological particulars and eccentricities of the individual languages work to limit the consistency of the alphabet used.

At any rate, and for what it's worth, here are some pointers for pronouncing the native-language words and names that readers will encounter in this book. Following them won't guarantee that you'll be right, just that you won't be egregiously wrong—a plausible rendition, if not a perfect one. For details on any particular language, consult the "Further Readings" section following each selection, which supplies references to grammars and teaching aids (if there are any for the language in question).

Most accepted orthographies for Native American languages are based on the Americanist Phonetic Alphabet (a North American variant of the International Phonetic Alphabet). Therefore the following suggestions will be valid for most of the Indian words you find in this (or any other) book.

The letter ʔ and the apostrophe both represent the glottal stop (the catch-in-the-throat sound spelled by the hyphen in "uh-oh!" or in the Cockney pronunciation of *bottle;* most likely your pronunciation of the word *apple,* when spoken forcefully in isolation, begins with this sound as well).

The letters *č* and *ǰ* represent the sound of the "ch" in *cheap* and the "j" in *jeep,* respectively.

The letter *c* may be pronounced either as "ch" or as "ts" (like the "zz" in *pizza*), depending on the language. (In old turn-of-the-century transcriptions, such as Sapir used for Yana, the *c* was used to represent a "sh" sound.)

The letters *p', t', c', č', k',* and *q'* are glottalized stops, pronounced as the base letter plus the simultaneous articulation of a glottal stop; likewise the letters *m', n', l', w',* and *y',* although these are sometimes written *ʾm, ʾn, ʾl, ʾw,* and *ʾy.* (If you say the phrase "Up-up-and-away" carefully, the first of the two *p*s you produce will come out sounding something like the glottalized *p';* likewise the negative murmur "Mm-mm" contains a glottalized *m'* in the middle.) These sounds are not easy to imagine, much less to produce, without first hearing someone do it.

The letter *q* stands for a voiceless uvular stop—somewhat like the "k" sound in English *car,* only farther back.

The letter *r* is usually pronounced as a flap, like the "r" in Spanish *María.*

The letter *x* represents a harsh "h" sound, like the "ch" in German *Bach.*

Raised or superscript letters can signify a variety of things. (1) A raised *ʰ* following a consonant indicates that a small puff of air (what phoneticians call "aspiration") accompanies the sound, like the "pʰ" in English *poor.* In orthographies where the *ʰ* is written, its absence (for example, plain *p* as opposed to *pʰ*) implies an absence of aspiration. (2) A raised *ʷ* following a consonant indicates the presence of lip-rounding or labialization, like the "kʷ" in English *queen* or *coop.* (3) A raised *ʸ* following a consonant indicates the presence of palatalization, like the "kʸ" in English *cute* or *keen.*

A dot underneath a consonant (primarily *ṭ, c̣,* and *ṣ*) indicates that the sound is retroflex—that is, the tongue is curled back in a slightly *r*-like fashion, like the initial consonants of English *tree* and *shrew.*

Other consonants should be pronounced more or less as expected.

Most vowels have their continental values: *a* as in *aha!*, *e* as in *gray*, *i* as in *bee*, *o* as in *show*, and *u* as in *boo*.

There are also three commonly found diphthongs, or complex vowels: *ay* as in *cry*, *aw* as in *cow*, and *oy* as in *coy*.

Some unfamiliar vowel symbols that you may encounter include the "barred" letters *i* and *u*, both of which represent a high back unrounded vowel (try saying *moo* while smiling), and the umlauted vowels *ü* and *ö*, which may be pronounced like their French and German counterparts (try saying "e" or "a" while rounding your lips as if to blow out a candle).

Many languages have a distinction between long and short vowels (a term that in phonetics refers to actual duration—long vowels are held longer than short vowels are). There are two common ways of indicating length: a colon or raised dot (*ba:nu* or *ba·nu*), or simply doubling the vowel (*baanu*). (*Baanu* is the Yana word for *basket*.) A few older orthographies use the macron for length.

Some orthographies indicate stressed or accented syllables with acute accents over the vowel (*á, é, í, ó, ú*, etc.) or immediately following it (*a', e', i', o', u'*). Others don't mark stress at all, in which case you'll just have to guess, unless you can locate a grammar that explains the rules for stress placement. (In a few languages, such as Karuk and Achumawi, the accent mark indicates high pitch rather than stress.)

An italicized or superscript vowel (*pat^i*) usually indicates that the vowel is whispered.

SURVIVING THROUGH THE DAYS

My heart, you might pierce it and take it,
You take it, you pierce it, you take it,
You might pierce it and take it,
You my older brothers here,
You Bear here,
You Mountain Lion here,
You Wildcat here,
You my older brothers,
My heart, you might pierce it and take it.

Song from a Quechan myth
Abraham Halpern
"Kukumat Became Sick"

General Introduction

When this volume was in its planning stages, I always described it to colleagues and editors as a "reader," a reader in the field of California Indian oral literature. It was to be a comprehensive anthology of both classic and contemporary works in translation, whose selections would feature as many of California's cultures and languages as possible. Indeed, my working title throughout these many years of putting it together was simply *A California Indian Reader.* The book has turned out pretty much the way I first saw it in my mind's eye, but the title itself has since then suffered a demotion. The reason why is worth the telling.

In truth, it wasn't long before I grew uneasy describing this book as a "reader." The term seems to promise that the book in hand will contain all of the essential readings on a given topic. And I will admit to believing, when Brian Swann first suggested I think about undertaking such a project, that this book could and would do just that. I actually thought I could examine and absorb *all* of what there was and select the essentials from a complete picture of the recorded literature. Looking back, bemused, I can only shake my head at such naïveté. There is so much material in so many sources, in so many different forms and places, that after many years of going through libraries and collections, talking to singers and storytellers, linguists, and archivists, and wearing out my welcome at my once-willing interlibrary loan department, I've still seen only a portion of what exists. What's more, I'm thrilled to admit it. My notion that this volume could actually *be* a reader, in the most restrictive sense of the term, is gone. In retrospect, I see that what I've really been putting together is more of a "sampler"—and that is the genre I have tried to make good.

There are several reasons why the task proved so overwhelming. The first thing to consider is the astounding diversity of language and culture that is Native California. Four markedly distinct culture areas—Pacific Northwest, Central California, Southern California, and Great Basin— lie within the cartographic confines of the state. With some seventy-five to one hundred distinct languages and tribal groups at the time of European contact, California was the single most populous and linguistically diverse area in all of North America. Indeed, Native California stands out as one of the richest, most linguistically complex areas in the world.[1] To find a corresponding depth and richness in its oral traditions and literatures should not be surprising. The sheer number of traditions alone makes any attempt at exhaustive coverage impossible in a single volume. A look at map 1 (p. 573) will show how much of the region has in fact been represented but will also reveal just how much has not.

Second, the University of California at Berkeley has been home to two of the most active Native American research programs in the country, in anthropology and linguistics. A. L. Kroeber took command of the newly founded Museum and Department of Anthropology in 1901 and, in his forty-five years as chairman of anthropology at Berkeley, wrote hundreds of articles and dozens of books and either sponsored or coordinated four decades of research by many of the great scholars and collectors of his time. In 1953, Mary R. Haas, the great Americanist, helped to found the Department of Linguistics, also at Berkeley. This program has had a major impact on the study of Native American—particularly Californian—languages. Both these scholars had the gift to inspire not just one but two or even three generations of students (many of whom serve as translators in this book) and, in the process, sent scores of researchers into the field to study California cultures and languages.

But the work on California language and literary traditions has never been an exclusively academic pursuit; it has come from within the Native community as well as without. Elders throughout the state have led family and tribal efforts to preserve local traditions, revive their languages, and tell their histories. From Lucy Thompson, the aristocratic Yurok elder who wrote *To the American Indian* in 1916—the most widely known example of this kind in California—to the latter-day efforts of people like the late Ray Baldy (Hupa), Villiana Calac Hyde (Luiseño), Goldie Bryan (Washoe), and Bun Lucas (Kashaya), to name just four out of so many little-sung heroes, California Indians have long been active in trying to sustain and document their own cultural and linguistic heritage.[2]

As a result of all this academic and grassroots activity, most of California's many cultures have received at least some documentary attention, though some to much greater degree than others. (Wintu and Yurok, for instance, have a rich, varied, and continuing history of documentation going back more than a hundred years, whereas so little is known of Esselen and Saclan that the extant materials on these languages amount to little more than a sheaf of papers.) Of course, only some of this wealth of material concerns traditional storytelling and song, but that fraction still turns out to be a great deal. In short, if a particular culture is not represented in this volume, it is not usually for want of material—though for all too many (Huchnom, Esselen, Tataviam, and Northeastern Pomo, to name a few) the shock of contact destroyed the continuity of language and tradition before anyone took an interest in trying to preserve or write down the literature.

Third, however long the bibliography of published accounts of Native California anthropology and linguistics, still more lies unpublished. Active fieldworkers generally gather far more material than they can ever hope to work up in a lifetime. The ultimate case in point is the legacy of John Peabody Harrington, whose fifty years of ceaseless fieldwork for the Smithsonian Institution focused almost exclusively on California. Harrington left behind not mountains but whole mountain *ranges* of information about California Indian cultures. The Smithsonian collection of his California and Great Basin fieldnotes (those that have been found, that is, for he was secretive and given to caching his notes in unlikely places) runs to 283 reels of microfilm—hundreds of thousands of pages. Very little of this work has ever been published, even now, some thirty-five years after his death.[3] It is only in the last few years, with the inauguration of the annual J. P. Harrington Conference, that researchers, Native and otherwise, have begun to sort through these priceless notes to see what they contain.

Harrington, of course, was an extraordinary case. In the last fifty years, though, hundreds of men and women have done work on California cultures, collecting photographs, recordings, notes, and artifacts. But scholars are just like everybody else. They get busy, or sidetracked, or interested in other things. They get burned out. They get discouraged and quit the field. They get married, find jobs in other sectors, or move away. The archives are overflowing with recordings and photographs and cartons of original fieldnotes going back to the early part of this century, much of which has never been published. And who knows how much material is dusting away in attics and offices across the country, saved for posterity, for a rainy day that never came, for the illusory free time of retirement—or just plain forgotten.

The same is true on the Native side of the equation. Affordable cameras have been around for sixty years at least, tape recorders for forty, and camcorders for ten or more. How many sons and daughters, how many grandchildren, have had the urge to document something of their parents' or grandparents' lives—record their stories and songs, their life histories, photograph them basketweaving or leaching acorns or dancing? Usually these private documentations are treasured and saved. Some even get made into locally distributed pamphlets or tribal learning materials. Often, though, human nature being what it is, the photos curl in a box somewhere, the tapes get jumbled up with the country-western or heavy metal or rap, always just a step or two away from destruction or loss. And because human life and times are always in a state of passing, all of it—everything we know, everything we have learned or gathered against the future, everything we are in danger of forgetting—is precious, no matter who we are.

There is a fourth reason, most important by far, why this volume cannot hope to draw from an exhaustive consultation of the literature: *the traditions are still alive, still growing.* Despite more than two centuries of occupation, assimilation, and outright genocide, they have never been fully stopped. (Hence the choice of title for this volume: *Surviving Through the Days.*) People adapt, and the appearance of things may change, but there's a deeper current, a continuity of difference, that the Native peoples of California have fought hard and paid dearly to preserve. New ways come to mingle with the old.

As a graduate student, I once attended a conference, the Fifth Annual California Indian Conference, in Arcata in the northwestern part of the state. On the last evening of the conference, the organizers arranged a traditional-style Yurok salmon roast at one of the beaches. Perhaps a hundred people attended, so this was not a small affair—the Yurok man (husband of one of the organizers) who put it on had been fishing for days prior to the feast. The charcoal pit was in fact a trench about fifteen feet long and a yard wide, banked with alder logs and ringed with dozens of slender, blade-like cedar stakes about eight inches apart around the entire perimeter of the fire. The stakes were stuck in the sandy ground like the pickets of a fence and spitted with huge chunks of salmon and snaky loops of eel. There was harmony everywhere: the red-orange glow of the fire matched the glow in the sky after sunset; the surf, and the breezes combing through the dark bank of pines and redwood along the hill leading down to the beach, alternately matched and masked the quiet sizzle of salmon juices pressed out by the heat of the coals.

Of course, I'm describing a still life here—a static scene, wonderfully idyllic for those of us enjoying the feast, and one that I have always remembered. But the reality was more than a simple picture postcard: it was a *performance*, and a masterful one at that, made possible only by a prodigious amount of labor and traditional skill on the part of the organizer's husband. But it is this scene that sets the background for the part of the story I'm really trying to tell.

Later, I wandered away from the party and walked along the beach. It was dark and a bit chilly. Down in a hollow between dunes I came across a little circle of people from the conference party—adults and a few youngsters, a mix of Indians and whites—sitting around a small driftwood fire. I stopped to say hello. One of the women had just finished telling a story as I walked up. After the silence ripened again, another woman, older than the first, began telling a new story. As I listened, I realized to my surprise that I knew the story she was telling: the traditional California tale of the Rolling Head. I recognized it because, by chance, I was in the process of translating a 1907 version of that tale from Yana, called "Rolling Skull."[4] Hers was definitely the same story, but different from the version I was familiar with in all sorts of interesting ways. Grad student that I was, when she was finished I mentioned the coincidence and described some of the differences. Before I knew it, I had been invited to contribute a story of my own to the circle. Lacking the skill and experience of telling a traditional story aloud, I knew I would make a hash of any tale I might try, so wisely but somewhat sheepishly, I declined the invitation. The point of all this is that the two women in that firelit circle *did* possess that skill. In another time, they would have been telling their stories in Karuk, say, or Yurok, but because of the mixed and mostly younger audience and the sad course that history took in Northern California, that night found them performing their repertoire in English. And so the traditions are still being carried forward—sometimes in English now instead of Karuk or some other Native language, but carried forward nonetheless.

So much of the spirit and particularity of a culture is embodied in its language that, when language is lost, in many and indefinable ways the patterns of the culture, of its poetics and worldview, are lost as well, or transformed. At the same time, koan-like, there is so much that transcends the particularity of language that in many and indefinable ways the culture flows on just as before. As a linguist, I mourn the loss of language more than anything—but people have to conduct their lives in whatever language they happen to share. If that language is now becoming English, where once it was Karuk (or Kawaiisu, or Konkow, or Kitanemuk), then so be it. At least the stories—their excitement, wisdom, and spirit intact—are still being told. As long as this remains true, as long as the precarious flame of tradition passes to a new generation, the body of Native California oral literature will remain open-ended and continue to grow.

So, all things considered, there is a tremendous wealth of material on the oral literatures of Native California, in libraries, in archives, in attics, and in the living minds of the people whose religious and literary heritage it is. Yet consider this: however overwhelming this literary wealth may appear to an unsuspecting scholar out to master the field, those same riches seem to dwindle when compared to the body of, say, Irish literature, or Persian or Japanese. Despite my mad, naive campaign to read and hear "all there is" in the oral-literary fields of Native California, I am left, in the end, with a sudden, keen perception of the rarity of material. Such rarity makes every scrap precious. And every piece of tradition that has been passed on, recorded, or written down is made that much more valuable, as it becomes—in consequence, for better or worse— emblematic of all that was not.

PRINCIPLES BEHIND THE SELECTION

Surviving Through the Days presents the reader with a solid sampling of these riches. As befitting a sampler, you will find something of nearly everything in this book. Though it is an impossible task in a collection this size, I have tried my best to cover the state geographically as thoroughly as possible—patchy though the result may be. And I have tried to represent as many different genres as possible, though here I faced my most intractable problems. I have also tried to represent different translational styles, different eras and methods of collection—even, in some cases, different versions of the same tale. Lastly, I have tried to feature at least a few of the best-known personalities in the field of California oral tradition, from its most indefatigable collectors to its most important singers and storytellers. (There was far from enough room on the ark for everyone, though . . .)

Yet all that I have tried to accomplish in making the selections for this book has been constrained by one overriding imperative: that each piece chosen, whatever its genre or translation style, be grounded in an actual performance—that there be an authoritative text behind each presentation, backing it up.[5] This means that every translation in this book (with two rather complicated exceptions) is both *verifiable* and *replicable*.[6] Not replicable in the scientific, experimental sense, of course, but replicable in the sense that there is an original text upon which to base a new translation, should anyone desire to do so. And verifiable in the sense that serious literary and linguistic scholars can examine the native-language text to judge the peculiar blend of conservatism and liberty in an individual translator's style, or examine the original language underlying some crux in a song or story.[7]

The reader may therefore be certain that these are honest, authoritative translations of authentic oral performances.[8] The singers and storytellers whose work is represented in these pages are all knowledgeable, sometimes even renowned, proponents of their cultural traditions, and finely skilled in their art. Likewise, their translators are all acknowledged experts in the language at hand—either native speakers themselves or linguists with a deep insight into its grammatical structure.

I had a second imperative, which was to follow the laudable standard of presentation established in Brian Swann's recent anthology, *Coming to Light* (1994). Too often, Native American and other oral literatures have been presented without context other than tribe of origin. Nothing is given of cultural background, the identity of singers or storytellers, the circumstances of collection, the methods of translation or transcription, clues as to significance and interpretation, and the like. Each selection here is therefore accompanied by an introductory essay providing background and contextual information helpful for approaching and appreciating the work.

Oddly enough, though, this documentary requirement—which I think an essential one—has led to a crisis in choosing materials for this book. The reader will notice that, while the narrative genres— myth, legend, folktale, and reminiscence—are amply represented, there are only a few selections of songs, and oratory is not represented at all by formal selections. Although there is very little authentic extended oratory in the California corpus to begin with, which explains its near absence here, there is a lot of song. Open almost any ethnographic treatment of California tribes, and you will find a few scattered songs and maybe even a snatch of oratory accompanying the description of a ceremony. This presents a problem: it is hard to justify space for a selection that consists of a four-page introduction followed by one or two couplets of song, yet that is precisely what the documentary spirit of this volume and its format requires. Unfortunately, there are very few extended collections of song, and those that do exist are either already well-known or were so poorly glossed and contextualized at the time as to defy reliable translation today.[9] Until quite recently, most songs were neither collected nor presented in the exemplary style that Alice Shepherd and Leanne Hinton have developed for the Wintu songs of Grace McKibbin (#13). So the genre of song, which is scattered everywhere in the notes and pages of California's many ethnographers, does not receive its full formal due in this volume. The same shortcoming holds for the bits and pieces of oratory that stud the ethnographic literature.

To compensate, I have sprinkled the volume with songs and speeches and quotations, unannotated except for the bare essentials of who, what, when, and where. As Beverly Crum, a well-known Shoshone singer and anthropologist, once said to me, sometimes the beauty of a song should be appreciated all on its own, just the sheer poetry of it, without the millstone of analysis and interpretation—in short, let the bare words speak for themselves. To honor that minimalist impulse in a book that otherwise goes out of its way to contextualize its selections, as well as to increase the presence of these slighted genres in this collection, I have gathered up handfuls of such gems and tucked as many as I could into its nooks and crannies to serve as epigraphs, as verbal artwork.

Some final words of caution. The reader should not presume that the selections in this volume necessarily represent what is typical of Native

California oral traditions. Some do, some do not. William Benson's "Creation" (#16) is not a typical Central California version of the Beginning, for instance, though its roots nevertheless reach deep down in Pomo cultural tradition. And James Knight makes no bones about how he has changed his telling of the widespread California Orpheus myth in "The Dead People's Home" (#19). The Orpheus myth is much more conventionally rendered in the Chawchila Yokuts selection, "Visit to the Land of the Dead" (#20a), yet even so, there are elements here (the startling cause of the young bride's death, for instance) that simply come shining out of nowhere. Outstanding works of verbal art may often be highly individualistic, while still evoking the tradition from which they emerge.

Nor should the reader presume that this book presents "the best" of California oral literature. It does not, it could not. Rather, you will find in these pages only *some* of the finest songs and stories that the Native cultures of California have to offer. Easily a dozen volumes of material could have been selected (and in time no doubt will be). Ultimately, despite all my earnest considerations and constraints, this is my own very personal selection of works—stories and songs that struck me, in one way or another, with their power, their subtlety, their humor, or their beauty.

A GUIDE TO THE BOOK

The order of selections could have followed any number of different organizations: genre, tribe, theme, language family, date, culture area, recording method, and so on. In the end, though, I chose to follow a geographic arrangement—not despite, but actually because of the artificiality of such an organization. That artificiality has one virtue: that it introduces an appealing randomness to the sequence and arrangement of the selections. (The cartographic approach—the book runs generally from north to south—is not entirely random. Neighboring cultures often, though not always, share cultural patterns and motifs, and geographic proximity lends a shared landscape to passing sections of the book. In any case, the book's division into regions—"Northwestern," "Southern," and the like—is based more on geography than on culture areas per se.) Readers interested in charting a different path through the material may certainly do so. To that end, tables 1–4 offer nonrandom ways of organizing the book's main selections—by genre, recording method, date of performance, and language of narration.

Since few readers will actually read this book through consecutively from beginning to end, let me say a few things about Darryl Babe Wilson's opening contribution, "Kwaw Labors to Form a World," which stands separate from the rest of the selections in two key ways. First, it has no introduction of its own, save this mention here. More important, it is not an oral composition. Darryl, a Native California writer of great power and ability, sent me this piece as part of his introduction to the story of "Naponoha" (#9). But I was so struck by the self-contained elegance of this section that I asked him if I could use it as a kind of narrative "myth-preface" to the body of the collection as a whole. He agreed, so that is where it now stands. All readers should enter the collection, whatever paths they choose to take inside, through this opening selection.

As for supporting materials, I have tried to be generous in providing critical, historical, and linguistic information on California languages and literatures. Immediately following this introduction is an essay, "Making Texts, Reading Translations," that examines the processes by which oral-literary texts are typically collected and produced and discusses the various schools and philosophies of translation that help shape the selections you will encounter here. This essay ends with a section, designed with beginning students of oral literature in mind, that explores some of the aesthetic features of Native American storytelling that new readers are sure to wonder about.

Following the translations themselves comes a suite of essays. The first, "A Brief History of Collection," offers historical background on text-collecting and fieldwork in California. The second, "Notes on Native California Oral Literatures," provides an overview of the distribution and stylistic characteristics of California oral literatures, including sections on genres of narrative, oratory, and song. The third, "Notes on Native California Languages," offers information on California language families, provides a historical perspective on the tragedy that has befallen California languages and their speakers in the years since European contact, and reviews contemporary efforts toward language revival. After the essays comes a section containing maps of California tribal territories, linguistic diversity, language families, and language endangerment. The bibliography section contains an article, "Selected Resources for Further Study,"

Table 1. Selections: Genre

Origins
"Kwaw Labors to Form a World" (#1)
"Test-ch'as (The Tidal Wave)" (#2)
"The Boy Who Grew Up at Ta'k'imiłding" (#6a)
"Creation" (#16)
"The Creation" (#23)
"An Account of Origins" (#27)

Myths
"The Young Man from Serper" (#3c)
"Naponoha (Cocoon Man)" (#9)
"Loon Woman" (#12)
"Mad Bat" (#15)
"The Trials of Young Hawk" (#17)
"The Dead People's Home" (#19)
"Visit to the Land of the Dead" (#20a)
"Condor Steals Falcon's Wife" (#20b)
"From 'The Life of Hawk-Feather'" (#25)

Coyote stories[a]
"Coyote and Old Woman Bullhead" (#4)
"The Contest between Men and Women" (#21)

Tales
"The Devil Who Died Laughing" (#5)
"The Stolen Woman" (#6c)
"It Was Scratching" (#6d)
"The Bear Girl" (#7)
"A Story of Lizard" (#10)
"The Dog Girl" (#22)

Songs
"A Selection of Wintu Songs" (#11)
"Four Songs from Grace McKibbin" (#13)
"A Harvest of Songs from Villiana Calac Hyde" (#24)

Personal reminiscences
"Blind Bill and the Owl" (#3a)
"Ragged Ass Hill" (#3b)
"Grandfather's Ordeal" (#6b)
"How My Father Found the Deer" (#8)
"How I Became a Dreamer" (#14)
"The Woman Who Loved a Snake" (#18)
"The Dead People's Home" (#19)

Historical epic
"In the Desert with Hipahipa" (#26)

[a]Other selections involving Coyote as an incidental or supporting character include numbers 1, 3 ("The Young Man from Serper"), 15, 20 ("Condor Steals Falcon's Wife"), and 23.

Table 2. Selections: Recording Method

Tape recording	"Blind Bill and the Owl" (#3a)
	"Ragged Ass Hill" (#3b)
	"The Young Man from Serper" (#3c)
	"'The Boy Who Grew Up at Ta'k'imiłding' and Other Stories" (#6)
	"How My Father Found the Deer" (#8)
	"Four Songs from Grace McKibbin" (#13)
	"The Woman Who Loved a Snake" (#18)
	"The Dead People's Home" (#19)
	"The Creation" (#23)
	"A Harvest of Songs from Villiana Calac Hyde" (#24)
	"From 'The Life of Hawk-Feather,' Part 1" (#25a)
Phonetic or verbatim dictation	"Coyote and Old Woman Bullhead" (#4)
	"The Devil Who Died Laughing" (#5)
	"The Bear Girl" (#7)
	"Naponoha (Cocoon Man)" (#9)
	"A Story of Lizard" (#10)
	"A Selection of Wintu Songs" (#11)
	"Loon Woman" (#12)
	"How I Became a Dreamer" (#14)
	"Mad Bat" (#15)
	"Creation" (#16)
	"The Trials of Young Hawk" (#17)
	"Visit to the Land of the Dead" (#20a)
	"Condor Steals Falcon's Wife" (#20b)
	"The Contest between Men and Women" (#21)
	"The Dog Girl" (#22)
	"From 'The Life of Hawk-Feather,' Part 2" (#25b)
	"An Account of Origins" (#27)
Interpreter translation	"In the Desert with Hipahipa" (#26)
Written composition	"Kwaw Labors to Form a World" (#1) [English]
	"Test-ch'as (The Tidal Wave)" (#2) [Tolowa]

Table 3. Selections: Date of Performance

1900s	"Mad Bat" (#15)
	"In the Desert with Hipahipa" (#26)
	"An Account of Origins" (#27)
1910s	"The Dog Girl" (#22)
	"A Story of Lizard" (#10)
1920s	"From 'The Life of Hawk-Feather,' Part 2" (#25b)
	"The Bear Girl" (#7)
	"Loon Woman" (#12)
	"A Selection of Wintu Songs" (#11)
1930s	"Creation" (#16)
	"Coyote and Old Woman Bullhead" (#4)
	"Condor Steals Falcon's Wife" (#20b)
	"Naponoha (Cocoon Man)" (#9)
	"Visit to the Land of the Dead" (#20a)
	"The Contest between Men and Women" (#21)
	"How I Became a Dreamer" (#14)
1940s	"The Trials of Young Hawk" (#17)
1950s	"The Devil Who Died Laughing" (#5)
	"The Young Man from Serper" (#3c)
1960s	"From 'The Life of Hawk-Feather,' Part 1" (#25a)
	"The Creation" (#23)
	"'The Boy Who Grew Up at Ta'k'imiłding' and Other Stories" (#6)
1970s	"How My Father Found the Deer" (#8)
1980s	"The Dead People's Home" (#19)
	"Four Songs from Grace McKibbin" (#13)
	"Test-ch'as (The Tidal Wave)" (#2)
	"Blind Bill and the Owl" (#3a)
	"Ragged Ass Hill" (#3b)
	"The Woman Who Loved a Snake" (#18)
1990s	"A Harvest of Songs from Villiana Calac Hyde" (#24)
	"Kwaw Labors to Form a World" (#1)

Table 4. Selections: Language of Narration

Achumawi	"How My Father Found the Deer" (#8)
Chimariko	"The Bear Girl" (#7)
Cupeño	"From 'The Life of Hawk Feather'" (#25)
English	"Kwaw Labors to Form a World" (Atsugewi) (#1) "Blind Bill and the Owl" (Yurok) (#3a) "Ragged Ass Hill" (Yurok) (#3b) "Naponoha (Cocoon Man)" (Atsugewi) (#9) "Four Songs from Grace McKibbin" (Wintu) (#13) "How I Became a Dreamer" (Nomlaki) (#14) "The Woman Who Loved a Snake" (Cache Creek Pomo) (#18) "The Contest between Men and Women" (Tübatulabal) (#21)
Hupa	"The Boy Who Grew Up at Taʼkʼimiłding" (#6a) "Grandfather's Ordeal" (#6b) "The Stolen Woman" (#6c) "It Was Scratching" (#6d)
Karuk	"Coyote and Old Woman Bullhead" (#4) "The Devil Who Died Laughing" (#5)
Lake Miwok	"The Dead People's Home" (#19)
Luiseño	"A Harvest of Songs from Villiana Calac Hyde" (#24)
Maidu	"Mad Bat" (#15)
Mojave	"In the Desert with Hipahipa" (#26)
Pomoan	"Creation" (Eastern Pomo) (#16) "The Trials of Young Hawk" (Southern Pomo) (#17)
Quechan	"An Account of Origins" (#27)
Serrano	"The Creation" (#23)
Tolowa	"Test-chʼas (The Tidal Wave)" (#2)

Table 4—*Continued*

Wintu	"A Selection of Wintu Songs" (#11)
	"Loon Woman" (#12)
	"Four Songs from Grace McKibbin" (#13)
Yahi	"A Story of Lizard" (#10)
Yokutsan	"Visit to the Land of the Dead" (Chawchila) (#20a)
	"Condor Steals Falcon's Wife" (Yowlumni) (#20b)
Yurok	"The Young Man from Serper" (#3c)

where interested readers may find an annotated list of important books, articles, websites, and other resources on California languages and literatures. This list prefaces the reference section, which collects full citations for all the works referred to in the essays and individual selections of the book.

NOTES

1. Johanna Nichols's *Linguistic Diversity in Time and Space* (1992) demonstrates this observation in great technical detail.

2. Nor is it just the elders who give their energies to rescuing their native languages and traditions. Parris Butler (Mojave), Nancy Richardson (Karuk), Terry and Sarah Supahan (Karuk), the late Matt Vera (Yowlumni), and Linda Yamane (Rumsien) are only some of a growing younger generation working hard to revive their languages and sustain their cultural traditions.

3. Harrington's Chumash notes alone run to nearly half a million pages, by most estimates. See Kathryn Klar's introduction to "The Dog Girl" (#22) for more information on Harrington's life and work.

4. This translation appeared along with another Yana tale in Brian Swann's *Coming to Light* (1994).

5. I very much would have liked this book to have been in a bilingual format, with the English and native-language texts on facing pages, but the realities of publishing and marketing such a volume—consider that its size would

have been nearly doubled—made that option impossible. I hope to see bilingual formats become the norm in this field someday.

6. The exceptions are selections #26, "In the Desert with Hipahipa," and #27, "An Account of Origins," which were interpreted from Mojave and Quechan, respectively, but recorded only in English.

7. Many of the stories here have been previously published, and their native-language texts are accessible or are stored in archives, as noted in their respective introductions. However, many of the newly commissioned translations are based on unpublished texts. Scholars wishing to examine the originals in these cases will have to get in touch with the individual translators to see if interlinear versions of the texts are available. As for the handful of stories narrated originally in English (see table 4), the version presented here *is* the text, for all practical purposes.

8. It must be kept in mind, though, that stories are rarely recorded "live" at actual ceremonies or storytelling sessions where the presence of a linguist with a tape recorder tends to be intrusive or even unwelcome, but instead are generally recorded "in the studio," as it were, where the researcher can better control sound quality and focus the interview. Not all storytellers can deliver living, natural performances under such circumstances, but many do rise to the occasion, as evidenced by the performances in this book. (For scholarly discussions of the differences between "live" and "studio" performances, see Hymes 1981, Sherzer 1987, and Tedlock 1983.)

9. An example of the former case would be the famous Wintu Dream songs collected by Dorothy Demetracopoulou and excerpted here as selection #11; an example of the latter (which I owe to Margaret Langdon) would be the Diegueño Eagle Ceremony songs published by T. T. Waterman in 1910, which do not appear here as a selection for precisely this reason.

Making Texts, Reading Translations

FROM PERFORMANCE INTO PRINT

In books like the one in hand—monolingual in format, without the presence of an original native-language text on each facing page as a reminder—it is entirely too easy for readers to forget that they are reading translations, that the performances behind most of the stories and songs they are reading were given first in another language, and that therefore the words they are reading are not the actual words of the singers and storytellers but approximations of them created by scholars who happen to speak or study those languages and who are presenting or "packaging" the works for their perusal. Just what and how much is inevitably lost in the process of translation is difficult even to imagine. It's not so much that information is lost—the journalistic facts of "who, what, where, and when" come through in any translation—but *sound* is lost, *nuance* is lost, the very substance of verbal art goes missing. If, as Pope once said, "The Sound must seem an Echo to the Sense," pointing to the interdependence of sound and meaning in a work of art, then when the sounds and connotations of English words replace the sounds and connotations of Chumash words or Pomo words or Karuk words, the "sense" in English can never be quite the same as it was in the original language, no matter how good the translation. Different sounds and rhythms and nuances take the place of the original.

For a translator, though, that is the challenge and the real pleasure in doing the work: learning how to carry into English the fullest possible share of what is present in the text. But that goal presumes being able to recognize what is there in the first place—what is said and what is unsaid, how it is said or unsaid, and why it all hangs together. And so the process of translation is always a voyage of discovery. Each word is a step along a trail that leads deeper and deeper into the unexplored country of the language and the culture that cradles it. Translation, therefore, makes an excellent discovery procedure for all aspects of linguistic study, as all the facets and resources of a language are brought to bear in making verbal art. The act of translation, then, forces the translator to grapple with the entire range of these resources and often leads to a deeper understanding of the linguistic patterns of the source language itself. At the same time, translation stretches the limits of the English language to embrace the resources of that other linguistic world—so it's a voyage of discovery into English, my own beloved language, as well.

Translations get made in a number of different ways, and in this collection I have tried to represent the most important of them. Perhaps the most primitive of these methods, from the point of view of accuracy, is what I will call *interpreter translation.* Common in the days before tape recording, this method was employed by collectors who either lacked the phonetic skill to take down texts in dictation, or who were too pressed for time (phonetic dictation was an exhausting and laborious process) to do so. Three parties are involved: the narrator and the collector (often monolingual speakers of their respective languages), and a bilingual interpreter who mediates between the two. Jeremiah Curtin's early collection of Yana and Wintu narratives, *Creation Myths of Primitive America* (1898), was made in this fashion.

In this volume, the Mojave migration epic, excerpted as the episode "In the Desert with Hipahipa" (#26), was collected this way, too, as was "An Account of Origins" (#27). Alfred Kroeber, who made the handwritten record of the former, is quite frank about the limitations of the process in his commentary (A. Kroeber 1951:133):

> In spite of my best efforts to record the full translation of the story, it is evident that I did not altogether succeed. It now contains between thirty and forty thousand words, whereas Inyo-kutavêre in six half-days must have spoken the equivalent of a hundred to a hundred and fifty thousand English words. I have already mentioned [see Kroeber's introduction to #26, this volume] that some of the shrinkage is due to my omitting verbal repetitions and otherwise trimming redundancy, primarily in self-de-

fense in trying to keep up with the interpreter—I wrote only in abbreviated longhand. Perhaps a fair estimate would be that the other half was a regrettable loss of vividness, concrete detail, and nuance. In short, condensation compacted the manner of telling, but also diminished something of such virtues of quality as it possessed. Verbal style in particular had little chance of penetrating through the double screen of Englishing and of condensed recording.

In this process, it is actually the Native interpreter—John Jones in this case, working on the fly without the opportunity for reflection or refinement—who should really be credited for the translation. It is the interpreter who does the hardest work, and whose linguistic and mnemonic skills primarily determine the integrity of the finished product. The collector merely writes it all down as best he can and edits the transcript later. Because the original text has thus had to pass through two different filters on the way from performance into print, narratives recorded by this method have to be appraised carefully. In addition, because no record of the original language is made or kept—it vanishes immediately, replaced by the interpreter's English rendering—such texts are unfit for all but the coarsest sorts of stylistic studies, however impressive and culturally sound they may be in other respects.

Almost any method of recording oral literature (save hearsay, I suppose, or hazy recollection) is preferable to interpreter translation, at least as far as the study of poetics is concerned. Texts taken down by *phonetic dictation* (or "verbatim" dictation if the text is given in English) are much more desirable, because they preserve the exact words of the original performance, in the exact order in which they were spoken. Before tape recorders became widely available, this was the preferred method for collecting texts. Once the story had been dictated and an accurate phonetic transcript made, the collector would read it back to the narrator, word by word or phrase by phrase, verify it, and obtain a running gloss of the meaning.[1] Needless to say, this second stage of the process could take even longer than the first—sometimes several days or weeks for a long story. The translation itself (and a great deal of linguistic analysis as a by-product) is produced by working back and forth between the phonetic text and this initial gloss. Roughly half of the stories and songs in this collection were taken down this way (see table 2 in the "General Introduction" for a complete list of selections categorized by method of recording).

The emergence of *tape recording* in the latter half of the century as the new (and still) primary method of documentation changed some aspects of the collection process drastically, and others not at all. Once the taped record of a performance has been made, the process of working it up as a text is largely similar to that of phonetic dictation. A phonetic transcription is made by listening (endlessly, endlessly!) to the tape, usually with the help of the narrator or another native speaker. Next, a running gloss of the text is made, this time with the crucial help of a native speaker, by playing the tape back a phrase or sentence at a time. (These two steps may, of course, be combined.) The process of translation itself works just the same as it did with the older method, except that in recent years it has become more common for contemporary singers and storytellers to take an active or collaborative role in producing the final literary translation of their work.[2]

Marianne Mithun's obituary remembrance of Frances Jack, a Central Pomo elder who died in 1993, while canted more toward the linguistic side of fieldwork, reveals something of what this kind of work is like and the closeness and warmth that can develop between people involved in the process of documentation (Mithun 1993):

Her knowledge of her traditional language, Central Pomo, was rich and vast. She was an exquisitely skilled speaker; her style could be dramatic and spellbinding, as she told of events from the past, or quick and full of wit, as she conversed with friends. Over the past nine years, as we worked together on a grammar and dictionary of the language, we certainly never came to the end of what she knew. Her memory was astounding. She easily came up with words that no one had used for decades.

At the same time, she was highly articulate in English, able to explain intricacies of the Central Pomo language in ways that few others could. She was aware not just of what could be said in her language, but also of what had been said, and under what circumstances.

One day we were discussing a suffix, *-way,* whose meaning is something like 'arrive.' This suffix appears with the verb root *mó-* 'crawl' in the verb *mó-way,* for example, to mean literally 'crawl-arrive.'

As she explained the meaning of that word, however, she went well beyond that definition, as usual, noting it would be used if someone feels sorry and crawls over to you like a dog, in a pitiful way.

She explained that *čá-way,* literally 'run-arrive,' would be used if a gust of wind hit you, or a child ran into you. The word *hlí-way,* literally 'several go-arrive,' would be used for moving in on someone, as when a woman sees a man sitting on a bench, sits down next to him, and moves in on him.

She was dedicated to creating as full a record as possible of her language. We found we worked best by staying together for four or five days at a stretch every few weeks, working steadily. What a tireless worker she was! First thing in the morning she would be eager to begin, brimming over with things she had thought of during the night. We would work late into the night, stopping only when I could no longer hold a pen.

The best working relationships have always been based on mutual respect and admiration, and that goes for linguistic fieldwork as well as anything else. But I think what shines through here most of all is the genuine love of the work itself, and the immense sense of commitment and urgency that both workers brought to this self-appointed task of documentation—the drive, not so much to "get it all" for posterity, which can never be done, but to get as much as humanly possible, and then to get it right, before it's gone. After preserving life itself and passing the seed of culture and language on to the next generation, no work is more important than this for Native American cultures at the beginning of the twenty-first century. It demands great knowledge and great skill to begin with, but ends as a labor of love.

SCHOOLS OF PRESENTATION

Of course, there is a big difference between the literal translations produced for linguistic publications and the literary translations created for a wider audience. In the earliest days of text publishing in California, in volumes of the old *University of California Publications in American Archaeology and Ethnology* series, the format was an interlinear one, where the native-language text was accompanied by a running word-for-word gloss. The following example from the story "Grizzly Bear and Deer" in Sapir's *Yana Texts* (1910), taken down by phonetic dictation, serves to illustrate this format.[3]

bamaꞌdu   waꞌwi   tꞌeꞌnna   mīkǃaꞌiᵋi   djūꞌtcǃilᵋaimāꞌdj
Deer place | house. | Grizzly Bear | she was angry. | "Cut it off for me

aidju   ba´cⁱ   mô´yau   djô´tc!ilᵋ aitc‘itᵋ atdi´nᵋt‘i
the your | flesh. | I shall eat it." | Now she cut it right off,

mô´citdinᵋt‘êᵋa   mô´ᵋatdinᵋt‘   djī´kithī´s   ‘itdjiha´mᵋ
now she roasted it, | now she ate it. | "It tastes good." | "I looked for your lice."

auwi´tdi´nᵋt‘   dji´na muitc!ila´uᵋatdint‘   baru´ll o‘pdjinᵋt‘
Now she got hold of it | louse | Now she bit her | neck, | she killed her.

djô´t!alditdinᵋt‘   mô´banᵋt‘   mô´banᵋt‘ⁱ   danᵋma´un
Now she split her up, | she ate up all, | she ate up all | being much.

o´pdjibanᵋt‘
She killed all.

Because the glosses are not, strictly speaking, "readable" with any fluency or certitude (much less enjoyment), texts presented in this manner were generally also accompanied by a "free" translation, wherein considerable liberties might be taken to bring the story into conventional English storytelling prose. Here is Sapir's turn-of-the-century free translation of the preceding passage:

> There was a house in which dwelt Deer. Grizzly Bear was angry. "Cut off some of your flesh for me," (she said to Deer). "I am going to eat it." Then (Deer) cut some of it right off and roasted it. (Grizzly Bear) ate it. "It tastes good," (she said. Some time after this, she was lousing Deer, and scratched her. Deer protested; but Grizzly Bear said,) "I was lousing you." Now she caught hold of a louse; now she bit (Deer's) neck and killed her. Then she cut up her belly and ate her up, ate up much. All (the Deer people) she killed.

Some of the liberties are obvious: the first sentence has been considerably contextualized, as has the clause *djô´t!alditdinᵋt‘* 'now she split her up, it is said'; and near the end, the exact repetition of *mô´banᵋt‘(ⁱ)* 'she ate her all up, it is said' has been obscured, thanks to a misreading of prosodic junctures (the word *danᵋma´un* goes with *o´pdjibanᵋt‘*, not with *mô´banᵋt‘ⁱ*). The remote-past quotative element *-nᵋt‘(ⁱ)* 'it is said' has not been translated at all, either in the translation or in the gloss line. Still, these liberties, good or bad, are afforded precisely because the native-language text has been presented in this fashion—it's there to check the translation against, since the interlinear presentation provides a running gloss of the forms and their meanings.[4]

Texts made and presented this way are often referred to as *ethnolinguistic* texts. Their practitioners, from Kroeber and his early Californianist colleagues all the way through to present-day scholars, all share the central Boasian belief in the primacy of the native-language text. Along with that insistence, however, often came a corresponding lack of interest in the translation of the text as an entity in itself—except insofar as it should reflect accurately the semantic and syntactic structures of the original. In short, the translation is just there as a "crib," a convenient key to the native-language text. And because Boasian ethnolinguistics focused on the ethnographic and linguistic aspects of the texts collected, not so much on their aesthetic or poetic aspects, the aesthetic and poetic dimensions are only indirectly reflected in the translations of ethnolinguistic texts.[5]

Over the last couple of decades, there has been a change—some say a revolution, others merely an evolution—in the way scholars go about collecting, translating, and presenting Native American texts. Today, we refer to this new approach as *ethnopoetics,* in explicit contrast to the more classically oriented school of ethnolinguistics. Pioneered by Dell Hymes and Dennis Tedlock in the 1960s and 1970s, ethnopoetics brings together the overlapping interests of linguistics, literary criticism, folklore, and anthropology. It makes the claim that a disciplined understanding of the aesthetic properties of an oral text, be it song or story or reminiscence, is essential to making a proper analysis—that there is an interplay between form and meaning that is ignored only at the risk of misinterpretation, misrepresentation, or both.[6] Such claims are taken for granted with written literary traditions. It should not be surprising to learn that these matters are just as relevant to oral literary traditions. Despite vast differences, both modes, written and oral, fall within the broad domain of verbal art.[7]

The criticism raised against older ethnolinguistic treatments is that they tend to ignore poetics—those aspects of structure, style, and performance that make a text a work of verbal art. Ethnopoetic approaches seek to reverse this tendency. (Contemporary ethnolinguistic translators, of course, are much more conscious of the aesthetic and rhetorical dimensions of their texts.) To illustrate some of the characteristics of an ethnopoetic approach, let's return to Round Mountain Jack's version of "Grizzly Bear and Deer." This time, the translation is my own and proceeds from Hymesian principles of ethnopoetic presentation and analysis. (To provide more in the way of illustration, I have gone beyond the short passage of interlinear glosses and translated the entire opening scene of the story. The right-margin notes supply interpretive information that is not present in the native-language text.)

1 There was a house at Deer's place.
 Grizzly Bear,
   she was angry:
 "Cut me off a piece of your flesh—   *Grizzly said to*
   I'm going to eat it."   *Deer*

2 Now right away she cut off a piece, they say. *Deer did*
 Now she roasted it.   *Grizzly did*
 Now she ate it.

3 "It tastes go-o-d!"

4 "I was just grooming you!"   *Grizzly protest-*
                 ed, when Deer
                 complained of
                 roughness

5 Now she plucked up a louse.
 Now she bit her through the neck—   *Deer's neck*
 she killed her.

6 Now she carved her up.   *Grizzly did*
 She ate her all up,
  she ate her all up, they say.

7 There being so many, she killed them all. *so many Deer*
                 people

8 She went off looking for them.   *for Deer's two*
 She didn't see them.   *children*
 She came back.

9 She went down into the south.
 She killed everything.
 She came back north.

10 Off in the west she ate up all of the deer.
 She came back east.

11   Off to the north she ate up all the elk.
      She ate them all up,
      she killed them all.

12   She headed back, they say, into the east.
      She killed all of the deer.
      She stood still, they say.

13   She looked around.
      "I have killed them all," she said.
      "Now then!" she said.

14   Then she went back home, they say.

The most obvious difference, of course, is the typographical format: this translation is presented in broken lines—akin to poetry, not to prose. Furthermore, many of the lines are grouped into units that look like stanzas or verses, making the result superficially even more like poetry. I will have more to say about the nature of this resemblance later on; for now, I merely want to point out a few of the oral-literary features of the Yana story that are reflected in this excerpt.

In making the translation above, I used syntactic constituency as my main criterion for dividing the text into lines. Each line of translation, therefore, represents a clause or predication in the original Yana. When I then looked more closely at the sequence of lines, I noticed that some of them seemed to be more tightly linked together than others in terms of thematic unity. To reflect that observation, I used blank lines to represent the existence of these groups of lines (numbered in the left margin to facilitate discussion) on the page. Groups 5 and 8, for instance, form units on the basis of related action: in 5, it's the tight action-sequence of plucking, biting, and killing that defines these lines as a single rhetorical entity; in 8, it's the sequence of going, looking around, and returning that defines them as a unit.[8] In fact, all of the line-groups in this excerpt are defined by patterns of action or speech, as examination will reveal. What is interesting is how frequently these units seem to come in triplets. Eight of the fourteen line-groups in this passage contain three clauses each—a high enough proportion to speculate that this pattern represents some kind of rhetorical ideal, one that the narrator actually strove for in his oral composition of the work. (Indeed, a preliminary examination of the entire text suggests that the overall proportion of triplet line-groups is even higher than in this excerpt.)

Furthermore, the four "singlet" groups (3, 4, 7, 14) seem all to carry a special rhetorical force: by virtue of their brevity, their singularity, they tend to punctuate the rhythm and add dramatic highlight to the information they convey. In contrast, the lone "doublet" group (10) simply seems underdeveloped, in that it fails to realize the three-fold rhetorical pattern established in group 8, of going, doing something, and coming back. Groups 9 and 12 fulfill this template (though in 12, "standing still" takes the place of "coming back"), while group 11 appears to be an incomplete variant of the basic design, perhaps deliberate, perhaps not.

Sometimes this latent trinary patterning even plays out at higher levels than the line-group, as in this passage translated from the middle of the story:

1   "Where are they?" she said.

Grizzly, looking for Deer's children

2a   She asked a poker;
      it didn't answer.

2b   She asked a stone;
          it didn't answer.

2c   She asked the earth,
              she asked the stick,
              she asked the fire.

3a   She asked the coals:

3b   "Yes, indeed," they said.
          "They have run south," they said.

3c   "Aha!" she said.

4   She bit the stone, angry.
      She bit the stick.
      She bit the fire.

5   She went right out.

Only two of the nine separate sets of line-groups in this passage (2c and 4) are actually triplets in their own right, but it is easy to see the way the overarching structure of the passage involves a three-fold organization of line-groups. Set 2 is defined by a three-stage action-sequence (the interrogation of various nonrespondent objects), just as set 3 is defined by the three-stage interrogation of the responding coals (the three stages being Grizzly's question in 3a, the coals' answer in 3b, and Grizzly's response in 3c). Similar complex hierarchical organizations may be found throughout the story.[9]

This type of organic literary patterning, which Hymes (1976) has termed *measured verse*, is obscured in the typical prose-format presentations of the ethnolinguistic school but is nicely revealed by the broken-line presentations of the ethnopoetic school. On the whole, ethnopoetic texts and translations are more amenable or accessible to stylistic analysis than the typical ethnolinguistic text—in part because considerable rhetorical analysis has gone into working up the text in the first place.

While some ethnopoetic presentations try to make explicit the underlying rhetorical and compositional patterns of the text, others try instead to capture various "live" aspects of the performance itself—such dynamic features of the living human voice as intonation, vocal quality (shouting, whispering, and the like), and pause-phrasing. Hymes is most often associated with the former, Tedlock with the latter. I often refer to these two different ethnopoetic styles, respectively, as the *structural* and *prosodic* approaches to the poetics of oral literature. Structural approaches focus on the rhetorical architecture of the narrative and are most common with texts taken down earlier in the century by the method of phonetic dictation, whereas prosodic approaches focus on the voice and necessarily require texts that have been tape-recorded or videotaped, because only taped performances can capture and hold the sound of the voice itself in delivery.[10]

As it happened, the first scholar to try for a synthesis of these two methods, William Bright, was himself a Californianist, working with Karuk myths. Today most ethnopoetic practitioners who have the luxury of working with tape-recorded texts aim for some combination of the two approaches. The following translation, the middle section (Bright calls them "acts") of a three-part myth, illustrates an integrated approach. The original was told in Karuk by Julia Starritt and translated by Bright. The story is a widespread myth, well-known in California and elsewhere in North America, called "Coyote Steals Fire." In this presentation, Bright uses a number of typographical conventions to represent aspects of his ethnopoetic analysis (1979:94–95). Capitals, for instance, represent "extra-loud material," and italics represent "extra-soft material." Each line-group ("verse" in Bright's terminology) starts at the left margin, with each succeeding line indented. Intonation contours are indicated by punctuation: falling final intonation by a period, marking the end of a verse; falling but nonfinal intonation by a comma or dash; final high or mid-pitch intonation by a colon. In act 1, Coyote devised a plan for getting back the fire the "upriver people" had stolen. Here, in act 2, he puts his plan into action:

SO THEN THAT'S HOW THEY WENT UPRIVER.
And Coyote arrived upriver.
And he saw it was empty.
And in the mountains he saw there were fires,
   there were forest fires,
     up in the mountain country.
And he went in a house.
And he saw only children were there.
And he said:
   "Where have they gone?
"Where have the men gone?"
And the children said:
   "They're hunting in the mountains."
And he said:
   "I'm lying down right here,
     I'm tired."
And he said to the children:
   "I'll paint your faces!
"Let me paint your faces.
"You'll look pretty that way."
And the children said:
   "Maybe he's Coyote."
They were saying that to each other.
And they said to him,
   to Coyote:
     "Maybe you're Coyote,"
And he said: "No.
"I don't even know
   where that Coyote is.
"I don't hear,
   I don't know,

the place where he is."
And he said:
 "Let me paint your faces!"
And when he painted all the children's faces,
 then he said:
   "<small>SEE, I'VE SET WATER DOWN RIGHT HERE,</small>
    <small>SO YOU CAN LOOK INTO IT.</small>
"Your faces will look pretty!
"<small>BUT I'M LYING DOWN RIGHT HERE,</small>
 <small>I'M TIRED.</small>"
In fact, he had stuck fir bark into his toes.
And then he stuck his foot in the fire.
And then finally it caught fire well,
 it became a coal,
  it turned into a coal.
And then he jumped up again.
And he jumped out of the house.
And he ran back downriver.
And when he got tired,
 then he gave the fire to the next person.
And he too started running.
And in the mountain country,
 where there had been fires,
  then they all were extinguished.
And then people said,
 "Why, they've taken it back from us,
  our fire!"

In an ethnopoetic presentation, the typographical layout of the text on the page (line breaks, indentations, font effects, and the like) is used to convey linguistic information (intonation boundaries, syntactic structure, pauses, voice quality, and so on)—information that is primarily of interest to the specialist. At the same time, though, it offers the nonspecialist a visually intuitive way into the flow and structure of the text as a verbal performance. Notice how the broken-line format of Bright's presentation works to slow the eye as it follows down the page and helps to re-create the pace or rhythm of the original. The vocal cues signaled by italics and caps add texture to the result.

 The notion that oral storytelling is delivered in lines—which in turn are organized into units resembling verses or stanzas, which in turn may be organized into larger and larger units resembling "scenes" and "acts"— is one of the foundational insights of modern ethnopoetics. It is also one of the most widely misunderstood. In ethnopoetic theory, the line is the basic unit of oral-literary composition, comparable in most respects to the cognitive-prosodic units of ordinary speech production (breath groups, intonation units, pause groups, idea units, and so on) that have been identified by linguists doing discourse analysis on conversational speech more generally (see Chafe 1980, 1994).[11] If you listen closely to the sound of people telling stories, lecturing, or just plain talking, you will notice that their speech doesn't come forth in a long, smooth, un- broken flow, like a river. Instead, it comes in pulses, rising and falling like waves on a shore, with each new spurt or "parcel" of information riding in on the crest of its own wave. The lines in ethnopoetic texts are meant to represent these waves or pulses of language.[12]

The misunderstanding comes about because, when these lines are de- lineated typographically by line breaks and further grouped into "stan- zas" by means of blank lines or indentation, the resulting text looks like modern written poetry. Looking at a story presented in this fashion, it's easy to jump to the conclusion that Native American myths and stories are not prose but poetry. But in fact they are neither. Prose is a written category, as is our default conception of poetry. Whatever *poetry* (or *prose*, for that matter) might mean in the context of oral storytelling, it is sim- ply not the same as what it means in the context of Western written lit- erary tradition. All this is not to say that Native American storytelling is not poetic—it most certainly is, often densely and intricately so. But I particularly wish to avert the conclusion, implied by the broken-line for- mats of most ethnopoetic presentations, that it is poetry in the sense that literate Europeans and their cultural descendants typically understand that term. The purpose of presenting texts and translations in broken- line format is to highlight the poetic and rhetorical structures organic to the original language and performance patterns of the text—not to sug- gest potentially misleading cultural parallels between oral and Western written traditions.

And yet, over the years there has been considerable, sometimes even acrimonious, disagreement over these ideas, and ethnopoetics remains somewhat controversial even to this day.[13] Both paradigms continue to stimulate useful contributions to the discipline. For that reason, in addition to presenting classic examples of ethnolinguistic work from the past, I have made it a point to represent a range of contemporary approaches, both ethnolinguistic and ethnopoetic in orientation, in the selections for this volume. In these pages, Dell Hymes's retranslation of the Wintu "Loon Woman" myth (#12) is a prime example of a structural ethnopoetic presentation. There are also two essentially prosodic presentations: Ken Hill's Serrano "Creation" (#23), and the second of Jane Hill's two Cupeño episodes in "From 'The Life of Hawk Feather'" (#25b). Other ethnopoetic treatments here include William Bright's "The Devil Who Died Laughing" (#5) and Leanne Hinton's "Four Songs from Grace McKibbin" (#13). On the ethnolinguistic side of the equation, we have Victor Golla's presentation of "'The Boy Who Grew Up at Ta'k'imiɫding' and Other Stories" (#6), Robert Oswalt's "The Trials of Young Hawk" (#17), Catherine Callaghan's "The Dead People's Home" (#19), Bruce Nevin's "How My Father Found the Deer" (#8), and Darryl Wilson's "Naponoha" (#9). The other contemporary translations in this volume steer more towards Bright's synthetic middle ground—for example, Luthin and Hinton's "A Story of Lizard" (#10), William Shipley's "Mad Bat" (#15), Richard Applegate's "The Dog Girl" (#22), and Ermine Wheeler Voegelin's "The Contest between Men and Women" (#21). Translations made prior to the 1970s, before the real advent of the ethnopoetics movement, are by definition ethnolinguistic presentations.

Both modes of translation are in active use today. Readers interested in comparing these two approaches will find that the difference between the two camps has nothing to do with their literary quality. All the translations in this volume are literary translations, after all—carefully crafted with the intent of re-creating as far as possible in English the style and artistry of the original songs and stories.

WHEN AESTHETIC WORLDS COLLIDE

First-time readers of Native American oral literature often feel confused, even alienated, by the narrative worlds they have entered. Without guidance and preparation, they may even turn away in bewilderment. The motivations for behavior may seem opaque; the timing of stories may seem "off"; their sense of outcome, of dramatic resolution, may seem to be missing entirely. By and large, these problems are simply due to a different style of storytelling—so similar in some ways to the fantastical myths we know from the Bible, or to the European folktales most of us know from childhood, yet so very different in others.

Sometimes the initial strangeness can obscure the common ground. In Ishi's "A Story of Lizard" (#10), when Lizard cuts open Grizzly Bear's stomach to rescue the gobbled-up Long-Tailed Lizard, try thinking of "Little Red Riding Hood." Or again, in the story behind "Sapagay's Song" (see pages 533–34), when Sapagay dives down into a pool to discover a shaman's underground realm, try thinking of Beowulf diving into the lake to confront Grendel's mother. At other times, the sensation of familiarity can obscure what is truly different. For instance, the average American reader will take the ending of the Yurok story "The Young Man from Serper" (#3c) right in stride:

> And so for this we say that it is not good if a person thinks too much, "I will have everything." But a man lives happily if somewhere he has plenty of friends, and has his money; then he does not go around thinking that he should have everything that does not belong to him, and wishing it were his own.

Most will automatically absorb this moral thanks to its familiar ring, so congruent with European folk wisdom regarding wealth and ambition. And in truth there is much here that can be taken at face value from Yurok into English tradition. But the idea and function of money, of personal wealth, in Yurok culture is ultimately quite different from its Western counterpart, and so this feeling of transparency is partly an illusion.

Other difficulties readers may encounter are caused by the nature of oral literature itself.[14] True oral storytelling—as opposed to reading aloud or acting out a story one has memorized (the usual fare at "story hour" in libraries and schools across the country)—is something that most of us in America today are completely unfamiliar with. When a child hears the story of "Goldilocks" or "Snow White" over and over again at bedtime, it's the same every time. Different readers may have different voices, some more animated than others, but the words written down are always the same. True oral storytelling very seldom involves the redaction of a fixed text, but rather, involves the re-creation of a living one. While some storytellers can produce versions of their stories that remain remarkably constant even when many years separate the tellings, others may dramatically alter the structure and even substance of their stories from one occasion to the next. Depending on factors such as audience, mood, setting, and personal style, oral narrators tailor their performances to suit the moment, expanding an episode here, truncating an episode there, highlighting this or that aspect to reflect what's going on in the here and now. Thus, in a living oral culture, there could never be just one "Goldilocks." Instead, there would be a different "Goldilocks" for every storyteller—with a great deal of consensus among the versions, to be sure, but with divergent versions as well. On top of that, each version will have its own variations, slight differences each time the story is told. In a sense, there is an ecology to what we find here, for in this very diversity lies the health of an oral tradition.

Native American stories will strike readers in many different ways. When you think about it, though, these stories *should* feel different. Native American traditions and cultures are as much a part of the grand galaxy of world human culture as any other group. But Native American cultures have also been growing independently on the American soil for at least fifteen thousand years. (By way of perspective, that's seventy-five thousand generations—at least ten times longer than the mere fifteen hundred years the English have dwelled in Britain.) In that wash of time, they have found their own paths of custom and philosophy, made their own worlds, alike yet unlike any other. So we must expect to encounter differences alongside the similarities. Therein lies what is special about Native American cultures and traditions.

Of course, Native American cultures are different enough from each other, let alone from other cultures around the globe. Even while we may speak of "European" culture, we are mindful of the differences between Germany and France, Hungary and Spain. So, too, with Sioux and Hopi, Nootka and Cherokee. If you, as a reader, come from some other tradition—European, Asian, African—and Native American stories *don't* seem just a little strange and different, then you should wonder whether the translator has gone too far in translating the stories into English.

The contributions to this book strike a balance between the need of the general reader to connect with the stories and the rights of the storytellers to be heard in their own voices. Here, then, are a few of the stylistic highlights that novice readers may look forward to when encountering Native American oral literature for the first time.

Anthropomorphism

Anthropomorphism, where animals and even inanimate objects take on characteristics and capabilities of human beings, is probably the easiest feature of Indian myths for contemporary Americans to adjust to. After all, anthropomorphism is nearly ubiquitous in our own culture today, from children's books and fairy tales to movies and advertising campaigns on TV. But it is important to understand the nature of Native American anthropomorphism, which is significantly different from what European descendants are accustomed to. In Western cultures, so very long separated from their mythic, animistic pasts, anthropomorphism carries largely an allegorical value, and today it performs the function of entertainment more than anything else. In the old-time Native American traditions, though, anthropomorphism is much more: it is also a consequence of cosmology and religion. Most Native cultures look back to a remote time when the difference between people and animals was blurred, before humans emerged as a distinct race of beings on earth. Animals (or "animal people") were thus our forerunners on this earth. The hard dichotomy between Man and Beast that characterizes Western worldviews is largely absent in Native America. People are distinct from animals, to be sure, but there is still an ancient kinship between them; the relationship is not one of alienation and dominion.

Annie Burke's way of opening her Southern Pomo story, "The Trials of Young Hawk" (#17), sums up the situation with a minimum of fuss: "A group of small birds and animals, who were all also people, used to live together in a big community," she begins. That's why, in so many myths and stories, it can be difficult to decide whether a character is an animal with human characteristics or a person with animal characteristics— or both, or each in alternation. In the end, the distinction is somewhat meaningless; at best, it is a sliding scale. Traditions, even individual narrators within local traditions, vary on how "human" or "animal" their characters appear to be. In "The Trials of Young Hawk," for instance, the characters are fairly concrete, remaining close to their animal natures. Thus Young Hawk has a "perch" high in his older brother's earthlodge, and the beaver brothers "gnaw" new eyes for him, and the fieldmouse sisters "nibble" off his hair. (Note that Young Hawk has hair, though, not feathers.) But in other stories, there is often little that is specifically "animal" about the characters, beyond their names, personalities, and a tendency to dwell in surroundings appropriate to the natural habitats of their namesakes, like Ouzel at the end of the Maidu story "Mad Bat" (#15). There is perhaps a tendency for minor characters to display more animal-like traits than do main characters, possibly because of the greater range of actions main characters are called on to perform, with the consequent drain that maintaining such restrictions (lack of hands, particularly) tends to place on the task of narration.

The core personalities of anthropomorphic characters are often drawn at least tangentially from the Book of Nature. Not surprisingly, there are parallels to be made between Native American folklore and the folklore of ancient and medieval Old World fables and beast tales (the *Panchatantra,* for instance, or closer to home, the fables of Aesop and a variety of Middle English poems, like *The Owl and the Nightingale,* "The Fox and the Wolf," and Chaucer's "Parliament of Fowls"). Just as, in a European folktale, when a fox or a nightingale comes on the scene, we already know what to expect from that character in terms of behavior and personality, so it is in Native American stories when Coyote or Eagle or Bluejay comes on the scene.

Coyote makes a superb example of a character whose behavior—curious, tricky, insatiable, and by turns noble and foolish—is based in part on close observations of the natural world. The Bear Girl in the Chimariko story (#7) is another example—she is crabby, unpredictable, and violent, just like a real bear. Still, different cultures can read the Book of Nature differently. There's a degree of arbitrariness in all bodies of folklore, so what we know about animal figures in one tradition is not always transferable to another. For instance, the loon is a giddy minor character, little more than a walk-on, in American folklore. (As our saying goes, "crazy as a loon.") But in the native folklore of Northern California, Loon is a much darker, much more serious character—a heavy. And the wolf, far from being the evil, rapacious killer that salivates its way through European folklore, is a stalwart, dependable character—a strong leader and good provider, maybe even a bit dull and unimaginative— in much Southern California mythology. Readers should look for both similarities and differences in the animal characters they meet in these stories.

All cultures, and especially oral cultures, make use of anthropomorphism. The mythologies of animistic hunting-and-gathering societies in particular are often heavily and crucially anthropomorphic. As the anthropologist Claude Lévi-Strauss once pointed out, animals are "good to think with." In Native California, animals have long been used, through systematic anthropomorphism in mythology, folklore, art, and religious ceremony, to express deep patterns of thinking about the world. It's a common mistake—and one the reader should guard against—to interpret anthropomorphic myths and stories as merely "children's fare"; they are not. These narratives are amenable to multiple levels of interpretation, at any degree of sophistication their audiences—traditional or modern—care to approach them with. In truth, anthropomorphism has always provided humankind a primary means for exploring one of the most enduringly important themes of inquiry and spirituality: the relationship between ourselves and the natural universe.

Repetition and Parallelism

Somewhere along the road to written culture, in becoming readers rather than listeners, we have lost our patience for repetition, or at least think we have. Yet some of our oldest and most fundamental literary texts—the books of the Old Testament Bible, for example—are alive with repetition, at all levels of rhetorical structure. That's because the writings of the Bible, like Homer, like Gilgamesh, are intimately grounded in oral tradition—and repetition is a cornerstone of oral composition.

In cases of *episodic repetition,* entire scenes or plot motifs get repeated, wholesale or piecemeal, sometimes with only minimal variation. Anyone raised on the Brothers Grimm knows all about episodic repetition. In "Cinderella," when the Prince takes the glass slipper on the road, searching for the foot that wore it, there's a scene at Cinderella's house where he tries it on the eldest sister's foot to no avail. This "Foot Trial" episode is repeated twice more. The first repetition, with the second sister, is virtually identical to that of the eldest sister's trial—except that where the eldest sister amputates her toe to make the slipper fit, the second sister amputates her heel. Both times, the slipper fills up with blood, and the Prince returns the impostor to her family. The third time around, of course, it's Cinderella's turn, and the outcome and content of this episode is significantly different from the first two—indeed, the third trial marks the culmination of the whole sequence and leads to the resolution of the tale. But this is often how episodic repetitions work: a sequence of more-or-less parallel episodes culminates in a final episode where it "all works out," where the tensions generated by the preceding episodes are resolved and their expectations gratified.

The Cinderella example points to an important ingredient of episodic repetition, namely, *pattern number.* In European and many other traditions, things happen in threes: three wishes, three obstacles, three magical helpers, and so on. The influence of the pattern number pervades not just our literature but also all aspects of our symbolic life, from sports (three strikes, three outs; the gold, silver, and bronze) to folk superstition ("third time's a charm," "three on a match," "disasters come in threes") to religion and poetry (the Trinity, Dante's *terza rima*), and all points in between.[15] Pattern numbers may be found in all the world's cultures, a predisposition that stems, perhaps, from a still more fundamental numeric capacity—part of our innate human cognitive endowment. After the manner of language itself, numbers provide human beings with an instrument for perceiving and controlling their world—for structuring and hence manipulating it. Indeed, the old Whorfian arguments concerning linguistic relativity and universalism may be just as apt (or just as overstated) where basic numerical perception is concerned.[16] But even though all cultures appear to possess a dominant pattern number, that number varies from culture to culture—that is, it is acquired through cultural transmission. In the Americas, fours and fives are more prevalent than threes, and this is true in Native California, too.

Examples of episodic repetition are everywhere in this volume. Myths like Ishi's "A Story of Lizard" (#10) and William Benson's "Creation" (#16) involve repetition at the macro level, with entire chapter-like structures repeated with either very minor or very major variation, respectively. Annie Burke's "The Trials of Young Hawk" (#17) is another story where episodic repetition forms a prominent feature of the narrative landscape. But really, this important rhetorical device is present at least in some measure, on large scales or small, in almost all the selections. Sometimes the patterns are played out in full, very strictly; other times, narrators choose merely to summarize some of the sequences. In this passage from Jo Bender's "Loon Woman" (#12, lines 52–89), the repeated episode begins with the mother's question about which brother to take for a companion and concludes with Loon Woman's rejection (or final acceptance) of the mother's suggestion:

Thinking of the man,
    "This morning I shall go west," so says that woman.
      "I want to take someone along to guide me.
"I am going to go," so she tells her mother.

"I am going to go west," so she says,
   thinking of the man, so she spoke.
"Hm," [her mother] says.

"Whom do you want to take with you?" she says.   *[first suggestion]*
She will not tell whom.

The old woman,
    "Well, surely take this little one, your younger brother."
Now that woman says,
    "I don't want to take him."

"Whom will you take with you?" so she says.   *[second suggestion]*
"I want to take another one with me."

"Take this one then."
"I won't," so said that woman.

She does this for a long time,   *[third and*
   she goes through them all.   *fourth suggestions,*
He-who-is-made-beautiful alone is left,   *conflated]*
   He-who-is-made-beautiful.
The little old woman sits,
   sits pondering it all, the old woman.

That woman measures that hair like that.
The hair of the rest does not match.
The one hair she had found is longer.

The old woman sits,
   sits pondering it all.
Suddenly,   *[fifth suggestion]*
    "Yes, surely take this one,"
      so she says,
        "He-who-is-made-beautiful,"
          her son.
"Yes," so she said.

The woman is happy she is going to take him along.
She measures the hair,

that hair matches.

"I'm going to take this one," she says.

From other evidence, the Wintu pattern number appears to be five, but here the full potential run of five episodic repetitions—four rejections capped by the final selection of He-who-is-made-beautiful—has, for one reason or another, been truncated in this telling.[17] (See Dell Hymes's introduction to the myth for a more detailed discussion of the numerical patterns operating in this complex narration.) As is often the case, the final episode here is considerably more elaborated than the lead-up episodes. In the hands of a skilled narrator like Jo Bender, episodic repetitions are far from mechanical.

For readers coming from a European or Europeanized background, pattern number is a common stumbling block.[18] Stories can seem repetitious simply because they are playing out a different pattern, a pattern based on fours or fives instead of threes. We are seldom consciously aware of the ways in which our sense of timing, of suspense and expectation, is in thrall to these deep-seated rhetorical patterns. Forewarned, though, readers can take an interest in looking for these cyclical patterns in myths and stories. Some of the translators have pointed out the presence of these patterns, where they are known or understood, in their introductions. Often, though, this aspect of linguistic structure hasn't even been studied yet for the narrative traditions in question. An astute reader may well spot rhetorical patterns in these translations that no one has yet described or documented.[19]

Another pattern, *formulaic repetition,* is found where a single phrase or line gets repeated several times, with or without slight variation. A typical example is this one from a Central Yana story I translated several years ago, called "Rolling Skull" (Luthin 1994). In the story this passage is taken from, Wildcat is up in a tree knocking pine cones down to his wife:

> He knocked one loose down to the east,
>> he knocked one loose down to the west,
>>> he knocked one loose down to the north,
>>> he knocked one loose down to the south.

Formulaic repetitions frequently involve an action repeated, as here, to each of the cardinal directions. The repetition suggests almost a ceremonial quality and often seems to mark the event it highlights as having special significance. (Here it foreshadows another action still to come, the real turning point in the story.) In part, this highlighting effect is a consequence of the simple, temporal "physics" of repetition itself: an action repeated twice formulaically is kept before the listener's consciousness twice as long; an action repeated four times, four times as long; and so on. The rhetorical device of repetition thus provides the narrator with a straightforward means of dwelling on the event in question—of slowing the action, and the story, down. However, it is not only strict formulaic repetitions that have this "lingering" effect.

Under the heading of *poetic repetition*—a rather loose and deliberately general term—come patterns of repetition that, through a variety of effects, seem especially to increase or enhance the linguistic resonance of the passages they adorn. In the "Loon Woman" passage cited previously, there's a great deal of such poetic repetition going on, even apart from the basic episodic patterns. Right at the outset, two lines, "Thinking of the man" and "This morning I shall go west," are repeated, but in reversed order—ab . . . ba—a simple chiasmus. A little later, the name "He-who-is-made-beautiful" is repeated, purely for the poetic and rhetorical effect of the echo. The next pair of lines, "The old woman sits, / sits pondering it all," is also repeated, with slight variations, the two occurrences separated only by the image of Loon Woman measuring the telltale hair—an image that is itself repeated at the end of the scene.

These repetitions serve to enrich the telling—phonetically, of course, since all these echoes make the language reverberate, but also in other ways. There is a cyclical, replay effect created by these repeated lines, as if the narrator were forcing us to linger in the scene by circling back through it again and again, visualizing and revisualizing key images, like the measuring of the hair, or the old woman sitting. It's a haunting, almost cinematic effect—though one that can be confusing to readers who aren't yet sensitized to the value of repetition in oral storytelling.

Akin to repetition, or a subset of it, is the literary device of *parallelism*. Although parallelism necessarily also involves some element of repetition, what I'm referring to here has more to do with iterated syntactic and semantic patterns than with exactly dittoed phrases or episodes. The emphasis is more on the variation than on the identity. This passage from Sally Noble's Chimariko story, "The Bear Girl" (#7), makes for a good illustration:

Her mother hired a good Indian doctor to ask
    what was the matter with the girl.
She was not like people.
She was not like our flesh.
She was not a person.
She was not a human woman.
She was going to turn out to be a bear.
That's what the matter was.

The parallelism of these four middle lines is straightforward, uncomplicated by other phenomena—in effect, a small litany. But things are not always so clearly laid out. The following passage, taken from María Solares's telling of the Chumash "Dog Girl" (#22), is one of the most complex and richly ornamented passages in this collection:

As for the dog girl:
    she had a bracelet,
        a bracelet of fine beads;
    she had a necklace,
        a pendant,
            a pendant of *api* beads,
               of *api* beads;
        a nose stick;
        a basket hat;
    she had many ornaments.
Her hair was all fixed up in a braid wrap—
    she had braid wraps—
        and her apron,
            her apron was of otterskin.
His wife was well dressed,
    she was adorned.

Notice how much of all this sheer poetic repetition is contained and organized within the framework of a single syntactic pattern—the template "she had _____" that introduces the various adornments in the Dog Girl's possession. This syntactic frame leads internally to a run of parallel object noun phrases in the sequence "she had a necklace, / a pendant . . . / a nose stick; / a basket hat." Though some storytellers and stylistic traditions employ more of this type of parallelism than others, there are numerous examples to be found in this volume's selections.

Finally, in this same "Dog Girl" passage, there's another pattern, *incremental repetition,* that has been exploited here by María Solares three separate times. First, "she had a bracelet, / a bracelet of fine beads"; then, "a pendant, / a pendant of *apɨ* beads"; and lastly, "and her apron, / her apron was of otterskin." Each of these repetitions takes the incremental form "X / X + Y," where the second line of the pair repeats the key element of the first and expands it with additional detail. Incremental repetition is a common feature of oral storytelling, and, along with formulaic repetitions, is often found in song as well. (For a more extended discussion of song aesthetics, see the "Notes on Native California Oral Literatures.")

I have tried to be indicative, rather than exhaustive, in this thumbnail sketch of repetition and parallelism in oral poetics. Certainly, there's no single function that repetitions and parallelisms serve. But with close attention and a bit of literary sensibility—a feel for rhythm, scene, and poetry—the careful reader can probably figure out some of the dramatic and rhetorical effects that the narrators are striving for in their performances. Suffice it to say that oral poetics can indeed be extremely intricate and that repetition is an important device in the narrator's toolkit.

As to why this might be so, why repetition, parallelism, and numerical patterning are so pervasive in oral literatures the world over, there is no simple, single reason. Their prevalence stymied nineteenth-century critics of Native American song and narrative, who typically saw these elements as signs of "primitivism" and inferiority. Even pioneering early-twentieth-century critics like Nellie Barnes lacked a sufficiently sophisticated theory of poetics to see them properly. It wasn't really until the 1950s, with Alfred Lord's work on the oral composition of epic poetry (*The Singer of Tales,* 1960), later augmented by developments in performance theory and ethnopoetics led by Hymes and others, that we have finally come to appreciate the significance of these devices, to understand their dynamic role in the process of oral composition itself.[20] For clearly one of the key functions of repetition, especially when abetted by numerical patterning, is to assist narrators in maintaining the structure of their compositions, in terms of both storage in memory and delivery in performance. This is most obviously true of the larger-scale episodic patterns, where the coarse mechanics of plot sequencing come into play, but scholars are increasingly amazed at how fine-grained the rhetorical patterns of oral composition really are. At least some of the smaller-scale repetitions—the poetic and formulaic repetitions, the syntactic parallelisms—may actually be motivated by subtle structural patterns operating at considerably more local levels, in keeping with what Hymes has called *measured verse*.[21] This possibility, though, does not diminish the other roles that repetition plays—in controlling flow, in heightening dramatic effect, in highlighting actions, and in elevating the sheer poetic resonance of the narrative language. Is it art or architecture? Improvisation or design? Poetry or technique? At some point, in the hands of a skilled narrator, the question becomes one of the chicken or the egg. Repetition and parallelism add dimensions of both beauty and intricacy to the performance of verbal art.

Motivation and Characterization

Motives for behavior are often taken for granted, because they are obvious within the culture. After all, when Jack grabs the golden goose and hightails it out the door, the story doesn't stop to explain why he does so. A European audience already knows it's because gold is valuable in that society; the audience shares the ever-present dream of getting rich. The same is true in Native American stories: storytellers don't bother to explain what is plainly understood by all. In fact, when we encounter stories that *do* provide this kind of explanatory information, it can sometimes be a clue that the story was performed in front of a mixed or nonnative audience, or before native listeners who weren't raised traditionally—or even before a solitary linguist.

One of the purposes of providing an introductory essay for each story is to anticipate such confusions and fill in some of the cultural gaps. Sometimes even the storytellers themselves try to do this. Loren Bommelyn added the opening section of his Tolowa story, "Test-ch'as (The Tidal Wave)" (#2), to remind people what precipitated the events he tells about. Over the phone one day, as we were talking through details of his translation, Loren suddenly realized I had been misinterpreting a key passage of dialogue. As a result, he decided to back the story up a bit, in order to frame the myth more formally. Apparently, the old-time narrators Loren learned it from, counting on other Tolowas' familiarity with the myth, picked up the storyline a bit further along, beginning in medias res. But now, thanks to his additions, we can know what happened: the improper behavior of some partying villagers triggered a cataclysmic imbalance of nature, in the form of an earthquake and tidal wave. The arrival of the widow, who should have been in mourning, was the last straw, scandalizing even the dog.

So characterization is often assumed, or "referred to," rather than being explicitly developed as it would be in a novel. Where traditional myths and stories are concerned, the audiences by and large already know what happens and are well acquainted with the quirks and motives of the characters taking part in them—a factor that gives narrators a great deal of latitude in shaping their performances. One consequence of stories being so familiar and oft-told is that characters can seem to behave as they do simply because they are destined to do so, being eternally in the process of acting out the events of the story they are in. Often they seem to have an eerie foreknowledge of their own fates, as if they already "knew their own stories." This quality probably stems from the nature of oral literature itself.

In the end, the stories and songs are just the tip of the iceberg. Many songs are specific to certain dances or ceremonies, performed only at the appropriate point of that one ceremony, whenever it might be held in the annual cycle. And storytelling, particularly of myths, is typically restricted by general cultural prohibition to certain seasons of the year—the rainy winter months in most California cultures. But there is a kind of running, ethnocritical discussion that's carried on by the people in the culture at large—a whole metaliterary conversation—that constantly explores and reexplores the themes of its great stories and the meanings that are to be taken from them. Oral storytellers draw and depend on this ongoing conversation at least as much as they contribute to it.

So human is this tendency to dwell on and in our stories, that it is even possible, with faith, imagination, and hard work, to revive that conversation once the flame has gone out. Ohlone culture, its language and oral literature along with it, was an early casualty of the Contact period in California. Its stories now are known only through the archived fieldnotes of collector J. P. Harrington and a handful of others. Linda Yamane, a Rumsien Ohlone artist, storyteller, and writer living in the Bay Area, speaks movingly about how those scratchy pages have begun to come alive for her, enriching not just her perceptions of nature, but her sense of place in the universe:[22]

> Finding these stories has changed the way I see the world. I can see it like a picture in my mind . . . [N]ow when I go hiking and see Crow, it's not just a crow, it's Crow person from the story, who did these things from our history. It's the same with Hawk—it's not a hawk from a natural history field guide, but Hawk, who with Eagle's help planted the feather in the earth at the bottom of the floodwaters, causing the waters to recede. I recently saw Golden Eagle for the first time, very close up, near my ancestral village site. I could see Eagle and it was just how I pictured him saving the world. The same with Hummingbird, it's all a part of our history.
>
> It's a connection to the ancestors and to this place, to this land where I live and where my ancestors lived. In the course of the work I have been doing [with Harrington's fieldnotes], what feels most important to me is that these stories can now be out in the world for other Ohlone people, so that they can have the same experience. It strengthens our sense of cultural community. . . .
>
> I think in a similar way the stories help non-Indians[, too]. It's not exactly the same, because there is not the ancestral connection, but it's similar in that the stories can help people to feel more connected to the place where they live. Feeling more connected to a place gives them a better understanding—not just a mental understanding, but an emotional understanding. An emotional understanding and connection helps people to feel they are more a part of things and to care for a place. It's easier not to care when you don't have a connection to a place.

In the final analysis, stories must have a place in people's hearts and minds, not just on their lips or in the pages of their books, to be truly part of a living tradition.

Stories are always more than just entertainment. Much of the conscience and philosophy of a culture is expressed, either directly or indirectly, in the myths of its people. It's no different than with the stories and characters of the Bible, the Koran, the Torah: if you are a Christian or a Muslim or a Jew, you have probably *heard* much more about the central events and characters—about Joseph or Mary Magdalen, Adaam or Gibreel, Eve or Noah, their thoughts, their feelings—than is written in the pages of the holy books themselves. Almost anyone raised in a Christian, Islamic, or Jewish culture could provide a more embellished account of the Flood than is actually given in Genesis. The same is true of aspects in Hindu tradition, or any other. No matter how rich the literary canon of a culture may be, the oral tradition that it grew out of, and that embeds it still, is richer by far. And the oral tradition surrounding an oral-literary canon is no different than that of a literary one in this respect.

As you read the translations in this book, then, remember: these are *traditional* songs and stories, most of them, heard time and time again in the course of a lifetime. Except when visitors from afar might be invited to give a telling in the roundhouse or sweat lodge (or in later days, around the kitchen table at home), most traditional stories were not new to their audiences, only newly told. And everybody—except for children, to whom everything is new, and for those readers encountering Indian stories here for the first time—everybody already *knows* what's going to happen, and who does what, and why.

The people these stories were originally intended for were wholly immersed in their world, at home with their own traditions. Readers should not figure they can play catch-up with California cultures—not really, anyway, and maybe not ever.[23] Even cultural outsiders, though, can listen in on the songs and stories as they are translated here—enjoy them and learn from them. The introductions will help readers through the roughest patches, and the notes on suggested readings will carry them further where problems nag or an interest is kindled. In the meantime, Jaime de Angulo's trademark advice to *his* readers may prove indispensable: "When you find yourself searching for some mechanical explanation, if you don't know the answer, invent one. When you pick out some inconsistency or marvelous improbability, satisfy your curiosity like the old Indian folk: 'Well, that's the way they tell that story. I didn't make it up myself!'" Sure, he's being a *bit* disingenuous. After reflection, you will want to know if your guess, the sense you have made of something puzzling, was on the mark. When that happens, you suddenly find yourself right back where you started from—but with one important difference: while you were pondering, you moved on. Keep reading, and after a while, you'll start to get the hang of it. And then, bit by bit, these worlds of song and story will open up for you.

1. Actually, good storytellers often don't have the patience for the work of analysis and translation that comes after the dictation is finished; in such cases, the collector usually works with a friend or relative of the narrator to make the translation.

2. Certainly this is true, in this volume, of Villiana Hyde's collaboration with Eric Elliott, from which is drawn her "Harvest of Songs" (#24). Indeed, we have finally reached a milestone stage of development—long overdue—in California, where some performers (Julian Lang and Loren Bommelyn spring to mind) have begun to translate themselves.

3. In Sapir's early Americanist orthography, *c* and *j* represent "sh" and "zh" sounds, respectively; the ᵉ represents a glottal stop; a *!* (exclamation mark) glottalizes the preceding stop or affricate; and the ' (open single quote) indicates aspiration. Both macron and circumflex indicate vowel length, and superscript vowels are "whispered."

With the exception of the first two lines, all the narrative verbs in this excerpt contain a quotative suffix, "they say" or "it is said." This element has been translated only in those lines where it appears to receive a special emphasis.

4. In later years, when typesetting costs began to chip away at the budgets of publication series like the *UCPAAE* and others, editors switched to another design format, that of facing pages. This format became the standard for subsequent text series, like *UCPAAE's* successor, UCPL. In consequence, the translation portion was constrained to become much more literal, because the loss of the interlinear element of the old-style format meant that the single, facing-page translation now became the only avenue to an accurate interpretation of the original. The result was the rise of a series of purely technical publications that were drastically less accessible and appealing to the casual reader or the student of literature than the interlinear publications of old (not that the latter were not technical and arcane-looking as well). Their volumes now contained only linguistic translations, not literary ones, despite the best efforts of most authors to serve both masters. As William Shipley says in the introduction to his 1963 *Maidu Texts and Dictionary* (UCPL 33), "Although I have done my best to practice the art of translation, . . . I have subordinated such efforts to my responsibility as a linguist—to the providing of a key for the forms of the original" (8). In the end, the need for utmost fidelity toward the source language will always outweigh considerations of aesthetics and felicity in the target language—and rightly so, where that choice must be made. But a price is always paid.

5. Indeed, some have claimed (Hymes 1981, Tedlock 1983) that such translations can actually impede our understanding of Native American songs and stories as works of verbal art.

6. Hymes argues this case very strongly in his book *'In vain I tried to tell you': Essays in Native American Ethnopoetics* (1981), as does Tedlock in *The Spoken Word and the Work of Interpretation* (1983), though the two writers come at the problem from very different directions. There are several important anthologies of ethnopoetic writings and translations: Brian Swann's *On the Translation of Native American Literatures* (1992) and *Smoothing the Ground: Essays in Native American Oral Literature* (1983), Swann and Arnold Krupat's *Recovering the Word: Essays on Native American Literature* (1987), Karl Kroeber's *Traditional American Indian Literatures: Texts and Interpretations* (1981), and Joel Sherzer and Anthony Woodbury's *Native American Discourse: Poetics and Rhetoric* (1987).

7. In short, the literary value of a text is inextricably intertwined with its formal poetic structure, which is in turn intertwined with the circumstances of its performance. Any treatment of a song or story that does not begin with the recognition that it is a work of verbal art, and does not recognize the effect of performance dynamics on form, and does not try in some way to reflect performance features in terms of presentational form, is bound to misrepresent the text on those levels.

8. Both these units, and many of the others besides, exemplify a common American Indian rhetorical pattern that Dell Hymes (1977) refers to abstractly as "Onset—Ongoing—Outcome." In group 5, the plucking is the Onset (it's the action that pushes Grizzly Bear over the edge), the biting is the Ongoing (the action of the group as a whole, seen in progress), and the killing is the Outcome. Such rhetorical "templates" help oral performers structure their compositions.

9. Dell Hymes's hypothesis (1981) that the world's oral-literary traditions tend to prefer rhetorical patterns based on groupings of threes and fives, for some, and twos and fours, for others, has been tested many times by many different scholars (for instance, Bright 1982 and Kinkade 1987). The evidence for Yana, to my mind, is somewhat ambiguous, though a tendency toward threes and fives (as in the passages under discussion here) is frequently apparent.

10. However, Luthin (1991) presents a methodology for recovering or reconstructing at least some live prosodic information from dictated texts.

11. Different practitioners have different criteria for defining lines, so this statement is meant to be a general one. Tedlock, for instance, typically works with a pause-based line defined by silence, whereas Hymes works with a syntactically based line defined largely by clause boundary. Others (Woodbury 1987, McLendon 1982) work with intonationally defined lines. Woodbury (1987) points out that all three of these phenomena (and others besides) are in fact interlocking components of a language's overall rhetorical system and that any ethnopoetic analysis of a text that does not take all such aspects into account is bound to be inadequate.

12. In the case of ethnopoetic analyses done on texts taken down by phonetic dictation, the lines are technically only reconstructions of what the actual lines of the original performance must have been, based on syntactic and structural clues such as repetition, particle placement, and the like.

13. For an extended discussion of some of the parameters of this disagreement and of the development of the ethnopoetics movement in general, see my *Restoring the Voice in Yanan Traditional Narrative* (1991).

14. We are not used to seeing genuine spoken language in print. Most interviews in books and magazines are either heavily edited or are given by people—politicians, actors, novelists, academics—who are professional writers or speakers themselves, whose speech is very "written" to begin with. Of course, storytellers are professional talkers, too, but their craft is entirely an oral one, not channeled into written grooves.

15. It's not that we don't have other significant numbers—sevens, fours, fives, twos, tens, and dozens all have roles to play in Western symbolism. It's just that the number three has premier cultural dominance; other numbers are subordinate to it.

16. I refer here to the dialectic between the Chomskyan theory of linguistic universalism and the earlier theory of linguistic relativity, also known as the "Sapir-Whorf Hypothesis"—surely two of the most exciting intellectual conjectures in the history of human thought, even given the ultimate failure of relativity in its strong form.

17. Our long-standing literary tradition has made us fairly impatient with full-blown episodic repetition, and there is a strong tendency in written literature for the second and third episodes in a sequence to be progressively truncated or even dropped entirely. The example here shows that the same thing can happen in oral performance. But whether the choice to do so stems from an intrinsic impatience (perhaps the mood of the storyteller or the attentiveness of the audience controls this) or marks a concession to presumed European narrative tastes (linguists and anthropologists must often seem to Native storytellers to be glancing at their watches—and they even pay hourly rates!), it is difficult to know.

18. More precisely, what we're talking about here is *global form/content parallelism,* in current ethnopoetic terminology (see Hymes 1981 and Sherzer and Woodbury 1987 for further discussions of this and related concepts).

19. Keep in mind, though, that you're just dealing with translations in this volume; if you really think you are on to something, the only ultimate arbiter is the original-language text.

20. These in turn built on Propp's earlier codification of episodic and motif patterning, *Morphology of the Folktale* (1968 [1928]).

21. The best single source for treatment of this notion is Hymes's *'In vain I*

tried to tell you': Essays in Native American Ethnopoetics (1981). Sherzer and Wood-bury's *Native American Discourse: Poetics and Rhetoric* (1987) makes a good source as well.

22. Linda Yamane, quoted in excerpt from Lauren S. Teixeira, "Like the Air We Breathe," *News from Native California* 9.4 (1995): 50.

23. As Bill Bevis (1974) has rather famously said, "We won't get Indian culture as cheaply as we got Manhattan."

I

SELECTIONS

Who is tending this sun, [this] moon?
Who moves them around?
There must be somebody to look after this world . . .

Nisenan prayer
Ralph Beals, "Ethnology of the Nisenan"

CREATION SONGS

1A
Deserted it was,
Deserted it was,
Deserted, the earth.

First they appeared,
First they came out,

First Mukat,
First Tamayowet,

First the chiefs,
First the ancients.

1B
His heart roared,
His heart thundered,
Water and mud roared.

Then outside, toward the door,
Themselves they lay down,
Mukat outside,
Tamayowet then,
Themselves they lay down:

Where it was bare, where it was lonely,
Themselves they laid down,
Where dust was, where mist was.

Cupeño song, Salvadora Valenzuela, 1920
Paul Faye, collector

1

Kwaw Labors to Form a World

ATSUGEWI
1996

DARRYL BABE WILSON

It is said by the old ones that a thought was floating in the vastness. Thought manifested itself into a voice. Voice matured into Yeja, an everlasting medicine song. Song sang itself into being as Kwaw, Silver Gray Fox. By continuing the song, Kwaw created all that we know. He sang the universe into being. His singing spawned Reason, but not sufficiently, so we shall never know all that moves within this universe.

It was Song, infusing itself with both beauty and power, that caused the outer world to tremble and the inner world to quake, and instructed the stars to become one with the vastness and the vastness to become one with the stars.

The "new" universe created a new kind of emptiness, within which Kwaw grew lonesome—wanting somebody to talk with. Laboring over what to do with so much nothingness, he decided to make another being, much like himself. Some haste on Kwaw's part caused that being to be created with a defect: vanity. That being came to my people as Ma'kat'da, Old Coyote.

Kwaw instructed Ma'kat'da to sleep while he busied himself with making "something shiny." Kwaw sang for a million years or more, and in the distance something shiny appeared, a mist. Mist contained no voice and no song, but it possessed a magic.

Kwaw kicked Ma'kat'da awake, showing him the shiny mist. They sang together and Mist moved ever to them. It approached silently, like a soap bubble on a summer afternoon, floating upon the breeze. Kwaw caught it in his hands and it rested there. Ma'kat'da thought that Kwaw could not possibly know what to do with Mist, so he grabbed for it. There was a struggle. In the conflict, Kwaw dropped the mist. Ma'kat'da and Kwaw wrestled over the possession of Mist for eons. Meanwhile, Mist dropped slowly down, ever down. And, just before Mist struck Nothingness, Kwaw broke free from Ma'kat'da, reached under it, and gently nudged it back into the safety of his hands.

Here, then, if there ever was one, is "the beginning," according to the keepers of our ancestral knowledge. For it was from the birth of the mist sung into being that all of the stars and moons of the universe were created; earth, also. Our earth, they say, is an infant, being fulfilled after all of the rest of the universe.

It is said that Mist took on substance, forming into something much more solid. It became more pliable, like bread dough, and they kneaded it and stretched it as they sang and danced. They danced harder and fragments separated from the mist-gel and moved out in a vast circle, tumbling ever away. These became the stars and the Milky Way.

Kwaw labored to form a world. But everything he created, Ma'kat'da changed. Vanity caused Ma'kat'da to think that he knew best. Kwaw created, Ma'kat'da changed. Then Ma'kat'da grew angry because all he could accomplish was "change." He became destructive.

Seeing that he could not teach Ma'kat'da, Kwaw decided to remove himself. He entered his *chema-ha,* his sweat lodge, lifted the center post, and dropped down through into this world, carefully replacing the center post so Ma'kat'da would not see where it was disturbed. When he arrived here, there was only water. Kwaw sang land into being, then sang a *chema-ha* to rest upon the land. He created himself a fresh home upon new earth—with no Ma'kat'da!

Then Kwaw set about making the world as we know it today, thinking that Ma'kat'da would be satisfied with the world beyond the sky and would never come to this one. He made all that we know: the geese and salmon, the mornings and the mountains, the rivers and streams, the seasons and the songs of all the birds. He made it wonderful and, it is said, he made it good.

Ma'kat'da searched for Kwaw in the world beyond the sky and could not find him. So Ma'kat'da, whose best power is fire, found a little basket in Kwaw's abandoned *chema-ha* and threatened it with cremation if it did not tell. Little Willow Basket, not wanting to perish in flames, said, "He went through there," pointing to the center post of the *chema-ha*. So Ma'kat'da, employing his own magic, came to this world like Kwaw after all . . .

This explanation came to me through Ramsey Bone Blake, who received it from White Horse Bob. White Horse Bob was given the song that Kwaw sang upon the inception of Life. The song was his *damagoomi,* his spirit helper. Ramsey couldn't remember the whole song, but often recalled fragments of it. However, he was not allowed to sing it, for the song already belonged to White Horse Bob.

Within this magic my people dwelled just a short time ago. More recently, our home has become the legal possession of strangers. We have been restricted from approaching our places of power and spirit. We have become mute witnesses while others despoil the air, the land, the wildlife, the rivers, and the ocean waters. It is said that Kwaw created this world for original native people, not for wanderers. But it is the wanderers who have brought a different rule, saying that our ancient laws are of no value.

This may be one of the reasons why we are in a spiritual quandary: not knowing how to become a functioning part of the invading American society, not remembering how to sustain a strict connection with the "knowing" that is our origin—and trembling in the presence of both.

With these thoughts in mind, then, proceed through the following "lesson-legends" realizing that it was not long ago that there was great magic in the land of my people—of all our Native people. That there was a wonder in the patterns of everyday life, and that there was much singing and dancing. For these were our instructions when the earth began turning around the sun, and the sun began moving with the universe, to a destination that may never be known to any of us but Kwaw.

NORTHWESTERN CALIFORNIA

You come upon a place you've never seen before,
and it has awesome beauty.
Everything above you,
   below you,
      and around you is so pure—

   that is the beauty we call *merwerksergerh,*
   and the pure person is also *merwerksergerh.*

            Yurok, Florence Shaughnessy, at Requa
        Peter Matthiessen, "Stop the GO Road"

Why is the water rough,
    by Rekʷoy at the river mouth?
Why is the water rough,
    by Rekʷoy at the river mouth?

By Rekʷoy at the river mouth,
    that is why they watch it,
        by Rekʷoy at the river mouth.
Near the houses the surf runs further up,
    by Rekʷoy at the river mouth.

Why is the water rough,
    by Rekʷoy at the river mouth?
Near the houses the surf runs further up,
    by Rekʷoy at the river mouth.

Why is the water rough,
    by Rekʷoy at the river mouth?
Near the houses the waves break further up,
        by Rekʷoy at the river mouth.

High in the air by Rekʷoy,
    that is why they watch it,
        by Rekʷoy at the river mouth.
Near the houses the surf runs further up,
        by Rekʷoy at the river mouth.

Why is the water rough,
    by Rekʷoy at the river mouth?
Near the houses the waves break further up,
    by Rekʷoy at the river mouth.

Yurok doctor dance song
R. H. Robins and Norma McCloud
"Five Yurok Songs: A Musical and Textual Analysis"

2

Test-ch'as (The Tidal Wave)

TOLOWA

1985

LOREN BOMMELYN, AUTHOR AND TRANSLATOR

INTRODUCTION BY LOREN BOMMELYN

The Tolowa are a Pacific Coast Athabascan-speaking people of Northern California and Southern Oregon. Their terrain is heavily wooded with climax redwood and Douglas fir forests and accustomed to heavy rainfall. The rivers of the past were choked with trout, steelhead, and several species of salmon. The ocean provided whale, sea lion, and innumerable species of fish. The coastal tide-pools produced a rich diversity of crustacea and bivalves. The land, too, yielded its plenty: the annual harvest of fruits, nuts, and herbs. The control-burned forests and prairies of the hills ran with great herds of elk and deer. And the skies were blackened with hundreds of thousands of fowl from the Pacific flyway.

The rich food supply afforded the Tolowa a heavy population and encouraged the development of high customs, elaborate protocol, and a complex legal system. They built their homes from hand-split and hand-hewed redwood planks. The Tolowa seagoing canoes were famous up and down the coast. Their exogamous marriage customs resulted in a multilingual society with a diverse system of religious practices. The Headmen controlled and protected their village districts, where dentalia currency ranked supreme in deciding all legal matters—torts, damages, marriages, and all the rest of it. These men were responsible for implementing and carrying out the high ceremonies surrounding our foremost responsibility: for men and women alike to walk in balance with creation.

But the life of the Tolowa changed forever in the 1850s with the arrival of the Europeans. Their rapacious passions and disease destroyed the Tolowa and their neighbors. Thousands of people perished. The Europeans pushed and drove the Tolowa population into two separate concentration camps, one at Siletz, Oregon, and the other at Hoopa, California. The Tututni and Chetco people are our northern divisions. The residual population—of no more than two hundred individuals who escaped the camps and returned to their homeland—established the basis for the current Tolowa population. Out of this painful past the Tolowa have survived. My great-grandparents survived the seven-year holocaust that began in 1853. Their children were born at the end of the nineteenth century, their children's children (my parents) in the 1920s and 1930s. I was born in 1956.

Aunt Laura was nineteen years older than my mother and served as my grandma. Auntie and Mom did everything together. The annual food cycles followed one after another. First was the spring routine of gardening, seaweed drying, beef fattening, and salmonberry and thimbleberry picking. Next was the summer routine of smelt drying, clamming, strawberry and blackberry picking, and peach, apricot, and pear canning. And last came the fall routine of acorn and herb gathering, the making of deer jerky, huckleberry picking, and the netting of steelhead and Chinook salmon. Every day after school, we would run down to Auntie's house. She fed us, and we played continental rummy and cribbage. Then Auntie would tell us stories. I could envision how our village looked during her youth. I could see how our village looked when Grandma Alice was young and when Great-grandma Deliliah was alive. Many times it would get dark, and we would sleep at Auntie's.

The fall nights were gillnet-setting time. The State of California had long since illegalized our livelihood, but this made no difference to us. "Paddle quietly. Never smoke out on the water: the game warden can see the red cherry from a long way off. Wear a sweatshirt: the buttons of a shirt will hang up in the net and drown you. Club the fish with a quiet sock to the head." No one could gut and fillet a salmon with the skill and finesse that Auntie and Mom had. Each salmon was carefully washed and scaled. The stomach was split open exactly, and the entrails and black blood removed with precision. The salmon's head and fins were removed, and then it was filleted. They stripped the fillets with care. Each jar was packed to perfection. They hung long strips of salmon in the smokehouse. A small, cool alder-wood fire sent the curing smoke wafting through the salmon strips. My favorite dish at fish-cleaning time was salmon-head and egg chowder.

The winter rains of Del Norte County were extremely marked during my youth. The rain would pelt out of the skies for ten days and nights from its high ceilings, while powerful winds and clouds cloaked the coastal plain. These winds pounded the top of Milichundun Mountain across the Smith River from our home place, Nelechundun. The air was warm and magical, astir and wild. Back in the eastern mountains at the headwaters of the river, the annual rainfall could reach twelve feet at Bear Basin Summit. These rains would send us scurrying over mountains, through redwood forests, fields, and the riparian habitats of the river and estuaries. Soaked to the bone, we panted, cheeks flushed and red, lost in time, lost to the eternity of our ancestors. Aunt Laura counted the days of rain and the swift slapping waves of the river to predict if it would flood.

"Gee, maybe we'll have the Great Flood again," she might say. "One time the people began to go against the laws of the Creator. That was the time when Dog spoke to the people. This is why in Grandma Deliliah's time you did not talk to dogs. If they were to answer you, the world might come to an end." You see, a dog speaking to humans is an indication of catastrophic destruction. A few years ago, someone had recorded the Christmas carol "Jingle Bells" with a dog barking out the tune of the song. The radio station owner, Bill Stamps, played it over the air. Ella Norris, one of our elders, called him up and chewed him out. "What are you trying to do, make the world come to an end?" (This belief had changed in my family during Grandpa Billie Henry's time, though. He and Grandma Alice always used to "dog talk" with the dogs. And we still "dog talk" with our own dogs today.)

The following account of Test-ch'as is an illustration of the powerful ethical values of the traditional Tolowa. The outside pressures of modern American socialization and religions are eroding these values. But the traditionalists have a strong sense of what living right means. "If you can't do it right, don't do it!" Each activity of daily life is presided over by the "One Who Watches Over Us." At the time of our genesis, K'wan'-lee-shvm laid out the universe and the laws we are to live by. To live correctly brings us blessings. To live outside these laws is to invite strife and trouble into one's life. The Test-ch'as account is a testimony and a warning to us of what happens when we fall outside the balance of the universe.[1]

The Test-ch'as account is a template of inspiration and replenishment. From the nearly complete annihilation of the Tolowas from the face of the earth during the 1850s, our population has now reached more than one thousand members. It has happened again as it did in Test-ch'as: that a man and his wife live together.

NOTES

1. The opening section of this story, set in italics, comes from a different version of the myth than that on which the rest of the translation is based. Because the main version of the story presented here begins with the disaster itself, leaving the "why" unspoken, Bommelyn added this scene onto the beginning to explain the events that precipitated the disaster.

The Tolowa place-name *Enmai* ('Big Mountain'; rhymes with "Hen-my") corresponds to the peak known as Mount Emily on maps of the region. ("Emily" is an Anglicization of the original Tolowa form.) The word *Chit-dvn* is pronounced "Cheat-done."— HWL

FURTHER READING

Philip Drucker produced an excellent ethnography of the Tolowa, *The Tolowa and Their Southwest Oregon Kin.* Richard Gould's article,

"Tolowa," in the California volume of the Smithsonian *Handbook* presents a useful summary. Jack Norton's *Genocide in Northwestern California* provides information on how the Tolowa fared in the post-Contact period. Bommelyn has two books of language-teaching materials, *Now You're Speaking Tolowa*, and *Xus We-Yo': Tolowa Language* (with Berneice Humphrey). (The latter contains the glossed Tolowa-language version of the story translated here.) Allogan Slagle's article, "The Native American Tradition and Legal Status: Tolowa Tales and Tolowa Places," explores the legal standing of territorial references contained in traditional tales. Finally, Bommelyn may be heard singing Tolowa songs on a recording made by Charlotte Heth, *Songs of Love, Luck, Animals, and Magic.*

TEST-CH'AS (THE TIDAL WAVE)

At Chit-dvn Village, all the young men and young women, they were partying there, at the center of town. At dusk they had partied. One alone of all of them told his sister, "Our grandmother teaches us, 'Don't you go outside at dusk.'"

A widow also joined with them, then. She, too, started laughing around with them there.

Truthfully, then, a dog sat up and spoke out loud: "You all will see what's going to happen!"

The young man and the young woman, they ran to their home.

"Gram! A dog has spoken here!"

"I knew it was going to happen this way," their grandmother said. "You two go to Mount Enmai now. Grab some dentalia, and a smelt net also. To Enmai you must go—quickly, both of you! Wait for no one."

"Gram, what are you going to do?"

"I am old. I am going to die. You must go quickly now, both of you . . ."

It was during the fall when the ground shook. Twice the ground had shaken.

"Well now! Something bad is going to happen. You had better go look now," the man said.

Then the ground shook again.

"You two run to the beach," he told the boys. "You two paddle the boat out to sea. Should the boat run aground on the sand, the ocean tidal wave will come that way. If it happens like that, you two return again quickly to this side. Then we will know what is going to happen."

The ocean was extremely smooth. Not a bit of wind blew. When those two paddled toward the beach, it happened just that way.

"We ran ashore almost to the sand," they said.

Then they put all the canoes in a safe place. Then the ground shook again.

"If it shakes the ground from east and west, the ocean will rise up."

Then the ground shook from the west. Everything standing on the ground fell over. The water began to rise in the rivers. The river ran over its banks.

One teenage girl amongst them was having her time of the month. With her brother, she ran up into the mountains. They kept looking behind them as they were running. As they ran, the ocean nearly caught them. Everything that lived there turned into snakes. The snakes all slithered into the ocean.

These two people ran up on top of a ridge. The water, rising up in a tide, nearly ran them over. Everyone who lived upon the earth ran toward the mountains. The water, too, rose up the mountain from the east—all the rivers were running over, is why. Everything alive was floating alongside the mountain. When the water ran over them, they all turned into snakes.

"Let's run along the ridge now," he told his sister.

Then they ran to the top of Mount Enmai, and saw that the water had flooded over the Earth. Then all this water began to boil.

When the water had run almost over the top of Mount Enmai, the boy told his sister, "Stick your nose ornament into the ground. The water will rise up no further than there."

Then she stuck her flicker feather in the ground. Really, the water rose up no further! The young man built a fire. Then all who did not drown stood on the mountaintop. The Eastern people, the Western people, all perished.

Everywhere the fog came in. Nowhere could land be seen. All night they could not sleep. All night they kept the fire going. When it was morning everywhere, they looked around. Only mountaintops were sticking out of the water. Mount Enmai's peak floated southward. These two stayed there ten nights.

All those dangerous ones who live in the forest, they, too, were standing on Mount Enmai's peak. All of them were afraid—they didn't want to go down to the foot of the mountain. Ten days passed by. The young man went to the foot of the mountain.

When he returned, he told his sister, "Many large creatures and small creatures are lying around everywhere."

The ocean had left them there.

"You and I will go down the mountain."

His sister told him, "All right."

They descended to the valley. The girl was afraid, until her brother told her, "Nothing will harm you. All of them everywhere are lying dead. Do not be afraid of it. Let's seek out our home."

When those two found their way back there, everything was nothing there. Their house was also gone. Everywhere only sand was lying. They recognized nothing. There, where they used to live, there was nothing. Everywhere they went, the dead ones had started to stink.

"Where will we live?" one asked. The other said, "Anywhere we live is going to be good."

Then this teenager told his sister, "You sit here. Wait for me. I am going to the bottom to see what I can see. Perhaps some people are living there."

Before he went, he prepared food. He took it there to a safe place. They found a piece of fresh whale tail. The whale meat was cut up for drying.

"This meat will be good for you," he said.

Then the young man walked to the south. He looked for people everywhere. As he was walking, he saw only dead ones. He walked far into the south. He saw not a soul still alive. Then he walked to the east. He walked all night and all day. He saw only small lakes. Then the lakes became a gully in there. In the east, he walked along the border of his land. There, also, he found not a soul alive. He also saw no deer tracks. He walked far to the north there. He saw coyote tracks there.

Then he thought, "I suppose another mountain poked out. Different people must still be alive. It will be good if I see some people."

He saw nothing. Then he walked to the beach. The beach was covered only with sand. As he walked southward, nothing stood. Not a fir tree stood. Finally he found one tree, a crabapple. It alone had not become a snake when the ocean washed over it. Then again he walked southward. He had walked almost to his home when the ocean began to look like blood.

Finally, he returned there to where his sister was living. He told her, "Nowhere did I see a man. Everywhere all of them were drowned, I suppose. I walked ten days and ten nights. I walked continually. All the water running down is not good. On the tenth night I thought, 'I wanted to find a man alive for you to marry. Also, I wanted to find a woman alive for me to marry. That is the reason I walked over the whole earth.' So let us marry each other. There is no one else anywhere still alive for us to marry."

They dug a round depression in the ground for a house. There they lived, those two, together.

In time she gave birth to a son.

"We shall make a better house. Let's go down to the beach," the man said.

Something was floating out on the ocean. All day they watched it. When it was about sunset they could still see it. Then they went together to their house.

"Let us look again," the man said.

When it was growing daylight outside, they went together. Really, there was a redwood log there! They went together to the edge of the shore. There were whale ribs and body bones piled there.

"Let's split the log," the man said.

They split the log into boards with the whale bones. They pounded the wedges with rocks. They made many planks. They packed the boards to the bank. There they built a house, a good one.

One day, he dipped for smelts there. Another woman came paddling along from the south in a canoe. They too married.

When again another year had passed, the head wife gave birth to another one. She gave birth to a girl child. When these two in turn became man and woman, they married. When it happened again and again this way, there came to be a great number of people. They scattered all over, everywhere. In every place, all the men lived together with their wives.

3

"The Young Man from Serper" and Other Stories

YUROK

1951, 1985–1988

FLORENCE SHAUGHNESSY, NARRATOR

R. H. ROBINS, COLLECTOR AND TRANSLATOR

JEAN PERRY, COLLECTOR

INTRODUCTION BY JEAN PERRY

These three stories come from the Yurok Indians, who still inhabit their ancestral homeland along the lower forty miles of the Klamath River and the surrounding coastline in Northwest California, near the Oregon border. Here they continue to harvest salmon, eels, and winter steelhead, to hunt deer and elk, and to follow many of the old lifeways and traditions along with other more modern pursuits.

All of these stories were told by Mrs. Florence Shaughnessy, a Yurok elder who was born in 1902 and lived in Requa, near the mouth of the Klamath. In 1951 Robert H. Robins was recruited as a young Ph.D. by the Survey of California Indian Languages at the University of California at Berkeley to come from London and do fieldwork on a California Indian language. Mary Haas assigned him to do a grammar, lexicon, and collection of texts of the Yurok language. He came to the

Klamath and worked with Mrs. Shaughnessy during the winter and spring of 1951, left for a time, then returned in the late summer, during the height of the salmon run, to finish his work. In 1958 he published *The Yurok Language.*

When I met him in 1986 and talked to him about his fieldwork, he still remembered the place, the people, and much of the language in detail and with great fondness. He told me many things about the circumstances of his work that year—that he spent part of his time in Michigan at the Linguistic Society of America's Summer Institute working up the grammar, lexicon, and texts, and that he used his return visit to check the details and fill in the gaps in his data. During that year the Survey was able to purchase its first tape recorder, which was shared among all the researchers in the field. He said that he (along with Bill Bright, who was then working on Karuk just upriver) was able to keep the recorder for two weeks, rather than the usual one. He told me that on his return visit, Mrs. Shaughnessy was very busy working on the Ark, her floating restaurant, and that he was worried that he might be bothering her, so he tried to minimize the bother. (Ironically, she once told me that Robins was sometimes in too much of a hurry to take down detailed explanations, that he would run into the kitchen and say, "What's the word for so-and-so?" and then run back out again.) "The Young Man from Serper" is one of the stories that Robins recorded with that tape recorder in the Yurok language and translated into English.

I, too, worked with Mrs. Shaughnessy, although much later in her life, from the end of 1985 until she passed away in 1988. I, too, was working for the Survey when I first came to Yurok country. The first goal of our work together was to record stories. The two stories I have selected here are reminiscences from her childhood, in contrast to the old, formal, and mythical "Young Man from Serper." Though she told them to me in both Yurok and English, I have decided to use the English versions here, because they directly reflect her voice and storytelling style in English, without the mediation of a translator. They are transcribed verbatim, with only minor editing.

When she told me the story about Blind Bill, we were sitting in her room, looking out the window at the hillside where it happened, and she was pointing out where the buildings once stood (most of them are gone now). So this story has always held a sense of immediate reality for

FIGURE 1. Florence Shaughnessy.
Copyright 1988 Jean Perry.

me, and conveys a feeling of Requa in its boomtown days when the canneries were still in operation, with the old Indian way of life mingling with that of the newcomers. The owl in the story, of course, foretells death, and one way to circumvent that message is to "kill the messenger," the owl.

"Ragged Ass Hill" is a steep mountainside leading down to the beach south of Crescent City, California. The name is derived from the experience of a settler in the 1860s. Wagon drivers would usually tie a log to the wagon to hold it back. The present Highway 101 is slightly east of the wagon road described in this story but is still quite steep. Nowadays as I drive through that area, I think of my daughter, who is Mrs. Shaughnessy's niece and who is about the same age as Mrs. Shaughnessy was then, and I wonder how she would manage such a trip. These stories show how rapid—just a few generations—the transition from the old ways to the frontier to modern times has been in this region of California, one of the last areas of the Continental United States to be settled.

"The Young Man from Serper" was one of Mrs. Shaughnessy's favorite stories. Her mother was from Serper, and this story was handed down within her family. I believe Mrs. Shaughnessy learned it from her grandmother, who spoke only Yurok. It is a mythical tale, a journey across a mythical geography during the time long ago when animals were like people and the idealized world that parallels this one on earth was more readily accessible than it is now. Such journeys often provide the framework for Yurok myths.

In the myth, the notion of the white deer is highly significant, because the Yurok regarded them as sacred. Likewise, the white sand on the other shore signals that it is a special place, since our local beaches have sand that is dark gray to black. Oregos is a tall, upright rock that stands at the mouth of the Klamath River. It is considered to have once been a person, a very long time ago, and there are stories about it as well. Going out the mouth on the eleventh breaker is not a case of number symbolism; the eleventh breaker is simply said to be the smallest one, the one on which it is easiest to pass through the rough place where the river current and the surf collide.

Oddly enough, Mrs. Shaughnessy was not entirely satisfied with the version of this story as it appears here, as she told it into Robins's tape recorder. Her main criticism was that parts of the story had been left out. Early in our work together, she told me a very different version of it in English. It seems that when the young man was leaving to return home, a few of the people there wanted to rescue Coyote, so "all the animals with teeth" went and chewed holes in their boats so that Coyote would be sure to leave. And when the young man returned home, his grandmother (and a grandfather) were still alive. The moral of the story as she told it to me was that it is good to take care of the old people—very different from the moral of the Robins version, which is that one should not want too much. We continued to work on this story on and off during our time together but never really completed a definitive version. It is clear to me that Mrs. Shaughnessy knew several different versions of this story.

These three stories are but a very small sample of the wealth and variety of Mrs. Shaughnessy's repertoire. She, in turn, was but one of a number of valued Yurok storytellers from her generation. Although the Yurok oral tradition continues on in various ways, the Yurok language is severely endangered today, because only the oldest people speak it fluently. And as the language is endangered, so this repertoire of stories—indeed, a whole way of *telling* stories—is endangered, too.

For a cultural overview, start with Arnold Pilling's article "Yurok" in the California volume of the Smithsonian *Handbook.* R. H. Robins combines grammar, eight texts (including "The Young Man from Serper"), and a Yurok-English vocabulary in *The Yurok Language: Grammar, Texts, Lexicon.* Alfred L. Kroeber's *Yurok Myths,* published posthumously, is a rich and important collection of traditional narratives, mostly told in English, drawn from a wide variety of Yurok storytellers; it includes some stylistic and folkloristic analysis of the texts.

"THE YOUNG MAN FROM SERPER" AND OTHER STORIES

BLIND BILL AND THE OWL

In the old days,
right up there,
there used to be a flat.
Brizzard's used to have a store there.
Above there they have a salt house,
and then above that they had a big hall house where people
   would dance.
They put on Christmas plays and everything in there.
And a little above that was a jail house.

When an owl comes and starts making noise around your home,
it's bad luck.
Mama's cousin was Blind Bill,
Starwen Bill.
He lived with us.
She came and got him.
She says,
   "There's an owl, now,
     making noise right out here."

And he says,
    "Pick me up some flat rocks,
    like that.
    I want three,
    three rocks."

So she went out with the lantern and picked up the rocks.
He said,
    "Don't bring them in the house.
    Give them to me when I get out there,
    and then you show me the direction,"
      because he was blind.
    "Show me the direction."

While he was getting his directions this owl made noise again,
so he knew right where.
I guess he had already said something to those rocks,
blessed them or whatever.
He threw them down there,
and then there was not another sound.

Early in the morning,
as soon as he got up,
he told Mom,
    "Get those kids up.
    I want them to get that owl."
And so we got up and went around there.
We looked in the hall there,
and we looked around by the jail,
all around.
And we found it,
we saw it.
By golly, he killed that owl!
That blind man killed that owl in the nighttime.

RAGGED ASS HILL

With us,
we lived here,

and it was only toward the last that we had hard times.
But at first Dad used to go out and gamble.
Sometimes he'd go to Crescent City and stay three or four nights
    playing Indian cards.
He'd take his drum,
and he was a good singer.
He'd take his team.
They'd go up there and play the Smith Rivers.
There were two or three different tribes of Indians up there all in
    the same area,
but they spoke their own different dialect.
They'd go up there and play them.
Sometimes they'd lose and come home pretty poor.
But then Dad had a lot of friends in Crescent City.
He always took his wagon and the team when he went.
So then he'd stop and borrow money from the friends,
and then stop the wagon and make all the friends walk up.

Oh! You don't know what they would call it—
Ragged Ass Hill!
Boy,
to bring freight up that hill!
Oh my goodness!
You almost had to get out and help the horses.

I must have been eight or nine years old,
because I was always a big girl for my age.
Something went wrong with Dad's eyes.
And there was nobody that could drive.
We had a little buggy,
one with those little tops like you see in pictures now,
a little black buggy.
Well, they said,
    "Florence is the only one that can drive,"
because I used to drive the team getting the hay in.
    "She can drive."

Well,
Dad said,

"What about Ragged Ass Hill?"
They said,
    "Florence will drive,"
and he had to take me because there was no one else.
His eyes were blind then,
they were hurt so bad.
So somebody said,
    "Jimmy,
    why don't you cut down a good-sized pine tree up at the top
        there?
    Take your saw and your axe and yank the rope and tie that in
        the back.
    Then the horses will have to pull that."

So that's how,
using the brakes,
I got down that hill.
We got down to Cushing Creek,
and even then we had Indians living there.
There used to be three little huts there,
and there were three Indians,
one old man and two women.
They looked like they were blind to me.
But Dad talked to them;
they knew Jimmy.
And they blessed him and wished him luck.

We still has five miles to go.
They say that beach is five miles long.
You see,
we had to make that beach while the tide was out.
Because at high tide you had to seek the sand roads in the back,
and sometimes they weren't even passable.
You'd get stuck.
So we had to hurry across there.
But we made it.
I got to the stable.

All I know is that they called that hill Ragged Ass Hill.

It seems that some men came down through there,
and it was so brushy that they just tore their pants to shreds
   by the time they got down to the bottom of the hill.
That's why they named it Ragged Ass Hill.
It was a bad one.
It's still there.

THE YOUNG MAN FROM SERPER

Once upon a time an old woman lived up the river, and she had her grandson there with her. It was difficult for her to look after her grandson. The
boy was very small, but as he began to grow up it turned out that all he
would do was to go down to the water's edge and was never done with
fishing for trout; whatever he caught he gave to his grandmother. And
then the old woman began to live better because the boy was always catching something in his fishing. He began to get bigger and then he would
catch all sorts of birds, and the old woman would say, "Child, this one's
feather is pretty; you will make something with this; we will put it away."

Then he quite grew up and became a young man, and it so turned out
that all he did was to hunt. And once it seemed as if something said to
him, "Go way up into the hills," and he saw lying there a tiny white
fawn. He took it and carried it away and felt very pleased. He said,
"Look, grandmother, I have caught this and will make it a pet." The
old woman was very glad. It so turned out that his pet ran around there;
whenever the young man went anywhere his pet would often run right
on ahead of him. The pet grew up and it often happened that it disappeared in these runs. He would look for it and frequently found it high
up in the hills.

Once the young man woke up, looked, and searched in vain for his pet.
It was not there. Then he ran straight off to look where else it could
have gone. He also asked his grandmother, "Haven't you seen my pet,
Grandmother?" She said, "No, child, I have not seen anything here this
morning." Then he ran off; and he had a friend, and so he went to him.
He said, "Let us both go together and look; my pet has disappeared."

And for a long time they looked everywhere, and they came back and lay down. In the evening he thought, "I believe that maybe it will come back now."

The following morning they looked for it again; but no, there was nothing moving about there. So it went on, and the young man mourned its loss and came to pine for his pet. Then one night it seems he was not sleeping soundly, and he heard something apparently talking to him. He was told, "Wake your friend up, and both of you go down to the water. Your friend is to sit in the front of the boat, and you stand behind. Don't touch your paddle; you are just to stand there."

So he did just as he was told. His friend woke up, and they went down to the water. His friend sat in the boat in front and watched; they did not speak. Then the boat moved and slid down into the water, and then sped along. The boat passed through patches of very rough water as though it was quite smooth as it seemed to move along on top of the water. Then he saw that it was being taken down the river.

From up in the hills Coyote had seen where something was moving along and had heard tell that the two young men were being carried down from across the river. Coyote thought, "Well I will not be left behind. There is bound to be plenty more to eat wherever they are going. Shouldn't I go too?" He ran along the bank, and whenever he got to any point on the riverside the boat was passing near him. And in this way Coyote jumped along and saw the boat floating down and moving toward the mouth of the river. Then Coyote ran and came along the bank to Hop'ew [Klamath]; he jumped and saw the boat already moving far down stream. Then Coyote ran for all his might along the bank to pass it and chased after the boat.

Then he leaped on to the rock Oregos as the boat was first breasting the breakers. It was just going to pass the rock, and Coyote jumped in and came crashing down from high up into it. Then he said, "Yes, my grandchildren, I will come with you wherever you are going, for I think you will not get on well if there is no one who will speak on your behalf wherever you may go."

Then the boat sped on; eleven times it broke through the waves at the mouth of the river, and then went on its way. So it was that it sped on; it sped on toward the west. Then it was dark for a long time, and the boat still sped on.

The next morning they looked and fancied they saw some things swimming ahead of them. Even Coyote was now afraid and did not talk, because he had been chattering and at last had felt drowsy where he was sitting, and was not the first to see that it looked like land in sight. Then they saw that it really was land lying right out in the ocean. And the sand was all white, and a crowd of people were standing on the shore to watch the boat bounding in there.

Then they landed. When they landed they saw that there were seals going ashore, and that it was they that had towed the boat. And then two girls arrived there and one said, "Come to our house; we will be going. I am sure you are tired, for your voyage here has been long."

Coyote went on ahead and ran to see how the people lived who lived there. The two young men went up to the house and entered, and there stood another young man. Then he said, "I am glad that you have come, Brother-in-law," and then he said, "Let us go and bathe ourselves." They went outside and were all together at the young man's dwelling.

Then Coyote thought, "How very pretty that girl is. I think I will get acquainted a little with her." They were sitting by the fire when the cooking was finished, and Coyote sat down right in the middle. No notice whatever was taken of him where he sat.

The two who had arrived had a meal when they came in. They could not but feel strange wondering where on earth they had come to at this place, for the sand was all white, and they had never seen people living like this. Then one of the girls said, "Now I will tell you in full why you have come here. I am your former pet. For a long time I stayed outside, and then I saw how you lived. I saw that you were good and loved you for it. It was I who engaged the seals, saying to each of them 'Go and fetch him.' I have a sister. I thought too that you would be lonely here if you did not bring your friend; and my sister may be his wife." He thought, "Well," and then he thought, "So this girl is my former pet, and that is why I loved her so much." Then they loved one another well, and were married, and lived long and happily, and had children.

Then gradually the woman noticed that it happened that her husband would go far up in the hills and sit somewhere there. For a long time he would gaze out over the water. And one day the woman followed him and said, "Alas, my husband, you seem to have something on your mind." He said, "No, I sit here, but I have nothing on my mind." Then his wife said, "I think, no I know, how you are; you keep sitting here and gazing. I think you are homesick here. Do you want to go back home?" Again he said, "No." She said, "Well, I know that really you are homesick. And I will tell you that if you decide to go home, I will arrange it that you shall go home."

Then he thought, "I will go and tell my friend, and I shall go home." He went in where his friend lived and said, "Let us both go home. Arrangements can be made for us to go home." Then his friend thought, "No, friend, I will not go with you. I now like living here; I have my children and I will not leave them." The other said, "Well, I shall go home; I shall return. Alas, alas that my grandmother's life is a burden to her, as I fear she does not know where I have disappeared to."

And so it came about that the boat was launched. And then they saw there was a crowd and that something was being dragged along there. It was Coyote being dragged along; he was all tied up, and thrown into the boat, because people were fed up with Coyote ever since he had been there. Whenever anyone was at home he leaped into the house and said, "Grandmother, isn't there anything lying here for me to eat?" And he was told, "Be off outside! Who are you and what on earth are you doing here?" Coyote ran up again; "Aha," he said. "It seems there is some soup in the pot here. I think I will have some." Then he gobbled it all up and heard the old woman pick up her stick. "Be off! You are just going to steal again. Ugh! I hate you. Don't come here again! Don't come to the house again to steal something!" So he was now hated by everyone, and therefore he was thrown into the boat. After a shout the boat was thrust out into the sea.

Then the young man came back again to this part of the world. At once he went up the river, and when he arrived there he saw that it was now a long time since his grandmother had died. His house was no more; it had fallen down, and nothing remained. Then he thought, "What a terrible thing has befallen me! Now I have come to be here alone. How happily I was living across the water, and I have left it all."

And so for this we say that it is not good if a person thinks too much "I will have everything." But a man lives happily if somewhere he has plenty of friends, and has his money; then he does not go around thinking that he should have everything that does not belong to him, and wishing it were his own.

4

Coyote and Old Woman Bullhead

KARUK
CIRCA 1930

MARGARET HARRIE, NARRATOR
HANS JØRGEN ULDALL, COLLECTOR
JULIAN LANG, TRANSLATOR

> *Springtime comes more quickly when we recite our creation stories.*
> *We lay down together for a long time*
> *and recite the stories to each other in turn.*
> *We answer each telling with a telling.*
> *And when we recite creation stories long into the night,*
> *daylight comes more quickly.*
>
> A Karuk elder's commentary, 1920s

INTRODUCTION BY JULIAN LANG

The Karuk are a Hokan-speaking people living in mountainous North-western California. Traditionally, they lived along the Klamath River be-tween their territorial boundary with the Yurok and the California-Ore-gon border. They lived by hunting, gathering, and especially fishing. Salmon and acorns were the staples of life, because these were what the land gave in abundance, as everywhere in Northern California. They were closely allied in social structure and worldview—though not in linguis-tic affiliation—with the Hupa and Yurok.

Then came the Europeans. The American "gold fever" of 1850 ended nearly as quickly as it began. It left behind widespread disruption of Karuk culture, destruction of many village sites and other lands, and death for many. As the placer mines petered out, the miners left in droves, leaving behind the Karuk to resume their lives, in relative peace, and still living within their aboriginal homelands. Today there are about twenty-eight hundred tribal members. Important religious and healing ceremonies continue to be held annually at the same sites ordained by the spirit race known through the tribal creation stories.

In pre-Contact times (prior to 1849) a Karuk creation story possessed a unique power to transport the teller and the listener from their present into myth-time. The word *uknîi* was a signal that a *pikva*, or creation story, was about to be told, and that the present was about to become one with the creation. The awesome power and energy of the Ikxaréeyav, the spirit inhabitants of myth-time, was unleashed with the telling. Cultural protocol insisted upon silence while the story was recited. Often recitations lasted well into the night. When special guests visited, the best *pikva* were recited: the stories of Ithyarukpíhriiv ('Across-the-Water-Widower'), Ikmahachram'íshiip Veekxaréeyav ('Sacred-Sweathouse-Spirit'), and Kahthuxrivishkúrutihan ('One-Upriver-Who-Carries-the-Network-Sack'). The best *pikva* were rarely told in mixed company, being considered the highest form of tribal knowledge. Only the wealthiest and most spiritually endowed families possessed such stories.

There are very few *pikváhaan,* or storytellers, today, in the pre-Contact sense. Rarely used to invoke the creation, today the *pikva* have become grist for elementary school education. For instance, in California the study of California Native peoples occurs during the fourth grade (when students are ten years of age), and only at that time. An arbitrary and distinctly non-Indian educational framework forces the conformity of *pikva,* trivializing medicine formulas and other important, orally transmitted cultural knowledge.

The very origin and design of the Karuk worldview is delineated by the *pikva.* They are the verbal chronicle of the prehuman era of the Ikxaréeyav, the Immortals, and their world, the Pikváhahirak ('Place-of-the-Creation-Stories'). As Yaas'ára, or Humanity, was about to come into existence, the Immortals were instructed to transform themselves into what is now the diversity of the Karuk natural world. Individually named and motivated, each Ikxaréeyav metamorphosed into an animal, a bird, a plant, a mountain, a constellation. Sometimes an Ikxaréeyav family transformed together. Whether alone or as a group, the Ikxaréeyav left behind their "story" (that is, their insights and instructions) for the benefit of Humanity.

The initial religious Karuk ceremony of the year, the First Salmon Ceremony, prominently featured *pikva* storytelling. In April of each year a spring salmon was ritually caught and cremated. The rising smoke of the fire served as Humanity's signal to the Heavens requesting that all eating and hunting taboos be erased, and that good fortune and good health descend upon the Earth. The Salmon Ceremony ritual was preceded by a month-long period during which the adolescent boys stayed in the sacred Ameekyáaraam ('Where-They-Make-the-Salmon') Sweat House, learning the *pikva* of Hookbill Salmon, Spring Salmon, Steelhead, Lamprey Eel, Summer Salmon, Fall Salmon, Trout, Sucker, the Old Spinsters, Buzzard, Grizzly Bear, and many others. Of these sweat house stories it was said, "*Kóovura vaa kooka píkva, áas va'avahapíkva*" 'all that kind of stories, stories of food from the river.'

The story included here concerns the now-familiar figure of Pihnêefich, Coyote. In Northwestern California, Coyote was regarded as "the craziest and nastiest man." Usually the stories told about him reveal his buffoonery and lascivious nature. This story is unique because it presents Coyote's darkest side. When recited, the story invariably causes both Native and non-Native audiences to squirm uncomfortably in their seats as their well-known, funny, crazy Coyote murders a child in cold blood, greedily eats the child's food, and physically and verbally abuses an old woman who has come to avenge the murder of her grandson. When finally she overcomes Coyote, she transforms.

This *pikva* was recited by Margaret Harrie, known as Mâakich (a diminutive of the English "Maggie"). She was from the village site of Asánaamkarak (Ike's Flat) on the Klamath River, which was the site of the First Salmon Ceremony. Her son, Benonie Harrie, became a highly respected *êem*—a shaman. The Danish linguist Hans Jørgen Uldall recorded the story in the early 1930s at Harrie's home in the Quartz Valley near Ft. Jones, California (see Lang 1994). Uldall, a noted phonetician of the day, was invited by Alfred Kroeber, the head of the anthropology department at U.C. Berkeley, to study California Indian languages and, incidentally, to trace the footsteps of the Spanish physician-linguist Jaime de Angulo, who had transcribed several creation stories from Margaret Harrie and texts from her son. I translated Uldall's phonetic transcriptions after finding them—handwritten, in pencil, on lined "filler" paper—in the archives of the Survey of California and Other Indian Languages in 1989.

Each *pikva* opens with the word *uknîii,* its only functional usage. The word means 'a story from the time of creation is about to be recited'. Once uttered, there should be no talking among the listeners, and no interruptions, because the *pikváhaan,* the *pikva*-teller, must render the story verbatim, just as it was previously taught to him or her. All creation stories take place during the era known as Pikváhahirak ('Place-of-the-Creation-Stories'). The word *kupánakanakana* (its only functional usage) ends the creation story and alerts the listeners that they have been returned to the present time. After bringing us back, the teller usually reminds us of the most significant deed of the story's protagonist. Finally, the teller recites a kind of word-medicine which she or he must speak after every recitation in order to hasten forth the springtime (stories are reserved for the winter months, as is the case with many tribes), by beckoning forth Spring Salmon and the brodiaea plants. The recitation also attests that the teller has been punctilious in his or her telling of the story. A sloppy telling might result in the teller having a *vasíhkuun* (a crooked back) in old age, or some other bad luck, such as a snake bite or broken leg. Some tellers elaborate their recitation (in fun) by saying that their "asses are wrinkled and shriveled" from lack of food.

The conventional recitation:

Cheemyâach ik Ishyâat imshiríhraavish!
Spring Salmon, you must shine upriver quickly!

Náyaavheesh ik!
You must hurry to me!

Cheemyâach ik Ataychúkinach i'uunúpraveesh!
Brodiaea, you must sprout upriver quickly!

Náyaavheesh ik!
You must hurry to me!

Nanivási vúra veekináyaach!
My back is straight!

The self-mocking coda:

Afupchúrax taneemchitátkoo!
My ass is all wrinkled and shriveled!

FURTHER READING

For a concise anthropological orientation to Karuk culture, the reader should consult William Bright's "Karok" article in the California volume of the Smithsonian *Handbook*. ("Karok" is an older spelling of the tribal designation.) Bright also has written a grammar, *The Karok Language,* and translated several Karuk stories into English, including "Coyote Gives Salmon and Acorns to Humans," "Coyote's Journey," and "Coyote Steals Fire." Harvey Pitkin presents a Wintu version of "Coyote and Bullhead" that is strikingly different from this one yet is not without parallels. More texts may be found in A. L. Kroeber and Edward Gifford's *Karok Myths*. Julian Lang's book, *Ararapíkva: Creation Stories of the People,* contains an introduction discussing Karuk culture and storytelling traditions, a pronunciation guide and notes on Karuk grammar, a glossary, and interlinear translations of six traditional stories and personal reminiscences.

COYOTE AND OLD WOMAN BULLHEAD

Uknîii . . .

A person lived there. He thought, "I'm going upriver. I'm tired of living here! I feel lonesome."

So, he left. He went a long ways upriver, to where a big creek flowed down. He looked up the creek, when suddenly he saw a boy walking about. The boy carried lots and lots of trout.

The man looked at the boy and said, "Geez, I like eating trout, I wish I was eating some of his." The man went over to the boy.

"Where did you find that trout?"

The boy said, "I caught them."

"You couldn't have caught that many fish! I bet you've been traveling with someone else!"

The boy said, "No-o-o. I have a willow seine. I was just there to see it. That's where I caught the trout."

Then the man said, "Are you telling me the truth?" The man was thinking to himself, "I'm going to murder him." And then he killed the boy.

"Hooray! I'm gonna eat trout!" The man built a fire, a big fire. Then he hid the one he had just murdered. There was a logjam nearby, and he hid the body under a log.

Then he went back to his fire, and he roasted the trout. He picked some herbs, and added them to his cooking.

Then he ate, finally devouring all the trout. Then he thought, "Hooray! I'm just full! Now I can travel a long ways upriver!" He said to himself, "I'm going to paint myself."

He saw smoke rising when he looked upriver. "Hey, I'm about to arrive at a village!" So he painted himself up good with red-earth paint.

Then he decorated his buckskin shoes. He painted red stripes running down his leather leggings, and he painted his buckskin blanket completely red with the earth paint. He put on an Indian-money necklace, and then he put on a new man's basketry cap.

Then he walked upriver.

After walking just a little ways, he looked upriver and saw an old woman standing in the trail. She was crying.

The man arrived where she stood, and asked her, "You're crying HERE, in the path?"

The old woman refused to answer him.

"Why don't you answer me!" the man asked. The old woman just kept on crying. Then he said, "YOU can't beat me up!"

The man started to walk upriver. He barely passed her by, when she grabbed him around the waist.

"Hey, let me go! Why did you grab me?" He tried hard to pry apart her grasp-hold, but he couldn't do it. She was slippery. He gave it his all, but she still held onto him.

Suddenly there were dark clouds! Before too long it was raining. The rain just flowed down. When he looked downhill toward the river, the water was rising.

And Coyote thought, "It's all right now! She'll let me go now, as soon as the river rises up to us here. She's so short! It's all right now."

Finally, the river rose right up to where they stood. The man said, "Hey! My nice shoes are getting wet! My little leggings are getting wet! Let me go!" She refused to answer; the water hit them. "It's all right now!" the man thought. "She'll let me go when she disappears under the water!"

Finally the water was up to her knees. He kept thinking, "I wish she'd let me go." He tried hard to pry her hands apart again. It was no use.

Finally the water was up to *his* waist. "All right! She'll be under water any moment!" Then she disappeared under the water.

Coyote started crying then—still she held onto him. Finally both of them disappeared under the water. The river rose to uphill of where they were. *Then,* she let him go.

The old woman poked her head out of the water. "Let it be so, that I become transformed here in the water!" And then she turned into Bullhead Fish.

As for Coyote, he drifted far downriver. The old woman found him stuck in among some willows. When the high water receded, the old woman hauled him out of there.

As for the old Spirit Woman, she came back to this world.*

And Coyote, he came back to life again!

Kupánakanakana.

Coyote did that. He killed the old woman's grandson . . .

Spring Salmon, you must shine upriver quickly!
You must hurry to me!

Brodiaea, you must sprout upriver quickly!
You must hurry to me!

My back is straight!

---

* That is, she came back to this mortal world, transformed as Bullhead.

5

The Devil Who Died Laughing

KARUK
1950

MAMIE OFFIELD, NARRATOR
WILLIAM BRIGHT, COLLECTOR AND TRANSLATOR

INTRODUCTION BY WILLIAM BRIGHT

My principal fieldwork on the Karuk language (previously called "Karok") was done in the spring of 1949 and the summer of 1950. During the latter period, in search of Karuk speakers who could tell traditional stories, I visited Mrs. Mamie Offield, an elderly woman living at her summer home on the slope of Mount Offield, near Somes Bar, in Siskiyou County. (During the winters, she lived in Los Angeles.) Some years before, she had served as a translator and consultant for the ethnographic fieldwork of Professor Edward W. Gifford, of Berkeley; people told me that she knew a lot, but that she was "kinda mean"—that is, unfriendly or uncooperative. I was apprehensive, but in fact she proved to be knowledgeable, friendly, and very cooperative. During that summer she dictated eighteen stories and helped me translate them. Most were myths, about the deeds of Coyote and the other Ikxaréeyavs—the First People who inhabited the earth before humans came into existence. But others were stories with human characters—sometimes involving supernatural occurrences, but believed to have happened in "modern" times.

Among these, the anecdote that I have called "The Devil Who Died Laughing" has always been one of my favorites. It involves no superhuman characters and no moral lesson: it's simply a funny story, which I have enjoyed retelling, and my Karuk friends have enjoyed hearing, for the last forty years. Years ago, I published the text (Bright 1957:274–75; there is a photo of Mrs. Offield on page 155) in a technical transcription system for linguists and other specialists. The spelling for Karuk used in this introduction is a more practical system, which I have recently developed for the Karuk tribe's language program.

To understand the story, one needs to know what the Indians of Northwestern California mean by a "devil" (Karuk *apurúvaan*). The term has nothing to do with demons from Hell, but rather refers to sorcerers: human beings, male or female, who practice malicious magic. (One could use the term "witch" except for the female connotation of the English word.) Devils get their power from magical objects called *ápuroon* 'devil machines'; armed with these, they prowl around human dwellings at night, sometimes emitting *machnat,* or small flashes of light (will-o'-the-wisps?), spying on the inhabitants and choosing their victims.

In Mamie Offield's story, a pair of devils come to spy on a man and his wife, who are occupying a temporary house in an acorn-gathering area. But the devils get a surprise and never have a chance to practice their sorcery. Stories in which devils are thwarted seem to be a recognized genre; Mrs. Offield told me three such stories on a summer afternoon in 1950 (see Bright 1957:274–77). The humor of such stories is perhaps enhanced by being at the expense of a hated and feared class of people; we might imagine a similar modern story in which the prowlers were tax collectors.

In spite of its secular nature, the story shows an ethnopoetic structure similar to that of Karuk myths and other narratives. It consists of fourteen "verses," most of which begin with a sentence-initial particle construction—usually *kári xás* 'and then', indicating sequentiality. As is typical in Karuk storytelling, the initial verse lacks this element. The following central passage shows a variation in the use of initial particles: verses 11–12, at the climax of the action, begin not with *kári xás,* but with the word *hínupa* indicating a surprise, translatable as 'and there . . . !' This initiates a kind of freeze-frame effect: the sequence of actions is suspended and previously unknown features of the situation are revealed.

5   Kári   xás   chámuxich   ú-ykar.
     And   then   sucker   he caught it.
     And then (the husband) caught a sucker.

6   Kári   xás   pa-asiktávaan   u-piip,   "Chími   kan-thimnûup-i."
     And   then   the woman   she said, "(intention)   I'll roast it."
     And then the woman said, "I'm going to roast it."

7   Kári   xás   u-thímnup,   pa-chámuxich.
     And   then   she roasted it,   the sucker.
     And then she roasted it, that sucker.

8   Kári   xás   pá-faan   u-yhúku-rishuk.
     And   then   the guts   she ripped them out.
     And then she ripped out the guts.

9   Kári   xás   pa-mukun-ikrívraam   u-súru-ruprin-ahi-ti,   yítha-kan.
     And   then   their house   there was a hole through,   at one place.
     Now then, there was a hole through their house-wall, at a certain place.

10   Kári   xás   vaa   kaan   u-ákith-rupri,   pá-faan.
     And   then   that   there   she flung them through,   the guts.
     And then she flung them through that hole, those guts.

11   Hínupa   vaa   káan   u-t-nûuprih-ti,   yítha   pa-apurúvaan.
     And there that   there   he was peeking through,   one   the devil.
     And there he was peeking through that hole, a certain devil!

12   Hínupa   yúp-yaach   t-u-ákith-tir.
     And there smack in the eye   she had flung them.
     And there she had flung them right smack in his eye!

Apart from the initial particle constructions, features of ethnopoetic structure in this passage include the following:

Word Order

There is regular alternation of preverbal and postverbal position for nouns to indicate new and old information, respectively. Thus we have, in verses 5–7, "He caught a sucker [NEW]—And then she roasted it, that sucker [OLD]"; then, in verses 8–10, "She ripped out the guts [NEW]— And then she flung them through that hole, those guts [OLD]." Along with the repeated *kári xás,* this pattern suggests an atmosphere of routine activity or "business as usual," serving as a background to the surprise that comes in verses 10–11.

Repetition

There is repetition of the verbal suffix meaning 'through a hole', with the three variants *-ruprin ~ -rupri ~ -nûuprih:* (9) "There was a hole through their house-wall"; (10) "She flung them through that hole, those guts"; (11) "He was peeking through that hole." Apart from the poetic echo effect of the partial phonetic repetition, the reiterated semantic element gives extra cohesion to the narrative at this point of climax.

For a translation of this text, I would have liked to present Mrs. Offield's own English version, but unfortunately, I have not preserved that—either in a verbatim transcript, or in an audio recording—so I've done my best to reproduce features of her colloquial storytelling style, as I remember it: short sentences, informal but totally clear vocabulary and syntax, and certain Karuk stylistic devices such as the movement of old-information noun phrases to the end of the sentence ("And then she roasted it, that sucker"). Where the Karuk text uses repetition, I've tried to reproduce that faithfully in English. Finally, at several points where the Karuk uses vocabulary items that are highly distinctive, semantically or phonologically, I've attempted to find correspondingly colorful English vocabulary. Thus, in verse 8, the verb-form *uyhúkurishuk* means 'she pulled (something) out' but can refer only to the guts of an animal; I translate "she ripped out the guts." In verses 10 and 12, the verb stem *ákith* means not simply 'to throw' but 'to throw something soft'—such as mud, dough, or (in this case) fish guts; I propose the translation "to fling." In verse 12, the alliterative *yúp-yaach,* literally 'eye-exactly', suggests not just 'right in the eye' but the more vivid "smack in the eye."

FURTHER READING

For an overview of Karuk culture, see William Bright's article "Karok" in the California volume of the Smithsonian *Handbook.* Concerning sorcery in Native Northwest California, see William J. Wallace and J. S. Taylor's article, "Hupa Sorcery." A Karuk grammar, text collection, and dictionary are presented by Bright's *The Karok Language.* For ethnopoetic analyses of Karuk narrative, see Bright's "A Karuk Myth in 'Measured Verse'" and "Coyote's Journey," both collected in *American Indian Linguistics and Literature;* see also Dell Hymes's "Particle, Pause, and Pattern in American Indian Narrative Verse."

THE DEVIL WHO DIED LAUGHING

1 A lot of people were gathering acorns,
    up in the mountains,
    in acorn season.

2 And then they had gone home,
    all those people.

3 Only one man was left,
    he and his wife.

4 And then he said,
    "I think I'll go spear some fish."

5 And then he caught a sucker.
6 And then the woman said,
    "I'm going to roast it."

7 And then she roasted it,
    that sucker.

8   And then she ripped out the guts.

9   Now then, there was a hole in their house-wall,
        at a certain place.

10 And then she flung them through that hole,
        those guts.

11 And there he was peeking through that hole,
        a certain devil!

12 And there she had flung them right smack in his eye!

13 And then that other devil burst out laughing.

14 And then he just laughed himself to death;
        the next day his friend saw him,
            he was lying there,
        he was still laughing,
            even though he was dead.

15 So then the other one told what happened.

6

"The Boy Who Grew Up at Ta'k'imiłding" and Other Stories

HUPA

1963–1964

MINNIE REEVES AND LOUISA JACKSON, NARRATORS

VICTOR GOLLA, COLLECTOR AND TRANSLATOR

INTRODUCTION BY VICTOR GOLLA

Together with their close neighbors the Yurok on the lower Klamath River, and the Karuk further upstream on the Klamath, the aboriginal Hupa of the lower Trinity River subsisted (and subsisted well) on the abundant spring and fall runs of salmon, which they supplemented by gathering acorns and berries, trapping eels, and hunting deer and small game. The modern Hupa people have been able to preserve a close attachment to this rich environment, since they are fortunate to possess a large reservation that includes the center of their traditional territory, Hoopa Valley. This spectacularly beautiful eight-mile-long stretch of bottomland, studded with oaks, is located on the Trinity a few miles above its confluence with the Klamath. In the Hupa language it is called *na:tinixw* 'where the trail goes back', and its geography is closely interwoven with traditional Hupa religion and story.

In addition to the people of Hoopa Valley (*na:tinixwe* 'those of *na:tinixw*'), there were several Hupa-speaking tribelets, all virtually identical in language. Two of these tribelets (known ethnographically as the Chilula and the Whilkut) were located on Redwood Creek, west of Hoopa Valley. There was at least one tribelet upstream on the Trinity River, centered on the village of Łe:lding where the Trinity and South Fork join.

Shortly before the turn of the century, Pliny Earle Goddard came to Hoopa as an interdenominational missionary. He built a church, which still stands, and learned Hupa sufficiently well to be able to preach in it. In 1900, however, he abandoned religious work to become an anthropologist. His ethnographic sketch "Life and Culture of the Hupa" is a classic, and he also published an important volume of traditional Hupa narratives, "Hupa Texts." These studies, together with Goddard's numerous publications on the language, made the Hupa one of the best described Indian cultures of California in the early decades of this century. In 1927 the great anthropological linguist Edward Sapir added even more to the documentation of Hupa traditional culture in a field study that focused on language and literature. He collected seventy-six narratives, some of them quite long and most of them full of cultural detail. This important collection is now being readied for publication in a forthcoming volume of *The Collected Works of Edward Sapir*.

I began my own work with the Hupa in the 1960s. My work was primarily linguistic, but I also collected a number of narrative texts. The four Hupa stories included here are translations of narratives collected on tape in 1963 and 1964 from Mrs. Minnie Reeves and her younger sister, Mrs. Louisa Jackson. Minnie Reeves (1880–1972) was well past eighty at the time, and Louisa Jackson (1888–1991) was in her late seventies. Although married into Hoopa Valley families, Minnie and Louisa were actually from the Chilula tribelet. Their father, Dan Hill, and grandfather Tom Hill had refused to resettle the family on the Hoopa Valley Reservation after its establishment in 1864; they continued to live in the traditional village of Nolehding ('waterfall place') on lower Redwood Creek, a few miles northwest of the reservation boundary. The family moved to Hoopa in 1888, and both sisters attended the boarding school there.

Minnie Reeves was a talented narrator, and her carefully told stories span several genres. Her sister Louisa Jackson had a smaller repertoire, but a vivacious style.

"The Boy Who Grew Up at Ta'k'imiłding" is the sacred charter of the two principal World Renewal dances. These ceremonies, the Hupa term for which is *ch'idilye,* are unique to the traditional cultures of the Yurok-Karuk-Hupa area and continue to be performed today. They focus on maintaining the equilibrium of the physical and social world through songs and dances pleasing to the *k'ixinay,* the supernatural inhabitants of the world before humans arrived who still exert influence on human affairs from a Heaven beyond the sky. The ceremonies are performed in two ten-day cycles, the White Deerskin Dance (*xonsił ch'idilye* 'summer World Renewal') and the Jump Dance (*xay ch'idilye* 'winter World Renewal'). The White Deerskin Dance takes place in August or early September at a series of dancegrounds in Hoopa Valley. The Jump Dance is performed in late September at a single site about one hundred yards upstream from the village of Ta'k'imiłding ('acorn cooking place'). Formerly the two dances may have been annual events; today they are biennial, held in odd-numbered years.

The story that Minnie relates is not in the strict sense a myth. Hupa myths relate events that happened in the days when the *k'ixinay* were still on earth, whereas this story has the character of a religious legend set in human times. In it the World Renewal dances are said to be the inspiration of a specific young boy, a child of the family that owns the *xontah nikya:w* ('big house'), the largest and most prestigious house in the principal Hoopa Valley village, Ta'k'imiłding. This boy is well-behaved and "sings all the time," an indication that he has been chosen by the *k'ixinay* as a vehicle of spiritual power. Then one day he disappears in a cloud to join the *k'ixinay* beyond the sky. After a long absence he briefly reappears to his father to convey to the Hupa people how and where the *k'ixinay* want the World Renewal dances to be performed. "I will always come back. . . . I will always be watching," he both promises and warns.

Minnie Reeves's telling of this sacred story was appropriately solemn and serious. Although her version was abbreviated and broken here and there by a hesitation or groping for words, it was clear that she was reciting well-known lines and phrases—a sacred text in the most real sense. (See the "Hupa Language Sample" at the end of this introduction for a closer look at the language behind the translation.)

The incident that Minnie Reeves relates in "Grandfather's Ordeal" probably occurred in the 1850s or early 1860s, when hostilities between white settlers and Hupas—particularly the Chilulas—were at their worst. Minnie's maternal grandfather and the Indian doctor he was escorting were by no means the only Indians gratuitously killed or wounded by whites on the trails between Hoopa Valley and the coast. The need to import a shaman from Hoopa Valley underscores the peripheral status of the Chilula tribelet.

"The Stolen Woman" is one of many legends whose theme is a raid on a peaceful Hupa village by "wild Indians" from the south. There is undoubtedly a historical kernel to these stories, and the raiders (usually called *mining'wiltach'* 'their faces-tattooed') may be either the Yuki of Round Valley or the Hayfork Wintu. A particular twist to this story is the implication that the wealth of Me'dilding, the leading village of the upriver (southern) half of Hoopa Valley, is based on stolen treasure. Not surprisingly, Minnie's connections were largely to Ta'k'imiłding and the downriver (northern) half of the valley.

"It Was Scratching" was told to me by Louisa Jackson. It belongs to a popular genre of "Indian Devil" stories, based on a widespread belief in witchcraft practices (*k'ido:ngxwe*). Devils are said to sneak around houses and graveyards in the night, peering through windows or catching people when they venture outside alone. They insert "pains" into people, causing illness, bad luck, and even death. Note how the woman in the story accuses the devil of having killed off her entire family (*ch'e'whinełya:n* 'he ate me up' is the Hupa idiom). In traditional times, suspicions and accusations of deviling were quite common, giving social life a distinctly paranoid tinge.

Hupa Language Sample

The following lines of Hupa, with their glosses and translations, come from the beginning of the first story presented here, "The Boy Who Grew Up at Ta'k'imiłding."

Ta'k'imiłding nat'tehłdichwe:n,
at Ta'k'imiłding he grew up
He grew up at Ta'k'imiłding;

xontah   nikya:w   me'   ts'isla:n—   kile:xich.
House   Big   in   he was born   a boy
he was born in the Big House—a boy.

Haya:ł   ang'   łahxw   na'k'iwing'ah   wehst'e';
then   it was   only/nothing but   he sang   continually
He would do nothing but sing all the time;

na'k'e'a'aw.
he would keep singing
he just kept singing.

Haya:ł   hay diydi   'a:ya:xołch'ide'ine',
then   whatever   they would tell him
Then, whatever they would tell him,

'aht'ingq'a'ant'e: mida'   q'eh   na'a'a'.
everything   its word/mouth   after   he carried it about
he minded it.

'e'ilwil   na'ky'a'ah'xw,
it would get dark   as he sang,
He would sing all day long,

xontah   nikya:w   me',   Ta'k'imiłding.
House   Big   in   at Ta'k'imiłding
in the Big House at Ta'k'imiłding.

FURTHER READING

Readers should consult William J. Wallace's entry, "Hupa, Chilula and Whilkut," in the California volume of the Smithsonian *Handbook.* For a more in-depth ethnography, there is Pliny Earle Goddard's classic "Life and Culture of the Hupa." Goddard's "Hupa Texts" is also an important collection of Hupa oral literature. The stories presented here are taken from *Hupa Stories, Anecdotes, and Conversations,* a booklet prepared by Golla for the Hoopa Valley tribe in 1984.

"THE BOY WHO GREW UP AT TA'K'IMIŁDING" AND OTHER STORIES

THE BOY WHO GREW UP AT TA'K'IMIŁDING

MINNIE REEVES

There once was a boy who grew up at Ta'k'imiłding—born into the Big House there.

He did nothing but sing all the time. He would always be singing. He was a good boy and did what he was told, but he would stay there in the Big House at Ta'k'imiłding, singing all day long.

One day his mother went down to the river to fetch water, leaving the boy singing in the house. She dipped up some water, and was on her way back up to the house when a sound stopped her. It sounded like someone was singing inside a cloud that hovered over her house. She put her water basket down and listened. She could hear it clearly: someone was singing there inside the hovering cloud. After a while the cloud lifted up into the air. She could still hear the singing. Eventually it vanished into the sky.

She went on back to the house. When she went inside, the boy was gone. It was clear that he had gone off inside the hovering cloud.

When her husband returned from hunting she told him what had happened. They had loved him very much, and they cried and cried.

A long time passed and there was no sign of the boy. Then, one day, many years later, the man went up the hill to hunt. After hunting for a while he got tired and decided to rest under a big tan oak. As he sat there smoking his pipe he was suddenly aware of a young man walking toward him out of the forest. Looking more closely he saw that it was the boy, now grown up. He leapt to his feet and ran to embrace his son.

"Stop there, Father! Don't come toward me," the young man said. "Don't try to touch me. I can't bear the scent of human beings any more."

Then he continued, "The only reason I have come back is to tell people the way things should be done in the future. When I went off to Heaven in that cloud, I found them dancing there, dancing without ever stopping, dancing the whole day long.

"And that is why I have returned—why you see me now. I have come to tell you about the dances. I am here to tell you the ways they should be danced, and the places where they should happen.

"You will dance downstream through Hoopa Valley, you will finish the dance over there on Bald Hill: that is where the White Deerskin Dance is to be danced.

"Ten days after the White Deerskin Dance is finished, you will dance the Jump Dance for another ten days. There behind the Jump Dance fence I will always be looking on. I will always come back for the Jump Dance, although you won't ever see me. Because I will be looking on from there, invisible though I am, don't let anyone go back of the fence, don't even let a dog go back there.

"I will always be watching."

That is the end of the story.

GRANDFATHER'S ORDEAL

MINNIE REEVES

I will tell you now about how my grandfather—my mother's father—got shot, a long time ago.

His mother had gotten sick. The Chilula Indian doctors who were treating her told him that she probably wouldn't pull through. They told him that he should go get this Indian doctor from Hoopa who had a good reputation. She might be able to save his mother.

My grandfather immediately set out on foot for Hoopa Valley. He found the Indian doctor and the two of them started back toward the Bald Hills.

The Indian doctor carried a lot of stuff in a pack basket, and my grandfather carried another pack basket. They crossed Pine Creek at the ford called Soaproot (*qos-ding*) and went up the Bald Hills past Birds Roost (*k'iya:wh-nondiłding*).

As they were heading down the far slope, my grandfather happened to look back along the trail and caught sight of a party of whites on horseback. The whites had seen the two of them and were pointing their rifles at them. My grandfather tried to raise his hands—he raised them straight up—but it did no good: the whites shot at them anyway. A bullet hit the Indian doctor and she fell down dead. Another bullet tore through the upper part of my grandfather's back. It didn't kill him, but his legs got caught in some berry vines and he too fell to the ground. Thinking that they had killed both of the Indians, the whites went off downstream.

My grandfather dragged himself back up the trail toward the ridge. He remembered that there was a cedar-bark hunting shelter up there. He finally found it and crawled inside, where he collapsed and fainted.

Meanwhile, the people back at home were getting worried. "They should have gotten back long before now," they thought. "Maybe something has happened. Somebody should go out looking for them." So a party went off to search for them. When they got to the hunting shelter, they saw my grandfather lying inside. It looked like he had been dead for some time. They took a piece of bark from the shelter and were going to lay him out on it, like a corpse, to carry him home for burial.

But when they started to handle him, he jumped up. The moment he leapt up, blood and matter spurted out of his wound and he started gasping for breath. He had been in a deep coma, near death, but he had seen a vision of a white grizzly bear pouncing on him and tearing open his infected wound. He had trained for power and had acquired a lot of it— he was a strong believer in all of those things. A vision came to him from Heaven, and he survived.

They carried him back home, where he recovered. And that is the end of the story.

THE STOLEN WOMAN

MINNIE REEVES

A long time ago, they were having a Brush Dance at the village of Me'dil-ding. In the middle of the night, when the dance was going strong, an extraordinarily handsome man showed up, carrying two valuable fisher hides. He went right into the pit and danced between two girls.

As they filed out of the pit at the end of the set of dances, he caught hold of one of the girls and ran away with her. He took her far off. She had been kidnapped.

He took her along with him from place to place, across the mountains. After a long while they arrived back at his home—a bark house, located at the base of a large rock. They lived there together, and eventually she had a child—a little boy.

When the man went out hunting he would take the woman with him. When he saw a good-sized deer, he would point a magic Jump Dance basket (*na'wehch*) at it and wiggle it around, and instantly the deer would fall over dead. He was always careful to keep the woman with him and would never let the magic basket out of his sight. They would then go back home. After the venison was all eaten up they would go out hunting again.

One time when they were doing this, the man incautiously put the magic basket down while he went to pick up a fallen deer. The unhappy woman thought that she saw a way of getting home to Me'dilding. She picked up the magic basket and pointed it toward him, wiggling it around the way he did when he was killing a deer. He didn't see her do this, and they went back home. That evening he complained of a headache, and before the first light of dawn appeared he was dead.

The woman searched the man's house. She found her child, now grown to be a fair-sized young man. She also found that the man had a large number of valuable things that he had stolen from people. She fixed up a pack basket full of such things and then she and the boy set off for home.

She thought hard about how they had come when she had been kidnapped, and the two of them traveled for several days. Finally they reached Me'dilding. The boy had never seen so many people before. It scared him, and he would run and hide behind the houses.

This is how there came to be rich people at Me'dilding. The kidnapped woman had brought back all sorts of valuable things.

This is the end of the story.

IT WAS SCRATCHING

LOUISA JACKSON

Once, a long time ago, when the harvest season came, a group of women went off to gather acorns. They camped in a bark hut at the place called Mortar Lies There (*me'ist-sitang-xw*). They had gathered lots of acorns, and when it came time to pack them home they decided it would be best to fetch a man to help. So they went back for someone, leaving one woman to stay with the acorns.

She spent the night alone in the bark hut. In the middle of the night she heard something making a noise, like an animal scratching the outside of the hut. She didn't get concerned about it. But when she got up in the morning she thought she'd look, and discovered scratch marks outside the hut next to where she had been sleeping. In spite of this she went out and spent the day gathering more acorns.

That evening she got ready to spend another night in the hut. Thinking that perhaps someone was trying to devil her, she placed a log where she had slept before. She covered it with a blanket and sat down beside it. In the middle of the night she again heard the noise of something scratching. As she watched, she saw someone put his hand into the hut. He kept pushing it in until his arm reached the log that was lying there like a person in the blanket. At that instant, the woman caught him around the wrist, held his arm down, and sawed it off with a knife. When it was severed, she hurled it aside.

When she got up in the morning she decided to go back to the village. She gathered some ferns and stuffed them in her pack basket. Throwing the severed arm on top of the ferns, she set off for home.

As she was coming down the ridge past the village of Xonsahding, she heard the sound of people crying. She wondered what was going on and decided to go down and see. When she got there she found a man laid out for burial and people mourning him. She asked what had happened.

"That poor man met with a great misfortune," they told her. (They also mentioned his name, but I won't repeat it here.) "A tree limb fell on him out in the woods."

"Yes," she said. "Of course. A tree limb fell on him."

She took her pack basket down, felt around in it, and pulled out the severed arm. She threw it on top of the body.

"This too," she said. "This too is his. He was the one who was coming after me, trying to devil me. Now I know who it was who killed off my family!"

And suddenly the mourners were silent.

7

The Bear Girl

CHIMARIKO
1921

SALLY NOBLE, NARRATOR

J. P. HARRINGTON, COLLECTOR

KATHERINE TURNER, TRANSLATOR

INTRODUCTION BY KATHERINE TURNER

The Chimariko language was once spoken on the Trinity River in Northwestern California, a heavily forested and mountainous country. Chimariko is classified by linguists as a Hokan language, but it is only distantly related to some of the other languages spoken in prehistoric California. To the west and northwest their neighbors were the Athabascan Whilkut and Hupa. Their neighbors to the south and east were Penutian-speaking Wintu people.

Sally Noble was the last known fluent speaker of the Chimariko language. She told the story of "The Bear Girl" to John Peabody Harrington in 1921. Mrs. Noble told Harrington several Chimariko stories as well as recounting historical events, describing customs such as tattooing and doctoring, and giving her personal reminiscences. There is no place in Harrington's notes of his work with her where she told a single story from start to finish. Sally Noble was remembering these stories from long before she told them to Harrington, and each time she told a story she would remember another detail or episode. Although she knew Chimariko, she had seldom spoken the language as an adult. By the time she told this story, she had not spoken Chimariko for many years, so she told it in many overlapping fragments. This story was pieced together from those fragments.

J. P. Harrington amassed more data about North American languages and cultures than any other person. An ethnographer and linguist, he was employed by the Bureau of American Ethnography. He recorded his notes on the Chimariko language from Sally Noble between September 1921 and January 1922. His notes are stored in the Smithsonian Institution in Washington, D.C. They have been photographed and microfilmed, making them more accessible to libraries around the world. By January 1922 Harrington had compiled several thousand pages of notes on Chimariko, and he planned to return to his work with Sally Noble in May. Mrs. Noble died in February 1922.

The story of "The Bear Girl" told here is my translation of Mrs. Noble's Chimariko, not her English versions of the story. She spoke in English at first, then in both Chimariko and English, and, finally, in Chimariko with an occasional English word or phrase. When she spoke English, Harrington wrote it down in English, and when she spoke Chimariko, he wrote it down phonetically because there is no alphabet for Chimariko. As Sally Noble got into the story of "The Bear Girl" in her own language, she added a wealth of detail absent from her English tellings.

In Chimariko the story is lyrical through its use of repetition to unfold the plot gradually. There is a majestic beauty in the repetitions. For most of the story, Mrs. Noble speaks one phrase and then partially restates it, adding just a little more detail before moving on to the next sentence. This is such a prominent feature that it is quite noticeable when Mrs. Noble does not exploit this device but moves straight ahead with her story, adding new information with each new sentence. For instance, in the scene where the Bear Girl abandons civilization for good (lines 60–73), there is very little repetition, and its absence underscores one of the climaxes of the story. We find the same pattern again near the end of the story (lines 96–104) at another dramatic moment, the scene where her brother shoots the Bear Girl.

FIGURE 2. Sally Noble.
Courtesy of the Bancroft Library,
University of California, Berkeley.

A few additional notes about the translation of Chimariko may be in
order. First, there is no difference between *he* and *she* in Chimariko, so
I have supplied the distinction for English-speaking readers; it would look
and sound odd had I translated the Chimariko pronouns as *it*. Second,
I have changed the order of the words from Chimariko word order to
that of English and moved descriptive words to where they would occur
in an English sentence.

This story gives us a glimpse of Chimariko culture and beliefs, as in the concept that there was a time long ago when a person could grow up or "turn out" to be an animal. In translating this story into English, I have tried to reflect the style and phrasing as Sally Noble told it in Chimariko. The line breaks are an attempt to suggest the controlled, rhythmic pace of delivery that seems implicit in the language of the original. I have not elaborated or filled in blanks, because that would alter the story told and add nothing of significance. This story speaks for itself.

FURTHER READING

Little is known about the Chimariko. Two articles in the California volume of the Smithsonian *Handbook*, Shirley Silver's "Chimariko" and William Wallace's "Hupa, Chilula and Whilkut," supply the most up-to-date information we have about the Chimariko people, their language, and their culture. Roland Dixon's "The Chimariko Indians and Language" provides an earlier but more extensive ethnography. C. Hart Merriam's "The New River Indians Tol-hom-tah-hoi" may also be of interest. James Bauman's "Chimariko Placenames and the Boundaries of Chimariko Territory" takes an interesting look at Chimariko ethnogeography. In addition to the few published sources, the Bancroft Library at the University of California at Berkeley has two small notebooks of fieldnotes on the Chimariko language recorded by A. L. Kroeber in 1901–1902. The American Philosophical Society in Philadelphia has the small amount of Chimariko linguistic data recorded by Edward Sapir in 1927.

THE BEAR GIRL

Long ago there was a cross Indian girl.
She was cross and angry all the time.
She did not like people.
She had no appetite for food.
She did not like the food her mother fed her.   5
She did not eat the food she was given.

They were afraid of her.
They could do nothing with her.
They wondered what she would amount to.
Everybody wondered how she would turn out.   10

Her mother hired a good Indian doctor to ask
    what was the matter with the girl.
She was not like people.
She was not like our flesh.
She was not a person.
She was not a human woman.   15
She was going to turn out to be a bear.
That's what the matter was.

Everybody was afraid of her because she was so cross.
She was always slapping.
She did not use a stick, not ever.   20
She always slapped with her hand.
She was not like the other children.
She always slapped.
When good children play,
they do not slap with their hands but use a stick.   25
Their mother told the children: "Don't hit her.
I am going to punish you if you hit the bear girl."
But they would sometimes hit her with a rock because she was so
    mean.

When she was still a little girl,
she already slept alone in a little house,   30
because everybody was afraid of her because she was so cross.
When the hazelnuts and berries got ripe,
she gathered wild blackberries,
but she did not eat them in the house.

She had only one brother.   35
Her brother watched his sister as she got a little bigger and
    crosser every year.
Everybody kept a watch on her.
Every year she got worse and worse.

When the old women went to gather hazelnuts,
she went with them.   40
Each time she went a little further.
She watched other people cracking the hazelnuts
and learned how to crack them too,
though she had been told not to.
She gathered lots of hazelnuts and cracked them,   45
but she did not eat them in the house.
Maybe she ate them out in the woods.
In the house she threw everything around.
She got worse and worse every year—bigger and crosser.

When the women went out to gather hazelnuts,   50
the girl went to get a drink further upstream.
When it was time to go home, the women called out:
"We are going home."
They called to her and hollered,
"Come on, let's go."   55
They hollered but she did not answer.
She went a little further every time.
She went further into the brush.
Finally she set the basket down on the trail and just kept going.

They say her brother followed her through the thick brush,   60
and found the basket.
She kept going, up into the mountains,
and she threw away her apron.
But she wore a nice fancy dress, well fixed up.
Her brother found the apron and put it in the basket.   65
She kept going, climbing higher and higher.
Her brother found her nice fancy dress.
He put it in the basket, laying it across her apron.
Then he found her hat.
Her brother kept following her upstream through the brush.   70
Finally he caught up with her.
She had already changed into a bear.

She looked back.
She said:

"My brother,   75
I thought I was a natural born person,
but I am a big bear.
Now I get where I want to go,
now I turn out to be a bear,
so that's how I turn out.   80
I have turned out to be a bear,
a cross female bear.
Remember what I say:
You will see me in a clover patch with lots of other bears.
I will be the biggest black bear.   85
I won't run.
That will be me.
Don't shoot."

She had become a bear, she ran away as a bear.
That is the reason why the little girl was so mean.   90

Her brother returned to the village and told the people what she
    said.
"I am going to be big and black,
don't shoot me," she told him.

Then, after a while, that boy got to be an old man.
All the men went bear hunting.   95
The old man saw a big patch of clover and went to look at it.
He saw lots of bears.
He shot one.
He shot a black bear twice.
Then he heard her: 100
"Don't you recollect?
I told my brother not to shoot me!"

The bear got away through the snow high up on the mountain.
The man looked for her,
but he never knew whether the bear died or not.   105
But that bear could talk Indian.

Finally, the man went home.
At supper time he wouldn't eat or say anything.

He looked like he'd been crying.
He wouldn't say anything.   110
He lay in bed for two days looking sick but saying nothing.

His wife asked him,
"What's the matter? Are you sick?"
But he wouldn't say anything.

After a while he told his wife,   115
"I shot her. I shot her twice."
And his wife said,
"Don't tell the old folks. Don't tell them."
His wife said,
"Well, what's the use to cry, you can't help it,   120
that part of it is done already,
that part of it is gone," she said.
"She is alive and that's all."

So, he never told any people at all.
He told nobody else.   125
He told only his wife.

NORTH-CENTRAL CALIFORNIA

Winter mosquitos go,
Summer mosquitos come—
Spring, hurry up!

Traditional story-closing
formula, Wintu

Dorothy Demetracopoulou
and Cora Du Bois, "A Study
of Wintu Mythology"

SPELL SAID BY A GIRL DESIROUS OF GETTING A HUSBAND

S·uwā´! May you think about me to yourself! May you turn back to look! Would that I might stand before his face! I just cry to myself. Would that I might see him every day!

I do just as you do. Sometimes I dream of him, and I rise when it is daylight, and I look about. Now, as I see him, my heart flutters. I look at him without raising my eyes. He gives me trinkets, and I take them, and I wear them for some time, until they are worn out.

Northern Yana, Betty Brown, 1907
Edward Sapir, *Yana Texts*

8

How My Father Found the Deer

ACHUMAWI

1970

LELA RHOADES, NARRATOR

BRUCE NEVIN, COLLECTOR AND TRANSLATOR

INTRODUCTION BY BRUCE NEVIN

Probably they ought to be called the Is, or the Ish, their word for "people." Anthropologists call them the Achumawi, from their word *ajúm:á:wí*, meaning dwellers on the *ajúm:á* or 'river', though the people themselves applied that term only to families who lived in the valley midway up the Pit River where the Fall River flows into it from the north. We will call them the Pit River people, for that is what they call themselves today.

Their territory overlaps two ecological zones. Traveling up the Pit River, one passes from deeply wooded intermountain declivities through valleys that are progressively higher, broader, and drier. Downriver from the place called *wíní'ha:'lí'wa* 'where it [the salmon] turns back', below the junction of the Fall River, one finds typically Californian deer and salmon, pine and oak. Upriver from that point, the land opens out to the high plateau ecology of sagebrush and juniper, jackrabbit and elk that one associates with Nevada and Eastern Oregon.

The people trapped animals in pits, hence the name. European explorers surely saw too the people's semisubterranean, earth-covered homes.

The ancestors of the Pit River people were evidently among the earliest settled inhabitants of California, speakers of Hokan languages whose descendants include Yana to the south, Shasta, Chimariko, and Karuk to the west, and others which are now separated from this northern group by intervening populations, such as the Pomo and Yuman groups of languages.

From ancient times they have maintained an annual cycle of land use: descending to the great rivers to fish for salmon in the spring; scattering to small family camps in the cooler foothills and mountains in the summer and autumn to hunt and to harvest crops planted for them, as they saw it, by the hand of God; retiring for the winter (*asjúy*) to separated villages of permanent earth-covered homes (*asjúy*) in sheltered mountain valleys; then returning to the riverside for the salmon run, cycle after yearly cycle of life in the Garden.

After centuries, or perhaps millennia, speakers of Penutian languages, whose descendants include the Wintu and the Maidu, brought different forms of land use and social affiliation. They occupied their riverside villages throughout the year, making expeditions for hunting and for the gathering of particular foods or craft supplies. When the Hokan people returning in the spring found a small Penutian settlement at some choice fishing spot, they shifted to another just as good, or almost as good. But the newcomers spread along the river into chains of villages whose inhabitants responded with quick allegiance to ties of blood and marriage if conflict arose with returning Hokan fishermen. The autonomous families and bands of Hokan speakers could not compete. Gradually, but with no evidence of settled warfare so far as we can tell today, the Hokan people retreated from the great Sacramento Valley to its periphery and outlying regions, where they continued their way of life, adapting to changed ecological conditions where they needed to.[1] The annual reunions for the spring salmon run, in which now both peoples were represented, continued to be the occasion of celebration, with feasting, dancing, singing, and gambling at the stick games.

At such a "big time" much trading was accomplished, and much courtship, for these were exogamous communities, proscribing marriage to relations calculated to a degree of remoteness that concerns only genealogists among us today. It was not uncommon for one of these small Pit River communities to include Modoc or Maidu or Wintu in-laws, and indeed one of these in-laws has an important role in our story. The fabric of communal life is woven of a thousand expectations and commitments that are as important to survival as the implements of hunt and harvest are for a small, highly interdependent community such as the one in which our story is set. So long as these mutual expectations are met, they scarcely rise to awareness. But this fabric is easily torn, and rifts put all parties at risk of privation and even death. As we shall see, the healing of relationships, the mending of reliability and reliance, was one of the responsibilities of a doctor or shaman.

Mrs. Lela Rhoades, whom it was my privilege and delight to call "Grandma," told me this story about her father's work as a shaman on November 28, 1970, at her home in Redding, California, when she was about eighty-seven years of age. I had met her that summer, not long after the beginning of my first experience of linguistic fieldwork. She lived alone in a large trailer home south of town. I say "alone," though her daughter and granddaughter were much present, her two sons lived nearby and visited, and before long her great-granddaughter's cradle was often at her feet as we sat and worked at her kitchen table—I with my tape recorder and notebook, she with her seemingly endless fund of stories and songs remembered from childhood. Once, she was singing me a song, remembering it, with her eyes closed, and she stopped suddenly and would not go on. "Something's looking at me," she said—a spirit animal, such as her father worked with. "I don't want to catch it." She explained that she could have been a doctor too, but she didn't want it, because it was an all-consuming profession. "People always want something from you," she told me, "or blame you for something."

Her father, Samson Grant, was of the Atsugewi or Hat Creek tribe.[2] These are close relatives of the Pit River people, living immediately to the south of them. Like many Atsugewi, he spoke both languages. Around 1852, when he was only a young boy, the majority of the Pit River and Hat Creek people were force-marched by soldiers to the concentration camp in Round Valley, Mendocino County. Indians from all over the state were confined there. After his parents died in the camp, he made his living by hunting and fishing for an elderly widow, who in turn cooked and provided a home of sorts. In his early teens he worked in various places around the Sacramento Valley as a ranch hand.

He knew that not all of his people had been captured. After a few years he returned to Pit River country. He found Buckskin Jack, the Hat Creek chief, who later arranged his marriage to Lela's mother. Her family had hidden themselves at Wé:'lá:mugí:'wa 'it gets shadowy early', a remote place near Goose Valley, north of Burney. To the north and west of this valley stands Yét, great Mount Shasta—"Lonely as God," in the celebrated words of Joaquin Miller, "and white as a winter moon." Southward, beyond lesser heights, stands its companion Ye:dí:jana 'the other Yét' (Mount Lassen). Except for the remoteness of their valley, and the fact that they were there year-round, they were much like other Pit River family groups that had dwelt under the watchful guardian spirits of the mountains for more than ten thousand winters past.

When Grandma Lela told the story to me in the Pit River language, it was somewhat as it might be told to one who knew the participants and their motivations, who was familiar with the customs and expectations of the community—the easiest and most natural way to tell it in Pit River. But when she retold the story in English, she provided background information interpreting one culture to the other—the easiest and most natural way to tell it in English. For example, in English she had to explain how Uncle Jack called Samson his son-in-law. In Pit River, she merely used a kinship term that, like many in the language, happens to apply reciprocally to both the elder and younger member of a relationship. This sort of difference of rendition is one of the thorniest and most disputed of the translator's problems. To present a story that is meaningful for English speakers, yet still reflects faithfully the teller's intentions and narrative skill, I have begun with her English rendition and have made it conform more closely to her Pit River rendition. Where new participants or new themes are introduced, the English version interjects more detail, some of which I have kept. This is especially obvious at the very beginning of the story. Here are the first few sentences, for comparison:[3]

Háné'gá	tól	chgí'wá:lujan	twijí:ní
Thence	for long	doctor	he was

qa	itú	wa'y:í:wíló'o.
the	my	late father

A long time ago my late father was a doctor.

Wíy:úmji	twijí:ní.
One who dwelt	he was

[An old Wintun man] was living there.

'Amqhágam   qa   dó:si   dét'wi,   dí:qá:lami,
When   a   deer   kill   carry home

 'lá:sa'ch   duji.
 happy   to do

When someone killed a deer, packed it home, he was happy.

The word *wíy:úmji* 'one who [characteristically] dwelt' has perhaps a bit
of the sense of a "roomer" or "boarder" in English. The old Wintun doctor was around seventy years old. The elderly were dependent on relatives for sustenance. In the opening two paragraphs of the English rendition we are told much more about him, about Uncle Jack, and about
their relationship.

The example shows the characteristic verb-subject-object word order
of this language, but scarcely any of the complexity of pronominal, ad-
verbial, and other prefixes and suffixes that Pit River verbs frequently have
(for instance, *twijí:ní,* t- 'EVIDENTIAL', w- '3RD PERSON', -jí- 'be, do', -n
'DURATIVE PAST'), and only hints of the sound system, with its tones, its
laryngealized consonants, and its uvular (q) sounds pronounced at the
back of the throat; but these are after all matters for another kind of discussion. A particular problem for translation is ambiguity as to the reference of pronouns. In this narration, Mrs. Rhoades makes frequent use
of a narrative infinitive construction, with no pronouns at all. This ambiguity was also a characteristic of the English rendition, which I have
tried to remedy without disturbing the vernacular tone of the original.

Three details in the story may require clarification. First, when Samson Grant accepts and smokes the tobacco, it seals a contractual agreement. In earlier days, it would probably have been in a pipe (*s'qoy'*), but
this was a rolled cigarette. Having served its ceremonial function, the tobacco cannot be used further, so the grandfather returns it to the earth.
Second, in the matter of who is at fault—the uncle or his wife—for neglecting the old man's portions, I would accept at face value the uncle's
claims about responsibility for the distribution of meat; he had presumably expressed his feelings to his wife about their elderly neighbor,
and she may well have shared those feelings. Third, a doctor commonly
worked with an assistant who "interpreted" the words of his song, but
Samson Grant did this for himself.

Mrs. Rhoades's gifts as a storyteller, long whetted on the myths and traditional stories of her people, are applied here to a piece of family history with grace and skill. Regardless of whether these events could be proven or disproven to have happened exactly as told, her narration is a true and vivid representation of the concerns and values of the community in which it arose.

NOTES

1. This account, which seems entirely plausible to me, is based on the work of Christopher Chase-Dunn of Johns Hopkins University and S. Edward Clewett and Elaine Sundahl of Shasta College in Redding.

2. "Atsugewi" is the anthropologists' term for this tribe, on analogy with the name "Achumawi." The actual Hat Creek word is *acug:e*, or "Atsuge."

3. The Achumawi forms cited in this article are given in a practical orthography, not a linguistic one.

FURTHER READING

A brief account of mostly physical aspects of Pit River culture is given in Alfred L. Kroeber's *Handbook of the Indians of California*. Jaime de Angulo's popular *Indians in Overalls* retells stories of his youthful encounters with a society in tragic disarray. He was primarily a raconteur, and his tales are colored by his personal preoccupations and his notions of "primitive psychology." The grammatical sketch of the language that he prepared with the help of L. S. Freeland ("The Achumawi Language") is not reliable. David Olmsted's *Achumawi Dictionary* is a compilation of earlier records, mostly de Angulo's, with elements of at least one other language mistakenly interspersed. Nevin treats the Achumawi sound system in his dissertation, "Aspects of Pit River Phonology." James Bauman's *Pit River Teaching Dictionary* represents upriver dialects.

HOW MY FATHER FOUND THE DEER

A long time ago my late father was a doctor. There was an old Wintun man who lived with us. He was married to my grandfather's sister. He didn't know how to talk Pit River, just a few broken words, but when he would sing for somebody, his words were just clear. He used to live aside of my uncle, my mother's brother, who had a lot of children.

My uncle used to be a good deerhunter. He didn't like this old fellow because he was a doctor. A doctor can do things to you, by just looking at you. He knows what you're going to do tomorrow, and who you did something to yesterday. He'd sing first, and his power would look back, trace you back. Then he'd tell you what you did and did and did, he'd pick up the tracks. He could see ahead too, maybe four or five years ahead, what you're going to do. But they don't do that until they sing.

So my uncle went out and killed a big deer. And the old man was happy, he was so happy. "We'll eat some meat tonight, they're going to give us a piece of meat." But no one came, they never gave him any meat. "He has to feed a lot of kids," he thought, so he didn't say anything, he didn't think anything about it, he didn't have bad thoughts.

In a week or so, my uncle brought in another deer. The old man was feeling very happy again. "This time he'll give us a piece of meat," he thought. And he was looking forward to sundown, for the evening meal. "I'm going to eat good tonight!" he thought. But he went to sleep without eating deer meat. And then in the morning no one came. That night, and next morning, no one came, and he didn't have any to eat. It went that way three times. And he thought, "Why does he do that? What's the matter, that he doesn't give me any meat?" And it grieved his heart, and then he cried.

"You won't eat, you won't eat deer meat," he thought. And then he sang, that night he sang. He called the *mák'má:ga*, the pileated woodpecker. He sang, "Drive away these deer and hide them! He didn't give me any," he sang, as though talking to the woodpecker. And then the woodpecker drove all the deer away and hid them.

After that, when my uncle went out, he didn't kill a deer. He didn't kill any deer all winter long. They went out, and none of them could find a deer. My father went out to hunt, my grandfather went out to hunt, they couldn't find even a track. And my uncles went out, but they couldn't find a track. For almost two years we never got any deer meat, we didn't eat any deer meat.

My uncle Jack's father, he knew something was the matter. "Something is wrong," he said. "Something is wrong someplace. I'll go and see my son-in-law." He called my father "son-in-law" because it was his brother's son-in-law. Of course, he knew my father was a doctor.

Just after dark he came, and he came in where we were all sitting around. He didn't come right in and sit down, he came in and stood. He rushed right in, talking, without stopping he talked. When he pulled out his tobacco, we knew something was wrong. He rolled some tobacco. He took just three puffs.* Then "Bi!" he said, "Here!" holding out his hand. My father looked at him. "What for?" he said. "You know what for!" he said. "There isn't any food, there isn't any meat, there isn't anything. There's no sign of a track," said my grandfather. "We haven't had any meat! What's wrong?" he said. "What's wrong with our country," he said, "that we don't have any meat? We've been hunting all winter, all this summer, and now we haven't got any meat, we can't find any meat. What's wrong? Look for it," he said. "I want you to have it searched for. That's why I've come in the evening," he said. And then he held out the tobacco again.

This time my father took the tobacco. He only drew three puffs, and he gave it back to him. After my father tasted it my grandfather didn't smoke it, he destroyed it. My grandfather never even sat down. And my father says, "You sit down and eat before sundown," he said. "I'll help sing right here," he said, "in my own house. Just before sundown I'll sit down. But don't invite anybody," he said. "Just you and your son and his two brothers, that's all." And that's all that came. But they didn't invite this old man, because he was a medicine man. "Before sundown, you eat. Then just before the sun touches the mountain, I'll sit down." And then without sitting down my grandfather went out and went home.

The next day in the evening they all came, they came to our house. And then, when the sun was just striking the mountain, my father went out. When he stepped out, they all came in, the three brothers, and sat

* Here, Mrs. Rhoades puffs three times.

down. We already had wood piled up inside, and pitch wood already split up and ready for us to use; my father had a chimney. They didn't allow a lamp to be lit, just the pitch. Then my father went out. I don't know where he went to. He just went out in the timber. And then when the sun was just about to disappear behind the mountain, he came in and sat down. Everything had to be very quiet. We were all to sit and be quiet, we couldn't even whisper. We children all sat in bed and watched.

Then he sang. Then he said, "I'm ashamed to say it. I'm ashamed to tell about it. I don't know," he said. And my grandfather said, "Don't be ashamed to tell us," he said. "Tell us," he said. "Tell us, tell us, tell us. We want to know," he said.

"Well," my father said, "OK, there's that old man, he was your brother-in-law, lives right there by you." He said, "He was sitting outside there, and he saw your son. This man," he said, "brought in a deer. And that old fellow was so happy that he was going to have some deer meat too. He thought maybe you'd give him a little of the ribs or something. But you didn't give it to him. You didn't take him over a piece of meat that evening, or the next day, or the next day. You didn't give him any. Then he thought, 'Well, he's got a big family, he's got lots of kids to feed. And of course, me, I'm nothing. So I guess that's why he didn't have any meat left over to give me any,' he thought. So he never thought any more about it. He forgot about it," he said. "He didn't think any more about it," he said.

"Then the next week, you killed another deer," he said. "You brought it in. He was happy when he saw you come in, he laughed to himself, he was so happy inside," he said. "And he thought he was going to get a piece of meat. But the same thing happened. You didn't give it to him. Three times you killed meat and he saw you. And you never gave any to him. And he cried," he said, "that night he cried. And he sang a song," he said. "He sang a song with ʼmákʼmá:ga. He sang this song," he said, "and this ʼmákʼmá:ga drove all the deer away and hid them. He's hiding them," he said, "and we can't find them."

And my uncle Jack said, "Yes, I did that. But I guess my wife never gave him anything," he said. "I have got nothing to do with it after I come home with that deer," he said. "She's the boss of the meat," he said.

Then my grandfather came again next night. They went home that night, and he came again, the same way. And then they knew something happened again, something was wrong again. My mother got kind of scared. Maybe he wanted my father to kill that old man, or maybe Uncle Jack killed him, or something. And he came again and he rolled that tobacco. And he gave it to my father. And my father says, "What for?" "Well," he said, "I want you to look for that meat and bring it back," he said. "Bring it back!" he said. "Where did he hide it? You look for it!" he said. "You, you're that kind too," he said. "Track that *mák'má:ga,*" he said. So my father took the tobacco, and he tasted it. "Yeah," he said. "The deer are still alive," he said. "They're still alive," he said. "They're not dead. He's just hiding it." And he gave the tobacco back, and my grandfather destroyed it.

Then, the same way, he had to sit down the same time. The same way, and that's why we had supper early, and they came again. They didn't invite the old Wintun man. And he sang that song again. And he couldn't find it. He hired this little screech owl spirit. "Did you see it go?" he asked, and he sent it out, and this little screech owl went out and looked for what was hiding the deer. And he said that the little screech owl said, "I can't find it." In just a short while, he came back. He says, "I can't find it. I can't even see the tracks," he said. Then he got another animal, I can't remember what. And that one came back right away, and said he couldn't find it either.

So then he sent out this little burrowing snake. It travels under the earth, like a mole burrowing, humping up the earth. He told it to go along under the earth. "Now go look for him, you go look for him in your earth," he said. And that little snake went along, and before long he came back. "It's there, I found it," he said. He found the deer bones. "But it's hot," he said. A big man was roasting all the deer bones in his *asjúy,* his winter house, that's how he kept the spirit of the deer there. "He's got it roasted," he said. "He's got it so hot that I can't pull it down," he said. "And this man was watching, and he had his bow ready and an arrow half drawn, ready to shoot anybody that looked down, looking for that deer meat. He was ready for him with his bow. He was ready to shoot," he said. "I just peeked in there, but it's too hot," he said. "I just peeked and I burned one of my eyes," he said. "I'm blinded in one eye." Blinded from the heat.

"Go again," my father said, "and take ice along with you. And as soon as he's not looking down," he said, "you look first, be very careful, don't make any noise," he said. "Look those bones over good, and you pull that one," he said, "you pull that bone down in the ground." He named a main bone in the deer's body, a special bone, but I don't remember what it is. "Take that bone from the fire with your mouth, holding it in your mouth," he said. So this little fellow went back again. He sang the song again, and it sounded like he went, that little snake. I heard that he went.

This little snake spirit went, he went under the ground. Then he peeked up with one eye, and he saw that man was looking right straight up there. While he was looking, he saw those bones, and with his one eye he saw that bone, the one to take. So he went out there and, holding ice in his mouth, he pulled it out from the fire and drew it down. He slipped the bone down under the ground, and that man never noticed it. He brought it back under the ground, though it was burning him, even as my father was singing. And he danced, he danced around the fireplace. They lit a stick of pitch. He had no shirt on, just his pants, barefooted, and he was dancing right by the chimney there. When that little snake was going to pull the bone down, my father had to be in that hot place there too. Then blood gushed out of my father's mouth, it just streamed down his mouth. The little snake was the one that was burned, that was what made blood come up. That's when the snake burned his mouth, that's why he did that. Then it looked like he came back. When he brought that bone back, "Here!" he said, and he gave it to my father. And he reached out and took it, it looked like he reached out and grasped something. My father took it. We couldn't see it. And he fainted, my father fainted. They had a bucket of water there, and they stuck that arm in the water, and they put water on his face, and he came to.

And then he sang and talked to the snake. And he said, "Now he brought back the deer." Then he said, "Treat that man good. Next time you kill meat, even a small one, don't be stingy, give him a ham. Even a ham, going to him with it, say 'Have some for breakfast,'" he said. That's what he said when he sang. And then he told it, he was the one who told about it, he didn't have an assistant to interpret for him. And he said, "Don't think anything bad, but doing in the right way, have compassion, treat him well. You should give some to him first," he said. "Not to us," he said. "We're young men yet, we can still hunt for ourselves, so don't think about giving meat to us. That one, you two give to that one," he said. "Well," said my uncle, "I'll tell my wife." And I guess he did.

The woodpecker was the one who drove all the deer away and hid them, piled the bones up in a ring of fire, piled the bones inside the fire so nothing was able to touch them. And he was waiting for someone to look down through the doorway in the roof of the *asjúy*, ready to shoot him in the heart, watching, determined not to give up the deer bones. That's why the screech owl was afraid, and the other one also was afraid, so he came back. But this little snake, burrowing through the earth, he's the one that brought back the deer.

And then we ate deer meat again. "For three days, you wait, and then you go hunting," said my father, "and you'll get your deer." So Uncle Jack went out there and he got his deer, and Uncle Jim went out there, and they all got deer. My father killed one deer. And so they gave the old Wintun man meat, and he was happy.

So I saw this, I saw it while I was still pretty young, but old enough to understand, and that's how it was that I listened. That's how my father used to do.

9

Naponoha (Cocoon Man)

ATSUGEWI
1931

JOHN LAMARR (DIXIE VALLEY), NARRATOR
SUSAN BRANDENSTEIN PARK, COLLECTOR
DARRYL BABE WILSON, EDITOR

INTRODUCTION BY DARRYL BABE WILSON

In 1931, Susan Brandenstein Park had just graduated from the University of California, in Berkeley's anthropology program, and had applied to be a part of an expedition to the Fiji Islands. She placed her name on the sign-up sheet, "somewhere near the bottom, but not off of the roster by any means whatsoever."[1] Then she, along with all the others, anxiously awaited its posting. Daily she rushed to the anthropology department. Finally, the roster was hanging on the door.

"There was a crooked line through my name. It was as if somebody had cut me across the heart with a knife. I never quite fully recovered." Although slashed, Susan was not defeated. Dr. Kroeber and her advisor, Robert Lowie, had strongly hinted that, if she first could accomplish some fieldwork, she would then have a good chance at the next Fijian expedition.

She dreamed of Fiji. Of the perfume from the jungle flowers in the morning sun, and the waves rushing in and smoothing back out. Of birds of every color flitting through the sunlit forest while she walked in the silver sand hunting seashells. Of listening to the drumming and singing in the night and watching the stars move softly across the powdery, warm heavens.

But Dr. Kroeber had advised her to cut her teeth on a "simpler culture" and directed her to the mountains of Northeastern California to work with the Atsugewi, my father's people, with the admonition that information that is not published "is worthless." So she packed her little coupe and headed north from San Francisco.

The Atsugewi ('People Who Live in the Pine Forest') live along Hat Creek, east of Mount Lassen and south of Mount Shasta, about sixty miles east of Redding. Susan found herself in very wild country, with lava beds, rattlesnakes, bears, mountain lions, and coyotes. "To me, it was like going to the moon," she said. This was because there was such disparity between American society and the Atsugewi culture. She was surrounded by huge mountains, rushing rivers, wild animals, some not-so-tame natives, and some not-so-civilized whites.

She rented a shack so the Atsugewi would not think of her as needing too many comforts. Then, after learning that the Cassel Post Office was the place to find "Indians," she walked there in the morning.

"There were many Indians there, sitting around. Not talking, just sitting. I do not know what they were waiting for, they never seemed to get any mail," Susan told me. She did not know that the post office was the local "Department of Employment" and a place for people to exchange news and information. Whenever a farmer wanted a fence built, he picked up an "Indian" from the post office. Loggers, ranchers, and construction companies all did the same.

Susan "did not know where to begin," so she simply talked with the first person who seemed to be friendly, Lee Bone. She failed to record her first conversation, but word got out quickly that she was paying a dollar a day for information—the same as the Atsugewi received for hard labor. Contrary to the opinion of her advisor, Susan had discovered that the Atsugewi were "not such a simple culture, after all." Although some people wondered about being paid "just for talk," Susan received many responses, recording over two thousand pages with her Number Two pencil and hardbacked notepads, from the people of Hat Creek, Dixie Valley, and Goose Valley.

One evening she decided to move out of her shack. "I returned to discover that a friendly rattlesnake had taken up domicile under my cot!" She promptly moved to Rising River Lodge and continued her research from there.

In 1989, I met Susan through *News from Native California,* a quarterly produced by Malcolm Margolin in Berkeley, California. Susan had been reading the magazine and had seen my name and my tribal identity, A-juma-wi/Atsuge-wi. "'Atsugewi' just leaped out of the page at me—the very people I had studied long ago," she stated.

Soon I was visiting her in Carson City, Nevada. We looked over the old narratives. There were my elders, peering back at me through the pages and through time. It was exciting to read the transcriptions of the old stories I had heard when I was just a child holding on to my father's legs in the midst of a gathering of grandmothers and grandfathers, in the darkness of winter evenings, long ago.

I asked her one day in 1992 if she had ever made it to Fiji. "No," she said, "I never did, but I hope to. Some day in the future, perhaps." Susan Park was born in 1908 and was in fragile health when we first met in 1989. She often said that she would not make it through the winter of 1993. She did not: she died just before Thanksgiving 1992. If she had lived just one more year, she might have seen her work published at last, in my master's thesis, *Yo-Kenaswi Usji (Necklace of Hearts).*

According to the legends of my people, Naponoha (Cocoon Man) changed into Night-Flying Butterfly during the "great transformation." This butterfly is not to be confused with the moth, but is the huge butterfly that appears to be a moth. Up close, it has all the markings of a monarch butterfly. It could be compared to the black jaguar: upon closer examination, the fur of the black panther reveals all of the patterns and markings of the "regular" jaguar, but black is very dominant.

The Night-Flying Butterfly is beautiful. When viewed in the sunlight, it shines with the most precious colors of camouflaged shadows. The powder on its body is thick, like fur, and it moves so softly! My boy Sonny, when he was five years old, once asked me, "Dad, do you know what happens to butterflies when they get old? I mean, when they get *really* old?" And then he answered his own question: "They turn into moths."

So, Naponoha may be the wise and creative butterfly that turned into something like a moth. But Naponoha is also much more than that, according to our legends. He also helped create much of the world and the universe.

Lela Rhoades, one of the very old wisdom-keepers of our history, gave our nation a song:

> Aboni-ka-ha, me-moo-ischi-ee
> Aboni-ka-ha, me-moo-ischi-ee
> Aboni-ka-ha, me-moo-ischi-ee

She sang the melody three times in a variety of tempos. Then she explained that it meant, "in American,"

> Great Wonder, we are your children,
> Great Power, we are your children,
> Great Spirit, we are your children.

It should not be surprising, then, that Naponoha possesses all of the abilities to dream and to have his dreams fulfilled. He can see all of the world around him. His vision goes through the mountains, deep into the universe, and far into the thoughts of his people. Naponoha is a prophet, a dreamer, a creator, a wonder. In this narrative, Naponoha takes the form of a leader of his people—a warrior.

Latowni is the ceremonial roundhouse at Pittville around which the people lived. The Mice brothers stay awake all night, get into the food, and cache or scatter it. They are mischievous. It is their "way" to stay awake at night and to sleep during the day. Weasel intends to scold the boys for their nocturnal troublemaking. What Weasel does not know is that Naponoha has a mission for the boys.

The Klamath people (Oregon, just north of the Modocs) have stolen three articles: the Pestle, used for grinding seeds and dried foods, and representing the labor of the people; the Sky Knife, a long sword made from clear obsidian, and representing the protection of the nation; and the Diamond, a lucky stone that contains a rainbow and brings goodness to those who honor its power. (Naponoha later uses the Sky Knife while riding his dog during the war, taunting the enemy.) Naponoha tells the Mice brothers that they should go north to the Klamath people and retrieve the tribal materials, which they do.

When the Mice brothers have completed their mission, they return home, make a lot of noise in camp at night, then sleep during the day. Their father is Coyote. The Mice frolic around, play war by shooting at each other, and wind up shooting their father in the ear. They think they are pretty tough.

A few days later, a Klamath man arrives at Latowni and says there is going to be a war to regain the articles. Naponoha sends for Frog to interpret his message, but Frog gets it wrong. When the messenger returns, Naponoha this time asks Lark to translate, which she does. After displaying the recovered articles, Naponoha agrees to have a war to settle the issue. So the Dixie Valley people and the Klamath people meet. The war lines are drawn in the Fall River valley. Twins do the interpreting for each side, carrying messages back and forth. Each side constructs rock fortifications in the forest and just beyond the ridge, but they actually meet face-to-face in the valley, the Dixie Valley warriors facing the Klamaths in a long line within arrow range. Naponoha has a huge dog that he rides like a horse, and he has the Sky Knife, which flashes in the sunlight, and his long hair shines. The Klamaths are bewildered. And so the war begins.

The Klamath people have a "witch" with them. Every time the arrow hits the witch, it glances off. Finally, the witch tells how he can be killed, and the Dixie Valley Indians use this information to kill him. The witch turns out to be a turtle, all the Klamaths are killed, and the war is over. Turtle, who is a powerful "doctor," revives. He takes a stick and brings all the Klamaths back to life. The Klamath people agree to abandon their war over the Diamond. Both sides smoke to seal the "word."

Naponoha then declares that the timber line will always be a reminder that there was once a war between the Klamath people and Dixie Valley. He also decides that he and the twin interpreters should stay beside the river for a while, telling the story, so the history might be told properly. Turtle and some of the other Klamaths want to stay in the Fall River valley, which Naponoha decides to allow. So Turtle and some of the Klamath people remain in the Pit River country, which is how the turtle came to be in the Fall River valley. It must have been the first time any of the Dixie Valley people had seen a turtle.

In the end, all of the Dixie Valley people return home to have a big sweat in their sweat house. Everybody gathers together and Naponoha makes a big smoke of many colors and many shapes. It is so beautiful that the people agree that, if there is ever any more trouble, there should be a big fire and a big smoke announcing the event, and all will assemble quickly.

All this was recorded to preserve the history of the conflict between the Dixie Valley and Klamath people and to show that it is not right to steal or claim something that belongs to another. The timber has long since been cut, and the rock fortifications removed by settlers—but the history, like the spirit of the people, remains.

NOTE

1. All quotes attributed to Susan Park in this introduction are drawn from conversations I had with her during the years 1989–1992.

FURTHER READING

See Thomas Garth's "Atsugewi Ethnography" and his "Atsugewi" article in the California volume of the Smithsonian *Handbook.* See also David Olmstead's *A Lexicon of Atsugewi.* Diane Walters presents an Atsugewi story, "Coyote and Moon Woman (Apwarukeyi)," in Victor Golla and Shirley Silver's *Northern California Texts.* Darryl Wilson has edited a collection of some forty-five narratives recorded by Susan Brandenstein Park from Atsugewi and Achumawi storytellers: see his *Yo-Kenaswi Usji (Necklace of Hearts).* He has also written an autobiography, *The Morning the Sun Went Down.*

NAPONOHA

Naponoha said this: "The Mice in Latowni, whatever grub they had, they changed it around all night. Next morning, Yas, the Weasel, got mad because they took their grub to another place." And Naponoha said, "Leave these boys alone. Don't scold them."

That night Naponoha said to the Mice, "You two ought to go north, get the Diamond and the Pestle. If you could get that . . ." And they listened and they whispered to one another, "What does he mean?" And, he said, "You might, too, get the Sky Knife at the same time. It's back north." And [the] Mice said, "Where about does he mean, anyway?"

They did the same thing that night—made lots of noise, changed the grub again. Along toward daylight they went, and everything was quiet after they left. And they went north, the two little Mice. They were brothers.

They kept going till they got there. They stopped overnight and then would keep going. They got to a great big river and they saw a lot of people on the other side, and the two little Mice said, "Maybe that's the place Naponoha meant. Maybe that's the place. And how are we going to get across?" the two little Mice said.

And they said, "We'll wait till dark comes and maybe someone will cross with a canoe and maybe we'll get across that way. And all night we'll do that."

And some people were waiting, and someone came across, and the Mice hid in the tules, and someone called to the man to come across and he went across. It was dark-time and he came up to shore. "There's a chance, there's a chance," one mouse said. "Now, get ready!"

And the man got in the canoe and the Mice jumped in under the man and they went across, and when they got to the shore on the other side, as soon as they hit shore, the two little Mice jumped out, and these two men didn't know that the Mice were in the canoe.

And the Klamath chief said, "Well, we better have a Big Time tonight. We'll look at the Diamond and the Pestle and the Knife. We better show them," he said.

"Now we got the right place," [the] Mice said when they heard it. Little Mice said, "There's our chance now, we must be sure now." And everybody came all to one place in the *chema-ha,* the sweat house, and they got ready and showed the Diamond and the Pestle and the Knife.

And the two Mice were behind the legs of the people. They hid and no one knew they were there. They watched while the Diamond and Pestle and Knife were being shown.

Oh! there was a big light over the sweat house when they showed the Diamond. And then everybody got through showing it and they put the Diamond and Pestle and Knife away, and the Mice wondered where they put them away.

Nobody went to sleep that night and the Mice began taking the grub that night the same as they did at home. And they went to look for the Diamond and the Pestle and the Knife.

They found them and they took them outside and they went all over the camp, all over where the people were living. They ran across Pi-jko, the Lark, who had a Klamath Indian for a husband.

They said, "Hello," and they pinched her and that woman said, "What's bothering me so much?" And [the] Mice said, "That's us two," and they went up and they talked to her, and she said, "Two bad brothers. How did you get over here?"

Well, they said, "Put us across. We want to go home." They told Pi-jko, and she did, she put them across, and they let her know what they took away, and they went to where the canoe was and all got in and went to the other side. And they said, "Good-bye," to Pi-jko and they came back, the two little Mice, and she went back to the other side in the dark.

And she called, "Brothers, be sure and get back." And the little Mice said, "All right," and they came back. They stopped over night, and they came and stopped and came, and they got home way in the middle of the night, and when they got back they made a noise and the Big Time chief felt everyone in Latowni was sorry. Naponoha was sorry for them, and they made the same noise, and when daylight came they slept.

They had a bow and arrow apiece, and they shot one another and then they shot Coyote in the ear. Coyote was Mice's father.

"Oh!" said Coyote. "You're hurting me." And Mice said, "That's what I'm going to do when I fight." 'Course they went to sleep, them two.

Oh, a few days after that he says, "Friends, *she-me-wolol, she-me-wolol.*"

That time the Klamath Indian came over to tell them they were going to have a war because the Mice stole the Diamond. And the Klamath Indian said, "*She-me-wolol, she-me-wolol.*" And he said this through the smoke hole of Latowni.

And Naponoha asked Ali-yem, Frog, who spoke all languages, what was meant by this. And Yas ran over there to Ali-yem to tell her that Naponoha wanted her to come over and say what the Klamath Indian meant. So, she came there inside, and the Klamath Indian said, "*She-me-wolol, she-me-wolol.*"

And Naponoha said to Ali-yem, "What does he mean?" "Oh," she said, "They are going to have a dance down here, that's what he means." And, of course, after she said this the Klamath Indian went back, and after he went back the Klamath people asked him, "What did they say?" And he said, "They didn't say anything to me."

They sent him back again to Naponoha's place. He came again to the same place and he said, "*She-me-wolol, she-me-wolol*" again. And Naponoha said, "What does he mean? You said he was saying they are going to have a dance. What did he come back for?"

So, Naponoha said, "You get Pi-jko now," and Yas went over to let her know again. So she came over, and the Klamath Indian said, "*She-me-wolol.*" And Pi-jko said, "He says the two Mice stole the Diamond, the Pestle, and the Knife. And he says there is going to be a war. That's what he's saying. They want the Diamond right back; otherwise there will be a war."

And the two little Mice were sleeping all the time. They would not get up. And then the Klamath Indian went back, and Naponoha said, "You two better get up. What did you do with the Diamond and Pestle and Knife? You stole them. We used to lose those things. It's a good thing you have them back. We're going to have a war with the Klamath Indians," he said.

The two little Mice jumped up and they shot their father, Coyote, in the ear again, the same way, and they said, "Yes, sir, right over there." "Go get them then," Naponoha said. "Where are they?"

They went and got them and gave the Diamond and Pestle and Knife to Naponoha, and they untied and untied and held the Diamond up and it was just like lightning. And the Klamath Indian saw it. Oh, the Klamath Indian saw that light, and they sent that same Indian over again, and he said, "*She-me-wolol, she-me-wolol.*"

And Pi-jko said, "You better get ready to fight. Hurry and get ready. If you ain't going to give the Diamond up, there is going to be a war!"

"All right," Naponoha said. Pi-jko can talk any language. And Naponoha, he told Pi-jko, "All right. We are going to have a war." And the Indian went back and he said, "Yes, they are willing to fight, and right away." That's what the Klamath Indian told his own people, and Naponoha's people got ready and they went down on the side of Fall River.

Naponoha's people were in that edge of timber there, and the Klamath Indians were on the other side of that ridge of timber, and each side got interpreters halfway between the Klamath Indians and Naponoha's Indians. There were two twins there and those were the interpreters for the two sides, and they went forth and back with what they said.

The Klamath Indians sent over a man who said, "If you don't give up that Diamond, we are going to have a war."

So then Naponoha's interpreter went back and told Naponoha, and he said, "They said for you to give up the Diamond, otherwise they're going to have a war." Naponoha sent him back. "Tell him I'm not going to give it up. Tell him we'll have a war."

And the interpreter told the Klamath interpreter, "They ain't going to give up. They are going to have a war."

So the Klamath Indians said, "All right, we'll have a war and we'll fight right away." And they all got ready and they fought.

They fought. They shot one another and Naponoha had a great big dog that hunted around, and he used it as a horse and he rode it with his hair flying (and Naponoha had great long hair, bright hair), and he had a great long knife in his hand, and when the Klamath Indians saw him they didn't know what to do.

And he told his people, "Go ahead and fight!" And they killed all the Klamath Indians. They killed every one of them.

But they couldn't kill To-ka-jisa, the witch. They didn't know how to. They shot him and the arrows just glanced off. And To-ka-jisa said like this to Naponoha: "I like this country." And he said to Naponoha, "If I stand straight up and you shoot down at me, that's the only way you can kill me."

So, he stood straight up, and they shot down into his mouth, and that was the only way they could kill him. "I don't like to go back to Klamath. I like this country, that's why I told you how to kill me. If I didn't tell you, I could clean you all up."

And To-ka-jisa took a stick and he hit the Klamath Indians, and they all came back to life. And Naponoha said, "You people better go back." And the Klamath Indians said, "All right. We give up. You whipped us all right."

So he said, "When you were [in] the war lines, [that was] good. That is our timber. It shows that you were Klamath Indians on that side. So it will be on my side, the same way." That's what Naponoha told them and that interpreter.

"Those two twin interpreters will be there along on the river. So the people would know what we did. So they can tell about it in history, what trouble we had, and it will settle it right." That's what Naponoha said. And the Klamath Indian said, "All right." And he said, the Klamath Indian said, "I'm sorry, but I can't help it. I would not think about it anymore. You can have the Diamond and Pestle and Knife for good."

"How about it," Naponoha said to To-ka-jisa. "Why are *you* going to stay here in this country?" And the Klamath chief said, "What can I do if they want to stay here? I cannot kick over them because you whipped us and asked me, that's the reason I have to let my man stay. I can't kick," he said.

"Well, let them stay here," Naponoha said.

And that's the reason that Hap-ej, the Turtle, is in the Fall River valley. Hap-ej belonged to the Klamath and he spread all the way down the Sacramento Valley. And they scattered all over. That was the Klamath Indians. There Hap-ej was, and they scattered him.

They sat down and smoked, and then they said, "Well, I go." And the Klamath Indian went back.

So, Naponoha came back where he belonged, and they got home, all on both sides. So they had a Big Time, Naponoha's people. And he let all his people see the Diamond and the Pestle and the Knife. He said, "We used to have this and we got it back." And Naponoha told his people, "We've got it back."

And it was all right. Everything was settled fine and dandy, and Naponoha was in the *chema-ha,* everybody was in the *chema-ha.* It was a great big sweat house. Naponoha told his people, "I'll show you what I can do." And he filled his pipe with tobacco, Naponoha did, and he smoked and he smoked like a cloud inside the sweat house. It was so pretty, and they all looked, and all the Indians said, "Ain't that pretty?"

It was a pretty color and all kinds of shapes, rings. And all the Indians said, "We'll all have to go back where we belong, and if anything happens let us know." So he said, "Whenever you have anything happen, build a big smoke so we will know."

That's what Naponoha told his people. And the people said, "All right." And they all scattered and went back.

That's what it is, Naponoha's history.

It shows plainly right now in the timber. That was all.

10

A Story of Lizard

YAHI

1915

ISHI, NARRATOR

EDWARD SAPIR, COLLECTOR

HERBERT W. LUTHIN AND LEANNE HINTON, TRANSLATORS

INTRODUCTION BY HERBERT W. LUTHIN

Ishi, the narrator of this story, is something of a legend in the history of post-Contact Native America and is a touchstone figure in California anthropology. His story is well-known—it's been told in books, articles, and films—so I won't do much more than summarize it here. But it's only fair to say that the "legend" of Ishi is nothing if not a conflicted one.

The subtitle to Theodora Kroeber's celebrated Ishi source book, *Ishi in Two Worlds,* provides us with a good starting point in this regard: *A Biography of the Last Wild Indian in North America.* Whatever he may have been to himself, for non-Indians Ishi, quite simply, stood as an icon of the natural man, a latter-day remnant of pre-Contact Native America. The irony, of course, is that Ishi lived anything but a natural human life, was anything but a pre-Contact "natural man."

Ishi was the last Yahi. His tribe (the southernmost division of the Yana group), after decades of conflict with settlers and prospectors, skirmishes with the U.S. Army, and what can only be called the wanton "poaching" of white vigilantes who killed for sport, was all but wiped out along with the rest of the Yana in a concerted campaign of genocide carried out by local militia groups. Ishi was born into this shattered world—probably in 1862—about two years before these "final solution" massacres took place.

Ishi survived because his band survived, decimated but intact, only to be surprised a year later by vigilantes in their Mill Creek camp and decimated once more. Only a handful, perhaps as many as a dozen, escaped—among them the little boy Ishi, his mother, and an older sister. This small group then went into deep hiding, vanishing almost without trace for forty years. Except for a few scattered incidents, as far as anyone knew, by 1872 the Yahi were functionally extinct. But life went on for Ishi's people in hiding. With no births, though (there were no marriageable children in the group when it slipped "underground"), the old just grew older, and the group gradually dwindled. By the time Ishi reached the age of forty, after nearly four decades of hiding, the last member of his group, his own aged mother, had died.

That year was 1908. On August 29, 1911, naked and starving, hair still singed off in mourning three years after the death of his last human companion, Ishi gave himself up outside a slaughterhouse in Oroville. Until he walked out of hiding and into the history of twentieth-century California, Ishi's entire life, from infancy to middle age, was spent in hiding—a sort of backcountry version of Anne Frank's concealment. The stress of that existence, a life of constant hardship and fear of discovery, is difficult for us even to imagine. Ishi was Yahi, all right—purely, deeply, fully so. But the Yahi life he knew was not the free, self-possessing, traditional existence of his ancestors; and it is a mistake to think that Ishi can represent for us—for anyone—some animistic "free spirit" or serve as a spokesman of untrammeled Native American life and culture.

Upon his discovery, Ishi became an overnight media sensation: a "wild Indian," a living Stone Age man—captured in the backcountry of modern California! When the news hit the stands in San Francisco, Alfred Kroeber, head of anthropology at the University of California, dispatched the linguist-anthropologist T. T. Waterman to Oroville to establish communication and bring him to the university. To protect him from exploitation (though let's not forget that Ishi was also the anthropological "find" of a lifetime), Kroeber gave him light employment as a live-in caretaker at the university's new Museum of Art and Anthropology, as a way of providing him with pocket money and safe lodging. His days were often filled with linguistic and ethnographic work, for there was an endless stream of scholars coming to work with him, and other interested visitors seeking audience. And on Sunday afternoons, he appeared as a kind of "living exhibit" in the museum itself, chipping arrowheads, drilling fire, and demonstrating other native Yahi crafts and techniques for the public. Thus did Ishi live out the last five years of his life—in truth, in relative contentment and ease, unlikely though this may seem. Those who knew him and became his friends came to love him. He died of tuberculosis in March of 1916.

Given this extraordinary life, it should come as no surprise to learn that Ishi's stories—which only now, eighty years after their narration, are finally being made available to scholars and the public alike—are strikingly unlike anything else known in California oral literature. In some respects, they are of a piece with known Yana tradition; in others, they are eccentric to an amazing degree. Yet we are extremely fortunate to have them, for they tell us a great deal about Yahi life and custom and even more about Ishi himself.

The story presented here was taken down by the great linguist Edward Sapir, who came to California in the summer of 1915 to work with Ishi in what was to be his last year. Ishi was probably already ill by the time Sapir arrived, but in August, after many weeks of steady work, his illness grew too pronounced to ignore, and he was placed in the hospital, where he died about six months later. Ishi's untimely death was no doubt the main reason Sapir never returned to his notebooks and worked up these texts for publication. And in truth, it would have been a daunting task, for much of the work of translation and verification was incomplete at the time Ishi was hospitalized. Sapir called his work with Ishi "the most time-consuming and nerve-wracking that I have ever undertaken," noting that "Ishi's imperturbable good humor alone made the work possible" (Golla 1984b:194).

Sapir recorded Ishi's stories the hard way: by hand, in detailed phonetic transcription. All told, he recorded at least six stories, filling five notebooks—more than two hundred pages of text. Most of the pages are only sparsely glossed at best (indeed, two entire notebooks contain only unglossed Yahi text), and this poses a challenge for linguists of the Yahi Trans-

FIGURE 3. Ishi.
Courtesy Phoebe Apperson Hearst Museum of Anthropology
and the Regents of the University of California.

lation Project, who are trying to reconstruct their meaning.[1] I present here the best-worked, best-glossed text, "A Story of Lizard." Even so, there are places (duly marked) where we are still not sure exactly what is going on.

Ishi's narrative style is often demanding, at least for those coming from a Western literary tradition. Readers may well find this to be the most difficult of all the selections in this volume, thanks to Ishi's stripped-down, elliptical approach to telling a story, even a long one, and the short, bulletlike bursts of his delivery. Compositionally, "A Story of Lizard" is more of a suite than a story. Rather than a single overarching plot, it contains a series of episodes and situations, each with its own interior form, all of which combine to form the larger whole. Some of these episodes and situations recur cyclically a number of times. For instance, the Ya'wi, or "Pine-nutting," episode occurs three times, in parts verbatim; and there are four separate "Arrow-making" episodes, some quite elaborately detailed. The remaining two episodes are unique: one, a "Grizzly Bear" adventure, is essentially a story-within-a-story; the second is a "Night Dance" episode that is not matched by other elements within the tale. Rather than recounting the story sequentially, I will briefly describe the individual episodes, then explain how they are pieced together to comprise the whole.

Arrow-making

Ishi opens his tale with a glimpse of Lizard making arrows, an activity that provides the background for the entire story. In some sense it is Lizard's unflagging industry that serves as the story's thematic center. Other adventures—the various alarms and excursions that make up the "plot"—may come and go, but the arrow-making is always there.[2] (It is something of a joke among those of us working on these stories, that the real reason Lizard always seems to be making arrows is because he keeps losing them all in his fights with the Ya'wi.) Ishi was himself a master arrow-maker, and reportedly loved to flake arrowheads, experimenting with all sorts of materials. Indeed, the arrowheads he made during his brief tenure at the old Museum of Anthropology in San Francisco are among the finest in the Lowie Museum's collection of artifacts. One can almost learn how to make arrows from Ishi's descriptions of the process in the four Arrow-making episodes.[3]

Pine-nutting

The "Ya'wi" is what the Yahi called the Wintun people to the west—enemies in ancient times. Lizard ventures into hostile territory to collect pine-nuts for his people, and is attacked by a band of Ya'wi warriors. He keeps his cool, pretending their war-whoops are "nothing but the wind," and shoots his arrows "straight into their faces." In the end, he makes it back home with a fresh supply of pine-nuts. The oral-formulaic style of patterned repetitions is very prominent within these sections, based primarily on the variation of Yahi directional elements ('to the west', 'to the east', 'across a stream', 'up a mountain', and so on) against a common stem, especially *mooja-* 'to shoot' and *ni- ~ ne-* 'to go'.

Grizzly Bear and Long-Tailed Lizard

This is the most complex episode of the story—a fully developed narrative in its own right. Lizard runs out of *baiwak'i* sticks for making the foreshafts of his arrows. He sends Long-Tailed Lizard to collect some more. Long-Tail is surprised by Grizzly Bear, who swallows him up and "grows pregnant." When Long-Tail fails to return, Lizard sets out after him. He finds the *baiwak'i* all scattered around, and Grizzly's tracks, and guesses the rest. Gathering up the sticks, he returns home. As a token of mourning, the sticks are not used, but burned. At daybreak, after cutting off his hair and smearing his face with pitch (further tokens of mourning), Lizard sets out to find the bear.

What happens next is unclear, because there are some thorny problems with the interpretation of Sapir's text and glosses throughout this section. But it appears as if Lizard travels to Grizzly Bear's favorite feeding ground and climbs up into a convenient tree toward evening to have a smoke and wait for her. In the morning she comes, as she seems destined to do, to feed on the *k'asna* vines (identified only vaguely as a vine growing near water). Lizard has prepared himself by draping one of the vines around his neck and letting it dangle down, the idea being (we think) that when Grizzly arrives and begins to feed, she will tug on the vine and alert him. In the morning she comes and starts to feed. Lizard puts a loop into his bowstring and lets Grizzly pull him down onto her back, whereupon he slips the loop around her neck and lets the strung bow strangle her. After gouging out her eyes (the revenge against a man-eating bear is always harsh), he slits her open and recovers Long-Tailed Lizard. (As Leanne Hinton points out, this is a familiar motif in folklore: Europeans know it from "Little Red Riding Hood.") In the morning it's back to making arrows.

The Night Dance

One day, as Lizard is "busy with his arrow-making," he breaks a shaft. The break in the shaft foretells a break in the routine: some neighboring people are having a dance. For the next three days, the domestic rhythms of the camp are inverted, as Lizard's people dance all night and—except for one attempt at gathering food, abandoned the next time around as too much hassle—sleep all day. We simply have no idea what all the "excrement" is about: the way the text reads, at the beginning of the Dance episode, Lizard's people are given some excrement (the stem *wak'i-* 'shit' is unambiguous on this point), which they smear all over themselves. After the last night of dancing, Lizard scolds them for being slug-a-beds, whereupon they all bathe themselves clean and get back to work. Life returns to normal, and Lizard resumes his arrow-making.

When we put all these episodes together, paying careful attention to their cycles of repetition, an overall pattern reveals itself—the true architecture of this fascinating tale. If we take the four Arrow-making episodes to be the thematic baseline or rhythmic "pulse" of the narrative, view the Pine-nutting episodes with their Ya'wi attacks as intermittent events that punctuate that baseline, and recognize the unique Grizzly Bear and Night Dance episodes as extraordinary happenings that stand far out against that background "hum," we might represent the narrative structure schematically as in figure 4:

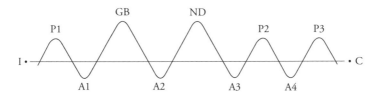

FIGURE 4. Narrative structure of Ishi's "A Story of Lizard." (I = Introduction; P = Pine-nutting; A = Arrow-making; GB = Grizzly Bear; ND = Night Dance; C = Conclusion.)

What seems at first a hopeless déjà vu of motifs and situations proves now to be quite the opposite: a carefully controlled narration of great balance and dignity.

When I first went to work on this story, nearly a decade ago, I felt it to be one of the bleakest accounts of survival I had ever seen—a relentless tale of repetitive drudgery and danger. Now, looking at it anew, I see it in a different light. Like a Beowulf or a Roland in European tradition, Lizard represents the essence of a Yahi culture-hero. Lizard provides for his people—unfailingly. Instead of despair, there is reassurance in these unvarying routines and in Lizard's unflappable reliability in a crisis.

And in truth, I think Ishi, as the only able-bodied man among his lost band of survivors for all those long, lean years of hiding, must have been something of a Lizard himself.

A NOTE ON THE TRANSLATION

Because so much has been said for and about Ishi, and so little has ever come forth from Ishi himself, we have felt a special urgency, in dealing with the records he left behind, to let Ishi be heard in his own voice and words at last. Granted, proclamations like this have a hollow ring when the end-result is a translation. After all, what Ishi *actually* said in "A Story of Lizard" (as in these lines from the very beginning of the myth) was this:[4]

Híri',
    héebil' k^h híri'mawna . . .
K'úllil'.
Niwílji',
    wísdu' gi iwílc^{hi}.   5
Nilóopji'.
Domjawáldi' k^h díitel^{la}
(Hóok'awdubalgu' gi wéeyump^{ha};
dóowayalcidibil' wéeyump^{ha}).
Bóot'an' c^h wísh^i.   10
Júspja',
    jóst'al'^{i}.
Jewóo' c^h yónbal'^{i}.
Jé^{h}duwoo' k^h báan^u.
Busdím' c^h Yáa'^{wi}!   15

Since there is no one left alive who can speak or understand this language, the need for translation is unimpeachable. Still, we have wanted to minimize the degree to which the voices of translation mingle with Ishi's own. So where, in most other literary translations, obscure or ambiguous sentences are silently clarified—with the addition of a phrase or transition here, a "she said" there—we have chosen another tack. Though this is still a literary—not a literal—translation, we have nonetheless tried to convey only what is present in the Yahi text, just as Ishi dictated it to

Sapir in 1915. That means that we have had to explore other methods of providing readers with the interpretive and textual information they need in order to follow the story. We have settled on two devices, footnotes and sidenotes, to help us "buy" this degree of fidelity.

The sidenotes (set in the right margin, in space fortuitously made available by the broken-line format of the translation) are used mostly to supply key missing information—primarily proper names or specific nouns that are referred to only by pronoun in the original, and which the reader might have trouble intuiting. Less-critical information—of a contextual, interpretive, linguistic, or philological nature—has been consigned to footnotes. To illustrate the way the sidenotes work (the footnotes should need no explanation), let's take a look at an excerpt (lines 138–149) from the translation:

> He made himself arrows in the morning.
> He rubbed them and smoothed them.   *the cane shafts of the arrows*
> He was busy at it all day—
>   finished.
> As he turned them on the ground,
>   he painted on the bands.
> He finished putting on the painted bands.
> He soaked them in water,   *the feathers*
>   wrapped them on with sinew—
>   finished.
> He trimmed the feather-vanes—   *with a flint blade*
>   finished.

At line 139, while the reader can certainly deduce that the pronoun "them" refers generally to the arrows of the preceding line, the sidenote allows us to provide a bit more specificity: it's the cane *shafts* of the arrows that Lizard is smoothing, as Sapir's fieldnotes indicate. At line 145, the reader may be forgiven for being puzzled as to the referent for the pronoun "them." But a quick glance to the side supplies that information right when it's needed, and saves us from having to falsify the text by interpolating the missing referent (either with distracting brackets, or, worse, without) into the line: that is, "He soaked the feathers in water." Our unembellished translation makes it clear that Ishi himself, to whom the process of arrow-making was second nature, thought the circumstances too obvious to spell out using the concrete noun. Finally, at line 148,

Sapir's own gloss for the Yahi sentence *Dee-wunii-'* (literally, 'cut some-thing-feather-NARRATIVE TENSE') reads "He cut off vanes with flint," but in fact the information about the flint blade is not there in the Yahi—it's only implied by context and cultural knowledge; the sidenote here allows us to provide this information (useful for helping readers visualize the action) without embellishing the translation itself.[5]

NOTES

1. The Yahi Translation Project was constituted at Berkeley in 1986, specifically to prepare Sapir's unpublished Yahi materials for publication. Victor Golla was the project director, and Leanne Hinton coordinated the Berkeley seminar that kicked off the project. Bruce Nevin and Ken Whistler served as special consultants. Other researchers who have kept involved in the project over the years include Jean Perry and this author.

2. In other of Ishi's stories, different sets of domestic activities such as leaching acorns and going for water take the place of arrow-making yet serve the same narrative function.

3. In order to determine the complete sequence of steps in arrow-making, it is necessary to build a composite sequence based on a collation of steps from the various episodes, because no one episode contains all the steps in the process.

4. This passage is cast in an informal practical orthography devised for the Yanan languages; it balances linguistic needs with the desire to be helpful with regard to pronunciation. Doubled characters represent length, stress is indicated with an acute accent over the vowel, and superscript letters are voiceless. Certain phonetic processes involved with prosody (final aspiration, devoicing, secondary and emphatic primary stress) are preserved in the transcription.

5. The text has been parsed into lines primarily on the basis of predication units (one per line), augmented by reference to prosodic features like final-syllable retention and Sapir's own field punctuation (see Luthin 1991 for a detailed discussion of these issues).

FURTHER READING

For an account of Ishi's two lives, Theodora Kroeber's *Ishi in Two Worlds* is indispensable as well as good reading; she covers the brutal years of extermination in great historical detail, as well as what is known of Ishi's life in hiding, and describes his last years at the museum. For those interested in Ishi's arrow-making, Saxton Pope's "Yahi Archery" gives a thorough description of the process (Pope was Ishi's doctor and closest friend at the university). The Ishi texts will eventually be published as volume 9 of *The Collected Works of Edward Sapir* (Sapir, forthcoming). Leanne Hinton, with artist Susan Roth, has excerpted this story in a stunningly illustrated children's book called *Ishi's Tale of Lizard*. Finally, there have been two recent films made about Ishi: the HBO production, *The Last of His Tribe* (Hook 1992), starring Graham Green as Ishi, and the Yahi Film Project's excellent documentary, *Ishi, the Last Yahi* (Riffe and Roberts 1994). A fair amount of Ishi collectanea is on more-or-less permanent display at the Hearst (née Lowie) Museum in Berkeley.

A STORY OF LIZARD

He made arrows,
   he was busy with his arrow-making . . .

I.	[PINE-NUTTING I]

He wanted to start back.
He went westward across a stream,
   went to gather pine-nuts west across a stream.   5
He went westward up a mountain.
He put his quiver down on the ground.
(He had just gone and gotten some old deer antlers;   *to use as a quiver*
he carried the antlers around on his shoulders.)
The one pine-nutting cracked the cones with a rock.   10
He was getting out the nuts,
   got them broken open.
And then he scooped them up in his hands.
He took up his storage basket again.
The Ya'wi shouted their war-whoops!   15
He took up his quiver again.
The Ya'wi whooped.
He drew his bow from his quiver.
"The wind is blowing," he said,

"It is storming," he said.   20
They rushed against him.*

Now he shot off his arrows,
    hit them straight in the face.
He went back east down the hill.
He shot off arrows to the north,   25
    shot off arrows to the south,
    shot off arrows to the east,
        hit them straight in the face.
He went back into the water at the river,
    went back east across the water,   30
    came out of the water at the river.
The Ya'wi scattered out of sight.

Now he stepped along the trail.
He got back home during the night.
He put his storage baskets away again.   35

II.   [ARROW-
                                                              MAKING I]
Early in the morning he smooths them down.   *the arrow shaft*
He made arrows,   *canes*
    rubbed the shafts smooth,
    worked at his arrow-making—
        finished.   40
He fitted the cane shafts tight around the arrow shafts—
    finished.
He socketed the foreshafts.
Turning them on the ground,
    he painted the bands.   45   *on the*
                                                                     arrow
Now he was busy all the day.   *butts*
He fletched the arrows—
    finished.
And then he trimmed the feathers—
    finished.   50
He charred the feathers black,

* Literally, "He was rushed at."

bound the shafts together with sinew—
    finished.

Now he smoothed the foreshafts.   *with a scouring*
He finished and put them aside for the night.   *rush*
                                                           55

III.   [GRIZZLY BEAR
"It seems there aren't enough to eat," he said.   EPISODE]
(Enough pine-nuts,
    for those coming to him for food.)
The woman shared them out.

"There are no more of my foreshaft sticks," he said.   60
"Let's have Long-Tail get some for me," he said.*
"Let's see you go get *báiwak'i!*" he said to him.†

And then the one getting *báiwak'i,*
    now he went off.
He twisted the *báiwak'i* shoots out of the ground,   65
    broke them off at the roots.
He laid the shafts down on the ground.
"There are plenty of sticks!" said Long-Tail.

Up jumped Grizzly Bear!
And then she eats him!   70
Grizzly Bear swallowed him down and grew pregnant.
She turned around,
    lumbered back down the middle of the trail.

When it was just too dark for gathering *báiwak'i,*
    Lizard took up his quiver.   75 *to go find*
Sure enough, there was the *báiwak'i*—   *out what*
    it was lying on the ground.   *happened*

Now he looked around all over.
Sure enough, there was the grizzly bear,
    her tracks.   80
"Little one,
    did you get eaten?" he said.

* Referring to *páat'elwalla,* a long-tailed lizard.
† A type of wood for making foreshaft sticks.

He gathered up the *báiwak'i*,
  carried it back to the house in his arms,
  placed the *báiwak'i* in the fire.*   85

In the morning,
  "What shall I do?" he said.
And then he cut off his hair.   *in mourning*
He took some pitch,
  finished smearing his face with pitch.   90

"Now how long will it take before you return?" he said.   *said Lizard, to*
  "Don't let it be long," he said.†   *absent Bear*
  "Aren't you getting hungry?" he said.

He strung a *k'asna* vine around his neck.‡   *as a necklace*
He smoked, then filled his pipe: 95
  "I'm having myself a smoke!
  How long before your return?
  Don't let it be long," he said.
  "These are your feeding grounds!" he said.
  "This is the one, all right!" he said.   100
He climbed up the *k'asna* tree,
  settled himself up in the grape vines
    as the sun went down.

When the sun came up,
  "I want to go back west," she said.   105 *Grizzly Bear*
  "He may be sleeping there," she said.   *at the* k'asna
                                                            place

Now Grizzly Bear went back west,
  pregnant with Long-Tail.
Lizard heard her to the east:
  "It must be her," he said.   110

Now she came padding from the east after *k'asna*.
The *k'asna* vine was hanging down from the tree,
  the one wrapped around his neck.

---

* Because of the death associated with it, the wood is now tainted and must be destroyed.
† This is just a wild guess as to the meaning of this difficult line.
‡ Sapir identifies *k'asna* as "wild grape."

She pulled down on the vine.
"Pull hard at me, you who bereaved me!   115
     It would be good if you would die," he said.
     "Pull me down on your back!" he said.
He loosened his bowstring.
"Let it be me who gets packed on your back," he said.
The pregnant one started to climb up.   120
He tied his bowstring into a noose,
     looped it back onto itself.
He was pulled back down from above.   *onto her back*
Grizzly Bear climbed down again,
     tumbled back down to the ground.   125
Grizzly Bear's head fell off,
     strangled in two by the bowstring.
He took his stone knife,
     gouged out her eyes.
He picked up his Long-Tail,   130
     placed him in water,
     bathed him.
He picked up his quiver again—
     put Long-Tail into his quiver.

He got back home.   135
He threw away the makeshift "necklace."
He got back home.

IV.   [ARROW-
                                                              MAKING 2]
He made himself arrows in the morning.
He rubbed them and smoothed them.   *the cane shafts of*
He was busy at it all day—   *the arrows*
     finished.   140
As he turned them on the ground,*
     he painted on the bands.
He finished putting on the painted bands.
He soaked them in water,   145   *the feathe*
     wrapped them on with sinew—
          finished.

* That is, while holding the brush stationary, he rotates the arrows to apply the paint bands.

He trimmed the feather-vanes—
    finished.

with a flint blade

Now he charred the feather-vanes,*
    finished putting them away.

150

Now he bound the joins with sinew—†
    finished.
He put the arrows in his quiver.

Early in the morning,
    she took up her fire-making,
        the woman.

155

Now he rubbed them—
    finished.

the arrows

Now he was busy with it.
He finished socketing the arrow shafts.
And then he painted on the bands.
He put them away finished.
He soaked the feathers in water.

160

Now he fletched the arrows,
    wrapped them on with sinew—
        finished.

165

the feathers

Now he was busy trimming the feathers—
    finished.
He charred the vanes,
    put them away finished.

170

Now he went ahead with putting on red paint.

Now he worked at it,
    put on the red paint,
    put them away finished.

175

Early in the morning,
    as he turned them on the ground,‡
        he flaked arrowheads.

made of obsidian

---

* With a hot stick, to "seal" them.
† Where the shaft fits into the foreshaft.
‡ Here, the action seems to refer to pointing arrowheads.

Now he chipped off flakes.
He finished at sundown.   180

Early in the morning,
    as he turned them on the ground,
        he attached the points to the foreshafts—
            finished.
His deer-horn quiver was slung over his shoulder.   185
He finished,
    put the arrows into it.
At night,
    he finished working.

Early in the morning,   190
    he went after more foreshaft sticks.
He packed home the new *baiwak'i* and put it down.

Now he started scraping the bark off: *with a stone*
    he scraped off the *baiwak'i*.   *scraper*
He finished at sundown.   195

Now he was busy with it—
    he finished working in the dark.

V.   [THE NIGHT
Early in the morning,   DANCE]
    he took his arrow shafts,
        spread them out in front of him.   200

Now he rubbed the arrow shafts smooth.
"What's the matter?" he said.
He broke it on the ground,   *the arrow he was*
    broke it in two on the ground.   *smoothing*

Now he just sat there, waiting.   205

"The women are dancing together," she said.*
"The men are dancing together," he was told.
"Aaah, and you would spread the news, too," he said.
    "That smoothing work of mine just broke for no reason."

* Unclear; Sapir's notes say, "not girls but 'story' creatures," whatever that means.

"They are going out there to dance," she said.　　　　　210
He put away his arrow-making things.

At sundown:
　　"Some funny kind of pitch—
　　　　it smells like that," he said.*
　　"They must be dancing," he said.　　　　　215
And then the pitch—
　　it was given to him,
　　　　the pitch.
"What's the matter?
　　Aaah, so that's what this is," he said—　　　　　220
　　　　"some funny kind of pitch."
"Evidently what it is, is excrement," a man said.†
He gave him the excrement.　　　　　*gave Lizard*
Lizard smeared it all over,
　　smeared the excrement smoothly over himself—　　　　　225
　　　　finished.
"Build a fire!
　　I'm going to dance and play!" he said.

Now they danced:
　　the young women danced, it is said,　　　　　230
　　the young women rested, it is said.

Now he sang out,　　　　　*Lizard did*
　　he went to sing the lead.
He called out the dance.‡

Now he sang along.　　　　　235
They danced.
"I'm just going to let it down, children!" he said.　　　　　*i.e., 'stop dancing'*

"Dance and play!" he said.
　　"Say it!" he said—
　　　　"your play-dancing song!"　　　　　240

* The smell is coming from where they are dancing.
† It's not clear who's speaking here.
‡ Or 'accompanied his dance-song with whispered shouts'.

The play-dancers sang.*
"Now the women shall dance," he said.

> "Henééyah, paneyáh,   [singing]
> Henééyah, henééyah, hiiyaa!"

"Say it!"   245
He called for a dance:
   "Children!
      Say your song!" he said.

Now they were dancing, dancing.
   "Say it!" he said.   250
   "Children!"
They're dancing to the south,
   they're dancing to the north,
      they're dancing to the south,
         they're dancing to the north.   255
"Hiiyaa!" he said.
He called for a dance:
   "Say it, children!" he said,
      "your play-dancing song," he said.
"I'm just going to let it down," he said.   260   i.e., 'stop
                                                 dancing'

Early in the morning:
   "Everybody go off to the woods!" he said;   to gather food
   they all went off and headed into the woods.

At night:
   "Dance, children!   265
   Dance!" he said.
[Then:] "To sleep, all of you!" he said.
   "Children!
   Let it down," he said.

Early in the morning,   270
   they got up.
"Guess I'll just stay home."   said Lizard
The young women danced.

* Or 'They sang and danced'.

At sundown:
    "Dance and play, children!" he said.   275
Again the dancers danced.

Early in the morning,
    they got up.
"All this sleeping is a bad thing," he said,
    "it's not good," said Lizard.   280
The woman went back home.*
They bathed themselves.   *Lizard and the woman*
He took up his arrow-making again.

VI.   [ARROW-MAKING 3]
He rubbed the arrows smooth all on his own.
He socketed shafts throughout the day—   285
    finished.

Now he painted on the bands during the day,
    put them away when they were finished.
He soaked them in water.   *the feathers*

Now he fletched the arrows—†   290
    now, while he was busy at it,
        he fletched the arrows—
            finished.
He turns them on the ground.
He trimmed the vanes—   295
    finished.
He charred the feathers—
    finished.
He put them away when they were finished.
He carried the deer antlers slung over his shoulder.   300
(That's what made his quiver:
    he just cut deer antlers off at the stump.)
He placed the arrows inside.

"Off to the woods, children!"   *for food*

---

* Sapir's gloss regarding the woman notes "little, but not child."
† By attaching the feathers with strips of sinew.

He took up his flints,*
    chipped off a piece.

Now he flaked away during the day.
He scoops the loose flakes into a basket.

"Eat, children!" he said at night.

Now they began eating their meal:
    they ate it,
        they finished eating.

"Off to the woods, children!" he said.
They went off and gathered food.
He inserted the arrowheads—
    finished.
He put his finished pointed shafts away.

"Eat, children!"

VII.
Early in the morning,
    he took up his quiver,
    he took up his net bag.

Now he went westward,
    went west across the water.
He put his quiver down on the ground.
He climbed up after pine-nuts,
    climbed back down.
And then he pounded out the cones.

Now he kept on pounding—
    finished.
He took up his net bag and scooped them in.
And he filled one up—
    finished.
And then his other bag—
    finished.

305

310

for food

315 *into the foreshafts*

[PINE-NUTTING 2]

320

325

330 *his net bag*

---

* *Xaka* 'flint' probably represents chert or obsidian.

Now, as they were spilling,
    he scooped them up from the ground. 335   *the pine-nuts*
They made a sound like the wind there, and the sound came
    down:
    the Ya'wi,
        they howled their war-whoops at him.
"I'll presume you're not just the wind blowing," he said. 340
He picked up his net bags,
    tied both his net bags together to carry home.
He reached for his bow.

Now he stepped along the trail.
He shot off arrows— 345
    shot to the north,
    shot to the east,
        hit them straight in the face.

Now he stepped along the trail,
    fired his bow down into them. 350
"You are just barely visible,
    scattered all around me," he said.
He shot to the south,
    shot to the east—
        he killed them off, these Ya'wi. 355
He went back home through the water.

Now he stepped along the trail.
He arrived back home at sundown.
"Here is plenty to eat, it seems," he said,
    as he was asked for food. 360
"It looks like it's really raining down out there, with the wind,"
    he said.

VIII. [ARROW-
MAKING 4]
Early in the morning,*
    "Off to the woods, children!" he said. *to gather food*

Now he was busy trimming feathers all day.

---

* Line inserted by translator.

"Eat, children!" he said.

Early in the morning,   430
    "Off to the woods, children!" he said.   *to gather food*
    "I won't be doing like the rest of you,
        as for myself," he said.
He finished his sinew-binding.

Now he was busy inserting the flaked arrowheads.   435
He put them away finished.

IX.   [PINE-
Early in the morning,   NUTTING 3]
    he took up his net bag.

Now he went westward,
    went west across the water,   440
        went westward up a mountain.
He put his quiver down on the ground.
He climbed up after pine-nuts,
    climbed down again.
And then he piled pinecones all around the fire.   445

Now he was busy with it,
    now he started pounding.
He pounded out the nuts—
    finished.
He took up his net bag,   450
    he took up his other net bag.

(*Not yet . . .*)*

Now, as they were spilling,   *the pine-nuts*
    he scooped them up from the ground.
They made a sound like the wind there, and the sound came
    down: 455
    the Ya'wi,
        they howled their war-whoops at him.
"Ho, I'll presume you're not just the wind!" he said.
    "It really looks like it's raining down, now—

---

* Perhaps a foreshadowing device: Lizard (and Ishi) anticipating the Ya'wi rush.

maybe I'll sit and shell some pine-nuts," he said. 460
He took up his net bags.
   "I have just seen you, everywhere down on the ground," he
     said.
He slung the bags over his shoulder again.
He took up his bow.

Now he stepped along the trail. 465

Now he shot at them:
   he shot to the east,
     he shot to the south,
       he shot to the north.

Now he stepped along the trail. 470
He fired his bow at them,
   hit them straight in the face.
He went into the water again,
   came back out of the water.
The Ya'wi scattered away. 475

Now he stepped along the trail at sundown.
He came into the clearing. *where his camp*
"Here is plenty to eat, it seems," he said. *was*
"It really looks like rain, coming down out there on the wind,"
   he said.

[*To Sapir:*]

"Be gone, now!" as they say. 480
Now he has finished talking . . .

11

A Selection of Wintu Songs

WINTU

1929–1931

FANNY BROWN, JENNIE CURL, HARRY MARSH,
SADIE MARSH, AND EDO THOMAS, SINGERS
DOROTHY DEMETRACOPOULOU, COLLECTOR AND
TRANSLATOR

INTRODUCTION BY DOROTHY DEMETRACOPOULOU

The songs presented here were collected in the summers of 1929, 1930, and 1931, during three field trips that were conducted under the auspices of the Department of Anthropology of the University of California.[1] I recorded them intermittently, chiefly as an expression of literary art, partly for their ethnographic value, partly for linguistic purposes. I secured them in text and translated them as literally as the discrepancy between Wintu and English would permit.

The Wintu who sing them live in California, along the northern reaches of the Sacramento, the Pit, and the McCloud. These rivers are in reality only mountain streams, swift and narrow, forming steep little canyons in the mountains. The mountainous country affords almost no valleys and only a few "flats" where the people could build their brush houses. The drainage runs north and south, and perhaps because of this, directional terms are indispensable to the Wintu when any purposeful going is to be described. One goes north along the river, south, east uphill, west along the ridge; or one just walks.

The songs that are sung most by the Wintu today are the so-called dream songs. At one time they formed the chief feature of the Dream Dance cult that was introduced circa 1872 and held sway for about forty years. Dream songs were given to men and women in their sleep by the spirit of some dead relative or friend. In the morning the dreamer sang the song and danced to it. The song then became common property, though the name of the dreamer was usually remembered. A split-stick rattle, struck against the thigh, accompanied the song and dance. The rattle, the dance, and the song each followed its own different rhythm.

Since dreaming afforded such an excellent opportunity for exhibitionism, the Wintu seem to have indulged in it, despite the prevalent belief that it brought bad luck and perhaps death to the dreamer. Dreaming stopped about forty years ago, but many songs are still remembered and danced to when Big Times are held. The most recent stimulus to the revival and preservation of the dream songs came when Miss Cora Du Bois and I began collecting them.

The dances of the Dream Dance cult show a wide range of variation, but the songs roughly follow certain set rules; this, despite the fact that they were genuinely acquired in a dream. The words treat of the land of the dead, as for example, the above, the west, the mythical earthlodge of the flowers, the Milky Way along which the spirits of the dead went to their final resting place. Flowers form an important theme. The references to nature are not lyrical expressions but simply an unquestioned conformation to the requirements of the song.

The arrangement of the verses as well as the tune follow a somewhat set pattern. Generally there is the introductory part, consisting of one or two verses that are repeated several times in a low key. Then the first verse with perhaps a new verse is sung in a variation of the theme in a higher key once, and a final verse, the completion or climax, is sung in the original low key.

The following song will serve as an illustration. First come two alternating verses in a low tone:

It is above that you and I shall go;
Along the Milky Way you and I shall go;

It is above that you and I shall go;
Along the Milky Way you and I shall go.

Then we have a variation of the theme in a higher key:

It is above that you and I shall go;
Along the flower trail you and I shall go.

Then we go back to the tune of the first verse:

Picking flowers on our way, you and I shall go.

This tune pattern seems to derive from the Southland Dance cult.[2] The only song that is remembered from the Southland Dance cult is one which is composed of the meaningless syllables *heyoyohene,* sung according to the tune pattern found in the dream songs.[3] Whether this tune pattern originated with the Southland Dance cult or was already present among the Wintu when this cult entered the territory, we do not know. Just now it occurs only in the singing of dream songs.

Individual variation is to be found in the particular arrangement of the verses within the tune pattern. It is not known how much unconscious revision of the words took place. Unfortunately, only one song was secured from two different informants. The two versions show a difference in the tune pattern as well as in the words. Miss Du Bois reports a case where the tune of a song was revised consciously. A singer of some note altered the tune to suit his taste, and it is his version that is known and sung now.

The words of the songs are important in themselves. My informants sometimes repeated them to me, exclaiming over their beauty; this, in spite of the poetic license that allows the dreamer to break from the ordinary Wintu phrasing and makes the meaning often hard to grasp. Miss Du Bois has even recorded a song whose words are remembered and liked although the tune has been forgotten.

NOTES

1. This selection is based on Demetracopoulou's famous 1935 article, "Wintu Songs" (*Anthropos* 30: 483–494). The text of her introduction and song notes

has been excerpted, rearranged, and edited (for continuity) for inclusion in this volume. Of the forty-nine songs included in the original article, twenty-nine have been selected here. The songs retain their original numbering, for the sake of reference.

In her publication of these songs, Demetracopoulou printed only the "gist" of each song, with notes indicating how many times each separate line was sung, and in what order. I have reconstructed the original order from her annotations and present the songs here in their full performance order.—HWL

2. This cult was introduced into Wintu territory circa 1871 and held sway for about a year. See Cora Du Bois, "Wintu Ethnography," for a fuller description. Most of the information about the ethnographic aspect of the songs contained in this essay has been supplied by Miss Du Bois.

3. These syllables may be simply a variation of *heninoiheni,* the introductory and final refrain of the girls' puberty songs, which is sung with slight variations by different singers.

FURTHER READING

Cora Du Bois's "Wintu Ethnography" and Du Bois and Demetracopoulou's "Wintu Myths" are important sources of information, as is Demetracopoulou and Du Bois's "A Study of Wintu Mythology." Demetracopoulou's "A Wintu Girls' Puberty Ceremony" (Lee 1940) might be useful for contextualizing the puberty songs selected here. Harvey Pitkin has published a *Wintu Grammar* and *Wintu Dictionary.*

A SELECTION OF WINTU SONGS

DREAM SONGS

1. Harry Marsh, dreamer; sung by Harry Marsh, 1929[*]

It is above that you and I shall go,
Along the Milky Way you and I shall go,

[*] Harry Marsh uses the inclusive dual that is found in practically all the dream songs where an address form is used. The song is considered to contain an amorous or at least a romantic flavor.

It is above that you and I shall go,
Along the Milky Way you and I shall go,

It is above that you and I shall go,
Along the flower trail you and I shall go,

Picking flowers on our way, you and I shall go.

2. Anonymous dreamer; sung by Harry Marsh, 1929

Above the place where the minnow maiden sleeps while her fins
    move gently in the water,
Flowers droop,
Flowers rise back [up] again.

3. Anonymous dreamer; sung by Harry Marsh, 1929

WHERE WILL YOU AND I SLEEP?

Where will you and I sleep?
Where will you and I sleep?
Where will you and I sleep?
Where will you and I sleep?
At the down-turned jagged rim of the sky you and I will sleep.

4. Jim Thomas, dreamer; sung by Harry Marsh, 1929*

Above [they] shall go,
The spirits of the people, swaying rhythmically,
Above [they] shall go,
The spirits of the people, swaying rhythmically,

---

* The word used for "swaying rhythmically" is applied to women swaying with bent elbows and
forearms pointing forward, as an accompaniment to the dancing of the men. During a performance of the Dream Dance, the men danced in a circle around a fire, while the women stood in
two lines on either side, swaying and waving flowers or handkerchiefs in their outstretched hands.
Jim Thomas, a shaman, introduced in his song the dandelion puffs as representing spirits that
float away. This conception was liked so generally that the song was dedicated to funerals. The
participants sway, holding dandelion puffs, and then with one accord, blow on them and make
them float away. Singing at funerals is an innovation and probably was initiated with the first use
of this song, at the death of Bill Popejoy, some twelve years ago.

Above [they] shall go,
Swaying with dandelion puffs in their hands,
The spirits of the people, swaying rhythmically.

5. Anonymous dreamer; sung by Harry Marsh, 1929

There above, there above,
At the mythical earthlodge of the south,
Spirits are wafted along the roof and fall,

There above, there above,
At the mythical earthlodge of the south,
Spirits are wafted along the roof and fall.

Flowers bend heavily on their stems.

8. Dum Du Bel, dreamer; sung by Harry Marsh, 1931

O me, your brother-in-law
Looks west.
All day long
He looks west.

O me, your brother-in-law
Looks west.
All day long
He looks west.

O me, your brother-in-law
Looks west.
Flowers of daybreak
He holds northward in his outstretched hands.
All day long
He looks west.

9. Mary Silverthorne, dreamer; sung by Harry Marsh, 1931

From the east he came west against the mountains and stopped.
Flowers he picked just now,
Flowers from my grave.
Flowers he picked just now.

11. Sadie Marsh, dreamer; sung by Sadie Marsh, 1929*

Down west, down west we dance,
We spirits dance,
Down west, down west we dance,
We spirits dance,

Down west, down west we dance,
We spirits weeping dance,

We spirits dance.

12. Mary Kenyon, dreamer; sung by Edo Thomas, 1929

From the old camping place
Comes a flash of flowers.

I love flowers.
Give me flowers.
Flowers flutter
As the wind raises them above.
I love flowers.
Give me flowers.

13. Dick Gregory, dreamer; sung by Edo Thomas, 1929†

Daybreak people have been chirping.
Daybreak people have been chirping.
Daybreak people have been chirping.
Daybreak people have been chirping.
Daybreak people have been chirping.

Above on the roof,
Alighting, they chirp.

* Sadie Marsh says that a few years ago her best friend died, and a little after came to her in a dream
 with a company of other female spirits, weeping, dancing, and singing this song.
† The daybreak people are sparrows. The roof is that of the mythical earthlodge.

GIRLS' PUBERTY SONGS*

21. Sung by Harry Marsh, 1931†

Heninoy, heninoy
Heninoy, heninoy

At Bare-Gap-Running-South-Uphill a girl has [come to] pu-
    berty,
We said to ourselves.
So from below, bringing eastward with us,
We brought puberty songs.

Heninoy, heninoy
Heninoy, heninoy

22. Sung by Harry Marsh, 1931‡

Heninoy, heninoy
Heninoy, heninoy

Where the eastern star emerged,
Fire comes up westward over the slope and falls in a shower.
To the edge of the mountains, to the foot of the pointed ridge,
Come southward along the mountain shore to [join] the dance!

Heninoy, heninoy
Heninoy, heninoy

---

* All songs other than dream songs and shamanistic songs are anonymous. There are many girls'
  puberty songs, of which I secured a few. Some time after the first menstruation, perhaps as long
  as three years after, a Big Time was called to give public recognition to this event. This was done
  for the daughters of the most important people. The headman of the village sent invitations to
  other villages, and as each group arrived, they danced down into the celebrating village, singing.
  Song 21 was sung by such a group. All girls' puberty songs begin and end with a refrain of *heni-*
  noy repeated an indefinite number of times.

† When I first recorded this song, I found it impossible to understand since it was sung for me starting with the second verse. Girls' puberty songs are generally supposed to be incomprehensible,
  full of obsolete words and involved as to style. From this generalization must be excepted the sala-
  cious songs that people take care to understand.

‡ This is an arrival song.

23. Sung by Harry Marsh, 1929*

Heninoy, heninoy
Heninoy, heninoy

Up the hill to the northwest
    an obsidian knife whizzes through the air,
        on the west slope.
It is the beautiful adolescent girl;
      to the place where the deer were scared out of the bush,
          listening, may I come back!

Heninoy, heninoy
Heninoy, heninoy

24. Sung by Harry Marsh, 1931

Heninoy, heninoy
Heninoy, heninoy

At the edge of the mountains she [came to] puberty.
Look along the curve of the mountain shore;
Fleas must be emerging!

Heninoy, heninoy
Heninoy, heninoy

26. Sung by Harry Marsh, 1931†
Heninoy, heninoy
Heninoy, heninoy

May I fall into the hole made by digging,
And there, fluttering about, may I remain!

Heninoy, heninoy
Heninoy, heninoy

---

* Songs 23–28. After the groups arrived there was feasting and dancing for several days. During this time, pertinent songs were sung, some of them incomprehensible to the singers, others referring to the fact that the girl was now ready for a lover or a husband. In Bald Hill, some extremely obscene songs were sung, usually upon arrival. Songs 26 and 28 were sung during the feasting period.

† This is a wish to join the girl where she sits.

27. Sung by Harry Marsh, 1931

Heninoy, heninoy
Heninoy, heninoy

In the southeast the adolescent girl comes seducing to get herself
   a man.
She comes crossing Sucker Creek which should not be crossed.

Heninoy, heninoy
Heninoy, heninoy

28. Sung by Harry Marsh, 1931

Heninoy, heninoy
Heninoy, heninoy

To the north behind the snow mountain,
Going up a bare ridge, feathers* are visible.
Going up a bare ridge north behind the snow mountain,
Going up a bare ridge, feathers are visible.

Heninoy, heninoy
Heninoy, heninoy

LOVE SONGS†

36. Sung by Harry Marsh, 1931

Hinini, hinini
Hinini, hinini

Where he walks about, where he walks about,
Pushing the deer decoy back away from his face,
Right there in front of him

---

* The feathers presumably belong to the headdress of a potential lover.
† The rest of the songs that I collected are love songs and songs from forgotten stories. Love songs are known as *nini*, from the introductory and final refrain *hinini*, which is repeated an indefinite number of times. They are complete in themselves or simply songs coming from love stories, which also are known as *nini*. These latter are often hard to understand, as they refer to incidents in the story. *Nini* tunes were sometimes played on a flute.

May I come gliding down and fall!

Hinini, hinini
Hinini, hinini

37. Sung by Harry Marsh, 1931

Hinini, hinini
Hinini, hinini

Please,
Teach me a word I don't know!

Hinini, hinini
Hinini, hinini

38. Sung by Harry Marsh, 1931

Hinini, hinini
Hinini, hinini

Long ago I wept for you,
But now I weep
For him who lives west, further west, I weep
For him who dwells in the west,
Under the sharp pinnacles of Lime Rock.

Hinini, hinini
Hinini, hinini

39. Sung by Harry Marsh, 1929

Hinini, hinini
Hinini, hinini

The sleeping place which you and I hollowed out will remain
    always,
Will remain always, will remain always, will remain always.

Hinini, hinini
Hinini, hinini

41. Sung by Fanny Brown, 1929

Hinini, hinini
Hinini, hinini

Before you go over the gap of the snow-mountain to the north,
Downhill toward the north,
O my, do look back at me!
You who dwell below the snow-mountain,
Do look back at me!

Hinini, hinini
Hinini, hinini

42. Sung by Fanny Brown, 1929

Hinini, hinini
Hinini, hinini

For some reason I dislike you.
I do not love you.

I dislike you because,
Like a snipe hopping on,
You crossed creeks ahead of me.

Truly I dislike you for good.
I love one who dwells there in the west.

Hinini, hinini
Hinini, hinini

43. Sung by Sadie Marsh, 1929*

Of course,
If I went to the McCloud
I might choke on a salmon bone . . .

---

* Songs 43–44. These two songs are referred to as *nini* sometimes. They are derisive songs. The
McCloud woman, who has been nurtured on juicy salmon and has to live on grasshoppers and
such small fry in the Stillwater subarea, sings to her husband.

44. Sung by Jennie Curl, 1930*

Of course,
If I went to Stillwater
I might choke on a grasshopper leg.

Yeah, but—
If I went to the Upper Sacramento
I might choke on the bone of a fawn . . .

SONGS FROM FORGOTTEN STORIES

45. Sung by Harry Marsh, 1929†

Down in the west, lying down,
Down in the west, lying down,
A beautiful bear I found,
Tearing up clover in fistfuls.

46. Sung by Jennie Curl, 1930

SONG OF THE PREGNANT WOMAN

On the north slope of Baqakilim
I was deserted.

Some flower made me heedless
And I was deserted.

A wild orange blossom made me heedless
And I was deserted.

* Another McCloud woman refuses her suitors with this ditty.
† Songs 45–47. The last three *nini* are songs coming from love stories. The stories, as myths, are forgotten or perhaps never have had any existence. Nowadays, they are told informally, only as explanations of the songs. There are *nini* tales containing songs that are told formally, but in these, the interest lies in the narrative and the song is merely part of the story, sung in the appropriate place.
   Song 45. This is, to my knowledge, the most popular Wintu song. It is said to have been composed by a lover rejected for his poverty, when he found his old love in circumstances so reduced that she had to live on a diet of clover. It is a song of derision, and the Wintu find it amusing.

47. Sung by Jennie Curl, 1930

SONG OF THE FORSAKEN BROTHER

Do not weep,
Do not weep,
Younger brother, do not weep.

She would have gone about,
She would just have gone about in the flat below.

Do not weep.
Do not let her come in front of the north side of our dwelling;
That is where Bead-bear will go about.

Do not let her get tiger-lily bulbs.
Do not weep, younger brother.

49. Sung by Sadie Marsh, 1929*

SONG OF THE QUAIL

I stroke myself, I stroke myself;
East of the camp site, where the earth is heaped,
On my back I lie.
I lie stroking myself,
In the summer, when sunshine falls deep in the northern
    canyons.

---

* The last song in this collection comes from a forgotten myth.

12

Loon Woman

He-who-is-made-beautiful, She-who-becomes-loon

WINTU
1929

JO BENDER, NARRATOR

DOROTHY DEMETRACOPOULOU, COLLECTOR

DELL HYMES, TRANSLATOR

INTRODUCTION BY DELL HYMES

This dramatization of incest, death, and renewal has drawn repeated attention since its publication in 1931.[1] It has been the focus of a special article (Demetracopoulou 1933), retold in a popular book (T. Kroeber 1959), and addressed at length in a major analysis of myth (Lévi-Strauss 1981).

The Source

We know the text because of the work of two women at the start of their careers, Dorothy Demetracopoulou (Lee) and Cora Du Bois. Both went on to become well-known for other work, Demetracopoulou-Lee for essays on languages as forms of thought (Lee 1944, 1959), Du Bois for study of culture and personality among the people of Alor (an island of Indonesia) and as the first woman professor of anthropology at Radcliffe (Harvard). In the summers of 1929 and 1930 the two women joined in an inquiry remarkable for its time. Among the Wintu, living along tributaries of the Sacramento River north and northwest of present Red Bluff, they sought not only good storytellers, but tellers of different abilities, under varied conditions, so as to shed light on change and stability. Because of this, we have converging perspectives on a community tradition, with specific information about tellers and their circumstances.[2]

Formerly myths were told only on winter nights. A good teller would have a good memory and be a good singer; evidently one could change voice with a change in characters or situation, and animate narration with gesture (Demetracopoulou and Du Bois 1932:376, 379, 497). The "Loon Woman" myth was told in the summer of 1929 by Jo Bender (Upper Sacramento). He was about eighty-five, esteemed as a teller by other Wintu (Demetracopoulou and Du Bois 1932:496, 498, 499) and by the two young anthropologists (379, 392).

I should explain this new translation. Demetracopoulou's transcriptions of Wintu texts are unpublished, and their location was not known to Herbert Luthin, the editor of this volume, or myself. Fortunately, Alice Shepherd had the text of "Loon Woman" and sent a copy to Luthin. It had only Wintu, no English, so the original translation must have been done separately. That translation was published twice, but the two are not quite identical.[3]

Thanks to the grammar and dictionary of Harvey Pitkin (1984, 1985), supplemented by the dictionary of Alice Shepherd (Schlicter 1981), I was able to match Wintu elements with English meanings and identify their grammatical roles. I could then look for further relations among them.

When "Loon Woman" was transcribed, such stories were thought to be prose. Division into larger units (paragraphs) was ad hoc. Recently it has been realized that stories may indicate ways of their own of going together. Intonation contours may indicate units (verses), which enter into longer sequences (stanzas, scenes). For "Loon Woman," the manuscript shows no contours, but patterns do emerge. It is common in stories for some sentence-beginning words to mark units, and that turns out to be true of "Loon Woman." So as to carry over the effect of the original, each such word has been translated always the same way, and each differently from the others: note "After," "After that," "And then," "At last," "At that,"

"For that," "Now," "Suddenly," and of course expressions such as "Next morning." (Interestingly, when "And then" [*uni-buha*] occurs, it tends to be second of a pair of units, or third of three. Parallelism is also a factor in particular cases. Repetition of a common verb of "being, residing" [*buha*] initiates the two opening scenes in part 1.)

Fundamentally, interpretation of the shape of the whole depends upon the hypothesis that, like many other oral narratives, Native American and English, the story makes use of certain kinds of sequence. The common alternatives among traditions are relations of three and five, or of two and four. A narrator may shift between them, to be sure, and one set may include something of the other. Awareness of such relations contributes to an appreciation of the rhythms of a story. This translation attempts to display them on the page.

Some texts in Shepherd (1989) suggest that Wintu narrators use relations of three and five; "Loon Woman" certainly does. But sequences of three and five are sometimes sequences of pairs: the scene in which the elder sister discovers the heart of the hero (part 3, scene [1]), and the final two scenes of the story as a whole, have each five pairs of stanzas (sets of verses). When units are paired, I put a single closing brace in the right margin to mark the end of the pair.

In such patterns a turn at talk is always a unit, and a sequence may consist of alternating turns, as in five pairs of interaction between mother and daughter (lines 56–68). Speeches count as a single unit (turn at talk) in large sequences, but may have internal patterning of their own. The long speech by the helpful bird in act 6 has three parts, each ending with a verb of speaking. (I mark these internal parts with the designations "E/1," "E/2," "E/3.")

Sometimes a three-step sequence has a sense of the onset, ongoing, then outcome of an action, or an object of perception, as when the daughter matures (21–23) and discovers a long hair (cf. 27–29, 30–32 and 33–35, 36–38). Repetition of words sometimes has one pair enclose another— what is called "chiasmus," as in lines 19–20, 234–35, 258–60, 497–98. Sometimes members of a pair alternate, as when twice the mother ponders and the daughter measures (73–74, 78–79 : 75, 87–88).

A run of three or five can elaborate a single action or activity. When the two boys set out, they "play, play, play" (430–32). The second time Loon Woman cries for her parents, she "cries, cries, cries" (236–38). When earlier she prepares a bed for herself and her brother, repetitious wording in a doubled set of five-line stanzas (122–31) seems to convey confusion, urgency, and excitement.

Translation as Retelling

Mr. Bender evidently controlled patterns in English as well as Wintu, and his translating was also in part retelling. When the sister first says, "Whose hair?" (34), the next line in Wintu means literally "she wants to know." Bender's translation is more dramatic: "I want to know."

When the sister and brother go, she calls for evening to come quickly, and then the two are said to "go" six times (given the doubling of "go" elsewhere, this presumably constitutes three pairs). The English has five verbs, not six: "They went, and went, and went, and went, and went."[4] Evidently Mr. Bender knew that English does not ordinarily multiply pairs but does multiply single words, and so he substituted a run. Even so, a run in English would usually be three; Mr. Bender goes to five. I suspect that in Wintu three pairs was a maximal effect, and that a run of five seemed an equivalent maximal effect in English.

In the five pairs of lines in which the brother wakes and leaves his sleeping sister, the third and fifth pairs (166–67, 170–71) exist in English only. The additions extend and do not disturb the pattern of the stanza.

It remains to be seen to what extent other Wintu narrators and translators have made use of possibilities such as those mentioned here.

Proportion

The whole of a story has to make sense in terms of a pattern of relations, and Jo Bender's "Loon Woman" does. Its verses, stanzas, and scenes combine into six acts, paired in three parts. (For other work of this kind, see Hymes 1992, 1994a, 1994b, 1995.) Recognition of such connections of form and content makes clear the proportions and emphases of the telling.[5]

Two acts present a beautiful boy, hidden, then discovered (part 1). Two central acts present incest and destruction (part 2). Two final acts present restorations and retribution (part 3). Within each part something accidental prompts what happens. The sister discovers a hair fallen from her brother's head, and so prepares for incest (act 2); Coyote, although warned, looks down as the family escape upward, and so they fall into the fire (act 4); the two boys wound a bird who tells them about the Loon, and so she is killed and the lost hearts recovered and restored (act 6).

Interpretations

Some of the meaning of the story involves understandings that members of the community would take for granted. Many are shared with other Native American traditions. Here are several such.

The opening and closing—"many people came into being" and "So they say it ends"—are conventional and show that the story was told by someone still conversant with such devices. (Young narrators were becoming less conversant during the period in which the story was taken down.) The opening sets the story in the earlier time when the human age was given shape. The closing indicates that the story is vouched for by what others have said. If it had been told in winter, someone would have followed the closing with words wishing for spring.

The sister's attention to a hair fits the first requisite for physical beauty, long, thick, shiny, black hair (Du Bois 1935:59; cf. restoration of such hair in Hymes 1983, and Lévi-Strauss 1981:389).

That the daughter goes west may foreshadow her transformation into a dangerous being. The word *nom-yo* ('west-?') describes persons likely to become animals, or "werebeasts" (Du Bois 1935:5).

When the mother at last accedes to the daughter's refusal to go except with the eldest son, it is not because she cannot recognize danger. One cannot forever refuse a kinsperson or partner.

That it is Coyote who looks down, causing escape to fail, is no surprise. He is the father in some versions of the story, but not here, and is not restored to life at the end. Having an isolated Coyote at just this point, a sort of walk-on numskull, fits well with the story's view of the family as not to blame. Given a boy so beautiful as to cause (illicit) desire, they hide him. That the daughter finds a telltale hair is accidental. A proper mother cannot at last keep her daughter from choosing her brother. The son leaves the sister as soon as he can awake, and the family do at once what he runs to tell them to do. A new generation kills what the daughter has become.

As for the two women who find the oldest son's lost heart, they are shown to be good at the very start (of act 5): they do useful work every day. And their first line inserts "human" (Wintu) before "women," contrasting them with what the woman just-mentioned, the sister, has become.

That the son's heart has song shows power. That there are deer tracks where it is found indicates a prototypical male power, hunting deer. Another version has his tears create a salt lick that attracts deer. Absence of that here may indicate that deer recognize power as such.

That the restored son has two women as wives indicates high status. Usually co-wives were sisters, and their husband slept between them.

Instruction from a wounded bird is a popular device in many traditions. The bird goes unnamed here, but perhaps its cry is an identification. The cry "Tuwétetek" is like a name for killdeer in the neighboring and related language, Nomlaki, *te-wé-dé-dik*.[6] Notice that the usual step of bandaging the wound, and being given advice in return, is absent. The bird is already on the side of the boys, somehow related to them, referring like their father to "she who made *us* kinless."

Title

In the manuscript and publications of the myth, the title has the name of the older brother in Wintu, but "Loon Woman" in English. In the story he is named, but she is not; not even a word for "loon" occurs. Perhaps that is because no loon survives. The story does not tell, actually, why a loon will look as it does in a world to come. One would have to speculate about that; this loon is different. The distinctive necklace has been taken back, the hearts are human beings again. So far as the story goes, the loon is an evil forever gone.[7]

I translate the hero's name with one of its possibilities (cf. Pitkin 1985: 36, 37, 38, 271). Shepherd (personal communication) says that the name could suggest most or all of those possible senses. Since the story is about what a sister as well as a brother becomes, lacking a Wintu name for her, I use "become" for her in the title.

Other Discussions

Demetracopoulou (1933) analyzes versions of "Loon Woman" in terms of some eighteen incidents and their distribution among versions from the Achumawi, Atsugewi, Maidu, Karuk, Modoc, Shasta, Wintu, and Yana.

She finds the story to have a sharply defined character in a limited area, integrating incidents intrinsically unrelated. Two incidents do seem original—that of the lost hair and the revivified heart—but neither would account for the story itself. The sequence of incidents, their dovetailing and remolding, is based first of all on the theme of catastrophic incest and secondarily on the punishment of the prime actors, linked with the widespread theme of a son revenging and reviving his father.

Theodora Kroeber (1959:39–65) reframes and retells the story, drawing on several of the same versions (Achumawi, Atsugewi, Karuk, Maidu, Shasta, Wintu, and Yana).

Lévi-Strauss (1981) makes the Loon Woman story an essential part of his great enterprise, to show the unity of myth throughout the New World. By way of a recently published Klamath myth, he connects the Loon Woman stories of Northern California to the bird-nester theme in South America, with which he began the four volumes of his *Mythologiques.* He takes the hidden child in Loon Woman to be an inversion of the bird-nester, and by a series of further inversions, oppositions, and transformations, he finds that "the whole northern part of North America is the scene of a vast permutation" (215), reaching as far as the Wabenaki of New England. His argument takes Demetracopoulou to task at several points (e.g., 60–62, 388–89)—for instance, for treating the hair incident as arbitrary and specific (389).

Lévi-Strauss's work is indispensable for its vast command of detail, its attention to natural history and geography as factors, and its recurrent sensitivity and insight. At the same time, its conception of mythical thought as often a playing out of formal possibility, its overriding concern for indications of the emergence of culture out of nature, and for certain kinds of coding—astronomical, gastronomical, and so forth—omit what may be perfectly good reasons for a story to be the way it is. In the case of Jo Bender's telling of Loon Woman, one reason may be pain felt for an intelligent, determined child cleaving to a fatal course. Another is to fit with a cultural cognitive style.

The two Wintu versions, this by Jo Bender, and another by Sadie Marsh (Du Bois and Demetracopoulou 1931:360–62) can be understood as alternative ways of portraying and thereby thinking about lust as a woman's motive. The daughter in the Marsh story is immediately impulsive, aggressive, and ultimately cannibalistic. The denouement takes little time. The denouement in the Bender story takes a generation. This daughter is complex. She holds to her goal in extended interaction with her mother, she plans and works and uses magic to make it happen, and later she grieves at length for the loss of her mother and father.

As to hair, having found the hair, she looks and looks, and later matches and measures. All this is in keeping with a Wintu concern for bases of knowledge, expressed in a recent development of a system of evidential suffixes (see the lucid analysis in Schlicter 1986). The first major action of the story is the scenes in which the daughter looks and looks to be sure of the source of a hair (act 2, scenes [1] and [2]). Visual knowledge, the kind most assured, is again in focus in lines in which her counterpart sees and hears speak the lost heart of that source (319–30). Even so, her conclusion as to who it must be (329) is marked as inference (-re:m). Sight is again in focus in the lines in which her younger sister sees what she has discovered (388–96), and when the boys who have killed Loon take their father to see. Hearing, to be sure, begins the long process by which she discovers, then nourishes, He-who-is-made-beautiful. The women at the center of the first and third parts, she who destroys and she who recovers, are akin in deliberate response to evidence.

In this respect the hair incident is indeed "important aesthetically to the form of the myth" (Demetracopoulou 1935:121) and is to be explained, not by distant analogues (Lévi-Strauss 1981:389), but from within Wintu language and culture. The myth as a whole is distinctive in its steady marshaling of detail to show a family almost destroyed and in the end surviving evil.

Native Language Passage

Here are lines 24–35 in Wintu, with word-by-word glosses and translation. The lines, in which the sister, She-who-becomes-loon, discovers the fateful hair, are taken from the incident that precipitates the main events of the story.[8]

'uni-r	p'o·q-ta	k'éte	hima	me·m-to·n	hará·,
they-say.SCA	woman-that	one	morning	stream-that.LOC	goes

After that one morning the woman goes to a certain stream,

me·m-tó·   me-s-to·   pi-to·n   hara·,
stream-that.OBJ   water-GEN-that.OBJ   she-that.LOC   goes
she goes to where they get water,

kćn·ła·   pi   p'o·q-ta.   Pómin-winé,   wine   tómoi,
sits-down   she   woman-that   ground-looks.at   sees   hair
she sits down that woman. She looks at the ground, she sees a hair,

číne·.   Wine·,   wine·   tómoi,   k'ete·m   tómoi.
catches/takes.it   looks.at.it   looks.at   hair   one.OBJ   hair
she takes it up. She looks, she looks at the hair, one hair.

Tómoi   niqa·'a   wíne: "Héket-un   tómoi?"   t'ipna·-s-kuya.
hair   find-STA   look.at   who-POSS   hair   know-STAT.INT-want
She looks at the hair she has found: "Whose hair?" she wants to know.

NOTES

1. I am indebted to Herb Luthin for inviting me to take on this challenging and rewarding task, and to Alice Shepherd for information and encouragement. She has caught mistakes and sparked recognition of the striking relation between categories of the language (Schlicter 1986) and the shape of this telling.

2. An example of such information as it bears on the present translation: to heighten action Mr. Bender used a special arrow-release gesture (not the one normal for arrow-release), whether or not an arrow was released in the story. The oldest teller, Jim Fender, age ninety, also actively used gesture, especially for directions and arrow-release. On the strength of this, two otherwise odd uses of a word that can mean "thus, like this" are taken here as marking gestures to show how Loon Woman scratched for hearts (lines 260, 264).

3. There is evidently incidental editing in the second publication (Demetracopoulou 1935) and slippage in the course of its reaching print. Part of the speech of the wounded bird is missing. Lines 456–68 here are in the first publication (Du Bois and Demetracopoulou 1931:359, lines 19–25), but absent in the second (Demetracopoulou 1935:107, line 3).

4. Wintu does not explicitly mark tense in the verb, and the past is the normal English narrative tense. In the translation itself (lines 111–13), I have used the present tense "going" at this point, thinking that it avoids the implication that the Wintu is the same as English, and because it has a certain freshness.

5. Following conventions I have established elsewhere (see Hymes 1992, 1994a, 1994b, 1995), I employ capital roman numerals (I, II, III) to designate

"acts," lowercase roman numerals (i, ii, iii) to designate "scenes," capital letters (A, B, C) to designate "stanzas," and lowercase letters (a, b, c) to designate "verses."

6. The information here comes from Alice Shepherd. Lévi-Strauss notes an analogous role for Killdeer in Klamath and Yana versions of the story (1981:49, 95) and for Meadowlark among the Shasta (133).

7. A giant bird called *wukwuk* was known among the Nomlaki, who live to the south of the Wintu and are their linguistic relatives (Goldschmidt 1951:353). The account of the bird that Goldschmidt obtained from Jeff Jones does not connect it with the loon or a myth.

8. The abbreviations used in this passage are as follows: GEN = 'generic', INT = 'intensive', LOC = 'locative', OBJ = 'objective', POSS = 'possessive', SCA = 'subordinating causal anterior', STA = 'subordinating temporal anterior', STAT = 'stative'.

FURTHER READING

The introduction points to numerous sources and readings. Frank LaPena's article "Wintu" in the California volume of the Smithsonian *Handbook* provides useful ethnographic background. Dorothy Demetracopoulou's "The Loon Woman Myth: A Study in Synthesis" is an essential comparative study. Theodora Kroeber, in *The Inland Whale,* retells the story in formal literary style. Lévi-Strauss, in *The Naked Man,* analyzes the myth from a structural perspective. For more on ethnopoetic approaches to oral literature, see Hymes's *'In vain I tried to tell you.'*

LOON WOMAN: HE-WHO-IS-MADE-BEAUTIFUL, SHE-WHO-BECOMES-LOON

[PART ONE]
[The Beautiful Boy]
[I] [Hidden]

They live there,
many people came into being.

After that two,
    a pair,

a man and wife live there,   5
they have many children,
    a lot of children,
nine boys,
    one girl,
        ten children.   10

The first born [is] a beautiful boy.
And then they leave him put away inside.
He-who-is-made-beautiful is what they name him,
they leave him put away inside,
they leave him to stay rolled up in a bear hide.   15

[II] [Discovered and Desired] [i]

They live there,   A
    live there,
        live there,
    some of the children walk around,
        children play around.   20

That "girl" lives there,   B
    the girl grows bigger,
        turns into a woman.   }

After that one morning the woman goes to a certain stream,   C
    she goes to where they get water,   25
        she sits down, that woman.
She looks at the ground,
    she sees a hair,
        she takes it up.
She looks,   30
    she looks at the hair,
        one hair.

She looks at the hair she has found: D
    "Whose hair?"
        she wants to know.   35
She looks at it long,
    looks at the hair,
        one long hair.

That woman thinks,
   she thinks, "Whose hair?"   40 }

That He-who-is-made-beautiful goes every morning to bathe.   *E*
No one has any idea that he goes to bathe.
That He-who-is-made-beautiful goes to that water,
   bathes,
      comes home.   45

One hair has come loose,   *F*
   comes off his head.
The woman finds it, the hair,
   finds the hair at the flat where they dip up water.
"I want to know whose hair it is," so she thinks.   50
   That woman keeps that hair.   }

Thinking of the man,   *A(ab) [ii]*
   "This morning I shall go west," so says that woman.
      "I want to take someone along to guide me."
"I am going to go," so she tells her mother.   55

"I am going to go west," so she says,   *(cd)*
   thinking of the man, so she spoke.
"Hm," [her mother] says.

"Whom do you want to take with you?" she says.   *(ef)*
She will not tell whom.   60

The old woman,   *B(ab)*
   "Well, surely take this little one, your younger brother."
Now that woman says,
   "I don't want to take him."

"Whom will you take with you?" so she says.   65   *(cd)*
"I want to take another one with me."

"Take this one then."   *(ef)*
"I won't," so said that woman.

She does this for a long time,   *C*
   she goes through them all.   70
He-who-is-made-beautiful alone is left,

He-who-is-made-beautiful.
The little old woman sits,
   sits pondering it all, the old woman.

That woman measures that hair like that.   75   D
The hair of the rest does not match.
The one hair she had found is long[er].   }

The old woman sits,   E
   sits pondering it all.
Suddenly,   80
   "Yes, surely take this one,"
      so she says,
         "He-who-is-made-beautiful,"
            her son.
"Yes," so she said.   85

The woman is happy she is going to take him along.   F
She measures the hair,
   that hair matches.
"I'm going to take this one," she says.   }

After that the woman prepares herself attractively,   90   *[iii]*
   paints herself,
      [gets] food to take along,
         everything—
           acorn soup,
           acorn bread,   95
           salmon flour.
She packs them on her back in a carrying basket.
She goes,
   taking him, He-who-is-made-beautiful, with her.
      (That woman is happy to take her older brother with her.)   100

                                            [PART TWO]
                                          [Incest,
                                          Destruction]
                                          [III] [Incest] [i]

The two go west,   A
   that He-who-is-made-beautiful goes ahead,
      that woman comes behind.

"Dearest, my husband," so speaks that woman.   B
That man, "What?" so he says.   105
"Oh elder brother, don't hurry,
    that is what I am saying to you," so she says.

So that woman says,   C
    "Hwaa," so she says,
        "Evening come quickly," so says that woman.   110

Going, going,   D
    going, going,
        going, going—
Evening comes.

The woman speaks thus: 115   E
    "Let's the two of us spend the night right here.
    It's evening."
"Yes," so he said.

After that she makes a fire.   A [ii]
And then the two eat,   120
    eat supper.

After [having eaten],   B
    she fixes a sleeping-place,
        she is the one who fixes it,
            makes it,   125
                that woman works hard—

Nicely she fixes [it],
    makes a bed,
        she fixes a sleeping-place nicely,
            all kinds of ferns she cuts,   130
                spreads them on the ground.

"Lie down here, elder brother.   C
    I finished making a bed for you to lie on,
        I finished making it."
After that,   135
    so she said,
    "As for me, I'll sleep anywhere on the ground."

After that the two lie down,   *A [iii]*
   He-who-is-made-beautiful lies down,
      sleeps,   140
         near the fire lies He-who-is-made-beautiful.
The woman lay there on the ground.

After that the woman says,   *B*
   "Hiwaa, go to sleep,"
so the woman says to He-who-is-made-beautiful,   145
   ["Go to sleep"].
They say then he sleeps,
   He-who-is-made-beautiful sleeps.

The woman, having gotten up,   *C*
   looks,   150
      he is sleeping.
Softly now she goes,
   lies on the ground,
      takes He-who-is-made-beautiful in her arms,
   on the ground now,   155
      that woman lies.

                                              [IV]
                                            [Destruction]
                                            [i]
He-who-is-made-beautiful wakes up,   *A*
   sees he is sleeping in his sister's arms.
That woman is sleeping,
   she lies snoring,   160
      asleep.

He-who-is-made-beautiful gets up,   *B*
      softly having gone and gotten pithy alder wood,
   brings it,
      leaves it on the ground,   165
gets pithy alder wood
   and leaves it there,
puts it in her embrace,
   leaves that wood.
[he,   170
   He-who-is-made-beautiful.]

Once he is done,   *C*
   he comes,
   comes toward the house,
     comes,   175
  comes rapidly,
    comes rapidly,
      comes rapidly.

The woman sleeps a long time.   *A [ii]*
That man comes,   180
   comes rapidly,
and then reaches the house,
   his mother's home,
     his father's home.

After he gets there,   185   *B*
   "Be quick, let's go," he said.
The old woman, the old man,
   "Yes, let's go," they say.
And then they set the earthlodge completely on fire,
   the earthlodge smokes.   190

At last at that spot they go whirling upward with that smoke.   *C*
Coyote they make sit at the very bottom.
"Don't look down!" they say to Coyote.
   "That woman will come and will cry,
     will say all sorts of things."   195
"Don't look down!" thus [they say] to Coyote.
Whirling upward,
   they go above.

That woman in that bed in the west wakes up.   *A [iii]*
Oh, and then she sees   200
   how the bed has held pithy alder.
She is angry,
   that woman is angry.
"I am going to kill you," she says.
She cries,   205
   that woman cries:
     "Anana, ɔñɔñɔñ,

Anana, ɔñɔñɔñ,
Omanuč anana,
Omanuč ɔñɔñɔñ!"   210

Singing, she comes toward the east.   *B*
Because of that the woman comes rapidly east.
She rushes to that earthlodge and stops,
     she sees the lodge burning,
          she truly doesn't know what to do.   215

She looks all about the country,   *C*
     she does not see anyone.
There she goes *completely* around the lodge.
Still she sees no one,
     she has no idea where they have gone.   220

She looks all about the country there,   *D*
     she looks all about.
"Where can Daddy have gone?
     Where can Mama have gone?"
          She thinks about them that way.   225

For that she cries,   *E*
     cries,
the woman cries,
     cries.

Suddenly she happens to look up,   230 *A [iv]*
     sees them going up,
          her mother, her father, her elder brother,
               she sees them going.

"I want to go, oh Mommy, oh Daddy,   *B*
     I want to go,"   235
          she cries,
               cries,
                    cries.   *}*

They almost get above,   *C*
     they almost get above into the clear sky.   240
The warned one,

Coyote,
    looks down,
everyone comes there to the fire,
    falls down to the earthlodge,   245
        burns up.

They fall down,   D
    they all fall into the fire.
He-who-is-made-beautiful falls into the fire,
    ah, everyone falls into the fire.   250
He-who-is-made-beautiful's heart pops off.   }

Because of that, that woman keeps walking around,   E
    keeps walking around,
        keeps searching.

It is cold,   255   F
    the fire gone out,
        the earthlodge burned down.   }

Now she takes a stick,   A(ab) [v]
    she searches there,
        she searches like this with the stick.   260
She finds her own mother's heart,
    her own father's heart she finds,
        all her younger brothers' hearts she finds.

Like that surely she scratches with both hands,   B(cd)
    she scratches in the ashes,   265
        trying to find He-who-is-made-beautiful's heart.
She does not find it.

After that, that woman strings the hearts on a cord,   C(ef)
    she strings them,
        hangs them on her neck.   270
She does not find He-who-is-made-beautiful's own heart.

For He-who-is-made-beautiful's own heart has exploded,   D(gh)
    going to another place,
        fallen.
No one knows about *his* kind of heart.   275

That woman,   *E(ij)*
    "I want to see *his* kind of heart," she says.
The woman, thinking a little,
    keeps walking around,
        hearts hung on her neck.   280

[PART THREE]
[Restorations,
Retribution]
[V] [Rediscovered
Restored] [i]

Far away two human women live.   *A*
The two go for wood early in the afternoon every day,
    the two sisters.
The older goes off ahead nearby.
The other girl breaks off wood,   285
    taking it home.

That older woman goes on ahead nearby,   *B*
    she seems to have heard singing,
        strange soft singing she hears.
That younger girl does not perceive   290
    what her older sister hears.
She listens,
    listens to the singing.

At last she turns around.   *C*
    "Let's take the wood," she says.   295
The two pack the wood on their backs in funnel-baskets,
    bring it to the house.
In the evening they sleep.

The next morning they get up,   *A [ii]*
    eat food,   300
        go for wood early in the afternoon.
At that, that woman hears singing,   *B*
    the singing she hears seems louder little by little.   *]*

And then she goes over there,   *C*
    she goes listening to that singing,
        she goes and goes.   305

That woman goes,   *D*
    goes over there,
        listening to the singing,
        listening ahead,   310
            goes on.   /

Stopping every now and then,   *E*
    she goes,
        comes up to the place,
            sees damp ground.   315
Having come up to it, she looks,   *F*
    she looks at the ground,
        nothing is there.   /

She keeps hearing singing.   *G*
She sees something black on the ground.   320
That black thing on the ground,
    that which sang, says,
        "Woman, come.
        Don't be afraid," it says.
That woman thinks,   325   *II*
    says,
        "This must be,
        this must be the one lost long ago.
        It must be that He-who-is-made-beautiful,"
            so she thinks.   330   /

At that, thinking, the woman looks at the ground.   *I*
The one on the ground says,
    "Ah, woman, don't be afraid of me,
    Come."
Now the woman says, "Yes."   335
At that she looks at the one who is on the ground.   *J*
Many deer had been there,
    it is dusty.
To the east of where that person lies,
    to the west,   340
        there are many deer tracks.   /

As soon as she had looked at him,   *A [iii]*
    she goes to carry her wood,
        where her younger sister is standing.
She goes,   345
    comes up to her.
When she came up to her,
    "Elder sister, where did you go?
    You were gone a long time," she says.
"I was off walking a while," she said.   350
Carrying the wood,
    the two brought it home on their backs.

And then in the evening the two went to bed,   *B*
    the two slept,
        the woman said nothing.   355

The next morning they got up.   *C*
As before they were about to go after wood.
She put a little soup into a basket cup,
    in the basket cup she carried it hidden in her clothes,
        she carried the soup.   360
The younger one gathers wood.
The woman gets the soup,
    carries it,
        does not let the younger sister see she is carrying soup.

She goes on,   365   *D*
    comes over to him there,
        feeds the soup to the one who lies on the ground.
The one who lies on the ground seems a little better,
    he is starting to be a person.
He eats soup,   370
    he eats soup,
        that woman feeds him,
            she feeds him.
Having finished feeding him,
    she gets wood ready,   375
        gets wood ready,
            gets wood ready.

At last she carries it on her back to the house,
    she brings it there,
        she brings the wood.   380

As before it became evening,   E
    they all slept.

After that the next morning those two women get up.   A [iv]
At last having eaten,
    she goes carrying the soup.   385
Then that younger girl,
    "What is going on?" so she thinks.

Her elder sister having gone,   B
    that younger girl follows.
She goes,   390
    she follows her elder sister's tracks,
        wanting to see.
She sees.
Her elder sister is sitting,
    feeding someone soup.   395
The younger girl sees.

At that she ponders about it,   C
as she sees she is feeding soup to someone.
"Have you discovered this one?" so says the younger girl.

And then the younger girl, going on,   400   D
    reaches her elder sister.
"Have you discovered this one?" she says.
"Yes," so she told her.
"The one who went away long ago,
    the person who was lost,   405
        the person not found,
            this is the one,"
                she said, speaking to her younger sister.
"Let's go home," she said.

The two go home,   410   E
    the two getting home,
        they sit.

It gets dark,   *A [v]*
   they eat,
      lie down,   415
   go to bed,
the two women sleep.

In the middle of the night the two women wake up,   *B*
   see a man lying between them,
      a beautiful man is lying. 420

For, they say, he has come back to life,   *C*
   come to the house,
      he who was found by the two women.

[VI] [Retribution and Family Restoration] [i]

And then he stays there,   *A*
   a little while he stays.   425
      At last the two women bear children.

The two boys,   *B*
   those their children,
      having grown little by little,
   play,   430
      play,
         play,
   shooting at birds.
Suddenly they see a bird,   *C*
   they shoot at it with an untipped arrow,   435
      they pierce its lower leg.

The bird,   *D*
   "Tuwétetek, tuwétetek!" it shrieks.
   "Oh why do you shoot at me, cousins?"
   "Come, you two, there is something I should tell you."   440

Now the two come to find a woman.   *E*
Having sat down,
   she talks:
      "Let me tell you.   *E/1*
         You two are getting older.   445
            There is a pool over there.

"You two, having gone to look,
   there will in fact be a raft,
      right there indeed on that deep pool.

"You two are *not* to shoot with this.   450
   You are to prepare good untipped arrows,
      You are to prepare good untipped pitchwood
         arrows," she said.

"There, to that deep pool, comes always every evening   E/2
   she who made us kinless.
      For that she comes from the east round the hill.   455

"You can hear her coming,
   there above she comes rushing,
      up there she'll come.   /

"She'll alight on that pool of water,
   she alights on the water,   460
      she alights,
         she who makes [us] kinless.
            There she glides on the water.

"After that she goes, 'Wuuuuk,'
   flaps her wings up in the air.   465   /

"And then she dives.

"And then she comes out of the water there near that raft.
   she always comes out close to it," she tells the two young
      men.   /

"And after she comes out,   E/3
   this is what she does,   470
      she always flaps her wings up in the air.

"Now look her straight in the eye, you two,
   and shoot.
Look carefully, you two,
   and shoot.   475
Just don't miss, you two, with your untipped pitch wood
   arrows.

"Do *not* miss, you two;
    Look her straight in the eye, you two,
      and shoot!"

When she is through talking,   480   *F*
    the two boys go to the house,
      come to their home,
    they come to the house playing.
      They do not say anything.

They stayed home the next day.   485   *A [ii]*
The next day, having gotten up,
    they eat,
        go,
            the two amuse themselves,
               the two amuse themselves.   490
And then the two arrive there at the pool.

At last it grows dark,   *B*
    the sun goes in.
      The two boys get up on the raft,
        row themselves about,   495
           shooting at the ducks in the pool.   *ʃ*

Suddenly they hear her coming with roaring wings.   *C*
"Here she comes, listen," they say.
She who is coming alights on the pool.
"Wuuuuk," she says.   500
And then she dives.

Those two boys, already prepared,   *D*
    sit watching, those two.
She comes close,
    gets out beside that raft.   505
And then, having gotten out,
    she flaps her wings in the air.   *ʃ*

The two boys are fully prepared,   *E*
    keep her in sight all the time,
      shoot with the untipped arrows of pitch wood   510
        exactly at the hollow of her armpit,

shoot,
    hit her.

Now she dives,   *F*
    into that pool she dives.   515
        The [two little] boys stand watching.   *⌡*

Suddenly she comes to the surface,   *G*
    rises bloated,
        dead.

Now the two take hold of her,   520   *H*
    drag her there to the edge of that raft,
        throw her on top,
    the two drag her out,
        the two throw her on top.   *⌡*

And then the two, having left,   525   *I*
    come to the house.
        The two finish eating.

And then they speak.   *J*
"Father," they say.
The old man says, "What?"   530
"We killed her," they say, "the Wukwuk."
The old man says, "Oh."   *⌡*

Early in the morning they have gotten up,   *A [iii]*
    the old man goes,
        the two boys go,   535
            leading their father,
                to show him the one they had killed.

They go,   *B*
    the old man sees who lies on that raft.
        "Yes," he says,   540
        "this is she who made us kinless," says the old man. *⌡*

And then he takes hold of her,   *C*
    sees she has on a necklace,
        she has on a necklace of human hearts.

At last the old man unties his father's heart,   545   D
   his mother's heart,
      the hearts of his younger brothers.   *}*

And then cutting the flesh into strips,   E
   he leaves it.

And then he goes,   550   F
   he cuts it into strips, leaving it,
      he goes to the house, his home.   *}*

He brings the hearts of his mother,   G
   his father,
      his younger brothers,   555
   he brings them to the house.

And then he weighs them down in water [with stones],   H
   he lies down in the evening.   *}*

In the morning, at dawn,   I
   his mother,   560
      his father,
         all his younger brothers,
            arrive,
   having come to life,
   those who had been soaked in water arrive early in the
      morning.   565

So they say it ends.   *J}*

13

Four Songs from Grace McKibbin

WINTU
CIRCA 1982

GRACE McKIBBIN, SINGER AND NARRATOR

ALICE SHEPHERD, COLLECTOR AND TRANSLATOR

LEANNE HINTON, ANALYSIS AND TRANSCRIPTION

INTRODUCTION BY LEANNE HINTON

Grace McKibbin was a great singer, with knowledge of hundreds of traditional Wintu songs. While there were many Wintu songs of ceremonial significance to be sung by trained religious leaders, the four songs transcribed and translated here are secular in nature and sung by plain folks. People among the Wintu and other tribes used to make up songs to express strong emotions in situations of great joy or pain. Three of these songs Grace called "love songs," and one was a "cry song." Although love songs sometimes speak about romance between a man and woman, they are more often about the strong bonds of family. Two of these songs express the pain of parents when their daughters leave them to marry; and the other love song displays the pride of a young girl in her brother-in-law. The cry song is also about family love: the lament of a newly widowed man trying to figure out what to do with his three small children.

FIGURE 5. Grace McKibbin.
Courtesy Alice Shepherd.

When Grace sang for Alice Shepherd, she always prefaced and ended her songs with some description of their history and meaning. I consider her words about the song to be part of the performance. Indeed, it must have been the case that even for Wintu listeners, most singings of these songs were also accompanied by explanations, because they were sung by people for generations after their first composition. I have therefore included Grace's explanations here as integral parts of the performance.

Since Grace was talking to an English-speaker, her explanations were in English, and are presented here verbatim. The songs were in Wintu, and in keeping with the requirements of this volume, they are presented in translated form. I present the songs with the exact number and arrangement of lines as the original performances. The translation tries to remain as true as possible to the meanings of the Wintu lines. When the lines contain vocables (meaningless syllables), they are presented as they are pronounced in the song. The spoken song explanations are formatted in keeping with pauses and sentential intonation (and punctuation therefore reflects phrasing rather than the conventions of English grammar). After each sentence-final falling intonation (whether terminal or not), a new left-adjusted line begins. A nonfinal pause at a clause boundary is signaled by a line break with the new line indented. A pause within a clause is signaled by a line break with the new line beginning just below the end of the previous line. Loudness is represented by capitalizing the words spoken loudly; italics indicate emphasis.

In general the song consists of only one or two different lines of text plus a line of vocables, sung to a longer melodic form (see p. 225). The same small set of lines is repeated many times in the song in different orders. Much of the artistry and listening pleasure comes from the weaving of the text lines into the different melodic phrases. Of course, no written transcript of a song text can do that song justice. Missing are the lilting melody, the startling rhythms, the fine glides and bursts and vocal ornaments that accompany the song performance. Songs on paper can sometimes seem strangely repetitive and dull. Nevertheless, the ideas being presented in the songs are profound. The line of text is an epigram, an epitome of a feeling, woven over and over into a melodic frame.

NOTES ON THE SONGS

1. First Love Song

Three brothers from a tribe in Oregon came to a Big Time, an intertribal celebration held in Wintu country and neighboring areas. They were the sons of Elc'o:di, named in the song as the "younger Elc'o:dis." They danced the *hisi* dance, and a young Wintu girl fell in love. As Grace McKibbin put it while explaining this song on another occasion:

And this young girl
    she fell in love with these brothers,
'Cause she didn't say which one she liked,
    but she
        she felt an awful lot for all three of them, I guess.

She decided to go home with them to Oregon, and this song is her farewell song to her father.

Love songs have a typical melody and rhythm that differ from *hisi* songs; but in this case, the young woman who made this love song used a *hisi* melody to frame her words, in commemoration of the event that caused her to fall in love. Two sets of vocables are used in the song: *henini ninini* is one variant of the standard vocable set used in love songs; and *heyano heyano* is the set used in *hisi* songs. In fact, after an earlier performance of this same song, Grace talked about the dual nature of the song and reminisced about the dancing itself:

It's a love song through *her,*
   but it's a dance song otherwise:
      hisi ča:wi.
They just go front,
   and backwards.
And the front [ones] go back,
   so that they—
         they *hold themselves same way:*
   my dad say they were,
     when they dance like that,
     they hold themselves SO straight,
     and so EVEN when they dance,
       they *step* even,
       step, go forward,
       and step back, you know?
They STEP EVEN.
They go side by side,
   whole big row of 'em.
That's just the way they dance that song.

2. Second Love Song

This love song shows the depth of family feeling among the Wintu and the joy that accompanies work in a well-integrated culture. The child who sings the song is expressing her pride in her brother-in-law who has killed a buck and gone with the girl's sister to bring it home. The girl is asked to take care of the cooking while the sister goes with her husband, and unlike children many of us no doubt know, this girl responds to the request with joy. She feels proud of her ability to help the family with adult tasks, and she sings with a welling sense of love. I have found a similar song and accompanying story among the Havasupais in Arizona, which makes me suspect that the song-type is very old and widespread among hunting cultures.

3. Third Love Song

In the first love song, a daughter sings a song of empathy for her father, who will be left alone without her when she heads off with her newfound lover. In this song it is the mother who sings to her daughter. This woman's daughter also met a man from a northern tribe and will go away with him. The mother likens the northerners to migrating geese, envisions the daughter flying north with the geese, and implores the daughter for one last backward look before she flies away. (Notice, by the way, that in Wintu one travels "down" north, rather than "up" north. The prepositions we choose to accompany the cardinal directions are culture-specific.)

4. Cry Song

Vocables (so-called nonsense syllables) actually carry some meaning. One aspect of their meaning is that they signal what kind of song is being sung. The vocables *hinini* are diagnostic of love songs. Cry songs are characterized by the lamenting exclamation *ani:*, or *ani: yo:*. In this cry song, there is a line of vocables sung many times, and then two lines of real words. The words are plain: "Which trail should I take to go over the hill? I guess I'll take the south trail over the hill." But meaning is multileveled: this grieving widower is trying to take his young children on a dangerous trip over the snowy mountain by horseback, and the wrong trail could mean the difference between life and death. On yet another level, he is expressing a general sense of being lost, not knowing what he and his family will do now that the mother of his children is dead.

FURTHER READING

Two essays in Hinton's *Flutes of Fire*—"Songs without Words" and "Song: Overcoming the Language Barrier"—should make good starting points for those interested in California Indian singing traditions. Cora Du Bois's "Wintu Ethnography" and Du Bois and Dorothy Demetracopoulou's "Wintu Myths" are both important sources of cultural information. Harvey Pitkin has published a *Wintu Grammar* and *Wintu Dictionary*. Alice Shepherd's *Wintu Texts* presents narratives in Wintu with English translations. Finally, there is the collection of McKibbin's singing and storytelling, *In My Own Words: Stories, Songs, and Memories of Grace McKibbin, Wintu*.

THREE LOVE SONGS AND A CRY SONG

1. LOVE SONG: "OH MY FATHER, WHAT WILL YOU DO?"

A good-size girl, must have been about seventeen or eighteen,
She fell in love with one of the guys
   and they had a Big Time
   and they belong some place up in Oregon, I guess,
      Oregon Indians it must have been.
And she fell in love with one of them
   and she was going to foller them,
   go where they go with them.
And she sing this song.
Told her dad, she said,
   "Dad," she said—
   "Name those guys's name,
   Indian name,"
   and she said, "I'm going too,"
   she said, "They're going up," she says,
   "My Dad," she say, "I don't know," she say,
      "don't know what you're going to do," she say.
   "I'm going to leave you."
And she sung this song:

henini ninini
henini ninini

EX. I. Musical transcription of first love song.

EX. 2. Musical transcription of second love song.

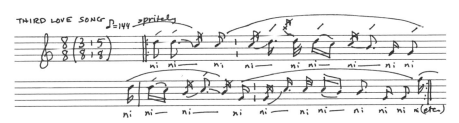

EX. 3. Musical transcription of third love song.

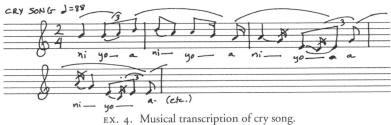

EX. 4. Musical transcription of cry song.

henini ninini
henini ninini

henini ninini
henini ninini

Oh my father, what will you do?
Oh my father, what will you do?

The younger Elc'o:dis danced, and I'm going north,
The younger Elc'o:dis danced, and I'm going north.

Oh my father, what will you do?
Oh my father, what will you do?

Heyano heyano. Oh my father,
Oh my father, what will you do?

2. LOVE SONG: "THERE! THERE! HE'S COMING!"

Well I'll sing that little girl's song again.
One that's maybe a love song for the brother-in-law . . .

hinini nini nini nini
hinini nini nini nini

hinini nini nini nini
hinini nini nini nini

There! There! He's coming!
There! There! He's coming!

My brother-in-law, my brother-in-law, he's coming,
There! There! He's coming!

Southwest upstream on the side of the hill,
Southwest upstream on the side of the hill.

My brother-in-law, my brother-in-law, he's coming,
There! There! He's coming!

My brother-in-law, my brother-in-law, he's coming,
There! There! He's coming!

hinini nini nini nini
hinini nini nini nini

hinini nini nini nini
hinini nini nini nini

My brother-in-law, my brother-in-law, he's coming,
There! There! He's coming!
Southwest upstream on the side of the hill.

Southwest upstream on the side of the hill,
My brother-in-law, my brother-in-law, he's coming.

There! There! He's coming!
There! There! He's coming!

hinini nini nini nini
hinini nini nini nini

My brother-in-law, my brother-in-law, he's coming,
There! There! He's coming!

Southwest upstream on the side of the hill,
There! There! He's coming!

[Alice Shepherd: That's one of my favorite songs.]

[*Laughter*]

That little girl she must have been about ten or twelve years old.
Her sister told her her husband killed this big buck
                                          way up in the canyon
And came home, said he wanted her to go [help him]
                                          pack that buck,

And his wife had acorn soup,
She was takin' the bitter out of it
    puttin' the water in it you know?
So she left her little sister to stay home,
    says, "I'm gonna help him pack this big buck,"
And she said to her,
    said, "You pour the water into the acorn soup,
    so it'll take all the bitter out."

She said it'll be late when they get back.
Meantime she said, "Try to get some wood,
    get some wood before it's dark."
So she's gatherin' the wood up
    and puttin' water in the acorn soup,
And she start about this song,
Make up this love song about her brother-in-law
    killin' that big buck, she's tickled. [*Laughs*]

So that's where brother-in-law's comin',
Around that hillside.
West Canyon,
She said he's comin' in,
He killed that buck,
That's where he's coming.
She's sing away.
And when they was comin' down close they could hear her sing,
Just as loud as she could sing.

[*Laughter*]

3. LOVE SONG: "FLYING NORTH WITH THE GEESE"

This is what old mother sing,
Kind of a sad song, I guess,
    she felt bad 'cause her daughter went off and left her,
Went to Klamath someplace.
She's gonna leave,
    she's leaving, and this
                        mother
    start to sing this song.

[*Hums*]

This song.

hiní niní niní ní niní
hiní ní niní niní ní niní

hiní ní niní niní ní niní
hiní ní niní niní ní niní

hiní ní niní niní ní niní
hiní ní niní niní ní niní

Flying down north with the geese,
Oh, my child, stop a while and look back at me!

hiní ní niní niní ní niní
hiní ní niní niní ní niní

hiní ní niní niní ní niní

hiní ní niní niní ní niní
hiní ní niní niní ní niní

Flying down north with the geese,
Oh, my child, stop a while and look back at me!

Oh, my child, stop a while and look back at me!
Flying down north with the geese,

hiní ní niní niní ní niní
hiní ní niní niní ní niní

hiní ní niní niní ní niní
hiní ní niní niní ní niní

Flying down north with the geese,
Oh, my child, stop a while and look back at me!

Oh, my child, stop a while and look back at me!
Flying down north with the geese.

hinini

[*Laughs*]

It's 'cause she done the same thing the girl [in the first song] did.
She had a boyfriend she's following and went down
                    north someplace.
Klamath Indian, I guess.

And this mother said,
    called them guys that,
    the way she sing called them guys that [were] there,
        GEESE.
Geese, when the geese fly down,
    the geese fly down
        north, she said—
            she's follerin' them, you know,
                her daughter is follerin' them,
        she said,
"Please look back before you go."
Said, "Please look back."
Yole means
    'Look
        back a while.'

4. CRY SONG: "WHICH TRAIL SHOULD I TAKE TO GO OVER THE HILL?"

My grandpa's song that he
                    lost his wife,
And he had—
    my dad was about four years old I guess, four to five years old,
    and my uncle must have been just about,
        no, my aunt was about
                        three,
    and my uncle was about,
        must have been going on two, he was a baby.
So he was living on the Wildwood Road, then he sold his horses,
    most of them,
And he sold his
                two cows he had;
Then he loaded up,
    he couldn't do nothing you know with them three kids;
    while he had his brother-in-law with him he babysat,
    and he sold his horses and cows,

And he
        got ready, and he
                        went to Shasta County with them
                        where his sister was.
Then they was going over the
                        mountain,
    up towards East Fork, and he couldn't go up there,
        on Chilula Trail
        over to Harrison Gulch, Shasta County, you know?
He went up the Wildwood, but,
There was snow,
    four foot of snow;
    hard to see where the horse stepped.
And he—
    he said,
    he telling me after I grew up, he said he didn't know what to do.
And he said he just started thinking about this song,
    singing a song,
    going over the mountain.
So he sing this song,
    about himself you know,
    which road,
    which trail would he go over,
    on the Hazelpatch Ridge or the
                        Wildwood Road.
South Trail,
And,
    he said he think he'd better take the South Trail,
        that's the way this sounds,
        the word is.
"I guess I'll take the South Trail and go over the hill.
I wonder which trail shall I take?"
So he took the Wildwood trail,
    the lower one you know,
    a little ways to go over the heavy snow.
He had
        one of the oldest boys,

packed right into the
                    pack horse, you know?
    Right in the middle, and had him tied down,
    bundled him up
        and tied him down.
Then he had the littler one sitting in the front of him,
    all wrapped up;
And one of them behind the saddle,
    all wrapped up.
So that's the way he led them.
He led the horses,
    the one the little boy is riding, my dad's riding.
And then one of the pack horses packing, and he followed.
So that's the way he went.
And
        he sing this song . . .

ní:yo: aní:yo:
aní:yo: aní:yo:

aní:yo: aní:yo:
aní:yo: aní:yo:

aní:yo: aní:yo:
aní:yo: aní:yo:

Which trail should I take to go over the hill?
I guess I'll take the South Trail over the hill.

Which trail should I take to go over the hill?
aní:yo: aní:yo:

aní:yo: aní:yo:
aní:yo: aní:yo:

Which trail should I take to go over the hill?
I guess I'll take the South Trail over the hill.

aní:yo: aní:yo:
aní:yo: aní:yo:

Which trail should I take to go over the hill?
I guess I'll take the South Trail over the hill.

aní:yo: aní:yo:
aní:yo: aní:yo:

Which trail should I take to go over the hill?
I guess I'll take the south trail over the hill.

I guess I'll take the south trail over the hill.
I guess I'll take the south trail over the hill.

Which trail should I take to go over the hill?
I guess I'll take the south trail over the hill.

Which trail should I take to go over the hill?

He didn't know which way to go.
Thinking about his little kids,
    little bitty ones.

He made it, though.

Snow was deep.
And he buried his wife in the deep snow, you know.
And there someplace where the
                                    sun hit and thawed out,
    under the trees,
    and he buried my grandmother up there,
        Wildwood Road,
        up there at
                    oh, Fox Farm,
        that's where he was staying.
To this day—
    well, before I got blind,
I tried to find that place, I couldn't find it.
He said it was at the other tree.
People lives there, I think they builded a shed on that grave.
But the Forest Service asked me if I
                            know where it was

they'd put a fence around it.
Only way to do is dig 'em out, I guess,
    and find out.

I don't know what she died from.
Just
    died.
Them days there used to be a lot of sickness you know.

14

How I Became a Dreamer

NOMLAKI
1935

CHARLES WATHAM, NARRATOR
CLARENCE CAMPBELL, COLLECTOR

INTRODUCTION BY BRIAN BIBBY

Late one evening, as I was conversing with Nomlaki elder Wallace Burrows in his home on the Grindstone Creek Reservation, nestled among the blue oak and bull pine that dot the rolling hills of western Tehama County, he brought up the name of Charley Watham. He had known Charley. Charley was a dance man who participated in the ceremonial life at Grindstone. He was also known for his regalia and, more specifically, as a maker of woven feather belts.

Wallace told me he remembered that Charley had owned a fine sheep dog who could manage a herd of sheep just about all by itself, leaving Charley free to relax, take a nap, eat lunch, or maybe make a feather belt. Sure enough, while the dog was watching the sheep, Charlie would sit up on a hillside where he had a good view of the animals and work away on his belts. These were woven in what is often described as a warp-face weave, using two-ply cordage. Although formerly the belts were made from native hemp, it's more likely that during this period of Charley's life he was using jute fibers he had unraveled from gunnysacks and then retwisted in the old style.

Tiny, brilliant scarlet-red feathers from the scalp of acorn woodpeckers and the iridescent green feathers from the head and neck of mallard ducks were woven securely into belts some five feet in length and often six to eight inches in width. White glass beads were woven into geometric patterns set against the sections of red feathering. This was no idle pursuit: the making of a woven feather belt required some very meticulous and demanding manipulation of thousands of feathers, usually less than a half inch long each. Feather belts were used in the Hesi ceremony and dance. In a photograph, one of several taken during the Hesi dance of July 1907 at Stonyford, a man identified by some as Charley Watham is wearing one such belt, perhaps of his own manufacture.

When the text of a 1935 interview with Mr. Watham recently came to light, I was greatly interested.[1] The only previous references to Watham I had heard were from a few people who had known him. All I really remembered, aside from the great sheep-dog story, was that he was a dance man. The places Charley went to dance are the same places I have heard about from other elders. These ceremonial dance houses—at Chico, Noweedehe (at Grimes), and Wyteedesla (near Princeton)—have long since ceased to exist. Only a few songs and the roundhouse at Grindstone still exist from his time.

There were some wonderful dances in those old places. Each of these communities had developed its own particular attributes relative to its ceremonial and religious life. Each had its own distinct flag (or flags) that flew during the Hesi. Cloth banners, reminiscent of the American flag in shape, materials, colors, and the use of stars and stripes, featured designs symbolic of images seen in a dream by the flag's originator. These villages also possessed their own songs for the Hesi: songs for each ceremonial outfit, songs for the flags, finishing songs, around-the-fire songs, and so forth. These songs were all born of dreams. Collectively they form a song-map of the region, part of the indigenous soundscape of the upper Sacramento Valley.

Remarkably, much of this fragile nineteenth-century oral literature has survived, and appears to be floating on into the twenty-first. The songs Charley Watham heard, and perhaps danced to, at Chico, Noweedehe,

FIGURE 6. Dancer believed to be Charles Watham.
Courtesy Phoebe Apperson Hearst Museum of Anthropology
and the Regents of the University of California.

and Wyteedesla continue to resonate in the four ceremonial roundhouses that still maintain the Hesi tradition. I remember very distinctly that, upon conclusion of a song, Wallace Burrows would always identify it according to its village-specific lineage. This was an important thing to know about a song, an essential aspect of a singer's professional knowledge. Moreover, Wallace often added his own personal remembrances of the songs: "You should have heard old So-and-so sing that," or "People used to dance that a lot in the old days," and so on. The association of a particular song with a particular place or individual is very strong in this tradition.

Charley Watham, like many before him and many since, was an initiated member of a dance society. At Chico, where he was of high standing or rank, the dance society was called the *Kumeh* (literally, 'of the dancehouse'). The term for a fully initiated member is *yeponi*. Participating in ceremonial dances such as the Hesi requires membership in the dance society. It is really quite a different experience from the contemporary powwow scene, where anyone with an outfit of any sort may participate. In other words, you didn't show up and dance, or even join; you were brought in at the discretion of the dance society's members and leadership.

As the autobiographical story told here suggests, dreams were a central and guiding factor in Charley Watham's life. Dreams played an important role, too, in the lives of the Native peoples he lived amongst. At one point in his narrative, Watham's wife tells him to reveal his dreams to a friend, because it would be better to have a confidant. By doing so, she says, he will not be bothered by troubling dreams. A special class of "doctor" among the Konkow was the *yom nedi,* or dream doctor. Such an individual helped interpret a dream's significance and advised the dreamer on how to take steps to follow the dream's directions. The *yom nedi* might also help the patient with advice on how to alleviate bad or troublesome dreams.

Within the religious society and the dance societies, the role of the dreamer was particularly significant. Dreams were the origin of most songs and dances, and certain people were more disposed to this kind of dreaming than others, although anyone might receive a dream about a song or a particular dance. The highest rank within the dance society was that of the Moki. The Moki wore a cloak of raptor feathers that covered the dancer's body from head to toe. A central part of the Moki's performance, given at intervals during the Hesi, was to relay messages and prophecies from the Creator and other spiritual entities. Much of this is connected to dreaming.

The reservation Charley Watham was probably born on was one of the first ever established in Northern and Central California. Nome Lackee Reservation was indeed located in Nomlaki country, although Native people were brought there forcibly from other tribal regions beginning in 1854. It is important to remember that Nome Lackee Reservation was established scarcely more than five years after most Nomlakis' first-ever encounter with European Americans. The corruption within this reservation is legendary and well documented and obviously led to its early demise. However, with the establishment of Round Valley a second and more devastating blow was dealt to Native people in Northern California. The "drive" to Round Valley, beginning in 1863, was brutal and deadly. It further removed the majority of Native people out of the upper Sacramento Valley, leaving it open to homesteaders and farmers who sought its fertile soils and plentiful waterways. It is unclear, in Watham's narrative, whether he and his father took part in this drive. He only states that his father "moved" to Round Valley around 1862.

When I visited with Wallace and Edith Burrows at Grindstone in the summer of 1976, Wallace told me that he had heard a rumor that Charley Watham might be living in Sacramento. Someone had supposedly seen him in the downtown area. At first I thought Wallace was pulling my leg again, but he was serious. Someone had seen Charley in Sacramento, and recently. We debated this unlikely news and later talked about traveling down the valley to find him. But we never made the trip.

Charley Watham's reminiscence was collected as part of a statewide Depression-era program (State Emergency Relief Administration Project) designed to provide temporary jobs for unemployed workers. While some such works-projects programs paid artists to paint murals in post offices and other public buildings, or laborers to cut trail in national parks and forests, this particular program—miraculous in its foresight and creativity—paid interviewers and translators to do "salvage ethnography" with knowledgeable Native Californians (Valory 1971: fn. 79). Frank J. Essene was the project supervisor for the Relief Administration and must have pursued his undertaking intently, for the Essene papers in the Bancroft Library Ethnological Archives amass some eighty cartons of ethnographic and oral-historical materials collected during this period.

Watham's interview was taken down by a man named Clarence Campbell, near Pinoleville, California, on the seventh and thirteenth of June 1935. Nothing is known of Campbell—where he came from, what his background was, or how he fell on hard times and came to seek out Charley Watham. Perhaps Campbell was a local resident, hired to conduct salvage ethnography in his own area, or perhaps he was merely directed by Essene to travel to Pinoleville and conduct an interview; we simply don't know, though we may now be grateful to him for performing—and to the inventive Roosevelt-style social programs of the thirties for offering—this service in a time of great hardship and need.

NOTE

1. This interview—a carbon typescript from original fieldnotes whose whereabouts are unknown (at least to me)—was found among the extensive Frank J. Essene papers in the Valory collection of the Bancroft Library at U.C. Berkeley. I've manipulated the original text of the interview in a number of different ways: (1) by supplying the title; (2) by reparagraphing the text, though location of the original paragraph boundaries is indicated by an extra line space between paragraphs; (3) by setting the first paragraph in italics, to reflect the fact that this paragraph is clearly in a different voice (the collector's alone) from the remainder of the text (a blend of two voices, narrator's and collector's, with the balance much in favor of the narrator—though that, of course, must remain a subjective assessment); and (4) by altering punctuation where needed for the flow or sense of the story. Other features of the text, including certain variant or nonstandard spellings and capitalizations, are presented as is.

The heading on the typescript in the Bancroft Library reads as follows:

> BOOK I pp. 1–133
> Charles Wathem, informant, age 77. Half or 3/4 breed Nom'laki
> Clarence Campbell, reporter
> Pinoleville, Calif.
> Work assignment from June 7, 1935 to—
> God Indian name Yeaphony.

Note that "Yeaphony" is not really Watham's "Indian" name, as Campbell mistakenly believed, but merely his title (*yeponi* 'initiated member') in the dance organization. There is also considerable variation in the spelling of Watham's name as found here and in other documents. ("Watham," "Wathen," "Wathem," and "Warthon" are all attested in the ethnographic literature.) Brian Bibby and I have regularized it in his introduction to the most common variant, "Watham."—HWL

For general information on the Nomlaki, begin with Walter Gold-schmidt's article "Nomlaki" in the California volume of the Smithsonian *Handbook;* there, too, will be found Lowell John Bean and Sylvia Brakke Vane's "Cults and their Transformations," with information on the Hesi and various other dance ceremonies. Cora Du Bois's fascinating research on "The 1870 Ghost Dance" includes interviews with Charley Watham ("Charlie Warthon" in her article). Robert Heizer and Alan Almquist's *The Other Californians* and James Rawls's *Indians of California* both contain information about Nome Lackee Reservation. Indian regalia of Northwest California was the focus of a full-color issue of *News from Native California,* which included Julian Lang's "The Dances and Regalia." Brian Bibby has written a richly illustrated book on California basketmaking, *The Fine Art of California Indian Basketry,* and had a number of articles in *News from Native California* concerning the roundhouses and dance ceremonies of Northern California, including one on "The Grindstone Roundhouse."

HOW I BECAME A DREAMER

A true story of an aged Indian, Charlie Wathen. Charlie's father arrived in California in the year 1849. He resided near the town of Weaverville until 1855 or 1856. He then moved to the Sacramento Valley near the old Nomlaki reservation. There he went to work for the government as an interpreter and stockman or cowboy. He could speak the Indian language as plainly as any Indian in the Tribe. "There he took up with my mother . . ."

[June 7, 1935.]

[First Day's Work.]

I was born during the year 1857, and shortly after my birth the Indian reservation was disbanded. My father moved to Round Valley some five or six years after this. This was somewhere between 1861 and 1862.

Now five years later, which brought my age up to about eleven, there came a call for what is known as catch-weight in racehorse riding. My father, being a horseman, owned some racehorses. I was successful in winning two races for my father that day. Then two years later, there was a man by the name of Max James, who picked me up and brought me here to Ukiah. He started me riding racehorses right; according to rules. I rode for thirty years during horse race seasons. These seasons took place in the fall of the year. My jockey days were spent all over the state of California, Nevada, and eastern Oregon.

Then after my jockey days I came to Chico to live. There I made the acquaintance of my first wife, whom I married. Two years later, I lost my wife through childbirth. After this had happened my life was very much changed.

Because of some strange occurrences, I took up the Indian ways. This I will try to explain.

I then went to dreaming. It made no difference what I did or where I went, these dreams came on every night. In these dreams, I and my wife were together all of the time. We would be going riding in our same buckboard driving the same horse. I had sold these belongings, but in my dreams they still lived. We would be going to an Indian dance or "Quomdee," this being a place to give sermons.* And always when we entered, we would be coming down through the top instead of through a side entrance. Somehow we would always find people dancing with no songs or music of any kind.

Being haunted with these dreams, I decided to leave my home, thinking this better for myself. I went to another rancheria, by the name of Noweedehe. There I remained for one year. But I went back to my former residence every year to shear sheep. While in Noweedehe, I instructed the younger folks in playing baseball. The reason for me doing this was that I tried in every way to fight off these dreams that had been with me. They troubled me very much, almost driving me insane.

---

* "Quomdee" is Campbell's untrained attempt at spelling *Kumdi* (pronounced "koom-dee"). *Kum* is the term for the ceremonial roundhouse.

At that time I knew nothing about the Indian ways, for I had always been among the white people and felt very much like a white person. But the Indian blood in me seemed to say that I must go back to the Indian ways.

Now, while I lived in Noweedehe there was a ceremonial dance every Sunday called the Ball Dance.* There was a feast or dinner connected with this, also brought in in a religious way.

So after these dreams, my conscience led me to begin to think over the Indian ways. Having lived among the Indians on a few reservations, I had a fair knowledge of how they conducted themselves and knew their habits and ways. But at that time I, myself, never took any part in their ways.

However, while my wife was living, she had told me to reveal my dreams to some friend, as it would be better to have a confidant. By doing this, she told me that I never would be bothered in any way.

She also told me to mourn her for only two months.† After that I could get married, do what I pleased, have any fun which ever I desired. She told me especially to dance, to go to the dances and enjoy myself. This I told her I could hardly do under two years' time.

She also told me to buy beads. So I went to Noweedehe to secure them. I bought over two hundred dollars' worth of beads. After making my purchase, I started to gamble‡ with the people of Noweedehe. I won two

---

* In the manuscript, there is a margin note regarding the name of this dance (two lines, penciled in by hand): "xxx [undecipherable] / bull-head." However, the Bullhead and the Ball are two separate dances. The Bullhead is equated with the Hesi; the Ball Dance was a more secular dance sometimes associated with Hesi ceremonies.
† Either Watham's wife had had early complications with her pregnancy, or she has had some premonition of her death. (Perhaps she herself was a dreamer.)
‡ The gambling Charley participates in is undoubtedly the traditional handgame played with two sets of bones, usually three inches in length, from the foreleg of a deer. Each set contains a marked bone and an unmarked one. Opponents try to guess which hand holds the marked bone, while the team holding the bones sings good-luck songs. Bets are placed before the game begins, each side putting into the center amounts of equal value. In Watham's day, people were still using clamshell disc beads as "property" or money.

hundred dollars' worth more of beads. When the gambling games broke up it was three o'clock in the morning. I retired for three or four hours, and while asleep I had a dream.

I dreamed that I went hunting and in this dream I saw two ducks come flying along. I raised my gun and fired. The two ducks came falling down to the ground. While falling they came down in a fast whirl. They fell near me. They were the most beautiful birds I had ever seen.

Having this dream interpreted by one of the dreamers of Noweedehe, I found out that the dream meant very bad luck for me. [So] I had my breakfast that morning about six o'clock. Before me, I had a trip of seventy-five miles to make before I reached home. This trip was made with a horse and small buggy called a buckboard. I had to drive my horse very fast and hard to make home by ten o'clock that evening.

On my return, I found my wife was very sick—on her deathbed. I went in and sat down by her bedside. She was asleep. There were some lady friends present who were taking care of her. They told me that some time before I had arrived, she was singing some Christian songs. After she had stopped singing, she told them that I was very near home, and that as soon as I arrived, she would bid me farewell and be on her way home. As soon as these ladies finished telling me the sad news, my only and dearest wife turned her head over to me, gave me her hand, and said, "Good-bye."

After my hard luck and the loss of my wife, I sold my horse and buckboard. The rest of my things I gave away. About two months later I left there thinking I could overcome these dreams. I moved to Noweedehe and, being a baseball player, I instructed the people in the game there. I made my home at that place about six months later.

Later, I made up my mind to start in the Indian way, by taking up the Indian dance ceremonies. The first dance I undertook was the Ball Dance. After my first experience at dancing, my dreams suddenly stopped.

After this event, I made up my mind that this is what my wife wanted me to do. So I danced with those people for several weeks doing the Ball Dance every Sunday. But I was not a success at this.

Now, the chief of this place took me and many mares out on a goose hunting trip. The meat was to be dried for winter, the oil saved, and the feathers. We were out on this hunting trip for one month.

One night I had a dream. I dreamed there were five little old people who took me into a dance house. They had a large basket, and we all sat around the basket. They sang a song and each was instructed to take it (the song) from one another and sing it all around the basket. Then one of these fellows told me to go over and take the drums and do the drumming while they sang. Then he told me to go to the floor and dance. Then one of these fellows took me by the arm with his two hands. He took me over to my place and told me to sit down and that I was all right then. This being a dream, on awakening, I gave it much thought.

Now, after this hunting trip, there came word from Wyteedesla calling for a big dance. So we went, a whole party of us. When we got to this place, Wyteedesla, the people from Chico had also come. The people from Wyteedesla had already taken me up to dance with them, but after the Chico people had seen me, they took me away from the Wyteedesla people and claimed me. So I had to dance with the Chico people.

Shortly after this dance at Wyteedesla, I went back to Chico and worked under those people for over seven years straight. They put me in a high standing or rank about the same as any white man's lodge would do. The first year I worked on the floor as leading dancer. This was to make me into a dance instructor. Then I began dancing Hessie.* Hessie was one of the leading Indian names for this one special ceremonial dance which took place in the spring of the year and in the fall of the year. We danced a different dance every two weeks during the seven years that I danced with them.†

---

* Campbell's spelling of *Hesi.*

† Some of the narrator's comments about rank and standing might at first blush seem like simple boastfulness. But the Hesi societies were in fact very rank-conscious: "Within the Hesi society there were as many as 10 or 12 ranks to be achieved by payment and performance. Members were

These people tore down the dance hall so as to fix it over, but got into a mixup and never did fix it. So I got discouraged there, and went to another place, a dance hall among my own people. They put me at the head of that hall and I remained there for five years.

[Stopped work at six o'clock.]

[Thursday, June 13.]
[Started work 8 o'clock A.M.]

This dance house which I was in charge of was located at Grindstone, another rancheria, of my people.

Now, while dancing at Grindstone, I would every other year have to go to the mountains to gather acorns. On the trip we would start out with a wagon, but on nearing the mountains we would have to leave our wagon and pack our horses. We had three pack animals. Getting to where we wanted to go was over deep canyons. After arriving at camp we would put in several days gathering acorns. When we had gathered enough and packed our horses, we would have to take another route home. This was through the high mountains.

On this [particular] trip back, we reached the summit after sundown and were forced to camp overnight. We staked our pack animals, made a quick meal, and retired for the night.

As I fell asleep, a dream came over me. I dreamed that the chief from Wyteedelso took me into a dance house and there showed me some of the most beautiful dancing customs that I had ever seen.* This man who

_____

paid for enacting ceremonial roles, the acting not requiring the acquisition of esoteric knowledge; they paid to learn the esoteric knowledge that permitted them to direct performances and for the right to sit in a hierarchy of seating sections within the dance house" (Bean and Vane 1978:667). Bean and Vane also comment on the "bewildering variety of dances" performed in the course of the ceremonies.

* "Customs" is undoubtedly a misspelling for *costumes*. Bean and Vane note that "the dance costumes [of the Hesi] were extremely elaborate" (1978:667).

showed me this outfit was a dead man from Wyteedelso. After this man had shown me this paraphernalia I dreamed that I fell asleep.

Another time, not long after this, I was herding sheep [on] the same mountain. While in camp one cold night, I retired early and fell right off to sleep. And another dream came over me. This time I dreamed that I was looking for my mule. I was tracking him along the ridge of a high mountain. While on this errand, I came across a very large snake track which was about twenty inches wide. Looking in the direction which he went, I saw him moving very slowly down the hill. His head was high in the air. It seemed to be about twenty feet high. As he crawled along he made a very loud noise. It sounded like a large body of water rushing through dry leaves. He was going down through a deep canyon, and just beyond him was a very big cliff of rocks. This cliff was just across the canyon from him. I stood there and watched him go. He seemed to run against this cliff of rocks and make a noise just the same as that of loud thunder. After this I crossed his track, lay under a shady sugar-pine tree, and fell off to sleep.

There are many other dreams that I could tell of, and what they meant to me. Some of these dreams put me where I am today, an Indian doctor.

15

Mad Bat

MAIDU
CIRCA 1902

HÁNC'IBYJIM (TOM YOUNG), NARRATOR
ROLAND DIXON, COLLECTOR
WILLIAM SHIPLEY, TRANSLATOR

INTRODUCTION BY WILLIAM SHIPLEY

One of the great adventures of my life began, during the winter holidays of 1954, when I went up into the Sierra of Northern California to seek out the last speakers of a dying California Indian language known as Mountain Maidu. I was a graduate student at Berkeley then, in the newly inaugurated Department of Linguistics. Research funds had been made available by the California State Legislature for sending qualified students out into the field to learn, record, and analyze data on as many native languages of California as possible before they all disappeared forever. Over the next few years, I got to spend some of those funds.

I found the speakers I was searching for: Lena Benner, who was ninety-something, and her daughter, Maym Benner Gallagher. It was actually Maym who turned out to be my great friend and teacher. She fully understood what I wanted to accomplish; she bonded enthusiastically with me in the service of our common enterprise. She put all her knowledge and talent at my disposal. I did the same for her in return. We had wonderful, vivid, and exciting times together and remained close friends until she died, many years later.

Before I started my work with Maym, I learned about the researches of Roland Dixon, a scholar who came out from the East at the turn of the century and investigated various California Indian languages, mainly Maidu. Among other things, he published, in 1912, a collection he had made of Maidu myths and stories, written in both Maidu and English on facing pages. He had collected this material in 1902–1903 from a young Maidu man whose American name was Tom Young. Dixon's achievement was truly remarkable in view of the inchoate state of ethnolinguistics at the time and the lack of any adequate mechanical recording devices.

When Maym and I were well along on our study of the language, I took Dixon's book up to the mountains with me. Maym remembered Tom Young very well, told me that he was noted among the Maidu as a storyteller, and said that his real name was Hánc'ibyjim (pronounced approximately like "HAHN-chee-buh-yim"). We looked through the book, noted the inadequacies of Dixon's Maidu transcriptions, and decided to reconstitute the section called "Coyote's Adventures," an example of what's known as a Trickster Cycle—a picaresque chain of short anecdotes. That was Maym's choice, actually. She and her mother were unspoiled pagans. I'm sure she was attracted to the bawdy, sexy subject matter so characteristic of Coyote stories all over North America. Unfortunately, we never worked through the rest of the book. I reconstituted, translated, and published most of the other stories in later years, including an unbowdlerized version of the Trickster Cycle (Shipley 1991).

"Mad Bat," however, was not among the stories that I translated. It appears here for the first time. Earlier on, I was daunted by some of Bat's speeches, which, as you will see, are essentially like the "word salad" talk of some schizophrenics and aphasics—an assemblage of valid bits and pieces of the language, jumbled together in an apparently meaningless potpourri. But as soon as I decided how to deal with those particular utterances, the rest of the translation came easily along.

The denouement of "Mad Bat" exemplifies a fairly common theme found in many Maidu stories: a powerful and malevolent creature—Bat, Frog Old Woman, and Muskrat are examples—finds himself deprived of his power and shrunken down to a small and innocuous animal. In this story, Bat commits murder and mayhem with grotesque abandon and without any immediate retribution or revenge, perhaps because the other people believe that his madness exempts him from responsibility for his actions.

My first impulse was to include only the first, longer and more elaborate, episode in the translation because the later—and much sketchier—adventure with Cloud and Ouzel seems, on the face of it, unrelated to what has gone before. However, it became clear to me that these later events resolve Bat's madness and restore order to the world. His death, followed by his demotion by Ouzel in the (Maidu) classical manner, involves what is, for us, a paradoxical situation. As Bat the individual he is dead, but as a stand-in for bats in general he lives on in the modern world, stripped of his power to do harm.

I should comment, parenthetically, on the brief irrelevant presence of Coyote in this story. Despite his appearance, this is not really a Coyote story; he's just here to liven the tale, a device which Hánc'ibyjim often used. Even the mention of Coyote could, in my day, move my Maidu friends to laughter. No matter that Coyote often "dies"; he always comes irrepressibly back to life again.

There are also a few contextual things that need to be explained or defined in order that the story may be more fully appreciated.

West Mountain (Táyyamanim) is the Maidu name for what is now called Mount Lassen, the southernmost peak of the Pacific Cascade range, a live volcano that dominates the skyline to the northwest of the Maidu homeland. It was thought that saying the name of the mountain out loud would cause it to erupt. Nakam Valley is the modern Big Meadows.

The ouzel, a bird that many people don't know about, is often called a water ouzel or a dipper bird (the Maidu name is *mómpispistom*). It lives along mountain streams and behind waterfalls and has the curious habit of walking along underwater in search of food. It is smallish and brown with a little white breast and a short tail.

There are four Maidu customs that appear in this story and require some explanation as well.

First, there is the way in which Bat and his brother seem to think of wives as (from our point of view) interchangeable objects. This is probably to be taken as part of Bat's heinousness. In fact, it seems certain that, in the old days, the woman's consent to a marriage was essential, though there was always a bride-price, and there were men who had two, three, or even four wives.

Second, the staple food all over Northern and Central California was prepared from ground and leached acorns. It was eaten as soup, bread, or mush. Therefore, it was perfectly reasonable for Bat's sister-in-law not to have gotten around to providing acorn soup. It's another example of Bat's madness.

Third, when people wanted to get various people together from some distance away, they sent out knotted buckskin strings with the knots matching the number of days before the event. The messengers and the recipients would untie one knot every day. That way, everybody came together on the same day. These strings are what I have called "invitation strings" in the story.

The fourth custom has to do with gambling. By contrast with our view of gambling as vaguely immoral or, for most people, trivial and peripheral, the Maidu held in high esteem an elaborate pastime known as the grass-game. It was more than a recreational event. Charms for luck in gambling were highly prized. A single game could go on continuously for many days and nights, sometimes with enormous wagers.

And now, here is how Hánc'ibyjim opened his telling of "Mad Bat," in Maidu, nearly a century ago:[1]

pótc'odem	májdym	sámbojekytom	hedéden
bat	person	sibling.group	very.close

mym	ínk'i-di	hybó	ky-dom;
that	alongside.place-at	house	make-ing

amá-di	myjím	bomóm-di-'im,
then-at	that. [HUMAN]	group-in-ish

syttim	májdym,	tetét	wasó-sa-pem	májdym,
one	person	very	angry-always-ish	person

ohéj-c'oj-am.
one.in.a.group-they.say-he.was

A very literal translation of these two sentences might read something like this:

A bat-person sibling-group making houses very close alongside each other; then, among this bunch of people, a very always-angry person was one of them, it is said.

Finally, here is the same opening passage in "good" literary English, as I have translated it for this collection:

Bat and his brothers built their houses right next to each other.
Now, among all the people around, there was one bad-tempered man.

A last suggestion. This story, of course, was always told and not written, and was, therefore, more like our theater than like our literature. I have tried to maintain this spoken quality in my translation, breaking the text into phrases, or lines, that suggest how Hánc'ibyjim may have told it. The best way to enjoy the story is to read it out loud, even if only to yourself.

NOTE

1. In Maidu, the letter *j* stands for a "y" sound, and the letter *y* stands for an umlauted vowel, "ü." Stressed vowels are marked with an acute accent.

FURTHER READING

For other Maidu myths and stories, see *The Maidu Myths and Stories of Hánc'ibyjim,* edited and translated by William Shipley and with a foreword by Gary Snyder, which contains most of the textual material collected at the beginning of the twentieth century. For a look at the original source materials from which *Maidu Myths* was reconstituted, see *Maidu Texts* by Roland Dixon. The only extensive ethnographic description of the Maidu is Dixon's beautifully illustrated "The Northern Maidu." For grammatical and lexical information, see Shipley's *Maidu Texts and Dictionary* and *Maidu Grammar.*

MAD BAT

Bat and his brothers built their houses right next to each other.
Now, among all the people around, there was one bad-tempered
  man.

Of all those pleasant folks, the mean and grumpy one was Bat!

One of Bat's brothers went off to find a wife.
But then, he never came back.   5
Bat just stayed there with his other relatives.

One of them said: "Let's go hunting!
We can make camp overnight somewhere and then come back.
But let Bat come along later behind us.
If he's with us, he'll just make trouble.   10
Let's go when everyone feels like it."
So they set off together, but Bat came along behind.

Now, when they got to the camping place and were all sitting
    down,
Bat arrived.

In the morning, they went off hunting here and there.   15
Along toward evening, one by one, they came back.
They skinned out the deer and divided up the meat.
It was a sight to see. But they didn't give Bat any.
They divided it among themselves. They didn't give Bat any.
When they had divided it up and tied it into bundles,   20
they went back home.

Later on, Bat came home too, following behind them.
Then he spoke to his sister-in-law.
"Make me some acorn soup," he said.
But the woman said: "Wait—the acorns aren't leached yet."   25
So he just shot her with an arrow!
He killed that woman! He killed his sister-in-law, just like that!

Later, as it began to get dark, his brother was crying.
And when his brother cried, Bat felt sorry for him.
And when his brother didn't stop crying, he too cried.   30
"Watery draggety, watery draggety, my dingalong," said Bat.
"Stop mourning for that woman!
I say that I will go and find you another woman to be with!"
So then, in the morning, Bat started off, they say.

He traveled along, coming to many places where people were
    living.   35
He looked all around in each and every dwelling.
And in one house, a couple of very beautiful women were living.
So, when Bat had sat outside the door for a while,
he tossed a couple of arrows in to the father of those women.
"I'll trade you these for the women," he said.   40

And then that old man said, "All right!
You two had better leave," he said.
"You two had better go with him, with this man."

And then the two women packed all their things into pack
    baskets,
and they all three set out,   45
and when they had traveled and traveled, they got there.

"You two go to that house over there," said Bat.
So those two women went over and crawled into his brother's
    house.
Thus Bat killed his sister-in-law,
brought those two women back, and made it up to his brother.   50

And after that, Bat went back to his own house and stayed there.
But, as it was getting dark, some people came along.
And when they had completely surrounded his house,
they burnt it down.

The house kept burning.   55
When it was almost completely burnt up,
Bat came rushing back out of the night shadows.

Then he spoke. "Why are you doing this?" he asked.

Then he shot at them.
And they kept shooting at each other until he had killed them   60
    all.
Then he stayed there.
The rest of the people didn't go away. They just stayed there too.

After a while, one of the men spoke.
"We used to always go hunting deer," he said.

Then the village headman said: 65
"Go hunting, but don't say anything about it.
That Bat fellow is a bad man,
so all of you go but don't talk about it.
Let him stay here."
So they packed up a midday meal and went.   70

But Bat, without their knowledge,
got to their camping place long before they did.
They came there,
and afterward, in the morning,
they went off hunting down the mountain.   75
Along toward dusk, they came back, one by one, carrying deer.
And then again next morning, they went off hunting
and straggled back toward evening.
They skinned out the deer and cut up the carcasses.
It was a fright to see!   80
The next day, they packed up their loads of meat
and got ready to go home.

Then Bat spoke.
"Go along think sinew more or less," he said.
"What do you mean?" they said.   85
He said, "Go along think sinew more or less."
Then one of them untied his pack and gave him some sinew.
He refused it. "Go along think sinew more or less," he said.
"What are you saying?" asked the other.
"Are you talking about this kind of sinew?"   90
He showed him leg sinew. He showed him back sinew.
Bat refused it. "Go along think sinew more or less," he said.
Then they gave him a look at a lung.
"Is this what you're talking about?"
They showed him a heart.   95
"Is this what you're talking about?" they asked.
He said, "No! Go along think sinew more or less!"
"He's bad-tempered. He's just going to say that.
Let him alone and go!"
It was one of his kinsmen who spoke.   100
So, when they had gotten their goods together, they went.

Meanwhile, Bat was flopped down on top of a rock.
Some deer's antlers were hanging down, hanging from a sapling.

The hunters went along until they got home.
When it was dark, they all went to sleep.   105
In the morning, they said,
"That magically powerful man never got back.
He was angry. It seems he must have run away somewhere.
That's the kind of thing he does!"
Then one said, "Well, then.   110
You all better go see what's going on with him." So they went.

They kept going until they got to another place, but he wasn't
    there.
When they looked all around,
they saw the antlers lying a little further on.
And one of them kicked them over.   115
Then, it seemed, Bat sprang up from under the antlers.
Then they set the antlers upright and went back home.
Antlers were the very things Bat was talking about,
but, the way he talked, the other men just didn't understand.
So it seems that when they got home they stayed there.   120

Then someone brought an invitation string and left again.
When a few days had passed, all the knots were untied.
Then, one by one, they went off to the feast.
"You mustn't let that bad man hear about the feast," someone
    said.
"If he knows about it, he'll go with us.   125
Let him stay here! He's a bad one!"

Then they sneaked away.
They went along and, when they were almost there,
they stopped to rest.
When they looked back from where they were sitting,   130
they saw that wicked fellow coming along.
"Why did you go away without telling me?" he asked.
"We came without thinking about it," they said.
So then they all went along and arrived at the feasting place.
They crawled into a large house.   135

Meanwhile,
Bat went across to the house where his brothers were staying.
When he got there, he crawled in. His brothers were there.
When he had crawled in there, he sat down.

Now, his sisters-in-law were there, many of them.   140
One of them put some manzanita berries on a plate
and set it in front of him.
"I'm not going to eat that kind of grizzly shit," he said.
And he gave the plate a kick.
And then those women, with scowling faces,   145
were terrifying to see, standing around staring at him.

He snapped them on the nose,
those who were looking down angrily at him.
Then they grabbed at him, but he dodged aside.
They all jumped to seize him but he dodged aside.   150
He kept dodging. He grabbed his bow and arrow and shot them.
Meanwhile, his brother stayed there and said nothing to him.
He kept shooting and dodging.
Then, after a while, he shot all his arrows. He killed them all.
And when he got over there, he stayed.   155

Taking no notice of him, his other brothers were gambling.
They all went on gambling. It got to be morning.
They gambled all day.
Along toward dark, they stopped gambling and set out for home.

Meanwhile, Bat, having come to the last house in the village,   160
got to the place where two women were weaving baskets.
Then he handed some arrows to the old man there.
"I'm trading you these for the women," he said.
"I'm giving them to you for these two women," he said.

"All right!" said the old man. "You two go now," he said.   165
Then those two packed up their basketmaking gear.

Now all the people were scared of Bat,
but there was nothing they could do.
They couldn't kill him. He was very powerful.
Though lots of people shot at him with arrows,   170

they couldn't hit him. They were very frightened.
Whatever he asked them for, they gave him.
They couldn't refuse him.

Those two women got all their things together,
and they all three went off.   175
And then they got there and Bat gave the women to his brother.
"You're going to stay here and be married to him," Bat said.
So his brother lived across the way from him with those two
    women.

Later, Bat ran a race with Cloud, they say. They raced.
They set out and raced toward where the sun goes down.   180
They raced.

Cloud floated up to a mountain.
Bat flapped up to a mountain further on.
Then Bat flew up to West Mountain,
and then Cloud drifted up to another, further on.   185
After that, Coyote saw Bat.
"Well, now, Cousin," he said,
"It looks to me like you're running a race.
When you're racing with somebody,
I'm not one to run along behind!"   190

Then Coyote got to his feet
and took off as fast as he possibly could.
He ran, staring up at them.

Meanwhile, Cloud drifted to another mountain,
and Bat flew to a mountain further on.   195

Coyote ran as fast as he could,
looking up at them all the time.
Then he tumbled over into a rocky river canyon.

Bat and Cloud hastened on,
but Coyote broke his neck and died.   200

Cloud floated to a distant ridge
while Bat flapped on to another mountain.

They went everywhere.
They came to where the sun goes down.

But they turned back from that place.   205
Bat was not left very far behind,
and, after the race, he went back home and stayed there.

Then, later on, he went somewhere to the south,
and he came to the place where Ouzel was fishing with a net.
Ouzel was netting all kinds of animals,   210
he was netting all kinds of creatures
that came floating down the river into Nakam Valley.

Then Bat went down to the river.
When he had gotten to the great waterfall,
he tried to catch fish as they came to the top of the water,   215
and he swooped and almost touched the water.
Just then, he fell into the net.

Bat died.

After he had killed Bat, Ouzel said:
"You'll never again be one of those people-killers.   220
After you fly around in the dark,
when morning comes, you'll stay in a hole in a hollow tree.
You'll be just an animal.
You'll not bother anyone.

That'll be the end of that," said Ouzel.   225

16

Creation

EASTERN POMO
1930

WILLIAM RALGANAL BENSON, NARRATOR
JAIME DE ANGULO, COLLECTOR AND TRANSLATOR

INTRODUCTION BY HERBERT W. LUTHIN

The work of recording this Eastern Pomo creation myth back in 1930
brought together two of the most remarkable figures in the annals of California oral literature: William Ralganal Benson, storyteller and artist ex-
traordinaire, and Jaime de Angulo, a wild and charismatic linguist who
became something of a cult figure in his own lifetime. Benson would
have been sixty-eight when he told this myth, and de Angulo forty-three.
In the latter's books on California Indian life and lore, Benson (or "Uncle William," as Jaime and his wife, L. S. "Nancy" Freeland, called him)
is the model for the character of Turtle Old Man. Because the two men,
friends for nearly twenty years, are such important figures in the history
of California folklore, I will briefly sketch their biographies before considering the myth itself.[1]

William Ralganal Benson

Benson was born in 1862 at Shaxai (now known as Buckingham Point) near the ancient town of Shabegok on the western shore of Clear Lake. It was, in de Angulo's words,

> a pleasant region of small fertile valleys where wild roots and seeds once grew in abundance; where acorns, laurel nuts, buckeye chestnuts were once plentiful; where the streams were once well stocked with fish; where the hillsides were once covered with numerous bands of deer. The lake itself, surrounded by mountains, teemed with fish, and flocks of aquatic birds of all kinds were constantly flying by. (de Angulo 1976a:103)

Benson was fortunate enough to have lived his boyhood years during the last decade in which Eastern Pomo speakers enjoyed a more-or-less traditional lifestyle. By the 1870s, the social and environmental disruptions caused by a growing local Anglo-American population would make traditional life impossible, as the lifeways of local Indians became increasingly marginalized.

Benson himself was of mixed-blood descent. His mother, Gepigul ("Sally" to local whites), came from a line of hereditary leaders of the Kuhlanapo (Water Lily People) and Habenapo (Rock People) tribes. His father was Addison Benson, one of the first white settlers in the Kelseyville area—by all local accounts, an intelligent and open-minded man who got along well with his Indian neighbors.[2] Indeed, Addison saw fit to learn the Eastern Pomo language of his wife's people, so despite his mixed heritage, William Benson still grew up in a household where Eastern Pomo was the language of choice. For this reason, Benson didn't really learn to speak English until later in his adult life. Something of a renaissance man, he even taught himself how to read and write.

Benson became not merely a tradition-bearer of his culture's arts and literature, but a master of them. Sally McLendon, who has worked on Eastern Pomo for many years and knew Nancy Freeland in Berkeley, tells me that everything Benson turned his hand to—basketry, regalia, storytelling—came out almost preternaturally ornate or beautiful: not just a mask, but a work of art; not just a basket, but the most beautiful basket you ever saw; not just a myth, but the most detailed and skillful version in the canon.

The Pomo were one of the very few California groups where baskets

FIGURE 7. William Ralganal Benson, circa 1936.
Courtesy Phoebe Apperson Hearst Museum of Anthropology
and the Regents of the University of California.

were made by men as well as women. Benson was already a skilled basketmaker when he met and married Mary Knight, a Central Pomo speaker
who was also expert in basketry. Together, they supported themselves by
making and selling their baskets to collectors and museums—perhaps the
first California Indians to make their living exclusively as artisans. They
even had their own exhibit at the 1904 St. Louis World's Fair, jointly weaving a basket that won the fair's highest award. Baskets made by the Bensons may be found not only in California museums like the Lowie in

Berkeley, but in the Smithsonian, the Field Museum in Chicago, and the National Museum of the American Indian in New York City.

An initiate into Eastern Pomo religion and ceremony, Benson, with his deep cultural knowledge and mixed-blood ancestry, was an ideal consultant for academic researchers—brilliant and informed, yet also familiar with the manners and expectations of the white world. Over the years, he worked and shared this knowledge (not without controversy) with a string of the most important figures in California linguistics and anthropology: Kroeber, de Angulo, Freeland, Loeb. He stands today as one of the most prolific and authoritative sources of information on the Northern California Indian world, particularly that of the Pomo.

William Benson died in 1937, at the age of seventy-five. Among the papers he left behind is a lengthy autobiography, written primarily in English, though with passages in Eastern Pomo. Sally McLendon is working on a scholarly edition and translation of this manuscript.

Jaime de Angulo

Cowboy in Colorado; failed silver miner in Honduras; medical student with a degree from Johns Hopkins; cattle rancher; army psychiatrist during World War I; novelist; gifted and largely self-taught linguist-psychologist-anthropologist-ethnomusicologist with a lifelong interest in the Indians of California—Jaime de Angulo was all these things and more. Born in Paris in 1887 of wealthy Spanish expatriate parents, de Angulo got fed up with his Jesuit schooling and came away to America at the age of eighteen, looking for adventure. He proved to have a talent for landing in the thick of things, like arriving in San Francisco in 1906 on the day of the great quake.

De Angulo had long been interested in anthropology, Jungian psychology, and linguistics, but it was through a mutual friend, Nancy Freeland, that he met Paul Radin and Alfred Kroeber at the University of California. (Freeland was then an anthropology student studying under Kroeber.) Kroeber quickly recognized his brilliance and—though the two men had an uneasy relationship throughout their careers (de Angulo's lifestyle was just too exuberantly bohemian for Kroeber's sense of propriety)—helped to get him established, inviting him to Berkeley to give lectures and, later, courses in anthropological psychology. (It was after his first such lecture, in 1919, that de Angulo met William

Benson, who was working in Berkeley that semester as a consultant; they soon became collaborators and firm friends.) In the end, de Angulo was too much of a "wild man" to find or hold a position in academia. For all of that, or because of it, he left a lasting mark on California studies.

During the twenties and thirties, de Angulo, often together with Freeland (whom he married in 1923—his second marriage), did significant fieldwork on a variety of California and Mexican languages, including Achumawi, Atsugewi, Karuk, Shasta, Sierra Miwok, Eastern Pomo, Mixe, Chontal, and Zapotec. But it was Achumawi, the language of the Pit River Indians of Northeastern California, that occupied center place in his life and life's work. From his deep personal and professional involvement with the Achumawi came a grammar, numerous mythological texts, ethnomusicological studies, and what has come to be his best-known book, *Indians in Overalls.*

Jaime de Angulo lived a colorful and in many ways tragic life—a life so rich and varied, so full of good times, hard work, and troubles, that I cannot even begin to portray it here. His work in linguistics and music alone (he was one of the pioneers of Native American ethnomusicology) would make him a seminal figure in California folklore and anthropology. But de Angulo was never merely an academic. He had the gift of a poet's ear, and used it to make books of translations and fictionalized retellings that far transcended other treatments of his day for the music, grace, and fidelity of the language, and for their wide-ranging accessibility and popular appeal.

As a writer, de Angulo managed to capture into English not just the contents of the texts he recorded, but something of their rhetorical style and, beyond that, of the worldview that informs them. It is a voice so distinctive as to be unmistakable among translators of Native American oral literature. Nowhere is this voice more evident than in his fictionalized settings of myths and tales jumbled together from his many field trips around California—in books like *Indian Tales, How the World Was Made,* and *Shabegok* (many of them ostensibly intended "for children"). It might be argued, perhaps, that de Angulo as much invented this voice in English as discovered it resident in the texts. There is something so easy-going, so engaging and seductive, about this voice that the dreary postmodernist inside us is all but incapacitated by its charm. In any case, he used this voice in his books and stories the way a musician uses his instrument, to convey what he perceived, from his long and intimate involvement with California Native peoples, as the key spirit—a kind of pragmatic joie de vivre—of California Indian life. He died in 1950, at the age of sixty-three.

Benson's Eastern Pomo "Creation"

This myth was first published in the *Journal of American Folklore* in 1935. De Angulo's commentary prefacing the text, which was presented first in Pomo and then followed by an English translation, was quite minimal. It is reproduced in near-entirety here:

> The text of this Pomo tale of the creation is in the Clear Lake dialect [of Eastern Pomo] and was dictated by W. Ralganal Benson. The translation was undertaken primarily as a linguistic study. In the first part of the myth [¶1–17] therefore the original Indian text has been adhered to most closely, and practically a literal rendering is given. This will be of advantage to students of linguistics, but a detriment to the general reader and folklorist. The general reader is likely to be repelled by the awkward English, as a result of the too close following of Pomo idioms and style. On the other hand he may perhaps welcome the guarantee of accuracy. If he is curious to know how the Indian mind [read: Pomo mind] shapes its thoughts in language and style, here he will find it. As the work of translation proceeded, it was deemed unnecessary to render the original so literally. The student of linguistics would by this time be familiar enough with morphology and semantics to supply or delete a few words here and there, by comparing with the original text. In this latter part of the tale the general reader will find a rendering that gives in reality a truer equivalent of the original Indian style with its slightly Homeric flavor.

Though de Angulo much later published a fictionalized setting of this text in a still freer translation that smooths away the "literal rendering" of the opening seventeen paragraphs, I have chosen to present the more scholarly version of the myth here because of its closer adherence to the original text. For contrast, though, here's how de Angulo opens the telling of this myth in *How the World Was Made* (1976b:41):

> *After the Kuksu left they were quiet in the Ceremonial-house for a long time. Then Old Man Turtle commenced the long tale of "How the World*

Was Made." He launched into it without any warning, as if he were just making an announcement of what had happened the day before.

Then Marumda pulled out four of his hairs. He held out the hairs, he held out the hairs to the east, he held out the hairs to the north, he held out the hairs to the west, he held out the hairs to the south. "Lead me to my brother," Marumda said to the hairs.

Readers who make the comparison will understand both how the overly literal version submits to change and why the fictionalized version, though more consistent in tone, was not chosen for inclusion in this volume.

Belying its tight cyclical structure, Benson's "Creation" reveals a sweeping, almost panoramic vision. Within its five gyres there is a great wealth of detail, as well as the continuing slight novelty of complex and nonformulaic variation. The particularity lends immense texture to each patch or passage of narrative ground, while the variation imparts a *through*-momentum to the story that carries it forward rather than backward, so that ultimately it transcends its own circularity. The cumulative effect of all this variation and detail is less déjà vu than daguerreotype: as in the development of a photographic plate the longer it is bathed in solution, with each pass at creation the image of the world fills in with richer and richer detail.

Though some plot elements exhibit less internal variation than others—for instance, the meetings between Marumda and the Kuksu are highly and ornately formulaic—variation is nevertheless the key to understanding the myth as a whole. Notice how each cycle of creation either involves different methods, focuses on different facets of culture and existence, or works at refining the establishments of the preceding creation.[3] In some rounds of creation, people are made from sticks or other inanimate objects; in others, like the second, they are simply thought or willed into being. In some creations, such as the first, Marumda's instruction is limited to basic survival skills, like what foods to eat and how to prepare them; in others, such as the third and fourth, in addition to survival instruction, Marumda sets up key social and governmental institutions. In some, he explains to people the fate of the previous creation; in others he does not. In some, he partakes of food with his people; in others he does not. In some, he establishes a dance ceremonial; in some, he decrees the division of labor between the sexes; in some, there is comic relief, like the encounters with Squirrel and Skunk; and so on. Even when two creations seem to cover essentially the same ground, like the third and fourth, Benson manages to impart to them a wholly different feel— a subtle shift in mood or sensibility.

On another level, Benson's "Creation" may be heard as an extended and unabashed love song to Marumda, the Eastern Pomo Creator. One of the most extraordinary features of this myth is the sophisticated way in which the portrait of Marumda is developed across the successive cycles of the world's resurrections. It is not so much Marumda himself but our perception of him as a character or deity that matures so profoundly during the course of the myth. He is lovingly portrayed as a revered and (for a deity) oddly human figure—not through didactic narration, as a lesser storyteller might have done, but obliquely, by showing the increasing respect, affection, and awe with which he is treated by the succession of peoples he creates and instructs. The belated discovery of generosity in the third creation (¶114–116), which is requited in the fourth (and codified culturally as the ideal of hospitality due a stranger), suggests something of this growth in stature and recognition. By the fourth and fifth creations, children are scolded for making fun of "the Old Man," as well as for fearing him—the knowledge of who he is and what he has done being passed on as lore from generation to generation.

There is ever an air of mystery surrounding Marumda. He always seems to be wandering off once his work is done, never to be seen again, leaving his people, his creations, behind to express their wonder and gratitude. Marumda reaps this loving adulation despite his role as avenging angel. Nowhere is this essential duality of character more evident than in the aftermath of Marumda's destructions, where we find him going along, inspecting the newly scorched or scoured earth, simultaneously ascertaining that no survivors have escaped his destruction *and* expressing shock and grief at their extinction. This behavior may seem quixotic to modern readers, given that it is Marumda who calls down their destruction in the first place. It helps, then, to learn that Marumda is historically an anthropomorphic development of a still more ancient mythological figure, Coyote, known across the whole of the California culture area. Once that connection is made, the disparate points of Marumda's personality begin to cohere into a well-known constellation of traits, and we can recognize in Marumda a reflection of Coyote's complex trickster nature in California religious cosmology.[4]

This is a masterful narration, surely with its place in the canon of world literature. The comments I have made here are merely suggestive of a myriad avenues of inquiry into this myth.

ADDITIONAL NOTES

The Kuksu Religion

The Kuksu religion was, at least in historic times, restricted to a portion of North-Central California, involving in one form or another all the Pomo groups, as well as the Coast, Lake, and Plains Miwok, the Maidu, the Patwin, the Yuki, and several other groups distributed around the northern end of San Francisco Bay and up the Sacramento and San Joaquin Valleys. The Kuksu (based on the Eastern Pomo term *kúksu*) was a godlike spirit figure—the focus of secret societies, initiation rituals, curing ceremonies, and dance cycles where the Kuksu and other spirit figures would be impersonated by society members wearing sacred, highly elaborate costumes. For the space of time that these supernatural figures were brought to life through impersonation during the ceremonies, they "re-created sacred time and in one way or another restored their people to the unsullied state that had prevailed at the time of creation" (Bean and Vane 1978:665). The Kuksu religion (often amalgamated with elements of other, prior or parallel, belief systems) has likely been indigenous to the region for thousands of years, though other more recent religions, such as the post-Contact Bole Maru and Ghost Dance cults, have wholly or partially overwritten its territory in historic times.

Marumda and Kuksu

One characteristic of the Kuksu region is the belief in a true creation of the world, instigated by an anthropomorphic Creator. Unlike the Kuksu, whose name takes essentially the same form throughout the region, this creator figure goes by many different names, including K'ódoyapè ('Earthmaker') among the Maidu, ʔolelbes among the Wintu, Nagayčo ('Great Traveler') among the Sinkyone, and Taikomal among the Yuki. In the present myth, this figure is Marumda (Ma·rúm'da). But Marumda and the Kuksu, who share in the planning of creation, have sharply diffcrent natures—one human-oriented and imperfect, caring but exacting; the other beyond human caring, and largely indifferent. The following passage of dialogue from *How the World Was Made* (de Angulo 1976b: 33–35), based on discussions between Benson and de Angulo, underscores this characterization. (The passage is long, but it happens to provide a prime example of the famous de Angulo "voice" discussed earlier. In the story, Tsimmu is a local boy, and Killeli is a young visitor from a more distant tribe. The character Coyote Old Man both is and is not supposed to be confused with the mythological Coyote.)

That evening they were all sitting around the fire. "Well, Tsimmu," Coyote Old Man was saying, "tonight you will get to attend the Kuksu ceremony, and hear the full story of how the Kuksu made the world. . . . "

"Kuksu didn't make the world," Turtle Old Man interrupted. "It was the Marumda who made the world. It happened like this. The Marumda went to see his elder brother, who was the Kuksu, and asked his advice about making the world. The Kuksu didn't care whether there was a world or not. He just sat in his cloud-house, and smoked his long pipe, and dreamed, and thought, and dreamed, and thought. Now he did give Marumda some wax . . . —but it was Marumda who went out and created the world."

"All right, all right," said Coyote. "Marumda made the world, but it was the Kuksu who first put the idea in his head."

"Has anybody ever seen the Kuksu," Tsimmu asked.

"Oh yes, from time to time," Old Man Turtle replied. "At least some people say that you can sometimes find him in the woods, hiding behind a tree, or at noon-time, just sitting in a clearing on a rock. . . . That was probably the Kuksu we saw hanging from the tree the other night."

"That was surely a frightening-looking figure," Killeli said. "Is the Kuksu a killer, like the Giants and the Imps over in my country?"

"Oh, of course not," Old Man Coyote said. "Why should he hurt anybody? The Kuksu doesn't care about people, one way or another. The Kuksu's no killer."

"But, Grandfather, doesn't the Kuksu take care of the world?" Tsimmu asked.

"No, Child. The world pretty much takes care of itself. When it doesn't, well, that's Marumda's job. Then that Old Man is liable to come along, and kick the world to pieces, and make a new one. . . . That Old Man is always worrying about the People, about whether they are behaving properly or not. . . . "

Bob Callahan, summing up the situation in his notes to the Turtle Island edition of *How the World Was Made,* observes that "the central characters of Kuksu and Marumda in the myth seem to function as the left and right hands, or the sons, of the ancestral Coyote figure of California Indian mythology" (de Angulo 1976b:100).

Incest

"Behaving badly," for Marumda and the Kuksu, means incest. Keep in mind that California's storied richness of habitat afforded high population density and a phenomenal linguistic-cultural diversity. Tribal units, correspondingly, tended to be demographically and territorially small, and the task of observing incest taboos and keeping bloodlines safely untangled was of no small moment. Exogamy was widely practiced (with bi- and even trilingualism a common consequence). It's an interesting subtheme that Marumda, dismayed that his creations keep "going wrong," comes up with one back-to-the-drawing-board remedy after another. In the fifth creation (¶153–154), he decides to make discrete languages, perversely hoping that the ensuing unintelligibility might isolate people into incest-proof groups. (Though clearly reminiscent of the myth of Babel, notice how this motif has an entirely different motivation from the biblical version.) And earlier, in the fourth creation, he thinks to establish *two* communities (¶141), the incest bans presumably being too difficult to uphold when there is but a single community. By the fifth and final creation, Marumda has strewn villages all over the place, thus maximizing the possibilities for exogamy, and the feeling is that this time people are finally going to be able to get it right.

Songs

Unfortunately, de Angulo did not record the numerous songs that embellished Benson's original narration. The reference to "archaic language" may indicate that the songs were in fact untranslatable, which might explain de Angulo's decision to remove them from the text. In any case, only their positions are noted in the myth.

Armpit Wax

I do not, nor does anyone else I've talked to, know what *damá-xahwé* 'armpit wax' really refers to. Clearly a potent mythological substance, its true nature remains a mystery. As in other creation myths, though, where the earth is formed from a dab of mud or sand or mist, the very insubstantiality of the original material serves to emphasize the awesome power of the beings who are able to make a world from such an unlikely substance.

Structure

Because the myth is so long, and because de Angulo was somewhat haphazard with his internal section-headings, here is a more detailed schematic of the text's major thematic movements:

PARAGRAPH	THEME
1–20	Meeting and Planning
21–33	Creation: The Making of the World
34–48	First Peopling of the World
49–57	First Destruction of the World (by Flood)
58–70	Second Peopling of the World
71–86	Second Destruction of the World (by Fire)
87–117	Third Peopling of the World
118–127	Third Destruction of the World (by Snow and Ice)
128–148	Fourth Peopling of the World
149–171	Fourth Destruction of the World (by Whirlwind)
172–239	Fifth and Final Peopling of the World
240–241	Narrator's Close

NOTES

1. Sources for the information contained in the following sketches include Gui de Angulo's "Afterword" to the City Lights edition of Jaime de Angulo's *Indians in Overalls;* Bob Callahan's "Notes" to the Turtle Island edition of Jaime

de Angulo's *How the World Was Made;* Sally McLendon's "Pomo Baskets: The Legacy of William and Mary Benson"; Victor Golla's *The Sapir-Kroeber Correspondence;* and review articles by Paul Apodaca ("Completing the Circle," a review of *My Dear Miss Nicholson . . . : Letters and Myths by William Benson*) and Victor Golla ("Review of *The Old Coyote of Big Sur*").

2. According to Sally McLendon, "Benson grew up in a world that was not 'wild' but seems to have been an interesting bi-cultural world of a few, mostly male, white settlers and their ways of doing things and the native world which had its own very rich and patterned way of doing things. The balance of power only shifted during Benson's adolescence, I think, but his first 13 years seem to have been fairly idyllic: sheltered, loved, protected by both parents, and protected from white racism by the standing of his father" (personal communication).

3. Strictly speaking, there is but one "true" creation here—where the physical substance or framework of the world is created out of wax, and beings are created to dwell on it—and this takes place near the beginning of the myth (¶21–33). Subsequent creations are really more like "re-peoplings," where Marumda adjusts local topography (a spring here, a mountain there) to create a suitable habitat, and then creates the community of people who will dwell in it.

4. In cognate and related myths among other California cultures, including the Pomo, the role of Marumda is sometimes played by Coyote. Indeed, Marumda (Eastern Pomo *ma·rúm'da*) is an esoteric name suggesting Coyote, most ancestral and important of all California mythological figures. As de Angulo notes, "Marumda alone, however, does not mean Coyote. Coyote in Lake Pomo, is *gunula.* Marumda is the name of the character in this myth. It may possibly be related to the adjective *maru* which has a series of very loose meanings, i.e., sacred, mysterious, traditional, dream omen, etc." (1976b:100–101).

FURTHER READING

On the Pomo culturally, see Sally McLendon and Michael Lowy's "Eastern Pomo and Southeastern Pomo" in the California volume of the Smithsonian *Handbook* and Edwin Loeb's *Pomo Folkways* (for which Benson was a major consultant). There are several collections of myths, especially S. A. Barrett's *Pomo Myths* (1933), Jaime de Angulo and Nancy Freeland's "Miwok and Pomo Myths"; see also McLendon's important ethnopoetic analysis of the Eastern Pomo myth "Grizzly Bear and Deer" in her article "Meaning, Rhetorical Structure, and Discourse Organization in

Myth." For language, try McLendon's *A Grammar of Eastern Pomo.* The myth presented here appears, with accompanying Eastern Pomo text, as de Angulo's "Pomo Creation Myth" in the *Journal of American Folklore* 48; later, he incorporated the translation into a fictionalized book called *How the World Was Made.* Gui de Angulo has recently written a biography of her father, called *The Old Coyote of Big Sur.* McLendon's article, "Pomo Baskets: The Legacy of William and Mary Benson," provides biographical information about Benson and his wife, Mary, and includes several photographs of the Bensons and their baskets. William Benson's "The Stone and Kelsey Massacre on the Shores of Clear Lake in 1849" is reprinted in Margolin's *The Way We Lived,* and also excerpted in "Notes on Native California Languages" (this volume). Extensive museum collections of Pomo materials may be found at the Milwaukee Public Museum, the Museum of the American Indian in New York, and the Field Museum in Chicago, among others. The Survey of California and Other Indian Languages archives several collections of Pomo fieldnotes by McLendon, Abraham Halpern, and others.

CREATION

THIS IS THE TRADITION OF HOW MARUMDA AND KUKSU MADE THE WORLD

1. He lived in the north, the Old Man, his name was Marumda. He lived in a cloud-house, a house that looked like snow, like ice. And he thought of making the world. "I will ask my older brother who lives in the south," thus he said, the Old Man Marumda. "Wah! What shall I do?" thus he said. "Eh!" thus he said.

2. Then he pulled out four of his hairs. He held out the hairs. "Lead me to my brother!" thus he said, Marumda the Old Man. Then he held the hairs to the east; after that he held the hairs to the north; after that he held them to the west; after that he held them to the south, and he watched.

3. Then the hairs started to float around, they floated around, and floated toward the south, and left a streak of fire behind, they left a

streak of fire, and following it floated the cloud-house, and Marumda rode in it.

4. He sat smoking. He quit smoking. And then he went to sleep. He was lying asleep, sleeping . . . , sleeping . . . , sleeping . . . , sleeping. . . . Then he awoke. He got up and put tobacco into his pipe. He smoked, and smoked, and smoked, and then he put the pipe back into the sack.

5. That was his first camp, they say, and then he lay down to sleep. Four times he lay down to sleep, and then he floated to his elder brother's house. His name was Kuksu. This Kuksu was the elder brother of Marumda.

6. The Kuksu, his was like a cloud, like snow, like ice his house. Around it they floated, four times they floated around it, the hairs, and then through a hole they floated into the house, and following them the Marumda entered the house.

7. "Around the east side!" said the Kuksu. Then around the east side he entered the house, and he sat down, he sat, and he took off the little sack hung around his neck. He took out his pipe and filled it with tobacco, he laid a coal on it, and he blew, he blew, and then he blew it afire. Then he removed the coal and put it back into his little sack. After that he smoked, four times he put the pipe to his mouth. After that he offered it to his older brother the Kuksu.

8. Then Kuksu received it. "Hyoh!" he said, the Kuksu, "hyoh! Good will be our knowledge, good will end our speech! Hyoh! May it happen! Our knowledge will not be interfered with! May it happen! Our knowledge will go smoothly. May it happen! Our speech will not hesitate. May it happen! Our speech will stretch out well. The knowledge we have planned, the knowledge we have laid, it will succeed, it will go smoothly, our knowledge! Yoh ooo, hee ooo, hee ooo, hee ooo, hee ooo! May it happen!" thus he said, the Kuksu, and now he quit smoking

9. Then Marumda sat up, he sat up, and then they both stood up. They stood facing east, and then they stood facing north, and then they stood facing west, and then they stood facing south, and then they stood facing the zenith, and then they stood facing the nadir. And now they went around each other both ways, they went around each other four times back and forth. Then Marumda went to where he had been sit-

ting before, and he sat down; and then Kuksu went to where he had been sitting before, and he sat down.

10. Then Marumda put tobacco into the pipe that he took out of his little dried-up sack. He felt in his little dried-up sack, he brought out some tobacco, and filled the pipe with it. Then he felt in his little dried-up sack and brought out a coal, he put the coal on top of the tobacco, he put it on top and he blew, he blew, and blew it afire. Four times he drew, and then he offered it to his brother Kuksu.

11. Four times he made as if to take it, and then he received it. Four times he drew, and then he offered it back to Marumda. He received it, and put it back into his little dried-up sack. He blew out the smoke four times. First he blew it toward the south, then he blew it toward the east, then he blew it toward the north, then he blew it toward the west. Then he blew it to the zenith, then he blew it to the nadir.

12. Then turning to the left, Kuksu gave an oration: "Ooo!" thus he said, "it will be true, our knowledge!" Then Kuksu poked him with the pipe, and Marumda received the pipe, he received it and put it back in his little dried-up sack.

13. And then the Marumda scraped himself in the armpits, he scraped himself and got out some of the armpit wax. He gave the armpit wax to the Kuksu. Then Kuksu received it, he received it, and stuck it between his big toe and the next. And then he also scraped himself in the armpits, he scraped himself, and rolled the armpit wax into a ball. His own armpit wax he then stuck between Marumda's toes.

14. Then Marumda removed it and blew on it, four times he blew on it. Then Kuksu also removed the armpit wax and blew on it four times, and after that he sat down. Then Marumda went around the Kuksu four times, and then he sat down. And then the Kuksu he got up, he got up, and four times around the Marumda he went. Then they both stood still.

15. Now they mixed together their balls of armpit wax. And Kuksu mixed some of his hair with it. And then Marumda also mixed some of his hair with the armpit wax.

16. After that they stood up; facing south, and then facing east, and then facing north, and then facing west, and then facing the zenith, and

then facing the nadir: "These words are to be right and thus everything will be. People are going to be according to this plan. There is going to be food according to this plan. There will be food from the water! There will be food from the land. There will be food from under the ground. There will be food from the air. There will be all kinds of food whereby the people will be healthy. These people will have good intentions. Their villages will be good. They will plan many things. They will be full of knowledge. There will be many of them on this earth, and their intentions will be good.

17. "We are going to make in the sky the traveling-fire. With it they will ripen their food. We are going to make that with which they will cook their food overnight. The traveling-fires in the sky, their name will be Sun. The one who is Fire, his name will be Daytime-Sun. The one who gives light in the night, her name will be Night-Sun. These words are right. This plan is sound. Everything according to this plan is going to be right!" thus he spoke, the Kuksu.

18. And now the Marumda made a speech. Holding the armpit wax, holding it to the south, he made a wish: "These words are right!" thus he said, the Marumda. And then he held it to the east, and then he held it to the north, and then he held it to the west, and then he held it to the zenith, and then he held it to the nadir: "According to this plan, people are going to be. There are going to be people on this earth. On this earth there will be plenty of food for the people! According to this plan there will be many different kinds of food for the people! Clover in plenty will grow, grain, acorns, nuts!" thus he spoke, the Marumda.

19. And then he blew tobacco smoke in the four directions. Then he turned around to the left, four times. Then he put the armpit wax into his little dried-up sack. After that he informed the Kuksu: "I guess I'll go back, now!" thus he said, and then he asked the Kuksu: "Sing your song, brother!" he said. And then the Kuksu sang: "*Hoyá, hohá, yugínwe, hoyá* [here comes a long SONG in archaic language] . . . "

20. After that Marumda floated away to the north, singing the while a wishing song: "*Hinaa ma hani ma* [another SONG in archaic language] . . . " Thus he sang, the Marumda.

21. With this song he traveled north, the Marumda, riding in his house,

in his cloud-house. He was singing along, holding the armpit wax in his hand and singing the song. Then he tied a string to the ball of armpit wax, passed the string through his own ear-hole and made it fast. Then he went to sleep.

22. He was lying asleep, when suddenly the string jerked his ear. He sat up and looked around but he did not see anything, and he lay down again to sleep. It went on like that for eight days, it went on for eight days, and then it became the earth. The armpit wax grew large while Marumda was sound asleep, and the string jerked his ear. At last Marumda sat up, he sits up, and he untied the string from his ear-hole. Then he threw the earth out into space.

23. It was dark. "What shall I do about it?" said Marumda. "Oh! . . . I know," and he took the pipe out of his little sack. He also brought out a coal, and applied it to the pipe. Then he blew on it, he blows, and set it afire. He sets it afire, and then he held the pipe to the south. Then he blew away the fire that was in the pipe. The fire traveled to the south, it grew large, and over the earth the sunshine spread.

24. Now Marumda walked around all over the earth. He walks around: "Here will be a mountain, here will be rocks, there will be clover, here will be a valley, there will be a lake, there will be crops, here will be a playground, there will be crops, here will be a clover flat, there will be a grain valley, on this mountain there will be acorns, on that one manzanita, juniper, cherries; on this mountain there will be potatoes, deer, hare, rabbits; on that mountain there will be bear, puma, cougar, fisher, coon, wolf, coyote, fox, skunk; on this mountain there will be rattlesnake, king-snake, gopher-snake, red-striped snake, mountain garter-snake, blue snake, big gopher-snake."

25. Marumda then walked over the hill; on the other side it was dark; he sat down; there was no light. He went on. Up in the sky there was light. Then he rolled the earth over, it turned over, he pushed it over: "This is the way you will perform," said the Marumda, "now it is dark, and now it is light, and now it is sunlight." Thus now it performed.

26. Thereupon he went on: "Here will be a valley, and in it there will be many villages. Here will be a river with water in it wherein the fish will run." Thereupon he went on and made a big pond, and then he

said: "Here the fish will come; this will be a fish-bend, a food larder, this pond." Thereupon he made a river: "This will be a roadway for the fishes," thus he said, the Marumda.

27. And then he went on and made a mountain: "On this there will be sugar-pine." And then he went on and made a pond: "Here there will be all kinds of fowl." And then he went on and made a mountain of flint: "This will be for arrowheads and spearheads." And then he went on and made a mountain of drill flint. After that he went on and made a spring and on either side he put sedges, rushes, redbud bushes: "This will be for the women to weave their baskets; dogwood, white willow, black willow, wherewith to weave." And then he went on and made wild nutmeg: "This will be bow-wood." After that he made another kind of dogwood: "This will be arrow-wood, mountain bitterweed."

28. After this Marumda went on the other way, he went on and on, and then he thought of making Big Mountain. He makes it, and on each side he made a large river: "This will be for the fish to come out to the lake." Thereupon he went on and made a wide valley: "Here will be all kinds of crops," thus he said, the Marumda.

29. And now he arrived at the lake, and going along the shore he made rocks, he makes them, and: "This will be a playground for the water-bears." Thereupon he went on and made a sand-flat, and then: "This will be a playground for people." Thereafter he went on and made a mountain: "Here people will not come! Men! Never approach this place!" thus he said, the Marumda.

30. Thus he was going along by the shore, and he found a river barring his way: "Wah!" he said, "what am I going to do?" he said standing on the shore. "Eh!" he said, and laying his walking-cane across he passed over to the other side. "Eh!" he said, "that was the way to do it, there was nothing else to do!"

31. Thus he walked along the shore making rocks, making sand-flats; thus he went around the lake, performing like that. Now he went back inland, and facing the lake he sat on a log. The water was calm: "Water! You will not be like that!" thus he called to the water. Then he went to the water and he splashed it toward the land: "This is the way you will behave!" he told her. Then the wind blew and the water became rough,

it becomes rough, and ran in waves over the shore, it ran in waves over the rocks: "Hyoh! Good! That's the way you will do!" thus he said. "Hyoh! Now I will go across," he said.

32. "Wah! What am I going to do? How am I going to go across? Wah!" he said. "Eh! that oak over there . . . " and going to a tree standing there he picked up from the ground an acorn shell, he took it to the shore and laid it by the side of the water. The water made waves and thereby the shell was pushed into the water. It floated, it grew large, it grew large, it floated toward the shore and became a boat. "Hyoh! That's a good boat for us!" thus he said.

33. He felt around in his little dried-up sack and took out his pipe; he filled it with tobacco; he laid the coal on top; he blew on it; he blew it afire; then he blew smoke in the four directions and a thick fog arose. He put the pipe back in his little sack and hung the sack around his neck, then he sat down in the boat and shoved off. It started to float away, it floated way off toward the center of the lake; then he whirled his cane in the air and that boat started to race, it went like a bird, and in no time at all it went across.

34. He sat down by the side of the water and he looked about, and then he thought to experiment at making people. "Wah! What shall I make people with?" he said. "Eh!" he said, and he picked up rocks: "These will be people!" These rocks became people. They spoke a language. They were short-legged, these rock-people. These rock-people lived in the mountains only. They did not walk about in the valleys.

35. Then he experimented making other kinds of people. The rock-people were mean, that's why he experimented making other people. He made people out of hair. These people were long-haired; the hair came down to their feet. They found the Old Man Marumda and came up to him: "What are you doing, Old Man?" they said. "I am eating food," he answered. He was eating clover. He also dug potatoes out of the ground, and ate them. Then the long-haired people took an object lesson and they also ate. "This is your food," said the Marumda, and then he went away.

36. Sitting down on a hill he looked back. After a while he went over to where there was a valley. And now the idea came to him to make another kind of people. He felt inside his little dried-up sack and brought

out some feathers. He split them, he splits them, and he broke them into small pieces. These he scattered over the plain.

37. "These will grow into people!" he said, and he sat down with his back to the valley. Then people also came to life and they too came to the Old Man and asked him: "Where do you come from?" These people were covered all over with feathers, like birds. "What are you doing?" "I am eating," he answered. Then they also took an object lesson and started to eat. "Thus you will eat! This is your food!" he said, and then he went away.

38. Then he experimented making more people. This time he went over to another mountain and he experimented making people out of wood. He gathered small sticks, he split them, and scooping out little hollows here and there, he planted them in [the ground]. "These will be people!" he said. Then he went off and turning his back to them he sat down. Soon he could hear them talking among themselves: "There is an old man sitting over there," they said.

39. They came over to him: "What are you doing, Old Man?" "I am eating," he answered. Then they also took a lesson and started to eat. "This is the food that you will eat! I made it for you!" said the Marumda. Then he departed and went around another mountain.

40. "Wah! This also looks like a good place for people." He pulled four hairs from his arm and scattered them over the plain, here and there, all over. Then he sat down on a knoll and listened. In no time they also turned into people. "Where do you come from?" they asked one another. The nearest one to the Old Man said: "There is a man sitting over there too," and they came up to him.

41. "And you, where do you come from?" they said. "Oh! I came from a distance," he answered. "Are there any other people?" they asked. "Yes, there are other people far away from here. You'll find them after a while." These people were hairy and cloven-hoofed, and they had horns. They were the deer-people. He didn't like their looks. "Eh! Over there I will make another kind of people," he said, and went off.

42. Then he went on, northward, and in the hills, in a little hollow he sat down: "And now I will make other people again," he said, the Marumda. And feeling in his little dried-up sack he brought out some sinew. This sinew he broke into little pieces, he breaks them, and then

he scattered them about over the hollow. "These will be people!" he said.

43. Then he sat down with his back to it. In no time they became people. Then the Old Man stood up: "Come over here," he said. Then the people came over to him. "This is your land where you will live," thus he said. These people were like ourselves; they had no hair, no feathers on their bodies, they were all slick. "Here you will eat your food! There is plenty of food on the ground over there; eat it!" thus he said, and he went away.

44. After this he went over to a hillock. There he took some hair out of his little dried-up sack, and this he scattered over the hill. Then he sat with his back to it and in no time they were people talking among themselves. Then he looked. They were big, hairy people, walking about. These were the bear-people; they had long claws.

45. And now he went over to them: "Here you will eat this kind of food," he said, and plucking some clover he ate it. Then these people they also imitated him and ate. Then he dug up some potatoes. "These also you will eat," he said. "Oo! That's good! And are there any other people around?" they asked. "Yes! There are going to be lots of people!" Marumda answered.

46. After this he experimented making still another kind of people: "Wah! What shall I make them of now?" he said. He went to a big valley toward where the sun rises. Here he made people out of flint. These people were the Gilak people. He made this people on the mountain where there are nothing but rocks.

47. These people were like birds flying in the sky. They used to swoop down on people. They had not been taught to do that way. They were mean people.

48. All these were the first people that the Marumda made.

DESTRUCTION OF THE FIRST WORLD

49. Then he went north to his abode. Time passed, time passed, time passed, time passed, and then Marumda saw in a dream that the people were behaving badly. So he decided to go to his elder brother. Then the

cloud-house started to float. Eight days it floated, the cloud-house, and then it reached the Kuksu's house.

50. Four times he floated around it, and then he knocked at the door. Then the Kuksu opened the door and Marumda went in. Then the Kuksu said: "What is it, younger brother?" thus he said, the Kuksu.

51. Then Marumda said: "Oo! It's all wrong! That's why I have come to consult you. The people that we made are behaving wrongly. They are intermarrying, they are turning into idiots, and their children grow puny. Therefore I will wash them away!" thus he said, the Marumda.

52. Then Kuksu spoke: "Wah! It's all wrong! We never taught them to do this!" Then Marumda spoke: "Our people have become like birds, they have become like deer! They sleep with their own children. This is too bad! Therefore I am going to wash them away!"

53. Then Kuksu: "Oo! That is right! They did not believe our wisdom! Well, you know what you must do!" thus he spoke, the Kuksu. Then Marumda filled his pipe, lit it, and offered it to Kuksu. Kuksu then smoked, he smokes, and he blew the smoke in the four directions. Then he returned the pipe to Marumda. Then Marumda he too smoked to the four directions.

54. Then in no time the skies clouded up, the thunder spoke, and rain began to fall. For four days it rained; it became a flood. Marumda himself was running around among the rocks. Finally he ran for refuge to the top of a mountain peak.

55. But the people followed him there. Then Marumda called for help to his grandmother: "Grandma! Grandma! Quick!" thus he cried running back and forth among the rocks. Then a spiderweb basket floated down to him from the sky, Marumda got in it, and with it he floated away, he floated up to the sky.

56. "Ride and don't look around!" said Old Lady Spider, "or you will fall . . . !" but as she said the words he looked down and out he fell. He falls, but already the Old Lady Spider she had thrown out her net, she caught him, she pulled him up, she pulls him up, and to the Kuksu's house she carried him.

57. She carried him, she carried him up to the door, and Marumda

went in. "Oo!" cried Kuksu, "how did it go? Did you wash them away?" "Yes!" said Marumda. "Oo! That was right!" said the Kuksu. "Now we will make a different kind of people."

58. Now Marumda called his grandmother again, and she sent the basket floating down to him. He got in and floated away. It floated for four days and landed on top of a mountain peak. "Here! Get off!" said Old Lady Spider.

59. Then Marumda got off and looked around the world, he wandered about. Then he gathered some sticks of wood and built a fire. Then he went off to look for people. But he couldn't find a single one. Then he called. Not a single person came out.

60. "Wah!" said the Marumda, "what am I going to do? Eh! On this mountain there will be people!" and he called: "Wulu! Wulu!" . . . But there did not remain a single person to come out.

61. Four times he called, then he went off toward the lake. He walked along the shore, he sat down, and looked around. "Here there will be a large village!" he said. Then he went on, he goes on, and again he returned, and once more he looked around.

62. Where a while ago there had been nobody now a big village existed. There were many people along the shore of the lake. Here goes the Chief-Woman. Boys, children, are playing along the shore. They are chasing one another playing tag. They play tag in the water.

63. Marumda stood watching the village he had made. "Hyoh! They will be good people. They will be healthy. Their village will be healthy. They will be kindly in their manners." Thus he spoke, and he went on.

64. He walked, he walked, he walked. "Eh!" he said, "here there will be a big mountain jutting out into the lake." Then the mountain arose. Then he went on. "Here there will be a valley. In this valley there will be a village and a dance house. In the dance house they will perform their dances, they will enjoy their dances, the boys, the girls, the women, the children, the old people!" Thus he spoke, and then he went away.

65. He goes on, he went on, and then he stood. "Here there will be a hillock!" Thus he spoke, and a hillock arose. Then he stood on the top, he stands, and he looked to where he had wished a village to be. And

now they came out, the boys, the girls, the men, the children, the women, they ran to bathe in the lake. They ran hither and yon along the shore, chasing one another. Out of the dance house they swarmed, the many people, the people whom he had wished into existence.

66. The Marumda sat on the ground. He unslung his little dried-up sack from around his neck, out of it he pulled his pipe, he put in a coal, on top of it he placed the tobacco, on top of that he placed another coal, he blew on it, he blew it afire, he smokes, he smoked and blew the smoke toward the village.

67. Then a fog arose and a drizzling rain began to fall. Then the people started to run toward the house. The older boys are telling the younger boys to run into the dance house. Thereupon the grown-up men started building individual houses out of dogwood. They set them all around the dance house. The houses of that village were so closely set together that a man could hardly walk between them.

68. Then the Marumda quit smoking, and he made a speech to call the people: "Gather for the dance! Gather for the dance!" he called. Then the people went into the dance house, they all went into the dance house. And then the Marumda went to the mountain he had just made. He stood on the top and listened. Soon after they began the ceremony.

69. Then he told the people of the village on the other side of the hill: "Over here they are dancing. Watch it. Come and watch it!" Then the boys, the girls, they came running, they came running over the hill. They ran to the door of the dance house and they peeped in.

70. Then Marumda made a speech. "'Come this way!' thus you must say when a visitor approaches. Claim him as a friend. 'Sit down here!' say to your friend. 'You are my relative! These are your people! Therefore you and I must dance together.'" Thus he spoke, the Marumda, and then he went away.

SECOND DESTRUCTION OF THE WORLD—BY FIRE

71. Time passed, time passed, time passed, time passed, and then the people began again their incestuous ways. And Marumda knew by a

dream that his people were doing wrong. "Wah! That's not the way I taught them to do! I will go and consult my elder brother about this!" Thus he said, and then the cloud-house floated south.

72. Eight days it floated, and then it arrived at the Kuksu's place. Four times it floated around the Kuksu's house. And then it floated to the door on the south side. Then Marumda knocked with his cane.

73. "Ooo!" called the Kuksu, and Marumda also called: "Ooo! Here I have come." "All right! Come in on the east side," said the Kuksu. Then Marumda sat down on the east side. Without saying anything he took his pipe out of his little dried-up sack; he placed a coal in it; on top of that he put tobacco; and on top of that he placed a coal. Then he blew on it, he blew it afire. He smoked four times and then he offered it to the Kuksu.

74. Four times he feigned to take it, then he accepted it, he accepts it, and with the pipe in his hand he went back to his seat. "Hyoh! Sumee!" he cried, "what's the matter? What's happened now? The people are doing wrong! Oo! You must tell me the truth!" Thus he spoke to the pipe before smoking.

75. Now he smoked, he smokes four times, and he gave the pipe back to Marumda. "They are doing wrong!" said the Marumda. "The people that we made, they are not obeying our teachings. They have started again their incestuous ways. That's all wrong! Therefore I will destroy them! This is what I have come to consult you about." Then the Kuksu answered: "Ooo! All right! Later on you will make more people!"

76. "Oh! I'll go back and I'll cook them!" "All right! That's fine!" said the Kuksu. "Right now you are going to do it!" "I am going back over there and I'll burn them with fire!" "Oh! that's good! Oh! that's fine! Go! Go!"

77. Then Marumda replaced his pipe in the little dried-up sack, he hung the sack around his neck, and he went away, he went away riding in his cloud-house. He went away, and the cloud roared like thunder as he went back north to his place.

78. After this he went west. Then he went south. Then he went east, he went east to where the sun rises. That was where the Fire-Man lived.

"You must burn the world!" Marumda told him. "Why should I burn the world?" he replied. "Eh! The people we made on the earth are behaving badly! They are incestuous with their own children! They are wrong! They are acting like animals! Therefore I will burn them!" Thus spoke the Marumda.

79. The Fire-Man was still refusing, saying: "And then, where will I live?" "Never mind! You are going to burn the world! You will start the fire from here. You need have no fear about starting the fire. I will not let it burn your house here!" said Marumda. "When shall I start this fire, then?" said the Fire-Man. "Right now you start the fire!" said the Marumda.

80. Then he took down his fire-bow, he took down his fire-arrows, and he went out. He goes out, and he shot to the north. Then he shot to the west, then he shot to the south, then he shot to the zenith. In the north where he had shot the fire commenced blazing, then in the west where he had shot the fire commenced blazing, then in the south where he had shot the fire commenced blazing, then from the sky where he had shot the fire came blazing down toward his house.

81. He was running around pouring water everywhere around his house. Marumda was crying: "That will not burn!" Then the fire spread in the west. Marumda was running around in his excitement. He ran up the mountain crying: "Grandmother! Grandmother! The fire is raging!" Then, just as the fire was reaching him, his grandmother floated her basket down to him.

82. Marumda dropped in it, and it started to float toward the sky. Then the people arrived down below at that spot after his grandmother had started to pull him up, and they cried to him: "Save us also!" "What can I do? We are all finished now!" he cried back.

83. Then he said to his grandmother: "Take me over there to my older brother's place." Then the Old Lady Spider took him to the Kuksu's house. Four times she floated him around, and then she floated him down.

84. Then he went up to the door. "The people are finished!" he said. "Oh!" said the Kuksu. "The fire spread all over the earth and cooked them!" said Marumda. "Oh! Now you will make a different kind of people!" answered the Kuksu.

85. Then he went back and made his grandmother take him to the Fire-Man. She carried him east to the Fire-Man's house, and when she got him there, "Get out now!" she said, and Marumda got out.

86. Then he found the Fire-Man. "Why! I thought all the people were finished," said the Fire-Man, "how is it that there is somebody left yet?" Marumda came up to him: "Yes indeed! All the people are finished everywhere in the north, everywhere in the west, everywhere in the south, the people have all been cooked!" "Well then, how do you happen to be saved?" "I had my grandmother carry me off, that's how I got saved." "Oh! Are there going to be any more people? Will more people come out somewhere now?" "Yes! You will see many people tomorrow in that valley close by." Thus he said, and he went off north to where there was a big valley.

THIRD CREATION

87. He went along the valley and built a fire . By the side of a river he dug a hole. Then he went off, and breaking off some willow wands he brought them back and planted them around the hole. It was evening.

88. To one of the sticks he tied a string. He passed the other end through his ear-hole and made it fast. Then he lay down with his back to the fire. He went to sleep, and while he slept the string jerked his ear. He sat up quickly.

89. He looked toward where he had planted the sticks, but there was nothing. Then he lay down again, he lies down, and he went to sleep. As he lay, the string jerked his ear. He sat up quickly. He looked toward where he had planted the sticks, but there was nothing. "Wah! Why is it that what I had in mind does not become true?"

90. He lay down again: "Wah! Something has got to happen!" thus he said and went back to sleep. While he was sleeping the string jerked his ear. He sat up quickly. He peered toward where he had planted the sticks: nothing whatever! Then he untied the string from his ear-hole, and going over to where he had planted the sticks he examined them. Some of them had fallen down. "I thought so!" said Marumda, and he planted them again.

91. Then he went back to his sleeping place, and passing again the string through his ear-hole he made it fast. Then he went to sleep. He was sound asleep when it jerked. This time he did not sit up. Then the string jerked and pulled him up.

92. Then he sat up and peered. It was dawn. He thought he could see people moving about. He rubbed his eyes and looked again. It looked like people moving about. Then he said: "Hm! I had better go." He went there.

93. It was little boys playing outside. The little boys saw him: "Somebody over there, coming this way!" they cried and ran into the house to tell the people inside. "Over there some man was coming this way!" they said.

94. Then the people went out also. "It's an old man!" they cried. "Who can that old man be, limping along, leaning on his cane?" He came, he came to the house, he sat near the entrance.

95. "Where do you come from?" one of the people asked him. "I have come a long ways. I camped over there last night. I have come to teach you something. That's what I have come here for, to teach you. The people who lived here before, they did wrong, and they are no more. That's why I have come: to teach you not to be that way."

96. Thus he said, and then he picked out four men: "These men will take care of you. What I am teaching you, you must not forget!" Then he led out the four men and stood them apart. He stood in front of them and spoke: "These four men will guard the law for you, they are your chief's lieutenants." He turned around and pointing to the foremost one: "This one is your Head-Chief. If you behave like the people before you, you also will be destroyed! Therefore, be good people! Keep the law! Do not commit incest! The people before you did it, and they were destroyed; therefore don't do likewise!"

97. Thus he spoke, and then he went off and brought back some straight sticks. One large stick he split, and in a trice he had made a bow out of it. Then he peeled the smaller sticks and made arrows. Then he went and brought back some flint. He warmed it in his mouth and chipped it and made arrowheads.

98. Then he felt inside his little dried-up sack and brought out some

sinew, and he rolled it into a string, a bowstring. Then he felt again, and bringing out some feathers he split them in two. Then in a trice he lashed the arrowheads to the arrows and tied the feathers.

99. Then he strung the bow. "That deer over there standing . . . shoot it!" The men looked at one another. Then the Old Man called a fellow who was standing behind the others: "Come over here! You have good strong arms . . . Try this bow!" The man came out and he gave him the bow. Taking the bow he stood looking at it: "What shall I do with it?" he said. "That deer standing over there . . . try it on him!" and he gave the man an arrow. Then: "Where is he standing?" "There . . . he is standing behind the bush . . . Go out toward that tree and then shoot!"

100. Then he went out and the Old Man accompanied him singing the deer-song while the rest of the people watched them. The deer was standing in a waiting attitude. Then the man went out toward the tree, then he shot and knocked him over dead.

101. Then the man who had shot the deer motioned toward the people, and two men came out, they loaded the deer on their backs and deposited him at the door of the house, but they did not know what to do further.

102. Then the Old Man came up, and taking out a piece of flint he skinned him right there and then: "This is the way!" he said. Then calling the man who had shot the deer: "Watch and learn!" he said, and he handed him the flint: "That's the way to skin. You will hunt deer for this village!" Thus he said.

103. After this he led the women to a spring to dig roots [for basketweaving]. He took out the roots, peeled them, split them, and spread them out on the ground. Then he brought out some willow shoots, split them, and commenced a basket. When he was starting to weave the upright part he called one of the women.

104. "This is what you women will do!" he said, and he gave the basket he had commenced to the woman he had called. That woman started weaving right away. Then the others they too started digging for roots, peeling them and drying them in the sun by the side of the willow shoots they had gathered.

105. Then Marumda built another basket and gave it to the same

woman. This was a pounding-basket. Then he went off and picking up a rock, in a trice he made a pestle out of it. Then he picked up a flat slab and brought it to the woman. "These are your tools for preparing food," he said, and then he went off toward the hills.

106. He looked for a spot where acorns had drifted in a pocket in the creek. "These you will gather, and with them you will make mush!" Then they commenced picking up acorns. They spread them on a rock and cracked them the way he taught them, and in no time they dried them. Then they took them home and commenced grinding them and took the meal out to the water.

107. Then Marumda went with the women. He dug a hole in the shape of a hopper and filled it with sand which he patted down, and over this he poured the meal. Then he brought some water and poured it over the meal. "This is how you must do to make it sweet!" thus he taught the women. Then the women they also dug pits in the ground and poured in the meal. They did as he had taught them.

108. Now the Old Man went back to the house with some willow wands and sat down at the entrance. Then he started a basket, a long fish-trap it was, and in no time he finished it. Then he made a little hoop, he wove it into a trap-inset, and when it was finished he set it in the mouth of the basket and braided it in.

109. The people were watching him. "Have you learned?" said the Old Man. "Yes!" they answered. Now he led them to the riverbank. He cut some fence palings, took them into the water, and stuck them into the bottom. The men were watching him. "This is the way to do it!" he said. The trapdoor that he had made, he blocked it on the sides. Then he took the basket-trap into the water and set it facing downstream, and he made it fast with long poles driven into the bottom.

110. He went ashore and after a while he looked back. "It's already filled with fish!" he cried, and: "Bring the trap ashore!" he cried. Then the young men waded into the water and they brought the fish-trap ashore. It was full of fish. They could hardly bring it ashore. Then more young men helped, and they rolled it ashore, and they poured out the fish.

111. Other men commenced weaving pack-baskets. They did it the

way the Old Man showed them. Now they put down their pack-baskets all around the pile of fish. Then the chief divided the fish. Meantime other men had placed the fish-trap back into the water and returned.

112. They carried the fish home. They built big fires. The women now leached the acorn-meal. They brought rocks, cooking-rocks, to the fire. They mixed the meal with water in a cooking-basket, and when the rocks were hot they threw them in. And in no time the mush was cooked.

113. Other women brought their mush-baskets to the fire and filled them with mush. And now they ate the fish they had cooked with the mush they had put on the fire. Meantime in another place they were eating the cooked venison.

114. They had forgotten that the Old Man also might be fond of food. Then the chief said: "Offer food also to the Old Man! Invite him to eat! Give him some fish, give him some venison!" One of the men who had brought the fish-trap ashore then said: "Maybe he is still over there in the creek . . . I'll go and see!" He went off toward the water but did not find him. Then he searched around, but he could not find him. Then he went back to the beach: "I can't find him!" he cried.

115. Then the boys quit eating: "We will all look for the Old Man!" they said. Along the river, in the brush, they searched for him. But they could not find him. "He may have gone off somewhere!" they said, and they returned home.

116. They returned home feeling badly. The chief harangued them: "That Old Man who went around teaching us, he is the one who made us. He was teaching us things that we did not know. In the same way he must have gone somewhere else to teach. He must have left us to teach other people somewhere else." Thus spoke the chief.

117. After a while the Marumda went back to his place in the north.

THE DESTRUCTION OF THE WORLD—
BY SNOW AND ICE

118. The time passed, the time passed, the time passed, the time passed, and then Marumda saw in a dream that the people he had made were

acting badly. "Wah! What's the matter with the world?" he said, and he lay down.

119. He took his pipe out of his little dried-up sack, he put tobacco in, he placed a coal on top, he blew on it, he blew it afire. He took the coal and put it back in the sack, and then he puffed smoke. "Yoh! Sumee!" he cried, "may this smoke spread like a cloud over the earth!" and then he quit smoking. "I will ask my elder brother why these people that I made are behaving badly." Thus he said, and he went to see the Kuksu.

120. He traveled for eight days, and then he got there. Four times each way he went around the Kuksu's house, and then he knocked at the door. "Ooo . . . !" he cried from inside, "Ooo . . . ! Come in on the east side! Come in on the east side!" thus spoke the Kuksu.

121. Marumda went in on the east side, and sat down in silence. He felt in his little dried-up sack and brought out his pipe. He filled it with tobacco and placed a coal on top. He blew on it, blew it afire, took the coal and put it back in the sack.

122. Then he smoked. Four times he drew, then: "Here, brother, take it!" The Kuksu made a motion four times as if to take it, then he accepted it, and said, "Yoo! Sumee! What's the matter with the world? They ought to be good, but they are acting wrongly! You made them and they ought to behave according to your plan! They are your people, therefore do as you like with them!"

123. Then he smoked. Four times he drew, and then he gave the pipe back to Marumda. Marumda said: "Oh! You have spoken well! You knew! You knew that the people I had made were behaving badly! Now I am going to destroy them with snow and with ice!" "All right," said Kuksu, "you may well destroy them. After a while you will try another kind." "Oh! That is why I came here: to get your approval. And now I will go back, and then I will make it snow!" And right away he left.

124. Then the cloud-house floated back to the north. It floated over above the earth, and the thunder roared in the north. After that snow and hail fell, and in no time the snow mantled the earth. The people were snowed in. Time passed. The people were exhausted from cold and starvation. Time passed. Marumda never looked back. He went on north.

125. After a while he dreamed that all the people were dead on the earth. "Wah!" he said, "I'll go and see if they are all exterminated . . ." and he went south. He went to the place where he had first made people and he looked around. There was no one; only birds walking around.

126. "Where are the people?" he asked the birds. The Thrasher answered: "All the people have been destroyed." The Meadowlark also put in a word: "*Yówal quhlíbi'its,* down they skipped!" he said, the Meadowlark.

127. Then Marumda walked around. "Ooo!" he said, "there will be people here again!"

FOURTH RE-CREATION OF THE WORLD

128. He walked around the valley. By the side of a mountain he made a spring. Then a little ways from there he dug a hole. Then he planted sticks around it. Then he went away from the spring. Then he built a fire, and with his back to it he lay down to sleep. Then he wished: "Over there where I wished it to be, people will be!" and then he lay down to sleep.

129. Just before dawn he woke up. He lifted his head quickly. It sounded to him like people talking. He held his head up and listened, but he could not hear anything. Then he lay down again and went sound asleep. While he was sound asleep some little boys came upon him. "Here is an old man lying asleep," said the little boys.

130. Then the Old Man woke up: "Is that you, little boys?" Then the little boys asked him: "Where do you come from?" "I camped a long way from here. Are there any people around here?" "Yes indeed! Over there there are lots of people!" "Lead me over there!" he said, and then the little boys they lifted him up, they pushed him up, and they pulled him up.

131. Then they led him to the people. The people gathered in front of the entrance to the dance house. "Over there the little boys are leading an old man . . . Where did they find him?" they were wondering. They led the old man to where the men were gathered. "Where did you find

that old man?" "Over there on the hillside he was lying down," the boys answered.

132. Marumda sat down by the entrance. "Men! Gather here!" he called. Then he sat up and walking among the people he took one of them by the hand and led him aside. "Stand here!" he said to him. "Let me teach you! You will be the Head-Chief of these people. You will teach them. You will make plans for them. You will harangue them. You will take care of them. This is your village. And they in turn will take care of you!" Thus he spoke.

133. And now, going again amid the crowd, he took one of the men by the arm. "Come!" he said, "and you also stand here!" And then he went back and took another man by the hand, and he led him to the side of the first one. "Stand here!" he said. And then he went back, and taking another one by the hand he led him to the side of the second one. "Stand here!" he said.

134. "You will be the Lieutenant-Chiefs of all these people! You will take care of them. You will teach them as children. You will take care of this village. Over there on yonder mountain there is deer. In that water over there, there is fish. Over there on that hill there are acorns; there are bay-nuts also; you will eat those. Over there on the lake there are birds; you will eat those. All this is your food." Thus spoke the Marumda.

135. After a while he went and got some milkweed. He laid it down by the fire, and when it was dry he cracked it with his teeth and scraped it. In no time he had rolled the milkweed into a string: "This is the way you must do." He whittled a stick and made it into a mesh-stick, then he made a shuttle out of another stick, and he wound the string on it. After that he tied the string to one end of another piece of wood and strung it in the shape of a bow. On this he commenced a net, and in no time he had it finished.

136. Then he went into the brush, broke off two straight sticks, and came back with them. One was for the cross-bow of the net. The other one was for the long handle. And now he led the people to the river. He took the net into the water. And the young men also helped to hold the net in the water. "Now, now! Splash the water!" he said. Then the young men splashed the water. Then the fish went into the net and filled it.

137. Then he called the young men. They ran to him. They took hold of the net and pulled it shoreward. All kinds of fish. The people who had remained on the bank were watching. Then: "Build a fire! Build a fire!" cried the Marumda.

138. Then they built a big fire. First they laid the fish on the fire. The very first batch they had pulled ashore, once it was cooked, was enough to supply the whole village. They did not know what to do with it. It stood in a pile by the side of the fire like a mountain.

139. Then the Old Man took some of the fish, he laid them on the ground, split them open while the people gathered around him, watching. The Old Man ate the fish, he ate it all up. Then: "That's the way to eat!" he said to them.

140. Then he acted as if he were going out for just a little way. But it was to be forever. After that they never saw him again.

141. After that he went over the hill to where there was a big valley, and he walked around. "Here also there will be a village," he said. He brought some willow wands to the center of the valley, and dug a small hole. He planted the wands around the hole and then he went away.

142. He stood a little way off and he made a wish: "Over there, there will be a dance house! In this dance house there will be people!" Thus he spoke and then he went away. He went away and built a fire on a hillside. He lay down to sleep by the side of the fire. He slept all night.

143. At sunrise the people came pouring out of the house, boys, young men, young women, grown-up men, women, they swarmed out. One of them saw the fire. "Over there . . . a fire!" he cried. Some of the boys ran over there. "Hey! Here is an old man lying down!" they cried. Thus they said and they ran back.

144. They told the grown-up people. Then the grown-up people, they went there. They went. "Why are you lying here?" they asked. Then the Old Man turned over on his side. "Is it you my people?" he asked. "Yes!" they answered. "Come over there and teach us!" they said, and they pulled him up.

145. Then they led him up, they continued to lead him, they led him toward the dance house, they led him into the house. They made him

sit down in front of the center-post. "May you live happily! May the food grow in this valley for you! On that mountain over there, there will be acorns for you, bay-nuts, manzanita, for you to eat, for you to store away. When your friends come, you will eat together. There are going to be many people like this. They may come to visit you from afar. When they come you must greet them thus: "In that river down there there is fish. Eat it! It is food for you. Over on that mountain there are deer. Hunt them! It is food for you. In that pond yonder there are birds. Eat them! They are food for you.

146. "You will build houses in which to dwell. This house will be a dance house in which to perform your ceremonies. Over there on that mountain there is flint. You will make arrowheads out of it so as to hunt deer." Thus he taught them, and then he went out.

147. He watched the boys playing. Then he called the men together. He took one of them by the arm and stood him aside. "This man will be your Head-Chief. He will make plans for you. He will place the knowledge for you." Thus spoke the Marumda.

148. And then he took another man by the hand, led him out of the crowd, and stood him by the side of the other one. Then he took another man by the hand, led him out, and stood him by the side of the last one. Then he took still another man by the hand, led him out, and stood him by the side of the others. "These people will advise you and harangue you. The first one I took by the hand, he will be your Head-Chief. You must not disobey his orders. These four men will take care of you." Thus spoke the Marumda.

FOURTH AND LAST DESTRUCTION
OF THE WORLD—BY A WHIRLWIND

149. Then Marumda went back to his abode. Time passed, time passed, time passed, time passed, and then he dreamed. "What is the matter with the world? Why don't they do as I teach them? They have thrown away the knowledge! Why have they turned again to incest? I forbade them to do that! I will have to see about it." Thus he said, and he started his cloud-house floating.

150. He made it float over the earth, and then he looked down to see what was going on. Then he floated toward the Kuksu. He floated out to the Kuksu's house. Four times he floated around it, and then he floated down to it. Then he got out of his cloud-house and knocked at the door. "Ooo!" cried the Kuksu from inside, and he opened the door. "Ooo! On the east side! On the east side!" he said.

151. Then Marumda went in on the east side and sat down against the wall on the east side. He felt in his little dried-up sack, he took out his pipe, he filled it with tobacco, he took out a coal and placed it on top of the tobacco, he blew on it, he blew it afire, he removed the coal and put it back in the little sack, and then he smoked.

152. Four times he drew, and then he gave the pipe to the Kuksu. "Brother, you test it now!" he said. He went out to him, and four times he made as if to take it, and then he took it, and then he went back to the place where he had been sitting before. "Ooo! Yo Sumee! May our conference be good, may we be well inspired!" Thus he said, and then he smoked.

153. Four times he inhaled, and then he returned the pipe to Marumda, and he went back to where he had been sitting. "Ooo . . . ! Now again they have been doing wrong, the people that we made! Therefore I want your consent to destroy them for the last time. Now, this is what we will do, we will teach them to speak different languages so that they cannot understand each other.

154. "Maybe it is because they speak only one language that they are incestuous with their own children, with their older sisters, and with their younger sisters. That is why they are begetting puny and deformed children. Therefore I want to destroy them!" Thus spoke the Marumda.

155. "Ooo . . . ! That is well. You know your own business. You made these people; therefore it is your right to destroy them. This time you had better blow them away with a whirlwind. You go and get the Whirlwind-Man where he lives in the east under the sun. He will blow them away for you. The people that you destroyed before, maybe they inherit their bad tendencies from the bones in the ground, and that is why they are not quitting their evil ways.

156. "Now therefore you will scatter them with the wind. After that

you will make new people, big ones. You will teach them different languages so that they may not understand one another." Thus spoke the Kuksu.

157. "Oh! That's good! That is what I came to hear. I will wipe off the whole world and then I will come back to you!" thus said the Marumda. "And then we will make a different kind of people. You will make people over there as you like them, and I will make people here as I like. Oh! I will find you somewhere! Oh! Now I will go!" "Oh! Go your way! Go your way!" said the Kuksu.

158. "You watch here! Whatever happens I will come back. If not, then I will call you, and you come to me in the north by the side of the water," thus said the Marumda. "Ooo!" answered the Kuksu, "I will come. Wherever you are I will come!" thus said the Kuksu. "Ooo, go your way, go your way!"

159. Then they separated. Then he got up in his cloud-house, and the house started to race like the wind, going eastward. In no time it arrived at the Whirlwind-Man's house. It stood whirling like a big mountain of smoke.

160. Four times he went around, and then downward he floated to it, and then he knocked at the door. "*Kling!*" it said, and the door opened. "Hey! hey!" said the Whirlwind-Man, "it looks like the Old Man! Must be something wrong that you came. Come in! Come in! On the east side! On the east side!"

161. "Oh! The people have gone wrong, they are acting badly. That's why I have come for you. Over there on the earth you must destroy the people. They are behaving badly. They practice incest with their children, with their sisters. That's why they are becoming puny and deformed, incapable of hunting their food. Therefore I want you to destroy these people. After that I will make different and better people." Thus spoke the Marumda.

162. "Ooo! All right! It's too bad for them to act that way, to disregard the rules, to forget what they were taught, to throw away their knowledge! All right then, I will blow them away!" Thus spoke the Whirlwind-Man. "All right," said Marumda. "Come! You will go with me." "All

right!" Then Marumda went out and got into his cloud-house, with the Whirlwind-Man following him.

163. Then the Whirlwind-Man whirled his cane, he made the cloud-house whirl, he whirled it to the north, and he himself followed. And as he went over the land the water stood up and the trees were uprooted.

164. Now the Whirlwind-Man was in the lead with Marumda following. "Now we are going to destroy! Now we are going to destroy!" he cried as he went ahead. Whenever the Whirlwind reached a village you could not see where the people went. Some ran into the dance house. The Whirlwind blew away the house and scattered the people everywhere. Thus he did and destroyed all the people.

165. Ground-Squirrel came out of his hole. "Why! all the people are destroyed and *titsik!*" he said. The Whirlwind heard him and he came back and pulled him out of his hole. "*Titsik!*" he said and threw him in the water. Then he whirled the water into a spout. Ground-Squirrel scooted back under the ground. "That's the way to treat people when they get fresh!" said the Whirlwind.

166. And now the Whirlwind was returning. The people were destroyed. Whirlwind-Man was going home still on the lookout for people. Then it was that he came across the Skunk. He ran up to him and said: "How do you happen to be walking about?" Then he grabbed him and started to whirl him around. Then Skunk farted, and Whirlwind threw him away. "If you were people I would throw you in the water!" he cried to him. Then he chased him into a hole in the rocks, and then he up-turned the rocks. That's the way Skunk beat the Whirlwind with his fart.

167. After this the Whirlwind left him and wended his way north, looking for people that might have escaped, but he found no one. "That's what happens to bad people!" he said, and then he started searching for the Old Man. "Maybe something went wrong with him . . . He was ahead of me . . . and then I didn't see him any more . . . I had better search for him . . ." and he went north. He ran north like lightning, and in no time he arrived at Marumda's house. "Oh! You are here!" he said.

168. "Yes!" said the Marumda. "And you are alive?" "Yes, I am lying down but I am alive." "Well, everything is finished, just exactly the way

you told me to do it." "All right . . . Have a smoke before you go," said the Marumda, taking his pipe out of the little dried-up sack. Then he filled it with tobacco, put a coal on top, blew on it, blew it afire, removed the coal, put it back into the sack, and then he smoked.

169. Then he passed the pipe to the Whirlwind. "Yooo! Sumee!" said the Whirlwind. "May it be well! May his knowledge be right! May whatever he does be fit! When he makes people they will be right, they will be fine, they will be thrifty, they will not practice incest with their own blood! If the people that he makes will listen to these words they will be all right! Yooo! Sumee!" thus he said.

170. Then he inhaled four times, and he gave the pipe back to Marumda. "Oh! That's good, my son, that's good! And now you may go back and you will hear whenever I make those people! Oh! You may go!" Then the Whirlwind got into his house. It made *"Klink!"* and then it raced, the Whirlwind's house, it raced like the lightning, and in no time he got home in the east, and it sounded plain as he went.

171. And now Marumda started to look for people. "Have all the people been destroyed?" he said to himself as he went along. And then: "Eh! What shall I do?" he said, walking along. "Oh! There must be people! This earth cannot stay naked! There are going to be many peoples on this earth. They will speak different languages. They will be different in color, the people on this earth!"

FIFTH AND LAST CREATION OF THE WORLD

172. And then he went eastward, the Marumda. He arrived at a large valley and walked around it. "Wah!" he said, "why are there no people here? Here there will be a village!" Then he brought some willow sticks to the middle of the valley. There he dug a small hole, and all around he planted the sticks.

173. "Yoh!" he said, and then he went off a little way, there he built a fire, and then he went back. And now to one of the sticks that he had planted he tied the end of a string that he took out of his little dried-up sack. Then he went back to the fire and lay down with his back to it after passing the other end of the string through his ear-hole and making it fast.

174. He was just dozing when it jerked, and he sat up. He looked back to where he had planted the sticks. He did not see anything. "Wah!" he said, and he lay back to sleep. He slept. In the middle of the night it jerked him, and he sat up. He looked to where he had planted the sticks, but nothing. He went back to sleep. Toward dawn it jerked him. He paid no attention. At daybreak it jerked and pulled him up. Then he sat up.

175. This time he peered. Where he had planted the sticks it sounded like people talking among themselves. "Eh! What I planned will stand true!" he said, and he went over. As he was nearing the roundhouse a man came out of the door. "Where are you going?" he asked.

176. "I have come to see how the villages are doing. In this valley you will hunt your food!" Then the man called to the people inside and then came out. "How are we to hunt food?" asked the leader.

177. "That's what I have come to teach you. Break off some of that wood over there and bring it here." Then the man who was in front of the others broke off some of the wood and brought it back. "Now break off some little ones and bring them here!" Then that man broke off some little sticks and brought them back.

178. Then Marumda split the large piece of wood and scraped it, and in no time he made a bow out of it. Then he peeled the little ones and made arrows out of them. Then: "Bring some flint from over there!" he said. He chipped the flint with his teeth, and in no time he made arrowheads out of it. Then he felt in his little dried-up sack and brought out some sinew.

179. He twirled a string, tied it to the bow, and pulled. "This is called a bow," he said. Then he felt in his little dried-up sack and brought out some feathers, he split them, and tied them to the end of the arrows. Then he fixed the flint arrowheads. "With this you will hunt deer," he said.

180. Then he said to the women: "Over there there is *kuhum* [basketweaving material]." "What is *kuhum?*" they asked. Then Marumda went to dig some and brought it back. "This is weaving material for you." He also brought some willow roots. "With these you will make baskets. Over on that mountain there are trees with acorns. These are food for you. In that river over there there is fish for you to catch with nets. Thus you will live."

181. He felt in the little sack hung around his neck and brought out a string. Then he started a net and in no time he wove a long one. "This is a *gunam* net [a seine]," he said. Then he wove a *buxal* [fish-trap]. "You will make a dam in yonder river, you will place this trap in it, and then you will drive the fish into it."

182. Then he picked up a rock and pecked it, and in no time he made a pestle. Then he brought out a flat rock. "This is called a *gushi-xabe* [metate], for pounding seeds and acorns." Then after a while he said: "Now I am going. Live righteously and your people will be healthy!" Thus he said, and he went on.

183. In this fashion he went around the world. Wherever there was a good place, there he made a village. He went where he had first made people. "Are you living well?" he asked. "Yes, we are living well. But where have you been?" "Just a little way." "Are there other people like us?"

184. "Yes, lots of them! There are people far from here whose language you don't understand. They speak different languages. They live on the other side of that mountain. They speak nearly like you. You must make friends with them."

185. Thus he said. Then the chief sent two young men over. The two young men went over the mountain and found a large village there, and they came back.

186. After this the Old Man went away somehow, and after this nobody ever saw him again in that village.

187. Then he went off. He went over the hill to where there was a big valley, and he walked around it. "Here also there must be a village!" he said. He brought some willow wands to the middle of the valley, and there he dug a little hole. Then he split the wands with his teeth, he took some charcoal and crushed it. Then he painted the sticks with it.

188. "This one will be the song leader. These will be the chorus. These will be the dancers. These will be the women dancers." He felt in his little dried-up sack and brought out a string. He tied one end to one of the sticks, and the other end he tied to his own ear-hole.

189. Then he lay down with his back to the fire. He was sound asleep when the string pulled him up. Then he got up. It was the dancers. The

people that he had wished, they got up to dance, and then it was that the string jerked him.

190. Then he also started to dance. And the boys, and the girls, and the chorus, they all watched him. They laughed at him: "Hurrah for the Old Man!" But the chief stopped them saying: "Don't do that! This is our Old Man Marumda! He is the one who made us!"

191. Four nights he made them dance. When the sun was high the people got out of the dance house and the chief harangued them: "Now you go and hunt deer so that we may have a feast!"

192. And then the women pounded acorns, and when they were done they carried the meal to the water. They scooped out the ground like a bowl and poured the meal in it. Then they poured water over it to leach it. And the boys brought out a large deer and put it down at the entrance.

193. They had already built a fire in preparation. Now the men quartered the deer. Now the women brought in the dough. The men had already heated the cooking-rocks in the fire. The women soon dissolved the dough. They dropped the cooking-rocks in a basket and cooked the mush.

194. After this the men cut the deer-meat into strings and put it on the fire. As soon as some of the meat was roasted they took it out of the fire and put it on the table while other people cut more venison into strings. Thus all the meat got cooked.

195. And now the chief called: "Gather hither!" Then all the people gathered. The women brought out the cooked mush and the meat. They brought it out, and then the women gathered in one place.

196. Then the chief chose four young men. He took the leader by the arm. Then he [the leader] took the next one by the hand. This one in turn took the next one by the hand. Thus he led them around the food four times back and forth. Then he placed the leader on the south side. The next one he placed on the east side. The next one he placed on the north side. The last one he placed on the west side.

197. Then the chief spoke: "These people I have chosen to be your guardians. They will make plans for you. They will address you in speeches."

198. Then the Marumda spoke: "This is what you people are going to do. You are going to gather your provisions, your venison-meat, your acorns, your valley-seeds. Then you will store it away, and on this you will live in abundance. You will hold festivals. When visitors come from a distance, take them into the house and partake of food with them. When your friends come from somewhere to visit you, that's the way you must provide them with food.

199. "There are going to be many of you people. Therefore you must take care of each other. Therefore you must claim one another as friends, you must claim one another as relatives. Thus you will live in happiness!" Thus spoke the Marumda. And then he departed.

200. Thus it was that people got acquainted with one another. They acknowledged one another as friends and relations. The young men hunted deer and caught fish. They gathered acorns. They married and brought food in dowry, and deer, and fish. Thus they did.

201. Thus he went, the Marumda, making villages on the shores of the lake, and he came around again to where he had made the first village. The little boys found him. "Here lies an old man!" they said. The older boys came near. "Where have you come from?" they asked him. "Oh! I have come from far away . . . Say, little boys, bring me an acorn shell." Then the biggest of the boys said, "I'll bring it!"

202. The boy ran home and came back with an acorn shell. "Are you going to eat it?" he asked the Marumda. "No, give it to me!" The boy gave him the shell. Then Marumda took it and threw it in the water. "Hey!" cried the boy, "what did you throw it away for? Now I won't give you any more. You threw it away! Now I won't give you any more."

203. "Look over there!" said Marumda. The boys went to the shore and looked at the shell. It was floating. Then they also threw in acorn shells. Marumda's shell floated on [the water] and became a boat. The boys' shells did not become boats. "Why is it that your shell became a boat but ours did not?" asked the boys.

204. "Are you going to ride in it?" they asked then. "Yes, I am going across the lake in it." "And you are not afraid?" "What should I be afraid of?" said Marumda. "Won't the water-bears eat you?" "The water-bears are my playmates," said the Marumda. "Look, boys, I am going now."

He pushed the boat into the water, he got in, with his cane he shoved off, then he whirled the cane, and that boat went off like a bird flying. In no time it was out of sight. "Oh, he is gone!" cried the boys.

205. Not far from there, there were some grown-up people watching. "Who was that old man?" asked the boys. "What did you ask him?" said the people. "That was no old man. He just made himself into an old man. And then he grew wings. His name is Marumda. He is the one who made the world. He made the lake. He made everything that you see. You saw how he made a boat out of that shell that he threw in the water. He made this big lake and he can dry it up. He also made us people. He made everything here on the earth. Understand that, boys!" Thus spoke the chief.

206. Marumda's boat was already across. It skidded ashore. There were some boys playing there who saw him land. "Hey! An old man just landed out of the water!" they cried. Then a crowd of people came out, men and women. "Why! Here is our Old Man! Give him food!" cried the chief.

207. Then the women went to the house to fetch food and they came back with meal and mush for the Old Man. "Thank you! Thank you!" he said, "I will freshen [i.e., initiate] the boys for you when I am through eating. Look toward the south!" The boys saw a monster running. "He is running this way!" they cried.

208. The monster approached nearer and nearer, and the boys ran away, but he headed them off. They ran toward the house. He rounded them up in one place and drove them into the house. Then he went around the house, four times to the right, and four times to the left, he went around. Then he went over to where Marumda was sitting.

209. "Oh!" said the Marumda, "that's my older brother the Kuksu!" "Younger brother, how are the people that you made? Are they behaving? Did everything come right as you wished? You haven't missed anything?" Thus spoke the Kuksu.

210. They were sitting facing the lake. "Yes, I made everything as I wanted, and then I crossed over." "Then I am happy! Now you must make the people hold a dance, a four-day dance." "I told them the same thing over there across [the water]. We will watch this dance and when

it is all completed and well performed, we will go over there." Thus said the Marumda.

211. "All right!" said the Kuksu. "You are right, your words are true. Good words, sound knowledge and straight. Therefore make a speech for them so that they may learn from you. Already they have their dancing costumes on." Thus spoke the Kuksu.

212. Then Marumda got up and went toward the dance house. He stood on top of the dance house and harangued the people: "Gather for the dance! Gather for the dance! My people, my boys, my girls! Gather for the dance! Go into the dance house!" Then the people, the boys, the girls, the children, everybody went into the dance house.

213. The men gathered in front of the center-post. The chorus sat down in front of them. And then Marumda came out in front of them. Then the people tried to sing the song, but they didn't know how.

214. Then Marumda himself sang it. [SONG.] "This is the sitting-down-song," said Marumda.

215. Meanwhile the men and the women were fixing their dancing costumes. Now they sang the dance-song. Men and boys together were fixing themselves. Women and girls together were fixing themselves. The dance house was crowded with dancers.

216. In the lead went the Marumda. He performed in front of them. Eight times he danced and stopped, and then they rested. They danced all night for four nights. They carried out the dance till just before dawn. Then they took off their dancing costumes and carried them around the dance house four times.

217. After this the men went to the lake to bathe. The young men went to the lake to bathe. The women went to the lake to bathe. The girls went to the lake to bathe. And then they came back to the shore.

218. Thereupon the singers went to the lake to bathe. They came out and started toward the dance house. The singers walked in the lead. Then came the men, then came the young men, then came the women, then came the girls.

219. Four times each way they went around the dance house, and then they went in. And now they went around the center-post four times each

way. After that they sat down inside the house. Marumda stood in front of the center-post and delivered a prayer. Four times he spoke.

220. Then he commanded: "Make donations of food!" Then everyone in the village brought out donations of food. Now Marumda selected assistant chiefs. He selected four of them to distribute the food. He selected four men, and he selected four women chiefs to distribute the food.

221. They first gave some to Marumda, a ball of mush. In no time he cleaned it up. And then he went off. That was forever that he departed. After that no one ever saw him. No one knows where he went. Thus it happened.

222. In this wise he visited every village, teaching them how to perform the dances. Eight days and eight nights he would perform, and then it was completed.

223. After this he walked about on a mountain, and he called together the coyotes: "You will watch over the villages that are strung out on the land. If enemies should approach, you must cry: *Guhmá a'a . . . guhmá a'a . . .* Enemies . . . enemies . . . " Thus the Marumda instructed the coyotes.

224. After this he called together the wolves of the woods: "You will travel in the woods, hunting your food!" Thus he instructed them. And then he called together the pumas: "You will travel on the mountains, hunting your food!" Thus he instructed them.

225. Then he called together the *wiq'a* [unidentified animal]: "You will travel amid the rocks, hunting your food!" Thus he instructed them. Then he called together the lynxes: "You will travel in the chamise brush, hunting your food!" Thus he instructed them. Then he called together the foxes: "You will live inside hollow trees amid the rocks!" Thus he instructed them.

226. Then he called together the skunks. He came out with his tail over his head. There was some noise, and he squirted in that direction. He made the whole land stink as he came. "You mustn't do that!" said Marumda. "Only if they threaten to kill you, then you may do it! You will live in holes in the rocks and in the trees." Thus he instructed them.

227. Then he called together the raccoons: "You will live in holes in the trees and there you will hunt your food!" Then he called together the squirrels: "You will build your nests high up in the trees and from there you will go and hunt your food!" Thus he instructed them.

228. Then he called together the martens: "Amid the rocks you will dwell. From there you will hunt your food." Then he called together the bears: "On the mountains you will travel. There you will dwell in caves. From there you will hunt your food!"

229. After that he called together the elk: "You will dwell in the hills and you will hunt your food in the valleys." Thus he instructed them. And then he called together the chamise-animals [the deer], and he addressed them: "You, in the hills you will dwell, amid the sagebrush. You are dwellers of the hills." Thus he instructed them.

230. Then he called together the rabbits: "You will live in the valleys and in the mountains." Thus he instructed them. After this he called together the ground-squirrels, the moles, the gophers, the field mice, the wood-rats, the badgers: "You will dwell under the ground, you will live in holes!" Thus he instructed them.

231. Then he called together the rattlesnakes, the large gopher-snakes, the small gopher-snakes, the milk-snakes, the red-striped snakes, the mountain garter-snakes, the snakes with green back and red belly, the big lizards, the common lizards, the salamanders, the giant salamanders, the snails: "You will live in the hills, amid the rocks, in the trees, in holes underground!" Thus he instructed them.

232. Then he called together the birds, the eagles, the condors, the hawks, the falcons, the goshawks, the kites, the big horned owls, the screech owls, the nighthawks, the little horned owls, the ground owls: "You will live in the hills, in hollow trees, in holes in rocks!" Thus he instructed them.

233. Then he called together the bluejays, the blackbirds, the quail, the crows, the flickers, the red-headed woodpeckers, the mountain jays, the grouse, the robins, the mountain robins, the towhees, the black-and-yellow finches, the mountain quail, the roadrunners, the ravens, the sapsuckers, the woodpeckers, the thrushes, the bluebirds, the mead-

owlarks, the orioles, the grosbeaks, the swallows, the black swallows, the shrikes, all of them he called together and instructed them: "You will live in the hills and the valleys, and in hollow trees!" Thus he instructed them.

234. Then he called together the water birds, blue heron, sand-hill crane, white crane, bittern, little green heron, swan, goose, mallard, cormorant, grebe, merganser, seagull, pied-billed grebe, little merganser, mud-hen, he called them together and addressed them: "In the water you will live, in the water you will seek your food!"

235. Then he called together the fishes: "Fishes who live in the water, all of you, come ashore!" Thus he spoke. Then Turtle came ashore first, and behind him came all the fishes. "You are not a fish!" said Marumda to the Turtle. "You will travel on the land. You fish, you are not to travel on land! You fish, you must live in the water. You will eat food from the water. And you too, Turtle!" Thus he spoke. Then the fish went back into the water, and Turtle floated back into the water.

236. Thus sitting on top of a mountain spoke the Marumda. Thus he instructed everything on the earth. How they were to behave, what they were to eat, where they were to live, he told them that way, everything. That's what he called them together for.

237. He sat on a large flat rock on top of the mountain, giving instructions to everything that lives. Then he got off and stood the rock on edge. "People must never come here!" Thus spoke the Marumda.

238. Then he departed. "If people come here this rock will fall and the people will live no longer! If anyone comes here he will die forever!" Thus spoke the Marumda.

239. After that he went to see the Kuksu. He arrived at the Kuksu's place and told him what he had done. "You have done the right thing!" said the Kuksu. "Sing a praying song, older brother!" said Marumda to Kuksu. Then: "All right!" he said. [SONG.] Thus spoke the Kuksu. Then Marumda spoke: "Oh! That's good! Ooo . . . Ooo . . . Ooo . . . Ooo!" And then the Marumda pulled out a song. [SONG.] Then he went back to his own abode. And the Kuksu also went back to his own place.

240. Four times he made us people. First he drowned them in the water. Then he destroyed them by fire. Then he destroyed them by snow. Then he destroyed them by a whirlwind. Thus he destroyed them four times. This tale I was taught by the old men, this tale of world-making, of making people, this is the tale as I was told.

241. This is the tale that I heard when I was little, when I was a boy.

17

The Trials of Young Hawk

SOUTHERN POMO

1940

ANNIE BURKE, NARRATOR

ABRAHAM M. HALPERN, COLLECTOR

ROBERT L. OSWALT, TRANSLATOR

INTRODUCTION BY ROBERT L. OSWALT

Historical Background

The terms *Pomo* and *Pomoan* refer to a family of seven related languages and to their speakers. The divergence among the seven languages is similar to that among the various Romance languages; at the extremes, the divergence is greater than that between English and German. At a more distant level, Pomoan is related to some languages classified as Hokan. The Pomo lived in an area stretching roughly from about fifty miles north of San Francisco northward for ninety miles, and from the Pacific Coast inland for fifty miles to include much of the shore of Clear Lake, with an offshoot to the northeast across the Inner Coast Range.

Estimates of the total population of the pre-Contact Pomo vary from eight thousand to twenty-one thousand. The Southern Pomo, who occupied the drainage system of the lower half of the Russian River, were one of the more numerous of the language groups, constituting about 30 percent of the Pomo total. They were not a political unit but lived in several independent village communities.

Aboriginally all the Pomo lived by hunting, fishing, and gathering plant foods. Acorns were the staple of their diet and required a great deal of preparation: gathering, drying, cracking, grinding, leaching (to remove the bitter tannic acid), and cooking. They clipped and ground clamshells into beads, which were strung and used as a store of wealth. Larger and much more valuable beads were made of magnesite (known as "Indian gold"). To keep account of the wealth represented by these beads, they developed a system for counting up into the thousands. However, the Pomo have been most famed for their basketry, which was woven with great skill in a wide variety of techniques. The women took pride in doing artistic work, often taking months to complete a fine, coiled six-inch basket. There has recently been a cultural renaissance, and a few younger women have learned to produce the fancy baskets.

Beginning in the early nineteenth century the Southern Pomo were disastrously affected by missionization, raids, disease, and settlement of their land by immigrants. By the early twentieth century, in the southernmost region, containing the present cities of Santa Rosa and Sebastopol, the surviving biological descendants of the Southern Pomo had lost their ancestral speech. Further to the north, two dialects survived, with, at midcentury, perhaps two dozen speakers each: Mihilakawna 'West Stream', spoken in the Dry Creek Valley (now filled with vineyards), and Makahmo 'Salmonhole', spoken in the area of the town of Cloverdale. By the early 1960s the number of speakers had dwindled to about a dozen for each of the two dialects. And by 1999, there was one speaker of each dialect. There are hundreds of descendants with some Southern Pomo blood, but they are much assimilated and racially mixed through intermarriage with other Indian groups, with Mexicans, and with white people. In the recent cultural revival many of the younger generations have learned their traditional songs and dances and perform them in public.

Salvage Workers

Into the situation in 1939 came Abraham M. Halpern (1914–1985), to collect, over a one-year period, lexical material and texts with free translations and some word-by-word translations in each of the seven Pomo languages. Halpern had spent considerable time studying Yuma (also called Quechan), spoken in far Southeastern California, and he eventually produced a grammar of that language as a doctoral dissertation. He brought northward with him a phonetic skill that enabled him to record in the Pomo languages the unusual sounds that had escaped the occasional earlier collector. For Southern Pomo, Halpern obtained seven Coyote stories, dictated by the one speaker, Annie Burke.

By 1963, I had completed a grammar and a volume of texts of the neighboring Kashaya Pomo language and turned my attention to salvaging as much as possible of the Southern Pomo language. My first principal consultant was Elizabeth Dollar (1895–1971), speaker of the Mihilakawna dialect, who was able to furnish some Coyote stories, as well as much lexical material. From the mid 1960s and for twenty years, Elsie Allen (1899–1990) and I worked together for a couple of weeks each year gathering lexical and grammatical material on her mother tongue. She did not know any Coyote stories, nor did any other surviving speaker of the Makahmo dialect, and thus those dictated by her mother, Annie Burke, remain the only real corpus for the genre in that dialect.

Annie Burke (1876–1960), born Annie Ramone, was raised in a relatively traditional way, speaking only the Makahmo dialect; she learned English later in life. She married George Comanche and with him had two daughters. She gave birth to her first while working in the hop fields and this child, Elsie, was to become a chief consultant on the Makahmo. Annie's second husband was Richard Burke, and with him she had one son, Salvador. The family lived on the Hopland Reservation, where the language was Central Pomo, a language about as different from Southern Pomo as French from Spanish, and that became the third language that Annie and Elsie learned to speak.

Annie Burke was a master basketweaver. Like many artists, she was also a collector of the creations of other masters in her medium. Earlier tradition had been that personal property should be buried with the deceased; however, Annie Burke requested that this not happen to her baskets and that they be preserved for later generations to see. Her daughter Elsie, who also became a master weaver (and wrote a booklet on Pomo basketweaving), made the same request for preservation, with the result that the family baskets are now on display in the museum in the town of Willits.

Narrative Structure

"The Trials of Young Hawk" is of a class of narratives that the Pomo call "Coyote stories," told of a time when animals had speech and other human attributes. Coyote often is the principal character, but, as here, it is not necessary for him to be a participant for the tale to be a Coyote story.

Ritual Numbers. The magical number among the Pomo and neighboring Indians is four: a ritual (submersion in water, in this story) may have to be performed four times, good or bad luck may come in fours, and the hero of a story may have to overcome four obstacles (compare three and seven in European tales). On occasion, half or twice four has special significance: duality, the occurrence of characters in pairs—two siblings, parent and child, two opponents—is fairly common in Pomo stories. This tale carries out the principle of duality to an exceptional degree. The tale begins with two hawk brothers but quickly turns to following the trials of the younger brother alone. He has encounters with various pairs, even pairs of pairs: two beaver brothers, then two gopher brothers; two red ant sisters, then two field mice sisters. There is a shift toward the end of the tale to two separate attacks from single opponents, an ogress and thunder. The story closes with revenge taken on the older brother.

Personal Names and Kinship Terms. Animal characters are identified in the Native text by species name. In other translations these have often been converted into proper names by capitalizing them. As a convention, that might well have been done here, but it is not, because the designations in Southern Pomo are not proper names. As a term of reference, *kaʔbekʼacʼ* 'sharp-shinned hawk' is used of either the older or younger hawk brother, not as the name of one of them. Real proper names of individuals cannot be used in ordinary secular situations; instead, a kinship term is almost invariably employed as a term of address.

Whether the characters are related or not, a kin term suitable to the age difference can be selected: someone two generations older might be called by one of the grandparent terms; a slightly older male might be addressed as "Older Brother." The Pomo languages all have distinct terms for the four grandparents, each of which is more inclusive than is suggested by the English translation; for example, the Southern Pomo term for "mother's father" includes all the brothers of the father of the mother. At two points in the tale the younger brother addresses the older, not by the relationship of the addressee to the speaker—that is, "Older Brother"—but by a tecnonym, a term based on the relationship of the addressee to a child, in this case the adopted hawk: "O Father of his Mother" (one word in Southern Pomo). It might be noted that the two pairs in the story addressed as "Mother's Father" are helpful, as older relatives should be. The two pairs of females are not addressed by a kin term because they are potential mates and it would be incestuous for them to be adopted into the equivalent of a close blood relationship. The single ogress is not a potential mate and can address the young hawk by the deceptively friendly "Grandson."

Sentence Connectors. Southern Pomo has an elaborate system of suffixes for subordinating one clause to another. When attached to the verb *ha:mini-* 'do thus' or 'do so' they form a word that links two sentences together, giving such information as the relative timing of the successive sentences and whether there has been a switch in subject between the prior sentence and the one with the connector. The narrative may proceed through several clauses and sentences with no subject expressed overtly; even so, the appropriate English pronouns can be deduced from the tracking system and supplied in the translation. In the native-language extract that follows, taken from the end of the fourth paragraph of the story, these characteristic features of Southern Pomo discourse are clearly on display.

šin:akʰle   heʔ:e   pʰaʔs'i-ba,
crown.of.head   hair   grabbed-having
Having grabbed the hair on the crown of the head,

ma:-ṭ'iki-n,   "ka:li-n-hkʰay huʔ:uci-n!"   nih:iw.
own-younger.brother-to up-to-ward   turn.face-IMPERATIVE said
he said to his younger brother, "Turn your face upward!"

ha:mini-ba,   ma:-ṭ'iki-n   huʔ:u-kʰbe ʔakʰ:o ba-:ciṭ'.
done.so-having own-younger.brother-to eye-rock   two   poke-out
Having done so, he poked out his younger brother's two eyeballs.

ha:mini-ba   kʰma:yow,   hidʔa   hwa:-ba,
done.so-having   after,   outside   gone.out-having
After having done so, having gone outside,

ʔahca -n-hkʰay   ho:liw.
house-to-ward   set.off
he set off homeward.

The closest English translations of these sentence connectors are phrases like "Having done so," "He having done so, the other," "While doing so," and "While he was doing so, the other." In the story, some of the connectors are fully translated, to convey the style of Southern Pomo narratives, but others are rendered more simply to avoid being excessively intrusive. "Then" and "and" are common translations but deliver less information than the Southern Pomo connector.

Definite and indefinite articles also are supplied to fit the context. Other major elements that have been inserted to clarify the translation, but are not in the original text, are put in square brackets.

Quotatives. Annie Burke's rendition is curiously at variance with what is typical among all other Pomoan traditional stories: She rarely employs the evidential suffix *-do* 'it is said, they say', used to mark that the narrator has been told of the events by someone else, and that they are not personal experiences. The suffix appears only in the fifth paragraph from the end.

FURTHER READING

The most accessible reference on the culture of the Pomo is the *Handbook of North American Indians,* volume 8, which, in three chapters, covers the seven branches of the Pomo and includes a good listing of sources for more information. Elsie Allen, the daughter of the narrator of this story, wrote a small well-illustrated book, *Pomo Basketmaking*, which also contains a biographical sketch of Elsie Allen by her granddaughter, Linda McGill. S. A. Barrett's *Pomo Myths* contains 108 tales in English only, from the Central, Northern, and Eastern Pomo, together with a motif index, a glossary of words in the three languages, and an introduction with a discussion of such topics as the methods of storytelling and the mythological system, and a description of the many supernatural beings. Robert Oswalt's *Kashaya Texts* contains eighty-two texts in the neighboring Kashaya Pomo language, together with English translations; twenty are Coyote stories, thirty more are tales with some supernatural element, nineteen are folk history, and thirteen are of miscellaneous genres. Oswalt's "Retribution for Mate-Stealing" is a story told by Elizabeth Dollar in Southern Pomo, Mihilakawna dialect, with word-by-word translation, free translation, and a grammatical sketch of the language.

THE TRIALS OF YOUNG HAWK

A group of small birds and animals, who were all also people, used to live together in a big community. A sharp-shinned hawk lived there along with his younger brother. The hawk's younger brother always perched up high in the earth lodge on the side with the fire. The older sharp-shinned hawk was married to a wildcat; his wife was a wildcat woman.

One time many of the people set off eastward to load up on fish. After they all had left, the wildcat woman went to her husband's brother down in the earth lodge and pulled her husband's brother down from where he was perched. Having pulled him down, she dragged him away. Then she scratched him, scratched him everywhere on his face, scratched his body too. When she had scratched him, he fled to where the earthlodge was and ran down in. There he perched up high where his bed was.

Those people who had gone off toward the east now started for home, bringing a load of fish. While they were on their way, the scrub jay told the older hawk, "Your wife scratched your younger brother."

In the morning, the older hawk went down there to the earth lodge. He then said to his younger brother, "Climb down! I'm going to brush your hair." He spread a hide for him to climb down onto. The younger brother, having climbed down, sat down on the hide. The older brother, the sharp-shinned hawk, having sat down near his younger brother, brushed his head hair with a louse brush. All of the head hair he brushed well. Having grabbed the hair on the crown of the head, he said to his younger brother, "Turn your face upward!" Then he poked out his younger brother's two eyeballs. After having done so, he went outside and set off homeward.

The younger brother cried and screamed and screamed, writhing around. But nobody at all saw this; he just suffered it alone.

Now night came on and, when the people all lay down to sleep, he, by crawling around, felt the door, the earth lodge doorway, and through there crept outside.

Now he just crawled away somewhere on all fours. He didn't know where he was crawling to. Weeping he crept along; groaning he crawled this way and that. Falling down into brush, he rolled down a steep incline. Having crawled around in this way, he clambered up onto an earth lodge.

When this happened, a beaver and his younger brother living there together both heard the movement on their earth lodge. The older beaver brother said to his younger brother, "Look outside there! Somebody is groaning a lot out there." When he said this, the younger brother said "All right" and went outside. When he did so, he found the eastern hawk and said, "My poor child! It must be our child who has been crawling around, O Father of his Mother!"

The older beaver brother also ran outside. The two of them carried that hawk down into the earth lodge. When they had done this, the mother's fathers wept. After they had wept, they built a fire and placed rocks in it. They filled a baby-bath basket with water, and, when the rocks had become hot, they dropped those hot rocks into that water-filled baby bath. They dropped the rocks, the hot rocks, into the baby-bath basket, in order to heat the water. When the water had become hot, they washed the hawk's body. They fixed up his hair as well, the head hair that had become so tangled, so full of dry grass, so full of foxtails and burrs. Twigs and leaves were all snarled with that once fine hair.

The two of them, sitting beside that place, fixed him up. They made everything good. After doing this, they next gnawed out round balls from wood and set these artificial eyes into the eyesockets. It didn't look good, because it was white, just white all over.

At night, when his mother's fathers had gone to sleep, he crawled back and forth on all fours and then crawled outside. He crawled away, not knowing where he was crawling. He just crawled here and there on all fours, crawling while crying. Having crawled around in this way, he crawled up onto a gopher's earth lodge.

A gopher lived there with his younger brother. The older gopher said to his younger brother, "Somewhere on top of the earthlodge I hear someone groaning. Go and look up there!" "All right, I'll go look. You are such a coward," said the younger, and he went outside.

When he did so, he found the hawk. He then said to his older brother, "The child must be ours, O Father of his Mother." When the younger said this, the older followed him out. The two of them picked [the young hawk] up and carried him down into the earth lodge. They set him down there where they had spread something out. When they had done this, the two of them wept over their grandchild.

When they had finished crying, they set rocks on their fire and put water in a baby-bath basket. Then, when the rocks had become hot, they dropped those hot rocks down into the water. The water heated up. Then they washed the hawk. They washed that body all covered with blood and scratched with brush. They also brushed his head hair well. They fixed him up good.

Then the older gopher said to his younger brother, "Pick some asters and let us try to make eyes out of them." The younger brother said, "All right" and went outside, snapped off the best aster blossoms, gathered them up, and carried them down into the earth lodge. Some of these flowers they prepared well and set into the eyesockets. They looked at their work and it seemed good. It was good. When they were finished, the hawk said, "I see things well. Thank you, Mother's Fathers, for giving me eyes."

His mother's fathers: "You should live here with us. Don't go away!" The hawk: "No, I will leave. I will just wander about. I will wander wherever I wander." When he said this, his mother's fathers said, "All right, it is good. We will give you presents." They gave him arrows, a bow, a duck-bow. The arrows had been placed down into a quiver.

Having picked these up, the hawk set out.

In this manner—wandering, wandering, wandering—he wandered all day long. Then he spied a small house standing. Two red ant women lived there, an older with her younger sister. Those women caught sight of that man. "Ey, a fine man is coming." The older sister: "He will be my man." The younger: "No, he is mine. You are old; I am the one who will marry him." "Come! Come here!" she said to the hawk. Then she had him come into the house.

The older sister: "I am the one who will marry him. I am the one he will lie down with." When she said this, the younger sister said, "No, I will have him lie with me. You are an old woman; I am the one who will marry him." The older sister: "No, we will have him lie in the middle. We will both marry him."

Having said that, night came, and the three lay down together. When they did this, these women didn't let the man sleep. All night long they were biting him. That's why the man, early next morning, when dawn was just brightening in the east, left. Having left, he wandered around.

All day long he walked. Then he spied a small house, a small house standing.

Two field mouse women lived there, an older with her younger sister. At twilight, this younger sister: "Older Sister, a man is coming. A fine man is coming." Then, having said, "Ey," they went out—both of the women went out.

Then, to the hawk, "Come! Come here! Now, where do you come from? Come on into the house!" They had him sit down in the house. Having done that, the older sister said, "I will marry him." Thereupon the younger sister: "But I saw him first. I am the one who should marry him. You are just an old woman." "No, I am the one who should marry him. You are way too immature."

It became night. [The older sister said], "No, we will lie down together in one place and we will have him lie in the middle." Having said this, they lay down and had that man lie in the middle. Because of this, the man was dying for sleep. Next, those women ate his head hair, chewed up his eyebrows, bit out his eyelashes, chewed up all his face hair, and nibbled off all the hair on his body.

In the morning the man awoke. That erstwhile head of hair was gone when he awoke; he arose entirely smooth. Even his duckbow had been eaten up. The quiver had been chewed up as well. Those women were gone; he arose alone. He tried feeling on himself with his hand for his missing hair, but there was nothing there; it was perfectly smooth. Then he went outside and set out.

Having done so, he discovered a pond lying still. Then he said, "You will cause my head hair to grow." And, "World lying around here, have pity on me and cause my head hair to grow! Four times I will submerge in the water."

Now, after having said that, he went down to the pond and into the water. Then he dove under. When he reached the limit of his breath, he lifted his head up out. There was nothing there when he lifted his head; he lifted a smooth head. Again he dove under; again he lifted his head up out. With nothing there, smooth, he lifted his head up. Again he dove under. When he reached the limit of his breath, he lifted his head up out.

Now that body hair had sprouted, and the head hair had sprouted as well. Again he dove under. For a long time he kept his head in the water. When he reached the limit of his breath, he lifted his head up out. Facial hair had grown. Eyebrows had grown. That head hair had become longer. All over the fine body hair was growing out. That wooden bow had become new. That quiver had become new. Everything was good.

Now he set out. He was just walking along. Looking here and there he wandered around. Then he spied a house, a small house standing.

One old woman was living there. Whoever visited there, she would kill. Of the people who visited that old woman, not even one ever left alive. Of the people who visited her, that blind old woman killed every single one. The old woman was blind.

The hawk arrived there.

"Sit down here! Sit down beside me, Grandson! Who have you been listening to that you come here to visit me, your mother's mother?" The hawk sat down near there. She picked up her rock walking stick and struck at the hawk with it. The hawk dodged, causing her to strike bare ground. The old woman missed.

When she did this, the hawk shot that old woman with one of his arrows. He killed her off, put her to death. After he had done this—put an end to that old woman, now dead in the house—he went outside. He put a torch to the house, burned it up. The old woman was burned up as well.

When he had done this, the hawk set out again. He just set out wandering around, set out looking at things here and there.

Now clouds formed and thunder sounded. It thundered very loud. The thunder man kept on failing to strike the hawk. While the thunder man was missing him, the hawk spied, high on a tree, an open woodpecker hole. When he did so, the hawk crawled away and into the hole. Then, the thunder man hovered around where the hole was. While he was doing so, the hawk shot the thunder in the soft spot above the front of the collarbone. When he shot, the thunder thudded onto the ground with the sound "Chol."

When this happened, the hawk crawled up and out from the hole. He looked at the thunder that he himself had shot. They say that the thunder wore all kinds of blankets: rain blanket, fog-rain blanket, hail blanket, snow blanket, wind blanket, fog blanket. In these, they say, the hawk dressed himself up, having removed them [from the thunder].

Then, next, he set out flying far away to where his own older brother had mutilated him. Having become the thunder, he set out flying.

Then he caused rain to fall where his older brother's people lived. He caused thunder to sound. He caused it to rain a lot. When it had rained a lot, the earth lodge filled with water. When this happened, his older brother knew [the cause].

The older brother: "Younger Brother, Younger Brother, make the rain end, make the rain end! I know it is you, Younger Brother, who make the rain fall." When he said this, he went away; the thunder went away.

That is the end.

18

The Woman Who Loved a Snake

CACHE CREEK POMO
1988

MABEL McKAY, STORYTELLER
GREG SARRIS, COLLECTOR AND NARRATOR

INTRODUCTION BY GREG SARRIS

Mabel McKay was born on January 12, 1907, in Nice, Lake County, California. Her father, Yanta Boone, was a Potter Valley Pomo Indian. Her mother, Daisy Hansen, was a Losel Cache Creek Pomo. Mabel was raised by her maternal grandmother, Sarah Taylor, and always considered herself a Losel Cache Creek Pomo. It was from her grandmother that Mabel learned the Losel Cache Creek language and the rich and extensive history, not just of her tribe, but of many surrounding Pomo and southwestern Wintun tribes.

But this knowledge was not what Mabel would become known for. She became an expert basketweaver, perhaps the finest of her time, weaving brilliantly colored feather baskets and miniatures, some no larger than eraserheads. And she became a medicine woman, what we call locally an Indian doctor. She was a "sucking doctor," the most highly valued of the local Indian doctors, and she would be the last sucking doctor, not just among the Pomo, but in all of California. Every aspect of her life was guided by the dictates of her Dream, her general term for her experience

FIGURE 8. Mabel McKay, October 1, 1971.
Courtesy Herb Puffer.

with and knowledge from the Spirit. These things—her basketweaving
and doctoring—made her famous. Other Indians, anthropologists, and
basket collectors all flocked to her, seeking information about this or that.
But she was uncanny, maddening in her replies.

"What do you do for poison oak?" a student once asked in a large au-
ditorium where Mabel was being interviewed as a Native healer. "Cala-
mine lotion," she answered.

At the time this story was recorded, in 1988, I had known her for more
than thirty years, since I was a child.[1] I was attempting to write her life
story, both because she wanted me to and because I had made her life
story my dissertation project at Stanford. I figured because I am Indian
(Kashaya Pomo/Coast Miwok) and because I knew her so well I would
be able to understand her wishes for her "book," as she called it, in terms
of its content and narrative structure. No such luck. "You just do [the
book] the best way you know how," she said. "What you know from me."

What I knew from her were narratives that circled around and around, connecting with one another in space and time in ways I couldn't make sense of, at least not for a book I might write. And when I countered with questions that might help me order these narratives in a way meaningful for me, I heard the same uncanny responses the student heard about poison oak.

"Mabel, people want to know about things in your life in a way they can understand. You know, how you got to be who you are. There has to be a theme."

"I don't know about no theme," she said.

"A theme is a point that connects all the dots, ties up all the stories," I explained.

"That's funny," she said. "Tying up all the stories. Why somebody want to do that?"

Eventually, I came to see and feel what she meant. The stories cannot be tied up, disconnected from one another, not her story, my story, any story. Stories live and change in contexts, with changing hearers and tellers. Mabel reminded me of this every step of the way. I became a part of the story the moment I heard it. In hearing stories, we begin to interpret, or "make sense," of them, and Mabel always seemed to remind me of that fact. Just as Mabel broadened the student's notion of a Native healer, letting the student understand that as an Indian doctor Mabel was also a contemporary woman, so Mabel continued to open my eyes, reminding me of who I was and what I was thinking as a participant in her storytelling. It was important that I remembered my life, my presence and history, as I attempted to understand Mabel.

As I learned more about Mabel, I learned more about myself. The stories, and the dialogue about the stories, served as a way to expose boundaries that shape and constitute cultural and personal worlds. Thus, I understood how I might write her story and her book. I had to chart not just her "story," but the story of my hearing her story. I had to expose the ever-widening world the story comes from and becomes.

Scholars familiar with my work with Mabel often question the fact that my conversations with her were always in English. Would the situation and outcome of the storytelling event be the same or different if she spoke Pomo? Of course, I don't know for certain, because I only know a few words and phrases of her language and could never converse with her at length in that language. But I suspect not. What Mabel invoked and inspired was an awe and respect for everything around her, a way of reminding oneself that the story, like everything in the world, was always more than what you thought, and perhaps more than you could ever imagine. More than the interesting facts of her life as a basketweaver and medicine woman, Mabel wanted to teach me that. English seemed to work just fine.

Others have asked if Mabel's talk—her narratives, conversations, and responses to questions—are typical of older, say traditional, Pomo-speakers. It seems in many ways Mabel was unique as a speaker, but I am not certain. I have known other Pomo storytellers who remind listeners of the context in which they are hearing stories. I have also known Pomo storytellers to implicate their listeners in what they are saying. None of the speakers I have known, however, was as consistent in these matters as Mabel. But I have not done a study or comprehensive survey. I have only looked at Mabel's talk in terms of its effect as I have known it, not in terms of the ways it may or may not represent traditional or typical Pomo discourse, whatever that may be. What I wrote, finally, was what I knew from Mabel, the best way I knew how.

NOTE

1. The present selection is taken from chapter 2 of Greg Sarris's book, *Keeping Slug Woman Alive: A Holistic Approach to American Indian Texts*. In that edition of the story, the transcribed text of "The Woman Who Loved a Snake" is broken up, its parts presented out of narrative sequence and embedded in a larger (and fascinating) exegesis of the context and story's meaning. For this collection, what Sarris and I have done is to extract the text of Mabel's narration from its critical matrix and restore it to the chronological order of its original telling. Greg has added a few sentences of transition here and there to compensate for the reordering of the text.

Sarris's experimentation with the framework of contemporary fiction to present this story strikes me as an ingenious way of contextualizing the narrative, of incorporating both expressive and interpretive information—"atmosphere" and explanation—directly into the presentation itself, rather than handling it through the medium of footnotes and introductory essays. As a method for presenting traditional narrative (one that Jaime de Angulo experimented with as well, though from a very different perspective), it holds great promise, at least for those editors and translators who have a "first-person" recollection of the original performance.

Though it is not reflected in the title of the piece, the reader will discover that Mabel McKay actually tells *two* stories here, not just one. The second story, about the first-Contact arrival of Europeans in Kashaya territory, is technically unrelated to the main story about the woman and the snake. What I find fascinating is how the two stories, separate until Mabel called them up on this occasion, seem to adapt *toward* each other in their new surroundings. It's as if all her stories were really one, part of an endless, multivocal braid. Once Mabel has brought the two stories into one light, they remain forever intertwined.—HWL

FURTHER READING

Greg Sarris has written a number of books, including *Keeping Slug Woman Alive: A Holistic Approach to American Indian Texts* (a collection of literary essays) and *Mabel McKay: Weaving the Dream* (a collaborative account of Mabel's remarkable life, the "book" referred to in this selection). He also has a collection of short stories, *Grand Avenue,* and wrote the screenplay for the HBO miniseries of the same name.

THE WOMAN WHO LOVED A SNAKE

One day I took a colleague of mine from Stanford University to the Rumsey Wintun Reservation to meet Mabel McKay. "I want to meet this famous Pomo medicine woman," my friend said. "I've heard her talk and I've seen her baskets in the Smithsonian." My friend, Jenny, had heard me talk about Mabel also. I had been recording Mabel's stories for a book about her life. As always, Mabel proved a gracious host. She served us hot buttered toast and coffee and, for lunch, tuna fish sandwiches with pickles and lettuce. As Jenny and I ate, Mabel told about the woman who loved a snake.

"See, her husband, he would work at night. 'Lock the door,' he'd tell her. 'Don't let nobody in.' Every night he'd go off saying that: 'Lock the door, keep everything locked up.' She would fix his dinner, then his lunch." Mabel chuckled to herself. "By lunch I mean what he takes to work. That's what I call lunch when I was working nighttime in the cannery.

"Anyway, this woman, she says 'OK.' And sometimes, after he would leave, she'd stay up for a while. She'd clean up around, maybe do the dishes, get things ready for the morning, for the breakfast. I don't know.

"Then ONE TIME she hears a knock on the back door. 'What is that?' she's thinking. First she thought maybe it was her husband; maybe he was coming home early; maybe he got sick or something. 'But then why doesn't he just come in?' she was saying. Well, then she thought maybe she was hearing things. She just kept working then.

"But it kept on, this knocking. Then she got scared. See in those days no phones up there. And this was far out, up on some white man's place there, where her husband worked. She could not yell, nothing. Nobody to hear her. Maybe she's thinking this to herself. I don't know.

"'Who is this?' she is saying. Then I don't know what he said. I forgot. Something, anyway. And she opens the door. Just a little bit. He comes in and she stands there looking at him. But she doesn't recognize him.

"Anyway, she fixes some coffee. I don't know. Gives him something to eat. They're talking around there. I don't know what.

"Next day, her husband comes home. 'What's this?' he is saying. He's standing there—by the bedroom—and he's looking down in some vase. Something there. It was on the table. 'What are you talking about?' she says. Then she goes and looks where he's looking. And she sees it, too: a snake, a little black snake all coiled up. 'What is this?' he says to her. Then he takes it out and puts it in the brush. He lets it out there.

"Next day, same thing happens. Then the husband, he gets suspicious of that snake. 'What is this?' he is saying. Then she gets worried; now she knows what the snake is. But she don't say nothing. 'I'm going to kill it,' he says, 'chop it to bits out in the brush.' He's testing her, but she don't say nothing. Then she got REAL worried, seeing him go out with that snake.

"But next day same thing it happens. Maybe she tried talking to that man. I don't know. 'Don't stay around here,' she might said to him. But it's there again, that snake. Now her husband, he shakes her; he knows something is going on. 'What is this?' he's saying. But he had an idea about it anyway. 'You come with me,' he says, 'and watch me kill it.' He starts pulling on her arm, shaking her, but she refuses him. She won't go. She's crying by this time.

"He takes the snake out, same way, coiled around his hand. She just sees him go. Then he comes back. She doesn't know what happened. Maybe this time he DID kill it. She's crying yet. Her husband, he comes in and says nothing. Just goes to bed.

"But he never did chop that snake up. Maybe he did. I don't know. Anyway, it went on like that . . . "

Jenny, a Ph.D. candidate in English, asked what the snake symbolized. Mabel didn't seem to understand the question. She looked at me, then turned to Jenny. "Well, it was a problem, I don't know."

"Why didn't he, I mean the husband, just kill the snake?" Jenny asked.

With an incredulous look on her face, Mabel focused on Jenny. "Well, how could he?" she asked. "This is white man days. There's laws against killing people. That man, he would go to jail, or maybe get the electric chair, if he done that."

Mabel mentioned that she knew the woman, that she often visited her when she lived in the same area north of Clear Lake. "Then one night I seen that man. He was handsome, too," she chuckled. "It was late. Lakeport grocery was closing and I seen him come out with groceries. He didn't take the road. He went the creek way, north. Then, I say to myself, 'I bet I know where he's going.'"

"Maybe he just carried the snake with him and left it in the vase each morning before he left," Jenny offered. "Like a sign."

Mabel laughed out loud. "Like a sign. That's cute. Why he want to do that?" She lit a cigarette. "See, I knew he was odd. He's moving in cold, late at night. Snakes don't do that."

"Well, was it man or snake? I mean when you were looking at it?" Jenny was desperate now.

"You got funny ideas," Mabel answered. "Aren't I sitting here?" She tapped her cigarette in the aluminum ashtray on the table. "You do crazy things like Greg. And he's Indian! He gets ideas where he wants to know this or that so he can write it all up for the people. Well, it ain't like that what I am saying."

About a month later, after my trip with Jenny, Mabel and I took a ride and parked along a road on the south side of Clear Lake, where we had a view of the lake and of Elem Rancheria, the old village site and present-day reservation of the Elem tribe of Pomo Indians. Mabel had been talking about her maternal grandmother, Sarah Taylor, and about how the Elem people initiated her into their dances and cult activities after Sarah's people, the Cache Creek Pomo, had been removed from their land and ceremonial grounds by the non-Indian invaders.

"'You will find a way, a way to go on even after this white people run over the earth like rabbits. They are going to be everywhere,' he was saying. That's Old Man, I forgot his name. He had only Indian name, Taylor's father, Grandma's grandfather. He's the one saying these things."

Mabel opened her purse, pulled out a cigarette. She lit her cigarette and exhaled a cloud of smoke. Below us, on the narrow peninsula of Elem, smoke rose from the rusted chimney tins of the small, dilapidated houses. A lone dog barked in the distance.

"Well, it was over here, below them hills," Mabel said, gesturing south over her shoulder with her chin. "This things, they come over the hill in a trail, long trail. So much that dust is flying up, like smoke wherever they go. And first to see them this people down there, where you are looking. 'What is this?' the people saying. Things with two heads and four legs, bushy tail, standing here on this hill somewhere, looking down at Elem people.

"Lots of people scared, run off, some far as our place, Cache Creek. They tell what they seen then. All Indians, Indians all over, talking about it then. 'What is it?' they is asking. Nobody knows. People is talking about it all over the place. Lot's scared. I don't know. People say different things.

"Some people somewhere seen them things come apart, like part man, then go back together. Then I guess maybe they knew it was people— white people. I don't know," Mabel said and chuckled. "They Indians dance and pray. I don't know. Then they was saying these things [was] mean, killing Indians and taking Indians."

Mabel drew on her cigarette and leisurely exhaled. "But he seen it in his Dream, Old Man. He said what was coming one day, how this would be."

"So they knew what it was coming down this hill," I ventured.

"Hmm," Mabel said, gazing across the lake. "They knew what he meant by 'white man.'"

"So why did they run? Why all the fuss?"

Mabel rubbed out her cigarette and looked at me as if she had not understood what I said. "If they knew from Old Man's prophecy that white people were coming, why didn't they know what was coming down the hill? Why all the fuss?"

Mabel started chuckling, then exploded with loud, uncontrollable laughter. She caught her breath finally and asked, "How can that be? You ever know white people with four legs and two heads? Maybe you do. You're raised around them—your mother's people, I don't know," she said, chuckling again.

She lit another cigarette, then straightened in her seat. "Sometimes takes time for Dream to show itself. Got to be tested. Now we know what he told about, Old Man. He was told . . . He said lots of things: trails, big trails covering the earth, even going into the sky. Man going to be on moon he was saying."

"But how did HE know that?"

"But sometimes Dream forgets, too. Like them snakes. Old Man come in MY dream, give me rattlesnake song. 'You going to work with this snakes; they help you,' he is saying. Then, after that, I seen them. All over my house I seen them: porch, closet, in my bathtub when it's hot, all over. Then I say to him, to that spirit, 'This is modern times, better take that song out of me . . . I don't want nothing to happen. People around here might call animal control place.'

"You know, peoples around here they don't always understand things like that."

After Mabel told the story about the people of Elem seeing non-Indian invaders coming "over the hill in a trail," we headed east, back to the Rumsey Reservation. On the way home, Mabel again told the story of "The Woman Who Loved a Snake."

"It was across there. Up in them hills where she lived. That time Char-lie* [was] running stock up there. By stock I mean the cattle. Charlie al-ways wanted to have the stock. That woman lived there. Sometimes she would come down the road the other side there and talk to me. Anyway, how it happened, she was alone at night. Her husband used to go off working, where it was I don't know. I forgot. How it happened, she hears this knocking one night, at her door . . . "

I was quieter now, listening.

"Well, you see, I know about them snakes," she said as she finished the story. "They can teach about a lot of things."

Mabel pulled her purse to her lap and began rummaging for her cig-

---

* Charles McKay, Mabel's husband.

arettes. I looked to the cold, damp winter hills. Too cold for snakes, I thought to myself.

"Hmm," she said. "Maybe you'll get some idea about the snakes." I looked at her and she was laughing, holding an unlit cigarette between her fingers. "I know you. You'll . . . you're school way. You'll think about it, then write something."

She was right.

19

The Dead People's Home

LAKE MIWOK
1980

JAMES KNIGHT, NARRATOR
CATHERINE CALLAGHAN, COLLECTOR AND TRANSLATOR

INTRODUCTION BY CATHERINE CALLAGHAN

This is a Lake Miwok story, told to me in the summer of 1980 by James (Jimmy) Knight, at Middletown Rancheria in Middletown, California. Lake Miwok was formerly spoken in a triangular area south of Clear Lake, about eighty miles north of San Francisco. This language is closely re-lated to Coast Miwok, once the language of the Marin Peninsula, and more distantly related to the Eastern Miwok languages, once spoken on the western slopes of the Sierra Nevada mountains from the Fresno River north to the Cosumnes River, as well as on the floor of the Great Valley between Ione and Mount Diablo.

Aboriginally, Lake Miwok culture resembled that of its Pomo and Wappo neighbors. Hunting, gathering, and trading expeditions took Lake Miwok Indians from the top of the Coast Range to Bodega Bay. Settle-ments were usually located along stream courses in fertile valleys. Acorns, harvested from a variety of oak trees, comprised the starch staple, and important game animals included deer, elk, rabbits, and squirrels, as well as several species of birds whose feathers were sometimes woven into elaborate basket designs.

Contact with the whites during the nineteenth century was traumatic. Ranchers to the south often kidnapped Lake Miwok Indians for use in work forces, and there were at least two massacres of Clear Lake Indians, one in 1843 and one in 1850. As a result, the Lake Miwok population, which might never have numbered more than five hundred, dwindled to forty-one by the turn of the century, and there are now probably fewer than half a dozen that remember the language, although many more can claim Lake Miwok ancestry.

Jimmy Knight was in his middle years when I first started working with him in the summer of 1956. I had met him through Mrs. Alma Grace, my first consultant, who was living in San Francisco. He and his brother, John Knight, conferred with me in Mrs. Grace's cabin on the Middletown Rancheria. Jimmy told the stories, which his brother later translated sentence by sentence into English. After John Knight's death in 1960, I worked with Jimmy alone, usually at his home.

This story is a version of the Orpheus Myth, common worldwide but surprisingly absent from Judeo-Christian or Islamic traditions. Briefly, the hero (or sometimes, the heroine) grieves over the loss of a loved one and finds a magical route to the Land of the Dead, but after a brief encounter with the dead relative, is forced to leave because he or she is still living.

I elicited an earlier version of this same story from Jimmy during the 1950s, in which the main character is a heroic figure from Lake Miwok history. Otherwise, the principal elements are the same. A brother grieves over the death of his sister, watches at her grave until she rises on the fourth night, and follows her to the top of Mount St. Helena, where her dead relatives greet her and accompany her to the Land of the Dead in the middle of the lake (or ocean). Her brother slips past the chief into the dead people's sweat house, but is forced to go back, following a brief visit. He returns to Cottonwood Place after stopping again on Mount St. Helena, becoming a powerful person who makes a hole through a tree. Although many elements are different, this account may be related to an earlier text that Lucy Freeland elicited from Maggie Johnson (Jimmy's aunt) in 1922, featuring a man who searches for a dead brother.

In the present version, Mr. Knight personalizes the account by casting his father and aunt as the principal characters. Ironically, Maggie Johnson is the dead sister. This version also includes extensive philosophizing, a feature that characterizes the texts Jimmy Knight gave toward the end of his life.

The Orpheus Myth reinforces belief in an afterlife where one will encounter dead relatives, as well as the hope of seeing them even in this life. I once elicited a Northern Sierra Miwok version in which a girl visits her dead mother. My consultant had heard this story after the death of her beloved grandmother, who had raised her from infancy. The heroine must walk across a swinging bridge on her way to the Land of the Dead, an element in a Yokuts Orpheus Myth (see #20a, this volume, for another example) in which the hero is following the ghost of his dead wife. This resemblance suggests a Yokuts origin for the Northern Sierra Miwok account. It is also evident that the Northern Sierra Miwok storyteller had altered its content to fit my consultant's needs—soothing the grief of a young girl whose grandmother has just died.

Versions of the Orpheus Myth were common throughout South-Central California. They were always localized to the storytellers' own tribes, indicating that they had at some previous time made conscious or unconscious alterations to render the accounts more relevant. Such traditions also facilitated the spread of the Ghost Dance during the 1870s, with the belief that dancing and good conduct would bring about the return of dead relatives in the immediate future.

James Knight was a great storyteller, and he brought verve to his art, so that it was a joy to work with him. His rare sense of irony colored the dialogue of his tales, rendering other versions flat by comparison. Especially in his later years, he believed that his mission was to transmit his cultural tradition to Lake Miwok children, and he was distressed over their apparent lack of interest.

It is impossible to reproduce his oral performance on the printed page, and I now regret that I made only tape recordings and no videos. Unfortunately, he is no longer with us (Jimmy died in 1988), and the opportunity is lost.

Translation of an oral account from a non-Western culture into readable English always presents a challenge. I have not included every instance of Lake Miwok words such as *'ekaal* 'then', *'aye* 'however', and *weno* 'they say', which often function as quotation marks or indicators of new sentences, but I have tried to remain as faithful as possible to the original, sometimes at the expense of English style.

In the native-language passage that follows, I present the opening sentences of the story just as Jimmy spoke them to me in Lake Miwok. Underneath the transcription runs a word-for-word gloss of the text. Underneath that comes a more literal translation of the sentence than is found in the translation proper.

Ném   'uṯél-yomi-n   húuni ka-líilaw   'ena.
This.is Magician-Home-of   story   I-tell   will.
This is the Magicians' [Dead People's] Home story I'm going to tell.

Kaníi 'aye   ka-líilaw miṯi kaníi 'aye,
I   however   I-tell   and   I   however
When I tell it, however,

ka-áppi,   ka-'enéene, ka-'únu,   ka-páapa,
my-father,   my-aunt,   my-mother, my-grandfather,
my father, my aunt, my mother, my grandfather,

ka-wée'ama-kon   ṣe   má-t   ka-hóoye.
my-relative-PLURAL also it-into   I-put
my relatives, too—I put them [all] in.

FURTHER READING

One text can only hint at the rich oral tradition Lake Miwok–speakers once enjoyed. Interested readers will find more Lake Miwok traditional stories in English translation in C. Hart Merriam's *The Dawn of the World.* Lucy Freeland's "Western Miwok Texts with Linguistic Sketch" provides two Lake Miwok texts in the original, accompanied by word-for-word running glosses and a free translation; these texts are "The Story of the Two Shamans" and "The Stealing of Hawk's Wife." Another of James Knight's texts, "Coyote the Impostor," appears in Victor Golla and Shirley Silver's *Northern California Texts,* and yet another, "Fire, Flood, and Creation," in William Bright's *Coyote Stories,* both of which include word-for-word translations of the Lake Miwok along with freer renditions. Readers interested in the Central California culture area might consult the appropriate chapters of Malcolm Margolin's *The Way We Lived*.

THE DEAD PEOPLE'S HOME

The story I'm going to tell is about the Dead People's Home. When I tell it, I put in my father, my aunt, my mother, my grandfather, and also my relatives. This way it's easy to tell the story. If I put in someone else, I can't tell it well. That's why I'm telling the truth. It'll come out nicely in the end.

I'm trying this; that's why I'm speaking Lake Miwok. This is Lake Miwok I'm speaking. The white people will translate this and understand it, the words that I'm saying.

They claim that dead people used to rise from the grave in three or four days. They rise up from there and land on the top of Mount St. Helena. That's what they said, the old people who knew. That's how they told it.

Then my aunt died. My father was distressed. "All right, I want to see my sister. That's why I'm going to the grave, and I'm going to sit there. And I'm going to wait for her," he said. Then he sat there about four days or five days, that many days.

He sat there day and night. He said he was sitting there four or five days, and something like wind came. Lots of wind. Then he already knew. My father was a dreamer. My aunt was a dreamer, too. So he just sat there. He didn't cry, he just listened.

In the meantime, something white appeared over his sister's grave. This was a ghost. "Sister! Sister!" he said. "Brother, what are you doing here?" said his sister. (His sister's name was Maggie Johnson; her husband's name was Johnson. So her name was Johnson.) "All right," she said. "You can't go with me, Brother. I'm going to the Chief's Home now, the Dead People's Home. I can't put you there," she said.

He tells it, my father, whose name was Henry, Henry Knight. Both whites and Indians knew he was a doctor, you see. He went doctoring all over. He went to Upper Lake—wherever someone was feeling bad or sick, he went there and doctored them. That's why they knew him all over. He made a lot of life on this earth.

Henry Knight grieved for his sister and went with his sister to the mountain top. From right there, they flew to the middle of the ocean, and they came down right there to the middle, right to the middle of the Pacific Ocean. At that place, there was a great man, a chief, standing inside the sweat house.

"All right, there's one person here that shouldn't have come. And that one will have to go back from here," he said, that's what he told them. Then his sister, Maggie Johnson, spoke to her brother Henry Knight, "All right, that's you. You can't go to the Dead People's Home. So you have to go back from here. You can't go around there. I'm going to leave. So I'm not going to see you again."

This is how they told the story many years ago.

Then he came back home from there, Henry did, from the middle of the ocean. He came out of that sweat house—a beautiful one, he said— the sweat house that was over there. He left his sister there. He came back to Cottonwood Place. He came to the top of the mountain and realized where he had come. He flew from there and hit a tree at Cottonwood Place; he claimed he hit a big tree right in the middle and made a hole there. That tree used to be standing there. But now they've pulled it out and destroyed it.

The chiefs and dreamers and doctors knew him, my father, Henry

Knight. "Where have you been?" they asked. "I've been to the Dead People's Home . . . I came from the Magician's Place, but they wouldn't have me because I'm not dead. They sent me back from the middle of the ocean." That's what he told them.

On that occasion, they danced for four days. For four days they gave a big feast. They celebrated four days. Everything used to go on for four days.

And that's how he became a great man. From then on, he became a doctor, because something was watching over him. That's why his sister was great, too, and helped him. She helped him through dreams. She guarded him with songs. They protected each other by talking. They were both great.

My mother was a doctor, too. My grandfather also was a dreamer. So everything they did came out wonderful, beautiful. They ran the land. They worked for the earth. They cured people. They even made dead people well. They did everything great. Something great granted them this power.

As for me, I claim that God has given them this, because they knew. Because they thought good things. Because they made good rules. Because they had many relatives. Because they did everything the nice way. That's why they were granted many gifts.

Because that's how it was, that's how they taught me. Since they explained it to me that way, here's what I'm telling you now. Now I'm putting what they told me a long time ago onto the tape. So [the tape] is telling you this. My friends and relatives can listen and say, "Yes, this is true." As for me, I'm happy about what I'm saying and what they know about the grave.

So what I'm saying is this. Everything used to happen four times. Look, now they die on this earth. From there they drop into the water. From there, they'll go to heaven. (Not that place, they couldn't put my father in because he hadn't died.) Pretty; up there everything is pretty. Look, this is what they teach us. So we should believe it. We should learn it, become aware of it. I'm sitting here, talking this way now. Here's the way I teach my children, because I feel sorry for them.

As for me, I'm happy to be talking like this today, just like those lying in the grave. My grandfather, my aunt, my relatives are lying in Already-My-Home, resting there. Someday I'm going to see them. That's what I feel. That's what I feel all the time. They are happy for me. And me, I keep dreaming about them.

Sometimes they come to help me. "We've come to help you," that's what they say; I see them night and day. They keep asking me questions, just like a string coming out. They come at me just like a dreamer. And me, I'm glad that something is watching over me. Look how many times I've gotten sick, how many times I could have died, but I haven't gone to the grave yet. I haven't yet gone to Already-My-Home.

Somehow they sympathize with me because of the way I talk and what I'm going to teach the little ones. The plan is still there. That's the way I'm going to work. That's why something great feels sorry for me from someplace.

As for me, I attribute this to God. And so, I'm grateful for this. I always get up in the morning and sleep in the evening. Oh, I'm grateful: make me dream pleasantly and wake up fine in the morning. What causes me pain—my arm, my eyes—press and fix everything.

"I wish." That's what I say for my little ones, too. "All right, watch over them wherever they are playing—they don't understand. They're this way because they don't know." I talk like this all the time, morning and evening.

And me, I'm grateful for what He has put in my head, my feelings, and my blood.

As for me, here's the way I'm going to be from now on. Look: my relatives are all there, my older and younger brothers, my father, my uncle, my grandmother, my aunt, my mother. When I get there, they'll welcome me, that's what I feel now. That's why I'm just sitting here not scared of anything.

I'm happy about what I'm going to do. I just say, "Thank you." I'm grateful and I say, "Thank you." I laugh because I'm happy. When I'm happy, I talk. When I'm happy, I tell things. I'm grateful for whatever they show me. When I'm happy, I'm grateful for everything: trees, birds, water, food.

Before I eat anything, before they help me, I talk to them. As for me, here's the way I'm going to travel: when I go somewhere, I talk to everything— all the cars, horses, carts.

"All right," I say. I've come this far and told this much. Now when I'm telling this, I'm enjoying myself. This far. All right, that's as far as I'm telling now.

My relatives are in the graveyard over there, filling it up. So I'm glad they're lying there peacefully. Some day when I see them, I'll teach them. I'll tell them how wonderfully I live, how He takes care of me here on earth. This is the reason I know. This is the reason I'm teaching the little ones. That's why I've been here a long time.

All right, I'm happy. That's all now.

SOUTH-CENTRAL CALIFORNIA

Kingfisher, kingfisher,
      cover me with your power,
Sho ho, sho ho, na na, het na na, het,
      I am circling around.

              Wikchamni song
           Anna Gayton, "Yokuts
    and Western Mono: Ethnography"

But Čiq'neq'š knew that the devil [*lewelew*] wanted to deceive him, and he began to sing:

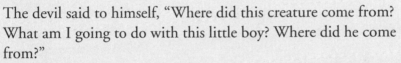

> *Now I am beginning,*
> *Beginning to make my defense.*
> *I have just put my plant in this soil.*
> *I don't know the end.*
> *I barely put my foot on land.*
> *I come from a great distance, from the clouds.*
> *I am the son of all the dead and*
> *That is why I'm hungry.*

The devil said to himself, "Where did this creature come from? What am I going to do with this little boy? Where did he come from?"

And the devil said to Čiq'neq'š: "Do you know that you are under this sun, and that you are seen by means of its light?"

And the boy started thinking, "This fellow is trying to get me all mixed up, but I'm going to make him cry."

So he said to the devil, "Do you know that we all see by the light in which we are?"

Excerpt from "The Čiq'neq'š Myth"
Ventureño Chumash, Fernando Librado
Thomas Blackburn, *December's Child*

20

Two Stories from the Central Valley
"Visit to the Land of the Dead"
and "Condor Steals Falcon's Wife"

YOKUTS

1931, 1930

JOHNNY JONES AND ROSS ELLIS, NARRATORS

STANLEY NEWMAN, COLLECTOR AND TRANSLATOR

INTRODUCTION BY GEOFFREY GAMBLE

The Yokuts people once inhabited the south-central portion of California from roughly the crest of the Tehachapi Range in the south to Stockton in the north and from the Coastal mountains in the west to the western slopes of the Sierra Nevada range in the east. This territory ranged about 350 miles from north to south and about 200 miles east to west and presented great variation in where the Yokuts people lived, from marsh lands and lakes such as Tulare and Kern Lakes to the lush banks of river canyons of the Tule, Kaweah, Kings and San Joaquin Rivers. The Yokuts people were divided into about forty small tribal groups with each tribe recognizable by its name and by its particular dialect. By and large these tribes were friendly to one another, and their dialects were similar enough that speakers from opposite ends of the territory could understand each other. Of the languages and dialects once spoken, no more than a few are spoken today, and many of those speakers live at the Yule Reservation near Visalia, California.

For most Yokuts people, disturbance by white soldiers and settlers did not come until the early 1860s. Such relatively late contact allowed the Yokuts culture and language to remain relatively intact for a much longer period of time than is seen among the coastal groups of California or in many other parts of North America. This means that the tellers of the two Yokuts stories presented here had learned them from speakers who had little or no contact with outsiders, thus considerably enhancing the fidelity of the material.[1]

Our knowledge of the Yokuts languages and dialects primarily comes from the work of Alfred L. Kroeber (1907, 1925), John P. Harrington (1914–1925), Stanley Newman (1944), and Geoffrey Gamble (1978). The Yokuts language group is included within the California Penutian stock, where it is thought to be most closely related to Costanoan and Miwokan and more distantly related to the Maiduan and Wintun families. Specific details of genetic affiliation and subgrouping are still being worked out. Yokuts is a relatively close-knit language family, and internal variation is most clearly seen among the languages and dialects of the southern-most speakers. The two stories here, "Visit to the Land of the Dead" and "Condor Steals Falcon's Wife," come from the Chawchila and Yowlumni dialects, which are fairly closely related linguistically.

The Chawchila people lived in the northern third of Yokuts territory, inhabiting both the Sierra foothills as well as the valley locations along the Fresno River. A large Chawchila village was situated near the present town of Friant where the Fresno River has now been dammed to form Millerton Lake. As with other Yokuts people, storytelling was an evening and winter activity. Good storytellers were clearly recognized by their ability to exploit the syntactic and semantic richness of the Yokuts language and to occasionally provide creative twists on the classic stories known to everyone.

"Visit to the Land of the Dead" is one of the best-known and frequently told stories among the Yokuts people and was also well-known by other tribes in the region. This version was collected by Stanley Newman in the summer of 1931 from Johnny Jones, who lived at Friant, California. A translation of the story was first published by Anna Gayton and Stanley Newman in 1940, but Newman had completed a rough translation, which forms part of his loose note sheets in the Newman collection, much earlier.

Jones's Chawchila version of the tale not only maintains all the features of this classic story, but also provides a richness that clearly indicates a skilled and talented storyteller. The main features of the story include a young couple, recently and happily married, who are punching at each other in playfulness. As the young woman cleans her ear with a small stick, her husband hits her arm and the stick pierces her ear, killing her. The distraught young man then follows his wife to the Land of the Dead, where he is challenged by the "Captain" of the dead people to identify his wife. He does so and is allowed to take his wife back to the land of the living under the condition that once they return they do not have sexual intercourse until after ten days have passed. Naturally, they do not wait the full ten days, and the young man dies. Jones's version includes the young man's confrontation with his mother about the death of his wife, a graveside vigil, a feast in the Land of the Dead, and a complex dialogue with the leader of the dead people.

The second myth, "Condor Steals Falcon's Wife," was told to Newman in the summer of 1930. Ross Ellis is the most likely storyteller, because so much of Newman's Yowlumni text material came from Ellis. This particular telling of the story, which was known not only among the Yokuts people but also by other tribes throughout the region, is unusually rich in detail and complexity. The story takes place in mythic times, when people and animal were one and the same. There is a gathering of the people to share food. While Falcon is away, Condor steals his wife. Falcon goes to the leader, Eagle, and asks for help in finding his wife. Eagle sends out a series of people to look for her (Bottlefly is the one who finally finds her), and eventually, after great daring and suspense, Falcon succeeds in rescuing his wife from the malevolent Condor.

Though the California condor today conjures up a precarious, split image of magnificence and vulnerability for those following its struggle against extinction, the Yokuts tradition as reflected in this telling appears to have focused more on the bird's enormous strength and tenacity. Here, Condor is little more than a monster, a brute who willfully kidnaps his kinsman's spouse and forces her to be his wife, keeping her in a house hidden so high among the crags that it takes magic for Falcon to reach it. Condor is so tough he can't be killed, not even cremated: though his body finally burns up, his head slips away during the night "by itself"

FIGURE 9. Ross Ellis with his son.
Courtesy of the Bancroft Library,
University of California, Berkeley.

and resumes its pursuit. Falcon, fleeing with his rescued wife, repeatedly smashes the head with a rock, but the head just keeps on coming. Taken as a latter-day ecological prophecy, this story lays down powerful odds for the condor's survival. But if the ongoing efforts at reintroduction ultimately fail, the story also leaves us a final monument: the "Echo Rock" where Condor's head finally turned to stone.

NOTE

1. The text of Newman's translations has been slightly altered in the following ways. First, as it is clearly a prominent feature of Valley Yokuts narrative style for storytellers to use what we call the "historic present" tense to highlight key moments and passages in the narrative, these sentences have been cast in italics, as a visual correlate of this special rhetorical heightening effect. Second, to conform more closely with the punctuational style of "Visit to the Land of the Dead," and also to improve readability, many cases of sentence-initial *And* in "Condor Steals Falcon's Wife" have been adjoined to the preceding sentence, either with a comma or a semicolon. For instance, in the second paragraph of that story, the sequence "And Coyote went to him. And he questioned him." becomes "And Coyote went to him, and he questioned him." Third, bracketed interpolations (some Newman's, some the editor's) have been allowed to supplant the pronominal form they clarify. For example, the sentence "But he [Condor] is already losing strength" becomes "But [Condor] is already losing strength." (This tactic has been applied to the first story as well.) Readers interested in checking Newman's original presentation of "Visit to the Land of the Dead" and "Condor Steals Falcon's Wife" may consult the versions in Gamble (1994) and Gayton and Newman (1940), respectively.—HWL

FURTHER READING

See William J. Wallace's "Southern Valley Yokuts" and "Northern Valley Yokuts" for a general overview of Valley Yokuts culture; also Anna Gayton's "Yokuts and Western Mono: Ethnography." For linguistic information, see Stanley Newman's *Yokuts Language of California,* Geoffrey Gamble's *Wikchamni Grammar,* and Alfred L. Kroeber's *Yokuts Dialect Survey.* Several important text collections have been produced: Gamble's *Yokuts Texts,* from which the story "Visit to the Land of the Dead" was taken; Gayton and Newman's "Yokuts and Western Mono Myths," from which the story "Condor Steals Falcon's Wife" was taken; Howard Berman's "Two Chukchansi Coyote Stories"; and Gamble's "How People Got Their Hands." Kroeber's "Indian Myths of South Central California" includes numerous Yokuts myths in English. In a rare stylistic study prior to 1960, Newman considers aspects of Yokuts poetics in "Yokuts Narrative Style." Stanley Newman's notes and field notebooks are housed at the Maxwell Museum of Anthropology, University of New Mexico. Before Newman, J. P. Harrington collected extensive manuscript materials on Yokuts.

VISIT TO THE LAND OF THE DEAD

CHAWCHILA YOKUTS

JOHNNY JONES

They were married six days. And they loved each other; they played with each other and punched each other in fun. And the woman got a little stick, and she twisted it around in her ear. And while she was cleaning her ear, her husband hit her with his hand; and the stick stuck there in her ear, and she died. At his wife's death, he went to tell his mother. "Mama," he said, "my wife died." And his mother said, "How did she die?" "I struck her while she was cleaning her ear." And his mother scolded him.

They mourned all night. And after mourning for two nights, they buried her. And, having buried her, the old ones went home to their houses. And they returned; and the man stayed all night at the grave, and he was taken home. And he returned to the grave and slept there on the foot of the grave. And his sister got him and took him home. And again he returned to that grave in the evening.

And he heard the dead one getting up shortly after sunset. *And she jumps up.* "Eeee," she says, jumping. And the husband saw her jumping and getting up. "I guess my wife is getting better," he says. *And his wife is standing up, shaking the dirt from her; and she goes north.*

And her husband follows. He is snatching at her in vain. And her husband puts his arms around her; he does not grasp her. When he snatched her, she melted away. He kept doing this while going along. And going far ahead, she says to her husband, "Why are you following me?" And her husband did not speak at his wife's words.

And the two of them keep going north. Already they have gone far. When daylight came, she disappeared. And at his dead wife's disappearance, he went to sleep. And toward dusk, he arose. And the dead one went north. He followed her; her husband went along behind her. He continued this while they were going. And she says to him, "Why do you keep following me? Return!" *Her husband does not hear what she is saying. And the two of them keep walking during the night.* And at daybreak he went to sleep where his wife disappeared. *And again evening comes. And the dead one gets up and walks. And they continue, her husband following her.* "Return!" she says to her husband.

And when they arrive at the bridge, [she says], "Don't get frightened. Crow will yell at us; Quail will fly; they will scare us. Don't be frightened at Quail's flying. Perhaps you will fall in the water and become a sturgeon." And her husband replies, "Yes. I don't think I shall fall in." And the woman went ahead; she crossed the bridge and arrived on the other side. And while she was looking back at her husband, he took a step on the bridge. And he shook the bridge, and he crossed over and reached his wife on the other side. And while they were going along, she advised her husband, "Don't follow me! You had better stay back there! Don't go in where the dancers are! You must stay back!" she says to the husband.

And the two of them arrived there where the dead people are. *He follows his wife in vain. He is stopped.* "That is a live man. Stop!" said the Captain to him. *He grasps [the man] with his hand.* And being spoken to, he stopped there; he stared at his wife. And when his wife reached the place where the dead people were dancing, she went in. And he stared at his wife.

And he is troubled there on his heart. "I am hungry," he says there on his heart. And the dead Captain heard his worrying there on his heart. And the Captain says to him, "Why are you troubled? You are hungry; you say you are troubled. Now I shall give you some food." And he gave him acorn mush full of acorn-heads. *And he is troubled there on his heart.* "I don't think I'll get full on this. There is too little." The Captain says to him, "Don't worry about that. You will get full soon." *And he drinks the acorn mush.* And while he was drinking it, it emptied; and again it filled up. *He keeps worrying all the time; doing this, he gets full.* "Here! I am already full doing this. Take your food away!" he says to [the Captain].

And he saw his wife dancing; he stared at his wife. And it became morning; and the dead dancers disappeared. *And her husband sits all day where he had been standing.* All the dead ones disappeared.

At sunset the messengers wake up. They call out; they are busy among themselves; they build a fire; they run around looking for wood. Some of them have already made a fire. Some [of the dead] have already emerged from the fire; they have already sat down, ready for their dance. And when the Captain saw it, he arose next to the place where the live man was. And the dead people emerged. And the messengers made a fire for the dead Captain. And the dead people danced.

And the Captain said to him, "Will you recognize your wife?" "Yes, I think I shall recognize my wife," he said to him. "If you will recognize your wife, then you will bring her [out]."

And there were five dead women, similar to one another. And they looked like recently dead women, but they had been dead a long time. The five dead women were alike beautiful. And the recently dead woman put on her dress. And the Captain said to him, "Recognize your wife!" "Yes, I shall recognize my wife," [said the husband].

At his saying this, the six women came out. *They are very similar!* In the middle, that recently dead woman was placed. And her husband saw her. And having come out, they danced around him. "Can you recognize your wife?" "Yes," he said. "Let us see. Go get your wife and bring her." And the one who was told went straight to his wife; he grasped her on the arm. "Come!" he said to his wife, looking back. "We shall go to the Captain."

And he brought his wife along to the Captain. "Yes," said the Captain. "Sit down!" And she sat by the side of her husband; and the Captain said to them, "You will go home." And they [started to] return. "Wait a little while! Listen to my words!" he said to them. And he advised them, "After arriving at your house, you must not have sexual intercourse for ten days. If you do so before ten days, you [the husband] will return here quickly. You must finish all the days as I am advising. And you will tell your people what you have seen here. You will tell your people, 'I have seen the dead.'"

And after he said that, they went to the road on which they had come; and they crossed the bridge that they had crossed before; and they went to sleep where they had slept before. And they walked all night; and they went to sleep during the day. [They continued this way until] near dusk they reached the place where she had died.

And in the morning he arose and got his people, his father. "I shall tell you what I saw where I went." And his father said, "Yes. Tell what you have seen!" And he related, "I saw many dead ones. They had a good time; they were always dancing; they had a lively time. Our life here is bad. I shall tell you everything that I saw." And his father said, "Yes, my son, tell everything that you saw there." [But] he did not tell [them], "Ten days have been counted for me." He did not relate that he was told, "Don't have sexual intercourse."

And after eight days he wanted to have sexual intercourse; and she would not permit him. [But] when there remained only one day to complete, she permitted him. After having sexual intercourse, he died.

And it became daylight. And his father said, "Tell your older brother to get up!" And being spoken to by her father, [the husband's] younger sister went. "Get up, Older Brother!" He did not wake up. "What's the matter with my older brother? I think he died." And his father came and shook him. "Wake up, my Son!" [But] he did not get up. "My son died," he said.

And they mourned, and his son was buried; he had died. And that is all.

CONDOR STEALS FALCON'S WIFE

YOWLUMNI YOKUTS

ROSS ELLIS

There they were living, above Xɔlmiu (Clover Place) at the foot of this mountain. *Their leaders are thinking about their meeting.* And Eagle said, "Tell Cougar and Big Eagle and his friend, the large Crow, and their crier, Dove, and Coyote and Falcon and Wolf." And Coyote was sent. *Now he is going to assemble the people.* "In seven days we will assemble." *Now they will be told—Wind and Thunder and Dog too.* And Coyote informed them, and Wind said, "Of course I can go anywhere. But tell Thunder. Will he go?" And, "I'm not sure that he can," he added.

And the seven days came, and already all the people were assembling there. And Thunder did not come. *The booming noise he makes is useless; he can't walk.* And Coyote went to him. And he questioned him, and Thunder said, "I can't go anywhere. Tell my friend and he will come." And Wind went to him, and there he arrived. And he said to him, "What's the matter with you! Aren't you able to walk? Haven't I been telling you, I'll see to it that you will go where they want you? Are you ready to leave now?" he says to him. "Stand up now, and you will speak," he says to him. "Ready?" Wind says to him. "Yes," then says Thunder. "Speak now," he says to him. "Will we go now?" And Thunder spoke. Just as soon as he spoke, the two of them walked off.

And they arrived there immediately, and their leader, Eagle, said to him, "Have you arrived already?" he says to him. And [Thunder] said to him, "This gathering of ours is certainly a small one. How is that?" Thunder says. "These are important people. I am thinking about our going west," says Eagle. "All the seeds are now getting ripe again." "Good," they say. "But who will go to look them over?" they say. "Antelope," they say. And Antelope said, "In the morning I will go." And he went, and there he arrived. To his surprise, there were a great many seeds. And he took a great many; he placed them in both his feet. And he arrived after sundown.

And, as before, Coyote assembled the people, and all the people assembled. A large covering was already spread over the ground. *On it he is now going to pour his load.* And he poured it, and they said, "There is certainly a lot." And, "Count these important people," they say to Dove. *Now they are going to divide it.* And each of them took his share, and the unimportant ones took what was left, and all of them were pleased. *Having taken their food, all of them will now prepare it.* And Falcon's friend, Crow, ate a lot of black seeds, and he turned black. "Well," says their leader, "in seven days we will go."

Now they are going to gather food. And the seven days arrived, and some of them asked their leader, "In how many days will we return?" "In three days." And they said, "There is food enough for our children."

And all the people went, and there they arrived; and they got many seeds. And in three days they returned.

And Falcon probably got a great many. And he said to his wife, "I'll take some of this, and I'll come right back." And his wife was working; she was getting more. And the woman heard him coming. *She looks about, but she does not see anything.* And Condor alighted close to her, and after alighting he said to her, "Are you the wife of my younger brother?" he says to her. "Is he your younger brother?" she says to him. "Yes," he says. "His name is Tsopnix." And the woman said to him, "What is your name?" she says. "Condor," he says. "So we will go now," Condor says to her. He says to her, "Take off your necklace." Her necklace was money—small beads and big dark beads and small bone beads. And she said, "No!" but it was useless. "Why should I?" she says to him. "I'm afraid he'll be angry," she says to him. "No," she says. "We will go now," [Condor said]. He took her away by force.

And then Falcon arrived after they had gone, and he couldn't find his wife. And in vain he looked for their footprints. He found nothing. And from there he returned. And he arrived at the leader's house, and the leader said to him, "Why are you alone?" "I can't find her," he says. And the leader said, "I think she has been stolen from you. Now we'll assemble the people," the leader says to him. And he sent Dove. "Assemble the people," he says. And Dove got all the people. "Falcon's wife has been stolen," he says. "Now Eagle will ask the people," he says. "Who's going to find her?" he says.

And all the people assembled, and he asked all of them, "Who can find out where she went?" And Buzzard said, "I'll try. But he must take me where she was stolen," Buzzard said. And there Falcon took him where she was stolen, and there they arrived. "For one day I will search for her," he says. And Buzzard searched all the ravines. *He looks down all the impassable places. He comes down. Where is she hidden? And in vain he goes up again. He finds nothing.*

He did not find anything. He worked for one day, and he returned. And, as before, all the people assembled, and they asked him, "What happened on your journey?" "I didn't find anything," he says. "I walked over the whole world, but it was useless," he says. "I didn't find anything."

And the leader said, "Now you," he says to Wind. "Yes," says Wind. "I think I can do something. I try to get in everywhere over the whole world," says Wind. And there Falcon took him, and they arrived there. "Is this it?" says Wind to him. "Yes," says Falcon. "Well, I'll walk now," he says. "I will arrive there after sundown," he says. And Falcon says to him, "Well, I am going now," he says. And Wind walked over the whole world. He did not find anything. He worked for one day. And he arrived late at the leader's house, and the leader asked him, "What happened on your journey?" he says to him. "I didn't find anything," he says.

"Now you," Bottlefly is told. And there Falcon took him, and they arrived there. "Did she go from here?" he says to him. And he stood right there where the woman had been sitting. And he said to Falcon, "You must not go anywhere. You must wait for me right here," he says to him. And Bottlefly says, "From here I'll find out where she went. I'll turn around here," he says. "East," and also, "North," he says, and also, "West," and also, "South." And Falcon said, "Where is she?" he says. "Not there," Bottlefly says. "She went far up," he says. "You must wait for me right here," he says.

And there he went far up, and there he remained. *He sniffs in all directions.* And he turned around, and he saw a house. It was the house of the thief. And there Bottlefly went. And on entering his house, he slipped. *He falls on his back.* His house was slippery. And it was quiet there. And he saw the woman. From there he returned. He seemed to be very quick.

He came there where Falcon remained, and he reached Falcon, and Falcon said to him, "Where?" And he said to him, "She is up there." "I have known it for a long time. I have been thinking," says Falcon. "It is best that we return, and I will go in the morning."

And they returned, and they arrived at the leader's house, and the people assembled. *Now they will listen to the one who found her.* And all the people assembled. And the leader questioned Bottlefly. "The two of us arrived there where she was stolen," he says. "We arrived there," he says. "And I couldn't find her east or north or west or south," he says. "Well! She went above," he says. "And there I arrived far up," he says. "There she was," he says, "that woman." And Coyote said, "I have known it for a long time," he says. And he named him. "That is his name," he says. "Condor," he says. "All of his body is stone, but his heart can be seen through his back," he says. And Eagle said to him, "Is he certain to fight us if he comes?" he says; and then he said, "Sparrow Hawk is Falcon's younger brother. Yayil is his name." And Falcon said, "In the morning I will get her," he says.

And in the morning Falcon went. He took his musical bow. And far off there he arrived, and there he placed it where his wife had been. And there he sat on his musical bow. And he went up. That musical bow of his took him up.

And far above he came out through a hole in the world, and after coming out he stood there. And there he saw the house. And there he went. And there he arrived at the door, and he said to her, "Come out." And she said to him, "Who are you?" And Falcon said to her, "It is I." "So it is you," she says to him. "Now I will come out," she says to him, and she came out with a string of human bones around her neck. And Falcon said to her, "Take off your necklace. Now we will go," he says to her. And from there they went to the place where he had come out, and they arrived there, and there he placed his musical bow. They sat in the middle of it. And from there they descended far below. And from there they went to their house where their leader was. There they arrived. *At their arrival, the people are happy.*

And then Condor, the fighter, arrived at his house, and there he saw their wife's necklace; she had thrown it on the door. And at that he immediately got ready to go. *Now he is going to follow his wife.* And he descended far below; and from there he went. *Now he will go toward them.* And far off there he arrived; and he asked them, "Where does Tsopnix live?" he says. And Falcon was told, "Condor is looking for you." "Has he come already?" he says. "Yes," says the speaker. And there went Falcon.

All the people are getting very frightened. "Hello," Tsopnix says to him; "It is really you." "Hello," says Condor. "So you took our wife," he says. "Therefore," Condor says to him, "therefore, we will settle it between ourselves. If you kill me, then you will take our wife. But if I kill you, then I will take her," he says. "Which one will shoot first?" he says. "I will be first," says Falcon.

And they went far off to an open plain. "Ready?" Falcon says to him. And it seems that he conjured up a fog. And "Ready?" says his opponent. And many stones fell where Falcon was standing. And Condor asked him, "Where are you?" his opponent says to him. "I'll take my turn with you. Now I come," Falcon says to him. And he conjured up a fog again. *Soon his younger brother will go in a circle around him. He has many wiregrass [cane] arrows now. He is shooting at the heart through Condor's back. There this heart of his could be seen.* "Well, get ready now," Falcon says to him. "Now I will shoot at you. Three times I will shoot at you," he says to him. "Ready," he says to him. "Get ready now. Now I will shoot at you." And he shot at him. Many stones dropped from his body when he shot. And he shot at him again; and, as before, stones dropped there. And, "Where are you?" Falcon says to him. "Here I am," he says.

"Now I will take my turn with you. I come next," Condor says to him. "Good," says Falcon. "Ready?" he says to him. "Ready," then says Falcon. *His younger brother still keeps shooting at him through his back.* And he conjured up a fog again, and many stones dropped where he was standing. And again he went far off to a different place. And he says to him, "Where are you?" "I am standing here," says Falcon.

"And now I will take my turn with you. I will come next again," Falcon says to him. *Already Condor is losing strength. Now he is going to shoot at him again.* And a lot of stones fell; they seemed to be very large ones.

"Again," Falcon says to him. And he shot at him again. "There is one more," he says to him. "Now I'll shoot at you again," he says to him. *But [Condor] is already losing strength.* And, "Again," he says to him. And finally he fell down. *Yet he does not stop talking.* And then they rested. *Now he does not get up. Now he has fallen.*

And, "What are we going to do with him?" says Coyote. "We will burn him," say all these people. And all of the people gathered wood. They piled it there where he had fallen, and it was set on fire, and the fire died out. Nothing was burning. "Hello," says Falcon to him. "Hello," then says Condor. "So! You are still alive," Falcon says to him. "There is nothing you can kill me with," [Condor] says to him. And another kind of wood was gathered; and, as before, it was again piled there where he is lying, and, as before, it was set on fire. It was not burning any longer. "Hello," Falcon says to him. "It is really you. Hello," he says to him. "I am well," he says. "So! You will not die," Falcon says to him.

And Coyote was asked, "What will we burn him with? He does not burn up," they say. And, "With grass," Coyote says; "with that he will burn," he says. And a lot of grass was brought. *Now he will be burned with it.* And it was set on fire. And all of his body was burning. *But his head still talks.* "We have probably killed him now. Leave him right there," he says.

And they stayed over night. And during the night the head, by itself, went away. His body was not there. And Falcon got the head and took it away. And the head got angry at being taken. *Now the head will try many times to harm him. And again Falcon takes it in his hands. Now he is going to keep smashing it down on these stones.* And again it kept trying to harm him.

And finally Falcon said, "We had better go to my father's sister." And Falcon and his wife went off. *Now they are going to run away.* And the two of them went. And now the head came again. It was trailing them now. And again it overtook them. Again it failed to do any harm to Falcon. And, as before, Falcon took it and kept smashing it down. He broke it in many pieces. And again the two of them went off. And again it overtook them as they were nearing his father's sister's house. And, as before, he again kept smashing it down. And with that the two of them went off again. And his father's sister shouted, "Run," she says to him. "You are coming close now," she says to him. They were getting very near. And now the head was approaching them again, and already it was overtaking them. Just as it approached, the rock closed shut. Just as it closed, the head arrived there. There the head broke. There it became Echo Rock.

And then Eagle was asked, "Where will you go?" he is asked. "Here in the mountain I am going to roam," he says then. And Cougar also was asked, "Where will you go?" he is asked. "Here in the mountain I am going to roam," he says. "I'll kill many deer," he says. Falcon also says, "I too will walk here in the mountain," he says. And Coyote was also asked, "Where will you go?" he is asked. "Here I will walk on the plains. Maybe I will steal something there," he says. And Crow also was asked. "I'll walk west," he says. "Maybe something will die, and I will eat its eyes," says Crow. That is the end.

21

The Contest between Men and Women

TÜBATULABAL
CIRCA 1932

MIKE MIRANDA, NARRATOR
ERMINIE WHEELER VOEGELIN, COLLECTOR

INTRODUCTION BY CHRIS LOETHER

The classic myth "The Contest between Men and Women" transcends
the cultural milieu of its origins in the universal, timeless appeal of the
issue at the heart of the story, the gender roles played out by men and
women in human societies.[1] The story was told to Erminie Wheeler
Voegelin, in English, by Mike Miranda during one of her summer field-
trips to Tübatulabal country in Central California between 1931 and 1933.
She had been collecting ethnographic information from Miranda, who
offered this myth in answer to her question of whether women had ever
had a role in hunting.

Mike Miranda, whose Tübatulabal name was Yukaya, was about forty-
three years old at the time he worked with Erminie. Although his mother
was from the neighboring Yokuts tribe, his father, Steban Miranda, was
the last hereditary chief of the Tübatulabal. (After his father's death in
1955, the Tübatulabal were ruled by a Council of Elders until the early
1970s. At that time they joined with the neighboring Koso Shoshone and

Kawaiisu tribes to form the Kern Valley Indian Community, which gained tax-exempt status in 1987, though they are still fighting for federal recognition by Congress.)

The Tübatulabal consisted of three bands in aboriginal times: the Pahkanapil, the Palagewan, and the Bankalachi, which occupied three connected valleys formed by the confluence of the Kern River and the South Fork Kern River in the southern Sierra Nevada mountains. The Tübatulabal have no migration myths such as the Mojave and Navajo have; according to their traditions, they have always lived in those three valleys. Linguistic and archaeological findings confirm that they have been right where they now are for a very long time indeed. The archaeological evidence indicates that the Tübatulabal's ancestors probably occupied Kern River territory as early as 1200 B.C. They are clearly distinguished archaeologically at this early time from their Numic-speaking neighbors in terms of settlement patterns, lithic materials, rock art, and milling equipment (Moratto 1984:559). And the comparative linguistic evidence indicates that, by 1500 B.C., the Tübatulabal were already becoming distinct in language from their closest linguistic relatives, the Numic-speaking peoples of the Great Basin, such as the Shoshone, Western Mono (Monache), Owens Valley Paiute, and Kawaiisu.

The Tübatulabal first encountered the whiteman in 1776—ironically, the American year of independence—with the arrival in their territory of two different Spanish expeditions. But the people were spared the brunt of outside immigration into Native California until the 1850s, when the California Gold Rush brought hordes of newcomers into their valleys. A turning point (though not a good one) came in 1863, when some thirty-five to forty innocent Tübatulabal men were massacred by the local white population in retaliation for cattle-raids by Indians in the Owens Valley. After this time it was no longer safe to be a Tübatulabal in Tübatulabal country.

The early California anthropologist Alfred Kroeber estimated the Tübatulabal population to have been between five hundred and one thousand at time of Contact (1925:608), though this figure may be low. By the early 1990s there were approximately four hundred Tübatulabal who still lived in the three valleys, and an additional five hundred living away from the traditional homeland (Holmes-Wermuth 1994:661). As of this writing, there are less than half a dozen fluent speakers of the language.

Culturally the Tübatulabal straddle the border between two Native culture areas: California to the west and the Great Basin to the east. The Tübatulabal show influences from both culture areas. In their three valleys the Tübatulabal had access to both acorns (the main staple of California Indian people) and pine-nuts (the main staple of Great Basin Indian people). Influences from these two culture areas seem to permeate all aspects of Tübatulabal culture. Their mythology has been classified as being Great Basin in character (Gayton 1935:588, 595), but their religious rituals and material culture are clearly more similar to their California neighbors, such as the Yokuts. These dual cultural influences are reflected in "The Contest between Men and Women" where, contrary to the norm in Tübatulabal society for each politically independent band to have but one chief, there are two chiefs, Eagle and Coyote. Eagle is the character who is most often the chief in Central California mythology, and Coyote is the culture-hero par excellence of Great Basin mythology.

The Tübatulabal yearly cycle was similar to that of their Sierran neighbors. They spent the winter in permanent villages along the rivers in the three valleys and then migrated to family camps in the mountains during the summer months. Sex roles were strictly determined in Tübatulabal society, with the men hunting and the women gathering. Contact between women and men was strictly limited during certain critical periods—particularly while women were menstruating, and for a several-day period before men went hunting. There were, however, special times when everyone participated in certain food gathering activities, such as fishing in July, the pine-nut harvest in early fall, the acorn harvest in late fall, or occasional rabbit and antelope drives.

Tübatulabal cosmology and worldview were similar to that of their neighbors in that they believed in a previous world that had been inhabited by animals with supernatural powers and very human characteristics. These mythological "animal people" became the animals of this world when the current world, along with humans, was created. The story given here is set in the world of myth-time.

Let us now look at some of the cultural aspects found in the myth itself, which addresses the age-old question of why the sexes play different roles that seem in some way inherently predetermined. In this myth, it appears that men and women were created equal in the beginning, since the story hints that, were it not for Coyote's magic at the last moment, the division of labor might well have turned out differently.

As the story opens, we find the men all living by themselves. While they are out hunting all day, Coyote stays home, gathering and stacking wood for each man's camp. (Coyote here is playing the traditional role of the *berdache,* the man who stays in camp and does women's work, such as gathering and preparing food, and therefore must wear women's clothes.) What is notable is that the men know *only* how to hunt—there is no mention of any plant foods (the product of women's labor) in their camp. The women, on the other hand, who are also living by themselves, enjoy both hunted *and* gathered foods.

When the men discover the women's camp, they send Road Runner to investigate.[2] Interestingly enough, after Road Runner has arrived in the women's camp and been offered food to eat, it is the chia, a plant food, that makes him sick. Despite its thematic symbolism, though, the scene where Road Runner loses his lunch also happens to be one of the best comic moments in the story:

> Pretty soon he vomited—
> oh, vomited!—
> and everything came up;
> Lizard came up;
> he vomited Lizard and the chia too.
> Lizard,
> he chased all those women;
> they got up,
> and ran,
> and those women said,
>   "What kind of food does this man *eat?*" they said.

The women, a sensible crew overall, are clearly disgusted by this startling turn of events. On top of it all, Lizard, once on the loose again, starts running around like a sex-starved maniac when he sees all the women standing around gaping at Road Runner.

After three days, the women move to the men's camp. Now begins the big adjustment for the men (which, one can argue, is still being played out among humans today). At first they take turns with the daily tasks. First the men go hunting, while the women stay at home and prepare the acorn, pine-nuts, and other plant foods. Next the women hunt, and the men stay at home. Unlike the previous day, though, the women are all successful in their hunting; furthermore, most of the men have problems in preparing the plant foods. This leads to a lot of grumbling on the part of the men, especially Coyote, who devises the final "shooting contest" to determine who gets to go out hunting and who has to stay at home to grind seeds.[3]

The women in this myth seem to be inherently superior, in overall competence, to the men. This portrayal in turn sets up the comic necessity for Coyote to have to "cheat" in order to win the contest, thereby garnering for men the "right" to hunt and establishing for all time the division of labor between the sexes—the gender roles that characterize Tübatulabal society in their native world. The Tübatulabal have traditionally believed that they should model their behavior on that of the previous world, because the mythological animal people were so much more powerful and knowledgeable than humans are today. After all, myths (in any culture) not only explain the origins of the world as we know it, but also validate its status quo.

Just as every story has a purpose, every storyteller has a reason for telling a particular story at a particular moment to a particular audience. This time, the story wasn't told to a Native Tübatulabal audience, but was told in English to a female anthropologist, who wrote it down in a notebook in the course of collecting ethnographic information. Before the advent of recording equipment, taking down a text was a very tedious and time-consuming process, involving constant breaks in the flow of the narration. Despite these difficult conditions, Mike Miranda managed to keep his mind in his story and present a coherent text, formally structured and richly detailed, with its comic flair intact.

One is always tempted to look for the storyteller in the story itself. If Mike Miranda is "in there" at all—his cultural beliefs, his chiefly family background, his sense of the world—it is probably his gift for humor that is best revealed in "The Contest between Men and Women."

NOTES

1. The only published source for this myth is in Erminie Voegelin's ethnography of the Tübatulabal (1937:53–55). The version of the story that appears here is taken from the Charles F. and Erminie Voegelin Papers (1931–1933:26–31) in the Bancroft Library at Berkeley. The two versions are virtually the same in text; the only significant change from either involves the presentational form of the story as it appears in this volume. The ragged-line format was discerned by the

editor, Herbert Luthin, based strictly on the transparently prosodic punctuation patterns in Erminie Voegelin's prose transcription. Punctuation therefore follows prosodic-intonational contours, rather than the usage rules of formal written English. (The paragraph boundaries of the original typescript are indicated by the conjunction of a line space and a flush-left margin.) Finally, in the Bancroft typescript, Voegelin notes occasional accompanying gestures and other performance cues that she recorded at various points in the story. These gesture notes, or their likely content, are presented in the right margin of the text.

2. We have opted not to normalize Erminie's rather charming spelling of Roadrunner's name.—HWL

3. This contest seems similar in some ways to public contests that were traditionally held between shamans to show off their skills and instill respect and awe in the lay population.

FURTHER READING

For those interested in further reading concerning the Tübatulabal, Erminie Voegelin's "Tübatulabal Ethnography" is the best primary source. The most complete published collection of Tübatulabal myths and legends is found in Carl F. Voegelin's "Tübatulabal Texts," including the bilingual autobiography of the storyteller, Mike Miranda (1935:223–241). There is also a collection of largely unpublished Tübatulabal stories in Voegelin and Voegelin's "Tübatulabal Myths and Tales" at the Bancroft Library in Berkeley. Other general sources that include sections on the Tübatulabal are Alfred Kroeber's *Handbook of the Indians of California,* Charles Smith's article "Tübatulabal" in the California volume of the Smithsonian *Handbook,* and Carol Holmes-Wermuth's article "Tübatulabal" in *Native America in the Twentieth Century: An Encyclopedia.*

THE CONTEST BETWEEN MEN AND WOMEN

There were a lot of people living,
    and Eagle and Coyote were chiefs—
    and all of them were men;
    there were no women.

And they hunted rabbits;
    every day.
    Coyote stayed home every time they went;
    he never went hunting,
    he just hauled wood for them;
    he hauled wood for every camp.
    That's all Coyote did all the time.

And when they got tired of rabbits, you know,
    they went to hunt deer for a change.
    And when all of them went to hunt deer the next day they
        went farther off,
    way up in the mountains.
    And they saw smoke from there,
    way across up on another mountain.
    And they said,
        "Maybe somebody is living over there—
        people."
    And one of them said,
        "I think we should tell Coyote about it,
        when we get home tonight."
    That's what he said.

And they came home in the evening;
    every one had a deer,
    and Coyote had all the wood,
    piled up at every camp.
    And they cut a little piece of meat,
    every one,
    and gave it to Coyote for his work.
    Coyote ate that.

And pretty soon they told Coyote after supper,
        "We saw smoke from the top of the mountain,
        across on a mountain,
        far away."

And Coyote said,
        "Maybe somebody is over there;
        let's send somebody tomorrow and find out."

And they picked one man;
they said,
   "This fellow—
   Road Runner.
   He goes fast," they said.

And next morning Road Runner went,
   after breakfast,
   and those fellows went again,
   to hunt deer.
   And Coyote stayed home,
   and hauled wood for the camp.

And that fellow, he went;   *[gesturing]*
   he went way up on the mountain,
   and when he saw Lizard running quickly,
   close to him,
   Road Runner ran close,   *[gesturing]*
   grabbed Lizard,
   picked him up,
   and ate him.
   Lizard was his life, I think—
   Road Runner just swallowed him.

And those women—
   lots of women over there at a big pit mortar bed—   *[nodding]*
   a long one;
   and there lots of women were grinding pine-nuts.
   They were all sitting down there,
   grinding them.
   There were no men;
   all women.

And pretty soon one woman said,
   "Oh!" she said,
   "the edge of my vagina is shaking,"
   and they laughed;
   all laughed.
   And pretty soon another woman over there said,   *[pointing]*
   "Oh! Mine too.

The edge of my vagina is shaking."
Pretty soon somebody said,
    "Maybe somebody is coming;
    some man is coming."
And they said,
    "Maybe."

And then one of these women looked that way and saw one
    man coming.   *[nodding]*
She said,
    "You see.
    I told you,
    somebody is coming,
    coming over there now."

And Road Runner saw those women,
    lots of women;
    he saw those women sitting down there,
    all of them.
    And Road Runner came there;
    he said, "Hello!"

All those women said, "Hello,"
    and they asked him what he was doing way up there.
    And Road Runner said,
        "Those fellows saw smoke yesterday," he said,
        "from a long way across the mountain;
        and they told me to come and find out if somebody
            were living here.
    All of them are men over there," he said.

    "And here no men,"
        they told Road Runner;
    "all women."

And pretty soon they all of them got up,
    and they called to Road Runner,
        "Come on;
    come on down to the house,"
    and Road Runner went with them.

When they came down to the house,
they told Road Runner,
    "Come in,"
and they took a big basket—
homol, you know—
and they mixed chia in there,
about full,
and they gave it to that man,
to eat;
and a piece of meat:
deer meat.

And Road Runner drank it all, you see,
and when he was through eating,
he sat down there for a while,
and pretty soon the chia made him sick;
he felt like vomiting,
that man.
Pretty soon he vomited—
oh, vomited!—
and everything came up;
Lizard came up;
he vomited Lizard and the chia too.   *[grimacing]*
Lizard,
he chased all those women;
they got up,
and ran,
and those women said,
    "What kind of food does this man eat?" they said.
Lizard was alive, you know.

And those women came back after the man got all right;
the man recovered, you know;
and those women came back.

And one woman went into the house and brought chia seeds,
tied up in a little bag.
She said,
    "When you get home,

give this to that Mountain Lion Man," she said.
And Road Runner said,
    "All right."

(That's a Mountain Lion Woman—
all that company of women,
were all different—
Hawk Woman,
Mountain Lion Woman,
Coyote Woman.
And it was just the same over there—   [pointing]
Mountain Lion Man,
Hawk Man,
and all the rest.)

And another woman—
    Hawk Woman—
came out,
and she had the same thing,
a little bag of acorns.
She gave it to that man;
    "When you get home you give this to that Hawk Man."
Road Runner said, "All right."

Well.
    All of them gave that man a little bag for those fellows.
    Road Runner said, "All right."
    And last of all came one big woman,
    a fat woman;
    she had a little bag,
    and she said,
        "You give this to Coyote."

And those women said,
        "After three days we will go over there;
        three days from now we will all go over there."
    Road Runner said, "All right,"
    and set off for home;
    he had a big load.

And Coyote, over there—   [pointing]
  Coyote looks all the time to watch for Road Runner's
    return;
  he is in a hurry,
  he wants to see.
  He goes up a hill and looks,
  every little while,
  to see when Road Runner returns.

Then he saw Road Runner coming,
  in the evening.
  Coyote went over to meet him;
  he was curious.
  Coyote said,
    "Did you find out,
    about everything over there?"
  And Road Runner said,
    "Oh," he said,
    "You'd better wait;
    you don't want to find out now;
    you'd better wait."

Coyote just came alongside of Road Runner;
  he said,
    "Hurry up—   [whispering]
    you'd better tell me!"
  Road Runner said,
    "Wait,
    until those fellows come home.
    Then you'll find out," he said.

Pretty soon those fellows came in in the evening;
  those men.
  And after supper they all gathered together;
  they are going to find out now.
  And Road Runner said,
    "They are all women over there,
    lots of them.
    And they gave me little bags," he said.

"They told me to give them to you."

(Well,
maybe that's a present—
something,
you know,
to give to the men.)

Road Runner gave all those men what the women had given
    him;
    Road Runner told those men,
        "Those women said they were going to come,
      in three days,"
    and Coyote said,
        "Good, good, good!" said Coyote.   *[laughing]*

And after three days, those women came,
    after three days.
    Every one of them had a load;
    some had acorns,
    chia,
    pine-nuts,
    all kinds;
    all different seeds.
    And all of them had bows and arrows;
    all of them had arrows,
    all those women.
    And Road Runner went to meet those women, you see;
    he was going to tell them about each man,
    where each was living, you see—
    in which house.

And Road Runner said,
        "There's that Mountain Lion Man's house over there;
      he is living over there,"
    and Mountain Lion Woman went over there.
        "And there's Hawk's house over there—
      Hawk's,"
    and Hawk Woman went over there.
    All those women,

every one,
went this way,   *[points]*
and that way,   *[points]*
and the last one—
oh!—
a big woman,
came,
and Road Runner said,
    "There's Coyote's house,
    way over there,"   *[pointing]*
and the big woman went over there.

The next day all those men went hunting, you know,
and those women,
all of them went to grind acorns,
and chia, you know.
And those men returned in the evening,
and those women had everything ready,
all cooked,
and those men came home and ate.

And the next day those women told those men,
    "We are going to hunt now,
    and you men go grind some acorns";
they told those men that, you know.

And those women returned in the evening and they had deer,
every one of them, you know—
those women.
And those men,
some of them,
had gotten through early;
they had returned home,
and some of them were still over there,
cooking acorns, you know—
they didn't know how to very well, you know.

And came sundown;
    Coyote hadn't come home yet;
    he was still up at the pit mortar working.

Coyote was pretty mad;
at sundown he hadn't come home yet,
and his wife went over there,
to help her man.
And they got through,
and came home.

And the next day all the men went up on the hill to hunt,
and all the women went to grind acorns;
all of the men went to hunt deer,
Coyote too.
He didn't haul any more wood;
he went to hunt deer.

When they got way up in the mountains,
Coyote said,
"You fellows wait," he said.
"We are going to talk about those women," he said,
and they stopped.
And Coyote said,
"These women,
they have arrows,
and they hunt,
and they send us over there to grind acorns,"
Coyote said.
"That's not right," he said.
"I think women better handle the mortar," he said,
(you know,
where they grind pine-nuts—)
"that's just right for them;
that's woman's work," he said.
"Not man's," he said.

"And tomorrow,"
Coyote said,
"we are going to talk;
to have a big talk," he said;
"we are going to shoot at a target," he said.
"If those women win,

then they can handle the arrow," he said,
    Coyote said.
"If *we* win,
then we keep hunting and handle the arrow,
and women keep handling the mortars,
all the time."

And everybody said,
    "All right,
    we'll do that."

When they returned home in the evening,
    after supper Coyote told those men and women,
    everybody,
    to gather;
    he said,
        "We are going to have a big talk here."
    And Coyote told them all,
        "Tomorrow we are going to shoot a target;
        if you women win then you can handle the arrows and
            we can handle the mortars,
        and grind acorns," he said.
        "But this way,
        you women hunt and we handle the mortars;
        that's not right,"
            said Coyote.
        "That's woman's work," he said.

        "Tomorrow morning,"
            Coyote said,
        "I will put up a target over there;
        we will shoot," he said.
    Those women said,
        "All right."

And Coyote didn't sleep that night, you know;
    he got up,
    at midnight;
    he went way up on top of the mountain, you know,
    and built a fire way up on top.

And when he came back home he said,
    "You fellows get up now;
    the morning star is up now;
    you get up,
    hurry."

And Road Runner looked and said,
    "Oh, that's not the morning star over there;
    that's a fire you built up there on top of the mountain,
    you devil,"
      Road Runner said.
  Coyote said,
    "Hurry up!"
but everybody went back to sleep again.

And when daylight came they all got up;
    and after breakfast Coyote went out,
    and set a target over there,
    and Coyote said,
      "Everybody line up," he said,
      "get ready."
  And one of those women,
  Mountain Lion Woman,
  was a pretty good shooter,
  pretty hard to beat with an arrow.

And every woman stood here with her husband,   *[gesturing]*
    and they were going to shoot together,
    each woman and her husband,
    at the same time.
    And Coyote and his wife stood way over there on the edge.
    And Coyote said,
      "I'm going first;
      I'm going to shoot first."   *[laughing]*
    He wanted to win, you know.   *[laughs]*

And Coyote said,
    "You ready?"
  and his wife said,
    "Yes,"

and they shot.
And they never hit the target;
Coyote missed the target,
and his wife too;
they didn't hit the target.

Coyote said,
    "Next,
    ready," he said,
and the next two shot,
and they never hit the target.
And all of them missed;
just two,
Mountain Lion and his wife,
had not yet shot.
And Coyote said,
    "You fellows next,"
and then Coyote, he came round to Mountain Lion;
he told Mountain Lion,
    "You shoot good;   *[gesturing]*
    your wife is a good one,
    but you shoot good," he said.

And when they were ready to shoot,
    one man shot—   *[pantomimes*
    that was Mountain Lion,   *drawing bow]*
    and his wife shot too.
Coyote said,
    "Break,
    you string,
    break!"
and Mountain Lion Woman's string broke,
and her arrow went to one side.
And that Mountain Lion,
Mountain Lion hit right in the center;
that man hit it.
And those women lost, you know;
the men won.
Coyote said,

"Now," he said,
"all right;
you women handle the mortars," he said,
"we will handle the arrows," he said.

"We are men,"
    said Coyote.

And those men won,
    and lived there.

That's the end.

the family established a home in the city that remained Harrington's main base of operations throughout his life. Following his graduation from Stanford University in 1905, Harrington spent his *wanderjahr* studying at the Universities of Leipzig and Berlin with linguistic giants such as Eduard Sievers and Karl Brugmann. He evidently planned to return to study with Franz Nikolaus Finck in Berlin, to whom he became close during this German year; the plan was cut short by Finck's untimely death in 1910. At this point, Harrington was seriously considering extended fieldwork among the languages of the Caucasus. Finck, both personally and through his published writings, may have been instrumental in shaping the young Harrington in his characteristic way of approaching unfamiliar languages. Finck's 1899 work on an Irish Gaelic dialect, *Die araner Mundart* (The dialect of the Aran Islands), is based upon the result of a brief, intensive period of living "in the field" with the islanders in the remote western extreme of Ireland. Finck stressed the need for work with remote dialects, even of relatively well-known languages (as Gaelic was at the time), in order to carry out comprehensive comparative work on related languages. These ideas are features of Harrington's work throughout his life.

Between 1906 and 1912, Harrington cast about for a purpose in life. He never seemed to want to venture far from his boyhood home for long (his letters home from Germany are touchingly domestic), and among other things, he taught modern languages (German and Russian) at Santa Ana High School, worked on Mojave and Yuman (at Kroeber's behest), worked in several southwest fields in connection with employment at the School of American Archaeology, helped Edgar Lee Hewett prepare exhibits for the 1915 Panama-California Exposition in San Diego, and gave several series of summer lectures on anthropology and linguistics in Colorado and Washington State. He considered some academic options: further study in Germany, a graduate fellowship in anthropology at Berkeley (arranged by Kroeber, but turned down by Harrington), work on Caucasian languages, and graduate study at the University of Chicago. In 1912, however, for some reason (had he heard that Kroeber was busy in the Chumash area?) he returned home and began the work that formed a focal point for much of the rest of his life: his Chumash fieldwork. He worked on every Chumash dialect for which he could find a speaker, in a frenetic attempt to record everything. He and his new bride, Carobeth, spent their June 1916 honeymoon working on Obispeño and Purisimeño!

FIGURE 10. María Solares.
Photograph by J. P. Harrington.
Courtesy Smithsonian Institution.

Harrington did most of his Incseño work between about 1914 and 1919. About his principal consultant, María Isabel del Refugio Solares, little is known; there is no good, extensive source of information on the field-work with her, only the linguistic notes themselves. She was born in 1842 at Monterey, and died in 1923, probably in Santa Inez. That she was a fluent Ineseño speaker and a master storyteller is clear from her story "The Dog Girl." She also apparently spoke some Purisimeño, though Harrington never recorded any text in that dialect from her or anyone else.

So much material has been preserved in various Chumash languages that we have an opportunity rare in California, that of getting some idea of both the range and depth of cultural experience and verbal dexterity of the people. "The Dog Girl" is the merest drop of this material; but like a drop of honey, it is very satisfying and leaves one craving more. Because the story has been left, as closely as the translator is able, in the style in which it was told, one senses the rhythm of the storyteller's art and the hearer's reception. As Leanne Hinton noted (about Yahi) in her introduction to *Ishi's Tale of Lizard,* "Some phrases are repeated a lot, and there is a rhythm in the telling that make it something like a poem. Read it out loud if you have a chance to: it sounds best that way." This applies as well to this story. It was paraphrased in Thomas Blackburn's *December's Child* (an extremely rich collection of Chumash narrative folklore), but because Blackburn worked only with Harrington's notes in translation, the full linguistic richness of the text was not realized. Blackburn's long, conjoined, written-English phrases are not characteristic of the Chumash oral storytelling style (as indeed they are not characteristic even of English oral style).

The short Chumash-language passage that follows (the nine opening lines that constitute the introductory scene of "The Dog Girl") should give readers a better sense of María's storytelling style, which can be formal, comic, and moving by turns. Here, the most striking rhetorical feature lies in the careful disposition of her phrases and the stately, almost processional rhythm that results:

Sikk'um'ewaš ahuču:	There were some very poor dogs;
šiyaqyaquyepš ašiyašɨn;	they scavenged to eat;
ma'uš'uškuyaš' šiyaqiyepš.	refuse, they scavenged.
Wahač' ač'ič'ihi':	There were lots of children:
kasilunan',	they grew,
siyoqʰo yila'.	they were all thin.
Šiyuxnišukutačiš:	They were quick to stand:
siyuqmawil;	they were suffering;
šiyaquyepš asʰese'.	they scavenged bones.

The fine, formal balance of this passage, based on increments of three, is readily apparent.

As Hinton said of Ishi's story, María's tale is something like a poem, with short narrative episodes full of concrete imagery strung together without a wasted word. Repetitions punctuate the narrative and draw attention to important actions.[1] This technique demands close attention by listeners; nothing is overtly explained, and the sequence of events must be closely observed. The tale is meant to be heard; take Hinton's advice, and your enjoyment—and understanding—will increase immeasurably.

NOTE

1. Readers will find a more extended discussion of the poetics of repetition in "The Dog Girl" in the essay "Making Texts, Reading Translations" (this volume)—HWL

FURTHER READING

For a people so populous in a land so abundant with a culture so rich, surprisingly little has been published (and remained in print) on Chumash for a general audience. A series of books published (with one exception) in the 1970s, all based primarily on Harrington's notes, remain the best compilations, though one may have to look for them in libraries. Campbell Grant's *Rock Paintings of the Chumash* is an excursion into the beautiful, mystical world of Chumash art and remains accessible and readable. Thomas Blackburn's *December's Child* brings together many shorter and longer Chumash stories from throughout the Harrington corpus; the overall organization of the material is Blackburn's, however, not that of Harrington or the storytellers. *The Eye of the Flute,* edited by Travis Hudson, Blackburn, Rosario Curletti, and Janice Timbrook, gathers materials about Chumash traditional ritual from Harrington's work with Fernando Librado. *Crystals in the Sky* by Hudson and Ernest Underhay may be of particular interest to a wide audience, because it deals with Chumash archaeoastronomy; it is a good interpretive companion piece to Grant's book on rock art. *Tomol,* edited by Hudson, Timbrook, and Melissa Rempe, offers a detailed look at the building of a Chumash plank canoe according to the instructions of Fernando Librado; it includes material on the cultural complex surrounding Chumash marine culture.

Reliable Chumash language materials tend to be unpublished; the best grammar is Richard Applegate's exemplary doctoral dissertation, "Ineseño Chumash Grammar." Published dictionaries and lexicons do not exist, though several are in preparation for various dialects.

For general overviews of Harrington and his work, one can read Carobeth Laird's remarkable *Encounter with an Angry God,* with the caveat that this is the former wife's version of events, told with more than fifty years of hindsight. Carollyn James's piece in *Smithsonian Magazine,* "A Field Linguist Who Lived His Life for His Subjects," is sketchy but accurate. More recently, Leanne Hinton's "Ashes, Ashes" from *News from Native California* gives some of the seldom-heard Indians' views on Harrington and his work. Much Harrington lore remains in the realm of oral tradition; a full-scale biography is being undertaken by Kathryn Klar.

THE DOG GIRL

There were some very poor dogs:
   they scavenged to eat;
      refuse, they scavenged.
There were lots of children:
   they grew,
      they were all thin.   5
They were quick to make themselves stand:*
   they were suffering;
      they scavenged bones.

One of the children (she was already grown)
   climbed a range of hills,   10
      and she saw many people.
The men were playing the hoop game.
There she sat:
   she watched the people.
She said: "So many people,   15
   so many people!
      A town!"
They called out: "Come, come!"
She didn't go down.
She said: "Tomorrow I'll go down there."   20

When it was evening she went home.

---

* The idiomatic meaning of this line is unknown. The Chumash text reads *šiy-uxni-šukuta-čïš: šiy-..-čïš* '3 PL.RFLX', *uxni-* 'quickly', *su-kuta* 'to cause to stand' (literally, then, something like 'They quickly made themselves to stand'). A wild guess as to the lost meaning of the expression might be "They were quick to beg"—but this interpretation makes some unverifiable assumptions, however plausible, about the way the Chumash interacted with their dogs.— HWL

She told her mother, she said:
  "Many people I saw;
    they were calling to me," she said.   25
      "I didn't go."
Said her mother: "Why didn't you go?
  Weren't they indulgent with you?*
    You're going to disgrace yourself.
      Go on over there."   30
"I'll go tomorrow."   *the girl said*
"Come here so I can comb you—   *her mother said*
  you will be going where there are people."
She combed her,
  she readied her by combing: 35
    the dog was beautiful.

Next day the girl got up before dawn.†
"Take heart," said her mother,
  "Don't disgrace yourself!
    You will see fine people."   40

She went,
  she came to her spot.
They saw her,
  they called out to her:
    "Quick, quick! Come, come!"   45
She went to them;
  they went to meet her.
It was good:
  the girl was beautiful,
    she was pretty.   50

* Harrington's notes provide a Spanish gloss for this line: *no te chiquéas!* 'Don't indulge (adorn?) yourself'. However, the Chumash text reads *'inišamuštiktikus,* which means something like 'They were not indulgent with her', making this a narrative line, not a line of dialogue. The Spanish gloss has been followed in this instance, because it appears to flow better and may have represented a revision on the narrator's part.—RA

† With respect to this and the preceding line, note that the dog girl is referred to sometimes as "the dog" and sometimes as "the girl"—perhaps depending on which aspect of the dog girl's character the narrator is emphasizing or sympathizing with at any given point in the story.—RA

"Come, come! Eat something!"
They took her to the chief's house;*
    they gave her food.†
She saw the food:
    acorn mush, islay, chia,   55
        many kinds of food;
    fish, deer meat—
        the hunters would go out to hunt,
            and bring it to the chief's house.‡
They gave her food.   60
She ate:
    there was a lot of food;
        she got full.

In the evening she said:
    "I have to go home already."   65
She was very full.
They said to her:
    "Be content,
        come back!"

Back at her house, she vomited.   70
The children ate it;
    the mother ate it, too.
She said to her: *the girl to her*
    "It's not enough,   *mother*
        not a lot of food."§   75
"My poor child,
    I made a mistake."   *said her mother*

---

* This was the old custom that a stranger was taken to the chief's house and given food, etc.—JPH

† For some reason this line was crossed out by Harrington.— RA

‡ Informant added that men were also in former times sent to the beach to bring ʔušqoyičaš 'shellfish'. They brought it to the captain's house, whereupon the chief paid them and women cooked it up for the people.—JPH

§ Literally, 'it's not good, lots of food', which doesn't quite make sense, though the words are simple and unambiguous. Perhaps 'This [referring to the dog-like act of regurgitation] is not good— [there was] lots of food', an interpretation that would tie in with the theme of dog behavior being "shameful"—in which case, the following line ("I made a mistake") might be interpreted as 'Sorry daughter, I was acting like a dog'.—RA

"I will go again tomorrow."   *said the girl*
"Be of good cheer;   *said her mother*
    I will comb you,   80
        come quick so I can comb you."

She went,   *in the morning*
    she sat down again at her spot.
They called: "Come, come!"
The chief's son took a fancy to the girl.   85
The chief's son no sooner saw her
    than he took a fancy to her,
        he fell in love with her.
He didn't speak to her,
    he just looked.   90
To his mother he said:
    "Mother, I like this girl."

That was the custom of the ancient people long ago.

He said to his mother:
    "I like the girl."   95
The old woman said:
    "Good,
        I will speak to her, my son."

As soon as the girl came, the old woman called her.
She said to her: 100
    "Be quick to eat,
        eat something!"
As soon as she had eaten, she said to her:
    "My child wants to marry you,
        he wants to marry.   105
            What do you say?" she said to her.
She didn't make a sound.   *the dog girl*
"Speak!" she said to her.   *to the girl*
She said: *to the chief's wife*
    "Oh!—I can't say!—   110
        Good people—
            No!—

I will tell my mother to see what she says."
Said the chief's wife: "Good."

In the evening (it was already late), she said: 115
   "I'm going already;
      I will tell my mother."
Said the old woman: "Good."
They gave her dinner,
   a good meal;   120
      she was full.
They gave her food to take to her house.

She got back home:
   she vomited;
      they ate what she had "carried."   125
Her mother said:
   "How did it go for you, my child?"
She said to her: "Good, my mother—
   the chief's son wants to marry me.
      What do you say, Mother?"   130
She said: "What am I to say?
   Good, good!" she said to her,
      "Marry him!"
"Tomorrow I will go,
   I will return."   135   *said the girl*
Said her mother: "Good."

She went;   *in the morning*
   he came out to meet her.
They were married:
   much food did the people eat at the house of the chief.   140
They were married at the chief's house;
   his wife was beautiful.

The boy had a sister;
   the sister liked her sister-in-law very much.
His mother said: 145
   "Don't let your wife go hungry."
      "Right," he said.

As for the dog girl:
    she had a bracelet,
        a bracelet of fine beads;   150
    she had a necklace,
        a pendant,
            a pendant of *apɨ* beads,
                of *apɨ* beads;
        a nose stick;   155
        a basket hat;
    she had many ornaments.
Her hair was all fixed up in a braid wrap—
    she had braid wraps—
        and her apron,   160
            her apron was of otterskin.
His wife was well dressed—
    she was adorned.

But after a while, she reverted to her old habit,
    of eating excrement.   165
And after a while, her sister-in-law saw her doing it,
    her sister-in-law saw her *šitoxčʰoš išpiliwaš.**
That's what the girl was doing:
    the girl was eating shit!
The sister stopped to look at her;   170
    she said nothing.
That's what the dog's sister-in-law saw;
    she just sat there.
The sister returned home.
"My mother," she said,   175
    "my sister-in-law has been eating excrement."
She was pounding something.†
"Don't speak of this," she told her.
    "Your poor brother!
        Stay here.‡   180
            Don't follow her where she goes."

---

* There are several words I can't figure out here—unfortunately crucial ones. The undecipherable
  words are simply retained in the original Chumash.—RA
† The chief's wife was preparing food, probably acorn meal or chia seeds.—HWL
‡ Literally, 'Sit'!—RA

As for the woman,
　　she stood up and went;
　　　　she hid.　　　　　　　　　　　　　　　　　　*the dog girl*
"I don't want to make my husband unhappy," she said.　　185
She took nothing;
　　there was nothing;
　　　　she took nothing.

He said to his sister:　　　　　　　　　　　　　　*the chief's son*
　　"Where did she go?
　　　　Call for her!"　　　　　　　　　　　　　　190
He looked around;
　　he couldn't find her.
"I don't know where she went," she said,
　　"nobody's there."　　　　　　　　　　　　　　195
The man went out himself:
　　he looked for his wife,
　　　　he didn't find her.
And his mother said to him:
　　"Maybe you scolded her."　　　　　　　　　　200
They looked for her.
She had already gone.

She went up the hill;
　　she headed back to her village;
　　　　she wept.　　　　　　　　　　　　　　　205
"I did it to myself:
　　there was lots of food,
　　　　but I had to go and eat excrement.

"If only I had worn my bracelet!　　　　　　　　*[singing]*
If only I had worn my necklace!　　　　　　　　210
If only I had worn my pendant!
If only I had worn my basket hat!
ʔiya yaya yaya!

"But I didn't.

"If only I had brought my apron, I would be happy!　　215　*[singing]*
If only I had brought my bracelet, I would be happy!

If only I had brought my braid wraps, I would be happy!
If only I had brought my otterskin, I would be happy!
ʔiya yaya yaya! *

"My otterskin apron—I didn't bring it.   220
My husband would be ashamed.
   What hope have I of being kept?
     My husband would be ashamed.
Now I will turn into an animal:
   when I get back home,   225
     I will turn into an animal."

She got back home.
"How did it go for you, my child?"
"I had bad luck:
   there was no lack of food,   230
     but I wanted to eat shit.
My sister-in-law saw me.
I don't want to go back there,
   but I'll be leaving soon."

They all turned into animals;   235
   they were ashamed, all of them.
The mother and the children,
   all of them, turned into animals.
The animals, in the old days, knew shame;
   nowadays, people do not know shame.   240

---

* The second song here is reconstructed from notes in Harrington's notebook, where he transcribed the first line ('If I had brought my *smɨlɨ,* I would be happy'), but merely alluded to the rest: "song goes on to mention *waštap', tik'otuš.*" A plausible object for the song's missing but structurally implied fourth line has been supplied.— RA

SOUTHERN CALIFORNIA

I have told you to come away from the shore,
Because the small crabs will bite you—
You [will] want to say, "Ai! Ai! Ai! Ai! Ai!"

Coyote song, San Buenaventura
(Ventureño Chumash)
Robert Heizer, "California Indian Linguistic Records"

Whatever is it,
   that stuff,
that smoke,
   when it goes—
it burns,
   and when the smoke goes,
   the person,
   the one who has come to an end and is finally gone
      goes into the sky as smoke,
he goes like this and like this,
   he is the one,
and they go back and describe it again:
   that one is cloudy,
   and it's windy,
   and it stays in the sky like this;

it's cloudy, like this;

it's windy, and it stays in the sky;

and as for the moon,
the moon is giving instructions,
that's the one,
it goes back like this,
it goes that far in time and it rains,
it goes that far in time and it's cold,
it goes that far in time and it's hot,
it goes that far in time and it's cloudy and shady,
and so,
   it goes along;

that's the tradition,
that's what it must be, they say,
    that's the tradition,
and it comes back like this.

Excerpt from an account of "The Soul"
Quechan, Tom Kelly, 1978
Abraham Halpern, *Kar'úk*

23

The Creation

SERRANO

1963

SARAH MARTIN, NARRATOR

KENNETH C. HILL, COLLECTOR AND TRANSLATOR

INTRODUCTION BY KENNETH C. HILL

Serrano is a Uto-Aztecan language formerly spoken around the San Bernardino Mountains in Southern California. With the advent of the missions, some speakers of this language retreated into the mountains, whence their name, Spanish for "mountaineer." Aboriginally, Serrano may have had around 1,500 speakers (A. Kroeber 1925:617), but at the time of my fieldwork in 1963 and 1964, on the Morongo Indian Reservation at Banning, California, there were only about half a dozen known speakers.

Mrs. Sarah Morongo Martin told me this story when I was working on the Serrano language with her in the summer of 1963. Mrs. Martin had learned this story from her mother, Rosa Morongo, who also told it to Ruth Benedict. Benedict published a version of this story in her "Serrano Tales" (1926).[1] Mrs. Martin had a copy of Benedict's publication, which she used to jog her memory before retelling it to me in Serrano.[2] (It was only many years later that I learned that the reason she felt she had to use the written copy to get her started on a story was probably a cultural constraint: I was working with her in the summer, and stories of this sort are normally supposed to be told only during the winter.)

She begins the story by citing her mother as her source. In this way it is overtly acknowledged that the narrator is not responsible for the content of the story. But then, neither is the person she learned the story from directly responsible: almost every story sentence is marked by a "quotative" modal particle (*kwun* 'it is said'), indicating that the content of the sentence comes not from personal experience, but rather from what someone has said. Except in the narrator's coda, I have represented the quotative force of each sentence either by the use of the English narrative tense (the simple past tense) or by "they say." Sentences that don't use *kwun* are rendered either as English present tenses or as appropriately modalized forms.

At one point in the narrative, the quotative marker is omitted for a couple of sentences. This seems to create a sense of immediacy:

Taaqtam *kwun*u poahu'k.
    Ama' puu-na' ovia uk hoonav.
    Ovia mumu'.
    Ovia-m maahoa'n.
Ama' *kwun* wahi'—
        ya'i.

The people were in a circle, it is said.
    Their father is already lying in the middle.
    He is already dead.
    They are already cremating him.
The coyote, it is said,—
        ran.

In the translation, such lines are set in italics, as a way of conveying this highlighting effect visually.

Mrs. Martin didn't like to translate sentence-by-sentence, but rather one word at a time, and she left it to me to understand the sentence structure. The translation offered here is my own, therefore, and is quite literal, though I have omitted the occasional false start. The division into lines is based on what the narration sounds like on the recording tape, and the indentation pattern is based on my understanding of the meaning of the text.

So that the reader may obtain some notion of the distance that separates an original oral text from its translation, I present the opening lines of the story here, as transcribed directly from the tape of Mrs. Martin telling the story.[3] The translation offered here is somewhat more literal than is the case in the finished translation. False starts are given in italics and do not appear in the finished translation.

Ni-yukchoi'v   a-päävchan   ivi'.
My late mother | her story | this
This [is] my late mother's story.

Hiita'u —/
Something-or-other

Oviht   moto'   *vum/*
Long ago | still | *(?)*

— ivi'   taamiat   kwu'l
this | sun | (?)

ivi'   tiüvaṭ
this | earth

— moto'   namaa'i   ñiaaw;
still | soft | being

kwunumu'   qaṭ   wöh.
QUOT-they-PAST | sit/dwell | two
there were two.

Puu-tuwan —
Their name(s) [were]

Paqöoktach   ami'   Kokiitach.
Paqöoktach | and | Kokiitach.

Kwunu   poyo —   tom   hiiti   icho'kin   iip   tiüvav—
QUOT-they | all | INT | something | make | here | on earth
It is said [that] they made everything here on earth.

Mia   tamu'   hiiñim —   päähavim —
May | they-PAST | something-or-other | supernaturally powerful beings
They must have been powerful beings.

Kwunu   icho'kin —   poyo tom hiiti.
QUOT-they | make | everything
It is said [that] they made everything.

Wii'wunai-kwunu —
Want-QUOT-they
They wanted, it is said,

Haokp —
[I mean that] one [of them]

ama'   Kokiitach   kwun   wii'wun —
the | Kokiitach | QUOT | want
Kokiitach, it is said, wanted

taaqtam   püü-qöi'va',
[that] people | upon their death

puvaipa' ta   qöi'v   ami' ta —   *mii'/* —   *ami'   tam/* —
if | they | will die | and | they | *(?)* | and | they*(?)*
should they die, when they

qöi'v
will die
might die,

ami(') ta möch   mana'qtoi'v,
and | they | will return
they should return again

iingkwa' iingkwa',
to here | to here
this way this way,

ivi' tiüvaika'.
this | to earth
to this earth.

As a final note on the translation, the characters in this story are rendered as "the frog" and "the coyote" rather than as "Frog" and "Coyote" because that is how Mrs. Martin spoke of them in English. Names are rarely used in Serrano stories. Even when individual names are known, characters tend to be referred to as "her older sister," "the boy," "that old woman," and so on.

NOTES

1. Benedict says of the stories she published: "These stories are recorded as told by old Rosa Morongo, who learned them from her father-in-law, chief of the Marina (Morongo) ['Maarunga'—KCH] local group, who died thirty-five years ago" (1926:1).

2. For comparison, here is Benedict's published version of Rosa Morongo's story (1926:1), the version that Sarah Martin referred to to jog her memory before she retold it to me:

THE CREATION

In the beginning was darkness. Then there were two: Pakrokítatc and Kúkitatc. They made the animals. They quarreled, and Pakrokítatc departed, and Kúkitatc lived with his people. Kúkitatc said: "When people die, they shall come back." But the people said, "If they come back, the world will fill up, and there will be no room. We will get rid of Kúkitatc."

They employed a powerful shaman to bewitch Kúkitatc. He watched and saw that Kúkitatc came out every night to defecate in the ocean. Therefore he sent Frog to bite his excrement. Kúkitatc heard that the excrement did not splash as it fell into the water, and he knew that Frog was below. Now he knew he was going to die. He told his people to send Coyote far away to the north for wood to burn his body, and he said, "Immediately, as soon as I am dead, burn my body." He died, and his people lighted the funeral pyre. Coyote had not yet gone far, when he saw the pyre burning, and he knew that Kúkitatc was dead.

The people were standing close together all around the funeral fire, so close nothing could get through, for they were prepared lest Coyote should come back before the body was burned. Coyote ran round and round the circle and could not get in. But at last he saw his chance. Badger was standing bow-legged (as always) and Coyote slipped in between his legs and snatched Kúkitatc's heart before it was burned. He ran away with it and ate it.

(All prayers in the old time were addressed to Kúkitatc.)

3. The letter *u* is used for the high back (or central) unrounded vowel, the "barred i" of most Uto-Aztecan studies; *o* represents the mid-to-high back rounded vowel; the apostrophe is the glottal stop; *ä, ö, ü* are retroflexed ("r-colored") vowels; *ʈ* is a *t*- or *ts*-like sound made with the tip of the tongue. Word stress is on the first syllable. The following abbreviations appear in the gloss lines: QUOT, "quotative"; INT, "intensifier."

FURTHER READING

For general information on the Serrano, see Lowell Bean and Charles Smith's entry "Serrano" in the California volume of the Smithsonian *Handbook.* J. P. Harrington collected fieldnotes on the Serrano, which are among his papers in the Smithsonian. Ruth Benedict published some "Serrano Tales" in English translation, as well as "A Brief Sketch of Serrano Culture." Kenneth Hill has written "A Grammar of the Serrano Language" and edited a couple of Serrano tales ("The Coyote and the Flood" and "The Seven Sisters").

THE CREATION

This is my late mother's story . . .

Long ago
   when this earth
   was still soft,
      there were two.
Their names
      [were] Paqöoktach and Kokiitach.
They made everything
   here on earth.

5

They must have been powerful beings.   10
  They made everything.

They wanted,
  I mean that one of them, Kokiitach, wanted
    that people, upon their death,
      should they die,   15
      when they might die,
    they should return again
      this way this way,
      to this earth.

"No," said his older brother,   20
  "because if they could return again,
    then you could be crowded here,"
      he said.

Well, they quarreled then,
  and that one went away.   25
That Paqöoktach went away,
  he went away somewhere.

And then his younger brother stayed with his relatives,
    with them,
    with the people.   30
  He stayed there.

He went on creating everything then.
  Then the people got tired of him.
    They didn't like him.
    They were unhappy.*   35

And then they said, "We ought to kill this one."
  Then, "Yes,"
    they said.

And then they must have sent the shaman to bewitch him.
  He became ill.   40
  Once he didn't even go to the edge of the water.

* This line is not intonationally separated from the next section.

He went there to relieve himself,
    always.

And so they said, "It looks like we can't do anything with him."
    "Yes, but we can tell the frog.   45
    Maybe he can swallow his excrement,"
        he said then.
    "Yes,"
        he said.

And then, he did go there to relieve himself.   50
And then that frog was there.
And then he swallowed his excrement.

He already knew.
    Kokiitach said, "Now indeed I'm going to die,"
        he said.   55
    "He has already eaten my excrement,"
        he said.
      He went away.
      He lay down at home.
      "I'm already dying,"   60
        he said.

And then he called the people.
And then he told them,
    "I am already dying,
    and you should send that coyote   65
      away to the edge of the earth.
    Over there is a dry stick.
    He [the coyote] should get it.
    You should cremate me with that,"
        he said.   70
    "Because he might do something,"
        he said.

And then they sent the coyote off.
      He went away.
      He ran off.   75
    But he knew.

"Something must have happened,"
    he said.
"My father must have died,"
    he said.   80
        (For that person was their father).
  Then he went.
    He went up on the mountain.

And then he looked back.
    He looked back as he went.   85
    He didn't see anything.

Suddenly he saw smoke.
  "My father has already died,"
    he said.
  He ran, grabbed the stick.   90

And then with it he returned.
  He arrived.
    The people were in a circle.
      Their father is already lying in the middle.
      He is already dead.   95
      They are already cremating him.
    The coyote—
      ran.

And then he said,
  "Let your hands go,   100
    so I can go in!"
    he said.
  "Move aside,
    move aside,
    so I can go in!"   105
    he said.
  Nobody moved.

He was running.
  He kept going around the circle.

The badger was standing there.   110
  His legs were spread far apart.

And then the coyote dived through there.
   He dives through.
   Now his father's heart was still not burning.
   He grabbed it and swallowed it.   115
      With it,
      with it he ran away.

Out of the circle and away he ran.
Up the mountain he climbed.

There this earth being still soft,   120
where he climbed, they say his footprints still show.
      The blood all spilled out from it.
      But he swallowed his father's heart.

Today they say he lives far off,
   far away.   125

"To the Pines" [Big Bear] we say now.
That is where, long ago, they stood in the circle.
      They stood in the circle.
    They say those pines were the people,
      who were standing crying,   130
        who were crying for their father,
            for their father.
    Now they are in our songs, the pine trees, far away at "To the
    Pines."

Long ago, it was different from the way it is now,
   because long ago they changed it.   135
It isn't there any more.
Long ago they cleared it all off.

This is the end.

24

A Harvest of Songs
from Villiana Calac Hyde

LUISEÑO

1988–1992

VILLIANA CALAC HYDE, SINGER AND TRANSLATOR

ERIC ELLIOTT, COLLECTOR

INTRODUCTION BY ERIC ELLIOTT

The following song texts were selected from *Yumáyk Yumáyk* (Hyde and
Elliott 1994), a compilation of personal memoirs and historical texts
narrated in Luiseño by Villiana Hyde.[1] Luiseño is a member of the Cupan branch of the Takic subfamily of the Uto-Aztecan family of languages. The Uto-Aztecan family includes languages spoken from the
American Northwest to Central America. The Cupan languages were
all spoken within the boundaries of modern California. Within the Cupan languages, Luiseño is most closely related to the now-extinct Cupeño language.

Born Villiana Calac, Mrs. Villiana Hyde was a native speaker of
Luiseño and a proud member of the Luiseño community at the Rincón
Reservation of San Diego County. In Luiseño orthography the name
"Calac" is spelled "Qáálaq" and literally means '(the earth) caves in'. In
complete contrast to the literal meaning of the family name, the Calac

family has a long history of never "caving in," but rather of standing tall and providing the community and the world beyond with prominent leaders.

True to the Calac family tradition of serving the community, Mrs. Hyde found her niche early on as historian and linguist. Forbidden to speak Luiseño at Sherman Indian School in Riverside, California, Mrs. Hyde became painfully aware at a young age that her language and culture were in peril. As a young woman she gained an acute understanding of what it means for a language and culture to die. Mrs. Hyde's own mother-in-law was a native speaker of Cupeño, Luiseño's closest geographic and linguistic neighbor. The Cupeño people, including Mrs. Hyde's mother-in-law, had been forcibly evicted from their home at Warner Springs. Mrs. Hyde watched as her mother-in-law, now living among Diegueño and Luiseño speakers, saw her language and culture fade into extinction as the few remaining Cupeño speakers passed away around her.

Mrs. Hyde thus had a clear understanding of the ominous task of preserving her language and culture for future generations. Her formal career as a linguist began in the 1960s, when she first collaborated with Professors Margaret Langdon and Ronald Langacker of the Department of Linguistics at the University of California, San Diego (UCSD). This work eventually culminated in the publication of Mrs. Hyde's first book, *An Introduction to the Luiseño Language* (1971). Among those who collaborated with Mrs. Hyde on the *Introduction* were Langacker and the linguists Pamela Munro and Susan Steele, all of whom have continued their linguistic research on Luiseño language to the present day.

As an undergraduate student at the University of California, Irvine, I had the good fortune to stumble onto Mrs. Hyde's *Introduction to the Luiseño Language.* Long fascinated by the indigenous languages of California, I also happened to sign up for a class on Amerindian languages offered by Professor Mary Key, a linguist who had spent decades working on various American Indian languages of Mexico and South America. Professor Key encouraged my interest in Native American languages, opening up her office and personal linguistic library to me. When I showed up with Mrs. Hyde's *Introduction,* Professor Key further encouraged me to contact Mrs. Hyde and Professor Margaret Langdon of the Department of Linguistics at UCSD.

At the time, Mrs. Hyde's telephone number was listed in the directory. I simply called up directory assistance, got her number, telephoned Mrs. Hyde, and asked her whether she would teach me more about her language. Mrs. Hyde graciously agreed. Armed only with the *Introduction*, my tape recorder, and William Bright's *Luiseño Dictionary*, I drove to Mrs. Hyde's house. Our technique was simple. I would ask Mrs. Hyde about a particular subject of interest. She would tell me details on tape in Luiseño. I would take the tape home, transcribe the Luiseño, analyze it morphologically, translate it into English as best I could, and bring the work back to Mrs. Hyde for editing. At first, the work was painstakingly slow. Mrs. Hyde, who opened up her home to me most Saturdays, thought nothing of working from nine o'clock in the morning until as late as five o'clock at night.

Mrs. Hyde and I ended up collaborating for more than eight years. Our work has thus far yielded *Yumáyk Yumáyk* ('long, long ago'), and we also have a dictionary and grammar in the making. Mrs. Hyde passed away in 1994, several weeks before *Yumáyk Yumáyk* was published. Mrs. Hyde was a good friend to me. She was also an ideal linguistic consultant. With her passing I lost a friend and also the possibility of further data collection or further clarification of material already gathered. The following excerpts from *Yumáyk Yumáyk* are therefore presented raw, as they appeared in the original—that is, with no further interpretation or explanation on my part. Mrs. Hyde provided explanations where she felt them necessary in *Yumáyk Yumáyk*. As with any culture's history, or as with any individual's own life story, there will always be facets of that history that are more readily comprehensible to outsiders, and other aspects that are less transparent. In order to fully understand the culture of a given community or individual, one has to be a member of that culture. I am not a member of the Luiseño-speaking culture presented in *Yumáyk Yumáyk*, a culture where speaking Luiseño and having one's gallstones removed by a shaman (Hyde and Elliott 1994:175–84) were as natural to Mrs. Hyde as speaking English and going to the dentist for a filling is to me. Yet, the more one reads of Mrs. Hyde's life and times, the better picture one forms of her culture, which really did exist not so long ago. It is my hope that these selections will provide readers with a glimpse of the grace and beauty of the language and culture that Mrs. Hyde worked so hard to document.

1. Song numbers here refer to text numbers in Hyde and Elliott's *Yumáyk Yumáyk* (1994). For the sake of reference, they have not been renumbered for this volume. The titles of songs given in Luiseño, in the absence of an explanatory phrase at the beginning, may be translated with reference to the first line of the song itself.—HWL

FURTHER READING

For a general orientation to Luiseño culture and history, see Lowell Bean and Florence Shipek's article "Luiseño" in the California volume of the Smithsonian *Handbook*. William Bright has written *A Luiseño Dictionary*. Helen Roberts's *Form in Primitive Music* contains numerous Luiseño songs collected in the 1930s. Villiana Hyde produced *An Introduction to the Luiseño Language*. Lastly, Hyde and Elliott's *Yumáyk Yumáyk (Long Ago)* contains hundreds of Villiana Hyde's stories, songs, and reminiscences, in interlinear text format.

A HARVEST OF SONGS
FROM VILLIANA CALAC HYDE

BADGER SONG (#138)

These are the ones who looked down
These are the ones who peered down

The badger and the vulture, long ago
These ones [are] the vulture . . .

Look at his stained hand with a ring around it
Look at his speckled hand

These are the ones who looked down
These are the ones who peered down

I speak of my [own] spirit
I try to speak of my heart

I try to speak of my spirit
I try to speak of my heart

"They too looked down. And that's why they look that way. That badger saw, he looked down." *

KÁÁMALA SONG (#145)

Child, *ʔáṣkat's* song:
The ones inside her rolled and moved
The ones in her chest,
 the ones in her chest rolled and moved
The ones inside her,
 their beloved sons, rolled and moved

TEMÉÉNGANISH SONG (#149)

THE DAWN SONG†

I speak of the East
I speak of the East
I tell my story, of how I was dying
In the first little month called *Táwsanmaytal*

The *chuyúkmal* star, the *kayá'mal* star
Made growling sounds
They opened their mouths when I was dying
In the first little month called *Táwsanmaytal*

The bullfrog and the angleworm . . .

I speak of the Antares star of the East

---

* These explanations were provided by Mrs. Hyde and are not part of the song itself. The remaining lines of the song are apparently lost.

† "They would sing this song toward dawn," Mrs. Hyde explained. (The star names *chuyúkmal* and *kayá'mal* may refer to animals. The Vulture Star is Arcturus.)

I speak of the Vulture star of the East
I tell my story of the East
I tell my story of the East

LULLABY IN IMITATION
OF A CRICKET CHIRPING (#153)

THE CRICKET'S SONG

The oak trees are standing there
The oak trees are standing there
In the house, in the house, in the house

PÍ'MUKVOL SONG (#162)

DEATH SONG*

1

The *mááxwala* hawk, the *wasíímal* hawk
They left speaking of their spirits, of their hearts
They left singing of their spirits, of their hearts

2

The *qáwqaw* bird, the kingbird and the *wasíímal* hawk
They left speaking of their spirits, of their hearts

PA'LÁÁKWISH SONG (#165)

THE PA'LÁÁKWISH BIRD'S SONG

My nephew, get your arrow
To shoot and kill someone

CHALÁÁWAAT SONG (#167)

THE CHALÁÁWAAT ("STANDING UP") DANCE

I suppose I've survived the first little month
I suppose I've survived the first big month

* The song has two parts, as numbered.

Oh, I am surviving through the days
I am surviving through the days

PIWÍÍSH SONG (#170)

THE MILKY WAY SONG (SECOND PART)*

It keeps waking me up
It keeps waking me up
It makes me spark
My rattle, my turtleshell rattle
My rattle keeps me awake

QAXÁÁL QAXÁÁWUT SONG (#171)

The valley quail and the mountain quail singed their hair†
They cut off their hair, with tears and lamentations
They singed their hair
The mountain quail singed off his hair
The mountain quail singed off his hair
They cut off their hair, with tears and lamentations

The flicker bird and the roadrunner
They cut off their hair, with tears and lamentations
They singed their hair
The flicker bird singed off his hair
The roadrunner singed off his hair
They cut off their hair, with tears and lamentations

PÍ' TÓÓWISH HULÚYKA SONG (#174)

And the spirit landed
And the little dove landed

---

* The phrase *makes me spark* is a poetic idiom meaning "keeps me awake." The word *rattle* at the
beginning of lines 3 and 4 translates literally as "my little fire."
† This is not the whole of the "Qaxáál Qaxááwut" song. The two stanzas presented here represent
two separate parts of the song. Neither part begins the complete song, but they are not necessarily sequential either.

And it stopped to warn
And so it wandered around to warn

And the coyote landed
And it stopped to warn
And so it wandered around to warn

The owl landed
And the fox landed
And it stopped to warn
And so it wandered around to warn

The screech owl landed
And the *péépimal* bird landed
And it stopped to warn
And so it wandered around to warn

The *páátapi* duck landed
And the *nóóchaqi* duck landed
And it stopped to warn
And so it wandered around to warn

The *pááwnat* bird landed
And the killdeer bird landed
And it stopped to warn
And so it wandered around to warn

TÓÓWISH MIXÉÉL SONG (#178)

The spirit, the dove
This spirit [cried] over me
This dove [cried] over me
And so it cried over our future death
Over my future death
Over my future disappearance
Over my future disappearance
The fox [cried] over me . . .

WUNÁL PÍ' TUMÁMKAWISH SONG (#181)

There was an earthquake in the north
Our future death rumbled
My storehouse was shaken up
Our hearts rumbled
Our future death rumbled
My darkness was shaken
My darkness was shaken
Our future death rumbled

There was an earthquake in the north
Our future death rumbled
My storehouse was shaken up
Our hearts rumbled
Our future death rumbled
My darkness was shaken
My darkness was shaken
Our future death rumbled

[*Singer begins dancing*]

Our future death rumbled
My storehouse was shaken up
Our house rumbled
My darkness was shaken
My darkness was shaken
Our house rumbled

SECOND KÁÁMALA SONG (#182)

THE CHILD SONG

The dust from the area around Pááyaxchi
Billowed up from their feet as they walked along
And erred along the way

CHALÁWYAX MILA MÓÓTA SONG (#190)

The gopher danced the *chaláwyax**
The meadow mouse danced
They danced the *chaláwyax* and the *yúngish*
After their father
They danced when their father died
They danced all night
They danced, *héé, héé,* amen . . .

---

* The *chaláwyax* and *yúngish* are dances. The gopher and meadow mouse's father is Móyla Wuyóót (the Moon). The vocables *héé héé* at the end of the song work in much the same way that the word *amen* does—by "sending the song to heaven."

25

From "The Life of Hawk Feather"
The Bear Episodes

CUPEÑO

1962, 1920

ROSCINDA NOLASQUEZ AND SALVADORA VALENZUELA,
NARRATORS

JANE HILL AND PAUL-LOUIS FAYE, COLLECTORS

JANE HILL, TRANSLATOR

INTRODUCTION BY JANE HILL

The "Bear Episode" is one part of a longer account of the life of Hawk
Feather, the greatest hero in Cupeño history. Roscinda Nolasquez told
me two parts of the "Bear Episode" when she was teaching me the Cupeño language during the summer of 1962. In 1920 Paul-Louis Faye collected several events from this episode in a single text. The teller was probably Salvadora Valenzuela, because, among the texts where Faye bothers
to note his consultants' names, she is consistently listed as the teller of the
longer and more elaborate stories. Salvadora Valenzuela comes from a lineage of storytellers and authorities on Cupeño culture; her mother, Mrs.
Manuela Griffith, was a principal consultant for William Duncan Strong.
Miss Nolasquez had known Mrs. Valenzucla and considered her to be a
particularly skilled narrator of Cupeño history. The 1920 text has some

elements that Miss Nolasquez's two later tellings lack, but hers includes some details that are absent in the text that Faye recorded. This publication gives us an opportunity to put the two parts of the Bear Episode together. In addition to bringing together versions by two narrators, we have inserted into the story the texts of the songs that a teller would have sung in a formal winter recitation. Faye apparently recorded the song texts separately from the story (and left us no musical notation for them), but on the story text itself, in Faye's fieldnotes, there are instructions about where the songs should be. I have placed them there, writing them in italics.

The story of Hawk Feather is in the genre that Cupeños refer to with the verb root *a'alxi* 'telling history'. Histories tell us how the world has come to be the way that it is today. The story of Hawk Feather is only one part of a longer history that begins in the creation of the world and continues into the present day. An important new history in the *a'alxi* genre includes stories about the removal of the Cupeño in 1902 from their ancestral communities at Pal Atingve 'Hot Springs' (which included the villages of Kupa 'Fire Place' and Wilakalpa 'Buckwheat Place'), known to non-Indians as Warner's Hot Springs.

Hawk Feather is born into chaos, as enemy warriors (Strong [1929] says that they were Diegueños) attack and burn the village of Kupa. His mother flees with her baby to live with relatives at Soboba, called Yuykat. The boy grows into a great hunter. But, perhaps because they are jealous of his accomplishments, people do not like him, and he hunts alone. It is in the Bear Episode that his special powers are first manifested, when he blows up the skin of the dead bear and brings it to life. In Salvadora Valenzuela's telling of how he did this, she says,

He carried the hide to the brush.
He gathered the softest grass that he could find.
He stuffed the hide.
He sewed up the hide into the shape of a body.
And then he blew it up.
And then it breathed.
And he tied it with cords,
for it was trying to run away.

Miss Nolasquez's segment of the narrative ends in the touching moment when Hawk Feather begs his mother not to be afraid of him. At this point in the story, we switch narrators, turning to Salvadora Valenzuela's telling from 1920. We pick up her story when the hero and his mother set forth with the bear to kill their enemies, traveling across a countryside punctuated with place-names that record the moments in their quest. But when they reach Kupa, the bear is killed by the terrified people. They manage to take away from him the magic stone that was his "heart" (according to Paul-Louis Faye's notes), and the women come and "cut his beads" from the carcass. The 1920 text (as well as the present version) ends there.

In her second set of episodes from the life of Hawk Feather, Miss Nolasquez narrates Hawk Feather's maturity—events in his life that occurred after the death of the magic bear. He takes two wives. They bear three sons, who are the founders of the three Cupeño lineages. Hawk Feather continues to exhibit magical powers: his dances control whether oak trees will bear the acorns that were the staple of the Cupeño diet.

One of the most delightful moments in Miss Nolasquez's part of the Bear Episode shows her special gift for sparkling narrative. This is the section where the hero tries to figure out who might be stealing his caches of meat. Miss Nolasquez seizes the opportunity to poke fun at Coyote, through the voice of the hero's mother. (Roscinda Nolasquez knew innumerable Coyote stories and took great pleasure in the humor in these texts.) Thus lines 48–54 of her story go like this in Cupeño:

Muku'ut aye peye peyik peyaqal,
  "Ishmi'ishep ne'ey ni'ituqa,"
    peyaqal ku'ut.
  "Ivi'aw ham iyaxwe,"
    peyaqal ku'ut.
Pi'isniqal pexuchi.
  "ISILYshepe"
    peyaqal ku'ut peye.
  "Isilyem pe' EYet!
  Meshepe isilya i'ITU'qa!"
    peyaqal ku'ut.

And then they say he said to his mother,
  "Something must be stealing from me,"
    they say he said.
  "Here is how it looks,"

they say he said.
He draws the outline of a footprint.
"It MUST be a COYOTE!"
they say his mother said.
"Coyote is SUCH a THIEF!
It must be Coyote who is STEALING from you!"
they say she said.

One interesting feature of Cupeño historical texts that we can see in this passage is that all narrative sentences (excepting those in quoted speech) contain the quotative particle *ku'ut* 'they say'. Here, I have translated all the quotatives, so that their frequency is obvious. In the main translation, only a few of these remain, but in Cupeño every sentence in a history is marked with this particle, reiterating again and again and again the authoritative force of the story and the teller's humility before tradition.

Another striking feature of Roscinda Nolasquez's storytelling style in part 1 is the exaggerated emphasis, with loud, drawn-out syllables (marked in the text in capital letters) that she gives to the speech of the mother as she diagnoses the footprint: *ISILYshepe* 'COYOTE must be him!', *pe'EYet* 'He is SUCH a THIEF!', *i'iTU'qa* 'He is STEALING from you!' This way of telling the story must have made audiences laugh out loud, thinking of all the times Coyote has foolishly stolen something that turned out to do him no good. The solemnity of history, thus punctuated with a good joke, is rendered delightful, and the serious privileges of humor are equally revealed.

There are any number of interesting problems in interpreting this story. One of them is why Miss Nolasquez finished her telling at the moment when Hawk Feather reassures his mother that she need not be afraid of him. Some are internal to the story; others are external to it, pointing to the interpersonal context of the recording session itself. Miss Nolasquez's story really centers around Hawk Feather's relationship with his mother. Miss Nolasquez herself had a very close relationship with her son and with her grandchildren. Indeed, Miss Nolasquez was known to everyone at Pala as "Grandma" Nolasquez. Furthermore, there was every reason for her to think about motherhood when she worked with me, because in August 1962 I was seven months pregnant with my first child. (The next summer, Eric went with me in his portable crib as a not-so-silent listener to Miss Nolasquez's teaching.) Finally, because I hardly knew any Cupeño, most of the stories Miss Nolasquez helped me with that summer were simple stories appropriate to children. The part of the Hawk Feather episode that she told is, in fact, excellent entertainment, with magic and humor. No enemies are killed in it—instead, Hawk Feather tricks them into using up all their arrows, which he adds to his own arsenal. However, the story grows darker when Hawk Feather, his mother, and the pet bear set out toward Kupa, slaughtering their enemies along the way. The death of the pet bear at the hands of the enemies who remained in Kupa is an especially sad moment in the history. This part of the episode might be frightening and confusing to little children, or inappropriate to an atmosphere of grandmotherly nurturing, as opposed to the solemn world-renewing ritual context of the winter tellings. Thus Miss Nolasquez's version of the Bear Episode suggests how she could use the story as a flexible resource, drawing from it for entertainment and for moral contemplation as a part of everyday life.

Another problem involves Hawk Feather's name. Miss Nolasquez used the name Kisily Pewik 'Hawk His-Wing/Plume' for this hero. Paul-Louis Faye's 1920 version calls him Kisily Pewish 'Hawk His-Down', and this is also the name recorded by Strong. The problem is, Miss Nolasquez had the latter word only in the meaning 'feces'. Apparently in her speech two ancient Uto-Aztecan words had merged in pronunciation. The first, listed by Wick Miller (1967) as Proto-Uto-Aztecan, is **_pi_ 'feather' (probably it was **_pi'wi:,_ with Cupeño retaining only the second syllable). The second word is listed as **_kwita_ 'to defecate'; its etymological reflexes often mean 'feces' (in Cupeño, the sound **_kw_ appears as /w/, and **_t_ as /sh/, yielding _wish_). This ambiguity gave Roscinda Nolasquez's son, Robert Lovato, the opportunity to tease me with a naughty bilingual pun—that the hero's name was really Kisily Pewish, or "Hawk His-Number Two"! For this translation, I have decided in favor of Kisily Pewik—that is, Hawk Feather rather than Hawk Down (or worse).

The monolingual format of this volume requires a final note or two on the translation. I wish that the text did not have to be translated at all; I wish that it were being told, every winter, in community gatherings, and being quoted with pleasure, and that its songs were being hummed, by speakers of the language. I hate having to put it in English, so my translation is in a way an act of resistance to my own language; it is as literal as possible, consistent with the joy and dignity of the original. I have left in as many quotatives as I could get away with, because I think that their drumbeat rhythm is part of the power of this history.

And about the lines. The division of the text into lines partly reflects the way that Roscinda Nolasquez divided her recitation into what linguists call "breath groups" or "intonation units"; that is, it reflects her pattern of slowing down, and speeding up, and pausing. For the 1920 text, I have simply guessed about this, based on my experience with Miss Nolasquez's speech. The line divisions also serve to open the text up and make it more readable—they represent the flow and phrasings of ordinary speech. However, they do not reflect the sort of rhythmic performance— Hymes's "measured verse"—that is found in some Native American languages, especially in the Pacific Northwest. This is, in my opinion, prose, not verse, and the narrative sentences are very different from those in songs.

FURTHER READING

Versions of the story of Hawk Feather are also found in William Strong's *Aboriginal Society in Southern California* (1929:270) and in Edward Gifford's "Clans and Moieties in Southern California" (1918:199). Alfred Kroeber briefly notes the story in *The Handbook of the Indians of California* (1925:692). Both Roscinda Nolasquez's two tellings and the 1920 version collected by Faye appear in Jane Hill and Nolasquez's *Mulu'wetam*, which also includes a brief grammatical sketch and vocabulary of Cupeño.

FROM "THE LIFE OF HAWK FEATHER": THE BEAR EPISODE, PART 1

ROSCINDA NOLASQUEZ, 1962

One young man, it is said, lived there,
    and he was always hunting.

He would go to the mountains,
and he would always kill deer,
and he would bring the carcass to his mother.   5
His mother never wanted to eat,
for of course it was not proper for a woman to eat such deer.
    "Take it to the chief in the Big House,"
        she would say;
    "To the chief's house."   10
And he would take it there,
to the chief's house,
for the people to eat the deer.
And he would gather his relatives together,
and they would all eat that deer.   15
But not his mother.
For if a person kills a deer, then he should not eat it.
And his mother never wanted to eat,
since her son was the one who had killed it.
And he would go off again.   20

He would go off, it is said, to a certain place,
    going looking here and there,
    and he would always kill something, a rat, or a rabbit,
    and he would take it off to his mother.
But she did not eat.   25
    "To the other place, to the Big House,"
        she would say;
    "They will eat it there."
And it is said that the people really did dine there,
    they ate what he had killed.   30
And then he would go out again.

He used to go hunting, it is said, at a certain place,
    and he would kill a deer,
    and he would leave it there.
And ALways, when he returned again in the morning,   35
    his cache would be gone,
    for something was always stealing it.
And the man said,

"I wonder who is stealing from me?"
    he would say.   40
And he would go off again.

It is said he would kill some rats somewhere,
    and bring them from there to his mother.
    But when he came around,
        "To the Big House," she would say.   45
    And he would take it there,
        even if it was only one thing.
    But he said to his mother,
        "Something must be stealing from me," he said.
        "Here is how it looks," he said.   50
    He draws the outline of a footprint.
        "It MUST be a COYOTE!" said his mother.
        "Coyote is such a THIEF.
        It must be Coyote who is STEALING from you," she said.
    And he went off again.   55

And it is said then he arrived again at that same place,
    and again he saw a footprint there.
    That footprint was huge!
    And he said to his mother,
        "Something is obviously coming around.   60
        I saw the track there," he said.
        "You'll catch it," she said,
        "in a trap," she said.
        "Here is how wide the foot is," he said.
    And his mother said,   65
        "It must be a BEAR!" she said.
    And he went off again.

Now, his mother, it is said, always stayed behind when he went
    hunting.
    And he killed that bear,
    and then he carried it back.   70
    It was a really big bear.
    But he carried it back from there,
    and he brought it to his mother.

And his mother said,
    "To the chief's house," she said,   75
    "I cannot eat this, for this is a human being," she said.

And then, it is said, he skinned it, the man skinned the bear.
    He took it ALL out,
        all of that flesh,
    and he prepared the hide.   80
    And he BLEW it up,
    he BLEW it up,
    until he made it really ENORMOUS.
    And his mother was there,
    and she was watching   85
        while he made the body of the bear.
    And then he played with it there.
    It was just like a dog;
    it was playing,
    it was jumping around.   90

And it is said his mother went off to tell the other people.
    On the way she crossed a stream,
    and she scratched up her feet,
    with all the sticks, SO many,
    where she crossed several times from this side to that.   95
    So her feet were completely scratched up.
    And still she kept going;
    she was looking back.
    She got home, and she said,
        "He is definitely over there," she said,   100
        "the Bear.
        He is just like a dog.
        The two of them are playing," she said.
    And so many people set off.

It is said they readied their bows and arrows.   105
    And they went off.
    And there he was, under a shelter.
    And from under there, a paw REACHED out.

And then it disappeared again.
And it came out—   110
it was the body of the bear.
And then it disappeared again.
And then the people shot at him,
their arrows flew everywhere.
Underneath the shelter he would duck,   115
he would turn into something different,
he would come out again,
and again they shot.
Back under the shelter he goes!
Then their arrows were used up,   120
    from all their shooting.
And then they went away.
And they said,
    "It is impossible for us to kill him," they said.
And then he came out.   125
He gathered up ALL those arrows.
And he piled them up.

Arrows in piles
You went looking around
You went crawling around   130
You went touching the ground
You were weak
That is all

And then, it is said, his mother came.
    And he said,
        "Where did you go?" said the son.   135
    And his mother said,
        "I went over there to the foot of the mountain."
        "You must have washed your feet.
        You got your feet all scratched up," he said.   140
        "My feet did get wet there," she said.
And then she kept standing there,
    she kept standing there.
His mother was afraid of that bear.
And her son said,   145

"Don't be afraid," he said to his mother.
"It was only me," they say he said.

FROM "THE LIFE OF HAWK FEATHER":
THE BEAR EPISODE, PART 2

SALVADORA VALENZUELA, 1920

And then, it is said, when the sun rose,
    all of those many warriors came again.
    Again they called him, and he came out as an old man.
    In the same way now they shot at him,
    but they could not hit him,   5
    since he would duck back under the shelter.
      "Mother," he said,
      "Now I am going to come out in the shape of a baby,
      and they're going to see me, and they're going to shoot
          at me,
      and all of them are going to grab at me.   10
    And I will come back in here,
    and you and my pet bear will come out.
    They have no arrows left.
    They are going to go away,
    they are going to say that they will come again tomorrow.   15
    And now I will say that I will show them my pet."
And then they said,
    "You won't show us your pet bear."
    "Now you will see it,
    and now you will kill me as I come out to you."   20
    "No," they said,
    "we will do it tomorrow."
And they say that he said to his mother,
    "Now we are going to chase them."
And he gave her his club.   25
And he said to his mother,
    "This pet of mine will come out of the bushes at them,

and I will shoot them from atop a level place,
    and you will hit them about the ears, breaking their jaws."

And then, it is said, they chased them, he and his mother,   30
    they caught up with them,
    he shot them,
    he killed them.
    When they tried to escape into the bushes,
    the bear then came out at them,   35
    reaching out his arms to them.
    The bear killed them,
    while the man came along shooting them
    while his mother came along clubbing them about the ears.

Halayla! Hahahalayla!   40
The bear, his paws!
Halayla! Hahalayla!
The bear, his paws!

One enemy would run to the south,
    another, in the same way, to the west,   45
    but it was no use,
    they could not pass.
    Now two of them appeared,
    and the man chased those two.
    He caught up with them,   50
    he grabbed them,
    and he dashed them repeatedly against a White Oak.
    And they say that he said,
        "You will all go and tell one another,
        so the name of this place will be   55
            'Where He Dashed Them against the White Oak,'
        and you will tell about me, how I finished them off."
    And they went away to tell.

And then, it is said, he and his mother returned to their victims,
    in order to scalp their heads.   60
    And they packed the scalps into their carrying net,
    to take them to their shelter,

to take them there.
And he said,
    "Mother, tomorrow I think that we will go home
        to Kupa."   65
In the morning they left, he and his mother,
carrying their burdens on tumplines.
And at a certain place he adjusted his burden.
And they say that he said,
    "This place will be called 'Where He Adjusted His
        Burden';   70
        its name will be thus."
And they went on.
And then at a certain place he was climbing,
and he caught his breath.
    "This place will be called, 'Where He Caught His Breath.'"   75
And they went on.
And at a certain place he stopped to eat.
And they say that he said,
    "'Meal Place' is its name."
And then they went on from there.   80
And then they came to Mekwashma,
and because of him its name is 'Flea Place.'

And then, it is said, while they rested there at Mekwashma,
    he turned his pet bear loose.
    And the bear killed women, and men, and children,   85
    those who remained of his enemies.
    And at Kelelva, the bear would come out in the morning,
    to graze in the meadow grass.
    And there also he killed those who remained.
    And so the old women went to the chief of the Teshvekinga
        Clan.   90
    They said to him,
        "You men must do something for us,
        you should kill that bear for us,
        for he has almost finished us off.
        When the sun rises, that is when he appears."   95

And it is said that there is a place where there are rocks on each
  side.
  And the men set off.
  One sat on this side, on top of one of the rocks.
  And another did the same on the other.
  And then the bear appeared.   100
  And they tried to shoot him.
  And he caught their arrows,
      he broke them in half.
  And then the bear shook his head.
  And a stone fell from the back of his neck.   105
  And he swallowed it.
  And then those men went away, for their arrows were
      exhausted.
      "Tomorrow, we will come again."

It is said that again, in the morning, they came.
  The ones on the rocks kept watch.   110
  And one of them said to the other,
      "Now I will tell you what he is carrying on the back of his
          neck.
      And you will shoot at it first; you are to shoot.
      And I will jump down from here,
      and I will knock that thing far away,   115
      so that he cannot swallow it,
      and when he tries to grab it,
      we will shoot him from both sides."

And then, it is said, the bear appeared.
  The man did as he was told,   120
  he shot him.
  The bear shook himself as before.
  And the man on top of the rocks jumped down,
  and knocked the stone away.
  They shot at the bear,   125
  they killed him.
  And they skinned him,
  and the place is named 'Bear-skinning Place.'
  And when the bear lay dead,

those old women came.   130
And the bear was cut,
they cut loose the bear's beads.
  "He was going to eat us, he was going to catch us."

The bear's beads
They were cut   135
They were cut loose
"He is going to eat us"
"He is going to take us"

26

In the Desert with Hipahipa

MOJAVE

1902

INYO-KUTAVÊRE, NARRATOR
JACK JONES, INTERPRETER
A. L. KROEBER, COLLECTOR

INTRODUCTION BY A. L. KROEBER

*[The text that follows is an excerpt from a much, much longer (yet still incomplete) Mojave migration epic collected by A. L. Kroeber in 1902. The portion reproduced here, "In the Desert with Hipahipa," is the ninth of eighteen sections distinguished by Kroeber.[1] The introduction is taken, with a few emendations and reductions, from Kroeber's own general introduction to the study as a whole. The orthographic conventions used for writing Mojave words and names have changed since Kroeber's time (as indeed has the spelling of "Mohave" itself, Mojave being the preferred form today). However, I have chosen not to modernize Kroeber's spelling system in the present selection, not only because they are appropriate to the era of collection (1902), but to avoid confusion for readers who may consult the remainder of this fascinating epic. Readers—particularly those who take the trouble to consult the original publication—may find that some of Kroeber's comments and evaluations of the text as a work of oral history seem unnecessarily dismissive. We must keep in mind, though, that he has come to his conclusions on the basis of quite exhaustive investigations into the substantive historical content of this and other versions of the narrative. Even so, I think that scholars today would be far less likely to dismiss the oral-historical basis of documents such as this one, seeking instead to understand better the nature of the interaction between dreaming and traditional knowledge.—*HWL*]*

Circumstances and Nature of the Tale

The story of the recording of this tale is this.

In a previous visit to the Mohave I had learned of their male-lineage clans or *simulye,* known each by the name which all the women born in the clan shared, these names in turn having totemic reference or connotation, though in most of the names no etymologic denotation of the totemic animal or object was apparent. There is no evidence that these clans functioned other than as regards coresidence and exogamy: they had no ritual associations. Settlements normally consisted of kinsmen in the male line, and thereby of men of the same clan; but there were said to be usually several places thus "belonging" to each clan, especially if it was large. I found it difficult to engage Mohave interest in reciting to me a list of such clan localizations: the *simulye* were now "all mixed up," they said, compared with old times. When I said it was the old times that I wanted to know about, the answer was, that how it was with the clans in the old days, how they came to be, was known only to certain old men who had dreamed about that and about the traveling and fighting of the Mohave. *Itš-kanavk* 'great-telling' was the name of that kind of story; people who had not dreamed that—that is, did not specialize in it— would know nothing of moment about it.

Several old men were mentioned as informants; but a train of ill luck accompanied my endeavors to secure from any one of them the full version of what he knew. The well-informed on the subject, or at any rate those generally reputed well-informed, were evidently all of an advanced age that made their mortality high in the first decade of this century. As this clan or migration legend also was not associated with a cycle which would be sung at festivals or funerals, the series of men inclined to "dream" it—to hear, learn, and refantasy it—would be pretty thoroughly and suddenly cut off when the remodeling of Mohave life by American contacts had reached a certain point. To men who had worked, however intermittently, on railway maintenance of way, in the locomotive roundhouse or in the ice plant, a legend about ancient migrations of bands that lived off the land must have seemed irrelevant and fairly pointless, and even more so to the prospective all-night audiences whose interest would provide much of the stimulus for dreaming up the tale. By contrast, singing has an appeal in itself, reinforced for the Mohave by the emotional associations of their custom of singing their cycles as a gift at impending deaths of kinsmen. Around 1903, accordingly, song-cycle myths were still being learned and dreamed by individual Mohaves; but I now suspect that no one had then learned and reelaborated a version of the migration legend in several decades. If this is a fact, it was the very last of the crop of aged migration dreamers that I encountered at Needles about 1900 to 1905.

However, in March 1902, my customary guide and interpreter, Jack Jones, took me across the river from Needles and some two or three miles inland, more or less to the settlement Ah'a-kwinyevai, . . . [on the] eastern side of Mohave Valley. I was purchasing ethnographical specimens on the way. At Ah'a-kwinyevai, in a sand-covered Mohave house, we found the old man whom we had come to see, Inyo-kutavêre 'Vanished-pursue', who was reputed to know about the origin of clans. He admitted that he did, and would tell me the story. It would take a day, he said when I asked the length. As that day was partly gone, I arranged to come back in the morning.

Of course he did not realize that it would take Jack about as long to English to me his telling in Mohave as that took him, and I overlooked the fact, or had long since learned not to be too concerned about inaccuracy of time estimates by natives. However, he went on for six days, each of three to four hours' total narration by him and as many of translation by Jack and writing by me.[2] Each evening he believed, I think honestly, that one more day would bring him to the end. He freely admitted, when I asked him, that he had never told the story through from beginning to end. He had a number of times told parts of it at night to Mohave audiences, until the last of them dropped off to sleep. When our sixth day ended, he still, or again, said that a day would see us through. But by then I was overdue at Berkeley; and as the prospective day might once more have stretched into several, I reluctantly broke off, promising him, and myself, that I would return to Needles when I could, not later than next winter, to conclude recording the tale.

By next winter Inyo-kutavêre had died, and his tale thus remains unfinished, though its central theme, the final conquest of Mohave Valley and the taking of lands by the clan leaders, is completed. I made efforts to find other old men who might continue where Inyo-kutavêre had left off. I came to realize soon afterward that no Mohave could "continue" the narration of another.[3] The versions differ too much through being after all individually refantasied, as I would construe the core to be of

FIGURE 11. Jack Jones.
Courtesy Phoebe Apperson Hearst Museum of Anthropology
and the Regents of the University of California.

what the Mohave mean by "dreaming." With a different informant it
would have been necessary to get a new version of the entire tale; only
in that sense could Inyo-kutavêre's tale have been "finished" by another.
However, I was given the names of two surviving old men who might
furnish a completion; and in the spring of 1903, and again of 1904, I re-

turned to Needles to look them up: only to find that one of them was speechless from a paralytic stroke. The other, I wrote on April 15, 1904, to my chief, F. W. Putnam, I had as yet been unable to go to see because he lived too far from the telegraph office at Needles, to which I was then tied by an expected message. I do not recall now why I was unable to connect with him later; and before long he too died.

In 1908 I was again at Needles. The Mohave seemed to think that their recognized dreamers of the clan migration were all gone. But meeting an old man called Kunalye, I asked him whether he knew anything of Hipahipa, the greatest hero in Inyo-kutavêre's version. He affirmed that Hipahipa was the name of a Kutkilye clan band living in Mohave Valley in ancient times, and proceeded to tell me their story on March 1. I returned to him on March 3 for another installment, in which as yet the warfare that was to be the central theme of the plot was only being threatened. The old man then became ill. I had to discontinue, and so another attempt remained fragmentary. . . . For the time spent in its recording, its text is proportionally briefer than Inyo-kutavêre's telling, owing probably in part to my having as interpreter Leslie Wilbur, younger and less accustomed to me and the work than Jack Jones was.

To return to Inyo-kutavêre. He was stone blind. He was below the average of Mohave tallness, slight in figure, spare, almost frail with age. His gray hair was long and unkempt, his features were sharp, delicate, [and] sensitive. . . . He sat indoors, on the loose sand floor of his house, for the whole of the six days I was with him, in the frequent posture of Mohave men, his feet beneath him or behind him to the side, not with legs crossed. He sat still whether reciting or awaiting his turn, but drank in all the Sweet Caporal cigarettes I provided. His housemates sat about and listened, or went and came as they had things to do.

The tale is discussed in detail in parts 4, 5, and 6 [of Kroeber 1951]. A few of its more salient qualities are mentioned here now by way of preliminary orientation.

Like almost all elder Mohave, the narrator asserted he had dreamed his narrative, had seen it. . . .

The story is wholly without songs.

It has "historical" appearance in that it might have actually happened almost as told. There is no magic or supernatural ingredient in the tale, beyond such occasional deeds as the Mohave believed living members of their tribe were able to perform or experience: sorcery, charming, omens. The strength or size of a leader is sometimes exaggerated, but almost never with any great extravagance. The story is therefore factually sober. As regards its content and form, it might well be history.

At the same time there is nothing to show that any of the events told of did happen, or that any of the numerous personages named ever existed. The type of events is largely drawn from Mohave pre-Caucasian actual tribal experience; but I doubt whether any of the specific incidents were really handed down by tradition. In short, the story is a pseudo-history. It is a product of imagination, not of recollection, and therefore [is] an effort at literature. In that circumstance lies perhaps its greatest interest. It can in effect be characterized as a prose epic, or at least an effort at one. It is also a secular epic: it contains neither mythology nor ritual elements, just as it is without trace of metrical or other formally stylized language, except to a very slight degree in the names of personages.[4]

In my opinion, the one item of possible historical fact in the tale is that it may reflect a time when the Mohave were not yet permanent residents of Mohave Valley but were in the process of occupying it. Beyond that, the enumeration and localization of totemic bands or subclans after the conquest of Mohave Valley, as given in paragraphs 174–176 [of Kroeber 1951], probably rests on fact. But this list is static: it reflects the landholdings as they were more or less remembered to have existed synchronously a few generations ago—probably within a century before the telling. All the people and events of the long story I consider to be a fantasy, produced as an end in itself by the dreamer-narrator—and, with analogous but largely independent content, by a few other like-minded individuals.

The successful attainment of an appearance of historicity in a fantasy creation within an unlettered tribe, especially one wholly lacking mnemonic devices, is significant as a cultural event because of its unexpectedness and near-uniqueness. The historic-mindedness of the story is further evidenced by the consistent "nativeness" of the culture depicted: wheat, chickens, red cloth, white men are never even hinted at, though they have crept both into origin myths and ritual song-cycle tales of the Mohave. No purist ethnographer reconstructing the old culture could have been any stricter than Inyo-kutavêre.

In our recording, Jack Jones allowed the old man to proceed—for perhaps five to ten minutes—until the interpreter had as much as he could remember, then Englished it to me. With omission of repetitions, condensation of verbiage, and some abbreviating of words, I nearly kept up writing in longhand. If Jack got too far ahead, I signaled him to wait. On the other hand, if names of new places or persons came too thickly, Jack would stop translating and ask Inyo-kutavêre to repeat the names slowly, directly to me.

NOTES

1. At the end of his introduction, Kroeber makes the following comments, which are important to understanding the format of the text as presented here:

> To give a narrative of the prolixity of this one some organization, I have divided it into 197 paragraphs, according to sense, and then grouped these into 18 sections designated A to R [of which the present excerpt is section I]. For orientation I have also prefixed to each paragraph a summary side-head of my own manufacture, as well as title headings to the 18 sections. These heads are arbitrary: but I am sure they will help the reader. The need of organization was greater in this narrative than for most Mohave myths, which come punctuated by songs so that the narrator, as he concludes each incident or topic, naturally says "so many songs" and comes to a pause.

The translation is heavily annotated in the original publication (A. Kroeber 1951); the section presented here, for example, contains 147 endnotes. Only the most literarily germane of these notes have been included here, as footnotes. In addition, to open up the page for the reader and help make section-internal rhetorical organizations more transparent, I have "sub-paragraphed" the text within the numbered sections of Kroeber's original presentation.—HWL

2. They were not continuous. I took about two days off to wander about and pick up specimens, believing that even so Inyo-kutavêre would finish by the date on which I ought to return to the university.

3. Unless possibly, in some degree, a young man who was still learning from a father or other kinsman.

4. Unfortunately, because Kroeber did not record the Mojave and greatly reduced the amount of repetition and "excess verbiage" (see remarks in the final paragraph of this introduction), there is no way today to verify or contradict his assertion here.—HWL

Besides Kroeber's *A Mohave Historical Epic,* from which this selection was taken, the reader might wish to look at Kroeber's *Seven Mohave Myths* and *More Mohave Myths,* Herman Grey's *Tales from the Mohaves,* George Devereux's "Mohave Coyote Tales," or the bilingual selection of Mojave texts in Leanne Hinton and Lucille Watahomigie's *Spirit Mountain.* Leslie Spier's *Mohave Culture Items* provides some ethnographical information, and Pamela Munro's *Mojave Syntax* provides information on aspects of Mojave grammar.

IN THE DESERT WITH HIPAHIPA

I. IN THE DESERT WITH HIPAHIPA

92. EMPTY HOUSES AND FOOTPRINTS

Maθkwem-tšutšām-kwilyêhe said: "We will not go east. We will follow this valley northward. I know these mountains ahead: I know their name. But we do not want to go there: we do not want to go east. We will go north." Then they went north, following the valley.

In the afternoon they turned eastward. Then they were in the center of the valley.* In the middle of the valley was a little gulch, but there was no water in it. There they found twenty houses. There were ten houses on the west side of the dry ravine and ten on the east side. Wells had been dug: ten of them. There were no paths about, but they saw tracks of boys and girls and women and men all about. They looked inside the houses but saw nobody. It was one man who lived there: he made his foot large and small—like a man's, like a woman's, like a child's. He owned these twenty houses and lived in them, but he was not there now: he had been gone five days.

His name was Hipahipa.† He used to hunt. He did not hunt deer

---

* They are in "Basin and Range" country.
† Our introduction to one of the great heroes of the tale. Hipa is the girls' name of the Coyote clan.

or rabbits, but rattlesnakes. The rattlesnakes did not bite him. He picked them up with his hands and hung them by their heads under his belt, with their tails hanging down and rattling.* In this way he took ten of them home. There he cooked them in the sand. Thus he lived.

93. A RATTLESNAKE DIET

There were two men. Cut-blood-knee and Ha-yeθa-yêθwa, who lived at Avī-ny-ūlka and Aha-kwa-hêl on rats and rabbits and jackrabbits. [Now, shortly before,] they had been hunting and had cooked their meat [near Hipahipa's home] when Hipahipa came to them.† They gave him meat and said: "Eat what we eat!" He put a piece into his mouth. He said: "I do not like to eat that: it is not good. What I eat are rattlesnakes: see, I have some with me." The two men took up their meat, made it into a bundle, put it on their backs again [and went home].

Then Hipahipa cooked his rattlesnakes and ate them. But he thought: "That was good food which Cut-blood-knee and Ha-yeθa-yêθwa gave me. Why did I not eat it? What I eat is not good; it is rattlesnakes.‡ I will go to their houses and see what they eat." Then he went to Avī-ny-ūlka and Ahe-kwa-hêl, arriving at sunset. Then they gave him their meat, he ate it, and liked it. He lived with them five days.

Then he said: "Today I want to go back. I have twenty houses and twenty wells and live alone. I do not live like you. You have women and children and many people. When I am at home you know what I eat. At night I bring home rattlesnakes: in the morning I eat them: that is how I live. Now I want to go back. But I want all of you to know this before I go." Then they all said: "It is well. You can go back."§ Hipahipa said: "I am ready." His houses were to the northwest, and he went northwestward.

---

* This is quite a picture—the lonely man wearing a rattling snake skirt, living in twenty empty houses, with footprints about as a whole village. He has gone wild; but why so, the story does not tell.

† This is going back to the time before the arrival of the traveling band, and is to explain why Hipahipa was away from his twenty houses when they arrived.

‡ He had refused their food childishly or, like a hermit, gone queer; now he begins to regret it.

§ Assent, not permission.

Then he saw people living in his houses: he saw smoke.* He thought: "I wonder who is living there? I was alone, but I see smoke. Well, I must go, for they are my houses." He came nearer and heard the noise of the people. He said: "I see women and boys and girls all living in my houses." Then he went near and saw children playing about.

They saw him and went and told Maθkwem-tšutšám-kwilyêhe: "We have seen someone." "You have seen someone?" "Yes. Over there." Then he sent a man to see Hipahipa. He saw him and returned. Maθkwem-tšutšám-kwilyêhe asked him: "Did you see him?" and he said: "Yes." "What did he look like?" "He looks good: he is as large as we are." Then the four leaders said, "We had better go to see him." Hipahipa shouted loudly twice, and the children said: "Do you hear him?" The men said: "Yes. He shouts like a man. We shout like that."†

Hipahipa was standing behind a bush. He did not want the people to come nearer to him. As they approached he drew back. Maθkwem-tšutšám-kwilyêhe said: "Why do you go back? Why do you not meet me so that we can talk?" Hipahipa continued to retreat.‡ Maθkwem-tšutšám-kwilyêhe said again: "Why do you go back? Meet me and we will talk." Then Hipahipa came out and they all stood together. Hipahipa said: "All those are my houses." Maθkwem-tšutšám-kwilyêhe said: "Well, if they are your houses, let us go inside."

Then the people were outside cooking. The sun went down. It became dark and all went indoors. Hipahipa said: "I think none of you know me. Do you not know me? You have seen me before. I was at Kohôye [near Barstow] with you. I was a young man then, and a bad man. I kicked and ran and fought. I dreamed that way: that is why I did it. I could not help it. I was young then. My name was Noise-unruly-night. Now I am called Hipahipa. I have come here from Kohôye. Kunyôr-'iko-rāvtši and his people went away from there and I went with them, going east. When we came to Kepetšiqô and Selye'aye-metši we crossed the [Colorado] river to this [eastern] side. We came to Amaṭya'āma and Ahaly-kuīrve. Then we came to Hatai-kwa'ī and Ahmo-ku-tšeθ'īlye. There we slept. Then we came to Avi-nye-hamokyê and Aqwawa-have. When

---

* Now he encounters the migrants.
† I.e., he is not a ghost.
‡ He has turned wild and shy in his isolation.

we came there it was nearly sunset and we camped. In the morning the rest went on, but I stayed there. I did not go on. I thought: 'Why do I go with them? I do not want to go with them. I will go another way.' Then I started alone and went east. I found this place. I thought: 'I will stay here and make a house and dig a well and live here. I will call my place Halyerave-kutšakyāpve. I will call it also Hanye-kwêva.'" Thus Hipahipa told it all to Maθkwem-tšutšam-kwilyêhe.

Then Maθkwem-tšutšam-kwilyêhe said: "Now we know you. We used to see you at Kohôye: you are the man." Hipahipa said: "Yes. I am the one." Maθkwem-tšutšam-kwilyêhe said: "Then you were a young man. Now you are large, as large as we. If you had not told us, we would not have known you; but I know you now. You were called Noise-unruly-night then. Now you have changed your name and are called Hipahipa.* That is why we did not know you. Well, we have come to your houses." Hipahipa said: "Very well. You say: 'Whatever you say we will follow it.'" Maθkwem-tšutšam-kwilyêhe said: "Yes, that is what I said." Hipahipa said: "Well, I do not eat what you eat. You eat melons and pumpkins and seeds. I am not eating those: I eat rattlesnakes. But I saw men living in that direction [pointing]. I will take you there. I want you to go with me. When I take your people there, perhaps those there will give them something to eat, and you will live there. In the morning we will go."

95. UNDESIRED VISITORS

In the morning Hipahipa said: "I will not go with you. I will go ahead to show the way." He had a crooked *tukoro* stick. He said: "I will go ahead and draw a line for you with this and you can follow it. There is a place [called] Hatšuvāvek-aha with a spring; when you reach it, drink. From there, tell your people to carry water. I will continue from there marking a line, and you follow it. As you go on farther, you will come to a valley and will see smoke there. That will be Aha-ku-hêl and Avī-ny-ūlka, where I want you to go." Thus he told them how to go.

Starting that morning, they came to the spring Hatšuvāvek-aha. Maθ–kwem-tšutšam-kwilyêhe said: "This is the spring he told of. Here we will drink and take water to carry." They went on a short distance and saw

* Mohave style: reaffirming what is known or has just been said.

smoke. "Those are the places Aha-ku-hêl and Avī-ny-ūlka." Then all knew those places. Hipahipa had gone ahead: he had begun to cut brush in order to make a house. "I want Maθkwem-tšutšām-kwilyêhe to live here," he thought. Then he went east and brought a load of wood. He went again and again and brought five loads. All about were men playing with [hoop and] poles, but Hipahipa did not speak to them. Some of them thought: "I wonder why he clears that place and why he is getting five loads of wood?" But they did not ask him; therefore he did not say a word. This was in midafternoon.

When Maθkwem-tšutšām-kwilyêhe approached from the northwest, those who were playing with poles looked up. They said: "Is it wind and dust? I think someone is coming." One of them told Ha-yeθa-yêθwa and Cut-blood-knee: "I think people are coming. There is dust over there." The two leaders said: "All come here to this house! All stand here! Yes, people are coming." Hipahipa said nothing. The two leaders said: "Those who are approaching come for war, I think. All you women and children climb the mountain! All you men stay here! Do not run off!"

Then all the women and girls and old men and children climbed up the mountain. Cut-blood-knee and Ha-yeθa-yêθwa said: "We will stay here and meet them and fight." These two leaders went to meet Maθkwem-tšutšām-kwilyêhe's people. Hipahipa saw them close together; they had nearly met: then he ran toward them. He ran in front of Maθkwem-tšutšām-kwilyêhe: then he turned and went toward Cut-blood-knee and Ha-yeθa-yêθwa; Maθkwem-tšutšām-kwilyêhe followed him. Then Cut-blood-knee and Ha-yeθa-yêθwa said: "I do not think that they want to fight: Hipahipa has brought them here." They called the women and children to come down from the mountain; and they came. Hipahipa led Maθkwem-tšutšām-kwilyêhe's people to the place which he had cleared off. Cut-blood-knee and Ha-yeθa-yêθwa said: "These people are travelers. They have come to my house: give them to eat." Then their people gave them rabbits and other meat and mescal. Now the newcomers had enough to eat.

96. WILL THERE BE FOOD ENOUGH?

Cut-blood-knee and Ha-yeθa-yêθwa thought: "I want to see the strangers," and went into Maθkwem-tšutšām-kwilyêhe's camp. He said to them:

"I wonder where you have come from. You know that we all started from one place.* Then you scattered over the mountains. And we have traveled, looking for you: now we have found you." Then one of the two said: "We are scattered over the country: we have taken all the springs: there is no place for you to stay.† Everywhere our tribes have made monuments of trees or brush to claim the land. There is no room for you."

Maθkwem-tšutšām-kwilyêhe said: "We are not looking for that. We are not looking for a place to live in [here]. You have heard of the fighting and how one party was beaten. We are on the way to take back our country. We want to fight with the people there: that is why we have come." Cut-blood-knee and Ha-yeθa-yêθwa said: "We do not wish war. We live well here: we support ourselves: our women and children like living here. We do not want to take them away: they might die in the desert." Hipahipa said: "Maθkwem-tšutšām-kwilyêhe, listen to what I tell you. I want you to build a house for your people. If it rains, all that is outdoors will be wet, but if you make a house and it rains you can go inside and make a fire and it will be well." Then they built houses and lived like the other people there.

97. ANTELOPE MAGIC

Cut-blood-knee and Ha-yeθa-yêθwa had a friend called Put-it-into-eagle-down. This man had no bow and arrows: he just went in any direction—north or east or south—and brought back rabbits and jackrabbits. He caught them with his hands, seizing them by the neck, without shooting: that is how he lived. Hipahipa told Maθkwem-tšutšām-kwilyêhe: "They [Cut-blood-knee and his partner] give you meat, but they do not give you enough. I am like that man: I hunt, but without a bow. I can catch anything I want with my hands. Let us go to Ahtatš-ku-ðauve and Aha-ku-pāka. We will all go to that mountain. Take this man with you who has no bow but can kill antelope,‡ and I will go with you. The antelope have tracks like this."

---

* This may mean Avikwame, when they were still with Mastamho, but more likely it refers to the time before the emigration from Mohave Valley.
† The springs would be crucial for occupation of this southeast desert tract.
‡ Now we rise from rabbits to antelope. The charming of the swift antelope which live in open plains is a Basin Shoshonean specialty, found also among the Yokuts. But mountain sheep (*ammo*), big horns, would be more appropriate to a mountain range than are antelope (*umul*).

When they came to the place, Hipahipa said to Put-it-into-eagle-down: "Sit here! You, Maθkwem-tšutšam-kwilyêhe, take your men and go around the mountain and drive the antelope this way. Then I will kill them. And this man sitting here will kill them too. Then we shall have antelope meat." So they started to go around the mountain to drive them.

Hipahipa thought about Put-it-into-eagle-down: "I do not think he is wise. I do not think he is a doctor. I think I can beat him." Thereupon Put-it-into-eagle-down could not get up. He was weak and sweaty: Hipahipa made him be thus. The antelope came by but he could not see them: they all went past him. Others came to Hipahipa and he seized their necks, broke their legs, and killed many. He killed them all and piled up the meat. Then all the people came back there. "What is the matter with this man?" they said. Put-it-into-eagle-down said: "I do not know: I am sick: I cannot work with my hands." Then they divided the meat, and all ate. Put-it-into-eagle-down returned, and at night he said to Cut-blood-knee and Ha-yeθa-yêθwa: "I have killed antelope for you, but I cannot kill them any more. I am sick. Tomorrow morning I am going back to my place at Avī-kwe-hunāke."

In the morning he ate mescal, took his crooked *tukoro,* and went off, walking like a sick man, slowly.

98. SKIN CLOTHING

The people of Cut-blood-knee and Ha-yeθa-yêθwa shot deer and rabbits: Hipahipa killed antelope as before. He did it a third time. Now the antelope hides lay piled up high. Then he said: "All you women and girls are poor. I see you wearing willow bark [as skirts]. You have worn it two years: It is worn thin. Today I will kill more antelopes: today we shall all stay home. I want to make buckskin." Then they put water into large dishes and baskets and laid the hides in to soak. Then they worked on them. It did not take them long to cure the skins: in one day they had prepared them all.

The next day they made women's dresses and moccasins: "So that you can go out away and get firewood," said Hipahipa. "All these people here have moccasins." Before this they had been afraid to go out far into the cactuses because they were barefooted. When they had made all the dresses, Hipahipa said: "Pick each the one that will fit you." Then all picked dresses that fitted them. Now all the women had dresses and moccasins, and all the men had moccasins and leggings and shirts, and they were all dressed.

99. HUNGER AND JEALOUSY

Now it was about two years [later]. In the night they gathered,* and Ha-yeθa-yêθwa said: "*Kwaθepilye* seeds and *maselye'aye* seeds, and deer and antelope, and mescal, and rabbits and rats: those are what we live on. When Hipahipa came here I told him what we ate: he knew it. Then the man Maθkwem-tšutšām-kwilyêhe came here. Now when Hipahipa kills antelope, why does he not give me meat? Why does he not treat me well? That man only wandered in here, but Hipahipa gives him much food."

Now these people [the old residents] were shooting their game with bows and arrows. Thus it happened that sometimes they did not have enough to eat, because sometimes they missed when they shot; whereas Hipahipa merely seized the animals, and so Maθkwem-tšutšām-kwilyêhe's people always had enough. Then Hipahipa said [to the newcomers]: "We have taken all the antelope that are here: there are none left. Let us go south to Avī-ka-hāyihāyi and Aha-talame: there we shall find more antelope. Another man lives there: he also hunts them, but only with bows and arrows."

That night the people [originally] living there came back angry because they did not have enough to eat, while Maθkwem-tšutšām-kwilyêhe's people had abundance.

100. DOCTOR'S SORCERY

The next day in the morning they went hunting again; the women and children stayed home. Now Red-sky was a doctor of Cut-blood-knee and Ha-yeθa-yêθwa. The children were playing about the houses. The boys took ground *maselye'aye* and *kwaθepilye* seed, threw it up into the air, and

---

* Cut-blood-knee and the old residents of the region. In spite of saying that they were on their way to war, the wanderers have by now stayed another two years.

caught it in their mouths. MaθKwem-kwapāive's boy was with them.*
Then Red-sky killed him:† the boy died right there. Then a boy went
and told the old men and women who had stayed at home: "MaθKwem-
kwapāive's boy is dead." The old people went to see. "Well, he is dead
indeed," they said. They stood by the body and cried. They said to
Tūkyet-nyi-hayi: "Follow the men and say: 'MaθKwem-kwapāive, your
boy is dead.' Tell them that." The men had come to Avīl-he-talame and
were drinking when Tūkyet-nyi-hayi arrived and told them: "MaθKwem-
kwapāive, your boy is dead."

Thereupon they did not hunt but all came back; by midafternoon they
returned to the houses. The boy was lying where he had fallen on the
ground. All stood around him and cried. Hipahipa took a rope, went
eastward, and gathered wood. He broke it with his hands or with stones
and, making a bundle, brought it back to the house. Then they burned
the boy. Hipahipa said: "If this boy had been sick, he would have died
after two or three days. But he was not sick. I know who did this: it was
the doctor. I know his name; it was Red-sky. Tonight I will kill him."
But MaθKwem-kwapāive said: "No, do not kill him. When we traveled
here, my daughter got married; it was the same as if we had lost her. We
knew that before. Now my boy is dead, and it is as if I had lost my son
and my daughter. So we will cry; that is all. Do not kill Red-sky." Then
they cried.

101. NOTIFICATION OF A DAUGHTER

In the morning MaθKwem-kwapāive said: "I told you to cry, and we have
cried all night. I am tired. Tonight we will cry again. In two days in the
morning I will go to tell my daughter. It will take me two days to go
there. The sun will be nearly down or it will be down when I arrive: I
do not know when I shall arrive there. I will stay there two nights. Then

* Up to now [MaθKwem-kwapāive was] a sort of second-in-command to MaθKwem-tšutšām-
 kwilyêhe; MaθKwem-kwapāive from here on replaces him in the tale. He had previously let his
 daughter go in marriage; now he loses his boy, then collects gifts from his people for funeral destruction, and, when the entry into Mohaveland finally takes place, he is Hipahipa's companion
 and dies in battle by him when Hipahipa is driven out. [In contrast], MaθKwem-tšutšām-kwilyêhe,
 though the first leader of all to be mentioned in the tale, is a singularly pallid personality throughout: he leads almost abstractly; nothing ever happens to him as an individual.
† By magic or mana.

I will come back. It will take me two days to come back again. That will be six days." All said: "Good. You say you will be away six days."

Then Maθkwem-kwapāive started. He slept at Hihô-kusave. The next night he slept at Kapotak-ivauve. The third day he followed the river. When he had nearly come to where his daughter lived, the people there saw him coming. The players came to the house and said:* "Maθkwem-kwapāive is coming; I think it is he." But some said: "No, that is not the man. Maθkwem-kwapāive has long hair."† Then he arrived and all saw that it was he. They said: "Maθkwem-kwapāive, is that you?" He said: "Yes, it is I. I have come to tell my daughter that my son died." Then the woman cried. White-dream, her husband, the head man of the place, cried, and all his people cried. All gave Maθkwem-kwapāive beads or other things to burn.‡

They gave him a large pile, and he burned it all. He said: "Tonight I will sleep here. Tomorrow morning it will be one night. Tomorrow I will stay, and sleep here again. That will be two nights. In the morning I will go back." The second morning he went back. He slept again at Ota-ke-vāuve and then at Hihô-kusave, and after two days [on the way] he returned when it was nearly sunset to where he lived. Then he said to his people: "I told you I would be gone six days. Now it is six days."

102. TO KŪTPĀMA

It was night. Hipahipa said: "We have lived here four years. Your son died here. You have burned your clothes and cut your hair. I do not feel good. I want to move from this place. I do not want to stay here. We will move to Kūtpāma and Ikwe-nye-va. We will go and live there and eat tule roots and beaver and *av'a* seeds."§ Maθkwem-kwapāive said: "As you say. If you say that we should move, we will move, because you have done good to us. When you want to go, we will go." Hipahipa said: "We will start in two days."

---

* As almost always in this tale, somebody is outdoors playing hoop and poles, and the settlement is referred to as if it consisted of one house.

† It is taken for granted that he had cut it shorter in mourning, but of course they did not yet know of the mourning.

‡ To express sympathy, and honor to the dead. The destruction of property at a funeral is called *tšupilyk*.

§ Tule is cattail rush, *Scirpus acutus*. Meal from the roots is a low-grade food.

After two days, in the morning they all started and came northwest. When it was nearly noon they came to Ovālyeha and drank there and rested. That night they slept at Ahtatš-ku-ðauve. That next night they slept at Ah'ā-kuva'ê: that was two nights. The next morning they started and came to Kūtpāma and Ikwe-nye-va. There is a stream there, a little river which empties into this [Colorado] river. Now they had come to this stream: that is where they were wanting to live. Then some boys would go fishing, the women went to gather av'a seeds; some men went to hunt deer, others to get rats, beaver, or tules.

103. EATEN OUT

Then Hipahipa said: "We have [now] lived on these things here for four years and there are not many of them left. I think we will move again. We cannot stay here without food: we cannot live without it. There are two places. Hatūi-meðau and Mastamho-tesauve. I think we will go there. We will go downstream to those places, and we will eat there the same things that we eat here." Then they went to those places. They stayed there two years. They ate the same things as at Kūtpāma: fish and beaver, and tules and av'a. Then Hipahipa said: "I think we have eaten it all out." He sent four or five men to go back to Kūtpāma: "Go and look around where we lived before." They found many fish and beaver and tules and av'a again.*

104. MEETING A STRANGER

Then the wife of Maθkwem-kwapāive went upstream to Kūtpāma to gather av'a.† When she came there she met a man, Put-mark-around-neck. He was sitting under the shade of a cottonwood tree and had four jackrabbits. He asked her if she wanted some. She said: "Yes," and he

* The subsistence margin is shown to have been both close and resilient, in these nonfarming areas, by the way in which a band could eat out a tract and it would then recuperate in some years. Psychologically, it is remarkable how interested and informed the farming Mohave were about these desert conditions. There is a parallel in the fact that in the [Mastamho and Origins] myths, more space is given to the institution of wild desert foods than agricultural ones. It may be that the Mohave interest rests on famine experiences at home, when groups of them temporarily lunged into the desert for subsistence.
† She is the third member of his family to whom something happens.

cooked some in hot sand. Then he took her into the shade [of the tree] and cohabited with her.* When the meat was cooked, he gave her of it and she ate. She said: "It is good. I like to eat this." Put-mark-around-neck asked her: "What will you do now?" She said: "I am going back." When she returned home, she brought no seeds with her.

105. A PASSION IN THE DESERT

In the morning the woman went out to gather seeds and she went to the same place. She had agreed to meet Put-mark-around-neck there. So she met him. [This time] he had six jackrabbits. Then he undressed [her] completely, and the same thing happened. He gave her the meat, and she said: "I am going home."

Now this woman had a little boy. All day he cried. Maθkwem-kwapāive carried him on his arm all day trying to quiet him; Hipahipa helped him. While the woman was returning she thought: "My husband might know. But in this way he will not know: I will leave my basket and take up a stick, and walk slowly like a sick woman. Then he will not know." So she arrived at the house and said to Maθkwem-kwapāive: "I do not know how it is: I am sick; I can hardly walk. I am very sick."

106. ELOPEMENT

In the morning all got up and the women went out to gather again. This woman went too. She said: "I am [still] sick, but I think I shall be able to gather seeds for mush to eat; I will not stay home." So she went off with the other women, but hid, and ran off from them, and went back to the same place as before. There she met Put-mark-around-neck the third time; he had four [jack]rabbits with him; and they did the same way. Then he said: "What will you do now?" She said: "I want to go back." But he said: "No, no. I am your husband now. Did you not take off your clothes, and I saw you, privates and all? When a man does that to a woman, she is married to him.† And you know that I am a man: I

---

* The term "cohabit" was a common euphemism for "copulate" at the time this text was taken down.—HWL.

† Intimacy implies marriage, escapades are furtive: such seems to be the sentiment.

am not a bird.* I will take you to my house. I want you to come with me." It was midafternoon; then he took her with him. They went southeastward past Amaṭ-akano to Opui-ku-tšumāka and Humθe-vinye-haliāva where he lived.

107. HIPAHIPA RECOVERS THE ERRANT WIFE

Now the woman was gone all night: she had not come back. Hipahipa said: "What is the matter with her? I thought she would come back at night. Now it is morning and she has not returned. Maθkwem-kwapāive, your wife has been gone all night. You and I will go to see." They ate and started off. They came to Kūtpāma and saw tracks. Then Maθkwem-kwapāive said: "I knew it. I knew that someone took my wife; but I was ashamed to say it.† That is why she went away." The woman had left her basket, and they found it. They tracked her and Put-mark-around-neck. Then they came near his house. Hipahipa said: "Stand here now. He would see you; but he will not see me. I will make all who live there blind so that they cannot see me. I will cause them to know nothing." Maθkwem-kwapāive said: "Good. I will stand here."

Now those people used seeds, and the woman was grinding them. She stood in front of the house at the east corner. Hipahipa came around the house, stood behind her, grasped her around [the middle], and ran off with her to where his friend stood. [Only] when he had gone some distance did the people there see him. The woman was unwilling and scratched Hipahipa's face. "I do not want to go with you," she cried. She tore out his nose ornament and threw it away. Then Hipahipa was angry: he tore off all her clothes,‡ till she had nothing on; still she struggled. Hipahipa said: "Do not struggle: let us go." Then they came to where Maθkwem-kwapāive was waiting and started back. They made her walk in front of them. They came to Kūtpāma and took willow leaves to make a dress for her. Then they returned to their house: it was afternoon.

---

* "He meant that he had a house to live in," the interpreter explained.

† A natural enough sentiment; but he gets and takes her back. There seems to be more public shame than personal resentment.

‡ Evidently in resentment, to humiliate her by her nakedness. [Or perhaps to negate the claim of "possession-by-exposure" advanced by Put-mark-around-neck.—HWL]

108. TO KŪTPĀMA AGAIN

Then they lived as before and ate the same food for a year.* Then Hipahipa said: "Let us go [back] where we were." So they all moved back to Kūtpāma. They made houses there and lived as they had before.

109. HIPAHIPA INCITES THEM TO RETURN

They were there at Kūtpāma two years. Then Hipahipa said: "We have eaten up all the food [about here]. The women have gone far and taken all the seeds. We have killed all the rabbits and rats and fish and other animals." Boys and girls were playing outside. They picked up handfuls of yellow gravel and said: "This is red beans. This is black beans. This is white beans." Hipahipa said: "There is no maize. I see no red beans or white or blue or yellow beans. I think these boys and girls say wisely. They have dreamed well. Soon we shall have that. In the place from which we came there are those things." The children playing said: "This is yucca. This is melon. This is watermelon." Hipahipa said: "They have dreamed well. After a time we shall have all those."

It was night. Hipahipa said: "There is another thing that I always think of. You know what made us angry. Let us be going against those people to fight. What do you say to what I say, Maθkwem-tšutšām-kwilyêhe and Maθkwem-kwapāive? You do not want your people to die somewhere out in the desert."† Maθkwem-tšutšām-kwilyêhe and Maθkwem-kwa-pāive said: "Good. As you say." Two, four, five times Hipahipa spoke thus.‡ He said: "Well. I am going to say the same thing. Let us go to fight them. They are rich. They have enough to live on. They laugh at us all. They say of us: 'Those in the mountains, they have died some-where. But we live well: we live better than they.' And they do have plenty. That is what makes me angry. [Though] when we go there we shall [per-haps] die before daylight."

---

* A year between talking of the move and making it! The chronology is in round numbers.

† "If you do not fight for better land, you are likely to starve here."

‡ Characteristic expression. The Mohaves are not afraid of numbers, either exact or approximate; and, according to situation, the numbers may be either formally "round" (ritual) or "odd" and specific. It is now Hipahipa, the converted and escapist hermit, who is urging invasion and war on the leaders who set out so full of purpose of reconquest.

Then Maθkwem-tšutšām-kwilyêhe and Maθkwem-kwapāive said: "It is well: we will go with you. We will follow you. You say that when you arrive there you shall not live until the next day, but that you shall die. Well, we shall die before another day. We are not afraid." Hipahipa said: "I want all of you women and girls and old men and all to come along. If all the strong men go and are killed there, the old people will not be able to live here: they are too old. If we die, perhaps they will die too; so we will all go. Perhaps they will kill all of us; perhaps half of us. But if they do that, it will be well." Then Maθkwem-tšutšām-kwilyêhe and Maθkwem-kwapāive told their people: "All of you [prepare to] go! No one stay here!" And Hipahipa said: "There is another thing that I want to tell you. I want to go east to Avī-ka-ha'sāle, to Kunyôre and Oskīive-tekyêre. I will see those who live there. I want to tell them that we are going, tell them before we start. Many live there. Then all will hear of it. After that we will go."

110. VISIT TO AN ALLY

Then Hipahipa started for Avī-ka-ha'sāle in the morning. He arrived there at nearly sunset. At night he told them why he had come; he spoke to Dusty-sunrise and Shadow-sun, who were the leaders there. "I am going to make war. I will take my people north. I wanted to inform you before I went to war. That is why I came here. When we arrive there, perhaps we shall die. If we die there, you will not have seen me for two or three years, when you will think of me, and remember how I looked." Before daylight, when the morning star was up, Dusty-sunrise stood and said [to his own people]:* "You know what Hipahipa says. He says: 'I am going to war. It is the last time you will see me.' You all hear what he says. He says that in the morning he is returning. I will tell you what to do. Give him something!"† Then all said: "It is good. We will give him something."

In the morning Hipahipa ate. When he had eaten, the women gave him small baskets and large baskets. They were piled as high as that. The men gave him woven blankets and woven sashes and cloth shirts. They

---

* "Standing up" means that he is orating formally, "preaching."
† Merely as an honored guest? Or in anticipation of his death in war?

piled these things as high as that. Hipahipa said: "Well. I do not know how to roll them into a bundle. Do it for me!" They said: "We will do it for you." Then they made two bundles and tied the baskets to the bundles by strings. Hipahipa took the bundles on his back. "Well, this is the last time you see me, I say."

III. GIFTS DISTRIBUTED

Then he returned to Kūtpāma where he lived, nearly at sunset. He left the bundles lying, without untying them. He said: "Tomorrow morning all of you come. All the women and girls take a basket. Let everyone take one that she likes, a large one or a small one. The men do the same. Some of you like feathers, some of you buckskin shirts and leggings, some woven blankets or coats or shirts. I will not give the things to you: take them yourselves; but not tonight: tomorrow morning take them."

In the morning the girls came and took small baskets, the women large ones. The men took blankets and clothes and feathers. Hipahipa said: "If this which I have brought is not enough [to go around], I will go again. But I will not go to the same place; and I will not go today. This is not enough perhaps. Have all something?" They said: "No, not all. Half have nothing." Hipahipa said: "I will go tomorrow. It will be two days. I will go to Huvalilyeskuva and Pakat-hôave. There are people there. To them I will go."

112. ANOTHER ALLY VISITED

After two days he went in the morning. He came again to Avī-kwa-ha'sāle nearly at sunset. Then they gave him to eat, and at night he went into the house, but he said nothing.* In the morning he started again. He came to Aspa-nye-va-ke-holêve and went past it. He came to Iðo-ke'āpe and again went past it, not resting. Then he saw smoke in the south. "That is the place to which I want to go." When it was nearly sunset he reached there. There were five leaders there: Earth-guts, Sky-guts, Hold-inside-mouth,

---

* Made no speech.

Hold-in-hands, and Lying-on-dust.* Hipahipa spoke to Lying-on-dust: "I know that you live here. I saw your people about the place. I have not come to stay here: I have come to tell you what I have to say. I have told my people: 'I want to go to war.' All those at the places from which I have come answered: 'Good.' That is what I wanted to come to tell you."

Lying-on-dust said to his people: "You hear what Hipahipa says. He says: 'I am going to war. This is the last time you will see me. I shall die somewhere in that country. Tomorrow I am returning.' That is what he says. In the morning I want you to give him something—baskets and small baskets and feathers and other things." Lying-on-dust gave him a bow and arrows and a quiver. "I give you this," he said. He also gave him a large bunch of long red feathers, saying: "Take this with you: you may die there." Hipahipa stayed there all day. The second day in the morning, after eating, he said: "Roll all the things for me! Make two bundles!" Then he took them on his back. "Now is the last time you see me," he said.

113. GIFTS TO GO AROUND

In the afternoon he came to Tenyi-ku-tanākwe and drank at the spring there. He stood and thought: "I will go by another way. The way I came is around; this way is straight." Then he went on. Near sunset he came to Ah'ā-kuvate. He made a fire, lay by it, and slept.

Early in the morning he started, going westward. When it was nearly noon he came to Ahtatš-kītše, where there is a spring, and he drank and rested. He went past Yamasāve-katakalālve to Aha-nye-viðūtše; there he also went by. From there he followed the gulch to Kwil-ke-holêve. He also went by that place and came to Kuya-ny-itáêrqe. There he stood a while.

Starting again, he reached Kūtpāma at sunset as all were coming home for the day. Then he said: "Tomorrow morning all of you come. All the women and girls take a basket. Let everyone take one that she likes, large or small. Let the men do the same. Some of you like feathers, some like deerskin shirts and leggings, some woven blankets or coats or shirts. I will not give the things to you. Take them yourselves, but not tonight. Tomorrow morning take them!"

---

* We have already encountered these five in E 50 [cf. the full text in Kroeber 1951] at the same place. They are tobacco clan, and apparently Mohave, since one of them participates in the reconquest.

In the morning the people came and took the things. Now all had something.

114. THE UNDERTAKING URGED AGAIN

Then Hipahipa said: "I do not want you to wear what I gave you. Do not wear the things out in this country. I am thinking of another country. When we come there, make friends with those people. If they do not follow what we say, if they wish something else, then we will make war on them. I know that they are many there, but they are not as brave as I am. I am a brave man. In two days we will go north."

27

An Account of Origins

QUECHAN (YUMA)
1908

TSUYUKWERÁU (JOE HOMER), NARRATOR
J. P. HARRINGTON, COLLECTOR AND TRANSLATOR

INTRODUCTION BY J. P. HARRINGTON

[*What follows is an excerpt from the introduction that accompanied Harrington's original publication in the* Journal of American Folklore *in 1908.[1] Some of Harrington's comments here on the Quechan reflect the times he lived in. Anthropologists today no longer believe in the old-fashioned distinction between so-called primitive and modern cultures, once a staple of anthropological discourse. All contemporary human cultures by definition are modern cultures, regardless of level of technology or social organization. In any case, what Harrington appears to mean here is more along the lines of "uncontaminated" (by European influences), rather than "primitive" per se, with all its negative connotations.*—HWL]

The Yuma occupy a central position in the Central Group.[2] They held both banks of the Colorado from fifteen miles south to sixty miles north of the Gila confluence. They are now nearly all settled on the Yuma Indian Reservation, California, where they number in 1908 about 960, including over sixty persons belonging to other tribes.

The Yuma are still primitive in religion, and largely so in life. The Christian influence has been slight. Two missions were established among them in 1780 by the military commander of Sonora, but were destroyed by the Yuma the following summer. They were then free from missionaries for over a hundred years. The present Catholic Church is attended by few Indians. The Protestants have as yet no mission building. The medicine-men, who have much influence over the people, talk openly against the missionaries and regard their traditions as a perverted form of the Yuma traditions.

The religion of the Yuma, like that of the other tribes of the Central Group, is based on revelations received in dreams. Dreaming is declared to be more real than waking. Every individual "can dream vivid dreams"; and whatever is dreamed is believed either to have once happened or to be about to happen. Only a few men, however, dream proficiently and professionally. These are known as "dreamers" (*sumátc*). They have power to reach in their dreams the ceremonial house on the summit of Avikwaamé, a gigantic flat-topped mountain thirty miles north of Needles, California, called "Ghost Mountain" by the whites. There the dreamer finds everything as it was in the mythic past. There he receives instruction from Kumastamxo, the younger of the two great gods of the Yuma. All singing and dancing ceremonies are taught by Kumastamxo and his assistants on the top of that mountain, and the dreamer of such a ceremony is bidden to teach the others who are to participate. The various practices for curing the sick may be learned there, and there only. Thus "doctor" (*kwasidhé*) and "dreamer" (*sumátc*) are synonymous. When a man dreams myths, he usually dreams his way first to the top of that mountain, and there perceives with his senses everything which is narrated in the myth.

The "best dreamer" among the Yuma is Tsuyukweráu, a man of the Xavtsáts "nation," whose English name is Joe Homer. He is about forty-five years old, and the syphilis has already affected his eyes so that he is almost totally blind. Besides the Yuma account of origins published herewith, which it takes him four days to tell, he knows a score of animal stories, some very long tales of adventure, and sixty-four ceremonial songs.[3] This material was collected by me at my own expense. It has been carefully revised by the narrator himself.

Joe Homer made to me at various times the following statements concerning his powers and training as a dreamer:

> Before I was born I would sometimes steal out of my mother's womb while she was sleeping, but it was dark and I did not go far. . . . Every good

doctor begins to understand before he is born, so that when he is big he knows it all. . . . When a little boy, I took a trip up to Avikwaamé Mountain and slept at its base. I felt of my body with my two hands, but found it was not there. It took me four days and nights to go up there. Later I became able to approach even the top of the mountain. At last I reached the willow-roof in front of the dark-house there. Kumastamxo was within. It was so dark that I could hardly see him. He was naked and very large. Only a few great doctors were in there with him, but a crowd of men stood under the willow-roof before the house. I tried to enter, but could not. The lightnings were playing all about. They hurt my eyes. Since then I have grown blind. . . . When I was a boy, I used to eat jimsonweed leaves (*smalʸkaapítᵃ*) plucked from the west side of the plant, in order to make me dream well. . . . I now have power to go to Kumastamxo anytime, tonight if I want to. I lie down and try hard, and soon I am up there again with the crowd. He tells me everything I want to know, and it takes only a little while to go there. . . . He teaches me to cure by spitting and sucking. . . . He tells me when I "speech" or sing wrong. . . . One night Kumastamxo spit up blood. He told me, "Come here, little boy, and suck my chest." I placed my hands on his ribs and sucked his sickness (*hirávᵃ*) out. Then he said, "You are a consumption dreamer.[4] When anybody has the consumption, lay your hands on him and suck the pain out continually, and in four months he will be well." When I returned home, I went to my nephew, whose lungs were all rotten. He spit all the time. I took him to my house for four months. I sucked his chest till I sucked the sickness out. Now he is well and is going to school. . . . It takes four days to tell all about Kwikumat and Kumastamxo. I am the only man who can tell it right. I was present from the very beginning, and saw and heard all. I dreamed a little of it at a time. I would then tell it to my friends. The old men would say, "That is right! I was there and heard it myself." Or they would say, "You have dreamed poorly. That is not right." And they would tell me right. So at last I learned the whole of it right.

This approval and disapproval by the old men, it would seem, tends to unify versions of the same myth originating in the dreams of various dreamers, rendering the Yuma myths less variable than those of some peoples who do not claim to dream their mythology.

Since the writer hopes to publish in a subsequent number of this journal shorter creation myths of the Cocopa, Mohave, and Wallapai, a discussion of Joe Homer's Yuma account will be reserved till then.[5] Let him here, therefore, merely hint at Christian influence, and point out how this myth differs from similar myths found among the Mohave.[6] The myth differs from any similar account which has been found among the Mohave in the prominence and creative activity of Kwikumat (in Mohave, Mataví^{lya}), who in Mohave mythology merely leads the people to Axavol^{y}pó, builds a house there, and dies; in the mention of Blind-Old-Man; in the doctrine of four destructions of the people; in the prominence of Marxokuvek, "the first Yuma Indian"; in the instruction of the people by Kumastamxo (in Mohave, Mastamxó) at Axavol^{y}pó as well as at Avikwaamé; and in the vivid description in the story of Rattlesnake and the account of the cremation of Kwikumat.

NOTES

1. I have done little to emend or modernize Harrington's 1908 text. Readers should note, therefore, that Harrington's spelling of Quechan words—as also his spelling of certain tribal designations, like "Mohave" and "Wallapai"—is no longer consistent with contemporary practice. (For a layperson's guide to modern Quechan orthography, see Hinton and Watahomigie 1984:296–97.)

In only three areas have I felt the need for editorial "tinkering." First, both introduction and translation are heavily footnoted in Harrington's original, mostly with etymological information; I have retained only those notes that are germane to the story itself. Second, for convenience of reference in such a long and complex myth, I have added numbering to Harrington's original paragraphs and, on occasion, seen fit to break some of the longer paragraphs into (unnumbered) "subparagraphs." Third, I have inserted section titles in brackets at three points in the narrative; these titles correspond to apparent divisions at the highest level of thematic organization and are intended as "guideposts" for the reader.

Finally, a word about the Latin passages encountered in the translation. In deference to the more delicate sensibilities of his time, Harrington translated the "dirty bits" of this myth into Latin, as was then customary in publications of this nature. Since few readers today are likely to be conversant in Latin, I have had these passages translated into English. Instead of silently replacing the Latin text with English, though, I have gathered the translated passages in a section of their own at the end of the myth—not out of some outmoded sense of decorum, but simply because I find the Latin passages of the original version pleasantly quaint. Harrington's translation—like all translations, whether we are aware of it or not—is very much a product of his literary time and fashion. To replace the Latin, I felt, would have damaged this translation's patina of age.—HWL

2. The "Central Group" that Harrington mentions here refers to an earlier classification (now no longer considered to be a single branch of Yuman) that included—in addition to Quechan (a.k.a. "Yuma") itself—Mojave, Maricopa, Diegueño, and Cocopa.—HWL

3. Only a few of these songs were recorded by me. They, as well as the songs which occur in the myths and animal stories, abound in archaic, mutilated, and repeated wordforms. Compare the song "*watᶜamár umár, wakʸ akʸér ukʸér*" ('the house will burn, the house will crackle') with Yuma prose, "*avatᶜ hamárk, hakʸérk.*"

4. A Yuma doctor usually treats only one class of diseases. He is a "specialist."

5. Harrington refers here to the *Journal of American Folklore,* where this myth originally appeared.—HWL

6. The Indians compare Kwikumat with the God, Blind-Old-Man with the Devil, and Kumastamxo with the Jesus of the Christians.

FURTHER READING

C. Darryl Forde's *Ethnography of the Yuma Indians,* besides being a primary source of Quechan (Yuma) cultural information, is full of songs and ethnographic texts. Joe Homer, the narrator of this myth, was the principal consultant for Edward Gifford's "Yuma Dreams and Omens," which contains extensive dream narratives and related commentary. Leanne Hinton and Lucille Watahomigie's bilingual anthology, *Spirit Mountain,* contains a selection of Quechan oral literature, including songs and reminiscences. Frances Densmore's *Yuman and Yacqui Music* is a classic study of California and Southwestern song traditions. Abraham Halpern published a much shorter version of part of the Quechan creation cycle, "Kukumat Became Sick—a Yuma Text," in Margaret Langdon's *Yuman Texts.*

AN ACCOUNT OF ORIGINS

[THE AGE OF KWIKUMAT]

1. There was water everywhere. There was no land. Kwikumat and another man who at that time had no name kept moving at the bottom

of the water. Suddenly with a rumbling sound Kwikumat emerged and stood on top of the water. The other man wished also to come to the surface. He asked Kwikumat, "How did you emerge from the water?" Kwikumat said, "I opened my eyes." He had really held them closed. When the other man opened his eyes, the waters fell into them and blinded him. As he emerged, Kwikumat gave him his name: Kweraák Kutár ('Blind-Old-Man').

2. All was dark. There were neither sun, nor moon, nor stars. Kwikumat was not pleased. He took four steps north, and four back. He then stepped in like manner west, south, and east. This made the water subside. He stirred the water with his forefinger as he sang four times—

> *I am stirring it around, I am stirring it around.*
> *It will be dry land, it will be dry land.*

The place about which he stirred became an island.

3. "Aqa," said Blind-Old-Man, "it is too small. There will not be room enough for the people."—"Be patient, you old fool!" said Kwikumat. Blind-Old-Man seated himself on the ground and took up some mud. He shaped out of it clay dolls (*hantapáp*) such as boys now make. He made them after his own fashion, asking Kwikumat for no instruction. He stood them in a row. Kwikumat stood behind Blind-Old-Man. "What are you trying to make?" asked he. "People," said Blind-Old-Man. "You must first watch how I make them," said Kwikumat. Blind-Old-Man said nothing. He was angry.

4. Kwikumat said, "I will make the moon first." He faced the east. He placed spittle on the forefinger of his right hand and rubbed it like paint on the eastern sky until he made a round, shiny place. Said Blind-Old-Man, "Something is coming."—"I call it the moon (*hal'á*)," said Kwikumat. He made just one star at the same time. Kwikumat said, "This moon shall not stand still. It shall move toward the west." Blind-Old-Man said, "But it will go into the water, and how will it get out again?"—"I shall turn the sky, so that the moon will move along the northern horizon and thus reach the east again."

5. "I do not believe that," said Blind-Old-Man, as he continued working on his mud people. Kwikumat sat down also and took up some mud.

He feared that Blind-Old-Man might anticipate him in creating people, and that Blind-Old-Man's people might be wrongly made. First he made a Yuma man, then a Diegueño man, then a Yuma woman and a Diegueño woman. Next he made a Cocopa man and a Maricopa man, a Cocopa woman and a Maricopa woman. They lay there on the ground.

6. Blind-Old-Man showed Kwikumat some of the people he had made. They had feet but not toes, hands but no fingers. "They are not right," said Kwikumat, "the fingers are webbed. How can your man use his hands? Like you, I made hands, but I also made fingers and finger-nails; like you, I made feet, but I also made toes and toenails." Blind-Old-Man felt grieved at this. "But my man is better, because, if he wishes to pick up anything, he can pick up plenty of it."—"No," said Kwikumat, "your man is not right. I made ten fingers. If my man injures some of them, he has still some left, and can use his hands; but when your man hurts his hand, it will become sore all over."

Saying this, he sprang toward Blind-Old-Man and kicked the figures which he had made into the water. Blind-Old-Man, raging with anger, sank into the water after them, making a great whirlpool which emitted all kinds of sicknesses. Kwikumat promptly placed his foot upon the whirlpool. But some foul wind still escaped. If none had escaped, there would be no sickness in the world. Blind-Old-Man remained beneath the water, emitting sickness. Kwikumat stood long on the shore, watching and listening.

7. When Kwikumat returned to the people he had formed, he picked up the Yuma man. Lifting him by the armpits, he swung him far north and back, west and back, south and back, east and back. Previously this man had been as long as a human hand. Now he was as long as we are. This man had all his senses, but he could not talk. Kwikumat commanded him to keep his eyes closed. Then Kwikumat animated the other people in the same way. He swung the Cocopa man south first, then east, west, but did not swing him north, for he was to dwell in the south. He swung the Maricopa man east, north, south, but did not swing him west, for he was to dwell in the east.

8. Kwikumat next gave the people speech. He took the Yuma man aside and thrice commanded him to speak. He understood, but could not speak. At the fourth command he spoke a few words. Then Kwiku-

mat gave him his name, Kwitcᵞánᵃ. In like manner Kwikumat made each of the other men talk. He named the Diegueño Kamyá, the Cocopa Kwikapá, the Maricopa Xatpá. Kwikumat did not teach the women to talk. They learned from the men.

9. The Yuma man looked into the face of the Diegueño, and the two became friends. The Cocopa man stood close to the Maricopa, and the two became friends.

10. The Yuma woman meditated, "Why did Kwikumat make women different from men? How shall children be born?" A man overheard her and said, "I will ask Kwikumat." But Kwikumat said to the woman, "I know already the thoughts which you are hiding in your heart. Why be bashful? Women alone cannot conceive children. You must marry that Yuma man." Hearing this, the woman felt happy. But she meditated again, "I want a good-looking husband. I do not want that Yuma man. The Cocopa man is handsomer." She wished to marry the Cocopa man. She looked very sweetly at him. Kwikumat said, "Do not marry the Co-copa man, for you and he are destined to dwell in different places."

The woman did not believe Kwikumat. She went aside and sulked. Blind-Old-Man arose out of the water and found her here. He said, "Do not believe what Kwikumat tells you. He can do nothing for you. But if you believe in me, you will have many possessions and eat six meals each day." Kwikumat had become aware of Blind-Old-Man's presence, although he did not see him. As he sprang toward the woman, Blind-Old-Man disappeared in the ground. Kwikumat said to the woman, "You did not believe what I told you. Therefore I shall destroy you and all the other people."

Kwikumat then faced the north and talked rapidly four times. Then it rained for four days. Water covered the earth. The people were still swimming about when the rain ceased. Kwikumat picked them up, and said, "I will make you into wild beasts." He made from the Cocopa the mockingbird (*sukwilʸlá*); from the Diegueño the deer (*akwák*); from the Maricopa the buzzard (*asé*). The Yuma man only he retained in human form, and named him Marxókuvék.* "I cannot accomplish much thus alone in the world," said Marxókuvék. Kwikumat said, "I will teach you

---

* Ancestor and especial friend of the Yuma Indians. In Yuma and Mohave, *marxó* means 'ground-squirrel'.

how to make other people, and how to help me fix up the world. I made earth, sky, moon, and star, and even the darkness of night, and I shall make other things also." Kwikumat was standing on the water. He sang four times—

> This water is not deep. I could drink all this water.
> This water is good. I could drink it.

He told Marxókuvék to close his eyes. As he did so, the water went down until they stood on the ground.

11. "I made eight people," said Kwikumat, "and they had no faith in me. This time I shall make twenty-four. And I shall make them right." He kept wandering about. He went west, then east. At last he said, "Here is the center of this world. Here I shall build my dark-house."* He picked four head-lice (*nʸiílʸ*) off himself and threw them on the mud. They became little black-abdomened ant (*xurû*), little red piss-ant (*xanapúk*), big red ant (*tcʸamadhúlʸ*), and big black ant that lives on the mesa (*tcʸa-madhulʸavi*). They dug holes. They drained the mud dry. "How will you build your house?" asked Marxókuvék. He did not have a stick or a pole or a cottonwood trunk. He created these by thought. Four posts were born in the darkness, then other material. Then he built his dark-house. "I call this place Cottonwood Post (Axavolʸpó)," he said.

12. Marxókuvék made a man out of mud. He asked for no instruction. His man looked good to ride on, so he jumped on his back. Kwikumat cried, "Now that you have ridden on him, he will never walk on his hind legs only. I call him the burro (*alavúr*)."

13. Kwikumat created a woman and a man. The man asked the woman, "Has Kwikumat told you any secrets?"—"None," said the woman, "but I am going to ask him." The woman went to the dark-house, and Marxókuvék called Kwikumat thither. "I want you to marry the Yuma man whom I have just made," said Kwikumat. "But I want to bear a child," said the woman, "and he does not know what to do." Kwikumat said, "I will show you, but do not tell anybody." He told Marxókuvék to prevent the Yuma man from coming about. The woman was frightened.

---

* In Yuma, *avakutinyám*—a house without openings, used, according to this myth, like any other Yuma house, both as a dwelling and for religious purposes.

She thought that she would conceive by merely standing there in the dark-house. *Ut virgo bene intellegeret, ipse ei quid facturum esset demonstravit. Cum ea enim humi concubuit et quater copulavit. Femina, multum sudans, sibi sudorem quater manibus abstersit.* [See p. 488, A.]

Kwikumat then named the woman Xavasumkul'í, and the man Xavasumkuwá. In four days the woman became sick. She wanted a doctor. There was none to be had. But the baby within her was already a wise doctor. He told her, "Lie down!" Then he made himself very small, so that he would not cause the woman pain. In a few days he could walk and talk. Kwikumat named him Kumastamxó, and told him that he was his son and assistant in fixing up the world.

14. "Is it to be dark always?" asked Kumastamxo. "The moon and the star shine dimly." Kumastamxo spit on his fingers and sprinkled the spittle over all the sky. Thus he made the stars. Then he rubbed his fingers until they shone, and, drawing the sky down to himself, he painted a great face upon it, rubbing till it shone brightly. "What are you going to call that?" asked Kwikumat. "This is the sun (*in'á*). The moon goes west and returns, it dies and in two days it is born again. But I have made the sun at a different time, and it shall move differently." Kumastamxo allowed Marxókuvék to make daylight and darkness. "Both eternal darkness and eternal daylight would strain our eyes. Therefore one half of the time it shall be night (*tin'ám*), and one half day (*in'ám'k*). Some creatures will sleep by day, some by night."

15. Kwikumat made another Yuma man and a Diegueño man and instructed them in the dark-house. Then he made a Cocopa man, a Maricopa, an Apache, a Wallapai, a Havasupai, a Chemehuevi, and a Kawia, and a wife for each. Marxokuvek said, "These are enough. If you make more people, this earth will be too small for them." Kwikumat told him that the earth was growing bigger all the time.

16. Kumastamxo stamped until he shook earth and sky. Everything was frightened. Kwikumat was in the dark-house. He knew that Kumastamxo was trying to make cracks in the earth, so that plants and trees might grow up. The arrow-weed (*isáv*) was the first plant to grow up through the cracks in the mud.

17. Kumastamxo talked north four times. He said, "It will hail." But the sky-kernels (*amain'etadhítc*) which fell were not hail-stones, but grains

of corn. The people began to eat them. "Do not eat them all," cried Kumastamxo. "Plant some."—"How shall we plant them? With our hands?" He sent the people north to get sticks. Each one found a sharp stick. "This is corn (*tadhíitc*)," said Kumastamxo. "Take it, plant it."

18. Kumastamxo then made seeds of the gourd (*axmá*) and melon (*tsemetó*). He made them out of spittle. He gave them to the Cocopa. He gave seeds of the prickly pear (*aá*) to the Maricopa. The people planted the seeds in the wet ground.

19. Nobody knew how to make it rain. "To the Maricopa man alone I give power to produce and to stop rain," said Kumastamxo. "When the people thirst, let them remember me, for I have power to cover up the face of the sun with a rain-cloud and to send a rain-wind every day. When a man plants upon dry ground, let him remember me. If he calls my name and sees me, it will rain four or five days, and he can plant his seed."

20. Kwikumat said, "I am tired. I think I shall take a rest. It is about time to have some darkness." Kumastamxo said, "I will give you all the darkness you want." He fastened the sky so that the sun could never rise again. But Kwikumat stamped four times. This jarred the sky free, and the sun came up. Kumastamxo was in the dark-house. He said, "I see the daylight coming. Who did that?"—"I did," said Kwikumat.

21. Marxókuvék tried to make some people. He made the coyote (*xatalʸwí*). Coyote began at once to look for something to eat. He would not stand still. Marxókuvék also made the raven (*akák*), the mountain-lion (*numéta*), and the cougar (*axatakúlʸ*). Kwikumat appointed Coyote as head man (*piipá xeʟtanák*) over these three. Marxókuvék next created a girl and a boy. He was about to name them when Coyote said that he wished to. Coyote named the girl Sakilʸkilʸnamá,* and the boy Ax'alʸesmetnʸitcʸót.

22. Kwikumat noticed that none of these people were behaving properly. Mountain-lion tried to catch Sakilʸkilʸnamá. Kwikumat told him to stop. After that he prowled about, trying to catch Marxókuvék and Kumastamxo, and even Kwikumat himself. "I must get rid of these animals," said Kwikumat. He assembled all the good people in the dark-house. He talked rapidly at each of the four corners, invoking a flood.

---

* Joe Homer tells a very long myth about Sakilʸkilʸnamá, who weds Madhemkwisám.

First came a blinding dust storm. Then it rained thirty days. No water entered the dark-house. In vain the wicked besought Kwikumat to let them in. Most of them were drowned. Burro has, since then, great white spots on his belly.

23. Raven flew up to heaven. He hung by his beak at the very top of the sky. The water rose until it wet his tail. One can see where the water touched it. Then Kumastamxo caused the water to subside, for he did not want to drown this bird, for he was so pretty. Raven was black at first, and was then called *akák;* but Kumastamxo gave him many-colored feathers, and then named him *kukó.** Kumastamxo built him a cage, and in this he floated on the subsiding waters. Kumastamxo built the cage out of nothing, because he loved Kuko so much. When the cage rested on the earth, Kuko wished for freedom. In return for his freedom, he promised to be a faithful servant of Kumastamxo. He accompanied Kumastamxo everywhere he went. He would ascend high in the air and, descending, report to him what he saw. He could hear the tread of an enemy a day's journey distant.†

24. When the water had subsided and the earth began to grow dusty again, Kwikumat told the people that they might go outside the dark-house. Far in the west the storm was disappearing over the ocean.

25. The water sank so low that little was left in the ocean. Blind-Old-Man feared it would dry up. He crawled out upon the northern shore. He found Xavasumkulʸí and Xavasumkuwá in the dark-house. He promised them many things if they would renounce Kwikumat. He told them, "Kwikumat is going to kill you by and by." Xavasumkuwá believed him. But Xavasumkulʸí showed that she did not believe him, and feared him. Blind-Old-Man tried to seize her. She ran. He caught her. He promised her six meals a day. "Bring them here, then," she said. "I would like to," he said, "but I fear Kwikumat." Kwikumat approached, and Blind-Old-Man sank into the earth. "He had a tail, and claws on his fingers," said Xavasumkulʸí. "He wishes to take you down under the earth," said Kwikumat. "How could you catch anything to eat down there?"

* In Wallapai, *kukwóka* means 'woodpecker'.
† In Joe Homer's version of the Kwiyu myth, Kuko guides Kumastamxo to the dwelling of Axalykutatc.

26. Xavasumkul^yí walked over to where the people were standing, and told them how to produce children. They did not believe her. *Nec invitus unus ex viris conatus est ea agere quae ipsa dixisset. Penem autem in anum et non in vaginam inseruit. "Mox pariam aliquid," dixit femina. Exspectavit parere infantem paene eodem temporis momento. Cum id non accederit ea femina et ceterae ira commotae sunt. "Cur in me incensae estis?" inquit Xavasumkul^yí. Atque iterum explicavit, "Vaginae penem insere!" At ille vir in vaginam quidem non penem sed testes inseruit.*

Turn rediens ea marito dixit illas mulieres numquam concepturas esse. Kwikumat eam incusavit quod dixisset ceteris ea quae ipse eam occultim docuerat. "Nec metuo ne intellegant," Xavasumkul^yí inquit. Kwikumat jussit: "Duc has mulieres gradus quattuor ad septentriones, ad occidentem, ad meridiem, ad orientem et ego, item, viros ducam." Hac saltatione facta imperavit omnibus ut humi jacerent et copularent. [See p. 488, B.]

27. Because Kwikumat had wearied in his work and had stamped the sun loose again, Kumastamxo felt anger against him and boasted that he was the greater of the two. Kwikumat said, "You are only my little boy, too young to do better." Kumastamxo went into the dark-house and dreamed Kwikumat and Marxókuvék sick.

28. Kwikumat became crazy. He tried to turn the sky north instead of west. Then he walked from the dark-house out into the desert. He walked east, then west. Since he had turned the sky the wrong way, it got stuck, and would not turn at all. "Can I assist you?" asked Kumastamxo.

29. Kwikumat seated himself on a mountain and thought that he would make some more people. So he picked up a little stick, and, taking mud on his forefinger, he plastered it upon one end. Then he threw the stick away. This made it angry. It became the rattlesnake (*avē'*). The mud became the rattle. Rattlesnake feared the people, and they feared him. But the people discovered him and surrounded him. He tried to catch a woman. But the Apache Indian seized him and tied him around his waist. Kwikumat gave him power to do this, and he in turn gave power to his friends. Rattlesnake bit several persons. Among those bitten was Marxókuvék. Everybody said, "Kill that snake." But Marxókuvék was unwilling to kill it, for he knew that this would displease the Apache. "I suppose that I am going to die," said Marxóku-

vék. "No, you will not die," said Kwikumat, who then bade the people catch Rattlesnake and pull off his rattle, so that if Rattlesnake should thereafter bite anybody, the bite would not poison. Kwikumat then threw Rattlesnake far to the north. There he made a roaring sound, trying to make his rattle grow again. A man said that Rattlesnake had other rattles in his mouth. Kwikumat caught him again and opened his mouth. He found no rattles, no teeth, no poison. He then hurled Rattlesnake so far to the north that he fell into the ocean. He swam swiftly through the water, but soon went to the bottom, where he dwelt and grew fat.

30. The people asked Kumastamxo, "If we fall sick, who will cure us?"—"Men who have been instructed," said Kumastamxo. "We do not believe that," said the people, "for when you get sick, you cannot even cure yourself." Kumastamxo called all the Yuma men into the dark-house. "You are my favorite people," said he, "and I will tell you all secrets." He then made a dust storm arise in the east. It covered up the sun. It became like night. "Now sleep," said Kumastamxo. Dreams came. One man noticed that Kumastamxo's eyes were sore. He rubbed spittle on them and cured them. Another man saw that Kumastamxo had rheumatism. He found the pain and pressed it out. To another man Kumastamxo appeared to have the diarrhea. Kumastamxo sang, and this man sang with him, till it became cured. When a man talked wrongly, Kumastamxo stopped him, and asked another man to talk. "Most of you fellows talk right," he said, "and will be great doctors. If a man gets sick, let him call a Yuma doctor."

31. Marxókuvék had died from the snakebite. Kwikumat said, "Come here, you doctors, and cure this man. It is a difficult case. He is already dead. Well, I will show you how." He grasped Marxókuvék's hands. He then made himself imagine that Marxókuvék was breathing. "This man is not dead, but sleeps. I shall awaken him." He then took a stride in each of the four directions, reaching the ocean which surrounds the earth each time. Then a whirlwind came and breathed upon Marxókuvék. He stood up with closed eyes. Kwikumat then called the thunder from the west. All the places about grew bright. Marxókuvék opened his eyes. "You were sleeping too long," said Kwikumat, "so I awakened you."—"The snake bit me, and I felt drowsy," said Marxókuvék. "You died," said Kwikumat, "but the whirlwind came and cured you." When the people

learned that medicine-men had such power, they were afraid that they might kill as well as cure.

32. All the women asked one another, "What is coming within me?" They asked Xavasumkulᵞí what was to happen, but she would not tell. All the children were born on the same day. The women were disappointed in them. "Why so small?" they said. "We wished to bear big men and women. These have not even hair on their heads, and cannot stand erect on their hind legs." They did not know that babies have to grow up. Kwikumat told them, "You will bear no more children unless you cohabit again."

33. Kwikumat created four more men—the Wallapai, Mohave, White, and Mexican. Some of these held themselves aloof from the other people. Kwikumat stamped four times in anger, and fire sprang up all over the earth. Kumastamxo saved the good people by covering them up with snow. The Mexican and the White escaped by flight. "This will not do," said Kumastamxo. "You make people and then destroy them, only because you yourself did not make them right." Kwikumat felt ashamed, and quenched the fires by rain.

34. Kwikumat took two whitish sticks. One he threw east, where it became a horse. The other he threw into the water, where it became a boat. He gave boat and horse to the whites.

35. Kumastamxo told the whites that if they would enter the dark-house, he would instruct them. But they distrusted him. They were rich and stingy. Kumastamxo told the Indians to drive them away. When the latter hesitated to do this, Kumastamxo invoked a hot windstorm, and the whites fled far to the west in a boat.

36. The people heard a great noise in the water. It seems that the figures made by Blind-Old-Man which Kwikumat had kicked into the water had come to life. The people were the duck (*xanamó*), the beaver (*apén*), the turtle (*kupéta*), and the wild goose (*yelák*). Their fingers and toes were webbed. "I fear they will kill us," said Kwikumat.

37. Kumastamxo made bow and arrows and gave them to the people. He then threw a handful of mud north, where it became a bird. "Shoot that," he said. The Cocopa man shot at it. But the arrow broke, for the bird was hard as stone. The man felt sad. He had no more arrows. Kumastamxo pulled up an arrow-weed and showed how to make arrows.

He then went west and turned himself into a deer. He asked the Yuma man to shoot the deer. He refused, for he knew it was Kumastamxo. The Apache, however, shot into the hindquarters of the deer, which fell to the ground. When he tried to skin it, Kumastamxo said, "Foolish man! That deer is of stone." This explains why the Apache kill deer. Kumastamxo was angry because the Apache shot at him and gave bow and arrows to the Yuma man alone, and forbade the others to use them. A big stone was coming out of the ground. That was the bow.

38. Kwikumat made another flood. The waves made the mountains and the high places as they now are. Before then the earth was flat. Kumastamxo lifted one man and one woman of each kind of people upon his shoulders. *Nonnulli refugium petierunt in ejus anum ascendentes.* [See p. 488, C.] Others stood on the top of Avihaatác Mountain. When these entreated Kumastamxo to save them, he turned them into rocks. It rained forty days. Kumastamxo spread his arms four times. The waters went down.

39. When the earth was dry again, Kwikumat created just one person more, Akoikwitcʸán ('Yuma-Old-Woman'). She belonged to the Xavtsats nation.

[THE DEATH OF KWIKUMAT]

40. Kwikumat had no wife, but he had a daughter, Xavasúmkulapláp ('Blue-Green-Bottom-of-her-Foot'). People now call her the Frog (Xanʸé). She was born in the water, like Kwikumat himself. They lived in the darkhouse. Kwikumat lay at the north wall of the house. Frog lay naked by the door. Kwikumat felt sick. He staggered outside to defecate. As he passed Frog, he touched her private parts with his hand. He went south and defecated. Frog straightway turned over and burrowed under the earth. Coming up under Kwikumat, she opened wide her mouth, into which fell four pieces of excrement. She then burrowed back to the hut and lay down as before. Kwikumat came back into the house dizzy and groaning. All his strength had left him. Frog said, "Father, what ails you?"

"I am sick, I am sick.
What made me sick? What made me sick?

Did rain-cloud make me sick?
Did foul-wind make me sick?
My head is sick, my belly is sick,
My limbs are sick, my heart is sick."

Kwikumat lay with his head turned successively in all four directions. The people squatted around. All the doctors together could not cure him.

41. The Badger (Maxwá) fetched cool sand and placed it on his breast. Although Badger was not a doctor and did not know the reason for his own action, Kwikumat said, "I think I am getting better." Then he grew sicker. He said, "I do not think I shall live long, I am going to die. But I shall feel all right again sometime, somewhere." The people did not understand what he meant by "die." His was the first death. Kwikumat sweated. His sweat is white pigment. They get it north of Yuma. Beaver threw some clothes over him, for he felt cold. That is why people wear clothes. Kwikumat called to Kumastamxo, "Little boy, come here!" The fourth time Kumastamxo heard him. Kwikumat told him, "I am going far away. I leave everything in your care. Complete my works! I have taught you long. Do everything right." Frog said, "He is nearly dead. I will flee from here." She burrowed under the earth.

42. When the dawn came, Kwikumat died. He lay in the dark-house. His head was toward the west. All the people were silent. They thought he was asleep. Wren (Xanavtcíp) said, "He is dead. He is a shadow. He is a wind. You will never know him more."

43. Kwikumat, when dying, told Coyote, "Since I placed you as chief over three, you must behave yourself and set a good example." Kwikumat knew that Coyote intended to steal his heart, and all the others knew it also. Wren said to Coyote, "You take my heart as a substitute" (*'Inyép iwá madháuk matsinyóxa'*).* And the people understood that Coyote would take Wren's heart instead of Kwikumat's.

44. Wren deliberated silently how he might thwart Coyote in his purpose. He asked himself, "Shall we hide the body? Shall we throw it into the water? Shall we burn it up?" Wren said to the people, "We must burn him up." Wren then told Beaver, "Fetch cottonwood-logs from the north,

---

* Often said at cremations in a figurative sense.

where you will find them standing dry, ready to burn." Beaver felled them with his teeth. He brought them back with his teeth. Wren told the ant-lion (*manisaár*), "Dig a hole here quickly; dig it as long, broad, and deep as a man." When the hole was finished, Wren commanded Beaver to fill it with dry arrow-weed, and then to lay three logs lengthwise across the hole, and two more on each side of these. Beaver had brought only four. He had to fetch three more. On these logs Beaver and others piled dry logs and arrow-weed.

45. There was no door nor opening in the dark-house. "Which side shall we tear open in order to take the body out?" asked Kumastamxo and Marxókuvék. They decided to bear it south. Wren said, "Because some of us are born in the north, bear it north." Wren said, "Lift him up!" They seized the body with their hands. They took one step north. Then they laid it down. They were still inside the house. Kumastamxo broke open the north wall without touching it. Then they took another step north and laid it down again. Thus with four steps they laid it, head south and face down, on the pyre, and piled wood and arrow-weed over it.

46. All was ready. But they had no fire. Wren sent Coyote east to get fire. He told him to run to the place where Kumastamxo had rubbed his spittle on the sky. He did not wish to have Coyote about. Coyote reached the dawn with four bounds. He rubbed his tail in the white fire. Meanwhile Wren directed two women to make fire. They were the House-Fly (Xalesmó) and Big-Blue-Fly (Kwixvacó). They took turns at twirling a dry arrow-weed stalk on a piece of willow-wood. They fed the sparks with willow-bark. Kumastamxo said that all people would make fire thus. Lizard (Kwaatul^y) lighted a wisp of arrow-weed. He lighted the south-east corner of the pyre first, and last of all the southwest corner.

Coyote came bounding back, his tail all light. He leaped straight for the burning pyre. He was angry. The light on his tail went out. That is why it is black on the end. "Stand close together!" all the people cried, "for he is going to jump." They crowded thickly about the fire. Badger and Squirrel (Xomir) were the shortest men. Coyote sprang over these, seized Kwikumat's heart in his teeth, and then, springing back again, ran swiftly southwest. Chicken-Hawk (Its'ór^a) was the best runner in the crowd. They sent him after Coyote. But Coyote left Chicken-Hawk far behind. Still he did not stop. Only when he had reached the Maricopa country did he lay the heart down and eat it. The heart became a mountain. It is called Greasy Mountain (Avikwaxós). It is greasy from the fat of the heart. It is always shady about this mountain.

47. After Coyote ate that heart, his mouth was black and his tongue blood-red. They were burnt by the heart. Kumastamxo said, "Coyote is not worthy of being called a man. He shall be wild. He shall have neither a friend nor a home. He shall sneak about the mountains and sleep with the jack-rabbits. I call him Xuksaraviyŏu."

Coyote was crazy. He tried to marry his own daughter. One day he noticed a girl among the bushes *cui erat vagina ulcerosa et putrida, quam omnes fugerent. Cum ad eam lupus decurreret, exterrita in manus genuaque descendit. Tum lupus cum ea copulavit.* [See p. 489, D.] He could not disengage himself. The girl carried him with her up to the sky. Coyote may still be recognized as the dark spot on the moon.

48. All sat in silent grief about the burning pyre. The old people felt saddest, for they knew they must soon share Kwikumat's fate. But none knew about crying. It was the Yuma man who cried first. His name was Xanavá. He is now a kind of red bug which cries, "Tci-tci!" He was sitting on a mesquite-tree, looking at the ground. He raised his little voice, and cried, "Tci-tci-tci-tci!" Then Tinʸamxworxwár joined in. He cried, "Xwurrxwurr!" He was sitting on a willow-tree. He is now a green bug. All the people began to cry, everything cried. The wind cried. The sky cried. Kumastamxo shouted, "Because we have lost our father, all people will lose their fathers. Our father dies. Everybody dies. People are born and must die. Otherwise there would be too many people. They would have to sleep on top of one another. Maybe somebody would defecate all over you." As he said these words, all the people trimmed their hair (or feathers) and threw it into the fire. Deer (Akwák), Jack-Rabbit (Akúlʸ), Cotton-Tail (Xalʸáw), and Bear (Maxwát) cut their tails off and threw them in. They found it hard to make their tails grow again. Roadrunner (Talʸpó) was the only man who kept his tail long. He needed it.

49. A whirlwind now blew all about. The people thought that Kwikumat was about to appear again. "No," said Kumastamxo, "that is the holy spirit-wind. Sometimes it will come very near you. But you will see nobody, only dust-laden wind." He sang four times—

The wind is wandering, is wandering.
The wind is wandering, is wandering.

Then all the people cried anew.

50. Kumastamxo said, "Wren was a poor manager. Henceforth I will attend to everything myself."

51. Frog kept burrowing beneath the earth with guilt and fear in her heart. She felt that she must emerge in order to open her mouth and cool it, for it was burning hot from the excrement which she had eaten. But hearing the wailing of all things, she burrowed under again, lest the people discover and kill her. She emerged four times—(1) at Amatkoxwítc, a round pit near Mellen, Arizona; (2) at Samkótcave,* a hole in the ground near Bill Williams Fork, three miles above its confluence with the Colorado; (3) at Avixᵃá, Cottonwood Mountain, a mile east of Yuma, Arizona; (4) at Avixanᵞé, Frog Mountain, near Tucson, Arizona. Frog was transformed into this mountain.

[THE AGE OF KUMASTAMXO]

52. Rattlesnake remained in the ocean. He feared to come on shore, lest the people take vengeance upon him for having bitten Marxókuvék. He grew to such enormous size that he could encircle the earth with his body. The people feared that if Kumaiavĕta were allowed to grow much larger, he might come on land and kill them all. Kumaiavắta was a powerful doctor. Kumastamxo feared that he might send forth pestilence from under the water, or that he might eat somebody's excrement, as Frog had done. Therefore Kumastamxo resolved to destroy Kumaiavĕta. "We will summon him to Axavolᵞpo," said Kumastamxo, "and I will manage the rest." Kumastamxo sent Spider (Xalᵞtót) to request Kumaiavĕta to come to Axavolᵞpo in order to cure a sick man there. Spider darted down and back. "Kumaiavĕta says that he does not wish to come."—"Tell Kumaiavĕta that the man will die if he does not hasten hither," said Kumastamxo to Spider.

When Spider delivered this message, Kumaiavĕta said, "It is my duty as doctor to go, although I know exactly what you fellows are trying to do. I have, however, one request. Grind corn and place some of it at four places on my way, that I may not famish on the long journey." When Kumaiavĕta reached the first stopping-place, he found more corn there

* In this hole the Yavapai are said to have married.

than he could eat. He thought, "I know now that they wish to kill me, since they have placed a lunch for me here. But it is my duty to go ahead." Spider said, "You had better hasten, lest the man die." At that Kumaiavĕta grew angry. He shook his tail, making a noise like thunder. Enveloped in storm-dust and lightning, he reached Axavolʸpo. The people all fled from the dark-house when they saw that Kumaiavĕta had four heads. Only Kumastamxo remained within. Kumaiavĕta smelled of the house. "Nobody is in there," said the people. "Yes, a sick man is there," said Kumaiavĕta. "That is true," said the people, "but we thought you would prefer not to have us about when you cure him, so we came outside."

Kumastamxo stood inside the house, west of the door. In his hand he held a great stone knife. There was no sick man there. He had merely thrown up earth in the center of the floor, so as to resemble a sick man. Kumaiavĕta tried in vain to wedge his heads through the door. Kumastamxo made the door wider. Kumaiavĕta then caught scent of Kumastamxo. He pushed his four heads inside the house. With a single blow Kumastamxo severed all four heads from the neck. Then he sprang outside, leaving the heads in the room. He brandished his knife before the people. "When you want to kill somebody, use this." This is why people have knives. He tossed it up and caught it. Kumastamxo said, "Because Kumaiavĕta has been killed, other bad doctors will be killed." There is blood and spittle in the mountains all along where Kumaiavĕta's body lay. The whites call the red "gold" and the white "silver." Kumastamxo took the four heads, cut them apart, and pounded up each one separately west of Axavolʸpo. They are now gravel-beds.

Kumastamxo said, "I know you all fear that there will be another flood. There have been four floods. There will never be another; for I shall take this great body and place it along the shore about the whole world, and above it the water shall not rise. But if you kill my bird Kuko, I will make the water rise and drown you all." When Kumaiavĕta was killed, he urinated freely. The ocean is his urine. That is why it is salty, has foam on [it], [and] is not good to drink.

53. Kumastamxo said, "This place is unclean. I shall burn the house." Marxókuvék said, "No, leave it there; for I will call the birds and wild animals, and they will dwell about there when we have already journeyed forth." [Song, repeated four times:—]

The house will burn, will burn.
The house will be crackling, will be crackling.
It will blaze.
We are going to [dance?].
It is going to be lighted.
It is going to be lighted.
It will blaze.
We are going to [dance?].
Something bird-like is coming.
Bird-like tracks will be about the place. *
We are going to light this unclean house.
It will blaze, blaze.

Kumastamxo took four steps, lighting the house at the four corners. Then they all danced. When they ceased, Kumastamxo called Night-Hawk (Wiú). He taught Night-Hawk to sing when the dawn is coming, so as to awaken the people. Kumastamxo promised him great wisdom if he would do this regularly. "Let me sleep a little longer," said Night-Hawk. After a while Night-Hawk called out, "Qrr′ rr′ rr′ rr′!" When he calls thus, the people know it is time to wake up.

54. Kumastamxo said, "Let us leave this place!" He took four great strides to the north. The people moved with him. He had a wooden spear. He made it out of nothing. He pressed the sharp end into the ground and moved the other end toward and from himself four times. Then he pulled it out toward the north. Water gushed forth and started to flow north. He stopped it without touching it. A second time he drew the spear out toward the west. He stopped the water. Then toward the east. He stopped the water. Then he threw it out toward the south. He let the water flow freely. He took four strides south. At each stride he made a great scratch with his spear in order to guide the water to the ocean. Where he held the spear-blade flat, the river is broad. Where he held it sidewise, the river-channel is narrow, and most of the water flows on one side. At Yuma he cut the mountains asunder to let the river through. Taking four more steps, he returned to the source. [Song, repeated four times:—]

---

* When a man dies, and his house is burned, seeds are thrown into the fire. Birds come later and pick them up.

This is my water, my water.
This is my river, my river.
We love its water.
We love its driftwood [foamwood].
It shall flow forever.
It shall flow forever.
When the weather grows hot,
It shall rise and overflow its banks.
It shall flow forever.

55. Kumastamxo made a raft of cottonwood-logs out of nothing. On it he placed four medicine-men—a Maricopa, Yuma, Diegueño, and Cocopa. On a second raft he placed four more medicine-men. One of these was a Mohave. The other people walked down.

56. They stopped first at a whirlpool near Kwiyuhitáp, north of Mellen, Arizona.* A great snake (Xikwír) was traveling southward "behind the river." He wanted to bite somebody. Kumastamxo caught him. That he might always stay in the water, and never become a man, Kumastamxo pulled the snake's teeth out.†

57. At Avikarután, south of Parker, they stopped a second time. Kumastamxo told the Yavapai to live there on the Arizona side. He forbade them to cross the river. They did not know how to swim. At last they crossed on a tule-raft. Kumastamxo made a bright light shine forth from Avikarután Mountain. But the California side was dark.

58. Kumastamxo said to the people, "Because you are good people, I want you to find a good place to stay. We are going to move up to the top of a high mountain, and I shall teach you everything up there. From there we can see far over the earth." He moved north with four steps. The people moved with him. "This is my homeland," said he, "this is High Mountain (Avikwaamé)."

59. "Here is the place for the dark-house," said he. He sent Beaver to bring four cottonwood-posts. Ant-Lion (Manisaár) dug four holes.

---

* Mohave, Kwayuhitápmave ('place [*ave*] where Kwayu was killed [*hitap*]'). Kwayu was a gigantic cannibal.

† My informant explains that his body is a red stratum on the California bank. Nearby is a cave. If one enters, Xikwír will not bite, but will make one sick. He stabs in the abdomen, and blood flows forth. All about lie Xikwír's teeth. They are shiny and as large as fingers.

Lizard (Kwaatúl^y) brought willow-poles. Big Red Ant (Tcamadhúl^y) brought sand and placed it on the roof.

60. Kumastamxo stationed the learners in the northeast corner, the good doctors in the southwest corner. Dead people stayed in the southeast corner, for they go in that direction when they die. The door was in the northern side. Kumastamxo made the bad "speechers" sit down. He did not allow them to bewitch one another. Kumastamxo alone bewitched, and gave only those sicknesses which others had power to cure.

61. Kumastamxo said, "I should like to keep all of you in here all the time. But it is so crowded that you cannot learn well. So I ask you to go outside." He sent them out. Only Ampot^axasarkwitin^yám remained within. Kumastamxo produced a great star and showed it to him there in the dark. "You are a good 'speecher.' With this find the road, with this find your own house in the darkest night. This is the great star (*xamasé vatái*).* Take this out when you cannot see well." Kumastamxo called in each of the great doctors separately. He taught some of them how to kill a man in four days.

62. Kumastamxo called all the people into the dark-house again. He made everything dark. All fell asleep. He ascended into the sky. The people could not find him. He entered the dark-house again, and they discovered him there. Then the sun, moon, and stars disappeared. There was consternation among the dreamers. Even Marxókuvék did not know how to make a light. But after a while a certain man pulled out the morning star. It shed light all about. Then Kumastamxo took the very sky away with him. They found him with it in the dark-house. He taught by alarming the people and then assisting them.

63. Kumastamxo made a cottonwood-tree grow up in the dark-house. He cut the roots with his mind. It fell toward the west. "Who wishes to have this tree?"—"We," said the Yuma. "We will tie feathers along the sides of it and make the sacred sticks (*xaukwíl^y*) used in Yuma fiestas."

64. Kumastamxo bade the people go outside. He taught them how to fix up and fight. He gave them bows and arrows and war-clubs as they went out.

---

* That is, the morning star.

65. He kept the people outside. He allowed only one Yuma man and one Diegueño man to enter. He taught them how to make fiesta houses (*avakarúk*).* That Yuma Indian was Pamavíitc, ancestor of all the women who bear the name Mavé. They had no cottonwood nor willow trees. They built it out of nothing. They made a shade-roof. Meanwhile all the other people were standing in a line east of the house, and facing east. Kumastamxo announced that all was finished. When the people turned about, they beheld not one but two fiesta houses, one for the Yuma, and one for the Diegueño. Kumastamxo led one half of the Cocopa under the Diegueño house and taught them how to make one for themselves. These told the other Cocopa people. Kumastamxo said, "When you lose a big man, you will have a fiesta some months after he is dead."

66. It became dark. Kumastamxo detailed Ampot^axasarkwitin^yám to take charge of the speeches. Kumastamxo gave him many songs. Then Kumastamxo changed the darkness into daylight. He knew what each Yuma man could do. He called each man to him separately. He was in the dark-house. He said to each man, "You know to what tribe you belong. Kwikumat told you not to forget. For if you forget, you will not be swung into the right place [?]."

67. To the first man thus called into the dark-house Kumastamxo said, "Since Frog was eldest-born, I call you 'Xavtsáts'; but since Frog fled, I call her 'Xan^yé'. Call your daughters 'Xavtsáts'."†

Then he called in Paxipátc and gave him his nation, too. He said, "Call your daughters 'Hipá'. But I now call Coyote 'Xatalwí'."

To Pagel^yótc [?] he gave the nation-name 'ʟ^aots', which is connected with rain-cloud. Rain-clouds are now known as *akwí*.

To Pamavíitc he gave the name 'Rattlesnake' (Maavě). Rattlesnake is now called 'Avě'.

To the next man he gave 'Red-Ant' (Ciq^upás). Red-Ant is now called 'Ikwís'.

---

* Shade-roofs built of cottonwood-poles and willow-branches for ceremonial use during the various "fiestas."

† The informant at first stated, and later denied, that [the first man] was Ampot^axasarkwitin^yám. Each Yuma man has one or more names of descriptive or fanciful meaning. Each woman, however, bears an inherited name, which is the same as that of her full sisters, father's sisters, and father's father's sisters. The Indians, when talking English, call such names of women "nations." A woman . . . is always known by the name of her nation, although this may be coupled with one or two other names which serve to distinguish her from other women of the same nation.

To the next man he gave 'Roadrunner' (Met'á). Roadrunner is now called 'Talʸpó'. Kumastamxo named him after he ran.

To the next man he gave 'Mesquite-Beans' (Alʸmō′s).*

To the next man he gave 'Deeɪ-Hide' (Sinʸkwáʟ).

To the next man he gave 'a kind of Brown Bug' (Èstamadhún), not an ant-lion.

When the next man came in, Kumastamxo had to stop and think. All the good names had been given. He gave him 'a bunch of shreds of willow-bark which had been soaked at least ten days in water' (Kwickú).

When the next man came, Kumastamxo said, "'Xalʸpŏ′t', call your girl thus." Xalʸpŏ′t means "already done."

One lone man came running up. "Am I too late?"—"No, I call your nation 'Hard-Ground' (Xakcí)."

68. Kumastamxo then called out the stones and trees, and gave each its nation.

69. Kumastamxo gave each man a gourd rattle and taught him to "throw the gourd." Then they all danced. They stood east of the house, grouped in tribes. Inside the house the Yuma stood north, the Diegueño west, the Cocopa south, the Maricopa east. Kumastamxo told the Wallapai and the Havasupai to go northeast, and he told the Chimehuevi to go northwest, and the Kawia to go west. Then he said to the others, "I send you four kinds of people south. Because I send you, you must remember me wherever you stay, for I am going to turn into something." The Mohave alone stayed there with Kumastamxo. They were little children, too young to march.

70. Marxókuvék led the Yuma and Diegueño people away first. The Cocopa and Maricopa followed. They marched west across the desert, crossing many mountains. When the Yuma and Diegueño reached Aviivéra, east of Riverside, they found the eastern slope wooded, and they held a fiesta there. There the Cocopa overtook them. Kumastamxo did not want them to fight. But soon they began to shoot at the Yuma and Diegueño. The Maricopa Indians stood close to the Cocopa and sided with them.

71. Kumastamxo tried to produce a thunderstorm. Only a few drops of rain fell. Then he said, "I must return to Avikwaamé." He took Marx-

---

* An old woman of this nation bears the additional name 'Akoiitchámál' ('Old-Woman-Something-White'), because the mesquite beans referred to by Kumastamxo were ripe and white.

ókuvék with him. When they neared Avikwaamé, Marxókuvék sickened. The people carried him down the Colorado river-valley, for they liked him. At Yuma the river was so swift that they could not carry him across. Kumastamxo knew their difficulty, and made the river shallow. Then they carried Marxókuvék across. At Avixolʸpó,* Marxókuvék said, "This is my homeland. Here we shall live. Burn my body by yonder mountain." Then he died, with his head to the south.

They burned him at the base of Mokwintaórv Mountain, at a place called Aauxʹrakyámp.† The rocks are still red from the fire. The people cried loudly, "He is dead, he is dead!" referring to Kwikumat and Kumastamxo, as well as to Marxókuvék. They burned Marxókuvék on top of that mountain. The Yuma go to that place,‡ and Marxókuvék shows them how to do wonderful things. He tells us everything. Men also climb this mountain. It takes four days to climb it. On its summit they fall into visions at midnight. Marxókuvék asks them what they want and satisfies them. But great doctors go up to Avikwaamé and see Kumastamxo. It takes four days to go up there. No songs are taught at Mokwintaórv.

72. Kumastamxo said, "Havíirk," meaning, "It is finished." He stood there. He thought, "I will sink into the ground." He sang four times—

Into the earth I go down, go down.
Nothing but earth will I be seeing, will I be seeing.
I sink down into the old riverbed,
Down into the interior.

The first time he sang thus, his feet sank into the earth; the second time, his thighs sank into the earth; the third time, his neck sank into the earth; the fourth time, he sank out of sight, and remained there in the interior of the earth four days.

73. Then he came up again. He stood there. He said, "I am going to ascend." He extended his arms horizontally toward either side. Then he sang four times—

I am springing, springing.
Wing-feathers!

---

* Now Castle Dome, on the Arizona side, near Laguna.
† Meaning 'fire all around'.
‡ In their dreams.

Body-feathers!
On my hands, wing-feathers.
On my body [?], body-feathers.

He flew awkwardly into the air as he sang this the fourth time. He flapped his wings four times. He said, "I shall be called 'the black eagle' (*aspakwaanʸílʸ*) in the west,* 'the high eagle' (*aspakwaamaí*) in the east,† 'fish eagle' (*aspaatsikwítc*) in the south,‡ 'white eagle' (*aspahamál*) in the north."

LATIN PASSAGES

A. So that the virgin might fully understand, he himself demonstrated to her what should be done. Indeed, he lay down on the ground and copulated four times. The woman, sweating profusely, four times wiped away the sweat from her body with her hands.

B. Not unwillingly, one of the men tried to do those things which [Xavasumkilʸi] herself had described. However, he inserted his penis into [his woman's] anus, not into her vagina. "Soon I will bear something," said the woman. She expected to bear a child at any moment. When it did not happen, she and the other women became greatly agitated. "Why are you all inflamed against me?" asked Xavasumkulʸi. And so she explained again, "Insert the penis into the vagina." This time, though, the man inserted not his penis but his testicles into her vagina.

Returning, [Xavasumkilʸi] told her husband that the women would never conceive. Kwikumat scolded her because she had told to the others those things that he himself had taught her in secret. "I am not afraid that they should learn," said Xavasumkulʸi. [Then] Kwikumat ordered: "Lead these women four steps toward the north, toward the west, toward the south, toward the east, and I will lead the men likewise." When this dance was done, he ordered everybody to lie down on the ground and copulate.

C. Some sought refuge by rising up into his anus.

---

* This eagle protects the whites. That is why they have it on their money.
† High eagle lives in the Maricopa country. It is seen by medicine-men only.
‡ About the gulf.

D. One day he noticed a girl among the bushes whose vagina was ulcerous and putrid, from which everything fled. When Coyote ran toward her, she fell down on her hands and knees, terrified. Then Coyote copulated with her.

II

ESSAYS ON NATIVE CALIFORNIA LANGUAGES AND ORAL LITERATURES

The acorns come down from heaven.
I plant the short acorns in the valley,
I plant the long acorns in the valley,
I sprout:
    I, the black-oak acorn, sprout—
      I sprout.

          Ceremonial acorn song, Maidu
       Stephen Powers, *Tribes of California*

WHEN I HAVE DONNED
MY CREST OF STARS

The deeds of the people,
   the way they were,
     the people who spoke those things are heard no longer.

This will surely be the end of all that.
   Those things that were said are no longer heard.
     None have lasted beyond.

Those who continue beyond into the future
   will surely say the same about me,
     when I have gone off wearing my crest of stars.

Nevertheless,
   what I've said and the way I have been
     will remain in this land.

Kiliwa, Rufino Ochurte, 1969
Mauricio Mixco, *Kiliwa Texts*

A Brief History of Collection

SALVAGE

In October of 1914, James Alden Mason, an anthropologist at the University of California at Berkeley, made a brief fieldtrip down to the Santa Cruz area in an effort to locate speakers of Costanoan, a group of closely related languages spoken, at the time of European contact, roughly from the San Francisco Bay down to Big Sur along the coast and coastal foothills. He was hoping to find fluent speakers who still used the language in everyday life and who could provide him with wordlists and grammatical information and texts—information that could help him answer questions about the structure of the language and the nature of its relationship to neighboring languages and develop a better picture of Costanoan mythology and culture. It wasn't much of an expedition— more of an overnight trip, really—but its outcome speaks volumes about the critical condition of California's native languages, both then and now, and provides insight into the imperatives of the collecting endeavor itself. When Mason returned from his trip, he filed the following report with his department head, A. L. Kroeber.[1]

REPORT

Reached San Juan in early evening. In morning had a talk with priest of mission and several other oldest inhabitants of the place. All agreed that there were no Indians remaining in San Juan, that the few remaining ones had sold their lands and moved to Gilroy where land seemed to be a little cheaper. Consequently decided to go to Gilroy. Reached there about 2.00 and hunted up Acension Solorsan, an elderly Indian woman.[2] She claimed to know absolutely nothing but referred me to a very old woman, Josefa Velasquez in Watsonville. As prospects seemed a little better there, went to Watsonville and arrived there in early evening.

Wednesday morning went out to see Dona Josefa. She lives out East Lake St. about a half hour's walk out on the road to Morgan Hill, at the first horse trough. Is an old woman born at Santa Cruz in 1833 but reared in the ranches around Watsonville. A stay of several days with her might reveal many important points of interest but she remembers very little and very slowly. Spoke the San Juan dialect originally but has had no one to talk to for many years so forgets most of it. Verified many of de la Cuesta's words which are surprisingly accurate and got a few sentences and other words but very little. Also got a myth herewith included. After several hours of work she professed to know many myths, songs, dances, etc. Returned in the afternoon and, while she continued to insist that she knew many myths, etc., she was unable to recall one all afternoon. I got a few more words, phrases and two Yokuts gambling songs from María Gomez who lives with her. I am inclined to think that with a few days['] experience the old woman could be induced to tell many myths and songs, possibly in text, but they came so slowly at the beginning I decided it was not worth while trying again.

She insisted that Acension in Gilroy knew more than she, but claimed, like all others, that these two [herself and Acension] were the only living persons who remembered anything of the language and customs. Refugio Castello spoke it well, and so did Barbara Solarsan, the mother of Acension, but these two died no more than three years ago. I could learn of no other old or middle-aged Indian in the whole country.

So Thursday morning I returned to Gilroy to see Acension again. She was born in San Juan in 1855 and her mother, who died only a few years ago[,] spoke the language well. But she [Acension] never knew it well and has not spoken it for years. With difficulty I got from her a few phrases and sentences, words[,] and corroboration of many of de la Cuesta's words[,] but as she remembered very little, I decided the result was not worth the while and took the afternoon train home. With practice she might be taught to give texts but she undoubtedly remembers very little. She knows much less than Josefa, though her memory is a little better. Jacinta Gonzales died a few years ago.

Attached to this sad report were approximately two pages of elicitation labeled "San Juan words and phrases." The wordlist was followed by two

Yokuts gambling songs and a page of desultory ethnological notes—precious little return for the hours spent in gleaning them.

Mason's dejected, disappointed tone is impossible to mistake. Yet what modern reader will not be dismayed that he did not stay with Doña Josefa for as long as it took to rekindle her memory and revive her former fluency? She was one of the last speakers of her language. Whatever myths and legends she might have been helped to recall, whatever songs she might have resurrected, whatever poetry she might have spun from reminiscences long locked away in her rusty native tongue, they are gone now, completely. "Later" is not a reliable option when your best consultant is eighty-one years of age. Surely he gave up too easily.

But when the house is afire, to use J. P. Harrington's famous metaphor, you have to rescue what can best be saved.[3] Mason judged that his limited time and energies were best spent elsewhere, working with other languages, other consultants, where the knowledge lay closer to the surface. In 1914 in California, a mere sixty-some years—a single life-span, in fact—after the ethnic catastrophe of the Gold Rush, fieldwork was too often an exercise in linguistic and cultural triage.[4] It is no less true today, and will be again tomorrow: the last, best generation of elders is always just passing through their children's hands.

So Mason returned to San Francisco disappointed in his slim pickings and no doubt depressed at finding yet another age-old California culture in such dire straits. In the midst of his notes, though, lies a scrap of text recorded in the form of a mock letter, unremarked at the time but for an oblique reference to "a few sentences" in the second paragraph of his report. I present the text just as it appears in Mason's report, surrounded by a portion of the wordlist it was embedded in.

kanša´wi	I sing
wa´tị ka	I am going
aru·´ta kawa´tị	tomorrow I will go
wakɨšaš	coyote
u´mụ	wolf
wa´tị ka u´ršị kaniš e´kwe ni´pa	I am going because you will not teach me
e´kwe kahi´nšu	I don't know
hī´nue e´kwe kahi´nšu	when I don't know
hi´nua kamšit haiwe´	when will I see you?
e´kwe kamišie´te oišu hai´we	I will not see you again

mi´šmin	nošo´	mišho´ke	hose´fa	kǫ´	men.e´kwe
Dear	heart,	thee sends	Josefa.	Says	thou not

pe´šio	hose´fa	še	katawa·´k	haiṭu´hiš
remember	Josefa	of	as she	every day.

hi´nuakše	wakiaṭ´a´kan	miš	hai´weni
Some day	she will come,	thee	to see

kutceke´kwe	se´mon	a´ram	mišminsire´	mensi´tnumak
if not	dies.	Give	thy regards	thy children.

hu´miṭ tapu´r	give me wood!
šu´nesteka	I am hungry
a´mai[x]	come!
šu´niešteka	I am filled
hiu´sęⁿ kame´š	Ah! how I love thee
hi´nuame ṭa´kan	when will you come?
e´kwe ka meš hole nipa	I cannot teach you
ni ekwe semon mumuri	here the flies won't die
xutceknis	dog
ekwe ka pe´sio kanri·´tca	I don't remember my language

A free translation of Doña Josefa's long-lost message runs as follows:[5]

> Dear heart,
> Josefa sends this to you!
> She says you don't remember her, Josefa,
> as she is every day.
> When will she come to see you—
> before she dies?
> Give me good wishes,
> you and your children!

What prompted Josefa Velasquez to compose this "letter" we'll never know. Probably Mason, in a desperate attempt to jump-start her dormant fluency, had asked Doña Josefa what she would say to family and friends if he were to carry back the message in Costanoan.[6] Whatever he was hoping for, he got a brief, emotional burst from the heart, straight from the ragbag of an old woman's worries and cares. It wasn't much, as texts go, and I'm sure Mason would have regarded his attempt as a failure. But today this little text has acquired such a force of eloquence, of poignancy, over the long years it has lain forgotten in the archives, that it fairly cracked open my brain like a nut when I stumbled across it—a voice from the past, leaping out from the detritus of a musty wordlist's bits and shards. *Because it's all there was,* and because it rings true, a kind of greatness is thrust upon it, the unintended plainsong of an old woman's words.

California has a rich and spectacular oral-literary heritage, as this book attests. But sometimes literature is simply where you find it, or when. Indeed, in the absence of any form of text at all, the wordlists themselves—*mother, father, acorn, sun*—take on an importance, a luminosity, well beyond their original mundane intention: they are the atoms of lost poetics.

WORKERS IN THE VINEYARD

Men and women, J. A. Mason among them, have been collecting and analyzing California myth, song, and ceremony for nearly two centuries in an effort to preserve the traditions before they are gone forever.[7] Yet I don't mean to give the wrong impression in stating this fact. Though commonplace in the discourse of Native American studies, such pronouncements throw the spotlight always onto the role of the fieldworker, the local historian, the interested amateur collector—an "outsider" role typically played by whites of European descent. Such statements tend to ignore the role of the performers themselves, who gave them the songs and stories in the first place. The performers, too, have dedicated their lives to preserving their traditions—but *their* efforts go back, ultimately, more than ten millennia in California: a hundred centuries of listening, learning, practicing, performing—and yes, refining, forgetting, adapting, and composing anew—the traditions that have passed from one generation to the next across the long reaches of time.

It is a mistake, and a bad one, to think that the act of recording in any way marks the culmination or fulfillment, much less the validation, of any given song or story. The arrival of a folklorist with microphone or notebook is not the "moment it's been waiting for"—as if, once it is written down, the people whose culture it portrays can breathe a sigh of relief and turn their attentions to something else. Writing a story down merely makes a record of its passing, like a single line of footprints tracked in the sand along a shore.[8] We all know just how much and how little that track can teach us. Nevertheless, without the collectors and their passion for writing things down, students of language and oral literature the world over—Native Californians included—would have less to marvel at, take pleasure in, draw wisdom from, and find beauty in.

Prior to the establishment of the University of California's Museum and Department of Anthropology at Berkeley in 1901, there was no systematic program of ethnographic research or collection in California—only a handful of men over the years who, driven by their interests, tried to record the folklore and verbal art of California narrators, and to do so faithfully (at least within the dictates of their era and training) rather than interpretively. Among the most important of these early works are Father Geronimo Boscana's record of Juaneño myth and religious ceremony, *Chinigchinich* (1933 [1846]); Alexander Taylor's enthusiastic but somewhat erratic series of articles on "Indianology" between 1860 and 1863 in *The California Farmer and Journal of Useful Arts* (an early California periodical conveniently owned by his father-in-law); Stephen Powers's important, indefatigable early work in Northern California during the 1870s, which culminated in his now badly dated *Tribes of California* (1877); and Jeremiah Curtin's large collection of Wintu and Yana myths in English (1898). Aside from these few mostly amateur collectors, prior to 1900 we have little but the passing anecdotal reports of travelers, settlers, and journalists, the occasional words and place-names recorded by early explorers (nautical expeditions by Cabrillo in 1542–1543 and Drake in 1579; overland explorations by Portolá in 1769, Frémont in 1846, and others), and the vocabularies and grammars compiled by Franciscan missionaries (for instance, de la Cuesta's early Salinan vocabulary [1825], or the later Costanoan materials [1861–1862] mentioned above in Mason's report).

With the dawn of the twentieth century, we enter a new stage in the documentation of California's native oral literature. Kroeber's Department of Anthropology was founded in 1901 with the specific goal of focusing and accelerating research on California cultures and languages—a goal that matured rapidly and with resounding success.[9] The next few decades saw a great explosion of scholars, students, and independent field-workers who contributed significantly to the corpus of California oral literature. In addition to Kroeber himself, these included such now-legendary collectors as Pliny Earl Goddard, Roland B. Dixon, Samuel Barrett, C. Hart Merriam, John Peabody Harrington, Carobeth Laird, Edward Sapir, Constance Du Bois, Edward W. Gifford, T. T. Waterman, Paul Radin, James A. Mason, Helen R. Roberts, Jaime de Angulo, L. S. Freeland, Susan Brandenstein Park, Dorothy Demetracopoulou, Anna Gayton, Stanley Newman, Gladys Reichard, Hans Jørgen Uldall, C. F. Voegelin, and Erminie Wheeler-Voegelin. A search through the published (and unpublished) work of any one of these researchers will lead the reader directly to important primary sources of California myth, song, and storytelling.

What distinguishes the work of these collectors from those who came before, and from the sundry amateur collectors who have tried their hand at presenting Indian stories in memoirs and magazines, is their attention to the actual words, not merely the gist, of the performances they recorded. All aspired to rigorous Boasian principles of textual documentation, and most had the phonetic training to take down texts in the original language, word-for-word as the narrator pronounced them. As a result of this care, this teneted belief in the primacy of the spoken word, the texts they later published from their fieldnotes are accurate records of actual narrative performances, not ex post facto re-creations of remembered events.[10] When it comes to the translations, of course, these are subject, like all translations the world over, to the whims of personal and period style—compare, say, Edward Sapir's translations from the Yana, made in 1910, with Jaime de Angulo's translations of Eastern Pomo (#16), made just twenty-five years later. But the texts themselves, the true legacy, stand always in testament to, or judgment of, their translators.[11]

Most of this early authoritative work was done by hand, laboriously, by taking manual dictation, a process that has stylistic consequences for the performance thus recorded. (See table 2 in the "General Introduction" for a list of the selections in this volume that were recorded by this and other methods.) A few researchers, notably J. P. Harrington, experimented with the early sound-recording technology, such as wax or wire cylinders and aluminum phonograph discs. Because of the awkwardness of the devices themselves—they were expensive, heavy, finicky, fragile, limited in capacity, and low in fidelity—machine recording was the exception rather than the rule. Kroeber and his colleagues at Berkeley made a great many recordings at the university, but the early machines were seldom practicable for use in the field (though Jack Marr, one of Harrington's intrepid young assistants, tells some hair-raising tales of trying to backpack phonographs and heavy cartons of aluminum discs across swaying rope bridges in the mountains of Northern California, on assignment from Harrington to reach important narrators).

The side effects of manual dictation on style are easy to predict: the pen, being slower by far than the voice, forces delivery to a crawl; at this slower pace, it is easy for narrators to lose the thread of their composition; longer, more complex sentence patterns may not be ventured, being rejected in favor of shorter, more direct phrasings that better suit the dribs-and-drabs progress of the dictation; and because it takes so long, there is a strong tendency toward truncation, so that the elaborate rhetorical patterns of episodic and incremental repetition that often characterize oral poetics are suppressed in the interests of economy. (The approach of evening after a grueling day of dictation must have hastened many a grand tale to a premature conclusion.) Time and again, though, in the earlier decades of this century, California's tribal narrators, answering the call of posterity, somehow managed to adjust to the limitations and artificiality of the work, minimizing its deleterious effects, and to deliver performances that transcended the special circumstances of their recording. In this volume, Jo Bender's "Loon Woman" (#12), William Benson's "Creation" (#16), and Johnny LaMarr's "Naponoha" (#9) all illustrate narrators who rose magnificently above the limitations of the collection methods of the time (though it remains true: we can still never know what performances they might have delivered had they been working with a tape recorder instead of dictation).

Later, when portable recording equipment became widely available, the dictation problem was effectively eliminated. But comparison of dictated and tape-recorded texts reveals that there is still an enormous range and diversity of style and helps validate the essential (if not the particular) stylistic integrity of the older texts. For instance, Minnie Reeves's crisply told "The Boy Who Grew Up at Taʼkʼimiłding" (#6a) and James Knight's wonderfully loose, rambling version of "The Dead People's Home" (#19) are both from tape-recorded texts. Similarly, Margaret Harrie's blunt "Coyote and Old Woman Bullhead" (#4) and Joe Homer's

FIGURE 12. *From left:* Sam Batwi, Alfred L. Kroeber, and Ishi.
Courtesy Phoebe Apperson Hearst Museum of Anthropology
and the Regents of the University of California.

densely detailed "An Account of Origins" (#27) are both from dictated texts.

Nevertheless, the advent of tape recording ushered in a new era in the collection of California oral literature. Under Mary Haas's direction of Berkeley's new Department of Linguistics, inaugurated in 1953, a new generation of researchers, trained in anthropological linguistics, began working the field. The tape recording of texts became the rule rather than the exception. (Nowadays, of course, videotaping is gradually becoming the new standard of documentation.) In 1951 Haas and Murray Emeneau founded the Survey of California and Other Indian Languages (initially as "The Survey of California Indian Languages"), which has sponsored research and archived tapes, fieldnotes, and other linguistic materials through the present day.[12] Inspired directly or indirectly by Haas and her colleagues and successors, dozens of students and scholars have made a vocation of California languages—among them Richard Applegate, Thomas Blackburn, William Bright, Sylvia Broadbent, Catherine Callaghan, James Crawford, Jon Dayley, Geoff Gamble, Victor Golla, Abe Halpern, Jane Hill, Ken Hill, Leanne Hinton, William Jacobsen, Richard Keeling, Martha Kendall, Kathryn Klar, Sidney Lamb, Margaret Langdon, Sally McLendon, Wick Miller, Mauricio Mixco, Julius Moshinsky, Pamela Munro, Mike Nichols, Mark Okrand, Robert Oswalt, Harvey Pitkin, R. H. Robins, Alice Shepherd, Hans Jacob Seiler, William Shipley, Shirley Silver, Len Talmy, Karl Teeter, Russell Ultan, and Ken Whistler.[13] Most of these scholars, in trying to honor Haas's demanding documentational goal of "grammar, texts, and dictionary," have made it a point to collect and publish oral-literary texts.

In the end, this storehouse of work recalls for us the hundreds of California singers and storytellers (without whom, nothing) who have dedicated their time and services—their personal repertoires, their cultural insight, their performing skills, and (perhaps above all) their patience—to the program of documentation over the last hundred years and more. Some were undoubtedly attracted to the idea initially by the pay, since it is customary for fieldworkers to compensate their consultants with a modest hourly wage. But truth be known, most would have carried on the work regardless. All too many elders have looked around to find themselves increasingly alone in language, among the last native speakers of their tribes, and they become as anxious as their linguists to help document its richness and repertoire before they themselves pass on.

Most language consultants, young or old, have a keen sense of posterity when it comes to the work they do. As James Knight observed, speaking "through" the tape in an aside while telling "The Dead People's Home" (#19), he had a compelling reason for recording his stories:

Because that's how it was,
　　that's how they taught me.
Since they explained it to me that way,
　　here's what I'm telling you now.
Now I'm putting what they told me a long time ago onto the tape.
　　So it [the tape] is telling you this.
My friends and relatives can listen and say,
　　"Yes, this is true."

Besides, singers and storytellers *like* to sing and tell stories. And the work they do with their field researchers often gives them the opportunity to focus on their art in a new way. Many also enjoy the intellectual pursuit of glossing and explicating their texts once they are recorded, and excel at this kind of linguistic work; others find the "drudge" work of analysis a burden to be avoided if possible. Of course, the sense of posterity "looking over your shoulder" that comes with making a permanent record of a song or story puts a special pressure on the performers. Jean Perry, in her introduction to "The Young Man from Serper" (#3), details the way Florence Shaughnessy would fret about getting her stories just right, reviewing her own work with a critical ear, knowing that the versions she taped were "for the record." She was not alone in feeling this way.

Unfortunately, we don't always know the identity of the singers and narrators of California's recorded literature. It wasn't always considered important information, owing to an early and flawed theory of folklore that viewed individual singers and narrators as passive and faceless "passers-on" of their traditions rather than as active and potentially idiosyncratic "shapers" of the traditional materials in their personal repertoires. Even so, fieldworkers always had a keen sense of their consultants as individuals, as personalities. Often the information is there, buried in the archived fieldnotes or correspondence of the linguist or anthropologist who collected the materials for publication. We know the names of many, many of the men and women who took the time to dictate or record their best work for the generations to come—names that we should hold in honor. The list is an amazingly long one—and open-ended, because the work is still going on—but a few among those who have contributed substantial bodies of their own art to the canon of California oral literature are Sam Batwi (Yana), Jo Bender (Wintu), William Ralganal Benson (Eastern Pomo), Annie Burke (Southern Pomo), Ted

Couro (Iipay Diegueño), Hanc'ibyjim (Maidu), Joe Homer (Quechan), Villiana Calac Hyde (Luiseño), Ishi (Yahi), Killeli (Yosemite Miwok), James Knight (Lake Miwok), George Laird (Chemehuevi), Fernando Librado (Ventureño Chumash), Harry and Sadie Marsh (Wintu), Mabel McKay (Pomo), Grace McKibbin (Wintu), Mike Miranda (Tübatulabal), Rufino Ochurte (PaiPai/Kiliwa), Lela Rhoades (Achumawi), Florence Shaughnessy (Yurok), María Solares (Ineseño Chumash), Robert Spott (Yurok), Tom Stone (Owens Valley Paiute), Lucy Thompson (Yurok), Lame Billy of Weitspus (Yurok), and Mary Yee (Barbareño Chumash).

Individually, each of the people named here, scholars and Indians alike, and so many unnamed others besides, have made significant contributions to the field of California oral literature. Collectively, the combined impact of their labors is enormous, and the value of their legacy, beyond measure.

NOTES

1. From papers in the ethnographic collection of the Bancroft Library, University of California at Berkeley (Valory Index, #23). The manuscript report is reproduced here in its entirety.

2. According to Catherine Callaghan, Ascensión Solarsano de Cervantes was J. P. Harrington's principal Mutsun (San Juan Bautista Costanoan) consultant. She was dying of cancer in the late 1920s but was still able to recall almost everything.—HWL

3. The phrase comes from a letter Harrington wrote in 1941 to his young neighbor and assistant, Jack Marr (who was just a teenager at the time). In full, and retaining Harrington's urgent underscores (now in italic), the passage reads:

> You've been a good friend if ever I had one, you just rushed at the work. You know how I look at this work, you and I are nothing, we'll both of us soon be dust. If you can grab these dying languages before the old timers completely die off, you will be doing one of the *few* things valuable to the people of the *remote* future. You know that. The time will come and *soon* when there won't be an Indian language left in California, all the languages developed for thousands of years will be *ashes,* the house is *afire,* it is *burning.* That's why I said to go through the blinding rain, roads or no roads, that's why I thanked God when you tried to cross the Mattole River, haven't I gone back even two weeks later to find them *dead* and the language *forever dead?*

4. The Gold Rush, which affected primarily the northern half of the state, followed upon a previous sixty-five years of Indian exposure to the Spanish mission system, whose main influence extended over the southern half of the state.

5. I am grateful to Catherine Callaghan for her help in making this translation. In return for her assistance, she has prevailed upon me to make the following corrections to the Costanoan language data reproduced here verbatim from Mason's unedited fieldnotes. (As she says, there may never *be* another opportunity to set this particular record straight.)

Corrected (and converted to modern orthography, where ʔ represents a glottal stop and doubled characters represent length), these forms should read.

OPENING WORDLIST

/kan šaawc/	'I am singing'.
/watti ka/	'I am going'.
/ʔaruuta ka watti/	'Tomorrow I will go'.
/wakšiš/	'coyote'
/ʔummuh/	'wolf'
/watti ka ʔussi kannis ʔekwe niipa/	'I am going because you will not teach me'.
/ʔekwe ka hinsu/	'I don't know'.
/hinwa ʔekwe ka hinsu/	'when I don't know'
/hinwa ka mes yete haywe/	'When will I see you'? [rapid speech]
/ʔekwe ka mes yete ʔoyšo haywe/	'I will not see you again'.

WORDS FROM TEXT

/mišmin/	'good one'
/nossow/	'soul, spirit; heart'
/mes/	'thee'
/hokke/	'to send away'
/hoseefa/	'Josefa'
/koo/	'to say'
/men/	'thou, thy'
/ekwe/	'not'
/pesyo/	'to think, remember'
/hoseefa-se/	'Josefa-OBJECTIVE CASE'
/kata/	'like, as'
/waak/	'he, she'

/hayi/	'all'
/ṭuuhis/	'day(s)'
/hinwa-kše/	'when-INDEFINITE(?)'
/wak/	'he, she'
/ya/	'also'
/ṭaakan/	'to come'
/mes/	'thee'
/hayweni/	'to come-see'
/koč/	'if, when'
/ʔekekwe/	'not' [intensified]
/semmon/	'to die'
/haram/	'you [PLURAL] give me'
/mišmin/	'good'
/sire/	'wishes' [*literally* "liver" (seat of emotions)]
/men/	'thy'
/sitnunmak/	'children'

CLOSING WORDLIST

/hummit tappur/	'Give me wood'!
/šunneste ka/	'I am hungry'.
/ʔammay/	'Eat'!
/sunyište ka/	'I am full'.
/hiwse ka mes/	'I love thee'.
/hinwa me ṭaakanʔ/	'When will you come'?
/ʔekwe ka mes holle niipa/	'I cannot teach you'.
/ni ekwe seemon muumuri/	'Here the flies won't die'.
/hučeknis/	'dog'
/ekwe ka pesyo ka riiča/	'I don't remember my language'.

6. Unfortunately, it is not entirely clear just who Doña Josefa is addressing in this text.

7. The whole concept of preserving a culture—or a literary tradition or a language—on paper is a vexed one. What does it mean to "preserve" a tradition? To what extent is the page merely the literary and cultural scholar's equivalent of formaldehyde? There has long been a tendency—a pernicious weakness, in truth—among American and European scholars steeped in the hyperliteracy

of the Western academic tradition to "confuse the map with the territory," as the saying goes. Would that scholars of American Indian cultures had always been as active in helping to preserve their people as their languages and traditions.

8. There's a fundamental difference, it seems, between the way a scholar thinks of preservation and the way a Native performer does: for the former, the goal is *documentation,* a record of what went on or what was said; for the latter, the goal is *continuation*—a preservation of the continuity of tradition and, most important of all, the people themselves, who bear that tradition into the future. This difference comes about not because the scholar is by nature indifferent, but simply from a difference in the underlying interests of scholars as opposed to Native peoples. It's no secret that a great deal of frustration and resentment has grown up in the chasm of this divide during the last few decades of interaction between these two parties, each of whom tends to view the other in a kind of client or worker relationship—researchers and "their" consultants, Indians and "their" researchers—and is surprised to feel underappreciated or exploited as a result.

9. A concise summary of the history and influence of this research program may be found in Robert Heizer's essay "History of Research" in the California volume of the Smithsonian's *Handbook of North American Indians* (1978), which he edited.

10. Absence of this rigor results in the myriad well-intentioned but bogus collections of Native American oral literature, such as Bertha Smith's *Yosemite Legends* (1904), which Stephen Medley, annotating a bibliography at the back of the recent and lovely *Legends of the Yosemite Miwok* (La Pena et al. 1993), describes as follows: "This is an attractively designed and presented selection of six Yosemite legends of suspect origin. Using Hutchings (1860) as a primary source, the author demonstrated her skill at the art of turning a short, concise legend into a longwinded and romantic epic. The writing is stylized and reflects a Europeanized concept of Native American thought" (94).

11. It must be said that when anthropologists and linguists took down texts *in English* before the advent of recording devices, they were not always so faithful to the word of their texts, feeling free—in ways they did not with native-language texts—to silently edit or recompose the words of their narrators. One is far less sure with English-language narratives (often signaled by the use of the words *myth* or *tale* in the title, as opposed to *text*) that they have not passed through the grammatical and stylistic filter of their collectors. Such filtering is always for the worse, never the better, as far as authenticity is concerned.

12. Though the *University of California Publications in Linguistics* series, which took over the burgeoning publication of linguistics monographs from the older *University of California Publications in Archaeology and Ethnology*

(1903–1969) in 1943, long ago widened its horizons to encompass the globe, it still publishes important monographs on California languages (see "Selected Resources for Further Study" for examples).

13. This list was compiled primarily from Victor Golla's obituary for Mary Haas in the *SSILA Newsletter* 15.2 (July 1996).

WOMEN'S BRUSH DANCE SONG

The owl cries out to me,
the hawk cries out to me as death approaches.

The killdeer, the mountain bird,
cry out to me as death approaches.

The black rattler, the red rattler,
cry out to me as death approaches.

The red racer, the gartersnake,
cry out to me as death approaches.

A large frog, a little frog,
cry out to me as death approaches.

An eagle, a condor,
cry out to me as death approaches.

Ceremonial song, Luiseño
Helen H. Roberts, *Form in Primitive Music*
(version by Brian Swann, *Song of the Sky*)

Notes on Native California Oral Literatures

No detailed, comprehensive survey of California's oral literature has ever been done. Accessible recent overviews include William Wallace's "Comparative Literature" (1978c) and William Bright's "Oral Literature of California and the Intermountain Region" (1994b), which the reader is urged to consult, along with Robert Heizer's "Mythology: Regional Patterns and History of Research" (1978b). Edward Gifford and Gwendoline Block's lengthy introduction to their *California Indian Nights Entertainments* (1930) still makes, even after seventy years, a reliable layperson's entry into California culture patterns, oral-literary genres, and storytelling customs.[1]

Most California cultures had no restrictions on who could perform verbal art. Men and women alike sang songs, recited myths, and told stories. (Though I'm aware of very few instances of speeches recorded from female orators, that doesn't mean—particularly when the record is so spotty and incomplete—that women never made speeches.) There does seem to have been an overall tendency for men to be the performers on the more public and formal occasions—to recount the stories of creation in the roundhouse at night when everyone is gathered, to conduct the ceremonies and dances, to make the public announcements, and so forth (Gifford and Block 1930:43). But in many cultures, women were involved in ceremonies as well, and curing rituals, and storytelling sessions. The pages of California's many text collections (this one included) attest to the great significance of women as bearers of their oral traditions and to their skill as narrators.

Songs by and large are closely tied to their occasions—that is, you wouldn't normally sing a hunting song except in the proper context of hunting, or a ceremonial song apart from its attendant ceremony—but there are so many different kinds of songs and song contexts, that few aspects of life are devoid of the opportunity for singing them. Myths, in contrast, at least the more serious ones, were typically restricted to the winter cold-rainy season, when they helped to pass the time during the long nights and spells of bad weather. (In a great many California cultures, telling a myth out of season, in summertime, tempted fate by aggravating Rattlesnake.)

Like songs, stories are performed in a great variety of settings and contexts, both public and private, from the most weighty and formal of ceremonies to the most lighthearted of entertainments. They are told in connection with dances and ceremonies, religious initiations, rainy days, moral instruction, and funeral rites, as well as parties, family gatherings, and children's bedtimes. They are told to affirm the deepest cultural verities, to conserve knowledge, to explain the world, to interpret human and animal behavior, to illustrate points in public or private debate—or just to pass the time, to get a laugh or make people think, to sound a warning or sugarcoat friendly advice. In short, they perform all the functions that stories, from Bible stories to fairy tales to personal narratives to traveling salesman jokes, perform in Western cultures—and every other culture, for that matter.

In terms of genre, it is customary to recognize at least three broad categories or oral-literary *phyla*—narrative, song, and oratory, each of which is eager for further subdivision. In the remainder of this essay, I take up each of these genres in turn, hoping to give the reader a general "lay of the land" for each broad category.

NARRATIVE

Narrative itself might be further subdivided into myths, tales, legends, and personal reminiscences, along with various minor genres. Scholars tend to draw more distinctions than do ordinary people—the "folk" themselves. Still, most cultures draw at least a loose distinction between myth and tale, myths being stories that relate the actions of the First People in the world before human beings came into existence, and tales being stories dealing with human beings and their doings. (Note that this is not a distinction between supernatural and realistic stories, because tales are often just as fantastical as their mythic counterparts.) Often, too, the distinction between the two is a blurry one.

Beginning with Alfred Kroeber's "Indian Myths of South Central California" (1907b), later refined and expanded by Anna Gayton's "Areal Affiliations of California Folktales" (1935), California's oral literatures have typically been classified loosely according to the pattern of their creation myths. These rough "mythological zones" correspond by and large to the main culture areas agreed on by anthropologists: that is, allowing for exceptions, we find a Northwestern California creation pattern, a Southern California creation pattern, and a Central California creation pattern (itself often divided into North-Central and South-Central subareas).

Briefly, in Central California we tend to find a variation of the "Earthdiver" motif, where the Creator, assisted by a handful of other original beings (Coyote among them, as a rule), manages to procure a little bit of mud or sand brought up by a helper from the bottom of the primordial ocean they find themselves in, and stretches it out to make the earth. One of the most powerful yet lyrical examples of this type in the California canon was narrated in 1902 or 1903 by a brilliant Maidu storyteller named Hánc'ibyjim. In William Shipley's fine translation (1991:19–20), this portion of the creation myth runs as follows:

And then, they say, Earthmaker sang.
"Where are you, my great mountain ranges?
O, mountains of my world, where are you?"

Coyote tried. He kept on singing.
"If, indeed, we two shall see nothing at all,
traveling about the world,
then, perhaps,
there may be no misty mountain ranges there!"

Earthmaker said:
"If I could but see a little bit of land
I might do something very good with it."

Floating along, then,
they saw something like a bird's nest.
Earthmaker said:
"It really is small.
It would be good if it were a little bigger,
but it really is small.
I wonder if I might stretch it apart a little.
What would be good to do?
In what way can I make it a little bigger?"

As he talked, he transformed it.

He stretched it out to where the day breaks;
he stretched it out to the south;
he stretched it out to the place where the sun goes down;
he stretched it out to the North Country;
he stretched it out to the rim of the world;
he stretched it out!

When Earthmaker had stretched it out,
he said, "Good!
You who saw of old this earth, this mud,
and made this nest, sing!
Telling old tales, humans will say of you:
'In ancient times, the being who was Meadowlark,
making the land and sticking it together in just that way,
built the nest from which the world was made.'"

Then Meadowlark sang—
sang a beautiful song about Earthmaker's creation.

In Hánc'ibyjim's version, there is no diving, and a floating scrap of bird's-nest takes the place of mud, but the basic design of the myth is the same. In this collection, Darryl Wilson's Atsugewi creation myth, "Kwaw Labors to Form a World" (#1), lies closest to this pattern, drawing on this notion of stretching or "kneading" out the earth from a small dollop of initial substance (in Wilson's case, mist). Similarly, in William Benson's Eastern Pomo "Creation" (#16), two brothers—the creator Kuksu and his brother-helper Marumda (one of Coyote's many mythical names)—create the world from a ball of "armpit wax" (whatever that might be) and hair, by singing and dreaming it into being.[2]

In the South-Central literatures, the role played by a nonhuman, nonanimal creator or "Earthmaker" figure in the northern myths is often filled by Eagle. Sometimes, even, Coyote himself is in charge of the creation, as in certain Pomo, Patwin, and Miwok traditions (A. Kroeber 1907b:195; Gayton 1935:584). Usually, though, Coyote is just a helper— and a bumbling, contrary one at that, who is more apt to tamper with the Creator's efforts, spoiling them, than to follow directions.

In contrast, the Northwestern literary complex is characterized by its technical absence of creation myths (A. Kroeber 1925). Instead, the world is seen as having always been in existence (though humans were not among the race of First People). The annual World Renewal ceremonies of the Yurok, Karuk, Hupa, Tolowa, and others were, and still are, conducted to ensure the proper continuance of this eternal world.[3] The following passage comes from Francis Davis's account of the Karuk version of the ceremony performed in 1938:[4]

Between Yusarnimanimas and the mouth of Clear Creek I take a swim
    in the Klamath River.
When I get into the water so it runs over my head, I pray.
I think the prayer,
I do not say it aloud.
When I sink my head into the water,
the world will recognize me and awaken everyone to a realization that
    it is the beginning of *irahiv*.
When I pray, I pray for all to have luck.

When I get out of the water,
I put my shorts on again and go down the west bank of the river
    to a bedrock flat.
As I walk along,
I pray that all people who believe will walk as easily as I walk along this
    rough place.
The *ixkareya animas* walked over this in mythical times.
As I walk over it, I tramp it down,
I make room for everyone to live well and for there to be no sickness in
    the world.

Near Yusarnimanimas the people have placed a stone,
which has lain there for long years.
With my hands I rotate it slightly to make it sit more solidly,
so that the world will be solid too.

Everyone,
when I move it around,
will have the same power that *ixkareya animas* has.
Then I sit on the stone.

While I sit on the stone,
people come to see me.
All who come to see me will be lucky.
Besides[,] I pray for everyone else.
Then the *ipnipavan* paints me while I sit on the stone.

In Northwestern California, in place of creation myths per se, what we find is a body of "institution myths" (so-called by Kroeber), which relate the story of how various customs and ceremonies were first established for humankind by the Spirit People. Minnie Reeves's account of the "The Boy Who Grew Up at Ta'k'imiłding" (#6a) is an example of this type of myth from the Hupa.

In Southern California, too, a very different creation pattern is found. In some traditions (summarizing Gayton 1935), an Earth Mother figure and her brother-lover, together with their dying son, create the sun and moon and other features of the physical universe, including people, to whom they give customs and cultural institutions, instructing them in the conduct of proper human lives. In other traditions, two brothers take the place of the divine brother and sister and emerge, quarreling, from a primordial ocean to complete the work of creation. In the process, one of the brothers dies, thereby introducing death to the world. Either way, the story of this "dying god," of his death and burial, serves as a focus of cathartic grief for the people of the cultures that worship him.

The collector Paul Faye took down a small set of creation and burial songs in 1920 from a Cupeño singer named Salvadora Valenzuela (coincidentally the narrator of one of the two "Hawk Feather" episodes translated by Jane Hill in selection #25), songs that dwell on the themes and characters of this creation. Two of these songs may be found on page 57, where they serve to open part 1 of this book. The remaining songs in this set are presented below.[5] (The reference to "hell" in the second song should not be taken as a reference to the Hell of Christian theology, although there may be a degree of cultural overlay involved, but to the traditional Cupeño underworld or land of the dead.)

DEATH SONG
OF MUKAT

Far away they died,
Mukat, Tamayowet,
Mukat, Tamayowet.

Their hair they cut,
Their hair they banged,
Red-Bird, Roadrunner.

BURIAL SONG

My heart gives out, gives out,
My heart turns over, turns over.

My heart goes down to hell,
My heart goes down to hell.

My heart goes to the ocean,
My heart goes to the ocean.

More recently, Villiana Calac Hyde, the late, lamented Luiseño tradition-bearer and educator, saw fit to record a great many of her own store of songs before she died, including several long and profoundly moving funerary songs. (These songs have since been published in Hyde and Elliott 1994.) Taken as a whole, the creation and burial songs point to the key intermingling of two griefs that is so characteristic of the Southern California culture area: a religious grief felt for the death of the god in the story and a personal grief for one's own mortality and the very real death of family and friends. In the lines of the Luiseño mourning song that follows (Hyde and Elliott 1994:#175), we can see this intermingling made explicit:[6]

POPÍ'MUKVOY NÓÓNKWA
PÍ'MUKQA SONG

I am dying his death
I am dying his death
I am dying his death
I am dying his death
His death is my death

The death of the Moon
It became foggy at the time of his death
It was foggy when he expired
I am dying his death
I am dying his death
His death, hóó, hóó, hóó, amen . . .

Some of Mrs. Hyde's less culturally sensitive songs are presented in "A Harvest of Songs" (#24), this volume.

There are two Southern California creation myths included in this volume: Joe Homer's "An Account of Origins" (#27) and the Serrano "Creation" told by Sarah Martin (#23). The stylistic contrast in the two narrators' handling of the same basic myth-type is profound: where Homer is formal and detached, Martin is emotional and immediate; where Homer is profuse of detail, Martin is sparing, even stark at times; where Homer is complex, Martin is simplicity itself.[7] Yet both are expressions of the same essential pattern.

But creation myths are not the be-all and end-all of a literary tradition. Besides creation myths specifically, there is a whole constellation of stories set in this myth-time of creation, before the race of human beings came to dwell upon the earth—stories like "Theft of Fire," "Origin of Death" (blame Coyote), "Theft of the Sun," and the many versions of the "Pleiades" myth.

Perhaps the most significant and extensive genre or body of traditional stories in California centers on the mythic persona of Coyote. Actually, it's probably wrong to label the Coyote story as a narrative genre in its own right, because Coyote stories run the gamut from core cosmological myths and creation elegies, through just-so stories and picaresque adventure yarns, all the way to tall tales and the cultural equivalent of the raunchy joke. You name it, and Coyote has poked his nose into it somewhere. In any case, there's no question that Coyote is a favorite subject of Native California's narrators and audiences alike. As readers will come to see as they explore the contents of this volume alone (see table 1 in the "General Introduction"), Coyote is a complex and multivarious personality: now hero, now fool, now trickster, now lech, now spoiler, now all of these things rolled up in one.[8]

Myths are often distinguished from legends and other narrative genres by literary and linguistic features. The Karuk story "Coyote and Old

Woman Bullhead" (#4) is a myth not just because it happens to be set in the time of the Ikxaréeyav, the 'Spirit People', but because its special opening and closing formulas—"*Uknîii*" and "*Kupánakanakana*"—declare it to be a myth. Myths are also very often marked as such by the presence of a special grammatical element, usually referred to as a remote-past "quotative." In Yana, a Hokan language of Northern California, this element takes the form of a verbal suffix, *-n't^h(i),* and indicates that the actions being related took place long ago, outside the direct experience of the narrator.[9] The use of this quotative (highlighted in boldface) is demonstrated in the following excerpt taken from a Northern Yana myth, "Coyote, Heron, and Lizard," narrated by Betty Brown in 1907 (Sapir 1910). In this passage, Coyote is seeking revenge on Heron Woman and all her companions for cuckolding him at a dance and for not sharing food with him.[10]

Sáadipsitdi**n't^h,**
They were all sleeping now, they say—

> ayji ʻiwílsapcʼⁱ,
> [all] across one another,

>> sáadipsiyaw,
>> all sleeping,

>>> petgáaʼayaw.
>>> all snoring.

Púllayʼatdi**n't^h** ay mícʼⁱ,
Now Coyote smeared pitch on it, they say,

> aygi wátguruᵂ.
> on the sweat house.

Púllayjiba**n't^h** ayk^h lalúuᵂki,
He smeared pitch all over their feet, they say,

> púulay**n't^h** aygic^h yàa.
> He smeared pitch on the people, they say.

"Kúuyawgummagat^h bátdiduwálsaʼaʼ!"
"May you not run out and save yourselves!"

Wáyrᵘ,
Now then,

híiram**n'tʰ** ay míc'ⁱ.
Coyote ran out of the house, they say.

Yámʰjatdi**n'tʰ** aycʰ yàa,
Now the people all burned up, they say,

    wátguruʷ.
    the sweat house [too].

"Túuma'ninj ayje asinj míik'áyʼⁱ.
"I have always done like this when I was angry.

"Wáyrᵘ,
"Now then,

    ditbílpaw' ayji c'áxaa'ays.
    cook for your loved one!

"K'un c'úps,
"So it's good,

    ayji túuyawna,"
    this doing of mine,"

        tíi**n'tʰ**.
        they say he said.

The passage shows how this suffix (translated as 'they say' or 'it is said') is typically attached only to the verbs in narrative clauses—that is, those statements the narrator is personally responsible for, which negotiate the temporal distance that separates myth-time from the present world—and not to the verbs in dialogue, which are made by the characters and are seen as statements belonging *to* that time.[11] In contrast, personal reminiscences, which relate events that the narrators themselves have been witness to, will not involve the use of a quotative, except perhaps incidentally. Many California traditions observe loose genre distinctions where the classification correlates with the appearance of a quotative element.

There are a great many narrative subgenres, both localized and widespread. Many Southern California repertoires reveal a great interest in legends of "witches" or sorcerers. Among the Northwest cultures, stories about the antics of Indian "devils," like "The Devil Who Died Laughing" (#5) and "It Was Scratching" (#6d), are a favorite genre. In

Central California, the Pomo stand out—even against a broader cultural background where birds like Falcon, Condor, Loon, Eagle, and Meadowlark are frequent and important characters in the mythic dramatis personae—as having an especial fondness for songs and stories featuring birds; Annie Burke's "The Trials of Young Hawk" (#17) is an example from Southern Pomo.

In contrast, so-called monster stories may be found pretty much everywhere; tales like "Mad Bat" (#15) and "Condor Steals Falcon's Wife" (#20b) are instances in this volume.[12] In the same way, most tribes tell stories about a culture hero—differently conceived for each group, it seems—who personifies the moral and physical ideals of his society. The Central Yana tale of "Flint Boy" (Sapir 1910) makes as good a template as any: a common outline might include the birth or arrival of a baby (often under supernatural circumstances, such as springing up from the ground like a plant, or from a clot of blood or spittle on the floor) who grows to maturity in a matter of days or weeks and sets off to right outstanding wrongs or kill monsters (marauding Grizzly Bear women in Flint Boy's case) or fight wars, rescuing his people by virtue of his physical prowess, cunning, and moral single-mindedness. Jane Hill's translation of episodes "From 'The Life of Hawk Feather'" (#25) provides an example of this genre here.

The distribution of tale-types can also make for interesting study. Some stories, like the "Grizzly Bear and Deer" myth, are known in the northern half of the state but not in the southern half, while others, like the "Visit to the Land of the Dead" myth (#20a), have the reverse distribution. Both stories are widespread favorites in their respective areas of California, yet are well-known outside the state as well. The "Loon Woman" myth (#12), in contrast, is unique to the North-Central region of California. Readers interested in such regional patterns should consult Gayton's "Areal Affiliations of California Folktales" (1935).

A final type of narrative, common in the primary literature but not represented formally in this collection, is the ethnographic text. It is an artificial genre, because these texts have been elicited in response to a direct question from the collector, usually an anthropologist or linguist seeking information about some aspect of culture: "What was an Indian funeral like?"—"How did people used to make acorn mush?"—"Describe a typical puberty ceremony"—and so on. Such narratives don't conform to any traditional genre; they would have no natural context in the Native culture, in which the answers are simply part of the fabric of life, and by and large they would never have been produced but for the inquisitiveness of the collector (though it's easy to imagine children asking their grandparents questions like "What games did kids play when you were growing up?" and getting what amounts to an ethnographically rich personal reminiscence in response).

Sometimes these ethnographic texts amount to little more than verbal descriptions of traditional activities, such as basketmaking or acorn preparation—activities that are better documented visually, language being rather a poor medium for this sort of task. (Try explaining how to tie a shoe over the phone.) Typically, such descriptions have been collected, in the untimely absence of a camera, purely for the sake of documentation, but often linguists will elicit them for reasons that have little to do with the nominal subject matter itself. Asking a consultant to describe *in words* some such procedure as arrow-making is a little like administering a stress test to the language itself: the unusual demands placed on the syntax and lexicon often reap unsuspected grammatical constructions and vocabulary items that might otherwise never have been observed in hours of conventional narrative or conversation. But even in scenarios like this, narrators will occasionally produce texts that manage to transcend their utilitarian origins. In the following passage, linguist Judith Crawford has asked Robert Martin, a Mojave, to describe the making of a cradleboard:[13]

CRADLEBOARD

I'm going to make a baby cradle now.
I go, I go, I look for mesquite root, mesquite root, mesquite root.
I dig anywhere up in the valley and I'll stay until I get one—if I'm
      lucky, if the tree "gives it to you."
If it is straight lying in the ground, then I take it. I bring it home, I
      bend it, I lay it down until it is dry, and in one week or so, I'll put
      the crosspieces on.
I'll go after some arrowweeds and put the crosspieces on, and I do it
      and then I finish.
Then I finish, then, I'm going again, after the [things for tying] on the
      cradle. I peel mesquite bark and I bring it home. That's all.
I tie it up and finish. Then that's all.
Then I finish the baby cradle. I finish in one week or so. That is a baby
      cradle, and that's the way I make them, and that's all.

Martin's account may not give much in the way of detail regarding the actual techniques of manufacture—no one could make a cradleboard on the strength of his description alone—but it does convey a nice sense of the speaker's state of mind as he goes about his imagined way, gathering his materials and working them. There's a personality here that shines through, despite the unlikely context and subject matter.

Artificial or not, these texts can often be quite interesting from a literary standpoint, as well, even apart from the cultural information they contain. The linguist Robert Oswalt recorded the following ethnographic "textlet" from Essie Parrish in 1959, one of many he collected in the course of his extensive work with Kashaya Pomo speakers. Mrs. Parrish would have offered it in response to queries from Oswalt regarding food preparation techniques (it is one of several such texts she contributed to *Kashaya Texts*).[14]

PRESERVING SHELLFISH

In the old days we could keep food without it rotting.

When winter came and the sea ran high, the Indians could not go to gather food along the coast for long periods. Before the water had already become rough, the leader would command, "Store away your food." Having had him say when [to go], they went up to the gravel beach, pried off mussels, gathered turban snails, packed them up the coastal cliffs, dug holes, poured the shellfish in there, packed up gravel, poured it on top, and poured ocean water over all that.

Then even when it rained, the mussels were still good and unspoiled for several days or even one week—turban snails they kept the same way. Because they did that, the old time people did not die off from starvation.

That is all there is of that.

Though this account may seem to be off-hand, the information conveyed is in fact quite carefully organized. It opens with a formulaic reference to "the old days," thereby situating the text in the realm of memory (paragraph 1), then moves into that time-frame for a sparse but detailed description of the season, social context, harvested species, physical setting, and steps involved in preserving shellfish (paragraph 2). She then closes the window she has opened into the past, returns us to the present with her reference once again to the "old time" people, and—storyteller that she is—finishes up with a "moral" about survival and the importance of diligence and know-how (paragraph 3), before terminating the topic at hand (paragraph 4). The sense of literary form and closure, even in so short a discourse, is unmistakable.

Indeed, sometimes narrators can deliver goods that far exceed the relatively narrow, prosaic expectations of the genre. Betty Brown, the Northern Yana consultant Edward Sapir worked with in 1907, dictated a series of ethnographic texts—ethnographic *vignettes* might be a better description—that soar far above most other texts of their kind. In this excerpt, from a much longer text Sapir called "Indian Medicine-Men," a frantic husband has just called in a powerful shaman to try to save his dying wife.[15]

> NARRATOR: [The medicine-man] has arrived.
>
> DOCTOR: "Put some water down on the ground!"
>
> NARRATOR: He offered him round white shell beads as payment, he offered him dentalia.
>
> HUSBAND, TO HIMSELF: "He will be glad because of these, when he sees them."
>
> DOCTOR: "I don't like these trinkets here—
> I like *p'aléhsi* shell beads."
>
> HUSBAND: "So you will doctor her!
> Doctor her during the night—
> perhaps she will recover."
>
> DOCTOR: "Oh, I am not afraid of doctoring the one who is sick.
> Why should I be afraid?
> I am a medicine-man!
> She will not cry.
> She will yet eat her own food."
>
> HUSBAND: "Go forth from the house!
> Shout!
> Call upon your dream-spirit!
> That's what a medicine-man always does."
>
> DOCTOR: "She will recover—I dreamed it.
> *Pray speak to the spring of water,*
>   my dream tells me.

Pray do not eat!
Go ahead and eat tomorrow when the sun is overhead.
You shall go to the spring to bathe.

[Thus] I dreamt.

Pray pass the night on the mountain!

Now then,
I shall return in the night.
Wake up the people.
They will help to sing.
I am a great medicine-man.

Pray ask the rocks!
Ask the trees!
Ask the logs!
Go about twice, and the owl will talk,
and the yellowhammer [too],
and pray roll tobacco between your hands and smoke it!
Eat nothing!
Pick up the round luck-stones!

Thus did I dream.
She will recover."

Rather than responding to Sapir's requests with the critically detached descriptions of the practiced cultural interpreter, she throws herself into the scene, re-creating not so much the details but the life and spirit of the occasion.[16] Her re-creation is so vivid and emotional, so immediate, that it essentially takes the form of a drama. Describe an Indian burial? Describe a curing ceremony? Betty Brown did that and more.

SONG

Songs were an integral part of life in Native California, and still are today. There were curing songs, love songs, dance songs, power songs, gambling songs, hunting songs, mourning songs, ritual songs, luck songs, dream songs, work songs, and traveling songs, to name just a few. Songs were sung publicly, to accompany dances, ceremonies, and games, or in smaller settings, to be shared with friends and family. The girls' puberty songs of the Wintu (#11), for instance, were public songs, sung by visiting parties as they entered the village where a puberty celebration was being held. Their dream songs, in contrast, typically would have been sung first for a more intimate audience—though once debuted, they could then be sung to accompany dances. Of course, songs were also sung privately, to help the singer think, pray, or focus an emotion. The Wintu cry song that Grace McKibbin sings—*"Which trail should I take to go over the hill? I guess I'll take the south trail over the hill"* (#13)—is an example of a song that originated as a private song, composed by her grandfather while traveling, and later was passed down through the singer's family as part of its oral tradition.

Songs are frequently incorporated into stories and myths. Four of the selections in this volume demonstrate this characteristic: William Benson's "Creation" (#16) from Eastern Pomo (sadly, the songs accompanying this myth were not preserved); the Chumash story of "The Dog Girl" (#22), told by María Solares; the older of the two Cupeño "Hawk Feather" episodes (#25b), dictated by Salvadora Valenzuela; and Joe Homer's "An Account of Origins" (#27). As this sampling suggests, myths and other sacred narratives are perhaps more likely than other genres to have a significant component of song, just as hymns and liturgical music form an integral part of Western (and other) religious ceremonial traditions. But the example of "The Dog Girl," a secular tale if there ever was one, shows that song may be associated with other genres as well.[17]

Leanne Hinton has observed, for Yuman storytelling traditions, that the songs often create key interludes of emotionality, which are set off like jewels against an essentially neutral or reportorial narrative background. Where the narrative portions of Yuman stories are invariably told from a third-person, remote-past quotative point of view, the songs tend to be first-person expressions of what the protagonist is feeling at that point in the story, giving the audience a view directly from the story's heart, its emotional core. Though Hinton's observations were originally made for Havasupai, they clearly have a wider application: for instance, it is easy to see exactly this same stylistic pattern—of inner versus outer experience, the subjective emotionality of song against the objective reportage of narration—at work in the Chumash story of "The Dog Girl."

Songs can vary greatly in terms of content, as well. A lot of California songs are actually wordless—that is, they consist entirely of nonsense syllables or vocables,[18] much like the Irish lilting tradition, or the burdens of so many English and Celtic folk songs (*hey-nonny-nonny, fol la diddle dido, down-a-down hey down-a-down,* and the like). For instance, one of the many Miwok gambling songs consists of the vocable phrases *Wa ni ni ni, wa ah ha, yo wa ha* sung in litany, over and over, until the singer's gambling turn is over (Angulo 1976a:85). It is not accurate, however, to call these vocable songs "meaningless." Although they may not have explicit lexical content, they carry an emotional weight and often tap into their true meaning by association with a particular ritual or story.

At the other extreme are the long, verbally complex song cycles of many Southern California tribes. For the most part these songs are connected with religious ceremonies. The following example, taken from the Quechan "Lightning Song" as sung by William Wilson (Halpern 1984), presents a sampling of eight song texts drawn almost at random from within the longer cycle. Each song, probably interwoven by strings of vocables, would be sung a specified number of times—or simply over and over until its particular segment of the ceremony was concluded. It took all night to sing the complete cycle.

He stands and looks from afar
He looks from afar and sees
He looks from afar and describes

He sees the quivering foggy cloud
He describes the quivering foggy cloud
He sees the cloud passing
He describes the cloud passing
He is looking at the clouds as they turn this way and that
He describes the clouds turning this way and that

He sees lightning
Lightning flashes in the darkness
He describes lightning

He sees its impossibility
He describes its impossibility

He clumps it together
He takes darkness and clumps it together
He describes taking darkness and clumping it together

You have mistaken it
He sees you mistake it

Coyote is there describing dawn
He describes you mistaking it

Stars pass overhead
Stars wandering overhead
Stars pass overhead
Stars trail across the sky
Stars trail across the sky
He describes stars sitting in the sky

He sees sunrise
He describes sunrise

The Luiseño songs of Villiana Calac Hyde, some of which are presented
in this volume (#24), likewise illustrate this more elaborate lyric tradition. In Northern California, the Karuk "Evening Star" songs, too, can
be quite involved, verging on a quasi-narrative form.[19]

The vast majority of known California songs are considerably less
complex, at least as far as their explicit verbal content is concerned. They
tend to consist of a few lines—often just one or two—of verse sung in
alternation with lines of vocables. Grace McKibbin's songs (#13) are good
examples of this most typical California pattern and have the advantage
of representing complete performances, including repetitions and vocables, rather than just the abstract of the words alone. Hinton's presentation gives us the full text of one particular performance—a bit different
each time the song is sung—as words and vocables intertwine.

Usually, though, the verbal abstract is all that is presented of a song;
the vocables are ignored, and the organic cycle of repetitions eliminated.[20]
What we see of a song then is merely the distillation of its verbal essence.
It doesn't mean that the song's text is not authentic—just a bit diminished, removed still further from its spontaneous musical and performance context. Here are some examples, striking nonetheless, drawn from
a variety of sources and singing traditions:[21]

Who is like me!
My plumes are flying—
They will come to rest in an unknown region
Above where the banners are flying.

                    Chumash song, from a story

Listen to what I am about to sing.
Listen to my breathing on high.
Listen to my stamping, I tear the ground up.
Listen to my groaning.
I am done.
I-ha-ya-a-ha-hu-ha!
I-ya-ka-mi-ha-mi!

Bear Dance song (Santa Rosa Island)

Jumping echoes of the rock;
Squirrels turning somersaults;
Green leaves, dancing in the air;
Fishes, white as money-shells,
Running in the water: green, deep, and still.
Hi-ho, hi-ho, hi-hay!
Hi-ho, hi-ho, hi-hay!

Modoc puberty song

I am traveling—me, me, me!
I go around the world—me, me!
I cause the mist—me, me!
When I climb the mountaintops
I cause [the] clouds,
I cause the rain.
Long live Coyote!
He will always be.

Coyote's song while traveling
(Chumash)

Going along singing,
Following the deer trail,
Hunting deer,
Going along singing,
Going along singing.

Yahi mouth-bow song

In this more common, stripped-down mode of presentation, California songs tend to resemble Japanese haiku more than anything—indeed, it's an obvious and striking connection to make. Consider these examples, again drawn from a variety of sources and singing traditions:[22]

> The dawn is dawning,
> a shadow—
> I come home, I come home.
> > Achumawi waking song

> Where we used to make love,
> the grass is grown up high now.
> > Hupa brush dance song

> I am the only one, the only one left—
> An old man, I carry the gambling board,
> An old man, I sing the gambling song.
> > Costanoan gambling song

> Come! Come!
> I mean you
> With the brown hat . . .
> > Costanoan love song
> > (post-Contact)

> Dancing on the brink of the world . . .
> > Costanoan dance song

> Jump, salmon, jump!
> So you may see your uncle dance!
> > Coyote's song to catch salmon (Chumash)

In truth, many of the songs *do* resemble haiku in terms of their imagery, as well as in their perceptual and emotional immediacy, the "here and now" of their subject matter. But, when we recall that these songs are typically sung over and over again, the words being repeated many times over, we see that they share some of the characteristics of the mantra, as well.

Because of their essential textual brevity, songs tend to be highly elliptical and allusive. It is often impossible to draw the true meaning of a song merely from its words alone. The impression of understanding that someone outside the tradition gets can well be a mistaken one: we only *think* we get it, because we are able to respond to the surface of the words as we do to any poetic image.[23] But songs presented this way are isolated from their context, and their context is often the primary place where their deepest meaning resides. Take this Tachi Yokuts song, "Dawis Sapagay's Song," recorded from Leon Manuel by James Hatch in 1957:

> Where will I go in?
> I will go in
> where green scum is on the pool.

Even knowing that Dawis Sapagay was a well-known Tachi shaman and that this was his personal power song does not take us very far along the path to understanding. Still, we form an impression, and after a while, feel that we have established some sort of connection with the song. What we don't know is that the song refers to a story, the story of how Sapagay received his doctor's power to cure sickness. Manuel told Sapagay's story this way:

> Looking for a doctor who would teach him curing power, Sapagay went to the edge of Wood Lake to find the underwater entrance to the place where the doctor lived. He dove in (at the place where the green scum is), and came up in a cave in which he met the guardians of the doctor. There was a man-sized spider with voracious jaws, and, afterward, a rattlesnake coiled ready to strike. Last, there was a puma and a bear who tore men to pieces. Sapagay used a kingsnake charm against the spider and the rattlesnake (kingsnakes eat spiders and rattlesnakes), while against the puma and the bear he used a weasel charm which made him small and agile. He thus passed them by.

At length he came to the end of the cave. It was a new and strange land which he had not seen before. After looking around, he came upon the doctor sitting steadfast as a stone and looking straight at him. After a time the doctor looked up and asked Sapagay, "What are you doing here? How did you get in? You must have some sort of power to get past my guardians." Sapagay told him of the charms he had used and the doctor approved of them. They were the right charms for the man who wanted doctor power.

Sapagay looked about and saw that there was no one around. He said, "This must be a very lonely place; there are no other people here." The doctor replied, "You don't seem to like it here; why did you come?" And he continued, "I will show you the people who live here." So he called, and a long line of deer came out of the black mountain to the west. Sapagay thought to himself, "These aren't real people, but just deer from the woods." But the deer came and formed a circle about him and lost their horns and hooves, and turned into beautiful girls dressed in string aprons, beads, and clamshell ornaments. The doctor then addressed the girls, "Now give him your songs, that he may have doctor power among his people." And the girls taught Sapagay their songs so that he could use their secret power.

When Sapagay learned all that he could, he asked the doctor how he could get back to his people. The doctor told him that the guardians would be asleep when he returned through the tunnel. And then Sapagay returned to his people and became a famous doctor who was called to all parts of California to cure the sick.

Without knowing the story, we can only aspire to the most superficial appreciation for the song—its words, perhaps, but not its meaning. Once we do know the story, we see just how far off-base our understanding really was. So much is implied here, that the song itself is merely an allusion. To be sure, there is a clear image captured in these words, the image of algae floating on the surface of a pond. But this image is actually a bit like the green scum in the song itself—its true meaning lies beneath it: the pool itself, and what was down there.

Examples like the Sapagay song serve as cautionary tales, warning us not to be too confident that we can ever fully understand the meaning of a song—even if it seems laid out before us in crystalline form. The words of a song are the looking-glass through which we, as readers, enter the world of the song—but they themselves are not that world, just its signifiers. When seen in this light, it is clear that a song composed mostly or even entirely of vocables will be as rich in meaning as a song composed with many verses of words.

ORATORY

This category, which variously includes prayers, eulogies, sermons, morning speeches (in some cultures given daily by the chief from atop the assembly house), public announcements, and instructional lectures, among other genres, is little documented in California and can only be touched on here. The print literature provides us with very few reliable examples (too often the content of the speeches has merely been paraphrased or summarized), and discussions of the topic therefore tend to draw from the same few published sources: Edward Gifford's "Central Miwok Ceremonies" (1955), Philip Sparkman's "Culture of the Luiseño Indians" (1908), C. Darryl Forde's "Ethnography of the Yuma Indians" (1931), Samuel Barrett's "Wintun Hesi Ceremony" (1919), and perhaps a few others. Further examples will yet turn up in private and archival collections of unpublished fieldnotes, as these are box-by-box uncovered. As if in proof of this belief, a careful examination of Richard Keeling's *Guide to Early Field Recordings (1900–1949) at the Lowie Museum of Anthropology* (1991) suggests that a considerable store of potentially retrievable oratory on wax cylinder and aluminum disc may lie waiting in the vaults.

Most of the oratory that has been published consists of either prayers or public speeches. Here and there may be found examples of other genres, though. The following passage forms the conclusion of the lengthy lecture or "counsel" given to initiates at the *Yuninish,* the girls' puberty ceremony of the Luiseño (Sparkman 1908:226):

See,
these old men and women,
these are those who paid attention to this counsel,
which is of the grown-up people,
and they have already reached old age.

Do not forget this that I am telling you,
pay heed to this speech,

and when you are old like these old people,
you will counsel your sons and daughters in like manner,
and you will die old.

And your spirit will rise northwards to the sky,
like the stars, moon, and sun.

Perhaps they will speak of you
and will blow three times
and thereby cause to rise your spirit and soul to the sky.

The dynamics of setting can contribute nearly as much to the structure of an oration as its content does. Numerous observers have commented on the peculiar vocal and rhythmic characteristics of public speaking as delivered by California orators. In Northern California, the Yana, like most people, even had a specific word, *gaac'an'i* 'to talk like a chief', to refer to this speaking style. Forde, describing the special effects of a Quechan funeral speech, noted that "normal word order is changed. Words are omitted and others repeated to produce the rhythm of the speech. They are sometimes abbreviated, sometimes expanded by the addition of consonants to increase the staccato of the speech" (1931:212). This example, from a Patwin Hesi oration, was described as being "delivered in very high voice and jerky phrases" (A. Kroeber 1925:389), and illustrates some of the features of this type of address:[24]

Be like this!
Be like this!
Be good!
Be good, good!
Be glad of it!
Rejoice in it!
Rejoice in this speech!
Rejoice in this!
Rejoice in these roses!
Rejoice in these healthy roses [you're wearing]!
Say yes!
Say yes!
We come approving!
We come approving!
We shall do it like that!

We shall approve!
We shall be glad!
Father will be glad!
Mother's brother will be glad!
Older brother will be glad!
When we gather like this!
When we gather like this!
We shall rejoice, therefore!
Our speech!
Our speech!
Be glad, therefore!
I was glad, was glad!
I rejoiced!
Rejoice and approve!
Rejoice and be glad!
Approve of it!
Rejoice in it!

It is easy to see how the economics of breath constrains the form of this oration. As everyone who has ever hollered at a friend or called a child to supper knows, the louder you shout, the less you can say on your lungful of air. The need to be heard, to broadcast the voice across the widest area, often to a dispersed audience, has certain predictable consequences for the shape of the message. We should *expect* to find short, jerky phrases and repetitions (for the sake of both emphasis and of euphony), distorted vocal qualities, and a powerful rhythmic drive. Most of the recorded examples of California public oratory exhibit these or similar signs. Indeed, when these features are less in evidence, it often turns out that the speech has been re-created "in the studio," as it were. Then again, it may simply represent a less bombastic genre appropriate to a smaller or more intimate or indoor audience— for instance, the girls' puberty lecture quoted earlier. Add to these physical constraints the purely stylistic tropes and quirks, embellishments and deviations, that accumulate in an art form with the most ancient of roots, and it's no wonder these examples command our attention.

What has survived of California oratory presents a tantalizing picture. But I look forward to a time when more examples of these marvelous verbal art forms have been found and brought to light, and we can begin at last to appreciate their multiplexity and discern something of their poetics. Still more, I look forward to the minting of *new* examples, to hearing how the living generations of California Indians have carried these traditions into modern life.

Indeed, that should make a fine "best hope" for the future of California's oral-literary heritage at large—the whole constellation of its indigenous verbal arts, of myth and song, chant and celebration—as this new century gets under way. In the meantime, let us "rejoice in these roses" that have come down, by some of the hardest paths imaginable, into the hands of posterity.

NOTES

1. Theodora Kroeber has a nice essay, "Some Qualities of Indian Stories," in *The Inland Whale* (1959), her book of literary "retellings" of five California stories.

2. Benson's version, though, contains ideas that are unusual in the Central California traditions: *cycles* of creation and destruction—by flood, fire, whirlwind, and the like—brought on by the Creator's dissatisfaction with the results of his labors. Versions by neighboring Pomo and Lake Miwok narrators (for example, Callaghan 1978) conform to the Earthdiver type. Such ideas are more common in Yuman literatures such as the Mojave and Halchidhoma, though they are not unheard of elsewhere. Alfred Kroeber (1925:206) speculates that this subordinate "cycles" pattern in Central California may be associated with the Kuksu religion.

3. Sources regarding the World Renewal ceremonies include A. Kroeber and Gifford (1949).

4. From A. Kroeber and Gifford (1949:14). This does not appear to be a verbatim record of Mr. Davis's account, because it shows clear signs of paraphrasing, probably introduced during the dictation process. The Karuk term *Írahiv* refers to the World Renewal Ceremony; *Ixkareyev Animas* is the name of one of the Spirit People from the prehuman myth-time.

5. The texts reproduced here and on page 57 come from a fair-hand copy found among Faye's notes in the Bancroft Library. Readers familiar with the literature will notice some variation from a version of these songs first published in Joughlin and Valenzuela (1953) and subsequently reprinted in a variety of sources.

6. Out of respect for the feelings of contemporary Luiseño singers who consider the funeral songs both sacred and private, I present only the first stanza of

this beautiful and powerful song—just enough to illustrate the point I make here. Readers interested in studying this and other such songs in their entirety may consult *Yumáyk Yumáyk (Long Ago)*, Mrs. Hyde's extraordinary collection of narratives and songs (Hyde and Elliott 1994).

7. There are other reasons besides stylistic choice why these two versions are so different—the foremost being the age of the narrations and the narrators themselves. Joe Homer told his myth in 1912, and Sarah Martin told hers in 1960. Many details, and indeed the practice of extended narration itself, would have "evaporated"—been lost from tradition during the generations that separated the two performances.

8. Coyote stories, of course, are not confined to California. Far from it: Coyote is an important mythic character throughout much of the American and Canadian West. William Bright's book, *A Coyote Reader* (1993), is a fascinating and very readable celebration of mythology's most notorious multiple-personality disorder; it will point the reader toward all kinds of interesting Coyote sources. Gary Snyder's essay, "The Incredible Survival of Coyote" (1975), is well-known but still rewarding. Most any collection of myths or stories you might pick up, especially from California, will contain at least a few stories featuring Coyote; it's actually hard to avoid him once you start looking. Indeed, because there are so many collections out there that focus on Coyote stories, I haven't gone out of my way to include examples in this volume—so if anything, the importance of Coyote to the oral-literary canon of California is underrepresented by the selections in this volume.

9. Actually, this element is a complex unit combining a remote-past tense suffix *-n'(i)* with the actual quotative *-t^h(i)*, each of which has an independent function. The former may be used for remembered events of long ago, whereas the latter may be used for reporting direct discourse or information acquired through hearsay. Together, though, they have this special narrative function in myth.

10. This Northern Yana passage is cast in an informal practical orthography designed to balance linguistic needs with the need for phonetic transparency. Doubled characters represent length, stress is indicated with an acute accent over the vowel, and superscript letters are voiceless. Certain phonetic processes involved with prosody (final aspiration, devoicing, secondary and emphatic primary stress) are preserved in the transcription. For a more detailed description of linguistic writing systems, see the "Pronunciation Guide" at the beginning of the book.

11. Often there is a poetics involved with the use of this element. Ken Hill, in his introduction to Sarah Martin's Serrano "Creation" (#23), points out that its occasional suppression seems to have a heightening or intensifying effect. And

sometimes narrators will deploy the quotative element in their stories tactically, controlling that element's placement so as to section the story into passages, rather like paragraphing in written prose.

12. Perhaps unwisely, I collapse two related but rather different types of story into this ad hoc designation. First are stories like "Grizzly Bear and Deer" (Whistler 1977a) and "Condor Steals Falcon's Wife" (#20b), where the "monster" is simply bad by disposition. For example, it is in Bear's nature to be violent—she's almost always the villain in her own stories and usually suffers the deadly revenge meted out for her actions; likewise, Condor appears to be "bad by nature." Second is a class of stories like "Rolling Skull" (Luthin 1994) and "Mad Bat" (#15), where an otherwise "normal" character begins behaving in a psychotic manner. In the Yana "Rolling Skull" story, Wildcat has a bad dream, which deranges him, sending him off on a terroristic rampage until someone (Coyote, in this instance) steps in to "end his career" and restore harmony. In Mad Bat's case, we don't know the cause of his deranged behavior, but eventually he, too, is stopped, and pays with his life for his actions.

13. In Langdon (1976:34), I have slightly altered Crawford's free translation, as indicated by brackets.

14. This text, in both Kashaya and English, may be found in Oswalt (1964:300–301).

15. The translation is my own, based on Sapir's 1910 free translation and the original Yana.

16. Sapir began eliciting ethnographic texts from Betty Brown because he was doubtful of her skill as a teller of traditional myths and stories. As it turned out, he was also less than satisfied with her ethnographic work. In a footnote to the present text, he comments on this matter: "In this and the following texts an attempt was made to secure from Betty Brown an account in her own language of some phases of Yana religious and social life. Owing to her tendency to use conversational narrative instead of general description, these texts are rather illustrative by means of real or imaginary incidents in the life of the Yana than ethnologically satisfying statements" (1910:178).

17. Some traditions seem to exploit this characteristic more than others. Mojave stories, for instance, are often densely interspersed with songs—so much so that their complete absence from the archaic migration epic (#26) strikes contemporary Mojaves as distinctly peculiar and un-Mojave-like. The Chumash, Chemehuevi (Laird 1984), and other Southern California cultures also seem to have a preference for this style of storytelling.

18. For a more detailed look at vocable elements in California song, see Hinton 1994d.

19. See William Bright's translation of one such song ("Myth, Music, and Magic: Nettie Reuben's Karuk Love Medicine") in Swann 1994.

20. This approach is typical of earlier ethnolinguistic collections, made before the field's relatively recent advances in ethnopoetics and performance theory.

21. Chumash song (Blackburn 1975); Santa Rosa Island Bear Dance song (Heizer 1955); Modoc puberty song (Powers 1877); Chumash Coyote song (Blackburn 1975); Yahi mouth-bow song (T. Kroeber 1964).

22. Achumawi waking song (Angulo 1990); Hupa brush dance song (Keeling 1985); Costanoan gambling song (A. Kroeber 1925); Costanoan love song (A. Kroeber 1925); Costanoan dance song (A. Kroeber 1925); Chumash Coyote song (Blackburn 1975).

23. This can be nearly as true for members of other California tribes—or even other family traditions *within* a tribe—as it is for people with no experience of Native culture at all.

24. I have taken the text as reported in A. Kroeber (1925) and "smoothed it up" a bit for use in this discussion. Though my alterations stick very close to the original English glosses, this still should not be considered an "authoritative" rendering of the Patwin original, for which the reader should consult the original text. For those who were wondering, the Hesi is a dance ceremony.

Oh, people!
Our hearts are good and strong!
We can work all day!
This sickness does go away, I know it!

I go off by myself.
Alone in the house, I lie down on the bed
And forget everything.
All this fades away.

All the people!
All our sick hearts will change!
This day is passing away,
Passing [away] from here.
We are all together.
Now will we think well,
Now will we think in this place,
Now that we are all together.

I tell you, when we lose a strong man,
Our hearts cannot be good—but now,
We must not think about it.

I will end right now,
I will end [it] well.

We [must] think now, about being here all together now.

People!
It will be good when this day has passed,
[That's what] we are thinking here.
I will find our strength, I will find our good.
It used to be that my body [felt bad],

When I lay down alone.
On that I rely:
We trust our sick hearts will change.
I rely on that!

I will finish.
Rightly we are thinking good things.

Quechan funeral speech
C. Darryl Forde, *Ethnography
of the Yuma Indians*

Notes on Native California Languages

LANGUAGE FAMILIES

Kelp-beds, redwoods, desert scrub, oak savannah: from the coastal waters of the Pacific to the crest of the high Sierras, from the Sacramento Delta to the dry sands of the Baja Peninsula, California has always been a land of abundance. Most of us are aware of the extremes of habitat, the tremendous biological and geographic diversity that California embraces. Not so many are aware that this exuberance extends to its Native cultures and languages as well. Yet aboriginal California was one of the most linguistically diverse places on earth, and its great abundance helped support the single highest population density in North America (A. Kroeber 1939:153)—that is, until the Spanish, and later the new "Americans," came and began to change the lives of its people forever, constraining their ways, restricting their freedoms, and dispossessing them of their lands. California was home to at least eighty to one hundred distinct languages—and probably more—at the time of European contact. (Each language reflects a cultural division, too; see map 2, p. 574.) As always, though, language is an early casualty in the forced assimilation of other cultures. It is a tribute to the tenacity of California Indians that some fifty of these languages are still spoken today.[1] The majority of these languages are severely endangered, however, and drastic measures need to be taken to ensure their survival into the next century.

Most of California's many languages were in turn spoken in different dialects as well, just as the English "accents" of Brooklyn, Atlanta, Dublin, Nairobi, Bombay, and Perth are different today. Our world

Englishes, though, have only been developing for a few hundred years, whereas California's languages have been rooted and changing, many of them, for thousands of years—and thus the dialect differences within a language can be quite profound. The three attested dialects of Yana, for instance—Northern, Central, and Yahi—vary from each other about as much as do the Romance languages, say Spanish, Portuguese, and Italian, which are themselves really just the modern descendants of medieval Latin dialects. (In truth, the Yanan dialects are not excessively differentiated. There are much greater differences to be found among the various Shastan and Chumashan "dialects," which are more properly classified as distinct languages than as dialects.) It is easy to see that the distinction between language and dialect is not always a straightforward one: sometimes it's just a matter of convention or historical accident or politics whether two related forms of speech are labeled as dialects or as separate languages.

So when linguists cite a figure like the conservative "eighty to one hundred distinct languages" figure for pre-Contact California, astonishing though it may be, the reality was even more complex: there are layers of diversity *within* that overall diversity that the general figure doesn't even hint at. Finally, as if this complexity were not enough in itself, the stability and relatively small size of most California tribal territories (and the close contact with neighboring groups through trading and intermarriage that this implies) means that bilingualism and even trilingualism must have been a commonplace. California truly was a linguistic land of plenty—a proud trait that modern California, thanks to its surviving native languages and the multilingual constellations of its major cities, preserves to this day.[2]

Given their tremendous diversity, it's unsurprising that California's languages bear genetic resemblances among themselves. (By *genetic resemblance* we mean that the languages in question trace back to a common ancestor language, just as Spanish, French, and Italian have evolved or descended from Latin.) There are approximately twenty language families in California (see table 5).[3] Some, like Pomoan or Utian, are relatively large families of languages, having many sibling members (fifteen in the case of Utian); others, like Karuk or Washoe, are "only children" within their respective families.

In turn, these twenty or so California language families may ultimately descend from five superfamilies, or stocks. (In the same way, the

Table 5. Language Families:
California Languages and Genetic Affiliations

YUKIAN
Yukian Family
  Yuki (Yuki/Coast Yuki/Huchnom)
  Wappo

CHUMASHAN
Chumashan Family
  Obispeño
  Purisimeño
  Ineseño
  Barbareño
  Ventureño
  Island Chumash

HOKAN STOCK (PROPOSED)
  Karuk
  Chimariko
  Yana (N. Yana/C. Yana/Yahi)
  Washoe
Shastan Family
  Shasta
  Konomihu
  New River Shasta
  Okwanuchu
Palaihnihan Family
  Achumawi
  Atsugewi
Pomoan Family
  Northern Pomo
  Central Pomo
  Northeastern Pomo
  Eastern Pomo
  Southeastern Pomo
  Southern Pomo
  Kashaya (Southwestern Pomo)
Salinan Family
  Antoniaño
  Migueleño

HOKAN STOCK *(continued)*
Yuman Family
  Ipai (Northern Diegueño)
  Tipai (Mexican Diegueño)
  Kumeyaay (Southern Diegueño)
  Mojave
  Halchidhoma (Maricopa)
  Quechan (Yuma)

ESSELEN
  Esselen

PENUTIAN STOCK (PROPOSED)
Wintuan Family
  Wintu (Wintu/Nomlaki)
  Patwin (Hill Patwin/River Patwin/
    Southern Patwin)
Maiduan Family
  Maidu
  Konkow
  Nisenan
Miwokan Family (Utian)
  Coast Miwok (Bodega/Marin)
  Lake Miwok
  Saclan (Bay Miwok)
  Plains Miwok
  Northern Sierra Miwok
  Central Sierra Miwok
  Southern Sierra Miwok
Costanoan Family (Utian)
  Karkin
  Chochenyo
  Ramaytush
  Tamyen
  Awaswas
  Chalon
  Rumsen
  Mutsun

Continued

Table 5—*Continued*

PENUTIAN STOCK *continued*
Yokutsan Family
Valley Yokuts
Far Northern (Yachikumne
[Chulamni]/Lower San
Joaquin/Lakisamni-
Tawalimni)
Northern Valley (Nopchinchi/
Chawchila/
Chukchansi/Merced/
Kechayi-Dumna)
Southern Valley (Wechihit/Nutunutu-
Tachi/Chunut/Wo'lasi-
Choynok/Koyeti-
Yowlumni)
Buena Vista (Tulamni/Hometwoli)
Gashowu
Kings River (Chukaymina/
Michahay/Ayticha/
Choynimni)
Tule-Kaweah (Wikchamni/Yawdanchi)
Palewyami
Plateau Penutian Family
Modoc

UTO-AZTECAN STOCK
Tübatulabal
Takic Family
Kitanemuk
Tongva (Gabrielino/Fernandeño)

UTO-AZTECAN STOCK *continued*
Serrano
Luiseño (Luiseño/Ajachmem
[Juaneño])
Cupeño
Cahuilla
Tataviam
Numic Family
Northern Paiute
Mono (Monache/Owens Valley
Paiute)
Panamint (California Shoshone)
Kawaiisu
Chemehuevi (dialect of Ute)

ALGIC STOCK
Ritwan Family
Yurok
Wiyot

NA-DENE STOCK
Athapaskan Family
Tolowa (Tolowa/Chetco)
Hupa (Hupa/Chilula-Whilkut)
Mattole (Mattole/Bear River)
Eel River (Nongatl/Lassik/
Sinkyone/Wailaki)
Cahto

SOURCE: Goddard (1996).

Germanic family—which includes English, Dutch, German, and the Scandinavian languages—is itself a member of the Indo-European superfamily of languages, a stock that incorporates such seemingly disparate languages as French, Armenian, Greek, Croatian, and Hindi under its umbrella.) Two of the five stocks, Penutian and Hokan, are closely or quintessentially associated with California and are so ancient that the resemblances among their constituent language families are barely discernible. Indeed, the resemblances are so hard to pin down, and the time-depth involved is so profound, that many linguists believe them to be chimerical. We may catch a glimmer here and there, as in the various words for 'two', but their interrelationships are deeply buried in time.[4] The other three stocks—Algic, Na-Dené, and Uto-Aztecan—are well accepted and have their primary distributions outside the California region.[5] In addition, there is one "family isolate" that can't be plausibly linked up with any of the other stocks: Yukian, which includes the Yuki, Coast Yuki, and Huchnom dialects of Yuki proper, together with the remotely related Wappo.[6] (Isolates are languages, like Basque in Europe, that have no known genetic affiliation to any other language groups.) Like the Hokan language families, Yukian represents an ancient presence in California. Map 3, page 575, shows the geographic distribution of these stocks and families.

The prehistory of the California languages makes for a challenging study. Of Penutian, Michael Silverstein has written, "There is, first, tremendous linguistic diversity, *equalling perhaps that of the entire continent,* encompassed within the proposed 'superstock'" (1979; italics mine). So much time has passed that the modern descendants of that original language—if we can even be sure there *was* but one such language—have metamorphosed dramatically. Yet, although Penutian is a venerable family in its own right (there are ten-thousand-year-old sites in southern Oregon, the presumed Penutian homeland, distributed along the shores of ancient lakes, that were probably Penutian sites), as a family presence in California proper it is not terribly old: on the order of forty-five hundred years or more, dating from the first incursions of Proto-Utians into the Sacramento Valley. Hokan, in contrast—or anyway, the distinct language families that traditionally comprise this grouping—is much, much older in California, going back beyond our ability to calculate with any certainty. Its ancestral speakers are, along with ancestral Yukian speakers, if not the first, certainly among the oldest inhabitants of California. We must presume they were already here—long in residence, families of an old and already divergent stock—when the earliest Period II archaeological sites begin to enter the record, some eight thousand years ago.[7] If demonstrable as a language family or superstock, Hokan would be much older than Indo-European, perhaps even older than Penutian itself. A rough general consensus puts its time-depth at twelve thousand years old.[8]

The presence of the other three groups (though ancient in and of themselves) in California is much more recent. Indeed, by taking a closer look at the family-and-stock map (map 3) of California, we can get a glimpse of its linguistic past. Like the residue of waves fossilized in the rippled sediments of an ancient shoreline, the contemporary language map of California (map 5, p. 573) reveals a tracery of ages-old patterns of migration. But first we have to learn to see that map as if in motion.

We can start by imagining a time, some five thousand years ago—consistent with the linguistic evidence—when long-resident, already divergent Hokan-affiliated peoples were spread pretty much across the coast and heartland of the Central California culture area, sharing parts of this territory with early Chumashan and Yukian peoples (and no doubt other groups as well, who have passed from the record without trace). Then, beginning around forty-five hundred years ago, Proto-Utian peoples—the Penutian ancestors of the Miwok and Costanoan families—began moving into California from the northeast along the great river-and-valley systems—first along the Klamath, then over to the Sacramento, following it all the way down into the Bay region and up its tributaries into the Sierra Nevada and south along the coast to Monterey—the very territories that they occupy today. As they went, they would have displaced some of the already-settled "Old California" peoples from these regions. The Utians were followed in time by ancestral Yokutsan peoples, who began their long move down into the Central Valley and southern Sierra foothills about thirty-five hundred years ago. Both these expansions into California would have taken place over the course of centuries, involving generations of geographic adaptation to new lands and the give-and-take of cultural accommodation with new neighbors.

Later, beginning around two thousand years ago, ancestors of the Wintuan peoples, probably pushed by Athabascan groups still farther to the north, made *their* move into California, following the by-now well-worn Penutian migration routes down into the upper Sacramento Valley, spreading slowly south over the course of the next thousand years (Whistler 1977b). At about the same time the Wintuan groups were beginning their descent, around two thousand years ago, ancestral Maiduan people, who had been living in the Tahoe region from about 4000 B.P., began expanding into their present territories, at the expense of the Washoe and Yana. All these waves of Penutian migrations have greatly enriched the linguistic tapestry of California.[9]

Looking again at the modern distribution of Hokan and other Old

California families (see map 4, p. 576), you will see them displaced in clumps and islands along the periphery of cartographic California, pressed outward in a great, broken ring around the central region of the state, beginning with Karuk, Chimariko, and Shasta in the northwest, over to Achumawi, Atsugewi, and Yana, and skipping down to Washoe in the east. Then comes a big gap in that ring, where Uto-Aztecan tribes from the interior much later flowed out of the Great Basin or southeastern Sierra into southern California, eventually reaching all the way to the Pacific. The pieces of the ring pick up again, hundreds of miles further on, with the Yuman tribes far to the south: Mojave, Halchidhoma, Quechan, Cocopa, and Tipai-Ipai.[10] Fragments of the great ring can be seen scattered northward along the coast, as well: beyond the Chumash we find Salinan and Esselen, and finally, north of the Penutian expansions into the San Francisco and Monterey Bay areas, the Pomoan languages and languages of the Yukian stock.

On the map, the Uto-Aztecan territory looks like nothing so much as a vast cultural and linguistic lava flow that has displaced or simply covered over the traces of whatever groups may have lain in its path. The Takic ancestors of modern-day California Uto-Aztecan peoples (the Serrano, Luiseño, Cupeño, Gabrielino, and others) began expanding westward into California from the southern Sierra Nevada about three thousand years ago, reaching the coast as early as 2500 B.P.[11] As they came, they would have pushed the resident Yuman groups out and away to the south and east, where they are found today. Behind them, and later, came Numic groups from further out in the Great Basin.

Following the many and staggered Penutian and Uto-Aztecan migrations, around one thousand years ago according to available evidence, the ancestors of the two Ritwan languages, Wiyot and Yurok, arrived (separately, it appears) to claim territory in the northwest—though how they came to be here, so far from their distant Algic relatives in the Algonquian family, is a mystery that may never be solved. Later still, as late as A.D. 900, the California Athabascan groups—the Tolowa, the Hupa/Chilula-Whilkut group, the Mattole, the Eel River cluster (Nongatl-Sinkyone-Lassik-Wailaki), and the Cahto—drifted down from Oregon, further displacing the descendant speakers of those original California language families.

Not many places on earth could sustain the diversity such repeated incursions have engendered in California.[12] In a different landscape—a land of more limited resources, of harsher climate, of less rugged and varied terrain—there would have been insufficient room, ecologically speaking, for new populations. In a more pitched competition for resources, the newcomers would have been repulsed, or the incumbents vanquished, else both groups would have risked starvation. In hostile environments—say, the Arctic or Great Basin regions of North America—human populations must be highly nomadic, requiring large territories to provide more than the meagerest sustenance of life. True to expectation, the linguistic and cultural diversity in both those regions is relatively minimal. From Alaska to Greenland, we find but a single language, Inupiaq, spoken in a long chain of dialects across the entire circumpolar region. A similar dialect continuum of closely related Numic languages (Northern Paiute, Mono, Shoshoni, Comanche, Southern Paiute, Chemehuevi, and Kawaiisu) spreads through the Great Basin from Wyoming and Montana in the north down through Utah and Nevada, all the way to Mexico.[13] But California's geography and rich ecology have afforded it an extraordinary carrying capacity for human cultures and the languages they bear with them.

CALIFORNIA LANGUAGES IN THE POST-CONTACT PERIOD

So what has become of this great diversity of tongues? Sadly, California's languages have been fighting for survival since the day the first Spanish mission was established in 1769 at what is now San Diego. Against all odds, some fifty ethnic groups still have active speakers of their native language (Hinton 1994a). Yet this situation, always a precarious one, is changing ever faster, as last speakers one by one pass on, taking their words and the music of their voices with them. (Map 5, based on a study reported in Leanne Hinton's *Flutes of Fire,* shows the areal distribution of these remaining speakers, by language.) Some of the losses have been recent indeed: for instance, when Laura Somersal, the last fluent speaker of Wappo, died in 1990, the Wappo language died with her. Of the fifty or so still-active languages, many are being taught to schoolchildren and young adults in the classroom, but not one is currently being passed on to the youngest generation of speakers, to be learned by children as their mother tongue, the language of home and family. How could this have happened? How could so many languages have fallen silent? In the end, the history of languages is inseparable from the history of the people who speak them.

The story of California's holocaust has been told many times, though still the truth of it is not yet common knowledge.[14] Estimates of the pre-Contact Native population of California range from a conservative 310,000 to nearly a million. By the end of the nineteenth century, that population had fallen to 20,000 or even less (Cook 1978). Even at the most conservative estimate, this represents a loss of more than 90 percent. (It takes a great deal of restraint to print a figure like this without an exclamation mark.) This catastrophic decline encompasses two main cycles or epicenters of destruction: one in the south from 1769 to about 1834, spreading inland and north along the coast with the expansion of the iniquitous Spanish mission system; the other in the north from 1848 (when gold was discovered at Sutter's Mill) to roughly 1865—the madness of the Gold Rush, which quickly spread throughout the mountainous regions of the state. The brief period between these cycles was no haven of recuperation. In addition to increased European-American encroachment on Indian lands amid the upheavals of the Mexican War, epidemics of malaria and smallpox decimated already stressed populations reeling from the onslaught of sustained contact begun a mere sixty years before. Cook (1978:92) mentions eyewitness reports of "entire villages of several hundred people being exterminated, of masses of skeletons found for years after."

It would be comforting to all of us—not just for those who must come to terms with the dark underside of their forebears' history of conquest, but also for those whose peoples have paid the price of that conquest—if we could believe that this waste and devastation was largely unintended, the sad but inevitable by-product of worlds in collision: microbial tragedies played out in the blood, ecological tragedies brought on by inexperience in a new environment, cultural tragedies kicked off by the discrepancy in medical and technological skills—all of which opened the way to a gradual abandonment of traditional ceremonies and crafts. Unfortunately, the reality of what happened between Indians and whites in California was not always so innocent. Genocide is a hard word but the only right one for what took place.

I don't mean to dwell on the issue here. This book is intended as a celebration, not a court-martial, still less a requiem. But certain facts must be faced squarely in order to understand the odds against *any* of the cultures represented here surviving into the twentieth century, let alone the twenty-first, with some semblance of their languages and traditions intact. Rather than attempt to cover this history discursively, I will take a testimonial approach, using the particulars of three short narratives to suggest the type and existence of more general conditions.

The Mission period, whatever the intentions of the Franciscan padres, was not a benign one for the Native cultures scorched by their influence. Forced labor, starvation, disease, rape, slavery, incarceration, torture, execution—these were commonplaces of Mission life. The brutality of the padres and soldiery is well-documented, through both eyewitness reports and archaeological findings (see Jackson and Castillo 1995). Needless to say, Native memory of the Mission era runs deep. Quite a few autobiographical and oral-historical accounts have been collected over the years, some published, most probably not. Even today, many Indian families have stories, passed down through the generations to the present, that date back to this period.

The text that follows was narrated by Rufino Ochurte, and describes the slow but inexorable process of Spanish enculturation among the Kiliwa down in the Baja Peninsula.[15]

THE FRIARS AT KILIWA

There were "pagan" Indians in this land. They were in these mountains. There was a friar, [but] no one came near him. When they least expected it he would seize one or two people. That's how he used to do it.

All of the people he had done that to went in, and when they had become acquainted they didn't flee anymore. "Well, it's very good, I tell you," they would report. In that manner one or two more would come in, and so it went until there were many people at the Mission.

The friars would make the people work. When they were disobedient, they whipped them. They gave them corn mush to drink so that they could work. They built houses. But they didn't earn anything. As for food, those with families they paid a sackful of corn. The others ate at the Mission. That's what they used to do. The disobedient ones were seized and beaten and dunked in water.

They used to baptize people. The friar would say, "What I am doing is a good thing. I'm going to do that to the others, also." The Indians would say, "I don't know about that." No one came near. It continued that way. Slowly the friar began to get more people. Everyone knew the friar. Then they were all pacified. They came to the Mission—not many, [just] a few. In that way, people kept arriving.

They saw what the friar did and spoke about it. Slowly, more people approached. So many came closer—[but still] not a large number. They would say, "This is queer." "It's evil," they said. "You never know," they said. The people remained at a distance, spread out; the friar pacified them.

Some understood a little Spanish. They translated [for those who didn't]: "He says 'such-and-such'." They told the others [about] what the friars did and what they said to those who did not understand. They began understanding one or two words.

The friars would sponsor the unbaptized as godparents. They gathered the non-Christians together.

It seems to me that they should have taught them something. If they had, these people would now be educated. They didn't do that; they just baptized everyone. They deceived these people. They didn't do anything good for them at all.

As this and numerous similar narratives show, even the most dispassionate and even-handed recollections of Spanish encroachment and coercion reveal the essential blindness and insensitivity at the heart of the Mission enterprise, even where large-scale atrocities did not occur.

Of course, California Indians did not take the Spanish assaults on their societies and sovereignty lying down. There must have been active resistance movements and renegade bands all up and down the California coast during the Mission period. Indians did lash back at their oppressors from time to time, though their efforts to control the Spanish were futile in the end. Native accounts of retaliation, like Mary Yee's Barbareño Chumash story of the 1824 Santa Barbara uprising or Lorenzo Asisara's account of the death, in 1812, of Father Quintana at Mission Santa Cruz, are relatively rare.[16] Yet these narratives paint a chilling picture of the prevailing mood of suspicion, threat, and violence that the warped Mission societies induced for everyone involved, Spaniard and Indian alike. Fear, stymied anger, paranoia—and something almost like a continuing disbelief that the Spanish could really commit the kinds of atrocities they did in fact, again and again, commit—these kept the Indians in check just as surely as the Spanish militias did with their muskets, swords, and cannon.

Less than a hundred years after the mission system began spreading in the south came the Gold Rush. If the devastation of the missions swept through the Southern and South-Central California cultures like a fire, the Gold Rush hit the Northern cultures like an atom bomb. Some of the most shameful passages in United States history took place in California during the decades immediately following the Gold Rush of 1849. Basic human rights, as far as Indians were concerned, were nonexistent. De facto slavery was institutionalized by the California legislature under the auspices of a variety of labor and indenture laws, such as an 1850 vagrancy law that allowed any white man, without burden of proof, to declare any Indian a "vagrant." Once so declared, Indians could be incarcerated, and the rights to their labor—up to four months without pay (Castillo 1978:108)—auctioned off to the highest bidder. The kidnapping of children and young girls for purposes of domestic and sexual servitude was also legally sanctioned and widely practiced (Cook 1943).

As if these offenses to civil liberties and human rights weren't bad enough, the legislature also allocated huge sums of money to fund military and paramilitary campaigns against Indian communities. The newspapers of the time are full of reports, both pro and con, of the so-called Indian wars. But the term *war* is misleading: the carnage of these vigilante campaigns was truly bestial in nature, shocking sometimes even to the citizenry they hypocritically claimed to "defend." Though often decried by reporters, scholars, federal agents, and a few righteous voices among the white community, the state nevertheless saw fit to sponsor them. According to Castillo (1978:108), "Almost any White man could raise a volunteer company, outfit it with guns, ammunition, horses, and supplies, and be reasonably sure that the state government would honor its vouchers." One of the most infamous of these many actions took place at Clear Lake in 1850 and became known as the Stone and Kelsey Massacre.

Most accounts of hostilities, even when sympathetic to the Indian plight, come from the reports of whites; rarely do we glimpse how the same events looked from an Indian point of view. The Stone and Kelsey Massacre is a notable exception. William Ralganal Benson, an Eastern Pomo man and narrator of the myth of "Creation" (#16) presented earlier in this volume, was born in 1862, some thirteen years after the killings that sparked the massacre, but he knew men who had taken part in the killings, suffered through the retaliation, and survived to tell the tale. To bear their witness, he wrote a detailed account based on their firsthand descriptions of what had transpired. Benson's account, originally published in 1932 in the *California Historical Society Quarterly,* begins: "The Facts Of Stone and Kelsey Massacre. in Lake County California. As it was stated to me by the five indians who went to stone and kelseys house purpose to kill the two white men. after debateing all night." (Benson, an extraordinary individual and something of a renaissance man, did not learn English until he was a young man and, without benefit of schooling, taught himself to read and write.) The first, and longer, portion of his account documents the brutal conditions on the Stone-Kelsey ranch—the starvation, whippings, torture, and executions—that motivated the killings; gives an account of the all-night debate that ultimately authorized the attack; and graphically details the killing itself. The remainder of his account describes what happened next: the inevitable retaliation, when government troops and vigilante militias "avenged" the killing of Stone and Kelsey. The following excerpt is taken from this latter section and is presented verbatim, without editorial change, in Benson's own words:[17]

one day the lake watchers saw a boat come around the point, som news coming they said to each others. two of the men went to the landing. to see what the news were. they were told that the white warriors had came to kill all the indians around the lake. so hide the best you can. the whites are making boats and with that they are coming up the lake. so they had two men go up on top of uncle sam mountain. the north peak. from there they watch the lower lake. for three days they watch the lake. one morning they saw a long boat came up the lake with pole on the bow with red cloth. and several of them came. every one of the boats had ten to fifteen men. the smoke signal was given by the two watchmen. every indian around the lake knew the soldiers were coming up the lake. and how many of them. and those who were watching the trail saw the infantrys coming over the hill from the lower lake. these two men were watching from ash hill. they went to stones and kelseys house. from there the horsemen went down torge the lake and the soldiers went across the valley torge lakeport. they went on to scotts valley. shoot a few shoots with their big gun and went on to upper lake and camped on Emmerson hill. from there they saw the indian camp on the island. the next morning the white warriors went across in their long dugouts. the indians said they would meet them in peace. so when the whites landed the indians went to wellcome them. but the white man was determined to kill them. Ge-We-Lih said he threw up his hands and said no harm me good man. but the white man fired and shoot him in the arm and another shoot came and hit a man staning along side of him and was killed. so they had to run and fight back; as they ran back in the tules and hed under the water; four or five of them gave alittle battle and another man was shoot in the shoulder. some of them jumped in the water and hed in the tuleys. many women and children were killed on around this island. one old lady a (indian) told about what she saw while hiding under abank, in under aover hanging tuleys. she said she saw two white man coming with their guns up in the air and on their guns hung a little girl. they brought it to the creek and threw it in the water. and alittle while later, two more men came in the same manner. this time they had alittle boy on the end of their guns and also threw it in the water. alittle ways from her she, said layed awoman shoot through the shoulder. she held her little baby in her arms. two white men came running torge the woman and baby, they stabed the woman and the baby and, and threw both of them over the bank in to the water. she said she heared the woman say, O my baby; she said when they gathered the dead, they found all the little ones were killed by being stabed, and many of the women were also killed stabing. she said it took them four or five days to gather up the dead. and the dead were all burnt on the east side the creek. they called it the siland creek. (Ba-Don-Bi-Da-Meh). this old lady also told about the whites hung aman on Emerson siland this indian was met by the soldiers while marching from scotts valley to upper lake. the indian was hung and alarge fire built under the hanging indian. and another indian was caught near Emerson hill. this one was tied to atree and burnt to death.

the next morning the solders started for mendocino county. and there killed many indians. the camp was on the ranch now known as Ed Howell ranch. the solders made camp a little ways below, bout one half mile from the indian camp. the indians wanted to surrender, but the solders did not give them time, the solders went in the camp and shoot them down as tho they were dogs. som of them escaped by going down a little creek leading to the river. and som of them hed in the brush. and those who hed in the brush most of them were killed. and those who hed in the water was over looked. they killed mostly women and children.

More than 135 Indians (60 at the island, another 75 along the Russian River) were indiscriminately killed in this campaign, according to the army's own report (Castillo 1978:108). Tribe after tribe during these bad California years came to know what it was like to be hunted down, and suffered crippling population losses to large- and small-scale "military" actions, as well as to disease and starvation.

By the 1880s this kind of direct physical assault, this war on Indian peoples and territories, had become more sporadic. In its place came more insidious modes of assault, directed at the languages and cultures themselves. We may think that the recent hysteria over "family values" is a new phenomenon in our public and political discourse. But the American people (that is to say, their legislators, policymakers, educators, and social critics, on their behalf) have long understood the importance of the family in the continuity of culture and preservation of ethnic identity. Unfortunately, this insight has all too often been used for ill as well as good: to *disadvantage* families—through politically motivated withholding of funds for key social programs in endangered communities, for instance—as well as to help them. The strategy is not new. One of the most devastating (and, sadly, effective) social policies this country has ever known was aimed at the heart of the Indian family—devised and implemented expressly to ensure its destruction.[18] I refer to the establishment of the federal Indian boarding school system in 1887, the year of the Dawes Act, which mandated the educational model pioneered by Richard Pratt at the Carlisle Industrial Training School in Pennsylvania.[19]

Carlisle-style boarding schools came to California in 1881 with the opening of a school on the Tule River Reservation in Tulare County. Numerous other schools followed over the course of the next twenty years. Given the high value Americans have always placed on education, at least until recently, it may be difficult to see the establishment of an Indian educational system as a destructive act. But when you consider that Indian children, by decree of state and federal law, were taken from their families (sometimes forcibly) and sent off to distant boarding schools where they were forbidden to speak their languages under penalty of physical punishment, where local white households could buy their labor as domestic servants for a pittance (Pratt 1964), and where the integrity of their Native culture was systematically demeaned—well, it's not so hard to see the destructive potential of such a program. Imagine, too, what it felt like for helpless parents to see their children taken from them, as if into custody, though they'd done no wrong; or what it felt like for the children themselves, frightened and homesick, stolen from their families and put down in a barracks with strange bunkmates far from home, to be whip-taught an alien standard by teachers who too often considered them barbarians. For that's what the boarding school system was, at its worst; and at its best, it was not much better—just less brutal. The federal Indian boarding school system was, and still is, a textbook illustration of how you break the spine of another culture. It's simple: remove its children from their families and home communities and keep them away long enough that they come back (if they do come back) something like strangers to their own people and traditions, to their own pasts, and to their own new futures. Fortunately, more liberal and humane heads prevailed, and critics eventually called a halt to the system before Native American cultures and communities were entirely flat-lined. But the reprieve came too late for all too many cultures. The damage done has proved immeasurable. And hardest hit were the languages—which is why the schools have garnered so much attention here.

What the boarding schools were most effective at killing was not the spirit of Native peoples—though the toll was heavy, the spirit survived—but their languages. As with a flame, as with a species, all it takes to extinguish a language forever is an interruption, however brief—just one broken link in the chain of transmission. And so it was that the generation "attending" the boarding schools during the first decades of the twentieth century turned out to be the last generation of speakers for hundreds of native languages across the United States. What may come as a surprise, though, is the conscious role this generation of parents took in the demise. The following personal reminiscence shows how the school-instilled psychology of persecution and humiliation could have brought this about. Few recollections could spell out the connection between language extinction and the boarding school experience as clearly as this one does. Elsie Allen, the narrator and a renowned Central Pomo basketmaker, was born in 1899 and got sent to Covelo Indian School in 1911. Her account, taken from an interview published in *News from Native California* in 1989, demonstrates just how successful the boarding schools were at alienating Indian children from their own cultures, especially their languages.[20]

BOARDING SCHOOL

When I went to school at that time [to the boarding school at Covelo,] there were three girls there from Hopland. I already knew some of their language, it's a different dialect from mine. I couldn't talk the English language in the school at Covelo, so I hollered at them when we lined up. Then one of the girls that was in my line reported me. They took me and strapped the heck out of me with a big leather strap. I didn't know what I got strapped for. Three days later those girls told me it was for talking the Indian language on the grounds, which I'm not supposed to do.

I was eleven years old [when I went to Covelo], and every night I cried and then I'd lay awake and think and think and think. I'd think to myself, "If I ever get married and have children I'll *never* teach my children the language or all the Indian things that I know. I'll *never* teach them that, I don't want my children to be treated like they treated me." That's the way I raised my children. Everybody couldn't understand that, they always asked me about it in later years. My husband has a different language. He can't understand me, but I learned his language much faster. I can talk it too, but I never taught my children. That's why they don't know. [My daughter] can understand it, but she can't speak the language.

In later years I found lots of ways they could have taught me in school but they didn't. They just put me in a corner and gave me a card with a lot of holes in it and a needle and yarn. They didn't say, "This is a needle." I would if I was teaching, if the child didn't know. Nobody said that. Well, I guess they just thought I was dumb or deaf or something. They treated me just like I was deaf and dumb. I was eleven years old, I wasn't a little kid, a baby. It should be easy to teach a person like that, but they didn't.

How I got to school in Covelo was every year the agent of the government school came around in the fall of the year and gathered the children to take them to the school. My mother signed a paper for me to go up there. In the morning [after a two-day trip to Covelo by wagon, flatbed railroad car, stage coach, and gravel wagon with six other children from the Hopland/Ukiah area], I just kind of stood around and watched the other girls, what they were doing and where to go. I didn't know what to say. I think I only knew two words of English, "yes" and "no." I never got to ask my mother why she sent me like that when I didn't know the English language.

I was scared, I had no one to talk to [because no one spoke my dialect]. That was sure hard. I felt that if I said something or fought against how we were treated, they might kill me. I cried every night. I couldn't talk to anybody or ask anybody anything because I didn't know how to. I was so dumb, that's the way I felt. They knew that I couldn't understand, so nobody talked to me. I was the only one that had my language.

California, because of its great diversity of languages, was perhaps especially affected by the federal program, as Elsie Allen's story suggests. Her experience—of doing time in communicative solitary confinement, not knowing anyone who shared her mother tongue—must have been a common one in California's gagged but polyglot boarding schools.[21]

In the end, though, governments and would-be conquistadores always underestimate the capacity of the human spirit to endure. Despite these two centuries and more of persecution and cultural devastation, California Indians have survived, their cultures strained and changed, but with the heart intact.

REVIVAL: A CALIFORNIA RENAISSANCE

Today in California, Native people and their cultures are experiencing a revival, a renaissance. Language is often at the center of the new interest, seen in some ways as the "book" in which the deep patterns of a culture, the life and heart's blood, are written. In language lies continuity with the past. It holds the keys to religion, ritual and ceremony, philosophy, art, song and story, healing, traditional crafts, and, through place-names, a centuries-deep sense of place. After all the decades of scorn and disparagement—and in the boarding schools, of active suppression—by white civilization, Indians are once again looking to their languages with pride. The turn has come not a moment too soon (and indeed, too late for real recovery in all too many cases). In the remainder of this essay, I will try as much as possible to allow those most closely involved in this revival to speak for themselves.

At a conference on Pomoan languages held in 1994, Edna Guerrero, a Northern Pomo elder, tells of her frustration and her commitment to the cause of language preservation:[22]

> My language is the thing that has always meant a lot to me. I became interested in it more and more because I resented the remarks made by (what we say) the white man. They say we grunted and nothing else; there were no words. And I thought to myself, "How can you [the white man] say that these people grunt, when there's an *entire conversation* being carried on in words that *they* [the Indians] understand!"

But now people are running around trying to find the languages . . . [S]o much of it is gone and will never be recovered . . . It's tragic. I think the young people are just beginning to realize what a tragedy it is. A well-known philosopher once said that when people lose their language, they lose their identity. You're nobody. And this is very true because the majority do not speak their language . . . What can be done about it? Where are you going to find the people that speak the language? There's no one left anymore. . . .

It's all that's interested me and I've done my best to preserve my share of it, and I hope that someone will benefit from it . . . I hope they continue . . . I don't know . . . That's all I can say. I've done the best I can; it's up to the rest.

Edna Guerrero speaks for many California elders, past and present, who have felt the same sense of loss and mystified resentment and have dedicated their energies to doing what they can to preserve their languages. More and more younger people have been taking up her challenge, following in these elders' footsteps. Nancy Richardson, in a 1992 essay, "The State of Our Languages," describes the dire situation this current generation of revivalists face, now that the torch is being passed:[23]

Since the first contact between the indigenous people of California and the western world, the original language and culture of this land have been endangered. Language has declined in a rapid, downward spiral from the very onset of that first contact. In my own experience, I have watched this painful loss of language in my tribe, the Karuk. In the early '70s, I began an optimistic journey of language work, recognizing and valuing the beauty and uniqueness found within my language. Twenty years ago, I kept hearing the language must be saved for the future. With 150 strong, fluent, tenacious Karuk elders in the background in those days, the urgency was not so apparent.

As I paid my last respects to my elders, one after another, as they crossed over to the next world, I began to directly feel the impact and the loss. I remember in 1981, how angry I was when Daisy Jacobs, 111, passed away. I thought, "How dare she die at one hundred and eleven. My work is not finished! I have so much still to learn from her." Then a few years later, when my teacher and the medicine man of the tribe, Shan Davis, passed away at a relatively early age, I was forced to come to terms with the reality of the situation. The details of this reality were simple, in that the death of each elder, each fluent speaker, was the death of my language.

The death of our language was inevitable and terminal . . . without new birth.

[The] Karuk language is considered by linguists and anthropologists as one of the oldest languages in California, spoken for many thousands of years, belonging to one particular place and one particular people. It is at the brink of extinction in the very immediate future, if drastic measures are not taken to reverse this trend. Currently there are 12 elderly fluent speakers of the Karuk language and approximately 40 more semi-fluent speakers at varying levels of speech competency. The Karuk language has reached a critical state. All of the languages in California have reached a similar state of language loss or passed beyond it.

Without immediate and proactive intervention, the majority of California's surviving native languages are doomed to extinction within the next twenty years. Richardson, along with dozens of other language activists, is keenly aware of this threat, but has taken it as a challenge, not a fait accompli. Her essay concludes with her hopes for the future:

In California, the children that are being born today are the seventh generation since first European contact. From out of this seventh generation will come the next fluent speakers of the indigenous languages of California. The number may be great or small; one alone is invaluable. But this effort will not be easy—it will involve a lot of work, commitment as well as courage and faith. It is a grim situation, that we as the indigenous people of California must face head on, yet I have no sadness, only faith. I look forward optimistically to the innovative challenges and the unknown possibilities.

One of the most promising of recent efforts to turn things around is California's own Master/Apprentice Language Learning Program. (The MALLP is conducted and administered by the Advocates for Indigenous California Language Survival [AICLS], which is an affiliate of the Seventh Generation Fund, an important umbrella organization for a number of Native American activist groups.) Nancy Richardson was one of the program's founding forces, along with people like Ray Baldy (Hupa), Mark Macarro (Luiseño), L. Frank Manriquez (Tongva/Acagchme), Parris Butler (Mojave), Darlene Franco (Wukchumni), Leanne Hinton, and others. Since its first season in 1993, the Master/Apprentice program has initiated training sessions for more than seventy master/apprentice pairs, involving (at the time of writing) twenty-five languages—most of them down to their last handful of fluent speakers—with more being added every year. Its success and the enthusiasm it generates have made it a model for similar programs around the country and abroad.

The AICLS, part of a larger revival that includes the California Indian Basketweavers Association and the California Indian Storytelling Association,[24] has initiated a number of other projects as well. One of these is the "Breath of Life" Native California Language Restoration Workshop, first held in 1996 at Berkeley and targeted at languages that now exist only in "fieldnote form."[25] The workshop answers a problem that the Master/Apprentice program, which presumes the existence of elders who still speak the language, cannot address. The problem is that not all tribal communities are lucky enough to have any native speakers left, and those who seek their languages must rely on the fieldnotes, recordings, and publications of the linguists who worked with the last generation of fluent elders. There are thirty or so such languages in California, languages that are sometimes described as "merely sleeping" (Hinton 1996). With this kind of proactive involvement, intelligence, and determination driving the California language revival movement, there is once again hope for the future of California's Native tongues.

There is still a long, long way to go, however, and California's remaining indigenous languages are not out of danger, by any stretch of the imagination. In truth, many of these flickering flames will yet be extinguished, despite the best efforts of Native communities and scholars combined. But the all-important start has been made, and at this point, it is only the road that matters. The people, programs, and communities fighting for their linguistic and cultural survival need all the help, understanding, and encouragement they can get. Which languages will survive and which pass into memory? No one knows. With the struggle for revival just enjoined, it is too soon to write the final chapter on California native languages. And with cooperation, faith, and hard work, that chapter will never need to be written. Here, in California at the beginning of the twenty-first century, in the seventh generation since European contact, we can find a new and thankful—if unintended—meaning in Villiana Calac Hyde's lovely translation of the Luiseño "Chaláawaat Song":

Tásmomaytal nevétiqankwa,
táásutal chulúpiqankwa.
'áá, temét nóó nevétqankwa,
temét nóó chulúpiqankwa.

I suppose I've survived the first little month,
I suppose I've survived the first big month.
Oh, I am surviving through the days,
I am surviving through the days.

NOTES

1. For a summary of the most recent data on language survival, see Hinton's "Living California Indian Languages" in her book *Flutes of Fire* (1994a); map 5 generalizes some of the information in this article.

2. Unfortunately, language diversity is not celebrated in all quarters. Beginning with Senator S. I. Hayakawa, California has seen more than its share of "English-Only" referendums in recent years. See Hinton's "The Native American Languages Act" in *Flutes of Fire* (Hinton 1994a). For a wider discussion of such matters, see James Crawford's book *Language Loyalties* (1992) or visit his website (http://ourworld.compuserve.com/homepages/JWCRAWFORD/). The University of Northern Arizona maintains a web-page on "Teaching Indigenous Languages" (http://jan.ucc.nau.edu/~jar/TIL.html) that contains a variety of links and resources related to this topic as well.

3. William Shipley's essay, "Native Languages of California" (Shipley 1978), in the California volume of the Smithsonian's *Handbook of North American Indians*—an indispensable reference found in most libraries—is probably the most accessible and concise scholarly introduction to the language families of California. For those with some linguistic training, there are detailed chapters on California language families in Lyle Campbell and Marianne Mithun's *The Languages of Native America* (1979) and the Smithsonian's *Handbook of North American Indians* (volume 17: *Languages,* ed. by Ives Goddard, 1996). I merely provide a general orientation here.

4. The names for these superstocks are separately based on similarities for the number 'two' within the languages of the individual families. For instance, the Atsugewi word *hoqi* (compare Achumawi *hak',* Shasta *xokwa,* Chimariko *xok'u,* Diegueño *xawok,* and Salinan *hakic,* all meaning 'two') gives rise to the term *Hokan.* (The phonetic letter [x] represents a velar fricative—the hard, *h*-

like sound in the German pronunciation of *Bach* or the Scottish *loch*.) The term *Penutian* is actually a compound of the Proto-Maiduan and Proto-Costanoan forms for 'two'—*pé·ne* and *uṭxi,* respectively (Shipley 1978).

5. Uto-Aztecan languages are found throughout the Great Basin and American Southwest (languages like Paiute, Shoshone, and Hopi) and in Mexico (Yaqui, Nahuatl, Huichol, and Pipil, to name a few). The main branch of Algic is Algonquian—a very large and widespread family of languages concentrated in the East (Delaware, Micmac, Abenaki, Passamaquoddy), the Midwest (Shawnee, Kickapoo, Fox, Potawatomi), and fanning west across Canada (Ojibwa and the great Cree continuum); the Ritwan languages, Wiyot and Yurok, are the two California representatives of this superstock. The large Athabascan family, part of the Na-Dené superstock (Haida, Tanaina, Koyukon, Carrier, Chilcotin, Dogrib, Chipewyan, and Umpqua, to name a few), is primarily concentrated in the Pacific Northwest, Alaska, and the Canadian North. Navajo and Apache are southwestern "walkabouts" of this same family.

6. And probably Chumashan as well, if Chumash proves to be unrelatable to other so-called Hokan languages. Yukian has long been chalked up as an isolate family, but Chumash, until recently, was presumed to be a member of the Hokan superstock. Current research, encouraged by a large-scale examination of Harrington's vast Chumash corpora now under way at the University of California, Santa Barbara, suggests that this long-standing assumption (going at least back to Sapir 1925) is becoming increasingly difficult to maintain (Foster 1996:86). Indeed, recent classifications (Ives Goddard 1996) do not include either Chumashan or Esselen within the proposed Hokan grouping. However, the dust has yet to settle on this reevaluation.

7. Foster's (1996) *Handbook* discussion of California linguistic prehistory, in "Language and the Culture History of North America," is an extremely valuable overview of the field, and I have relied heavily on his synthesis of past and present scholarship in the account that follows. (See especially his sections on Yukian, Hokan, Penutian, and Uto-Aztecan, pp. 83–95.) Other useful resources include Shipley (1978), Wallace (1978a), Whistler (1977b), and Moratto (1984).

8. Should conclusive linguistic evidence for the Hokan grouping remain beyond the reach of our methodological grasp, the term *Hokan* may yet survive as a kind of shorthand for referring to some of these "Old California" languages and language families. Indeed, informed speculation (for example, Moratto 1984) associates ancestral Yukian and "Hokan" peoples with the ancient Western Fluted Point tradition, which dates to 9,000–10,000 B.P.

9. This model of Penutian southern expansion echoes what has come to be called the "Multiple Entry Hypothesis." A great deal of new work has come out in the past couple of decades (see Foster 1996 for summary and orientation),

work which has largely dismantled the prevailing older notion that there was ever a genetically unified "California Penutian" subgroup from which the contemporary California Penutian families evolved. Rather, the Penutian incursions into California seem to have come in distinct and chronologically separate waves, as outlined here.

Furthermore, if Mike Nichols (1981) is correct, and the long and complex Pre-Uto-Aztecan dispersal can in fact be traced out of the Basin and Southwest, back through the Central Valley and Southern Sierra and north toward Oregon, then it may have been Pre-Uto-Aztecan peoples who actually pioneered the ancient Penutian route south out of Oregon, down through the river systems of northern California, and into the Central Valley and foothills of the Sierra, long before the ancestral Yokutsan, Utian, and Wintuan peoples, who by turns followed in their footsteps.

10. The southern distribution of Hokan, in the form of Yuman-family languages, continues down into the Baja peninsula with PaiPai and Kiliwa, and back into the Southwest with the other Yuman tribes (Havasupai, Walapai, Yavapai, and Maricopa). There are also distant "Hokan" languages in Mexico: for instance, Seri and Chontal-Oaxaca.

11. California Uto-Aztecan groups include Tataviam; Tübatulabal in the mountain foothills; the Takic group (Luiseño, Gabrielino, and Juaneño along the coast; Serrano, Kitanemuk, Cupeño, and Cahuilla inland); and the Numic group (Mono, Owens Valley Paiute, Panamint, Kawaiisu, Southern Paiute, and Chemehuevi) out in the Basin proper, beyond the boundaries of the California culture area per se. For discussions of California Uto-Aztecan prehistory, see Bean and Smith (1978), Nichols (1981), Moratto (1984), and Foster (1996).

12. The discussion here owes much to Johanna Nichol's pioneering work on the geographical aspects of linguistic diversity, *Linguistic Diversity in Space and Time* (1992).

13. In effect, this tendency holds true even within California itself. The linguistically least diverse area of California—the desert territories of its closely related Uto-Aztecan tribes—is also the most inhospitable.

14. I would urge the interested reader to look for Robert Heizer's *The Destruction of California Indians* (1993), Robert H. Jackson and Edward Castillo's *Indians, Franciscans, and Spanish Colonization: The Impact of the Mission System on California Indians* (1995), Rupert and Jeannette Henry Costo's *The Missions of California: A Legacy of Genocide* (1987), and Albert Hurtado's *Indian Survival on the California Frontier* (1988), among other works on this subject.

15. This account is taken from Mauricio Mixco's "Kiliwa Texts." The only editorial liberties I have taken—as this is not a technical publication—is to remove the brackets and clause numbers from Mixco's free translation and supply occasional punctuation marks where they seemed appropriate. The brack-

etted words and phrases in the text here are my own insertions, provided for clarity.

16. Yee's narrative, which was brought to my attention by linguist Suzanne Wash, was collected in the 1930s by J. P. Harrington; it is unpublished, but may be found among Harrington's voluminous Barbareño fieldnotes at the Santa Barbara Museum of Natural History. Asisara's account, collected in 1877 but dating to 1818, is reprinted in Malcolm Margolin's *The Way We Lived*.

17. Margolin reprints Benson's account in its entirety in *The Way We Lived: California Indian Stories, Songs, and Reminiscences* (1993).

18. True, many of the most disastrous Indian policies and programs were conceived with "the best of intentions." It's just hard to understand, today, how a program that intentionally dismembers families can be seen in a humanitarian light. We are left with a historical view of a society so blinded by its own presuppositions and prejudices that up is seen as down, and a sow's ear is taken for a purse of gold. Let our forebears be a lesson to us today, where such reactionary and mean-spirited public policies as immigrant health-care bans or English Only movements are concerned, and examine our ethnic legislations with a true humanitarian eye.

19. See Hamley 1994 for a comprehensive treatment of the history and cultural effects of the federal boarding school system.

20. *News from Native California* 4.1 (1989):40–41. The interview was conducted by Vic Bedoian and Roberta Llewellyn, and transcribed by Vera Mae Fredrickson.

21. Margolin, in a postscript to this interview as excerpted in *The Way We Lived,* writes: "Elsie Allen did have children, and true to her resolve she, like so many of her generation, did not teach them her Pomo language. She did, however, become a masterful weaver of baskets, and until her death in 1990 she was tremendously important in passing along traditional skills and knowledge to her children and to many others" (1993:183).

22. From an article published in *News from Native California* 8.4 (1994): 40.

23. This essay appeared in *The Advocate* (the newsletter of the Advocates for Indigenous California Language Survival), published as an inset to *News from Native California* 7.1 (winter 1992–1993): 40–41.

24. See Lauren Teixeira's "California Indian Stories and the Spirit" in *News from Native California* 9.4 (1996).

25. See Leanne Hinton's "Breath of Life/Silent No More: The Native California Language Restoration Workshop" in *News from Native California* 10.1 (1996). Sixteen languages were represented: Rumsien, Mutsun, Awaswas, Coast Miwok, Patwin, Nomlaki, Nisenan, Central Pomo, Northern Pomo, Chimariko, Salinan, Ventureño Chumash, Tongva (Gabrielino), Ajachmem (Juaneño), Wiyot, and Mattole.

MAPS

Do you come from the north?
Do you come from the east?
Do you come from the west?
Do you come from the south?
Do you come from above?
Do you come from below?

Hai´-kut-wo-to-peh's song
Ceremonial acorn song, Maidu

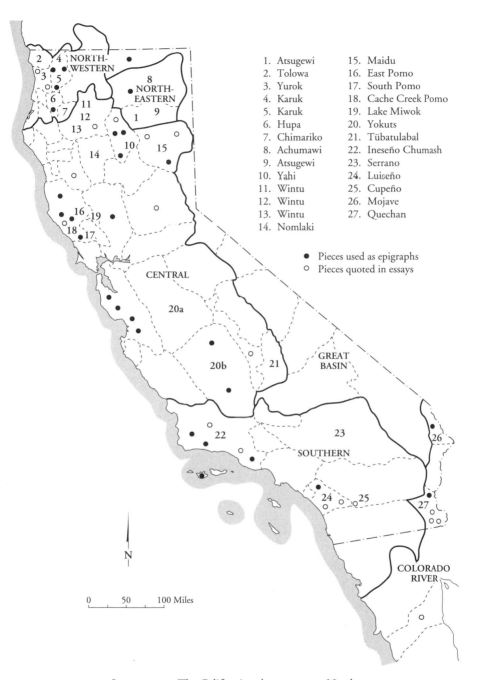

1. Atsugewi	15. Maidu
2. Tolowa	16. East Pomo
3. Yurok	17. South Pomo
4. Karuk	18. Cache Creek Pomo
5. Karuk	19. Lake Miwok
6. Hupa	20. Yokuts
7. Chimariko	21. Tübatulabal
8. Achumawi	22. Ineseño Chumash
9. Atsugewi	23. Serrano
10. Yahi	24. Luiseño
11. Wintu	25. Cupeño
12. Wintu	26. Mojave
13. Wintu	27. Quechan
14. Nomlaki	

● Pieces used as epigraphs
○ Pieces quoted in essays

MAP 1. Locator map. The California culture areas are Northwestern,
Northeastern, Central, and Southern. Parts of the Great Basin and Colorado
culture areas are also shown. The numbers correspond to the selections in the text.
Divisions based on Kroeber (1936), in Heizer and Elsasser (1980).

MAP 2. California linguistic diversity.

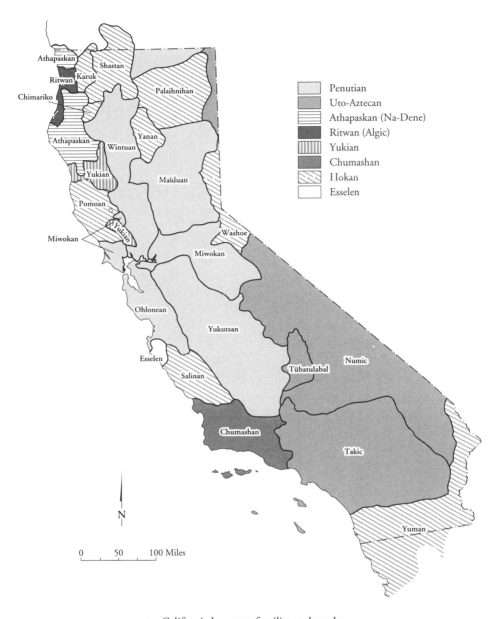

Legend:

- Penutian
- Uto-Aztecan
- Athapaskan (Na-Dene)
- Ritwan (Algic)
- Yukian
- Chumashan
- Hokan
- Esselen

Labels on map: Athapaskan, Shastan, Ritwan, Karuk, Chimariko, Palaihnihan, Athapaskan, Yanan, Wintuan, Yukian, Maiduan, Pomoan, Yukian, Miwokan, Washoe, Miwokan, Ohlonean, Yukutsan, Esselen, Salinan, Tübatulabal, Numic, Chumashan, Takic, Yuman

N

0   50   100 Miles

MAP 3. California language families and stocks.

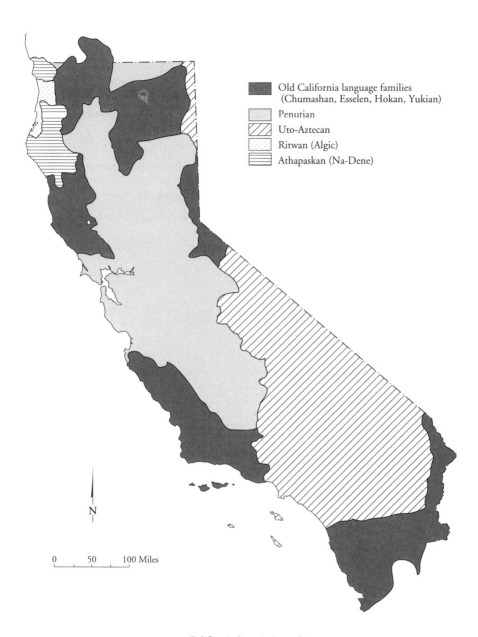

Old California language families
(Chumashan, Esselen, Hokan, Yukian)
Penutian
Uto-Aztecan
Ritwan (Algic)
Athapaskan (Na-Dene)

N

0   50   100 Miles

MAP 4. California linguistic prehistory.

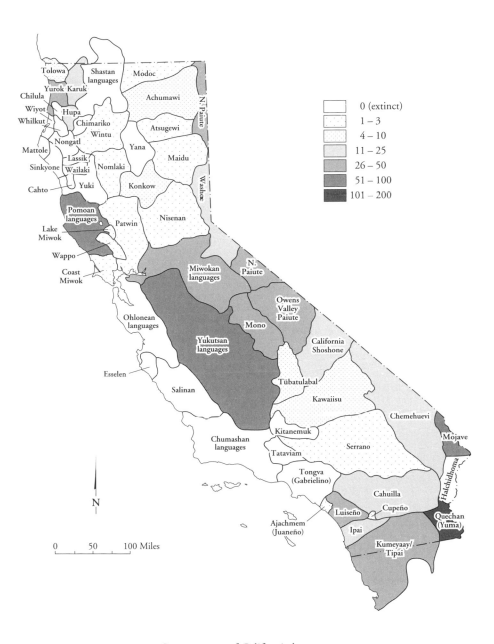

Legend:

- 0 (extinct)
- 1 – 3
- 4 – 10
- 11 – 25
- 26 – 50
- 51 – 100
- 101 – 200

Labels on map:

Tolowa, Shastan languages, Modoc, Yurok, Karuk, Chilula, Achumawi, N. Paiute, Wiyot, Hupa, Whilkut, Chimariko, Atsugewi, Wintu, Nongatl, Yana, Mattole, Lassik, Maidu, Sinkyone, Nomlaki, Wailaki, Washoe, Cahto, Yuki, Konkow, Pomoan languages, Lake Miwok, Patwin, Nisenan, Wappo, Miwokan languages, N. Paiute, Coast Miwok, Ohlonean languages, Owens Valley Paiute, Mono, Yukutsan languages, California Shoshone, Esselen, Salinan, Tübatulabal, Kawaiisu, Chemehuevi, Kitanemuk, Chumashan languages, Mojave, Tataviam, Serrano, Halchidhoma, Tongva (Gabrielino), Cahuilla, Luiseño, Cupeño, Ajachmem (Juaneño), Ipai, Quechan (Yuma), Kumeyaay/Tipai

N

0   50   100 Miles

MAP 5. Current status of California languages.

BIBLIOGRAPHY

There is an entire world of information on California Native cultures, languages, and oral literatures for interested readers to explore. Some of it is in books, some in magazines and journals, some in archives, some on websites. Some of it is geared more toward a general audience, as this book is, and some of it is technical or scholarly in nature. But all of it will help to illuminate, in one way or another, the selections of California oral literature contained in these pages. All items mentioned here are listed in full in the "References" section.

A. General-Interest Books

Malcolm Margolin's *The Ohlone Way* is perhaps the best possible popular introduction to the unique Native California patterns of life and worldview— beautifully written and evocative rather than academic in nature. (Margolin is also the publisher of *News from Native California,* a quarterly magazine providing "an inside view of the California Indian world," and Heyday Books, which has a fine line of general-audience books celebrating Native Californian peoples and cultures.) Leanne Hinton's *Flutes of Fire,* a collection of articles originally written for her regular "Language" column in *News for Native California,* provides an accessible and engaging introduction to the world of California languages through a miscellany of essays on place-names, songs, language legislation, basketry terms, language families, writing systems, and many other topics, including a variety of fascinating grammatical features of California languages. If you only read two popular books on California Indians, these would be the two I recommend.

There are several biographies of real interest to the general reader: Theodora Kroeber's *Ishi: In Two Worlds,* which documents the life of California's so-called last wild Indian and provides a good bit of Yahi ethnography and contact history in the process; Carobeth Laird's *Encounter with an Angry God,* an extended reminiscence of her not-so-happy life as J. P. Harrington's wife; Gui de Angulo's *The Old Coyote of Big Sur,* a biography of her famous linguist father, Jaime de Angulo; Lucy Thompson's *To the American Indian: Reminiscences of a Yurok Woman,* an early Indian autobiography; *The Autobiography of Delfina Cuero,* a Kumeyaay woman, as told to Florence Shipek; Darryl Babe Wilson's *The Morning the Sun Went Down;* Victor Golla's edition of *The Sapir-Kroeber Correspondence,* which gives a fascinating inside view of the early days of anthropology and linguistics in California, including quite a few letters concerning Ishi; and Greg Sarris's *Mabel McKay: Weaving the Dream,* a captivating blend of biography and oral autobiography telling the life story of his remarkable and provocative aunt, a basketmaker and one of the last Pomo doctors.

Other general-interest books include Greg Sarris's *The Sound of Rattles and Clappers,* an anthology of contemporary poetry and fiction by Native California writers; Jaime de Angulo's classic *Indians in Overalls,* an account of the author's first season of fieldwork among the Pit River Achumawi; Thomas Mayfield and Malcolm Margolin's *Indian Summer: Traditional Life among the Choinumne Indians of California's San Joaquin Valley;* Brian Bibby's *The Fine Art of California Indian Basketry;* and Jeannine Gendar's *Grass Games and Moon Races: California Indian Games and Toys.*

Regarding the post-Contact history of California Indian peoples, there are a number of important and useful works, including Robert Heizer's *The Destruction of California Indians,* Robert Jackson and Edward Castillo's *Indians, Franciscans, and Spanish Colonization: The Impact of the Mission System on California Indians,* Albert Hurtado's *Indian Survival on the California Frontier,* and Rupert Costo and Jeannette Costo's *The Missions of California: A Legacy of Genocide.*

B. Collections of Story and Song in Translation

There is a surprising amount of California oral literature in English translation. Malcolm Margolin's *The Way We Lived: California Indian Stories, Songs, and Reminiscences* is a fine and wide-ranging newer collection, drawn from authentic sources, with enlightening commentary on each selection. Earlier anthologies include Frank Latta's *California Indian Folklore* and Edward Gifford and Gwendoline Block's *California Indian Nights.* Theodora Kroeber's *The Inland Whale* contains literary reworkings of authentic traditional stories. One of the oldest sources is Jeremiah Curtin's *Creation Myths of Primitive America,* originally published in 1898 and containing a large body of Yana and Wintu myths. Beyond these, there are quite a number of collections focused on particular tribes and languages: Thomas Blackburn's *December's Child: A Book of*

Chumash Oral Narratives; Alfred Kroeber's *Yurok Myths, A Mohave Historical Epic, Seven Mohave Myths,* and *More Mohave Myths;* Alfred Kroeber and Edward Gifford's *Karok Myths;* Robert Spott and Alfred Kroeber's *Yurok Narratives;* Istet Woiche's *Annikadel: The History of the Universe as Told by the Achumawi Indians of California;* Julian Lang's *Ararapíkva: Creation Stories of the People;* Jaime de Angulo's *How the World Was Made, Shabegok,* and *Indian Tales* (fictionalized settings of mostly retold Achumawi, Miwok, and Pomo tales); William Shipley's wonderful translations of *The Maidu Indian Myths and Stories of Hánc'ibyjim;* Leanne Hinton and Susan Roth's children's-book version of *Ishi's Tale of Lizard;* and Carobeth Laird's *Mirror and Pattern,* a collection of Chemehuevi stories (with commentary) told by her second husband, George Laird.

Two publications stand out for their pure loveliness as books to have and hold: *Mourning Dove, a Yurok/English Tale* (a chapbook put out by Heyday Books); and the Yosemite Association's *Legends of the Yosemite Miwok,* edited by Frank LaPena, Craig D. Bates, and Steven Medley.

Finally, though they do not focus exclusively on California traditions, the following works incorporate significant California materials: Brian Swann's *Song of the Sky* and *Wearing the Morning Star,* which contain the poet's versions of several classic and beautiful California songs; Leanne Hinton and Lucille Watahomigie's *Spirit Mountain,* which presents bilingual (and occasionally trilingual) versions of Yuman oral literature, including Mojave, Diegueño, Quechan, and Kiliwa; William Bright's *A Coyote Reader,* which contains translations of Coyote tales from a number of different California traditions; and Brian Swann's mammoth anthology *Coming to Light: Contemporary Translations of the Native Literatures of North America,* which includes selections from Yana, Karuk, Atsugewi, and Maidu.

C. Studies of Native California Oral Literature

There are a few studies that focus specifically or largely on California traditions: Greg Sarris's collection of literary essays, *Keeping Slug Woman Alive: A Holistic Approach to American Indian Texts;* Richard Applegate's "Chumash Narrative Folklore as Sociolinguistic Data"; Carobeth Laird's *Mirror and Pattern;* and Thomas Blackburn's *December's Child: A Book of Chumash Oral Narratives,* an extended folkloristic analysis. Anna Gayton's "Areal Affiliations of California Folktales" and Alfred Kroeber's "Indian Myths of South Central California" are both useful attempts at areal classification. Dorothy Demetracopoulou and Cora du Bois's "A Study of Wintu Mythology" is an important early work of stylistic analysis, as is Anna Gayton and Stanley Newman's "Yokuts and Western Mono Myths." Studies of Native California song include Richard Keeling's

Cry for Luck, which focuses on Northwestern California singing styles; George Herzog's "The Yuman Musical Style"; Bruno Nettl's "The Songs of Ishi: Musical Styles of the Yahi Indians"; R. H. Robins and Norma McLeod's "Five Yurok Songs: A Musical and Textual Analysis"; and Helen Roberts's *Form in Primitive Music: An Analytical and Comparative Study of the Melodic Form of Some Ancient Southern Californian Indian Songs.*

For readers wishing to broaden the scope of their exploration, there are many useful and important studies of Native American oral literature. Seminal works include Melville Jacobs's *The Content and Style of an Oral Literature: Clackamas Chinook Myths and Tales;* Dell Hymes's *'In vain I tried to tell you': Essays in Native American Ethnopoetics;* and Dennis Tedlock's *The Spoken Word and the Work of Interpretation.* Other important studies from the linguistic or ethnopoetic side are Karl Kroeber's recently reissued *Traditional American Indian Literatures: Texts and Interpretations;* Brian Swann and Arnold Krupat's *Recovering the Word: Essays on Native American Literature;* Leanne Hinton's *Havasupai Songs: A Linguistic Perspective;* Brian Swann's *Smoothing the Ground: Essays in Native American Oral Literature* and *On the Translation of Native American Literatures;* and Joel Sherzer and Anthony Woodbury's *Native American Discourse: Poetics and Rhetoric.*

On the more literary side of the equation are Arnold Krupat's *Ethnocriticism: Ethnography, History, Literature* and *New Voices in Native American Literary Criticism,* an anthology of critical essays; David Brumble's *American Indian Autobiography;* and Gerald Vizenor's *Narrative Chance: Postmodern Discourse on Native American Indian Literatures.*

D. Linguistic Text Collections

Linguistic editions of texts collected in the field are the foundation, the documentary base on which the study of Native American oral literature is built. As far as California cultures are concerned, most of these primary text collections are published as volumes in serial publications like the *University of California Publications in American Archaeology and Ethnology (UCPAAE),* which in 1943 shifted its specifically linguistic monographs over to the *University of California Publications in Linguistics* (UCPL).

Major book-length collections are Samuel A. Barrett's *Pomo Myths;* James Crawford's *Cocopa Texts;* Grace Dangberg's *Washo Texts;* Roland Dixon's *Maidu Texts;* L. S. Freeland's *Freeland's Central Sierra Miwok Myths* (edited by Howard Berman); Pliny Earl Goddard's "Hupa Texts," "Kato Texts," and "Chilula Texts"; Jane Hill and Roscinda Nolasquez's *Mulu'wetam (The First People): Cupeño Oral History and Language;* Wick Miller's *Newe Natekwinappeh: Shoshoni Stories and Dictionary;* Robert Oswalt's *Kashaya Texts;* Paul Radin's *Wappo Texts: First Se-*

ries; Gladys Reichard's *Wiyot Grammar and Texts;* Edward Sapir's *Yana Texts;* Hansjakob Seiler's *Cahuilla Texts;* William Shipley's *Maidu Texts and Dictionary;* and Stuart Uldall and William Shipley's *Nisenan Texts and Dictionary.* (Many of these scholars have also produced grammars and dictionaries for their respective languages, and most grammars also contain a few texts as well.) Certain volumes in the *Native American Texts Series* (both the new series and the old) also feature texts from a variety of California literary traditions: William Bright's *Coyote Stories;* Geoffrey Gamble's *Yokuts Texts;* Margaret Langdon's *Yuman Texts;* Victor Golla and Shirley Silver's *Northern California Texts;* and Martha Kendall's *Coyote Stories II.*

Many important linguistic texts and short collections also appear in journal format, among them Jaime de Angulo's "Pomo Creation Myth"; Jaime de Angulo and L. S. Freeland's "Karok Texts"; Madison Beeler's "Barbareño Chumash Text and Lexicon"; L. S. Freeland's "Western Miwok Texts with Linguistic Sketch"; Pliny Earl Goddard's "Wailaki Texts"; John Peabody Harrington's "Karok Texts" and "Karok Indian Myths"; Robert Lowie's "Washo Texts"; William Seaburg's "A Wailaki (Athapaskan) Text with Comparative Notes"; and Carl Voegelin's "Tübatulabal Texts."

E. Handbooks, Bibliographies, and Archives

The single most useful reference work—your bible for beginning research or simply seeking information on California Indians—is the California volume of the Smithsonian's *Handbook of North American Indians* (volume 8, edited by Robert Heizer). Next come Alfred Kroeber's *Handbook of the Indians of California,* Robert Heizer and M. A. Whipple's *The California Indians: A Source Book,* and Lowell Bean and Thomas Blackburn's *Native Californians: A Theoretical Retrospective.* Stephen Powers's *Tribes of California,* important and even groundbreaking in its day (1877) and still a valuable source of information and firsthand observation, has not aged well. (It is entirely too easy to stumble across sentences like the following, which introduces the text of a Konkow song: "The reader will understand, if he knows anything about Indian habits, that there was a great deal introduced into this performance which no man can describe or imitate—unutterable groans, hissings, mutterings, and repetitions, with which the savage so delights to envelop his sacred exercises" [307].)

William Bright's annotated *Bibliography of the Languages of Native California* is an invaluable reference tool, though it runs out at its date of publication, 1982, and much new work has been produced since then; an updated version is available on the web (see section I here). Robert Heizer, Karen Nissen, and Edward Castillo's *California Indian History: A Classified and Annotated Guide to*

Source Materials is likewise an useful tool, as is Richard Keeling's *Guide to Early Field Recordings (1900–1949) at the Lowie Museum of Anthropology.* One of the most comprehensive bibliographic sources is on-line at the California Indian Libraries Collection website (see section I here). This site provides fairly comprehensive bibliographics organized by tribe and draws on historical, anthropological, and linguistic sources; unfortunately, the project has not yet been expanded to cover Southern California cultures.

For those interested in archival materials, the Bancroft Library at Berkeley has a vast collection of California ethnographic and linguistic holdings, including the A. L. Kroeber Papers and the Frank J. Essene collection. (Researchers should ask for Dale Valory's "Guide to Ethnological Documents" [CU-23.1]—the "Valory Guide," for short.) The Phoebe Appleton Hearst Museum of Anthropology (formerly the Lowie) at Berkeley has a collection of sound recordings and an extensive photographic collection now in the process of being catalogued electronically. The archives of the Survey of California and Other Indian Languages, also at Berkeley, is administered by the Department of Linguistics; the Language Lab with its tape archives is conveniently located in the same building. Other important archival sites for California materials include the American Philosophical Library in Philadelphia, the Huntington Library in San Marino (especially the Wieland collection), the Santa Barbara Museum of Natural History, the Southwest Museum in Los Angeles, and the Malki Museum at the Morongo Indian Reservation.

Finally, researchers should be aware of the huge Harrington collection archived at the National Anthropological Archives at the Smithsonian Institution in Washington, D.C. There is a complete microfilm edition of the Harrington papers (running to 283 reels) distributed by Kraus International. Many university libraries own at least selections from this microfilm collection; larger universities and institutions, such as U.C. Berkeley and the University of Pittsburgh, are likely to possess the entire set.

F. Magazines and Newsletters

For more than a decade, the quarterly magazine *News from Native California* has been an important forum for news and views of California's Native communities and a major force in encouraging the current renaissance of contemporary California languages and cultures. Another lively and informative periodical, *The Masterkey,* put out by the Southwest Museum, is sadly now defunct. Two newsletters provide useful and engaging sources of information on California languages: the *SSILA Newsletter* (where SSILA stands for the Society for the Study of the Indigenous Languages of the Americas), which occasionally mentions topics germane to California, including conference schedules; and the occasional *Newsletter of the J. P. Harrington Conference,* which serves as a clearing-house of information for scholars working with the Harrington materials.

There are several California-oriented conferences that convene annually: the California Indian Conference, an "interdenominational" gathering of people—specialist and nonspecialist, Native and non-Native—to read papers and give talks on topics and issues of interest to Native California studies; the Hokan/Penutian Workshop, a gathering of linguists specializing in Hokan and Penutian languages (watch for announcements in the *SSILA Newsletter*); and the California Indian Storytelling Festival, which was inaugurated in 1995 (check their website for information).

G. Tribal Booklets and Instructional Materials

Many tribes, sometimes working in cooperation with linguists, sometimes working on their own, produce documentary and pedagogical materials for their languages, in the form of text collections, teaching grammars, vocabularies and dictionaries, videos, and so forth. These materials tend to be geared more toward the classroom and the community—practical applications—than to the specialist audience of professional linguists and language consultants. Sometimes these materials are readily available, but often they are distributed only locally and can be very difficult to obtain. Accessible or not, they do exist, and it seems worthwhile to list them here.

Some examples I've run across include Lucy Arvidson's *Alaawich (Our Language): First Book of Words in the Tübatulabal Language of Southern California;* James Bauman, Ruby Miles, and Ike Leaf's *Pit River Teaching Dictionary;* Ruth Bennett's *Hupa Spelling Book;* Catherine Callaghan and Brian Bibby's *Northern Sierra Miwok Language Handbook* and *Let's Learn Northern Sierra Miwok;* Ted Couro and Christina Hutcheson's *Dictionary of Mesa Grande Diegueño;* Ted Couro and Margaret Langdon's *Let's Talk 'Iipay Aa: An Introduction to the Mesa Grande Diegueño Language;* Victor Golla's *Hupa Stories, Anecdotes, and Conversations;* Villiana Hyde's *An Introduction to the Luiseño Language;* Roscinda Nolasquez and Anne Galloway's *I'i Muluwit: First Book of Words in the Cupeño Indian Language of Southern California;* Jesús Ángel Ochoa Zazueta's *Ya'abú ti'nñar jaspuy'pai (Esta es la Escritura Pai'pai);* Thomas Parsons's *The Yurok Language, Literature, and Culture;* and Katherine Saubel and Pamela Munro's *Chem'ivillu': Let's Speak Cahuilla.*

H. Films and Documentaries

Several recent movies and documentaries have focused on California Indian cultures. Two of them concern Ishi: the Ishi Documentation Project's excellent documentary *Ishi, the Last Yahi,* and the considerably more popularized HBO production *Ishi, Last of His Tribe,* starring Graham Green as Ishi and Jon Voight as A. L. Kroeber. Ken Burns's PBS series *The West* contains a good bit of California coverage, including (for once) some Indian perspective on the Spanish Mission period and the Gold Rush. Finally, Greg Sarris's miniseries *Grand Avenue,* which follows the lives of contemporary Indians in Northern California (and is based on his short-story collection of the same name), aired on HBO in 1996.

I. Internet Sites and Discussion Groups

The Survey of California and Other Indian Languages maintains a website with a searchable database indexing its holdings, along with pointers to other relevant addresses. The California Indian Library Collections site mentioned in section E provides maps, pictures, and basketry information, in addition to the tribal bibliographies. The UC Berkeley linguistics department has a homepage that includes information about conferences and California language courses, sometimes even including data gathered from ongoing classes in linguistic field methods. The California Indian Storytelling Festival also has a website, with information on upcoming festivals and other issues. Addresses for these and other relevant sites, as of time of publication, are as follows:

The California Indian Storytelling Festival:
   http://www.ucsc.edu/costano/story1.html

California Indian Library Collections:
   http://www.mip.berkeley.edu/cilc/brochure/brochure.html

Survey of California and Other Indian Languages:
   http://www.linguistics.berkeley.edu/lingdept/research/Survey/SCOIL.html

The Cahto (Kato) Language Page:
   http://www.geocities.com/Athens/Parthenon/6010/

Costanoan-Ohlone Indian Canyon Resource:
   http://www.ucsc.edu/costano/

UC Berkeley Department of Linguistics:
   http://www.linguistics.berkeley.edu/lingdept/

Society for the Study of the Indigenous Languages of the Americas:
   http://www.trc2.ucdavis.edu/ssila

This bibliography contains the full citations for all works referred to in this volume, including the "Further Reading" sections found with each individual introduction.

Abbreviations

CAL-HB *California,* ed. Robert F. Heizer. Vol. 8 of the Smithsonian *Handbook of North American Indians,* ed. William C. Sturtevant (1978). Washington, D.C.: Smithsonian Institution.

IJAL *International Journal of American Linguistics.* Chicago: University of Chicago Press.

IJAL-NATS *International Journal of Linguistics,* Native American Texts Series. Chicago: University of Chicago Press.

JAF *Journal of American Folklore.* Boston and New York: Houghton, Mifflin and Co. for the American Folklore Society.

NNC *News from Native California. An Inside View of the California Indian World.* Berkeley: Heyday Books.

RSCOIL *Reports from the Survey of California and Other Indian Languages.* Berkeley: Survey of California and Other Indian Languages, University of California.

UCAR *University of California Anthropological Records.* Berkeley: University of California Press.

UCPAAE *University of California Publications in Archaeology and Ethnology.* Berkeley: University of California Press.

UCPL *University of California Publications in Linguistics.* Berkeley: University of California Press.

Allen, Elsie. 1972. *Pomo Basketmaking: A Supreme Art for the Weaver.* Healdsburg, Calif.: Naturegraph Publishers.
———. 1989. "Boarding School." *NNC* 4.1.
Angulo, Gui de. 1995. *The Old Coyote of Big Sur: The Life and Times of Jaime de Angulo.* Berkeley: Stonegarden Press.
Angulo, Jaime de. 1935. "Pomo Creation Myth." *JAF* 48.189: 203–262.
———. 1953. *Indian Tales.* New York: A. A. Wyn.
———. 1976a. *Shabegok.* Old Time Stories 1. Berkeley: Turtle Island Foundation.
———. 1976b. *How the World Was Made.* Old Time Stories 2. Berkeley: Turtle Island Foundation.

———. 1990. *Indians in Overalls.* San Francisco: City Lights Books.

Angulo, Jaime de, and L. S. Freeland. 1930. "The Achumawi Language." *IJAL* 7: 77–120.

———. 1931a. "Karok Texts." *IJAL* 6.3–4: 194–226.

———. 1931b. "Two Achumawi Tales." *JAF* 44.172: 125–136.

Apodaca, Paul. 1997. "Completing the Circle." Review of *My Dear Miss Nicholson . . . Letters and Myths*, by William R. Benson. *NNC* 11.1 (fall): 32–34.

Applegate, Richard. 1972. "Ineseño Chumash Grammar." Ph.D. diss., University of California at Berkeley.

———. 1975. "Chumash Narrative Folklore as Sociolinguistic Data." *Journal of California and Great Basin Anthropology* 2: 188–197.

Arvidson, Lucy. 1976. *Alaawich (Our Language): First Book of Words in the Tübatulabal Language of Southern California.* Banning, Calif.: Malki Museum Press.

Barrett, Samuel A. 1919. "The Wintun Hesi Ceremony." *UCPAAE* 14.1: 437–448.

———. 1933. *Pomo Myths.* Bulletin of the Public Museum of the City of Milwaukee 15. Milwaukee.

Bass, Howard, and Green Rayna, prods. 1995. *Heartbeat: Voices of First Nations Women.* Washington: Smithsonian/Folkways Records (CD SF 40415).

Bauman, James. 1980. "Chimariko Placenames and the Boundaries of Chimariko Territory." In *American Indian and Indo-European Studies: Papers in Honor of Madison S. Beeler,* ed. Kathryn Klar, Margaret Langdon, and Shirley Silver, 11–29. The Hague: Mouton Publishers.

Bauman, James, with Ruby Miles and Ike Leaf. 1979. *Pit River Teaching Dictionary.* National Bilingual Materials Development Center, Rural Education, University of Alaska.

Baumhoff, Martin A., and David L. Olmsted. 1964. "Notes on Palaihnihan Culture History: Glottochronology and Archaeology." In *Studies in Californian Linguistics,* ed. W. Bright. UCPL 34: 1–12.

Beals, Ralph. 1933. "Ethnography of the Nisenan." *UCPAAE* 31.6: 335–414.

Bean, Lowell John, and Thomas Blackburn. 1976. *Native Californians: A Theoretical Retrospective.* Socorro, N.Mex.: Ballena Press.

Bean, Lowell John, and Florence C. Shipek. 1978. "Luiseño." CAL-HB: 550–563.

Bean, Lowell John, and Charles R. Smith. 1978. "Serrano." CAL-HB: 570–574.

Bean, Lowell John, and Sylvia Brakke Smith. 1978. "Gabrielino." CAL-HB: 538–549.

Bean, Lowell John, and Sylvia Brakke Vane. 1978. "Cults and Their Transformations." CAL-HB: 662–672.

Bedoian, Vic, and Roberta Llewellyn. 1995. "Interview with Edna Guerrero." *NNC* 8.4 (spring): 40.

Beeler, Madison. 1979. "Barbareño Chumash Text and Lexicon." In *Festschrift for Archibald A. Hill,* vol. 2, ed. M. A. Jazayery et al., 171–193. The Hague: Mouton.

Benedict, Ruth. 1924. "A Brief Sketch of Serrano Culture." *American Anthropologist* n.s.26:366–394.

———. 1926. "Serrano Tales." *JAF* 39.151: 1–17.

Bennett, Ruth S. 1981. *Hupa Spelling Book.* Arcata, Calif.: Center for Community Development, Humboldt State University.

Benson, William Ralganal. 1932. "The Stone and Kelsey Massacre on the Shores of Clear Lake in 1849." *Quarterly of the California Historical Society* 11.3: 266–273.

———. 1997. *"My Dear Miss Benson . . .": Letters and Myths.* Ed. Maria del Carmen Gasser. Pasadena, Calif.: Bickley Printing Company.

Berman, Howard. 1980. "Two Chukchansi Coyote Stories." In *Coyote Stories II*, ed. Martha B. Kendall. *IJAL*-NATS, Monograph 6: 56–70.

Bevis, William. 1974. "American Indian Verse Translations." *College English* 35: 693–703.

Bibby, Brian. 1992. "The Grindstone Roundhouse." *NNC* 6.3 (summer): 12–13.

———. 1996. *The Fine Art of California Indian Basketry.* Sacramento: Crocker Art Museum in association with Heyday Books.

———, ed. 1992. *Living Traditions: A Museum Guide for Native American People of California.* Vol. 2: *North-Central California.* Sacramento: California Native American Heritage Commission.

Blackburn, Thomas. 1975. *December's Child: A Book of Chumash Oral Narratives.* Berkeley: University of California Press.

Blackburn, Thomas, and Kat Anderson, eds. 1993. *Before the Wilderness: Environmental Management by Native Californians.* Ballena Press Anthropological Papers 40. Menlo Park, Calif.: Ballena Press.

Bommelyn, Loren, and Berneice Humphrey. 1985. *Booklet of Tolowa Stories.* 2d ed. Crescent City, Calif.: Tolowa Language Committee and the Del Norte County Title IV-A American Indian Education Program.

———. 1987. *Xus We-Yo': Tolowa Language.* 2d ed.. Crescent City, Calif.: Tolowa Language Committee.

———. 1995. *Now You're Speaking Tolowa.* Happy Camp, Calif.: Naturegraph Publishers.

Boscana, Geronimo. 1933 [1846]. *Chinigchinich: A Revised and Annotated Version of Alfred Robinson's Translation of Father Geronimo Boscana's Historical Account of the Belief, Usages, Customs, and Extravagencies[!] of the Indians of This Mission of San Juan Capistrano Called the* Acagchemem *Tribe.* Ed. P. T. Hanna. Santa Ana, Calif.: Fine Arts Press.

Bright, William. 1957. *The Karok Language.* UCPL 13.

———. 1968. *A Luiseño Dictionary.* UCPL 51.

———. 1977. "Coyote Steals Fire (Karok)." In *Northern California Texts,* ed. Victor Golla and Shirley Silver. *IJAL*-NATS 2.2: 3–9.

———. 1978a. *Coyote Stories. IJAL*-NATS, Monograph 1.

———. 1978b. "Karok." CAL-HB: 180–189.

———. 1979. "A Karuk Myth in 'Measured Verse': The Translation of a Performance." *Journal of California and Great Basin Anthropology* 1: 117–123.

———. 1980a. "Coyote Gives Salmon and Acorns to Humans (Karok)." In *Coyote Stories 2,* ed. Martha Kendall. *IJAL*-NATS, Monograph 6: 46–52.

———. 1980b. "Coyote's Journey." *American Indian Culture and Research Journal* 4.1–2: 21–48.

———. 1982a. *Bibliography of the Languages of Native California.* Native American Bibliography Series 3. Metuchen, N.J.: The Scarecrow Press.

———. 1982b. "Poetic Structure in Oral Narrative." In *Spoken and Written Language,* ed. Deborah Tannen, 171–184. Norwood, N.J.: Ablex Publishing.

———. 1984. *American Indian Linguistics and Literature.* Berlin: Mouton de Gruyter.

———. 1993. *A Coyote Reader.* Berkeley: University of California Press.

———. 1994a. "Myth, Music, and Magic: Nettie Reuben's Karuk Love Medicine." In *Coming to Light,* ed. Brian Swann, 764–771. New York: Random House.

———. 1994b. "Oral Literature of California and the Intermountain Region." In *Dictionary of Native American Literature,* ed. Andrew Wiget, 47–52. New York: Garland Press.

Brumble, H. David. 1988. *American Indian Autobiography.* Berkeley: University of California Press.

Burns, Ken. 1996. *The West.* Dir. Steven Ives. Alexandria, Va.: PBS Video.

Callaghan, Catherine A. 1977. "Coyote the Impostor." In *Northern California Texts,* ed. Victor Golla and Shirley Silver. *IJAL*-NATS 2.2: 10–16.

———. 1978. "Fire, Flood, and Creation." In *Coyote Stories,* ed. William Bright. *IJAL*-NATS 1: 62–86.

Campbell, Lyle, and Marianne Mithun. 1979. *The Languages of Native America: History and Comparative Assessment.* Austin: University of Texas Press.

Castillo, Edward. 1978. "The Impact of Euro-American Exploration and Settlement." CAL-HB: 99–127.

Chafe, Wallace. 1980. *The Pear Stories: Cognitive, Cultural, and Linguistic Aspects of Narrative Production.* Norwood, N.J.: Ablex Publishing.

———. 1994. *Discourse, Consciousness, and Time: The Flow and Displacement of Consciousness in Speaking and Writing.* Norwood, N.J.: Ablex Publishing.

Chase-Dunn, Christopher, and Mahua Sarkar. 1993. "Place Names and Intersocietal Interaction: Wintu Expansion into Hokan Territory in Late Prehistoric Northern California." Paper presented at the Thirteenth Annual Meeting of the Society for Economic Anthropology, Durham, N.H., April 23, 1993.

Chase-Dunn, Christopher, S. Edward Clewett, and Elaine Sundahl. 1992. "A Very Small World-System in Northern California: The Wintu and Their Neighbors." Paper presented at the Fifty-Seventh Annual Meeting of the Society for American Archaeology, Pittsburgh, Pa., April 8–12.

Cook, Sherburne F. 1943. "The Conflict between the California Indian and White Civilization, 1: The Indian versus the Spanish Mission." *Ibero-Americana* 21. Berkeley.

———. 1978. "Historical Demography." CAL-HB: 91–98.

Costo, Rupert, and Jeannette Henry Costo. 1987. *The Missions of California: A Legacy of Genocide.* San Francisco: Indian Historical Press for the American Indian Historical Society.

Couro, Ted, and Christina Hutcheson. 1973. *Dictionary of Mesa Grande Diegueño: 'Tipay Aa–English / English–'Tipay Aa.* Banning, Calif.: Malki Museum Press.

Couro, Ted, and Margaret Langdon. 1975. *Let's Talk 'Tipay Aa: An Introduction to the Mesa Grande Diegueño Language.* Ramona, Calif.: Ballena Press.

Crawford, James. 1983. *Cocopa Texts.* UCPL 100.

———. 1992. *Language Loyalties: A Source Book on the Official English Controversy.* Chicago: University of Chicago Press.

Crawford, Judith. 1976. "Seven Mohave Myths." In *Yuman Texts,* ed. Margaret Langdon. IJAL-NATS 1.3: 31–42.

Crozier-Hogle, Lois, and Darryl Babe Wilson. 1997. *Surviving in Two Worlds: Contemporary Native American Voices.* Austin: University of Texas Press.

Cuero, Delfina. 1970. *The Autobiography of Delfina Cuero, a Diegueño Indian.* As told to Florence C. Shipek. Banning, Calif.: Malki Museum Press and the Morongo Indian Reservation.

Curtin, Jeremiah. 1898. *Creation Myths of Primitive America, in Relation to the Religious History and Development of Mankind.* Boston: Little, Brown. (Reprint, New York: Benjamin Blom, 1967.)

Dangberg, Grace. 1927. "Washo Texts." *UCPAAE* 22.3: 391–443.

Demetracopoulou, Dorothy. 1933. "The Loon Woman Myth: A Study in Synthesis." *JAF* 46: 101–128.

———. 1935. "Wintu Songs." *Anthropos* 30: 483–494.

Demetracopoulou, Dorothy, and Cora Du Bois. 1932. "A Study of Wintu Mythology." *JAF* 45.178: 375–500.

Densmore, Frances. 1932. *Yuman and Yacqui Music.* Bureau of American Ethnology Bulletin 110. Washington, D.C.: Government Printing Office.

Devereux, George. 1948. "Mohave Coyote Tales." *JAF* 61: 233–255.

Dixon, Roland. 1902. "Maidu Myths." *Bulletin of the American Museum of Natural History* 17.2: 33–118. New York: The Knickerbocker Press.

———. 1905. "The Northern Maidu." *Bulletin of the American Museum of Natural History* 17.3: 119–346. New York: The Knickerbocker Press.

———. 1910. "The Chimariko Indians and Language." *UCPAAE* 5.5: 293–380.

———. 1912. *Maidu Texts.* Publications of the American Ethnological Society 4: 1–241. Leyden: E. J. Brill.

Dozier, Deborah. 1997. *The Heart Is Fire: The World of the Cahuilla Indians of Southern California.* Berkeley: Heyday Books.

Drucker, Philip. 1937. "The Tolowa and Their Southwest Oregon Kin." *UCPAAE* 36: 221–300.

Du Bois, Cora. 1935. "Wintu Ethnography." *UCPAAE* 36.1: 1–148.

———. 1939. "The 1870 Ghost Dance." *UCAR* 3.1: 1–151.

Du Bois, Cora, and Dorothy Demetracopoulou. 1931. "Wintu Myths." *UCPAAE* 28.5: 279–403.

Eargle, Dolan H. 1986. *The Earth Is Our Mother: A Guide to the Indians of California, Their Locales, and Historic Sites.* San Francisco: Trees Company Press.

———. 1992. *California Indian Country: The Land and the People.* San Francisco: Trees Company Press.

Finck, Franz Nikolaus. 1899. *Die Araner Mundart: Ein Betrag zur Erforschung des Westirischen.* Marburg: N. G. Elwert'sche Verlagsbuchhandlung.

Forde, C. Darryl. 1931. "Ethnography of the Yuma Indians." *UCPAAE* 28.4: 83–278.

Foster, Michael K. 1996. "Language and the Culture History of North America." In *Languages,* ed. Ives Goddard. Vol. 17 of the Smithsonian *Handbook of North American Indians,* ed. William Sturtevant. Washington, D.C.: Smithsonian Institution.

Freeland, Lucy S. 1947. "Western Miwok Texts with Linguistic Sketch." *IJAL* 13.1: 31–46.

———. 1982. *Freeland's Central Sierra Miwok Myths,* ed. Howard Berman. RSCOIL 3.

Gamble, Geoffrey. 1978. *Wikchamni Grammar.* UCPL 89.

———. 1980. "How People Got Their Hands." In *Coyote Stories II*, ed. Martha B. Kendall. *IJAL*-NATS, Monograph 6: 53–55.

———, ed. 1994. *Yokuts Texts.* Native American Texts Series [n.s.] 1. Berlin: Mouton de Gruyter.

Garth, Thomas R. 1953. "Atsugewi Ethnography." *UCAR* 14.2: 129–212.

———. 1978. "Atsugewi." CAL-HB: 236–243.

Gayton, Anna. 1935. "Areal Affiliations of California Folktales." *American Anthropologist* 37.4: 582–599.

————. 1948. "Yokuts and Western Mono: Ethnography." *UCAR* 10.1–2: 1–302.

Gayton, Anna, and Stanley Newman. 1940. "Yokuts and Western Mono Myths." *UCAR* 5.1: 1–110.

Gendar, Jeannine. 1995. *Grass Games and Moon Races: California Indian Games and Toys.* Berkeley: Heyday Books.

Gifford, Edward Winslow. 1918. "Clans and Moieties in Southern California." *UCPAAE* 18: 1–285.

————. 1926. "Yuma Dreams and Omens." *JAF* 39.151: 58–69.

————. 1955. "Central Miwok Ceremonies." *UCAR* 14.4: 261–318.

Gifford, Edward W., and Gwendoline Block. 1930. *California Indian Nights Entertainments: Stories of the Creation of the World, of Man, of Fire, of the Sun, of Thunder, etc.; of Coyote, the Land of the Dead, the Sky Monsters, Animal People, etc.* Glendale, Calif.: Arthur H. Clark. (Reprint, Lincoln: University of Nebraska Press, Bison Books, 1990.)

Goddard, Ives. 1996. "Introduction." In *Languages,* ed. Ives Goddard. Vol. 17 of *The Handbook of North American Indians.* Washington, D.C.: Smithsonian Institution Press.

————, ed. 1996. *Languages.* Vol. 17 of the Smithsonian *Handbook of North American Indians,* ed. William Sturtevant. Washington, D.C.: Smithsonian Institution.

Goddard, Pliny Earle. 1903–1904. "Life and Culture of the Hupa." *UCPAAE* 1.1: 1–88.

————. 1904. "Hupa Texts." *UCPAAE* 1.2: 89–368.

————. 1909. "Kato Texts." *UCPAAE* 5.3: 65–238.

————. 1914. "Chilula Texts." *UCPAAE* 10.7: 289–379.

————. 1921–1923. "Wailaki Texts." *IJAL* 2.3/4: 77–135.

Goldschmidt, Walter. 1951. "Nomlaki Ethnography." *UCPAAE* 42.4: 303–443.

————. 1978. "Nomlaki." CAL-HB: 341–349.

Golla, Victor. 1984a. *Hupa Stories, Anecdotes, and Conversations.* Told by Louisa Jackson, Ned Jackson, and Minnie Reeves. Recorded, transcribed, and translated by Victor Golla. Arcata, Calif.: The Hoopa Valley Tribe.

————. 1996. "Mary Haas." [Obituary.] *SSILA Newsletter* 15.2 (July). Arcata, Calif.: Society for the Study of the Indigenous Languages of the Americas.

————. 1996. "Review of *The Old Coyote of Big Sur.*" *SSILA Newsletter* 15.1: 7–8. Arcata, Calif.: Society for the Study of the Indigenous Languages of the Americas.

————, ed. 1984b. *The Sapir-Kroeber Correspondence: Letters between Edward Sapir and A. L. Kroeber, 1905–1925.* RSCOIL 6.

Golla, Victor, and Shirley Silver, eds. 1977. *Northern California Texts.* IJAL-NATS 2.2.

Gould, Richard A. 1978. "Tolowa." CAL-HB: 128–136.

Grant, Campbell. 1965. *The Rock Paintings of the Chumash: A Study of California Indian Culture.* Berkeley: University of California Press.

Grey, Herman. 1970. *Tales from the Mohaves.* Norman: University of Oklahoma Press.

Halpern, Abraham M. 1976. "Kukumat Became Sick—a Yuma Text." In *Yuman Texts,* ed. Margaret Langdon. *IJAL*-NATS 1.3: 5–25.

———. 1984. "Quechan Literature." In *Spirit Mountain: An Anthology of Yuman Story and Song,* ed. Leanne Hinton and Lucille Watahomigie. SunTracks 10. Tucson: Sun Tracks and University of Arizona Press.

———. 1988. "Southeastern Pomo Ceremonials: The Kuksu Cult and its Successors." *UCAR* 29.

———. 1997. *Kar'úk: Native Accounts of the Quechan Mourning Ceremony.* Ed. Amy Miller and Margaret Langdon. UCPL 128.

Hamley, Jeffrey Louis. 1994. "Cultural Genocide in the Classroom: A History of the Federal Boarding School Movement in American Indian Education, 1875–1920." Ph.D. dissertation, Harvard University.

Harrington, John Peabody. 1907–1957. The Papers of John Peabody Harrington in the Smithsonian Institution, 1907–1957. National Anthropological Archives, Washington, D.C. (Microfilm edition, Millwood, N.Y.: Krauss International, 1984.)

———. 1908. "A Yuma Account of Origins." *JAF* 21: 324–348.

———. 1921–1922 and 1928. Chimariko Field Notes. The Papers of John Peabody Harrington in the Smithsonian Institution, 1907–1957. National Anthropological Archives, Smithsonian Institution, Washington, D.C. (Microfilm edition: Vol. 2, Northern and Central California, Chimariko/Hupa, Reels 20–24, 31, and 35. Millwood, N.Y.: Krauss International, 1984.)

———. 1930. "Karok Texts." *IJAL* 6.2: 121–161.

———. 1932. "Karok Indian Myths." Bureau of American Ethnology Bulletin 107. Washington, D.C.: Government Printing Office.

Hatch, James. 1958. "Tachi Yokuts Music." *Kroeber Anthropological Society Papers* 19: 47–66. Berkeley.

Heizer, Robert F. 1978a. "History of Research." CAL-HB: 6–15.

———. 1978b. "Mythology: Regional Patterns and History of Research." CAL-HB: 654–657.

———. 1993. *The Destruction of California Indians: A Collection of Documents from the Period 1847 to 1865 in Which are Described Some of the Things That Happened to Some of the Indians of California.* Lincoln: University of Nebraska Press.

———, ed. 1955. "California Indian Linguistic Records: The Mission Indian Vocabularies of H. W. Henshaw." *UCAR* 15.2: 85–202.

———, ed. 1978. *California.* Vol. 8 of the Smithsonian *Handbook of North*

American Indians, ed. William Sturtevant. Washington, D.C.: Smithsonian Institution.

Heizer, Robert F., and Alan J. Almquist. 1971. *The Other Californians: Prejudice and Discrimination under Spain, Mexico, and the United States to 1920.* Berkeley: University of California Press.

Heizer, Robert F., and M. A. Whipple, eds. 1951. *The California Indians: A Source Book.* Berkeley: University of California Press.

Heizer, Robert F., Karen N. Nissen, and Edward Castillo. 1975. *California Indian History: A Classified and Annotated Guide to Source Materials.* Ballena Press Publications in Archaeology, Ethnology and History 4. Ramona, Calif.: Ballena Press.

Herzog, George. 1928. "The Yuman Musical Style." *JAF* 41.160: 183–231.

Heth, Charlotte. 1992. *Songs of Love, Luck, Animals, and Magic: Music of the Yurok and Tolowa Indians.* Recorded Anthology of American Music. New York: New World Records (NW 297).

Hill, Jane H., and Roscinda Nolasquez. 1973. *Mulu'wetam (The First People): Cupeño Oral History and Language.* Banning, Calif.: Malki Museum Press.

Hill, Kenneth C. 1967. "A Grammar of the Serrano Language." Ph.D. diss., University of California at Los Angeles.

———. 1978. "The Coyote and the Flood." In *Coyote Stories,* ed. William Bright. *IJAL*-NATS, Monograph 1: 112–116.

———. 1980. "The Seven Sisters." In *Coyote Stories 2*, ed. Martha Kendall. *IJAL*- NATS, Monograph 6: 97–103.

Hinton, Leanne. 1984. *Havasupai Songs: A Linguistic Perspective.* Tübingen: G. Narr.

———. 1994a. *Flutes of Fire: Essays on California Indian Languages.* Berkeley: Heyday Books.

———. 1994b. "Ashes, Ashes: John Peabody Harrington—Then and Now." In *Flutes of Fire: Essays on California Indian Languages,* 195–210. Berkeley: Heyday Books.

———. 1994c. "Song: Overcoming the Language Barrier." In *Flutes of Fire: Essays on California Indian Languages,* 39–44. Berkeley: Heyday Books.

———. 1994d. "Songs without Words." In *Flutes of Fire: Essays on California Indian Languages,* 145–151. Berkeley: Heyday Books.

———. 1996. "Breath of Life/Silent No More: The Native California Language Restoration Workshop." *NNC* 10.1 (fall): 13–16.

Hinton, Leanne, and Susan L. Roth. 1992. *Ishi's Tale of Lizard.* New York: Farrar, Straus and Giroux.

Hinton, Leanne, and Lucille Watahomigie, eds. 1984. *Spirit Mountain: An Anthology of Yuman Story and Song.* SunTracks 10. Tucson: Sun Tracks and University of Arizona Press.

Holmes-Wermuth, Carol. 1994. "Tübatulabal." In *Native America in the Twentieth Century: An Encyclopedia*, ed. Mary B. Davis, 660–661. New York: Garland Publishing.

Hook, Harry, dir. 1992. *The Last of His Tribe*. A River City Production.

Hudson, Travis, and Ernest Underhay. 1978. *Crystals in the Sky: An Intellectual Odyssey Involving Chumash Astronomy, Cosmology, and Rock Art*. Socorro, N.Mex.: Ballena Press.

Hudson, Travis, Thomas Blackburn, Rosario Curletti, and Janice Timbrook, eds. 1977. *The Eye of the Flute: Chumash Traditional History and Ritual*. As told by Fernando Librado Kitspawit to John P. Harrington. Santa Barbara: Santa Barbara Museum of Natural History.

Hudson, Travis, Janice Timbrook, and Melissa Rempe, eds. 1978. *Tomol: Chumash Watercraft as Described in the Ethnographic Notes of J. P. Harrington*. Socorro, N.Mex.: Ballena Press.

Hurtado, Albert L. 1988. *Indian Survival on the California Frontier*. New Haven: Yale University Press.

Hyde, Villiana Calac. 1971. *An Introduction to the Luiseño Language*. Ed. Ronald Langacker et al. Banning, Calif.: Malki Museum Press.

Hyde, Villiana Calac, and Eric Elliott. 1994. *Yumáyk Yumáyk (Long Ago)*. UCPL 125.

Hymes, Dell. 1976. "Louis Simpson's 'The Deserted Boy.'" *Poetics* 5.2: 119–155.

———. 1977. "Discovering Oral Performance and Measured Verse in American Indian Narrative." *New Literary History* 8: 431–457.

———. 1980. "Particle, Pause, and Pattern in American Indian Narrative Verse." *American Indian Culture and Research Journal* 4.4: 7–51.

———. 1981. *'In vain I tried to tell you': Essays on Native American Ethnopoetics*. Philadelphia: University of Pennsylvania Press.

———. 1983. "'Gitskux and His Older Brother': A Clackamas Chinook Myth." In *Smoothing the Ground: Essays on Native American Oral Literature,* ed. Brian Swann, 129–170. Berkeley: University of California Press.

———. 1992. "Use All There Is to Use." In *On the Translation of Native American Literatures,* ed. Brian Swann, 83–124. Washington, D.C.: Smithsonian Institution.

———. 1994a. "Helen Sekaquaptewa's 'Coyote and the Birds': Rhetorical Analysis of a Hopi Coyote Story." *Anthropological Linguistics* 34: 45–72.

———. 1994b. "Ethnopoetics, Oral Formulaic Theory, and Editing Texts." *Oral Tradition* 9.2: 330–370.

———. 1995. "Reading Takelma Texts: Frances Johnson's 'Coyote and Frog.'" In *Fields of Folklore: Essays in Honor of Kenneth Goldstein,* ed. Roger D. Abrahams, 90–159. Bloomington, Ind.: Trickster Press.

Jackson, Robert H., and Edward Castillo. 1995. *Indians, Franciscans, and Span-*

ish Colonization: The Impact of the Mission System on California Indians. Albuquerque: University of New Mexico Press.

Jacobs, Melville. 1959. *The Content and Style of an Oral Literature: Clackamas Chinook Myths and Tales.* Chicago: University of Chicago Press.

James, Carollyn. 1989. "A Field Linguist Who Lived His Life for His Subjects." *Smithsonian Magazine* 15.1 (April): 153–174.

Jeffers, Robinson. 1983. *Cawdor.* California Writers of the Land 1. Covello, Calif.: Yolla Bolly Press.

Joughlin, Roberta, and Salvadora Valenzuela. 1953. "Cupeño Genesis." *El Museo* [n.s.] 1.4: 16–23.

Keeling, Richard. 1985. "Contrast of Song Performance Style as a Function of Sex Role Polarity in the Hupa Brush Dance." *Ethnomusicology* 29.2: 185–212.

———. 1991. *Guide to Early Field Recordings (1900–1949) at the Lowie Museum of Anthropology.* Berkeley: University of California Press.

———. 1992. *Cry for Luck: Sacred Song and Speech among the Yurok, Hupa, and Karuk Indians of Northwest California.* Berkeley: University of California Press.

Kendall, Martha. 1980. *Coyote Stories 2. IJAL*-NATS, Monograph 6.

Kinkade, M. Dale. 1987. "Bluejay and His Sister." In *Recovering the Word: Essays on Native American Literature,* ed. Brian Swann and Arnold Krupat, 255–296. Berkeley: University of California Press.

Kroeber, Alfred L. 1907a. "Shoshonean Dialects of California." *UCPAAE* 4.3: 65–166.

———. 1907b. "Indian Myths of South Central California." *UCPAAE* 4.4: 167–250.

———. 1917. "California Kinship Systems." *UCPAAE* 12.9: 339–396.

———. 1925. *Handbook of the Indians of California.* Berkeley: California Book Company.

———. 1932. "Yuki Myths." *Anthropos* 27.5–6: 905–939.

———. 1939. "Culture and Natural Areas of Native North America." *UCPAAE* 38: 1–242.

———. 1951. "A Mohave Historical Epic." *UCAR* 11.2.

———. 1953. "Seven Mohave Myths." *UCAR* 11.1.

———. 1963. "Yokuts Dialect Survey." *UCAR* 11.3: 177–251.

———. 1972. "More Mohave Myths." *UCAR* 27.

———. 1976. *Yurok Myths.* Berkeley: University of California Press.

Kroeber, Alfred L., and Edward Gifford. 1949. "World Renewal: A Cult System of Native Northwest California." *UCAR* 13.1: 1–156.

———. 1980. *Karok Myths.* Ed. Grace Buzaljko. Berkeley: University of California Press.

Kroeber, Karl. 1981. *Traditional American Indian Literatures: Texts and Interpretations.* Lincoln: University of Nebraska Press.

Kroeber, Theodora. 1959. *The Inland Whale.* Bloomington: Indiana University Press.

———. 1963. *Ishi in Two Worlds: A Biography of the Last Wild Indian in North America.* Berkeley: University of California Press.

———. 1964. *Ishi, Last of His Tribe.* Berkeley: Parnassus Press.

Krupat, Arnold. 1992. *Ethnocriticism: Ethnography, History, Literature.* Berkeley: University of California Press.

———. 1993. *New Voices in Native American Literary Criticism.* Washington, D.C.: Smithsonian Institution Press.

Laird, Carobeth. 1975. *Encounter with an Angry God: Recollections of My Life with John Peabody Harrington.* Banning, Calif.: Malki Museum Press.

———. 1984. *Mirror and Pattern: George Laird's World of Chemehuevi Myth.* Banning, Calif.: Malki Museum Press.

Lang, Julian. 1993. "The Dances and Regalia." *NNC* 7.3 (fall–winter): 34–41.

———. 1994. *Ararapíkva: Creation Stories of the People.* Berkeley: Heyday Books.

Langdon, Margaret. 1976. *Yuman Texts. IJAL*-NATS 1.3.

LaPena, Frank R. 1978. "Wintu." CAL-HB: 324–340.

LaPena, Frank, Craig D. Bates, and Steven Medley, eds. 1993. *Legends of the Yosemite Miwok.* Yosemite National Park, Calif.: The Yosemite Association.

Latta, Frank. 1936. *California Indian Folklore, as told to F. F. Latta by Wah-nom-kot, Wah-hum-chah, Lee-mee [and others].* Shafter, Calif.: Shafter Press.

Lee, Dorothy [Demetracopoulou]. 1940. "A Wintu Girl's Puberty Ceremony." *New Mexico Anthropologist* 4.4: 57–60.

———. 1944. "Linguistic Reflection of Wintu Thought." *IJAL* 10.4: 181–187.

———. 1959. *Freedom and Culture.* Englewood Cliffs, N.J.: Prentice-Hall.

Lévi-Strauss, Claude. 1981. *The Naked Man.* Introduction to a Science of Mythology 4. New York: Harper and Row. (Translation of *L'Homme Nu* [Paris: Plon, 1971].)

Loeb, Edwin. 1926. "Pomo Folkways." *UCPAAE* 19.2: 149–405.

Lord, Alfred. 1960. *The Singer of Tales.* Harvard Studies in Comparative Literature 24. Cambridge: Harvard University Press.

Lowie, Robert H. 1963. "Washo Texts." *Anthropological Linguistics* 5.7: 1–30. Bloomington: Indiana University Press.

Luthin, Herbert W. 1991. "Restoring the Voice in Yanan Traditional Narrative: Prosody, Performance, and Presentational Form." Ph.D. diss., University of California at Berkeley.

———. 1994. "Two Stories from the Yana: 'The Drowning of Young Buzzard's Wife' and 'A Story of Wildcat, Rolling Skull.'" In *Coming to Light,* ed. Brian Swann, 717–736. New York: Random House.

Manriquez, L. Frank. 1998. *Acorn Soup*. Berkeley: Heyday Books.

Margolin, Malcolm. 1978. *The Ohlone Way*. Berkeley: Heyday Books.

———. 1993. *The Way We Lived: California Indian Stories, Songs, and Reminiscences*. Berkeley: Heyday Books.

Margolin, Malcolm, and Yolanda Montijo, eds. 1995. *Native Ways: California Indian Stories and Memories*. Berkeley: Heyday Books.

Matthiessen, Peter. 1979. "Stop the GO Road." *Audubon Magazine* 81.1 (January): 49–84.

Mayfield, Thomas Jefferson, and Malcolm Margolin. 1993. *Indian Summer: Traditional Life among the Choinumne Indians of California's San Joaquin Valley*. Berkeley: Heyday Books and The California Historical Society.

McKibbin, Grace, and Alice Shepherd. 1997. *In My Own Words: Stories, Songs, and Memories of Grace McKibbin, Wintu*. Berkeley: Heyday Books.

McLendon, Sally. 1975. *A Grammar of Eastern Pomo*. UCPL 71.

———. 1982. "Meaning, Rhetorical Structure, and Discourse Organization in Myth." In *Analyzing Discourse: Text and Talk*, ed. Deborah Tannen, 284–305. Washington, D.C.: Georgetown University Press.

———. 1990. "Pomo Baskets: The Legacy of William and Mary Benson." *Native Peoples* 4.1: 26–33.

McLendon, Sally, and Michael J. Lowy. 1978. "Eastern Pomo and Southeastern Pomo." CAL-HB: 306–323.

McLendon, Sally, and Robert L. Oswalt. 1978. "Pomo: Introduction." CAL-HB: 274–288.

Merriam, C. Hart. 1910. *The Dawn of the World: Myths and Weird Tales Told by the Mewan Indians of California*. Cleveland: Arthur H. Clark.

———. 1930. "The New River Indians Tol-hom-tah-hoi." *American Anthropologist* 32: 280–293.

Miller, Wick. 1967. *Uto-Aztecan Cognate Sets*. UCPL 48.

———. 1972. *Newe Natekwinappeh: Shoshoni Stories and Dictionary*. Anthropological Papers 94. Salt Lake City: University of Utah Press.

Mithun, Marianne. 1993. "Frances Jack, 1912–1993." [Obituary.] *NNC* 7.3 (summer): 11–13.

Mixco, Mauricio. 1983. *Kiliwa Texts: 'When I have donned my crest of stars.'* Anthropological Papers 107. Salt Lake City: University of Utah Press.

Moratto, Michael J. 1984. *California Archaeology*. Orlando, Fla.: Academic Press.

Mourning Dove, a Yurok/English Tale. 1993. Berkeley: Heyday Books.

Munro, Pamela. 1976. *Mojave Syntax*. New York: Garland.

Nettl, Bruno. 1965. "The Songs of Ishi: Musical Styles of the Yahi Indians." *Musical Quarterly* 51.3: 460–477.

Nevin, Bruce E. 1991. "Obsolescence in Achumawi: Why Uldall Too?" In *Papers from the American Indian Languages Conferences, Held at the University of California, Santa Cruz, July and August 1991.* Occasional Papers on Linguistics 16: 97–127. Carbondale: Department of Linguistics, Southern Illinois University.

———. 1998. "Aspects of Pit River Phonology." Ph.D. diss., University of Pennsylvania.

Newman, Stanley A. 1940. "Linguistic Aspects of Yokuts Narrative Style." *UCAR* 5.1: 4–8.

———. 1944. *Yokuts Language of California.* Viking Fund Publications on Anthropology 2. New York: Viking Fund.

Nichols, Johanna. 1992. *Linguistic Diversity in Time and Space.* Chicago: University of Chicago Press.

Nichols, Michael P. 1981. "Old California Uto-Aztecan." RSCOIL 1: 5–41. Berkeley: Survey of California and Other Indian Languages, University of California.

Nolasquez, Roscinda, and Anne Galloway. 1979. *I'i Muluwit: First Book of Words in the Cupeño Indian Language of Southern California.* Pala, Calif.: Alderbooks.

Norton, Jack. 1979. *Genocide in Northwestern California: When Our Worlds Cried.* San Francisco: Indian Historian Press.

Ochoa Zazueta, Jesús Ángel. 1976. *Ya'abú ti'nñar jaspuy'pai (Esta es la Escritura Pai'pai).* Cuadernos de Trabajo 2. Mexicali: Colección Paisano, Universidad Autónoma de Baja California.

Olmsted, David L. 1966. *Achumawi Dictionary.* UCPL 45.

———. 1984. *A Lexicon of Atsugewi.* RSCOIL 5.

Oswalt, Robert. 1961. "A Kashaya Grammar." Ph.D. diss., University of California at Berkeley.

———. 1964. *Kashaya Texts.* UCPL 36.

———. 1975. *K'ahšáya cahno kalikakh [Kashaya Word Book].* Rohnert Park: Kashaya Pomo Languages in Culture Project, Department of Anthropology, California State University at Sonoma.

———. 1977. "Retribution for Mate-Stealing." In *Northern California Texts,* ed. Victor Golla and Shirley Silver. *IJAL*-NATS 2.2: 71–81.

Parsons, Thomas, ed. 1971. *The Yurok Language, Literature, and Culture.* Textbook, 2d ed. (mimeo). Arcata, Calif.: Center for Community Development, Humboldt State College.

Pilling, Arnold R. 1978. "Yurok." CAL-HB: 137–154.

Pitkin, Harvey. 1977. "Coyote and Bullhead." In *Northern California Texts,* ed. Victor Golla and Shirley Silver. *IJAL*-NATS 2.2: 82–104.

———. 1984. *Wintu Grammar.* UCPL 94.

———. 1985. *Wintu Dictionary.* UCPL 95.

Pope, Saxton T. 1918. "Yahi Archery." *UCPAAE* 13.3.

Powers, Stephen. 1877. *Tribes of California.* Contributions to North American Ethnology 3. Washington, D.C.: U.S. Geographical and Geological Survey of the Rocky Mountain Region.

Pratt, Richard H. 1964. *Battlefield and Classroom: Four Decades with the American Indian, 1867–1904.* New Haven: Yale University Press.

Propp, Vladímir. 1968. *Morphology of the Folktale.* Austin: University of Texas Press.

Radin, Paul. 1924. "Wappo Texts: First Series." *UCPAAE* 19.1: 1–147.

Rawls, James J. 1984. *Indians of California: The Changing Image.* Norman: University of Oklahoma Press.

Reichard, Gladys. 1925. "Wiyot Grammar and Texts." *UCPAAE* 22.1: 1–215.

Richardson, Nancy. 1992. "The State of Our Languages." *NNC* 7.1 (winter): 40–41.

———. 1994. "Indian Language Is Happening in California." *NNC* 8.3 (winter): 47–49.

Riffe, Jeff, and Pamela Roberts, prods. and dirs. 1994. *Ishi, the Last Yahi.* Written by Ann Makepeace. Newton, N.J.: Shanachie Entertainment Corp.

Roberts, Helen H. 1933. *Form in Primitive Music: An Analytical and Comparative Study of the Melodic Form of Some Ancient Southern California Indian Songs.* New York: W. W. Norton.

Robins, R. H. 1958. *The Yurok Language: Grammar, Texts, Lexicon.* UCPL 15.

Robins, R. H., and Norma McLeod. 1956. "Five Yurok Songs: A Musical and Textual Analysis." *Bulletin of the School of Oriental and African Studies* 18: 592–609. University of London.

Sackheim, Daniel, dir. 1996. *Grand Avenue.* Santa Monica, Calif.: Wildwood Enterprises and Elsboy Entertainment.

Sapir, Edward. 1910. "Yana Texts (together with Yana Myths, collected by Roland B. Dixon)." *UCPAAE* 9.1.

———. 1925. "The Hokan Affinity of Subtiaba in Nicaragua." *American An-*

————. 1994b. *Mabel McKay: Weaving the Dream.* Berkeley: University of California Press.

————, ed. 1994c. *The Sound of Rattles and Clappers: A Collection of New California Indian Writing.* Tucson: University of Arizona Press.

Saubel, Katherine Siva, and Pamela Munro. 1981. *Chem'ivillu': Let's Speak Cahuilla.* Los Angeles: American Indian Studies Center, University of California.

Schlicter, Alice. 1981. *Wintu Dictionary.* RSCOIL 2.

————. 1986. "The Origins and Deictic Nature of Wintu Evidentials." In *Evidentiality: The Linguistic Coding of Epistemology,* ed. Wallace Chafe and Johanna Nichols, 46–59. Norwood, N.J.: Ablex Publishing.

Seaburg, William. 1977. "A Wailaki (Athapaskan) Text with Comparative Notes." *IJAL* 43: 327–332.

Seiler, Hansjakob. 1970. *Cahuilla Texts, with an Introduction.* Indiana University Language Science Monographs 6. Bloomington: Indiana University Press.

Shepherd, Alice [Schlicter]. 1989. *Wintu Texts.* UCPL 117.

Sherzer, Joel. 1987. "Poetic Structuring of Kuna Discourse: The Line." In *Native American Discourse: Poetics and Rhetoric,* ed. Joel Sherzer and Anthony C. Woodbury, 103–139. Cambridge: Cambridge University Press.

Sherzer, Joel, and Anthony C. Woodbury. 1987. *Native American Discourse: Poetics and Rhetoric.* Cambridge Studies in Oral and Written Culture. Cambridge: Cambridge University Press.

Shipley, William. 1963. *Maidu Texts and Dictionary.* UCPL 33.

————. 1964. *Maidu Grammar.* UCPL 41.

————. 1978. "Native Languages of California." CAL-HB: 80–90.

————. 1991. *The Maidu Indian Myths and Stories of Hánc'ibyjim.* Berkeley: Heyday Books.

Shipley, William, and Richard Alan Smith. 1979. "The Roles of Cognation and Diffusion in a Theory of Maidun Prehistory." *Journal of California and Great Basin Anthropology—Papers in Linguistics* 1: 65–74.

Silver, Shirley. 1978. "Chimariko." CAL-HB: 205–210.

Silverstein, Michael. 1979. "Penutian: An Assessment." In *The Languages of Native America,* ed. Lyle Campbell and Marianne Mithun, 650–691. Austin: University of Texas Press.

Slagle, Allogan. 1987. "The Native American Tradition and Legal Status: Tolowa Tales and Tolowa Places." *Cultural Critique* 7: 103–118.

Smith, Bertha. 1904. *Yosemite Legends.* San Francisco: Paul Elder and Co.

Smith, Charles R. 1978. "Tübatulabal." CAL-HB: 437–445.

Snyder, Gary. 1975. "The Incredible Survival of Coyote." *Western American Literature* 9: 255–272.

Sparkman, Philip Stedman. 1908. "Culture of the Luiseño Indians." *UCPAAE* 8.

Spier, Leslie. 1955. "Mohave Culture Items." *Museum of Northern Arizona Bulletin* 28. Flagstaff, Ariz.: Northern Arizona Society of Science and Art.

Spott, Robert, and Alfred L. Kroeber. 1942. "Yurok Narratives." *UCPAAE* 35.9: 143–256.

Strong, William Duncan. 1929. *Aboriginal Society in Southern California.* (Reprint, with an introduction by Lowell John Bean, Banning, Calif.: Malki Museum Press, 1972.)

Swann, Brian. 1993. *Song of the Sky: Versions of Native American Song-Poems.* Amherst: University of Massachusetts Press.

———. 1996. *Wearing the Morning Star: Native American Song-Poems.* New York: Random House.

———, ed. 1983. *Smoothing the Ground: Essays in Native American Oral Literature.* Berkeley: University of California Press.

———, ed. 1992. *On the Translation of Native American Literatures.* Washington, D.C.: Smithsonian Institution Press.

———, ed. 1994. *Coming to Light: Contemporary Translations of the Native Literatures of North America.* New York: Random House.

Swann, Brian, and Arnold Krupat, eds. 1987. *Recovering the Word: Essays on Native American Literature.* Berkeley: University of California Press.

Taylor, Alexander. 1860–1863. "Indianology of California." Column in *The California Farmer and Journal of Useful Arts,* vols. 13–20, February 22, 1860, to October 30, 1863.

Tedlock, Dennis. 1983. *The Spoken Word and the Work of Interpretation.* Philadelphia: University of Pennsylvania Press.

Teixeira, Rachel. 1996a. "California Indian Stories and the Spirit." *NNC* 9.4.

———. 1996b. "Like Air We Breathe." *NNC* 9.4.

Thompson, Lucy. 1991 [1916]. *To the American Indian: Reminiscences of a Yurok Woman.* Berkeley: Heyday Books.

Uldall, Stuart, and William Shipley. 1966. *Nisenan Texts and Dictionary.* UCPL 46.

Valory, Dale, comp. 1971. "Guide to Ethnographic Documents (1–203) of the Department and Museum of Anthropology." University of California Archives, Bancroft Library, Berkeley.

Vizenor, Gerald. 1989. *Narrative Chance: Postmodern Discourse on Native American Indian Literatures.* Albuquerque: University of New Mexico Press.

Voegelin, [Carl] Charles F. 1935. "Tübatulabal Texts." *UCPAAE* 34.3: 191–246.

Voegelin, Carl F., and Erminie Wheeler Voegelin. 1931–1933. "Tübatulabal Myths and Tales." [Unpublished Manuscript #73.] Ethnological Documents of the Department and Museum of Anthropology. University of California Archives, Bancroft Library, Berkeley.

Voegelin, Erminie [Wheeler]. 1937. "Tübatulabal Ethnography." *UCAR* 2.1: 1–90.

Wallace, William J. 1978a. "Post-Pleistocene Archaeology, 9000 to 2000 B.C." CAL-HB: 25–36.

———. 1978b. "Hupa, Chilula and Whilkut." CAL-HB: 164–179.

———. 1978c. "Southern Valley Yokuts." In CAL-HB: 448–461.

———. 1978d. "Northern Valley Yokuts." In CAL-HB: 462–470.

———. 1978e. "Comparative Literature." CAL-HB: 658–661.

Wallace, William J., and J. S. Taylor. 1950. "Hupa Sorcery." *Southwestern Journal of Anthropology* 6: 188–196.

Walters, Diane. 1977. "Coyote and Moon Woman (Apwarukeyi)." In *Northern California Texts,* ed. Victor Golla and Shirley Silver. *IJAL*-NATS 2.2: 147–157.

Waterman, T. T. 1910. "The Religious Practices of the Diegueño Indians." *UCPAAE* 8.6: 271–358.

Whistler, Kenneth W. 1977a. "Deer and Bear Children." In *Northern California Texts,* ed. Victor Golla and Shirley Silver. *IJAL*-NATS 2.2: 158–184.

———. 1977b. "Wintun Prehistory: An Interpretation Based on Linguistic Reconstruction of Plant and Animal Nomenclature." *Proceedings of the Annual Meeting of the Berkeley Linguistics Society* 3: 157–174.

Whittemore, Kathrine. 1997. "To Converse with Creation: Saving California Indian Languages." *Native Americas,* 1 14.3 (fall 1997): 46–53.

Wilson, Darryl Babe. 1998. *The Morning the Sun Went Down.* Berkeley: Heyday Books.

———. Forthcoming. *Yo-Kenaswi Usji (Necklace of Hearts).* Tucson: Sun Tracks and the University of Arizona Press.

Woiche, Istet. 1992 [1928]. *Annikadel: The History of the Universe as Told by the Achumawi Indians of California.* Recorded and ed. C. Hart Merriam. Tucson: University of Arizona Press.

Woodbury, Anthony C. 1987. "Rhetorical Structure in a Central Alaskan Yupik Eskimo Traditional Narrative." In *Native American Discourse: Poetics and Rhetoric,* ed. Joel Sherzer and Anthony C. Woodbury, 176–239. Cambridge: Cambridge University Press.

Yamane, Linda. 1995. *When the World Ended—How Hummingbird Got Fire—How People Were Made: Rumsien Ohlone Stories.* Told and illustrated by Linda Yamane. Berkeley: Oyate Press.

ACKNOWLEDGMENTS
OF PERMISSIONS

Grateful acknowledgments are made to the following for permission to reprint or excerpt copyrighted or archival materials:

Gui de Angulo, for permission to reprint the song "The dawn is dawning" from *Indians in Overalls* by Jaime de Angulo (City Lights, 1990).

Anthropos, for permission to reprint selections from "Wintu Songs" by Dorothy Demetracopoulou (*Anthropos* 30, 1935).

The Bancroft Library, for permission to use or translate "Mason's Report," Paul Faye's Cupeño "Creation Songs," "A Story of Lizard," and "How I Became a Dreamer."

The California Historical Society, for permission to reprint sections of "The Stone and Kelsey Massacre on the Shores of Clear Lake in 1849" by William Ralganal Benson (*Quarterly of the California Historical Society* 11.3, 1932).

Larry Evers, Leanne Hinton, and Lucille Watahomigie, for permission to reprint excerpts from "Lightning Song" by Abraham Halpern, in *Spirit Mountain: An Anthology of Yuman Story and Song,* edited by Leanne Hinton and Lucille Watahomigie (Sun Tracks and University of Arizona Press, 1984).

Heyday Books, for permission to reprint an excerpt from "In the Beginning" in *The Maidu Indian Myths and Stories of Hánc'ibyjim* by William Shipley (Heyday, 1991)—as well as excerpts from the following articles in *News from Native California:* "Boarding School" by Elsie Allen (*NNC* 4.1, 1989); "The State of Our Languages" by Nancy Richardson (*NNC* 7.1, 1992); "Frances Jack, 1912–1993" by Marianne Mithun (*NNC* 7.3, 1993); "Interview with Edna Guerrero" by Vic Bedoian and Roberta Llewellyn (*NNC* 8.4, spring 1995); and the Linda Yamane commentary from "Like Air We Breathe" by Rachel Teixeira (*NNC* 9.4, 1996).

Houghton Mifflin, for permission to reprint "Yahi mouth-bow song" from *Ishi, Last of His Tribe* by Theodora Kroeber (Parnassus Press, 1964).

The Journal of American Folklore, for permission to reprint "A Yuma Account of Origins" by J. P. Harrington (*JAF* 21, 1908); "Creation" from "Serrano Tales" by Ruth Benedict (*JAF* 39.151, 1926); "Winter mosquitos go" from "A Study of Wintu Mythology" by Dorothy Demetracopoulou and Cora Du Bois (*JAF* 45.178, 1932); and "Pomo Creation Myth" by Jaime de Angulo (*JAF* 48.189, 1935). These four items are not for further reproduction.

Mouton de Gruyter, for permission to reprint "Journey to the Land of the Dead" from *Yokuts Texts* by Geoffrey Gamble (Native American Texts Series 1, Mouton de Gruyter, 1994).

Oxford University Press, for permission to reprint the Yurok doctor dance song "Why is the water rough" from "Five Yurok Songs: A Musical and Textual Analysis" by R. H. Robins and Norma McLeod (*Bulletin of the School of Oriental and African Studies* 18, 1956).

Jean Perry, for permission to quote Florence Shaughnessy's recitation of "You come upon a place you've never seen before," which appeared in "Stop the GO Road" by Peter Matthiessen (*Audubon Magazine* 81.1 January 1979).

The Smithsonian Institution, for permission to use the "House Is Afire" excerpt (letter from J. P. Harrington to Jack Marr, 1941), as well as to retranslate the following materials from "The Papers of John Peabody Harrington in the Smithsonian Institution, 1907–1957" (National Anthropological Archives, Smithsonian Institution, Washington, D.C.): "The Bear Girl" (Chimariko fieldnotes, 1921–1922); "The Dog Girl" (Ineseño fieldnotes, 1919).

The University of California Press, for permission to reprint "The acorns come down from heaven" and "Do you come from the north?" both from *Tribes of California* by Stephen Powers (reprinted 1976); "Chalááwaat Song" from *Yumáyk Yumáyk* by Villiana Calac Hyde and Eric Elliott (text #167, 1994); excerpt from "The Čiq'neq's Myth," in *December's Child* by Thomas Blackburn (1975); "I have told you to come away from the shore," from "California Indian Linguistic Records: The Mission Indian Vocabularies of H. W. Henshaw" by Robert Heizer (*UCAR* 15.2, 1955); "Kingfisher, kingfisher," from "Yokuts and Western Mono Ethnography: I" by Anna Gayton (*UCAR* 10.1, 1948); Quechan funeral speech from "Ethnography of the Yuma Indians" by C. Darryl Forde (*UCPAAE* 28.4, 1931); excerpt from an account of "The Soul" in *Kar'uk: Native Accounts of the Quechan Mourning Ceremony* by Abraham Halpern, edited by Amy Miller and Margaret Langdon (*UCPL* 128, 1997); "Spell said by a girl desirous of getting a husband" from *Yana Texts* by Edward Sapir (*UCPAAE* 9.1, 1910); Nisenan prayer from "Ethnography of the Nisenan" by Ralph Beals (*UCPAAE* 31.6, 1933).

The University of Chicago Press, for permission to reprint "Cradleboard" by Judith Crawford, song from the myth "Kukumat Became Sick" ("My heart, you might pierce it") by Abraham Halpern, and "The Coming of the Friars" by Mauricio Mixco, all from *Yuman Texts,* edited by Margaret Langdon (*International Journal of American Linguistics—Native American Texts Series* 1.3, 1976).

University of Illinois Press, for permission to reprint the song "Where we used to make love" from "Contrast in Song Performance Style as a Function of Sex Role Polarity in the Hupa Brush Dance" by Richard Keeling (*Ethnomusicology* 29.2, 1985).

The University of Massachusetts Press, for permission to reprint "Women's Brush Dance Song" from *Song of the Sky: Versions of Native American Song-Poems* by Brian Swann (1993).

The University of Utah Press, for permission to reprint "When I Have Donned My Crest of Stars" from *Kiliwa Texts* by Mauricio Mixco (*University of Utah Anthropological Papers* 107, 1983).

INDEX

A'alxi genre of stories ("telling histories"), 422

"An Account of Origins" (Quechan), 20n6, 461–89; alterations of Harrington's original text, 464n1; collection and translation of, 15(table 1), 22, 503; as example of Southern California creation pattern, 520, 539n7; Latin passages in, 489–90

Achumawi: geographical territory, 127; "How My Father Found the Deer," 127–38; waking song, 532

Achumawi language: Jaime de Angulo's work on, 264; sample passage, 130–31, 132n3

Acorns: ceremonial acorn song (Maidu), 491; as food, 90, 104, 204, 251, 334, 365, 390; gathering, 102, 113, 246; leaching and cooking, 227–28, 290, 291, 303, 376; shell transformed into Marumda's boat (Eastern Pomo), 279, 304

Advocates for Indigenous California Language Survival (AICLS), 564–65

Aisisara, Lorenzo, 555

Algic stock, 548, 549, 567n5

Algonquian language family, 551, 567n5

Allen, Elsie (Central Pomo), 313, 560–62, 569n21

Animals: anthropomorphism of, 38–40; as both characters and part of nature, 39, 49; creation of, in Eastern Pomo origin myth, 277; creation of, in Quechan origin myth, 468, 471, 473; creator's instructions to (Eastern Pomo), 307–9; as food for Lake Miwok, 334–35; made by Kwaw (Atsugewi), 60–61; named by Kumastamxo (Quechan), 485–86; people growing up to be (Chimariko), 118; people turned into (Chumash), 395; tails cut in mourning (Quechan), 479; trapped in pits (Achumawi), 127. *See also specific animals*

Antelope, killed without bow for food (Mojave), 448–49

Anthropomorphism, 38–40

Applegate, Richard, 504; "The Dog Girl" (translator), 382–95

"Areal Affiliations of California Folktales" (Gayton), 515, 523

Arrow-making, in "A Story of Lizard" (Yahi), 155, 156, 161n3, 163–64, 166–68, 171–72, 173–76. *See also* Bow and arrow

Arrowweeds: cradleboard made of (Mojave), 524; as first plant (Quechan [Yuma]), 470

Arroyo de la Cuesta, Father Felipe, 500

Athabascan language family, 548, 551, 567n5; bascan on, 551

Atsugewi, 129, 132n2; geographical
  territory, 140; "Kwaw Labors to Form
  a World," 14, 59–61; "Naponoha
  (Cocoon Man)," 14, 139–51; song
  given by Lela Rhoades, 142
Av'a seeds, as food for Mojave, 452, 453
Avikwaamé (Ghost Mountain), 462, 463

Badgers: "The Creation" (Serrano),
  406n2, 409–10; "The Death of
  Kwikumat" (Quechan [Yuma]), 477
Baldy, Ray (Hupa), 7, 564
Barnes, Nellie, 46
Barrett, Samuel, 501; "Wintun Hesi
  Ceremony," 535
Baskets: Eastern Pomo's uses for, 290–
  91; feathers in (Lake Miwok), 335; for
  fetching water (Hupa), 109; magic
  Jump Dance, 112; Marumda teaches
  making and use of (Eastern Pomo),
  289–91; Southern Pomo, 312, 313,
  318, 319; talking, 61; woven by Annie
  Burke, 313; woven by Elsie Allen,
  313, 569n21; woven by Mabel McKay,
  324–25; woven by William Benson
  and wife, 261–63
Bat, "Mad Bat" (Maidu), 248–59
Bathing, baby-bath basket for (Southern
  Pomo), 318, 319
Batwi, Sam (Yana), 503(fig. 12), 505
Beads, clamshell and magnesite (Pomo),
  312
"The Bear Girl" (Chimariko), 115–22;
  anthropomorphism in, 39; parallelism
  in, 44–45
Bears: "The Bear Girl" (Chimariko),
  39, 115–22; "Grizzly Bear and Deer"
  (Yana), 25–26, 28–29, 30; "The Life
  of Hawk Feather: The Bear Episodes"
  (Cupeño), 426–35; "A Story of Lizard"
  (Yahi), 155, 156–57, 164–66; white
  grizzly (Hupa), 111
Beauty, 63
Beavers: "The Death of Kwikumat"
  (Quechan [Yuma]), 478; as food for
  Mojave, 452, 453; "The Trials of Young
  Hawk" (Southern Pomo), 318–19
Belts, feather (Nomlaki), 235–36

Bender, Jo (Wintu), 505; "Loon Woman"
  (narrator), 43, 192–218, 200n2
Benedict, Ruth, version of Serrano
  creation story, 401, 405n2
Benner, Lena (Maidu), 248
Benson, Addison, 261
Benson, William Ralganal (Eastern
  Pomo), 262(fig. 7), 505; biography of,
  261–63, 272n2; "Creation" (narrator),
  13, 260–310; Stone and Kelsey Mas-
  sacre account by, 556–58
Bevis, Bill, 54n23
Bibby, Brian, 235–41, 564
Birds: as both character and part of
  nature, 49; inventory of, in Eastern
  Pomo myth, 308–9; in Pomo nar-
  ratives, 523; wounded, in "Loon
  Woman," 197, 201n6, 214–18. *See also
  specific birds*
Blackburn, Thomas, 504; *December's
  Child*, 386
Blake, Ramsey Bone, 61
"Blind Bill and the Owl" (Yurok), 78–79,
  81–82
Block, Gwendoline, *California Indian
  Nights Entertainments,* 513
Boarding-school system, 559–62; impact
  on languages, 560–62; underlying
  philosophy of, 559, 569n18
Bommelyn, Loren, 51n2; "Test-ch'as (The
  Tidal Wave)" (author and translator),
  47–48, 67–76
Bone, Lee, 140
Boone, Yanta (Pomo), 324
Boscana, Geronimo, *Chinigchinich,* 500
Bottlefly, "Condor Steals Falcon's Wife"
  (Yowlumni Yokuts), 358–59
Bow and arrow, Marumda teaches people
  to make (Eastern Pomo), 288–89, 301.
  See also Arrow-making
"The Boy Who Grew Up at Ta'k'imił-
  ding" (Hupa), 35, 104–110; collected
  by tape recording, 16(table 2), 502; as
  ethnographic text, 35; as "institution
  myth," 518
Brandenstein, Susan, "Naponoha
  (Cocoon Man)" (collector), 14, 139–51
Bright, William, 78, 504; *A Coyote*

Reader, 539n8; "Coyote Steals Fire" (translator), 31–33; "The Devil Who Died Laughing" (collector and translator), 98–103; integrated ethnopoetic approach of, 31–33, 35; *Luiseño Dictionary,* 413; "Oral Literature of California and the Intermountain Region," 513

Broadbent, Sylvia, 504

Brodiaea plants, Karuk, 93, 97

Brown, Betty (Yana): "Coyote, Heron, and Lizard" (narrator), 521–22, 539n10; "Indian Medicine-Men" (narrator), 526–27, 540n16; "Spell Said by a Girl Desirous of Getting a Husband," 125

Brown, Fanny, "A Selection of Wintu Songs" (singer), 178–81, 189

Brugmann, Karl, 384

Bryan, Goldie (Washoe), 7

Buckskin Jack, 129, 130, 131

Bullhead, transformation of, 97

Burial songs, Cupeño, 518–19, 538n5

Burke, Annie Ramone (Southern Pomo), 505; biography of, 313; "The Trials of Young Hawk" (narrator), 38, 311–23

Burke, Richard, 313

Burke, Salvador, 313

Burrows, Wallace (Nomlaki), 235, 237, 239

Butler, Parris (Mojave), 19n2, 564

Butterfly, Night-Flying, Naponoha's transformation into (Atsugewi), 141–42

Buzzard, "Condor Steals Falcon's Wife" (Yowlumni Yokuts), 358

Cabrillo, João Rodrigues, 500

The California Farmer and Journal of Useful Arts, articles on "Indianology" (Taylor), 500

California Indian Conference, story-telling at, 8–9

California Indian Nights Entertainments (Gifford and Block), 513

Callaghan, Catherine, 504; "The Dead People's Home" (collector and trans-lator), 13, 334–42; Costanoan data provided by, 507–8n5

Callahan, Bob, 270

Campbell, Clarence, 239–40; "How I Became a Dreamer" (collector), 235–47

Canoes, seagoing, Tolowa, 67, 72

Castillo, Edward, 556

Central California creation pattern, 515–17, 538n2

Central Group, 461, 462, 465n2

"Central Miwok Ceremonies" (Gifford), 535

Ceremonies: ceremonial acorn song (Maidu), 491; for spring salmon run (Achumawi), 128; girls' puberty (Lui-seño), 535–36; Hesi (Nomlaki), 74, 236–38, 243n, 245n; Hesi, Patwin, 536–37, 541n24; seasonal, First Salmon Ceremony (Karuk), 92; seasonal, salmon roast (Yurok), 8–9; World Renewal, 517; World Renewal, Hupa, 106; World Renewal, Karuk, 517–18, 538n4. *See also* Dances

"Chalááwaat Song," vii, 416–17, 565–66

Characters: anthropomorphism of, 38–40; motivation for behavior of, 47–48. *See also names of specific characters*

Chawchila Yokuts. *See* Yokuts

Chemehuevi, songs in stories of, 540n17

Chetco (Tolowa), 68

Chia: "The Contest between Men and Women" (Tübatulabal), 366, 372, 375, 376; as food for Chumash, 390

Chico, 236, 238, 245

Childbirth, 470

Chilula (Hupas), 105, 107, 110

Chimariko: "The Bear Girl," 115–22; geographical territory, 115

Chinigchinich (Boscana), 500

Chumash: Barbareño Chumash, Santa Barbara uprising, 555; Coyote songs, 397, 531, 532; geographical territory, 382; Harrington's fieldnotes on, 19n3; Ineseño Chumash, "The Dog Girl," 382–95; songs in stories of, 530, 540n17; Ventureño Chumash, "The Čiq'neq's Myth" (excerpt), 345

Chumashan language family, 546, 547, 567n6

Chumash languages, 382–83; sample passage (Ineseño), 386

"The Čiq'neq's Myth" (excerpt), 345

Clear Lake, Stone and Kelsey Massacre at, 556–58

Clothing: belts (Nomlaki), 235–36; jewelry (Chumash), 393; men's (Karuk), 95; skin (Mojave), 449–50; willow bark for women's skirts (Mojave), 449

The Collected Works of Edward Sapir (Sapir), 105

Collectors: preservation of traditions by, 499–500, 508n7, 509n8; at University of California at Berkeley Department of Anthropology, 500–501; at University of California at Berkeley Department of Linguistics, 503–4; unpublished material of, 7–8. *See also names of specific collectors and scholars*

Comanche, George, 313

Coming to Light (Swann), 11

"Comparative Literature" (Wallace), 513

Condors, 349–51

"Condor Steals Falcon's Wife" (Yowlumni Yokuts), 349–51, 356–62, 523, 540n12

"The Contest between Men and Women" (Tübatulabal), 35, 363–81

Cook, Sherburne F., 553

Corn, as food for Quechan (Yuma), 471

Costanoan language: dance song, 532; fieldtrip to record, 495–99, 506n2, 507nns,6; gambling song, 532; love song, 532; wordlist and text, 497–98, 507n5

Cottonwood: for funeral pyre (Quechan [Yuma]), 477–78; sacred sticks for Yuma fiestas made from, 484; shade-roofs constructed of (Quechan [Yuma]), 485

Couro, Ted (Iipay Diegueño), 505–6

Covelo, Indian boarding school at, 560–61

Coyote: in Central California creation myths, 515, 516, 517; Coyote songs (Chumash), 397, 531, 532; Coyote stories, 15(table 1), 520–22, 539n8;

creator's relationship to (Eastern Pomo), 267, 272n4; personality of, 39, 92; Trickster cycle (Maidu), 249

Coyote, selections and excerpts involving, 15(table 1); "Condor Steals Falcon's Wife" (Yowlumni Yokuts), 356–57, 359, 361; "The Contest between Men and Women" (Tübatulabal), 365–67, 368–69, 373–81; "Coyote, Heron, and Lizard" (Yana; excerpt), 521–22; "Coyote and Old Woman Bullhead" (Karuk), 92, 94–97; "Coyote Steals Fire" (Karuk; excerpt), 32–33; "The Creation" (Serrano), 405, 405n2, 408, 409–10; "The Death of Kwikumat" (Quechan), 477–79; "The Life of Hawk Feather: The Bear Episodes" (Cupeño), 423–24, 428; "In the Beginning" (Maidu; excerpt), 515; "Kwaw Labors to Form a World" (Atsugewi), 59–61; "Loon Woman" (Wintu), 195, 196, 207, 208–9; "Mad Bat" (Maidu), 250, 258; "Naponoha (Cocoon Man)" (Atsugewi), 143, 146–47; "The Young Man from Serper" (Yurok), 80, 86–89

"Coyote and Old Woman Bullhead" (Karuk), 90–97, 502–3, 520–21

"Coyote, Heron, and Lizard" (Yana), 521–22, 539n10

A Coyote Reader (Bright), 539n8

"Coyote Steals Fire" (Karuk), ethnopoetic presentation of, 31–33

"Cradleboard" (Mojave), 524–25

Crawford, James, 504

Crawford, Judith, "Cradleboard" (collector), 524–25

Creation: of animals, 277, 468, 471, 472; of humans, 279–81, 466–68, 469, 470; of plants, 278, 470

"Creation" (Eastern Pomo), 13, 260–310, 502; episodic repetition in, 41; as example of Central California creation pattern, 516, 538n2; published versions of, 265–68; songs in, 270–71; thematic structure of, 271

"The Creation" (Serrano), 35, 401–10;

alternate version of, 401, 405n2; as example of Southern California creation pattern, 520, 539n7

Creation myth patterns: Central California, 515–17; Northwestern California, 517–18; Southern California, 518–20. *See also* Destruction of the world

Creation myths. *See* Origin myths

Creation Myths of Primitive America (Curtin), 22

Creation songs (Cupeño), 57, 538n5

Crescent City, "Ragged Ass Hill" near, 79, 82–85

Crow, "Condor Steals Falcon's Wife" (Yowlumni Yokuts), 356, 357, 362

Crum, Beverly (Shoshone), 12

Cry songs (Wintu), 219, 223, 225, 230–34, 528

"Culture of the Luiseño Indians" (Sparkman), 535

Cultures, Native California: dominant pattern numbers of, 41, 53n15; geographic distribution of, 6, 573(map 1); language as embodying, 10, 563; oral literature's link to, 47–50; preservation of, 508n7; variation in documentation of, 7

Cupan languages, 411

Cupeño: burial songs, 518–19, 538n5; creation songs, 57, 538n5; "The Life of Hawk Feather: The Bear Episodes," 421–35

Cupeño language: extinction of, 411, 412; quotatives in, 424; sample passage, 423–24

Curl, Jennie, "A Selection of Wintu Songs" (singer), 178–81, 190–91

Curtin, Jeremiah, 500; *Creation Myths of Primitive America,* 22

Dances: Ball (Nomlaki), 243, 243n, 244–45; Brush (Hupa), 112; Bullhead (Nomlaki), 243n; Dream (Wintu), 179–80, 181nn2,3, 182n; Hesi (Nomlaki), 236, 238, 245, 245n, 246–47; *hisi* (Wintu), 221, 222; Jump (Hupa), 106, 110, 112; Marumda's (Eastern Pomo

Creator) instruction on, 283–84, 302–3, 305–7; Night (Yahi), 155–56, 157–58, 168–71; White Deerskin (Hupa), 106, 110. *See also* Ceremonies

Dance songs: Bear Dance song (Santa Rosa Island), 531; brush dance song (Hupa), 532; brush dance song (Luiseño), 511; Chaláawaat Song (Luiseño), vii, 416–17, 565–66; Costanoan, 532; Yahi, 170; Yurok doctor dance song, 65

Davis, Francis, account of Karuk World Renewal ceremony, 517–18

Davis, Shan (Karuk), 563

"Dawis Sapagay's Song" (Tachi Yokuts), 533–34

Dayley, Jon, 504

"The Dead People's Home" (Lake Miwok), 13, 35, 334–42, 502

De Angulo, Jaime, 501; advice to readers, 50; biography of, 263–65; "Creation" (collector and translator), 13, 260–310; fictionalized publications of, 264; *How the World Was Made,* 264, 265–66, 269–70; Karuk creation stories transcribed by, 92–93

Death song (Luiseño), 416

December's Child (Blackburn), 386

Deer: antlers as quiver (Yahi), 171; cooking (Wintu), 222–23, 227–28; "Grizzly Bear and Deer" (Yana), 25–26, 28–29, 30; hunting (Maidu), 255; hunting and skinning (Eastern Pomo), 289; killed by magic (Hupa), 112; necessity of sharing meat (Achumawi), 132–38; not eaten by one who kills deer (Cupeño), 427; shot by Apache, 476; tracks of, as sign of male power (Wintu), 197, 211; white, as sacred (Yurok), 80, 85, 87–88

Deities, in Native California religions: Aboni-ka-ha (Atsugewi), 142; anthropomorphic Creator figures (North-Central California), 268–69; Blind Old Man (Quechan), 464, 465n6; Coyote, 267, 272n4, 515, 516, 517; "dying god" (Southern California), 518–20; Eagle (Southern California), 517; Earthmaker (Maidu), 515–17;

Deities *(continued)*
  Earth Mother (Southern California),
    518; God (Christian), 340, 341;
    Kumastamxo (Quechan), 465n6,
    480–88; Kuksu (North-Central Cali-
    fornia), 268–70, 516; K'wan'-lee-shvm
    (Tolowa), 70; Kwaw (Atsugewi), 59–
    61; Kwikumat (Quechan), 464, 465n6,
    465–80; Marumda (Pomo), 267–70,
    272n4, 516; Mukat and Tamayowet
    (Cupeño), 57, 519; Paqöoktach and
    Kokiitach (Serrano), 405–10. *See also*
    Coyote
Demetracopoulou, Dorothy, 501; "Loon
    Woman" (collector), 192–218; "A
    Selection of Wintu Songs" (collector
    and translator), 178–91, 180n1; Wintu
    Dream songs, 20n9, 181–84
Destruction of the world: by fire, 284–
    87; by flood, 281–83, 468, 471–72, 476,
    481; by whirlwind, 296–300; by snow
    and ice, 291–93
Devils: "The Devil Who Died Laughing"
    (Karuk), 98–103, 522; excerpt from
    "The Čiq'neq's Myth" (Ventureño
    Chumash), 345; "It Was Scratching"
    (Hupa), 107, 113–14, 522; as sorcerers,
    99, 522; stories about, 99, 522
"The Devil Who Died Laughing" (Karuk),
    35, 98–103, 522; ethnopoetic structure of,
    99–102
Dictation, phonetic/verbatim, 23, 51n1;
    limitations of, 502; lines in texts de-
    rived from, 53n12; selections collected
    by, 16(table 2), 502–3
Diegueño Eagle Ceremony songs, 20n9
Dixie Valley, 140; people, conflict with
    Klamath people, 142–51
Dixon, Roland B., 501; "Mad Bat"
    (collector), 248–59
Doctors (shamans): "Dawis Sapagay's
    Song" (Tachi Yokuts), 36, 533–34;
    death by gunshot wounds (hupa),
    110–11; dream doctor (Nomlaki),
    238; dreamers as (Quechan [Yuma]),
    462–63, 465n4, 474–75; "Indian
    Medicine-Men" (Yana; excerpt), 526–
    27; Lake Miwok, 339–40; Mabel

McKay as "sucking doctor," 324–25;
    relationships healed by (Achumawi),
    129, 132–38. *See also* Dreamers
"The Dog Girl" (Ineseño Chumash), 35,
    382–95; parallelism in, 45–46; repeti-
    tion in, 46, 386; songs in, 394–95, 528
Dogs: "The Dog Girl" (Ineseño Chu-
    mash), 35, 382–95; talking (Tolowa),
    69–70, 71
Dollar, Elizabeth (Southern Pomo), 313
Dove, "Condor Steals Falcon's Wife"
    (Yowlumni Yokuts), 356, 357
Drake, Sir Francis, 500
Dream Dance cult, 179
Dreamers: Lake Miwok, 338, 339, 340,
    341; Mojave, 437, 438, 439, 440;
    Nomlaki, 235–47; Quechan, 462–
    63, 465n4, 474–75. *See also* Doctors
    (shamans)
Dreams: "How I Became a Dreamer"
    (Nomlaki), 235–47; "Indian Medicine-
    Men" (Yana), 526–27; of Mabel McKay
    (Cache Creek Pomo), 324–26; Marum-
    da (Eastern Pomo Creator) sees state
    of people on earth, 281, 291–92, 293,
    296; role of, in Quechan religion, 462;
    as source of authority for narration
    (Mojave), 437, 440; of white people
    coming (Cache Creek Pomo), 331–32;
    Yana spell for girl wanting husband,
    125
Dream songs (Wintu), 20n9, 179–80,
    181–84, 181nn2,3
Du Bel, Dum (Wintu), 183
Du Bois, Constance, 501
Du Bois, Cora, 179, 180, 192–93
Ducks: dream about (Nomlaki), 244;
    mallard, feather in feather belts, 236

Eagle: "Condor Steals Falcon's Wife"
    (Yowlumni Yokuts), 349, 356, 357, 359,
    362; "The Contest between Men and
    Women" (Tübatulabal), 365, 368; in
    South-Central creation myths, 517
Eagle Ceremony songs, Diegueño, 20n9
Earthdiver motif, 515–16
Earthmaker, 515–17
Earthquake, as causing tidal wave, 71–72

Elders: contribution of, to oral literature documentation, 504–5; as diminishing resource for languages, 497, 506n3; necessity of sharing food with (Achumawi), 130–31, 132–38

Elem Rancheria, 330

Elliott, Eric, 51n2; "A Harvest of Songs from Villiana Calac Hyde" (collector), 411–20; on Villiana Calac Hyde (Luiseño), 411–13

Ellis, Ross (Yowlumni Yokuts), 350 (fig. 9); "Condor Steals Falcon's Wife" (narrator), 349–51, 356–62

Emeneau, Murray, 504

Enmai (Mount Emily), 70n1, 71, 73–74

Episodic repetition, 40–43, 46–47, 53n17; in "Creation" (Eastern Pomo), 41; pattern numbers as element of, 41, 43, 53nn15,18; in "A Story of Lizard" (Yahi), 41, 155–58; in "The Trials of Young Hawk" (Southern Pomo), 41. *See also* Repetition

Esselen language, 7, 547, 567n6

Essene, Frank J., 239

Ethnographic texts, examples of: "Cradleboard" (Mojave), 524; "Four Songs from Grace McKibbin" (Wintu), 224–34; "Indian Medicine Men" (Yana; excerpt), 526–27; "Preserving Shellfish" (Kashaya Pomo), 525; "The Soul" narrative (Quechan; excerpt), 399–400; World Renewal narrative (Karuk; excerpt), 517–18; "You come upon a place" (Yurok), 63. *See also* Narrative

"Ethnography of the Yuma Indians" (Forde), 535

Ethnolinguistic translations, 25–27, 51nn4,5; example of, 25–27, 51n3; selections exemplifying, 35; of songs, 530, 541n20

Ethnopoetic translations, 27–35, 52nn6,7; example of, 28–31, 52nn8,9; integrated approach to, 31–33, 35; lines in, 33–34, 52n11, 53n12; prosodic approach to, 31, 35, 52n10; selections exemplifying, 35; structural approach to, 31, 35

Europeans: Atsugewi restricted by, 61;

creation of (Quechan), 475; folk stories of, 36; foreknowledge of (Cache Creek Pomo), 331–32; Hupa grandfather wounded by, 111; Karuk culture disrupted by, 91; Lake Miwok contact with, 335; Native California cultures destroyed by contact with, 7; Tolowa life changed by, 68; Tübatulabal encounters with, 364; Yokuts contact with, 348. *See also* Gold Rush; Mission system

"Evening Star" songs (Karuk), 530

Facing page formats, 51n4

Fages, Pedro, 382

Falcon, "Condor Steals Falcon's Wife" (Yowlumni Yokuts), 349, 351, 357–62

Fall River: Achumawi, 127; Atsugewi, 143, 150

Fauna, inventory of (Eastern Pomo), 307–9

Faye, Paul-Louis, 518; Cupeño creation and burial songs (collector), 57, 518–19, 538n5; "The Life of Hawk Feather: The Bear Episodes" (collector), 421–35

Feathers: in basket designs (Lake Miwok), 335; belts made of (Nomlaki), 235–36; flicker, as nose ornament (Tolowa), 73

Federal boarding schools. *See* Boarding-school system

Fender, Jim (Wintu), 200n2

Fieldmice, "The Trials of Young Hawk" (Southern Pomo), 320–21

Field notes: Harrington's, 7, 19n3, 383; unpublished, 7–8, 19n3

Field trip, Mason's Costanoan, 495–99, 506n2, 507n5

Fieldwork, accounts of: Achumawi (Nevin), 129; Central Pomo (Mithun), 24–25; Cupeño (J. Hill), 424–25; Karuk (Bright), 98; Luiseño (Elliott), 413; Maidu (Shipley), 248–49; Mojave (A. Kroeber), 438–40; Southern Pomo (Oswalt), 313; Yurok (Robins), 77–78

Fieldwork, relationship between people involved in, 24–25. *See also* Collectors

Finck, Franz Nikolaus, 384

Fish: Marumda (Eastern Pomo Creator) teaches how to catch, 290–91; "Preserving Shellfish" (Kashaya Pomo), 525–26

Fishing nets (Eastern Pomo), 294–95, 302

Fishing practices (Tolowa), 68–69

"Five Yurok Songs: A Musical and Textual Analysis" (Robins and McCloud), 65

Flicker feathers, used as nose ornament (Tolowa), 73

"Flint Boy" (Yana), 523

Flood, caused by tidal wave (Tolowa), 71–76

Food: Achumawi, 128; Chimariko, 119, 120; Chumash, 390; Eastern Pomo, 276, 279, 280, 281, 289–91, 294, 295, 296; Hupa, 104, 113; Karuk, 90, 94, 102; Lake Miwok, 334–35; Maidu, 251, 253; Mojave, 444, 449, 450, 452, 453, 456; Quechan (Yuma), 471; shared with elders (Achumawi), 132–38; shared with strangers (Chumash, Eastern Pomo), 304, 390; theft of (Karuk), 94–95; Tolowa, 67, 68, 74; Tübatulabal, 365, 370, 372, 373, 375, 376; Wintu, 204, 227–28; Yurok, 77. *See also specific plants and animals*

Forde, C. Darryl: "Ethnography of the Yuma Indians," 535; Quechan funeral speech, 536, 543–44

Formulaic repetition, 43–44

Formulas, story opening and closing: in Karuk, 93–94, 520–21; in Wintu, 123, 196, 201, 218

"Four Songs from Grace McKibbin" (Wintu), 12, 35, 219–34, 528, 530

Fox, "Kwaw Labors to Form a World" (Atsugewi), 59–61

Franco, Darlene (Wukchumni), 564

Freeland, Lucy S., 335, 501

Freeland, Nancy, 260, 261, 263, 264

Frémont, John Charles, 500

"The Friars at Kiliwa," 554–55, 568–69n15

Frog: "The Creation" (Serrano), 405, 405n2, 408; as daughter of Kwikumat (Quechan [Yuma]), 476, 477, 480;

"Naponoha (Cocoon Man)" (Atsugewi), 143, 147

Gallagher, Maym Benner (Maidu), 248–49

Gamble, Geoffrey, 504; on Yokuts, 347–51; Yokuts language work by, 348

Gambling: Maidu, 251, 257; Nomlaki, 243–44, 243n; Yurok, 83

Gambling songs: Costanoan, 532; Miwok, 529; Yokuts, 496

Games: hoop game (Chumash), 388; hoop and poles (Mojave), 447, 452; tag (Eastern Pomo children's), 283

Gayton, Anna, 348, 501; "Areal Affiliations of California Folktales," 515, 523

Geese, "Flying North with the Geese" (Wintu), 223, 228–30

Gender roles: baskets made by both men and women (Pomo), 261–62; "The Contest between Men and Women" (Tübatulabal), 363, 365–81; Marumda's (Eastern Pomo Creator) teachings on, 289–91; for performing verbal art, 513–14

Generosity, consequences of not sharing deer meat (Achumawi), 132–38

Genocide: in California, 553–54, 556–59; of Tolowa, 68

Genre, oral-literary, 514; of selections, 15(table 1). *See also* Narrative; Oratory; Songs; *specific genres*

Genres, native: a'alxi (Cupeño; "telling histories"), 422; cry songs (Wintu), 219, 223; "devil" stories, 107, 522; dream songs (Wintu), 179; girls' puberty songs (Wintu), 105n1; *itš-kanavk* (Mojave; "great-telling"), 437; *nini* (Wintu; "love songs"), 187n2, 219, 222

Gepigul (Eastern Pomo), 261

Ghost Dance, 336

Gifford, Edward W., 501; *California Indian Nights Entertainments*, 513; "Central Miwok Ceremonies," 535; Mamie Offield's work with, 98

Global form/content parallelism, 53n18

Goddard, Pliny Earle, 105, 501

Gold Rush: impact on Native California cultures, 91, 497, 556; geographic area impacted by, 507n4, 553

Golla, Victor, 504; "The Boy Who Grew Up at Taʼkʼimiłding" (collector and translator), 104–110; "Grandfather's Ordeal" (collector and translator), 107, 110–11; "It Was Scratching" (collector and translator), 107, 113–14; "The Stolen Woman" (collector and translator), 107, 112–13; Yahi Translation Project, 161n1

Gomez, María, 496

Gophers, "The Trials of Young Hawk" (Southern Pomo), 319–20

Gourds, grown by Quechan (Yuma), 471

Grace, Alma, 335

"Grandfather's Ordeal" (Hupa), 107, 110–11

Grant, Samson, 129, 130, 131

Gregory, Dick (Wintu), 184

Grief. See Mourning

Griffith, Manuela, 421

Grindstone Creek Reservation, 235, 239, 246

"Grizzly Bear and Deer" (Yana), 540n12; ethnolinguistic presentation of, 25–27, 51n3; ethnopoetic presentation of, 28–31, 52nn8,9; geographic distribution of, 523

Ground-Squirrel, "Creation" (Eastern Pomo), 299

Guerrero, Edna (Northern Pomo), 562–63

Guide to Early Field Recordings (1900–1949) at the Lowie Museum of Anthropology (Keeling), 535

Haas, Mary R., University of California at Berkeley Department of Linguistics work of, 6, 503–4

Halpern, Abraham M., 504; studies of Quechan (Yuma) language, 313; "The Trials of Young Hawk" (collector), 311–23

Hánc'ibyjim (Tom Young; Maidu), 506; "Mad Bat" (narrator), 248–59; Maidu creation myth (excerpt), 515–16

Hansen, Daisy (Pomo), 324

Harrie, Benonie (Karuk), 92

Harrie, Margaret (Karuk), "Coyote and Old Woman Bullhead" (narrator), 90–97

Harrington, John Peabody, 501; "An Account of Origins" (collector and translator), 20n6, 22, 461–89; "The Bear Girl" (collector), 115–22; biography of, 116, 383–84; Chumash work by, 382, 383, 384–85, "The Dog Girl" (collector), 382–95; early sound recordings by, 501–2; Ohlone culture fieldnotes of, 48–49; unpublished fieldnotes of, 7, 19n3; on urgency of Indian language fieldwork, 497, 506n3; Yokuts language work by, 348

"A Harvest of Songs from Villiana Calac Hyde" (Luiseño), 51n2, 411–20, 530

Hat Creek, Atsugewi, 129, 140

Hat Creek people. See Atsugewi

Hawk, sharp-shinned, "The Trials of Young Hawk" (Southern Pomo), 317–23

Hazelnuts, as food (Chimariko), 120

Heizer, Robert, "Mythology: Regional Patterns and History of Research," 513

Hesi: dance ceremony (Nomlaki), 236–37, 234n1; oration (Patwin), 536

Hewett, Edgar Lee, 384

Hill, Dan, 105

Hill, Jane, 504; "The Life of Hawk Feather: The Bear Episodes" (collector and translator), 421–35

Hill, Kenneth C., 504; "The Creation" (collector and translator), 401–10

Hill, Tom, 105

Hinton, Leanne, 12, 385–86, 504, 564; "Four Songs from Grace McKibbin" (analysis and transcription), 219–34, 530; on songs in Yuman stories, 528; "A Story of Lizard" (translator), 152–77; Yahi Translation Project, 161n1

Historical epic, selection classified as, 15(table 1)

Hokan languages, 90; Chimariko as, 115; speakers of, geographical retreat of, 128

Hokan stock, 547, 567n6; age of, 549, 567n8; geographic expansion of, 550, 568n10; similarities among language families of, 548–49, 566–67n4

Homer, Joe. *See* Tsuyukweráu (Joe Homer)

Hoopa reservation, 68, 104

Hoopa Valley, 104, 105, 106, 107, 110–11

Hopland Reservation, 313

"How I Became a Dreamer" (Nomlaki), 235–47

"How My Father Found the Deer" (Achumawi), 35, 127–38

How the World Was Made (de Angulo), 264, 265–66, 269–70

Huchnom language, scant documentation of, 7

Humans, creation of, 466–68, 469, 470

Hupa: "The Boy Who Grew Up at Taʼkʼimiłding," 104–110; brush dance song, 532; geographical territory, 104–5; "Grandfather's Ordeal," 107, 110–11; "It Was Scratching," 107, 113–14; "The Stolen Woman," 107, 112–13

Hupa language, sample passage, 107–8

Hyde, Villiana Calac (Luiseño), 7, 51n2, 506; "Chaláawaat Song," vii, 416–17, 565–66; "A Harvest of Songs from Villiana Calac Hyde" (singer and translator), 411–20, 530; *An Introduction to the Luiseño Language,* 412, 413; language work by, 411–13; mourning song, 519–20, 538n6; *Yumáyk Yumáyk,* 413, 414n1

Hymes, Dell: ethnopoetics pioneered by, 27, 31; lines as defined by, 52n11; "Loon Woman" (translator), 192–218; measured voice concept of, 47; rhetorical patterns identified by, 31, 52nn8,9

Ikxaréeyavs (Karuk First People), 91–92, 98

Imaginary beings: with four legs and two heads (Cache Creek Pomo), 331–32; ghost, "The Dead People's Home (Lake Miwok)," 338; monster in "Cre-

ation" (Eastern Pomo), 305; monster stories, 523, 540n12

Incest: as "behaving badly" (Eastern Pomo), 270, 281–82, 284–85, 291–92, 296, 297, 298; in "Loon Woman" (Wintu), 195, 204–6

"The Incredible Survival of Coyote" (Snyder), 539n8

Incremental repetition, 46

"Indian Medicine-Men" (Yana; excerpt), 526–27, 540n16

"Indian Myths of South Central California" (A. Kroeber), 515

Indians in Overalls (de Angulo), 264

Indian Tales (de Angulo), 264

Indian wars, 556–59

Ineseño Chumash. *See* Chumash

"Institution myths," 518

Interlinear formats, 25–26, 51n4

Interpreter translation, 22; limitations of, 22–23; selections collected by, 16(table 2), 22

"In the Desert with Hipahipa" (Mojave), 20n6, 22–23, 436–60

An Introduction to the Luiseño Language (Hyde), 412, 413

Inupiaq language, 552

Invitation string (Maidu), 251, 256

Inyo-Kutavêre: description of, 440; "In the Desert with Hipahipa" (narrator), 20n6, 22, 436–60

Ishi (Yahi), 155(fig. 3), 503(fig. 12), 506; biography of, 152–54; "A Story of Lizard" (narrator), 152–77

Ishi in Two Worlds (T. Kroeber), 152

"It is said." *See* Quotatives

"It Was Scratching" (Hupa), 107, 113–14, 522

Jack, Frances (Central Pomo), 24–25

Jackson, Louisa, "It Was Scratching" (narrator), 105–6, 107, 113–14

Jacobs, Daisy (Karuk), 563

Jacobsen, William, 504

Jimsonweed leaves, to encourage dreaming (Quechan [Yuma]), 463

Johnson, Maggie, 335, 336, 338, 339

Jones, Jack, 439(fig. 11); "In the Desert

with Hipahipa" (interpreter), 20n6, 22–23, 436–60
Jones, Johnny (Chawchila Yokuts), "Visit to the Land of the Dead" (narrator), 348–49, 352–55

Karuk: "Coyote and Old Woman Bullhead," 90–97; "Coyote Steals Fire," 31–33; "The Devil Who Died Laughing," 98–103; ethnopoetic structure of myths, 99–102; "Evening Star" songs, 530; geographical territory, 90; surviving population, 91; World Renewal ceremony, 517–18, 538n4
Karuk language: Hokan affiliation of, 546; loss of, 563–64; opening and closing formulas for stories, 93–94, 520–21; sample passage, 93–94
Kashaya, "Preserving Shellfish," 525–26
K'asna vines, 157, 165–66
Keeling, Richard, 504; Guide to Early Field Recordings (1900–1949) at the Lowie Museum of Anthropology, 535
Kendall, Martha, 504
Kenyon, Mary (Wintu), 184
Key, Mary, 412
Kiliwa: "The Friars at Kiliwa," 554–55, 568–69n15; "When I Have Donned My Crest of Stars," 493
Killdeer, "Loon Woman" (Wintu), 197, 201n6, 214–18
Killeli (Yosemite Miwok), 506
Kingfisher, addressed in song (Wikchamni), 343
Klamath people, conflict with Dixie Valley people, 142–51
Klamath River: Karuk, 90, 92, 104; Yurok, 77, 86, 104
Klar, Kathryn, 504; on Ineseño Chumash, 382–86
Knight, Henry, 339–40
Knight, James (Lake Miwok), 504–5, 506; "The Dead People's Home" (narrator), 13, 334–42
Knight, John, 335
Knight, Mary, 262
Kokiitach (Serrano deity), 406, 407, 408
Kroeber, Alfred L., 263, 503(fig. 12);

Chumash work by, 382, 384; on "cycles" pattern in Central California creation myths, 538n2; ethnolinguistic presentation used by, 27; "In the Desert with Hipahipa" (collector), 20n6, 22, 436–60; "Indian Myths of South Central California," 515; on "institution myths," 518; as Ishi's employer, 153–54; on limitations of interpreter translation, 22–23; Patwin Hesi oration (collector), 536–37, 541n24; and Susan Brandenstein Park, 139, 140; as source of Tübatulabal population estimate, 364; University of California at Berkeley Department of Anthropology work of, 6, 92, 495, 500–502, 509n9; Yokuts language work by, 348
Kroeber, Theodora: Ishi in Two Worlds, 152; "Loon Woman" version, 198; "Some Qualities of Indian Stories," 538n1
Kuksu (Eastern Pomo spirit figure), 266; "Creation," 273–310; Marumda contrasted with, 268–70
Kuksu religion, 268, 538n2
Kumastamxo (Quechan [Yuma] deity), 462, 463, 465n6; "An Account of Origins," 470–89
"Kwaw Labors to Form a World" (Atsugewi), 14, 59–61, 516
Kwikumat (Quechan [Yuma] deity), 463, 465n6; "An Account of Origins: The Age and Death of Kwikumat," 465–80; "Kwikumat Became Sick," 3

Laird, Carobeth, 501
Laird, George (Chemehuevi), 506
Lake Miwok. See Miwok, Lake
Lamarr, John, "Naponoha (Cocoon Man)" (narrator), 14, 139–51
Lamb, Sidney, 504
Lame Billy of Weitspus (Yurok), 506
Lang, Julian, 51n2; "Coyote and Old Woman Bullhead" (translator), 90–97
Langacker, Ronald, 412
Langdon, Margaret, 20n9, 412, 504

Language diversity, 566n2, 574(map 2); California's ecology as enabling, 552, 568n13; extent of, 6, 545; geographical history of, 549–51; within superstocks, 549

Language families, 546–52, 547–48(table 5); geographic distribution of, 575(map 3). *See also* Language stocks

Language revival, 6–7, 412, 562–65

Languages: bilingual format for collection of oral literature, 19n5; boarding schools' impact on, 560–62; current status of, 545, 552, 577(map 5); dialects in, 545–46; elders as diminishing resource for, 497, 506n3; as embodying culture, 10, 563; geographic distribution of, 573(map 1); multiple, in "Creation" (Eastern Pomo) myth, 297, 300, 302; of narration of selections, 18–19(table 4); prehistory of, 549–52, 576(map 4); pronunciation guide for, xix–xxi; renaissance of, 562–66. *See also specific languages*

Language samples: Achumawi, 130–31; Cupeño, 423–24; Hupa, 107–8; Ineseño Chumash, 386; Karuk, 93–94; Lake Miwok, 337; Maidu, 251; Northern Yana, 521–22; Serrano, 402, 403–5; Southern Pomo, 315–16; Wintu, 199–200; Yahi, 159

Language stocks, 546–49, 566–67n4; geographic distribution of, 575(map 3); history and geographical expansion of, 549–52. *See also* Language families

Lark, "Naponoha (Cocoon Man)" (Atsugewi), 146, 147, 148

Lassen, Mount: Táyyamanim (West Mountain), 250, 258; Ye:dí:jana, 130

Legal system, Tolowa, 67–68

Legends, as genre of narrative, 514

Lévi-Strauss, Claude, 40; "Loon Woman" analysis by, 198, 201n6

Librado, Fernando (Ventureño Chumash), 506

"Life and Culture of the Hupa" (Goddard), 105

"The Life of Hawk Feather: The Bear Episodes" (Cupeño), 35, 421–35, 523; problems in interpreting, 424–26; songs in, 430, 432, 435, 528

"Lightning song" (Quechan [Yuma]; excerpt), 529–30

Line breaks in ethnopoetic presentations, criteria for, 34, 52n11, 53n12; "The Bear Girl," 118; "The Contest between Men and Women," 367–68n1; "Coyote Steals Fire," 31–33; "Creation" (Serrano), 402–3; "Four Songs from Grace McKibben," 220–21; "From 'The Life of Hawk Feather,'" 426; "Mad Bat," 252; "A Story of Lizard," 161n5. *See also* Typographical conventions

Lizards: "The Contest between Men and Women" (Tübatulabal), 366, 370, 372; Long-Tailed, 155–77; "A Story of Lizard" (Yahi), 162–77

Loeb, Edwin, 263

Loether, Chris, on Tübatulabal, 363–68

Loon: "Loon Woman" (Wintu), 192–218; personality of, 39

"Loon Woman" (Wintu), 192–218, 502; geographic distribution of, 523; interpretations of, 196–99; numerical patterns in, 43, 194–95; repetition in, 41–43, 44, 53n17

Lord, Alfred, 46

Love songs: Costanoan, 532; Wintu, 187–90, 187n, 219, 221–23, 224–30

Lowie, Robert, 139

Lucas, Bun (Kashaya), 7

Luiseño: "Chaláawaat Song," vii, 416–17, 565–66; "A Harvest of Songs from Villiana Calac Hyde," 411–20; lecture at girls' puberty ceremony, 535–36; mourning song, 519–20, 538n6; "Women's Brush Dance Song," 511

Luiseño Dictionary (Bright), 413

Luiseño language, 411–13

Luthin, Herbert W.: on "Creation" (Eastern Pomo), 260–72; "A Story of Lizard" (translator), 152–77; Yahi Translation Project, 161n1

Macarro, Mark, (Luiseño), 564

"Mad Bat" (Maidu), 35, 39, 248–59, 523, 540n12

Magic: antelope killed without bow and arrow (Mojave), 448–49; deer killed with supernatural basket (Hupa), 112

Maidu: ceremonial acorn song, 491; creation myth (excerpt), 515–16; customs of, 250–51; "Mad Bat," 248–59

Maidu language, 252n1; sample passage, 251

Makahmo 'Salmonhole' dialect of Pomo language, 312, 313

Ma'kat'da (Old Coyote of Atsugewi), 59–61

Manriquez, L. Frank (Tongva/Acagchme), 564

Manual dictation. See Dictation, phonetic/verbatim

Margolin, Malcolm, 141

Marr, Jack, 502

Marriage: Chumash, 391–92; exogamous (Eastern Pomo, Tolowa), 67, 270; food as dowry (Eastern Pomo), 304; intimacy resulting in (Mojave), 454; multiple wives (Maidu), 250

Marsh, Harry (Wintu), 506; "A Selection of Wintu Songs" (singer), 178–83, 181n, 185–88, 190

Marsh, Sadie (Wintu), 506; "Loon Woman" version, 198; "A Selection of Wintu Songs" (singer), 178–81, 184, 184n, 189, 191

Martin, Robert (Mojave), "Cradleboard" (narrator), 524–25

Martin, Sarah Morongo (Serrano), "The Creation" (narrator), 401–10, 520, 539n7

Marumda (Eastern Pomo Creator): Benson's portrayal of, 266–67, 272n3; Coyote's relationship to, 267, 272n4, 516; "Creation," 273–310; Kuksu contrasted with, 268–70

Marxokuvek (first Quechan Indian), 464; bitten by rattlesnake, 473–74; creations by, 469, 470, 471; death of, 487

Mason, James Alden, 501; Costanoan fieldwork, 495–99, 506n2, 507nn5,6

Master/Apprentice Language Learning Program, 564–65

McCloud River, 178, 189

McKay, Charlie, 332

McKay, Mabel (Pomo), 325(fig. 8), 506; biography of, 324–26; "The Woman Who Loved a Snake" (storyteller), 324–33

McKibbin, Grace (Wintu), 220(fig. 5), 506; "Four Songs from Grace McKibbin" (singer and narrator), 219–34

McLendon, Sally, 504; on William Benson, 261, 263, 272n2

Meadowlark: "Creation" (Eastern Pomo), 293; Maidu creation myth, 516; Shasta version of "Loon Woman," 201n6

Measured verse, 31, 47, 426

Medicine men/women. See Doctors (shamans)

Me'dilding (Hoopa Valley village), 107, 112–13

Medley, Stephen, 509n10

Melon, as food for Quechan (Yuma), 471

Merriam, C. Hart, 501

Mescal, Mojave, 449, 450

Mesquite, cradleboard made of (Mojave), 524

Mice: fieldmice, "The Trials of Young Hawk" (Southern Pomo), 320–21; "Naponoha (Cocoon Man)" (Atsugewi), 142, 143, 144–48

Middletown Rancheria, 334, 335

Mihilakawna dialect of Eastern Pomo, 312, 313

Milkweed, rolled into string (Eastern Pomo), 294

Miller, Wick, 504

Miranda, Mike (Tübatulabal), 506; "The Contest between Men and Women" (narrator), 363–81

Miranda, Steban, 363

Mission system, 554–55; California Indian resistance to, 555; geographic area impacted by, 507n4, 553; Native Californians' accounts of, 554–55, 568–69n15

Mithun, Marianne, on relationship in linguistic fieldwork, 24–25

Miwok: gambling songs, 529; Northern Sierra, Orpheus Myth, 336

Miwok, Lake, "The Dead People's Home," 13, 334–42; geographic territory, 334; surviving population, 335

Miwok languages, 334, 335; sample passage (Lake Miwok), 337

Mixco, Mauricio, 504

Modoc, puberty song, 531

Mojave: "Cradleboard," 524–25; "In the Desert with Hipahipa," 20n6, 436–60; songs in stories of, 540n17

Moki, 238

Monsters: in "Creation" (Eastern Pomo), 305; monster stories, 523, 540n12

Morongo, Rosa (Serrano), 401, 405n1

Morongo Indian Reservation, 401

Mortar and pestle (Eastern Pomo), 290, 302

Moshinsky, Julius, 504

Mountain lions (pumas), 307; as characters, 372–73, 380

Mourning: burial songs (Cupeño), 518–19, 538n5; Chawchila Yokuts, 352; cry song (Wintu), 219, 223, 225, 230–34, 528; hair cut (Mojave and Yahi), 165, 452; Luiseño mourning song, 519–20, 538n6; tails cut by animals (Quechan [Yuma]), 479

Mouth-bow song (Yahi), 531

Munro, Pamela, 504

Myth: creation patterns, cultural classification based on, 515–20; excerpts from, 28–29, 30, 32–33, 512–22; flood (Tolowa), 71–76; as genre of narrative, 514; geography and (Hupa), 104; "institution," 518; literary and linguistic features of, 520–22, 539nn9,10, 539–40n11; selections classified as, 15(table 1); songs in, 528, 540n17; vs. tales, 515. See also Origin myths; Orpheus myth

"Mythology: Regional Patterns and History of Research" (Heizer), 513

Myth time: in Karuk, 93; grammatical reflections of, 521–22

Na-Déné stock, 548, 549

Nakam Valley (Big Meadows), 250, 259

Naming, 485–86

"Naponoha (Cocoon Man)" (Atsugewi), 14, 35, 139–51, 502

Narrative, 12, 514–27; categories of, 514–15; Coyote stories, 15(table 1), 520–22, 539n8; epic, 437, 440–41; ethnographic texts, 523–27; institution myths, 106, 518; opening and closing formulas, Karuk, 93–94, 520–21; opening and closing formulas, Wintu, 123, 196, 201, 218; oral reading of, 386; poetry vs. prose debate, 33–35; repetition in, 41, 155–58; set in time of creation, 520; settings and contexts for, 514; songs in, 528, 540n17; translation of, 159–61, 161nn4,5; Trickster cycles, 249. See also Myth; Stories; Tales

Narrative, examples of less well-known genres: autobiography, 241–47; Coyote stories, 32–33, 368–81, 521–22; "devil" stories, 102–3, 113–14; epic, 443–460; ethnographic texts, 63, 224–34, 399–400, 517–18, 524, 525, 526–27; family history, 110–11, 388–95, 554–55; hero tales, 426–31, 431–35; institution myths, 109–10; legends, 112–13, 118–22, 345, 533–54; oral history, 557–58; personal reminiscence, 81–82, 82–85, 132–38, 328–33, 338–42, 493, 560–62, 563–64; tales, 162–67

Narrative genres. See Coyote stories; Ethnographic texts; Myth; Narrative; Origin myths; Stories; Tales

Native California Language Restoration Workshop, 565, 569n25

Native California Network, 564

Native Californians: contributing to oral literary work, 6–7, 19n2, 24–25, 504–6; population decline of, 553; private documentation of culture by, 8. See also Elders; names of specific Native Californians

Nevin, Bruce: "How My Father Found the Deer" (collector and translator), 127–38; Yahi Translation Project, 161n1

Newman, Stanley, 501; "Condor Steals Falcon's Wife" (collector and translator), 349–51, 351n1, 356–62; "Visit to the Land of the Dead" (collector and translator), 348–49, 351n1, 352–55; Yokuts language work by, 348

News from Native California, 141

Nichols, Mike, 504

Nisenan prayer, 55

Noble, Sally, 117(fig. 2); "The Bear Girl" (narrator), 115–22

Nolasquez, Roscinda, "The Life of Hawk Feather: The Bear Episodes" (narrator), 421–35

Nome Lackee Reservation, 238–39

Nomlaki: birds of, 197, 201n7; "How I Became a Dreamer," 235–47

Northwestern California: creation myth pattern, 517–18; linguistic prehistory of, 351

Noweedehe, 236, 242, 243

Numerical patterning. *See* Pattern numbers

Numic languages, 552

Ochurte, Rufino (PaiPai/Kiliwa), 506; "The Friars at Kiliwa" (narrator), 554–55, 568–69n15; "When I Have Donned My Crest of Stars," 493

Offield, Mamie, "The Devil Who Died Laughing" (narrator), 98–103

Ohlone culture, 48–49

Okrand, Mark, 504

"Old California" language families, 550–51

Oral literature, Native California: anthropomorphism in, 38–40; categories of, 514; confusion when first reading, 35–37, 50, 53n14; continuing growth of, 8–10, 48; creation myth classification of, 515–20; culture's link to, 47–50, 54n23; difficulties in producing collections of, 6–10; Europeanized collections of, 509n10; gender of performers of, 513–14; history of documentation of, 499–506, 509nn9–11, 509–10n12; overviews of, 513; parallelism in, 44–46; pattern numbers in, 41, 43, 53nn15,18; pronunciation guide for, xix–xxi; repetition in, 40–44, 46–47, 53n17. *See also* Narrative; Oratory; Songs

"Oral Literature of California and the Intermountain Region" (Bright), 513

Oratory, 12, 535–38; sources of, 535; vocal and rhythmic characteristics of, 536–37. *See also* Speeches

Oratory, examples of, by genre: interviews, 63, 562–63; prayers, 55; speeches, 535–36, 536–37, 543–44; spells, 125

Oregos (rock at mouth of Klamath River), 80, 86

Origin myths: selections classified as, 15(table 1); Atsugewi, 59–61; Eastern Pomo, 273–310; Hupa, 109–10; Maidu (excerpt), 515–16; Quechan, 465–89; Serrano, 405–6, 406–10; Tolowa, 71–76. *See also* Creation

Orpheus myth, 13, 335; Chawchila Yokuts version, 13, 336, 348–49, 351n1, 352–55; Northern Sierra Miwok version, 336. *See also* "The Dead People's Home" (Lake Miwok)

Oswalt, Robert L., 504; "Preserving Shellfish" (collector), 525–26; "The Trials of Young Hawk" (translator), 311–23

Ouzel, "Mad Bat" (Maidu), 39, 250, 259

Owl: in doctor's dream (Northern Yana), 527; as messenger of death (Yurok), 79, 81–82; screech, hired to track deer (Achumawi), 136, 138

Paqöoktach (Serrano deity), 406, 407

Pal Atingve 'Hot Springs' (Warner's Hot Springs), 422

Parallelism, 44–47; global form/content parallelism, 53n18

Park, Susan Brandenstein, 501

Parrish, Essie (Kashaya Pomo), "Preserving Shellfish" (narrator), 525–26

Pattern numbers, 41, 43, 53nn15,18; in "Grizzly Bear and Deer" (Northern Yana), 29–31; identified by Dell Hymes, 31, 52nn8,9; Lake Miwok, 340; in "Loon Woman" (Wintu), 194–95; Pomo, 314

Patwin, Hesi oration, 536

Penutian stock, 547–48; geographic expansion of, 550, 567–68n9; similarities among language families of, 548–49; speakers of, contact with Hokan speakers, 128

Performances: date of, of selections, 17(table 3); "live" vs. "in studio," 20n8; personal and period style's effect on recording of, 501, 509n11; selections based on, 11; transformed into printed word, 21–25

Performers: contribution of, 504; gender of, 513–14; preservation of traditions by, 499, 509n8

Perry, Jean: "Blind Bill and the Owl" (collector), 78–79, 81–82; "Ragged Ass Hill" (collector), 79, 82–85; Yahi Translation Project, 161n1; "The Young Man from Serper" (collector of alternate version), 78, 79–80, 85–89, 505

Personal reminiscences: absence of quotatives in, 522; as genre of narrative, 514; selections classified as, 15(table 1)

Philologists, 383

Phonetic dictation. See Dictation, phonetic/verbatim

Pikva (Karuk creation stories), 91–93

Pine-nuts: Tübatulabal, 365, 370, 375; Yahi, 155, 156, 162, 172–73, 176–77

Pine trees, Serrano, 410

Pitkin, Harvey, 193, 504

Pit River: Achumawi, 127, 128; Wintu, 178

Pit River people. See Achumawi

Plants, created by Marumda (Eastern Pomo Creator), 276, 277, 278. See also specific plants

Poetic repetition, 44

Pomo: baskets woven by, 261–63, 312, 313, 324–25, 569n21; birds in narratives of, 523; Central Pomo, relationship developed doing linguistic fieldwork among, 24–25; quotatives in, 316; geographical territory, 311; historical overview of, 311–12; Marumda (deity) of, 266–67, 272nn3,4; Northeastern Pomo, scant documentation of, 7; pre-Contact population, 311–12

Pomo, selections and excerpts: Cache Creek Pomo, "The Woman Who Loved a Snake," 324–33; Eastern Pomo, "Creation," 13, 260–310; Kashaya Pomo, "Preserving Shellfish," 525–26; Southern Pomo, "The Trials of Young Hawk," 311–23

Pomoan languages, 546; 311, 312; Hokan affiliation of, 311; quotatives in, 316; preservation of, 562–63; Southern Pomo, 312, 313, 314–16

Popejoy, Bill, 182n

Portolá, Gaspar de, 500

Potatoes, as food for Eastern Pomo, 279, 281

Powers, Stephen, Tribes of California, 500

Prayer, Nisenan, 55

Prehistory, linguistic, 549–52, 576(map 4)

Preservation: of languages, 6–7, 412, 562–65; of traditions, 499–500, 508n7, 509n8

Prickly pear, as food for Quechan (Yuma), 471

Puberty songs: Modoc, 531; Wintu, 185–87, 185nn, 186n, 527–28

Purity, 63

Putnam, F. W., 440

Quechan (Yuma): "An Account of Origins," 20n6, 461–89; Central Group relationship to, 461, 465n2; dreamers (doctors), 461–62, 465n4; funeral speech, 536, 543–44; geographical territory, 461; Halpern's studies of, 313; "Kwikumat Became Sick," 3; "Lightning Song" (excerpt), 529–30; religion of, 461–62, 465n6; songs, 3, 462, 465n3; "The Soul" (excerpt), 399–400; surviving population, 461

Quotatives: absence or suppression of, 522, 539n11; in Cupeño, 424; in Pomo, 316; in Serrano, 402; in Yana, 26, 51n3, 521–22, 539nn9,10

Radin, Paul, 263, 501

"Ragged Ass Hill" (Yurok), 79, 82–85

Rancherias. See Reservations

Rattlesnakes: "An Account of Origins"

(Quechan [Yuma]), 473–74, 480;
aggravated by summertime telling
of myths, 514; as food (Mojave), 444;
worn as skirt, 444n1

Recording methods, 16(table 2). *See also*
specific methods

Redwood Creek, 105

Reeves, Minnie: biography, of, 105; "The
Boy Who Grew Up at Taʾkʾimiɫding"
(narrator), 105–110; "Grandfather's
Ordeal" (narrator), 107, 110–11; "The
Stolen Woman" (narrator), 107, 112–
13; as storyteller, 105–6

Reichard, Gladys, 501

Repetition, 40–44, 46–47; in "The Bear
Girl" (Chimariko), 116; in "The Devil
Who Died Laughing" (Karuk), 101–2;
in "The Dog Girl" (Ineseño Chumash), 385, 386; episodic, 40–43,
46–47, 53n17; formulaic, 43–44;
incremental, 46; in "Loon Woman"
(Wintu), 41–43, 44, 53n17; and pattern
numbers, 41, 43, 53nn15,18; poetic, 44;
in "Rolling Skull" (Yana), 43–44; in
"A Story of Lizard" (Yahi), 41, 155–58;
in "The Trials of Young Hawk"
(Southern Pomo), 41

Requa (Rekʾwoy), 77, 79

Reservations: Elem Rancheria, 330;
Grindstone Creek, 235, 239, 246;
Hoopa, 68, 104; Hopland, 313;
Middletown Rancheria, 334, 335;
Morongo, 401; Nome Lackee, 238–
39; Rincón, 411; Rumsey Wintun,
328, 332; Siletz (Oregon), 68; Yule,
348; Yuma, 461

Revival of California languages, 6–7, 412,
562–65

Rhetorical patterns. *See* Pattern numbers

Rhoades, Lela (Achumawi), 506; Atsugewi song, 142; "How My Father
Found the Deer" (narrator), 127–38

Richardson, Nancy (Karuk), 19n2, 564;
"The State of Our Languages," 563–64

Rincón Reservation, 411

Ritwan language family, 548, 551, 567n5

Roadrunner: "An Account of Origins"
(Quechan [Yuma]), 479, 486; "The

Contest between Men and Women"
(Tübatulabal), 366, 370–76, 379

Roberts, Helen R., 501

Robins, Robert H., 77–78, 504; "The
Young Man from Serper" (collector
and translator), 78, 79–80, 85–89;
The Yurok Language, 78

Rolling Head tale type, 9

"Rolling Skull" (Yana), 9, 43–44, 540n12

Round Valley, Mendocino County, 129,
239, 241; Nomlaki people, 239, 241;
Pit River and Hat Creek people, 129

Rumsey Wintun Reservation, 328, 332

Saclan language, scant documentation
of, 7

Sacramento River, 178, 190, 193

Salmon: Coyote's song to catch (Chu-
mash), 532; First Salmon Ceremony
(Karuk), 92; as food (Hupa, Karuk,
Wintu), 90, 104, 204; gillnet fishing
of (Tolowa), 68–69; salmon roast
(Yurok), 8–9

Salvage linguistics, 239, 312–13, 495–99,
506n3

San Juan Costanoan language: fieldtrip
to record, 495–99, 506n2, 507nn5,6;
wordlist and text, 497–98, 507n5

"Sapagay's Song," 36, 533–34

Sapir, Edward, 501; *The Collected Works
of Edward Sapir*, 105; "Grizzly Bear
and Deer," 25–27, 51n3; "Indian
Medicine-Men" (excerpt; collector),
526–27, 540n16; "A Story of Lizard"
(collector), 152–77; Yahi Translation
Project, 154–55, 161n1

Sarris, Greg, "The Woman Who Loved
a Snake" (collector and narrator),
324–33

Schools. *See* Boarding-school system

Seals, boat towed ashore by (Yurok), 87

Seiler, Hans Jacob, 504

"A Selection of Wintu Songs" (Wintu),
178–91

Selections: criteria for choice of, 10–13,
20n7; performance dates, 17(table 3);
ethnolinguistic and ethnopoetic presentation of, 35; genre of, 15(table 1);

Selections *(continued)*
  language of narration of, 18–19(table
  4); methods of recording, 16(table 2),
  22–25; order of, 13–14. *See also titles
  of specific selections*
Serrano: "The Creation," 401–10; geo-
  graphical territory, 401
Serrano language: number of speakers
  of, 401; quotatives in, 402; sample
  passages, 402, 403–5
Seventh Generation Fund, 564
Sexual intercourse: instruction in, 488;
  prohibition of, 355
Shabegok (de Angulo), 264
Shamans. *See* Doctors (shamans)
Shape-shifting. *See* Revelations;
  Transformations
Shasta, Mount (Yét), 130
Shastan language family, dialects in, 546
Shaughnessy, Florence (Yurok), 79(fig. 1),
  505, 506; "Blind Bill and the Owl"
  (narrator), 78–79, 81–82; "Ragged Ass
  Hill" (narrator), 79, 82–85; remarks
  from Matthiessen interview, 63; "The
  Young Man from Serper" (narrator),
  78, 79–80, 85–89
Shepherd, Alice, 12, 504; "Four Songs
  from Grace McKibbin" (collector and
  translator), 219–34; "Loon Woman"
  version, 193, 194, 197
Shipley, William, 504; "Mad Bat" (trans-
  lator), 248–59; Maidu creation myth
  (excerpt; translator), 515–16; on published translations, 51n4
Sievers, Eduard, 384
Siletz (Oregon) reservation, 68
Silver, Shirley, 504
Silverstein, Michael, 549
Silverthorne, Mary (Wintu), 183
Skunk, as character in "Creation"
  (Eastern Pomo), 299
Smith, Bertha, *Yosemite Legends,*
  509n10
Snakes: all living things turned into
  (Tolowa), 72–73; dream of (Nomlaki),
  247; hired to find deer (Achumawi),
  136–38; inventory of (Eastern Pomo),
  308; "The Woman Who Loved a

Snake" (Cache Creek Pomo), 328–33.
  See also Rattlesnakes
Snyder, Gary, "The Incredible Survival
  of Coyote," 539n8
Social structure: of dance societies
  (Nomlaki), 238, 245n; role of chief
  and assistants (Eastern Pomo), 294,
  296, 303; Tolowa, 67–68
Solares, María (Ineseño Chumash),
  385(fig. 10), 506; biography of, 385;
  "The Dog Girl" (narrator), 382–95
Solarsan, Barbara, 496
Solarsano de Cervantes, Ascensión, 496,
  506n2
"Some Qualities of Indian Stories"
  (T. Kroeber), 538n1
Somersal, Laura (Wappo), 552
Song cycles, 529
Songs, 527–35; content of, 528–35;
  ethnolinguistic presentation of, 530,
  541n20; for Hesi ceremony (Nomlaki),
  236–38; minimal information accompanying, 12; occasions linked to, 514,
  527–28; reader's treatment of, 12;
  selections classified as, 15(table 1);
  types of, 527; vocables in, 528–29, 530.
  See also specific types of songs
Song selections, 15(table 1); "Four Songs
  fron Grace McKibben" (Wintu),
  224–34; "A Harvest of Songs from
  Villiana Calac Hyde" (Luiseño),
  414–20; "A Selection of Wintu Songs,"
  181–91
Songs incorporated into essays, 519,
  529–30, 530–31, 532, 533, 759
Songs incorporated into stories and
  myths, 528, 540n17; "An Account
  of Origins" (Quechan), 466, 469,
  476–77, 479–80, 482, 483, 487–88,
  528; from Chumash stories, 345, 530;
  "Creation" (Eastern Pomo), 270–71,
  276, 306, 309, 528; "The Dog Girl"
  (Ineseño Chumash), 394–95, 528;
  from forgotten stories (Wintu), 190–
  91, 190n; "The Life of Hawk Feather:
  The Bear Episodes" (Cupeño), 430,
  432, 435, 528
Songs used as epigrams: acorn song

(Maidu), 491; "Chalááwaat Song" (Luiseño), xviii; creation songs (Cupeño), 57; doctor dance song (Yurok), 65; "I warned you" (Chumash), 397; "Kingfisher, Kingfisher" (Wikchamni), 343; "My heart, you might pierce it and take it" (Quechan), 3; song from "The Čiq'neqš Myth" (Chumash), 345; women's brush dance song (Luiseño), 511

"The Soul" (Quechan; excerpt), 399–400

Southern California creation pattern, 518–20

Southern Pomo language: kinship terms, 314–15; proper names in stories, 314; sample passage, 315–16; sentence connectors, 315–16; surviving dialects, 312, 313

Southland Dance cult, 180, 181n2

Spanish mission system. *See* Mission system

Sparkman, Philip, "Culture of the Luiseño Indians," 535

Speakers, last: Chimariko, 115; Wappo, 552; Yahi, 152–53

Speakers, native: of California languages generally, 552–53, 577(map 5); of Karuk, 563–64; of Lake Miwok, 335; of Serrano, 401; of Southern Pomo, 312; of Tübatulabal, 364; of Yokuts, 348; of Yurok, 80

Speeches: by Dusty-sunrise (Mojave), 457; by Eastern Pomo chief on Marumda (Creator), 291; by Hipahipa (Mojave), 457, 458–59, 460; by Kuksu in Eastern Pomo creation myth, 274, 275, 276; lecture at girls' puberty ceremony (Luiseño), 535–36; Lying-on-dust (Mojave), 459; by Marumda in Eastern Pomo creation myth, 276, 277–79, 283, 284, 288, 289, 290, 294, 296, 304, 306, 307–9; Patwin Hesi oration, 536–37, 541n24; Quechan funeral speech, 536, 543–44. *See also* Oratory

"Spell Said by a Girl Desirous of Getting a Husband" (Yana), 125

Spider: "Creation" (Eastern Pomo), 282–83, 286–87; "An Account of Origins" (Quechan), 480–81

Spott, Robert (Yurok), 506

Starritt, Julia (Karuk), "Coyote Steals Fire" (narrator), 31–33

State Emergency Relief Administration Project, salvage ethnography work by, 239–40, 240n1

"The State of Our Languages" (Richardson), 563–64

St. Helena, Mount, 335, 338

Stinginess, consequences of (Achumawi), 132–38

"The Stolen Woman" (Hupa), 107, 112–13

Stone, Tom (Owens Valley Paiute), 506

Stone and Kelsey Massacre, 556–58

Stories: about culture heroes, 523; about devils, 522; about monsters, 523, 540n12. *See also* Narrative

Storytelling: California Indian Storytelling Festival, 565; Native American vs. European, 36–37; true oral, 36–37, 53n14; as wintertime activity, 93, 193, 402, 514

Strong, William Duncan, 421

Sucker fish, as food (Karuk), 102–3

Supahan, Sarah (Karuk), 19n2

Supahan, Terry (Karuk), 19n2

Survey of California and Other Indian Languages, 504; phonetic transcriptions of Karuk creation stories, 93; work on Yurok language, 77–78

Swann, Brian, 5; *Coming to Light*, 11

Sweat house: Atsugewi, 60, 61, 145, 146, 150; Lake Miwok, 339

Tachi Yokuts. *See* Yokuts

Taʾkʾimiłding (Hoopa Valley village), 106, 109–10

Tales: as genre of narrative, 514; geographic distribution of types of, 523; vs. myths, 515; selections classified as, 15(table 1)

Tale types, 523. *See also* Orpheus myth

Talmy, Len, 504

Tape recording: as collection method, 24–25, 51nn1,2; early, 501–2, 503–4; "live" vs. "in studio," 20n8; selections collected by, 16(table 2), 502; of Yurok stories, 78

Tataviam language, scant documentation of, 7

Taylor, Alexander, *The California Farmer and Journal of Useful Arts* articles on "Indianology," 500

Taylor, Sarah (Cache Creek Pomo), 324, 330

Tedlock, Dennis: ethnopoetics pioneered by, 27, 31; lines as defined by, 52n11

Teeter, Karl, 504

"Test-ch'as (The Tidal Wave)" (Tolowa), 67–76; cultural understanding behind, 47–48

"They say." *See* Quotatives

Thomas, Edo, "A Selection of Wintu Songs" (singer), 178–81, 184

Thomas, Jim (Wintu), 182–83, 182n

Thompson, Lucy (Yurok), 6, 506

Thrasher, "Creation" (Eastern Pomo), 293

Thunder: "Condor Steals Falcon's Wife" (Yowlumni Yokuts), 356; "The Trials of Young Hawk" (Southern Pomo), 322–23

Tobacco smoking: by Marumda during Creation (Eastern Pomo), 277, 279, 284, 292, 300; in meeting of deities (Eastern Pomo), 274–75, 276, 282, 285, 292, 297; by Naponoha (Atsugewi), 150; as sealing contractual agreement (Achumawi), 131, 134, 136

Tolowa: geographical territory, 67; history and culture, 67–70; surviving population, 70; "Test-ch'as (The Tidal Wave)," 67–76

To the American Indian (Thompson), 6

Traditions, preservation of, 499–500, 508n7, 509n8

Transformations: of acorn shell into Marumda's boat (Eastern Pomo), 304; of girl into bear (Chimariko), 118–22; of girl into white fawn (Yurok), 87–88; of handsome man into snake and back into handsome man (Cache Creek

Pomo), 329–30; of Immortals into elements of natural world (Karuk), 91–92; of Kumastamxo into eagles (Quechan), 487–88; of Mad Bat into ordinary bat (Maidu), 250, 259; of Naponoha into Night-Flying Butterfly (Atsugewi), 141–42; of old woman into Bullhead (Karuk), 92, 96–97; of people into animals (Ineseño Chumash), 395

Translations: based on unpublished texts, 20n7; interpreter, 16(table 2), 22–23; methods of making, 21–25, 51nn1,2; modes of presenting, 25–35; personal and period styles' effects on, 501, 509n11; replicability of, 11; verifiability of, 11. *See also* Ethnolinguistic translations; Ethnopoetic translations

"The Trials of Young Hawk" (Southern Pomo), 35, 311–23, 523; anthropomorphism in, 38; episodic repetition in, 41

Tribes of California (Powers), 500

Trinity River, 104, 105, 115

Trout, caught by boy (Karuk), 94–95

Tsuyukweráu (Joe Homer; Quechan), 506; "An Account of Origins" (narrator), 20n6, 22, 461–89, 520, 539n7; biography of, 462–63

Tübatulabal: "The Contest between Men and Women," 363–81; cultural influences, 365; geographical territory, 364; surviving population, 364

Tule, as food for Mojave, 452, 453

Turner, Katherine, "The Bear Girl" (translator), 115–22

Turtle, "Naponoha (Cocoon Man)" (Atsugewi), 143, 150

Tututni division of Tolowa, 68

Typographical conventions, 28–29, 33; Bright's early, 31–32, 33; in "The Contest between Men and Women," 367–68n11; in "The Creation" (Serrano), 402–3; in "Four Songs from Grace McKibbin," 220–21; in "From 'The Life of Hawk Feather,'" 424, 426; in "Loon Woman," 200–201n5; in "A Story of Lizard," 160; in "Two Stories from the Central Valley," 351n1.

See also Line breaks in ethnopoetic translations, criteria for

Uldall, Hans Jørgen, 501; "Coyote and Old Woman Bullhead" (collector), 90–97
Ultan, Russell, 504
University of California at Berkeley: Bancroft Library, Frank J. Essene papers, 239, 240n1; Department of Anthropology, 6, 500–502, 509nn9,11; Department of Linguistics, 6, 503–4; Survey of California and Other Indian Languages, 77–78, 93, 504
University of California Publications in American Archaeology and Ethnology (UCPAAE), 25, 51n4, 509n12
University of California Publications in Linguistics (UCPL), 51n4, 509n12
Utian language family, 546
Uto-Aztecan language family, 548, 549, 567n5; California groups, 568n11; geographic expansion of, 551, 567–68n9, 568n13; Serrano and Luiseño as members of, 401, 411

Valenzuela, Salvadora: Cupeño creation and burial songs, 57, 518–19, 538n5; "The Life of Hawk Feather: The Bear Episodes" (narrator), 421–35
Vanity, as defect of Coyote (Atsugewi), 59–61
Velasquez, Josefa, 496–99, 507nn5,6
Ventureño Chumash. *See* Chumash
Vera, Matt (Yowlumni), 19n2
Verbatim dictation. *See* Dictation, phonetic/verbatim
Videotaping, 504
"Visit to the Land of the Dead" (Chawchila Yokuts), 348–49, 351n1, 352–55; geographic distribution of, 523; as Orpheus myth, 13, 336
Vocables, 223, 420n1, 528–29, 530, 535, 541n20
Voegelin, C. F., 501
Voegelin, Erminie Wheeler, 501; "The Contest between Men and Women" (collector), 363–81

Waking song (Achumawi), 532
Wallace, William, "Comparative Literature," 513
Wappo language, death of, 552
Washoe language, 546
Waterman, T. T., 20n9, 153, 501
Watham, Charles, 237(fig. 6); feather belts made by, 235–36; "How I Became a Dreamer" (narrator), 235–47
Wealth, desire for (Yurok), 36, 89
Weasel, "Naponoha (Cocoon Man)" (Atsugewi), 142, 144
West Mountain (Mount Lassen), 250, 258
Whales: bones used to split logs (Tolowa), 75–76; dried meat as food (Tolowa), 74
Wheeler-Voegelin, Erminie. *See* Voegelin, Erminie Wheeler
"When I Have Donned My Crest of Stars" (Kiliwa), 493
Whilkut, 105
Whistler, Ken, 16n1, 504
White Horse Bob, 61
Whites. *See* Europeans
Wikchamni song, 343
Wilbur, Leslie, 440
Wildcat Woman, "The Trials of Young Hawk" (Southern Pomo), 317
Willits, 313
Willow: bark for women's skirts (Mojave), 449; as basket-weaving material (Eastern Pomo), 301; branches for constructing shade-roofs (Quechan [Yuma]), 485; seine made of (Karuk), 95; sticks of, with string to detect movement (Eastern Pomo), 287–88, 300
Wilson, Darryl Babe: "Kwaw Labors to Form a World," 14, 59–61; "Naponoha (Cocoon Man)" (editor), 14, 139–51
Wilson, William (Quechan), "Lightning Song" (singer), 529–30
Wind, "Condor Steals Falcon's Wife" (Yowlumni Yokuts), 356, 358
Winter, as time for storytelling, 93, 193, 402, 514
Wintu: abundant documentation of, 7; cry songs, 219, 223, 225, 528; dream songs, 20n9, 179–80; elderly, living

Wintu *(continued)*
with Achumawi, 130–31, 132–38;
geographical territory, 178–79, 193;
Hayfork, 107; love songs, 187n, 219,
221–23; puberty songs, 185nn1,2, 186n1,
527–28; songs from forgotten stories,
190n2
Wintu language: opening and closing
formulas for stories, 123, 196, 201, 218;
prehistory of, 550; sample passage,
199–200
"Wintun Hesi Ceremony" (Barrett), 535
Wintu selections and excerpts: "Four
Songs from Grace McKibbin," 219–34;
"Loon Woman," 192–218; "A Selection
of Wintu Songs," 178–91; "Winter
mosquitos go," 123
Witches: among the Hupa, 107; of
Klamath people, 143, 149–50. *See also*
Devils
"The Woman Who Loved a Snake"
(Cache Creek Pomo), 324–33, 326n1
"Women's Brush Dance Song" (Luiseño),
511
Woodbury, Anthony C., 52n11
Woodpecker: acorn, belts constructed
from feathers of (Nomlaki), 236; deer
driven away by (Achumawi), 133, 135,
136, 138
Wren, "The Death of Kwikumat"
(Quechan [Yuma]), 477–78, 480
Written composition, selections collected
by, 16(table 2)
Wukwuk bird (Nomlaki, Wintu), 201n7,
217
Wyteedesla, 236, 237, 245, 246–47

Yahi: mouth-bow song, 531; "A Story of
Lizard," 152–77
Yahi language, sample passage, 159, 161n4
Yahi Translation Project, 154–55, 161n1
Yamane, Linda (Rumsien), 19n2; on
Harrington's fieldnotes, 48–49
Yana: "Coyote, Heron, and Lizard," 521–
22, 539n10; "Flint Boy," 523; "Grizzly
Bear and Deer," 25–27, 28–31, 51n3,

52nn8,9; "Indian Medicine-Men,"
526–27, 540n16; public speaking style,
536; "Rolling Skull," 9; "Spell Said
by a Girl Desirous of Getting a
Husband," 125
Yana language: dialects of, 546; quotatives in, 26, 51n3, 521–22, 539nn9,10;
sample passage, 521–22
Yee, Mary (Barbareño Chumash), 506;
account of Santa Barbara uprising, 555
Yokuts: Chawchila, "Visit to the Land of
the Dead," 348–49, 351n1, 352–55;
geographical territory, 347–48; record-
ing of two gambling songs, 496–97;
Tachi, "Dawis Sapagay's Song," 533–
34; Wikchamni "Kingfisher" song, 343;
Yowlumni, "Condor Steals Falcon's
Wife," 349–51, 351n1, 356–62
Yokutsan languages, 347–48; linguistic
prehistory of Penutian affiliation of,
550
Yosemite Legends (Smith), 509n10
Young, Tom. *See* Hánc'ibyjim (Tom
Young)
"The Young Man from Serper" (Yurok),
36, 78, 79–80, 85–89
Yowlumni Yokuts. *See* Yokuts
Yukian language family, 547, 549, 567n6
Yuki of Round Valley, 107
Yule Reservation, 348
Yuma. *See* Quechan (Yuma)
Yuma Indian Reservation, 461
Yuman language family, songs in stories
of, 528
Yumáyk Yumáyk (Hyde and Elliott), 413,
414n1
Yurok: abundant documentation of,
7; "Blind Bill and the Owl," 78–79,
81–82; current storytelling by, 9–10;
doctor dance song, 65; geographical
territory, 77; "Ragged Ass Hill," 79,
82–85; salmon roast, 8–9; "You come
upon a place of awesome beauty," 63;
"The Young Man from Serper," 78,
79–80, 85–89
The Yurok Language (Robins), 78

Designer:	Sandy Drooker
Cartographer:	Bill Nelson
Indexer	Jean Mann
Compositor:	Integrated Composition Systems
Text:	11/14 Adobe Garamond
Display:	Lithos
Printer and binder:	Edwards Brothers, Inc.

California
Political
Almanac

1991-1992

Published By
California Journal Press

California

Political

Almanac

1991-1992

Stephen Green, Editor

With
Amy Chance, Thorne Gray, Rick Kushman,
James Richardson and Rick Rodriguez

Foreword by Dan Walters

John L. Hughes, Production Editor
Lori Korleski Richardson, Cover Design & Graphics
Mary Elizabeth Buchin, Copy Editor

Published By
California Journal Press

ISBN 0-930302-74-5

Contents

1 California–a state of change
A foreword by Dan Walters   1

2 A budget mess of historic proportions   21

3 Governors command attention   30

4 The big bad bureaucracy   59

5 The California judiciary   83

6 Legislature   91
    Senate   104
    Assembly   181

7 Congress–Gulliver and the Lilliputians   305

8 Lobbyists–a vital link in the process   379

9 California's movers and shakers   403

10 County government–at the crossroads   418

11 Press vs. politicians–never-ending war   478

    Index   498

Charts, graphs and maps

Assembly district maps 181-182

Assembly speakers 208

Attorneys general since 1950 43

Budget, income and expenses 24-25

California demographics 10

Congressional delegation growth 378

Congressional district maps 310-311

Counties, 20 fastest growing 421

Governors 34

Governor elections since 1902 35

Lt. Governors since 1950 41

Salaries 32

Secretaries of state since 1950 49

State bargaining agents and units 62

State Senate district maps 104-105

State Senate presidents pro tem 146

State work force 61

Superintendents of public instruction since 1950 51

Treasurers since 1950 47

U.S. senators 314

Voter profile 12

Voter turnout, 1912-1990 6

Voting patterns, governor and U.S. Senate '64-'90 8

Preface

In the summer of 1989, a team of writers and editors at The Sacramento Bee was assembled by longtime political columnist Dan Walters. Our goal was to produce a book that would give California what The Almanac of American Politics provides on the national scene – a reliable and comprehensive source book on the issues, the players and the political process. The result was the California Political Almanac, published the following winter.

We all knew there would be demand for such a book. But few of us expected it would instantly gain acceptance as the standard reference on California politics. That was underscored in dramatic fashion on Jan. 2 of this year when Gov.-elect Pete Wilson plucked state Sen. John Seymour from obscurity and named Seymour as his replacement in the U.S. Senate. News reports nationwide cited the California Political Almanac as their source for information on Seymour's record.

This second edition contains all the background and insight of the first. But we've expanded and updated old chapters, and added new ones on the state's finances and the judiciary. The results of the 1990 elections have been incorporated. New officeholders and appointees have been profiled. The latest data from the once-a-decade census has been analyzed in terms of the social change in the Golden State and for what it means in the coming battles over reapportionment. Throughout, the reader will find more charts, better maps and an expanded index.

The writing and editing team, meanwhile, has changed slightly. But it still includes some of the most knowledgeable political journalists in the state. They account for more than 150 years of combined experience covering government at all levels, from local cemetery districts to the halls of Congress.

We are indebted to the editors, librarians and managers of The Sacramento Bee who have given us moral support and generously allowed us to use the newspaper's computer systems. The Bee also has given us advertising support. We received excellent counsel from the staff of California Journal magazine, a subsidiary of our publisher. Many readers also sent us comments and thoughtful suggestions for updating the work. And finally, we wish to thank our spouses, families and significant others who tolerated the long nights and weekends that were spent away from them while we completed this project. It is to them that we dedicate this book.

Stephen Green
Sacramento
May 1991

1

California–a state of change

A foreword by Dan Walters

California is the planet's most diverse society. At no time in mankind's history have so many people gathered in one place from so many ethnic and national groups, practicing so many different religions, speaking so many languages and engaged in such diverse economic activities. It would follow, therefore, that California's politics would be equally complex. And they are, but not exactly in the ways that one might think.

Rather than reflecting the incredible socioeconomic and demographic diversity, the state's politics have become the almost exclusive province of California's relatively affluent and middle-aged, Anglo – non-Hispanic white – population.

Proposition 13, the successful campaign to oust liberals from the state Supreme Court and a seeming lock on the state's electoral votes by Republican presidential candidates are just three indications that California's politics have been edging to the right in recent years, thus creating a growing tension between the aspirations of the emerging majority and the limits laid down by the politically dominant soon-to-be minority. That tension manifests itself in an untold number of specific struggles and issues, ranging from reapportionment to fiscal policy, that form the murky political climate as the state approaches the 21st century.

As it functions as a living social laboratory, so does California test the ability of the traditional American system of government to cope with social and economic change beyond the wildest imagination of the system's creators. A major question for the 1990s and beyond is whether features of government developed in the 18th and 19th centuries – the two-party system, separately elected legislative and executive branches of government, counties and cities formed along traditional lines – can function amid such a range of values.

To understand the political currents flowing through California in the late 20th century, one must first understand its social and economic currents. And if one accepts the wave theory of social development – each wave consisting of economic

1

change, followed by social change, followed by political change – California is in the third, or political phase, of its third wave.

The first wave lasted for roughly a century, from the early days of white settlement in the 1840s to the onset of World War II. The gold rush aside, that century was one in which California was a relatively unimportant place in the larger scheme of things. Its economy was resource-based – mining, agriculture, timber – and it had a decidedly rural ambiance. Los Angeles, with its orange groves, vegetable fields and low buildings, resembled an overgrown Midwestern farm city, the presence of the Pacific Ocean and a few movie studios after World War I notwithstanding. San Francisco had a more cosmopolitan reputation, but it was the socioeconomic exception. California was white, Republican and quiet. It was largely ignored by the rest of America, whose population was centered in the East and had, if anything, a European outlook.

All of that changed, suddenly and dramatically, on Dec. 7, 1941, when the Japanese bombed Pearl Harbor and plunged the United States into world war. Suddenly, America was forced to consider Asia as a factor in its future, and the window through which the nation viewed the war in the Pacific was California. Overnight, seemingly, the state was transformed into an industrial giant to serve the war effort, sprouting countless dozens of aircraft assembly lines, shipyards, steel mills and military installations. And it became a staging point for the war, a training ground for soldiers, sailors and airmen.

A WAR BRINGS ECONOMIC AND SOCIAL CHANGE

It was war, but it was also a sudden economic change for the state; California was jerked into the industrial 20th century. And that economic transformation had an equally rapid social impact: hundreds of thousands and then millions of Americans were drawn or sent to the state to participate in the war effort.

While there had always been a steady flow of domestic emigrants to the state, it was nothing compared to what happened during World War II and continued almost unabated after the war. "Gone to California" became a terse explanation for the sudden absence of families in hundreds of Midwestern, Southern and Eastern communities. It was one of history's great migrations, and one that actually began a few years before the war when refugees from the Dust Bowl, as chronicled in John Steinbeck's Grapes of Wrath, came to California in a desperate search for work. These Depression-era migrants formed the nucleus of life and politics in agricultural areas of the state, such as the Central Valley.

As the expanding industrialism created jobs, it drew emigrants and they, in turn, formed the nucleus of a new industrial middle class. These young emigrants had vast ambitions. They wanted schools, highways, parks and homes. And they provided, during the post-war years, the core backing for politicians who promised to fulfill those desires. A political change was under way.

California's prewar Republicanism was of a particular variety. Rooted in the abolitionism of the Civil War era and the prairie populism of such men as William Jennings Bryan and Robert LaFollette, California's Republicans were reformist and progressive. The state's great Republican reformer, Hiram Johnson, set the tone for the 20th century when he led efforts to break the stranglehold that Southern Pacific Railroad and other entrenched interests had on the state Legislature. Small farmers had battled for decades with the railroad over freight rates, the clashes being both political and, in one instance, violent. With Johnson – governor and later a U.S. senator – marshaling public opinion, California enacted a series of pioneering political reforms that included the initiative, referendum and recall, all designed to increase popular control of politicians. Decades later, the initiative was to become a tool of special interests, rather than a barrier, but that was after social and political developments beyond Johnson's ability to foresee. Johnson set a tone of high-minded Republicanism that survived for decades. Democrats were weak, electing a single one-term governor, Culbert Olsen, in 1938, despite the dramatic rise of the Democratic Party nationally after Franklin Roosevelt became president.

Olsen's Republican successor, Earl Warren, was out of the Johnson mold, and he became the only governor ever elected three times, going on to even greater fame as chief justice of the U.S. Supreme Court from 1953 to 1969. Warren was governor during and immediately after World War II, when the state underwent its big economic and social evolution. He responded to the demand with far-reaching investments in public infrastructure, schools, highways, parks and other facilities that not only served the state's fast-growing population but laid the foundation for even greater public works.

THE POLARIZATION OF POLITICS

During this period California began developing a national reputation for political unpredictability as it became a battleground for the ideological wars sweeping through America. Post-war California politics revolved mainly around Cold War issues, typified by the 1950 U.S. Senate contest between a young Republican congressman named Richard Nixon and a liberal political activist named Helen Gahagan Douglas, wife of actor Melvyn Douglas. Nixon won after a brutal campaign in which he implied, at least, that Douglas was sympathetic to communism. It was a polarizing political battle that launched Nixon on his way toward political immortality – and some would say, immorality. And it marked a turn away from centrist politics by both parties.

The Democrats began veering to the left through such organizations as the California Democratic Council, which was established by Alan Cranston and other liberals to strengthen party identification in a state where "cross-filing" allowed candidates to obtain the nominations of both parties and to do battle with the more conservative elements then in control of the party. And the Republicans took a turn to the starboard, with conservatives such as U.S. Sen. William Knowland, an Oakland newspaper publisher, assuming a larger role in the party as moderates of the Earl Warren-Goodwin Knight faction fell from grace in the absolutist atmosphere of the day.

At the time, in the mid- and late-1950s, social change favored the Democrats. The immigrants who had come to California to take jobs in the expanding industrial economy, their ranks swollen by returning veterans, put down roots and became politically active. As they did, they expanded the Democratic Party's base – especially since the Republicans were in the process of alienating voters who had supported centrists such as Warren.

THE NEW BREED

Jesse Unruh was archetypical of the new breed. He came to California from Texas during the war, remaining to attend the University of Southern California, where he became active in campus politics as leader of a band of liberal veterans. Within a few years, Unruh was heavily involved in politics on a larger scale and won a seat in the state Assembly in 1954. It was the ideal territory for the consummate political animal, and his arrival coincided perfectly with the general rise of Democratic fortunes in the 1950s.

The 1958 election was the pivotal event in the postwar rise of the state's Democratic Party, a direct result of the social and economic changes brought about by World War II. Sen. Knowland, who led the right-wing Republican contingent in the Senate during the early- and mid-1950s, was openly hostile to President Dwight Eisenhower's "modern Republicanism," which included Warren's appointment to the Supreme Court. Knowland saw Eisenhower, Warren, Thomas Dewey and other Republican leaders from the East as leading the party, and the nation, astray, refusing to confront expansionist communism around the globe and temporizing on such domestic issues as labor union rights and welfare spending.

Knowland wanted to take the party back to the right and hoped to do it by running for president in 1960, when Eisenhower's second term would end. But he thought the governorship of California would be a more powerful platform for a presidential campaign than the Senate. Knowland's major impediment was the moderate Republican governor of the time, Goodwin Knight, who didn't want to give up his office. Knight had been Warren's lieutenant governor, had inherited the top spot when Warren was appointed to the Supreme Court and had then won a term on his own in 1954. He wanted to run for re-election in 1958.

Knowland solved his problem by simply ordering Knight to step aside. With the rightists firmly in control of the party machinery, Knight was forced to obey, agreeing, with reluctance, to run for Knowland's Senate seat. But Knowland, in his preoccupation with Eisenhower, Communist expansionism and other weighty matters, didn't bother to consider how his forced switch with Knight would sit with California voters. With an arrogance that bordered on stupidity, he assumed that the voters would do whatever he wanted them to do. He was wrong. Democrat Edmund G. "Pat" Brown Sr., the liberal attorney general, was elected governor and

Democratic Rep. Clair Engle was elected to the Senate. Knight might have been re-elected governor and Knowland given another term in the Senate, but the voters retired both.

It was a banner year for Democrats. In addition to winning the top two spots on the ballot, they also took firm control of the Legislature. Over the next eight years, during this peak of Democratic hegemony, the most ambitious policy agenda in California history became reality. The early Brown years saw a torrent of liberal, activist legislation ranging from an ambitious water development scheme to pioneering civil rights and consumer protection measures.

While Unruh sharpened the ideological focus of the Assembly, taking it to the left, the state Senate remained a bastion of rural conservatism. For a century, the Senate's 40 seats had been distributed on the basis of geography, rather than population, in a rough approximation of the U.S. Senate's two-to-a-state system. No senator represented more than two counties and giant Los Angeles County, with a third of the state's population, had just one senator. With most of California's 58 counties being small and rural, it gave the Senate a decidedly rural flavor. Conservative Democrats and Republicans formed a solid majority. Even so, Pat Brown guided much of his progressive legislative agenda through the upper house, using his unmatched skills of personal persuasion.

In 1966, as Brown was winding up his second term, the U.S. Supreme Court, still under the leadership of Earl Warren, handed down its far-reaching "one-man, one-vote" decision requiring legislative seats to be apportioned on the basis of population, even though the U.S. Senate retained its two-to-a-state makeup. As the state Senate's districts were redrawn in response to the ruling, there was a huge shift of power from rural counties to urban areas, strengthening not only Democrats generally but liberals within the party. But that didn't take effect until after another man had assumed the governorship, the result of another clash between two big-name politicians.

THE RISE OF RONALD REAGAN

Brown wanted to run for a third term in 1966 but Jesse Unruh thought – or so he said later – that Brown had promised to step aside in his favor. Whatever the truth of the matter, there was a big rupture between the two most powerful California politicians of the day, and in the long run, both suffered. Brown ran for his third term, but his break with Unruh, some public fumbles, a rising level of social unrest and the appearance of an ex-movie actor named Ronald Reagan spelled disaster for that ambition.

Reagan, a moderately successful B-movie leading man and television actor, was enticed to run against Brown by a consortium of wealthy Southern California businessmen. At the time, television had become a new and powerful factor in campaigning. Televised debates had doomed Richard Nixon's bid for the presidency in 1960, which was followed by a hopelessly desperate run against Brown for the governorship in 1962. In 1964, Reagan made a powerful television speech for Barry Goldwater, the Republican presidential candidate. Reagan was, the businessmen decided, just the man to take on the non-telegenic Pat Brown in 1966.

They were right, in more ways than one. Even though the Democratic phase of the postwar era was not yet concluded, and even though a large majority of California voters were Democrats, Reagan buried Pat Brown and his bid for a third term by emphasizing Brown's shortcomings and stressing a conservative, get-tough attitude toward civic and campus unrest. The strength of Reagan's win swept several other Republicans into statewide offices.

Two years earlier, Reagan's old chum from Hollywood, song-and-dance-man George Murphy, had defeated Pierre Salinger for a California U.S. Senate seat. Salinger, who had been John Kennedy's press secretary, had won his party's nomination in June 1964 and was appointed to the U.S. Senate by Pat Brown after Clair Engle died in July at the end of his first term in office.

With Murphy in the Senate (he was defeated in his second-term bid by John Tunney in 1970), Reagan in the governor's office and Republicans holding other statewide offices, the GOP appeared once again to be on the ascendancy. But it all proved to be a short-term spurt. It would take another socio-economic cycle for the Republicans to begin a real, long-term rise in influence among the voters.

The GOP won control of the Assembly (for two years) in 1968, but for most of Reagan's eight years as governor, he had to deal with a Democratic-controlled

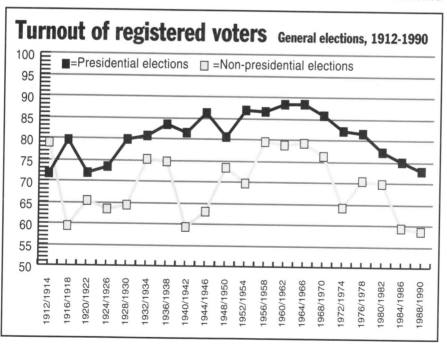

Turnout of registered voters General elections, 1912-1990

■=Presidential elections □ =Non-presidential elections

Legislature. Unruh was gone after losing his own bid for governor in 1970, but another Southern California liberal, Bob Moretti, took his place. There were occasional compromises between the conservative governor and the liberal legislators, most notably on welfare reform, but it was a period remarkable for its dearth of serious policy direction from Sacramento. The Pat Brown-Jesse Unruh legacy was not undone, Reagan's rhetoric notwithstanding. But neither could liberals advance their agenda. It was a time of stalemate.

Even as Reagan and Moretti did battle in Sacramento, another economic-social-political cycle, largely unnoticed at the time, was beginning to manifest itself. The period of intense industrialization in California began to wind down in the 1960s. Asia, principally Japan, had risen from the devastation of the war to become a new industrial power. Californians began buying funny-looking cars stamped "Made in Japan" and domestic automakers began shutting down their plants in California. The steel for those cars was made not in Fontana but in Japan or Korea. Even tire production began to shift overseas. One factory at a time, California began to de-industrialize.

California was not the only state to experience damaging foreign competition in basic industrial production in the 1960s and 1970s, but what happened here was unusual. The state underwent a massive economic transformation, from a dependence on basic industry to an economy rooted in trade (much of it with the nations of Asia), services and certain kinds of highly specialized manufacturing, especially of the high-tech variety centered in the Silicon Valley south of San Francisco. Computers and associated devices and services – including a huge aerospace industry tied to Pentagon contracts – became the new backbone of the California economy. By the late 1980s, in fact, California's economy, on a per capita basis, was probably the most productive in the world, even more so than that of much-vaunted Japan. But there was a period of adjustment between the apex of the industrial era and the onset of the post-industrial period. That occurred in the 1970s, and it resulted in a social lull as well.

The rapid population growth of the postwar years, driven by domestic immigration, slowed markedly in the 1970s as industrial job opportunities stagnated. California was still growing, even growing a bit faster than the nation as a whole, but it was much less dramatic than what had occurred earlier. And California began to experience another phenomenon: an outflow of residents.

A DIFFERENT KIND OF POLITICIAN

In retrospect, that lull in population growth may have been politically misleading. It persuaded the state's political leaders, first Reagan and then his successor, Democrat Jerry Brown, that the infrastructure of services and facilities that had been built after World War II was adequate; that it was time to retrench, to tighten budgets and cut back on public works. It was a collective and indirect policy decision that was to have adverse consequences in later years.

California voting patterns–gubernatorial races

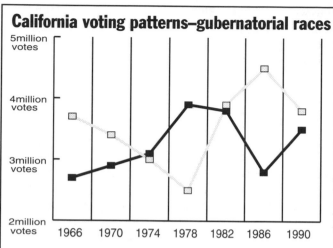

■ =Democrats

☐ =Republicans

The candidates:
1966
Reagan(R)
Brown(D)
1970
Reagan(R)
Unruh(D)
1974
Brown(D)
Flournoy(R)
1978
Brown(D)
Younger(R)
1982
Deukmejian(R)
Bradley(D)
1986
Deukmejian(R)
Bradley(D)
1990
Wilson(R)
Feinstein(D)

California voting patterns–senate races

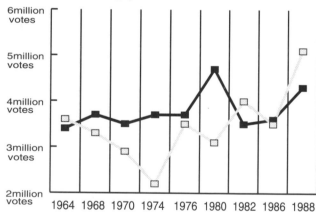

■ =Democrats

☐ =Republicans

The candidates:
1964
Salinger(D)
Murphy(R)
1968
Cranston(D)
Rafferty(R)
1970
Tunney(D)
Murphy(R)
1974
Cranston(D)
Richardson(R)
1976
Hayakawa(R)
Tunney(D)
1980
Cranston(D)
Gann(R)
1982
Wilson(R)
Brown(D)
1986
Cranston(D)
Zschau(R)
1988
Wilson(R)
McCarthy(D)

Jerry Brown, son of the governor Reagan had defeated in 1966, burst into state politics in 1970 by getting himself elected secretary of state, a mostly ministerial office with few opportunities for publicity. But Brown, a young former seminarian who was the personal antithesis of his back-slapping father, seized the moment.

The Watergate scandal that erupted in 1972 and destroyed Richard Nixon's presidency two years later focused attention on political corruption. Brown grabbed the issue by proposing a political reform initiative and shamelessly pandering to the media, especially television. He bested a field of relatively dull rivals, including Assembly Speaker Moretti, to win the party's nomination for governor and then took on Houston Flournoy, the Republican state controller, who was a throwback to the earlier era of Republican moderation.

Even so, it was a whisker-close race. Ultimately, Brown was elected not so much because of his political acumen as because of his name and because the post-Watergate climate had raised Democratic voter strength to near-record levels. At the height of Democratic potency in California, which occurred during the early years of Jerry Brown's governorship, 59 percent of California voters identified themselves as Democrats in an annual party preference poll while just over 30 percent said they were Republicans. Democrats ran up huge majorities in the Legislature; at one point, after the 1976 elections, Republicans fell to just 23 seats in the 80-member Assembly. Even Orange County, the seemingly impregnable bastion of Republicanism, had a Democratic registration plurality.

With the younger Brown as governor and big Democratic majorities in the Legislature, there was a spurt of legislative activity, much of it involving issues such as farm labor legislation and bread-and-butter labor benefit bills, that had been stalled during the Reagan years. Brown preached a homegrown political philosophy that defied easy categorization. It was liberal on civil rights, labor rights and environmental protection, but conservative on taxes and spending. Brown defined the philosophy in a series of slogan-laden speeches in which he spoke of teachers being content with "psychic income" rather than salary increases and California facing an "era of limits." His philosophy contrasted directly with the expansionist policies of his father and most post-war governors.

THE PROPERTY TAX REVOLT

At first, Brown was a hit. The words and a rather odd personal lifestyle that included late-night visits to Mexican restaurants drew attention from national political reporters starved for glamour in the post-John F. Kennedy world of Jerry Ford and Jimmy Carter. Soon, there was a steady stream of pundits to Sacramento and a flurry of effusive praise in the national media. Brown was a star, it seemed – a Democratic Reagan. Brown believed it. And scarcely more than a year after becoming governor, he was running for president. As Brown turned his political attention eastward – or skyward, according to some critics – Brown neglected California politics. And they were changing again.

While the state's economy roared out of a mid-1970s recession, property values soared. And as they rose, so did property tax bills. It was an issue too prosaic for Jerry Brown, whose sights by then were firmly fixed on the White House. But it was just the ticket for two aging political gadflies, Howard Jarvis and Paul Gann.

Raising the specter of Californians being driven out of their homes by skyrocketing tax bills, Jarvis and Gann placed on the ballot a radical measure to slash property taxes and hold them down forever. Republican candidates, seeking an issue to restore their political power, seized upon Proposition 13, as the measure was numbered on the June 1978 ballot. Belatedly, Brown and legislative leaders devised a milder alternative for the same ballot.

Proposition 13 was enacted overwhelmingly and Brown, then running for re-election against the state's terminally dull attorney general, Evelle Younger, did a 180-degree turn. Sensing that the tax revolt could be his political downfall, Brown proclaimed himself to be a "born-again tax cutter" and pushed a state tax cut as a companion to Proposition 13. Younger failed to exploit the opening and Brown breezed to an easy re-election victory. Almost immediately, Brown began plotting another run for the White House in 1980, this time as an advocate of balanced

Social and political demographics

	1970	1980	1990*	1990 voters**
Population	20 million	23.8 million	29.7 million	7.7 million
White	15.6 million 78%	15.8 million 66.4%	17.2 million 58%	81%
Hispanic	2.4 million 12%	4.6 million 19.3%	7.3 million 24.7%	5%
Asian	.6 million 3.2 %	1.6 million 6.6%	2.9 million 9.7%	4%
Black	1.4 million 6.9%	1.8 million 7.5%	2.2 million 7.5%	9%

* Preliminary 1990 census data   ** Exit polls of voters, November 1990 election, by Voter Research and Surveys

budgets, spending limits and tax cuts. Brown was nothing if not ambitious and opportunistic, qualities that were to be his political undoing in the long run.

Brown's re-election aside, the 1978 elections marked the beginning of a long slide for the Democratic Party after it had enjoyed two decades of dominance. Democrats suffered major losses in legislative races that year and a flock of conservative Republicans, dubbing themselves "Proposition 13 babies," came to Sacramento – out of caves, liberals said – prepared to conduct ideological war.

In years since, Republicans have both gained and lost legislative seats, with a net increase even in the face of a Democratic reapportionment plan in 1982 that was designed specifically to keep the Democratic Party in power. And the Democrats have suffered a massive hemorrhage of voter strength. Since the Democrats' high point in the California Poll's annual survey of party identification, 59 percent to 32 percent in 1976, the margin has eroded year by year. In the most recent polls, the parties are tied at about 45 percent each.

In the mid-1970s, registration favored Democrats by, at most, a 57 percent to 34 percent margin. But in more recent years it has dipped to about 50 percent to 40 percent on the official rolls. Democrats even lost a fraction of a point in 1988, when they committed $4 million to a huge voter registration drive in support of Michael Dukakis' presidential campaign, and fell below 50 percent in 1989 for the first time in more than a half-century. The fractional slide continued in 1990 and contributed to Democrat Dianne Feinstein's narrow loss to Republican Pete Wilson in their duel for the governorship.

THE DEMOCRATS' CRISIS

The unofficial voter registration numbers are even worse for the Democrats. It's estimated that at least 1 million, and perhaps as many as 2 million, of California's 14 million registered voters don't exist. The official euphemism for those phantom names is "deadwood," and it exists because California's registration laws make it relatively difficult to drop people from the rolls when they die or move. Some mobile Californians may be counted two or three times as registered voters in different jurisdictions. And because Democrats are more likely to change addresses than Republicans, an adjustment for the deadwood tends to reduce their ranks more.

It's generally acknowledged among political demographers and statisticians that stripping the voter rolls of duplicate or missing names would reduce official Democratic registration to 47 percent or 48 percent and raise Republican registration to well above 40 percent. That's why Democratic legislators have resisted efforts to purge the rolls of non-persons. Adjustment to a true figure would bring registration closer to the 45 percent to 45 percent identification margin in recent polls. The state's leading public pollster, Mervin Field, adjusts the voter registration split to 48 percent to 42 percent in his polling, saying the number is based on surveys of actual registration.

Whatever the real number, Democrats have been declining and Republicans gaining. And some Democratic officials, most notably Secretary of State March Fong Eu, are warning that the party is in danger of slipping into minority status. The big question asked among political insiders in California is why the Democrats are failing. Democratic leaders ask the question themselves, even though most deny the existence of the trend.

The roots of the trend may be found in the socioeconomic currents evident in California during the late 1970s and 1980s. As the state's post-industrial economy shifted into high gear in the late 1970s, it created millions of jobs and, like the postwar period of industrialization, began attracting new waves of immigrants to fill them. But these immigrants didn't come from Indiana, Tennessee and Texas with their political consciousness already formed. They came from Mexico, Taiwan, Korea and the Philippines.

By the late 1980s, California's population was growing by some 2,000 people a day and half of them were immigrants, mostly from Pacific Rim nations with whom California was establishing ever-stronger economic relations. California was developing, in short, into the new American melting pot.

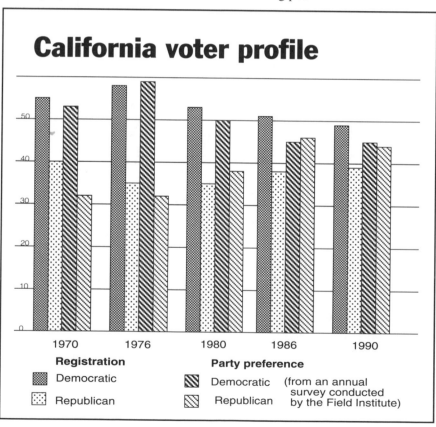

As the newcomers poured into the central cities, especially Los Angeles, San Francisco and San Jose, there was a commensurate outpouring of Anglo families to the suburbs. And as those suburbs filled and as their home prices soared, there was an even more dramatic movement into the new suburbs in former farm towns such as Modesto and Stockton in the north and Riverside and Redlands in the south. These newly minted suburbanites – white and middle-class – shifted their political allegiance to the Republicans and their promises of limited government and taxes. Areas that had once been dependably Democratic in their voting patterns, such as Riverside and San Bernardino counties, evolved into Republican registration majorities as they suburbanized and exploded with population. Prosperity encouraged the conversion, as did the popularity of Ronald Reagan in the White House.

A 1988 California Poll revealed that Anglo voters favored Republicans by a 50 percent to 41 percent margin. And that was critical because non-Anglos, while identifying with the Democratic Party by substantial margins, were not voting in numbers anywhere close to their proportions of the population. Exit polls in the 1980s elections revealed that more than 80 percent of California's voters were Anglos, even though they had dipped to under 60 percent of the population.

At the other extreme, Asians doubled their numbers in California between the late 1970s and late 1980s, surpassing blacks to become almost 10 percent of the population. Yet Asians accounted for just 2 percent of the voters. The fast-growing Hispanic population was approaching one-fourth of the total by the late 1980s, but they were only 6 percent or 7 percent of the voters. Among non-Anglo minorities, only blacks voted in proportion to their numbers – roughly 8 percent of both population and electorate. But they also are the slowest-growing minority population.

THE CHARACTERISTIC GAP

Thus, the 1980s saw a widening gap between the ethnic characteristics of California and those of voters, who not only were white but better educated, more affluent and – perhaps most important – markedly older than non-Anglo non-voters. By 1986, half of California's voters were over 50 years old, a reflection of the rapid aging of the Anglo population, and the aging process continued as the state entered the 1990s and the baby boomers edged into middle age.

In brief, while California's population was moving in one direction – toward a multiracial, relatively young profile – the electorate was moving in another. And this gap was driving California politics to the right, toward a dominant mood of self-protection and reaction. Republicans scored well among these older voters with appeals on crime and taxes. Democrats, hammered on these and other hot-button issues, scrambled to find some response and were mostly unsuccessful.

The characteristic gap makes itself evident in a wide variety of specific issues and contests, but is most noticeable when it comes to issues of taxes and spending. The Proposition 13 property tax revolt in 1978 and the subsequent passage of a public spending limit measure promoted by Paul Gann in 1979 were the first signs that the climate had changed. Republican George Deukmejian's 1982 election as governor on a no-new-taxes, tough-on-spending platform (along with tough-on-crime) was another indication. Deukmejian, a dull-as-dishwater attorney general and former legislator, represented a 180-degree change of style from the unpredictable Brown.

The demands for more spending were coming from and for a growing, relatively young non-Anglo population, while the political power was being held by a relatively old, Anglo bloc of voters. By the late 1980s, a majority of California school children were non-Anglo, but less than a quarter of California's voters had children in school – one example of how the gap affected political decision-making.

A 1987 poll conducted for the California Teachers Association revealed that older voters would kill any effort to raise state taxes for education. A CTA consultant told the group that even "arguments about grandchildren and overall societal need don't work." And if education was losing its basic political constituency – voters with children in public schools – other major spending programs, such as health and welfare services for the poor, had even smaller levels of support.

Gov. Deukmejian resisted new taxes, vetoed Democratic spending bills, trimmed the budget and saw his popularity among voters soar. He was re-elected by a landslide in 1986, defeating for the second time Los Angeles Mayor Tom Bradley. Even Deukmejian, who gloried in the "Iron Duke" image, relented in 1989 as the Gann spending limit enacted by voters 10 years earlier gripped the state budget. He was under pressure from business interests to spend more to relieve traffic congestion, but he refused to raise fuel taxes. And even if he had agreed, the spending limit would have prevented the money from being spent.

Finally, the governor and legislative leaders reached agreement on a complex package that placed a measure to loosen the Gann limit and increase the gasoline tax directly before voters in 1990. The transportation measure passed, but other tax measures on the ballot were summarily rejected, indicating that only something as universally used and popular as transportation could overcome the continuing resistance of voters to higher taxes.

The essential public policy question facing California in the 1990s, therefore, is whether an aging Anglo population will continue to dominate the political agenda, even in the face of pressure from business executives for more spending on infrastructure to maintain the state's business climate.

OPTIONS FOR THE DEMOCRATS

One might think the solution to the Democrats' political woes would be to register and organize millions of non-Anglo voters, rather than continue to face an erosion of support among white middle-class Californians. Ex-Gov. Jerry Brown, who went into political exile after losing his U.S. Senate bid in 1982, returned to the stage in 1989 by winning the state Democratic Party chairmanship on a promise to bring minorities and economically displaced whites into the party in record numbers. The unfaithful, Republican-voting Democrats would, in effect, be banished from the party as it took a couple of steps to the left.

But as simple as that sounds, it's a very complex task. There are barriers of citizenship, of language and of a tendency among refugees from authoritarian regimes not to stick their necks out politically. That's a tendency most evident among Asians, who have very high levels of education and economic attainment but very low levels of political involvement.

There are problems for the Democrats, too, in creating a party image that is attractive to minorities who may be social and political conservatives. Republicans regularly garner about 40 percent of the Hispanic vote, for instance, and some Democratic Party positions, such as being pro-choice on abortion, are hard-sells among Hispanics. GOP candidates do even better among Asian voters, as few as they may be.

There are also internal barriers, such as the traditionally powerful role of blacks in the Democratic Party. Rhetoric about a "Rainbow Coalition" notwithstanding, minority groups do not automatically cooperate on matters political, and there is, in fact, some friction. If these weren't serious enough problems, Brown also faced continued skepticism among traditional elements of the party, who see him as a loser with an image that repels many voters. Brown's attempt to centralize fund-raising activities as one step toward his goal of creating a powerful party apparatus has been rebuffed by other influential figures, who insist on running their own fund-raising.

While Brown raised millions of dollars during the first two years of his party chairmanship, he also spent millions on staff and infrastructure and when Democrats narrowly lost the governorship in 1990, Brown was blamed by many supporters of Dianne Feinstein. She had consciously attempted to woo middle-class white voters back from the Republicans and her failure touched off another round in the Democrats' perennial debate over positioning and tactics.

Political number-crunchers generally believe that in the short run – to the mid- or late-1990s at least – Republicans will continue to gain market share and Democratic strength will continue to erode. A major question is whether that trend will be reflected in real power.

REAPPORTIONMENT REDUX

Democrats maintained their hold on the Legislature and expanded their control of the state's congressional delegation with a highly partisan reapportionment plan after the 1980 census. In effect, they preserved their power in the face of real-world trends. The plans were approved by then-Gov. Brown and a state Supreme Court dominated by liberal Brown appointees. Conditions for the Democrats are not as favorable for the post-1990 census reapportionment and the stakes are much higher.

The relative lull in California population growth during the 1970s meant that the state was awarded only two new congressional seats after the 1980 census, increasing its delegation from 43 to 45. Prior to reapportionment, the delegation had been divided 22-21 in favor of Democrats. It was a fair division of the seats in terms of both overall party identification and total congressional vote in the state, both of which were evenly divided between the parties. But after the late Rep. Phil Burton completed what he called "my contribution to modern art," a plan rejected by voters via referendum but ordered into use by the state Supreme Court for the 1982 elections, the delegation was 28-17 in favor of Democrats. That result was stark evidence that gerrymandered reapportionment of district boundaries works. And it was so well done that Republicans were able to gain only two seats in subsequent elections, leaving the delegation at 26-19. The margin held even though the total vote for Democrat and Republican congressional candidates in California continued to run almost dead even (and in some elections the GOP ran ahead).

California's population growth spurted in the 1980s, especially in relationship to the rest of the nation. The state's 6 million growth in population between 1980 and 1990 was roughly a quarter of all U.S. population growth. That means the state has been awarded seven new congressional seats, giving it not only the largest congressional delegation in the nation but the largest of any state in the nation's history.

Republicans want redress. They believe, with statistical evidence on their side, that they should have roughly half of the California seats, which would mean that they would receive all of the new ones. And it will be very, very difficult for the Democrats to pull a repeat of 1982, not only in congressional reapportionment, but in the redrawing of Assembly and state Senate districts.

Initially, Republicans pinned their hopes vis-a-vis reapportionment on Deukmejian's running for a third term in 1990. Thus, he would have been available to veto any gerrymander drawn by majority Democrats in the Legislature. But after dropping hints that he was interested in a third term, Deukmejian eventually announced in early 1989 that he would retire after his second term was completed.

GOP leaders, stretching as high as the White House, then engineered a strategic coup. They persuaded Pete Wilson, the one-time mayor of San Diego who had defeated Jerry Brown for a U.S. Senate seat in 1982 and had won a second term handily in 1988, to run for governor in 1990. Wilson was seen as the GOP candidate with the best chance of retaining the governorship.

The selection of a Democratic candidate didn't go as easily. Attorney General John Van de Kamp, a liberal with strong environmental and consumer protection credentials, was the early favorite and it seemed for awhile as if he would have a clear path to the nomination. But his only declared rival, former San Francisco Mayor Dianne Feinstein, refused to drop out.

Feinstein fashioned a decidedly more centrist image for herself, arguing that a liberal such as Van de Kamp was headed for certain defeat by Wilson. Among other things, she supported the death penalty, a litmus test issue for many Democrats. Van de Kamp, meanwhile, had made a strategic decision that turned out to be an error. Taking his own nomination for granted, Van de Kamp committed many of his campaign dollars to promoting three initiative measures – on political reform, the environment and crime – that he planned to use as the basis of his campaign against Wilson.

That left Van de Kamp strapped for cash when the duel with Feinstein became close, while she tapped her wealthy husband, financier Richard Blum, for critical millions. Feinstein won the nomination, but narrowly lost an expensive shootout with Wilson.

Although the Wilson and Feinstein campaigns spent well over $40 million combined in 1990, the less than-overwhelming Republican victory (Wilson won less than 50 percent of the total vote) indicated that the two wound up in November almost exactly where they had been tens of millions of dollars and nine months earlier, with Wilson holding a narrow edge in the polls.

The Wilson-Feinstein contest reaffirmed a corollary about California politics that first emerged in the 1970s and has continued in the 1980s: a generic Republican advantage in top-of-the-ticket elections. From 1980 to 1990, there were 10 such contests in California – for president, governor and U.S. senator – and Republican candidates won eight of them, often, as with Wilson, by extremely narrow margins. Deukmejian defeated Bradley in 1982, for instance, by fewer than 100,000 votes.

Given the closeness of popular support for the two parties and a higher level of turnout and party loyalty among Republicans, the GOP seems to have an overall generic advantage of about a quarter-million votes in an otherwise equal matchup of candidates, and that's almost exactly the margin by which Wilson defeated Feinstein.

ARE REPUBLICANS READY?

So far, however, that generic advantage hasn't translated into big gains in lesser offices or in the Legislature, thanks in part to skewed reapportionment, but one of Wilson's goals will be to improve GOP fortunes down the line in the 1990s.

A final factor in reapportionment are the minority groups, especially Hispanics, who believe they too were damaged by the 1982 reapportionment. They will be pressuring Democrats for new representation in both congressional and legislative seats. For all of those reasons, reapportionment is likely to be a nastier squabble than it was a decade earlier. And given the underlying trends, Republicans could become the dominant party by the mid-1990s if they get a fair shake on reapportionment.

Expansion of the Republican Party's share among voters in California has meant a subtle broadening of the party's base, and that has brought internal discord. Right-wingers, who were dominant in the party for years, have seen their influence slip in the 1980s. The 1982 elections were a watershed of internal party power. Deukmejian, denounced by some rightists at the time as a "closet liberal," defeated then-Lt. Gov. Mike Curb for the gubernatorial nomination and went on to win the election. Wilson, who is a little to the left of Deukmejian in ideological terms, defeated several conservatives to win the nomination, and then won his U.S. Senate seat.

With patronage from the governor's office and the Senate, Republican moderates have enjoyed a rebirth of influence within the party, and right-wingers have been complaining about being ignored. Their only bastion is the Assembly Republican caucus, which continues to be dominated by the "Proposition 13 babies" or "cavemen," as some dub them.

The conservatives have stopped short of open revolt and the party has remained relatively unified at the top. Conservatives didn't balk, for instance, about having Wilson as their candidate for governor in 1990 because they wanted a winner. But there are certain issues that could divide the party bitterly and thus lessen its chances of taking full advantage of the opportunity to become dominant in state politics.

One big issue is abortion. The right-wingers want laws to make it illegal. But the newer recruits to the party, as well as the moderate leaders, favor Wilson's pro-choice position. The issue was moot as long as national law favored abortion rights. But that changed in 1989, when the U.S. Supreme Court ruled that states could make their own abortion laws. It had an immediate impact. There was vicious in-fighting among Republicans in the summer of 1989 over abortion as they vied to fill a vacant state Assembly seat from San Diego County in a special election. What happened in San Diego, a contest between pro-life and pro-choice Republicans (the pro-choicer won in a district of white suburbanites) could be repeated dozens of times if abortion becomes an issue for the Legislature to decide.

Success, then, may become a Catch-22 for Republicans. They can only become the majority party by expanding their base to include a wider variety of cultural and ideological viewpoints. But that expansion could mean Republicans will squabble more among themselves as the Democrats have been doing. Wilson had scarcely been inaugurated when the sniping began. Conservatives were irritated by Wilson's selection of moderate state Sen. John Seymour – a former conservative himself – as Wilson's successor in the Senate, and they were put off by Wilson's advocacy of some new taxes to balance the state budget. In the early days of his governorship, the GOP right-wing loomed as Wilson's peskiest opponents while Democrats embraced his moderate policies.

Conversely, if the Democrats slip into minority status in the 1990s, they may find it easier to project a unified and integrated philosophical image, having rid themselves of elements – conservative whites – who are unhappy with the party's liberal ideology. Party chairman Jerry Brown, undaunted by criticism of his organizational efforts for the 1990 elections, has been preaching a new politics of grass-roots liberalism in apparent preparation for another U.S. Senate bid in 1992, saying the Democrats need a better message to attract minorities and dispossessed whites. That puts him on a collision course, figuratively if not literally, with Feinstein, who is preparing for a Senate campaign of her own and continues to advocate middle-of-the-roadism. "The party can't depend on minority votes to pull it through a general election," she said after her narrow loss to Wilson.

In the last decade, reapportionment, as partisanly slanted as it may have been, was one of the Legislature's few decisive actions. Increasingly, the Legislature drew within itself, preoccupied with such games of inside baseball as campaign strategy, fund-raising and partisan and factional power struggles. It seemed unable, or unwilling, to cope with the huge policy issues raised by the dynamics of the real world outside the Capitol: population growth, ethnic diversification, transportation congestion, educational stagnation, environmental pollution.

The Legislature, which Jesse Unruh had recast as a full-time professional body in the 1960s, had once been rated by most authorities as the finest in the nation. The 1980s saw not only policy gridlock but a rising level of popular disgust with the antics in the Legislature, fueled by several official investigations into corruption and a more critical attitude of the Capitol press corps.

California's political demography is at least partially responsible for the Legislature's lethargy. Legislators are torn between the demands and aspirations of California's new immigrant-dominated population and the limits set by white, middle-class voters. But the very professionalism that was Unruh's proudest achievement also has contributed to the malaise. Full-time legislators, many of them graduates of the Legislature's staff, are naturally preoccupied with their personal careers. Thus, legislative duties that conflict with career goals are shunted aside.

Throughout the decade, reformers proposed institutional changes to restore the Legislature's luster, such as imposing limits on campaign spending and fund raising (which have increased geometrically) and providing public funds to campaigns. Voters endorsed a comprehensive reform initiative in 1988, but they also approved a more limited version placed on the ballot by some legislators and special-interest groups. The first provided public funds for campaigns while the second barred such spending, and the second gained more votes. The result was that most of the first initiative was negated, but nearly all of the second was invalidated by the courts.

As a years-long federal investigation of Capitol corruption erupted in indictments in 1989, the Legislature itself began drafting reforms designed to raise its standing with an increasingly cynical public. These reforms – a tightening of conflict of interest rules, including a ban on receiving speaking fees from outside groups – were approved by voters in 1990. But voters, expressing obvious disgust with legislative antics and corruption, also approved an initiative that would, if it clears the courts, impose tough term limits on lawmakers, eliminate their pensions and sharply reduce spending on legislative operations.

Mostly, however, the impotence of the Legislature manifested itself in an explosion of initiative campaigns that took issues directly to voters, bypassing the Capitol altogether.

THE INITIATIVE EXPLOSION

The "initiative entrepreneurs," as some dubbed them, emerged during the decade as powerful new political figures, and the Legislature was reduced to reacting to their policy directives. The syndrome began when Howard Jarvis and Paul Gann sponsored Proposition 13, demonstrating how initiative campaigns could be self-financing through direct-mail appeals, and continued unabated through the 1980s, with causes emerging from both ends of the political spectrum. Voters finally rebelled during the 1990 election at the overloading of the ballot, rejecting most of the ballot measures.

The most notable example of the syndrome was auto insurance, the subject of no fewer than five measures in 1988. Four were defeated but one, championed by a consumer group coalition in sometime alliance with trial lawyers, won approval. Proposition 103 was only slightly less revolutionary than Proposition 13, the prototype for bomb-thrower initiatives. It promised big cuts in insurance rates and created an entirely new state regulatory system for insurers, including an elective insurance commissioner's position.

Proposition 103 also was something else: an indication that the political left might score points with a generally conservative electorate if it picked its issues carefully. Proposition 103, like Proposition 13, appealed to personal economic motives. Other initiatives from the left side of the political spectrum, such as a series of special tax and bond measures to benefit health and environmental causes, also were successful until the 1990 backlash that left the fate of all big initiative campaigns in doubt. Harvey Rosenfield, the young consumer activist who promoted Proposition 103, tried to establish a permanent initiative factory by proposing a measure to change Proposition 13, removing limits on property taxes for non-residential property but keeping them for homes. Rosenfield, however, fell well short of the signatures required and financial troubles forced him in 1990 to shut down much of his organization.

But the right wasn't silent. Republicans and conservatives pushed their own prescriptions for public ills, including two reapportionment initiatives in 1990 that failed after a massive opposition campaign by Democrats. The right's major victory at the polls in 1990 was the legislative term-limit measure.

Even though initiatives drove political policy in the 1980s, the future of the initiative industry is in doubt after the rejections of 1990. Many observers saw that, coupled with the election of a new governor, as an opportunity for the Legislature to redeem itself in the minds of voters by addressing fundamental policy issues.

California politics, having undergone so many evolutions in the past two generations, remains in a state of flux. In the immediate future, the state is likely to continue its slow movement toward the right as the dominant Anglo electorate ages. In the longer run, a major factor may be the development of some charismatic leaders among Hispanics and Asians who could move their latent political power in one direction or another, much as Martin Luther King and Jesse Jackson mobilized the latent power of blacks. But so far, none has emerged. Thus, the real story of California's 21st century political development will be the extent to which today's newcomers become tomorrow's voters and how their cultural values change the political landscape.

2

A budget mess of historic proportions

After eight years of claiming he had brought California's fiscal situation from "I.O.U. to A-OK," Gov. George Deukmejian found an economic downturn had left his final balance sheet for the 1990-91 fiscal year looking as tattered as one from a failing savings and loan institution.

The problem was simple to define: as the economy weakened, the state's revenues dropped and gobbled up the outgoing governor's reserve funds – and then some. State finances suffer quickly in a recession. Consumers spend less, prompting a slump in sales taxes, and state costs increase as more people call upon welfare, unemployment and other safety-net programs. In 1991, California's big economic engine could still be counted on to generate more revenue than had been available in the previous year, but nowhere near enough to keep pace with the state's rising Medi-Cal, welfare, school and prison populations.

Early evidence suggested Deukmejian's administration would leave the state foundering in more than $800 million in red ink by the end of the 1990-91 fiscal year – and that was before the Persian Gulf war began. Nothing in the state's 140-year history compared to the financial disarray incoming Gov. Pete Wilson confronted in 1991 as he took the podium in the state Assembly to deliver his State of the State message as California's 36th governor.

"Now more than ever, to lead is to choose," Wilson said. "And our choice must be to give increasing attention and resources to the conditions that shape children's lives. The emphasis must be more preventative than remedial – a vision of government that is truly as uncomplicated as the old adage that an ounce of prevention is worth a pound of cure."

Wilson's message represented a sharp shift from Deukmejian's approach to California's problems, and it was well received among Democrats as well as most Republicans in the Legislature. Where Deukmejian had fought to close a $3.6 billion gap between anticipated revenues and spending demands for the 1990-91 budget, Wilson was faced with a recession-driven shortfall of monster proportions.

Wilson had first estimated the 1991-92 budget deficit to be $7.1 billion, but Legislative Analyst Elizabeth Hill had said the shortfall between anticipated revenues and spending demands could hit $9.9 billion, absent action by the governor and the Legislature to curb expenses, raise taxes or both. By the end of March 1991, Wilson was declaring a "budget emergency" and projecting a $12.6 billion shortfall.

Furthermore, Wilson faced most of the same problems Deukmejian had faced in shaping a state budget to fit his priorities. State finances have been in a turmoil for years, ever since Proposition 13, the famous property tax limitation initiative, had gutted local government finances and prompted a redistribution of state revenues in 1978. More tax measures followed, among them one to index the income tax to inflation to protect Californians against "bracket creep," the automatic tax hikes that occurred as inflation pushed taxpayers into higher tax brackets. Inheritance and gift taxes were repealed, the business inventory tax was wiped out and new tax credits were invented and spread around. The loss to state government between 1978 and the 1988-89 fiscal year exceeded $190 billion, according to a study by Hill. Most notably, voters approved Proposition 4 in 1979, writing a state and local spending limit into the Constitution. The cap became known as the Gann limit after its main sponsor, tax critic Paul Gann. Spending would be tied to population growth and inflation. Excess revenue would be returned to taxpayers.

The Gann limit meant little until the 1986-87 fiscal year, when California's always powerful economy produced an unexpected surge in revenue. After nearly a decade of Proposition 13 austerity, the state's public schools and universities needed the money, but the spending cap dictated otherwise. Just over $1 billion was returned to the state's taxpayers during the Christmas season of 1987-88.

Those were the years of federal tax reform, state tax conformity, deficit spending on the federal level and unpredictable peaks and troughs for California's revenues. Shortage followed surplus. Teachers, school administrators, parents and other educators, with the exception of those representing the state's two university systems, launched an initiative campaign designed to protect themselves from Deukmejian's vetoes and the state's wavering finances.

In June 1988, they failed at the polls. In November, however, the voters approved Proposition 98, a school and community college spending guarantee, by 50.7 percent, the barest of majorities. The public schools and community colleges would henceforth get some 40 percent of the state's general fund budget. When revenues exceeded the Gann limit, half of the excess money would go to elementary, high school and community college education, not back to the taxpayers. Neither the Legislature nor the governor could take the money away.

WILSON'S FIRST BUDGET PROPOSAL

To Wilson, the state's finances must have resembled a windshield just after an encounter with a good-sized bug – some cleaning up would be necessary before he could even see where he wanted to go.

On all sides, Wilson could see the problems he would confront and he mentioned many – overstuffed schools, more and more homeless, workers without health insurance, growing welfare and Medi-Cal caseloads, swollen prisons, overwhelming child abuse and neglect problems and failing counties. To complicate matters, the Wall Street firm of Standard & Poor's placed California on a "credit watch" before Wilson had been in office a month. The Triple AAA credit rating that Deukmejian had so jealously guarded was clearly in jeopardy.

Where were the solutions? By 1991, there were some answers, and they helped a little. A trigger was in place to automatically trim welfare grants and other cost-of-living increases when state revenues lagged. The trigger was a victory for Deukmejian and the Assembly Republicans, who won it as part of the settlement that ended the longest budget stalemate in state history the previous year. The savings for Wilson's budget amounted to $800 million, of which less than $150 million would come from the Aid to Families with Dependent Children program.

Proposition 98 also had been amended under provisions of Proposition 111, the omnibus budget reform and transit tax measure approved in June 1990, to cut school spending in proportion with other budget cuts when state revenues are lagging. The savings here totalled $500 million in the 1990-91 fiscal year, giving a boost to Wilson's upcoming spending proposals. In addition, the voters, in approving Proposition 111 in June 1990, had agreed to double state motor vehicle fuel taxes, part of an $18.5 billion 10-year transportation plan that would keep the Caltrans budget, at least, from contributing to the fiscal mess. The Caltrans budget sprang to life, and so did the state's highway and mass transit programs.

Beyond those features, Wilson proposed to suspend the education spending guarantee for 1991-92 so he could cut the schools and community colleges by $1.4 billion. He pledged to cover increased enrollments and caseloads, but without granting any cost-of-living adjustments. He asked for legislation to shift responsibility for mental health and public health programs to the counties, along with new taxes to pay for them. He called for rolling back welfare grants to 1989-90 levels.

In all, Wilson proposed to:

●Raise vehicle license fees for local governments: $781 million.

●Raise alcoholic beverage taxes for local governments: $190 million.

●Make independent contractors withhold taxes: $290 million.

●Reduce the renters' tax credit: $210 million.

●Impose withholding on bonuses: $80 million.

●Impose withholding on estates and trusts: $42 million.

●Close tax loopholes for candy, snack foods, newspapers and magazines: $384 million.

●Give local voters the authority to raise sales taxes by as much as a half-cent to fight crime and drugs, and give them the authority to approve school and jail facilities by a simple majority vote rather than the two-thirds vote required under Proposition 13.

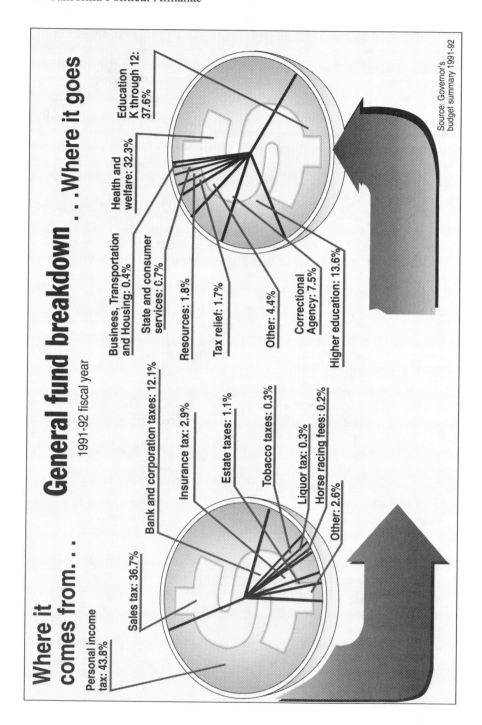

Where it comes from. . .

General fund breakdown . . .Where it goes

1991-92 fiscal year

Personal income tax: 43.8%

Sales tax: 36.7%

Bank and corporation taxes: 12.1%

Insurance tax: 2.9%

Estate taxes: 1.1%

Tobacco taxes: 0.3%

Liquor tax: 0.3%

Horse racing fees: 0.2%

Other: 2.6%

Business, Transportation and Housing: 0.4%

State and consumer services: 0.7%

Resources: 1.8%

Tax relief: 1.7%

Other: 4.4%

Correctional Agency: 7.5%

Higher education: 13.6%

Health and welfare: 32.3%

Education K through 12: 37.6%

Source: Governor's budget summary 1991-92

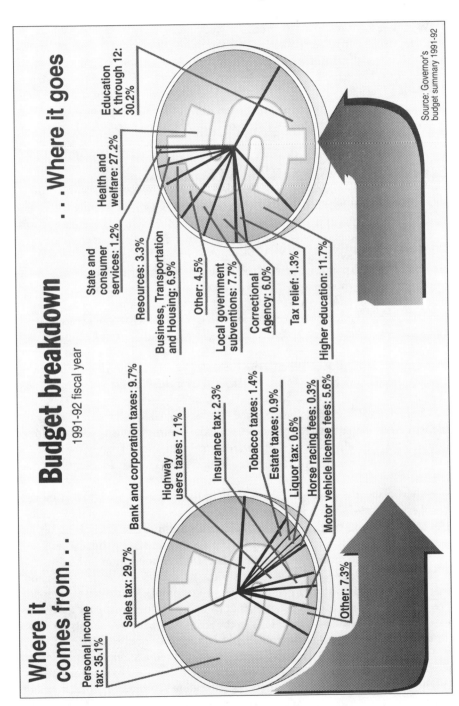

Where it comes from . . .

Budget breakdown

1991-92 fiscal year

. . .Where it goes

Personal income tax: 35.1%

Sales tax: 29.7%

Bank and corporation taxes: 9.7%

Highway users taxes: 7.1%

Insurance tax: 2.3%

Tobacco taxes: 1.4%

Estate taxes: 0.9%

Liquor tax: 0.6%

Horse racing fees: 0.3%

Motor vehicle license fees: 5.6%

Other: 7.3%

State and consumer services: 1.2%

Resources: 3.3%

Business, Transportation and Housing: 6.9%

Other: 4.5%

Local government subventions: 7.7%

Correctional Agency: 6.0%

Tax relief: 1.3%

Higher education: 11.7%

Health and welfare: 27.2%

Education K through 12: 30.2%

Source: Governor's budget summary 1991-92

Wilson also proposed raising fees for students, drivers, Medi-Cal patients, the handicapped, fishing licenses and even adoptions to bring in another $207 million a year. Along with measures to reform Medi-Cal and other areas of government, the goal was to close what had become known as the "structural" revenue gap facing California year after year. The cyclical gap, caused by recession, presumably would take care of itself once the economy began to recover.

The question was, how long will it take California to recover from the downturn and the Deukmejian years?

EDUCATION AND THE STATE BUDGET

By any measure, education spending has been woefully inadequate in California since the advent of Proposition 13. By the end of the Deukmejian administration in January 1991, California had effectively consigned many of its children to stiff prison sentences in place of solid educational skills. School districts floundered in deficits and fiscal uncertainty. Classes remained overfilled and buildings were in disrepair. Music, sports and driver's education programs were being cut. Schools were running year-round. Spending as a percent of income on elementary and high school education had dropped to 44th in the nation, according to the Advisory Commission on Intergovernmental Relations. The state struggled to provide classrooms to house some 230,000 new students who arrived in California each year, many of whom could speak little or no English. To serve them and get them on the road to being productive citizens, the state faced a $7 billion to $8 billion task. The state needed to build 14 new classrooms every day of the year for the next decade.

The results of California's educational failures could be measured in many ways. Industries complained that the work force could not learn new tasks, often could not even read. The public assistance rolls were climbing. Teen pregnancies were on the rise. Jails and prisons were full and getting fuller. In the meantime, teachers, school nurses, counselors and administrators were being laid off.

Superficially, the problem did not seem at first glance to be a lack of money. Teachers in 1991, for instance, were making substantially more than they made in 1982-83, the bottom of the recession and the end of former Gov. Jerry Brown's last term in office. It was also the year Brown's big budget surplus finally vanished, leaving the state no money with which to backfill for Proposition 13 losses.

That year, too, educators sounded the alarm for the whole country: The nation was at risk, the schools had to be reformed. A key problem involved teacher pay. The schools were not offering enough money to lure college graduates away from industries and businesses – especially in the sciences. There was simply no future for anyone interested in teaching math, biology, physics or chemistry.

In California, the response was SB 813, a sweeping educational reform measure by Sen. Gary K.Hart, D-Santa Barbara, and AB 70, by Assemblywoman Teresa Hughes, D-Los Angeles, the chairs of the education committees. Their measures were pushed by the California Business Roundtable, among others. They had Deukmejian's support. They raised the salaries for beginning teachers, lengthened the school day and the school year, tightened up on the curriculum, toughened academic standards and handed teachers and principals more power to impose classroom discipline. Budgets improved. State schools chief Bill Honig seemed to be pumping his own Adrenalin into the system. Test scores began to climb.

Then in 1987 the state's constitutional spending limit came into play. Instead of pursuing reforms, the state ended up refunding $1 billion. Elementary, high school and community college educators responded with Proposition 98, a school spending guarantee that the voters approved in 1988. Two years later, lawmakers softened that measure with Proposition 111. Net result: Elementary, high school and community colleges get about 40 percent of the general fund budget. In tight years, they automatically get less. In fat years, when revenues exceed the spending limit, most of the money would go to education rather than rebates.

In reaction to Wilson's plan budget proposal, school districts issued budget cuts and dire warnings. San Francisco faced the closure of two high schools. Other districts were looking at huge deficits. Some 30 or 40 faced bankruptcy.

The Legislature and Wilson met the challenge with a characteristic sideshow, plunging into a partisan donnybrook over whether to suspend teacher collective bargaining rights. Teachers, the Republican thinking went, should forgo their contract right to pay increases because all other state employees were being asked to make that sacrifice. The powerful California Teachers Association did not share that viewpoint.

Ironically, the depth of the fiscal crisis showed promise of being the state's salvation. The consequences of inaction, or partisan action, seemed too overwhelming to contemplate. Legislators from both parties were genuinely alarmed. Wilson remained open minded, accessible and ready to find solutions. He started by calling on key legislators to meet in working groups to assess the dimension of the problems and to come up with possible solutions.

They, in turn, had a plateful of productive ideas, many of which were framed by the non-partisan legislative analyst's office. Maybe some tax loopholes could and should be closed. Maybe the schools should and could be reformed, both to save some money and to provide better education. Maybe Proposition 98 could be suspended, but the full $2 billion cutback could be avoided. Maybe the state's two tax agencies could be combined. Maybe non-violent prisoners could serve their sentences on parole instead of in prison.

THE BUDGET PROCESS

Politicians love to declare that government should be "run like a business." They are fond of insisting the state should "live within its means." They insist state finances can be managed like a frugal "family bank account." Statements like those may pave the high road in fiscal debates for elective office, but against the reality of California's annual budget bill they are about as valid as assertions that groundhogs can predict the weather.

The California economy is the sixth or seventh largest in the world. The state's budget is by far the largest in the nation. The business of collecting and spending more than $55 billion a year on schools, welfare, health, prisons, parks, highways and a myriad of other governmental functions is complex, tedious, politically intricate and a task that requires the expertise of hundreds of people. The money flows in from taxes, fees, tideland oil royalties, multinational corporations and even the poor, who make co-payments for Medi-Cal and other services. Much of it goes exclusively into one or another of nearly 1,000 special funds, earmarked for specific needs. Sales taxes, personal income taxes and bank and corporation taxes flow to the biggest pot of all, the $43.3 billion general fund.

All of that complexity is compressed into a single legislative vehicle, the annual budget bill, which is introduced by the governor within the first 10 days of each calendar year.

By January, of course, the budget has been months in the making. Department heads, agency heads and the governor's Department of Finance have been shaping it since the previous April to balance it with anticipated revenue. Reams of calculations have been completed. Programs are trimmed or expanded to conform to the governor's priorities. There will be winners and losers. If there is any fight left in the losers, and there always is, they will take their case to the Legislature.

In practice, the budget is introduced separately in both the Senate and the Assembly. The governor may be a Republican, Democrat, independent or a Martian, but his budget bills are always authored by the chairmen of the Senate and Assembly fiscal committees, both of whom are members of the majority party. In 1991, as for the past decade, they were Assemblyman John Vasconcellos, D-Santa Clara, chairman of the Assembly Ways and Means Committee, and Sen. Alfred Alquist, D-San Jose, chairman of the Senate Budget and Fiscal Review Committee. They reshape the governor's proposals, following guidance from their colleagues. They are in effective command of the most important bill of any legislative session, a two-volume document that lists appropriations for virtually every function of state government.

Much has to be done, of course, before the budget bills even begin to take shape for consideration by the full Legislature.

In late February, the non-partisan legislative analyst reports on the governor's budget proposal. The study commonly exceeds 1,400 pages of detail distilled from the work of dozens of specialists drawing upon the expertise throughout the government and the state as a whole. The budget subcommittees start on the smaller budgets first, particularly those that depend on special funds and have the money they need to confront the problems they manage. Programs that rely on the general fund come later. The final revenue estimates arrive in May, once the April tax bills are opened and the money is counted.

Eventually, the Assembly and Senate bills must pass by a two-thirds majority in each house (a constitutional requirement that gives the minority party, or minority coalitions, the power to block the budget). Differences are worked out in a six-member conference committee. In the end, a unified product must be approved, again by a two-thirds majority.

The Constitutional deadline for final legislative action is supposed to be June 15. The governor is supposed to sign the bill by the beginning of the new fiscal year, July 1. He can use his line-item veto authority to reduce appropriations set by the Legislature, but he cannot restore any spending levels the lawmakers cut. Usually the governor is able to sign the budget on time, but occasionally the deadline is missed. Major budget delays occurred in 1978, 1979, 1980 and 1983. The longest budget stalemate in state history occurred in 1990, when lawmakers went 28 days into the new fiscal year before reaching a compromise that closed a $3.6 billion

3

Governors command attention

To be governor of California in recent decades is to stand in the wings of the national political stage. Ronald Reagan proved most adept at moving into the spotlight, and George Deukmejian did his best to avoid it altogether. But the state's chief executive automatically commands attention, owing largely to the 54 electoral votes that make California enormously important in any presidential election.

Earl Warren, elected three times as governor, sought the Republican presidential nomination twice before going on to preside for 16 years as chief justice of the U.S. Supreme Court. Edmund G. "Jerry" Brown Jr. shone in a string of 1976 primaries as he made a characteristically tardy bid to seize the Democratic presidential nomination from Jimmy Carter, then tried to unseat Carter in 1980.

Brown's father, Edmund G. "Pat" Brown Sr., had been governor for two years when he first flirted with the possibility of a vice-presidential nomination. The former state attorney general, who defeated Republican William Knowland for the governor's job in 1958, was eventually frustrated in his hopes for higher office. He turned his attention instead to the less glamorous business of building the staples of government known collectively as the "infrastructure." Three decades later, the elder Brown's accomplishments – a bond issue to increase water supplies to Southern California, more investment in the university system, faster freeway construction for a rapidly growing state –are remembered fondly by elected officials facing a new crush of growth.

Brown's terms as governor also are memorable for their contribution to capital punishment history in a state where voters have demanded that political leaders be willing to put violent criminals to death. An opponent of capital punishment who nevertheless believed it was his job as governor to carry out state law, Brown described the agony of his clemency decisions in death penalty cases in a book published in 1989. "It was an awesome, ultimate power over the lives of others that no person or government should have, or crave," he wrote. "Each decision took something out of me that nothing –not family or work or hope for the future –has ever been able to replace."

Brown, whose defeat of Republican gubernatorial candidate Richard Nixon in 1962 prompted Nixon's infamous "you won't have Nixon to kick around anymore" press conference, was looking forward in 1966 to running against a political neophyte named Ronald Reagan. But the mediagenic actor, railing against disorder on college campuses and appealing to an electorate unnerved by the Watts riots, denied Brown a chance to join Warren as a three-term governor. Reagan continued while governor to fine-tune the conservative message that would propel him to the presidency, but he was largely unsuccessful in matching his fiscal actions with his anti-government rhetoric. The former Democrat, who bashed the bureaucracy and welfare state in his public appearances, signed what was the largest tax increase in state history in order to shore up the sagging budget he inherited from Pat Brown.

Reagan was replaced by Jerry Brown, a self-proclaimed spokesman for a younger generation demanding change and imagination in government. If Jerry Brown followed his father's footsteps to the governor's office, he seemed determined to carve out his own path once he got there. The father was a consummate political mingler; the son standoffish. Pat was a spender; Jerry a relative tightwad. Pat laid pavement; Jerry discouraged freeway construction in favor of car pooling and mass transit. Similarly, the younger Brown's contributions as governor were less concrete. More than anything else, he is remembered for his personal idiosyncrasies: his refusal to live in the governor's mansion, the mattress on the floor of his austere apartment, his 1979 trip to Africa with singer Linda Ronstadt.

Brown used his appointment power to fill state jobs with a more diverse group of people, but some of those appointments became enormous liabilities with voters. Transportation Director Adriana Gianturco defended the much-hated "diamond lanes" imposed on drivers, who resented being forced to share rides. Supreme Court Chief Justice Rose Bird, ultimately ousted by voters in 1986, came to symbolize a criminal justice system seen as too sympathetic to the people it was supposed to punish. Deukmejian used both to score points in his gubernatorial campaigns.

Yet even Deukmejian, acknowledging that the state could not simply build its way out of its traffic congestion problem, would later emphasize car pooling as a necessary gridlock-reduction tool. Brown also takes credit for influencing his Republican successor on other fronts, including energy and technology. His emphasis on minority hiring, he says, helped push the Deukmejian administration in that direction

In 1982 voters, fed up with Brown's slapdash style and nearly perpetual campaign for president, elected a governor who would give them some rest. They chose Courken George Deukmejian Jr., who joked about his own lack of charisma, demonstrated little interest in higher office and didn't hobnob with rock stars.

Deukmejian preferred to stay at home with his pet beagles and play an occasional game of golf. His public passions, which were few, included a weakness for jamoca almond fudge ice cream. People likened him to Ward Cleaver, and in his more casual moments, he did wear sweaters that would have looked right at home on the Beaver's dad.

Deukmejian decided from the beginning to stick to the basics. He didn't bombard Californians with many new ideas. He said he was convinced voters wanted a competent manager, and he did little to deviate from that mission. He did his best to avoid revenue-raising measures that might be labeled tax increases, built prisons and appointed judges whom he said took a "common-sense" approach to fighting crime.

His first election was the closest race for California governor since 1902. He beat Los Angeles Mayor Tom Bradley by just 1.2 percent of the votes cast, actually losing to Bradley in Election Day votes and winning on absentee ballots cast before

SALARIES

Governor	$120,000
Lt. Governor	$90,000
Attorney General	$102,000
Secretary of State	$90,000
Controller	$90,000
Treasurer	$90,000
Supt. of Public Instruction	$102,000
Insurance Commissioner	$95,052
Member, Board of Equalization	$95,052
Speaker of the Assembly	$63,000
Senate President Pro Tem	$63,000
Assembly/Senate Floor Leaders	$57,750
Legislator	$52,500
Chief Justice, Supreme Court	$127,104
Associate Justice	$121,207
Appellate Court	$113,632
Superior Court Judge	$99,297
Municipal Court Judge	$90,680
President, University of California	$243,500
President, state college or university	$96,480-$130,620
Chancellor, state universities	$149,040

Legislators receive other direct compensation, including per diem pay of $92 a day for attending legislative sessions (about $18,580 a year tax free) and their $4,800 car allowance. They also receive health, dental and vision benefits.

the election. Four years later, Deukmejian trounced Bradley in a rematch, winning by more votes than any governor since Warren locked up both the Republican and Democratic nominations before his re-election victory in 1946.

In the interim, Deukmejian bragged repeatedly that he had taken the state "from IOU to A-OK" by erasing a $1.5 billion budget deficit he inherited from Brown. He spent much of the campaign denouncing liberal members of a state Supreme Court that had overturned dozens of death penalty decisions. Voters responded by dumping three members of the court.

By the time Deukmejian finished his two terms, he believed he had accomplished much of what he had set out to do. He had said no to billions of dollars in state spending proposals, racking up one-year records for vetoing both bills and budget items. He could point to a state unemployment rate half of that facing the state when he took office, thanks to job development he attributed to his no-new-taxes posture.

He had reconstructed the Supreme Court with justices willing to impose a voter-approved death penalty, leaving the stage set for California's first execution since 1967. At the close of his two terms, nearly two-thirds of California's judges were Deukmejian appointees, including five of the seven members of the state Supreme Court. He also had pushed a massive construction program to more than double the number of state prison beds.

Yet as the country entered a recession, Deukmejian also watched his carefully cultivated fiscal legacy unravel. He left behind a state budget shortfall of unprecedented proportions, saddling his successor, Pete Wilson, with a far larger financial crisis than the one he had inherited from Jerry Brown.

California also was beginning to want more in a governor than a warrior against taxes and crime. As Deukmejian entered the "lame-duck" phase of his political career, complaints that he was bland, boring and stubborn escalated into a more serious charge: that he lacked the vision or leadership qualities needed to move the state into the 21st century with its prosperity intact.

Deukmejian wore out his welcome with business leaders, who liked lower tax bills as long the state provided the services they needed. At a time when businesses were increasingly finding they couldn't move their products and services freely on California's congested highways, the governor had to be coaxed into supporting a hike in the state's road-building tax on gasoline.

In addition, a population explosion and the accompanying demand for state services were blowing the lid off a voter-imposed spending cap that Deukmejian defended. Rather than raise the state's gas tax, Deukmejian initially shifted more responsibility for road-building to local government, signing a 1987 bill that gave counties the power to ask voters for sales tax increases to pay for transportation. But by 1989, even Republicans who shared Deukmejian's determination to hold the line on state spending chafed at what they saw as a lack of gubernatorial activism, and Deukmejian successfully campaigned for a measure to raise the state's gas tax and adjust the spending limit.

CALIFORNIA GOVERNORS

Governor	Party	Inauguration
Peter H. Burnett	Independent	December 1849
John McDougal	Independent	January 1851
John Bigler	Democrat	January 1852
John Bigler	Democrat	January 1854
J. Neeley Johnson	American	January 1856
John B. Weller	Democrat	January 1858
Milton S. Latham	Lecompton Democrat	January 1860
John G. Downey	Lecompton Democrat	January 1860
Leland Stanford	Republican	January 1862
Frederick F. Low	Union	December 1863
Henry H. Haight	Democrat	December 1867
Newton Booth	Republican	December 1871
Romualdo Pacheco	Republican	February 1875
William Irwin	Democrat	December 1875
George C. Perkins	Republican	January 1880
George Stoneman	Democrat	January 1883
Washington Bartlett	Democrat	January 1887
Robert W. Waterman	Republican	September 1887
Henry H. Markham	Republican	January 1891
James H. Budd	Democrat	January 1895
Henry T. Gage	Republican	January 1899
George C. Pardee	Republican	January 1903
James N. Gillett	Republican	January 1907
Hiram W. Johnson	Republican	January 1911
Hiram W. Johnson	Progressive	January 1915
William D. Stephens	Republican	March 1917
William D. Stephens	Republican	January 1919
Friend Wm. Richardson	Republican	January 1923
C. C. Young	Republican	January 1927
James Rolph Jr.	Republican	January 1931
Frank F. Merriam	Republican	June 1934
Frank F. Merriam	Republican	January 1935
Culbert L. Olson	Democrat	January 1939
Earl Warren	Republican	January 1943
Earl Warren	Rep.-Dem.	January 1947
Earl Warren	Republican	January 1951
Goodwin J. Knight	Republican	October 1953
Goodwin J. Knight	Republican	January 1955
Edmund G. "Pat" Brown	Democrat	January 1959
Edmund G. "Pat" Brown	Democrat	January 1963
Ronald Reagan	Republican	January 1967
Ronald Reagan	Republican	January 1971
Edmund G. "Jerry" Brown Jr.	Democrat	January 1975
Edmund G. "Jerry" Brown Jr.	Democrat	January 1979
George Deukmejian	Republican	January 1983
George Deukmejian	Republican	January 1987
Pete Wilson	Republican	January 1991

In 1978, anti-tax crusaders Howard Jarvis and Paul Gann had tapped into an underlying anger about government spending with Proposition 13. Proposition 13 and its follow-up, a voter-imposed limit on government spending promoted by Gann, still shape California politics today, forcing any aspiring officeholder who wants to be taken seriously to tiptoe around the subject of taxes. Failure to display enough tax-cutting zeal in 1978 cost several state legislators their seats and created a new corps of "Proposition 13 babies" in the state Legislature.

The anti-tax movement also marked the beginning of the end for Jerry Brown, who irreparably damaged his credibility by campaigning against the initiative, then embracing it with enthusiasm once it passed. Brown was defeated by Republican Pete Wilson in his 1982 bid for the U.S. Senate and left the political scene for a six-year sabbatical.

As the political pendulum began to swing back toward the middle, Brown returned to campaign for and win the chairmanship of the state Democratic Party. "The time," he told party members, "is ripe for resurgence." Ultimately, it became clear that he was most interested in reviving his own political career, and he resigned from the job two years early to plan a run for the U.S. Senate in 1992.

Whether the Democratic Party would continue its decade-long, post-Proposition 13 fade in voter registration or re-establish itself in California was one of the unspoken themes of the 1990 campaign for governor, one in-

ELECTIONS 1902-1990

Year	Candidate	Vote
1902	George C. Pardee (R)	48.06%
	Franklin K. Lane (D)	47.22%
1906	James Gillett (R)	40.4%
	Theodore Bell (D)	37.7%
1910	Hiram Johnson (R)	45.9%
	Theodore Bell (D)	40.1%
1914	Hiram Johnson (Pg)	49.7%
	John Fredericks (R)	29.3%
	J.B. Curtin (D)	12.5%
1918	William Stephens (R)	56.3%
	Theodore Bell (I)	36.5%
1922	Friend Wm. Richardson (R)	59.7%
	Thomas Lee Woolwine (D)	36%
1926	C.C. Young (R)	71.2%
	Justus Wardell (D)	24.7%
1930	James Rolph Jr. (R)	72.1%
	Milton Young (D)	24.1%
1934	Frank Merriam (R)	48.9%
	Upton Sinclair (D)	37.7%
1938	Culbert Olson (D)	52.5%
	Frank Merriam (R)	44.2%
1942	Earl Warren (R)	57%
	Culbert Olson (D)	41.7%
1946	Earl Warren (R &D)	91.6%
	Henry Schmidt (Prohibition)	7.1%
1950	Earl Warren (R)	64.8%
	James Roosevelt (D)	35.2%
1954	Goodwin Knight (R)	56.8%
	Richard Graves (D)	43.2%
1958	Pat Brown (D)	59.8%
	William Knowland (R)	40.2%
1962	Pat Brown (D)	51.9%
	Richard Nixon (R)	46.8%
1966	Ronald Reagan (R)	56.6%
	Pat Brown (D)	41.6%
1970	Ronald Reagan (R)	52.8%
	Jesse Unruh (D)	45.1%
1974	Jerry Brown (D)	50.2%
	Houston Flournoy (R)	47.3%
1978	Jerry Brown (D)	56%
	Evelle Younger (R)	36.5%
1982	George Deukmejian (R)	49.3%
	Tom Bradley (D)	48.1%
1986	George Deukmejian (R)	60.54%
	Tom Bradley (D)	37.37%
1990	Pete Wilson (R)	49.25%
	Dianne Feinstein (D)	45.79%

I: Independent; Pg: Progressive.

tertwined with growing concern among Californians about a widely perceived deterioration in the quality of their lives.

Republicans –Deukmejian being the chief example –prospered during the 1980s by aligning themselves with the Proposition 13-inspired mood of limited taxation and government spending; Democrats, who ordinarily favor a more activist government, were left befuddled by the onset of tax-cut fever. Republican Pete Wilson won election as governor by finding a middle ground, denouncing Democrat Dianne Feinstein as a "tax and spend liberal" while refusing to rule out tax increases himself –shunning the "read my lips" school of campaigning that helped put George Bush in the White House.

Within weeks of Wilson's inauguration, it was clear that he had been wise to avoid an anti-tax pledge. To cope with a budget shortfall estimated at 12.6 billion, he proposed tax increases coupled with major cuts in welfare and education spending. At the same time, he called for more "preventive" government programs to keep children in school and out of prison.

THE WILSON ERA BEGINS

More than 20 years ago, as Pete Wilson contemplated leaving his state Assembly seat to run for mayor of San Diego, his administrative assistant sketched out the pros and cons on a yellow legal pad. There were big problems in San Diego, a city racked by government scandal and rampant growth. The Navy town, tucked away near the Mexican border, was hardly noticed by most Californians. The job was probably a political cul-de-sac. On the other hand, managing a city might demonstrate executive ability, experience that Wilson could point to if he someday ran for governor. "I knew he wanted to be governor, and I wanted him to be governor," said Bob White, who has been Wilson's top aide ever since.

So Wilson pulled up his Sacramento stakes and went south to take charge of San Diego. Two decades later, that decision and the way he made it continue to say a lot about him. Having fulfilled his ambition to become governor, Peter Barton Wilson remains essentially a legal-pad kind of guy.

"Mostly, he works," says John Davies, who has remained close to Wilson since the two were law school classmates at Boalt Hall, University of California, Berkeley. Everyone who knows Wilson, who gets by on five hours of sleep a night, can tell a similar story about his driving work habits and stamina. Mike Madigan, in his first year as a policy aide to Wilson in the San Diego mayor's office, kept track of how many complete days he had off. "It turned out to be one," Madigan said. "It was either Christmas or New Year's, and Pete worked that day. He's a workaholic, and he expects that of the people that work for him."

A former Marine who completed his undergraduate studies at Yale University, Wilson still comes across as someone who wears starched shirts on Saturdays. When he does relax, he smokes a cigar, puts some Broadway show tunes on the stereo and knocks back a couple of scotches. But he rarely unwinds before 9 p.m., said Gayle Wilson, who recalls her exhaustion in the early days of their marriage. "I remember going in to my doctor and saying, 'God, I'm so tired.' He said, 'Don't try to keep up with Pete.' "

The former Gayle Graham, Wilson's second wife, is an energetic campaigner herself. A singer with the nerve to enliven a listless campaign rally by belting out a Wilson campaign tune without musical accompaniment, she often draws more enthusiastic applause than her husband. The impression left in San Diego circles is that Gayle is the gung-ho political wife that Wilson's first spouse never wanted to be. Pete and Betty Wilson divorced in 1982, following a separation of more than a year. But Wilson publicly shoulders the blame for the split, saying it

Pete Wilson

had less to do with Betty's lack of interest in politics than his own workaholic habits. He fiercely protects her privacy, and friends say all couples who split should do so in such an upbeat and dignified way.

It is true that Wilson was principally devoted in those years to making his mark on city government. Unsuccessful at convincing voters to institute a strong-mayor form of government at the ballot box, he used the force of his own personality to accomplish the same goal.

Wilson's father, James, a hard-charging advertising executive whom Wilson describes as one of his heroes, never wanted his son to go into politics. But ironically it was at the dinner table, when his dad would deliver "mini-lectures" on obligation to society, that Wilson said his interest in public service began. The senior Wilson, who dabbled in local politics himself, ran for local office after retiring to Florida. He won in a landslide, then failed to win re-election to a second term after offending constituents opposed to putting a day-care center in a local church.

Wilson, too, is not always one to watch his tongue when convinced that right is on his side. In 1989, Wilson penned his own scathing reply to a letter from a constituent who suggested Wilson's support for John Tower's nomination as defense secretary was motivated by political cronyism. If the constituent wasn't interested in his true reasons for supporting Tower, he wrote, "to hell with you."

In public-speaking settings, Wilson's self-confident attitude can border on smug. A long line of aides has tried to convince him to shorten his speeches, criticism he listens to but rejects. He does not suffer fools gladly, those close to him say. Yet in a business where loyalties can come and go with the election cycle, Wilson was surrounded in his gubernatorial campaign with aides who have been with him for years.

Wilson is also persistent. He failed the bar exam twice before passing on his third try. He practiced law only briefly, however, before grabbing a seat in the Assembly, devoting much of his time after law school to a series of political jobs. He was an advance man for Richard Nixon's gubernatorial campaign in 1962, a paid staff member for a local Republican club and executive director of the San Diego Republican Party Central Committee in 1964.

Wilson's plan to catapult from San Diego into statewide office failed in 1978, when he finished fourth in a bid for the GOP gubernatorial nomination. Four years later he considered another try, but settled instead for a successful U.S. Senate race against outgoing Gov. Jerry Brown.

Through most of Wilson's career, he's been more centrist than conservative. He has courted the environmental vote with consistent stands on coastal protection, limits on offshore oil drilling, expansion of transit systems and planned growth. On other matters, Wilson as a U.S. senator generally supported Reagan administration policies and was an early backer of George Bush's candidacy. In the U.S. Senate he worked for California industry, particularly agriculture, aerospace and computer electronics. One early success has also turned into a fund-raising plus. He backed Hollywood studios in a fight with the Federal Communications Commission over plans to allow television networks to own programs they broadcast. The plan was effectively killed when Wilson announced President Reagan's opposition at a 1983 hearing. Producer Lew Wasserman, a longtime fund-raiser for Democrats, thanked Wilson by throwing a Beverly Hills party that brought Wilson more than $100,000 in campaign contributions. More importantly, it gave Wilson entree to a number of show business personalities who seldom, if ever, had supported Republicans. Wilson's entertainment industry connections have muted the support Democratic foes expect from the liberal Hollywood community, a factor that helped Wilson win a second Senate term in 1988 and the governor's job in 1990.

Probably the most memorable moment of Wilson's Senate years came when he was recovering from an emergency appendectomy. The Senate was considering a complex budget measure, which included a freeze on cost-of-living increases for Social Security recipients, and it appeared that Vice President Bush would be needed to break a tie. At the critical moment, pajama-clad Wilson was wheeled onto the Senate floor to cast the deciding vote in favor. The episode surfaced again in the closing days of the gubernatorial campaign, when Democratic opponent Dianne Feinstein ran a television ad in which Senate Republican leader Bob Dole joked about Wilson's post-surgery appearance, saying he "does better under sedation."

Wilson also was embarrassed by revelations that he accepted round-trip air fare from defense contractors and others who regularly lobbied committees on which he served. His wife flew gratis on a number of the flights as well. Most of the trips were coast-to-coast and involved legitimate speaking engagements requested by the firms involved, Wilson contended. "What votes are those (trips) tied to, what actions?" he asked. "Senators do it routinely, and they do it because it is entirely within the law."

Wilson had never been a favorite of many state Republicans; he endorsed Gerald Ford over Ronald Reagan in the 1976 presidential campaign. At the 1985 Republican state convention, conservatives almost booed him off the stage. In November 1988, however, Wilson did something that none of his predecessors had been able to do for 36 years: He held onto his Senate seat for a second term. His re-election opponent, Lt. Gov. Leo McCarthy, had gotten nowhere with his campaign charge that Wilson "left no footprints" in Washington, and it appeared that the "jinxed seat" from California finally had an occupant who would make a career of the Senate.

Then came Deukmejian's announcement that he wouldn't seek a third term. GOP leaders, desperate to have a Republican in the governor's chair when the state was reapportioned after the 1990 census, cast about for someone electable. With no other Republicans holding statewide office, most agreed that only Wilson fit the bill. He was quick to hit the campaign trail again. "I see it very likely as a career capper –and a damn good one," he said in the midst of the campaign.

He was less definitive about his future career plans once in office. Keenly aware that California's governor is automatically catapulted into the ranks of potential presidents, he appeared ready to cultivate a national image.

PERSONAL: elected 1990; born Aug. 23, 1933, in Lake Forest, Ill.; home, San Diego; education, B.A. Yale University 1955, J.D. UC Berkeley 1962; wife, Gayle; Protestant.

CAREER: U.S. Marine Corps, 1955-58; attorney, 1963-66; Assembly, 1966-71; San Diego mayor, 1971-83; U.S. Senator, 1983-91.

LEO McCARTHY EYES SECOND SENATE RACE

Leo McCarthy, long considered a cut above most California politicians, found in 1988 that his squeaky-clean reputation and proven performance on a list of liberal issues were not enough to defeat incumbent Republican Sen. Pete Wilson in a lackluster U.S. Senate race.

In early 1989, the two-term lieutenant governor, his senatorial campaign still in debt, announced he was not willing to step back onto a round-the-clock fund-raising treadmill in order to run for governor. Instead, to the disappointment of several younger Democrats who had been waiting for him to move up or out, McCarthy opted to run for re-election. By early 1991, however, McCarthy was back in the hunt for higher office. Buoyed by poll results that showed voters had largely forgotten his political thrashing by Wilson, the three-term lieutenant governor announced he would mount a second try for the U.S. Senate. This time he is seeking the seat held by retiring U.S. Sen. Alan Cranston.

A workaholic and conscientious to a fault, McCarthy can also be sanctimonious and stubborn, qualities that rose to the surface during the prolonged strain of his last Senate campaign. But he had endured defeat before, most notably in an agonizing power struggle with then-Assemblyman Howard Berman, which ended McCarthy's six years as Assembly speaker in 1980. The

Leo McCarthy

fight ultimately handed the speakership to fellow San Franciscan Willie Brown after McCarthy and Berman battled to a draw.

McCarthy went on to become lieutenant governor in 1982 and won re-election in 1986 at a time when he was one of the few candidates willing to openly support state Supreme Court Chief Justice Rose Bird during her losing bid to retain her post. By then he had changed his position on the death penalty –the issue that led to Bird's defeat –after years of opposition to capital punishment. Kidnapped as a college student by a man who had just murdered a police officer, McCarthy said his views on violent crime began to change years later when he met the officer's widow.

McCarthy has used his post to pursue such issues as environmental protection and nursing-home reform. But his most visible moment as lieutenant governor came on Oct. 17, 1989, when a 7.1-magnitude earthquake struck Northern California. Gov. George Deukmejian was out of the country at the time, leaving McCarthy capably in charge of the early stages of the disaster.

Born in New Zealand, McCarthy grew up in San Francisco as the son of a tavern owner and attended Catholic seminary as a teenager. He served on the San Francisco

Board of Supervisors from 1963 to 1968. From there, he moved to the Assembly, where he soon earned a reputation as a family man who commuted home to San Francisco nearly every night rather than pursue Sacramento's political night life.

McCarthy's latest Senate try is likely to pit him against his longtime political foe, former Gov. Jerry Brown, as well as two or more Democratic members of Congress. His hopes for winning the seat may hinge on how many Democrats join the crowd. Too many candidates could divide the vote and hand the nomination to Brown and thwart McCarthy's hopes for escaping his powerless post.

PERSONAL: elected 1982; re-elected 1986 and 1990; born Aug. 15, 1930, in Auckland, New Zealand; home, San Francisco; education, B.S. University of San Francisco, J.D. San Francisco Law School; wife, Jacqueline Burke; children, Sharon, Conna, Adam and Niall.

CAREER: legislative aide to Sen. Eugene McAteer, 1959-1963; San Francisco Board of Supervisors, 1963-1968; Assembly 1969-1982; Assembly speaker 1974-1980.

OFFICES: Capitol (916) 445-8994; San Francisco (415) 557-2662; Los Angeles (213) 620-2560; San Diego (619) 238-3489.

LIEUTENANT GOVERNORS SINCE 1950		
Goodwin J. Knight	Republican	elected 1950
Harold J. Powers	Republican	appointed 1953
Harold J. Powers	Republican	elected 1954
Glenn M. Anderson	Democrat	elected 1958, '62
Robert Finch	Republican	elected 1966
Ed Reinecke	Republican	appointed 1969
Ed Reinecke	Republican	elected 1970
Mervyn Dymally	Democrat	elected 1974
Mike Curb	Republican	elected 1978
Leo T. McCarthy	Democrat	elected 1982, '86, '90

DANIEL LUNGREN LAUGHS LAST

The state Senate Democrats who dumped Dan Lungren, Gov. George Deukmejian's first nominee for state treasurer, had hoped to avoid creating a future formidable candidate for governor. But Republicans may have had the last laugh in 1990, when Lungren was elected in his own right to be attorney general, an even more prominent constitutional office. Aided by a massive voter-turnout program conducted by Republican gubernatorial candidate Pete Wilson, Lungren narrowly defeated San Francisco District Attorney Arlo Smith to become the state's chief law enforcement official.

It was a nasty, name-calling election that left many capital insiders wondering whether they should write in Van de Kamp's name for re-election instead of casting a vote for either candidate. Perhaps the lowest point came when an argument between the two candidates led to a pushing match between Smith's campaign manager and Lungren's driver in the hallway of a San Francisco television station. Theatrics continued after the campaign, as Smith, who had survived a tough primary battle against Los Angeles District Attorney Ira Reiner, refused to acknowledge that he had lost a close vote to Lungren and vainly sought to contest the outcome in the courts. It was January 1991 before he conceded.

Lungren, who spent 10 years in Congress as a law-and-order conservative, had abandoned an exploratory candidacy for the U.S. Senate in 1986 because he was unable to raise enough money. When his hopes of becoming state treasurer following the death of long-time Democratic Treasurer

Dan Lungren

Jesse Unruh in 1987 were dashed by the Democratic-controlled state Senate, Lungren returned to private practice in a Sacramento law firm and began to plan a campaign for attorney general instead.

Lungren, who at 6 years old began walking precincts for a GOP congressional candidate, isn't the only member of his family with political ties. His father was Richard Nixon's personal physician, and his younger brother, Brian, is a political consultant who managed his campaign for attorney general. Lungren served as an assistant to Republican U.S. Sens. George Murphy of California and Bill Brock of Tennessee in 1969 and 1970, and was a special assistant to the Republican National Committee from 1971 to 1972. He practiced law in Long Beach from 1973 to 1978, when he was elected to Congress. Watchdog groups consistently classified his congressional votes as conservative, and he earned the wrath of Japanese-American groups for voting against reparations to Japanese-Americans who were interned during World War II.

Lungren is an entertaining and dynamic public speaker, and his competitive nature and intense personality make him a candidate to be reckoned with should he seek higher office. The attorney general's office has long been a trampoline for those aspiring to be governor. While Van de Kamp's loss shows the route is not infallible, Earl Warren, Pat Brown and, most recently, George Deukmejian bounced into the chief executive's chair by that route. In a state where voters are solidly pro-choice, however, Lungren's political Achilles' heel is abortion. While he says his strong anti-abortion stance will not have much impact on state law –he argues the issue occupies an infinitesimal amount of the attorney general's time –he has also said he will not take "a vow of silence" on the subject.

PERSONAL: elected 1990; born Sept. 22, 1946; home, Roseville; education, B.A. University of Notre Dame, J.D. Georgetown University Law School; wife, Barbara "Bobbie" Lungren; children, Jeffrey, Kelly and Kathleen.

CAREER: U.S. Senate aide, 1969-70; Republican National Committee staff, 1971-72; private law practice in Long Beach, 1973-78, and in Sacramento 1989-1991; U.S. House of Representatives 1979-1989.

OFFICES: Sacramento (916) 445-9555; San Francisco (415) 557-2544; Los Angeles (213) 736-2304.

ATTORNEYS GENERAL SINCE 1950		
Edmund G. "Pat" Brown	Democrat	elected 1950, '54
Stanley Mosk	Democrat	elected 1958, '62
Thomas C. Lynch	Democrat	appointed 1964
Thomas C. Lynch	Democrat	elected 1966
Evelle J. Younger	Republican	elected 1970, '74
George Deukmejian	Republican	elected 1978
John Van de Kamp	Democrat	elected 1982, '86
Dan Lungren	Republican	elected 1990

GRAY DAVIS: TREADING WATER

As a California assemblyman, Gray Davis campaigned to find missing children and remove asbestos from school buildings. As state controller, he has promoted the return of unclaimed property to Californians and lobbied against offshore oil drilling. But Davis is best known in California political circles for two prominent traits: his impressive fund-raising talents and his unbridled ambition for higher office.

Like Lt. Gov. Leo McCarthy, Davis was forced to tread water politically in 1990, running for re-election rather than joining a tough Democratic primary battle for governor. Long believed to covet the governor's post, Davis nonetheless was weighing the possibility of a 1992 campaign for the U.S. Senate.

Born Joseph Graham Davis Jr. in New York, Davis moved to California with his family at age 11. A graduate of Stanford University and Columbia University law school, he served two years in the U.S. Army in Vietnam.

In 1974, with a stint as finance director for Tom Bradley's successful mayoral race under his belt, the slim and soft-spoken Davis made his first run at statewide office. He filed for the Democratic nomination for state treasurer, then learned to his dismay that former Assembly Speaker Jesse Unruh had decided to enter the race. It was no contest. "I was the doormat Jess stepped on in his road back to political prominence," Davis later recalled.

Davis then went to work as the chief of staff for Jerry Brown, who became governor that year. Putting aside his own ambitions for the moment, he helped forge Brown's thrifty image and ran interference with the Legislature, surviving a continual power struggle among the young governor's

Gray Davis

top aides. By 1981, however, Davis was restless and ready to run for the state Assembly. Elected to the 43rd District representing West Los Angeles in 1982, he won re-election two years later.

Those years laid the groundwork for Davis' second statewide run. When veteran state Controller Kenneth Cory announced his retirement just days before the filing deadline in 1986, Davis was already sitting on a $1 million campaign fund that enabled him to dash in and win the race. His 1985 effort to encourage companies to picture missing children on milk cartons, grocery bags and billboards had publicized his name, too. The program featured prominently in his campaign ads.

Although controversial Supreme Court Chief Justice Rose Bird presided at Davis' 1983 wedding, he sidestepped the issue in his race for controller, saying he did not want to prejudice cases involving the controller's office that someday could come before the court. He emerged largely unscathed by the Bird-bashing and Brown-battering leveled at Democratic candidates that year. He later narrowly escaped prosecution for using state staff and equipment in his 1986 campaign for controller. Attorney General John Van de Kamp, another Democrat, concluded taxpayer funds were used in the campaign, but found insufficient evidence to accuse Davis of any criminal intentions.

The controller's office gives Davis a seat on 52 boards and commissions, including the State Lands Commission, where he has been able to express his strong environmental views. He also sits on the state Board of Equalization, signs the state's checks and has a voice in managing some $86 billion in state employee and teacher pension funds.

Since his 1986 election, Davis has used the office as a platform to fight offshore oil drilling, defend the state's family planning program, hunt for people whom the state owes money and, on two occasions, press corporations to donate wetlands to the public. It's a safe bet, however, that he is not interested in serving indefinitely as the state's fiscal watchdog.

PERSONAL: elected 1986; born Dec. 26, 1942, in New York; home, Los Angeles; education, B.A. Stanford University, J.D. Columbia University Law School; wife, Sharon Ryer Davis.

CAREER: chief of staff to Gov. Jerry Brown 1974-1981; Assembly 1983-1986.

OFFICES: Sacramento (916) 445-3028; Los Angeles (213) 852-5213.

CONTROLLERS SINCE 1950		
Thomas H. Kuchel	Republican	elected 1950
Robert C. Kirkwood	Republican	appointed 1952
Robert C. Kirkwood	Republican	elected 1954
Alan Cranston	Democrat	elected 1958, '62
Houston I. Flournoy	Republican	elected 1966, '70
Kenneth Cory	Democrat	elected 1974, '78, '82
Gray Davis	Democrat	elected 1986, '90

A DIFFERENT SHADE OF BROWN

In 1990, a year in which voters sent one of their strongest anti-politician signals yet by imposing term limits on legislators, most candidates for statewide office did their best to portray their opponent as the politician in the race. In that context, Kathleen Brown's bid to become state treasurer might have been expected to be an uphill battle at best. Sitting Treasurer Thomas Hayes, a career civil servant, had never run for office before. Appointed by Gov. George Deukmejian to fill out the unexpired term of Jesse Unruh, who had died in office in 1987, Hayes prided himself on his money-management skills. He said he was asking voters to elect a financial manager –not a politician.

Enter Brown, a member of one of the state's most colorful and controversial political families. The daughter of former Gov. Pat Brown and sister of former Gov. Jerry Brown, her political ties were impossible to hide, and she didn't try. Arguing that the elected office called for a candidate who was more than a pencil-pusher, she said she would be a treasurer who didn't stay in the vault.

Brown, who had been a lawyer at O'Melveny and Myers, a powerhouse in government bond law, capitalized on her family's formidable political connections and her own network as an attorney to beat Hayes at the fund-raising game. In her talking-head TV ads, she came across as steady and sincere. The result was the election of a third Brown to statewide office, bringing the list of constitutional posts the family has held to four –governor, attorney general, treasurer and secretary of state.

Brown was quick to acknowledge that the assets she brought to the campaign –her gender, her political party and her family ties –were also liabilities. Hayes' television strategist, Republican image-maker Roger Ailes, called her "Sister Moonbeam," a refer-

Kathleen Brown

ence to the "Gov. Moonbeam" label that captured her brother's image at the close of his two terms as governor. But Kathleen said she was "a different shade of Brown." She preferred to discuss her father's record as governor, recalling his push to build highways, universities and water systems. She charged that Hayes had moved too slowly to sell voter-approved bonds for schools and other facilities.

Brown was elected to the Los Angeles Board of Education in 1975 and re-elected in 1979, the year her marriage to George Rice ended in divorce. The following year, she married television executive Van Gordon Sauter and resigned from the board to join her new husband in New York. The couple returned to California in 1987.

Brown's election as treasurer gave rise to great expectations in political circles. Washington Post columnist David Broder suggested that California at last had a Democratic officeholder capable of taking a place on the national ticket. At the very least, most believed she eventually would follow the Brown family tradition of using a lesser constitutional office as a launching pad for a gubernatorial campaign.

PERSONAL: elected 1990; born Sept. 25, 1945, in San Francisco; home, Los Angeles; education, B.A. Stanford University, J.D. Fordham University School of

Law; husband, Van Gordon Sauter; children, Hilary Rice, Sascha Rice, Zebediah Rice, Mark Sauter and Jeremy Sauter.

CAREER: Los Angeles Board of Public Works 1978-1989; attorney, 1985-87; Los Angeles Board of Education 1975-1980.

OFFICE: Sacramento (916) 445-5316.

TREASURERS SINCE 1950		
Charles G. Johnson	Progressive	elected 1950, '54
Ronald Button	Republican	appointed 1956
Bert A. Betts	Democrat	elected 1958, '62
Ivy Baker Priest	Republican	elected 1966, '70
Jesse M. Unruh	Democrat	elected 1974, '78, '82, '86
Thomas Hayes	Republican	appointed 1987
Kathleen Brown	Democrat	elected 1990

MARCH FONG EU STANDS PAT

March Fong Eu's own press releases bill her as the winningest woman in California politics. The first and only Asian-American to be elected to state constitutional office, Eu has served as California's chief elections officer since 1975. She was a four-term assemblywoman when she won the secretary of state's post in 1974. She was re-elected in 1978, 1982, 1986 and 1990.

In her last race, however, Eu withstood an unexpectedly strong challenge from Los Angeles City Councilwoman Joan Milke Flores, who campaigned with the slogan "Where was Eu?" Flores complained that Eu has been a chronic violator of the very campaign laws she is supposed to enforce and has done nothing to stem the decline in California voter par-

March Fong Eu

ticipation. In particular, she noted Eu reduced fines against her own campaign in 1986 and 1987 from $26,200 to just $650. Eu agreed in early 1990 to pay the Fair Political Practices Commission $8,000 to settle a complaint involving 95 reporting violations that could have resulted in penalties for her campaign totaling $190,000. Eu, who readily concedes waiving penalties for late campaign reporting on a bipartisan basis unless a pattern of willful violations is found, called the failures "inadvertent, but not excusable."

Eu cites a long list of accomplishments in office, including a record of fraud-free elections, efficient election reporting and an attack on the national media projections used to forecast election results long before the California polls close.

She has failed, however, to use her job as a launching pad for higher office. Jerry Brown, who served one term as secretary of state on his way to becoming governor, made the post a bully pulpit to push for political reform in the post-Watergate era. Eu largely sticks to more mundane tasks, including a thankless effort to boost voter registration and turnout in a state where campaigns dominated by money and media are driving voters away from the polls. She has warned fellow Democrats that the party is in danger of slipping into minority status if Democrats don't do a better job of registering members of the state's burgeoning Asian and Hispanic populations.

Eu tried to move up in 1987, when she declared herself a Democratic candidate for the U.S. Senate seat held by Republican Pete Wilson. But she demonstrated sketchy knowledge of federal issues in her early meetings with reporters and struggled in her efforts to mount a fund-raising operation. Eu, who had been beaten by a robber in her Los Angeles area home one week after winning election to her fourth term, put her Senate campaign on hold to launch a signature drive for a proposed initiative she called Dimes Against Crimes. The crime initiative was one way to keep her name in the news, a technique she had used to great advantage as an assemblywoman campaigning to ban pay toilets in public buildings. But she failed to raise enough money to qualify her initiative.

Ultimately, her biggest political liability proved to be her wealthy husband. Henry Eu, one of 13 sons of one of the wealthiest men in the Far East, refused to reveal details of his business interests, making it impossible for Eu to comply with the disclosure requirements of federal campaign law. She abandoned her Senate campaign in 1987 before it truly began, saying she was forced to choose between her candidacy and her marriage.

A third-generation Californian of Chinese descent, Eu was born in Oakdale, Calif., the daughter of a laundry owner. Eu began her own career as a dental hygienist and eventually earned a doctor of education degree at Stanford University. She moved in 1966 from a position on the Alameda County Board of Education to become the state's first Asian assemblywoman.

PERSONAL: elected 1974; re-elected 1978, 1982, 1986 and 1990; born March 29, 1922, in Oakdale, Calif.; home, Los Angeles; education, B.S. University of California, Berkeley, M.Ed. Mills College, Ed. D. Stanford University; husband,

Henry Eu; children, Matthew Fong Jr., Suyin Fong.

CAREER: Dental hygienist for Oakland public schools 1945-48; chairwoman, division of dental hygiene, University of California Medical Center in San Francisco 1948-51; supervisor of dental health education for Alameda County Board of Education 1956-66; Assembly 1967-74.

OFFICES: Sacramento (916) 445-6371; San Francisco (415) 557-8051; Los Angeles (213) 620-4382; San Diego (619) 237-6009.

SECRETARIES OF STATE SINCE 1950

Frank M. Jordan	Republican	elected 1950, '54, '58, '62, '66
Pat Sullivan	Republican	appointed 1970
Edmund G. "Jerry" Brown Jr.	Democrat	elected 1970
March Fong Eu	Democrat	elected 1974, '78, '82, '86, '90

BILL HONIG: THE EDUCATION WARRIOR

With reform as his battle cry, state schools chief Bill Honig marched into the 1980s waging political war on behalf of California school children. He crusaded relentlessly for the new money and new attitudes that he said were needed to bring about wholesale changes in the state's classrooms, and he spent much of the decade alternately feuding and making peace with Gov. George Deukmejian over spending for education.

Born Louis William Honig Jr. in San Francisco, he abandoned a career as a lawyer to become a teacher and was named to the state Board of Education by Gov. Jerry Brown in 1975. By 1982, he said he was angry enough about the lack of education leadership in California to challenge three-

Bill Honig

term incumbent Wilson Riles for state superintendent of public instruction. Upon his election, Honig plunged into a massive legislative dispute over education funding, emerging with Deukmejian's commitment to a plan that provided hundreds of millions in extra dollars for schools. The landmark package also enacted a series of reforms: a longer school day and year, stricter school discipline, higher pay for entry-level teachers and more stringent high school curriculum requirements for English, social science, science and math.

But maintaining the progress proved difficult as enrollment grew and California experienced an influx of young immigrants requiring extra classroom attention. The demands coincided with new state spending constraints as California began to experience the effects of a budget-capping formula approved by voters in 1979. Honig again martialed his political forces to demand a "fair share" of the state budget for schools. He lost a major round with Deukmejian in 1987, when legislators decided to return a $1.1 billion surplus to taxpayers rather than find a way to divert the money to education. He returned in 1988 to win voter approval of Proposition 98, an initiative that guarantees a minimum state funding level for schools. Passage of the measure, however, immediately threatened to isolate Honig politically when it ignited a storm of counterlobbying from doctors, university officials, state employees and others who said it paid for education at the expense of other vital state services.

Honig also has come under fire from members of the state Board of Education, who have complained that he has shut them out of key decisions. Honig ultimately agreed to give the board more authority, but members said he hadn't gone far enough and the power struggle continued to unfold.

Negative publicity also focused on a non-profit educational foundation established and run by Honig's wife. Known as the Quality Education Project, the foundation holds training sessions for parents and teachers on how they can work together to help their children succeed. Critics, however, began to question the propriety of school districts purchasing services from the wife of the superintendent of public instruction. Nancy Honig denied any improprieties and said no local superintendent felt obligated to subscribe to the program because of her husband.

In 1988, after declining to state his party affiliation for six years, Honig rejoined the Democratic Party and was rumored to be in line for a federal post if the Democrats had won the White House. When the defeat of Democratic presidential candidate Michael Dukakis denied him that opportunity, most Capitol observers expected Honig to run for governor in 1990. But he bowed out of the 1990 race before it began, announcing that he would concentrate on winning a third term. He said he had an obligation to remain in the post and continue to wage budgetary battles for schools.

Honig, always seen by Deukmejian as a potent political threat, welcomed the opportunity to work with newly elected Gov. Pete Wilson. He sees Wilson as more interested in education and more willing to forge political compromise, and for the moment has stopped threatening to mount his own campaign for the governor's seat.

PERSONAL: elected 1982; re-elected 1986 and 1990; born April 23, 1937, in San Francisco; home, San Francisco; education, B.A. and J.D. University of California, Berkeley, M.Ed. San Francisco State University; wife, Nancy Catlin Honig; children, Michael, Carolyn, Steven and Jonathan.

CAREER: clerk for Chief Justice Matthew Tobriner 1963-1964; associate counsel in state Department of Finance 1964-1966; San Francisco corporate and individual lawyer beginning in 1967; elementary school teacher 1972-1976; superintendent of the Reed Union Elementary School District 1979-1982; state Board of Education 1975-1982.

OFFICES: Sacramento (916) 445-4688; San Francisco (415) 557-0193.

SUPERINTENDENTS OF PUBLIC INSTRUCTION SINCE 1950

Roy Simpson	elected 1950, '54, '58
Max Rafferty	elected 1962, '66
Wilson Riles	elected 1970, '74, '78
Bill Honig	elected 1982, '86, '90

JOHN GARAMENDI'S OPPORTUNITY

For years, John Garamendi has been one the Capitol's most ambitious figures. And why not? Garamendi would appear to be the dream candidate: handsome ex-college football star with degrees from Harvard and the University of California; Peace Corps volunteer with his wife in Ethiopia; son of Basque-Italian parents who carved out a rugged living on ranches in Nevada and the Sierra foothills; bank officer; and devoted father of a handsome family. Yet, until he beat a large field of Democrats in the primary and an unknown Republican insurance agent in the general election to become California's first elected insurance commissioner, Garamendi's career seemed a collection of promising roads that had become dead-ends.

Garamendi won election to the Assembly in 1974 then moved up to the Senate two years later. In 1980, he became majority leader, the No. 2 spot in the Senate, in a leadership shake-up that made David Roberti president pro tem. But from that quick start, Garamendi's political career tripped and stumbled along, often because he tried to move it too fast. He was victimized, paradoxically, by his overweening ambition and a stubborn unwillingness to play the political game by the rules.

Garamendi's first fall was in 1982, when his quixotic bid for the Democratic nomination for governor got his ears boxed. He could, and probably should, have run for a lesser statewide office but insisted on going for the top. He also passed up a chance to run for Congress. As Garamendi's reputation for ambition grew in the Senate, he was accused by Democratic colleagues of neglecting his duties as majority floor leader. In 1985, he found himself replaced by Barry Keene. Garamendi made himself look foolish to many in the Capitol when he tried to dump Roberti as pro tem and found himself standing alone. His run for state controller in 1986 was an equal failure.

When Proposition 103, the 1988 insurance reform initiative, changed the insurance commissioner from an appointed to an elected post, Garamendi's career prospects were given new life. Here was a high-profile, statewide job attracting only low-profile candidates. Although his credentials as a consumer advocate were weaker than many others in the race, he alone had any name identification. He outspent his opponents, said very little during the campaign and sailed into office.

In a weird way, Garamendi's honest efforts to separate himself from common politics have led to his reputation for unreliability. He has

John Garamendi

been so afraid of being tainted that he refuses to admit to making the sort of deals that any politician, especially one brimming with ambition, must make to survive. That has made his explanations to everyone –lobbyists, legislators, Capitol staffers or reporters –sound like a 10-year-old trying to lie to his parents.

There was no better example than when he resigned his Senate seat early, in fact before he won the insurance commissioner race, to give his wife, Patti, a boost in her efforts to win his seat. By quitting early, it forced the primary to be consolidated with the November general election, meaning Patti Garamendi's opponent (and the eventual winner) Patrick Johnston had to run for his Assembly seat and the Senate seat simultaneously. Garamendi said to anyone who would listen that he only wanted to save voters money.

Since taking the commissioner's post, Garamendi has waged a battle against the insurance industry to enforce Proposition 103 and has been trying to badger the Legislature into passing some form of low-cost auto insurance. The consensus among California politicos is that if Garamendi hopes to advance his career, he must do something to lower the price of auto insurance.

In the meantime, he has a unique opportunity to capitalize on the legacy of his predecessor, appointed Commissioner Roxani Gillespie. She came from the insurance industry, was accused of siding with it against consumers and had a prickly personality that angered many. Almost anything Garamendi does that appears to be pro-consumer will make him look heroic.

PERSONAL: elected 1990; born Jan. 24, 1945, in Camp Blanding, Fla.; home, Walnut Grove; Peace Corps; education, B.S. business UC Berkeley, M.B.A. Harvard University; wife, Patricia Wilkinson; children, Genet, John, Christina, Autumn, Merle and Ashley; Presbyterian.

CAREER: Banker and rancher; Assembly 1974-76; Senate 1976-1990.

OFFICES: San Francisco (415) 557-1126; Los Angeles (213) 736-2572; Sacramento (916) 322-3555.

BOARD OF EQUALIZATION

The 1849 California Constitution advanced the notion that "taxation shall be equal and uniform throughout the state," and by 1879 the people made the Board of Equalization a constitutional agency to see to it. Today, the board boasts of its powers to affect "virtually every aspect of commerce and government in California," including the taxes paid by more than 900,000 businesses, 300 private utilities and some 4.5 million homeowners.

Operating in a quasi-judicial capacity, the board hears tax appeals and sets assessments on pipelines, flumes, canals, ditches, aqueducts, telephone lines and electrical systems –in a word, utilities. It acts in a quasi-legislative fashion to adopt rules, regulations and guidance for county tax assessors, and as an administrative body that adopts capitalization rates, classifies properties, sets the electrical energy surcharge rate and administers taxes on sales, fuel, alcoholic beverages, cigarettes, insurance, timber, hazardous waste, telephone services and city, county and transit district sales and use taxes. The board collects more than $16 billion each year in business tax revenues for the state and is the state's main revenue agency.

But does the board fairly administer these responsibilities? Or do politics and the influence of campaign donations seep into the board's decisions? Is the board a model agency for tax administration? Or is it an anachronism, outmoded, outdated and outpaced by the events it governs? As the board has assumed a more overtly political atmosphere in recent years, these and other questions are being raised.

The board consists of state Controller Gray Davis and four members elected to four-year terms from districts so extensive that few of the electorate can be expected to know who their representative is. Each board member represents one quarter of the state, or roughly seven million people. The board in the past has been a backwater, albeit a well-paid one, where members could expect to win re-election and serve comfortably until they retired. But in the 1980s, some board members began to demonstrate a bent toward political ambition and an interest in using the job as a rung toward higher office. Some accepted political contributions from

Board of Equalization districts

District
1

District
2

District
3

District
4

District 1

Alameda	Humboldt	Sonoma
Alpine	Lake	Sutter
Amador	Lassen	Tehama
Butte	Marin	Trinity
Calaveras	Mendocino	Tuolumne
Colusa	Modoc	Yolo
Contra Costa	Napa	Yuba
Del Norte	Nevada	
El Dorado	Placer	
Glenn	Plumas	
	Sacramento	
	Santa Clara	
	Shasta	
	Sierra	
	Siskiyou	
	Solano	

District 2

Fresno
Kings
Los Angeles
(Western and
San Fernando areas)
Madera
Mariposa
Merced
Monterey
San Benito
San Francisco
San Joaquin
San Luis Obispo
San Mateo
Santa Barbara
Santa Cruz
Stanislaus
Tulare
Ventura

District 3

Imperial	Orange
Inyo	Riverside
Kern	San Bernardino
Mono	San Diego

District 4

Los Angeles
(Southern and
Central areas)

public utilities and other donors who later won favorable board consideration on tax appeals. The board also saw a serious and often publicly acrimonious split, often pitting William Bennett, its senior member, against the other four. Bennett argued that the others were making tax decisions based on political considerations, often overruling staff recommendations. The board's reputation deteriorated further in 1990, when state and local officials began investigating Bennett himself for a pattern of questionable expense-account charges and credit-card misuse.

Member Paul Carpenter, meanwhile, was convicted in September 1990 on political corruption charges stemming from his previous service in the state Senate. He was sentenced to 12 years in prison. Voters re-elected him despite his conviction, however, and he continued to argue that he was entitled to remain on the board. He had himself sworn into office and offered to serve without pay while he appealed his conviction. State officials maintained, however, that the conviction made him ineligible to hold office, and Gov. Pete Wilson appointed Los Angeles lawyer Matt Fong to the post.

Turmoil on the board, coupled with the political scandals involving Carpenter and other lawmakers, did have one productive result. The state Legislature approved legislation prohibiting board members from voting on any issue in which they have received a campaign contribution of $250 or more in the last 12 months.

William M. Bennett
1st District

In April 1991, William Bennett was charged with 23 counts of filing false expense reports with the state. If convicted, he could face six years in jail and up to $230,000 in fines. Bennett protested his innocence, although it was widely reported that he had been attempting to negotiate a plea bargain with the Sacramento County district attorney. Bennett's problems surfaced almost a year earlier when one of his Democratic primary opponents audited his expense accounts and accused him of a widespread pattern of abuse. Despite that, Bennett easily won both the primary and the runoff.

William Bennett

The accusations aimed at Bennett were especially surprising in light of his long history as a public-interest critic of his fellow board members. Unlike his colleagues, Bennett accepts no campaign contributions, and often was in the forefront of those who advocate reforming the board. "The practice of money and votes continues," he declared in a public letter in 1988. "And if, indeed, we continue to render tax decisions based upon purchased votes, then the agency properly should go into the pages of history."

The outspoken Bennett began his sixth term on the board in January 1991. First elected in 1970, he served his first term as chairman in 1972. When board chairman John Lynch died in office in December 1975, Bennett was elected to complete the term, and was re-elected chairman through 1983.

Bennett, who flew 50 missions over Europe in World War II, began his government career with 12 years as a deputy attorney general, followed by appointment in 1958 as chief counsel to the Public Utilities Commission. He became a member of that commission in 1962. He has taught administrative law and consumer protection at Hastings College of Law.

Bennett represents the counties of Alameda, Alpine, Amador, Butte, Calaveras, Colusa, Contra Costa, Del Norte, El Dorado, Glenn, Humboldt, Lake, Lassen, Marin, Mendocino, Modoc, Napa, Nevada, Placer, Plumas, Sacramento, Santa Clara, Shasta, Sierra, Siskiyou, Solano, Sonoma, Sutter, Tehama, Trinity, Tuolumne, Yolo and Yuba.

PERSONAL: elected 1970; re-elected for the fifth time in 1990; born Feb. 20, 1918 in San Francisco; education, B.A. University of San Francisco, L.L.B. Hastings College of Law; wife, Jane Bennett; children, William Jr., James, Michael and Joan.

CAREER: deputy attorney general of California 1946-1958; chief counsel, California Public Utilities Commission 1958-1962; member, California Public Utilities Commission, 1962-1968.

OFFICE: 1020 N St., Sacramento 95814 (916) 445-4081.

Brad Sherman
2nd District

Brad Sherman, a Democrat, replaced Conway Collis, who unsuccessfully sought the Democratic nomination for insurance commissioner in 1990. A tax lawyer and certified public accountant with a Harvard law degree who refers to himself as "a bit on the nerdish side," Sherman won the Democratic nomination for the job with an upset win over former Assemblyman Lou Papan. Two months after Sherman was sworn in the Democratic majority on the board elevated him to chairman, replacing Ernest J. Dronenburg, Jr., who had been the first Republican chairman in decades.

Brad Sherman

Sherman ran for the board on a political reform platform, saying he wanted to "give people more confidence in the board and in the property tax process." One of his first actions as a board member, however, was to put three of his campaign workers and a campaign aide to Democratic gubernatorial candidate Dianne Feinstein on the state payroll as his "transition" team.

Sherman, who served as a board member of California Common Cause from

1986-1989, also is a Democratic Party activist who estimates he has walked precincts, registered voters, stuffed envelopes and worked in other capacities in more than 40 campaigns in the last 20 years. He also worked as an intern for Secretary of State Jerry Brown in 1973.

His district includes the counties of Fresno, Kings, Madera, Mariposa, Merced, Monterey, San Benito, San Francisco, San Joaquin, San Luis Obispo, San Mateo, Santa Barbara, Santa Cruz, Stanislaus, Tulare, Ventura and the northern and western portions of Los Angeles County.

PERSONAL: elected 1990; born Oct. 24, 1954; education, B.A. University of California at Los Angeles, J.D. Harvard Law School; single.

CAREER: private practice in areas of tax law, business law and estate planning; certified public accountant.

OFFICES: 901 Wilshire Blvd, Suite 210, Santa Monica 90401; (213) 451-5777, (818) 360-3186; 50 Fremont St., Suite 1403, San Francisco 94105; (415) 396-9880; 1020 N. St., Room 107, Sacramento 95814; (916) 445-4154.

Ernest J. Dronenburg Jr.
3rd District

Ernest J. Dronenburg Jr. is a staunch defender of the board and the system it represents, arguing that citizens prefer elected rather than appointed tax officials. When he was elected in 1978 Dronenburg became the first Republican to sit on the partisan board in 24 years.

Before his election, Dronenburg was an auditor and field audit supervisor in the board's business taxes department. In off-hours, he and two friends began and operated a racquetball equipment manufacturing and distribution firm in San Diego. He

Ernest Droneburg Jr.

served as president of the manufacturing company and vice president of the distribution company until he resigned after his election to the board.

In the mid-1980s, Dronenburg became a director of Seapointe Savings & Loan, which became one of the nation's fastest and most spectacular S&L failures. When state and federal regulators seized it in May 1986, the S&L had been in business for only 13 months. It had never hired a loan officer and had lost $24 million gambling investors' money on bond futures. Dronenberg, nonetheless, has never suffered politically for the failure.

Active in Republican Party politics, Dronenburg is also president of the Federation of Tax Administrators and an executive board member of the National Tax Association.

His district includes the counties of Imperial, Inyo, Kern, Mono, Orange, Riverside, San Bernardino and San Diego.

PERSONAL: elected November 1978 and re-elected in 1982, 1986 and 1990; born Aug. 9, 1943, in Washington, D.C.; lives in East San Diego County; San Diego State University, B.S.; wife, Kathy; three daughters.

CAREER: auditor and field audit supervisor, state Board of Equalization, 1971-1978.

OFFICES: 110 West C St., Suite 1709, San Diego 92101; (619) 237-7844, 1020 N St., Sacramento 95814, (916) 445-5713.

Matthew K. Fong
4th District

Matthew K. Fong waged an unsuccessful campaign in 1990 for state controller, but soon thereafter was appointed by Gov. Pete Wilson to the Board of Equalization. He was named to replace Paul Carpenter following Carpenter's conviction on corruption charges, and was considered likely to win legislative confirmation to the post. Fong will have to work hard, however, to win re-election in a district with a history of electing Democratic members.

Wilson, seeking to build bridges with the state's Asian-American community, had encouraged Fong to run for state controller in 1990 against incumbent

Matthew Fong

Gray Davis. Fong's decision to do so created an unusual mother-son combination on the state ballot. Fong, a Republican, is the son of longtime Democratic Secretary of State March Fong Eu. His grandfather, who had a pharmacy in San Francisco's Chinatown, was also the first Chinese-American to work for the Board of Equalization. Fong says his grandfather was recruited by the board to explain its laws to the Chinese community and collect their sales taxes.

His district includes the southern and central sections of Los Angeles County, including most of the city of Los Angeles and 74 other incorporated cities.

PERSONAL: appointed 1990; born Nov. 20, 1953 in Oakland; home, Hacienda Heights; education, B.S. U.S. Air Force Academy, M.B.A. Pepperdine University, J.D. Southwestern University School of Law; wife, Paula; children, Matthew and Jade.

CAREER: unsuccessful GOP candidate for state Controller in 1990; attorney, 1985-present; U.S. Air Force (currently a major in the reserves); manager, 1982 re-election campaign for his mother, Secretary of State March Fong Eu, a Democrat.

Gray Davis

State Controller Gray Davis is a member at large of the board and declines to vote on tax matters relating to his campaign contributors. (Davis' biographical information appears in this chapter, pages 43-45.)

4

The big bad bureaucracy

At 276,714 employees, the state bureaucracy that carries out the decrees of the governor and the Legislature still represents less than 1 percent of the state's population. There are, of course, another 250,000 county employees, hefty school district and special district payrolls and a substantial sprinkling of federal workers toiling at the countless chores that keep the state's people educated and healthy, its streets and work places safe and its commerce bustling. And behind all of them stands a virtual army of non-profit and profit-making entrepreneurs hired to undertake the state's pursuits–clinics, emergency rooms, hospitals, janitorial services, security specialists, mental health programs, drug treatment centers and a host of councils, commissions, think tanks and task forces.

Yet taken together, they hardly represent the threat to freedom or the drain on resources that some politicians like to portray. While bureaucrats may be constrained by red tape and devoted to the evenhanded distribution of blame for their failings, their numbers are not overwhelming.

Nevertheless, the first task of any governor is to tame the previous administration's bureaucracy and to put those countless workers to his or her own use. The Civil Service is designed to protect voters and taxpayers against political exploitation of the work force, but a carefully tailored system of Civil Service exemptions and gubernatorial appointments gives the chief executive the authority he needs to take the reins of government in hand.

When Gov. George Deukmejian took office in 1983, for instance, he had approximately 550 exempt positions to fill in his executive offices and another 100 or so on state boards and commissions. In addition, governors can generally reshape the state's judiciary according to their views as appointments become available – in all a significant pool of patronage that becomes theirs to dispense.

Gov. Pete Wilson, Deukmejian's successor, toiled at filling roughly the same list of appointments in the early months of his new administration in 1991. Within days of his Nov. 6 victory, Wilson named defeated Republican state Treasurer Thomas Hayes to be his director of finance. The appointment signaled that the state budget crisis would be Wilson's top priority. His selection put a key person in place to work with the outgoing administration on Wilson's 1991-92 budget proposal. Hayes quickly assembled his own budget team for the transition: Russ Gould and Susanne Burton, his assistants from the treasurer's office, and Steve Olsen, a budget expert from Senate Republican leader Ken Maddy's office.

Moving into the governor's office with Wilson on Jan. 7 were his right-hand man, Bob White, 48, who served the new governor during Wilson's eight years in the U.S. Senate and his 12 years as mayor of San Diego; Otto Bos, 47, the transition director of communications; and Loren Kaye, 34, who served in the Deukmejian administration and became policy director for the transition.

The pace at which Wilson filled key posts in the first months of 1991 was criticized as too slow by some. Wilson's transition advisory council was headed by Bill Hauck, executive vice president of a Sacramento information services company, and Kirk West, president of the California Chamber of Commerce. Democrat Maureen DiMarco of Cyprus, president of the California School Boards Association, was another member of the committee. Wilson later tapped her to fill a new position in his Cabinet, secretary for child development and education. She would help him forge his new preventive care policies for children.

WHITTLING AT THE BUREAUCRACY

The actual size of the state government work force is measured in "personnel-years," which represent the number of full-time positions or their equivalent. For example, a position that was filled only half of the year would represent 0.5 personnel-years, while three half-time jobs that were filled would represent 1.5 personnel-years. The concept sounds simple enough, but the politicians have been able to find ingenious ways to manipulate the numbers to their advantage.

In 1983, for example, the state work force stood at 228,489 personnel-years – a slight reduction from the year before. Although growth in the work force had been lagging behind the state's population growth for years – a product of the post-Proposition 13 budget crunch – and even behind the growth in state operational expenses, incoming Gov. Deukmejian was determined to pare back the bureaucracy even more. His budget called for a reduction of 1,016 personnel-years, a half-percent cut. He wanted to achieve the cut while increasing the state's prison and juvenile corrections work force by 1,078 personnel-years. Critics would argue that the staff cutbacks represented reductions in service to the state's neediest people, the poor and unemployed. The administration insisted it was trimming fat, not muscle, and that services remained intact or even improved.

In the succeeding years, Deukmejian proposed cutback after cutback in state personnel, all the while balancing the reductions with increases for the growing correctional system. As the state's population continued to balloon, the work force as measured as a ratio of employees per 1,000 residents declined. Most of the cuts came in the health and welfare programs, including the Employment Development Department. The towering Sacramento buildings that housed those programs became emptier as the state built more and more prisons to support the governor's crackdown on crime. Not until 1986-87 did the governor relent. He proposed a 3,253 personnel-year increase, including a 31 percent boost for prisons.

Throughout, the legislative analyst's office repeatedly identified what amounted to a political numbers game the governor played with staffing statistics. By introducing budgets with inflated midyear work force estimates, the analyst said, Deukmejian was able to give the appearance of paring back staff when, in fact, the number of personnel-years proposed for the budget exceeded the number of actual personnel-years in the prior year. By 1987-88, Legislative Analyst Elizabeth Hill concluded Deukmejian had, in effect, lost the war. His work force that year grew by more than 6,515 personnel-years. The staffing level the governor proposed for 1987-88 was the largest request in the state's history, Hill reported.

AFFIRMATIVE ACTION IN STATE SERVICE

Deukmejian had made some progress toward hiring minorities and females in numbers approaching their proportions in society at large. By the end of 1988, the State Personnel Board reported that the labor force overall either met or exceeded the 1980 parity standards for blacks, Asians, Filipinos, Pacific islanders, other minorities and females.

THE STATE WORK FORCE			
Year	Governor	Employees	Employees per 1,000 population
1976-77	Brown	213,795	9.7
1977-78	Brown	221,251	9.9
1978-79	Brown	218,530	9.6
1979-80	Brown	220,193	9.5
1980-81	Brown	225,567	9.5
1981-82	Brown	228,813	9.4
1982-83	Transition	228,489	9.2
1983-84	Deukmejian	226,695	9.0
1984-85	Deukmejian	229,845	8.9
1985-86	Deukmejian	229,641	8.7
1986-87	Deukmejian	232,927	8.6
1987-88	Deukmejian	237,761	8.6
1988-89	Deukmejian	248,173	8.8
1989-90	Deukmejian	254,589	8.8
1990-91	Transition	268,634	est. 9.1
1991-92	Wilson	276,714	est. 9.1

Other minorities had not achieved occupational parity. Hispanics, at 13.8 percent of the state work force compared to 17.2 percent of the population, remained underrepresented, as did American Indians and the disabled. The board also found women significantly underrepresented in all occupations except clerical work. The disparity in female representation in the state work force was particularly evident in a 1989 study by the Senate Rules Committee, which examined the prevalence of women on state and local boards and commissions. At the state level, women held only 27.6 percent of all board and commission appointments. In a sample of 18 counties, women held 34.3 percent of the positions, and in a sample of 24 cities, they held 35.5 percent. Women make up 51 percent of the state's population.

BARGAINING AGENTS AND BARGAINING UNITS

Union	Number of employees	Percent who pay dues
California State Employees' Association		
Administrative, financial and staff services	27,506	40%
Education and library	2,267	66%
Office and allied	35,114	65%
Engineering and scientific technician	2,566	54%
Printing trades	753	77%
Custodial and services	5,360	71%
Registered nurses	2,625	71%
Medical and social services support	2,162	44%
Misc. educational, maritime, library, consultants	613	60%
Alliance of Trades and Maintenance		
(buildings, grounds, roads, equipment)	10,767	70%
Association of California State Attorneys		
(attorneys and hearing officers)	2,301	69%
California Association of Highway Patrolmen	5,314	100%
California Correctional Peace Officers Association	18,839	92%
California Union of Safety Employees	5,728	76%
California Department of Forestry Employees		
Association (firefighters)	2,570	95%
Professional Engineers in California Government	7,016	64%
California Association of Professional Scientists	1,966	70%
International Union of Operating Engineers	695	92%
Union of American Physicians and Dentists	1,266	64%
California Association of Psychiatric Technicians	7,713	52%
American Federation of State, County and		
Municipal Employees	3,337	64%

The days have long since passed when state employees depended upon the largess of the governor and the Legislature to increase their pay or improve their benefits. Under the Ralph C. Dills Act of 1977, the administration now negotiates memorandums of understanding on working conditions and wages with 21 recognized bargaining units, represented by 13 employee associations. The MOUs are legal contracts that may remain in force for as long as three years.

California's bureaucracy includes everything from the Abrasive Blasting Advisory Committee to the Yuba-Sutter Fair Board. There are commissions on the status of women, government efficiency, water and heritage preservation, councils on the arts and job training, and offices for small business, tourism and community relations. The most significant offices, however, fall under the nine umbrella agencies and departments whose leaders comprise the governor's Cabinet.

BUSINESS, TRANSPORTATION, HOUSING AGENCY

Carl Covitz

This superagency oversees 13 departments dealing with housing, business and regulatory functions and transportation, including the California Highway Patrol, the state Department of Transportation (Caltrans) and the Department of Motor Vehicles.

Secretary Carl D. Covitz, 50, was appointed on Dec. 19, 1990. A Republican, Covitz was the founder, owner and president of Landmark Communities Inc., of Beverly Hills, a national real estate investment company. His contact with Wilson extends back to the governor's days as San Diego mayor, when Covitz belonged to the Young Presidents Organization. From 1987 to 1989, he was undersecretary for the U.S. Department of Housing and Urban Development, a period during which HUD officials were accused of offering grants to former HUD officials or their clients or to projects endorsed by prominent Republicans. Covitz himself was never implicated.

Covitz also served on the executive committee of the President's Private Sector Survey on Cost Control (the Grace Commission) as co-chairman of the Department of Defense Task Force.

Covitz was chairman of the board of the Federal Home Loan Bank in San Francisco when Wilson tapped him for state service, and he had recently served as chairman of the Los Angeles Housing Authority, a post he had accepted at the request of Los Angeles Mayor Tom Bradley. He also served as a commissioner for the Los Angeles Convention Center and was chairman of the Los Angeles Delinquency and Crime Commission.

Before starting his real estate firm in 1973, Covitz held marketing and development positions with ITT, Canada Dry, Rheingold Breweries and Bristol-Meyers. He earned his bachelor of science degree from the Wharton School of Finance and Commerce at the University of Pennsylvania and a master's degree in business administration from Columbia University. Salary: $106,410; Office: 1120 N St., Room 2101, Sacramento 95814; (916) 445-1331; Employees: 40,959; Fiscal '91-'92 budget: $5.7 billion (including federal funds mostly for transportation).

Department of Alcoholic Beverage Control

Licenses and regulates the manufacture, sale, purchase, possession and transportation of alcoholic beverages within the state. Director: Jay R. Stroh, Deukmejian holdover; Salary: $99,805; Office: 1901 Broadway, Sacramento 95818; (916) 445-6811; Employees: 393; '91-'92 budget: $24,471,000.

State Banking Department

Protects the public against financial loss from the failure of state-chartered banks and trust companies, including foreign banking corporations, money order or traveler's check issuers, and business and industrial development corporations. Superintendent: vacant; Salary: $99,805; Office: 111 Pine St., Suite 1100, San Francisco 94111; (415) 557-3232; Employees: 204; '91-'92 budget: $15,461,000.

Department of Corporations

Regulates the sale of securities, licenses brokers and agents, and oversees franchises, various financial institutions and health plans. Also controls the solicitation, marketing and sale of securities, oversees companies that lend money or receive funds from the public, and deters unscrupulous or unfair promotional schemes. Commissioner: Christine Bender, Deukmejian holdover; Salary: $99,805; Office: 1107 Ninth St., 8th Floor, Sacramento 95814; (916) 324-9011; Employees: 414; '91-'92 budget: $26,366,000.

Department of Commerce

Primary department that promotes business development and job creation to improve the state's business climate. Director: (interim) Anne Sheehan; Salary: $99,805; Office: 1121 L St., Suite 600, Sacramento 95814; (916) 322-1394; Employees: 146; '91-'92 budget: $42,514,000.

Department of Housing and Community Development

Guides and supports public- and private-sector efforts to provide decent homes for every Californian, administers low-income housing programs, administers standards for manufactured homes and manages the state's Proposition 77 and Proposition 84 bonded earthquake safety and homeless housing programs. Director: Tim Coyle; Salary: $99,805; Office: 1800 Third St., Suite 450, Sacramento 95814; (916) 445-4775; Employees: 719; '91-'92 budget: $341,141,000.

Department of Real Estate

Guarantees real estate agents and developers are competent and qualified, protects the public in offerings of subdivided property and investigates complaints. Commissioner: (acting) John Liberator; Salary: $99,805; Office: 2201 Broadway,

P.O. Box 187000, Sacramento 95818; (916) 739-3600; Employees: 398; '91-'92 budget: $34,407,000.

Department of Savings and Loan

Protects the $96 billion in funds deposited in savings accounts held in state associations to ensure the saving and borrowing public is properly and legally served and to prevent conditions or practices that would threaten the safety or solvency of the institutions or be detrimental to the public. Commissioner: William Davis, Deukmejian holdover; Salary: $99,805; Office: 600 S. Commonwealth Ave., Suite 1502, Los Angeles 90005; (213) 736-2798; Employees: 43; '91-'92 budget: $4,263,000.

California Department of Transportation (Caltrans)

Builds, maintains and rehabilitates roads in accord with the State Transportation Improvement Program, manages airport and heliport safety and access, helps small- and medium-sized communities obtain and maintain air service, regulates airport noise, helps local governments provide public transportation and analyzes transportation questions. Director: Robert Best, Deukmejian holdover; Salary: $99,805; Office: 1120 N St., Sacramento 95814; (916) 445-4616; Employees: 19,429; '91-'92 budget: $5.2 billion.

California Highway Patrol

Patrols state highways to ensure the safe, convenient and efficient transportation of people and goods, monitors school bus and farm labor transportation safety and oversees the transportation of hazardous wastes. Commissioner: M.J. Hannigan; Salary: $106,410; Office: 2555 First Ave., P.O. Box 942898, Sacramento 94298-0001; (916) 445-7473; Employees: 9,022; '91-'92 budget: $622,624,000.

Department of Motor Vehicles

Registers vehicles and vessels, issues and regulates driver's licenses and over-sees the manufacture, delivery and disposal of vehicles. Director: Frank Zolin; Salary: $99,805; Office: 2415 First Ave., Sacramento 95818; (916) 732-0250; Employees: 8,716; '91-'92 budget $509,096,000.

DEPARTMENT OF FOOD AND AGRICULTURE

This is one of three superdepartments whose directors (food, finance and industrial relations) are in the governor's Cabinet. This department is responsible for regulating – some would say protecting – California's food industry, governing everything from pesticide registration and enforcement to raw milk inspections. Other duties include weights and measures enforcement, assessment of environmental hazards for agricultural chemicals and other pollutants, protecting farm workers, keeping foreign insects and weeds out of the state or eradicating them, maintaining plant inspection stations, checking the safety of meat and poultry, predatory animal control, animal health programs and livestock drug controls, and marketing, statistical and laboratory services for agriculture.

Director Henry Voss was appointed by Gov. George Deukmejian on May 1, 1989, after serving seven years as the chairman of the California Farm Bureau Federation. By the following March, the department was bogged down in an aerial spraying attack against a stubborn Mediterranean fruit fly infestation in the Los Angeles area. With an angry Los Angeles delegation of state Senators opposing him, Voss barely won confirmation on a 22-7 vote, just one vote more than needed. In spite of the Medfly controversy, Gov. Wilson extended Voss' appointment on Dec. 3, 1990. To appease critics, however, Wilson said he would give responsibility for monitoring and regulating pesticides to a new California

Henry Voss

Environmental Protection Agency that he hoped to establish. The conflict of interest, in which the Department of Food and Agriculture was responsible both for promoting agribusiness and regulating key elements of its safety, would end.

A farmer's son born in San Jose in 1932, Voss was forced by urbanization to move to Stanislaus County, where the Voss family currently owns 500 acres of peaches, prunes, walnuts and almonds near Ceres. Voss is a specialist in agricultural marketing and has led trade missions on behalf of California agriculture to Europe, Japan, Southeast Asia and Israel. In 1986, he was appointed by President Reagan to the national Commission on Agriculture and Rural Development, a blue-ribbon panel set up to assess the 1985 farm bill. Upon Gov. Deukmejian's recommendation, he was named by U.S. Senate Republican leader Bob Dole to the Commission on Agricultural Workers. He is a member of Sunsweet Growers, Blue Diamond Almond Growers and Tri-Valley Growers, three of the state's leading agricultural cooperatives, and is a past president of the Apricot Producers of California and past chairman of the California Apricot Advisory Board. Salary: $106,410; Office: 1220 N St., Sacramento 95814; (916) 445-7126; Employees: 2,134; '91-'92 budget: $226,675,000.

DEPARTMENT OF FINANCE

The Department of Finance serves as the governor's chief fiscal policy agency, prepares the governor's January budget proposal and his annual May budget revision, reviews all state spending practices and proposals, administers the state budget after it has been adopted and signed, monitors all legislation that has fiscal implications for the state and recommends which bills and budget provisions should be adopted or vetoed. The department also conducts research, produces revenue estimates, analyzes tax policy and tracks population changes.

The director, Thomas Hayes, was appointed Nov. 20, 1990, after his narrow defeat by Kathleen Brown for the office of state treasurer.

Born in New York, Hayes moved to California with his Air Force father. Hayes is a Marine veteran who holds the Navy commendation medal for Vietnam service. He earned a master's degree in business from San Jose State University after leaving the military. He worked in the U.S. General Accounting Office before joining the California legislative analyst's office in 1977. He moved to the auditor general's staff as an assistant auditor general in 1977 and became the auditor general in 1979.

Thomas Hayes

In all that time, Hayes remained politically neutral, but he reregistered as a Republican in 1988 when Gov. Deukmejian tapped him to replace the late Jesse Unruh as treasurer. (Unruh died in August 1977.) As finance director, Hayes will develop and manage the state's $55.7 billion budget and serve on more than 60 authorities, boards and commissions. Salary: $106,410; Office: State Capitol, Room 1145, Sacramento 95814; (916) 445-4141; Employees: 366; '91-'92 budget: $30,123,000.

DEPARTMENT OF INDUSTRIAL RELATIONS

The Department of Industrial Relations is responsible for enforcing California's occupational safety and health laws, administering the compulsory workers' compensation insurance law, adjudicating workers' compensation claims, negotiating in threatened strikes, enforcing laws and promulgating rules on wages, hours and conditions of employment, and analyzing and disseminating statistics on labor conditions. Director: Lloyd Aubry; Salary: $106,410; Office: 1121 L St., Suite 307, Sacramento 95814; (916) 324-4163; Employees: 2,631; '91-'92 budget: $193,639,000.

HEALTH AND WELFARE AGENCY

This superagency, which covers 11 state departments, administers the state's health, welfare, employment and rehabilitation programs serving people who are poor, mentally ill, developmentally disabled, elderly, unemployed or who have alcohol and drug addiction problems. The agency also administers Proposition 65, the Safe Drinking Water and Toxics Enforcement Act of 1986; is the state's lead agency in administering the Immigration Reform and Control Act of 1986; and manages the state's emergency medical services program. Five departments within the agency oversee long-term care services in residential and institutional settings for the aging, disabled, mentally ill and other needy citizens. Director: Russell Gould; Salary: $106,410; Office: 1600 N St. Room 450, Sacramento 95814; (916) 445-1722; Employees: 37,694; '91-'92 budget: $29.2 billion (including both state and federal funds and local assistance).

Office of Statewide Health Planning and Development

Responsible for developing a statewide plan for health facilities, ensuring construction plans for health facilities conform to state building codes, maintaining a uniform system of accounting and disclosure for health facility costs and ensuring available federal and state assistance is provided to develop needed facilities. Director: Larry Meeks, Deukmejian holdover; Salary: $99,805; Office: 1600 Ninth St., Sacramento 95814; (916) 322-5834; Employees: 340; '91-'92 budget: $43,386,000.

Department of Aging

State focal point for federal, state and local agencies that serve more than 4 million elderly Californians, working through 33 Area Agencies on Aging. The agencies manage programs that provide meals, social services and health-insurance counseling and act as advocates for senior citizen issues. The department also manages the state's adult day health care centers, the Alzheimer's Day Care Resource Centers and the multipurpose senior services program, an experimental effort to keep the frail elderly from being unnecessarily admitted to skilled nursing homes or intermediate care facilities. Director: Chris Arnold, Deukmejian holdover; Salary: $88,062; Office: 1600 K St., Sacramento 95814; (916) 322-3887; Employees: 153; '91-'92 budget: $137,110,000.

Department of Alcohol and Drug Programs

Coordinates planning and development of a statewide alcohol and drug abuse prevention, intervention, detoxification, recovery and treatment system, serving 300,000 Californians largely through programs operated by counties. The department is responsible for licensing the state's methadone treatment programs, multiple-offender drinking driver programs and alcoholism recovery facilities. In addition, the department manages programs aimed at alcohol and drug abuse prevention, particularly among youth, women, the disabled, ethnic minorities and the elderly. The department expects to receive an increase of $22.5 million in the current fiscal year from the federal Alcohol, Drug Abuse and Mental Health Administration. Director: Andrew Mecca; Salary: $99,805; Office: 111 Capitol Mall, Sacramento 95814; (916) 445-1940; Employees: 269; '91-'92 budget: $300,730,000.

Department of Health Services

Manages 11 health programs including the state's $11.4 billion Medi-Cal program (serving an average of 4.3 million people monthly), the Office of AIDS and the Family Planning program. The department is in charge of preventive medical services, public water supplies, toxic substance control, environmental health, epidemiological studies, rural and community health, radiologic health, maternal and child health and the early detection of genetic disease and birth defects in newborns. The Food and Drug Program seeks to protect consumers from adulterated, misbranded or falsely advertised foods, drugs, medical devices, hazardous household products and cosmetics and to control botulism in canned products. A licensing office regulates care in some 6,000 public and private health facilities, clinics and agencies. Director: Kenneth Kizer, MD, Deukmejian holdover; Salary: $99,805; Office: 744 P St., Sacramento 95814; (916) 445-1248; Employees: 5,232; '91-'92 budget: $13.3 billion.

Department of Developmental Services

Coordinates services under the Lanterman Developmental Disabilities Services Act of 1977 for people with developmental disabilities, such as mental retardation, autism or cerebral palsy, to meet their needs at each stage of their lives through individual plans for treatment within their home communities where possible. The department provides 24-hour care for more than 6,000 severely disabled clients through seven state developmental hospitals (Agnews, Camarillo, Fairview, Lanterman, Porterville, Sonoma and Stockton) and indirect care for 93,000 clients through a statewide network of 21 private, non-profit regional centers. Director: Dennis Amundson; Salary: $99,805; Office: 1600 Ninth St., Sacramento 95814; (916) 322-8154; Employees: 11,293; '91-'92 budget: $1.2 billion.

Department of Mental Health

Administers the Lanterman-Petris-Short Act, the Short-Doyle Act and other federal and state statutes governing services to the mentally ill through county and community non-profit agencies and through the direct operation of the Atascadero, Metropolitan, Napa and Patton state hospitals and treatment programs for 600 clients at the Department of Developmental Services' Camarillo State Hospital. Services to the mentally ill include community education and consultation, crisis evaluation and emergency care, 24-hour acute care, 24-hour residential treatment, day-care treatment, outpatient care, case management and resocialization. The department also manages special programs for the homeless mentally ill, for mental illness associated with AIDS and other special categories. Gov. Wilson proposed shifting responsibility for community mental health treatment to the counties (with a new revenue source) in 1991-92 for a state savings of $432 million. Director: vacant; Salary: $99,805; Office: 1600 Ninth St., Sacramento 95814; (916) 323-8173; Employees: 7,554; '91-'92 budget: $812,241,000.

Employment Development Department

Assists employers in finding workers and workers in finding jobs through a statewide database, manages the unemployment insurance program, collects payroll taxes that support worker benefit programs, provides economic and labor market data and administers the Job Training Partnership Act. Under federal guidance, the department manages 130 field offices that provide job placement, employment counseling, vocational testing, workshops and referral services, targeted at groups such as veterans, older workers, the disabled, youth, minorities, welfare families and migrant and seasonal farm workers. Director: Thomas Nagle; Salary: $99,805; Office: 800 Capitol Mall, Sacramento 95814; (916) 445-8008; Employees: 10,727; '91-'92 budget: $5.8 billion.

Department of Rehabilitation

Helps rehabilitate and find employment for people with mental and physical handicaps. Director: Bill Tainter; Salary: $99,805; Office: 830 K Street Mall, Sacramento 95814; (916) 445-8638; Employees: 1,874; '91-'92 budget: $269,011,000.

Department of Social Services

Administers the state's $7.7 billion welfare program for poor children, disabled and elderly residents; provides or manages social services, community care licensing and inspections, disability evaluations, refugee assistance and adoption services; manages the federal food stamp program; regulates group homes, nurseries, preschools, foster homes, halfway houses and day-care centers; administers programs designed to protect children, the disabled and the elderly from abuse or neglect, and manages the state's Greater Avenues for Independence (GAIN) workfare program. Director: vacant; Salary: $99,805; Office: 74 P St., Sacramento 95814; (916) 445-2077; Employees: 3,768; '91-'92 budget: $10.9 billion.

SECRETARY OF ENVIRONMENTAL AFFAIRS

Gov. Pete Wilson has said he plans to "take charge of California's environment in the 1990s." To that end, Wilson called James Strock, a veteran from the U.S. Environmental Protection Agency to his side in California. Strock, an environmental lawyer and award-winning author, is California's third secretary for the environment, and he was expected to be a more formidable environmental proponent than his successors. Wilson's environmental efforts also included the appointment of an environmentalist to manage his Resources Agency and a small proposed increase for the Coastal Commission budget.

James Strock

Wilson also proposed a full-fledged California EPA under Strock's command. Previous secretaries have been responsible for coordinating offshore oil and toxic waste issues. They also advised the governor on environmental policy and appointments to the Air Resources Board, the Water Resources Control Board and the Waste Management Board. Strock was expected to handle many of those duties and play a coordinator's role among independent environmenta agencies. He also would oversee pesticide regulation, which Wilson has pledged to remove from the Department of Food and Agriculture. Salary: $106,410. Office and budget to be arranged.

Air Resources Board

Holds the primary responsibility for California air quality, including the establishment of clean air standards, research into air pollution, emissions enforcement and smog limitations on automobiles and industries. Chairwoman: Jananne Sharpless (who had been Gov. George Deukmejian's Cabinet secretary for environmental affairs); Salary: $106,410; Members: San Diego County Supervisor Brian Bilbray; Gilroy Mayor Roberta Hughan; Orange County Supervisor Harriett Wieder; Dr. Eugene Boston, M.D.; Betty Ichikawa; San Bernardino County Supervisor Barbara Riordan; Dr. Andrew Wortman; Office: 1102 Q. Street, Sacramento 95814; (916) 322-4203; Employees: 835; '91-'92 budget: $96,907,000.

State Water Resources Control Board

Regulatory agency with responsibility for administering and granting water rights, maintaining state water quality through monitoring and waste discharge permits, managing toxic cleanups and administering grants for waste treatment facilities. Chairman: W. Don Maughan; Salary: $95,403; Members: E.H. Finster, Eliseo Samaniego, John Caffrey and one vacancy, Salaries: $92,465; Office 901 P St., Sacramento 95814; (916) 322-3132; Employees: 1,305; budget '91-'92: $363,234,000.

California Integrated Waste Management Board

Responsible for promoting waste reduction, recycling and composting, including environmentally safe transformation of wastes into harmless or useful products or land disposal. Manages landfills through local agencies and administers the California Tire Recycling Act of 1989 to reduce the number of used tires in landfills. Members: Wesley Chesbro of Sacramento, Sam Egigian of La Habra, Michael Frost of Folsom, Jesse Huff of Fair Oaks and Kathy Neal of Oakland; Salaries: $95,395; Office: 1020 Ninth St., Suite 300, Sacramento 95814; (916) 322-3330; Employees: 321; '91-'92 budget: $62,376,000.

YOUTH AND ADULT CORRECTIONAL AGENCY

This superagency oversees the Department of Corrections and the Youth Authority, which are charged with responsibility for the control, care and treatment of convicted felons and civilly committed addicts, and the confinement and rehabilitation of juvenile delinquents. The agency managed the biggest prison and prison camp construction program in the world during Gov. George Deukmejian's years, although the inmate population continues to grow more quickly than prisons can be built. By February 1991, the state prison system housed 98,137 inmates and the Youth Authority had more than 8,000 wards. The agency also manages state parole programs and oversees the state Board of Corrections, the Youthful Offender Parole Board and the Board of Prison Terms. The agency considers itself the largest law enforcement organization in the United States.

Joe Sandoval

Secretary Joe Sandoval was appointed on Oct. 12, 1988, having been Gov. Deukmejian's chief of the California State Police, and was reappointed Feb. 25, 1991, by Gov. Pete Wilson. Sandoval is a veteran of 26 years with the Los Angeles Police Department. He was the primary law enforcement officer at the University of Southern California athletes village for the 1984 Olympics. His last assignment in Los Angeles was commander of some 235 officers in the Hollenbeck area, a community of 300,000. Salary: $106,410; Office: 1100 11th St., Sacramento 95814; (916) 323-6001; Employees: 37,309; '91-'92 budget: $3.4 billion.

Department of Corrections

Manages 21 correctional facilities including eight reception centers. The department also manages parole programs, prison camps and a community correctional program designed to reintegrate released offenders to society. Director: James H. Gomez; Salary: $99,805; Office: 630 K St., Sacramento 95814; (916) 445-7682; Employees: 31,886; '91-'92 budget: $2.7 billion.

Youth Authority

Provides programs in institutions and the community to reduce delinquent behavior, help local agencies fight juvenile crime and encourage delinquency prevention programs. The department operates reception centers and clinics as well as 18 conservation camps and institutions for males and females throughout the state. Director: B.T. Collins; Salary: $99,805; Office: 4241 Williamsbourgh Dr., Sacramento 95823; (916) 427-6674; Employees: 5,170; '91-'92 budget: $413,794,000.

RESOURCES AGENCY

This superagency is responsible for departments and programs that manage the state's air, water and land resources and wildlife. The main departments are Forestry and Fire Protection, Parks and Recreation, Conservation, Fish and Game, Boating and Waterways, the Conservation Corps and the Department of Water Resources, which among its many duties includes the state's Drought Center (and, on occasion, its Flood Center). The agency also oversees or provides backup for the Tahoe Regional Planning Agency, the Wildlife Conservation Board, the Santa Monica Mountains Conservancy, the state Coastal Conservancy, the San Francisco Bay Conservation and Development Commission, the Colorado River Board of California and the environmental license plate fund.

Douglas Wheeler

Keeping his pledge to bring "an environmental ethic" to state government, Gov. Pete Wilson chose Douglas P. Wheeler, 48, vice-president of the World Wildlife Fund and Conservation Foundation, to be his secretary for resources. Wheeler was appointed on Dec, 26, 1990, to replace outgoing Secretary Gordon Van Vleck, the cattleman who managed state resources throughout former Gov. George Deukmejian's two terms.

Wheeler has held positions in the U.S. Department of Interior, the American Farmland Trust, the National Trust for Historic Preservation and the Sierra Club, where he was executive director in 1985-86 (he left the position amicably, deciding he was not the activist that the Sierra Club seemed to want).

Wheeler, however, inherited a troubled agency. The Department of Fish and Game has suffered some of the most intense budget difficulties of any state agency. The Coastal Commission, after years of Deukmejian budget cuts, was under attack for not protecting the coastline. Environmentalists were turning to the initiative, with varying success, to protect state forests and wildlife and to launch aggressive mass transit programs. Salary: $106,410; Office: 1416 Ninth St., Room 1311, Sacramento 95814; (916) 445-3758; Employees: 16,697; '91-'92 budget: $2.4 billion.

California Conservation Corps

A work force of some 2,000 young men and women who perform nearly 3 million hours of conservation work each year, including flood patrol, fire restoration, tree planting, stream clearance, trail building, park maintenance, landscaping, home weatherization and wildlife habitat restoration. Director: Bud Sheble, Deukmejian holdover; Salary: $88,056; Office: 1530 Capitol Ave., Sacramento 95814; (916) 445-8183; Employees: 439; '91-'92 budget: $57,728,000.

Department of Conservation

Promotes the development and management of the state's land, energy, mineral and farmland resources, and disseminates information on geology, seismology, mineral, geothermal and petroleum resources, agricultural and open-space land, and container recycling and litter reduction. Director: Ed Heidig; Salary: $88,062; Office: 1416 Ninth St., 13th Floor, Sacramento 95814; (916) 322-7683; Employees: 571; '91-'92 budget: $337,248,000.

Department of Forestry and Fire Prevention

Provides fire protection and watershed management services for private and state-owned watershed lands. Responsibilities include fire prevention, controlling wildlife damage and improving the land and vegetative cover for economic and social benefits. Director: Harold Walt, Deukmejian holdover; Salary: $99,805; Office: 1416 Ninth St., Sacramento 95814; (916) 445-3976; Employees: 4,573; '91-'92 budget: $399,436,000.

Department of Fish and Game

Responsible for maintaining all species of wildlife; providing varied recreational use of wild species, including hunting and fishing, providing for the scientific and educational use of wildlife; and protecting the economic benefits of natural species, including commercial harvesting of wildlife resources. The department also has charge of the newly enacted oil-spill prevention and cleanup program. Director: Peter Bontadelli Jr., Deukmejian holdover; Salary: $99,805; Office: 1416 Ninth St., 12th Floor, Sacramento 95814; (916) 445-3531; Employees: 1,844; '91-'92 budget: $145,569,000.

Department of Boating and Waterways

Responsible for public boating facilities, water safety, water hyacinth control, beach erosion, small-craft harbor development (through loans and grants) and yacht and ship brokers licensing. Director: William Ivers, Deukmejian holdover; Salary: $80,726; Office: 1629 S St., Sacramento 95814; (916) 445-2615; Employees: 63; '91-'92 budget: $58,160,000.

Department of Parks and Recreation

Acquires, designs, develops, operates, maintains and protects the state park system; helps local park agencies through loans and grants; and interprets the natural, archaeological and historical resources of the state. State parks, recreation areas and historic monuments are designed to provide recreation, improve the environment and preserve the state's history and natural landscapes. The department is involved in underwater parks, a statewide trail network, state beaches and piers, coastal and Sierra redwood parks, an off-highway vehicle system and management of the Hearst San Simeon Castle and the Anza-Borrego Desert State Park. Director: Henry Agonia, Deukmejian holdover; Salary: $99,805; Office: 1416 Ninth St., Sacramento 95814; (916) 445-6477; Employees: 2,981; '91-'92 budget: $206,531,000.

Department of Water Resources

Responsible for managing, developing and conserving the state's water, from flood control to drought responses and drinking water safety, under the provisions of the California Water Plan. The department operates Oroville Reservoir, the California Aqueduct and related facilities, and manages the key Delta water supply in conjunction with the U.S. Bureau of Reclamation. Director David Kennedy has undertaken a massive effort to resolve the state's long-standing water supply conflicts through private negotiation and has achieved some success. Salary: $99,805; Office: 1416 Ninth St., Sacramento 85814; (916) 445-9248; Employees: 2,756; '91-'92 budget: $1 billion.

STATE AND CONSUMER SERVICES AGENCY

This superagency covers an array of departments and programs that include the departments of Consumer Affairs, Fair Employment and Housing, General Services and Veterans Affairs and the Fair Employment and Housing Commission, Building Standards Commission, State Personnel Board, State Fire Marshal, Franchise Tax Board, Museum of Science and Industry, the Public Employees Retirement System and the State Teachers Retirement System.

Secretary Bonnie Guiton, an official in the Bush administration, was appointed on Feb. 8, 1991, becoming the second woman in the Wilson Cabinet and the first black. Wilson called protecting consumers "the ultimate and most noble mission" of the State and Consumer Services Agency and Guiton pledged that the department, which had become nearly moribund under the previous administration, would differ from "business as usual." She placed enforcement of consumer protection laws among her top priorities, although she also reassured business leaders that she would continue to seek a "balance between the needs of business and the needs of consumers."

Bonnie Guiton

Guiton was president and chief executive officer of the Earth Conservation Corps, a non-profit conservation organization, when Wilson called her to Sacramento. The previous September, she left the Bush White House, where she had been a special adviser on consumer affairs and director of the U.S. Office of Consumer Affairs. Guiton served as chairwoman of the Consumer Affairs Council, an organization of federal agency consumer representatives. Before joining Bush's staff, she had been assistant secretary for vocational and adult education in the U.S. Department of Education. In 1984, President Ronald Reagan appointed her to the U.S. Postal Rate Commission. She attended Mills College and the University of California, Berkeley. Salary: $106,410; Office: 915 Capitol Mall, Suite 200, Sacramento 95814; (916) 323-9493; Employees: 14,383; '91-'92 budget: $642,271,000.

Department of Consumer Affairs

Oversees the Bureau of Automotive Repair, the Contractors' State License Board and the Board of Medical Quality Assurance, the Division of Consumer Services and 27 more small boards, bureaus and commissions that for the most part license and regulate "professional" services. They are the boards of Accountancy, Architectural Examiners, Barber Examiners, Behavioral Science Examiners, Cosmetology, Dental Examiners, Funeral Directors and Embalmers, Geologists and Geophysicists, Guide Dogs for the Blind, Landscape Architects, Examiners of Nursing Home Administrators, Optometry, Pharmacy, Polygraph Examiners, Professional Engineers, Registered Nursing, Certified Shorthand Reporters, Structural Pest Control, Examiners in Veterinary Medicine, Vocational Nurse and Psychiatric Technician Examiners and the Cemetery Board; the bureaus of Collection and Investigative Services, Electronic and Appliance Repair, Personnel Services and Home Furnishings; the Tax Preparers Program; and the Athletic Commission. Director: James Conran; Salary: $99,805; Office: 1020 N St., Sacramento 95814; (916) 445-4465; Employees: 2,302; '91-'92 budget: $209,375,000.

Department of Fair Employment and Housing

Enforces the state civil rights laws that prohibit discrimination in employment, housing and public services and endeavors to eliminate discrimination based on race, religion, creed, national origin, sex, marital status, physical handicap, medical condition or age (over 40). Complaints are pursued before the Fair Employment and Housing Commission. Director: Dorinda Henderson; Salary: $88,062; Office: 2016 T St., Suite 210, Sacramento 95814; (916) 739-4616; Employees: 235; '91-'92 budget: $14,098,000.

Office of the State Fire Marshal

Coordinates state fire services, adopts and enforces minimum statewide fire and panic safety regulations, controls hazardous materials and helps the film industry with special effects. State fire marshal: James McMullen; Salary: $88,062; Office: 7171 Bowling Drive, Suite 600, Sacramento 95823; (916) 427-4161; Employees: 216; '91-'92 budget: $16,116,000.

Franchise Tax Board

Administers the personal income tax, the bank and corporation tax laws, the homeowners and renters assistance program, and performs field assessments and audits of campaign expenditure reports and lobbyist reports under the Political Reform Act of 1974. The members are state Controller Gray Davis; the chairman of the state Board of Equalization, Brad Sherman; and state Director of Finance Thomas Hayes. Executive officer: Gerald Goldberg; Salary: $99,805; Office: 9645 Butterfield Way, Sacramento 95827; (916) 369-4543; Employees: 4,205; '91-'92 budget: $221,159,000.

Department of General Services

Manages and maintains state property, allocates office space, monitors contracts, insurance and risks, administers the state school building law and helps small and minority businesses obtain state contracts. Also has jurisdiction over the state architect, the offices of Telecommunications, Local Assistance, Procurement, Energy Assessments and Buildings and Grounds, and the state police. Director: John Lockwood; Salary: $99,805; Office: 915 Capitol Mall, Suite 590, Sacramento 95814; (916) 445-5728; Employees: 4,580; '91-'92 budget: $604,866,000.

State Personnel Board

Manages the state civil service system including the Career Opportunities Development Program. Members: President Richard Chavez, Alice Stoner, Clair Burgener, Lorrie Ward and Richard Carpenter. Executive officer: Gloria Harmon; Salary: $86,640; Office: 801 Capitol Mall P.O. Box 944201, Sacramento 94244-2010; (916) 322-2530; Employees: 223; '91-'92 budget: $16,068,000.

Public Employees' Retirement System

Administers pension, disability, health, Social Security and death benefits for more than 1 million past and present public employees. Participants include state constitutional officers, legislators, judges, state employees, most volunteer fire fighters, school employees (except teachers) and others. Executive officer: Dale Hanson; Salary: $99,804; Office: 400 P St., P.O. Box 942701, Sacramento 94229-2701; (916) 326-3829; Employees: 762; '91-'92 budget: $54,622,000.

State Teachers Retirement System

Administers the largest teacher retirement system in the United States with 340,700 members and 123,900 receiving benefits. Chief executive officer: James Mosman; Salary: $99,804; Office: 7667 Folsom Blvd., P.O. Box 15275-C, Sacramento 95851-0275; Employees: 374; '91-'92 budget: $28,316,000.

Department of Veterans Affairs

Administers the Cal-Vet farm and home loan program, helps veterans obtain benefits and rights to which they are entitled and supports the Veterans Home of California, a retirement home with nursing care and hospitalization. Director: Jesse Ugalde, Deukmejian holdover; Salary: $99,804; Office: 1227 O St., Sacramento 94295; (916) 322-1796; Employees: 1,277; '91-'92 budget: $1.3 billion.

SECRETARY OF CHILD DEVELOPMENT, EDUCATION

Maureen DiMarco

Declaring children to be the state's most precious resource, Wilson pledged to give them a healthy start in life and in school. His Cabinet would include a new position, secretary for child development and education, a post for which he chose Maureen DiMarco, a Democrat who had endorsed his campaign.

Wilson gave DiMarco the task of restructuring the state's delivery of social, health and mental health services to children in a period of severe budget constraints. She would also chair a new Inter-Agency Council for Child Development. Wilson said his approach would be preventive rather than corrective for the state's educational and children's needs. He considered such expenses to be investments in the future rather than costs.

DiMarco, of Cyprus, was immediate past president of the California School Boards Association and outgoing president of the board of the Garden Grove Unified School District in Orange County. In 1983, she worked as a consultant for state schools chief Bill Honig, and she was frequently critical of former Gov. George Deukmejian's education policies. DiMarco was expected to be paid the Cabinet-level secretary's salary of $106,410. Her office is in the Senator Hotel Office Building, 1121 L St., Sacramento 95814; (916) 323-0611.

BOARD OF EDUCATION

Establishes policy and adopts rules and regulations for the kindergarten through 12th grade, where authorized by the Education Code. Major duties include selecting textbooks for grades kindergarten through eight, developing curriculum frameworks, approving district waivers from regulations and regulating the state testing program, teacher credentialing and school district reorganizations. In practice, the board is subsidiary to state Superintendent of Public Instruction Bill Honig, who is a constitutional officer elected by the voters and who was constantly at odds with Gov. George Deukmejian over education spending.

The feud between Honig and Deukmejian spilled over to the board, the members of which were all appointed by Deukmejian. Well into 1991, the 11 board members – President Joseph Carrabino, Dorothy Lee, William Malkasian, Peter Mehas, Raga Ramachandran (student member), Joseph Stein, Gerti Thomas, Marion McDowell, Kenneth Peters, David Romero, Kathryn Dronenburg – were attempting to assert the board's power over Honig's budget and other Department of Education functions. Office: 721 Capitol Mall, Room 532, Sacramento, 95814.

DEPARTMENT OF EDUCATION

Administers the state's kindergarten through high school education system for 5.1 million pupils by coordinating and directing the state's local elementary and high school districts. The primary goal is to provide education policy to local districts, approve instructional materials and offer curriculum leadership. Superintendent Bill Honig; Salary: $102,000; Office: 721 Capitol Mall, Room 524, Sacramento 95814; Employees 2,423; budget '91-'92: $26.6 billion (including $16.2 billion from the state general fund, $8 billion from property taxes and other local sources, $1.8 billion in federal funds and $614 million from the state lottery).

UC BOARD OF REGENTS

Governs the nine campuses of the University of California, five teaching hospitals and three major laboratories operated under contracts with the U.S. Department of Energy. The 18 members have been appointed to 12-year terms since 1974, when terms were reduced from 16 years. The same amendment reduced the number of ex-officio members from eight to seven. The long-term appointment of a regent is considered to be among the most prestigious civic positions in California, much prized by the wealthy and politically well-connected. And because of their long terms, regents often survive the terms of the governors who appointed them. The regents (and the end of their current terms) are Gov. Pete Wilson, president; Frank Clark Jr., chairman (2000); David Gardner, president of the university; Assembly Speaker Willie Brown Jr.; Roy Brophy (1998); Clair Burgener (2000); Yvonne Brathwaite Burke (1993); W. Glenn Campbell (1996); Tirso del Junco (1997); Jeremiah Hallisey (1993); Willis Harman (1990); state schools chief Bill Honig; Meredith Khachigian (1990); Leo Kolligian (1997); Vilma Martinez (1990); Lt. Gov. Leo McCarthy; Joseph Moore (1990); William French Smith (1998); Yori Wada (1992); Dean Watkins (1996); Harold Williams (1994); Jacques Yeager (1994); and student regent Guillermo Rodriguez. President's salary: $243,500; Office of the secretary of the regents: 650 University Hall, Berkeley 94720; (415) 642-0502. The state investment in the UC system is $2.8 billion to serve an enrollment of 155,000 students.

University of California Chancellors

David Gardner, University System President; Chang-Linn Tian, Berkeley; Theodore Hullar, Davis; J.W. Peltason, Irvine; Charles Young, Los Angeles; Rosemary Schraer, Riverside; Richard Atkinson, San Diego; Julius Krevans, M.D., San Francisco; Barbara Uehling, Santa Barbara; Robert Stevens, Santa Cruz; Charles Shank, Director, Lawrence Berkeley Laboratory; John Nuckolls, Director, Lawrence Livermore National Laboratory; and Siegfried Hecker, Director, Los Alamos National Laboratory.

TRUSTEES OF THE STATE UNIVERSITIES

Sets policy and governs collective bargaining; personnel matters, including appointment of the system president and university chancellors, budget decisions and capital outlays. Members are appointed by the governor for eight-year terms. The trustees (and their terms) are Gov. Pete Wilson; Lt. Gov. Leo McCarthy; Assembly Speaker Willie Brown Jr.; state schools chief Bill Honig; Barry Munitz, chancellor; Claudia Hampton (1994); Willie Stennis (1991); Marianthi Lansdale (1991); Dean Lesher (1993); Dr. John Kashiwabara (1994); Roland Arnall (1990); Martha Falgatter (1995); William Campbell (1995); Dr. Lyman Heine (1989); Marian Bagdasarian (1996); R. James Considine (1992); Terrance Flanigan; James Gray (1998); Gloria Hom (1992); Ralph Pesqueira (1996); Ted Saenger (1997); J. Gary Shansby (1992); Scott Vick (1991) and Anthony Vitti (1997). Chancellor's salary: $149,040; Office: 400 Golden Shore, Long Beach, 90802; (213) 590-5506. Enrollment: 372,000. System budget '91-'92: $2.1 billion.

California State University Presidents

Barry Munitz, University System Chancellor; Tomas Arciniega, Bakersfield; Robin Wilson, Chico; Robert Detweiler, Dominguez Hills; Harold Haak, Fresno; Milton Gordon, Fullerton; Norma Rees, Hayward; Alistair McCrone, Humboldt; Curtis McCrae, Long Beach; James Rosser, Los Angeles; James Cleary, Northridge; Hugh La Bounty, California State Polytechnic University, Pomona; Donald Gerth, Sacramento; Anthony Evans, San Bernardino; Thomas Day, San Diego; Robert Corrigan, San Francisco; Gail Fullerton, San Jose; Warren Baker, California Polytechnic State University, San Luis Obispo; Bill Stacy, San Marcos; David Benson, Sonoma; John Moore, Stanislaus;

GOVERNORS, CALIFORNIA COMMUNITY COLLEGES

California's 71 community college districts comprise the largest postsecondary education system in the nation with 107 campuses statewide serving approximately 1.4 million students. Each district is managed by a locally elected governing board, but a statewide Board of Governors and chancellor provide leadership, a presence before the Legislature and policy guidance.

Board members are President Timothy Haidinger, John Parkhurst, Borgny Baird, David Lee, Phillip Bardos, Arthur Margosian, Karen Grosz, Ernest Mobley,

Shirley Ralston, William Kolender, Robert Rivinius, Thomas Sayles, Larry Toy, Duane Thompson and Scott Wylie. Chancellor: David Mertes; Salary: $106,404; Office: 1107 9th Street, Sacramento 95814; (916) 445-8752; '91-'92 budget (all campuses): $3.2 billion.

FAIR POLITICAL PRACTICES COMMISSION

Established by the voter-approved Political Reform Act of 1974, the commission enforces campaign expenditure reporting, conflict-of-interest statements, other disclosure rules and campaign restrictions imposed by statute and the voters. Propositions 73 and 68, rival initiatives both of which were approved in 1988, fell largely under the commission's jurisdiction but were gutted by court decisions in 1990. Proposition 68 was sponsored by Common Cause and Proposition 73 was sponsored by the unlikely alliance of Assembly Republican leader Ross Johnson of La Habra, Sen. Quentin Kopp, I-San Francisco, and Sen. Joseph Montoya, D-Whittier. (Montoya later was sentenced to prison on political corruption charges.)

In the first of the court decisions, U.S. District Court Judge Lawrence Karlton ruled in September 1990 that Proposition 73's contribution limits and its ban on fund transfers among candidates unfairly limited political speech. Two months later, the state Supreme Court ruled that no provisions of Proposition 68 could take effect because Proposition 73 had won more votes and provided a "comprehensive regulatory scheme related to the same subject."

The decisions meant that California no longer had any restrictions on how much money individuals or organizational political action committees could contribute to political candidates, and fund transfers between candidates for the Legislature, once banned, were permissible, according to one analysis. The decisions also meant Proposition 73's restrictions against public campaign financing were thrown out, too, but so far no one has stepped up to enact such a provision.

In the meantime, the Legislature passed an ethics package that included restrictions on travel, health-related expenses, vehicle, gift and other purchases with campaign proceeds and reimbursements of unused campaign funds. A significant part of the package became Proposition 112, approved in the June 1990 primary election, further restricting gifts and honorariums for lawmakers and personal use of campaign funds while establishing an independent Citizens Compensation Commission to set the pay for legislators and constitutional officers.

Within this framework, the FPPC adopts regulations governing disclosure of conflicts of interest, campaign finances and lobbyist activities and is empowered to fine public officials and candidates. Other elements of campaign enforcement are the responsibility of the secretary of state and the attorney general. Chairman: Ben Davidian; Members: Frank Aparicio, Joseph Rattigan, Donald Vial and George Fenimore (filling a vacancy as a holdover from the Deukmejian years); Office: 428 J St., Suite 800, Sacramento 95814; (916) 322-5660; Employees: 91; budget '91-'92: $6,039,000.

CALIFORNIA CITIZENS COMPENSATION COMMISSION

Created by Proposition 112 of June 1990 to hold the exclusive authority for setting the annual salaries and benefits for the governor, lieutenant governor, attorney general, controller, insurance commissioner, secretary of state, superintendent of public instruction, treasurer, members of the board of equalization and legislators. After a series of public hearings, the commission acted on Nov. 30, 1990, raising the governor's pay from $85,000 to $120,000, granting a separate pay category for the Senate president pro tem and the Assembly speaker, among other changes. (See chart page 32.) Lawmakers would continue to get free cars, health insurance and roughly $17,000 a year in tax-free living expenses. Under the pay commission statute, the increases took effect in December, a month before Gov. George Deukmejian left office. The change had the effect of raising his pension by $21,000 a year above what he would have received at his former level of pay.

The seven commission members were appointed by the governor. They serve without pay (except for $100 per diem and travel expenses). Salaries and benefits they approved will be in effect until Dec. 31, 1991, after which they may make annual pay adjustments.

The commissioners are: Chairman: Paul Brinigar; Members: George Nesterczuk, John Ohanesian, Ricky Izumi, Janice Baird, Steven Hayward and Frank Grimes.

TRANSPORTATION COMMISSION

Administers state highway planning and construction and other state transportation programs, including mass transit and rail transportation services. Chairman: Bruce Nestande; Members: Joseph Duffel, J. Thomas Hawthorne, Daniel Fessler, Assemblyman Richard Katz, Kenneth Kevorkian, William Leonard Sr., Joseph Levy, Sen. Quentin Kopp, Elaine Freeman and Jerome Lipp. Office: 1120 N St., Sacramento 95814; (916) 445-1690.

CALIFORNIA ENERGY RESOURCES CONSERVATION AND DEVELOPMENT COMMISSION

Responsible for siting major power plants, forecasting energy supplies and demands, developing energy conservation measures and conducting research into questions of energy supply, consumption, conservation and power plant technology. Chairman: Charles Imbrecht; Salary: $95,403; Members: Barbara Crowley, Richard A. Bilas, Art S. Kevorkian, Sally Rakow; Salaries: $92,465; Office: 1516 Ninth St., Sacramento 95814; (916) 324-3000; Employees 461; budget '91-'92: $110,752,000.

PUBLIC UTILITIES COMMISSION

Responsible for providing the public with the lowest reasonable rates for utilities and transportation services, and assures that utilities and transportation companies render adequate and safe services. President: Patricia Eckert; Salary $95,403;

Commissioners: G. Michel Wilk, John D. Ohanian, Daniel Fessler, Norman Shumway; Salaries: $92,465; Office: 505 Van Ness Ave., San Francisco 94102-3298; (415) 557-2444; Employees: 1,063; budget '91-'92: 82,285,000.

SEISMIC SAFETY COMMISSION

Responsible for improving earthquake safety in California; inventories hazardous buildings, sponsors legislation, pursues programs to strengthen state-owned buildings. Executive Director: L. Thomas Tobin; Salary: $78,276; Office: 1900 K St., Suite 100, Sacramento, 95814; (916) 322-4917; Employees: 12; '91-'92 budget: $989,000.

STATE LANDS COMMISSION

Administers state interest in more than 4 million acres of navigable waterways, swamp and overflow lands, vacant school sites and granted lands and tidelands within 3 miles of the mean high tide line (one of few state agencies not controlled by the governor). Members: State finance director Thomas Hayes, Republican; Lt. Gov. Leo McCarthy, Democrat; and Controller Gray Davis, Democrat. Executive Officer: Charles Warren; Salary: $88,056; Office: 1807 13th St., Sacramento 95814; (916) 322-7777; Employees: 260; '91- '92 budget: $19,175,000.

CALIFORNIA COASTAL COMMISSION

Charged with the state management of coastal resources, an area extending generally about 1,000 yards inland (but as much as 5 miles inland in some areas) and 3 miles seaward for the 1,100-mile length of the California coast, excluding San Francisco Bay. The commission was established in 1976 to succeed the California Coastal Zone Commission, a temporary agency created by the voters in 1972. The 15-member commission certifies local governments to manage the coastal zone in accordance with state-approved plans. Gov. Deukmejian attempted to abolish the agency in the early years of his administration and then cut budgets sharply. Executive director: Peter Douglas; Salary: $83,364; Office: 631 Howard St., San Francisco 94105; (415) 543-8555; Employees: 116; '91-'92 budget: $10,066,000.

MAJOR RISK MEDICAL INSURANCE PROGRAM

New program designed to provide health insurance for residents who are unable to find insurance in the open market by supplementing the cost of premiums with $30 million from tobacco taxes. Chairman: Cliff Allenby; Members: Soap Dowell, Rita Gordon, Ron Kaldor, Dr. Ralph Schaffarzick, M.D., and Anne Eowan; Office: 744 P St., Room 1077, Sacramento 95814; Employees: 9; '91-'92 budget: $103 million.

5

The California judiciary

California voters' confirmation of the five state Supreme Court justices on the ballot in 1990 was notable for its complete lack of controversy. Just four years earlier, an electorate enraged by the court's failure to affirm death sentences had ousted three sitting justices – Chief Justice Rose Elizabeth Bird and Associate Justices Cruz Reynoso and Joseph Grodin. All had been appointed by former Democratic Gov. Jerry Brown and all were the targets of crime victims groups' demands for swift executions.

"We need the death penalty. We don't need Rose Bird," Gov. George Deukmejian told audiences as he campaigned for re-election in 1986. Voters agreed, handing him the opportunity to replace the three liberal jurists with conservatives.

By the time Deukmejian left office in 1991, he had sealed the sweeping influence on the state's judiciary that he had sought to exert when he became governor. As a state senator in 1978, Deukmejian authored the law reinstating the death penalty. Later, as attorney general, he cited the governor's ability to appoint judges as his principal reason for wanting the job. Deukmejian had appointed a majority of the Supreme Court justices and about two-thirds of the roughly 1,500 sitting judges in lower courts by the end of his second four-year term in office. Most of his appointees were white males from prosecutorial backgrounds.

To fill the Supreme Court vacancies created by the 1986 election, Deukmejian selected three Court of Appeal justices – John Arguelles, David Eagleson and Marcus Kaufman. The governor elevated Associate Justice Malcolm Lucas, his former Long Beach law partner, to the chief justice's seat. All three of Deukmejian's new associate justices stayed scarcely long enough to fatten their pensions with the salary base provided by the state's top judicial post. They were replaced by Associate Justices Joyce Kennard, Marvin Baxter and Armand Arabian.

The ousted justices, meanwhile, did not go quietly. In the emotional campaign to remove Bird and the others, crime victims groups had argued that the justices were allowing their personal views against capital punishment to influence their interpretations of the law. Bird, who had been the subject of controversy since her 1977 appointment as the first woman on the court, herself aired television campaign ads, something previously unheard of in a Supreme Court election. She attacked Deukmejian for using the "politics of death" to advance his career.

In Grodin's first speech after removal from office, he argued that the political nature of the campaign had undermined the court's independence. Lucas, however, described the circumstances that led to Bird's departure and his elevation as "some very unusual times" and said the court would not preside over a "rush to death." It hasn't. The court instead entered a less controversial period. The Bird court had reversed all but a handful of the death penalty judgments it reviewed, and the new justices moved quickly to begin affirming death sentences. The Lucas court has given more latitude to trial courts and has been less likely to reverse cases for what prosecutors had argued for years were inconsequential errors.

Although the death penalty was reinstated in 1978, legal challenges have prevented anyone from being executed. No one has died in the gas chamber since 1967, when convicted police killer Aaron Mitchell was executed. In 1990, the gas chamber at San Quentin was readied for Robert Alton Harris, who was sentenced to death for the 1978 murders of two San Diego teenagers. But with the execution just days away, a federal appeals judge granted an indefinite stay. As of early 1991, California had 297 men and two women under the penalty of death.

While the justices have shown considerable independence on other matters – even to the point of reversing or refusing to hear cases favored by Deukmejian – gubernatorial candidates continued in 1990 to debate just how far they would go to determine the views of the judges they would appoint. Interpreting the 1986 elections as evidence that Californians want judges who agree with them on major political questions, Democrat Dianne Feinstein had promised to appoint a "pro-choice" Supreme Court. Republican Pete Wilson had argued that he would appoint judges who would apply the law as written, and that justices' personal views on abortion shouldn't matter.

The chief justice earns $127,104 a year. The salary for associate justices is $121,207.

State Supreme Court Justices

455 Golden Gate Avenue, Room 3200, San Francisco 94102; 415-557-1867.

Malcolm Millar Lucas

Lucas, the 26th chief justice of the court, was Gov. George Deukmejian's first appointee to the state Supreme Court in 1984. A longtime resident of Long Beach, Lucas practiced law there with Deukmejian from 1962 to 1967. He was then appointed by Gov. Ronald Reagan to the Los Angeles County Superior Court, and named by President Richard Nixon to the U.S. District Court in Los Angeles in 1971.

A native of Berkeley, Lucas earned both his undergraduate and law degrees from the University of Southern California. His great-grandfather was a two-time governor of Ohio and later the first territorial governor of Iowa.

PERSONAL: born April 19, 1927, in Berkeley; wife Joan Fisher; children, Gregory and Lisa.

CAREER: appointed by Gov. Deukmejian 1987; associate justice, state Supreme Court 1984-1987; U.S. District Court, Central District of California 1971-1984; Superior Court judge, Los Angeles County 1967-1971; private law practice 1954-1967.

Malcolm M. Lucas

Stanley Mosk

Mosk, who was state attorney general when Gov. Edmund G. "Pat" Brown named him to the court in 1964, was widely considered the front-runner to move up when Chief Justice Donald Wright retired in 1977. But Pat Brown's son, Gov. Jerry Brown, instead chose Rose Bird, a close friend and political ally with no prior judicial experience. The philosophically liberal Mosk had been one of four state Supreme Court justices originally targeted for defeat by conservative organizations. But crime victims groups ultimately opted not to pursue Mosk, and he is now the court's senior member.

Mosk earned his bachelor's and doctorate of law degrees at the University of Chicago. Before his

Stanley Mosk

election as state attorney general, he served as a Los Angeles County Superior Court judge.

PERSONAL: born Sept. 4, 1912, in San Antonio, Texas; wife Edna Mitchell; son, Richard Mitchell.

CAREER: appointed by Gov. Pat Brown 1964; state attorney general 1959-1964; Superior Court judge, Los Angeles County 1943-1959; executive secretary to Gov. Culbert Olson 1939-1943; private law practice 1935-1939.

Allen Edgar Broussard

Broussard announced in early 1991 that he intended to retire, leaving court observers to speculate that he had grown lonely as the court's only black member and the only remaining appointee of Gov. Jerry Brown. Although Broussard wrote the controversial pair of opinions prohibiting the death penalty unless a jury finds an "intent to kill," he escaped the wrath of crime victims groups in the 1986 election. He was the only member of the court not subject to voter confirmation that year. Broussard is considered one of the court's best scholars. As the last liberal, he'll be leaving with a viewpoint that may not be seen on the court again for years.

Broussard received his bachelor's degree from the University of California, Berkeley, and his law degree from UC's Boalt Hall.

Allen E. Broussard

PERSONAL: born April 13, 1929, in Lake Charles, Louisiana; wife Odessa James; children, Eric (deceased), Craig and Keith.

CAREER: appointed by Gov. Jerry Brown 1981; Superior Court judge, Alameda County 1975-1981; Municipal Court judge, Oakland-Piedmont Judicial District, Alameda County 1964-1975; private law practice 1956-1964.

Edward A. Panelli

A judicial moderate, Panelli was nominated by Gov. George Deukmejian to replace retired Supreme Court Justice Otto Kaus and won confirmation by the state's voters in the 1986 general election. Panelli was a Santa Clara County Superior Court judge for 11 years before joining the Court of Appeal in 1983. Before that, he practiced civil and criminal law in San Jose.

His bachelor's and law degrees are from the University of Santa Clara.

PERSONAL: born Nov. 23, 1931, in Santa Clara; wife Lorna Mondora; children, Tom, Jeff and Michael.

Edward A. Panelli

CAREER: appointed by Gov. Deukmejian 1985; presiding justice, Court of Appeal, Sixth Appellate District, 1984-1985; associate justice, Court of Appeal, First Appellate District, Division Four 1983-1984; Superior Court judge, Santa Clara County 1972-1983; general counsel, University of Santa Clara 1963-1972; private law practice 1955-1972.

Joyce Luther Kennard

Kennard, the first Asian-born nominee and second female justice in the court's history, grew up in the Japanese-occupied Dutch East Indies, where she spent three years of her childhood in a Japanese internment camp. She has said she never "used a telephone or saw a television set" until she was 14. As a teenager she lost a leg to an infection. She attended high school in Holland, and at age 20 immigrated alone to the United States in 1961. She became a naturalized citizen in 1967 in Los Angeles, where she eventually became a trial judge with a reputation as a tough sentencer. Appointed by Gov. George Deukmejian, she succeeded Associate Justice John A. Arguelles, who retired.

Joyce L. Kennard

She earned bachelors' and masters' degrees in public administration and her law degree from the University of Southern California.

PERSONAL: born May 6, 1941, in West Java, Indonesia; husband Robert Kennard.

CAREER: appointed by Gov. Deukmejian 1989; Superior Court judge, Los Angeles County 1987-1989; Municipal Court judge, Los Angeles Judicial District 1986-1987; senior attorney for former Associate Justice Edwin F. Beach, Court of Appeal, Second Appellate District 1979-1986; deputy attorney general, California Department of Justice, Los Angeles 1975-1979.

Armand Arabian

Arabian, a longtime friend of Gov. George Deukmejian, was the first Armenian-American to be named to the court. Appointed to replace Associate Justice Marcus M. Kaufman, a Deukmejian appointee who served just three years, Arabian has pledged to remain in his job for at least eight years. An outspoken and conservative jurist who is a recreational parachutist in his leisure time, Arabian has won a reputation as a judicial maverick. As a trial judge in a rape case, he once refused to give the jury the instruction, required at the time, that testimony of rape victims should be viewed skeptically. When the case reached the state Supreme Court, the justices chided Arabian for failing to comply with precedent.

Armand Arabian

But they then ordered that the instruction be barred in all future cases. His action in that case, coupled with his extensive writings on rape law reform, won Arabian the strong backing of women attorneys at his confirmation hearing for the state's highest court. He has law degrees from both the Southern California Law School and Boston University in addition to a bachelor's degree from BU.

PERSONAL: born December 12, 1934, in New York City; wife Nancy Megurian; children, Allison and Robert.

CAREER: appointed by Gov. Deukmejian 1990; associate justice, Court of Appeal, Second Appellate District, Division Three 1983-1990; Superior Court judge, Los Angeles County 1973-1983; Municipal Court judge, Los Angeles Judicial District 1972-1973; private law practice 1963-1972; deputy district attorney, Los Angeles County 1962-1963.

Marvin Ray Baxter

As appointments secretary to Gov. George Deukmejian, one of Baxter's chief responsibilities was recommending judges. As Deukmejian's second term drew to a close, Baxter became one himself, accepting an appointment to the Fifth District Court of Appeal in Fresno. In 1990, he became the second Armenian-American appointed to the state Supreme Court, replacing retiring Justice David Eagleson. Baxter, who was co-chairman of Deukmejian's 1982 campaign for governor, grew up in a farming community outside Fresno.

He has a bachelor's degree from Fresno State College and a law degree from Hastings College of Law.

Marvin Ray Baxter

PERSONAL: born January 9, 1940, in Fowler, Calif.; wife Jane Pippert ; children, Laura and Brent.

CAREER: appointed by Gov. Deukmejian1990; Fifth District Court of Appeal 1988-1990, governor's appointments secretary 1983-1988; private law practice 1969-1983; deputy district attorney, Fresno County 1967-1969.

California Appellate Court Justices

Court of Appeal, First Appellate District, Division One, 455 Golden Gate Avenue, San Francisco 94102; (415) 557-9580.

Presiding Justice John T. Racanelli; Associate Justices Robert L. Dossee, William A. Newsom and William D. Stein.

Court of Appeal, First Appellate District, Division Two, 455 Golden Gate Avenue, San Francisco 94102; (415) 557-9580.

Presiding Justice J. Anthony Kline; Associate Justices John E. Benson, J. Clinton Peterson and Jerome A. Smith.

Court of Appeal, First Appellate District, Division Three, 455 Golden Gate Avenue, San Francisco 94102; (415) 557-9580.

Presiding Justice Clinton W. White; Associate Justices Ming W. Chin, Robert W. Merrill and Gary E. Strankman.

Court of Appeal, First Appellate District, Division Four, 455 Golden Gate Avenue, San Francisco 94102; (415) 557-9580.

Presiding Justice Carl West Anderson; Associate Justices James F. Perley, Marcel Poche and Timothy A. Reardon.

Court of Appeal, First Appellate District, Division Five, 455 Golden Gate Avenue, San Francisco 94102; (415) 557-9580.

Presiding Justice Harry W. Low, Associate Justices Zerne P. Haning III and Donald B. King.

Court of Appeal, Second Appellate District, Division One, 300 South Spring Street, Los Angeles 90013; (213) 346-3002.

Presiding Justice Vaino H. Spencer; Associate Justices Robert R. Devich, Reuben A. Ortega and Miriam A. Vogel.

Court of Appeal, Second Appellate District, Division Two, 300 South Spring Street, Los Angeles 90013; (213) 346-3002.

Presiding Justice Lester William Roth; Associate Justices Morio L. Fukuto, Donald N. Gates and Michael G. Nott.

Court of Appeal, Second Appellate District, Division Three, 300 South Spring Street, Los Angeles 90013; (213) 346-3002.

Presiding Justice Joan Dempsey Klein; Associate Justices H. Walter Croskey, George E. Danielson and Edward A. Hinz Jr.

Court of Appeal, Second Appellate District, Division Four, 300 South Spring Street, Los Angeles 90013; (213) 346-3002.

Presiding Justice Arleigh Woods; Associate Justices Norman L. Epstein, Ronald M. George and Jack E. Goertzen.

Court of Appeal, Second Appellate District, Division Five, 300 South Spring Street, Los Angeles 90013; (213) 346-3002.

Presiding Justice Paul A. Turner; Associate Justices Herbert L. Ashby, Roger W. Boren and Margaret M. Grignon.

Court of Appeal, Second Appellate District, Division Six, 1280 South Victoria, Room 201, Ventura 93003; (805) 654-4502.

Presiding Justice Steven J. Stone; Associate Justices Arthur Gilbert and Kenneth R. Yegan.

Court of Appeal, Second Appellate District, Division Seven, 300 South Spring Street, Los Angeles 90013; (213) 346-3002.

Presiding Justice Mildred L. Lillie; Associate Justices Earl Johnson Jr. and Fred Woods.

Court of Appeal, Third Appellate District, 914 Capitol Mall, Sacramento 95814; (916) 445-4677.

Presiding Justice Robert K. Puglia; Associate Justices Coleman A. Blease, Frances N. Carr, Rodney Davis, Fred W. Marler Jr.,George Nicholson, Vance W. Raye, Arthur G. Scotland, Richard M. Sims III and Keith F. Sparks.

Court of Appeal, Fourth Appellate District, Division One, 750 B Street, Suite 500, San Diego 92101; (619) 237-6558.

Presiding Justice Daniel J. Kremer; Associate Justices Patricia D. Benke, Charles W. Froehlich Jr., Richard D. Huffman, Gilbert Nares, William L. Todd Jr., Howard B. Wiener and Don R. Work.

Court of Appeal, Fourth Appellate District, Division Two, 303 West Fifth Street, San Bernardino 92401; (714) 383-4442.

Presiding Justice Manuel A. Ramirez; Associate Justices Howard M. Dabney, Thomas E. Hollenhorst, Art W. McKinster and Robert J. Timlin.

Court of Appeal, Fourth Appellate District, Division Three, P.O. Box 1378, Santa Ana 92701; (714) 558-6779.

Presiding Justice David G. Sills; Associate Justices Thomas F. Crosby Jr., Henry T. Moore Jr., Sheila Prell Sonenshine and Edward J. Wallin.

Court of Appeal, Fifth Appellate District, P.O. Box 45013, Fresno 93721; (209) 445-5491.

Presiding Justice Hollis G. Best; Associate Justices James A. Ardaiz,Tim S. Buckley, Nicholas J. Dibiaso, Thomas A. Harris, Robert L. Martin, William A. Stone, James F. Thaxter and Steven M. Vartabedian.

Court of Appeal, Sixth Appellate District, 333 West Santa Clara Street, San Jose 95113; (408) 277-1004.

Presiding Justice Nat A. Agliano; Associate Justices P. Bamattre-Manoukian, Walter P. Capaccioli, Christopher C. Cottle, Franklin D. Elia and Eugene M. Premo.

6

California Legislature:

Unrepresentative and unrespected

"I've been on a tour of state legislatures. ... Mostly they are a bunch of fat white guys pretending to hurt each other."
–Satirist Mark Russell at a private dinner for California legislators hosted by Gov. Pete Wilson, Jan. 9, 1991.

"What's happened to me is like being traded from the Toledo Mud Hens to the Oakland A's."
–John Seymour on his elevation from the California state Senate to the U.S. Senate, February 1991.

California's Legislature was a grim place as the 1991-92 session began to unfold. It was an institution that got no respect.

Two former members – Democrats Paul Carpenter and Joseph Montoya – had recently been convicted of a slew of federal corruption charges for taking bribes while in office. More indictments of sitting legislators were expected. Policy had taken a back bench as the institution largely frittered away the 1980s without finding solutions to modernizing the state's water system, fixing a declining education system or making the streets safe from crime. And in November 1990, voters provided the capper: They approved Proposition 140, an initiative imposing strict term limits on legislators, cutting off their pension plan and requiring deep cuts in the legislative operating budget. The message was clear: California voters were fed up with their Legislature.

Two facts crystallized the nature of the California Legislature of the 1980s and early 1990s. First, it cost an average of $700,000 to win a seat in the state Senate – more than twice as much as it did to win a seat in Congress. That fact alone meant legislators spent considerable time and energy courting those who could write the checks to fill campaign coffers.

91

Second, the Legislature's membership did not reflect the state's demographics. The 1990 federal census showed California had a population that was 43 percent non-white. Yet white males held 73 percent of the seats (86 of the 120). Hispanics comprised more than a quarter of all state residents, but there were just seven Hispanics in the Legislature, or 6 percent. Asians nearly doubled their percentage of the state population to an estimated 10 percent, but the Legislature had no Asians. There were nine blacks, 8 percent of the Legislature, which nearly matched their population in California. Of the Legislature's top four leaders, only one – Assembly Speaker Willie Brown – was not white.

The occupational backgrounds of legislators were hardly representative of the population, either. There was some variety. Among California's lawmakers were two ex-cops, a doctor, a dentist, a nurse, farmers, small business owners, a law professor, a handful of Vietnam veterans and a reservist whose unit was activated for Operation Desert Shield. There also was a founder of the radical-but-defunct Students for a Democratic Society and a survivor of the Jonestown massacre in Guyana. But increasingly legislators' resumes listed "professional legislative aide" as their previous occupation, reflecting an institution that was becoming self-perpetuating. Some seats were held by a third generation of aides, handed down from one legislative assistant to the next. Lawyers, who once comprised half of the Legislature, had steadily declined to less than one-third by the end of the 1980s.

One reason for the disparity was that the reapportionment of the Legislature in the early 1980s had allowed Democrats to maintain a solid majority throughout the decade even as Democratic voter registration slipped below 50 percent. Legislative leaders maintained that term limits were not necessary because voters could always dump their representatives. But, in reality, districts were so skewed that for most legislators the idea of a competitive election remained a fiction.

More than half the seats could be considered safe for the incumbents of one party or the other. At the time of the November 1990 election, 23 out of 40 districts in the Senate had a registration edge of 20 percent or greater favoring the party of the incumbent; in the Assembly, there were 41 such seats out of 80. The number of districts with a 10 percent party advantage – still considered safe seats by most measures – stood at 29 in the Senate and 61 in the Assembly. What competition there was for incumbents was most often generated by local issues or because the incumbents themselves had come under a cloud for questionable activities.

THE CONSTANT CAMPAIGN

While in office, legislators live their life on a constant campaign, much like their congressional counterparts in Washington. "It is the nearest thing to Congress outside Washington, D.C.," said political scientist Alan Rosenthal of Rutgers University in New Jersey, an authority on state legislatures. "California is way out there beyond where any other legislatures are in terms of political partisanship, full-time campaigning and the cost of campaigns. California is almost another nation."

When the Legislature is in session – generally eight to nine months of the year minus vacation recesses – lawmakers usually arrive Monday morning and are gone by midafternoon Thursday. By day, legislators juggle committee assignments, floor sessions and their own bills. By night, many take part in the fund-raiser circuit at Sacramento watering holes frequented by lobbyists and staffers. They spend weekends toiling in their districts doing "constituent work," which is not very different from campaigning. Those from Southern California spend much of their life getting to and from airports.

Getting the money to get elected – and stay there – has become the dominant activity. Campaign spending studies, however, consistently showed legislators spent comparatively little money on actual electioneering. Mostly, they spent money being a politician – junkets, meals to schmooze donors and power-brokers, tickets to sports events, gifts for supporters, charitable contributions to make a favorable impression in the community and donations to other politicians.

FEDERAL PROBES UNDER THE DOME

In the first half of the decade, the Legislature endured a massive federal investigation into the passage of a bill that sought to overturn local ordinances banning fireworks. The probe of the activities of former fireworks mogul W. Patrick Moriarty yielded convictions of several Southern California officials, but only one legislator – Democratic Assemblyman Bruce Young of Norwalk. His conviction was later overturned.

Legislators had no sooner caught their breath from the Moriarty affair when the FBI lifted the lid in August 1988 on an even bigger investigation, officially code-named Brispec for "Bribery Special Interest." Beginning in 1985, undercover agents posed as Southern businessmen in search of a bill to benefit their sham companies in return for campaign contributions. They spread more than $50,000 among Capitol figures.

Agents gathered enough evidence in their "sting" to obtain search warrants of the offices of Patrick Nolan, the Assembly's Republican leader at the time; his close associate, Assemblyman Frank Hill, R-Whittier; Assemblywoman Gwen Moore, D-Los Angeles; and Sen. Joseph Montoya, D-Whittier. Montoya eventually was convicted and sentenced to federal prison on bribery and money-laundering charges. Former Sen. Paul Carpenter, by then a member of the state Board of Equalization, was convicted on similar charges soon thereafter. Moore eventually was cleared but others, including Sen. Alan Robbins, D-Encino, were drawn into the widening investigation.

The Legislature tightened its ethical standards by placing Proposition 112 on the June 1990 ballot. Once approved, the measure subjected legislators for the first time to enforceable conflict-of-interest laws, banned honorariums and restricted gifts to $250 a year in value from any single source.

In comparison with other high-achievers in society, legislators were not particularly well paid. They got a raise for the 1991-92 session from the Citizens Compensation Commission created by Proposition 112. Legislative pay went from $40,816 to $52,500 a year coupled with an additional $17,000 in living allowances, or $92 a day for each day the Legislature is in session and the member attends (an amount set by the state Board of Control). Legislative leaders were given a pay differential: the speaker of the Assembly and Senate president pro tempore were given $63,000 a year while the majority and minority leaders of each house got $57,750. Many lawmakers, however, still earned lower salaries than their aides.

Capitol life remains a hothouse with its own hybrid flowers. "The people who control the legislative process have become so wrapped up in the game – power for the sake of power – they've lost sight of the purpose the Legislature was created for: dealing with matters of public policy for the people of California," said Assembly Republican leader Ross Johnson in 1989.

While in Sacramento, a typical legislator would find issues flying in an endless succession. Even the best could expect to have no more than a shallow understanding of most bills, and all had to rely on the Legislature's army of 2,400 staffers to point out the nuances. Details and compromises were often worked out by the staff and later blessed by the elected officials. Legislators, armed with a huge staff, seemed compelled to legislate on a wide variety of issues, often creating a gridlock of bills. Many called the place a "bill mill."

LEGISLATIVE ACHIEVEMENTS

The Legislature has not been devoid of achievement. Since 1985, the Legislature has approved sweeping measures to reduce smog and garbage, passed a modest revision in workers disability compensation and taken a step toward modernizing the state's transportation system by placing a successful measure on the June 1990 ballot to raise gasoline taxes. Legislators also passed a mandatory seat-belt law, lowered the blood-alcohol standard for drunken driving and summoned the political courage to approve restrictions on the sale of semiautomatic weapons.

In the wake of the Exxon Valdez oil spill in Alaska, the Legislature approved a landmark oil spill cleanup law with a $100 million emergency fund. State lawmakers also garnered enough votes to enact the first far-reaching welfare reform since Ronald Reagan was governor, approving in 1985 a "workfare" plan. And lawmakers and the governor stiffened numerous criminal laws and appropriated hundreds of millions of dollars throughout the decade for the most massive prison building program in world history.

To be sure, the Legislature always was willing to go farther than Gov. George Deukmejian in a number of areas. The Legislature approved sweeping measures for health and work safety, parental leave to care for ill children and environmental regulations only to see them vetoed by Deukmejian.

But efforts to reorganize the Los Angeles transit system foundered under its own weight with the cross currents of intra-L.A. rivalries. The state's school system gradually slipped from the top half to the bottom half in the nation. Fees shot up at state colleges and universities – shutting out many promising students – and those who could afford it were being told the lack of professors and classrooms would force most of them to spend five years earning a bachelor's degree.

The state turned increasingly to deficit spending in the form of floating interest-bearing bonds, and passing a state budget each year became an act of supreme political will. In the summer of 1990, legislators and the governor sat in a steaming hot Sacramento for nearly a month trading insults after the constitutional deadline had passed for adopting a budget. As Republican Gov. Pete Wilson took office, the state faced a projected deficit of up to $12.6 billion.

Of the 5,000 or so bills before the Legislature each session, the fact remained that most dealt with mundane district issues or tinkered with business regulations. Indeed, the Legislature had become largely a regulatory body, spending considerable time refereeing "scope of practice" disputes between various medical professions (podiatrists and orthopedic surgeons waged one memorable battle over the right to perform surgery on the ankle) and dealing with licensure matters ranging from building contractors to interior decorators.

INITIATIVES ABOUND

The Legislature's biggest achievements were usually under the threat of a more Draconian initiative from the outside. A number of organizations found it easier – and cheaper than lobbying the Legislature – to draft their own law, gather enough signatures and take their measure directly to the voters. The result was a bewildering array of ballot proposals, some by outsiders, many by individual lawmakers and some by the Legislature itself. Voices and tempers have been raised in favor of reform, but whose voices, what reforms?

Maybe there's nothing wrong with the California initiative process that a good dose of voter skepticism wouldn't cure. And maybe the voters administered their tonic in November 1990 when they just said "no" to all but six of 28 ballot measures.

California became the 10th state in the nation to enact the initiative and referendum by special election on Oct. 10, 1911, during the term of reformist Gov. Hiram Johnson. Petitions designed to enact or reform statutes can be placed on the ballot with the valid signatures of 5 percent of the total number of votes cast for governor in the most recent gubernatorial election. Constitutional amendments can be placed before the voters with the backing of 8 percent of the total vote. In theory, they are restricted to making one change at a time in the Constitution, not wholesale revisions. There are signs that the courts may begin to enforce that single-subject rule. An appellate court struck down Proposition 105, the consumer's right-to-know act, on grounds that it was too broad. Legislators hope the state Supreme Court will make the same finding about Proposition 140, the term-limit initiative.

Other reforms are in the wind. Should paid signatures be banned? One court has already ruled otherwise. Should initiatives that propose bond issues be outlawed?

Should proponents be forbidden to write initiatives that would distribute tax proceeds to themselves? The dangers lie, no doubt, in the law of unintended consequences. Tampering with the people's right to place initiatives on the ballot by raising the signature requirement, for example, might do nothing more than protect the paid signature gatherers. They have the most to lose, the most chance of protecting themselves and the most interest in keeping their industry alive. The voters themselves may be sending the message that matters. Keep them simple and short. Write them honestly. Otherwise, the answer is "no."

TERM LIMITS

The voters did say "yes" to term limits, but they picked an initiative that may prove more problematic than if they had said "no." Proposition 140, the brainchild of retiring Los Angeles County Supervisor Pete Schabarum and pushed by the remnants of the organization founded by anti-tax crusaders Howard Jarvis and Paul Gann, passed by 53 percent – not exactly a resounding mandate. The initiative imposed the following limits:

●Constitutional officers, like the governor, are limited to two terms of four years each, or eight years. The initiative did not mention the newest constitutional officer, the insurance commissioner, thus that position has no term limit.

●State senators elected in 1990 – the even-numbered seats – are limited to two terms of four years each, or eight years. State senators who were not up for election in 1990 get one more term if they are re-elected in 1992. That anomaly in the initiative creates a paradox: state Sen. William Leonard, R-Big Bear, first elected to the Senate in 1988, must leave by 1996. However, Sen. Ralph Dills, R-Garden Grove, first elected to the Legislature in 1938 and re-elected to the Senate in 1990, is not required to leave until 1998.

●Assembly members, who face election every two years, are limited to three terms in office, or six years.

All limits were imposed for life, thus legislators and constitutional officers cannot sit out a term before running for their old offices. But they can seek a new office. Some Senators predicted that at the end of their terms they might run for Assembly seats. Other legislators wasted no time in seeking new career opportunities after the 1990 election. Among the first to go was Assembly Speaker Pro Tem Michael Roos of Los Angeles, who took a job heading an educational foundation.

Proposition 140 also shut down the Legislature's retirement system and cut its operating budget by 38 percent. Meeting the new budget restrictions required a massive reduction in personnel and to accomplish that lawmakers offered staffers severance pay equivalent of five months salary in what became known as the "golden kiss-off." Many of the most talented people took the offer, creating critical vacancies on key committee staffs. Their departure also contributed to one of the rockiest – and most unproductive – starts for a legislative session in modern times. Critics, however, maintained that legislators made a difficult situation worse by failing to eliminate unnecessary jobs in order to save the most essential members of the staff. In February 1991, legislative leaders sued to overturn Proposition 140, arguing, in part, that the Legislature had been rendered a less-than-equal branch of government with the executive branch because of the staff cuts required to meet the measure's budget limitation.

DECENNIAL REAPPORTIONMENT

As 1991 unfolded, legislators and Republican Gov. Wilson readied themselves to redraw legislative and congressional districts. The last time around, the master of the gerrymander, the late Rep. Phil Burton of San Francisco, had directed the crafting of congressional district lines and Democrat Jerry Brown had been waiting in the governor's office to sign the legislative and congressional district bills before leaving office. But after a decade of taking the brunt of criticism for Burton's handiwork, state legislators swore they would control the 1991 reapportionment. They also had another reason for wanting to take control of congressional reapportionment: With an eye mandatory term limits, some state lawmakers were expected to carve a nice congressional district in which to run in 1992 or later.

Wilson threatened to veto any reapportionment plan that was unfair and promised political doom to any Republican who tried to cut a deal for a safe district. This time, Democrats promised, they would be fair and conduct open hearings.

Added to the equation were other new factors not seen in the last reapportionment, namely off-the-shelf technology. In 1991, ethnic and economic interests outside the Legislature could draft their own reapportionment plans with easily obtained computer programs. Further, the federal Voting Rights Act required that districts favoring racial minorities be drawn first. A number of predominantly non-white areas of the state have long been represented by white Democrats. Reapportionment has the potential of creating rifts between such officeholders and their traditional supporters.

One certain effect of reapportionment will be in moving the center of political power further south, reflecting growth trends of the 1980s. And that spells bad news for Northern California Democrats. Some Northern California legislative districts must be merged so that more districts can be created in Southern California (the state constitution requires the Legislature remain at a constant 120 seats). Such a collapse of districts could push into retirement several aging Democratic legislators such as Milton Marks or Nicholas Petris.

With lawyers for every party and interest group readying their computers, most political insiders believed that – baring a political miracle – the 1991 reapportionment plan is destined for resolution by the courts. And this time, unlike the Rose Bird court of a decade earlier, the state Supreme Court is dominated by Republicans.

BIOGRAPHICAL SKETCHES

Following the biographical sketches are election results for the previous two campaigns, where applicable. To the right of the results is the money raised for the campaign. Where no figure is given, the amount was unavailable.

Ratings from nine lobbying organizations also are given. A score of 100 indicates the officeholder voted in agreement 100 percent of the time on bills of interest to that organization. Lower scores indicate fewer votes in agreement. All of the ratings are for the 1989-90 legislative session. Where "NR" is listed, the legislator was not rated by that organization, usually because the legislator did not cast enough votes for a fair rating or because the legislator was elected late in the session. The rating methodology used by each organization varies. For a complete analysis of how each organization compiled its ratings, the reader should contact the organization and request a copy of its ratings. The organizations are:

AFL–The California American Federation of Labor-Congress of Industrial Organizations (AFL-CIO), the largest labor federation in the nation, based its ratings on 33 bills for senators, 40 bills for Assembly members. The issues included expanded rights for collective bargaining, workplace safety, health care, farm labor and child care. (916) 444-3676; (415) 986-3585.

PIRG–California Public Interest Research Group, a non-profit consumer and environmental organization founded in 1972, based its ratings on 20 bills for senators, 22 bills for Assembly members. Issues included expanded environmental protections, recycling, landlord-tenant relations, health insurance, voter registration and consumer contracts. (916) 448-4516; (213) 278-9244.

CLCV–The California League of Conservation Voters, an environmental-legal defense coalition of more than 100 organizations, based ratings on 17 bills for senators, 20 bills for Assembly members. Issues included air and water pollution, waste disposal, recycling, wildlife protection, coastal protection, water conservation, and timber harvesting. (415) 896-5550; (213) 826-8812.

NOW–California National Organization for Women, Inc., a prominent women's rights group, based its ratings for members of both houses on 10 bills. The issues included abortion funding for the poor, sex discrimination in private clubs, sexual abuse, child and pregnancy care. (916) 442-3414.

CTA–The California Teachers Association, the largest single labor union in the state, based its ratings on 24 bills, varying on whether the member had an opportunity to vote on a selected bill in committee. Issues included crime safety in the classroom, collective bargaining, banning assault weapons, pension issues, school board election procedures, extended disability leave and various budget issues. (916) 442-5895; (415) 697-1400.

CofC–The California Chamber of Commerce, a statewide business group, based its ratings on 24 bills for senators, 25 bills for Assembly members. Bills included employment termination procedures, housing, health care, environmental regulation and regulations on labor unions. (916) 444-6670.

CFB–The California Farm Bureau, representing agricultural interests, based its ratings on five bills for senators, 12 bills for Assembly members. Issues included opposition to greater coastal protections, water use audits, and supporting measures for farmland protection and swifter pest eradication. (916) 446-4647.

NRA–The National Rifle Association, based its ratings on its opposition to nine bills in the Senate and 12 bills in the Assembly. (916) 446-2455

FPAC– Free Market Political Action Committee ("FREEPAC"), an organization dedicated to laissez-faire economic policy founded by former Republican state Sen. H.L. Richardson. The ratings were based on 25 bills for senators, 27 for Assembly members. Issues included opposition to a mandatory health insurance, family leave for illness, prevailing wage rules, merger regulation, air pollution regulation and support for repealing rent control. No telephone available.

KEY VOTES

A selection of 18 votes is given for each legislator on a range of issues since 1986. The issues and votes were selected by the editors and explanations for YES and NO are given below. If a lawmaker was not yet serving in the Legislature at the time of the vote, the vote is not shown. If the legislator was serving, but abstained or missed the vote, the absence is noted with a dash (–).

Divest S. Africa: AB 134 by Assemblywoman Maxine Waters, D-Los Angeles; signed by Deukmejian – The bill required the state to divest its investment portfolio from companies doing business in South Africa to protest that country's racial separation policy. The bill passed the Senate on Aug. 25, 1986, on a 27-11 vote and passed the Assembly on Aug. 27, 1986, on a 50-28 vote. YES favored divesting; NO was against.

Insurance reform: SB 103 by Sen. Alan Robbins, D-Encino; failed in the Assembly – The bill would have put into law the insurance reform provisions of Proposition 103's rate-rollbacks and other consumer-oriented insurance regulations. The bill was seen as a test of legislative opinion on the consumer-oriented initiative. The bill passed the Senate on Feb. 9, 1989, by 27-9 and lost in the Assembly on April 6, 1989, by 49-22. The bill was granted reconsideration and voted on again on May 8, 1989, and again failed 49-21. The Assembly vote given here is for April 6, the first vote. YES was for the bill; NO was against.

Child sick leave: AB 681 – by Assemblyman Terry Friedman, D-Los Angeles; vetoed by Deukmejian – The bill would have allowed employees to use sick leave for attending ill children. Proponents said the bill recognized a modern economic fact of life – many families have two wage-earners. Without the bill, many employees would have to choose between their jobs and leaving children unattended while ill. The bill was opposed by business groups, which contended it would force them to pay employees to care for their sick children. The bill passed the Assembly on June 26, 1989, by 43-29 and passed the Senate on Sept. 11, 1989, by 21-17. YES favored using sick leave to care for ill children; NO was against.

Assault gun ban: SB 292 by Sen. David Roberti, D-Los Angeles, and AB 357 by Assemblyman Michael Roos, D-Los Angeles; signed by Deukmejian – Two interlocking bills restricting the sales of semiautomatic, military-style assault weapons were passed in 1989. The bills were bitterly opposed by the National Rifle Association, and their passage marked a major setback to its political clout. The bills gained momentum after the massacre of children in a Stockton schoolyard. Since the bills were part of a package, the vote given here is a combination of the votes on both bills (no member voted in favor of one and against the other). The vote is shown if the member voted on at least one bill. Absences or abstentions are only noted if a member missed voting on both bills. The Roberti bill (SB 292) passed the Assembly on April 17, 1989, by 41-34 and the Senate on May 4, 1989, by 29-8. The Roos bill (AB 357) passed the Assembly on May 18, 1989, by 41-35 and in the Senate on the same day, 27-11. YES favored the restrictions; NO was against.

Parent consent abortion: AB 2274 – by Assemblyman Robert Frazee, R-Carlsbad; signed by Deukmejian – The bill required minor girls to have parental permission to get an abortion. However, the state has been under a court restraining order preventing enforcement. That order was upheld by the state Court of Appeal in October 1989. The bill passed the Assembly on June 25, 1987, by 46-28 and the Senate on Sept. 10, 1987, by 25-11. YES was in favor of parental consent to get an abortion; NO was against.

Ban AIDS discrimination: AB 65 – by Assemblyman John Vasconcellos, D-San Jose; vetoed by Deukmejian – The bill would have banned discrimination in employment against anyone stricken with acquired immune deficiency syndrome. Proponents argued that those with AIDS are sometimes fired from their jobs by fearful employers even though the disease is not easily transmitted. Opponents said the bill went too far in restricting businesses, such as restaurants that have lost business when patrons learned a cook had AIDS. The bill passed the Assembly on June 29, 1989, by 46-32 and passed the Senate on Sept. 11, 1989, by 25-6. YES favored banning discrimination against AIDS victims; NO was against.

Clean Air Act: AB 2595 – by Assemblyman Byron Sher, D-Stanford; signed by Deukmejian – The landmark bill expanded the powers of local air quality districts and required a phased reduction of smog-causing emissions into the 21st century. Those in favor contended it marked a major step toward clean air; opponents argued it allowed too much intervention by unelected officials into business and local land-use. The bill passed the Senate on Aug. 29, 1988, by 25-4 and the Assembly on Aug. 31 by 47-27. YES was in favor of the new smog restrictions; NO was against.

Ban insurance donations (Senate only): SB 205 – by Sen. Gary K. Hart, D-Santa Barbara; failed in Senate – The bill would have banned candidates for state insurance commissioner from accepting contributions from insurance companies. The bill was seen as a major test of the Senate's ability to clamp down on special-interest money in campaigns. Opponents argued a ban for insurance commissioner candidates could set a precedent for other offices – like their own. The bill needed a two-thirds majority (27 votes) to pass the Senate but was defeated on a 15-19 vote on June 29, 1989. YES was in favor of banning insurance company contributions to candidates for insurance commissioner; NO was against.

Cutting old trees (Assembly only): AB 390 by Assemblyman Byron Sher, D-Stanford; failed in Assembly – The bill would have begun a three-year moratorium on cutting old-growth timber on the state's North Coast. The measure was ambushed by the timber industry. The fight over the bill was played out with a set of "killer" amendments offered by Democratic Assemblyman Dan Hauser, who represents the North Coast and had received timber industry campaign contributions. The key amendment, requiring an appropriation for a University of California study on the old-growth timber, had the effect of converting the bill from a majority-vote measure to one requiring a two-thirds vote – a standard it could never meet. The bill died in the Assembly a day after the amendments on a 42-27 vote, well short of the 54 votes needed for passage. The vote given here is on the killer amendment on June 29, 1989, that converted the bill into a two-thirds-vote bill. The amendment was adopted on a 40-29 vote. YES was for approval of the amendment, in effect voting to kill the bill and continue the cutting of old growth trees; NO was against the amendment.

Expand death penalty: Efforts to expand the death penalty to include more "special circumstance" crimes have won majorities in both houses but have been thwarted from becoming law through parliamentary maneuvering in committees. Thus, two bills are given reflecting death-penalty votes, one for each house.

In the Senate: SB 1156 – by Sen. William Lockyer, D-Hayward; died in the Assembly – the Senate passed the bill by 26-5 on June 19, 1987, but it stalled in the Assembly Public Safety Committee. YES was in favor of expanding the death penalty to include new crimes; NO was against the bill.

In the Assembly: SB 44 – by Lockyer; died in the Senate – because the Assembly Public Safety Committee would not let a death-penalty bill leave its jurisdiction, a Senate bill awaiting a vote in the Assembly was amended on the floor to include expanding the death penalty. As amended, the bill passed the Assembly June 23, 1988, by 60-9 but died in the Senate without a vote. YES was in favor of expanding the death penalty to include new crimes; NO was against.

Limit product tort: SB 241 – by Sen. William Lockyer, D-Hayward; signed by Deukmejian – The bill contained a series of procedural and substantive changes in liability laws reached as part of a "peace accord" between doctors, lawyers and insurance companies. The bill was not seen by legislators until the final night of the year's session, and a number of lawmakers complained – to no avail – that they wanted more time to review it. The bill was seen as a test of Speaker Brown's ability to ramrod a bill and he succeeded. The bill passed in both houses on Sept. 11, 1987, approved by the Senate by 25-1 and the Assembly by 63-10. YES favored limiting liability laws; NO was against.

Ban offshore oil: AB 284 – by Assemblyman Dan Hauser, D-Arcata; vetoed by Deukmejian – The bill would have required establishment of a "sanctuary" prohibiting offshore oil drilling within three miles of the Northern California coastline. Proponents argued the northern coastline was too environmentally sensitive to risk disaster from offshore drilling. Opponents, including Deukmejian, argued that California was not doing its share to provide the nation with oil and was too dependent on Alaskan crude for its own needs. The bill would not have affected oil leases within federal jurisdiction beyond the state's three-mile limit. The bill passed the Assembly on June 23, 1987, by 43-34 and passed the Senate on Aug. 12, 1988, by 28-6. YES favored banning offshore drilling; NO was against.

Restrict abortion funds: budget amendments 1990-91 – by Sen. John Doolittle, R-Rocklin, and Assemblyman Phillip Wyman, R-Tehachapi; failed passage – Doolittle and Wyman, in their respective houses, proposed amendments to the state budget that would have restricted state-funded Medi-Cal abortions to cases of rape, incest, fetal abnormality or danger to the mother's life. The amendment, in the wake of U.S. Supreme Court rulings tightening restrictions on abortion, was seen as a test on where each California legislator stood on the issue. Doolittle's amendment failed in the Senate on June 11, 1990, by 12-24; Wyman's Assembly amendment failed on July 19, 1990, by 30-36. YES is in favor of restricting Medi-Cal abortions; NO is in favor of maintaining Medi-Cal abortions.

Lower alcohol std: SB 408 – Sen. William Leonard, R-Big Bear; signed by Deukmejian – the bill lowered the standard for drunken driving from .10 percent blood alcohol to .08 percent. The lower standard made it easier to win convictions. Those opposed argued it was a manifestation of "neo-prohibitionism" and would lead to other anti-alcohol laws. The bill passed the Senate on Sept. 6, 1989, by 24-3; and the Assembly on Aug. 31, 1989, by 67-5. YES was in favor of lowering the blood alcohol standard; NO was against.

Basic health care: Efforts to establish a basic health care insurance program for those who are not covered by their own or employer-supported plans have won majorities in both houses. But no such bill has reached the governor's desk because of differences between the Senate and Assembly. Two bills are listed, one for each house, to show the support for such a plan. YES was in favor of a state-run basic health program for employees; NO was against.

In the Senate: AB 1521 – Assemblyman Burt Margolin, D-Los Angeles – This version passed the Senate on June 14, 1990, by 32-4. A subsequent vote in the Assembly was designed to create a conference committee on the bill, thus that vote does not indicate actual support or opposition to the bill. The conference committee was never convened.

In the Assembly: AB 328 – Assemblyman Margolin – This was Margolin's health plan in its purest form. It passed the Assembly on June 27, 1989, by 43-32, but was not taken up for a final vote by the Senate.

Oil spill prevent: SB 2040 by Sen. Barry Keene, D-Benicia; signed by Deukmejian – The bill set up a $100 million contingency fund for coastal oil spills, imposed new fees on the oil industry and provided for a number of safety measures designed to prevent oil spills. The bill was prompted by the disastrous Exxon Valdez oil spill. Much of the work was done in a bill by Assemblyman Edward Lempert, D-San Mateo, and the Keene bill represented a merging of the measures. Opponents maintained the bill was unnecessary and represented a cost to consumers. The bill passed the Senate on Aug. 31, 1990, by 35-1; and the Assembly on Aug. 31, 1990, by 74-1. YES favors the oil spill prevention measures; NO is against.

Ethics reform: SCA 32 by Sen. David Roberti, D-Los Angeles; placed on the ballot as Proposition 112, approved by voters June 5, 1990 – the constitutional amendment imposed ethics restrictions on legislators, including an enforceable conflict-of-interest code, a ban on honorariums for speeches, restriction on travel paid for by others and a limit on gifts to $250 in value a year from any single source. The amendment also created the Citizens Compensation Commission appointed by the governor to set the salaries of legislators and constitutional officers. Those favoring the amendment maintained it was needed to restore confidence in the Legislature. Those against maintained variously that it went too far, did not go far enough and/or that it meant an automatic pay raise for legislators. The bill passed the Senate on Sept. 15, 1989, by 33-3; and the Assembly on Sept. 15, 1989, by 68-7. YES favored the ethics constitutional amendment; NO was against.

Work cancer stds: AB 1469 by Assemblyman Burt Margolin, D-Los Angeles; vetoed by Deukmejian – The bill would have required the state Occupational Safety and Health Standards Board to expand the list of carcinogenic substances and industrial processes covered by work safety health standards. The bill was a centerpiece for environmentalists' efforts to regulate environmental safety in the workplace. Opponents argued it was unneeded and scientifically unproved. It passed the Senate on Aug. 28, 1990, by 22-11; and the Assembly on Aug. 29, 1990, by 49-26. YES favored expanded health standards; NO was against.

Earthquake insure: SB 2902 by Sen. Frank Hill, R-Whittier; signed by Deukmejian – would require homeowners and others to purchase earthquake insurance. The measure came in the wake of the destructive Northern California earthquake in October 1989, although Hill had been promoting such a law since the 1987 devastating earthquake in Whittier. Because of a drafting error, the measure was not enforceable and was subject to new legislation in the 1991-92 session. The bill passed Senate on Aug. 31, 1990, by 28-3; and passed Assembly on Aug. 31, 1990, by 52-21. YES was in favor of mandatory quake insurance; NO was against.

COMMON ABBREVIATIONS

AI – American Independent Party
CSU – California State University
J.D. – Juris doctor (modern law degree)
L – Libertarian party
M.P.A. – Masters, Public Administration
NR – Not rated
P&F – Peace and Freedom party
UC – University of California
USC – University of Southern California
USMC – U.S. Marine Corps

Senate distirct maps

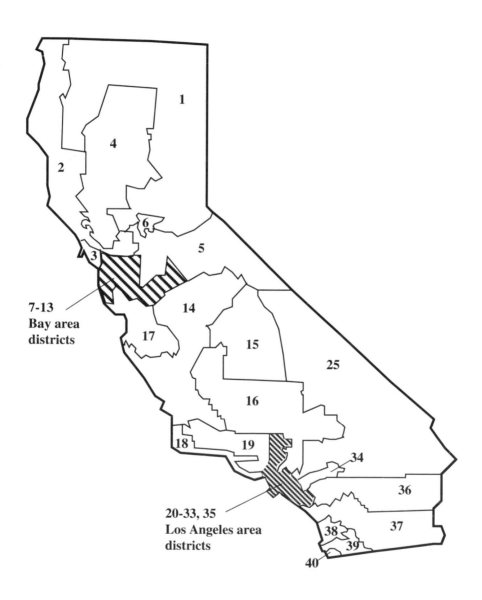

7-13
Bay area
districts

20-33, 35
Los Angeles area
districts

Los Angeles area Senate districts

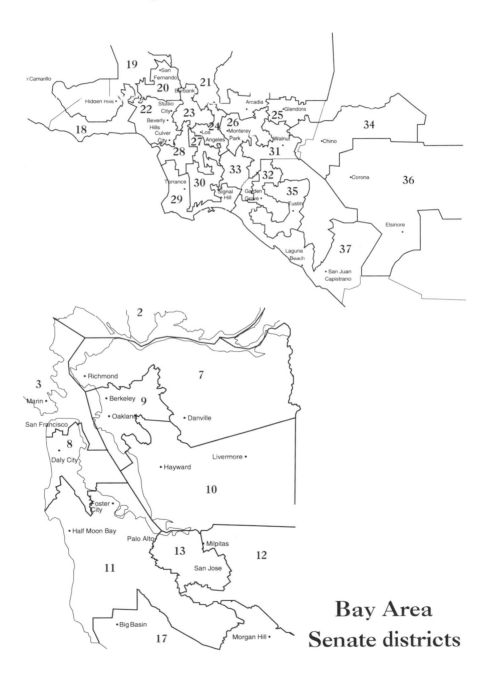

Bay Area
Senate districts

SENATE
Vacant
1st Senate District

This northernmost district loops from the Trinity Alps and Klamath Valley, across the top of the state, taking in snow-capped Mount Shasta, to the northeastern California border with Oregon and Nevada. It then moves south through the mountain counties of Lassen, Plumas, Sierra, Nevada, Placer and El Dorado along the northern reaches of the Sierra, including the Lake Tahoe Basin. The district hooks eastward again, taking in the suburbs of Sacramento, Yuba City and Yolo County, including the university town of Davis. It is a district with widely divergent political and economic forces. And it was one of the messiest political battlegrounds of the 1980s and remained so into the 1990s.

In recent years, the seat was held by John Doolittle, who moved on to Congress in 1991 (see 14th Congressional District). The special-election race to replace him attracted Assemblyman Tim Leslie of Carmichael (see 5th Assembly District), who had the backing of the state's Republican leadership. Only one problem – Leslie didn't live in the district. So he rented a home in Auburn in order to run. Despite a spirited challenge from Republican Bob Dorr, an El Dorado County supervisor, Leslie got 43 percent of the vote in the March primary. Democrat Patti Mattingly of Yreka, a moderate Siskiyou County supervisor who received 31 percent, was to face Leslie in the May 14 runoff.

The race held special interest for Democrats since a victory by Mattingly would give Democrats 27 votes in the Senate, enough to override a gubernatorial veto. However, Republicans still control enough votes in the Assembly to uphold a veto.

REGISTRATION: 44.4% D, 44.5% R

Barry D. Keene (D)
2nd Senate District

The craggy north coast with its dwindling stands of old-growth forest remains outside the economic mainstream of the state. Illegal marijuana growing may be its biggest cash crop. Quaint bed-and-breakfast inns dot the Mendocino and Humboldt county coastlines. The district has a national park – Redwoods – though residents nearby have always resented it as a symbol of a lost timber industry. The new Pelican Bay state prison in Crescent City has brought a new economic base for some, but the unlikely spot for a prison is awkward for transporting prisoners, and it has brought urban problems with it.

A generation ago, California's scantly populated north coast voted Republican most of the time, even though it had a majority of nominally Democratic voters. But its politics began to change in the late 1960s, when the decline of the timber industry was accompanied by an influx of counterculture urban refugees. As loggers became fewer and the newcomers more numerous, the political pendulum made a slow but steady swing to the left, with environmental and lifestyle issues becoming dominant in local politics. By the late 1980s, the region, stretching from the Oregon border nearly to San Francisco, was voting solidly Democratic.

The harbinger of that change occurred in 1972, when a young Democratic attorney from Santa Rosa named Barry Keene was elected to a vacant state Assembly seat. Keene spent six years in the Assembly before moving into the region's state Senate district, which includes the counties of Del Norte, Humboldt, Mendocino and fast-growing Solano. The district takes in much of Sonoma County and reaches nearly to Sacramento.

Barry Keene

Keene is one of the Capitol's most paradoxical figures, perhaps reflecting better than anyone realized the political tensions within the region. In his earlier legislative days, he was the archetypal young man on the make, climbing up the committee ladder and openly positioning himself to run for statewide office with high-profile moves, mostly in the medical field. An unabashed admirer of the Kennedys, Keene patterned himself – even his speaking style – on his idols. But sometime after moving to the Senate, Keene lost his political zeal. The tall young man stooped and grayed. He tried to persuade then-Gov. Jerry Brown to appoint him to the appellate court to no avail. In 1985, after helping Senate President Pro Tem David Roberti solidify his grip on the Senate's top political post, Keene moved to the No. 2 slot as majority floor leader.

Keene, the idealistic legislator, became Keene the apparatchik, hitting up lobbyists for campaign money and otherwise playing the inside game. And he also developed a reputation for personal erraticism, occasionally erupting into rages and firing his staff in wholesale lots. A magazine listed him as one of the worst bosses in California. Publicly, Keene displays a diffident, almost shy manner, but his problems were indirectly confirmed when a newspaper revealed that he had been spending campaign funds on psychological counseling services.

Since turning his attention to party affairs, Keene has authored only a handful of major bills and, at times, appears mostly interested in taking care of local matters. One recent stab at major legislation was noteworthy. In 1990, Keene authored the Senate's version of a bill to provide for oil-spill prevention and a $100 million response fund for cleanups. The bill, with major help from Assemblyman Ted Lempert, D-San Mateo, was signed into law.

Republican strategists targeted Keene in 1986, but Keene won handily and seemed in little danger of losing his seat until the region's politics reached a boiling point in 1990. "Redwood Summer" – a series of environmental protests against logging led by the radical Earth First! – deeply angered the district's loggers, who accused the environmentalists of trying to destroy their livelihoods. Keene backed the loggers and managed to ride out the political tide that swept the region's Democratic congressman, Doug Bosco, out of office. Although hardly a landslide, Keene won with 8 percentage points to spare over the well-financed Republican, Margie Handley, a Willits businesswoman.

PERSONAL: elected 1978; born July 30, 1938, in Camden City, N.J.; home, Benicia; education, B.A. prelaw and J.D. Stanford University; divorced; children, Susan, Mitchell, Joe, Tony, Patricia; Protestant.

CAREER: Sonoma County deputy district attorney 1967-1968; lawyer; businessman; school board member; Assembly 1972-1978; Senate majority leader.

COMMITTEES: Business & Professions; Governmental Organization; Insurance, Claims & Corporations; Judiciary; (Select) Calif. Wine Industry; Maritime Industry; Pacific Rim; (Joint) Fisheries & Aquaculture (vice chair); Legislative Retirement.

OFFICES: Capitol, (916) 445-3375, FAX (916) 443-4739; district, 631 Tennessee St., Vallejo 94590, (707) 648-4080; 317 3rd St., 6, Eureka 95501, (707) 445-6508; P.O. Box 1014 Ukiah 95482, (707) 468-0504; 50 D Street, 120-A, Santa Rosa 95404, (707) 576-2774.

REGISTRATION: 56.2% D, 31.5% R

1990 CAMPAIGN:	Keene - D	53.9%	$1,436,170
	Margie Handley - R	46.01%	$474,023
1986 CAMPAIGN:	Keene - D	56%	$853,502
	Richard Brann - R	41%	$667,306

RATINGS:

AFL	PIRG	CLCV	NOW	CTA	CofC	CFB	NRA	FPAC
91%	70%	NR	90%	90%	33%	20%	54%	19%

KEY VOTES:

Divest S. Africa:	YES	Insurance reform:	YES	Child sick leave:	YES
Assault gun ban:	YES	Parent consent abortion:	NO	Ban AIDS discrim:	YES
Clean Air Act:	YES	Ban insure donations:	YES	Extend death penalty:	–
Lmt product tort:	YES	Ban offshore oil:	YES	Restrict abortion funds:	NO
Lower alcohol std:	YES	Basic health care:	–	Oil spill prevent:	YES
Ethics reform:	YES	Work cancer stds:	YES	Earthquake insure:	YES

Milton Marks (D)

3rd Senate District

This district, which includes Marin County and northern San Francisco, appears tailor-made for a Democrat – or a Milton Marks.

Marks has represented the area for 22 years, the first 19 as a moderate-to-liberal Republican. Throughout his career, which began in the Assembly in 1958, Marks has been a maverick. He is a tireless campaigner who has built support through personal contact at myriad district events.

Marks took a brief respite from the Legislature in 1966, when Democratic Gov. Pat Brown appointed him to a San Francisco Municipal Court judgeship. But he returned to politics the following year, when California's new Republican governor, Ronald Reagan, supported Marks' successful effort to fill a vacant state Senate seat in a special election. In the subsequent years, Marks steered an independent course in the Senate, often voting with Democrats on environmental, civil liberties and social issues, much to the consternation of Republican colleagues. His credentials as a Republican got a brief boost in 1982, when, at the coaxing of the Reagan White House, he unsuccessfully ran against powerful Democratic Rep.

Milton Marks

Phil Burton, who died shortly after his re-election victory. Democrats, infuriated at Marks' challenge of Burton, targeted him in 1984, supporting Lia Belli, the wife of a prominent San Francisco attorney, but Marks won easily.

Marks' switch to the Democratic Party came in January 1986, when he cut a deal with Senate President Pro Tem David Roberti. In exchange for his change in affiliations, Marks, who had had little clout inside the Republican caucus, was immediately made caucus chairman, the No. 3 position among Senate Democrats. Some Republicans weren't bothered by Marks' defection. "It's like losing a hemorrhoid," quipped ultraconservative Sen. H.L. Richardson, who once punched Marks when both were Republicans in the Senate. Yet Marks' defection was significant. It put a damper on Republican moves to take control of the Senate before reapportionment in 1991.

Recent legislation by Marks reflects both his position as chairman of the Elections and Reapportionment Committee and the concerns of his liberal district. He has carried bills to prohibit posting guards at polling places – a direct response to that practice by Orange County Republicans in 1988 – and to purge voter rolls of non-voters in combination with programs aimed at increasing registration. He also has proposed making it a crime to raise veal calves in enclosures that do not meet minimum requirements and to give tax advantages to artists, a measure vetoed by Gov. George Deukmejian. Marks was one of the few state legislators to vote in July 1989 against a resolution urging that flag burning be made a crime.

In 1991 Marks will preside over the Senate's once-a-decade redistricting for legislative and congressional seats. He has promised open and fair hearings, but Republicans are skeptical. Meanwhile, Capitol insiders believe – or hope – Marks will retire at the end of his term in 1992, thus helping Democratic mapmakers by allowing them to use his Democratic territories to make seats safe for others.

PERSONAL: elected 1967 (special election); born July 22, 1920, in San Francisco; home, San Francisco; Army WWII (Philippines); education, B.A.

Stanford University, J.D. San Francisco Law School; wife, Carolene Wachenheimer; children, Carol, Milton III and Edward David; Jewish.

CAREER: lawyer; Assembly 1958-1966; municipal court judge 1966.

COMMITTEES: Elections & Reapportionment (chair); Banking & Commerce; Housing & Urban Affairs; Judiciary; Natural Resources & Wildlife; (Select) Maritime Industry (chair); Calif. Wine Industry; Citizen Participation in Government; Pacific Rim; (Special) Developmental Disabilities and Mental Health; (Joint) Fisheries & Aquaculture; Legislative Budget; Refugee Resettlement, International Migration & Cooperative Development; State's Economy.

OFFICES: Capitol, (916) 445-1412, FAX (916) 327-7229; district, 711 Van Ness, 310, San Francisco 94102, (415) 474-0308; 30 N. San Pedro Road, 160, San Rafael 94903, (415) 479-6612.

REGISTRATION: 58.4% D, 25.3% R

1988 CAMPAIGN: Marks – D   66.4% $578,897

                     Carol Marshall – R   30% $155,500

RATINGS:

AFL	PIRG	CLCV	NOW	CTA	CofC	CFB	NRA	FPAC
89%	100%	88%	90%	97%	25%	20%	0%	5%

KEY VOTES:

Divest S. Africa:	YES	Insurance reform:	YES	Child sick leave:	YES
Assault gun ban:	YES	Parent consent abortion:	NO	Ban AIDS discrim:	YES
Clean Air Act:	YES	Ban insure donations:	YES	Extend death penalty:	NO
Lmt product tort:	YES	Ban offshore oil:	YES	Restrict abortion funds:	NO
Lower alcohol std:	YES	Basic health care:	YES	Oil spill prevent:	YES
Ethics reform:	YES	Work cancer stds:	YES	Earthquake insure:	–

Michael Thompson (D)
4th Senate District

Cutting across all or portions of eight north-central California counties, the 4th Senate District takes in Butte, Colusa, Glenn, Lake, Napa, Shasta, Tehama and Sonoma. It includes the flatlands of the northern Central Valley and Redding, the largest city north of Sacramento. And it takes in the spectacular river country, including the wild McCloud, and a slowly dying timber industry.

With Democratic registration under 50 percent, this district was made to order for a Republican when boundaries were drawn in 1982. More specifically, it was made to order for Jim Nielsen, who had seen the district he was elected to in 1978 carved up during the reapportionment process. Nielsen, who relocated

Mike Thompson

from Woodland to Rohnert Park, won handily in 1982 and 1986 and served a stint as Senate Republican leader before he was ousted following GOP election losses. In the process, he underwent some unusual personal changes. Twice-divorced and thrice-married, Nielsen became a fundamentalist Christian. He created a stir in 1989 by declaring during a radio show that AIDS "may be God's way" of punishing "mankind (for) what kind of promiscuous society we've become." All of that contributed heavily to his narrow loss in 1990 to Mike Thompson of St. Helena.

Thompson worked for seven years as an aide to Assemblywoman Jacqueline Speier, D-South San Francisco, and Assemblyman Lou Papan, D-Millbrae, both liberals. He also has been a political science lecturer at state universities. Thompson, a Vietnam veteran who won a purple heart for his wounds as a platoon leader in the 173rd Airborne Brigade, will have to avoid the liberal label in order to hold onto this seat in what is a marginal region for Democrats. He pledged to serve no more than two terms if elected, but if Proposition 140's term limits are upheld by the courts, that will not be an issue.

In the campaign, Thompson won farm votes by opposing the "Big Green" environmental initiative and by charging that Nielsen sided with interests wanting to ship more water from the north to the south. He also tried to take a hard line on crime. Although Thompson said he supports the death penalty, he noted, "the taking of any life disturbs me." Nielsen, who was the only Senate incumbent to lose in 1990, outspent Thompson by almost 3 to 1, but that was not enough to overcome his personal and political baggage. Thompson also won endorsements from Republican-inclined newspapers that were fed up with Nielsen.

Sacramento has not seen the last of Nielsen. He was appointed by Gov. Pete Wilson to a high-paying seat on the Agricultural Labor Relations Board.

PERSONAL: elected 1990; born Jan. 24, 1951, in St. Helena, Calif.; home, St. Helena; Army, Vietnam; education, B.A. public administration CSU Chico, course work for M.S. public administration CSU Chico; wife Jan; children, Chris and John.

CAREER: chief of staff, Assemblyman Louis Papan 1984-1987; chief of staff, Assemblywoman Jacqueline Speier 1987-1990.

COMMITTEES: Agriculture & Water Resources; Banking & Commerce; Health & Human Services; Local Government; Veterans Affairs; (Select) Calif. Wine Industry; Children & Youth; Fairs & Rural Issues.

OFFICES: Capitol, (916) 445-3353, FAX (916) 323-6958; district, 1040 Main St., 101, Napa 94559, (707) 224-1990; 50 D St., 120A, Santa Rosa 95404, (707) 576-2771; 196 Memorial Way, Chico 95926, (916) 895-1990; 1443 West St., Redding 96001, (916) 225-2090.

REGISTRATION: 48.2% D 40.8% R

1990 CAMPAIGN:		
Thompson – D	48%	$598,322
Jim Nielsen (incumbent) – R	46.4%	$1,516,132
Juanita Hendricks – L	3.6%	
Irv Sutley – P&F	2.1%	

RATINGS and **KEY VOTES**: Newly elected

Patrick W. Johnston (D)

5th Senate District

This sprawling district covers all or part of eight counties, from the rural foothills of Alpine, Amador, Calaveras, Tuolumne and Mono to the city of Stockton and nearby delta communities of San Joaquin County. It also has part of Yolo County and an urbanized area of south Sacramento County.

In the mid-1970s, some newcomers burst onto the political scene in Stockton and surrounding areas. A young rancher named John Garamendi won an Assembly seat and then quickly moved into the state Senate. He hired another young man, Patrick Johnston, as his aide. Johnston won election to the Assembly in his own right in 1980 and by 1990 he found himself face-to-face not only with John Garamendi, who was

Pat Johnston

on his way to becoming the first elected state insurance commissioner, but his wife, Patti, who was eager to replace her husband in the Senate.

In fact, Garamendi quit his seat early – more than two months before the November election for insurance commissioner – in an attempt to give his wife an edge over Johnston. The plan was to have the special election for his seat consolidated with the general election. Since Johnston could not have his name removed as a candidate for re-election to the Assembly, it was hoped that he would look overly ambitious as he technically ran for two offices. But the maneuver backed-fired. The Garamendis were accused of trying to manipulate the process to create a family dynasty. Johnston beat Patti Garamendi and nine others in the first round, then easily won the run-off from the top Republican vote-getter, Philip Wallace. Patti Garamendi spent $621,122 on her effort, which included more than $500,000 she loaned her campaign from personal funds.

It wasn't Johnston's first tough election. In 1980, he challenged a Democratic incumbent, Assemblyman Carmen Perino, in the June primary. It was a nasty battle that was made nastier by a power struggle for the speakership of the Assembly that year and by the personal nature of local politics. Johnston defeated Perino but his struggle was just beginning. His November tussle with Republican Adrian Fondse was one of the sleaziest in California history, complete with anti-Johnston mailings appealing to racial prejudices and other dirty tricks. The initial vote count showed Fondse winning, but a recount, certified by Johnston's fellow Democrats in the Assembly, unseated Fondse and declared Johnston the victor by 35 votes out of about 84,000 cast.

Johnston, a former journalist who once aspired to the priesthood, has achieved a reputation as a liberal reformer and as one of the state's brighter legislators. He proved his adaptability while chairing the Assembly's Finance and Insurance Committee, a major "juice committee" with jurisdiction over banks and insurance companies and whose members are showered with attention from industry lobbyists. Johnston has not been shy about accepting campaign contributions, trips and other goodies from special interests, but he has earned kudos from affected industries and consumers alike for his honesty and evenhanded operation of the committee.

Johnston put himself in the thick of the battles over auto insurance and was a critic of both the industry and its self-appointed reformers in what seemed to be a politically dangerous move during California's wild, five-way insurance initiative war in 1988. Since then, he has continued to avoid the populist road paved by Proposition 103, the winner of that initiative war, and instead has joined with consumer groups in pushing a no-fault system that he has said holds out the best chance to control insurance rates and service.

However, no one will accuse Johnston of ignoring popular feelings. He was one of the first in the Capitol to react to the savings and loan industry scandals, but he was also one of the few who pushed investigations and reforms that were actually substantive.

PERSONAL: elected 1991 (special election); born Sept. 3, 1946, in San Francisco; home, Stockton; education, B.A. philosophy St. Patrick's College, Menlo Park; wife, Margaret Mary Johnston; children, Patrick and Christopher; Roman Catholic.

CAREER: Reporter for a Catholic newspaper; probation officer, Calaveras County; chief of staff to Sen. John Garamendi 1975-1980; Assembly 1980-1991.

COMMITTEES: Education; Banking and Commerce; Public Employment and Retirement; Natural Resources; Energy & Public Utilities.

OFFICES: Capitol, (916) 445-2407; district, 31 E. Channel St., 440, Stockton 95202, (209) 948-7930.

REGISTRATION: 53% D, 37.5% R

JAN. 8, 1991 SPECIAL ELECTION:

Johnston – D	56.9%	$564,924
Philip Wallace – R	38%	$58,234

RATINGS: (based on Assembly votes)

AFL	PIRG	CLCV	NOW	CTA	CofC	CFB	NRA	FPAC
89%	95%	95%	100%	86%	32%	33%	0%	4%

KEY VOTES: (all Assembly votes)

Divest S. Africa:	YES	Insurance reform:	YES	Child sick leave:	YES
Assault gun ban:	YES	Parent consent abortion:	NO	Ban AIDS discrim:	YES
Clean Air Act:	YES	Cutting old trees:	NO	Extend death penalty:	–
Lmt product tort:	YES	Ban offshore oil:	YES	Restrict abortion funds:	NO
Lower alcohol std:	YES	Basic health care:	YES	Oil spill prevent:	YES
Ethics reform:	YES	Work cancer stds:	YES	Earthquake insure:	YES

Leroy F. Greene (D)

6th Senate District

The Capitol is not only where Leroy Greene spends most of his working hours, it is also the middle of his district. The 6th District, which encompasses all of the city of Sacramento and much of the unincorporated area, was tailored to Greene's political specifications by Democratic leaders after the 1980 census.

Leroy Greene

In 1980, conservative Republican John Doolittle had stunned the Senate by upsetting one of its best-liked members, Democrat Al Rodda. What had been the Rodda district was reconfigured to lop off the most Republican suburbs and to concentrate strength in Democratic city precincts. And a clever change of district numbers forced Doolittle to stand for re-election in 1982, just two years into his first term.

Greene had spent 20 years in the Assembly representing a mid-Sacramento district, and with the change of boundaries, he was well-positioned to take on Doolittle. Greene defeated Doolittle, but another change of district lines after the election created another new district in which Doolittle successfully ran in 1984.

Greene represents one of the state's fastest-growing and fastest-changing metropolitan areas, one that is on the verge of assuming big-city status. Sacramento's traditional dependence on government payrolls is giving way to a surge in private industry, and with that change has come a shift to the right politically. The district, however, should remain solidly Democratic because most of the new industrial and commercial development is occurring in the suburbs outside the district.

As an assemblyman, Greene was an often acerbic, highly active legislator with a particular interest in education. A civil engineer who practiced in Sacramento for many years, Greene became chairman of the Assembly Education Committee and carried numerous bills to finance construction, reconstruction and operation of public schools. Since moving to the Senate, Greene has moved into the background, no longer playing a leading role in shaping major legislation, seemingly content to support the Democratic Party line on issues and to carry local-interest bills. He chairs the Senate Housing and Urban Affairs Committee, but it has not been a generator of major bills.

Greene survived a stiff challenge from Republican Sandra Smoley, a Sacramento County supervisor, in 1986. But with only token opposition four years later, he had no trouble keeping his seat in 1990.

PERSONAL: elected 1982; born Jan. 31, 1918, in Newark, N.J.; home, Carmichael; Army WWII; education, B.S. civil engineering Purdue University; wife, Denny Miller; daughter, Denny Lee Mazlak; no religious affiliation.

CAREER: civil engineer 1951-1978, owned firm; Assembly 1962-1982; newspaper columnist; radio talk show host.

COMMITTEES: Housing & Urban Affairs (chair); Banking & Commerce; Business & Professions; Education; Energy & Public Utilities; Industrial Relations; Appropriations; (Joint) School Facilities (chair); Rules.

OFFICES: Capitol, (916) 445-7807, FAX (916) 327-6341; district, P.O. Box 254646, Carmichael 95825, (916) 481-6540.

REGISTRATION: 56.1% D, 34.9% R

1990 CAMPAIGN:	Greene – D	53.7%	$507,849
	Joe Sullivan – R	40.4%	$8,745
1986 CAMPAIGN:	Greene – D	61%	$1,023,365
	Sandra Smoley – R	40%	$1,108,081

RATINGS:

AFL	PIRG	CLCV	NOW	CTA	CofC	CFB	NRA	FPAC
88%	80%	83%	70%	97%	29%	20%	0%	7%

KEY VOTES:

Divest S. Africa:	YES	Insurance reform:	YES	Child sick leave:	YES
Assault gun ban:	YES	Parent consent abortion:	NO	Ban AIDS discrim:	YES
Clean Air Act:	–	Ban insure donations:	NO	Extend death penalty:	YES
Lmt product tort:	YES	Ban offshore oil:	YES	Restrict abortion funds:	NO
Lower alcohol std:	YES	Basic health care:	YES	Oil spill prevent:	YES
Ethics reform:	YES	Work cancer stds:	–	Earthquake insure:	–

Daniel E. Boatwright (D)

7th Senate District

As the San Francisco Bay Area has grown into the fourth-largest metropolitan region in the United States, that growth has oozed out "through the tunnel" in the Berkeley Hills into Contra Costa County. The Diablo Valley, once a sleepy string of towns connected by two-lane roads, is now covered with concrete-and-glass towers. Walnut Creek even has a skyline.

In the 1930s, it was a long train ride to Oakland for basic services – like doctors – for the oil refinery workers in Avon, and not much in-between. Now the massive Bishop Ranch industrial park houses high-tech industry and housing tracts cover the hillsides and valleys. The headquarters of Chevron is here, and its executives live nearby in places like the exclusive

Dan Boatwright

walled community of Blackhawk with its nearby classic car museum and a supermarket with brass carts and a pianist. The region has a conservative bent more akin to Orange County than the rest of Northern California, reflected in the editorial pages of the newspapers belonging to aging right-wing publisher Dean Lesher.

Combative Democrat Dan Boatwright has been a central figure in Contra Costa politics for three decades. He has survived tough elections, a 1980s Internal Revenue Service investigation that sought $112,000 in back taxes for 1976 and a 1984 civil trial in which he was acquitted of taking money for official favors. Newspapers have written about the $10,000 Boatwright's law firm received from a client who also was seeking an $8.7 million tax break through a Boatwright bill. His girlfriend was a featured witness in his civil trial. Along the way, Boatwright has been called the "Teflon senator" in honor of his ability to slough off negative media coverage without its damaging his political career – an ability much on display in 1988, when he easily turned back a Democratic primary challenge from popular Contra Costa County Supervisor Sunne McPeak.

In the arena of the state Capitol, Boatwright has been one of the Legislature's biggest bullies. He and his assistant, Barry Brokaw, are known as two of the savviest operators "inside the building." When Boatwright was chairman of the Appropriations Committee, he arbitrarily killed without a hearing dozens of Assembly bills in a single day in 1986, setting off howls of protests from offended lawmakers. David Roberti stuck up for his demagogic chairman, but was repaid a year later when Boatwright tried to line up enough votes to depose Roberti as the leader of the Senate. Roberti swiftly sacked Boatwright as chairman of Appropriations, setting off a vintage Boatwright outburst: "If he wants to sit up in his little ivory tower and be besieged every day for the rest of his term, he's come to the right guy," said Boatwright of Roberti. "I was a combat infantryman in Korea – had my ass shot off, and I know how to fight a war. If he wants war, he's got war ... I'll throw hand grenades, go get a big bazooka. I mean, I know how to fight a war."

But no amount of public invective got Boatwright his job back (and he was not, by the way, wounded in Korea). Roberti, who eventually brings those he punishes back inside the tent, reached a detente with Boatwright in 1988. Roberti poured in thousands of dollars and drafted innumerable Senate staffers to help Boatwright meet McPeak's challenge. Roberti bolstered Boatwright's status by giving him a new job, chairmanship of the new Bonded Indebtedness Committee. After the conviction of Sen. Joseph Montoya on federal corruption charges, Boatwright moved into one of the Senate's best assignments – chairman of the Business and Professions Committee, with its authority over regulatory legislation.

Since his acceptance back into the fold, Boatwright appears to be a changed man. Unlike Montoya, Boatwright does not appear to be shaking down campaign contributions from those with business before the committee. At the start of the 1991-92 session, Boatwright authored a sweeping bill to close tax loopholes.

PERSONAL: elected 1980; born, Jan. 29, 1930, in Harrison, Ark.; home, Concord; Army 1948-1952 (Korea); education, B.A. political science and J.D. UC Berkeley; separated; children, Daniel Jr., David and Donald; Protestant.

CAREER: lawyer; Contra Costa deputy district attorney 1960-1963; Concord City Council 1966-1972, mayor 1966-1968; Assembly 1972-1980.

COMMITTEES: Business & Professions (chair); Budget & Fiscal Review; Transportation; Banking & Commerce; Elections & Reapportionment; Revenue & Taxation; (Select) State Procurement & Expenditure Practices (chair); (Joint) Prison Construction & Operations.

OFFICES: Capitol, (916) 445-6083, FAX (916) 456-7367; district, 1000 Burnett Ave., 130, Concord 94520, (415) 825-3321, 420 W. Third, Antioch 94509, (415) 754-3011; 2560 Macdonald Ave. Richmond 94804, (415) 236-3620; 2680 Bishop Drive, 105, San Ramon 94583, (415) 830-2871.

REGISTRATION: 53.1% D, 35.4% R

1988 CAMPAIGN: Boatwright – D 63% $1,215,545
William Pollacek – R 37% $243,386

RATINGS:

AFL	PIRG	CLCV	NOW	CTA	CofC	CFB	NRA	FPAC
84%	75%	85%	100%	100%	29%	0%	74%	12%

KEY VOTES:

Divest S. Africa:	YES	Insurance reform:	YES	Child sick leave:	–
Assault gun ban:	YES	Parent consent abortion:	YES	Ban AIDS discrim:	YES
Clean Air Act:	YES	Ban insur donations:	YES	Extend death penalty:	YES
Lmt product tort:	–	Ban offshore oil:	YES	Restrict abortion funds:	NO
Lower alcohol std:	YES	Basic health care:	–	Oil spill prevent:	–
Ethics reform:	YES	Work cancer stds:	YES	Earthquake insure:	–

Quentin L. Kopp (independent)
8th Senate District

Starting in San Francisco generally south of Market Street, this district takes in many of the city's older neighborhoods, the slums surrounding Hunter's Point and then stretches to the fog-shrouded suburb of Pacifica. Moving south, the district includes upscale Burlingame and Hillsborough, and the middle-class communities of South Francisco, Milbrae, Daly City and part of San Mateo. Heavily Democratic, this district is as sure a bet for Democrats as there can be in politics, which is to say strange things can happen.

The Assembly's "Lead-foot" Lou Papan (so named for his speeding tickets while commuting between the Bay Area and Sacramento) thought he was such a shoo-in for the seat in 1986 when Sen. John Foran

Quentin Kopp

retired that he had practically picked out his new office. But Republicans, mortified at the prospect of having the highly partisan Papan in the Senate, deserted their own candidate and threw their money behind San Francisco Supervisor Quentin Kopp, who ran as an independent. Papan's campaign tactics also offended Jewish voters (Kopp is Jewish). So, Kopp became the Legislature's only independent.

Kopp always has been more interesting in San Francisco politics than in the Capitol. His scraps with Dianne Feinstein are legion (Kopp actually had a date with Feinstein in their younger days). In fact, his scraps with nearly every San Francisco political figure from Willie Brown on down are legion. In March 1987, Kopp hinted he might (again) run for mayor with typical Kopp elocution: "Many people are importuning me to make the race." Instead, one of his aides managed the mayoral campaign of San Francisco Examiner columnist Warren Hinkel. With the approach of another mayoral election in 1991, Kopp toyed with running but again bowed out.

In the Capitol, Kopp has shown shrewdness. Although still registered as an independent, Kopp votes with the Democrats on leadership issues and a number of key budgetary matters. His sharpest move earned him a powerful post – and the wrath of Gov. George Deukmejian. A day before the 1988 confirmation vote on Deukmejian's hand-picked nominee for state treasurer, Dan Lungren, Kopp said he was behind Lungren all the way. On the day of the vote, Kopp switched, providing one of the last nails in Lungren's coffin and earning himself the gratitude of Senate President Pro Tem David Roberti. Democrat Wadie Deddeh, however, voted for Lungren and found himself stripped of the powerful chairmanship of the Transportation Committee. Kopp got Deddeh's job.

As a senator, he has continually pushed for an early presidential primary date. Kopp successfully authored a bill that tightened the conflict-of-interest rules for members of the state Board of Equalization, the state's tax commission. Among his unsuccessful efforts in 1990 was a measure that would have required landlords to pay 5 percent interest on security deposits held for at least a year.

In 1988, after Kopp was unsuccessful with a bill to ban transfers of campaign funds between candidates and to limit donations, he joined forces with Republican Assemblyman Ross Johnson and Democratic Sen. Joe Montoya to write the bill into Proposition 73. That initiative was approved by the voters in June 1988 but was ruled unconstitutional by a federal judge in 1990, providing no end of confusion in California's campaign laws.

Kopp maintains his friendship with Montoya, who is now in a federal prison for his conviction on corruption charges. Kopp and Sen. Ruben Ayala visited Montoya over the 1990 holidays.

PERSONAL: elected 1986; born Aug. 11, 1928, in Syracuse, N.Y.; home, San Francisco; USAF 1952-1954; education, B.A. government & business Dartmouth College, J.D. Harvard University; wife, Mara; children, Shepard, Bradley and Jennifer; Jewish.

CAREER: lawyer; San Francisco Board of Supervisors 1972-1986.

COMMITTEES: Transportation (chair); Housing & Urban Affairs; Local Government; Revenue & Taxation; Toxics & Public Safety Management; (Select) Maritime Industry.

OFFICES: Capitol, (916) 445-0503, FAX (916) 327-2186; district, 363 El Camino Real, 205, South San Francisco 94080, (415) 952-5666.

REGISTRATION: 63.2% D, 22.4% R

1990 CAMPAIGN:	Kopp – independent	72.7%	$1,227,499
	Patrick Fitzgerald – D	18%	$0
	Robert Silvestri – R	9.3%	
1986 CAMPAIGN:	Kopp – independent	47%	$749,203
	Louis Papan – D	46%	$1,731,002
	Russell Gray – R	8%	

RATINGS:

AFL	PIRG	CLCV	NOW	CTA	CofC	CFB	NRA	FPAC
68%	75%	76%	70%	87%	42%	20%	13%	38%

KEY VOTES:

		Insurance reform:	YES	Child sick leave:	NO
Assault gun ban:	YES	Parent consent abortion:	YES	Ban AIDS discrim:	YES
Clean Air Act:	YES	Ban insure donations:	YES	Extend death penalty:	–
Lmt product tort:	NO	Ban offshore oil:	YES	Restrict abortion funds:	NO
Lower alcohol std:	YES	Basic health care:	YES	Oil spill prevent:	YES
Ethics reform:	YES	Work cancer stds:	YES	Earthquake insure:	YES

Nicholas C. Petris (D)
9th Senate District

Lining the middle section of San Francisco Bay's eastern shoreline, the 9th Senate District takes in a polyglot that includes the affluent, white Piedmont hills, the intensely poor black neighborhoods of Oakland and the zany leftist environs of Berkeley and its University of California campus. The district includes parts of Alameda County, the one county where Tom Bradley did well in his rematch with George Deukmejian in the 1986 race for governor. Stretching over the Berkeley hills, the district takes in the Contra Costa County bedroom communities of Lafayette, Orinda and Moraga. The district is more than one-third black.

Nicholas Petris

Democrat Nicholas Petris, one of the last unbending liberals in the Capitol, is the only senator this district has known since the inception of the full-time Legislature in 1966. For years, the silver-haired, courtly Petris has railed against growers for their treatment of farm workers; pushed, without success, bills requiring warning signs in fields where pesticides have been sprayed; and championed the rights of criminal defendants, mental patients, the poor and the elderly. And he is a vocal champion of the state's influential trial lawyers, standing against all efforts to tighten the state's "deep pockets" tort liability laws, efforts he sees as victimizing consumers. Petris has one characteristic rare in a Legislature of plodding speakers – he is eloquent.

But the Deukmejian years were not kind to Petris. It has been two decades since he authored landmark legislation like the Lanterman-Petris-Short Act, which brought major changes to the mental-health system, and the post-Proposition 13 world has not been receptive to his pleas to spend more on health care and education.

The cantankerous right-wing Sen. H.L. Richardson, now retired, once claimed that Petris pulled the strings of Senate President Pro Tem David Roberti. Although that's a vast overstatement, Petris' influence in keeping the Senate Democrats left of center should not be underestimated. He still uses his position on the Judiciary Committee as a bully pulpit and he also sits on the all-powerful Rules Committee.

Beyond policy matters, one of Petris' major interests is Greece. He quotes from the Greek classics during his floor speeches and serves as the unofficial leader of the equally unofficial caucus of Greek-American legislators, often authoring resolutions that support that nation in its squabbles with Turkey.

Although Gov. Pete Wilson may be kinder to the ideas championed by Petris, many in the Capitol think Petris will retire at the end of his term in 1992, thereby making it easier on the Democratic architects of redistricting.

PERSONAL: elected 1966; born Feb. 25, 1923, in Oakland; home, Oakland; Army 1943-1946 WWII; education, B.A. UC Berkeley, J.D. Stanford University; wife, Anna S. Vlahos; no children; Greek Orthodox.

CAREER: lawyer, Assembly 1958-1966.

COMMITTEES: Budget & Fiscal Review, and budget subcommittee 1 – education (chair); Industrial Relations; Judiciary; Rules; (Select) Calif. Wine Industry; (Joint) Rules; Legislative Budget; Mental Health Research.

OFFICES: Capitol, (916) 445-6577, FAX (916) 327-1997; district, 1970 Broadway, 1030, Oakland 94612, (415) 464-1333.

REGISTRATION: 66.2% D, 20.8% R

1988 CAMPAIGN:	Petris – D	74.7%	$342,680
	Greg Henson – R	21.4%	$0

RATINGS:

AFL	PIRG	CLCV	NOW	CTA	CofC	CFB	NRA	FPAC
94%	80%	88%	70%	100%	29%	20%	0%	5%

KEY VOTES:

Divest S. Africa:	YES	Insurance reform:	YES	Child sick leave:	YES
Assault gun ban:	YES	Parent consent abortion:	NO	Ban AIDS discrim:	–
Clean Air Act:	YES	Ban insure donations:	NO	Extend death penalty:	NO
Lmt product tort:	–	Ban offshore oil:	YES	Restrict abortion funds:	NO
Lower alcohol std:	–	Basic health care:	YES	Oil spill prevent:	YES
Ethics reform:	–	Work cancer stds:	YES	Earthquake insure:	YES

William Lockyer (D)

10th Senate District

Taking in San Francisco Bay's eastern shoreline south of Oakland, this Alameda County district includes the middle-class cities of San Leandro, Fremont and

Hayward before extending over the hills to the Livermore Valley, with its housing tracts and nuclear weapons lab. Although it's a Democratic district, it has a conservative bent.

Democrat William Lockyer was elected in 1982 after serving a decade in the Assembly. He had earlier worked as an aide to one of the Legislature's most powerful figures of the 1960s, Assemblyman Robert Crown. Lockyer, as chairman of the Senate Judiciary Committee, has been a major force in the big issues of the last few sessions, including repeal of the business inventory tax, abortion, the death penalty and gun control. In 1990, he authored – or, more precisely,

William Lockyer

spearheaded – SB 25, the first major legislative overhaul of sentencing laws in years. But Gov. George Deukmejian vetoed the comprehensive bill at the close of the 1989-90 session. Lockyer reintroduced the bill at the start of the 1991 session hoping that the new governor, Pete Wilson, would be more amenable to its innovative sentencing concepts. Interestingly, Lockyer had served as chairman of the judiciary committee for several years before he got around to taking the State Bar exam, passing it in 1988.

Lockyer was among lawmakers and lobbyists who drafted a peace pact between major economic forces on a napkin at Frank Fat's restaurant two days before the end of the legislative session in September 1987 – a fabled meeting that culminated months of negotiations between doctors, lawyers and insurance companies over the state's liability laws. Lockyer got the related bill bearing his name through the Senate with little difficulty. Speaker Willie Brown ramroded it through the Assembly over the strenuous objections of several liberal Democrats. And Lockyer proudly displayed the napkin on the Senate floor.

Lockyer can be charming, though sometimes ponderous, but his behavior is erratic. His temper has gotten him in trouble – and kept Bay Area headline writers employed. During a particularly tedious committee hearing in 1985, Lockyer cut short fellow Democrat Diane Watson of Los Angeles, leaving her sputtering, "Can I finish my thought?" Lockyer retorted, "Well, if you had a thought it would be great," and added that he was fed up with her "mindless blather." Lockyer later apologized, but Watson has barely spoken to him since. His temper also got the best of him during the last week of the 1990 legislative session. In a hallway outside the Senate chambers, Lockyer began baiting trial lawyer lobbyist Bob Wilson, an ex-senator who was Lockyer's predecessor as chairman of the judiciary panel. Wilson lost his cool and the two got into a shoving match (Lockyer later said Wilson threw a "girlie punch" at him). And Lockyer also threw a temper tantrum during the Senate's 1990 ethics workshop. It wasn't anything about ethics that bothered him – it was the bright lights being used to video-tape the session.

Although Lockyer has been an insider on more major legislation than most of his colleagues, he still behaves as though he is being slighted as an outsider. In June 1989, Lockyer barged into a private meeting between Roberti and a handful of other senators working out which big-ticket bills would move out of the Appropriations Committee. To their wonderment, Lockyer protested that he wanted a chance to make a pitch for his bills.

Lockyer once told the Oakland Tribune, "I would like people to know that I am a lovable eccentric and not a dysfunctional, strange one."

PERSONAL: elected 1982; born May 8, 1941, in Oakland; home, Hayward; education, B.A. political science UC Berkeley, teaching credential CSU Hayward, J.D. McGeorge; divorced; daughter, Lisa; Episcopalian.

CAREER: teacher; school board member; legislative assistant to Assemblyman Bob Crown 1968-1973; Assembly 1973-1982.

COMMITTEES: Judiciary (chair); Appropriations; Elections; Governmental Organization; Industrial Relations; Revenue & Taxation; Toxics & Public Safety Management; (Select) Infant & Child Care & Development.

OFFICES: Capitol, (916) 445-6671; district, 22300 Foothill Blvd., 415, Hayward 94541, (415) 582-8800; 4725 Thornton Ave., 104, Fremont 94536, (415) 790-3605; 6140 Stoneridge Mall Road, 515, Pleasanton 94566, (415) 847-6041.

REGISTRATION: 55.3% D, 32.2% R

1990 CAMPAIGN:	Lockyer – D	60.6%	$1,037,242
	Howard Hertz – R	39.4%	$528
1986 CAMPAIGN:	Lockyer – D	71%	$445,583
	Bruce Bergondy – R	29%	$0

RATINGS:

AFL	PIRG	CLCV	NOW	CTA	CofC	CFB	NRA	FPAC
94%	95%	88%	100%	94%	25%	20%	0%	15%

KEY VOTES:

Divest S. Africa:	YES	Insurance reform:	YES	Child sick leave:	YES
Assault gun ban:	YES	Parent consent abortion:	–	Ban AIDS discrim:	YES
Clean Air Act:	YES	Ban insure donations:	NO	Extend death penalty:	YES
Lmt product tort:	YES	Ban offshore oil:	YES	Restrict abortion funds:	NO
Lower alcohol std:	NO	Basic health care:	YES	Oil spill prevent:	YES
Ethics reform:	YES	Work cancer stds:	YES	Earthquake insure:	YES

Rebecca Q. Morgan (R)

11th Senate District

On its western shore, the 11th Senate District includes Half Moon Bay and then loops over the San Andreas fault to the bedroom communities of the San Francisco peninsula – San Mateo, Belmont, San Carlos, Redwood City, Woodside. Dropping into the San Francisco Bay's basin, the district takes in California's fabled Silicon Valley, with its microchip industries, like Intel, that have grown up around Stanford University. Voters here are business oriented, but they lean to the left in their outlook and are decidedly environmentalist. The area has produced Republicans like maverick Pete McCloskey, moderates Ed Zschau and Tom Campbell, and Shirley Temple Black.

The success of the Silicon Valley has come with a price. Once thought of as "clean industry," high-tech manufacturing has proved to be a big polluter. The valley holds a number of toxic waste sites on the federal Superfund cleanup list. Fairchild Camera, among the first polluters discovered, used highly toxic solvents in its processing that leaked into the groundwater supplies.

Republican Rebecca Morgan is very much a product of her district. Her husband, James C. Morgan, is

Rebecca Morgan

a millionaire president of Applied Materials Inc., one of the Silicon Valley firms on the toxic cleanup list. The San Jose-based environmental organization Silicon Valley Toxics Coalition once accused Sen. Morgan of having a conflict of interest by chairing an important toxics subcommittee in the Senate. Nonsense, she replied.

Soon after Pete Wilson was elected governor, Morgan seemed to be under consideration to fill his U.S. Senate seat. She looked a good bet – a moderate woman, pro-choice on abortion and a solid fund-raiser. However, her husband, James, did her no favors when he told an interviewer from Forbes Magazine in October 1990 about why he was building a $100 million expansion in Austin, Texas, and not in California. "The cost of land in northern California is excessive and the attitude of state and local government toward industry is pathetic," James Morgan said. After much press speculation, state Sen. Morgan asked Wilson to take her name off the list for U.S. senator – if there really was a list (Wilson eventually said he picked his first choice: John Seymour).

Morgan has steered an independent course, sometimes going against the Republican grain in the Senate by voting to restrict semiautomatic weapons and to uphold abortion rights. Morgan made her own quiet protest against the U.S. Supreme Court's 1989 abortion rulings by removing from her office wall an autographed portrait of Associate Justice Anthony Kennedy.

She is popular among her colleagues, although she is inconsistent on her feet and is noted for missing some of the nuances in legislation. She has a reputation for vote-switching during roll calls – not out of any scheme but because she did not understand the bill.

Morgan, a former teacher, has focused on education issues. She won passage of a bill to tighten restrictions on "diploma mills" in 1989 and has pushed for a $207 million pilot project in the schools. Gov. George Deukmejian signed into law her 1988 measure that appropriated $29.9 million in transit improvements statewide.

She has maintained strong ties to the business community. At the start of the

1991-92 session, she began pushing SB 103 to give a property tax break to Luz International Corp., the operator of a huge solar electricity plant in the Mojave Desert. The Wilson administration, however, said the bill would cost San Bernardino County millions, one-third of which would have to be replaced by the fiscally strapped state general fund to support schools.

PERSONAL: elected 1984; born Dec. 4, 1938, in Hanover, N.H.; home, Los Altos Hills; education, B.S. home economics Cornell University, M.A. business administration Stanford University; husband, James C. Morgan; children, Jeff and Mary; Protestant.

CAREER: teacher; banker; school board member; Santa Clara County Board of Supervisors 1981-1984.

COMMITTEES: Education (vice chair); Budget & Fiscal Review; Energy & Public Utilities; Revenue & Taxation (vice chair); Transportation; (Select) Infant & Child Care & Development (chair); Source Reduction and Recycling Market Development; (Joint) Science & Technology.

OFFICES: Capitol, (916) 445-6747; district, 750 Menlo Ave., 100, Menlo Park 94025, (415) 688-6330.

REGISTRATION: 45.7% D, 41.1% R

1988 CAMPAIGN:

Morgan – R		60.7%	$640,868
Tom Nolan – D		36.1%	$90,629

RATINGS:

AFL	PIRG	CLCV	NOW	CTA	CofC	CFB	NRA	FPAC
41%	79%	27%	50%	94%	67%	20%	14%	75%

KEY VOTES:

Divest S. Africa:	NO	Insurance reform:	NO	Child sick leave:	YES
Assault gun ban:	YES	Parent consent abortion:	NO	Ban AIDS discrim:	YES
Clean Air Act:	YES	Ban insure donations:	NO	Extend death penalty:	YES
Lmt product tort:	–	Ban offshore oil:	YES	Restrict abortion funds:	NO
Lower alcohol std:	YES	Basic health care:	YES	Oil spill prevent:	YES
Ethics reform:	YES	Work cancer stds:	NO	Earthquake insure:	YES

Daniel A. McCorquodale (D)

12th Senate District

This district – created by Democratic reapportionment craftsmen in 1982 to maximize the party's position – straddles two counties on either side of the Coast Ranges, one urban, the other rural. To the east lies Stanislaus County, a mostly flat, agriculture-dominated region that includes the cities of Modesto, Turlock and Ceres. The area is becoming urbanized, epitomizing the land-use balancing act between farmland and subdivisions facing much of the rest of the San Joaquin Valley. To the west, in the Santa Clara Valley, the district takes in the Silicon Valley bedroom communities of Campbell, Milpitas and the southern third of San Jose.

Representing those diverse constituencies is Democrat Dan McCorquodale. The former Marine had an early political career in the San Diego area, once serving as the mayor of Chula Vista, but changed direction after his first wife committed suicide. He abandoned politics to champion programs for the disabled. Later, McCorquodale returned to political life after relocating in the San Jose area and developed the practice of personally walking every precinct during every campaign. It's a good technique for the naturally friendly McCorquodale.

Dan McCorquodale

In 1982, McCorquodale narrowly defeated incumbent Republican Sen. Dan O'Keefe. In 1986, Republicans tried bouncing back by waging a $1.3 million campaign to defeat McCorquodale, who is generally more liberal than his district. But McCorquodale worked hard and handily won a bruising re-election battle over his GOP challenger, Santa Clara County Supervisor Tom Legan. And in 1990, he buried his Republican opponent, Lori Kennedy, by 18 percentage points.

As chairman of the Natural Resources and Wildlife Committee, McCorquodale has taken an active role in trying to settle major disputes between environmentalists, hunters and business interests. An ardent fisherman, he pushes environmental causes in the area of fisheries, parks, offshore oil drilling, timber harvesting, and clean air. And he's waged a years-long battle to try to establish a powerful centralized agency to write and enforce air pollution controls for an eight-county area in San Joaquin Valley, a proposal that has encountered county opposition and which was vetoed in 1990 by Gov. George Deukmejian. In the wake of the Lincoln Savings and Loan failure, McCorquodale pushed unsuccessfully to consolidate the state's major financial regulatory agencies into a single department.

McCorquodale came under criticism in 1990 for carrying a bill that would have changed testing procedures for raw milk. State health officials charged that in carrying the measure, McCorquodale was rewarding a financial contributor in a way that could result in more illnesses and deaths from salmonella poisonings. The bill failed. McCorquodale also came under fire for allowing a staff member who runs a travel business on the side to use his name to promote a two-week South American tour. In exchange for the use of his name, McCorquodale got a free vacation.

PERSONAL: elected 1982; born Dec. 17, 1934, in Longville, La.; home, San Jose; USMC 1953-1956; education, B.A. education San Diego State University; wife, Jean; children, Daniel, Michael and Sharon; Protestant.

CAREER: special-education teacher; Chula Vista City Council and mayor; Santa Clara County Board of Supervisors.

COMMITTEES: Natural Resources & Wildlife (chair); Transportation (vice chair); Agriculture & Water Resources; Budget & Fiscal Review, budget subcommittee 2 – justice, corrections, resources & agriculture (chair); Business & Professions; Insurance, Claims & Corporations; Public Employment and Retirement;

(Select) Citizen Participation in Government (chair); Calif. Wine Industry; Maritime Industry; Mobile Homes; (Special) Developmental Disabilities & Mental Health (chair); (Joint) Energy Regulation & the Environment; Mental Health Research; State's Economy.

OFFICES: Capitol, (916) 445-3104, FAX (916) 327-8801; district, 4 N. 2nd St., 590, San Jose 95113, (408) 277-1470; 1020 15th St, B, Modesto 95354, (209) 576-6231.

REGISTRATION: 53% D, 36.3% R

1990 CAMPAIGN:

McCorquodale – D		59%	$802,650
Lori Kennedy – R		41%	$2,224

1986 CAMPAIGN:

McCorquodale – D		56%	$1,480,626
Tom Legan – R		44%	$1,384,357

RATINGS:

AFL	PIRG	CLCV	NOW	CTA	CofC	CFB	NRA	FPAC
97%	90%	100%	100%	97%	42%	60%	47%	17%

KEY VOTES:

Divest S. Africa:	YES	Insurance reform:	YES	Child sick leave:	YES
Assault gun ban:	YES	Parent consent abortion:	NO	Ban AIDS discrim:	YES
Clean Air Act:	YES	Ban insure donations:	NO	Extend death penalty:	YES
Lmt product tort:	YES	Ban offshore oil:	YES	Restrict abortion funds:	NO
Lower alcohol std:	YES	Basic health care:	YES	Oil spill prevent:	YES
Ethics reform:	YES	Work cancer stds:	YES	Earthquake insure:	YES

Alfred E. Alquist (D)

13th Senate District

Lying in the core of Santa Clara County, the 13th Senate District takes in the heart of San Jose and portions of Santa Clara, Sunnyvale and Mountain View. The area has mirrored the transformation and growth of California in the last 30 years. Where once there were orchards and canneries, now there are housing tracts, high-tech industries, traffic and smog.

Democrat Alfred Alquist, the oldest member of the Legislature, has served long enough to see all those changes. Elected to the part-time Assembly in 1962, Alquist was among the first class of "full-time" legislators elected to the Senate in 1966.

Alquist has had a generally successful career, though one with plenty of ups and downs. His land-

Alfred Alquist

mark legislation created the Energy Commission and the Seismic Safety Commission and established earthquake construction standards for hospitals. Alquist has had his stamp on every major piece of earthquake preparedness legislation of the last three decades. He could take grim satisfaction in knowing that many of the laws he authored doubtlessly saved lives in the Oct. 17, 1989, Bay Area earthquake.

Alquist, however, has become the Andrei Gromyko of the Legislature – iron-faced, publicly devoid of humor (although wryly funny in private), well past his prime, but still a force not to be crossed lightly. At his peak, Alquist was chairman of the all-powerful Appropriations Committee. But in 1986, he agreed to relinquish his post to mollify critics of Senate President Pro Tem David Roberti within his own party. Roberti split Alquist's committee in two. Alquist kept his imprint on the immensely complicated state spending plan as chairman of a new Budget and Fiscal Review Committee, a panel chiefly responsible for the Senate version of the state budget each year, but lost power over the daily workings of legislation, which go before the reduced Appropriations Committee now chaired by Sen. Robert Presley, D-Riverside. Each year, Alquist and Assembly Ways and Means Chairman John Vasconcellos take turns chairing the budget conference committee, where the final budget legislation is shaped.

Alquist is known for a stormy temper, much in evidence in 1985, when he had a fabled shouting match with enfant terrible Assemblyman Steve Peace over an Alquist bill to establish a nuclear waste disposal compact with other states. Exactly what was said is still disputed; some witnesses (including Sen. Ken Maddy) claim Peace called Alquist a "senile old pedophile" while thrusting his right index finger toward him. Peace claims that he (only) called the elder senator a "pitiful little creature." Whomever was right was unimportant; an outraged Senate responded by killing all of Peace's remaining bills for the year.

Although Alquist has authored his share of major legislation, he has also had his share of petty, narrow-interest bills. In 1985, Alquist, an ex-railroad employee, won passage of a bill that would have required freight trains longer than 1,500 feet to have a caboose. Deukmejian vetoed it.

Alquist's wife, Mai, died in 1989. Outspoken, and a character in her own right in the Legislature, she was her husband's political mentor and confidant for years. Without her, he may well choose to retire at the end of his term in 1992 if not sooner.

PERSONAL: elected 1966; born Aug. 2, 1908, in Memphis, Tenn.; home, Santa Clara; Army WWII; education, attended Southwestern University; widower; son, Alan Russell; Protestant.

CAREER: railroad yardmaster; transportation supervisor; Assembly 1962-1966.

COMMITTEES: Budget & Fiscal Review (chair); Constitutional Amendments (vice chair); Appropriations; Energy and Public Utilities; Governmental Organization; (Select) Calif. Wine Industry (chair); Maritime Industry; Pacific Rim; (Special) Solid & Hazardous Waste; (Joint) Fire, Police, Emergency & Disaster Services; Legislative Audit; Legislative Budget (chair).

OFFICES: Capitol, (916) 445-9740; district, 100 Paseo de San Antonio, 209, San Jose 95113, (408) 286-8318.

REGISTRATION: 54.2% D, 32.3% R

1988 CAMPAIGN: Alquist – D 64.8% $592,405
Daniel Bertolet – R 31.4% $66,314

RATINGS:

AFL	PIRG	CLCV	NOW	CTA	CofC	CFB	NRA	FPAC
88%	75%	87%	90%	97%	36%	20%	0%	11%

KEY VOTES:

Divest S. Africa:	YES	Insurance reform:	YES	Child sick leave:	YES
Assault gun ban:	YES	Parent consent abortion:	NO	Ban AIDS discrim:	YES
Clean Air Act:	YES	Ban insure donations:	YES	Extend death penalty:	NO
Lmt product tort:	–	Ban offshore oil:	–	Restrict abortion funds:	NO
Lower alcohol std:	YES	Basic health care:	YES	Oil spill prevent:	YES
Ethics reform:	YES	Work cancer stds:	YES	Earthquake insure:	

Kenneth L. Maddy (R)

14th Senate District

This sprawling district takes in a big chunk of the farm-dominated San Joaquin Valley as well as some of the most scenic areas in the Sierra Nevada and Pacific Coast. From Yosemite in the east, to the Carmel Valley in the west and south to the northern tip of Santa Barbara County, the district includes all of four counties and parts of three others, and was tailored to the man who has represented it for the past decade, Republican Ken Maddy.

Republicans outnumber Democrats in three of the counties: Monterey, San Luis Obispo and Santa Barbara. But Democrats dominate in the remaining four counties: Madera, Mariposa, Merced and Fresno County, which includes the western part of the city of

Ken Maddy

Fresno. Clearly, Maddy has won successive elections by garnering support from many Democrats, which is not uncommon in the San Joaquin Valley. A political moderate who is popular with colleagues on both sides of the aisle, Maddy has parlayed his agricultural roots, concerns about health care and lifelong love for horses and horse racing into legislative successes.

Mixed in along the way came tough campaigns and a couple of political and personal setbacks. In 1978, while still an assemblyman, he made a bid for governor with a campaign that got him nearly a half-million votes despite being an unknown entity from Fresno. Having given up his Assembly seat to run for governor, Maddy was out of politics for a few months. But the resignation of Sen. George Zenovich quickly brought him back, and he won a hard-fought special election to fill the seat.

Maddy's first marriage foundered after he won his Senate seat, and he later married the wealthy heiress to the Foster Farms chicken fortune, Norma Foster. That gave him the resources to pursue his intense passion for thoroughbred horse racing.

The Maddys have become A-list socialites, not only in Sacramento and the San Joaquin Valley, but in the playgrounds of the wealthy along Orange County's gold coast where they maintain a weekend residence.

Handsome and articulate, Maddy saw his star rise quickly in the Senate, especially since his longtime pal, Bill Campbell, was the minority leader. Maddy became caucus chairman, the No. 2 party position, but he and Campbell lost a power struggle several years later to a conservative faction. In 1987, Maddy returned in a countercoup and became minority leader.

Maddy has been on everyone's list of rising Republican stars since his better-than-expected shot at the governorship in 1978. But while he has toyed with seeking statewide office again, he's never taken the plunge, except to apply for a gubernatorial appointment as state treasurer.

Maddy is a star campaign fund-raiser and also is a pragmatic and effective legislator. He has forged a cordial working relationship with the leader of the Democrats, Senate President Pro Tem David Roberti. Maddy and Roberti stumped the state together talking with editorial boards to win passage of Proposition 112 in June 1990, imposing sweeping ethical standards on legislators in the wake of federal probes and corruption horror stories in the Legislature.

Maddy was among the leaders attempting to solve a record-long budget stalemate in 1990 and has tried to find common ground with Democrats to hold the state's presidential primary earlier in the year. In addition, Maddy, unlike some of the Republican colleagues, has pushed to guarantee basic health care for 3.2 million working Californians and their families although he's differed with Democrats on how such a program should be financed.

Maddy was under some pressure from supporters to run for governor in 1990 after George Deukmejian announced he would retire, but decided against it and now seems content to end his active political career in the Senate. He has said publicly he intends to retire when he's 60 – or when there's a Maddy-supported highway bypass through Livingston, site of the only traffic light on Highway 99 in California and headquarters of the Foster Farms chicken empire Maddy now shares. Capitol insiders speculate that Maddy may retire after his current term is completed.

Until he retires, his clout will be enhanced by the election of Gov. Pete Wilson. They have an excellent personal relationship and seem like-minded on many issues.

PERSONAL: elected 1979 (special election); born May 22, 1934, in Santa Monica; home, Fresno and ranch east of Modesto; USAF 1957-1960; education, B.S. agriculture CSU Fresno, J.D. UCLA; wife, Norma Foster; children, Deanna Hose, Don, Marilyn Geis, and stepchildren Jayne Waters, Ron Foster, Laurie Wesenberg, Suzi Sutherland, Janet Foster and Carrie Foster; Protestant.

CAREER: lawyer; horse breeder; Assembly 1970-1979; minority leader 1987.

COMMITTEES: Health and Human Services (vice chair); Governmental Organization (vice chair), Constitutional Amendments; Elections; (Select) Business Development; Calif. Wine Industry; Fairs & Rural Issues; Governmental

Efficiency; Infant & Child Care & Development; Pacific Rim; (Joint) Revision of the Penal Code (chair); Legislative Audit (vice chair); Arts; Refugee Resettlement, International Migration & Cooperative Development.

OFFICES: Capitol, (916) 445-9600; district, 2503 W. Shaw Ave., 101, Fresno 93711, (209) 445-5567; 19901 W. First St., 2, Hilmar 95324, (209) 667-3781; 895 Napa Ave., A-6, Morro Bay 93442, (805) 772-1287.

REGISTRATION: 48.6% D, 40.3% R

1990 CAMPAIGN:	Maddy – R	100%	$815,745
1986 CAMPAIGN:	Maddy – R	69%	$423,828
	Michael LeSage – D	31%	$15,955

RATINGS:

AFL	PIRG	CLCV	NOW	CTA	CofC	CFB	NRA	FPAC
42%	58%	35%	50%	70%	75%	80%	90%	79%

KEY VOTES:

Divest S. Africa:	YES	Insurance reform:	NO	Child sick leave:	NO
Assault gun ban:	NO	Parent consent abortion:	YES	Ban AIDS discrim:	–
Clean Air Act:	–	Ban insure donations:	NO	Extend death penalty:	YES
Lmt product tort:	YES	Ban offshore oil:	–	Restrict abortion funds:	NO
Lower alcohol std:	–	Basic health care:	YES	Oil spill prevent:	YES
Ethics reform:	YES	Work cancer stds:	NO	Earthquake insure:	YES

Rose Ann Vuich (D)
15th Senate District

Agriculture is synonymous with this rural district in the southeastern corner of the San Joaquin Valley. The district encompasses Tulare County and eastern Fresno County, including part of the city of Fresno.

Without ever having set foot in the Capitol, Rose Ann Vuich became the first woman elected to the state Senate in 1976. She had entered the race almost on a dare when the expected Democratic candidate backed out the day before the filing deadline. She upset the GOP nominee, longtime Assemblyman Ernest Mobley, by helping create the perception that he had done little to help Fresno get state money for a long-awaited cross-town freeway.

Rose Ann Vuich

Vuich continues to practice the politics of local issues. The daughter of Yugoslav immigrants, she works her district religiously and capitalizes on strong ethnic and social ties throughout the region. Since arriving in Sacramento, she has easily won re-election, and in 1988 ran unopposed. As she says at every district speech, the 15th District is Vuich country.

During her early Senate years, Vuich handled her status with aplomb. She sought a woman's restroom for the house, and when a speaker would refer to the "gentlemen of the Senate," she'd ring a little bell. As the novelty faded (there are now five women senators) Vuich settled into her self-defined roles as advocate for the district, defender of agriculture and chairwoman of the banking committee.

Considered to be independent and strong-willed, Vuich has scratched out a reputation as a plain-speaking, tell-me-what-it-means legislator known to say, "All right, I won't vote" if pressed to take a position before all her questions have been answered. It was that attitude that led to Vuich's name being brought up in an FBI probe of Capitol corruption – in a good way. On one tape, a former legislative aide who turned informant after being caught selling influence warned an undercover FBI agent pushing a special interest bill that they should seek to keep it out of the Senate Banking and Commerce Committee chaired by Vuich.

"The problem with banking and commerce is they don't play ball," the aide said. "That's Rose Ann Vuich. . . . Dot every I, cross every T. . . . She is so very straight-laced." Despite that reputation, she allowed bills deregulating the savings and loan industry to slip through her committee in the early 1980s. Many of those so-called reforms paved the way for the industry's billion-dollar excesses a few years later.

Vuich once called herself "probably the best Democratic vote" Republicans had in the Senate. But that changed when her independence crossed paths with Gov. George Deukmejian. She refused to support the governor's bottom-line issues: a Los Angeles prison bill and his initial nominee for state treasurer, Dan Lungren.

Amid persistent rumors of ill health in early 1991, Vuich told a reporter that she might consider stepping down before her term expires in 1992, noting, "I am just tired." She subsequently denied that she would retire. But it is clear that her age and the recent health problems of her brother, who has devoted his later life to her political career, are weighing heavily in deliberations about her future.

When she does leave, Democrats could have problems holding the seat in a district that is becoming increasingly Republican.

PERSONAL: elected 1976; born Jan. 27, 1927, in Cutler, Calif.; home, Dinuba; education, completed a business college accounting course; single; Serbian Orthodox.

CAREER: owner of accounting firm.

COMMITTEES: Banking & Commerce (chair); Agriculture and Water Resources; Transportation; (Select) Fairs & Rural Issues (chair); Calif. Wine Industry; Pacific Rim; (Special) Solid & Hazardous Waste (chair); (Joint) Rules (vice chair); Arts; Fairs Allocation & Classification.

OFFICES: Capitol, (916) 445-4641; district, 120 W. Tulare St., Dinuba 93618, (209) 591-5005.

REGISTRATION: 49.9% D, 41.6% R

1988 CAMPAIGN: Vuich – D   100% $204,335

RATINGS:

AFL	PIRG	CLCV	NOW	CTA	CofC	CFB	NRA	FPAC
65%	89%	57%	70%	100%	75%	100%	41%	57%

KEY VOTES:

Divest S. Africa:	YES	Insurance reform:	YES	Child sick leave:	YES
Assault gun ban:	YES	Parent consent abortion:	YES	Ban AIDS discrim:	YES
Clean Air Act:	YES	Ban insure donations:	YES	Extend death penalty:	YES
Lmt product tort:	YES	Ban offshore oil:	YES	Restrict abortion funds:	–
Lower alcohol std:	YES	Basic health care:	YES	Oil spill prevent:	YES
Ethics reform:	YES	Work cancer stds:	NO	Earthquake insure:	YES

Donald A. Rogers (R)

16th Senate District

With its population centered in Bakersfield, this expansive agricultural district is one of the nation's leading producers of food and oil. It covers Kings and Kern counties; the Mojave Valley and the high desert area of San Bernardino County, including much of Barstow; parts of Los Angeles County, including Lancaster, Palmdale and the eastern section of the Antelope Valley; sections of Pasadena and Altadena.

After the 1980 census, the district was gerrymandered to take in more Democratic voters south of the Tehachapis near Pasadena as a desperate effort to save one of the last Democratic seats in a strongly conservative, increasingly Republican region. The gerrymander worked for one election, saving veteran Democratic Sen. Walter Stiern's seat in 1982.

Don Rogers

But when Stiern retired four years later, Don Rogers, a former city councilman and four-term assemblyman from Bakersfield, won the seat. It was one of the few victories in the GOP's failed strategy to regain control of the Senate before the 1991 reapportionment. The district's voters, many of them conservative descendants of the Oklahoma migration, went with the Louisiana-born man who first built a career as an oil geologist.

As a legislator, Rogers has marked himself as perhaps the Senate's strongest opponent of environmental legislation, particularly affecting the oil industry. His knee-jerk opposition is so strong it is taken for granted by his colleagues, thus diluting whatever persuasive powers he might have. In 1990, he was the lone "no" vote in the Senate against a bill to set up a $100 million fund for oil-spill clean ups (in the Assembly, the single "no" vote was cast by fellow Bakersfield legislator Trice Harvey). Rogers' floor speech against the bill on Aug. 31, 1990, left many in the chamber gasping.

"Sure, we're probably going to have more oil spills," he began. "But let's state fact. The ones that have occurred – the one that occurred in Santa Barbara, it was too bad. That was a blow out. However, the effect did not last very long. It wasn't but a few months until all effects, all evidence of the spill, had disappeared due to the work of mother nature and the work of the response people....Even up in Alaska, you go there now and you have to look pretty hard to find any evidence of the spill up in Prince William Sound."

Rogers was a vocal opponent of a ban on semiautomatic assault weapons. He didn't endear himself to his Democratic colleagues when he mailed a fund-raising appeal billing himself as the "commanding officer and founder of the Republican Air Force." The plea went on: "The RAF has remained high above the quagmire of Socialism and has effectively stayed the evils constantly trying to invade the California Legislature."

In 1991, Rogers uttered what may have been the legislative non sequitur of the year. Apparently trying to point out the ignorance of his colleagues during discussions of the Persian Gulf War, he claimed that no senator could name more than two cities in Iraq. Sen. Wadie Deddeh, D-Chula Vista, a native of Iraq, rose from his seat and began rattling off Iraqi cities in alphabetical order. So much for the senator from Bakersfield.

PERSONAL: elected 1986; born April 22, 1928, in Natchitoches, La.; home, Bakersfield; USMC 1946-1948; education, B.S. geology Louisiana State University; wife, Marilyn L. Miller; children, Mallorie, Grayson and Douglas; Mormon.

CAREER: oil geologist; owner of a geological consulting firm and partner in a petroleum firm; Bakersfield City Council 1973-1978; Assembly 1978-1986.

COMMITTEES: Veterans' Affairs (vice chair); Agriculture & Water Resources; Budget & Fiscal Review; Insurance, Claims & Corporations; Natural Resources & Wildlife; Public Employment & Retirement; (Select) Fairs & Rural Issues.

OFFICES: Capitol, (916) 445-6637, FAX (916) 443-4015; district, 1326 H St., Bakersfield 93301, (805) 395-2927; 804 N. Irwin, Hanford 93230, (209) 582-2549; 528 Barstow Rd., Barstow 92311, (619) 256-5805; 1050 N. Norma, Ridgecrest 93555, (619) 446-4176.

REGISTRATION: 49.7% D, 40.5% R

1990 CAMPAIGN:	Rogers – R	52%	$492,674
	Ray Gonzales – D	44%	$120,072
1986 CAMPAIGN:	Rogers – R	52%	$860,607
	Jim Young – D	48%	$1,414,015

RATINGS:

AFL	PIRG	CLCV	NOW	CTA	CofC	CFB	NRA	FPAC
8%	30%	12%	20%	65%	75%	80%	100%	90%

KEY VOTES:

Divest S. Africa:	NO	Insurance reform:	NO	Child sick leave:	NO
Assault gun ban:	NO	Parent consent abortion:	YES	Ban AIDS discrim:	–
Clean Air Act:	NO	Ban insure donations:	NO	Extend death penalty:	YES
Lmt product tort:	YES	Ban offshore oil:	NO	Restrict abortion funds:	YES
Lower alcohol std:	YES	Basic health care:	NO	Oil spill prevent:	NO
Ethics reform:	YES	Work cancer stds:	NO	Earthquake insure:	NO

Henry J. Mello (D)
17th Senate District

This is one of the most diverse Senate districts, not only geographically but politically and demographically. It contains some of the state's most beautiful beach communities – Carmel, Monterey, Pacific Grove and Santa Cruz – and some of the state's most productive farmland – Salinas, Watsonville and San Benito County.

Henry Mello

The political spectrum ranges from the ultraliberal Santa Cruz to the conservative farm-area politics of Hollister. Its residents include the wealthy and movie stars – Clint Eastwood was briefly mayor of Carmel – as well as burgeoning Hispanic populations in cities like Salinas, Soledad and Watsonville.

Henry Mello, a farmer and businessman, has attempted to walk a tightrope in response to his diverse constituency. He is a moderate Democrat and a bit of a nervous one. On some controversial issues, he tries to give a little to each side. In 1989, for example, he voted in favor of a virtual ban of semiautomatic military-style assault weapons despite heavy pressure in his district from members of the National Rifle Association. Later in the year, when a key vote came up to require purchasers of rifles to wait 15 days between the time they buy rifles and the time they can be picked up, Mello, again under pressure from the NRA, called the waiting period "outrageous" and voted against it.

Mello's moderate course has made him, in effect, the swing vote on the powerful five-member Rules Committee. The committee routes legislation to committees and can block confirmation of gubernatorial appointees. Mello on occasion has sided with the two Republicans on the committee.

One area of particular interest for Mello has been senior citizens. He carried a bill to create the Senior Legislature, an annual gathering of senior citizens from throughout the state at which they set their legislative priorities. And Mello has frequently carried Senior Legislature proposals, measures ranging from housing and day care to lunch programs and nursing homes. He's also taken a special interest in victims of Alzheimer's.

Mello has, on occasion, generated controversy in his district by carrying bills to help local developers and other businesses in ways that some believe might have adverse environmental effects or benefit big contributors. In 1990, for example, a timber company controlled by Orange County developer Donald Koll, a large contributor to legislative and statewide campaigns, couldn't get a harvesting permit and subsequently couldn't find a buyer for its land. Mello carried a bill to have the state purchase the 1,500 acres of forest in the Santa Cruz mountains for $6 million, claiming the move would save a grove of redwoods. But the purchase, inserted in a statewide park bond, was voted down in November 1990.

In 1991 when the state was facing an unprecedented budget deficit requiring cuts in many vital programs, Mello was criticized for proposing a $3.5 million allocation for the state to participate in the 1992 World's Fair in Spain. Mello also is open to charges that he is the Senate's big spender, having used $618,022 in state funds in 1987 on his office and staff, more than any other member. As the Democratic whip, Mello has built a political organization around staffer Larry Sheingold, who has been lent out to win elections for Dan McCorquodale, Cecil Green and Lucy Killea.

PERSONAL: elected 1980; born March 27, 1924, in Watsonville, Calif.; home, Watsonville; education, attended Hartnell Junior College; wife, Helen; children, John, Stephen, Michael and Timothy.

CAREER: farmer; Santa Cruz Board of Supervisors 1967-1974; Assembly 1976-1980; Senate Democratic whip.

COMMITTEES: Rules; Agriculture & Water Resources (vice chair); Energy & Public Utilities; Governmental Organization; Health & Human Services; Natural Resources & Wildlife; (Select) Calif. Wine Industry (vice chair); Bilingual Education (chair); Business Development; Citizen Participation in Government; Mobile Homes; (Joint) Arts (chair); Rules; Fairs Allocation & Classification; Fisheries & Aquaculture.

OFFICES: Capitol, (916) 445-5843, FAX (916) 448-0175; district, 1200 Aquajito Road, 102, Monterey, 93940, (408) 373-0773; 701 Ocean St., 318A, Santa Cruz, 95060, (408) 425-0401; 240 Church St., 115, Salinas, 93901, (408) 757-4169; 92 Fifth St., Gilroy, 95020, (408) 848-1437.

REGISTRATION: 52.8% D, 33.6% R

1988 CAMPAIGN:

Mello – D		71%	$603,760
Harry Damkar – R		29%	$115,863

RATINGS:

AFL	PIRG	CLCV	NOW	CTA	CofC	CFB	NRA	FPAC
86%	85%	87%	90%	100%	29%	20%	54%	13%

KEY VOTES:

Divest S. Africa:	YES	Insurance reform:	YES	Child sick leave:	YES
Assault gun ban:	YES	Parent consent abortion: YES	Ban AIDS discrim:	YES
Clean Air Act:	–	Ban insure donations:	NO	Extend death penalty:	YES
Lmt product tort:	–	Ban offshore oil:	YES	Restrict abortion funds:	NO
Lower alcohol std:	–	Basic health care:	YES	Oil spill prevent:	YES
Ethics reform:	YES	Work cancer stds:	YES	Earthquake insure:	YES

Gary K. Hart (D)

18th Senate District

Running along a narrow coastal corridor from Lompoc to Malibu, the 18th Senate District includes growth-controlled Santa Barbara, Oxnard, Ventura and the laid-back communities surrounding UC Santa Barbara. The district runs along the spine of the low but rugged Santa Ynez Mountains. The district has an environmentalist tilt but is decidedly upscale and has a low Democratic registration, making it an increasingly volatile battleground.

Gary K. Hart

Democrat Gary K. Hart – he has taken to using his middle initial to distinguish himself from that other Gary Hart – has managed to balance the sometimes conflicting political tendencies of his district. A former teacher, Hart is popular among growth-controllers and environmentalists. He gets high marks among his colleagues for intellect and integrity. He has ably chaired the Education Committee and authored numerous education bills, including school bond acts in 1986 and 1988. While many child-care proposals died or were vetoed in 1988, Gov. George Deukmejian signed a Hart bill offering tax credits to employers who establish programs for the use of their employees' children. Many employers are beginning to take advantage of the Hart bill.

Hart chaired the Senate Select Committee on AIDS, becoming the Legislature's chief expert since Art Agnos left the Assembly to become mayor of San Francisco. Hart authored a bill to require AIDS education in the schools as suggested by U.S. Surgeon General C. Everett Koop, but Deukmejian vetoed it.

Hart also has fought to close and cleanup the Casmalia Resources hazardous waste dump in his district, a site facing a $6 million fine from the U.S. Environmental Protection Agency. Hart's toxics legislation got under the skin of the Deukmejian administration. One of his laws required the Department of Health Services to hold public hearings on dumps such as Casmalia.

When the political infighting gets rough, Hart often bows out – a trait that has contributed to his inability to move into a leadership role. Perhaps that's one of the reasons he seems bored with the Legislature. He ran for Congress in 1988 in one of the hardest fought congressional contests in the nation, falling less than 1 percentage point short of beating longtime Republican Rep. Robert Lagomarsino. Both national parties threw everything they could muster into the race. Ronald Reagan came down from his ranch (in nearby Ed Davis' Senate district) to stump for Lagomarsino. In the end, Lagomarsino won but was wounded. Hart doubtlessly was encouraged to try again, but rather than give up his state Senate seat in 1990, he took a predictably safe course by first running for re-election. With that success behind him – and a four-year "free ride" in the Legislature in hand – Hart has given every indication that he will run again for Congress in 1992.

PERSONAL: elected 1982; born Aug. 13, 1943, in San Diego, Calif.; home, Santa Barbara; education, B.A. history Stanford University., M.A. education Harvard University; wife, Cary Smith; children, Elissa, Katherine and Laura; Protestant.

CAREER: teacher; Assembly 1974-1982.

COMMITTEES: Education (chair); Natural Resources & Wildlife (vice chair); Constitutional Amendments; Budget & Fiscal Review; Business & Professions; Energy & Public Utilities; (Select) Children & Youth; Source Reduction and Recycling Market Development; (Joint) Legislative Audit; School Facilities.

OFFICES: Capitol, (916) 445-5405, FAX (916) 322-3304; district, 1216 State St., 507, Santa Barbara 93101, (805) 966-1766; 801 S. Victoria Ave., 301, Ventura 93006, (805) 654-4648.

REGISTRATION: 46.4% D, 40.1% R

1990 CAMPAIGN:	Hart – D	60.4%	$506,361
	Carey Rogers – R	35.4%	$16,252
1986 CAMPAIGN:	Hart – D	65%	$583,271
	DeWayne Holmdahl – R	33%	$166,150

RATINGS:

AFL	PIRG	CLCV	NOW	CTA	CofC	CFB	NRA	FPAC
94%	100%	94%	100%	97%	17%	20%	0%	0%

KEY VOTES:

Divest S. Africa:	YES	Insurance reform:	YES	Child sick leave:	YES
Assault gun ban:	YES	Parent consent abortion:	NO	Ban AIDS discrim:	YES
Clean Air Act:	YES	Ban insure donations:	YES	Extend death penalty:	–
Lmt product tort:	–	Ban offshore oil:	YES	Restrict abortion funds:	NO
Lower alcohol std:	YES	Basic health care:	YES	Oil spill prevent:	YES
Ethics reform:	YES	Work cancer stds:	–	Earthquake insure:	YES

Ed M. Davis (R)

19th Senate District

The canyons and badlands of the northwestern San Fernando Valley hold amusement parks, old citrus groves and Highway 101. The 19th Senate District is made to order for Republicans, with new housing tracts and old money. Ronald Reagan's ranch is in the district that stretches along the eastern rim of the Santa Ynez Mountains to include most of Santa Barbara and Ventura counties plus the Los Angeles County communities of Newhall, Chatsworth and Granada Hills.

Representing the region is Ed Davis, a Republican who seems never to have hesitated to say exactly what he thinks and do exactly as he pleases. It is hard to imagine California politics without him. As Los An-

Ed Davis

geles police chief, Davis wanted to hang hijackers at the airport, and he once wore a gag for the TV cameras when Mayor Tom Bradley tried to shut him up.

Liberals shuddered when Davis got elected to the state Senate after an earlier attempt for the U.S. Senate flopped. But pipe-puffing Davis has followed a more diplomatic course, though he is just as independent. Davis incurred the wrath of conservatives by voting to protect homosexual rights, and he branded as "un-American" those who asked him to refuse support from homosexual groups.

As a member of the Senate Judiciary Committee, Davis has steadily argued to do away with the state's determinant sentencing laws and return to the indeterminate sentencing procedures that he was familiar with as a police chief. Davis has begun to acquire a following on the issue. And although he voted against restricting the sale of semiautomatic weapons, Davis scolded lobbyists from the National Rifle Association for their unbending stubbornness on gun issues. Davis also was outspoken against Proposition 126, an alcohol-industry sponsored initiative on the November 1990 ballot that would have slightly raised liquor taxes while freezing them in place in the state constitution. Davis joined state schools chief Bill Honig, a pariah of Republicans, in denouncing the initiative as "fraudulent." Although Pete Wilson supported the initiative, Davis and Honig won the day on the issue.

Davis' continued aspirations for the U.S. Senate led to one of the most celebrated fiascoes in recent GOP history. In 1986, he was locked in a multicandidate race for the Republican U.S. Senate nomination. Cross-town rival Rep. Bobbi Fiedler allegedly offered to pay off his campaign debt if he would withdraw from the race. He considered it a bribe offer, and instead of taking the money he reported the incident to Los Angeles District Attorney Ira Reiner, who prosecuted Fiedler under an obscure state law. Davis and Fielder were irreparably damaged by the affair, and Ed Zschau won the nomination. Davis found himself booed at state party conventions and Fiedler beat the rap.

PERSONAL: elected 1980; born Nov. 15, 1916, in Los Angeles; home, Santa Clarita; Navy 1942-1945 WWII; education, B.S. public administration USC; wife, Aileen "Bobbie" Trueblood; children, Chris, Michael, Mary Ellen; Episcopalian.

CAREER: Los Angeles Police chief; professor.

COMMITTEES: Judiciary (vice chair); Appropriations; Banking & Commerce; Insurance, Claims & Corporations; Natural Resources & Wildlife; (Select) Governmental Efficiency; Motion Picture, TV, Commercial & Recording Industries; Source Reduction and Recycling Market Development; (Joint) Fire, Police, Emergency & Disaster Services; Legislative Ethics; Prison Construction & Operations.

OFFICES: Capitol, (916) 445-8873, FAX (916) 324-7544; district, 11145 Tampa Ave., 21B, Northridge 91326, (818) 368-1171.

REGISTRATION: 37% D, 52.4% R

1988 CAMPAIGN: Davis – R   72% $329,974
                   Andrew Martin – D   25.1% $0

RATINGS:

AFL	PIRG	CLCV	NOW	CTA	CofC	CFB	NRA	FPAC
41%	84%	69%	50%	74%	50%	40%	40%	50%

KEY VOTES:

Divest S. Africa:	NO	Insurance reform:	NO	Child sick leave:	NO
Assault gun ban:	NO	Parent consent abortion:	YES	Ban AIDS discrim:	YES
Clean Air Act:	–	Ban insure donations:	YES	Extend death penalty:	YES
Lmt product tort:	YES	Ban offshore oil:	YES	Restrict abortion funds:	NO
Lower alcohol std:	–	Basic health care:	YES	Oil spill prevent:	YES
Ethics reform:	YES	Work cancer stds:	–	Earthquake insure:	YES

Alan E. Robbins (D)

20th Senate District

The smog-shrouded eastern San Fernando Valley holds the middle-class communities of Van Nuys, Reseda, Panorama City, Mission Hills, Pacoima and other towns that blend one into the other. With pockets of Jewish, working-class and upscale voters, the valley votes generally Democratic with a conservative tinge.

When Democrat Alan Robbins first ran for the Senate as a 30-year-old upstart in a 1973 special election, he slung his coat over his shoulder, a la Bobby Kennedy, and heard hoots that he was a phony who would never get anywhere. He won and has become a power-broker in the San Fernando Valley.

Alan Robbins

Robbins has spent all of his adult life in and around the Legislature. He worked on an Assembly committee staff when he was 19. After he graduated from law school, he went to Assemblyman Tom Bane and said he wanted to seek office. Bane advised Robbins that he should first become a millionaire. He did. By the time he was in his late 20s, Robbins was reportedly worth about $3.5 million.

Robbins has skated on the edge of political, personal and legal disaster more than once – and always come back from the brink. He stood trial in 1981 on charges that he engaged in sex with two 16-year-old girls, and was acquitted; the FBI tried to sting him in its "Brispec" undercover operation in 1988 but failed; his former business associates have sued him, but settled out of court.

He is one of the shrewdest politicians in the Legislature and routinely carries one of the heaviest bill loads. By the end of the 1987-88 session, he had authored more than 120 bills, many enacted into law. He dives into such divergent subjects as animal rights, the death penalty, insurance, transportation and interstate banking.

Politically, Robbins is a chameleon, mirroring the political issue of the moment, be it opposition to busing for school integration, traffic jams or insurance rates. In so doing, he has become one of the most disliked and distrusted lawmakers among his colleagues. Robbins is a master at amending bills with hidden catches during the final end-of-session crush each year, so clever that Sen. Robert Presley once stood up on the floor and asked his colleagues to keep a sharp eye for Robbins' tricks. That distrust has had a detrimental effect on his legislation. For instance, Robbins' effort at reorganizing the Los Angeles transit district fell apart not just from cross-town conflicts (and greediness) but because many senators just did not trust Robbins.

As chairman of the Senate's insurance committee, Robbins has set himself up as the chief defender of Proposition 103's insurance regulation and rate rollbacks. For a time, he seemed to be positioning himself to run for state insurance commissioner. But with so many of his colleagues expressing their distrust, he was forced to say he would not run for the office.

No one is ever quite sure whose water Robbins is carrying, as, for example, when he authored a banking bill to limit interstate banking to Western states – a bill rivaling one carried by then-Assemblyman Charles Calderon to open up California banking to the rest of the country. At first it appeared Robbins was on the side of California bankers worried about Eastern encroachment. But when California banks lifted their opposition, Robbins continued to push his bill. As it turned out, he was working for the savings and loan industry. His role in banking legislation and other issues attracted the attention of the FBI, which subpoenaed batches of legislative records on interstate banking bills in June 1989. Robbins testified at the grand jury that indicted Sen. Joe Montoya, the first legislator convicted in the scandal. Among the most widely quoted pieces of testimony at the trial was an audio tape secretly recorded by the FBI in which Robbins was overheard telling a federal informant, "I don't need to be taken care of on every bill that comes through."

Robbins' Encino home was searched under federal warrant in November 1990. Agents reportedly sought evidence of an alleged scheme in which Robbins and state Coastal Commissioner Mark Nathanson extorted $250,000 from San Diego hotel developer Jack Naiman. Nathanson's Beverly Hills home also was searched. Naiman, who lobbied unsuccessfully against a competing hotel that was approved by the Coastal Commission, reportedly told investigators that he was put in "a squeeze" by Robbins and paid most of the money.

PERSONAL: elected 1973 (special election); born Feb. 5, 1943, in Philadelphia; home, Encino; education, B.A. political science and J.D. UCLA; divorced; children, Jacob and Leah; Jewish.

CAREER: lawyer.

COMMITTEES: Insurance, Claims & Corporations (chair); Banking & Commerce; Budget & Fiscal Review and budget subcommittee 4 – legislative, executive, business, transportation, housing & general government (chair); Transportation; (Select) Governmental Efficiency (chair); Motion Picture, TV, Commercial & Recording Industries; (Joint) Courthouse Financing and Construction (chair); Legislative Budget.

OFFICES: Capitol, (916) 445-3121, FAX (916) 324-7072; district, 6150 Van Nuys Blvd., 400, Van Nuys, 91401, (818) 901-5555.

REGISTRATION: 56.9% D, 33.3% R

1990 CAMPAIGN: Robbins – D   58.3% $2,045,100
                   David Podegracz – R   34.1% $0
1986 CAMPAIGN: Robbins – D   65% $1,134,771
                   Lynn Davis – R   35% $1,775

RATINGS:

AFL	PIRG	CLCV	NOW	CTA	CofC	CFB	NRA	FPAC
89%	85%	92%	60%	91%	29%	20%	100%	9%

KEY VOTES:

Divest S. Africa:	YES	Insurance reform:	YES	Child sick leave:	YES
Assault gun ban:	NO	Parent consent abortion:	–	Ban AIDS discrim:	–
Clean Air Act:	YES	Ban insure donations:	YES	Extend death penalty:	YES
Lmt product tort:	–	Ban offshore oil:	YES	Restrict abortion funds:	NO
Lower alcohol std:	YES	Basic health care:	YES	Oil spill prevent:	YES
Ethics reform:	YES	Work cancer stds:	YES	Earthquake insure:	YES

Newton R. Russell (R)

21st Senate District

Democrats needn't apply in this Los Angeles County District that includes Glendale, Lancaster, Palmdale, San Marino, Arcadia, Monrovia and part of Pasadena. Republican registration stands at 55 percent, 20 points higher than the Democrats.

Newton Russell has been in the Legislature for a quarter of a century, beginning his career in the Assembly in 1964 and moving to the Senate 10 years later. His late brother, actor John Russell, was best known in the title role of television's "The Lawman."

Newton Russell

The senator is a hard-working, consummate conservative, rarely breaking from the Republican caucus line. In fact, it was something of a mild surprise when Russell reversed himself in 1989 and supported a bill that would have heavily fined insurers who illegally canceled automobile policies following the passage of Proposition 103.

In recent years, Russell has been most visible for his involvement in bills dealing with sex education at schools. In 1988, he successfully pushed a bill, signed into law by then-Gov. George Deukmejian, that requires schools to encourage students to abstain from intercourse until they are ready for marriage and to teach respect for monogamous, heterosexual marriage. Russell said that measure was "not intended to preach morals. It is intended to give teens useful, factual tips." The following year, he introduced a bill that would require written parental consent for children to receive sex education, and another to prohibit schools from providing counseling to students other than career, academic or vocational without the same written consent.

Russell also is one of the Senate's resident parliamentarians, frequently rising to object to breaches of rules. And those protests about parliamentary games led to a series of procedural reforms in the Senate, designed to prevent legislation from slipping into law without notice and full airing. Russell has been mentioned in Republican legislative circles as a replacement for Ken Maddy as minority leader should he step aside or falter politically.

PERSONAL: elected 1974 (special election); born June 25, 1927, in Los Angeles; home, Glendale; Navy WWII; education, B.S. business administration USC, attended UCLA and Georgetown University; wife, Diane Henderson; children, Stephen, Sharon Sclafani and Julia Gans; Protestant.

CAREER: insurance agent; Assembly 1964-1974.

COMMITTEES: Banking & Commerce (vice chair); Energy & Public Utilities (vice chair); Local Government; Transportation; (Select) Calif. Wine Industry; Children & Youth; Pacific Rim; (Special) Developmental Disabilities & Mental Health; (Joint) Mental Health Research (vice chair); Rules; State's Economy; Energy Regulation and the Environment.

OFFICES: Capitol, (916) 445-5976; district, 401 N. Brand Blvd., 424, Glendale 91203-2364, (818) 247-7021.

REGISTRATION: 34.9% D, 55.3% R

1988 CAMPAIGN: Russell – R 68.4% $284,413
Louise Gelber – D 28.3% $121,146

RATINGS:

AFL	PIRG	CLCV	NOW	CTA	CofC	CFB	NRA	FPAC
22%	45%	18%	30%	74%	79%	80%	77%	79%

KEY VOTES:

Divest S. Africa:	NO	Insurance reform:	YES	Child sick leave:	NO
Assault gun ban:	NO	Parent consent abortion:	YES	Ban AIDS discrim:	NO
Clean Air Act:	–	Ban insure donations:	NO	Extend death penalty:	YES
Lmt product tort:	–	Ban offshore oil:	NO	Restrict abortion funds:	YES
Lower alcohol std:	–	Basic health care:	YES	Oil spill prevent:	YES
Ethics reform:	YES	Work cancer stds:	NO	Earthquake insure:	NO

Herschel Rosenthal (D)

22nd Senate District

The heart of the liberal West Side in Los Angeles, the 22nd Senate District includes Santa Monica, West Los Angeles, Sherman Oaks, Pacific Palisades, Beverly Hills and the posh Brentwood and Bel Air neighborhoods. Democrat Herschel Rosenthal is a product of the liberal political organization led by Reps. Henry Waxman and Howard Berman, and he is one of the most consistent liberals in the Legislature, although not nearly as articulate as Sen. Nicholas Petris. Rosenthal was among six senators who voted against a July 1989 anti-flag-burning resolution.

Rosenthal has made his legislative mark primarily in utilities law. He was the Senate Democrats' negotiator in breaking a tricky two-year stalemate over how to spend $154 million that California received from a national $2.1 billion judgment against several oil companies for overcharging during the 1974 oil crisis. The agreement reached in spring 1989 earmarked $60 million to start replacing about one-third of the state's unsafe school buses, and the rest was used to help poor people meet their utility bills and other energy and traffic projects.

Herschel Rosenthal

Rosenthal's yearly financial disclosure statements are among the more entertaining for their restaurant and travel listings. He is among the more traveled lawmakers, enjoying a steady stream of junkets courtesy of corporations, most of which have business pending before the public utilities committee he chairs. On the side, Rosenthal is a horse racing fanatic who owns all or part of several horses. This would appear to have influenced his choice of attire; he often wears plaid jackets that look as if they were tailored from horse blankets .

Rosenthal, who was among the Democrats underwhelmed with his party's crop of candidates for governor in 1990, won notoriety in an otherwise boring summer of 1989 by trying to get actor James Garner to run for governor. Garner declined, reportedly telling Rosenthal it would mean giving up his $6 million a year income.

PERSONAL: elected 1982; born March 13, 1918, in St. Louis, Mo.; home, Los Angeles; Navy; education, attended UCLA; wife, Patricia Staman; children, Joel and Suzanne; Jewish.

CAREER: partner ADTYPE Service Co. Inc.; Assembly 1974-1982.

COMMITTEES: Energy & Public Utilities (chair); Business & Professions; Elections & Reapportionment; Governmental Organization; Health & Human Services; Industrial Relations; Toxics & Public Safety Management; (Select) Motion Picture, TV, Commercial & Recording Industries (chair); (Special) Developmental Disabilities & Mental Health; (Joint) Energy Regulation and the Environment (chair).

OFFICES: Capitol, (916) 445-7928; district, 1950 Sawtelle Blvd., 210, Los Angeles, 90025, (213) 479-5588.

REGISTRATION: 58.4% D, 30.6% R

1990 CAMPAIGN: Rosenthal – D					64.6%		$875,866	
Michael Schrager – R					30.9%		$4,671	
1986 CAMPAIGN: Rosenthal – D					68%		$488,292	
Daniel Sias – R					29%		$0	

RATINGS:

AFL	PIRG	CLCV	NOW	CTA	CofC	CFB	NRA	FPAC
96%	85%	100%	100%	92%	25%	20%	0%	5%

KEY VOTES:

Divest S. Africa:	YES	Insurance reform:	YES	Child sick leave:	YES
Assault gun ban:	YES	Parent consent abortion:	NO	Ban AIDS discrim:	YES
Clean Air Act:	–	Ban insure donations:	NO	Extend death penalty:	NO
Lmt product tort:	YES	Ban offshore oil:	YES	Restrict abortion funds:	NO
Lower alcohol std:	NO	Basic health care:	YES	Oil spill prevent:	YES
Ethics reform:	YES	Work cancer stds:	YES	Earthquake insure:	YES

David A. Roberti (D)

23rd Senate District

On a rain-soaked Monday in January 1991, David Roberti stood in the rotunda of the state Capitol and greeted his third governor as president pro tempore of the Senate, the top post in the state's upper legislative house. On the day of Pete Wilson's inaugural, Roberti's grip on power was as firm as it had ever been and showed not the slightest sign of weakening. It was very much a day when Wilson needed David Roberti more than David Roberti needed Pete Wilson.

If he cared to, Roberti could look back on his two decades-plus in the Legislature with the satisfaction of a successful politician who has steadily risen in strength and stature. Republican numbers in the 40-

David Roberti

member Senate had steadily declined to 11. The 26 Democrats in the Senate were just one seat short of having the two-thirds vote to override gubernatorial vetoes (a largely academic point since the Democratic majority in the Assembly was much slimmer).

However, huge challenges faced Roberti and his colleagues. The state was groaning under a recession and a projected $12.6 billion budget deficit. And the institution led by Roberti and Assembly Speaker Willie Brown had just received the biggest body blow of a generation – the passage of Proposition 140, requiring state senators to step down after two terms, Assembly members after three terms, and forcing a huge reduction in the Legislature's operating budget.

Roberti, the son of Italian immigrants, has represented central Los Angeles in the Legislature since he was elected to the Assembly in 1966, then the youngest legislator at age 27. He moved up to the Senate in a 1971 special election. Roberti's district looks like the Democratic coalition personified, taking in Jewish Beverly-Fairfax, gay-dominated West Hollywood, the older Catholic immigrant neighborhoods of the Wilshire District and Los Feliz (where Roberti lives) and some of the state's newest immigrants in Chinatown and Koreatown.

No one has given Roberti re-election trouble, although feminist lawyer Gloria Allred once threatened to challenge him in his primary over his anti-abortion stance.

Roberti's anti-abortion rights view is the one issue that puts him at odds with his caucus. His tirades against Planned Parenthood are legendary. Even so, he enthusiastically supported the winning candidacy of Lucy Killea in a 1989 special election dominated by her pro-choice stance and conflict with her Catholic bishop.

Roberti and Brown were sworn-in as the leaders of their respective houses on the same December 1980 day, their coups triumphant. Forces that brought both to power were the same – the advent of the full-time Legislature in 1966 and the highly partisan atmosphere it engendered over the years. But their styles and personalities could not be more different.

Brown had noisily grabbed power by forming a coalition with Republicans (who thought he would be a weak speaker), while Roberti had quietly arranged the overthrow of President Pro Tem Jim Mills, who was planning to step aside anyway. Roberti had taken advantage of Senate Democratic fears following the 1980 election loss of Senate dean Al Rodda of Sacramento in a highly partisan, and decidedly ungentlemanly, contest with John Doolittle. While Mills, a Milquetoast Democrat, had entertained notions of handing off his mantle to the genteel Robert Presley, Senate liberals had other designs and elevated Roberti to pro tem on his promise to protect their seats in the upcoming reapportionment. There would be no more Rodda incidents if Roberti could help it.

Holding power in the Senate became dependent not on legislative prowess but on keeping incumbents re-elected, something Roberti first demonstrated in 1982, when he defended then-Sen. Alex Garcia, who was known mostly for his prolonged absences from the Capitol, against a Democratic primary challenge from then-Assemblyman Art Torres. Garcia lost anyway, but Roberti had demonstrated his fidelity to incumbents.

In recent years, Roberti's political machine has shown spectacular prowess in special elections, winning seats for Democrats Killea and Cecil Green of Norwalk in districts that should have gone to Republicans. In the 1990 election, Democrats knocked off former Republican Senate leader Jim Nielsen.

Although Roberti gained power on a partisan wave, he has proven a more complex politician. He enjoys cordial relations with many of his Republican colleagues, particularly with Republican leader Ken Maddy – a relationship in marked contrast to the poisoned blood among Democratic and Republican leaders in the Assembly. Some Republicans are even Roberti confidants, particularly Oceanside's Bill Craven, who sits with Roberti on the Rules Committee that governs Senate operations.

Roberti and the Rules Committee seem to have chosen a different path than Speaker Brown in the wake of Proposition 140. Roberti moved quickly, without complaining, to trim the Senate staff while Brown whined to the bitter end in making cuts. Roberti hired an outside ethics expert, Michael Josephson, to conduct an all-day ethics workshop for senators. Brown, on the other hand, hunkered down in his bunker and blamed the press for his troubles.

In contrast to Brown's flashy clothes, fast cars and pretty women, Roberti is a pet-loving homebody who wears dark suits and is devoutly Catholic. Roberti's weaknesses are for hearty food and travel, particularly to Italy.

His wife, June, is considered his closest political adviser.

Presidents pro tempore of the Senate

Name	P*	Year(s)	Name	P*	Year(s)
E. Kirby Chamberlain	–	1849	R.F. Del Valle	D	1883
Elcan Haydenfeldt	W	1851	Benjamin Knight Jr.	D	1885
Benjamin F. Keene	D	1852-1854	Stephen M. White	D	1887, 1889
Royal T. Sprague	D	1855	Thomas Fraser	R	1891
Delos R. Ashley	A	1856	R.B. Carpenter	R	1893
Samuel H. Dosh	D	1857	Thomas Flint Jr.	R	1895-1903
Samuel A. Merritt	D	1858	Edward I. Wolfe	R	1905-1909
W.B. Dickenson	D	1859	A.E. Boyton	R	1911,1913
Isaac N. Quinn	D	1860	N.W. Thompson	R	1915
Richard Irwin	DD	1861	Arthur H. Breed	R	1917-1933
James Safter	R	1862	William P. Rich	R	1935, 1937
A.M. Crane	U	1863	Jerrold L. Seawell	R	1939
R. Burnell	U	1864	William P. Rich	R	1941
S.P. Wright	U	1866	Jerrold L. Seawell	R	1943, 1945
Lansing B. Misner	U	1868	Harold J. Powers	R	1947-1953
Edward J. Lewis	D	1870	Clarence C. Ward	R	1954-1955
James T. Farley	D	1872	Ben Hulse	R	1955-1956
William Irwin	D	1874	Hugh M. Burns	D	1957-1969
Benjamin F. Tuttle	D	1876	Howard Way	R	1969-1970
Edward J. Lewis	D	1878	Jack Schrade	R	1970
George F. Baker	R	1880	James R. Mills	D	1971-1980
William Johnston	R	1881	David Roberti	D	1980-

Key to parties: A=American, D=Democrat, DD=Douglas Democrat, I=Independent, P=Progressive, R=Republican, U=Union; – denotes no party.

But the introverted Roberti has never been as prominent in politics outside the Capitol as Willie Brown. The San Francisco Chronicle once headlined a story about Roberti: "The Unknown Man Running the Senate." He disdains dabbling at presidential king-making, unlike Brown, and has been openly skeptical of advancing California's June presidential primary to March. He seems to believe presidential politics are a political distraction from policy making in California.

While the speaker has gallivanted around the country and bragged he is the "Ayatollah of the Assembly," Roberti has steadily racked up a more solid legislative record than Brown. Roberti's bills have run the gamut from consumer protection to child welfare, hazardous waste, energy and crime. By throwing his full weight as leader of the Senate behind it, Roberti won passage in 1989 of a law restricting semiautomatic assault weapons and, later that year, convinced his nervous colleagues to embrace ethics reforms limiting outside income. Those reforms were embodied in Proposition 112, approved by voters in June 1990. Roberti, often accompanied by Maddy, stumped for the measure. By contrast, the speaker kept his distance, showing no enthusiasm for the reforms and disdainfully declaring he would do nothing to help it pass. Roberti also authored the implementing legislation for Proposition 112, without which the ethics reforms would have had no teeth.

But while Roberti has shown tremendous skill in wielding and keeping power, he has exhibited twinges of jealousy toward the speaker. He tweaked Brown in a 1984 letter for mailing fund-raising appeals that referred to himself as "Speaker of the California Legislature."

"We don't have a unicameral legislature in California – yet," Roberti huffed. "If the vote were taken in the state Senate, you wouldn't have the votes to be elected Speaker of the Legislature."

By November 1990, Brown was reportedly furious with Roberti for not doing enough to defeat Proposition 140's term limits. The two were barely on speaking terms as the new session began.

When George Deukmejian became governor, he was taken in by Willie Brown's reputation for legislative acumen and behaved as if the speaker was the source of all his troubles. As it turned out, Deukmejian's nemesis was Roberti. When the Senate rejected Deukmejian's first nominee for state finance director, Michael Franchetti, Deukmejian's relationship with Roberti quickly soured.

Relations between Deukmejian and Roberti were never worse than when the Senate in 1988 dealt the death blow to Deukmejian's effort to name his own successor. After the death of Democratic state Treasurer Jesse Unruh in 1987, Deukmejian named Dan Lungren, an obscure Republican congressman from his hometown of Long Beach, to fill the post. The plan was for Lungren to serve as treasurer for the remainder of Unruh's term, then run for governor or re-election as treasurer in 1990 or 1994, depending on Deukmejian's career plans. Brown and the Assembly went along, confirming Lungren. But Roberti called in every chit he had in defeating Lungren's confirmation in the Senate. After that defeat, Deukmejian displayed his ill humor thusly: "It is obvious that deals were made to ensure that Dan would be rejected in the Senate. It is also obvious that David Roberti is behaving more like a dictator than a statesman."

Deukmejian took the argument to the state Supreme Court, contending that Assembly confirmation was enough for Lungren to take office. But the court – dominated by Deukmejian appointees – rejected Deukmejian's arguments and upheld Lungren's rejection. In retrospect, the Democrats may now regret torpedoing Lungren as treasurer. Lungren went on to successfully run for attorney general, a position in which he is far more dangerous to Democratic positions and programs.

Roberti also exacted several pounds of flesh from Deukmejian over building a prison in downtown Los Angeles, a subplot that dominated much of Deukmejian's tenure as governor. Initially, Roberti favored the administration plan to build a prison in an industrial section of downtown near the largely Hispanic neighborhoods of East Los Angeles. When residents raised objections with Sen. Art Torres, and he took their side, Roberti reversed position.

The politics and heat of those battles masked something that cynics sometimes fail to see about David Roberti – his idealism. In the Los Angeles prison battle, nearly everyone in both parties grew ever more impatient as the fight dragged into a special session in an election year. But Roberti held to a genuine belief that Deukmejian and the Department of Corrections were running roughshod over the residents of East Los Angeles. Roberti was willing to stake his leadership post on that proposition. The more Deukmejian appeared to be shoving a prison down the residents' throats, the more irate Roberti became. The prison battle became, in Roberti's view, a class struggle between country club Republicans and immigrant Democrats. For Deukmejian, it was a fight between the crime-fighting Republicans and the crime-coddling Democrats.

Incoming Gov. Wilson has appeared more cognizant of Roberti's power and went out of his way to soothe legislative egos. During inaugural week, Wilson hosted a party for legislators and tried to help them ease the pain of Proposition 140, with its huge staff budget cuts. Wilson began his administration free of the Senate fireworks that marked the start of Deukmejian's. However, Roberti will doubtless remain a vigilant protector of the Senate's constitutional prerogatives, particularly its veto over gubernatorial appointees.

On another level, Roberti is the head of a huge organization that keeps the Senate lurching along. As pro tem, Roberti has built a highly skilled staff, ruled initially with an iron-fist by Jerry Zanelli, who as executive officer of the Senate Rules Committee became a czar over the lives of lesser senators and staffers. However, Roberti fell out with Zanelli, who became a lobbyist, and replaced him with Clifford Berg, an icy bureaucrat who has become the most powerful staffer in the Legislature, administering Roberti's huge staff, doling out office space and committee assignments to senators, and overseeing Roberti's policy analysts. Berg is known as one of the Capitol's "Valley Boys" – a clique of staffers from the San Fernando

Valley cutting across party lines (others have included Republican Jerry Haleva, now a lobbyist, and Democrat Barry Brokaw, top aide to Sen. Dan Boatwright).

Roberti has faced three senatorial challenges to his leadership post, emerging from each struggle even stronger than before. Where Brown has sometimes dallied when challenged and then overreacted, Roberti has not hesitated. He isolates his opponents quickly and ruthlessly cuts them down. But Roberti, not wanting to surround himself with malcontents, also brings the chastened rebels back into his fold after a measured time of exile. His challengers at various times – Paul Carpenter, John Garamendi and Dan Boatwright – were all later given committee chairmanships.

Despite Roberti's lack of media appeal, he has sometimes entertained ambitions of moving into statewide office. But it's more likely that he will continue as the Senate's top leader until well into the 1990s. During the 1990 election cycle, although he was not up for re-election, Roberti raised $4,935,217, doling most of it out for initiatives and causes.

PERSONAL: elected 1971; born May 4, 1939, in Los Angeles; home, Los Angeles; education, B.A. political science Loyola University, J.D. USC; wife, June Joyce; Roman Catholic.

CAREER: lawyer; law clerk; deputy attorney general 1965-1966; Assembly 1966-1971; Senate president pro tempore 1980.

COMMITTEES: ex officio member of all standing and joint committees; Rules (chair); Agriculture & Water Resources; Elections & Reapportionment; Judiciary; (Select) Infant & Child Care & Development; Motion Picture, TV, Commercial & Recording Industries; (Joint) Fire, Police, Emergency & Disaster Services; Refugee Resettlement, International Migration & Cooperative Development; Revision of the Penal Code; Rules.

OFFICES: Capitol, (916) 445-8390; district, 3800 Barham Blvd., 218, Hollywood 90068, (213) 876-5200.

REGISTRATION: 58.4% D, 28.9% R

1988 CAMPAIGN:	Roberti – D	67.8%	$3,920,485
	Tom Larkin – R	26.3%	$0

RATINGS:

AFL	PIRG	CLCV	NOW	CTA	CofC	CFB	NRA	FPAC
96%	90%	94%	80%	80%	29%	40%	0%	5%

KEY VOTES:

Divest S. Africa:	YES	Insurance reform:	YES	Child sick leave:	YES
Assault gun ban:	YES	Parent consent abortion:	YES	Ban AIDS discrim:	YES
Clean Air Act:	YES	Ban insure donations:	–	Extend death penalty:	YES
Lmt product tort:	YES	Ban offshore oil:	YES	Restrict abortion funds:	YES
Lower alcohol std:	YES	Basic health care:	YES	Oil spill prevent:	YES
Ethics reform:	YES	Work cancer stds:	YES	Earthquake insure:	YES

Art Torres (D)
24th Senate District

East Los Angeles is an area where one is just as likely to hear people speaking Spanish as English. More than 70 percent of the residents in cities such as South Pasadena, Eagle Rock, Maywood, Commerce and Vernon are Hispanic. This is also the Senate district with the lowest number of registered voters – further testament to its reputation as a haven for new immigrants, both legal and illegal.

In Art Torres, the residents of East Los Angeles have a bright, articulate and passionate representative. He is mediagenic, one of the best speakers in the Legislature, a devoted father and an affable-but-shrewd political operator. It is those qualities that for years have prompted political insiders to anoint Torres as the Hispanic with the best chance of being elected to statewide office.

Art Torres

Yet Torres' political future has been clouded by personal problems, including a divorce and two arrests for drunken driving within 14 months. At the time of his first arrest in 1988, Torres was carrying a bill to take away the licenses of minors convicted of alcohol and drug-related offenses. Torres, who publicly confessed to being an alcoholic and who went through treatment, had no problem being re-elected in 1990, gaining 69 percent of the vote.

Torres is ambitious and when a court-created seat on the Los Angeles County Board of Supervisors came up for election in early 1991, he entered a crowded field in the hopes of becoming the first Hispanic to sit on that powerful board in this century. For Torres, it was more than an attempt to win the vaunted seat. It was a test of his personal appeal in light of his problems and he met with mixed results. Although Torres was one of the top two vote-getters in the primary election, he lost the run-off by 10 percentage points to Los Angeles City Councilwoman Gloria Molina, who once worked for him.

Still, in a Ted Kennedy-like way, Torres is courted by national Democrats for endorsements. He has the ability to appeal to Hispanic voters and mainstream Anglos. Torres also remains an active and effective legislator. He has fought for causes of importance to Hispanic voters, such as bilingual education and to block the siting of a prison in his district, and he has seized on statewide issues. He has pressed for a crackdown on the disposal of toxic wastes, to improve child nutrition, to ban the importation of foreign produce tainted with pesticide residues, to raise the minimum wage and to set up a system to destroy vicious dogs and fine their owners.

PERSONAL: elected 1982; born Sept. 24, 1946, in Los Angeles; home, Los Angeles; education, B.A. government UC Santa Cruz, J.D. UC Davis; John F.

Kennedy teaching fellow Harvard University; divorced; children, Joaquin and Danielle.

CAREER: lawyer; Assembly 1974-1982.

COMMITTEES: Toxics & Public Safety Management (chair); Appropriations; Education; Elections; Governmental Organization; Insurance, Claims & Corporations; Judiciary; (Select) Pacific Rim (chair); Bilingual Education; Business Development; (Joint) Science & Technology.

OFFICES: Capitol, (916) 445-3456; district, 107 S. Broadway, 2105, Los Angeles 90012, (213) 620-2529.

REGISTRATION: 65.6% D; 23% R;

1990 CAMPAIGN:	Torres – D	69%	$753,582
	Keith F. Marsh – R	25%	$0
1986 CAMPAIGN:	Torres – D	72%	$378,993
	Lee Prentiss – R	24%	$0

RATINGS:

AFL	PIRG	CLCV	NOW	CTA	CofC	CFB	NRA	FPAC
95%	95%	100%	100%	99%	25%	20%	0%	0%

KEY VOTES:

Divest S. Africa:	YES	Insurance Reform:	YES	Child sick leave:	YES
Assault gun ban:	YES	Parent consent abortion:	YES	Ban AIDS discrim:	YES
Clean Air Act:	YES	Ban insure donations:	YES	Extend death penalty:	YES
Lmt product tort:	YES	Ban offshore oil:	YES	Restrict abortion funds:	NO
Lower alcohol std:	–	Basic health care:	YES	Oil spill prevent:	YES
Ethics reform:	YES	Work cancer stds:	YES	Earthquake insure:	YES

William R. Leonard Jr.(R)
25th Senate District

This district was carved out of cactus and rock by Democrats trying to gerrymander right-wing guru Bill Richardson into retirement. He did not see it that way and easily won the seat again in 1984 before deciding to retire on his own accord four years later. The district takes in the upscale end of the eastern Los Angeles basin, including Redlands and Claremont, then bridges the rugged San Gabriel and San Bernardino mountains to span the Mojave Desert. Running north along the eastern edge of the Sierra, the district includes the remote towns of Bishop, Big Pine and other Owens Valley communities that depend on ranching, mining and tourism for their existence. The district is so immense that it abuts a district represented by a senator from Stockton.

Bill Leonard

Richardson's successor is William Leonard, who is both smoother and more intellectual than the gun-toting Richardson. But Leonard's conservatism is just as rigid – with some innovations. The San Bernardino native son won the seat after serving 10 years in the Assembly. He had originally come to Sacramento as one of the "Proposition 13 babies," elected the same year the property tax limitation initiative passed. His father, William Sr., has been a longtime figure in area politics and serves on the state Transportation Commission. After his Senate election, Leonard successfully passed off his Assembly seat to former aide Paul Woodruff.

With his intellect and gentlemanly ease, Leonard has moved swiftly through the ranks of Senate Republicans. He was elevated to the second ranking position as Senate Republican Caucus Chairman soon after John Doolittle vacated the post to run for Congress in 1990. As such, Leonard is responsible for the Senate GOP election machinery. He did not prove particularly effective in saving former Senate Republican leader Jim Nielsen from himself in the 1990 election, but then, probably no one could have and Leonard's colleagues do not seem to blame him for that defeat. It could be a different story if the GOP loses one or two more Senate seats.

As a legislator, Leonard is unwavering in his opposition to gun control and is intensely anti-abortion. He has opposed anything that looks like a tax increase. But unlike some of his Assembly Republicans, Leonard is not anti-government.

While in the Assembly, Leonard for years introduced legislation to ban the internal combustion engine. He honed the idea into a serious bill that won Assembly approval in 1987. That measure would have phased in clean-burning methanol vehicles in the 1990s. The bill was supported by major auto manufacturers. But after opposition from oil companies, the bill was buried in the Senate by Democratic Sen. Ralph Dills of Gardena, chairman of the Governmental Organization Committee. Leonard also has supported Democratic efforts to toughen smog laws, a subject of major concern to the eastern end of the Los Angeles basin he represents.

Leonard quickly asserted himself in his first Senate term, authoring SB 408, which lowered the drunken driving blood alcohol level standard to 0.08 percent. He also authored SB 1241 to end rent control laws on new mobile home spaces, a measure that displayed his economic conservatism.

In 1990, Leonard succeeded in moving through the Senate SCA 1, which would have allowed local school districts to approve bonds with a majority vote instead of two-thirds. The constitutional amendment was defeated largely by Republicans in the Assembly who pulled the measure down on a 43-28 vote. However, some months later, Leonard's idea was enthusiastically embraced by incoming Gov. Pete Wilson, who prominently mentioned it in his first state-of-the-state address.

At the start of the 1991-92 session, Leonard's bill introductions were tilted toward tougher criminal laws, including SB 136 that would suspend the driver's license of anyone 21 or older for six months upon conviction of any drug violation, and SB 139 that would give law enforcement authorities the power to seize the assets of anyone caught cultivating or harvesting marijuana. Also at the start of the 1991-92 session, he was appointed to a seat on the powerful Appropriations Committee.

Leonard has a promising future in the Legislature. But with term limits forcing him to make career choices, he has said he will consider running for one of the new congressional seats that will emerge from the 1991 reapportionment.

PERSONAL: elected 1988; born Oct. 29, 1947, in San Bernardino; home, Big Bear; education, B.A. history UC Irvine, graduate work CSU Sacramento; wife, Sherry Boldizsar; children, Michael, Tim and Jacob; Presbyterian.

CAREER: Real estate management; director San Bernardino Valley Municipal Water District 1974-1978; Assembly 1978-1988; Republican Caucus Chairman 1990.

COMMITTEES: Housing & Urban Affairs (vice chair); Appropriations; Industrial Relations; Toxics and Public Safety Management (vice chair); (Select) Business Development (chair); State Procurement & Expenditure Practices; (Joint) School Facilities.

OFFICES: Capitol (916) 445-3688, FAX (916) 327-2272; district, 400 N. Mountain Ave., 109, Upland 91786, (714) 946-4889.

REGISTRATION: 37.6% D, 52% R

1988 CAMPAIGN: Leonard – R   66% $402,887
                   Sandra Hester – D   34% $70,153

RATINGS:

AFL	PIRG	CLCV	NOW	CTA	CofC	CFB	NRA	FPAC
20%	40%	24%	10%	70%	83%	80%	100%	95%

KEY VOTES: (includes votes in the Assembly)

Divest S. Africa:	NO	Insurance reform:	NO	Child sick leave:	NO
Assault gun ban:	NO	Parent consent abortion:	YES	Ban AIDS discrim:	NO
Clean Air Act:	NO	Ban insure donations:	NO	Extend death penalty:	YES
Lmt product tort:	YES	Ban offshore oil:	NO	Restrict abortion funds:	YES
Lower alcohol std:	YES	Basic health care:	NO	Oil spill prevent:	YES
Ethics reform:	YES	Work cancer stds:	NO	Earthquake insure:	YES

Charles M. Calderon (D)
26th Senate District

This eastern Los Angeles County district is mostly Hispanic, taking in Alhambra, San Gabriel, Monterey Park, Rosemead, Montebello, Pico Rivera, Irwindale and part of Whittier. The district also has a sizable and growing Asian population that could eventually produce an Asian-American legislator. The Southern California Edison mega-utility is headquartered in the district, as is a large gravel pit that the city of Irwindale wanted to convert into a football stadium for the Los Angeles Raiders. It is also the home of the Operating Industries Inc. dump, a mountain of Los Angeles' garbage sitting astride the Pomona freeway that is on the federal Superfund list as one of the most polluted corners of the U.S.

Joe Montoya held this Senate seat for 12 years and probably would have been re-elected indefinitely. But Montoya, one of the Capitol's biggest "juice players," was convicted on federal bribery and racketeering charges in 1990, the first legislator

imprisoned in the FBI's on-going "Brispec" undercover investigation.

During Montoya's travails, an ambitious Assembly member, Charles Calderon, moved from Monterey
Park to Whittier and in so doing perfectly positioned
himself to grab off Montoya's seat. Calderon had
little trouble winning the seat in an April 1990 special
election. His only formidable opponent, Assemblywoman Sally Tanner, decided not to run.

Calderon, an ex-prosecutor, could not have left
the Assembly at a better time. He had fallen in with
four other youngish Assembly members who hung
out at Paragary's restaurant in midtown Sacramento.

Charles Calderon

The group eventually plotted the overthrow of Speaker
Willie Brown and became known as the "Gang of Five." At the start of the 1989
session, the rebels formed a brief alliance with Republican Assembly leader Ross
Johnson that had Republicans voting for Calderon for speaker. The effort failed.

Calderon had no trouble winning a full Senate term in November 1990. But not
even a year into his new job, Calderon ran for the Los Angeles County Board of
Supervisors in January 1991. His theory was that the San Gabriel Valley held the
balance of votes in the new, court-ordered Hispanic seat. While his theory may have
been right, he did not make the run-off.

Aside from his involvement in the endless petty intrigues of the Capitol, Calderon
is generally a competent legislator. His chief legislative accomplishment has been
in shepherding interstate banking legislation through to Gov. George Deukmejian's
signature – and dodging obstacles thrown in his way by Sen. Alan Robbins, D-
Encino, and the savings & loan industry, then riding on the peak of its clout.
Calderon's bill opened California to out-of-state banks over a phased-in period.

PERSONAL: elected 1990 (special election); born March 12, 1950, in
Montebello, Calif.; home, Whittier; education, B.A. political science CSU Los
Angeles, J.D. UC Davis; divorced; children, Charles and Matthew James; unaffiliated
Christian.

CAREER: lawyer; city attorney's prosecutor; school board member 1979-
1982; legislative aide to Assembly members Richard Alatorre and Jack Fenton;
special consultant to Secretary of State March Fong Eu; Assembly 1982-1990.

COMMITTEES: Veterans Affairs (chair); Housing; Health & Human Services; Local Government; Banking & Commerce.

OFFICES: Capitol, (916) 327-8315; district, 11001 E. Valley Mall Dr., 204, El
Monte 91731, (818) 450-6185.

REGISTRATION: 60.1% D, 29.6% R

1990 CAMPAIGN:			
Calderon – D		62.8%	$106,931
Joe Urquidi – R		32%	$1,190

APRIL 10, 1990, SPECIAL ELECTION:

Calderon – D	68.1%	$166,039
Joe Urquidi – R	27.1%	$6,104

RATINGS: (scores partially based on Assembly votes)

AFL	PIRG	CLCV	NOW	CTA	CofC	CFB	NRA	FPAC
91%	91%	71%	80%	93%	25%	40%	13%	10%

KEY VOTES: (includes votes in the Assembly)

Divest S. Africa:	YES	Insurance reform:	–	Child sick leave:	YES
Assault gun ban·	YES	Parent consent abortion:	YES	Ban AIDS discrim:	YES
Clean Air Act:	YES	Cutting old trees:	NO	Extend death penalty:	YES
Lmt product tort:	YES	Ban offshore oil:	YES	Restrict abortion funds:	NO
Lower alcohol std:	YES	Basic health care:	YES	Oil spill prevent:	YES
Ethics reform:	YES	Work cancer stds:	–	Earthquake insure:	YES

Bill Greene (D)

27th Senate District

South-central Los Angeles is among the poorest and most crime-beleaguered areas of the state, and the 27th Senate District lies in its heart. Sandwiched between the Harbor and Long Beach freeways, the district includes South Gate, Compton, Huntington Park, Bell and Cudahy. More than half the residents are black; almost 40 percent are Hispanic. Gangs roam freely in this district. By midyear 1989, the area had the highest homicide rate in Los Angeles, with 177 killings out of 395 committed in the entire city.

Bill Greene

The district's troubles are mirrored in the man who represents it, Bill Greene. A bombastic senator with a gravely voice and short fuse, Greene has one of the worst attendance records in the Legislature. In 1989, he missed more than 40 percent of his floor and committee votes, an average that only told part of the story. He has missed most of the key votes on major legislation in the last three years. Although he was around to vote for David Roberti's bill banning semiautomatic assault weapons, he missed the vote on Mike Roos' bill that was the second part of that legislative package.

In midsummer 1989, Greene finally admitted what Capitol insiders had long suspected – he was an alcoholic. Greene was arrested for drunken driving in Turlock, after being spotted urinating beside his car. He served two days in jail, then admitted himself into a 28-day treatment program, only to check out after two days. Shortly before the Legislature resumed for its late summer session, Greene entered the Betty Ford Center in Palm Springs.

A former labor organizer, Greene has been chairman of the Industrial Relations Committee and a member of the powerful Governmental Organization Committee that oversees gambling and liquor legislation. However, Greene has been chiefly noted not for his legislation – which is negligible – but for his severe tongue-lashings directed at witnesses coming before his committees.

By being out of commission for much of 1989, he missed having any involvement in an issue in which he had a long-standing interest – workers compensation reform. Greene lent his able staff to Assemblyman Burt Margolin, D-Los Angeles, who engineered the pact signed by the governor. After he emerged from treatment, Greene said he was turning over a new leaf and would apply himself to legislation.

Greene has not always shown much regard for the niceties of campaign finance laws. He has never had to worry about re-election, racking up 87 percent of the vote in 1988. Instead, he has operated his campaign fund almost like a personal bank, paying himself $102,442 out of campaign funds in the last decade with scant explanation on his disclosure forms.

He has been fined twice by the state Fair Political Practices Commission for running afoul of campaign finance laws, the most serious offense in 1980, when Greene was fined $36,000 for using $5,208 in campaign funds to pay his personal income taxes. He paid the FPPC fine out of campaign funds. Why does the district continue to re-elect him? With an 83.5 percent Democratic registration – the highest in a Senate district – Greene seems to have little to worry about with his voters.

At the start of the 1991-92 legislative session, rumors continued to abound in the state Capitol that Greene would quit the Legislature before his term expires. He had a heart attack soon after his discharge from the Betty Ford Center and has remained in ill-health. Although the Legislature reconvened in December 1990, Greene didn't appear until mid-March of 1991.

PERSONAL: elected 1975 (special election); born Nov. 15, 1931, in Kansas City, Mo.; home, Los Angeles; USAF; education, attended Lincoln Junior College, Kansas City, University of Michigan; wife, Yvonne La Fargue; children, Alisa Rochelle and Jan Andrea.

CAREER: first black clerk of the Assembly; consultant to Speaker Jesse Unruh; legislative Assembly assistant to Lt. Gov. Mervyn M. Dymally; lobbyist for a labor union; Assembly 1967-1975.

COMMITTEES: Industrial Relations (chair); Elections; Governmental Organization; Revenue & Taxation; (Select) Governmental Efficiency; State Procurement & Expenditure Practices; (Joint) Arts; Legislative Budget.

OFFICES: Capitol, (916) 445-2104, FAX (916) 327-5703; district, 9300 S. Broadway, Los Angeles 90003, (213) 620-5600.

REGISTRATION: 83.5% D, 9.3% R

1988 CAMPAIGN:

Greene – D		87.4%	$308,654
Johnnie Neely – R		9.6%	$0

RATINGS:

AFL	PIRG	CLCV	NOW	CTA	CofC	CFB	NRA	FPAC
94%	50%	82%	70%	100%	13%	0%	0%	0%

KEY VOTES:

Divest S. Africa:	YES	Insurance reform:	YES	Child sick leave:	–
Assault gun ban:	YES	Parent consent abortion:	–	Ban AIDS discrim:	–
Clean Air Act:	–	Ban insure donations:	–	Extend death penalty:	–
Lmt product tort:	–	Ban offshore oil:	–	Restrict abortion funds:	NO
Lower alcohol std:	–	Basic health care:	YES	Oil spill prevent:	–
Ethics reform:	–	Work cancer stds:	YES	Earthquake insure:	YES

Diane E. Watson (D)
28th Senate District

This southwest-central Los Angeles district is a mixture of new-money harbor condos and old working-class neighborhoods. Roughly half black, the district includes Inglewood, Hawthorne, Lawndale, Venice, Marina del Rey and Los Angeles International Airport. Democrat Diane Watson has never had any trouble getting re-elected here, although she once introduced a bill to eject predominantly white Lawndale from her district.

Watson, who spent three short years on the Los Angeles school board as one of its most vocal (and most televised) members in the 1970s during a period of high racial tensions involving the district's forced busing plan, made a splash when she first came to

Diane Watson

Sacramento in 1975. She was the first black woman elected to the Senate, a club heretofore comprised primarily of old white men set in their ways (symbolized by the high leather chairs in the back of their chambers). In those years, she seemed to specialize in crashing the party and opening the windows. But Sacramento has gotten used to her. Most of the old boys have retired or died, and many of the more recent newcomers are better at grandstanding than Watson.

Though she can still cause havoc, Watson doesn't generate much warmth from her colleagues and has increasingly found herself isolated with few allies. She has crossed swords with her colleagues on numerous issues, ranging from welfare revision to setting ethical standards – and lost. Her snits with Democratic Sen. Bill Lockyer are fabled, with the two trading insults across the dais in the Judiciary Committee. She is also known as one of the most difficult bosses in the Capitol, treating legislative staffers with disdain. Watson has, however, shown her loyalty to David Roberti during leadership tussles, and he has returned the loyalty – even to the point of paying off her delinquent credit cards.

As chairwoman of the Health and Human Services Committee, Watson oversees the welfare system in the state, enabling her to position herself as one of the chief critics of Republican social program slashing. In 1985, she filibustered a bipartisan legislative package for major welfare reforms (dubbed GAIN) that set up a "workfare" program for 190,000 recipients, most of them single mothers. Watson called it a "forced labor program," and held a lengthy committee hearing in the waning hours of that year's session, but the bill passed over her objections.

With Pete Wilson as governor, Watson has vowed to block his welfare cutting proposals in her committee. "We had a wonderful two or three days with him. The honeymoon is over," she huffed not long after his inaugural. However, her vows may only prompt her colleagues to make end runs around her.

Her dogma notwithstanding, Watson has looked for new solutions to some of the more vexing problems of her urban district. At the start of the 1991-92 session she introduced SB 224, which would enact procedures for the establishment of graffiti abatement districts with taxing powers to attack vandalism. And she has fought hard to protect Family Planning funds.

Watson's career has been marked by brushes with scandal. The circumstances surrounding her Ph.D. in education administration were called into question in 1989 when the Sacramento district attorney's office investigated allegations that she had used state staff and equipment to prepare her dissertation. District Attorney Steve White concluded that legislative record keeping was so shoddy that the allegations could not be proved or disproved and the matter was dropped.

She has not escaped scrutiny from the Fair Political Practices Commission. In December 1989, Watson agreed to pay a penalty of $21,075 for using campaign funds to pay for such expenses as a family reunion, credit card charges, airline tickets and a party. Watson takes numerous junkets worldwide from trade associations and others with business in the Legislature. She routinely uses her campaign fund for a wide range of expenses not traditionally associated with campaigning – like buying flowers for friends. She voted against the 1989 ethics reform package that ultimately tightened the rules for such spending, telling her colleagues that it "went too far." During an ethics workshop for senators in January 1991, Watson made clear her standards. "We're not ordinary people," she said.

PERSONAL: elected 1978; born Nov. 12, 1933, in Los Angeles; home, Los Angeles; education, A.A. Los Angeles City College, B.A. education UCLA, M.S. school psychology CSU Los Angeles, Ph.D. educational administration Claremont Graduate School; single; Roman Catholic.

CAREER: teacher; school administrator; textbook author; Los Angeles Unified School District board 1975-1978.

COMMITTEES: Health & Human Services (chair); Budget & Fiscal Review; Education; Judiciary; Toxics & Public Safety Management; (Select) Children & Youth; Citizen Participation in Government; (Special) Developmental Disabilities & Mental Health.

OFFICES: Capitol, (916) 445-5215, FAX (916) 327-2599; district, 4401 Crenshaw Blvd., 300, Los Angeles 90043, (213) 295-6655.

REGISTRATION: 73% D, 18.2% R

1990 CAMPAIGN: Watson – D   85.2% $291,369

1986 CAMPAIGN: Watson – D   72% $304886
                  Armand Vaquer – R   21% $1.925

RATINGS:

AFL	PIRG	CLCV	NOW	CTA	CofC	CFB	NRA	FPAC
96%	75%	93%	70%	98%	25%	20%	0%	5%

KEY VOTES:

Divest S. Africa:	YES	Insurance reform:	YES	Child sick leave:	YES
Assault gun ban:	YES	Parent consent abortion:	NO	Ban AIDS discrim:	YES
Clean Air Act:	YES	Ban insure donations:	NO	Extend death penalty:	NO
Lmt product tort:	–	Ban offshore oil:	YES	Restrict abortion funds:	NO
Lower alcohol std:	NO	Basic health care:	YES	Oil spill prevent:	YES
Ethics reform:	NO	Work cancer stds:	YES	Earthquake insure:	YES

Robert G. Beverly (R)

29th Senate District

Hooking along the Los Angeles Harbor shoreline, on through the Palos Verdes Peninsula, the 29th Senate District takes in the beach towns of surfing safari yore, including El Segundo, Redondo Beach, Palos Verdes, San Pedro and parts of Long Beach. In more recent years, however, property in the district has become too valuable for surfers' huts and the once-seedy beach towns are building glitzy hotels and malls. The district also has a base of high-tech industries, oil refineries, tourism and fishing.

Republican Bob Beverly, a former GOP leader in the Assembly, has never had much trouble holding this seat, though Republican Assemblyman Gerald

Bob Beverly

Felando has long coveted it, leading to stormy relations between the two. That aside, Beverly is the insider's insider in the Capitol. He is one of two GOP representatives serving on the Senate Rules Committee; he sits on the cushy Governmental Organization Committee, the overseer of liquor and gambling legislation; and he is vice chairman of Appropriations.

Beverly is generally considered a moderate. He was a key swing vote for David Roberti's bill banning semiautomatic assault weapons, but he has voted with conservatives on such issues as divesting the state from investments in South Africa. Labeling Beverly, however, does not do justice to the role he plays in the Senate. He shows himself motivated to a great extent not by ideology but by personal relationships. Beverly often presides over the Senate, his quick rulings and even temper at the rostrum are richly valued by Roberti and his colleagues.

Beverly may be in the minority, but he is certainly in the club that runs the Legislature. When Sen. Bill Lockyer crashed a meeting in David Roberti's office in the spring of 1989 to complain about secret budget deals, he found Beverly among those inside. When Assembly Speaker Willie Brown went to Lloyd's of London in 1986, among those he took with him was Beverly. The jovial Beverly carries water for a lot of people. He authored the bill for Gov. George Deukmejian that rebated $1.1 billion to taxpayers. A 1987 Beverly bill restored $86.6 million in aid to the state's urban school districts previously cut by Deukmejian.

Other, lesser bills by Beverly are worthy of note. In the waning days of the 1989 session, he pushed a measure allowing members of the Signal Hill City Council to circumvent conflict-of-interest laws so they could vote on a proposed development that could boost their property values. He has pushed hard on a measure to exempt certain over-the-counter stock transactions from state regulation. One of the most hotly contested measures behind the scenes was a Beverly bill to exempt employees of mortgage banking firms from having to hold a real estate license.

At the start of 1991, Beverly reportedly sought appointment to the Board of Equalization seat held by Paul Carpenter, who was convicted on federal corruption charges. But Beverly was passed over by Gov. Pete Wilson in favor of political neophyte Matt Fong, the GOP son of Democratic Secretary of State March Fong Eu.

PERSONAL: elected 1976; born July 1, 1925, in Belmont, Mass.; home, Manhattan Beach; USMC 1943-1946; education, attended UCLA 1946-1948, J.D. Loyola University; wife, Bettelu; children, Bill, Bob, Brian and Barbara; Protestant.

CAREER: city attorney; Manhattan Beach City Council, mayor 1958-1967; Assembly 1967-1976.

COMMITTEES: Appropriations (vice chair); Rules; Banking & Commerce; Elections; Governmental Organization; Veteran's Affairs; (Select) Business Development; Calif. Wine Industry; Maritime Industry; Motion Picture, TV, Commercial & Recording Industries; (Special) Solid & Hazardous Waste; (Joint) Fisheries & Aquaculture; Legislative Audit; Legislative Budget; Revision of the Penal Code; Rules; State's Economy.

OFFICES: Capitol, (916) 445-6447; district, 1611 S. Pacific Coast Highway, 102, Redondo Beach 90277, (213) 540-1611; 638 S. Beacon St., 508, San Pedro 90731, (213) 548-0651.

REGISTRATION: 40.2% D, 48.4% R

1988 CAMPAIGN:

Beverly – R		67.2%	$248,232
Jack Hachmeister – D		29.5%	$0

RATINGS:

AFL	PIRG	CLCV	NOW	CTA	CofC	CFB	NRA	FPAC
53%	60%	56%	60%	96%	63%	60%	40%	50%

KEY VOTES:

Divest S. Africa:	NO	Insurance reform:	NO	Child sick leave:	NO
Assault gun ban:	YES	Parent consent abortion:	YES	Ban AIDS discrim:	YES
Clean Air Act:	YES	Ban insure donations:	NO	Extend death penalty:	YES
Lmt product tort:	YES	Ban offshore oil:	YES	Restrict abortion funds:	NO
Lower alcohol std:	–	Basic health care:	YES	Oil spill prevent:	YES
Ethics reform:	–	Work cancer stds:	–	Earthquake insure:	YES

Ralph C. Dills (D)

30th Senate District

This Los Angeles County district is a blur of used car lots, tacky shopping centers and vast stretches of old and new working-class neighborhoods spanning Gardena, Compton, Lawndale, Lynwood, Harbor City and part of Long Beach. Stand-up comics joke about this part of the Los Angeles basin.

Ralph Dills

It is hard to think of the Legislature without Gardena's Ralph Dills, who arrived in the Assembly during the second term of Franklin D. Roosevelt and who once was known mostly as one of the Dills Brothers. His brother, Clayton, was an assemblyman until his death. Another was a Capitol elevator operator. He is not the oldest legislator; that distinction goes to Al Alquist of San Jose.

Dills has had several careers, nearly all of them lengthy. He was a saxophone player working jazz clubs in the 1930s, then a teacher. An organizer in Democratic New Deal worker leagues, he won an Assembly seat in 1938. In his first 10 years in the Assembly, Dills authored the legislation creating California State University, Long Beach. He quit to accept a judicial appointment in 1949, then returned to Sacramento as a senator in 1967 in the first class of "full-time" legislators. "He's quite a guy!" his campaign literature proclaims.

Dills became chairman of the powerful Governmental Organization Committee in 1970, a panel with an ironclad grip on liquor, horse racing, labor unions, oil leases and gambling legislation. Dills has long been known as the liquor industry's best friend in Sacramento. He has pushed legislation to give beer and wine distributors regional monopolies – bills vetoed with a vengeance by Gov. George Deukmejian as reeking with special-interest odor.

Dills also has helped bury anti-smog bills, incurring the wrath of environmentalists, who are left wondering why the bills went to his committee in the first place. At the start of the 1991-92 session, Dills was given a seat on the Revenue & Taxation Committee, where he has been a voice to maintain tax loopholes for various interests, including the snack food, newspaper and candy industries.

As the most senior senator, Dills is entitled by protocol to preside over the floor sessions of the Senate, a largely ceremonial post but with power to gum up the works. His parliamentary calls and flowery mannerisms have irritated some of his younger colleagues, who have persuaded him to preside less often. Dills looks like a caricature of a politician – or used car salesman – from a bygone age, with blue-rinsed hair, outrageously colored polyester suits and unfashionably wide ties. He has responded by toning down his dress a little.

Dills does not visit his district as often as most of his colleagues visit theirs, preferring to make his real home in the Sacramento suburbs. His voters do not seem to mind for Dills had no problem getting re-elected. But whether Democratic re-apportionment drafters have the desire to give him a safe district for another decade remains an open question.

PERSONAL: elected 1966; born Feb. 10, 1910, Rosston, Tex.; home, Gardena; education, graduate of Compton College and UCLA, M.A. from USC, J.D. Loyola University; wife, Elizabeth "Bette" Lee; three children, Leighton, Wendy and Gregory.

CAREER: saxophone player; teacher; lawyer; Assembly 1938-1949; municipal judge 1952-1966.

COMMITTEES: Governmental Organization (chair); Appropriations; Education; Revenue & Taxation; Veterans' Affairs; (Select) Calif. Wine Industry; Governmental Efficiency; Mobile Homes; Pacific Rim; Source Reduction & Recycling Market Development; (Special) State's Economy (chair); Solid & Hazardous Waste; (Joint) Courthouse Financing & Construction; Fairs Allocation & Classification; Refugee Resettlement, International Migration & Cooperative Development; Rules.

OFFICES: Capitol, (916) 445-5953; district, 16921 S. Western Ave., 201, Gardena 90247, (213) 324-4969.

REGISTRATION: 66.4% D, 23.8 % R

1990 CAMPAIGN:	Dills – D	68.3%	$615,454
	Timothy Poling – R	31.7%	$0
1986 CAMPAIGN:	Dills – D	72%	$432,111
	Anthony Gray – R	25%	$2,325

RATINGS:

AFL	PIRG	CLCV	NOW	CTA	CofC	CFB	NRA	FPAC
92%	90%	56%	100%	99%	50%	20%	0%	24%

KEY VOTES:

Divest S. Africa:	YES	Insurance reform:	YES	Child sick leave:	YES
Assault gun ban:	YES	Parent consent abortion:	NO	Ban AIDS discrim:	YES
Clean Air Act:	YES	Ban insure donations:	YES	Extend death penalty:	YES
Lmt product tort:	YES	Ban offshore oil:	NO	Restrict abortion funds:	NO
Lower alcohol std:	–	Basic health care:	YES	Oil spill prevent:	YES
Ethics reform:	YES	Work cancer stds:	YES	Earthquake insure:	–

Frank Hill (R)

31st Senate District

Shaped something like a map of Vietnam, the 31st District bulges and stretches from Los Angeles County through Orange County, stopping just short of San Juan Capistrano. The district takes in La Habra, West Covina, part of Whittier, La Habra Heights, El Toro – and its Marine Corps base – Mission Viejo and Laguna Niguel. It was once the heart of orange grove country. Though there are still vegetable farms and groves tucked here and there, the district is now a vast stretch of housing tracts, high-tech industries, military bases and shopping centers.

For years, the district was represented by the corpulent, good-natured Republican Bill Campbell. But in 1989 – less than a year after being re-elected – Campbell abruptly announced he would resign to become president of the California Manufacturers Association. In so doing, he set off a sharp free-for-all among Republicans for his seat (Campbell has not left the Capitol scene; he frequently takes advantage of his ex-member floor privileges to schmooze with his former colleagues in both houses).

Frank Hill

Two Assembly Republican "cavemen" – so dubbed for their right-leaning politics – were among the crowded field of eight in a 1990 special election to fill the seat: Assemblymen Gilbert Ferguson, the ex-Marine tormentor of Tom Hayden, and Frank Hill, a young politician with slick black hair who looks like the man on the wedding cake. Ferguson moved into the district in December 1989 soon after Campbell's resignation. But Hill got the immediate backing of Assembly Republican leader Ross Johnson, who also lives in the senate district and could have run for the seat. Better financed, Hill bested Ferguson in a special primary. The April 10, 1990, run-off was a foregone conclusion against the top Democratic vote-getter, Janice Graham, a retired Laguna Hills teacher.

Hill should have a bright political future. But a cloud continues to shadow him. Hill's office was one of the four searched in 1988 by federal agents as part of its undercover "sting" investigation into influence peddling in the state Capitol. Hill reportedly remains subject to the probe. Although his opponents attempted to capitalize on the investigation in the Senate special election, the voters of this district were evidently unimpressed.

The 35-year-old Hill has been in the Legislature since he was 28 and he is generally well-liked on both sides of the aisle. He has been in politics even longer, having served as the Whittier office manager for former Rep. Wayne Grisham and as an aide in Washington, D.C., to then-U.S. Sen. S.I. Hayakawa. In Sacramento, Hill used his political skills to move quickly into a leadership post among Assembly Republicans, eventually serving as their liaison with Gov. George Deukmejian.

In the Senate, Hill moved quickly to establish credentials as a legislating legislator. He authored a mandatory earthquake insurance bill, SB 2902, signed by Deukmejian. After an opinion by Legislative Counsel Bion Gregory that the mandatory clause of the new law was unenforceable, Hill introduced a new bill to make the coverage mandatory for all owners of the state's 6.5 million homes.

Hill gained some statewide exposure as a leader in the successful initiative drive to declare English the state's official language in 1986. While he supports more education funding in general, he also has become known for his opposition to mandatory bilingual education, arguing for local control over those decisions.

Hill is considered a strong voice for the liquor industry in the Capitol. In the closing days of the 1989 session, he made an impassioned floor speech in the Assembly against fellow Republican Bill Leonard's bill lowering the blood-alcohol standard to 0.08 for drunken driving. The bill passed overwhelmingly and was signed by Deukmejian.

PERSONAL: elected 1990 (special election); born Feb. 19, 1954, in Whittier; home, Whittier; education, A.A. political science Mt. San Antonio College in Walnut; B.A. political science UCLA; M.A. public administration Pepperdine University; wife, Faye; children, Jenny and Greg; Episcopalian.

CAREER: Washington office manager U.S. Sen. S.I. Hayakawa 1976-1978; field director Rep. Wayne Grisham 1978-1982; Assembly 1982-1990.

COMMITTEES: Budget & Fiscal Review (vice chair); Governmental Organization; Local Government.

OFFICES: Capitol, (916) 445-2848, FAX (916) 943-2690; district, 15820 Whittier Blvd., H, Whittier 90603, (213) 947-3021; 111 Pacifica, 210, Irvine 92718, (714) 727-9544.

REGISTRATION: 35.1% D, 54.5% R

APRIL 10, 1990 SPECIAL ELECTION:

Hill – R	60.8%	$701,053
Janice Graham – D	35.6%	$39,270

RATINGS: (scores partially based on Assembly votes)

AFL	PIRG	CLCV	NOW	CTA	CofC	CFB	NRA	FPAC
13%	35%	50%	20%	66%	42%	60%	100%	80%

KEY VOTES: (includes votes in the Assembly)

Divest S. Africa:	–	Insurance reform:	NO	Child sick leave:	NO
Assault gun ban:	NO	Parent consent abortion:	YES	Ban AIDS discrim:	NO
Clean Air Act:	YES	Cutting old trees:	YES	Extend death penalty:	YES
Lmt product tort:	YES	Ban offshore oil:	NO	Restrict abortion funds:	YES
Lower alcohol std:	NO	Basic health care:	NO	Oil spill prevent:	YES
Ethics reform:	YES	Work cancer stds:	NO	Earthquake insure:	YES

Edward R. Royce (R)

32nd Senate District

Curving through Orange County like a horseshoe, the 32nd Senate District has traditionally voted Republican, but with a growing Asian and Hispanic population it could prove a politically volatile area in the future. The district takes in Westminster, Stanton, Fullerton and parts of Anaheim and Santa Ana. It was supposed to be a "Hispanic seat," according to the Democratic drafters of a 1982 reapportionment plan. Instead, it went to an Anglo Republican, and a very conservative one at that.

Winning his first elective office in 1982, Ed Royce is one of the quieter members of the Senate. He seldom speaks during Senate debates and generally seems to stay out of harm's way. He got the seat after he unexpectedly won a GOP primary in 1982. Royce has said he will run for Congress in 1992 to fill the seat held by William Dannemeyer if Dannemeyer follows through on his promise to run for the GOP nomination to the U.S. Senate against John Seymour.

A very serious conservative, Royce has said his favorite television show is William F. Buckley's Firing Line. His heroes are Adam Smith and Milton Friedman. Royce's legislative accomplishments include a 1987 bill sponsored by Mothers Against Drunk Driving requiring automatic revocation of a driver's license of anyone who refuses to take a roadside sobriety test.

Ed Royce

Royce also won passage of a bill requiring the Board of Medical Quality Assurance – the agency that licenses doctors – to review applications of University of Saigon Medical school graduates. The measure helped 33 influential Vietnamese doctors in his district, the center of the largest concentration of Southeast Asian refugees in the nation.

Other Royce bills have been aimed at protecting the privacy of crime victims. As chairman of the Senate Constitutional Amendments Committee, he has tried to leave his mark on ballot proposals, including one to alter the state's Gann spending limit. Royce, however, chairs a committee in which he does not control a majority and has found himself out-voted 3-2 by the Democrats on major issues.

Royce has skirted the edges of a few low-grade controversies. Democrats accused him in the 1988 election of circumventing federal campaign laws to give $5,000 from his campaign fund to Republican Rep. Wally Herger of Yuba City. Herger gave the money back, and the Federal Election Commission – not untypically – dropped the matter.

PERSONAL: elected 1982; born Oct. 12, 1951, in Los Angeles; home, Anaheim; education, B.A. accounting and finance CSU Fullerton; wife, Marie Porter; no children; Roman Catholic.

CAREER: corporate tax manager and controller.

COMMITTEES: Constitutional Amendments (chair); Public Employment & Retirement (vice chair); Budget & Fiscal Review; Business & Professions; Health & Human Services; Industrial Relations (vice chair); Judiciary; (Select) Governmental Efficiency; (Joint) Refugee Resettlement and International Migration; State's Economy.

OFFICES: Capitol, (916) 445-5831; district, 305 N. Harbor Blvd., 300, Fullerton 92632, (714) 871-0270.

REGISTRATION: 42.3% D, 48.3% R

1990 CAMPAIGN:	Royce – R	61.3%	$654,347
	Evelyn Becktell – D	38.7%	$29,209
1986 CAMPAIGN:	Royce – R	66%	$520,485
	Francis Hoffman – D	34%	$3,450

RATINGS:

AFL	PIRG	CLCV	NOW	CTA	CofC	CFB	NRA	FPAC
28%	40%	13%	30%	68%	75%	80%	100%	91%

KEY VOTES:

Divest S. Africa:	NO	Insurance reform:	–	Child sick leave:	NO
Assault gun ban:	NO	Parent consent abortion:	YES	Ban AIDS discrim:	NO
Clean Air Act:	YES	Ban insure donations:	NO	Extend death penalty:	YES
Lmt product tort:	–	Ban offshore oil:	YES	Restrict abortion funds:	YES
Lower alcohol std:	YES	Basic health care:	NO	Oil spill prevent:	YES
Ethics reform:	YES	Work cancer stds:	NO	Earthquake insure:	–

Cecil Green (D)
33rd Senate District

Straddling the border between Los Angeles and Orange counties, this district is decidedly industrial and working class. Homes are old but well-maintained. Residents work at such places as Rockwell International and Powerine Oil Co., and they live in cities named Bellflower, Downey, Artesia, Norwalk and Buena Park. The district is cross-hatched with five freeways and its population is about one-fourth Hispanic. Koreans also are a growing presence. Voter registration has steadily slipped for the Democrats in the last decade, a circumstance that set the stage for a special election in 1987 that broke the records for legislative campaign spending in a special election.

Cecil Green

The conditions for campaign insanity ripened in 1986, when Democrat Paul Carpenter – seeing his hold on the district slipping – abandoned the seat for a cushy position on the state Board of Equalization. (Carpenter has since been convicted on federal corruption charges stemming from activity while a senator.) Looking at the registration figures, Republican strategists thought they had an excellent chance of winning in the subsequent special election. By the time the campaign was over, the two major parties had spent $3 million, mobilized hundreds of legislative employees going door-to-door, leased fleets of vans with car phones to ferry voters to the polls and purchased thousands of doughnuts to give voters as a reward for voting. In the aftermath, Republicans in the Senate laid the blame for the loss on their leaders, and unceremoniously dumped Sens. Jim Nielsen and John Seymour from their positions.

The winner was Democrat Cecil Green, ex-mayor and city councilman from

Norwalk and the anointed candidate of Senate President Pro Tem David Roberti. Green heeded the advice of professional managers, while his opponent, Assemblyman Wayne Grisham of Norwalk, spent much of his campaign days on the golf course and could never adequately cope with charges that he had made sexual passes at a woman on his staff. Green's victory was the first in a string of improbable triumphs engineered by consultant Larry Sheingold in the late 1980s. Green fought an equally tough re-election race in 1988 and won a full four-year term. As a political footnote, Grisham so enraged his own supporters in that 1987 special election that his campaign manager, Dale Hardeman, opposed him in the primary the following year. Grisham won his primary but went on to lose his Assembly seat.

As a senator, Green has done little more than keep a seat warm for the Democrats. Soon after arriving in Sacramento, he was rewarded with the chairmanship of the dull-but-important committee that oversees the public employee retirement system. And he was a leader in the 1988 fight to restore the Cal-OSHA worker safety system, which Gov. George Deukmejian had cut from his budget. But Green has shown no signs of bucking his patron Roberti. When Green signaled he had an open mind on the nomination of Dan Lungren as state treasurer, he was quickly braced into line.

PERSONAL: elected 1987 (special election); born Sept. 24, 1924, in Riverside; home, Norwalk; Navy 1942-1952 WWII, Korea; education, attended CSU Long Beach; wife, Mary; daughter, Janyce; Lutheran.

CAREER: carpenter; contractor; commercial pilot; flight instructor; corporate manager; mayor; Norwalk City Council 1974-1987.

COMMITTEES: Public Employment & Retirement (chair); Agriculture & Water Resources; Education; Insurance, Claims & Corporations; Local Government; Transportation.

OFFICES: Capitol, (916) 445-5581, FAX (916) 327-2187; district, 17100 Pioneer Blvd., 170, Artesia 90701, (213) 924-2116.

REGISTRATION: 51.5% D, 40.1% R

1988 CAMPAIGN:			
	Green – D	50.8%	$3,729,844
	Don Knabe – R	49.2%	$1,054,985

MAY 12, 1987 SPECIAL ELECTION:			
	Green – D	53.8%	$1,942,810
	Wayne Grisham – R	44.8%	$811,051

RATINGS:

AFL	PIRG	CLCV	NOW	CTA	CofC	CFB	NRA	FPAC
98%	80%	67%	60%	100%	37%	20%	74%	37%

KEY VOTES:

		Insurance reform:	YES	Child sick leave:	YES
Assault gun ban:	YES	Parent consent abortion:	YES	Ban AIDS discrim:	YES
Clean Air Act:	YES	Ban insure donations:	NO	Extend death penalty:	YES
Lmt product tort:	YES	Ban offshore oil:	YES	Restrict abortion funds:	YES
Lower alcohol std:	YES	Basic health care:	YES	Oil spill prevent:	YES
Ethics reform:	YES	Work cancer stds:	YES	Earthquake insure:	YES

Ruben S. Ayala (D)
34th Senate District

Tucked into the eastern end of the Los Angeles basin, this bow-tie-shaped district includes the communities of Pomona, the dairy farms and prisons of Chino and the boom towns along the I-10 corridor: Fontana, Upland, Ontario and San Bernardino. Fontana, in particular, has undergone a remarkable turnabout. Facing economic collapse when Kaiser Steel closed its World War II-vintage mill, the working-class town has come back from the dead with housing tracts and new businesses.

Ruben Ayala

Democrat Ruben Ayala has held the seat without much trouble until recently. The overheated growth of western San Bernardino County has brought new residents who don't know Ayala and who tend to vote Republican, and the core of his labor union support has faded as a local power. The western county just isn't the working-class valley it once was.

In 1990, Ayala faced a strong challenge from Republican Assemblyman Charles Bader of Pomona. The race represented the best chance Republicans had of wresting a seat away from the Democrats that year. Ayala and Bader raised and spent monumental amounts of cash and fought a bare-knuckled race. In the end, Ayala raised more money and was able to pull out a narrow victory with the help of Larry Sheingold, the Senate staffer most responsible for Democratic wins in recent years.

Ayala is an energetic legislator, jealously guarding the parochial interests of his district. He has kept a state building in San Bernardino by warding off the encroachments of Riverside's legislators to the south, and sought new escape-proofing measures for the cluster of prisons in Chino at the behest of middle-class homeowners terrified by the bloody massacre of a family by an escapee in 1984.

Ayala's choice committee assignments have given him a powerful weapon. But the former Marine's short temper and lack of patience are his worst enemies. As chairman of the principal committee on water issues, Ayala has labored to expand and modernize the state's water system with little success. To be sure, the task might defy even the most diplomatic and clever of lawmakers. But in the hands of the bullheaded Ayala, the effort in 1987-1988 took on the trappings of a personal war.

Backed by Gov. George Deukmejian, Ayala worked out a limited proposal to upgrade levees in the Sacramento River Delta. The plan also included rehabilitation projects at the Salton Sea and elsewhere in the southern end of the water system. But the proposal met unexpected opposition from Northern California Republican Sen. Jim Nielsen, and that was just too much for Ayala. Giving up in a burst of fury on the Senate floor, Ayala lashed out at all who had differences with him on the details

– and the state entered its worst drought in decades with few significant improvements to its water system.

PERSONAL: elected 1974 (special election); born March 6, 1922, in Chino; home, Chino; USMC 1942-1946 WWII (South Pacific theater); education, attended junior college and UCLA Extension, graduated electronics school; wife, Irene; children, Bud, Maurice, Gary; Roman Catholic.

CAREER: Insurance; Chino School Board 1955-1962; Chino City Council 1962-1964; Chino Mayor 1964-1965, San Bernardino County Board of Supervisors 1965-1973.

COMMITTEES: Agriculture & Water Resources (chair); Appropriations; Local Government (vice chair); Revenue & Taxation; Transportation; Veterans' Affairs; (Select) Fairs & Rural Issues; State Procurement & Expenditure Practices; (Special) Solid & Hazardous Waste; (Joint) Fairs Allocation & Classification; Legislative Audit; Organized Crime & Gang Violence; Rules.

OFFICES: Capitol, (916) 445-6868, FAX (916) 445-0128; district, 505 N. Arrowhead Ave., 100, San Bernardino 92401, (714) 884-3165; 2545 S. Euclid Ave., Ontario 91762, (714) 983-3566.

REGISTRATION: 52.1% D, 39.6% R

1990 CAMPAIGN:	Ayala – D	51.8%	$1,032,997
	Charles Bader – R	48.2%	$761,778
1986 CAMPAIGN:	Ayala – D	66%	$307,332
	Steve Turner – R	34%	$12,250

RATINGS:

AFL	PIRG	CLCV	NOW	CTA	CofC	CFB	NRA	FPAC
82%	90%	80%	80%	99%	38%	20%	0%	19%

KEY VOTES:

Divest S. Africa:	YES	Insurance reform:	YES	Child sick leave:	NO
Assault gun ban:	YES	Parent consent abortion:	YES	Ban AIDS discrim:	NO
Clean Air Act:	YES	Ban insure donations:	YES	Extend death penalty:	YES
Lmt product tort:	YES	Ban offshore oil:	NO	Restrict abortion funds:	YES
Lower alcohol std:	YES	Basic health care:	YES	Oil spill prevent:	YES
Ethics reform:	YES	Work cancer stds:	YES	Earthquake insure:	–

Vacant

35th Senate District

This district is part of the Republicans' magic kingdom of Orange County. It includes Tustin, Costa Mesa, Fountain Valley and parts of Santa Ana, Orange, Huntington Beach, Westminster, Irvine and Anaheim, the home of Disneyland.

The district was represented by John Seymour beginning in 1982 until Republican Gov. Pete Wilson chose him to fill his U.S. Senate seat. A special election in March 1991 pitted three Republican Assembly members against each other. Assemblyman John Lewis (see 67th Assembly district) had the party backing and easily beat Nolan Frizzelle and Doris Allen with 30 percent of the vote.

He faced a May 14, 1991, runoff with Frank Hoffman, the only Democrat in the 10-way race, who won 10 percent of the vote. Barring some unforeseen catastrophe, Lewis was all but assured of winning the runoff.

REGISTRATION: 32.4% D, 56.8% R

Robert B. Presley (D)
36th Senate District

Riverside County's 36th Senate District stretches from the suburban environs of Riverside through the earth-toned stucco housing tracts of Moreno Valley, then to the San Jacinto Badlands, out through ritzy desert communities and pockets of rural poverty to the Colorado River in Blythe.

When Robert Presley won the seat in 1974, there were considerably fewer people living in that vast expanse. In the years since it has become the fastest-growing region of the state, and that creates no end of political problems for the Democratic incumbent.

The newest residents, labeled disdainfully by those who have been there awhile as the Dreaded Orange County Influx, tend not to know their state legislators.

Bob Presley

And they are increasingly voting Republican. Presley, however, has managed to win handily every four years through hard work and a dash of cleverness.

A former Riverside County sheriff's deputy who rose through the ranks to become second in command, his law-and-order credentials are impeccable – and his exploits as a detective are still the stuff of local lore. He won a Bronze Star in Italy in World War II for staying behind enemy lines with the wounded until an American counteroffensive came to the rescue.

As a senator, Presley is the area's preeminent politician – practically Riverside County's unofficial "mayor," resolving disputes between competing local power interests. He has cultivated the old power structure, personified by the "Monday Morning Group" of Riverside businessmen, and it has shown him unmatched loyalty. Presley's power on the local scene has long eclipsed Riverside County's other legislators, David Kelley and Steve Clute, who sometimes show tinges of jealousy, and all of the area's mayors and county supervisors.

Politically, Presley calls himself a conservative and hints periodically that he will become a Republican. In 1982, he ran a write-in campaign for the Republican nomination and won, thus enabling himself to run as the nominee of both major parties.

Presley has cemented his relationship with Democratic President Pro Tem David Roberti, and reaped considerable benefits, not the least being the chairmanship of Appropriations, the Senate's second most powerful committee next to Rules. As chairman he has won plaudits for fairness, but he is not as fast with the gavel – or as ruthless – as his predecessor, Democratic Sen. Dan Boatwright of Concord.

Presley's legislative achievements are considerable and wide-ranging – and he has been free of the taint of special-interest scandals that have plagued many colleagues. His legislation has included the state's vehicle smog-check program, reorganizing and strengthening the South Coast Air Quality Management District, bringing reason to chaotic child welfare laws and stiffening numerous criminal laws. Another bill toughened ethical standards for lawyers and forced the State Bar association to begin addressing its lengthy backlog of complaints against member lawyers. Presley has also embarked on an effort to strengthen the discipline system of the medical profession.

As chairman of the joint prison committee, Presley also has carried the legislation authorizing the construction of every new prison of the last decade. And he has become a potent critic of wasteful spending, inadequate health care and outdated practices in the prison system.

Occasionally, Presley has hinted he would run for Congress if longtime Democratic Rep. George Brown ever retires. With term limits in place on his tenure in the Legislature, some locally speculate that Presley will run for Congress in 1992 regardless of what Brown does.

PERSONAL: elected 1974; born Dec. 4, 1924, in Tahlequah, Okla.; home, Riverside; Army 1943-1946 WWII (Italy); education, A.A. Riverside City College, FBI National Academy; wife, Ahni Ratliff; children, Marilyn, Donna and Robert; Baptist.

CAREER: Riverside County Sheriff's department 24 years, undersheriff.

COMMITTEES: Appropriations (chair); Agriculture & Water Resources; Judiciary; (Select) Children & Youth (chair); Pacific Rim (vice chair); Business Development; Fairs and Rural Issues; Infant & Child Care & Development; Mobile Homes; (Special) Solid and Hazardous Waste; (Joint) Prison Construction and Operations (chair); Legislative Ethics (vice chair); Fire, Police, Emergency & Disaster Services; Legislative Audit; Revision of the Penal Code.

OFFICES: Capitol, (916) 445-9781; district, 3600 Lime Street, 111, Riverside 92501 (714) 782-4111; 72-811 Highway 111, 201, Palm Desert 92260, (619) 340-4488.

REGISTRATION: 45.9% D, 44.7% R

1990 CAMPAIGN:	Presley – D	53.6%	$964,484
	Raymond Haynes – R	46.4%	$70,527
1986 CAMPAIGN:	Presley – D	61%	$401,632
	Anne Richardson – R	39%	$22,969

RATINGS:

AFL	PIRG	CLCV	NOW	CTA	CofC	CFB	NRA	FPAC
68%	90%	71%	60%	95%	42%	40%	74%	39%

KEY VOTES:

Divest S. Africa:	YES	Insurance reform:	YES	Child sick leave:	NO
Assault gun ban:	YES	Parent consent abortion:	YES	Ban AIDS discrim:	YES
Clean Air Act:	YES	Ban insure donations:	YES	Extend death penalty:	YES
Lmt product tort:	YES	Ban offshore oil:	YES	Restrict abortion funds:	YES
Lower alcohol std:	YES	Basic health care:	YES	Oil spill prevent:	YES
Ethics reform:	YES	Work cancer stds:	YES	Earthquake insure:	YES

Marian C. Bergeson (R)

37th Senate District

This huge district, so large it would be unwieldy for any lawmaker, takes in a strip of upscale beach communities in Orange County – Newport Beach, Balboa Island, Laguna Beach – and then roughly one-third of Riverside County, including the mini-metropolis of Rancho California, Temecula and Hemet. To the south and east, it includes most of North San Diego County, and all of fertile Imperial County. Its population is growing fast and the district, with an overwhelmingly Republican voter edge, doubtless will be carved up in the 1991 reapportionment.

Republican Marian Bergeson, a member of the Assembly for eight years, won the seat in 1984 after falling from favor with the ideologically rigid As-

Marian Bergeson

sembly Republican leaders. Bergeson has flourished in the Senate. She has shown an independent streak at times, and although conservative on issues like abortion, she has a practical bent.

But Bergeson is another of those lawmakers who have grown weary of the Legislature. She made a major pitch with Gov. George Deukmejian to appoint her treasurer after Democrat Jesse Unruh died in 1987. He passed her over twice.

With her Orange County base, Bergeson has proven herself an able fund-raiser and she used this in 1990 in an unsuccessful bid for lieutenant governor. Bergeson did surprisingly well in the GOP primary, upsetting fellow Orange County state Sen. John Seymour (who got the last laugh when Pete Wilson appointed him to fill his U.S. Senate seat). Bergeson, although rigidly against abortion rights, may have benefited from women voters who somehow thought that because she is a woman she was pro-choice. In any case, Bergeson won the primary, but Lt. Gov. Leo McCarthy easily bested her in the runoff.

Bergeson, a favorite of Democrat David Roberti, chairs a major committee in the Senate. As head of the Senate Local Government Committee, Bergeson presided over difficult hearings to reorganize the South Coast Air Quality Management District, and has attempted for years to streamline Caltrans' contracting policies for highway construction. She has put herself in the middle of major school construction financing fights and has tried to deal with thorny growth-control issues. She also has been on the two-house budget conference committee that irons out differences between the Senate and Assembly versions of the state's spending plan.

In the 1991-1992 session she again focused on education legislation and shown herself a serious-minded legislator.

Bergeson has had a thankless time balancing the needs of her district. She tends to tilt toward Orange County – where her political roots and major contributors are – although the bulk of her district is in Riverside, San Diego and Imperial counties. She has been caught more than once in the cross-fire of conflicting interests in her district. For example, in the fight over reorganizing the basin's smog district, she was drawn between Orange County and Riverside County – both wanting more representation on the district's board. She did her best to push for Orange County, but in the end acquiesced in letting smaller Riverside County have equal representation largely because the bill's author was Riverside Sen. Robert Presley.

Having tasted a statewide campaign, Bergeson likely will try again. She has said she is uninterested in running for Congress, primarily because she does not want the weekly commute to Washington.

PERSONAL: elected 1984; born Aug. 31, 1925, in Salt Lake City; home, Newport Beach; education, B.A. elementary education Brigham Young University; graduate studies UCLA; husband, Garth Bergeson; children, Nancy, Garth Jr., Julie and James; Mormon.

CAREER: Newport Mesa school board 1965-1977; president of California School Boards Association; Assembly 1978-1984.

COMMITTEES: Local Government, (chair); Appropriations; Elections & Reapportionment; Health & Human Services; Natural Resources & Wildlife; Transportation; (Select) Infant & Child Care; Source Reduction & Recycling Market Development; (Joint) School Facilities.

OFFICES: Capitol, (916) 445-4961, FAX (916) 324-0901; district, 140 Newport Center Dr., 120, Newport Beach 92660, (714) 640-1137; 27403 Ynez Rd., 217, Temecula 92390, (714) 676-6808.

REGISTRATION: 32.8% D, 56.8% R

1988 CAMPAIGN:

Bergeson – R	71.1%	$374,806
Pat McCabe – D	26.6%	$16,358

RATINGS:

AFL	PIRG	CLCV	NOW	CTA	CofC	CFB	NRA	FPAC
29%	50%	54%	50%	92%	50%	60%	40%	63%

KEY VOTES:

Divest S. Africa:	NO	Insurance reform:	NO	Child sick leave:	NO
Assault gun ban:	YES	Parent consent abortion:	YES	Ban AIDS discrim:	–
Clean Air Act:	NO	Ban insure donations:	NO	Extend death penalty:	YES
Lmt product tort:	YES	Ban offshore oil:	YES	Restrict abortion funds:	YES
Lower alcohol std:	YES	Basic health care:	YES	Oil spill prevent:	YES
Ethics reform:	YES	Work cancer stds:	–	Earthquake insure:	YES

William A. Craven (R)
38th Senate District

Sliced out of the upscale beach communities of northern San Diego County, the safely Republican 38th District stretches along I-5 from the horse track of Del Mar to the Marine Corps base at Camp Pendleton. Much of San Diego County's growth over the last decade has been here and North County politics tend to focus on growth control. It is a land of checker-board development, strawberry farms and quick-buck artists. It is one of the most livable corners of the state, where life is easy and homes expensive.

Bill Craven

Republican Bill Craven has long been a figure in North County's civic and political life. An ex-Marine major, he epitomizes the Californians who have found their paradise in North County. Craven came from Philadelphia, settled in North County and served on the Oceanside Planning Commission – the town just to the south of Camp Pendleton. He won a seat on the county Board of Supervisors in 1970. Five years later, he was in the Assembly, and three years after that he was in the Senate.

Craven is often called David Roberti's favorite Republican. Democrat Roberti often looks to Craven for advice. The two have built a cordial, trusting friendship verging on a cross-party alliance. Craven is one of the barons of the five-member Rules Committee that runs the Senate. The chain-smoking Craven often presides over the committee in Roberti's absence.

Craven has served as a bridge between the ideological poles of an increasingly fractured Senate. He helps the house work. And the Republicans can't take Craven's vote for granted; more than once Roberti has won a swing vote from Craven.

Craven's legislative accomplishments are solid though not flashy. In 1990, he successfully authored SB 2475, which restricts advertisements for adult videos to sections of stores reserved for adults only. After years of labor, he won approval of a state university campus for his district, which is being established in San Marcos. The administration building will be named for Craven. As chairman of the Select Committee on Mobile Homes, Craven is considered the Legislature's expert on such legislation, an area of major interest to many of his older constituents.

Craven was publicly outraged at the behavior of fellow Republican John Lewis, an assemblyman charged with forgery for faking Ronald Reagan's name on campaign literature in 1986. Although the charges were thrown out, Craven moved to close loopholes in the law that helped Lewis. Craven authored SB 1865 in 1990, signed by Gov. George Deukmejian, that prohibited a person from publishing the signature of another on a campaign advertisement without authorization.

Craven was ill with respiratory problems for stretches of the 1989-1990 session. Although he was back at his desk at the start of the 1991-1992 session, his friends and colleagues continued to worry about his health.

PERSONAL: elected 1973; born June 30, 1921, in Philadelphia; home, Oceanside; USMC 1942-1946, 1950-1953;education, B.S. economics Villanova University; wife, Mimi; children, William Jr., Patricia Worley and John; Roman Catholic.
　　CAREER: leather busines; Assembly 1970..

COMMITTEES: Rules (vice chair); Elections (vice chair); Agriculture & Water Resources; Business & Professions; Local Government; (Select) Mobile Homes (chair); Business Development; Citizen Participation in Government; Maritime Industry; (Special) Border Issues (chair); (Joint) Arts; Courthouse Financing & Construction; Fire, Police, Emergency & Disaster Services; Legislative Ethics; Legislative Retirement; Refugee Resettlement & International Migration; Rules.
　　OFFICES: Capitol, (916) 445-3731; district, 2121 Palomar Airport Road, 100, Carlsbad 92008, (619) 438-3814.
　　REGISTRATION: 32.6% D, 52.6% R

1990 CAMPAIGN:	Craven – R	66.7%	$442,621
	Jane Evans – P&F	18.2%	$0
	Scott Olmsted – L	15.1%	
1986 CAMPAIGN:	Craven – R	85%	$272,425
	Betsy Mill – L	15%	$0

RATINGS:

AFL	PIRG	CLCV	NOW	CTA	CofC	CFB	NRA	FPAC
51%	61%	NR	40%	100%	25%	0%	33%	33%

KEY VOTES:

Divest S. Africa:	NO	Insurance reform:	–	Child sick leave:	NO
Assault gun ban:	YES	Parent consent abortion: YES	Ban AIDS discrim:	YES
Clean Air Act:	YES	Ban insure donations:	NO	Extend death penalty:	–
Lmt product tort:	–	Ban offshore oil:	–	Restrict abortion funds:	–
Lower alcohol std:	–	Basic health care:	–	Oil spill prevent:	–
Ethics reform:	YES	Work cancer stds:	YES	Earthquake insure:	–

Lucy L. Killea (D)
39th Senate District

Starting on Coronado Island, the 39th District hooks north across a narrow stretch of water to Point Loma. Then the district heads east by southeast, taking in the heart of San Diego's featureless bedroom neighborhoods on the bluffs overlooking San Diego's sports stadium, including Democratic pockets in Hillcrest and Mission Hills. Extending past San Diego State University and La Mesa, the district roughly follows I-8 and the Mexican border into eastern San Diego County. It includes the Republican strongholds of El Cajon, Santee, Lakeside and Alpine.

Republican Larry Stirling was elected to this seat in 1988, but to the total surprise of Capitol insiders, he quit after less than a year to take a judgeship in the San Diego Municipal Court. Stirling's 1989 resignation set off one of the most improbable political events in modern state history: a special election that became a national referendum on abortion rights and the bounds of the Catholic Church's involvement in politics.

Lucy Killea

At first glance, it looked as if Lucy Killea stood no chance of winning. Republican registration stood at 50 percent to 39 percent for the Democrats. With such a GOP edge, Democrats usually would not have even tried. But Killea was solidly pro-choice on abortion and her rival, Assemblywoman Carol Bentley – then in her first term – was anti-abortion. Polls showed that while the San Diego region was conservative, more than two-thirds of adults were pro-choice. And polls also showed Killea was better known.

The special election snoozed along as a local affair until Catholic Bishop Leo T. Maher sent Killea a letter (by fax machine) informing her that she could no longer receive communion at her parish. His actions were clearly designed for maximum political – rather than pastoral – impact. He leaked the letter to a television station.

If Maher hoped his actions would defeat Killea, they soon backfired. Pundits condemned him for interfering in an election. Killea's campaign became an overnight national media event. She took a quick trip to New York to appear on the Phil Donahue show with Geraldine A. Ferraro (Bentley declined Donahue's invitation). Killea was the subject of stories in USA Today, the Washington Post and the New York Times. Her election night headquarters in an El Cajon union hall was covered not just by local media but by national networks and live on CNN. It was more than Bentley could overcome.

Killea actually lost on Election Day. The margin of her narrow victory was provided by absentee ballots in a sophisticated operation engineered by consultant Larry Sheingold, a legislative staffer to Henry Mello who has become the election genius to Senate Democrats. The Democrats' absentee voter drive peaked just as the controversy over Maher's sanctions reached a crescendo. Killea won about 17,000 absentee ballots to 12,000 for Bentley. (Bishop Maher died of cancer in 1991).

It should also be noted that Killea vastly outspent Bentley even though Proposition 73's campaign contribution limits were still in place. Killea spent $570,603 to Bentley's $217,389 (figures below show how much money was raised by each; the difference between the amounts generally reflects how much in restricted campaign funds each was able to transfer from older campaign funds under the complicated restrictions).

Killea's route to the Legislature was a bit unusual. Her resume was bulging before she got to Sacramento. Killea was an Army intelligence officer in World War II and was then detailed to the State Department as an aide to Eleanor Roosevelt during the first general assembly of the United Nations. She went on to serve nine years in the CIA in the 1950s. Killea later lectured in history, and is an expert on Mexican border affairs, having served as executive director of Fronteras de las Californias. Although a Democrat, she was appointed by Republican Mayor Pete Wilson to the San Diego City Council to fill a vacancy in 1978. She has remained cordial with Wilson and his chief of staff, Bob White, over the years.

While in the Assembly, Killea toyed with running for mayor after the demise of Roger Hedgecock in 1985, but she stepped back for another Democrat, the more charismatic – and enigmatic – Maureen O'Connor.

As an Assembly member, Killea focused primarily on her committee work, devoted to the tedium of solid and hazardous waste issues. She authored numerous bills in that area, and was among the many parents in the 1985 legislative effort that brought forth the state's "workfare" program. She has also concentrated on international trade incentives and Mexican border issues, both of major interest to the San Diego area.

In the Senate, Killea made it clear that after tasting the national spotlight, she was not content to slip back into legislative obscurity. She soon complained that while every other Democrat chaired a committee, she had none. Senate President Pro Tem David Roberti reshuffled committee assignments and gave her the chair of the Senate Bonded Indebtedness Committee. At the start of the 1991-92 session, the panel was made into a subcommittee of the Appropriations Committee, a downgrade in status but with a side benefit of giving Killea a slot on the powerful Appropriations Committee.

Killea also has begun a politically risky quest – she has been pushing for a state constitutional convention to reform the California Legislature into a unicameral legislature. And she has again suggested that she would like to run for mayor, this time to succeed O'Connor.

Meanwhile, Republican Jim Ellis, who retired from the seat in 1988, has said he wants it back and will challenge Killea if she is still around in 1992.

PERSONAL: elected 1989 (special election); born July 31, 1922, in San Antonio, Tex.; home, San Diego; Army 1943-1948 WWII; education, B.A. history Incarnate World College, Tex.; M.A. history University of San Diego; Ph.D. Latin

American history UC San Diego; husband, John F. Killea; children, Paul and Jay; Roman Catholic.

CAREER: State Department personal secretary and administrative assistant to Eleanor Roosevelt (delegate to United Nations 1946); Central Intelligence Agency 1948-1957; U.S. Information Agency 1957-1960; vice president Fronteras de las Californias; university lecturer; research and teaching assistant; San Diego City Council 1978-1982; Assembly 1982-1989.

COMMITTEES: Appropriations and sumcommittee on bonded indebtedness (chair); Education; Transportation; Housing; Energy & Public Utilities; (Select) Source Reduction & Recycling Market Development (chair).

OFFICES: Capitol, (916) 445-3952, FAX (916) 327-2188; district, 2550 5th Ave., San Diego 92103-6691, (619) 696-6955; 1651 E. Main St., 206, El Cajon 92021, (619) 440-4460.

REGISTRATION: 36.9% D, 49.7% R

DEC. 5, 1989 SPECIAL ELECTION:

Killea – D	51%	$474,703
Carol Bentley – R	48.9%	$195,689

RATINGS: (scores based partially on Assembly votes)

AFL	PIRG	CLCV	NOW	CTA	CofC	CFB	NRA	FPAC
92%	82%	100%	80%	92%	29%	20%	13%	10%

KEY VOTES: (includes votes in the Assembly)

Divest S. Africa:	YES	Insurance reform:	YES	Child sick leave:	YES
Assault gun ban:	YES	Parent consent abortion:	NO	Ban AIDS discrim:	YES
Clean Air Act:	YES	Cutting old trees:	NO	Extend death penalty:	YES
Lmt product tort:	YES	Ban offshore oil:	YES	Restrict abortion funds:	–
Lower alcohol std:	YES	Basic health care:	YES	Oil spill prevent:	YES
Ethics reform:	YES	Work cancer stds:	YES	Earthquake insure:	YES

Wadie P. Deddeh (D)

40th Senate District

The last decade has brought the transformation of downtown San Diego from fleabag sailor-bars to glistening waterfront hotels and gleaming towers crowned by the unconventional Horton Plaza shopping center. Southward, arrayed along I-5 are the South Bay communities of Chula Vista, National City, Imperial Beach, Bonita and San Ysidro (part of the city of San Diego). Like downtown San Diego, much of the South Bay also has undergone monumental change in the last decade, but pockets remain amazingly untouched. National City is still an expanse of shipyards and the "Mile of Cars." Chula Vista, just to the south, is breaking out of its mold with ambitious plans for waterfront hotels and housing tracts. Imperial Beach is what

California beach towns used to be – laid-back and a bit seedy – but also is going broke as a municipality. And all have one overriding denominator – their proximity to Mexico, with its steady flood of illegal aliens, drugs and Tijuana's sewage system polluting beaches and farms.

Wadie Deddeh

Wadie Deddeh was elected to the Assembly in 1966, the year the Legislature went full-time. Deddeh won a seat in the Senate after the last reapportionment in 1981. His attention to legislating, however, has waxed and waned over the years.

Born and educated in Iraq, he spent much of the 1980s entreating President Ronald Reagan to appoint him ambassador to his native land – to no avail. When war began with Iraq in 1991, Deddeh found himself in the uncomfortable position of being the most prominent Iraqi-American in California. Despite keeping a studiously low profile, he has been the subject of threats. With relatives in Baghdad, the Iraqi war was a particularly painful period for Deddeh. But he made it clear that his loyalties were not divided. A week after Operation Desert Storm began, Deddeh gave an emotional floor speech in the Senate.

"There is no doubt," he said, "that our troops with God's help shall prevail – will prevail. As I stand before you at this moment, there's a great pain because on both sides of this armed camp in the Middle East, personally I'm touched because I have relatives – cousins, aunts, uncles, from whom we haven't heard, and probably when this is all over, who knows that some of them will perish." He evoked tremendous sympathy from his colleagues, who stood for a minute of silent prayer following his speech.

Deddeh has had a rather up-and-down time with internal Senate politics. When longtime Transportation Committee Chairman John Foran decided to retire at the end 1986, Deddeh ascended to the chairmanship of the committee – one of supreme importance to his district with its creaky infrastructure.

Less than two years later, Deddeh squandered his chairmanship by supporting Deukmejian's ill-fated nominee for state treasurer, Republican Dan Lungren. Senate President David Roberti sacked Deddeh as Transportation chairman and appointed in his place independent Sen. Quentin Kopp of San Francisco, who in the last hours before the Lungren vote switched from support to opposition.

Roberti later resurrected Deddeh by creating a new committee on veterans affairs for him to chair. In 1990, Roberti further elevated Deddeh to the chairmanship of the powerful Senate Revenue and Taxation Committee, a post used historically as a "juice committee" to extract campaign contributions from special interests. But, to the delight of public-interest organizations, Deddeh has been attempting to use his chairmanship to block new loopholes in the tax code – with limited success. In 1991, Deddeh began pushing a major tax bill through the Legislature to close tax loopholes for snack foods, newspaper publishers and other industries. But his colleagues threw up many roadblocks.

Throughout the 1980s, Deddeh was one of the Senate's biggest junketeers, accepting free trips to the Middle East, Europe and throughout the Pacific. Although he considers himself a foreign policy buff, Deddeh has shown minimal interest in Mexico. He has left major border issues, like trade and pollution, to San Diego-area colleagues Sen. Lucy Killea and Assemblyman Steve Peace.

PERSONAL: elected 1982; born Sept. 6, 1920, in Baghdad, Iraq; home, Chula Vista; education, B.A. English University of Baghdad 1946, M.A. University of Detroit 1956, graduate work economics, government and political science San Diego State University; wife, Mary-Lynn Drake; son, Peter; Roman Catholic.

CAREER: political science teacher, Southwestern Community College, Chula Vista; Assembly 1966-1982.

COMMITTEES: Revenue & Taxation (chair); Budget & Fiscal Review and subcommittee No. 3 on health, human services and labor (chair); Education; Health & Human Services; Veterans Affairs; ; (Select) Pacific Rim; (Joint) Legislative Retirement.

OFFICES: Capitol, (916) 445-6767; district, 430 Davidson St., C, Chula Vista, 91910, (619) 427-7080.

REGISTRATION: 50.8% D, 36.4% R

1990 CAMPAIGN:	Deddeh – D	56.6%	$603,086
	Muriel Watson – R	36.6%	$2,871
	Roger Batchelder – P&F	3.6%	
1986 CAMPAIGN:	Deddeh – D	69%	$450,384
	William Hoover – R	29%	$7403

RATINGS:

AFL	PIRG	CLCV	NOW	CTA	CofC	CFB	NRA	FPAC
89%	100%	70%	40%	100%	13%	20%	41%	25%

KEY VOTES:

Divest S. Africa:	YES	Insurance reform:	– Child sick leave:	YES
Assault gun ban:	YES	Parent consent abortion: YES	Ban AIDS discrim:	YES
Clean Air Act:	YES	Ban insure donations:	– Extend death penalty:	–
Lmt product tort:	YES	Ban offshore oil:	YES Restrict abortion funds:YES
Lower alcohol std:	YES	Basic health care:	YES Oil spill prevent:	–
Ethics reform:	–	Work cancer stds:	– Earthquake insure:	–

Assembly districts

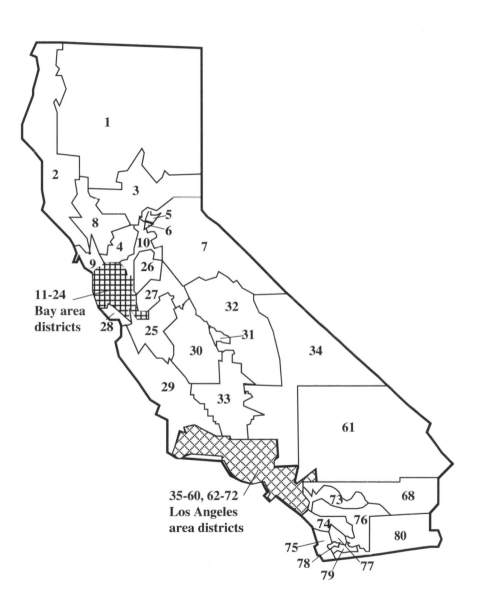

11-24
Bay area
districts

35-60, 62-72
Los Angeles
area districts

Los Angeles area Assembly districts

Bay Area
Assembly districts

ASSEMBLY
R. Stan Statham (R)

1st Assembly District

There's a little sign outside Assemblyman Stan Statham's Capitol office informing visitors that he represents "the 51st state." That's not quite true, but the nine-county 1st Assembly District covers some 30,000 square miles of northeastern California, almost a fifth of the state and an area nearly as large as Maine. As its size implies, the 1st District is mostly sparsely populated stretches of agricultural fields, rangeland, mountains and timber. There are few communities larger than small towns, the most prominent city being Redding.

Stan Statham

Although the district has a slight Democratic voter registration edge, it tends to vote Republican. Statham, who became known in the area during a decade as a local television anchorman, won the seat in 1976 after Democratic Assemblywoman Pauline Davis retired. He has won re-election easily ever since.

Despite his relative seniority among the fast-changing Republican membership of the Assembly, Statham has never achieved much power. That's because he comes from a rural backwater district and because his politics are decidedly more moderate than the prevailing slant in the GOP caucus. Statham is part of a loose confederation of Republican rebel moderates known as the "Magnificent Seven" and has been mentioned as a candidate for GOP leader should the faction become more powerful.

Being a minority within a minority means that Statham isn't a player on major legislative matters. His wife, Lovie, however, has carved out a semicareer of her own as an organizer of political fund-raising events not only for Statham but other politicians. Given the Republican bent to his district, Statham can probably remain in the seat for as long as he wants – which will be until a state Senate or congressional district becomes available.

PERSONAL: elected 1976; born April 7, 1939, in Chico; home, Chico; Army 1956-1959; education, attended CSU Chico; wife, Lovie Plants; children, Devin and Jennifer; no religious affiliation.

CAREER: finance and banking; radio disc jockey; television anchor; news and public affairs director, KHSL-TV Chico, 1964-1975.

COMMITTEES: Televising the Assembly (chair); Agriculture; Governmental Organization; Health; Insurance; (Joint) Courthouse Financing & Construction.

OFFICES: Capitol, (916) 445-7266, FAX (916) 448-6040; district, 410 Hemsted Drive, 210, Redding 96002, (916) 223-6300.

REGISTRATION: 46.4% D, 42% R

1990 CAMPAIGN:	Statham – R	56.5%	$271,554
	Arlie Caudle – D	42.9%	$19,802
1988 CAMPAIGN:	Statham – R	69.8%	$263,356
	Arlie Caudle – D	30.2%	$17,463

RATINGS:

AFL	PIRG	CLCV	NOW	CTA	CofC	CFB	NRA	FPAC
28%	53%	53%	50%	70%	59%	67%	63%	83%

KEY VOTES:

Divest S. Africa:	NO	Insurance reform:	NO	Child sick leave:	–
Assault gun ban:	NO	Parent consent abortion:	–	Ban AIDS discrim:	YES
Clean Air Act:	NO	Cutting old trees:	YES	Extend death penalty:	YES
Lmt product tort:	YES	Ban offshore oil:	–	Restrict abortion funds:	–
Lower alcohol std:	YES	Basic health care:	NO	Oil spill prevent:	YES
Ethics reform:	YES	Work cancer stds:	YES	Earthquake insure:	NO

Daniel E. Hauser (D)
2nd Assembly District

California's northwestern coast is so thinly populated that one state Assembly district stretches from
the Oregon border 300 miles southward to within
commuting distance of San Francisco. The area once
voted Republican with some regularity, but as the
traditional industries of lumber and fishing have
faded, and as flower children of the 1960s moved in
and established roots, the politics of the area have
crept leftward.

Dan Hauser

Democrats have replaced Republicans in all local
legislative seats, including the 2nd Assembly District, which covers all or parts of Del Norte, Humboldt,
Mendocino and Sonoma counties. Barry Keene captured the seat for the Democrats in 1972, and he was
followed four years later by Doug Bosco. Keene went to the state Senate and Bosco
to Congress in 1982. The third Democrat to win in the district was Dan Hauser, a
one-time insurance adjuster and mayor of Arcata.

Hauser chairs the Assembly Housing Committee. He has labored to produce a
stream of housing bills, but much of his time is occupied with avoiding being
chewed up by the ceaseless environmental controversies that buffet his scenic and
resource-rich district. Environmentalists and logging and mining companies battle
endlessly over regulations and laws. Hauser came into office as a Sierra Club
candidate. He routinely offers bills and resolutions to ban offshore oil drilling. But
in more recent years, Hauser has gravitated more toward the timber industry.
Matters came to a head in 1989, when an environmentalist-sponsored bill to put a
three-year moratorium on logging old-growth forests came to the Assembly floor.

Hauser successfully offered industry-supported amendments that gutted the bill. The bill then died. That and other instances have driven a wedge between Hauser and the increasingly militant environmentalists. His re-election prospects continue to grow more problematic.

PERSONAL: elected 1982; born June 18, 1942, in Riverside; home, Arcata; education, B.A. American history Humboldt State University; wife, Donna Dumont; children, Dawn and Doug; Lutheran.

CAREER. insurance claims representative; Arcata City Council, 1974-1978, mayor, 1978-1982.

COMMITTEES: Housing and Community Development (chair); Governmental Organization; Natural Resources; Water, Parks & Wildlife; (Joint) Fisheries and Aquaculture (chair); Fairs Allocation & Classification; School Facilities.

OFFICES: Capitol, (916) 445-8360, FAX (916) 322-5214; district, 510 O St., G, Eureka 95501, (707) 445-7014; 50 D St., 450, Santa Rosa 95404, (707) 576-2526.

REGISTRATION: 56.7% D, 30.8% R

1990 CAMPAIGN:	Hauser – D	55.2%	$233,187
	Tim Willis – R	31.4%	$1,080
	Bruce Anderson – P&F	13.4%	
1988 CAMPAIGN:	Hauser – D	74.9%	$173,396
	Rita King - R	25.1%	$1,286

RATINGS:

AFL	PIRG	CLCV	NOW	CTA	CofC	CFB	NRA	FPAC
95%	91%	94%	100%	80%	36%	33%	24%	16%

KEY VOTES:

Divest S. Africa:	YES	Insurance reform:	YES	Child sick leave:	YES
Assault gun ban:	NO	Parent consent abortion:	NO	Ban AIDS discrim:	YES
Clean Air Act:	YES	Cutting old trees:	YES	Extend death penalty:	YES
Lmt product tort:	YES	Ban offshore oil:	YES	Restrict abortion funds:	NO
Lower alcohol std:	YES	Basic health care:	YES	Oil spill prevent:	YES
Ethics reform:	YES	Work cancer stds:	YES	Earthquake insure:	YES

Christopher R. Chandler (R)

3rd Assembly District

Farms, mountains and wide-open spaces are the main characteristics of this conservative, rural district that includes the Northern California counties of Colusa, Nevada, Sierra, Sutter and Yuba.

Chris Chandler, a Yuba City lawyer and Realtor, was hand-picked by Assembly Republican conservatives to succeed Wally Herger, who was elected to Congress in 1986. The substantial financial support given to Chandler by Assembly GOP leaders in the contested Republican primary that year temporarily angered party moderates who were supporting other hopefuls. But the schism was patched up and Chandler handily won a seat that Democrats had some fleeting hopes of capturing.

Chandler has been true to the conservative ideals of his backers and has rarely strayed from the caucus line. In the Legislature he has concentrated primarily on carrying bills to benefit interests in his district. In 1988, for example, he pushed a bill to suspend California water quality and toxics laws to allow rice farmers to use a specific chemical fungicide. He pushed a measure to prohibit the administration at California State University, Chico, from taking over student-run businesses. And he has adamantly opposed measures by San Joaquin Valley and Southern Californian legislators to increase water shipments from his district to theirs. On budgetary issues, he has remained staunchly opposed to any tax increases and remains deeply suspicious of expanding government programs.

Chris Chandler

Chandler is among a group of a dozen legislators who were given "Free Speech" awards by Common Cause, a political watchdog organization, for refusing to take honorariums. He can be counted among those with an eye toward a congressional seat if an opportunity arises.

PERSONAL: elected 1986; born Jan. 20, 1951, in Marysville, Calif.; home, Yuba City; education, B.A. English UC Davis; J.D. McGeorge; wife, Cindy; children, Carolyn, Jessica and Emily; Episcopalian.

CAREER: lawyer.

COMMITTEES: Environmental Safety & Toxic Materials; Local Government; Natural Resources; (Joint) Fairs Allocation & Classification.

OFFICES: Capitol, (916) 445-7298, FAX (916) 323-3550; district, 1227 Bridge St., E, Yuba City 95991, (916) 673-2201.

REGISTRATION: 43% D, 45% R

1990 CAMPAIGN:	Chandler – R	54%	$369,765
	Lon Hatamiya – D	46%	$292,349
1988 CAMPAIGN:	Chandler - R	60.2%	$481,811
	Bruce Conklin - D	36.7%	$15,985

RATINGS:

AFL	PIRG	CLCV	NOW	CTA	CofC	CFB	NRA	FPAC
11%	36%	16%	30%	58%	73%	92%	100%	84%

KEY VOTES:

	Insurance reform:	NO	Child sick leave:	NO
Assault gun ban:	NO	Parent consent abortion:	YES	Ban AIDS discrim:	NO
Clean Air Act:	NO	Cutting old trees:	YES	Extend death penalty:	YES
Lmt product tort:	YES	Ban offshore oil:	NO	Restrict abortion funds:	YES
Lower alcohol std:	YES	Basic health care:	NO	Oil spill prevent:	YES
Ethics reform:	YES	Work cancer stds:	NO	Earthquake insure:	NO

Thomas M. Hannigan (D)

4th Assembly District

This district is being transformed into a series of commuter cities for people who work in the San Francisco Bay Area. It contains all of Solano County, most of the city of Vallejo and southern Yolo County, including the college town of Davis.

Former Realtor Tom Hannigan has developed a reputation as a thoughtful, honest and hard-working legislator since he was elected to the Assembly in 1978. He began his political career in local government, serving as mayor of Fairfield and later as chairman of the Solano County Board of Supervisors. Accordingly, Hannigan has shown interest in trying to help solve local government funding problems. He was among the early legislators who suggested that

Tom Hannigan

Proposition 13 and the state's spending limits needed some adjusting. He has proposed giving counties more money to encourage preservation of agricultural lands under the Williamson Act. He also has been acutely aware of his district's changing status, backing proposals to get rail service between Auburn and San Jose. And he pushed to help fund construction of the Vietnam Memorial in Capitol Park through a checkoff on the state income-tax form.

For most of his Assembly career, Hannigan has been recognized as an expert in tax and financial matters, serving a stint as chairman of the Assembly Revenue and Taxation Committee. In 1986, Hannigan set in motion a move to reform the state income tax. The following year, however, Hannigan relinquished control over the committee when Assembly Speaker Willie Brown named him to replace Mike Roos of Los Angeles as the Democrats' majority leader, one of the top leadership posts. At the time, Democrats were suffering from charges that they were putting politics over policy. Hannigan had a reputation for being more interested in issues than back-room maneuvering and campaign strategy. Since then, there has been some indication that part of Brown's naming of Hannigan to the post was aimed more at image polishing than substantive reform. In fact, much of the overtly political work of raising money and getting candidates elected has simply been shifted to others.

Still, Hannigan's reputation has remained intact. He is considered among the straight-arrows in the Capitol. He told the speaker to back off from his effort to help a law client, Norcal Solid Waste Systems Inc., to site a garbage transfer station in Solano County. Brown's role in the episode has become the subject of an FBI probe.

Hannigan is consistently mentioned when speculation arises about a successor to Brown as Assembly speaker. Yet he leaves even his admirers wondering if he has enough fire in the belly to become speaker. And in the wake of voter-approval of term limits, Hannigan is among the legislators known to be thinking about bailing out of politics altogether.

PERSONAL: elected 1978; born May 30, 1940, in Vallejo; home, Fairfield; USMC 1963-1966 Vietnam; education, B.S. business University of Santa Clara; wife, Jan Mape; children; Erin, Matthew and Bridget; Catholic.

CAREER: Fairfield City Council, 1970-1972; mayor, 1972-1974; Solano County Board of Supervisors, 1974-1978; owner and broker of Hannigan & O'Neill Realtors; Assembly majority floor leader.

COMMITTEES: Elections, Reapportionment & Constitutional Amendments; Local Government; Revenue & Taxation; Ways & Means; (Joint) Legislative Retirement; Rules.

OFFICES: Capitol, (916) 445-8368, FAX (916) 327-9667; district, 844 Union Ave., A, Fairfield 94533, (707) 429-2383.

REGISTRATION: 55.1% D, 32% R.

1990 CAMPAIGN:	Hannigan – D	57.9%	$300,291
	John Ford – R	35.6%	$2,495
1988 CAMPAIGN:	Hannigan - D	67.3%	$354,580
	John Ford - R	32.7%	$0

RATINGS:

AFL	PIRG	CLCV	NOW	CTA	CofC	CFB	NRA	FPAC
96%	95%	95%	100%	96%	23%	50%	0%	0%

KEY VOTES:

Divest S. Africa:	YES	Insurance reform:	YES	Child sick leave:	YES
Assault gun ban:	YES	Parent consent abortion:	NO	Ban AIDS discrim:	YES
Clean Air Act:	YES	Cutting old trees:	NO	Extend death penalty:	YES
Lmt product tort:	YES	Ban offshore oil:	YES	Restrict abortion funds:	NO
Lower alcohol std:	YES	Basic health care:	YES	Oil spill prevent:	YES
Ethics reform:	YES	Work cancer stds:	YES	Earthquake insure:	–

Robert Timothy Leslie (R)
5th Assembly District

The evolutionary nature of politics in the Sacramento suburbs is crystallized in the 5th Assembly District. Republican Jean Moorhead (later Duffy) won the seat in 1978, but she later switched to the Democratic Party after a blowup with Republican leaders, and in 1986 she retired. The district was altered in the post-1980 reapportionment to include more of fast-growing Placer County. Although that shifted voting emphasis toward Republicans, Moorhead agreed to the change. It now includes Sacramento County's northeastern suburbs, plus Roseville and Auburn.

Moorhead's decision to retire sparked a high-octane campaign by both parties because the district's registration at the time – about 49 percent Democratic to 42 percent Republican – made it potentially winnable by either party. The Republicans went with Tim Leslie, a former lobbyist and legislative aide who had tried to unseat Moorhead in 1984 and had lost by just 1,379 votes. Democratic leaders rebuffed a bid by Placer County Supervisor Terry Cook and anointed what they called "a macho man," Jack Dugan, a one-time New York policeman and retired Army colonel who had helped develop the California Conservation Corps. But Dugan had an Achilles heel that didn't surface until a showdown debate: He had never voted in a state election. Leslie blew out Dugan on Election Day.

As a legislator, Leslie has been a back-bencher who votes as GOP leaders decree. He was the pick of Gov. Wilson and other party leaders to replace John Doolittle in the 1st Senate District. Leslie was the top vote-getter in a March 19, 1991, special election, and he was set to face Patti Mattingly of Yreka, a moderate Siskiyou County supervisor, in a May 14 runoff.

Tim Leslie

Leslie has gotten into some spats with Democrats on the Assembly floor over symbolic resolutions and other non-substantive issues, but he is otherwise little noticed. His biggest problem seems not to be with Democrats, but with right-wing Republicans and the hostility of their house-organ, the Sacramento Union.

PERSONAL: elected 1986; born Feb. 4, 1942, in Ashland, Ore.; home, Auburn; education, B.S. political science CSU Long Beach; M.A. public administration USC; wife, Clydene; children, Debbie and Scott; Presbyterian.

CAREER: real estate; Assembly Ways & Means Committee consultant 1969-1971; lobbyist for County Supervisors' Association of California 1971-1980.

COMMITTEES: Higher Education; Judiciary; Labor & Employment; Public Employees, Retirement & Social Security.

OFFICES: Capitol, (916) 445-4445; district, 315 Main Street, Roseville 95678-5133, (916) 969-3660.

REGISTRATION: 46.3% D, 43.9% R

1990 CAMPAIGN:	Leslie – R	62.5%	$477,751
	Joe Buonaiuto – D	37.5%	$28,548
1988 CAMPAIGN:	Leslie - R	58.9%	$899,397
	John Byouk - D	41.1%	$625,766

RATINGS:

AFL	PIRG	CLCV	NOW	CTA	CofC	CFB	NRA	FPAC
13%	32%	11%	40%	68%	77%	58%	76%	92%

KEY VOTES:

		Insurance reform:	–	Child sick leave: NO
Assault gun ban:	NO	Parent consent abortion:	YES	Ban AIDS discrim: NO
Clean Air Act:	NO	Cutting old trees:	YES	Extend death penalty: YES
Lmt product tort:	YES	Ban offshore oil:	NO	Restrict abortion funds: YES
Lower alcohol std:	YES	Basic health care:	NO	Oil spill prevent: YES
Ethics reform:	YES	Work cancer stds:	NO	Earthquake insure: NO

Lloyd G. Connelly (D)
6th Assembly District

During the four terms Lloyd Connelly has represented this Sacramento district, he has developed a
reputation as one of the most honest and hardest-
working legislators at the Capitol, and also one of the
most controversial. It is not uncommon to find the
lawyer and former Sacramento city councilman at his
office before dawn or after midnight. It also wouldn't
be out of character to find him sleeping at a homeless
shelter to take a first-hand look at the vexing social
problem or running a marathon for relaxation.
Connelly has used his seemingly limitless energy on
measures to clean up the environment, improve public health and protect consumers. And he has been
generally effective.

Lloyd Connelly

Connelly has been able to shepherd through the Legislature a number of bills
aimed at cutting down on the use of potentially harmful pesticides on produce or
chemicals that may seep into groundwater supplies. He fought to establish a tumor
registry designed to warn public health officials of cancer clusters that might be
traced to environmental problems. He also pushed a bill aimed at reducing lead
levels in paint that might poison children. In 1989, he pushed for a bill to extend to
rifles and shotguns the 15-day waiting period and background checks required of
handgun purchasers. But that bill was killed in the Senate under pressure from gun-
owner groups. Connelly also has tended to local affairs when needed, for instance
successfully blocking moves by lawmakers from water-strapped regions that would
force Sacramento to install water meters on homes and businesses.

In addition to legislative accomplishments, Connelly has become a successful
guru of statewide initiative drives, attempting to get voters to accept a broad liberal
agenda that the Legislature has stalled. As such, he has been a key player in a loose
consortium of initiative writers associated with Gerald Meral of the Planning and
Conservation League. Connelly's success has been mixed. In 1986, he helped lead
the charge for Proposition 65, a sweeping initiative to control toxic waste. The
measure passed by a wide margin. In 1988, he successfully pushed Proposition 99,
which raised the state's tobacco tax in an attempt to curb smoking and at the same
time raise money for health programs. However, Connelly & Co. were singularly
unsuccessful in 1990 with their "nickel-a-drink" alcohol tax initiative. The measure
went down in flames at the polls after the liquor and food industries poured millions
into its defeat. Connelly was one of a handful of legislators to support Proposition
131, the milder of two term limit initiatives on the November 1990 ballot. That
initiative also lost while the more stringent Proposition 140 passed.

Connelly's tendency to turn to initiatives has brought on criticism that he is impatient and that he gives up on the legislative process too soon. And his candid, independent and tenacious style has not endeared him to some of his colleagues. Yet Connelly seems oblivious to most of the internal jockeying and posturing that goes on in the Legislature. In fact, sometimes Connelly seems oblivious to all that is happening around him – he is renowned for his absentmindedness. But when it comes to voting on bills, Connelly rarely lets a questionable one pass by. He carries around a list of such bills and others frequently ask to look at his "cheat sheets."

Connelly generally only gets token opposition from Republican candidates every two years. Decidedly restless with the Legislature, Connelly has said he wants to run for Congress in 1992 to replace Robert Matsui, who has said he will be giving up the seat to run for the U.S. Senate.

PERSONAL: elected 1982; born Dec. 31, 1945, in Sacramento; home, Sacramento; Army 1969-1970; education, A.A. American River College; B.A. government and speech CSU Sacramento; J.D. McGeorge; wife, the Rev. Jean Shaw; children, George and Keele; Roman Catholic.

CAREER: lawyer; administrative assistant to Sacramento County Board of Supervisors 1971-1974; Sacramento City Council 1975-1982.

COMMITTEES: Insurance; Judiciary; Natural Resources; (Special) Medi-Cal Oversight; (Joint) Revision of the Penal Code (vice chair); Arts.

OFFICES: Capitol, (916) 445-2484, FAX (916) 324-2782; district, 2705 K St., 6, Sacramento 95816, (916) 443-1183.

REGISTRATION: 55.6% D, 35.2% R

1990 CAMPAIGN:	Connelly – D	57.9%	$393,708
	George Marsh – R	36.8%	$584
1988 CAMPAIGN:	Connelly – D	61.3%	$296,574
	Mike Gates – R	38.7%	$0

RATINGS:

AFL	PIRG	CLCV	NOW	CTA	CofC	CFB	NRA	FPAC
96%	100%	100%	100%	93%	27%	42%	0%	0%

KEY VOTES:

Divest S. Africa:	YES	Insurance reform:	YES	Child sick leave:	YES
Assault gun ban:	YES	Parent consent abortion:	NO	Ban AIDS discrim:	YES
Clean Air Act:	YES	Cutting old trees:	NO	Extend death penalty:	YES
Lmt product tort:	NO	Ban offshore oil:	YES	Restrict abortion funds:	NO
Lower alcohol std:	YES	Basic health care:	YES	Oil spill prevent:	YES
Ethics reform:	YES	Work cancer stds:	YES	Earthquake insure:	YES

David C.H. Knowles (R)
7th Assembly District

Democrat Norman Waters narrowly dodged a political bullet in the November 1988 election when he defeated mortgage banker David Knowles by some 700 votes in this rapidly growing and rapidly changing district. But in the 1990 rematch,

Knowles put Waters, a third-generation cattleman who campaigned as "the last rancher," out to pasture. Although outspent, Knowles defeated the seven-term incumbent by 4,372 votes out of more than 161,000 in a contest that reprised many of the issues and insults of their previous encounter.

Knowles clearly benefited from the district's constantly changing political landscape. It encompasses the rural counties of Alpine, Amador, Calaveras, El Dorado, Mono and Placer plus parts of Tuolumne and Sacramento. Most of the newcomers live in the fast-growing foothills east of Sacramento. The percentage of registered Republicans has steadily climbed. Knowles also benefited from anti-incumbent senti-

David Knowles

ment, using every opportunity to link Waters to controversial Assembly Speaker Willie Brown, who was a major financier of Waters' campaigns. And while Knowles may have been correct in portraying Waters as ineffective and beholden to the Democratic leadership, he certainly wasn't the "liberal" Knowles claimed.

Waters, on the other hand, portrayed Knowles as a "right-wing nut." And while the derisive tone of Waters' comment may have been uncalled for, there is no doubt that Knowles espouses the views of the far right. For example, after a Sacramento abortion clinic was rammed by an old military vehicle in 1985, Knowles said the act was, "the answer to a prayer." And during the 1990 campaign, Knowles received substantial financial support from independent groups opposing abortion, against gun control and backing other conservative causes.

Knowles has offered few suggestions on how to deal with the problems facing the district. Instead, he has spoken in the generalities favored by bedrock conservatives, pledging to fight tax increases and crime, wipe out pornography and oppose gun control and abortion-upon-demand.

Knowles got off to a stormy start as a freshman legislator, loudly interrupting a hearing of the Assembly Labor Committee in March 1991 to protest a gay rights bill – that, after he had resigned from the committee. After much histrionics, Knowles stomped out of the hearing.

PERSONAL: elected 1990; born Sept. 5, 1952, Cleveland, Ohio; home, Cameron Park; education, B.A. Oral Roberts Univ.; wife, Anne; children, Robbie, David, Margaret, Peter, Jonathan; Protestant.

CAREER: mortgage banker.

COMMITTEES: Utilities & Commerce; Education; Consumer Protection, Governmental Efficiency & Economic Development.

OFFICES: Capitol, (916) 445-8343, FAX (916) 327-2210; district, 3161 Cameron Park Drive, 214, Cameron Park 95682, (916) 676-5953.

REGISTRATION: 48.9% D, 41.1% R

1990 CAMPAIGN: Knowles – R   51.4% $131,409
                  Norman Waters (incumbent) – D 48.6% $691,016
1988 CAMPAIGN: Norman Waters (incumbent) – D   50% $797,929
                  David Knowles – R   50% $889,671
RATINGS and **KEY VOTES**: Newly elected

Beverly K. Hansen (R)

8th Assembly District

Bev Hansen

The 8th Assembly District is the heart of the California wine region of Sonoma, Lake and Napa counties. It's scenic country, not only the center of the wine-making industry but a vacation destination with places such as Lake Berryessa attracting an increasing number of tourists whose presence, in turn, is sparking a debate over growth and development.

The district was represented for six controversial years by the scion of a well-known wine-making family, Don Sebastiani. When he stepped down in 1986 to run unsuccessfully for state controller, a nasty fight erupted among Republicans. The Assembly's conservative Republican leaders anointed 26-year-old goat rancher Martin McClure. But Bev Hansen, an aide to Republican state Sen. Jim Nielsen, wouldn't accept that decree. Hansen whipped McClure and then triumphed over a Democratic candidate, Mary Jadiker, who had been tabbed by Democratic leaders to capture the Sebastiani seat after a strong showing two years earlier.

With her double upset behind her, Hansen came to Sacramento with an independent mind-set that she has not relinquished. A moderate in a Republican caucus dominated by conservatives, Hansen initially joined forces with other moderates in the so-called "Magnificent Seven" to steer their own course on such hot-button issues as abortion. But by 1990, Hansen had moved into the Republican leadership circle, evidently to help placate caucus members who have been less than pleased with the leadership of Ross Johnson. She has gotten along well with the sometimes-blustery Johnson, even joining him and his family on a Mexican vacation.

Hansen joined Johnson and Bill Baker in representing the caucus to Gov. George Deukmejian during the monthlong budget impasse in July 1990. More graceful than Johnson, and not as acerbic as Baker, Hansen displayed a level of diplomatic quality that could well bring her the minority leader slot at some point – or even the speakership if Republicans somehow move into the majority. She is well-liked by colleagues, including Democrats. Only Proposition 140's term limits stand in her way of becoming a greater force in the Assembly.

Although she had no Democratic opponent in 1990, a measure of the voters' discontent with incumbents was on display in her district. Eric Roberts, a libertarian candidate, won more than 23 percent of the vote against Hansen.

PERSONAL: elected 1986; born, Aug. 18, 1944, in Oroville, Calif.; home, Santa Rosa; education, political science major UC Berkeley, no degree; divorced; children, Joe, Tim, Brett, Rick and Heather; Presbyterian.

CAREER: real estate; aide to Sen. Jim Nielsen 1981-1985.

COMMITTEES: Education; Elections, Reapportionment & Constitutional Amendments; Transportation; Ways & Means; (Joint) Legislative Budget.

OFFICES: Capitol, (916) 445-8102; district, 50 D Street, 301, Santa Rosa 95404, (707) 546-4500; 1700 Second St., 260, Napa 94559, (707) 255-9084.

REGISTRATION: 48.9% D, 41.1% R

1990 CAMPAIGN:	Hansen – R	76.5%	$373,259
	Eric Roberts – L	23.5%	$0
1988 CAMPAIGN:	Hansen – R	63.6%	$543,967
	Bruce Ketron – D	32.7%	$10,811

RATINGS:

AFL	PIRG	CLCV	NOW	CTA	CofC	CFB	NRA	FPAC
25%	45%	25%	40%	80%	86%	75%	100%	88%

KEY VOTES:

	Insurance reform:	YES	Child sick leave:	NO
Assault gun ban:	NO	Parent consent abortion: YES	Ban AIDS discrim:	NO
Clean Air Act:	NO	Cutting old trees:	YES	Extend death penalty:	YES
Lmt product tort:	YES	Ban offshore oil:	YES	Restrict abortion funds:	YES
Lower alcohol std:	YES	Basic health care:	NO	Oil spill prevent:	YES
Ethics reform:	YES	Work cancer stds:	NO	Earthquake insure:	YES

William J. Filante (R)
9th Assembly District

Marin and southern Sonoma counties have a well-deserved reputation as the laid-back land of expensive homes, a beautiful coastline, rolling vineyards, white wine and hot tubs. But the person those voters have chosen to represent them is anything but laid-back. Dr. William Filante is the only physician in the state's Legislature, and he still maintains a part-time ophthalmology practice.

What's more, Republican Filante represents a district that, judging from the numbers, should be in the hands of a Democrat. That makes Filante a moderate out of political necessity. He regularly breaks away from the conservative Assembly Republican caucus line on issues, most notably on the environ-

William Filante

ment – a must in this scenic district – and those involving health. In 1989, he was one of two Assembly Republicans to buck the National Rifle Association and vote for the ban on semiautomatic military assault-style weapons.

Filante, as could be expected, is the Legislature's resident medical expert and is often looked on to provide colleagues with his best scientific view on bills. He also is a fiscal conservative and regularly backs bills of interest to business.

Even though Filante's moderate views are closer to the Democrats' own than most Republicans', the Democrats regularly target his seat because of the registration numbers. Republicans, on the other hand, tolerate his occasional breaks, making occasional snipes at him behind his back. They only hope that Filante won't decide that practicing medicine full-time is more enjoyable than participating in politics.

PERSONAL: elected 1978; born Oct 22, 1929, in Brooklyn, N.Y.; home, Greenbrae; USAF flight surgeon 1955-1957; education, B.A. and M.D. University of Minnesota; internship Detroit Receiving Hospital; ophthalmology residency Los Angeles County General Hospital; wife, Margaret; children, Dave, Steve and Jan; Jewish.

CAREER: general practitioner; ophthalmologist; assistant clinical professor UC San Francisco; assistant chief, Department of Ophthalmology, Mt. Zion Medical Center; instructor Pacific Medical Center, San Francisco; director Marin Municipal Water District; trustee Marin Community College District.

COMMITTEES: Health; Rules; Utilities & Commerce; Water, Parks & Wildlife; (Joint) Rules.

OFFICES: Capitol, (916) 445-7827, FAX (916) 324-6869; district, 30 North San Pedro Road, 135, San Rafael 94903, (415) 479-4920; Post & English streets, Petaluma 94952, (707) 762-5706.

REGISTRATION: 53.1% D, 33.4% R

1990 CAMPAIGN:	Filante – R	51.4%	$516,572
	Vivien Bronshvag – D	42.5%	$183,627
	Bill Bright – L	3.8%	
	Coleman Persily – P&F	2.4%	
1988 CAMPAIGN:	Filante – R	55.9%	$792,488
	Francis Parnell – D	44.1%	$184,089

RATINGS:

AFL	PIRG	CLCV	NOW	CTA	CofC	CFB	NRA	FPAC
32%	77%	79%	60%	64%	64%	58%	33%	77%

KEY VOTES:

Divest S. Africa:	YES	Insurance reform:	YES	Child sick leave:	–
Assault gun ban:	YES	Parent consent abortion:	YES	Ban AIDS discrim:	YES
Clean Air Act:	YES	Cutting old trees:	NO	Extend death penalty:	YES
Lmt product tort:	YES	Ban offshore oil:	YES	Restrict abortion funds:	NO
Lower alcohol std:	YES	Basic health care:	NO	Oil spill prevent:	YES
Ethics reform:	YES	Work cancer stds:	YES	Earthquake insure:	YES

Phillip L. Isenberg (D)

10th Assembly District

This politically and geographically diverse district stretches from downtown Sacramento to the Sacramento-San Joaquin Delta. It includes the rural Sacramento County cities of Galt and Walnut Grove, Lodi and the farm areas of northern San Joaquin County and the Antioch area of Contra Costa County.

Democrat Phillip Isenberg, the former mayor of Sacramento, has represented the district since 1982, when he won the open seat by a landslide after the district was tailored to his needs by friendly Democrats. For instance, the boundary was altered slightly to include Isenberg's home.

Isenberg had his toughest re-election race in 1988, when his Republican opponent tried to paint him as

Phil Isenberg

soft on crime and as too close to liberal Assembly Speaker Willie Brown, who has served as something of a mentor to Isenberg. In 1990, Isenberg faced an easier opponent in Republican Tom Griffin, a Sacramento businessman and former general counsel for the state Department of Education. Griffin dropped out of the race complaining that it was too hard for political newcomers to compete against incumbents. Even so, Griffin won 38 percent of the vote.

Isenberg remains a top lieutenant to Brown, who gave him his first job as a lawyer and for whom he once served as chief of staff to the Assembly Ways and Means Committee. As assistant speaker pro tem, Isenberg is one of the Assembly Democrats' top political strategists, and he plays a key role in trying to maintain the Democratic majority in the lower house.

Some speculate that he may be among those in line to succeed Brown. Should Tom Hannigan leave the Assembly – as he has hinted he might – Isenberg probably will be considered the front-runner to be elected speaker. Others believe Isenberg will run for state Senate if and when Leroy Greene steps down. He has steadily moved up in the Democratic hierarchy, becoming chairman of the Judiciary Committee at the start of the 1988 session, a panel with responsibility over such issues as abortion and liability laws.

The owlish-looking Isenberg can be charming and witty or arrogant, impatient and dogmatic. And while other politicians might prefer splashy headlines, Isenberg seems to relish the nuts and bolts of the government process. He is a political insider, knows parliamentary rules and is adept at quietly maneuvering behind the scenes.

While politics are clearly Isenberg's passion, he has made some significant policy contributions as well. In 1989, he pushed through a new law to provide a state-subsidized health insurance program for Californians with pre-existing illnesses who would otherwise be uninsurable. He also played key roles in negotiating compromises on how to spend money from the state's tobacco tax and in the 50-year-old dispute over water diversions from Mono Lake.

No other issue generates more passion in Northern California than water and Isenberg has been in the middle of the continuing war of words between the north and the central and southern parts of the state. Isenberg is considered a major player on water issues, and a maverick one at that. He has argued that less water from the north should go to San Joaquin Valley farms so that more would be available for fast-growing urban areas in Southern California. The position has shaken what has traditionally been a rock-solid alliance between southern and central California interests against the north.

As the drought intensified in 1991, Isenberg made the following prediction: "I don't have any doubt in my mind that by the middle of this year, barring a miracle, there will be mandatory rationing throughout California – Northern and Southern."

PERSONAL: elected 1982; born Feb. 25, 1939, in Gary, Ind.; home, Sacramento; Army 1962-1968; B.A. social science CSU Sacramento; J.D. UC Berkeley; wife, Marilyn Araki.

CAREER: lawyer; Sacramento City Council 1971-1975, mayor 1975-1982; aide to Assemblyman Willie Brown 1967-1968; Ways & Means consultant 1971; assistant speaker pro tem.

COMMITTEES: Judiciary (chair); Health; Revenue & Taxation; Water, Parks & Wildlife; (Joint) Courthouse Financing & Construction; Legislative Budget; Legislative Ethics; Refugee Resettlement, International Migration & Cooperative Development.

OFFICES: Capitol, (916) 445-1611, FAX (916) 327-1788; district, 1215 15th St., 102, Sacramento 95814, (916) 324-4676; 625 W. 4th St., 4, Antioch 94509, (415) 778-4510; 1200 W. Tokay, Room D, Lodi 95240, (209) 334-4945.

REGISTRATION: 55.9% D, 34.8% R

1990 CAMPAIGN:	Isenberg – D	56%	$393,571
	Tom Griffin – R	38.4%	$8,467
1988 CAMPAIGN:	Isenberg – D	57.2%	$2,099,545
	Larry Bowler – R	42.8%	$649,193

RATINGS:

AFL	PIRG	CLCV	NOW	CTA	CofC	CFB	NRA	FPAC
97%	100%	100%	90%	96%	32%	33%	0%	4%

KEY VOTES:

Divest S. Africa:	YES	Insurance reform:	YES	Child sick leave:	YES
Assault gun ban:	YES	Parent consent abortion:	NO	Ban AIDS discrim:	YES
Clean Air Act:	YES	Cutting old trees:	NO	Extend death penalty:	YES
Lmt product tort:	YES	Ban offshore oil:	YES	Restrict abortion funds:	NO
Lower alcohol std:	YES	Basic health care:	YES	Oil spill prevent:	YES
Ethics reform:	YES	Work cancer stds:	YES	Earthquake insure:	YES

Robert J. Campbell (D)
11th Assembly District

Robert Campbell is one of the most consistently liberal members of the Assembly. And with the high percentage of blue-collar workers and minority residents of a Bay Area district that stretches from Richmond to Pittsburg, he can afford to be. Although Democratic registration in the district has gone down slightly, Democrats still outnumber registered Republicans by nearly 40 percentage points.

Campbell, a former insurance broker and Richmond city councilman, has only drawn token opposition – when he has any – since his election in 1980. One of Campbell's key interests is education funding. As chairman of the Assembly budget subcommittee that deals with education, he has significant influence

Robert Campbell

on where education dollars are spent. He has fought to restore funding cuts for community colleges and state universities as well as to limit increases in tuition. His efforts have made him popular with the University of California Student Association.

Campbell's liberal leanings also have been evident on environmental legislation, civil liberties issues and measures to help minorities and recently arrived immigrants. And he was one of only a few legislators who had an announced policy of refusing to take fees for speeches before the practice was outlawed.

But Campbell has not been adept at playing the inside game; several legislators with less seniority have more clout.

PERSONAL: elected 1980; born Dec. 20, 1937, in Los Angeles; home, Richmond; Army, National Guard Reserves 1961-1972; education, B.A. social science and history San Francisco State University, post-graduate studies UC Berkeley; divorced; children, Lisa and Kirk; Roman Catholic.

CAREER: insurance broker; Richmond City Council 1975-1982.

COMMITTEES: Higher Education; Revenue & Taxation; Water, Parks & Wildlife; Ways & Means and subcommittee 2 – school finance (chair); (Joint) Legislative Audit; Legislative Budget; School Facilities.

OFFICES: Capitol, (916) 445-7890; district, 2901 MacDonald Ave., Richmond 94804, (415) 237-8171; 604 Ferry St., 220, Martinez 94553, (415) 372-7990.

REGISTRATION: 63.7% D, 25.1% R 1988

1990 CAMPAIGN:	Campbell – D	100%	$133,972

1988 CAMPAIGN:	Campbell – D	72.9%	$200,094
	David Williams – R	27.1%	$2,234

RATINGS:

AFL	PIRG	CLCV	NOW	CTA	CofC	CFB	NRA	FPAC
98%	95%	100%	90%	95%	23%	25%	0%	0%

KEY VOTES:

Divest S. Africa:	YES	Insurance reform:	YES	Child sick leave:	YES
Assault gun ban:	YES	Parent consent abortion:	NO	Ban AIDS discrim:	YES
Clean Air Act:	YES	Cutting old trees:	NO	Extend death penalty:	NO
Lmt product tort:	NO	Ban offshore oil:	YES	Restrict abortion funds:	NO
Lower alcohol std:	NO	Basic health care:	YES	Oil spill prevent:	YES
Ethics reform:	YES	Work cancer stds:	YES	Earthquake insure:	NO

Tom H. Bates (D)
12th Assembly District

If the incumbent had had more pull with Democratic mapmakers, the 12th Assembly District probably would be more homogeneous. Instead the district, which covers portions of Alameda and Contra Costa counties, seems to have been composed of the bits left over after Democratic leaders of the Assembly had drawn districts to the specifications of others.

Tom Bates

The 12th District includes the upscale portions of Oakland and some affluent suburbs in Contra Costa County, such as Pleasant Hill and Kensington. The center of the district is Berkeley, home of the University of California and the spiritual center of all that is left-of-center in California politics. The bifurcated nature of the district is demonstrated in voter registration figures. The Alameda County portions, including Berkeley, have a 4-1 ratio favoring Democrats while the Contra Costa portions are about 3-2. Overall, it is safely Democratic.

The man who has represented the 12th District since 1976 is Tom Bates, and there's no question that the Alameda segment is his spiritual, as well as actual, home. Bates is perhaps the Assembly's most consistently liberal member and his credentials have been solidified by his marriage to Loni Hancock, the mayor of Berkeley.

Although Bates ranks near the top in Assembly seniority, he has never wielded first-rank power, a reflection of his own rather quiet personality and the extremity of his politics. Bates, an Alameda County supervisor for four years, has concentrated on liberal issues such as health care and only in recent years has he achieved a modicum of authority by becoming chairman of the Assembly Human Services Committee, which deals with welfare-related legislation.

Bates is a member of the "Grizzly Bears," an ad hoc coalition of liberals who congregate in the rear of the Democratic section of the house. His membership in the group has boosted his career of late because the group, as a whole, has gained influence.

The 12th District's strong Democratic bent means that Bates can probably continue getting elected in whatever configuration the 1991 reapportionment fashions his district. He'll most likely stick around until state Sen. Nicholas Petris retires, allowing Bates to move up to the Senate, or until a congressional seat becomes available.

PERSONAL: elected 1976; born Feb. 9, 1938, in San Diego; home, Berkeley; education, B.A. communications and public policy UC Berkeley; wife, Loni Hancock; children, Casey and Jon; no religious affiliation.

CAREER: real estate; Alameda County Board of Supervisors 1972-1976.

COMMITTEES: Human Services (chair); Governmental Organization; Higher Education; Natural Resources; Public Safety.

OFFICES: Capitol, (916) 445-7554, FAX (916) 445-6434; district, 1414 Walnut St., Berkeley 94709; (415) 540-3176.

REGISTRATION: 62.7% D, 23.1% R

1990 CAMPAIGN:	Bates – D	67.7%	$149,527
	Jonathan Gear – R	26.1%	$1,700
1988 CAMPAIGN:	Bates – D	73.9%	$219,047
	Jerald Udinsky – R	23.8%	$0

RATINGS:

AFL	PIRG	CLCV	NOW	CTA	CofC	CFB	NRA	FPAC
96%	95%	100%	100%	87%	23%	25%	0%	0%

KEY VOTES:

Divest S. Africa:	YES	Insurance reform:	YES	Child sick leave:	YES
Assault gun ban:	YES	Parent consent abortion:	NO	Ban AIDS discrim:	YES
Clean Air Act:	YES	Cutting old trees:	NO	Extend death penalty:	NO
Lmt product tort:	NO	Ban offshore oil:	YES	Restrict abortion funds:	NO
Lower alcohol std:	NO	Basic health care:	YES	Oil spill prevent:	YES
Ethics reform:	YES	Work cancer stds:	YES	Earthquake insure:	YES

Barbara Lee (D)

13th Assembly District

The eastern shore of San Francisco Bay is a region of contrasts: of great wealth and great squalor, mind-bending scientific research and mind-destroying drug traffic, industry and social inertia. Oakland lies at the heart of the region, a city that contains all of its contrasts and contradictions. It has a deeply troubled school district that has teetered on financial and political collapse. But with underdog pride it also has witnessed a rebirth of its downtown.

The center of Oakland is also the center of the 13th District, which takes in nearby Alameda and Emeryville. The seat was occupied for more than a decade by Elihu Harris, who was elected mayor of Oakland in 1990. The district's Democratic registration, more than 70 percent, is among the highest in the Assembly.

Harris' seat went to Barbara Lee, a former political consultant and aide to Rep. Ron Dellums. Lee had two decades of political experience before running for office herself. She was a key aide to Shirley Chisholm's 1972 president campaign and a fundraiser for Dellums and other Democrats over the years. She was active in Jesse Jackson's presidential campaigns. In so doing, Lee has been on a first-name basis with all of the East Bay's most prominent Democratic politicians.

Barbara Lee

Once Harris announced that he was considering running for Oakland mayor, Lee began running for his Assembly seat – 18 months before the primary, well before any other contenders came onto the scene. For all practical purposes, the election was decided in the primary. Lee picked up endorsements of virtually the entire East Bay Democratic legislative delegation and the Dellums progressives. Her most serious primary opponent, Aleta Cannon, an Oakland City Council member, was an ally of Oakland Mayor Lionel Wilson. But Wilson's wing of the Democratic party took a drubbing in 1990. Wilson fell so far from favor that he did not make it past his re-election primary and Cannon fell with him. In the general election, the GOP's Barbara Thomas, an Alameda City Council member, did not stand a prayer against Lee and garnered barely 20 percent of the vote.

As a rookie legislator, Lee already has weighed in with bills on issues such as abortion. Her AB 1097 would make it a misdemeanor to obstruct a health-care facility, such as an abortion clinic. Nor has she been shy on the fund-raising circuit, sending out invitations to a fund-raiser with tea bags attached. Lee appears to be among the brighter – and more ambitious – members of the Assembly Class of '90 and bears watching as her career progresses.

PERSONAL: elected 1990; born July 16, 1946, in El Paso, Tex.; home, Oakland; education, B.A. Mills College, M.A. social welfare UC Berkeley; divorced; children, Tony and Craig; Baptist.

CAREER: administrative assistant Rep. Ronald Dellums; owned private consulting business.

COMMITTEES: Education; Environmental Safety & Toxic Materials; Higher Education; Labor & Employment; Public Safety; Transportation.

OFFICES: Capitol, (916) 445-7442, FAX (916) 327-1941; district, 405 14th St., 715, Oakland, 94612, (415) 464-0339.

REGISTRATION: 72.4%, 15.1%

1990 CAMPAIGN:			
Lee – D		79.4%	$324,071
Barbara Thomas – R		20.6%	$0

RATINGS and **KEY VOTES**: Newly elected

Johan M. Klehs (D)

14th Assembly District

Democrats don't worry much about the possibility of losing this East Bay blue-collar district, which includes the cities of San Leandro and Hayward, Castro Valley and part of Oakland. Johan Klehs, a former aide to Sen. Bill Lockyer, has used his knowledge of how the legislative and political system work to his advantage. He has risen rather quickly to positions of political power, first as chairman of the Assembly Elections and Reapportionment Committee and now as chairman of the Assembly Revenue and Taxation Committee. In that post, he has attempted to head off efforts to open new loopholes in the state tax code – a refreshing change – but has had only limited success. With the state facing an unprec-

Johan Klehs

edented fiscal crisis in 1991, it fell to Klehs to fashion the Assembly Democrats' response to Gov. Pete Wilson's budget revenue proposals.

Klehs is generally liberal, but at times can be unpredictable. He is an archetypical political animal, the staffer who learned how to push buttons and then used that knowledge for his own benefit. In recent years, he has proposed many high-profile tax-related bills on a variety of subjects. He teamed with Controller Gray Davis to propose a constitutional amendment to give tax credits to individuals and corporations contributing toward research for an AIDS vaccine. He joined Attorney General John Van de Kamp in proposing that corporate tax loopholes be closed to fund anti-drug programs. He's also proposed letting first-time home buyers use Individual Retirement Accounts to purchase their homes without tax penalties and taking away tax-exempt status from social clubs that discriminate in membership.

Count Klehs as another who will be looking for a congressional seat should the opportunity present itself.

PERSONAL: elected 1982; born June 27, 1952, in Alameda; home, Castro Valley; education, B.A. political science and M.A. public administration CSU Hayward, attended Harvard University John F. Kennedy School of Government; single; Lutheran.

CAREER: Legislative assistant to Assemblyman Bill Lockyer 1973-1976; San Leandro City Council 1978-1982; salesman for a direct-mail advertising firm.

COMMITTEES: Revenue & Taxation (chair); Elections, Reapportionment & Constitutional Amendments; Insurance; Labor & Employment.

OFFICES: Capitol, 445-8160, FAX (916) 445-0967; district, 2450 Washington Ave., 270, San Leandro 94577, (415) 464-0847.

REGISTRATION: 63.1% D, 25.4% R

1990 CAMPAIGN: Klehs – D   65.8% $542,134
                          Don Grundmann – R   26.6% $0
1988 CAMPAIGN: Klehs – D   72.7% $489,698
                          Elliot Eaton – R   27.3% $0

RATINGS:

AFL	PIRG	CLCV	NOW	CTA	CofC	CFB	NRA	FPAC
98%	100%	100%	100%	98%	32%	25%	0%	4%

KEY VOTES:

Divest S. Africa:	YES	Insurance reform:	YES	Child sick leave:	YES
Assault gun ban:	YES	Parent consent abortion:	NO	Ban AIDS discrim:	YES
Clean Air Act:	YES	Cutting old trees:	NO	Extend death penalty:	–
Lmt product tort:	YES	Ban offshore oil:	YES	Restrict abortion funds:	NO
Lower alcohol std:	YES	Basic health care:	YES	Oil spill prevent:	YES
Ethics reform:	YES	Work cancer stds:	YES	Earthquake insure:	YES

William P. Baker (R)
15th Assembly District

There aren't many Republican enclaves in the east San Francisco Bay Area, but Democratic line-drawers made sure most of them were in the 15th Assembly District. It includes the Contra Costa County communities of Danville, Walnut Creek, San Ramon, Orinda, Lafayette, Moraga and part of Concord as well as the Pleasanton area of Alameda County.

William Baker fits this upscale, conservative district to a tee. A former budget analyst with the state Department of Finance, he has made tax and money matters his specialty. He is the Assembly Republicans' acknowledged fiscal expert and serves as the point man for them in virtually all major tax and budget negotiations.

William Baker

Along with his indisputable budget expertise, comes an acid wit. Baker is known to have angered more than a few of his colleagues after he has stared them down through his wire-rimmed glasses and dressed them down with sharp-tongued barbs. "The only difference between a Boy Scout camp and this Legislature," he once quipped, "is the Boy Scout camp has adult leaders." In a Capitol hallway, a young girl, wide-eyed with wonder, once asked him if he was a legislator. "No," Baker told her. "Do I look like a crook?"

Baker came to Sacramento with a mission to cut spending and limit taxes. While he has become more willing to negotiate over the budget with leaders of the Democratic-controlled Legislature, he has stuck close to his mission. In 1989, for example, he carried a bill that would have required pharmaceutical companies to discount the prices they charge the state for drugs that are regularly prescribed to Medi-Cal patients. The measure was killed by high-powered lobbyists, but Baker saw it as a way to save the state millions. Baker also has pushed to eliminate renters credit on state income taxes – a credit dear to the hearts of Democrats.

Because of his position in the GOP leadership, Baker was often called upon by Gov. George Deukmejian to carry bills for the administration. In 1989, Baker carried the governor's unsuccessful bill to let convicts in state prisons work for private employers. But Baker grew increasingly restive with the Deukmejian administration, which he viewed as selling out conservative ideals for political expediency. Baker became ever harsher in his public criticism of colleagues during the prolonged 1990 budget impasse. During one of the aborted attempts to pass a budget, Baker said the Senate "left us with a bag of dog doo on our doorstep, lit it on fire, rang the doorbell and ran away." A few days later, Baker pronounced a new proposal "Dog Doo II."

He has minded his tongue at the start of Pete Wilson's administration, but no one expects Baker to mind it long.

PERSONAL: elected 1980; born June 14, 1940, in Oakland; home, Danville; Coast Guard Reserve (six months active duty); education, B.S. business and industrial management San Jose State University, graduate study international marketing research CSU Long Beach; wife, Joanne Atack; children, Todd, Mary, Billy and Robby; Protestant.

CAREER: businessman; assistant to secretary of the Senate; budget analyst state Department of Finance.

COMMITTEES: Ways & Means (vice chairman); Elections, Reapportionment and Constitutional Amendments; Transportation; (Joint) Legislative Budget; Revision of the Penal Code.

OFFICES: Capitol, (916) 445-8528, FAX (916) 327-2201; district, 1801 N. Calif. Blvd., 103, Walnut Creek 94596, (415) 932-2537.

REGISTRATION: 36.9% D, 50.1% R

1990 CAMPAIGN:	Baker – R	55.1%	$462,532
	Wendell Williams – D	44.9%	$97,654
1988 CAMPAIGN:	Baker – R	68%	$724,002
	Wendell Williams – D	32%	$38,669

RATINGS:

AFL	PIRG	CLCV	NOW	CTA	CofC	CFB	NRA	FPAC
11%	19%	10%	30%	56%	77%	67%	100%	96%

KEY VOTES:

Divest S. Africa:	NO	Insurance reform:	–	Child sick leave:	NO
Assault gun ban:	NO	Parent consent abortion:	YES	Ban AIDS discrim:	NO
Clean Air Act:	NO	Cutting old trees:	YES	Extend death penalty:	YES
Lmt product tort:	YES	Ban offshore oil:	NO	Restrict abortion funds:	YES
Lower alcohol std:	YES	Basic health care:	NO	Oil spill prevent:	YES
Ethics reform:	YES	Work cancer stds:	NO	Earthquake insure:	YES

John L. Burton (D)
16th Assembly District

This district takes in some of the best – and the worst – that is San Francisco. It includes the eastern-most portion of the city, encompassing the downtown business district, Chinatown, the waterfront (including Fisherman's Wharf), the seedy Tenderloin, the industrial area and the poor and mostly black Hunter's Point neighborhood. Given the variety one can find within the 16th District, it's perhaps fitting that its representative is John Burton, the Capitol's only self-acknowledged ex-drug abuser.

John Burton

Burton, his late brother Philip, Willie Brown and George Moscone, who became mayor of San Francisco and was assassinated in 1978, were the founders of a political organization that has dominated San Francisco's major league politics for more than a generation.

John Burton and Willie Brown began in politics together as idealistic young men and close friends. They went to the Assembly, where Brown flourished, and Burton moved on to Congress. The two, along with Dolores Huerta of the United Farm Workers, were the co-chairs of the 1972 California delegation to the national Democratic convention that nominated George McGovern and made Willie Brown semifamous.

By 1980, Brown was speaker. And the organization's greatest triumph came in the 1981 reapportionment in which brother Philip made his "contribution to modern art" by carving up congressional districts in such a manner that lopsided majorities for the Democrats were preserved throughout the 1980s.

But then the Burton machine faltered. John Burton suddenly quit his seat in Congress, admitting publicly that he had a cocaine and alcohol problem. In 1983, Philip Burton died. His wife, Sala, took over his congressional seat but she died in 1987. The organization was brought back to life in 1987 to move then-Assemblyman Art Agnos into the mayor's office, which in turn opened the door for John Burton to run for the Assembly again.

The 1988 special election for Agnos' seat pitted Burton, who had undergone extensive and, he says, successful therapy for his substance abuse problems, against Roberta Achtenberg, an activist for lesbian and gay rights who was bidding to become the state's first openly lesbian legislator. She spent $333,383 in a sometimes bitter campaign. In the end, Burton's name and the organization's professional-class efforts (and heavier spending) won out and he returned to Sacramento.

Burton may have been the least fresh freshman ever to enter the Assembly, given his long political career and his close association with Brown. Those attributes paid off with a series of important committee assignments, including chairmanship of the Public Safety Committee, which deals with always sensitive crime legislation.

Burton is, of course, a liberal and by nature an outspoken one, so he has evolved into one of the Legislature's most distinct characters, a man who prowls the chambers and the hearings rooms constantly, usually shunning a tie, making loud and often rude commentaries on events as they unfold. He is known for having one of the shortest attention spans in the state Capitol.

He also has become louder in statewide Democratic circles. After gubernatorial candidate Dianne Feinstein lost in 1990, Burton publicly blamed Democratic Party Chairman Jerry Brown for failing to follow through on promises of a big voter registration and get-out-the-vote drive. Burton demanded that Brown step down as party chairman. Brown stood his ground, but only for awhile, eventually quitting to run for the U.S. Senate.

Burton's impact on the Assembly is more often theatrical than legislative. But he functions as a member of Brown's inner circle and the two represent a potent political force on behalf of San Francisco's parochial issues. As Public Safety chairman, Burton gleefully kills Republicans' lock-'em-up anti-crime bills while crafting Democratic measures that give his party the edge on crime legislation.

PERSONAL: elected 1988 (special election); born Dec. 15, 1932, in Cincinnati, Ohio; home, San Francisco; Army 1954-1956; education, B.A. social science San Francisco State University, J.D. University of San Francisco Law School; divorced; daughter, Kimiko.

CAREER: lawyer; Assembly 1964-1974; U.S. House of Representatives 1974-1982.

COMMITTEES: Public Safety (chair); Health; Ways & Means; (Joint) Legislative Budget.

OFFICES: Capitol, (916) 445-8253, FAX (916) 324-4899; district, 711 Van Ness Ave., 300, San Francisco 94102, (415) 557-2253.

REGISTRATION: 68.7% D, 14.9% R

1990 CAMPAIGN: Burton – D   100% $381,864

1988 CAMPAIGN: Burton – D   77.5% $845,156
                    Brian Mavrogeorge – R   14.6% $16,779

RATINGS:

AFL	PIRG	CLCV	NOW	CTA	CofC	CFB	NRA	FPAC
97%	90%	100%	80%	95%	23%	25%	0%	4%

KEY VOTES:

Insurance reform:	YES	Child sick leave:	
Assault gun ban:	YES	Ban AIDS discrim:	
Lower alcohol std:	–	Basic health care:	
Ethics reform:	YES	Work cancer stds:	

YES	Cutting old trees:	NO
YES	Restrict abortion funds:	NO
YES	Oil spill prevent:	YES
YES	Earthquake insure:	YES

Willie L. Brown Jr. (D)

17th Assembly District

Willie Lewis Brown Jr. is the ranking state legislator in seniority, arguably the most powerful and certainly the most interesting. He has been in the Assembly for more than a quarter of a century, rising to heights far beyond his humble origins. And, arguably, he is the most beloved and the most hated of California's politicians.

Willie Brown

However flashy he may be, Brown is not just another legislator. He has held center court in California's ornate Capitol for most of his career and for nearly a decade has been the Assembly's speaker, breaking all records for longevity.

A fiery orator and a brilliant strategist, Brown has an explosive temper and an equally sharp, urbane wit. But he leaves many, even those who admire him, wondering if he has any core beliefs other than holding power and enjoying to the hilt all that comes with it. Brown often behaves as if all that counts is Willie Brown.

Brown's district is almost an afterthought in his political career. It encompasses the more affluent western and northern sections of the city, but is so overwhelmingly Democratic that Brown need not spend more time on it than it takes to file his re-election papers every two years. Brown is a star, and not just in San Francisco and the tight little world of Sacramento politics. He was the Rev. Jesse Jackson's national campaign chairman in 1988.

His roots were modest – a black youth who had shined shoes in Mineola, Tex. He left the Lone Star State and never looked back. He went to college at San Francisco State and earned a law degree at Hastings. Brown was a man who seemed destined for big things from the moment he walked onto the Assembly floor as a freshman legislator in 1965, a flamboyant, left-leaning, angry-talking young street lawyer who had formed a homegrown political organization with like-minded liberals, the Burton brothers (Philip and John) and George Moscone, the son of a local fisherman. Brown had an opinion on everything and would voice it to anyone who would listen. One of his first votes was against the re-election of the legendary Jesse Unruh as speaker of the house. But Unruh tolerated Brown, perhaps because both were raised dirt poor in Texas, both emigrated to California after World War II and both began their political careers as rabble rousers.

"It's a good thing you aren't white," Unruh remarked to Brown one day after the latter had made an especially effective floor speech early in his career.

"Why's that?" Brown asked.

"Because if you were, you'd own the place," Unruh replied.

Speakers of the Assembly

Name	P*	Year(s)	Name	P*	Year(s)
Thomas J. White	–	1849	John C. Lynch	R	1895
John Bigler	D	1849,51	Frank L. Coombs	R	1897
Richard P. Hammond	D	1852	Howard E. Wright	R	1899
Isaac B. Wall	D	1853	Alden Anderson	R	1899
Charles S. Fairfax	D	1854	Cornelius W. Pendleton	R	1901
William W. Stow	W	1855	Arthur G. Fisk	R	1903
James T. Farley	A	1856	Frank C. Prescott	R	1905
Elwood T. Beatty	D	1857	R.L. Beardslee	R	1907
N.E. Whiteside	D	1858	P.S. Stanton	R	1909
William C. Stratton	D	1859	A.H. Hewitt	R	1911
Phillip Moore	D	1860	C.C. Young	R-P	1913-17
R.N. Burnell	DD	1861	Henry W. Wright	R	1919,21
George Barstow	R	1862	Frank Merriam	R	1923,25
Tim Machin	U	1863	Edgar C. Levey	R	1927-31
William H. Sears	U	1864	Walter J. Little	R	1933
John Yule	U	1866	F.C. Clowdsley	R	1934
Caisas T. Ryland	D	1868	Edward Craig	R	1935
George H. Rogers	D	1870	William Moseley Jones	D	1937
Thomas B. Shannon	R	1872	Paul Peek	D	1939
Morris M. Estee	I	1874	Gordon H. Garland	D	1940,41
G.J. Carpenter	D	1876	Charles W. Lyon	R	1943,45
Campbell P. Berry	D	1878	Sam L. Collins	R	1947-52
Jabez F. Cowdery	R	1880	James W. Silliman	R	1953-54
William H. Parks	R	1881	Luther H. Lincoln	R	1955-58
Hugh M. Larue	D	1883	Ralph M. Brown	D	1959-61
William H. Parks	R	1885	Jesse M. Unruh	D	1961-68
William H. Jordan	R	1887	Robert T. Monagan	R	1969-70
Robert Howe	D	1889	Bob Moretti	D	1971-74
Frank L. Coombs	R	1891	Leo T. McCarthy	D	1974-80
F.H. Gould	D	1893	Willie Brown Jr.	D	1980-

Key to parties: A=American, D=Democrat, DD=Douglas Democrat, I=Independent, P=Progressive, R=Republican, U=Union; – denotes no party.

Civil rights was the early focus of Brown's legislative career and no matter what the event, he was ready with a quote. When black athletes Tommy Smith and John Carlos raised their fists in a "black power" salute at the 1968 Olympics, Brown said, "They will be known forever as two niggers who upset the Olympic Games. I'd rather have them known for that than as two niggers who won two medals."

Despite statements of that sort, Brown was developing a reputation among Capitol insiders for smart political work. In 1970, he took his first big step up the ladder when friend Bob Moretti became speaker and elevated Brown into the chairmanship of the powerful Ways and Means Committee. Brown became a master of arcane matters of state finance, including the budget, and recruited a staff of young advisers who today form the nucleus of his Assembly senior staff.

California's political establishment was beginning to respect, if not like, the young politician. He took the national stage in 1972 as the leader of the George McGovern faction from California at the Democratic National Convention during complex and bitter credentials fights.

Moretti was planning to step down in 1974 to run for governor and wanted to lateral the speakership to Brown. But Brown was to make the worst tactical error of his career in counting on the support of Hispanic and black members. Secretly, San Francisco's other assemblyman, Leo McCarthy, had courted the minority lawmakers, promising them committee chairmanships and other goodies. When the vote came, they stood with McCarthy, who snatched the speakership from under Brown's nose.

That was the beginning of an in-house exile for Brown, one that became even more intensive when he and some supporters plotted an unsuccessfully coup against McCarthy. At one point, Brown was given an office so small that he had to place his filing cabinets outside in the hall.

The exile lasted for two years, during which, Brown said later, he underwent intense self-examination and concluded that he had been too arrogant in dealings with colleagues – like calling one member a "500-pound tub of Jello" in public. McCarthy resurrected Brown's legislative career in 1976 by naming him chairman of the Revenue and Taxation Committee, a fairly substantial job, and that gesture paid off in 1979, when another bloc of Democratic Assembly members, led by Howard Berman of Los Angeles, tried to oust McCarthy from the speakership. Brown declared loyalty to his old rival and maintained it during a year of often bitter infighting that culminated during the 1980 elections. Berman had seemingly won enough contested seats in 1980 to claim the speakership but the desperate McCarthyites cut a deal with Republicans to name Willie Brown as speaker. The Republicans, who openly feared a Berman speakership, were promised some extra consideration by the new regime. Although they later were to claim that Brown reneged, he always maintained that he stuck to the letter of the agreement.

Brown's speakership has been controversial. He has seen Democratic ranks whittled down due to Republican victories, but that may have resulted more from larger political trends over which he had no control. He has been accused of neglecting policy for politics, of shaking down special interests for millions of dollars in campaign funds, of presiding over a blatantly partisan reapportionment of legislative districts and of being too consumed with the inside game. Brown lists making life easier for legislators as his chief accomplishment as speaker. He has had a paucity of major legislative achievements. His principal legislative triumph as speaker, some think, was his authorship of the state's mandatory seat-belt law.

Brown has not remade the speakership, as Unruh did. Rather, he took the vast inherent powers of the office and shaped them into a personal tool. He is less innovator than implementer. He says that he appoints competent people to staff and committee positions and gives them the tools to work.

Despite aging, Brown has lost little of his controversiality among members of the larger public. But as speaker, he's answerable to only two constituencies: the voters of the 17th Assembly District and the 79 other members of his house. Brown could not be elected to statewide office, but he doesn't aspire to it. Republicans use Brown as a tool to stir up their troops and raise money, portraying him as the political devil incarnate. He says – with some validity – that it's thinly veiled racism. Likewise, he pins the racist label on critics, in and out of the media.

So it was not surprising that Brown took it very personally when the voters in November 1990 passed Proposition 140, imposing term limits on legislators and forcing them to cut staffs. Voter antipathy toward the Legislature was aimed, in part, at Speaker Brown – and he knew it. As a new session unfolded in the wake of Proposition 140, Brown bitterly lashed out at the press, calling reporters "despicable" and moving their desks from the side of Assembly chambers to the rear. Brown viewed the passage of term limits as an image problem – and not as the result of a more deep-seated institutional malaise.

One of his most nettlesome and frequent critics, Sherry Bebitch Jeffe, a political scientist with the Claremont Graduate School and a former Unruh staffer, maintains that Brown has become increasingly worried about how history will view his speakership. "My guess is that he has decided there is some truth to the charges about what has happened to the image of the institution," Jeffe said. "That indicates to me a shred of decency, a shred of understanding that he has had a role in its decline. ... If his legacy is that he helped destroy the legislative institution, I don't believe that is something he can live with."

At least some of the controversy stems from his high-style personal life. The $1,500 Italian-cut suits, the low-slung sports cars and the flashy parties that he throws for personal and political reasons all contribute to the image, as do his liaisons with a string of attractive women (he's long separated from his wife, Blanche, a reclusive dance teacher).

But it's what Brown does to support that lifestyle that raises the most eyebrows. He represents, as an attorney and quasi-lobbyist, a number of well-heeled corporations. His blue-chip client list includes one of the largest landowners in California, the Santa Fe-Southern Pacific Realty (renamed Catellus Inc.). Developers such as the East Bay's Ron Cowan and bond adviser Calvin Grigsby also have put the speaker on retainer. Occasionally, some of those clients also do business in Sacramento. Brown's activities on behalf of one of his law clients, Norcal Solid Waste Systems Inc., attracted the attention of the FBI in 1990. The company has increasingly come to dominate the garbage business in Northern California. The FBI, it became known, began looking into allegations that Brown attempted to help the company override local opposition to placing a garbage transfer station in Solano County. In December 1990, federal agents served a new round of subpoenas in the state Capitol for legislation involving the garbage business. Among the bills subpoenaed was a measure that became law allowing a Norcal subsidiary to relocate a dump near Marysville over the objections of local residents.

Regardless of what he does in Sacramento, Brown is a power in and around San Francisco – and especially so since Art Agnos became mayor with Brown's active assistance. Former San Francisco Supervisor Terry Francois put it this way a few years ago, even before Agnos became mayor: "He engenders fear like you wouldn't believe. I have just become enthralled at the way he wields power. I don't know a politician in San Francisco that dares take him on."

The greatest threat to Brown's hold on the speakership came in 1987 when five Democratic members, all of whom had enjoyed close relations with the speaker, declared their independence. The "Gang of Five," as the group was immediately dubbed, demanded procedural changes they said were reforms to lessen the power of the speaker. Before long they were actively demanding that Brown step down as speaker. They could have formed a new majority with Republicans, but the GOP leader at the time, Pat Nolan, also had established a close relationship with Brown and protected the speaker's right flank. Brown stripped the five of their best committee assignments and the war of nerves went on for a year. Eventually, the Republicans agreed to form a coalition with the Gang of Five. But Brown bolstered his loyalists with enough victories at the polls in 1988 to eke out a paper-thin re-election as speaker. When the Democrats increased their majority in the Assembly in 1990, Brown's grip on the speakership was assured.

The question of how long Brown will remain as speaker has become one of the most often asked in the Capitol. There is no definite answer. Sometimes it seems as if the only reason Brown is still speaker is that his colleagues cannot agree on a replacement. The bitterness of the Berman-McCarthy fight of 1980 – and the Gang of Five – is an experience many Assembly members do not savor repeating. For his part, Brown says he wants to be speaker for the indefinite future. The betting in the Capitol is that he will remain at least through the 1991 reapportionment.

PERSONAL: elected 1964; born March 20, 1934, in Mineola, Tex.; home, San Francisco; National Guard Reserves 1955-1958; education, B.A. San Francisco State University, J.D. Hastings College of Law; wife, Blanche Vitero; children, Susan, Robin and Michael; Methodist.

CAREER: lawyer, maintains a law practice while in office with major corporate clients including Catellus Inc., Olympia & York, Underwater World at Pier 39, Towers Collection Service, Inc., Doric Development, Harbor Bay Isle, Davies Medical Center; board of directors, American Shared Hospital Services Inc. 1984 to present; speaker of the Assembly 1980 to present.

COMMITTEES: the speaker of the Assembly is a member of all Assembly committees; (Joint) Courthouse Financing & Construction; Fire, Police, Emergency & Disaster Services; Rules.

OFFICES: Capitol, (916) 445-8077, FAX (916) 445-4189; district, 1388 Sutter St., San Francisco 94109, (415) 557-0784; Southern California, 107 S. Broadway, 8009, Los Angeles 90012, (213) 620-4356.

REGISTRATION: 63.4% D, 19.7% R

1990 CAMPAIGN:	Brown – D	64.2%	$6,770,364
	Terence Faulkner – R	27.1%	$0
1988 CAMPAIGN:	Brown – D	71.5%	$6,988,137
	Curt Augustine – R	23.2%	$0

RATINGS:

AFL	PIRG	CLCV	NOW	CTA	CofC	CFB	NRA	FPAC
94%	91%	95%	100%	99%	32%	42%	0%	8%

KEY VOTES:

Divest S. Africa:	YES	Insurance reform:	YES	Child sick leave:	YES
Assault gun ban:	YES	Parent consent abortion:	NO	Ban AIDS discrim:	YES
Clean Air Act:	YES	Cutting old trees:	–	Extend death penalty:	NO
Lmt product tort:	YES	Ban offshore oil:	YES	Restrict abortion funds:	NO
Lower alcohol std:	YES	Basic health care:	YES	Oil spill prevent:	YES
Ethics reform:	YES	Work cancer stds:	YES	Earthquake insure:	YES

Delaine Eastin (D)
18th Assembly District

This is a district where Republicans once thought they had a chance to win. Although the numbers clearly favored Democrats – 54 percent to 32 percent – many of those Democrats are conservatives, living in the cities of Fremont, Union City, Newark, Milpitas and parts of San Jose and Pleasanton. Delaine Eastin fought a tough race in 1986 to keep the seat in the Democratic column after the retirement of Alister McAllister. The campaign was among the most expensive for both sides that year.

Since winning the seat, Eastin has become a rising star in Democratic politics. In her first re-election bid in 1988, she blew away her Republican opponent, gaining two-thirds of the votes. Republicans did not

Delaine Eastin

even bother to challenge her in 1990. Eastin is hard-working and ambitious. At the start of the 1991-92 session, she was given the chairmanship of the Assembly Education Committee, a highly visible and important plum. Eastin supplanted longtime Chairwoman Teresa Hughes of Los Angeles, who was demoted without explanation to a Ways and Means subcommittee chair.

The difference between Hughes and Eastin was subtle but important. Hughes had opposed a compromise in 1989 that shifted some school funding from urban to suburban schools. Eastin supported it. In fact, by selecting Eastin to chair the education committee, Speaker Willie Brown appeared to be trying to shore up a weakness in the suburbs on the politically vital issue of education. And in picking Eastin, the speaker signaled that the balance of power on education issues was shifting away from Los Angeles. Ray Edmand, president of the Small Schools Association, welcomed Eastin's appointment, saying she "is out of that Los Angeles aura, that Los Angeles sphere of influence."

Some have talked of Eastin as a future speaker. She has become more partisan – and liberal – as she has progressed as a legislator, in marked contrast to when she walked a moderate line to get elected in 1986. For example, she declined until late in the 1986 campaign to say whether she supported retention of Chief Justice Rose Bird, a litmus test to many conservatives. She ultimately announced her opposition to Bird, causing the National Organization for Women to drop its endorsement of her. By 1990, however, Eastin had earned a 100 percent rating from NOW.

Eastin kept her distance from Dianne Feinstein's gubernatorial bid in 1990. She publicly stated that Feinstein had snubbed her initial bid for office so she was returning the favor. Eastin instead endorsed John Van de Kamp in the Democratic gubernatorial primary to the displeasure of a number of her women colleagues.

In the Legislature, Eastin has carried a solid list of bills including those aimed at helping consumers, such as pushing for a pilot project to see if it is feasible and economical to keep the Department of Motor Vehicles open on Saturdays to better serve drivers. She is a favorite of environmentalists and has become an advocate for senior citizens. She has also pushed hard for streamlining the San Francisco Bay Area's tangled web of transit districts. Eastin's AB 4 was part of the waste management package signed into law by Gov. George Deukmejian in 1989, setting up market incentives for recycled products. At the start of the 1991-92 session, Eastin reintroduced measures to provide $10,000 grants to cash-strapped school libraries and to reorganize the state's approval process for designing and constructing public buildings – measures vetoed by Deukmejian.

Eastin's intensity, however, can be annoying. Her speaking style often crosses the line into loud lectures rather than gentle persuasion – and her colleagues grumble about it.

PERSONAL: elected 1986; born Aug. 20, 1947, in San Diego; home, Union City; education, B.A. political science UC Davis, M.A. political science UC Santa Barbara; husband, Jack Saunders; no children; non-denominational Christian.

CAREER: corporate planner; political science professor De Anza Community College; City Council Union City.

COMMITTEES: Education (chair); Consumer Protection, Governmental Efficiency & Economic Development; Elections, Reapportionment & Constitutional Amendments; Transportation.

OFFICES: Capitol, (916) 445-7874, FAX (916) 324-2936; district, 39650 Liberty St., 160, Fremont 94538, (415) 791-2151.

REGISTRATION: 53.7% D, 32.4% R

1990 CAMPAIGN:	Eastin – D	100%	$410,523
1988 CAMPAIGN:	Eastin – D	67.3%	$452,117
	Tom Curry – R	32.7%	$64,741

RATINGS:

AFL	PIRG	CLCV	NOW	CTA	CofC	CFB	NRA	FPAC
96%	94%	100%	100%	85%	27%	33%	0%	4%

KEY VOTES:

	Insurance reform:	YES	Child sick leave:	YES
Assault gun ban:	YES	Parent consent abortion: NO	Ban AIDS discrim:	YES
Clean Air Act:	YES	Cutting old trees:	NO	Extend death penalty:	YES
Lmt product tort:	YES	Ban offshore oil:	YES	Restrict abortion funds:	NO
Lower alcohol std:	YES	Basic health care:	YES	Oil spill prevent:	YES
Ethics reform:	YES	Work cancer stds:	YES	Earthquake insure:	YES

K. Jacqueline Speier (D)
19th Assembly District

This safely Democratic district takes in the foggy, slightly funky, suburb of Pacifica and a southwestern corner of San Francisco. Then it moves down the peninsula to include Daly City, South San Francisco and Milbrae. Older housing tracts dot the hillsides while the flat areas are dominated by industry, Candlestick Park and the Cow Palace.

Jackie Speier

This district gave California Louis J. Papan, a man noted for his Rambo approach to politics, who gave up the seat in 1986 for an unsuccessful run against Quentin Kopp for an open seat in the state Senate. Assembly Speaker Willie Brown tried to fill the seat with a hand-picked candidate in the Democratic primary, Mike Nevin. More than half of Nevin's $300,000 primary budget came from Brown or contributors associated with him.

But neither Papan nor Brown calculated well in 1986. Papan lost to Kopp and an underfinanced San Mateo County supervisor, Jackie Speier, won a close Democratic primary and then the general election. Speier was an aide to Rep. Leo Ryan on that ill-fated trip in 1978 to Jonestown, Guyana. Ryan was killed and Speier was shot five times. She lay wounded on an anthill for 22 hours until, near death, she was rescued by the U.S. Air Force. She spent months in a hospital recovering and is still partially paralyzed. She ran unsuccessfully for Ryan's congressional seat.

Speier has turned out to be among the savviest of the newer crop of legislators. She is known as a sharp questioner of administration officials and is easily a match for the acid tongue of Republican Bill Baker during floor debates and committee hearings. Speier has waded into health issues with numerous bills. One of her major efforts in 1988 and 1989 was a measure that would have required cholesterol labeling on food products. It ran a heavy gauntlet of lobbyists from the food and agriculture industries before it died in a committee in July 1989. Many of the bills that she managed to get out of the Legislature did not fare well with Gov. George Deukmejian, who vetoed measures that would have beefed up measles vaccine programs, improved drug abuse and pregnancy programs.

In the 1991-92 session, Speier pushed bills to ban doctors from profiting from lab tests given to their patients or from conducting heart bypass operations without a review board's consent. Another bill would provide Medi-Cal payment for alcohol and drug treatment for pregnant and postpartum women. Speier also is among the Legislature's most vocal protectors of Family Planning and abortion rights.

However, Speier has also begun to get a reputation as a "player" in the Capitol, particularly after the San Francisco Chronicle published a story in July 1990 that reported that Speier had lobbied vigorously for state and federal approval of a dump proposed by a political donor who had given her more than $116,000 in campaign contributions. Although the contributions from Browning-Ferris Industries broke no laws and she has maintained that she was working on behalf of her district, the episode left its tarnish on Speier.

Speier has voted with Speaker Brown in leadership tests, but she has shown an independent streak at times in floor votes. She generally allies herself with the Assembly's "Grizzly Bear" liberals. If she stays in the Assembly, Speier has shown herself bright enough – and adept enough – to eventually move into a leadership position, possibly even becoming the Assembly's first woman speaker. However, many insiders have long suspected Speier has set her sights on Leo Ryan's old congressional seat, which currently is held by Rep. Tom Lantos.

Speier was an early and enthusiastic supporter of Dianne Feinstein's gubernatorial candidacy and was among the most active legislators in her campaign.

PERSONAL: elected 1986; born May 14, 1950, in San Francisco; home, South San Francisco; education, B.A. political science UC Davis, J.D. Hastings College of Law; husband, Steve Sierra; son, Jackson Kent; Roman Catholic.

CAREER: lawyer; San Mateo County Board of Supervisors 1981-1986; staff of Rep. Leo Ryan 1969-1978.

COMMITTEES: Consumer Protection, Governmental Efficiency & Economic Development (chair); Agriculture; Health; Judiciary; Water, Parks & Wildlife; (Joint) Mental Health Research; Rules.

OFFICES: Capitol, (916) 445-8020, FAX (916) 445-0511; district, 220 So. Spruce Ave., 101, South San Francisco 94080, (415) 871-4100.
REGISTRATION: 59.8% D, 25.6% R

1990 CAMPAIGN:	Speier – D	100%	$277,456

1988 CAMPAIGN:	Speier – D	77.2%	$409,857
	Robert Silvestri – R	20.8%	$0

RATINGS:

AFL	PIRG	CLCV	NOW	CTA	CofC	CFB	NRA	FPAC
100%	100%	95%	100%	92%	27%	33%	0%	0%

KEY VOTES:

	Insurance reform:	YES	Child sick leave: –
Assault gun ban: YES	Parent consent abortion:	NO	Ban AIDS discrim: YES
Clean Air Act: YES	Cutting old trees:	NO	Extend death penalty: YES
Lmt product tort: –	Ban offshore oil:	YES	Restrict abortion funds: NO
Lower alcohol std: YES	Basic health care:	YES	Oil spill prevent: YES
Ethics reform: NO	Work cancer stds:	YES	Earthquake insure: YES

Edward T. Lempert (D)
20th Assembly District

No Democrat had been elected to represent this San Mateo County area in 100 years until 1988, when young, idealistic Ted Lempert shocked first-term Republican Bill Duplissea. It was an upset of major proportions in a system that has been left with few political surprises because of redistricting.

Few Republicans or Democrats gave Lempert, an attorney who at 26 was already a longtime political activist, much of a chance to beat Duplissea. In fact, local Democrats casting about for a candidate asked his mother to run first, but she declined. Lempert, a cheery, earnest, boyish sort, took his opportunity seriously. He pounded the sidewalks in hundreds of precincts in Burlingame, Hillsborough, Foster City, Belmont, San Mateo, San Carlos and Half Moon Bay.

Ted Lempert

He scored points questioning his opponent's ethical standards by concentrating on a bill Duplissea carried to benefit a local car dealer – a potent issue in the midst of a Capitol scandal over influence-peddling. As part of his campaign, Lempert pledged to push for higher ethical standards in the Legislature and during his first term, he was true to his word. He introduced a package of eight bills to make major changes in the way the Legislature operates. Many of his ideas were incorporated into Proposition 112, a constitutional amendment on legislative ethics approved by voters in June 1990.

Lempert also pushed several other measures during his first term, including ones that would allow prosecution for misleading advertising and would require video stores to maintain separate areas for adult films. In 1990, Lempert co-authored one of the few major bills of the session – an oil spill prevention measure that included a $100 million fund for cleanups. The final version of the bill was authored by Senate Majority Leader Barry Keene, but Lempert was the Assembly's point man on the issue. In his first term, Lempert proved himself an able legislator of substance.

PERSONAL: elected 1988; born June 14, 1961, in San Mateo; home, San Mateo; education, B.A. public policy Princeton University; J.D. Stanford University; single; Jewish.

CAREER: lawyer.

COMMITTEES: Education; Environmental Safety & Toxic Materials; Housing & Community Development; Transportation.

OFFICES: Capitol, (916) 445-8188, FAX (916) 324-0012; district, 1650 Borel Place, 229, San Mateo 94402, (415) 571-9521.

REGISTRATION: 45.8% D, 41.5% R

1990 CAMPAIGN:	Lempert – D	63.4%	$408,908
	James Rinehart – R	32.2%	$160,194
1988 CAMPAIGN:	Lempert – D	52.4%	$515,944
	Bill Duplissea (incumbent) – R	44.4%	$1,543,437

RATINGS:

AFL	PIRG	CLCV	NOW	CTA	CofC	CFB	NRA	FPAC
92%	91%	95%	100%	92%	32%	33%	0%	0%

KEY VOTES:

Insurance reform:	YES	Child sick leave:	YES	Ban AIDS discrim:	YES
Assault gun ban:	YES	Cutting old trees:	NO	Restrict abortion funds:	NO
Lower alcohol std:	–	Basic health care:	NO	Oil spill prevent:	YES
Ethics reform:	YES	Work cancer stds:	YES	Earthquake insure:	YES

Byron Sher (D)

21st Assembly District

The microchip empire of the Silicon Valley grew up around Stanford University. Thus it may be appropriate that a Stanford professor represents this generally upscale district that includes Mountain View, Palo Alto, East Palo Alto and portions of Redwood City, Menlo Park and Sunnyvale. Bearded Professor Byron Sher was mayor of Palo Alto for two terms before his election to the Assembly in 1980. He has continued to teach law at Stanford during the fall term, perhaps illustrating that the "full-time" Legislature is not exactly full time.

As chairman of the Assembly Natural Resources Committee, Sher has emerged as one of the Legislature's chief environmentalists. He has pushed for adding rivers to the Scenic Rivers Act and he unsuccessfully tried to pass a three-year moratorium on lumbering old-growth stands along the North Coast. He was outmaneuvered by fellow Democratic Assemblyman Dan Hauser, who inserted killer amendments.

Sher's major legislative accomplishment has been in authoring the state's landmark Clean Air Act that gave new powers and responsibilities to local smog districts and requires localities to begin a phased reduction of smog emissions. He took a similar approach in his 1989 legislation revamping the state's garbage management board, a law that is pushing local governments into curbside recycling. The law requires local governments to cut in half the trash sent to dumps by the year 2000. The measure, however, was a mixed bag in another respect: It established a full-time, lavishly paid board. The positions have proven to be political plums. One of the parting acts of Gov. George Deukmejian was to appoint his chief of staff, Michael Frost, to the state garbage board.

Byron Sher

Sher took on the glass industry – and the Assembly speaker – with a bill beefing up recycling fees on glass manufacturers in 1990. The speaker backed a campaign contributor, the Glass Packaging Institute, which had given his campaign $8,000 in the previous two years. But after a public tussle that proved embarrassing, Brown gave in and Sher's AB 1490 was sent to the governor. The higher deposits mandated have since been credited with nearly doubling recycling of containers in California.

On a local level, Sher fought for years against Deukmejian's vetoes of bills to clean up leaking underground storage tanks, an issue of considerable concern to the Silicon Valley with its many toxic waste sites. Sher and his seatmate, Lloyd Connelly, collaborate in ferreting out special-interest bills and voting against them. The two are aligned with the Assembly's "Grizzly Bear" faction of liberals. They're frequently joined by Assemblyman Ted Lempert, a former law student of Sher's.

At the start of the 1991-92 session, Sher kept his committee chairmanship despite his up-and-down relations with the speaker. Sher also enjoyed cordial relations with Gov. Pete Wilson's administration. Sher's staff drafted legislation to make a reality Wilson's campaign pledge for a "California Environmental Protection Agency."

PERSONAL: elected 1980; born Feb. 7, 1928, in St. Louis, Mo.; home, Palo Alto; education, B.S. business administration Washington University, St. Louis; J.D. Harvard University; wife, Linda; children, Adrienne, Benjamin and Katherine; Jewish.

CAREER: law professor, Stanford University; Palo Alto City Council 1965-1967 and 1973-1980; mayor, 1974-1975 and 1977-1978; commissioner of the San Francisco Bay Conservation and Development Commission 1978-1980.

COMMITTEES: Natural Resources (chair); Consumer Protection, Governmental Efficiency & Economic Development; Environmental Safety & Toxic Materials; Insurance; (Joint) Arts; Energy Regulation & the Environment (vice chair); Prison Construction & Operations.

OFFICES: Capitol, (916) 445-7632, FAX (916) 324-6974; district, 785 Castro St., C, Mountain View 94041, (415) 961-6031.

REGISTRATION: 53% D, 32% R

1990 CAMPAIGN:
Sher – D		70.9%	$190,630
Eric Garris – R		29.1%	$0

1988 CAMPAIGN:
Sher – D		87.8%	$138,338
Bob Goodwyn – L		12.2%	

RATINGS:

AFL	PIRG	CLCV	NOW	CTA	CofC	CFB	NRA	FPAC
95%	91%	100%	90%	86%	27%	17%	0%	0%

KEY VOTES:

Divest S. Africa:	YES	Insurance reform:	YES	Child sick leave:	YES
Assault gun ban:	YES	Parent consent abortion:	NO	Ban AIDS discrim:	YES
Clean Air Act:	YES	Cutting old trees:	NO	Extend death penalty:	–
Lmt product tort:	NO	Ban offshore oil:	YES	Restrict abortion funds:	NO
Lower alcohol std:	YES	Basic health care:	YES	Oil spill prevent:	YES
Ethics reform:	YES	Work cancer stds:	YES	Earthquake insure:	YES

Charles W. Quackenbush (R)

22nd Assembly District

Voter registration figures make this district a Republican stronghold. But residents of the affluent San Jose suburbs of Los Altos, Cupertino, Los Gatos, Campbell and Saratoga are not hard-core conservatives, although they are not quite moderates, either.

Enter Charles Quackenbush, a tall, youthful-looking ex-Army captain and high-tech entrepreneur who is conservative with a bit of an independent streak. Quackenbush wasn't the first choice of the dominant conservative faction of the Assembly Republican caucus when he was elected to office in 1986, replacing Ernest Konnyu, who went on to a brief career in Congress. In fact, then-Assembly Republican leader Patrick Nolan pumped more than $164,000 into the

Charles Quackenbush

campaign of an Assembly staffer in an effort to defeat Quackenbush in the GOP primary. But Quackenbush won the primary, bested Democrat Brent Ventura in the general election and now appears solidly entrenched in the seat, aligning himself with moderates in the Assembly Republican caucus.

During his first two terms, Quackenbush hasn't been in the forefront of many major legislative issues, save one. His was the key committee vote in support of the landmark bill to outlaw semiautomatic assault weapons in the state. Without his vote, the measure, which ultimately became law, could have died in committee. In exchange for his vote, he got Democrats to outlaw weapons by specifically listing them rather than flatly banning all semiautomatic rifles. Quackenbush also was just one of two Republicans who supported the measure during the Assembly floor vote.

In 1990, Quackenbush tried unsuccessfully to tinker with the state's adoption laws with a bill that would have made it easier for grown adopted children to find their birth parents. The bill was beaten back by adoption organizations, but Quackenbush vowed to try again in the 1991-1992 session.

PERSONAL: elected 1986; born April 20, 1954, in Tacoma, Wash.; home, Cupertino; Army 1976-1981; education, B.A. American Studies, Notre Dame University; wife, Chris; children, Carrey and Charles; Roman Catholic.

CAREER: owner, Q-Tech, an electronics industry employment service, 1979-1989.

COMMITTEES: Elections, Reapportionment & Constitutional Amendments; Natural Resources; Public Safety; Ways & Means; (Joint) Science & Technology.

OFFICES: Capitol, (916) 445-8305; district, 456 El Paseo de Saratoga, San Jose 95130, (408) 446-4114.

REGISTRATION: 40.7% D, 46.2% R

1990 CAMPAIGN:	Quackenbush – R	59%	$199,841
	Bob Levy – D	34.7%	$20,017
1988 CAMPAIGN:	Quackenbush – R	63.2%	$554,594
	Robin Yeamans – D	36.8%	$17,188

RATINGS:

AFL	PIRG	CLCV	NOW	CTA	CofC	CFB	NRA	FPAC
11%	32%	37%	50%	73%	64%	50%	46%	85%

KEY VOTES:

	Insurance reform:	–	Child sick leave:	NO
Assault gun ban:	YES	Parent consent abortion: YES	Ban AIDS discrim:	NO
Clean Air Act:	NO	Cutting old trees:	YES	Extend death penalty:	YES
Lmt product tort:	YES	Ban offshore oil:	YES	Restrict abortion funds:	NO
Lower alcohol std:	YES	Basic health care:	NO	Oil spill prevent:	YES
Ethics reform:	YES	Work cancer stds:	NO	Earthquake insure:	YES

John Vasconcellos (D)
23rd Assembly District

The city of Santa Clara and the Hispanic neighborhoods of East San Jose comprise the bulk of this South Bay Democratic stronghold, which also includes Campbell and Alum Rock. Roughly one-third of the district is Latino.

For a quarter-century, this district in its various permutations has sent John Vasconcellos to the state Assembly. Only one other Assembly member has more seniority, Speaker Willie Brown. When Vasconcellos complained that the FBI had invaded "my house," he was not kidding; Vasconcellos has spent so much of his adult life in the Legislature that he is body and soul a part of it. And after voters had approved a term limit initiative in November 1990 that also forced deep cuts in legislative staff, a bitter Vasconcellos threatened to quit just months after having been re-elected saying he didn't "see any point in killing myself for people who apparently don't care if they have decent government or not."

The transformations of John Vasconcellos practically mirror the social history of California since World War II. He began as an aide to Gov. Pat Brown and was eventually favored with an Assembly seat. He traded his dark suits and crew cut for leather jackets and long hair in the '60s, storming the Capitol's halls with all the anger of the protest era. In the '70s and '80s, Vasconcellos became a convert to the inward-looking human awareness movement.

John Vasconcellos

Some consider Vasconcellos a visionary, others consider him a flake. Whatever he is, Vasconcellos is nothing if not interesting. He was lampooned by the Doonesbury comic strip for his legislation fathering the state's self-esteem commission. He routinely talks not in the language of politics, but in the lingo of encounter groups. The San Jose Mercury News once dubbed him "Mister Touchy Feely."

In the midst of the record budget deadlock in 1990, Vasconcellos carried on a one-way letter writing campaign with Gov. George Deukmejian, confessing his deepest feelings about the governor's proposals. In one letter, he told Deukmejian he went home crying because he was so depressed about the budget impasse. Vasconcellos also was one of the few public officials who sought to force the 1990 gubernatorial candidates to answer tough questions about how they would handle the state's impending budget crisis. His efforts met with some success, forcing Republican Pete Wilson and Democrat Dianne Feinstein to grapple at least peripherally with some issues they had sought to avoid. At the beginning of the 1991-92 legislative session, he sent a letter to colleagues telling them they can begin to solve many of the state's problems if they improve their own self-esteem.

But first and foremost, Vasconcellos is the chairman of the vastly powerful Ways and Means Committee, which rules on the state budget and all proposals to spend money. Although Vasconcellos embraces raising the self-esteem of citizens in the abstract, his iron-fisted temperamental management of his committee does not do much for the self-esteem of many who come before it or for the committee's staff. Vasconcellos is a difficult boss and he once threatened to run a reporter over with his car. During floor debates, he has been known to call those who disagree with him "stupid," which even by the Assembly's low standards of decorum goes too far. Assembly Speaker Willie Brown was said to have tried to ease Vasconcellos out of his Ways and Means post in 1987 but Vasconcellos would not go.

Vasconcellos has been one of the "Grizzly Bear" liberals who have been trying to keep the speaker true to his liberal religion. Vasconcellos is one of the rare voices in Capitol life against the influence of special interest money.

With the Legislature's image increasingly tarnished because of federal investigations and less-than-flattering news coverage, the speaker in 1989 turned to Vasconcellos to chair a special committee on ethics. After months of labor, the committee produced a comprehensive package of institutional reforms. However, Senate President Pro Tem David Roberti upstaged the Assembly version with a proposal of his own and the speaker allowed it to pass. Vasconcellos was said to be privately furious with Brown for pulling the carpet out from under him.

PERSONAL: elected 1966; born May 11, 1932, in San Jose; home, Santa Clara; Army; education, B.A. and J.D. from University of Santa Clara; single.

CAREER: lawyer; aide to Gov. Pat Brown.

COMMITTEES: Ways & Means (chair); Education; Higher Education; (Joint) Legislative Audit; Legislative Budget; Science & Technology.

OFFICES: Capitol, (916) 445-4253, FAX (916) 323-9209; district, 100 Paseo de San Antonio, 106, San Jose 95113, (408) 288-7515.

REGISTRATION: 59% D, 28.6% R

1990 CAMPAIGN:	Vasconcellos – D	62.7%	$368,161
	Monica Valladares – R	37.3%	$0
1988 CAMPAIGN:	Vasconcellos – D	65.6%	$470,323
	Lynn Knapp – R	30.9%	$0

RATINGS:

AFL	PIRG	CLCV	NOW	CTA	CofC	CFB	NRA	FPAC
91%	82%	100%	90%	95%	27%	17%	0%	4%

KEY VOTES:

Divest S. Africa:	YES	Insurance reform:	YES	Child sick leave:	YES
Assault gun ban:	YES	Parent consent abortion:	–	Ban AIDS discrim:	YES
Clean Air Act:	YES	Cutting old trees:	–	Extend death penalty:	–
Lmt product tort:	–	Ban offshore oil:	YES	Restrict abortion funds:	NO
Lower alcohol std:	–	Basic health care:	YES	Oil spill prevent:	YES
Ethics reform:	YES	Work cancer stds:	YES	Earthquake insure:	YES

Dominic L. Cortese (D)

24th Assembly District

Dominic Cortese spent 12 years on the Santa Clara County Board of Supervisors before he was elected to the Assembly in 1980. It prepared him well for what has become his primary role in the lower house: an advocate for local government.

For years, Cortese was chairman of the Assembly Committee on Local Government, figuring out ways for local governments to operate in the wake of the property tax-cutting Proposition 13. One of his proposals was to permit – with voter approval – creation of county "service areas" that would have allowed assessments on residents for increased police protection. It was vetoed.

Cortese successfully authored several major – though obscure – laws regulating land development. In 1990, Cortese moved onto a more daunting challenge: He became chairman of the Assembly Water, Parks and Wildlife Committee. As such, he is emerging as a major player on water issues. In 1990, he introduced a bill that sent shivers up the backs of developers. It would have required them to identify "a long-term, reliable supply of water" before permits could be issued for a project. At the behest of the wine industry, he proposed a modest increase in the state's liquor tax, an industry-sponsored constitutional amendment designed to head off a steeper tax also on the November 1990 ballot. Both failed.

Dominic Cortese

Cortese, who comes from a third-generation San Jose area farm family and is independently wealthy through his family grocery, is a political moderate who fits his district well. Still , Cortese faced a stiff challenge in 1988 from Republican Buck Norred, who attempted to tie Cortese to liberal Assembly Speaker Willie Brown. Cortese had less trouble in 1990.

Lawmaking aside, Cortese was charged in August 1990 by the Sacramento County district attorney with receiving a gift exceeding $10 "that was made and arranged by a lobbyist," between Jan. 1, 1987, and June 1, 1988. Cortese allegedly contacted Carl Burg, a lobbyist for the Painting and Decorating Contractors of California, about bids for a house-painting job when Cortese was sponsoring a bill of interest to painters and decorators. Burg contacted a contractor who bid $3,740 and painted the house. Prosecutors said the contractor wasn't paid, and Cortese later listed it as a gift. He denied any wrongdoing but eventually pleaded no contest in April 1991 and was fined $7,050 and ordered to do 100 hours of community service.

Cortese also owns the San Jose Jammers, an expansion team in the minor league continental Basketball Association.

PERSONAL: elected 1980; born Sept. 27, 1932, in San Jose; home, San Jose; Army 1954-1956; education, B.S. political science University of Santa Clara; wife, Suzanne; children, David, Rosanne, Mary, Thomas and James; Roman Catholic.

CAREER: businessman and farmer, part-owner of Cortese Bros. grocery chain; Santa Clara County Board of Supervisors 1968-1980.

COMMITTEES: Water, Parks & Wildlife (chair); Agriculture; Governmental Organization; Housing & Community Development; (Joint) Legislative Audit; Refugee Resettlement, International Migration & Cooperative Development.

OFFICES: Capitol, (916) 445-8243, FAX (916) 323-8898; district, 100 Paseo de San Antonio, 300, San Jose 95113, (408) 269-6500.

REGISTRATION: 53.4% D, 34.7% R

1990 CAMPAIGN:	Cortese – D	56.2%	$302,671
	Ron Granada – R	38.1%	$27,934
1988 CAMPAIGN:	Cortese – D	53.6%	$328,759
	Buck Norred – R	46.4%	$642,940

RATINGS:

AFL	PIRG	CLCV	NOW	CTA	CofC	CFB	NRA	FPAC
95%	100%	89%	90%	92%	27%	33%	15%	8%

KEY VOTES:

Divest S. Africa:	YES	Insurance reform:	YES	Child sick leave:	YES
Assault gun ban:	YES	Parent consent abortion:	YES	Ban AIDS discrim:	YES
Clean Air Act:	YES	Cutting old trees:	YES	Extend death penalty:	YES
Lmt product tort:	YES	Ban offshore oil:	YES	Restrict abortion funds:	–
Lower alcohol std:	YES	Basic health care:	YES	Oil spill prevent:	YES
Ethics reform:	YES	Work cancer stds:	YES	Earthquake insure:	YES

John Rusty Areias (D)

25th Assembly District

When framers of the post-1980 census reapportionment created the 25th Assembly District from other districts, they dubbed it the "Steinbeck seat" because it encompassed the agricultural areas featured in John Steinbeck's novels. The district straddles both sides of the coastal range, encompassing San Benito County, Gilroy and Morgan Hill in Santa Clara County, the Salinas area in Monterey County and western Merced County, including Los Banos.

Rusty Areias

Rusty Areias, a wealthy dairy farmer from Los Banos, fits the district well and never has been seriously challenged after winning his seat in 1982. Without Areias, however, the seat might be vulnerable to Republican penetration due to conservative voting patterns and relatively low Democratic registration.

Areias gained notoriety in 1988 as a member of the so-called "Gang of Five," a group of Democrats who challenged Assembly Speaker Willie Brown's authority despite having been favored by Brown with choice committee assignments. The challenge was turned back after months of bickering and Areias, who toyed briefly with running for the congressional seat vacated by Rep. Tony Coelho of Merced, has returned to the fold as a player on the Democratic team. Evidence of Areias' return to Brown's good graces was his appointment to chair the Assembly Agriculture Committee in 1991, replacing longtime chairman Norman Waters, who lost his re-election bid. The committee chairmanship has the potential to solidify Areias' already strong ties to agriculture and to make him a more influential political player as Democrats continue in their efforts to court moderate Central Valley residents.

Beyond balancing the sometimes diverse interests of his district, Areias has tried to carve out a role for himself as an advocate of consumer interests, being one of the few legislators to oppose hikes in consumer loan rate ceilings. Two new laws he authored that took effect in 1991 were aimed at curbing credit-card crimes. One prohibits merchants from writing credit card numbers on the backs of checks. The second bans businesses from asking customers to write their telephone numbers and addresses on credit card receipts. Areias unsuccessfully sought to have landlords pay interest to renters on security deposits. He also proposed a bill to require handgun buyers to go through a brief safety course – a proposal not well-received by the National Rifle Association, of which he is a member. The bill was vetoed.

With his personal wealth, good looks, sharp suits and fast cars, Areias challenges Speaker Brown's position as the Legislature's party animal. Cosmopolitan magazine once named him one of the nation's leading bachelors. But Areias has come under some criticism as a legislator who has misused the services of the Assembly's sergeant-at-arms. He has reportedly had them act as chauffeurs from the early morning hours to well past midnight – some say to squire him and his dates.

Areias is also ambitious and during a special session in the wake of the 1989 Bay Area earthquake, he served as chairman of a high-profile select committee on earthquake preparedness. He has tinkered with the idea of running for statewide office, perhaps secretary of state, or may take another look at Congress if reapportionment, as expected, creates some new valley seats. To that end, he has hired a high-powered staff of advisers who are trying to remake and refine his image.

PERSONAL: elected 1982; born Sept. 12, 1949, in Los Banos; home, Los Banos; education, B.S. agriculture CSU Chico; single; Roman Catholic.

CAREER: managing partner family business, Areias Dairy Farms, Los Banos.

COMMITTEES: Agriculture (chair); Banking, Finance & Bonded Indebtedness; Consumer Protection, Governmental Efficiency & Economic Development; Higher Education; Transportation; (Joint) Refugee Resettlement & International Migration.

OFFICES: Capitol, (916) 445-7380, FAX (916) 327-7105; district, 7415 Eigleberry, B, Gilroy 95020 (408) 848-1461; 545 J St., 14, Los Banos 93635 (209) 826-6100; 140 Central Ave., Salinas 93901, (408) 422-4344.

REGISTRATION: 53% D, 35.6% R

1990 CAMPAIGN:	Areias – D	63%	$306,478
	Ben Gilmore – R	32%	$22,676
1988 CAMPAIGN:	Areias – D	75%	$473,434
	Ben Gilmore – R	23%	$20,659

RATINGS:

AFL	PIRG	CLCV	NOW	CTA	CofC	CFB	NRA	FPAC
90%	75%	100%	90%	96%	41%	25%	13%	19%

KEY VOTES:

Divest S. Africa:	YES	Insurance reform:	YES	Child sick leave:	YES
Assault gun ban:	YES	Parent consent abortion:	YES	Ban AIDS discrim:	YES
Clean Air Act:	–	Cutting old trees:	NO	Extend death penalty:	YES
Lmt product tort:	–	Ban offshore oil:	YES	Restrict abortion funds:	NO
Lower alcohol std:	YES	Basic health care:	–	Oil spill prevent:	YES
Ethics reform:	YES	Work cancer stds:	YES	Earthquake insure:	YES

Vacant
26th Assembly District

This district takes in most of San Joaquin County, including Escalon, Linden, Manteca, Tracy, Ripon and Stockton. The main population center is Stockton, one of the most ethnically diverse and politically complex cities in California and one that's in the middle of a growth boom born of the outward push of the Bay Area.

For years, Stockton's politics were tightly controlled by a tiny, semisecretive oligarchy. That changed in 1974, when John Garamendi, then an outsider, broke through to win the 26th District seat. Two years later, Garamendi hopped to the Senate, and was replaced by another Democrat, Carmen Perino. In 1980, Perino was challenged in the primary by Garamendi's aide, Patrick Johnston, and a vicious fight ensued. Johnston won the primary, but nearly lost the general election in November. It was only after a recount that Johnston was declared the winner by 35 votes.

Johnston held the seat until 1991, when he followed Garamendi into the Senate. But to get to the Senate he had to fight a bitter battle with Patti Garamendi, who wanted to succeed her husband. After her loss in the Senate race, Patti Garamendi, a Democrat, moved from Walnut Grove to Stockton and campaigned for Johnston's Assembly seat. She won 26 percent of the vote at a March 19, 1991, primary, making it into a May 14, 1991, runoff with Stockton businessman Dean Andal, who won the GOP nomination with 28 percent of the vote. Andal is a former aide to former Rep. Norman Shumway of Stockton.

REGISTRATION: 56.2% D, 35.4% R

Salvatorre Cannella (D)
27th Assembly District

This district, one of the fastest-growing in the San Joaquin Valley, is comprised of all of Stanislaus County and the Atwater-Snelling region of the northern tip of Merced County. The population center is Modesto, which in recent years has become a boom town for Bay Area commuters, with dozens of housing subdivisions sprouting in former fields.

The conservative-Democrat tone of the 27th District is being altered in ways that are still not clear as the new residents sink roots. They may, or may not, shift the ideological tone of the district, but they move its orientation away from agriculture and toward more urban, or suburban, concerns.

The district was the scene of two hard-fought

Sal Cannella

races in 1990 prompted by the election of its former occupant, Gary Condit, to Congress. The winner both times was Sal Cannella, a tool and die maker, who for the third time followed Condit in an elective office. The walk in Condit's footsteps started when he succeeded Condit as mayor of Ceres in 1980. In 1982, Cannella was appointed to the Stanislaus County Board of Supervisors to replace Condit after he was elected to the Assembly. Cannella was twice re-elected to the supervisorial seat. Still, Cannella was considered an underdog to the Republican candidate, Modesto City Councilman Richard Lang, a well-known high school principal, when the two met in a special election in January 1990. Cannella and Lang offered moderate views, differing little on major issues. Both were pro-choice. Both opposed the Big Green initiative. Both argued to restore family planning funds. And both favored a ban on semiautomatic military-style assault weapons. Cannella, a longtime trade unionist, received his heaviest financial support from labor.

An overconfident Assembly Republican leader Ross Johnson hailed Lang in December as in a "solid position" to defeat Cannella, saying a poll showed him with a 17-point lead. But the election proved to be one place where state Democratic Party Chairman Jerry Brown made good on his pledge to mount aggressive voter registration and vote-by-mail drives. The Democratic hustle propelled Cannella to a rather easy victory. In the November rematch, the results were nearly the same.

In his short time in the Legislature, Cannella has been low-key and removed from the power structure. He got points for dedication when he left a hospital bed in 1990 to cast a crucial vote in favor of a compromise ending a 28-day stalemate between Gov. George Deukmejian and the Legislature on the budget.

His most visible statewide legislation – to increase civil penalties and criminal fines assessed for work place safety and health violations – was vetoed in 1990.

PERSONAL: elected 1990 (special election); born Sept. 23, 1942, in Newark, N.J.; home, Ceres; National Guard 1960-1966; education, Modesto Community College; wife, Donna, children Emily, Vincent and Nicole; Roman Catholic.

CAREER: tool and die maker.

COMMITTEES: Agriculture; Consumer Protection, Governmental Efficiency & Economic Development; Housing & Community Development; Local Government.

OFFICES: Capitol, (916) 445-8570, FAX (916) 445-8849; district, 950 10th Street, 8, Modesto 95354, (209) 576-6211.

REGISTRATION: 53.8% D, 37.4% R

1990 CAMPAIGN:

Cannella – D		51.4%	$293,367
Richard Lang – R		45.2%	$103,040

JAN. 30, 1990 SPECIAL ELECTION:

Cannella – D		53.1%	$475,159
Richard Lang – R		46.9%	$542,063

RATINGS:

AFL	PIRG	CLCV	NOW	CTA	CofC	CFB	NRA	FPAC
NR	NR	93%	90%	NR	36%	42%	50%	16%

Only two bills were scored for NRA rating

KEY VOTES:
Restrict abortion funds: NO Oil spill prevent: YES Work cancer stds: YES
Earthquake insure: YES

Samuel S. Farr (D)

28th Assembly District

There are those who believe that the Central California coast is the most beautiful spot on earth. The political custodian of that stretch of California, and its many contradictory forces, is Sam Farr, whose 28th Assembly District runs along the coast from Santa Cruz to south of Monterey. It's an area in which the forces favoring development and those favoring environmental preservation are locked in mortal combat. Farr tries to sidestep as much of the controversy as possible, although he defines himself as an environmental protectionist.

Sam Farr

The son of a state legislator and a one-time legislative staffer himself, Farr was a Monterey County supervisor before winning the Assembly seat in 1980. Given the high rate of turnover in the Assembly, that gives him a fairly high level of seniority, but he has seen the plums of power passed into other hands. To observers of the Assembly, Farr is known mostly as a talented amateur photographer who snaps pictures of his colleagues during floor sessions. He seems to lack the fire to engage in the sometimes brutal politics that lead to power.

Farr has taken over the chairmanship of the Local Government Committee from Dominic Cortese, who moved into the chairmanship of the water committee. The Local Government Committee shapes legislation defining the relationship between the state and local governments. Growth-related issues in the 1990s likely will be fought out on Farr's committee, including increasingly voguish proposals to set up regional growth-management agencies.

Farr doesn't have any trouble getting re-elected in a district with an above-average Democratic voter registration and he would be a leading candidate for the state Senate if Democrat Henry Mello decides to retire.

PERSONAL: elected 1980; born July 4, 1941, in San Francisco; home, Carmel; Peace Corps; education, B.S. biology Willamette University, attended Monterey Institute of Foreign Studies and Santa Clara School of Law; wife, Sharon Baldwin; daughter, Jessica; Episcopalian.

CAREER: assistant administrative analyst for the legislative analyst's office 1969-1971; chief consultant to Assembly Constitutional Amendments Committee 1972-1975; Monterey County Board of Supervisors 1975-1980.

COMMITTEES: Local Government (chair); Education; Higher Education;

Natural Resources; Televising the Assembly; (Joint) Arts (vice chair); Fisheries & Aquaculture; Refugee Resettlement, International Migration & Cooperative Development; Science & Technology; Quincentennial of the Voyages of Columbus.

OFFICES: Capitol, (916) 445-8496, FAX (916) 327-5914; district, 1200 Aguajito Road, Monterey 93940, (408) 646-1980; 701 Ocean St., 318B, Santa Cruz 95060, (408) 425-1503.

REGISTRATION: 54.7% D, 31.1% R

1990 CAMPAIGN:	Farr – D	71.5%	$296,236
	West Walker – R	28.5%	$99
1988 CAMPAIGN:	Farr – D	71.1%	$342,052
	Jack Skillicorn – R	28.9%	$21,790

RATINGS:

AFL	PIRG	CLCV	NOW	CTA	CofC	CFB	NRA	FPAC
94%	100%	95%	90%	88%	27%	33%	0%	0%

KEY VOTES:

Divest S. Africa:	YES	Insurance reform:	YES	Child sick leave:	YES
Assault gun ban:	YES	Parent consent abortion:	NO	Ban AIDS discrim:	YES
Clean Air Act:	YES	Cutting old trees:	NO	Extend death penalty:	YES
Lmt product tort:	YES	Ban offshore oil:	YES	Restrict abortion funds:	–
Lower alcohol std:	YES	Basic health care:	YES	Oil spill prevent:	YES
Ethics reform:	YES	Work cancer stds:	YES	Earthquake insure:	YES

Andrea Seastrand (R)
29th Assembly District

This scenic Central California coastal district includes San Luis Obispo and parts of Monterey and Santa Barbara counties. It has farm-based communities such as King City in the Salinas Valley and Santa Maria, and sleepy coastal towns of Pismo Beach and Morro Bay.

Andrea Seastrand had little trouble being elected to the seat her late husband, Eric, had held since 1982. He died of cancer in 1990. During Eric's eight years in office and several prior unsuccessful election tries, Andrea Seastrand was heavily involved in her husband's career while raising the couple's two children. She has spent 25 years working for conservative causes and took leadership roles in Monterey County Republican Party organizations.

Andrea Seastrand

A former teacher, she has taken special interest in youth issues. Like her husband, Seastrand has pledged to continue to support a strongly conservative agenda and remain a staunch supporter of agriculture. Her biography, for example, describes her as "holding dear to family values," conservative jargon for among other things, opposing abortion.

In her first months in the Legislature, Seastrand joined six of the most conservative members of the Assembly in sending a letter to Gov. Pete Wilson opposing any tax hike to combat the state's dire budget problems.

PERSONAL: elected 1990; born Aug. 5, 1941, in Chicago; home Salinas; education, B.A. education DePaul University; widow; children, Kurt and Heidi; Roman Catholic.

CAREER: teacher.

COMMITTEES: Agriculture; Consumer Protection, Governmental Efficiency & Economic Development; Education; Housing & Community Development.

OFFICES: Capitol, (916) 445-7795, FAX (916) 324-5510; district, 523 Higuera St., San Luis Obisbo 93401, (805) 549-2281.

REGISTRATION: 39% D, 48% R

1990 CAMPAIGN:

Seastrand – R	64.7%	$183,467
John Jay Lybarger – D	35.3%	$27,510

RATINGS and **KEY VOTES**: newly elected

James M. Costa (D)
30th Assembly District

The 30th Assembly District is mostly rural, but any resemblance to small family farming is purely coincidental. The game is agribusiness – agriculture on a large and scientific scale. The district covers all of Kings County, plus portions of Fresno, Madera and Merced counties, including Chowchilla, Madera, Mendota and part of the city of Fresno. The district's growers supply foreign and domestic markets with cotton, raisins, grapes, dairy products and beef cattle. Although agriculture is the backbone of the district, over half of its population resides in an urban setting, albeit one closely tied to the agricultural industry.

Jim Costa

Jim Costa, who was once referred to as congressional timber, is a tenacious and skillful politician who works hard for his district. But he is also weighed down by political baggage that could limit his career. For example, he decided against a 1989 race for the congressional seat vacated by Tony Coelho of Merced. Yet he may eye a congressional bid in 1992 should reapportionment create another valley seat.

Costa began his career working for Rep. B.F. Sisk, then was an assistant to Rep. John Krebs and, finally, was administrative assistant to Assemblyman (now congressman) Richard Lehman before winning a seat in the Assembly. During his more than 10 years in the Assembly, Costa has become an ace legislative technician and one of Assembly Speaker Willie Brown's lieutenants. In 1990, he was chosen by his fellow Assembly Democrats as caucus leader, the No. 4 party position in the lower house. To accept the job, however, Costa gave up chairmanship of the Assembly Water, Parks and Wildlife Committee, where he had protected his district's water interests since 1983.

On the upside of Costa's career, he's carried several major bond issues, including one that voters approved in 1990 that will result in the expenditure of $1 billion on upgrading rail transportation. He also has doggedly pushed – so far unsuccessfully – to move up the state's presidential primary to March in an effort to give California more clout in the selection of candidates.

On the downside, Costa has become one of the Capitol's big juice players, carrying legislation for special-interest groups and accepting large amounts of campaign contributions, gifts and speaking fees. He unsuccessfully pushed several anti-rent-control bills for landlords, as well as a measure for beer wholesalers that would have guaranteed them territorial monopolies, which eventually was vetoed by Gov. George Deukmejian.

But it was Costa's arrest on the last night of the 1986 legislative session that brought him his greatest notoriety. Just weeks before he was to face voters for re-election, and while traveling in a state-leased car with a known prostitute at his side, Costa offered $50 to an undercover woman police officer to join them in a three-way sex act, Sacramento police said. Nearly a week later, with his mother nearby, Costa admitted during a press conference in his home district that he had made an error in judgment. Later that month, he was fined $1 and given three years' probation. The episode would have spelled the end of a political career for anyone from a district with a different makeup of voters. But Republicans failed to capitalize on the incident and Costa easily won re-election. In 1990 Costa's margin of victory slipped by nearly 10 percentage points, but he still won handily.

PERSONAL: elected 1978; born April 13, 1952, in Fresno; home, Fresno; education, B.S. political science CSU Fresno; single; Roman Catholic.

CAREER: aide to Rep. B.F. Sisk 1974-1975 and Rep. John Krebs 1975-1976; assistant to Assemblyman Richard Lehman 1976-1978; Assembly Democratic Caucus Chair 1991-1992.

COMMITTEES: Agriculture; Elections, Reapportionment & Constitutional Amendments; Governmental Organization; Transportation; Water, Parks & Wildlife; Ways & Means; (Joint) Energy Regulation & the Environment; Fisheries & Aquaculture.

OFFICES: Capitol, (916) 445-7558, FAX (916) 323-1097; district, 1111 Fulton Mall, 914, Fresno 93721, (209) 264-3078; 512 N. Irwin, A, Hanford 92320, (209) 582-2869.

REGISTRATION: 58.8% D, 32.4% R

1990 CAMPAIGN:			
Costa – D	62.4%	$407,911
Gerald Hurt – R	37.6%	$8,070

1988 CAMPAIGN: Costa – D   71.8% $427,944

Gerald Hurt – R   28.2% $11,297

RATINGS:

AFL	PIRG	CLCV	NOW	CTA	CofC	CFB	NRA	FPAC
80%	89%	89%	80%	96%	45%	50%	0%	22%

KEY VOTES:

Divest S. Africa:	YES	Insurance reform:	YES	Child sick leave:	YES
Assault gun ban:	YES	Parent consent abortion:	YES	Ban AIDS discrim:	YES
Clean Air Act:	YES	Cutting old trees:	–	Extend death penalty:	YES
Lmt product tort:	YES	Ban offshore oil:	NO	Restrict abortion funds:	NO
Lower alcohol std:	YES	Basic health care:	YES	Oil spill prevent:	YES
Ethics reform:	YES	Work cancer stds:	YES	Earthquake insure:	YES

Bruce C. Bronzan (D)
31st Assembly District

This district centers on the heart of Fresno, the most strongly Democratic and liberal bastion, such as it is, in the San Joaquin Valley. It includes central Fresno County and most of the city of Fresno and surrounding cities of Clovis, Parlier, Sanger, Reedley and Selma. Republicans maintain a strong presence and Bruce Bronzan, recovering from early stumbles, is careful not to offend his moderate-to-conservative, staunchly pro-agriculture constituency.

Articulate, friendly and energetic, sometimes to the point of being hyperactive, Bronzan is surrounded by loyal staff members and has quickly risen through the ranks of the Assembly. He has honed health-related issues into a specialty with the speed of an X-

Bruce Bronzan

ray. After Assemblyman Curtis R. Tucker Sr. of Los Angeles died, Bronzan was named in early 1989 by Assembly Speaker Willie Brown to replace Tucker as Health Committee chairman.

Bronzan, a loyal Brown lieutenant, has a strong liberal bent but he also has been the point person on conservative issues critical to his district. For instance, after the Alar food scare, and with threats of a statewide initiative banning many pesticides in the wings, Bronzan proposed a measure to expand food testing. Opponents in environmental groups described it as a shrewd maneuver designed to pre-empt their initiative drive.

Bronzan also has carried numerous measures to revamp state health care systems, fix the workers compensation morass, cut exposure to cancer-causing asbestos, upgrade public safety, help AIDS victims and improve the lot of the disabled and the mentally incompetent. In 1990, he successfully helped lead a move to restore $20 million in state funds that Gov. George Deukmejian had cut from the budget six months early. Yet another Bronzan bill to restore $15 million in mental health funds for local governments was turned back by Deukmejian.

Politically, Bronzan weathered his most bruising campaign in 1988, when his Republican challenger, Doug Haaland, tried to keep Bronzan on the defensive by repeatedly focusing on Bronzan's open willingness to accept honorariums and gifts from many of the same special-interest groups that have a stake in bills he carries, votes on or hears as chairman of the health committee. Bronzan defended his practices as essential to representing his constituency and to keep from going personally bankrupt. Bronzan also was criticized for his campaign and personal finances, including accepting $16,000 from a Sacramento lobbyist as part of a secured home loan. The state's Fair Political Practices Commission cleared Bronzan of any wrongdoing but the agency warned him it was not ruling out reconsidering similar cases in the future. Bronzan worked hard to offset the negatives and won re-election easily. And in 1990, no one even challenged his re-election bid.

His articulation and drive – coupled with his ability to win in a district more conservative than he is – mark Bronzan as a Democratic comer who is likely to pop into a state Senate or congressional seat at the first opportunity and then explore statewide office.

PERSONAL: elected 1982; born Sept. 28, 1947, in Fresno; home, Fresno; education, B.S. political science and teaching credential CSU Fresno; M.A. in urban studies Occidental College; wife, Linda Barnes; children, Chloe and Forest; Protestant.

CAREER: teacher; Fresno County Board of Supervisors 1975-1982; head of a drug and alcohol treatment program for Fresno Community Hospital.

COMMITTEES: Health (chair); Agriculture; Insurance; Human Services. (Joint): Legislative Audit.

OFFICES: Capitol, (916) 445-8514, FAX (916) 324-7129; district, 2550 Mariposa Mall, 5006, Fresno 93721, (209) 445-5532.

REGISTRATION: 56.4% D, 35.8% R

1990 CAMPAIGN: Bronzan – D		100%	$455,329
1988 CAMPAIGN: Bronzan – D		71%	$413,564
Doug Haaland – R		29%	$37,774

RATINGS:

AFL	PIRG	CLCV	NOW	CTA	CofC	CFB	NRA	FPAC
91%	100%	94%	100%	87%	36%	33%	13%	0%

KEY VOTES:

Divest S. Africa:	YES	Insurance reform:	YES	Child sick leave:	YES
Assault gun ban:	YES	Parent consent abortion:	–	Ban AIDS discrim:	YES
Clean Air Act:	YES	Cutting old trees:	NO	Extend death penalty:	YES
Lmt product tort:	YES	Ban offshore oil:	YES	Restrict abortion funds:	NO
Lower alcohol std:	YES	Basic health care:	YES	Oil spill prevent:	YES
Ethics reform:	YES	Work cancer stds:	–	Earthquake insure:	YES

William L. Jones (R)

32nd Assembly District

Another agriculture-dominated district in the San Joaquin Valley, the 32nd District includes Mariposa County and the mountainous portions of Tulare, Fresno and Madera counties. It also has the cities of Dinuba, Porterville, Visalia and part of Clovis, plus the Kings and Sequoia Canyon National Parks. Business, farming and ranching are key bywords here, and Republican Bill Jones, a businessman, row-crop farmer and cattle rancher, speaks the language. Smart but reserved, Jones has carefully built a political career watching out for district interests such as agriculture, health, workers compensation, water, wine production, parks, education and local govern-

Bill Jones

ment. He was among those who helped draft the state's widely copied "workfare" program, where welfare recipients work to receive benefits. He has pushed measures to help reduce prison costs, increase highway funding for rural counties, keep rural hospitals open, recoup welfare overpayments and expand food inspections. He has tangled with Democratic Assemblyman Byron Sher on water pollution issues, generally siding with farm interests that have sought a lenient approach to health standards for water.

Part of a conservative-to-moderate faction of GOP Assembly members known as the "Magnificent Seven," Jones has openly challenged the Republican leadership for striking deals with Assembly Speaker Willie Brown, a San Francisco Democrat. On the day after his re-election in 1988 to a fourth two-year term, he met with fellow party members in an effort to capture the minority leader's job. He lost to Ross Johnson of La Habra. Jones made another unsuccessful run at Johnson in 1990, just two days after the Nov. 6 election. He only received nine out of 32 votes despite the fact that Assembly Republicans under Johnson's leadership lost more ground to Democrats in the election. Although Jones is hard-working and knows the art of behind-the-scenes compromise, some of his colleagues say his leadership ambitions are stymied by his less-than-aggressive style. Jones is a marked contrast to the volatile and bombastic Johnson. He chooses his words carefully and rarely says anything controversial.

Jones remains ambitious and is already considering running for Congress should reapportionment create another valley seat in 1992, or for state Senate should Democrat Rose Ann Vuich step down.

PERSONAL: elected 1982; born Dec. 20, 1949, in Coalinga, Calif.; home, Fresno; education, B.S. agribusiness CSU Fresno; wife, Maurine; children, Wendy and Andrea; Methodist.

CAREER: Chairman of the board of California Data Marketing Inc., a computer service and direct mail firm; family partner in a 3,000-acre ranch and an investments firm.

COMMITTEES: Agriculture; Environmental Safety & Toxic Materials; Water, Parks & Wildlife.

OFFICES: Capitol, (916) 445-2931, FAX (916) 445-3832; district, 2929 W. Main St., J, Visalia 93291, (209) 734-1182; 2497 W. Shaw, 106, Fresno 93711, (209) 224-7833.

REGISTRATION: 43.2% D, 47.6% R

1990 CAMPAIGN:	Jones – R	68.8%	$421,830
	Bernie McGoldrick – D	31.2%	$17,844
1988 CAMPAIGN:	Jones – R	72.5%	$421,382
	Aden Windham – D	27.5%	$0

RATINGS:

AFL	PIRG	CLCV	NOW	CTA	CofC	CFB	NRA	FPAC
14%	38%	6%	20%	61%	86%	92%	100%	85%

KEY VOTES:

Divest S. Africa:	NO	Insurance reform:	NO	Child sick leave:	–
Assault gun ban:	NO	Parent consent abortion:	YES	Ban AIDS discrim:	NO
Clean Air Act:	YES	Cutting old trees:	YES	Extend death penalty:	–
Lmt product tort:	YES	Ban offshore oil:	NO	Restrict abortion funds:	YES
Lower alcohol std:	YES	Basic health care:	NO	Oil spill prevent:	YES
Ethics reform:	YES	Work cancer stds:	NO	Earthquake insure:	NO

Trice J. Harvey (R)
33rd Assembly District

This district covers the western portions of Tulare and Kern counties and the cities of Delano, Taft and parts of Bakersfield and Tulare. The chief industries are agriculture and oil, and its politics are steadfastly conservative. Even Hispanic voters, who comprise 30 percent of the population, often vote Republican.

If Republican leaders had had their way, Trice Harvey would not represent this rural-conservative district. In 1986, Harvey, then a Kern County supervisor, was the anointed GOP candidate for the Assembly to replace Don Rogers, who had been elected to the Senate. Harvey had been endorsed by virtually all local GOP leaders when then-Assembly Republican leader Pat Nolan abruptly turned against Harvey and

Trice Harvey

backed his rival in the primary. Apparently, Harvey's alliance with Bakersfield Rep. Bill Thomas, a bitter rival of Nolan in past internal power struggles, prompted the turnabout. Harvey beat Nolan's candidate, Anna Allen, and won the seat.

Having isolated himself from the Republican leadership, Harvey has concentrated on district issues such as oil and agriculture. Harvey and Rogers are the two staunchest defenders of the oil industry in the Legislature, voting against all environmental regulation affecting the industry – sometimes long after the oil industry has agreed to a compromise. On one occasion Harvey and Rogers stood alone against the 1990 oil spill prevention bill.

Unlike Rogers, however, Harvey is not doctrinairily against all environmental legislation. He has pushed efforts to limit importation of hazardous wastes into his district, a sensitive local issue. His bill to expand state efforts to learn the cause of high cancer rates among children in the city of McFarland was vetoed by Gov. George Deukmejian, who said it duplicated existing efforts. Harvey also has remained sensitive to the concerns – and burdens – of local governments.

Harvey has been among those who advocate special-tax treatment for pet projects. He floated an unsuccessful bill in 1990 to give ostrich breeders a sales-tax exemption and vowed to push the bill again in 1991 despite a record state budget deficit. He won legislative passage of a bill giving the artist Christo a sales tax break for purchasing art materials to construct sculptured yellow umbrellas along Interstate 5. Deukmejian vetoed it.

Harvey's also had a role in helping write a happier ending to the "Onion Field" saga. Karl Hettinger was one of two Los Angeles officers kidnapped in 1963. Hettinger's partner was killed by the kidnappers in an onion field outside of Bakersfield while Hettinger escaped, only to suffer years of emotional turmoil. Harvey befriended Hettinger, made him his aide for 10 years and persuaded Deukmejian to appoint Hettinger to complete the remaining 21 months of his term on the Kern County Board of Supervisors. Hettinger later won election on his own.

A native of Arkansas who still speaks with a southern twang, Harvey also is known as one of the gabbiest members of the Legislature. He delays hearings with seemingly endless banter – much of which has nothing to do with the subject at hand.

PERSONAL: elected 1986; born July 15, 1936, in Paragould, Ark.; home, Bakersfield; B.A. education CSU Fresno; wife, Jacqueline Stussy; children, Nick and Dinah Marquez; Morman.

CAREER: County health sanitarian; pharmaceutical salesman; school board member; Kern County Board of Supervisors 1976-1986.

COMMITTEES: Agriculture; Governmental Organization; Human Services; Water, Parks & Wildlife.

OFFICES: Capitol, (916) 445-8498, FAX (916) 395-3883; district, 1800 30th St., 101, Bakersfield 93301, (805) 324-3300; 115 South M St., Tulare 93274, (209) 686-2864.

REGISTRATION: 49.3% D, 41.9%

1990 CAMPAIGN:	Harvey – R	100%	$296,383
1988 CAMPAIGN:	Harvey – R	66.5%	$561,442
	Mike Powell – D	33.5%	$10,572

RATINGS:

AFL	PIRG	CLCV	NOW	CTA	CofC	CFB	NRA	FPAC
10%	23%	5%	30%	56%	86%	58%	87%	92%

KEY VOTES:

	Insurance reform:	NO	Child sick leave:	NO
Assault gun ban:	NO	Parent consent abortion: YES	Ban AIDS discrim:	NO
Clean Air Act:	YES	Cutting old trees:	YES	Extend death penalty:	YES
Lmt product tort:	YES	Ban offshore oil:	NO	Restrict abortion funds:	YES
Lower alcohol std:	YES	Basic health care:	NO	Oil spill prevent:	NO
Ethics reform:	NO	Work cancer stds:	NO	Earthquake insure:	NO

Phillip D. Wyman (R)

34th Assembly District

Phil Wyman

This district includes rugged Inyo County, the desert areas of eastern Kern County, the rapidly developing Antelope Valley of Los Angeles County and a portion of Bakersfield. It was already conservative when Phil Wyman, a rancher and attorney, was elected to the Assembly in 1978. That translates into an extremely safe district for Wyman, a thin man with a chalky complexion who was once chided by some of his colleagues for his meek manner in a Legislature where aggressive behavior is often valued.

Wyman flirted with the idea of running for state controller in 1986, but after five months abandoned his campaign and announced that he would once again run for re-election. That abandoned campaign, in turn, came five months after he indicated he would run for the state Senate, another thought he later reconsidered. And while the two false starts hurt his credibility in some GOP circles, it did nothing to hurt Wyman's Assembly re-election bids. He continues to win by huge margins.

As a legislator, Wyman is an orthodox conservative, rarely, if ever, breaking from the party line. He has been most visible as an anti-abortion advocate, helping to push through a law requiring minors to get parental consent before they can have abortions. The law has been stayed pending challenges in the courts.

Wyman was among the stalwart Assembly Republicans who held up passage of the budget in 1990. Wyman and Richard Mountjoy led the opposition against it on the grounds that the bill sponsored by Gov. George Deukmejian had $14 million earmarked to cover abortions for women who are on Medi-Cal and $700,000 for enforcing the state's ban on semiautomatic military-style assault rifles. Although Wyman occasionally succeeds at stalling tactics, he is not particularly successful in advancing his agenda. In June 1990, for instance, the Assembly Health Committee defeated one of his pet bills, AB 3792, which would have prohibited abortion for the purpose of selecting sex. Aligning himself with the farthest right-wingers in the Assembly, Wyman was among four Republicans to vote for a resolution in August 1990 by Gil Ferguson that sought to justify the internment of Japanese-Americans during World War II as a military necessity.

And Wyman is the Republican Willie Brown most loves to taunt. Once during a committee hearing Wyman claimed the speaker's proposal to require vapor-recovery systems on cars would cause them to "blow up like the Hindenburg." That brought a pyrotechnic display from Brown, who told Wyman he was the Republican he would most like to get rid of and told him to report to his office for a private chat.

PERSONAL: elected 1979 (special election); born Feb. 21, 1945, in Hollywood; home, Tehachapi; USAF 1969-1973; education, B.A. political science UC Davis, graduate studies international law Ateneo de Manila University, Philippines, J.D. McGeorge; wife, Lynn Larson; children, Andrea Dee, Elizabeth Frances and David Elliott; Protestant.

CAREER: lawyer; rancher; vice chair, Assembly Republican Caucus.

COMMITTEES: Agriculture; Higher Education; Insurance; Water, Parks & Wildlife; (Joint) State's Economy.

OFFICES: Capitol, (916) 445-3266, FAX (916) 323-8470; district, 5393 Truxtun Ave., Bakersfield 93309, (805) 395-2673; 556 W. Lancaster Blvd., 1, Lancaster 93534, (805) 945-3544; 540 Perdew, A-1, Ridgecrest 93555, (619) 446-3484.

REGISTRATION: 39.9% D, 49.9% R

1990 CAMPAIGN:	Wyman – R	76.1%	$229,616
	Ronald Tisbert – L	$23.9%	$0
1988 CAMPAIGN:	Wyman – R	68.7%	$258,646
	Earl Wilson – D	29.4%	$0

RATINGS:

AFL	PIRG	CLCV	NOW	CTA	CofC	CFB	NRA	FPAC
11%	23%	11%	30%	53%	77%	67%	100%	93%

KEY VOTES:

Divest S. Africa:	NO	Insurance reform:	NO	Child sick leave:	NO
Assault gun ban:	NO	Parent consent abortion:	YES	Ban AIDS discrim:	NO
Clean Air Act:	NO	Cutting old trees:	YES	Extend death penalty:	YES
Lmt product tort:	YES	Ban offshore oil:	NO	Restrict abortion funds:	YES
Lower alcohol std:	YES	Basic health care:	NO	Oil spill prevent:	YES
Ethics reform:	NO	Work cancer stds:	NO	Earthquake insure:	NO

Jack O'Connell (D)

35th Assembly District

Republicans believe they might be able to win this district, which stretches from affluent Santa Barbara south to the farming community of Oxnard in Ventura County – but not until Jack O'Connell moves on. O'Connell is a hard-working, quietly effective legislator who has built a following in his moderate, environmentally conscious district through personal appearances and attention to local issues.

A few years earlier, GOP strategists thought they could turn him out of office. Now, they're waiting for state Sen. Gary K. Hart, another popular Democrat from the area, to run for higher office so that O'Connell will run for the Senate and open up the Assembly district, whatever it looks like after reapportionment.

O'Connell, a longtime resident of the area, served as an aide to former state Sen. Omer Rains of Ventura. He, like Hart, is a former teacher. O'Connell's bills have focused on education and children's issues. He pushed to extend programs for gifted and develop-

Jack O'Connell

mentally disabled students at a time when they were threatened by partisan politics. He has sought increased penalties on drunken drivers who have children in their cars and for drug dealers who sell near schools. O'Connell drew the ire of gun enthusiasts in 1989, when he voted in favor of a bill to virtually ban semiautomatic military-style assault weapons. An unsuccessful recall drive was started. He also got involved in the controversial animal-rights issue when he proposed making it a crime to use animals in certain laboratory tests.

At the start of the 1991-92 session, O'Connell sponsored one of the high-priority proposals of incoming Gov. Pete Wilson's administration. He proposed a constitutional amendment, ACA 6, which would allow local school bond approval by a simple majority of voters rather than the two-thirds required under provisions of Proposition 13.

O'Connell became speaker pro tem upon the departure of Michael Roos, who resigned from the Assembly early in 1991. The job entails presiding over the daily floor sessions and has been a stepping stone to the speaker's job in the past.

PERSONAL: elected 1982; born Oct. 8, 1951, in Glen Cove, N.Y.; home, Carpinteria; education, B.A. history CSU Fullerton, teaching credential CSU Long Beach; wife, Doree Caputo; daughter, Jennifer Lynn; Roman Catholic.

CAREER: high school teacher; speaker pro tempore 1991.

COMMITTEES: Education; Insurance; Rules; Ways & Means and subcommittee 3, resources, agriculture & the environment (chair); (Joint) Rules; School Facilities.

OFFICES: Capitol, (916) 445-8292; district, 228 W. Carrillo St., F, Santa Barbara 93101, (805) 966-2296; 300 South C St., 4, Oxnard 93030, (805) 487-9437.

REGISTRATION: 48.7% D, 36.7% R

1990 CAMPAIGN:	O'Connell – D	66.9%	$443,918
	Connie O'Shaughnessy – R	33.1%	$62,845
1988 CAMPAIGN:	O'Connell – D	92.7%	$328,580
	Robert Bakhous–L	7.3%	

RATINGS:

AFL	PIRG	CLCV	NOW	CTA	CofC	CFB	NRA	FPAC
97%	100%	95%	100%	94%	27%	33%	0%	0%

KEY VOTES:

Divest S. Africa:	YES	Insurance reform:	YES	Child sick leave:	YES
Assault gun ban:	YES	Parent consent abortion:	NO	Ban AIDS discrim:	YES
Clean Air Act:	YES	Cutting old trees:	NO	Extend death penalty:	YES
Lmt product tort:	YES	Ban offshore oil:	YES	Restrict abortion funds:	NO
Lower alcohol std:	YES	Basic health care:	YES	Oil spill prevent:	YES
Ethics reform:	YES	Work cancer stds:	YES	Earthquake insure:	YES

Thomas M. McClintock (R)

36th Assembly District

Tom McClintock

Not too many years ago, Ventura County was a quiet corner of California, a place of orange groves and oil wells separated from Los Angeles by a string of low mountains. But freeways were punched through the mountains and Ventura County has, albeit with mixed feelings, become part of the Los Angeles-centered megalopolis. And as it has evolved from bucolic backwater to suburbia, Ventura County has moved rightward in its politics, becoming a dependable citadel of Republican voters.

Tom McClintock was eight years old when Willie Brown was first elected to the state Assembly in 1964. But McClintock, like Ventura County, grew up quickly. In 1982, at the relatively tender age of 26, he was elected to the Assembly. A one-time aide to Republican state Sen. Ed Davis, McClintock got started in politics young, claiming the chairmanship of the county GOP central committee at 22. He was the youngest legislator when elected and still comes across as boyish, although that doesn't hinder his self-proclaimed role as the Republicans' chief parliamentarian. It's McClintock who arises on the Assembly floor to question points of parliamentary order that often place him in open conflict with Speaker Brown. McClintock doesn't win many of those parliamentary squabbles since the majority Democrats retain the ultimate authority over conduct, but he keeps on raising his points.

He was one of the loudest objectors to passing the state budget during the 1990 fiscal impasse because it contained tax-increase proposals. McClintock rose from his desk daily to recite an endless series of statistics on the tax burden to the average California family, to the point where many of his colleagues began doing parodies of McClintock-style statistics in their own speeches. He also got under the skin of Republican leader Ross Johnson, who fired off an angry note to McClintock telling him that if he wanted to keep complaining he ought to do the work.

The 36th District is so lopsidedly Republican that McClintock need not worry about re-election every two years. He's free to concentrate on his parliamentary procedures and his interest in political history. And, scarcely into his 30s, he also can explore higher rungs on the political ladder. He came close to running for Congress in 1986 and is a likely candidate for a House seat after districts are re-shuffled, or perhaps for the state Senate.

PERSONAL: elected 1982; born July 10, 1956, in White Plains, N.Y.; home, Newbury Park; education, B.A. political science UCLA; wife, Lori; daughter, Shannah; Protestant.

CAREER: administrative assistant to Sen. Ed Davis 1980-1982.

COMMITTEES: Environmental Safety & Toxic Materials; Judiciary; Labor & Employment; Transportation.

OFFICES: Capitol, (916) 445-7402, FAX (916) 324-0013; district, 350 N. Lantana, 222, Camarillo 93010, (805) 987-9797.

REGISTRATION: 37.2% D, 50.6% R

1990 CAMPAIGN:	McClintock – R	58.6%	$320,114
	Ginny Connell – D	35.8%	$54,341
1988 CAMPAIGN:	McClintock – R	69.9%	$456,723
	George Webb – D	27.5%	$0

RATINGS:

AFL	PIRG	CLCV	NOW	CTA	CofC	CFB	NRA	FPAC
9%	12%	5%	30%	56%	68%	58%	100%	81%

KEY VOTES:

Divest S. Africa:	NO	Insurance reform:	NO	Child sick leave:	NO
Assault gun ban:	NO	Parent consent abortion:	YES	Ban AIDS discrim:	NO
Clean Air Act:	NO	Cutting old trees:	YES	Extend death penalty:	YES
Lmt product tort:	YES	Ban offshore oil:	NO	Restrict abortion funds:	YES
Lower alcohol std:	YES	Basic health care:	NO	Oil spill prevent:	YES
Ethics reform:	NO	Work cancer stds:	NO	Earthquake insure:	NO

Cathie M. Wright (R)
37th Assembly District

The Los Angeles suburbs continue to push out, filling geographic nooks with houses, shopping centers, schools and highways. Simi Valley, northwest of Los Angeles and straddling the Ventura County line, is one of those nooks, and it is also the center of the 37th Assembly District, which takes in portions of three counties. Los Angeles suburbs tend to be Republican, and the 37th District is no exception, with its 52 percent-plus GOP registration. That has made it easy for Republican Assemblywoman Cathie Wright to win re-election – despite her troubles – since first taking the seat in 1980.

Wright hasn't played a big role in shaping legislation. But her extracurricular activities have made headlines at home and in Sacramento. In 1989, there were a series of published reports that Wright had interceded with state motor vehicle and judicial authorities in early 1988 to prevent her daughter, Victoria, from losing her driver's license for a series of traffic tickets. Wright denied doing anything wrong, but a report from the Ventura County district attorney's office concluded that she had tried to fix Victoria's tickets on several occasions and even solicited help in contacting judicial officials from the Assembly's top Democrat, Speaker Willie Brown. That incident led to another. In December 1988, Wright refused to go along with Republican efforts to deny Brown re-election as speaker, and for that, there were demands among Republicans that Wright be stripped of her seat on the Assembly Rules Committee. The GOP caucus voted to drop Wright from the committee but Brown, invoking another rule, protected her from being dumped.

Cathie Wright

Wright has aligned herself with the far right. She was one of four Republicans to vote in August 1990 for a resolution by Gil Ferguson that sought to justify internment of Japanese-Americans during World War II as a military necessity.

PERSONAL: elected 1980; born May 18, 1929, in Old Forge, Penn.; home, Simi Valley; education, A.A. accounting Scranton Community College, Penn.; widow; daughter, Victoria; Roman Catholic.

CAREER: insurance underwriter; school board; City Council and mayor Simi Valley 1978-1980.

COMMITTEES: Banking, Finance & Bonded Indebtedness; Utilities & Commerce; Environmental Safety & Toxic Materials; Rules; Ways & Means; (Joint) Rules.

OFFICES: Capitol, (916) 445-7676, FAX (916) 324-5321; district, 3655 Alamo St., 301, Simi Valley 93065, (805) 522-2920.

REGISTRATION: 36.3% D, 52.5% R

1990 CAMPAIGN:			
	Wright – R	54.7%	$535,301
	Dennis Petrie – D	38.9%	$0
1988 CAMPAIGN:	Wright – R	72.8%	$340,086
	Jeffrey Marcus – D	24.9%	$0

RATINGS:

AFL	PIRG	CLCV	NOW	CTA	CofC	CFB	NRA	FPAC
13%	18%	10%	30%	67%	91%	67%	100%	100%

KEY VOTES:

Divest S. Africa:	NO	Insurance reform:	NO	Child sick leave:	NO
Assault gun ban:	NO	Parent consent abortion:	YES	Ban AIDS discrim:	NO
Clean Air Act:	NO	Cutting old trees:	YES	Extend death penalty:	YES
Lmt product tort:	YES	Ban offshore oil:	NO	Restrict abortion funds:	YES
Lower alcohol std:	YES	Basic health care:	NO	Oil spill prevent:	YES
Ethics reform:	YES	Work cancer stds:	NO	Earthquake insure:	NO

Paula L. Boland (R)

38th Assembly District

The further north and west one goes in the San Fernando Valley, the more Republican it becomes. The 38th Assembly District lies at the west extremity of the valley, encompassing such communities as Woodland Hills, Northridge, Canoga Park and Calabasas. With its 48 percent to 42 percent registration edge in favor of Republicans, there's no question that GOP candidates have a decided advantage here.

Paula Boland

When Marian La Follette, who had represented the district since 1980, decided not to seek re-election in 1990, there was a scramble on the Republican side to fill the seat. And the winner was Paula Boland, a real estate broker and former Granada Hills Chamber of Commerce president, who was backed by, among others, La Follette's longtime rival in the lower house, Assemblywoman Cathie Wright, R-Simi Valley. Boland got a tougher-than-expected challenge in the general election, however, from Democrat Irene Allert, who hammered away at Boland's anti-abortion views.

A staunch conservative, Boland has worked in the trenches for Republican Party causes for 25 years, and her 1990 race was her first for elective office. She has experience in government, however, having served on the Los Angeles County Local Agency Formation Commission, an influential agency that oversees city incorporations and annexations.

During her campaign, some critics predicted that she would never be more than a back-bencher in the Assembly. But Boland now has a safe seat from which she can prove them wrong.

PERSONAL: elected 1990; born Jan. 17, 1940, in Oyster Bay, N.Y.; home, Northridge; education, San Fernando Valley High School; husband, Lloyd; three children; Roman Catholic.

CAREER: owner real estate brokerage firm, husband continues to manage.

COMMITTEES: Housing & Community Development; Local Government; Public Safety; Utilities & Commerce.

OFFICES: Capitol, (916) 445-8366, FAX (916) 322-2005; district, 10727 White Oak, 124, Grenada Hills, 91344, (818) 368-3838.

REGISTRATION: 42% D, 48.3% R

1990 CAMPAIGN:			
	Boland – R	52.5%	$353,601
	Irene F. Allert – D	44%	$112,511

RATINGS and **KEY VOTES**: newly elected

Richard D. Katz (D)
39th Assembly District

Republicans once thought they had a good chance of winning back this moderate San Fernando Valley district, which includes the largely Latino and black neighborhoods of San Fernando and Pacoima, working-class Sepulveda, rural Sylmar and upper-middle-class areas of Northridge. But Democrat Richard Katz has cruised to lopsided victories in his last three elections. Now, Katz, who once worried about just getting re-elected, is a key player in the Legislature and is seriously thinking about running for mayor of Los Angeles in 1993. And if he doesn't try that, don't be surprised to see him run for a statewide office in 1994, perhaps for lieutenant governor.

Richard Katz

Katz, who was running a graphic arts and printing company when he was elected in 1980, is a pragmatist. He is generally conservative on crime issues, tends to be moderate on fiscal issues and is liberal on social issues such as abortion and the environment. That middle-of-the-road record has allowed him to brush away GOP attempts to exploit his position as one of liberal Assembly Speaker Willie Brown's top lieutenants, a favorite tactic in swing districts.

Katz, in fact, has used his influence and skills to help elect more moderate Democrats. He was an outspoken critic of the Democratic Party's choice of former Gov. Jerry Brown as state chairman. Brown quit in 1991 to run for U.S. Senate.

Aside from his role as political strategist, Katz also is a key player in the legislative arena. As chairman of the Assembly Transportation Committee, he was a driving force behind the successful effort to get voters to raise the gas tax in 1990 to provide money for the state's highways and mass transit.

A few years earlier, at the height of statewide concern about toxic pollutants, Katz pushed a tough law regulating the way toxic waste can be stored and dumped. He also has seized on issues with which the general public can relate, successfully sponsoring legislation to require gravel trucks to cover their loads with tarps to protect the windshields of cars traveling behind, raising the speed limit to 65 mph on rural highways and making it easier for law enforcement officials to confiscate the assets of drug dealers.

Although generally affable, he is prone to occasional tantrums, and his ambition has caused friction with colleagues. In fact, there was speculation that one reason Assembly Speaker Brown ordered press desks off the sides of the Assembly floor at the start of the 1991-92 session was that a potential opponent for Los Angeles mayor, fellow Democratic Assemblyman Mike Roos, was worried about the time Katz spent talking to reporters. Katz, meanwhile, makes no secret of his desire to run for a high-profile office. He announced in 1989 he would seek the Democratic nomination for lieutenant governor in 1990, but then pulled out when Lt. Gov. Leo McCarthy said he would seek re-election.

PERSONAL: elected 1980; born Aug. 16, 1950, in Los Angeles; home, Sylmar; education, B.A. political science San Diego State University; wife, Gini Barrett; no children; Jewish.

CAREER: graphic artist and printer.

COMMITTEES: Transportation (chair); Elections, Reapportionment & Constitutional Amendments; Environmental Safety & Toxic Materials; Water, Parks & Wildlife.

OFFICES: Capitol, (916) 445-1616, FAX (916) 324-6860; district, 9140 Van Nuys Blvd., 109, Panorama City 91402, (818) 894-3671.

REGISTRATION: 57% D, 33.9% R

1988 CAMPAIGN:	Katz – D	73%	$818,914
	Jim Rendleman – R	25%	$76,285
1990 CAMPAIGN:	Katz – D	68%	$542,221
	Sam Ceravolo – R	32%	$0

RATINGS:

AFL	PIRG	CLCV	NOW	CTA	CofC	CFB	NRA	FPAC
86%	86%	100%	100%	83%	32%	17%	31%	15%

KEY VOTES:

Divest S. Africa:	YES	Insurance reform:	YES	Child sick leave:	NO
Assault gun ban:	YES	Parent consent abortion:	NO	Ban AIDS discrim:	YES
Clean Air Act:	YES	Cutting old trees:	NO	Extend death penalty:	YES
Lmt product tort:	YES	Ban offshore oil:	YES	Restrict abortion funds:	NO
Lower alcohol std:	YES	Basic health care:	YES	Oil spill prevent:	YES
Ethics reform:	YES	Work cancer stds:	YES	Earthquake insure:	YES

Thomas J. Bane (D)
40th Assembly District

The more celebrated side of the Santa Monica Mountains is the southern slope, which includes the communities of Beverly Hills, Laurel Canyon, Coldwater Canyon and Hollywood. The northern side of the mountains is a relatively quiet collection of residential communities that flow into the San Fernando Valley: Studio City, Sherman Oaks, Encino and Van Nuys. There are pockets of great wealth on the northern slope, but it lacks the show-business glitter of the south side. Some stars, such as singer Michael Jackson, and second-echelon performers, executives and professionals who spend their working hours over the hill make up much of the area's population. It's affluent and Democratic in its voting patterns.

Democrat Tom Bane has represented the district for many years. He first won election to the Assembly in 1958, just as the legendary Jesse Unruh was transforming it into a powerful political instrument. As part of Unruh's closest circle of friends and advisers, Bane quickly became chairman of the Rules Committee, which handles Assembly housekeeping functions and also directs the flow of legislation. He quickly established himself as a hardball player, using his power over office space, staff and other matters to enforce discipline on Unruh's behalf.

Bane left the Assembly in 1964 to make an unsuccessful bid for Congress, then operated a savings and loan. He returned to the Legislature 10 years later from the 40th District. Almost immediately, he found himself embroiled in a battle over the Assembly speakership and, as part of the losing faction, spent the rest of the 1970s in exile. In another speakership battle in 1980, this one between Speaker Leo McCarthy and Howard Berman, Bane again backed the loser,

Tom Bane

Berman. Willie Brown emerged from the confrontation as speaker. Bane's star slowly rose again. He resumed the chairmanship of the Rules Committee in 1986.

Bane is one of the Capitol's more controversial figures, not for what he says or does publicly, which is little, but because of his legislation and his high-handed, almost solitary operation of the Rules Committee. Even other members of the committee are kept in the dark about what Bane is doing in their name. As Willie Brown once said of him: "Tom's theory is kind of like mine. Someone may do something bad to you. The first time, it's an accident, you have to figure. So the only way to avoid it again is to constantly be reminded of it. Tom does that." His "reminders" take the form of using the Rules Committee chairmanship to reward loyalists and punish those who oppose him.

Bane is notable as the savings and loan industry's most loyal legislative ally in California. The S&L industry has reciprocated by contributing lavishly to Bane's campaign treasury, one that he rarely needs because of his safe district. According to one study, S&Ls gave more than $4 million in donations to California legislators over a 10 year period – and Bane was by far the top recipient, pulling in $513,000. He used much of that money to dole out to other Democrats, thus increasing his power and standing in the Legislature.

A Bane-authored bill in 1983 allowed for out-of-state ownership of California-chartered S&Ls. Common Cause has maintained that it was this law that allowed Charles Keating Jr. to purchase Lincoln Savings and Loan in March 1984. Lincoln was eventually seized by federal regulators and Keating was indicted in what has become the biggest financial scandal in American history.

Controversy has also swirled around Bane's personal business affairs. In 1986, it was revealed that Bane had been promoting a computer software package for Assembly offices that had been developed by a firm jointly owned by his wife, Marlene. No account of Bane's career is complete without mentioning Marlene, his one-time campaign manager and legislative aide whom he married in 1981. Marlene

Bane has had a small office near her husband's in the Capitol and has established a lucrative political fund-raising business on the side, drawing hundreds of thousands of dollars in fees from Speaker Brown and other politicians to tap into her extensive network of would-be contributors.

She also suffers from lupus, a potentially fatal genetic disorder, and her husband has carried a number of bills dealing with lupus research. But even that has been controversial. Marlene Bane chairs a three-member state board that doles out grants for lupus research and there have been published reports that scientists applying for the money also have been hit up for campaign contributions for Bane's and Brown's campaign treasuries.

PERSONAL: elected 1958, resigned 1964 to run for Congress, elected Assembly 1974; born Dec. 28, 1913, in Los Angeles; home, Van Nuys; wife, Marlene; Jewish.

CAREER: president of board, managing investment fund of Los Angeles City Employees Retirement System; savings & loan business.

COMMITTEES: Rules (chair); Banking, Finance & Bonded Indebtedness; Elections, Reapportionment & Constitutional Amendments; Insurance; (Joint) Rules (chair); Fire, Police, Emergency & Disaster Services.

OFFICES: Capitol, (916) 445-3134, FAX (916) 323-5397; district, 5430 Van Nuys Blvd., 206, Van Nuys 91401, (818) 986-8090.

REGISTRATION: 55.7% D, 34.1% R

1990 CAMPAIGN:	Bane – D	65.8%	$1,044,132
	Helen Gabriel – R	28%	$11,864
1988 CAMPAIGN:	Bane – D	73.1%	$1,124,576
	Bruce Dahl – R	25.1%	$6,357

RATINGS:

AFL	PIRG	CLCV	NOW	CTA	CofC	CFB	NRA	FPAC
88%	91%	95%	90%	88%	27%	25%	0%	8%

KEY VOTES:

Divest S. Africa:	YES	Insurance reform:	YES	Child sick leave:	YES
Assault gun ban:	YES	Parent consent abortion:	–	Ban AIDS discrim:	YES
Clean Air Act:	YES	Cutting old trees:	YES	Extend death penalty:	YES
Lmt product tort:	YES	Ban offshore oil:	YES	Restrict abortion funds:	–
Lower alcohol std:	YES	Basic health care:	YES	Oil spill prevent:	YES
Ethics reform:	–	Work cancer stds:	YES	Earthquake insure:	YES

Patrick J. Nolan (R)
41st Assembly District

With a solid Republican majority, this district skirts the flatlands and canyons of the north-eastern Los Angeles basin, including La Canada, parts of Altadena, Glendale and Pasadena. The growth of the Los Angeles area has extended up into the San Gabriel Mountain canyons, which periodically let loose torrential avalanches of rock and mud that wipe the homes away. The homes are re-built, are more expensive than ever and no one seems any wiser.

Republican Pat Nolan has never had any trouble in this district. He has used it as his home base for trying to win a Republican majority in the Assembly and expand his own political horizons. One of a batch of Republicans elected to the Assembly in 1978, Nolan deposed Bob Naylor as Republican leader in 1984. He patterned his leadership after that of his Democratic counterpart, Speaker Willie Brown, by raising vast campaign sums and choosing candidates. Even while bashing Brown as a campaign theme, Nolan reached an accommodation with the speaker that allowed him to pick the committee assignments for Republicans.

Pat Nolan

Nolan saw Republicans pick up three Assembly seats in 1986, despite his controversial penchant for attempting to override local party leaders and anoint GOP candidates from Sacramento. He claimed full credit for the Republican victories, even though Democratic miscues were important factors, and predicted that the GOP was on its way toward capturing control of the lower house in time for the 1991 reapportionment. Nolan insiders talked of his running for state attorney general in 1990.

Then Nolan ran into big troubles. His heavy-handed fund-raising came to the attention of the FBI, which was conducting an undercover investigation of Capitol influence-peddling. Nolan's Capitol office was among those raided in August 1988 by federal agents armed with search warrants. It seemed that Nolan had accepted $10,000 in campaign contributions from a sham undercover FBI company that was making the rounds in the Capitol looking for help on a bill. The FBI has continued its investigation of Nolan, among others, through 1991 giving no indication whether he will be prosecuted or cleared.

When three Republican incumbents – Paul Zeltner, Bill Duplissea and Wayne Grisham – lost in 1988, Nolan saw the writing on the wall and resigned as Assembly Republican leader. He managed to hand the job to a close associate, Ross Johnson of LaHabra. Both were embarrassed when one of their lieutenants, Assemblyman John Lewis, was indicted on forgery charges stemming from the distribution of letters of endorsement for Republican Assembly candidates carrying an unauthorized signature of President Ronald Reagan. There was testimony that both participated in the strategy sessions that led to issuance of the letters. One of the side-effects of the affair was to poison relations between Nolan and the Reagan White House. Lewis eventually had the forgery charge tossed out by an appellate court and never went to trial.

Despite those setbacks, Nolan has not slid very far into the background. He has remained a key strategist for Assembly Republicans. A few short months after he quit as their leader, GOP Assembly members followed Nolan in holding up passage of the budget in 1989 while he fought to redefine the distribution of school money for gifted and disadvantaged programs to get more for the suburbs and less for the inner cities. During the 1990 budget impasse, Nolan circulated a letter pledging to not tamper with Proposition 98's education financing formulas. His actions gave the protection of Proposition 98 a non-partisan patina, and thus backed Gov. George Deukmejian into a corner. Faced with such opposition – in large measure because of Nolan – Deukmejian had no other choice but to bitterly drop his proposal to deeply cut the education budget.

In the 1991-92 session, Nolan can be expected to play a major role in the reapportionment battle as the Assembly Republican point man on the Elections and Reapportionment Committee. He likely will strive to strike a hard bargain with both Democrats and Gov. Pete Wilson.

If Nolan can rid himself of the lingering federal investigation, he doubtless will renew his statewide political ambitions. However, Nolan may also be hobbled by his close relationship to the savings and loan industry. A study by Common Cause identified him as one the top legislative recipients of S&L campaign contributions in the last decade, garnering $154,000 in a 10-year period. A Nolan-authored bill in 1982 allowed California-chartered S&Ls to invest 100 percent of their assets in "virtually any type of venture, regardless of the risk," Common Cause said.

PERSONAL: elected 1978; born June 16, 1950, in Los Angeles; home, Glendale; education, B.A. political science and J.D. USC; wife, Gail Zajc-MacKenzie; children, Courtney and Katie; Roman Catholic.

CAREER: lawyer; reserve deputy sheriff, Los Angeles County.

COMMITTEES: Elections & Reapportionment; Elections, Reapportionment & Constitutional Amendments; Insurance; Ways & Means; (Joint) Legislative Budget; Fire, Police, Emergency and Disaster Services; Rules.

OFFICES Capitol, (916) 445-8364; district, 143 S. Glendale Ave., 208, Glendale 91205, (818) 240-6330.

REGISTRATION: 40.4% D, 49.6% R

1990 CAMPAIGN:	Nolan – R	56.4%	$814,638
	Jeanette Mann – D	38%	$62,749
1988 CAMPAIGN:	Nolan – R	58.1%	$1,797,131
	John Vollbrecht – D	38.3%	$30,237

RATINGS:

AFL	PIRG	CLCV	NOW	CTA	CofC	CFB	NRA	FPAC
11%	27%	15%	30%	60%	86%	58%	100%	100%

KEY VOTES:

Divest S. Africa:	NO	Insurance reform:	NO	Child sick leave:	NO
Assault gun ban:	NO	Parent consent abortion:	YES	Ban AIDS discrim:	NO
Clean Air Act:	NO	Cutting old trees:	YES	Extend death penalty:	YES
Lmt product tort:	YES	Ban offshore oil:	NO	Restrict abortion funds:	–
Lower alcohol std:	YES	Basic health care:	NO	Oil spill prevent:	YES
Ethics reform:	YES	Work cancer stds:	NO	Earthquake insure:	YES

Richard L. Mountjoy (R)

42nd Assembly District

The residential uplands of the San Gabriel Valley east of Los Angeles vote Republican and the 42nd Assembly District is the heart of the region. Arcadia, Azusa, Glendora, Irwindale, Monrovia and San Marino are just a few of the dozen-plus communities contained within the district.

The 42nd District's man in the Assembly, Richard Mountjoy, fits his district perfectly: a middle-aged, white Republican businessman who joined the Legislature in 1978 as one of the self-proclaimed "Proposition 13 babies" and has lost none of his zeal for political infighting in the decade-plus since.

He has become a point man for the Republicans in their ceaseless partisan wars with Democrats over

Richard Mountjoy

legislative procedure, and he helped write a 1984 ballot measure aimed at curbing Speaker Willie Brown's powers. Given that preoccupation, Mountjoy participates only rarely in policy matters and devotes much of his time to plotting strategy.

In 1990, Mountjoy single-handedly campaigned against Proposition 112, the Legislature's ethics reform package. Mountjoy and Ruth Holton, a lobbyist for Common Cause, faced-off on countless radio talk shows on the issue. Mountjoy maintained that while the ethical standards were desirable, the measure had a catch: a commission that, he said, almost certainly would give lawmakers a pay raise. He was right. The measure passed, and lawmakers got a raise.

Mountjoy owns a construction company and was a city councilman and mayor of Monrovia. Mountjoy usually flies his own plane between Southern California and Sacramento and survived a crash-landing at Sacramento's Executive Airport.

PERSONAL: elected 1978; born Jan. 13, 1932, in Monrovia; home, Monrovia; Navy 1951-1955 Korea; wife, Earline; children, Michael, Dennis, Judy; Protestant.

CAREER: general contractor; commercial pilot; Monrovia City Council and mayor 1968-1976.

COMMITTEES: Elections, Reapportionment & Constitutional Amendments; Governmental Organization; Rules; Utilities & Commerce; (Joint) Rules.

OFFICES: Capitol, (916) 445-7234; district, 208 N. First Ave., Arcadia 91006, (818) 446-3134.

REGISTRATION: 39.1% D, 50.7% R

1990 CAMPAIGN:	Mountjoy – R	57.9%	$247,724
	Evelyn Fierro – D	38.6%	$101,060
1988 CAMPAIGN:	Mountjoy – R	70.8%	$168,224
	Richard Boyle – D	29.2%	$0

RATINGS:

AFL	PIRG	CLCV	NOW	CTA	CofC	CFB	NRA	FPAC
8%	21%	26%	40%	52%	82%	42%	100%	96%

KEY VOTES:

Divest S. Africa:	NO	Insurance reform:	–	Child sick leave:	NO
Assault gun ban:	NO	Parent consent abortion:	YES	Ban AIDS discrim:	NO
Clean Air Act:	NO	Cutting old trees:	YES	Extend death penalty:	YES
Lmt product tort:	YES	Ban offshore oil:	NO	Restrict abortion funds:	YES
Lower alcohol std:	YES	Basic health care:	–	Oil spill prevent:	YES
Ethics reform:	NO	Work cancer stds:	NO	Earthquake insure:	NO

Terry B. Friedman (D)
43rd Assembly District

Deep in the heart of the liberal Democratic machine of Reps. Henry Waxman and Howard Berman, this district includes the upscale neighborhoods of West Los Angeles, Brentwood, Westwood and the "student ghetto" surrounding UCLA. Then it extends east along Wilshire Boulevard to take in Beverly Hills. The seat was once held by Jerry Brown's ex-chief of staff, Gray Davis, who was elected state controller in 1986.

Terry Friedman

Speaker Willie Brown tried to break the Berman-Waxman machine by backing his own candidate for the seat in the 1986 Democratic primary. Brown failed and the victor was Terry Friedman, a poverty housing lawyer who had long labored in the political trenches for Berman and Waxman. As a law student in 1972, Friedman was one of the organizers in West Los Angeles for George McGovern's presidential campaign.

As an Assembly member, Friedman has kept a close alliance with other "Grizzly Bear" liberals and is personally close to Burt Margolin. He showed early legislative ability, including winning passage of a bill to force employers to give sick time to employees to care for ailing family members. The bill was vetoed, but it marked Friedman's emergence as a serious legislator.

Friedman carried a successful measure for Los Angeles District Attorney Ira Reiner during the later's unsuccessful bid for attorney general in 1990. The Friedman-authored law imposes criminal charges on employers and their managers if they fail to notify employees of dangerous working conditions or don't disclose concealed product hazards to consumers.

At the start of the 1991 session, Friedman was appointed chairman of the Assembly Labor Committee, supplanting Tom Hayden. Among the bills Friedman is pushing in the session include AB 101, which would prohibit employment and housing discrimination against gay men, bisexuals and lesbians by granting them the same status as minorities and other groups under the state's Fair Employment and Housing Act. The bill's first hearing in March was full of fireworks.

PERSONAL: elected 1986; born Sept. 14, 1949, in Pasadena; home, Los Angeles; education, B.A. American studies UCLA, J.D. UC Berkeley; wife, Elise Karl; no children; Jewish.

CAREER: staff lawyer Western Center on Law & Poverty 1976-1978; executive director Bet Tzedek Legal Services 1978-1986.

COMMITTEES: Labor & Employment (chair); Judiciary; Natural Resources; Public Employees, Retirement & Social Security.

OFFICES: Capitol, (916) 445-4956, FAX (916) 323-7600; district, 14144 Ventura Blvd., 100, Sherman Oaks 91423, (818) 501-8991.

REGISTRATION: 54.6% D, 35% R

1990 CAMPAIGN:	Friedman – D	60.5%	$155,378
	Gary Passi – R	32.7%	$9,359
1988 CAMPAIGN:	Friedman – D	61.8%	$311,905
	Tom Franklin – R	34.3%	

RATINGS:

AFL	PIRG	CLCV	NOW	CTA	CofC	CFB	NRA	FPAC
100%	100%	100%	90%	88%	27%	25%	0%	0%

KEY VOTES:

	Insurance reform:	YES	Child sick leave:	YES
Assault gun ban:	YES	Parent consent abortion:	NO	Ban AIDS discrim:	YES
Clean Air Act:	YES	Cutting old trees:	NO	Extend death penalty:	NO
Lmt product tort:	NO	Ban offshore oil:	YES	Restrict abortion funds:	–
Lower alcohol std:	YES	Basic health care:	YES	Oil spill prevent:	YES
Ethics reform:	YES	Work cancer stds:	YES	Earthquake insure:	YES

Thomas E. Hayden (D)
44th Assembly District

This Los Angeles County coastal district includes comfortable Pacific Palisades, the beach houses and canyons of Malibu, portions of liberal West Los Angeles and the left-of-center environs of Santa Monica. The district should be safe for any Democrat, but the particular Democrat who occupies its seat happens to be one of the nation's most controversial figures, Tom Hayden.

To the public, Hayden is probably the best known member of the California Legislature, with the possible exception of Willie Brown. Hayden is the subject of scores of books, magazine and newspaper articles spanning three decades. He is certainly the only legislator whose comings and goings are charted

Tom Hayden

by People magazine. Hayden has a life that transcends the narrow world of the Legislature. Whatever he does in Sacramento is almost beside the point.

As a founder of Students for a Democratic Society, and as one of the authors of the New Left's manifesto, The Port Huron Statement, Hayden's place in postwar American history is assured. He was put on trial as one of the Chicago Eight, accused of fomenting the riot at the 1968 Democratic convention and sentenced to five years in prison. Back then, Hayden was urged to go underground because friends feared he would be murdered in prison. Those were the days when Hayden vented speeches calling for "revolutionizing youth" through "a series of sharp and dangerous conflicts, life and death conflicts." But Hayden drew back from the revolutionary life. His Chicago conviction was overturned in 1972. His marriage to Jane Fonda won him star status and something the New Left had lacked: a sizable bank account. With Fonda's money, Hayden rejoined the mainstream by running for the U.S. Senate in 1976 against Democratic incumbent John Tunney. Hayden lost and incurred the wrath of many Democratic leaders, who accused him of weakening Tunney, leaving him vulnerable to Republican S.I. Hayakawa. In the wake of his Senate campaign, Hayden created the Campaign for Economic Democracy (which became Campaign California.) Hayden's groups have won success at the ballot box, most notably the Proposition 65 chemical purity measure and in helping to close Sacramento's troubled Rancho Seco nuclear power plant. The organization has pockets of strength in the Bay Area, Chico, Sacramento and, of course, in Hayden's home base of Santa Monica.

But his organizations have also suffered notable setbacks. Hayden was one of the major backers of the "Big Green" environmental initiative in 1990 that would have created a new elected statewide position of "environmental advocate." Some thought the position tailor-made for Hayden. He and his organizations poured money into the initiative. However, the initiative went down in flames after multimillion spending by industrial and agribusiness opponents.

Hayden's fame and success have come with a heavy price. There are those who will always consider him a traitor for having supported the Communist side during the Vietnam War and believe he should have been put on trial for treason. Some of Hayden's colleagues, particularly Gil Ferguson, routinely refuse to vote for a Hayden bill regardless of its merits because his name is on it. And legislative life appears to have contributed to the breakup of his marriage with Fonda.

Hayden is the Legislature's loner. He counts only a handful of his colleagues as his friends, chief among them his seatmate, Tom Bates, who represents Berkeley. While Hayden has made little of a dent on the Legislature, it can safely be said that the Legislature has made little of a dent on him. In his autobiography, "Reunion," he made only scant mention of the Legislature. His close friends remain outside the Capitol as do the central events of his life.

Although Hayden at times seems bored in a sea of mediocrity, he remains one of the Legislature's more astute observers and original thinkers. He occasionally votes with Republicans on crime issues and favors the death penalty. Hayden has concentrated on toxic waste and higher education issues, particularly strengthening the state's community colleges. He also has focused on oversight of the University of California's Lawrence Livermore nuclear weapons lab, much to its discomfort.

Hayden was an indirect beneficiary of the 1987-1988 "Gang of Five" rebellion against Willie Brown. In sacking rebel Democrat Gary Condit as chairman of the Governmental Organization Committee, the speaker had to reshuffle other chairmanships. To Hayden went the chairmanship of the Labor Committee. However, he did not prove a very effective chairman, and the speaker shunted him aside at the start of the 1991-92 session. Hayden was instead appointed chairman of a new Higher Education Committee, a subject of more comfort-and-fit with Hayden.

Hayden may well run for statewide office again or decide it is time to climb back onto the national stage by running for Congress in the 1990s.

PERSONAL: elected 1982; born Dec. 11, 1939, in Detroit; home, Santa Monica; education, B.A. history University of Michigan; divorced; children, Troy and step-daughter Vanessa; Roman Catholic.

CAREER: founder Students for a Democratic Society; founder Campaign for Economic Democracy, Campaign California; author; teacher.

COMMITTEES: Higher Education (chair); Banking, Finance & Bonded Indebtedness; Natural Resources.

OFFICES: Capitol, (916) 445-1676, FAX (916) 447-4457; district, 227 Broadway, 300, Santa Monica 90401, (213) 393-2717.

REGISTRATION: 59.2% D, 29.2% R

1990 CAMPAIGN:	Hayden – D	56.2%	$188,614
	Fred Beteta – R	38.3%	$57,035
1988 CAMPAIGN:	Hayden – D	61.4%	$538,413
	Gloria Stout – R	38.6%	$41,526

RATINGS:

AFL	PIRG	CLCV	NOW	CTA	CofC	CFB	NRA	FPAC
97%	88%	100%	90%	86%	23%	25%	0%	0%

KEY VOTES:

Divest S. Africa:	YES	Insurance reform:	YES	Child sick leave:	YES
Assault gun ban:	YES	Parent consent abortion:	NO	Ban AIDS discrim:	YES
Clean Air Act:	YES	Cutting old trees:	NO	Extend death penalty:	–
Lmt product tort:	NO	Ban offshore oil:	YES	Restrict abortion funds:	–
Lower alcohol std:	YES	Basic health care:	YES	Oil spill prevent:	YES
Ethics reform:	–	Work cancer stds:	YES	Earthquake insure:	YES

Burt M. Margolin (D)
45th Assembly District

This heavily Jewish district extends along Sunset Boulevard to include Hollywood, North Hollywood, Fairfax (and CBS's Television City) and the posh homes of Laurel Canyon. It extends over the hills to include part of Burbank. Overwhelmingly Democratic, the district is a base for the liberal Democratic organization of Reps. Howard Berman and Henry Waxman, which dominates politics on the West Side. Thus it's not surprising that one of its proteges has held this Assembly seat since 1982.

Burt Margolin has become a masterful legislative technician with a clear, liberal agenda. He had good training. Margolin was Waxman's chief of staff in Washington and Berman's legislative aide when he was an assemblyman in Sacramento. He is aligned with the "Grizzly Bear" bloc of liberals in the Assembly and is a dependable vote for environmental and consumer protection bills.

Burt Margolin

Margolin moved into his own in 1986, when he engineered the state's bottle and can deposit law. Coaxing reluctant environmentalists and industry lobbyists, Margolin fashioned a complicated compromise that set up the state's recycling container program – and allowed the battling interests to avoid thrashing it out with a costly ballot initiative.

In 1989, Margolin moved on to an even more arcane area of law – workers compensation. After marathon negotiations that lasted all summer, Margolin worked out a bill that increased benefits to injured workers and trimmed lawyer fees. In 1990, he successfully expanded his container recycling law to increase deposits and include wine and liquor bottles. He was unsuccessful, however, in efforts to forge a health-care insurance bill for those not covered by any insurance. He moved bills out of both houses, but by the end of the 1990 session, neither house could come to terms. In all likelihood, Gov. George Deukmejian would have vetoed any agreement anyway. Margolin may try again with Gov. Pete Wilson, who appears more interested in health issues.

PERSONAL: elected 1982; born Sept. 28, 1950, in Chattanooga, Tenn.; home, Los Angeles; education, UCLA, no degree; wife, Laurie Post; son, Joshua David; Jewish.

CAREER: chief of staff to Rep. Henry A. Waxman 1975-1977 and 1980-1982; legislative consultant to Assemblyman Howard Berman 1978-1979.

COMMITTEES: Insurance (chair); Elections, Reapportionment & Constitutional Amendments; Health; Natural Resources.

OFFICES: Capitol, (916) 445-7440, FAX (916) 445-0119; district, 8425 W. 3rd, 406, Los Angeles 90048, (213) 655-9750.

REGISTRATION: 58.9% D, 28.3% R

1990 CAMPAIGN:			
	Margolin – D	65.2%	$198,254
	Elizabeth Michael – R	29%	$7,419
1988 CAMPAIGN:	Margolin – D	69%	$307,664
	David Frankel R	26.9%	$0

RATINGS:

AFL	PIRG	CLCV	NOW	CTA	CofC	CFB	NRA	FPAC
98%	91%	100%	100%	80%	27%	25%	0%	0%

KEY VOTES:

Divest S. Africa:	YES	Insurance reform:	YES	Child sick leave:	YES
Assault gun ban:	YES	Parent consent abortion:	NO	Ban AIDS discrim:	YES
Clean Air Act:	YES	Cutting old trees:	NO	Extend death penalty:	NO
Lmt product tort:	NO	Ban offshore oil:	YES	Restrict abortion funds:	NO
Lower alcohol std:	YES	Basic health care:	YES	Oil spill prevent:	YES
Ethics reform:	YES	Work cancer stds:	YES	Earthquake insure:	YES

Vacant

46th Assembly District

The locals call it "midtown," a swatch of Los Angeles west of downtown and east of Beverly Hills. It may be the most ethnically and culturally diverse portion of Los Angeles. The district contains Asian, Hispanic, Anglo, straight and gay neighborhoods whose residents range from the very wealthy to the very poor, plus the daytime, power-tie occupants of Wilshire Boulevard skyscrapers.

One of the few unifying factors in midtown is that when it comes to politics, the overwhelming majority of its voters are party-line Democrats. Michael Roos easily held the seat until he resigned in March to take a job as president of an education-oriented business organization.

There aren't very many voters in the 46th Assembly District. Its 65,000 registered voters are the second lowest total for any of the 80 Assembly districts, less than half the average Assembly district contains (the district actually has had a net loss of 10,000 registered voters since 1988). Moreover, the district consistently has had one of the lowest voter turnouts in the state.

REGISTRATION: 58.4% D, 27.8% R

Teresa P. Hughes (D)

47th Assembly District

Roughly nine out of 10 residents of this district, which includes central Los Angeles and the cities of Huntington Park, Bell and Cudahy, are either Latino or black. The percentage of registered Democrats is almost as high. Nonetheless, this is a district where residents are dropping out of the political process in droves. Only 79,700 residents were registered to vote in 1990, nearly 11,000 fewer than two years before (the average Assembly district in the state had 168,500 registered voters).

Teresa Hughes, former social worker, teacher, school administrator and college professor, was first elected to represent the district in a special election in 1975. With the district so solidly Democratic, Republicans sometimes don't even bother putting up anyone against her.

Hughes was most visible in the Legislature as chairwoman of the Assembly Education Committee. But at the start of the 1991-92 session, she was summarily booted out by Speaker Willie Brown and replaced with Delaine Eastin of Union City, a suburb south of Oakland. The move marked a major power shift on the education panel away from the gorilla-sized Los Angeles Unified School District and toward suburban schools. The speaker never publicly explained why he canned Hughes. Privately, those close to Brown said he thought Hughes was plodding and ineffective. Brown also was under pressure from more aggressive and intellectually supple liberals in the Democratic caucus who wanted a crack at forging education policy.

Teresa Hughes

Hughes was never as successful in the fractious Assembly as the Senate education leaders were in shaping consensus on controversial issues and innovative programs. Brown threw Hughes a bone by appointing her to chair a Ways and Means subcommittee on state administration, a not-insignificant post but one with considerably less clout and visibility. The grumpy Hughes made it clear she did not like the demotion and she hesitated before accepting the subcommittee chair.

Hughes has pushed several AIDS-related bills, including a 1987 measure signed into law that allows doctors to disclose AIDS test results to spouses of people who have been tested. She also has backed legislation to require condom standards to make sure that the prophylactics block the AIDS virus.

PERSONAL: elected 1975 (special election); born Oct. 3, 1932, in New York City; home, Los Angeles; education, B.A. physiology and public health Hunter College; M.A. education administration New York University; Ph.D. educational administration Claremont College; husband, Frank Staggers; children, Vincent and Deirdre; Roman Catholic.

CAREER: teacher, school administrator; professor of education, CSU Los Angeles; aide to Sen. Mervyn Dymally 1973.

COMMITTEES: Elections, Reapportionment & Constitutional Amendments; Local Government; Utilities & Commerce; Ways & Means and subcommittee 4, state administration, (chair); (Joint) State's Economy.

OFFICES: Capitol, (916) 445-7498, FAX (916) 327-1789; district, 3375 S. Hoover Ave., F, Los Angeles 90007, (213) 747-7451.

REGISTRATION: 80.6% D, 11.5% R

1990 CAMPAIGN: Hughes – D		100%	$152,310
1988 CAMPAIGN: Hughes – D		94.5%	$166,858
Bryan Riley – R		5.5%	

RATINGS:

AFL	PIRG	CLCV	NOW	CTA	CofC	CFB	NRA	FPAC
95%	100%	95%	100%	98%	32%	25%	0%	4%

KEY VOTES:

Divest S. Africa:	YES	Insurance reform:	YES	Child sick leave:	YES
Assault gun ban:	YES	Parent consent abortion:	NO	Ban AIDS discrim:	YES
Clean Air Act:	YES	Cutting old trees:	–	Extend death penalty:	YES
Lmt product tort:	–	Ban offshore oil:	YES	Restrict abortion funds:	NO
Lower alcohol std:	YES	Basic health care:	YES	Oil spill prevent:	YES
Ethics reform:	YES	Work cancer stds:	YES	Earthquake insure:	YES

Marguerite Archie-Hudson (D)

48th Assembly District

Republicans are an endangered species in the 48th Assembly District, which cuts across the heart of economically depressed south-central Los Angeles, Lynwood and South Gate. Voters are also an endangered species. The district has had a net loss of 13,800 registered voters since 1988, and there are just barely 100,000 registered voters left.

The 48th is California's most heavily Democratic assembly district, with a whopping 83.2 percent registration – actually down 1 percent from 1988 but still more than eight times the Republican registration. It is about 50 percent black and 37 percent Hispanic.

For the past 14 years, the district was represented by Maxine Waters, an aggressive protege of Assem-

M. Archie-Hudson

bly Speaker Willie Brown. But she moved on to Congress in 1991, and was replaced by Marguerite Archie-Hudson, a former administrator at the University of California, Los Angeles, who really won the seat when she defeated Los Angeles City Councilman Robert Farrell in the Democratic primary in June. The Republican candidate in the November general election got only 15 percent of the vote.

It wasn't an easy campaign, however, at least not in the Democratic primary. Archie-Hudson, herself a former aide to Speaker Brown, had to battle charges that she didn't live in the district and was illegally allowed to use the offices of Waters, who endorsed her.

At the start of the Democratic primary campaign, Archie-Hudson downplayed the importance of endorsements. Endorsements had already haunted her once – after spending nine years on the Los Angeles Community College District board of trustees, she lost re-election in 1987 largely on the strength of teachers' union opposition. But in her race for Assembly, she eventually got strong support from labor and other key officials.

Archie-Hudson pledged to end busing of students, opting to keep them close to neighborhood schools. She promised to offer tax incentives to attract business to south-central Los Angeles and proposed to establish a community plan that would integrate services from government agencies, schools and churches.

PERSONAL: elected 1990; born Nov. 18, 1937, on Younges Island, S.C.; home, Los Angeles; education, B.A. psychology Talladega College, Ala., PhD education UCLA; husband, G. Bud Hudson.

CAREER: Board of Trustees, Los Angeles Community College District; Southern California chief of staff for Assembly Speaker Willie Brown; district chief of staff Rep. Yvonne Brathwaite-Burke; associate dean and director for educational opportunity for CSUS; program director, Occidental College; program director, UCLA.

COMMITTEES: Banking, Finance & Bonded Indebtedness; Elections, Reapportionment and Constitutional Amendments; Human Services; Judiciary; Labor & Employment.

OFFICES: Capitol, (916) 445-2363, FAX (916) 323-9640; district, 8510 S. Broadway, Los Angeles 90003, (213) 751-1087.

REGISTRATION: 83.2% D, 9.9% R

1990 CAMPAIGN:			
Archie-Hudson – D	79.5%	$273,747
Gloria Salazar – R	15.1%	$0

RATINGS and **KEY VOTES**: newly elected

Gwen A. Moore (D)
49th Assembly District

This Democratic stronghold is both a combination of working-class and heavily black sections of Los Angeles and Culver City as well as fashionable oceanfront communities such as Marina del Rey. It has had one of the steepest declines in voter registration in the state, with a net loss of more than 15,000 voters since 1988.

Gwen Moore

Gwen Moore, a former deputy probation officer and community college instructor, regularly receives more than two-thirds of the votes every two years. For several years Moore has been the Assembly person out front on public utility and cable television issues as chairwoman of the Utilities and Commerce Committee. In that role, she has generally pushed utilities to justify proposed rate increases. And she successfully established a low-cost "lifeline" telephone rate for low-income people.

Moore, along with fellow Los Angeles Democrat Maxine Waters, was at the forefront of a movement to get the Legislature to prohibit investments of state pension funds in corporations doing business in South Africa. In 1990, she pushed legislation that would have allowed prosecutors to charge females with statutory rape as well as males, a measure that was vetoed by Gov. George Deukmejian. She also tried again on a bill that would require medium and large businesses to give unpaid leave to workers who want to care for sick children or parents, but the measure met the same fate in 1990 than it did in 1987 – a veto from Deukmejian. Moore has reintroduced the bill for the 1991-92 legislative session hoping that Gov. Pete Wilson will take a different view.

In October 1990, federal prosecutors announced that Moore had been cleared of wrongdoing in connection with an ongoing political corruption probe at the Capitol by the U.S. Justice Department. Moore had been living under a cloud for more than two years since she was the author of two bills that federal agents pushed through the Legislature that would have benefited two sham companies set up by the FBI to track influence peddling. Her office was one of several raided by the FBI, and one of her aides was indicted on corruption charges and faced a trial in June 1991.

With her connections to the political organization of Reps. Howard Berman and Henry Waxman, Moore is being readied to run for Congress when the opportunity arises – perhaps when Rep. Julian Dixon seeks a seat on the Los Angeles County Board of Supervisors.

PERSONAL: elected 1978; born Oct. 28, 1940, in Detroit, Mich.; home, Los Angeles; education, B.A. sociology CSU Los Angeles, graduate study at USC, teaching credential UCLA; husband, Ron Dobson; child, Ronald; Protestant.

CAREER: probation officer; Los Angeles Community College trustee 1975-1978.

COMMITTEES: Utilities & Commerce (chair); Consumer Protection, Governmental Efficiency & Economic Development; Education; Governmental Organization; Insurance; Televising the Assembly; (Joint) Energy Regulation & the Environment.

OFFICES: Capitol, (916) 445-8800, FAX (916) 324-6862; district, 3683 Crenshaw Blvd., 5th Floor; Los Angeles 90016, (213) 292-0605.

REGISTRATION: 72.5% D, 18.4% R

1990 CAMPAIGN:	Moore – D	72.9%	$229,170
	Eric Givens – R	21.9%	$4,130
1988 CAMPAIGN:	Moore – D	77%	$312,599
	Eric Givens – R	23%	$4,126

RATINGS:

AFL	PIRG	CLCV	NOW	CTA	CofC	CFB	NRA	FPAC
95%	100%	95%	100%	90%	27%	33%	0%	0%

KEY VOTES:

Divest S. Africa:	YES	Insurance reform:	YES	Child sick leave:	YES
Assault gun ban:	YES	Parent consent abortion:	NO	Ban AIDS discrim:	YES
Clean Air Act:	YES	Cutting old trees:	–	Extend death penalty:	YES
Lmt product tort:	–	Ban offshore oil:	YES	Restrict abortion funds:	NO
Lower alcohol std:	YES	Basic health care:	YES	Oil spill prevent:	YES
Ethics reform:	YES	Work cancer stds:	YES	Earthquake insure:	YES

Curtis R. Tucker Jr. (D)

50th Assembly District

This district, encompassing the El Segundo-Inglewood area of Los Angeles, is about 55 percent black and 20 percent Latino. It is one of the most heavily Democratic districts in the state, with only 16 percent Republican registration. The number of voters registered has declined sharply to 130,000 – roughly half the size of other Southern California districts. The district has had a net loss of more than 15,000 voters since 1988, reflecting a rampant alienation from the political process by those who live here.

Curtis Tucker

For 14 years, the district was represented by Curtis R. Tucker Sr., a former health department worker and Inglewood city councilman. He died in October 1988 of liver cancer, but it was too late to remove his name from the November ballot. Even in death, Tucker Sr. easily defeated his Republican opponent, gaining 72 percent of the vote. That set up a February 1989 special election, and Curtis R. Tucker Jr., a former Pacific Bell manager who was working as an aide to Assemblywoman Gwen Moore, emerged as the easy winner. With backing from Assembly Speaker Willie Brown and utilizing the name identification of his father, Tucker pulled away from a field of four, winning 71 percent of the vote.

Tucker has expressed interest in improving health care, the area in which his father specialized. A proponent of the death penalty, Tucker also listed cracking down on drugs and gang warfare among his priorities. But, so far, he has remained a quiet occupant of the back bench.

PERSONAL: elected 1989 (special election); born April 6, 1954, in New Orleans; home, Inglewood; education, B.A. history CSU Dominguez Hills; wife, Dianne; children, Christopher and Nicole; Roman Catholic.

CAREER: consultant to Assemblyman Michael Roos 1983-1988; aide to Assemblywoman Gwen Moore 1988; manager Pacific Bell.

COMMITTEES: Labor & Employment; Ways & Means; Health; Utilities & Commerce.

OFFICES: Capitol, (916) 445-7533, FAX (916) 327-3517; district, 1 Manchester Blvd., Box 6500, Inglewood 90306. (213) 412-6400.

REGISTRATION: 76.5% D, 16% R

1990 CAMPAIGN:			
Tucker – D		84.7%	$103,300
Michael Long–PF		15.3%	
FEB. 7, 1989 SPECIAL ELECTION:			
Tucker – D		71%	$218,720
Mike Davis – R		19%	$5,000

RATINGS:

AFL	PIRG	CLCV	NOW	CTA	CofC	CFB	NRA	FPAC
93%	91%	95%	100%	90%	27%	25%	0%	4%

KEY VOTES:

Insurance reform:	YES	Ban AIDS discrim:	YES	Child sick leave:	YES
Assault gun ban:	YES	Cutting old trees:	–	Restrict abortion funds:	NO
Lower alcohol std:	–	Basic health care:	YES	Oil spill prevent:	YES
Ethics reform:	YES	Work cancer stds:	YES	Earthquake insure:	YES

Gerald Felando (R)

51st Assembly District

In the Los Angeles area, the value of property is based largely on how close it is to the water – and thus how far upwind of the smog. The people who live in the 51st Assembly District are, therefore, residing on some of the area's most valuable real estate, the stretch of coastal land south of Los Angeles International Airport and north of Long Beach. Within the district are more than a dozen upscale communities – Rolling Hills, Rancho Palos Verdes, Manhattan Beach, Redondo Beach – and a couple of working-class towns whose property values have been skyrocketing in recent years, Torrance and a part of San Pedro.

Gerald Felando

It's a solidly Republican district, and the local political battles, therefore, pit Republican against Republican. A whale of a battle occurred in 1988, when the district's 10-year veteran, Gerald Felando, was challenged by Deane Dana Jr., who spent $777,106 on his primary campaign. His father, Los Angeles County Supervisor Deane Dana Sr., the local political powerhouse, poured tons of money into his son's campaign. Felando's rough personality had opened the door for the challenge, but he survived and won re-election handily. In 1990 he did not have a serious primary challenge.

Felando is a dentist who grew up in San Pedro and maintains close ties to the commercial fishing industry, which has been one of his prime legislative interests. He is known in the Assembly for speaking bluntly and for flashes of temper. It is not unusual to see Felando berating a staff member in public.

Although one of the "Proposition 13 babies" elected in 1978, Felando is somewhat less conservative than many members of the group. He underwent chemotherapy for cancer in 1989, but his disease seems to be in remission, and at the start of the 1991-92 session he was back to being his usual charming self.

PERSONAL: elected 1978; born Dec. 29, 1934, in San Pedro; home, San Pedro; Coast Guard 1953-1957; education, D.D.S USC; wife, Joyce; children, Cynthia, Nicholas and Steven; Roman Catholic.

CAREER: dentist.

COMMITTEES: Governmental Organization; Health; Ways & Means; (Joint) Fisheries & Aquaculture; Legislative Audit.

OFFICES: Capitol, (916) 445-7906; district, 3838 Carson St., 110, Torrance 90503, (213) 540-2123.

REGISTRATION: 36.6% D, 52% R

1990 CAMPAIGN:	Felando – R	58.3%	$420,912
	Marilyn Landau – D	37.6%	$50,625
1988 CAMPAIGN:	Felando – R	62.4%	$721,099
	Mark Wirth – D	34.5%	$27,160

RATINGS:

AFL	PIRG	CLCV	NOW	CTA	CofC	CFB	NRA	FPAC
21%	53%	35%	30%	72%	73%	50%	100%	95%

KEY VOTES:

Divest S. Africa:	YES	Insurance reform:	–	Child sick leave:	NO
Assault gun ban:	NO	Parent consent abortion:	YES	Ban AIDS discrim:	NO
Clean Air Act:	NO	Cutting old trees:	YES	Extend death penalty:	YES
Lmt product tort:	YES	Ban offshore oil:	NO	Restrict abortion funds:	–
Lower alcohol std:	–	Basic health care:	YES	Oil spill prevent:	YES
Ethics reform:	YES	Work cancer stds:	YES	Earthquake insure:	YES

Paul V. Horcher (R)
52nd Assembly District

This suburban Los Angeles County district in-cludes La Mirada, Walnut, La Habra Heights, Diamond Bar and portions of West Covina and Whittier. Although voter registration has slipped for both parties in this district, it has slipped worse for the Democrats since 1988.

The seat was held for eight years by Frank Hill until he moved to the state Senate in 1990 during a round of musical chairs begun when Bill Campbell left the Senate. The new occupant of the 52nd District seat, Paul Horcher, a lawyer and former city council-man from suburban Diamond Bar, is a Republican more in the mold of John Seymour than the ultracon-servative Hill. In fact, Horcher's biggest problems

Paul Horcher

have been with Republicans. Horcher was against state-funded abortions for the poor, but he changed his position to run for the Assembly as a pro-choice Republican. Horcher nosed out Kenneth Manning – an anti-abortion rights candi-date – by less than 100 votes in the GOP primary. Manning toyed with waging a write-in campaign in November but thought better of it.

In the general election, Horcher's Democratic opponent, Gary Neely, a Diamond Bar marketing consultant, tried to pin Horcher with the label of flip-flopper, a la

Seymour. Two loosely knit groups of Republicans also opposed Horcher. One campaigned directly for Neely while the other group asked Republicans to refrain from voting for Horcher because of his stance on abortion. Neither group proved effective. Horcher also courted environmentalists and picked up the endorsement of Californians Against Waste, one of the principal groups that has pushed for recycling laws. But he also tried to mend fences with conservatives, saying his votes in the Assembly would not differ much from Hill.

Horcher outspent Neely in spades. As extra insurance, Horcher loaned his campaign $237,000. With the district's registration favoring Republicans, Horcher won the general election by a healthy margin.

PERSONAL: elected 1982; born Feb. 19, 1954, in Whittier, Calif.; home, Diamond Bar; education, A.A. political science Mt. San Antonio College in Walnut; B.A. political science UCLA; M.A. public administration Pepperdine University, Malibu; wife, Faye; children, Jenny and Greg; Episcopalian.

CAREER: lawyer; Diamond Bar City Council.

COMMITTEES: Higher Education; Insurance; Judiciary; Utilities & Commerce.

OFFICES: Capitol, (916) 445-7550, FAX (916) 324-6973; district, 16209 E. Whittier Blvd., Whittier 90603, (213) 947-9878.

REGISTRATION: 41.9% D, 48.% R

| **1990 CAMPAIGN**: | Horcher – R | 58.9% | $513,681 |
| | Gary Neely – D | 41.1% | $35,372 |

RATINGS and **KEY VOTES**: newly elected

Richard E. Floyd (D)
53rd Assembly District

With a strong working-class bent, the district includes Gardena, Hawthorne and Carson with portions of the San Pedro area – though it never reaches the water. This Democratic district has grown increasingly conservative, and it has tempted the Republicans to try to oust its incumbent, the bad-boy of the Assembly, Dick Floyd. The Republicans probably should have thought the better of it for all the trouble Floyd has caused them. Floyd never forgets a grudge.

In 1986, Republicans targeted him for defeat and mailed letters to voters in his district calling him a friend of drug dealers – which he assuredly was not. The letters bore the forged signature of Ronald Reagan.

Dick Floyd

Livid, Floyd demanded criminal prosecution – and he did not let up until state Attorney General John Van de Kamp won an indictment of Assemblyman John

Lewis, the Assembly GOP's chief election strategist. Authorities said Lewis OK'd the use of Reagan's name after the White House balked at allowing it to be used. Lewis eventually got an appellate court to throw out the charge, but at no small cost or inconvenience.

Floyd is easily the loudest, most profane member of the Legislature – and proud of it. Not a last-night-of-the-session has gone by without Floyd bellowing a profanity directed at one of his Republican colleagues. Among his more polite expressions has been to address Republican Pat Nolan as "the fat man" during floor debates. He dismisses as "whiners" those who complain that Floyd's chain-smoking on the Assembly floor violates house rules. He opposed the state's beverage-container deposit law as a tax, and called its author, fellow Democrat Burt Margolin, an "aging hippie." And when John Vasconcellos sent around a letter urging legislators to get on the bandwagon of his self-esteem movement, Floyd reacted, "If he is going to keep sending me this stuff, I wish he would print it on a roll of toilet paper so it would be useful for something."

Floyd's histrionics aside, he is a serious legislator. He was Sen. Ralph Dills' legislative assistant for years, and like his mentor, knows liquor and horse racing legislation inside and out. In 1988, he was promoted to the chairmanship of the Assembly's governmental organization committee – the Assembly panel chiefly responsible for gambling and liquor legislation. He and Dills now hold full reign over what are politely called "sin bills." Floyd carried a full load of horse racing bills in 1989, including an unsuccessful measure to link the state Lottery with horse racing by having an Irish Sweepstakes-type lottery game tied to a race.

At the start of the 1991-92 session, Floyd introduced a three-bill package to overhaul the neurological examinations given to all boxers and to investigate the California Athletic Commission's boxer pension plan. He renewed his push to require that motorcycle riders wear helmets – a cause that he has pursued for years. He managed to get a helmet bill on Gov. George Deukmejian's desk, where it was vetoed. Floyd apparently believes he will have better luck with Gov. Pete Wilson.

Floyd has been perhaps the most vocally bitter legislator over the passage of Proposition 140's term limits and staff cuts. "I'm depressed," Floyd said in an interview soon after the session began. "There's no future for me. There's no future for my staff. ... Who (cares) whether I leave in two years or I'm not allowed to run (for office) in four years."

PERSONAL: elected 1980; born Feb. 3, 1931, in Philadelphia; home, Carson; Army 1948-1952 Korea; divorced; children, Lorene and Rikki; Protestant.

CAREER: Western regional sales manager for a tape manufacturer and propane equipment firm, 1957-1969; administrative assistant to Sen. Ralph C. Dills 1969-1980.

COMMITTEES: Governmental Organization (chair); Labor & Employment; Insurance; Judiciary; (Joint) Fairs Allocation & Classification; Prison Construction & Operations.

OFFICES: Capitol, (916) 445-0965, FAX (916) 327-1203; district, 16921 S. Western Ave., 101, Gardena 90247, (213) 516-4037.

REGISTRATION: 59.2% D, 29.7% R

1990 CAMPAIGN: Floyd – D   60.3% $401,647
                    Kevin Davis – R   39.7% $589

1988 CAMPAIGN: Floyd – D   58.9% $742,227
                    Charles Bookhammer – R   41.1% $421,075

RATINGS:

AFL	PIRG	CLCV	NOW	CTA	CofC	CFB	NRA	FPAC
94%	73%	88%	90%	88%	32%	8%	82%	17%

KEY VOTES:

Divest S. Africa:	YES	Insurance reform:	YES	Child sick leave:	YES
Assault gun ban:	–	Parent consent abortion:	–	Ban AIDS discrim:	YES
Clean Air Act:	YES	Cutting old trees:	–	Extend death penalty:	YES
Lmt product tort:	YES	Ban offshore oil:	YES	Restrict abortion funds:	NO
Lower alcohol std:	NO	Basic health care:	YES	Oil spill prevent:	–
Ethics reform:	YES	Work cancer stds:	YES	Earthquake insure:	YES

Willard H. Murray Jr. (D)

54th Assembly District

Willard Murray

When Republican Paul Zeltner won this largely minority and blue-collar district in 1986 – thanks mostly to a tactical blunder by Assembly Speaker Willie Brown – Brown quickly proclaimed that Zeltner's days as a legislator were numbered. Brown's prediction came true. Willard Murray, a former aide to Rep. Mervyn Dymally, edged the first-term lawmaker to reclaim a seat that had traditionally gone to Democrats. It didn't take Murray long to get in the middle of controversy.

Murray, whose southeast Los Angeles district includes cities plagued by Uzi-toting gangs, refused to support a measure that would restrict semiautomatic military-style assault weapons. In so doing, he was sticking by the National Rifle Association, which had given him a key endorsement against ex-cop Zeltner, and going against the wishes of many in his district. Ironically, shortly after he was elected, Murray came under fire from the NRA for sending out an endorsement letter without their permission.

Murray also was the subject of controversy before he was elected. During his campaign, he acknowledged that he had never graduated from UCLA despite campaign literature that said he had received a degree in mathematics. Nevertheless, Murray squeaked by Zeltner in a district that includes his hometown of Paramount, Lakewood, Compton, Bellflower and a portion of Long Beach.

In his first term, Murray concentrated on anti-crime bills, introducing a measure that would increase penalties for possession of a machine gun. He has proposed improved services for veterans and a program to encourage college students to become teachers. None of his legislation is particularly earthshaking, and he shows all the earmarks of being a permanent back-bencher.

PERSONAL: elected 1988; born Jan. 1, 1931, in Los Angeles; home, Paramount; USAF 1951-1954 Korea; education, attended CSU Los Angeles; widower; children, Kevin and Melinda Jane; Methodist.

CAREER: engineering; legislative consultant Rep. Mervyn Dymally; chief deputy Los Angeles City Councilman Robert Farrell; executive assistant Los Angeles Mayor Sam Yorty; senior consultant Assembly Democratic Caucus.

COMMITTEES: Higher Education; Local Government; Utilities & Commerce; Ways & Means.

OFFICES: Capitol, (916) 445-7486; district, 16444 Paramount Blvd., 100, Paramount 90723, (213) 516-4144.

REGISTRATION: 64.1% D, 28.1% R

1990 CAMPAIGN:	Murray – D	50%	$185,212
	Emily Hart-Holifield – R	41.2%	$22,554
	Arthur Olivier – L	5.9%	
	Norman Lynn – P&F	2.9%	
1988 CAMPAIGN:	Murray – D	51.9%	$636,352
	Paul Zeltner (incumbent) – R	48.1%	$512,847

RATINGS:

AFL	PIRG	CLCV	NOW	CTA	CofC	CFB	NRA	FPAC
100%	86%	95%	100%	82%	23%	50%	97%	7%

KEY VOTES:

Insurance reform:	YES	Child sick leave:	YES	Cutting old trees:	YES
Assault gun ban:	NO	Ban AIDS discrim:	YES	Restrict abortion funds:	NO
Lower alcohol std:	NO	Basic health care:	YES	Oil spill prevent:	YES
Ethics reform:	YES	Work cancer stds:	YES	Earthquake insure:	YES

Richard G. Polanco (D)

55th Assembly District

When then-Assemblyman Richard Alatorre was named to preside over the reapportionment of legislative and congressional districts after the 1980 census, he didn't neglect his own. The 55th Assembly District is a compact, overwhelmingly Democratic and predominantly Hispanic portion of East Los Angeles. Alatorre didn't remain in the 55th District seat very long. A federal lawsuit resulted in the redrawing of Los Angeles City Council districts, creating two Hispanic seats, and he quickly claimed one of those in 1985. He has since become a City Council power and has been mentioned as a future candidate for mayor.

When Alatorre left his Assembly seat, a serious split developed among local Hispanic politicians over his successor, who was to be chosen by special election.

Alatorre endorsed Richard Polanco, as did Assembly Speaker Willie Brown, and after a rough campaign and two elections Polanco emerged as the winner.

A one-time aide to Alatorre and several other politicians, Polanco made a big mistake on his very first day in the Assembly. He was placed on the Public Safety Committee and voted for a bill to authorize a new state prison in East Los Angeles. There was, however, heavy opposition to the prison in the community and Polanco quickly reversed course.

Polanco doesn't display the same gutsy political instincts as Alatorre and has yet to climb out of back-bencher status, although he tried to carve off a piece of the auto insurance controversy for himself by carrying some insurer-sponsored bills.

Richard Polanco

In 1990, Polanco won some plaudits in his district for carrying a bill – albeit unsuccessfully – to ban aerial spraying of malathion to combat the Mediterranean fruit fly in urban areas. Yet he came under heavy criticism for carrying a tobacco industry-sponsored bill that would have created a law to regulate free promotional distribution of tobacco products statewide. He dropped the bill after health and local government groups argued that the statewide standards would prevent tougher local ordinances. He began the 1991 session carrying a package of important bills on desalination of water. If successful, his legislation could have a lasting impact on Californians.

Given the nature of his district, Polanco probably can remain in the seat until term limits catch up with him, awaiting an opportunity to move up to the Senate or Congress, or perhaps even the Los Angeles County Board of Supervisors, if it is expanded to seven members from its present five.

PERSONAL: elected 1986 (special election); born March 4, 1951, in Los Angeles; home, Los Angeles; education, attended Universidad Nacional de Mexico and University of Redlands, A.A. East Los Angeles Community College; wife, Olivia; children, Richard Jr., Alejandro Gabriel and Liana Danielle; Methodist.

CAREER: special assistant Gov. Jerry Brown 1980-1982; chief of staff Assemblyman Richard Alatorre 1983-1985.

COMMITTEES: Banking, Finance & Bonded Indebtedness; Governmental Organization; Health; Rules; Utilities & Commerce; Ways & Means; (Joint) Mental Health Research (chair); Rules.

OFFICES: Capitol, (916) 445-7587, FAX (916) 324-4657; district, 110 North Ave., 56, Los Angeles 90042, (213) 255-7111.

REGISTRATION: 65.6% D, 22.9% R

1990 CAMPAIGN:		
Polanco – D	78.3%	$362,504
Dale Olvera – L	21.7%	$0

1988 CAMPAIGN: Polanco – D   75.3% $530,367
Evelina Alarcon – P&F   15.6%
William Wilson – L   9.1%

RATINGS:

AFL	PIRG	CLCV	NOW	CTA	CofC	CFB	NRA	FPAC
99%	100%	94%	100%	90%	27%	17%	0%	0%

KEY VOTES:

Divest S. Africa:	YES	Insurance reform:	YES	Child sick leave:	YES
Assault gun ban:	YES	Parent consent abortion:	NO	Ban AIDS discrim:	YES
Clean Air Act:	YES	Cutting old trees:	YES	Extend death penalty:	YES
Lmt product tort:	NO	Ban offshore oil:	YES	Restrict abortion funds:	NO
Lower alcohol std:	YES	Basic health care:	NO	Oil spill prevent:	YES
Ethics reform:	YES	Work cancer stds:	YES	Earthquake insure:	YES

Lucille Roybal-Allard (D)

56th Assembly District

There are 57,500 registered voters – the lowest of any Assembly district – in this predominantly Latino district, which includes part of east Los Angeles and the cities of Bell Gardens, Commerce, Maywood and Vernon. Since 1988, the district has had a net loss of 5,400 voters – proportionally, a huge drop. Moreover, only one-third of the district's voters – 14,000 – voted in the 1990 election.

Lucy Roybal-Allard

Those who voted had only one choice on their ballot for the Assembly: Democrat Lucille Roybal-Allard, a former United Way planner and the daughter of a legendary figure in East Los Angeles politics, Rep. Edward Roybal. Roybal-Allard came out of nowhere in 1987 to overwhelm a crowded field in a special election to fill the seat vacated by Gloria Molina when she was elected to the Los Angeles City Council. (Molina has since moved on to the county Board of Supervisors.) But the family name proved unbeatable in a district that included areas represented by her father for nearly four decades. Roybal-Allard leaves little doubt that she's grooming herself to take over her father's congressional seat whenever he decides to retire – and that may be as early as 1992.

In the meantime, she has emerged as a liberal, though a quiet one. She often sides with an informal group of Democrats known as the "Grizzly Bears," who share information on bills and ideas on how to vote on issues. Roybal-Allard has spent a good chunk of her time working to protect her district. She has helped Sen. Art Torres in the effort to keep the state from building a prison there.

She authored a bill to crack down on companies that constantly violate pollution laws, primarily because a company with a history of violations wanted to build a hazardous waste incinerator in her district. That bill was vetoed by Gov. George Deukmejian.

At the start of the 1991-92 session, Roybal-Allard took over the chair of the Ways & Means subcommittee on health. Although Assemblyman Bruce Bronzan remains the Assembly's lead legislator on the subject, Roybal-Allard's subcommittee gives her some say over the budgets of some of the state's largest bureaucracies.

PERSONAL: elected 1987 (special election); born June 12, 1941, in Boyle Heights; home, Los Angeles; education, B.A. speech therapy, CSU Los Angeles; husband, Edward T. Allard III; children, Lisa Marie, Ricardo; step-children, Angela and Guy-Mark; Roman Catholic.

CAREER: planning associate; past executive director, National Association of Hispanic Certified Public Accountants; past assistant director, Alcoholism Council of East Los Angeles.

COMMITTEES: Health; Rules; Utilities & Commerce; Ways & Means and subcommittee 1–health & human services (chair); (Joint) Refugee Resettlement, International Migration & Cooperative Development.

OFFICES: Capitol, (916) 445-1670, FAX (916) 445-0385; district, 1255 S. Atlantic Blvd., Los Angeles 90022, (213) 266-2772.

REGISTRATION: 59.8% D; 30.5% R

1990 CAMPAIGN:	Roybal-Allard – D	100%	$234,235
1988 CAMPAIGN:	Roybal-Allard – D	79.7%	$303,993
	Stephen Sheldon – R	13.7%	$0

RATINGS:

AFL	PIRG	CLCV	NOW	CTA	CofC	CFB	NRA	FPAC
100%	95%	100%	100%	89%	32%	25%	0%	4%

KEY VOTES:

	Insurance reform:	YES	Child sick leave:	YES
Assault gun ban:	YES	Parent consent abortion:	NO	Ban AIDS discrim:	YES
Clean Air Act:	YES	Cutting old trees:	NO	Extend death penalty:	NO
Lmt product tort:	–	Ban offshore oil:	YES	Restrict abortion funds:	NO
Lower alcohol std:	YES	Basic health care:	YES	Oil spill prevent:	YES
Ethics reform:	YES	Work cancer stds:	YES	Earthquake insure:	YES

Dave A. Elder (D)
57th Assembly District

The 57th Assembly District is an island in a sea of Republicanism, created by Democratic leaders to include loyalist neighborhoods in the Long Beach and San Pedro area. Dave Elder, a one-time budget analyst for the city of Long Beach and executive for the Port of Long Beach, won election in this district in 1978 and, with a 60 percent-plus Democratic registration, has had little trouble holding the seat.

Elder is something of a loner in the clubby Capitol, specializing in arcane bills dealing with taxes, government finance and public employees' pensions. He chairs the committee on public employees and retirement, among the lowest-visibility committees in the house. Periodically, Elder arises on the floor to ask some complicated question about a particularly complicated bill. If he has any hope of moving beyond the Assembly, it's probably to run for Glenn Anderson's congressional seat when Anderson retires.

Dave Elder

At the start of the 1991-92 session, Elder achieved some unwanted notoriety. His ex-wife, Linda Proaps, published a novel about the Legislature entitled "Capitol Punishment." While the book was not exactly headed for the New York Times best-seller list, it was hot copy among Capitol denizens. The main character, a fictional Assemblyman Eric Darcy from Long Beach, was described as "a tall proportioned man, although tending to be a little on the heavy side" with light-gray hair in "a slight wave" who wears three-piece suits, fancies himself a sexual athlete, uses his campaign funds for personal expenses and shakes down lobbyists for payoffs.

PERSONAL: elected 1978; born Feb. 10, 1942, in Los Angeles; home, San Pedro; education, B.A. political science CSU Long Beach; divorced; children, Jonathan and Nicholas; Roman Catholic.

CAREER: budget analyst; general manager of the Port of Long Beach.

COMMITTEES: Public Employees, Retirement and Social Security; Banking, Finance & Bonded Indebtedness; Elections, Reapportionment & Constitutional Amendments; Revenue & Taxation; (Joint) State's Economy.

OFFICES: Capitol, (916) 445-7454, FAX (916) 324-6980; district, 245 W. Broadway, 300, Long Beach 90802, (213) 590-5009; 638 S. Beacon St., 307, San Pedro 90731, (213) 548-7991.

REGISTRATION: 60.9% D, 28.6% R

1990 CAMPAIGN:	Elder – D	67.2%	$253,647
	Rodney Guarneri – R	32.8%	$0
1988 CAMPAIGN:	Elder – D	69.4%	$430,515
	David Ball – R	26.8%	$2,245

RATINGS:

AFL	PIRG	CLCV	NOW	CTA	CofC	CFB	NRA	FPAC
91%	100%	95%	90%	92%	23%	33%	44%	4%

KEY VOTES:

Divest S. Africa:	YES	Insurance reform:	YES	Child sick leave: –
Assault gun ban:	NO	Parent consent abortion:	YES	Ban AIDS discrim: YES
Clean Air Act:	YES	Cutting old trees:	YES	Extend death penalty: YES
Lmt product tort:	YES	Ban offshore oil:	YES	Restrict abortion funds: NO
Lower alcohol std:	YES	Basic health care:	YES	Oil spill prevent: YES
Ethics reform:	YES	Work cancer stds:	YES	Earthquake insure: YES

Thomas J. Mays (R)
58th Assembly District

This Southern California shoreline district, which includes a part of Long Beach, Signal Hill and the Orange County communities stretching from Huntington Beach to Seal Beach, was long safe for Republican Dennis Brown, an Assembly member who was chiefly noted for pushing his "no" button more than anyone else. Brown, one of the "Proposition 13 babies" elected in 1978, grew tired of politics and left the Legislature in 1990. His successor, Tom Mays, came to Sacramento after winning bipartisan kudos for his public handling of the Huntington Beach oil spill as mayor of that city in February 1990. Orange County Republicans consider Mays a bright rising star.

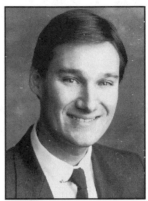

Tom Mays

Mays got his start working for the election campaign of Nolan Frizzelle and was his field representative for a time. Most of Mays' professional career has been spent as an aerospace systems analyst. For a Republican, Mays has had a decidedly environmentalist tilt, although he first won his City Council seat as a pro-development candidate. As a member of the Huntington Beach City Council, Mays voted for measures to protect the city's wetlands and to join Los Angeles in a lawsuit to ban malathion spraying in the battle against the Mediterranean fruit fly.

Mays may not pause long in the Assembly. He may run for a seat in Congress, depending on what new districts are created in Orange County from the 1991 reapportionment.

PERSONAL: elected 1990; born Feb. 6, 1954, in Huntington Park, Calif.; home, Huntington Beach; education, B.A. political science UCLA, M.A. political science University of Chicago; wife, Sydne; children, Kellsey and Lindsey; Roman Catholic.

CAREER: staff manager, McDonnell-Douglas Space Systems Co. 1978-1990; mayor Huntington Beach 1986-1990.

COMMITTEES: Banking, Finance & Bonded Indebtedness; Consumer Protection, Governmental Efficiency & Economic Development; Higher Education; Revenue & Taxation.

OFFICES: Capitol, (916) 445-8492, FAX (916) 322-0674; district, 4510 E. Pacific Hwy., 550, Long Beach 90804, (213) 493-5514.

REGISTRATION: 38.5% D, 50.5% R

1990 CAMPAIGN:		
Mays – R	55.1%	$246,269
Luanne Pryor – D	40.3%	$65,465

RATINGS and **KEY VOTES**: Newly elected

Xavier Becerra (D)

59th Assembly District

This San Gabriel Valley district is largely Hispanic but has seen a substantial influx of Asians in recent years. It includes Alhambra, Pico Rivera, parts of Whittier, South El Monte, Monterey Park and Montebello. The latter two cities, in fact, are not the best of friends. They've battled for years over a smelly dump and other issues.

Xavier Becerra

The district experienced another battle after Assemblyman Charles Calderon was elected to replace state Sen. Joseph Montoya, who was convicted on corruption charges. Calderon's successor in the Assembly was pretty much decided in the primary in this heavily Democratic district, and the surprise winner was Xavier Becerra, a deputy attorney general and former aide to state Sen. Art Torres.

Becerra was often called the "unknown candidate" in the campaign. After all, he had only been a resident of the district for about three years and a registered Democrat for about the same time. Moreover, he was facing a formidable field in the Democratic primary including Diane Martinez, daughter of Rep. Matthew Martinez, D-Monterey Park; and Marta Maestas, Calderon's district aide. With Torres' backing, Becerra ran an aggressive campaign, using strong grass-roots organizing and direct mail while portraying himself as an outsider who would emphasize ethics in government and using his deputy attorney general background to bolster his promise to crack down on crime.

Some attributed his win in the Democratic primary to Martinez and Maestas splitting the women's vote. Others said Becerra's election represented the voters' desire to break from the old tradition of outgoing Latino politicians anointing a relative or an aide to succeed them.

PERSONAL: elected 1990; born Jan. 26, 1958, in Sacramento; home, Monterey Park; education, B.A. and J.D. Stanford University; wife, Dr. Carolina Reyes.

CAREER: lawyer; deputy attorney general; aide to Sen. Art Torres.

COMMITTEES: Environmental Safety & Toxics; Human Services; Local Government; Revenue & Taxation.

OFFICES: Capitol, (916) 445-0854, FAX (916) 323-7179; district, 112 Taylor Ave., Montebello 90640, (213) 721-2904.

REGISTRATION: 61.4% D, 28.5% R

1990 CAMPAIGN:			
Becerra – D		61.3%	$272,000
Leland Lieberg – R		34.5%	$14,909

RATINGS and **KEY VOTES**: newly elected

Sally M. Tanner (D)

60th Assembly District

This heavily Democratic district in Los Angeles County is also mostly Latino – over 50 percent – and working class. It includes the cities of Baldwin Park, Bassett, El Monte, City of Industry, Valinda, La Puente, Rosemead and part of West Covina. Democrat Sally Tanner, a former commercial artist and an administrative aide to an assemblyman and a congressman, replaced Joseph Montoya in the seat. He moved on to the Senate and thence to federal prison. It is a district that Democratic Party officials say someday will likely be represented by a Hispanic, but for the time being, Tanner seems firmly entrenched, having defeated Latino Republican challengers in 1986, 1988 and 1990.

Sally Tanner

Tanner has focused largely on environmental issues during her tenure. As chairwoman of the Assembly Committee on Environmental Safety and Toxic Materials, Tanner has made a major mark on toxic waste and air quality laws in the state. Respected by members of both parties, Tanner has authored many of the major toxic laws of the last decade and helped craft those carried by others. Tanner's interest is natural; her smoggy district suffers from very real pollution difficulties. The underground water of the San Gabriel Valley is polluted from years of industrial abuses and there are several federal Superfund toxic sites in her district.

However, Tanner in 1985 was cheated out of what could have been her crowning legislative achievement by a fellow Democrat. After months of stormy negotiations with Deukmejian officials and nearly every industrial and environmental lobbyist in Sacramento, Tanner was on the verge of winning bipartisan passage for a total reorganization of the state's duplicative toxic cleanup agencies. But on the last night of that year's session, the Assembly's Rules Committee chairman, Lou Papan of Milbrae, held the bill hostage until Republicans would vote for an unrelated bill giving welfare cost of living increases to the elderly, blind and disabled. Despite Deukmejian's personal entreaties to Assembly Republicans, they would not budge and Tanner's bill died without a vote in a gridlock of stuck bills. Deukmejian never tried again. But Pete Wilson has given the reorganization idea something of a reincarnation with his proposal for a California Environmental Protection Agency.

Tanner has had serious battles with cancer, but appears to have won. She toyed with running for the Senate seat vacated in 1989 by Montoya but moved out of the way for the more politically ambitious Charles Calderon.

PERSONAL: elected 1978; born Dec. 12, 1928, in East Chicago, Ind.; home, El Monte; education, attended Pasadena City College and the Art Center College of

Design in Los Angeles, no degree; divorced; children, Timothy and Christopher; Roman Catholic.

CAREER: newspaper graphic artist; department store advertising director; campaign manager and administrative aide, Assemblyman Harvey Johnson 1964-1974 and Rep. George Danielson 1974-1977.

COMMITTEES: Environmental Safety and Toxic Materials (chair); Agriculture; Governmental Organization; Labor & Employment; (Joint) Fire, Police, Emergency and Disaster Services.

OFFICES: Capitol (916) 445-7783, FAX (916) 445-2840; district, 11100 Valley Blvd., 106, El Monte 91731 (818) 442-9100.

REGISTRATION: 59.8% D, 30.5% R

1990 CAMPAIGN:	Tanner – D	61.2%	$261,740
	Ron Aguirre – R	38.8%	$92,932
1988 CAMPAIGN:	Tanner – D	65.5%	$345,202
	Henry Valasco – R	33.2%	$50,859

RATINGS:

AFL	PIRG	CLCV	NOW	CTA	CofC	CFB	NRA	FPAC
95%	100%	94%	90%	90%	27%	25%	0%	0%

KEY VOTES:

Divest S. Africa:	YES	Insurance reform:	–	Child sick leave:	YES
Assault gun ban:	YES	Parent consent abortion:	YES	Ban AIDS discrim:	YES
Clean Air Act:	–	Cutting old trees:	–	Extend death penalty:	YES
Lmt product tort:	YES	Ban offshore oil:	YES	Restrict abortion funds:	–
Lower alcohol std:	YES	Basic health care:	YES	Oil spill prevent:	YES
Ethics reform:	NO	Work cancer stds:	YES	Earthquake insure:	YES

Paul A. Woodruff (R)
61st Assembly District

This expansive San Bernardino County district includes Redlands, Loma Linda and Yucaipa and the high desert towns of Barstow, Victorville, Needles and Crestline. Also included are the San Bernardino Mountain resorts of Big Bear and Crestline.

When longtime Assemblyman Bill Leonard decided to run for the state Senate in 1988, he set off a free-for-all. Seven Republicans announced in a district where the GOP nominee is the all-but-certain winner. In the end, Leonard's hand-picked successor, Paul Woodruff, won. Woodruff worked for Leonard as an administrative aide and campaign manager. Woodruff's main primary opponent was David Hansberger, who spent $143,221 on his losing effort.

Paul Woodruff

Woodruff, who still maintains a campaign consulting business, is a young, baby-faced legislator who spent his first term quietly sitting on the Republican back benches. Near the end of the 1989 session Woodruff was among those pushing for the inclusion of an open meeting requirement in the ethics reform package.

Woodruff has generally followed the Assembly Republican pack in his voting record. Should his patron, Leonard, move on to Congress in 1992, Woodruff probably will attempt to move into his state Senate seat.

PERSONAL: elected 1988; born Feb. 13, 1960, in San Bernardino; home, Forest Hills; education, B.A. political science CSU San Bernardino; single; Protestant.

CAREER: aide, Assemblyman William Leonard 1981-1988.

COMMITTEES: Banking, Finance & Bonded Indebtedness; Higher Education; Televising the Assembly; Transportation; Ways & Means.

OFFICES: Capitol, (916) 445-7552, FAX (916) 445-7650; district, 300 E. State St., 480, Redlands 92373, (714) 798-0337.

REGISTRATION: 39.4% D, 49.6% R

1990 CAMPAIGN:	Woodruff – R	56.5%	$298,736
	Raynolds Johnson – D	37.8%	$10,112
1988 CAMPAIGN:	Woodruff – R	62.3%	$264,332
	Wesley Ford – D	35.5%	$3,824

RATINGS:

AFL	PIRG	CLCV	NOW	CTA	CofC	CFB	NRA	FPAC
5%	23%	24%	30%	50%	86%	33%	100%	92%

KEY VOTES:

Insurance reform:	NO	Child sick leave:	NO	Assault gun ban:	NO
Cutting old trees:	YES	Ban AIDS discrim:	NO	Restrict abortion funds:	YES
Lower alcohol std:	YES	Basic health care:	NO	Oil spill prevent:	YES
Ethics reform:	YES	Work cancer stds:	NO	Earthquake insure:	–

William H. Lancaster (R)
62nd Assembly District

The 62nd Assembly District covers a patch of middle-class suburbia east of Los Angeles, and the man who has represented the area for nearly two decades fits it perfectly. Bill Lancaster, the highest-seniority Assembly Republican, is the Johnny Lunchbucket of legislators. He carries his quota of bills, diligently attends committee hearings and floor sessions and otherwise pays attention to his duty. He puts in his time, takes care of district concerns and is rewarded with re-election every two years.

Lancaster is chairman of the Joint Legislative Ethics Committee, a panel that seldom meets and is not to be confused with the Assembly Select Committee of Ethics, which was chaired by Democrat John Vasconcellos and churned out a comprehensive ethics proposal in 1989. It remains to be seen if Lancaster and his panel will be entrusted with enforcing the Legislature's new ethical standards – or simply abolished with other joint committees as a cost-cutting move.

Lancaster was a Duarte city councilman and mayor, a field representative for the

California Taxpayers Association and an aide to then-Rep. Charles Wiggins shortly before the latter won fame as one of the last defenders of Richard Nixon in the House Judiciary impeachment hearings in 1974. Lancaster left congressional employ after he was elected to the Assembly in 1972. He rarely engages in any of the partisan or factional infighting that marks the Assembly and seems content to punch the clock each morning and go home each night.

Term limits aside, Lancaster can probably hold his seat for as long as he wants. At some point, he may try to hand off his seat to his son, Chris, who is mayor of Covina and an ex-aide to former Sen. Bill Campbell.

Bill Lancaster

PERSONAL: elected 1972 (special election); born April 29, 1931, in Bakersfield; home, Covina; wife, Treece Whitaker; children, Cort, Christopher and Dianne; Protestant.

CAREER: City council, mayor of Duarte 1958-1965; aide to Rep. Charles Wiggins 1967-1972.

COMMITTEES: Banking, Finance & Bonded Indebtedness; Local Government; Transportation; (Joint) Legislative Ethics (chair); Legislative Audit.

OFFICES: Capitol, (916) 445-9234; district, 145 Badillo St., Covina 91723, (818) 332-6271.

REGISTRATION: 40.6% D, 49.9% R

1990 CAMPAIGN:	Lancaster – R	64.1%	$300,620
	Selma Calnan – D	35.9%	$3,081
1988 CAMPAIGN:	Lancaster – R	67.8%	$217,187
	Wayne Wendt – D	28.6%	$10,176

RATINGS:

AFL	PIRG	CLCV	NOW	CTA	CofC	CFB	NRA	FPAC
16%	36%	37%	30%	55%	82%	75%	87%	81%

KEY VOTES:

Divest S. Africa:	NO	Insurance reform:	NO	Child sick leave:	NO
Assault gun ban:	NO	Parent consent abortion:	YES	Ban AIDS discrim:	NO
Clean Air Act:	NO	Cutting old trees:	YES	Extend death penalty:	YES
Lmt product tort:	YES	Ban offshore oil:	NO	Restrict abortion funds	–
Lower alcohol std:	YES	Basic health care:	NO	Oil spill prevent:	YES
Ethics reform:	YES	Work cancer stds:	NO	Earthquake insure:	NO

Robert D. Epple (D)
63rd Assembly District

Reapportionment has eliminated all but a few truly competitive districts, where neither Democrat nor Republican has a clear advantage over the other. This is one of them, and in 1988, Democrat Robert Epple, a Norwalk attorney, was the surprise winner. He didn't win by much – 220 votes – but his defeat of incumbent Wayne Grisham helped solidify the Democrats' majority in the Assembly.

Epple represents the kind of district that would appear Democratic. It is comprised of the mainly blue-collar cities of Artesia, Cerritos, Downey, Hawaiian Gardens, Norwalk and part of Santa Fe Springs. But Democrats here are conservative to moderate.

Grisham, a former congressman, seized the seat in 1984 after Democrat Bruce Young, under investigation for his financial dealings with a campaign contributor, decided not to seek re-election. Grisham, however, had proven to be a lackadaisical campaigner in a 1987 special election to fill a vacant

Bob Epple

Senate seat. Assembly Speaker Willie Brown and other Democratic leaders smelled blood. They poured money and staff into the district and came out winners.

At the start of his first term, Epple went to great lengths to walk the moderate line and not give his opponents ammunition to tag him as a Brown puppet. He bucked the Democratic leadership by voting against restricting semiautomatic military-style assault weapons, one of six Democrats to do so. However, in time Epple has taken a decidedly more liberal line as evidenced by his 100 percent rating scores by three generally liberal organizations.

Among his bills, Epple carried a measure to increase the maximum home loans for Cal-Vet loans, a popular issue in his district. But he has remained a low-profile member.

PERSONAL: elected 1988; born Sept. 18, 1947, in Hollywood; home, Norwalk; Army 1966-1970; education, Cerritos Community College and CSU Dominguez Hills, J.D. American College of Law; wife, Cheryl; child, Nicole; Protestant.

CAREER: lawyer; tax consultant; Cerritos Community College board of trustees 1981-1988.

COMMITTEES: Banking, Finance & Bonded Indebtedness; Judiciary; Utilities & Commerce; Ways & Means.

OFFICES: Capitol, (916) 445-6047, FAX (916) 327-1784; district, 8221 E. Third St., 206, Downey 90241 (213) 861-5966.

REGISTRATION: 56.6% D, 36.3% R

1990 CAMPAIGN:	Epple – D	59.6%	$502,411
	Diane Boggs – R	40.4%	$77,811
1988 CAMPAIGN:	Epple – D	50%	$1,414,084
	Wayne Grisham (incumbent) – R	50%	$1,636,766

RATINGS:

AFL	PIRG	CLCV	NOW	CTA	CofC	CFB	NRA	FPAC
100%	100%	94%	100%	83%	36%	17%	32%	4%

KEY VOTES:

Insurance reform:	YES	Child sick leave:	YES	Ban AIDS discrim:	YES
Assault gun ban:	NO	Cutting old trees:	–	Restrict abortion funds:	NO
Lower alcohol std:	YES	Basic health care:	YES	Oil spill prevent:	YES
Ethics reform:	YES	Work cancer stds:	YES	Earthquake insure:	YES

J. Ross Johnson (R)
64th Assembly District

There's nothing mysterious about the 64th Assembly District. It's a hard-line conservative district in the heart of northern Orange County suburbia, covering such communities as Fullerton and Anaheim. But Ross Johnson, the man who has represented the 64th District for the past decade-plus, is something of an enigma. With a political intelligence that sometimes borders on brilliance, Johnson seems well-suited to his role as the Assembly's Republican leader. But lurking just beneath the surface of his public personality is an anger that bubbles up, rendering Johnson virtually incoherent with rage – a trait that leads some Democrats to bait him in public.

Ross Johnson

Johnson, an attorney who was active in local civic affairs prior to embarking on a political career, was part of the huge class of Republicans elected to the Assembly in 1978, a group that quickly dubbed itself the "Proposition 13 babies" and vowed to wage ideological war on liberals and Democrats. The group asserted itself within months by supporting a coup against the relatively moderate Republican leader of the time, Paul Priolo. That brought Carol Hallett into the leadership position. Johnson helped Pat Nolan, the de facto leader of the Proposition 13 babies, engineer another coup on Hallett's successor, Robert Naylor, in 1984 and wound up as one of Nolan's top lieutenants.

But in November 1988, after Republicans lost several seats to the Democrats and Nolan had become entangled in an FBI investigation of Capitol corruption, Nolan lateraled the leader's position to Johnson. The switch from Nolan to Johnson – which staved off rumblings from moderates in the Republican caucus – had nothing to do with ideology. The new leader was every bit as conservative as the old one.

Johnson has devoted his energies to overhauls of the political system, although his precise motives for that interest, like so many aspects of Johnson's persona, have never been clear. He joined with two other legislators – a Democrat and an independent – to sponsor a campaign finance reform initiative (Proposition 73) in 1988 that imposed limits on contributions and transfers of funds between candidates. That measure remains mired in the courts. Some reformers saw Proposition 73 as a poison pill for a broader reform initiative (Proposition 68) on the same ballot. Since Proposition 73 received more votes, it superseded Proposition 68 in areas of conflict, such as Proposition 73's ban on public financing of campaigns. And its anti-transfer provisions seemed aimed at Speaker Brown's political powers. Johnson, however, has resented the implication that he had ulterior motives. He has maintained that Proposition 73 was a genuine effort at campaign reform and fiercely lashed out at Common Cause for suggesting otherwise.

The styles of the two Republican leaders are far different. Whereas Nolan was gregarious and loved the public stage, Johnson is a semi-introvert, who, aides say, dislikes the limelight. And while Nolan developed a mutually beneficial, cooperative relationship with Speaker Willie Brown – one that protected Brown from being dumped during a squabble with critics within his own party – Johnson has proclaimed a more adversarial attitude.

While Nolan seemed to be consumed with politics as a game, Johnson displays a greater interest in political policy-making. He sat at the table as Gov. George Deukmejian and legislative leaders hammered out a series of agreements on major policy issues in early 1989 after years of unproductive wheel-spinning. But Johnson's skills at policy were no match for the total meltdown in the Legislature during the monthlong budget impasse in 1990. More than other legislative leaders, the usually articulate Johnson was unable to compose a public position on the budget. Other legislative leaders complained that he was not much different in private, reflecting the deeply divided nature of the caucus that sent him. Johnson proved near impotent in leading his caucus on the issue. At one point during the budget fiasco, Johnson lost his temper with GOP colleague Tom McClintock over a press release McClintock wrote that criticized nearly everyone. Johnson scrawled across the top: "Tom, if you want to insult the staff and me, you do the work – Ross."

Johnson has had no better luck than Nolan at winning at the polls. The 1990 election was nothing short of a disaster. Although the Republicans finally succeeded at picking off Democrat Norm Waters, the Assembly Republicans had a net loss of two seats. Reapportionment notwithstanding, the promise of a Republican majority in the Assembly is more distant than it was at the beginning of the 1980s.

Why then do Assembly Republicans keep the brittle Johnson as leader? Probably because, like the Assembly Democrats, the fractured caucus cannot agree on a replacement. At the start of the 1991-92 session, Johnson survived another vote of confidence in his caucus by a 23-9 vote. But the lopsided margin meant little. Given the volatile history of internal Republican politics in the Assembly – four leadership changes in a decade – Johnson may go at a moment's notice.

PERSONAL: elected 1978; born Sept. 28, 1939, in Drake, N.D.; home, Brea; Navy 1965-67; education, B.A. history CSU Fullerton, J.D. Western State; wife, Diane Morris; children, Susan and Molly; Protestant.

CAREER: iron worker; lawyer; legislative aide to Assemblyman Jerry Lewis, 1969-1973; Assembly Republican Floor Leader, 1988.

COMMITTEES: As Assembly Republican leader, Johnson does not serve on any standing committees. He is a member of the Joint Rules Committee.

OFFICES: Capitol, (916) 445-7448; district, 1501 N. Harbor Blvd., 201, Fullerton 92635, (714) 738-5853.

REGISTRATION: 34.6% D, 55.7% R

1990 CAMPAIGN:	Johnson – R	66%	$535,106
	Kevin Gardner – D	34%	$0
1988 CAMPAIGN:	Johnson – R	72.3%	$450,780
	Donald Heuer – D	27.7%	$3,035

RATINGS:

AFL	PIRG	CLCV	NOW	CTA	CofC	CFB	NRA	FPAC
12%	9%	0%	30%	52%	82%	67%	100%	100%

KEY VOTES:

Divest S. Africa:	–	Insurance reform:	NO	Child sick leave:	NO
Assault gun ban:	NO	Parent consent abortion:	YES	Ban AIDS discrim:	NO
Clean Air Act:	NO	Cutting old trees:	YES	Extend death penalty:	YES
Lmt product tort:	YES	Ban offshore oil:	NO	Restrict abortion funds:	YES
Lower alcohol std:	YES	Basic health care:	NO	Oil spill prevent:	YES
Ethics reform:	YES	Work cancer stds:	NO	Earthquake insure:	YES

Jim Brulte (R)

65th Assembly District

The west end of the San Bernardino Valley has experienced some of the most explosive growth of the last decade. Roughly following old Route 66, this district hardly resembles the ticky-tack conglomeration of towns immortalized in the song of the same name. The district includes the old, upscale neighborhoods of Ontario and the new stucco housing tracts of Rancho Cucamonga, Montclair, Chino and Pomona. The district extends north into the desert, including the small community of Adelanto that has been begging for years to get a state prison and talking about legalized gambling, both without success.

Jim Brulte

The district was once competitive. But after the 1981 reapportionment it became safely Republican. The seat was held for a time by Republican Charles Bader, who vacated it to run for the Senate against incumbent Ruben Ayala in 1990. After a mega-buck race, Ayala kept his seat and Bader was sent into political retirement, at least for the moment.

Meanwhile, Bader passed his Assembly seat to his chief of staff, Jim Brulte, an imposing man at 6-foot-4 and 260 pounds. Brulte is the quintessential politician of the era. He worked his way into the Legislature not through service to the community but by service to other politicians. Brulte had been active in political campaigns since he was 10. He was an aide to S.I. Hayakawa and an advance man for George Bush. Brulte's resume is stuffed with political jobs.

Brulte ran a typically modern campaign with direct mail, computerized fund-raising lists and humming fax machines. He overwhelmed an underfunded opponent in the GOP primary, Mark Nymeyer, a Pomona city councilman and Baptist preacher. The general election was a cinch for Brulte. His Democratic opponent, Robert Erwin, a counselor with the San Bernardino Probation Department and Vietnam veteran, was no match for Brulte's heavy backing from the area's building industry and all of its Republican legislators and congressmen.

Brulte began his elective career with a bipartisan idea: forming an "Inland Empire Caucus" with legislators from the San Bernardino and Riverside areas. Democrat Jerry Eaves of Rialto was elected the caucus's first chairman. But there was no mistaking where the idea came from – a freshman well-versed in playing the Capitol game.

PERSONAL: elected 1990; born April 13, 1956, in Glen Cove, N.Y.; home, Ontario; Air National Guard Reserve 1974-present; education, B.A. political science Cal Poly Pomona; single.

CAREER: Staff, U.S. Sen. S.I. Hayakawa in Washington D.C; staff, Republican National Committee; staff, Assistant Secretary of Defense for Reserve Affairs; advance staff, Vice President George Bush; executive director, San Bernardino County Republican Party; chief of staff, Assemblyman Charles Bader 1987-1990; owns management consulting firm.

COMMITTEES: Environmental Safety; Governmental Organization; Insurance; Natural Resources.

OFFICES: Capitol, (916) 445-8490, FAX (916) 323-8544; district, 10681 Foothill Blvd., 325, Rancho Cucamonga 91730, (714) 466-9096.

REGISTRATION: 40.7% D, 50.1% R

1990 CAMPAIGN:	Brulte – R	59.9%	$275,634
	Robert Erwin – D	40.1%	$34,208

RATINGS and **KEY VOTES**: Newly elected

Gerald R. Eaves (D)

66th Assembly District

Few districts in the state have undergone as much change in the last decade as the 66th Assembly District. Once solidly working class, the dusty neighborhoods of Fontana, Rialto, Colton and Ontario grew up around big factories, chief among them Kaiser Steel's huge plant in Fontana. The mill was put inland during World War II to escape shelling from Japanese submarines. After the war, the outlaw Hell's Angels motorcycle gang began there. But in the 1970s the mill fell on hard times and closed. The future looked bleak. Housing prices remained stagnant.

In the 1980s, western San Bernardino County boomed precisely because those housing prices had stayed low. Big developers came in, built instant neighborhoods and new businesses grew around them. And political loyalties just weren't what they used to be. When the state Fair Political Practices Commission found that

Democrat Terry Goggin had committed a raft of financial indiscretions, he got dumped in a Democratic primary by Rialto Mayor Gerald Eaves, who went on to win the general election.

In Sacramento, the bearded Eaves has been chiefly noted for one thing – his membership in that rebel group known as "The Gang of Five." The five waged war for a year on Speaker Willie Brown for a variety of political and personal reasons. Eaves' fellow rebel, Steve Peace, described Eaves as the most thoughtful among the bunch. Of the five, Eaves was the quietest.

Eaves was the last of the five to be stripped of his committee assignments, apparently because the speaker was trying to woo him away from the others.

Jerry Eaves

But after that failed, Brown threw support behind a 1988 primary challenger, Joe Baca. Eaves won his primary, and re-election, and the Gang of Five made an uneasy peace with Brown in 1989. Eaves has not been heard from much since, other than being elected chairman of the "Inland Empire Caucus" of legislators representing the Riverside and San Bernardino area.

PERSONAL: elected 1984; born May 17, 1939, in Miami, Ariz.; home, Rialto; education, San Bernardino Valley College and CSU San Bernardino, no degree; wife, Susan; children, Cheryl, Michael and Laura; Protestant.

CAREER: Steel-mill laborer and manager; insurance agent; Rialto City Council and mayor 1977-84.

COMMITTEES: Elections, Reapportionment & Constitutional Amendments; Governmental Organization; Rules; Transportation; Ways & Means; (Joint) Rules.

OFFICES: Capitol, (916) 445-4843, FAX (916) 443-6812; district, 224 N. Riverside Ave., A, Rialto 92376, (714) 820-1902.

REGISTRATION: 56.9% D, 35.3% R

1990 CAMPAIGN:	Eaves – D	59.3%	$507,919	
	Steven Hall – R	40.7%		$16,975
1988 CAMPAIGN:	Eaves – D	55.2%	$1,108,967	
	David Masters – R	40.5%		$443,068

RATINGS:

AFL	PIRG	CLCV	NOW	CTA	CofC	CFB	NRA	FPAC
95%	86%	89%	90%	89%	45%	33%	19%	13%

KEY VOTES:

Divest S. Africa:	YES	Insurance reform:	YES	Child sick leave: –
Assault gun ban:	YES	Parent consent abortion:	YES	Ban AIDS discrim: –
Clean Air Act:	–	Cutting old trees:	YES	Extend death penalty: YES
Lmt product tort:	YES	Ban offshore oil:	YES	Restrict abortion funds: NO
Lower alcohol std:	YES	Basic health care:	YES	Oil spill prevent: YES
Ethics reform:	YES	Work cancer stds:	YES	Earthquake insure: YES

John R. Lewis (R)

67th Assembly District

This major GOP stronghold includes Tustin, Orange, Yorba Linda, Villa Park and portions of Anaheim. The heart of Orange County, this is where Richard Nixon was born and the John Birch Society prospered. Since 1980, the district has been represented by John Lewis, whose roots in business have made him one of the most conservative members of the Legislature.

He rarely rises to make a speech on the floor, instead making his statement by pushing his red button – for "no" – on bill after bill. He carries a relatively light bill load, not out of laziness but out of conviction that government should be minimal. Lewis has a dry wit and is sharply analytical about the

John Lewis

Legislature – a detachment born, perhaps, of the fact that Lewis is one of the wealthiest members as the heir to a dog-food fortune.

Lewis is a major force in the Assembly Republican caucus, one of the "cavemen" who dominated the GOP caucus in the 1980s. Despite a poor win/loss record, Lewis continues to be the principal strategist in the effort to wrest control of the Assembly away from the Democrats. He is a much-in-demand designer of election tactics.

The 1986 campaign was a watershed for the Assembly Republicans, the closest they have come to getting a majority by picking up several seats from the Democrats. But the effort cost Lewis dearly. In 1989, he was indicted by a Sacramento County grand jury and accused of forgery for sending out letters bearing the faked signature of President Ronald Reagan during the '86 campaign. Going to households in several hotly contested races, the letters accused Democratic incumbents of favoring drug dealers. Lewis contended that the indictment was political, arguing that Democratic state Attorney General John Van de Kamp ignored campaign dirty tricks committed by Democratic legislative candidates in seeking charges against him. The state Court of Appeal in Sacramento threw out the indictment on the grounds that a faked signature on campaign literature did not constitute legal forgery. Although Lewis beat the rap, fellow Republican Bill Craven from the Senate said Lewis' behavior was reprehensible and pushed legislation to fill the loophole.

In 1991, Lewis was expected to join Craven in the Senate. In March, he beat seven other Republicans in a special primary election to take over the seat vacated by John Seymour upon his appointment to the U.S. Senate. He was to face Democrat Frank Hoffman in the May runoff, but in this part of Orange County, such contests are pro-forma activities.

PERSONAL: elected 1980; born Nov. 2, 1954, in Los Angeles; home, Orange; education, B.A. political science USC; wife, Suzanne Henry; no children; Protestant.

CAREER: aide to Assemblyman Dennis Brown; investment manager.

COMMITTEES: Banking, Finance & Bonded Indebtedness; Elections, Reapportionment & Constitutional Amendments; Revenue & Taxation; Ways & Means.

OFFICES: Capitol, (916) 445-2778; district, 1940 N. Tustin, 102, Orange 92665, (714) 998-0980.

REGISTRATION: 30% D, 59.9% R

1990 CAMPAIGN:	Lewis – R	67.1%	$228,623
	Fred Smoller – D	32.9%	$0
1988 CAMPAIGN:	Lewis – R	74.4%	$285,834
	Bruce Fink – D	25.6%	$1,690

RATINGS:

AFL	PIRG	CLCV	NOW	CTA	CofC	CFB	NRA	FPAC
3%	14%	11%	30%	62%	77%	50%	100%	100%

KEY VOTES:

Divest S. Africa:	NO	Insurance reform:	NO	Child sick leave:	NO
Assault gun ban:	NO	Parent consent abortion:	YES	Ban AIDS discrim:	NO
Clean Air Act:	NO	Cutting old trees:	YES	Extend death penalty:	YES
Lmt product tort:	YES	Ban offshore oil:	NO	Restrict abortion funds:	YES
Lower alcohol std:	–	Basic health care:	NO	Oil spill prevent:	–
Ethics reform:	YES	Work cancer stds:	NO	Earthquake insure:	NO

Steve W. Clute (D)
68th Assembly District

Winding like a desert serpent, the 68th District weaves and bobs through the Democratic neighborhoods of Riverside near the University of California campus and into Moreno Valley – an instant city created by developers stymied in their efforts to build in growth-controlled Riverside. The district weaves through the San Gorgonio Pass communities of Banning and Beaumont, then turns north through unpopulated Joshua Tree National Monument, avoiding the Republican territory of Palm Springs. Turning south again, the district includes the rich farmlands of the Coachella Valley and stretches across the desert to the Colorado River in Blythe. It will surely look nothing like this after reapportionment.

Steve Clute

The seat was vacated by the sharp-tongued and personally troubled Walter Ingalls in 1982, when he fell from favor by backing the wrong horse in the speakership wars of the early '80s. Steve Clute, an ex-Navy pilot, ex-airport manager – and total unknown – got the nod from Speaker Willie Brown and won the seat. Clute was such an outsider that he walked precincts in the wrong district in his first campaign and was labeled – somewhat unfairly – a carpetbagger. He did have some claim as a near-native; he was schooled in Pasadena and is a graduate of the University of California, Riverside.

It is easy to mistake Clute's aw-shucks, flyboy-jock manner as that of a less-than-serious politician. He seems more interested in triathlon competitions than legislative competitions. He does, at times, appear out of place and not particularly well versed on issues or legislation. He is, at best, an awkward speaker. But Clute is a tenacious, energetic campaigner, continually underestimated by his Republican foes, who every two years make him a target for defeat.

Clute appears unfailingly honest and exhibits a remarkably thick skin. Generally, he sticks to himself when in Sacramento. At home he is more at ease, working the district nearly every weekend in his state-leased four-wheel-drive truck with his wife, Pam, a math instructor at UC Riverside. Clute has preferred to stick to local issues like attempting to win a veterans' home in his district and efforts to block plans for a tire burning incinerator just outside his district in Rialto. He has labored in the shadow of a more powerful and successful Democrat, Sen. Robert Presley.

Clute chairs the Ways & Means subcommittee on transportation, which gives him some clout over the Caltrans budget. So far, however, he has not shown the touch Ingalls had at coaxing highway projects for his district.

He is often taken as a lightweight by some colleagues, and he hasn't been accepted by Riverside's snooty old families and press. He has made some headway on both fronts but has a distance to go. And he did not help his cause any by skipping out on the last night of the session in 1989 when a bill to restore $24 million to family planning fell a few votes short because of absent Democrats.

Clute has been more careful since then. He is known to have his eye on one of the new congressional seats that surely will be carved in his area, given its explosive growth of the last decade. Clute's political fortunes were only enhanced at the outbreak of the Persian Gulf War, when he attempted to get back into the Navy as a pilot. He was turned down as too old.

PERSONAL: elected 1982; born Dec. 8, 1948, in Chicago, Ill.; home, Riverside; Navy 1971-1977; education, B.S. social sciences UC Riverside, M.A. management Webster College, St. Louis; wife, Pamela Chaney; no children; Methodist.

CAREER: airport manager city of Rialto 1980-1982.

COMMITTEES: Agriculture; Governmental Organization; Transportation; Ways & Means and subcommittee 5–transportation (chair); (Joint) Arts.

OFFICES: Capitol, (916) 445-5416, FAX (916) 323-5190; district, 1650 Spruce St., 310, Riverside 92501, (714) 782-3222.

REGISTRATION: 53.4% D, 37.9% R

1990 CAMPAIGN:			
Clute – D	57.5%	$324,301
Clay Hage – R	42.5%	$118,817

1988 CAMPAIGN: Clute – D 55.4% $694,857
Brian Carroll – R 44.6% $1,228,735

RATINGS:

AFL	PIRG	CLCV	NOW	CTA	CofC	CFB	NRA	FPAC
85%	91%	60%	90%	97%	41%	58%	25%	33%

KEY VOTES:

Divest S. Africa:	YES	Insurance reform:	YES	Child sick leave:	–
Assault gun ban:	YES	Parent consent abortion:	YES	Ban AIDS discrim:	NO
Clean Air Act:	YES	Cutting old trees:	NO	Extend death penalty:	–
Lmt product tort:	YES	Ban offshore oil:	YES	Restrict abortion funds:	NO
Lower alcohol std:	YES	Basic health care:	YES	Oil spill prevent:	YES
Ethics reform:	YES	Work cancer stds:	YES	Earthquake insure:	NO

Nolan Frizzelle (R)

69th Assembly District

Bedrock conservative country is the best way to describe this Orange County district, which includes Irvine, Fountain Valley and parts of Santa Ana, Costa Mesa and Huntington Beach. Nolan Frizzelle is every bit as conservative as his district. He is an optometrist who has long been active in GOP politics and is a past president of the California Republican Assembly.

Since his election in 1980, Frizzelle has, for the most part, remained on the back benches in the Assembly, consistently voting the GOP caucus line. He is irascible, staunchly defends his point of view and is almost impossible to budge on an issue. One local issue of statewide importance with which Frizzelle is identified is toll roads. In an effort to alleviate Orange

Nolan Frizzelle

County's horrible traffic congestion, Frizzelle for years proposed authorizing privately built toll roads. His early advocacy eventually led to the passage of bills authorizing toll roads operated by a joint-powers agency.

Another bill of note that carried Frizzelle's name was a 1986 measure to give to legislators the same health benefits that state workers received. The provisions of the measure were actually amended into a bill introduced by Frizzelle under an agreement between Democratic and Republican leaders.

PERSONAL: elected 1980; born Oct. 16, 1921, in Los Angeles; home, Fountain Valley; USMC WWII; education, attended Stanford University, UC Berkeley, UCLA and USC School of Optometry; wife, Ina; children, Roger, David, Diane, Robert, Sabina and Tim; Protestant.

CAREER: Optometrist.

COMMITTEES: Governmental Organization; Natural Resources; Ways & Means. (Joint): Legislative Audit; State's Economy.

OFFICES: Capitol, (916) 445-8377, FAX (916) 323-5467; district, 17195 Newhope St., 201, Fountain Valley 92708, (714) 662-5503.

REGISTRATION: 31.7% D, 56.6% R

1990 CAMPAIGN:	Frizzelle – R	63.2%	$188,156
	Jim Toledano – D	36.8%	$21,868
1988 CAMPAIGN:	Frizzelle – R	70.4%	$179,093
	Marie Fennell – D	29.6%	$4,574

RATINGS:

AFL	PIRG	CLCV	NOW	CTA	CofC	CFB	NRA	FPAC
10%	27%	17%	20%	52%	77%	75%	100%	88%

KEY VOTES:

Divest S. Africa:	NO	Insurance reform:	NO	Child sick leave: –
Assault gun ban:	NO	Parent consent abortion: YES	Ban AIDS discrim: NO
Clean Air Act:	NO	Cutting old trees:	YES	Extend death penalty: YES
Lmt product tort:	YES	Ban offshore oil:	NO	Restrict abortion funds:YES
Lower alcohol std:	YES	Basic health care:	NO	Oil spill prevent: YES
Ethics reform:	YES	Work cancer stds:	NO	Earthquake insure: YES

Gilbert W. Ferguson (R)
70th Assembly District

Imbedded on the tony beachfront of Orange County, this district includes Newport Beach, Balboa Island, Mission Viejo, Laguna Beach, San Clemente and San Juan Capistrano – towns that are the epitome of upscale California suburbanization. Condos, hotels and estates are jammed along the bluffs above the beach. Development here is one of the major reasons voters statewide approved the Coastal Protection Act in 1972, setting up the Coastal Commission and a system for growth control along the shoreline.

Gil Ferguson

Not surprisingly, this stronghold of BMWs and cellular phones has been the most Republican district in the state during the 1980s. But there are pockets of Democratic voters, particularly in Laguna Beach, which has a politically active gay community and turned out by the thousands when Michael Dukakis made a campaign stop in 1988.

The district is so safe for Republicans it appears incumbent Gil Ferguson can do all sorts of outlandish things and still not be in trouble with voters. He can vote against the interests of Orange County on transportation issues. He can attempt to rewrite school books to reflect an ultraconservative view of history. And he can even say outrageous things about every non-Anglo community and his gay constituents.

Ferguson was elected to the Assembly in 1984 and became a core member of the conservative "cavemen" who made Pat Nolan the Republican Assembly leader.He tends to shoot from the hip. The retired Marine railed against resolutions to make amends for interning Japanese-Americans in World War II. "The veterans of Pearl Harbor have read this, and they are outraged!" he said in August 1989, bringing Assemblyman Phil Isenberg to his feet, whose wife was among those interned in the war. "You should be ashamed!" huffed Isenberg.

Toward the end of the 1990 session, Ferguson fought back with his own resolution, ACR 181, calling on state schools to teach "an honest, objective and balanced" version of history that excuses America for requiring 120,000 Japanese-Americans and Japanese immigrants to live behind barbed-wire fences during World War II. It was obvious Ferguson was directing his resolution toward an audience somewhere other than in the Assembly when, in his floor speech, he told cable TV viewers: "I'd advise you to tape this." He got four votes in the Assembly: his own, Cathie Wright, Phil Wyman and Marian LaFollette, who has since retired.

Ferguson is best known for his effort to oust Tom Hayden from the Legislature. Ferguson has called Hayden a traitor for supporting the North Vietnamese during the war and refuses to vote for any bill with Hayden's name on it. Ferguson came close to winning enough votes to have Hayden bounced in 1986.

Aside from his pyrotechnics in the Assembly, Ferguson is a lackluster legislator, authoring little legislation of any note and showing scant interest in learning much about the bills before him in committees. He instead spins off elaborate theories about the forces of evil, which usually means Democrats and Communists. He insists that Republican U.S. Attorney David Levi was manipulated by Democrats into investigating the Republican honchos in the Assembly. Nevermind that, so far, only Democrats have been prosecuted.

Despite his loss of a special state Senate election to Frank Hill in 1990, Ferguson's ambitions are unabated. He may run for statewide office at his first opportunity or for a congressional seat in 1992.

PERSONAL: elected 1984; born April 22, 1923, in St. Louis, Mo.; home, Balboa Island; USMC 1942-1968 WWII, Korea and Vietnam; education, attended USC, University of Maryland, B.A. Akron University; wife, Anita Wollert; children, Mark, Rhonda, Darrel and Jay; Protestant.

CAREER: career officer USMC; president of Corporate Communication, a Newport Beach advertising and public relations firm; corporate vice president of The Gilita Co., a housing development firm; newspaper publisher; columnist for Freedom Newspapers, including the Orange County Register; artist.

COMMITTEES: Education; Housing & Community Development; Insurance; Revenue & Taxation; (Joint) School Facilities.

OFFICES: Capitol, (916) 445-7222, FAX (916) 324-3657; district, 4667 MacArthur Blvd., 201, Newport Beach 92660, (714) 756-0665.

REGISTRATION: 27.2% D, 61.7% R

1990 CAMPAIGN:			
Ferguson – R		64.7%	$406,651
Howard Adler – D		35.3%	$1,448

1988 CAMPAIGN: Ferguson – R 70.5% $506,593
Michael Gallups – D 29.5% $0

RATINGS:

AFL	PIRG	CLCV	NOW	CTA	CofC	CFB	NRA	FPAC
6%	27%	17%	30%	50%	77%	50%	100%	100%

KEY VOTES:

Divest S. Africa:	NO	Insurance reform:	NO	Child sick leave:	NO
Assault gun ban:	NO	Parent consent abortion:	YES	Ban AIDS discrim:	NO
Clean Air Act:	NO	Cutting old trees:	YES	Extend death penalty:	YES
Lmt product tort:	YES	Ban offshore oil:	NO	Restrict abortion funds:	–
Lower alcohol std:	YES	Basic health care:	NO	Oil spill prevent:	YES
Ethics reform:	–	Work cancer stds:	NO	Earthquake insure:	NO

Doris J. Allen (R)

71st Assembly District

Democrats enjoyed a brief period of dominance in Orange County politics during the 1970s, but one-by-one, Democratic legislators fell to Republican challenges beginning in 1978. The 71st Assembly District, in the central portion of the county, was one of the last Democratic bastions left. In 1982, incumbent Chester Wray was beaten by Doris Allen, who had gained local prominence as a school district trustee and leader of an anti-busing campaign.

Doris Allen

Allen, as a woman and a Republican, has not been part of the Assembly's ruling circles. In fact, she's feuded publicly with one of the more influential Republican leaders, Gerald Felando. The issue that divides Allen and Felando is the one that has become her legislative preoccupation: mismanagement of the state Fish and Game Department (another male-dominated bastion) and, in particular, its regulation of commercial fishing. She sees Felando, who represents San Pedro, as pushing the interests of commercial fishermen over those of sports fishermen. Allen embarrassed Gov. George Deukmejian's administration by exposing several management scandals in the Fish and Game Department. But few in her caucus have shown any interest in supporting her attempts to make the agency more accountable. On a shoestring budget, Allen successfully promoted Proposition 132 on the November 1990 ballot, which banned use of gill nets in coastal waters. Commercial fisherman opposed the measure. Her proposition was the only one of six environmental measures to pass.

Early in 1991, she was one of three Assembly members who ran for a state Senate seat vacated by John Seymour, who was appointed to Gov. Pete Wilson's post in the U.S. Senate. But she lost in the primary to John Lewis.

PERSONAL: elected 1982; born May 26, 1936, in Kansas City, Mo.; home,

Cypress; education, University of Wyoming, no degree, Golden West College, IBM School in Kansas City, Long Beach Community College and Hallmark Business School; divorced; children, Joni and Ron; Protestant.

CAREER: co-owner lighting business, Lampco; trustee, Huntington Beach Union School District.

COMMITTEES: Governmental Organization; Health; Natural Resources.

OFFICES: Capitol, (916) 445-6233; district, 5252 Orange Ave., 100, Cypress 90630, (714) 821-1500.

REGISTRATION: 40.7% D, 49.7% R

1990 CAMPAIGN:	Allen – R	60.5%	$98,098
	Peter Mathews – D	39.5%	$54,621
1988 CAMPAIGN:	Allen – R	69.5%	$197,575
	Art Brown – D	30.5%	$16,512

RATINGS:

AFL	PIRG	CLCV	NOW	CTA	CofC	CFB	NRA	FPAC
15%	45%	35%	30%	57%	64%	42%	100%	85%

KEY VOTES:

Divest S. Africa:	NO	Insurance reform:	NO	Child sick leave:	NO
Assault gun ban:	NO	Parent consent abortion:	YES	Ban AIDS discrim:	NO
Clean Air Act:	YES	Cutting old trees:	YES	Extend death penalty:	YES
Lmt product tort:	YES	Ban offshore oil:	NO	Restrict abortion funds:	YES
Lower alcohol std:	YES	Basic health care:	NO	Oil spill prevent:	YES
Ethics reform:	YES	Work cancer stds:	NO	Earthquake insure:	NO

Thomas J. Umberg (D)

72nd Assembly District

The 72nd Assembly District is entirely in Orange County, the bastion of conservatism of California politics. Yet because of its working-class and minority enclaves in cities such as Stanton, Westminster, Garden Grove, Santa Ana and Anaheim, this is one Orange County district where either a Democrat or a Republican has a chance to win.

Tom Umberg

For 12 years, the district – tailored by Democratic leaders to maximize their chances of holding it – was represented by Democrat Richard Robinson, who left office to seek a congressional seat in 1986. Republican businessman Richard Longshore, who in 1984 had come close to unseating Robinson, won the seat in 1986, but died in 1988. That set the scene for a furious partisan tug-of-war that has not ceased. The current holder of the seat, Tom Umberg, is the third to have it since Robinson. Umberg unseated Curt Pringle, a boyish-looking Republican whose short tenure was dominated by the controversy surrounding his 1988 win over Democrat Christian F. Thierbach, a Riverside County deputy district attorney.

Pringle won by fewer than 800 votes out of more than 63,000 cast. But the Orange County Republican Central Committee hired uniformed guards to patrol polling places in heavily Hispanic precincts. Democrats charged that the guards were posted in an attempt to intimidate Hispanics. Pringle withstood legal challenges to his election, but he was so distracted by them that he had no impact as a legislator in Sacramento.

Umberg has gotten off to a smoother start. A former prosecutor with the U.S. attorney's office in Santa Ana, Umberg's campaign was interrupted when his Army Reserve unit was called up for Operation Desert Shield. Umberg's wife, Robin, a reservist nurse, also was called to active duty during the Persian Gulf crisis and continued to serve during Operation Desert Storm. The resulting publicity was worth more than any campaigning could possibly have produced and Umberg ousted Pringle to retake the seat for Democrats.

PERSONAL: elected 1990; born Sept. 25, 1955, in Cincinnati, Ohio; home, Garden Grove; Army 1973-82, reserve; education, B.A. political science UCLA, J.D. Hastings; wife Robin; children, Aaron, Brett, and Tommy; Roman Catholic.

CAREER: lawyer; assistant U.S. attorney, Santa Ana; Army Reserve.

COMMITTEES: Public Safety; Environmental Safety & Toxic Materials; Education; Transportation; Housing & Community Development.

OFFICES: Capitol, (916) 445-7333, FAX (916) 327-1783; district, 12822 Garden Grove Blvd., A, Garden Grove 92643, (714) 537-4477.

REGISTRATION: 51.7% D, 39.5% R

1990 CAMPAIGN:	Umberg – D	51.9%	$535,506
	Curt Pringle (incumbent) – R	48.1%	$612,632

RATINGS and **KEY VOTES**: Newly elected.

David G. Kelley (R)
73rd Assembly District

Falling within fast-growing Riverside County, the oddly configured district includes Norco's horse ranch country on the county's west end and affluent sections of Riverside and Corona. The district is sharply bisected by the Democratic 68th Assembly district, lopping off the bedroom community of Moreno Valley for neighboring Steve Clute. After circling to the south, the 73rd District picks up again in the farmland of San Jacinto and the mobile home parks of Hemet, stretching through the exclusive environs of Palm Springs and other decidedly Republican desert resorts.

Republican David Kelley has never had to work hard to stay elected in this district. Kelley coasts through legislative life, heard from occasionally with outbursts against farm-worker unions and the leaders of the Republican Assembly caucus (whomever they may be at the time). Kelley's intrigue against then-

Republican leader Pat Nolan got him temporarily stripped of his one important assignment, a slot on the Assembly Agriculture Committee, where his bona fide expertise on farming and water issues allowed him to make a contribution. Kelley later got the committee assignment back after he toned down his comments, but recently he seems just as dead-set against GOP leader Ross Johnson.

David Kelley

Kelley came to the Legislature relatively late in life. He is a wealthy citrus farmer with acres of productive trees in the Hemet-San Jacinto Valley. He was instrumental in helping George Deukmejian gain the trust of agricultural interests in the 1982 GOP gubernatorial primary, but Kelley got little in return.

In 1990, Kelley persuaded the state Department of Fish and Game to propose a 2,800-acre "wildlife area" next to his ranch in an unsuccessful attempt to protect his irrigation supply. Although the agency staff drew up a proposal to buy the $4.1 million property, the proposal died when a review board found nothing environmentally sensitive about the land – clearing the way for a huge housing development. The housing developer accused Kelley of a conflict of interest because he was the ranking Republican on the Assembly Water, Parks and Wildlife Committee, which oversees the Fish and Game department. "Well, it wasn't necessarily in my interest," Kelley responded to an interviewer. "It's an interest of a lot of growers out there, too, because they don't want to lose the water that they have for their farming operations."

Kelley makes occasional noises about running against Democratic Sen. Robert Presley but has never risked trying. Kelley's ranch is actually in the senatorial district of Republican Marian Bergeson, but Kelley is registered to vote at a mobile home he owns in Presley's district. He appears to be patiently waiting for Presley to move on.

PERSONAL: elected 1978; born Oct. 11, 1928, in Riverside; home, Hemet; education, B.S. agriculture, Calif. State Polytechnic University, Pomona; USAF 1949-1953; wife, Brigitte; children, Sharon Marie, Bridget Ann, Margaret Elizabeth, and Kenneth; Lutheran.

CAREER: citrus farmer.

COMMITTEES: Agriculture; Health; Labor & Employment; Water, Parks & Wildlife; (Joint) Fairs Allocation & Classification.

OFFICES: Capitol, (916) 445-7852, FAX (916) 324-1393; district, 6840 Indiana Ave., 150, Riverside 92506, (714) 369-6644.

REGISTRATION: 40.3% D, 50.5% R

1990 CAMPAIGN:			
Kelley – R		56.2%	$212,563
Ray Strait – D		43.8%	$17,519

1988 CAMPAIGN: Kelley – R   66.9% $259,569
                    Erlinda Parker – D   30.1% $1,435
                    Charles Beers – L   2.9%

RATINGS:

AFL	PIRG	CLCV	NOW	CTA	CofC	CFB	NRA	FPAC
14%	27%	26%	30%	62%	86%	83%	100%	96%

KEY VOTES:

Divest S. Africa:	NO	Insurance reform:	NO	Child sick leave:	NO
Assault gun ban:	NO	Parent consent abortion:	YES	Ban AIDS discrim:	NO
Clean Air Act:	YES	Cutting old trees:	YES	Extend death penalty:	YES
Lmt product tort:	YES	Ban offshore oil:	NO	Restrict abortion funds:	YES
Lower alcohol std:	YES	Basic health care:	NO	Oil spill prevent:	YES
Ethics reform:	YES	Work cancer stds:	NO	Earthquake insure:	YES

Robert C. Frazee (R)
74th Assembly District

Upscale communities in southern Orange County and northern San Diego County like San Clemente, Camp Pendleton, Oceanside, Rancho Santa Fe and Carlsbad make up this district. Robert Frazee is another conservative who mirrors his district. Frazee was president of a family-owned, fresh-flower growing business when he was elected to the Assembly in 1978. Prior to that, he had been on the Carlsbad City Council for six years, including a stint as mayor.

Bob Frazee

Quiet and courtly, Frazee is generally a pro-business, pro-development vote in the traditional Republican mold. But on a few occasions he has broken away to try and find solutions for social problems. He backed state funding for farm-worker housing, in large part because he has been made aware of the problem in his hometown of Carlsbad. Frazee also has worked to try to rescue financially troubled trauma centers and emergency medical centers, problems that plague big cities.

The issue on which Frazee has been most visible, however, was his 1987 bill to require minors to get parental consent before getting abortions. His bill was signed into law but has been hung up in the courts. In upholding a preliminary injunction in October 1989, the Court of Appeal in San Francisco ruled teenagers have the same privacy rights – and, therefore, the same abortion rights – as adults.

PERSONAL: elected 1978; born Sept. 1, 1928, in San Luis Rey, Calif.; home, Carlsbad; USMC 1950-1952; wife, Delores Hedrick; children, Susan Marie Kurner and Nancy Anne; Congregational.

CAREER: construction; horticulturist; Carlsbad City Council, mayor 1972-1978; chairman, Assembly Republican caucus.

COMMITTEES: Consumer Protection, Governmental Efficiency & Economic Development; Local Government; Rules; Transportation; (Joint) Legislative Retirement.

OFFICES: Capitol, (916) 445-2390, FAX (916) 324-9991; district, 3088 Pio Pico Drive, 200, Carlsbad 92008, (619) 434-1749.

REGISTRATION: 31.7% D, 55.8% R

1990 CAMPAIGN:	Frazee – R	56.9%	$220,253
	Gerald Franklin – D	31.3%	$2,208
1988 CAMPAIGN:	Frazee – R	69.3%	$98,119
	James Melville – D	27.1%	$0

RATINGS:

AFL	PIRG	CLCV	NOW	CTA	CofC	CFB	NRA	FPAC
17%	41%	22%	30%	53%	82%	75%	87%	96%

KEY VOTES:

Divest S. Africa:	NO	Insurance reform:	NO	Child sick leave:	NO
Assault gun ban:	NO	Parent consent abortion:	YES	Ban AIDS discrim:	NO
Clean Air Act:	YES	Cutting old trees:	YES	Extend death penalty:	YES
Lmt product tort:	YES	Ban offshore oil:	NO	Restrict abortion funds:	YES
Lower alcohol std:	YES	Basic health care:	NO	Oil spill prevent:	YES
Ethics reform:	YES	Work cancer stds:	NO	Earthquake insure:	NO

Deirdre W. Alpert (D)
75th Assembly District

The most exclusive – and Republican – sections of coastal San Diego County comprise this district, taking in Coronado, La Jolla, Del Mar and its race track. The district extends eastward to take in the horse country of Poway, rich avocado groves and North County housing tracts. This is the land of retired admirals, old money and the newly rich. It is also where scam artists like J. David Dominelli have worked their devious magic.

Deirdre Alpert

Sunny Mojonnier's 1988 Democratic opponent spent less than $500 on his campaign, and she breezed to an easy, third-term re-election as the district's Assembly member. But that was 1988. In the succeeding two years, Mojonnier ran into a world of trouble. She was fined $13,000 by the state Fair Political Practices Commission for double billing the state and her campaign fund for personal expenses. She used campaign funds to send staffers to a fashion consultant. She used Assembly sergeants-at-arms to do personal chores like pick her son up at school. And she skipped out of Sacramento in July 1990 to take a vacation in Hawaii during the bitter summer budget impasse.

There should have been no way Deirdre "Dede" Alpert could win this seat. Voter registration favored Republicans by 20 percent. But all of Mojonnier's well-publicized gaffs caught up to her. Mojonnier barely won her GOP primary, with only 39 percent of the vote in a four-way race. The weakened Mojonnier could not hang on in the general election.

Alpert, a travel agent and a member of the Solana Beach School District Board, skillfully capitalized on Mojonnier's flakiness. Alpert's patrician manners and upscale looks also helped in this middle- to upper-middle class district. Soon after the election, Alpert's husband, Michael, half-joked that he hoped his wife becomes a Republican because he figured that is the only way she can hold the seat.

Contributing to Alpert's victory was the general anti-incumbent mood in 1990, particularly in San Diego County, which gave its incumbents the smallest vote margins proportionally of anywhere in the state.

Alpert's vote will be stronger for abortion rights than Mojonnier's, who said she was pro-choice but voted against Medi-Cal funded abortions. Alpert said she will vote against any such restrictions on abortions. But short of her changing parties or a miraculous reapportionment, it remains a long-shot that Alpert can serve more than one term. Within 24 hours of her election, embarrassed Republican leaders were plotting her defeat in 1992.

PERSONAL: elected 1990; born Oct. 6, 1945, in New York City; home, Del Mar; education, Pomona College; husband, Michael; three daughters.

CAREER: Pacific Bell 1966-1969; travel agent 1985-1989; Solana Beach School Board 1983-1990, president 1990.

COMMITTEES: Education; Health; Housing & Community Development; Transportation.

OFFICES: Capitol, (916) 445-2112, FAX (916) 445-4001; district, 3262 Holiday Court, La Jolla 92037, (619) 457-5775.

REGISTRATION: 32.8% D, 52.2% R

1990 CAMPAIGN:	Alpert – D	45.7%	$57,403
	Sunny Mojonnier (incumbent) – R	41%	$304,100
	John Murphy – L	10.9%	
	Vi Phuong Huynh – P&F	2.4%	

RATINGS and **KEY VOTES**: Newly elected

Patricia Rae Hunter (R)
76th Assembly District

The district stretches from the plush suburbs northeast of San Diego, including Escondido, up the spine of "North County," with its avocado groves and housing tracts roughly following Interstate 15, and into the hot desert of Riverside County. It includes some of the state's fastest-growing suburbs, desert retirement communities and small towns in the hills that seem a thousand miles removed from California's coast. The area is staunchly Republican.

It hardly seemed the place where a special election would attract national attention, but when Republican Tricia Hunter won her seat in 1989 she did just that. The reason – hers was among the first elections in America after the U.S. Supreme Court gave states more power to restrict abortion. Forces on both sides of the issue poured money and people into the campaigns, and said a victory by their side would be a harbinger of things to come. Hunter, a Bonita nurse and former president of the state Board of Registered Nursing, narrowly survived the primary, then won the run-off, mostly on the strength of her pro-choice stand. She was the only pro-choice Republican in the field and got a big boost to her campaign from the California Abortion Rights Action League, the National Organization for Women and the California Nurses Association. Although the electoral fires cooled a bit around the state in 1990, Hunter faced another anti-abortion opponent in her re-election campaign, but that time the race was less dramatic and fairly easy for her.

Tricia Hunter

Hunter's tenure in the Assembly so far also has been much less noteworthy than her first campaign. She has been a quiet rookie, carrying little of substance. But Hunter, who spent much of her two campaigns insisting she has good Republican credentials, nonetheless is relatively moderate. That presents some problems for Assembly GOP leader Ross Johnson, who promised to remain neutral in Hunter's initial Assembly race and then raised money for her primary opponent. Johnson mended a few fences by endorsing Hunter in the general election and did nothing to cause her any problems in the 1990 campaign.

PERSONAL: elected 1989 (special election); born June 15, 1952, in Appleton, Minn.; home, Bonita; education, B.S. nursing UC San Diego, M.A. nursing UCLA; husband, Clark Hunter; Lutheran.

CAREER: surgical nurse; director surgical services Chula Vista Community Hospital; appointed by Gov. Deukmejian to state Board of Registered Nursing.

COMMITTEES: Education; Health; Human Services; Revenue & Taxation; (Joint) Mental Health Research.

OFFICES: Capitol, (916) 445-8211, FAX (916) 323-9420; district, 365 W. 2nd Ave., 208, Escondido 92025, (619) 489-8924.

REGISTRATION: 31.4% D, 55.5% R

1990 CAMPAIGN:	Hunter – R	58%	$312,655
	Steve Thorne – D	27.7%	$0
OCT. 3, 1989 SPECIAL ELECTION:			
	Hunter – R	49%	$362,875
	Dick Lyles – R write-in	38%	$315,103
	Jeannine Correia – D	13%	$0

RATINGS:

AFL	PIRG	CLCV	NOW	CTA	CofC	CFB	NRA	FPAC
NR	NR	28%	40%	NR	68%	58%	76%	71%

The NRA rated only two bills for Hunter and downgraded her for public statements construed as negative to NRA positions.

KEY VOTES:

		Restrict abortion funds:	NO
Oil spill prevent: YES	Work cancer stds: YES	Earthquake insure:	NO

Carol J. Bentley (R)
77th Assembly District

Carol Bentley

Following the east-west artery of Interstate 8, this district includes the settled portions of eastern San Diego County, including El Cajon, La Mesa and portions of San Diego proper. The district is in the heart of San Diego's middle-class Republican communities and was represented for nearly a decade by Larry Stirling. Stirling moved to the Senate in 1988 after Sen. Jim Ellis retired. Stirling's successor, Carol Bentley, a personable – though unaccomplished – aide to Ellis, won a GOP primary against San Diego City Councilwoman Gloria McColl. Bentley's election also signaled the shift in the district's center of gravity to El Cajon and the suburbs.

Thus was born from total obscurity a new San Diego area political figure, who in less than a year tried to go still further. At the end of the 1989 session, Stirling abruptly quit the Senate to accept a judgeship in San Diego. Republican leaders quickly – maybe too quickly – endorsed Bentley in a special election. With nearly an 11-point registration margin, Republicans should have taken the Senate seat for the price of a filing fee. But two things happened on the way to the polls. First, Bentley's opponent was the more experienced, better known – and pro-abortion rights – Democrat Lucy Killea. Bentley was – and is – against abortion rights in an area that is conservative on some issues but decidedly libertarian on social issues. Second, the December 1989 special election was unexpectedly transformed into a national referendum on abortion when Catholic Bishop Leo T. Maher of the San Diego diocese banned Killea, a Catholic, from receiving communion because of her abortion views. While Killea capitalized on the resulting backlash, Bentley seemed paralyzed. Bentley, afflicted with the flu, virtually dropped from sight until the closing week of the campaign. Although she finally seemed to regain her balance – she actually won more votes than Killea on Election Day – Bentley could not overcome the damage wrought by the bishop.

Killea's absentee ballot operation, peaking at the crescendo of publicity over the bishop's action, provided the election margin.

PERSONAL: elected 1988; born Feb. 26, 1945, in Riverside; home, El Cajon; education, B.S. business San Diego State University; divorced; Presbyterian.

CAREER: administrative assistant to Sens. Jack Schrade and Jim Ellis 1980-1988; political campaign consultant.

COMMITTEES: Elections, Reapportionment & Constitutional Amendments; Judiciary; Natural Resources; Public Employees, Retirement & Social Security; Public Safety.

OFFICES: Capitol, (916) 445-6161, FAX (916) 327-5297; district, 2755 Navajo Road, El Cajon 92020, (619) 464-7204.

REGISTRATION: 36.3% D, 50.8% R

1990 CAMPAIGN:	Bentley – R	53.7%	$225,228
	Thomas Connolly – D	35%	$5,666
1988 CAMPAIGN:	Bentley – R	64%	$358,736
	Sam Hornreich – D	32.4%	$86,645

RATINGS:

AFL	PIRG	CLCV	NOW	CTA	CofC	CFB	NRA	FPAC
6%	27%	13%	30%	54%	91%	58%	87%	92%

KEY VOTES:

Insurance reform:	NO	Child sick leave:	NO	Ban AIDS discrim:	NO
Assault gun ban:	NO	Cutting old trees:	YES	Restrict abortion funds:	YES
Lower alcohol std:	YES	Basic health care:	NO	Oil spill prevent:	YES
Ethics reform:	YES	Work cancer stds:	NO	Earthquake insure:	YES

Michael J. Gotch (D)
78th Assembly District

This compact San Diego district includes older neighborhoods near the zoo and Balboa Park, plus largely gay Hillcrest. It also extends eastward into black sections of East San Diego. The district has had the largest numerical drop in registered voters of anywhere in the state since 1988 – a net loss of 20,000. Still, the area is above average, with 185,000 voters. Democratic and Republican registration is virtually even, which means the district is marginal for the Democrats. And that has prompted one of the most topsy-turvy political thrill-rides of recent times.

Mike Gotch

The seat was held by Democrat Lucy Killea for seven years until she won a seat in the state Senate in a special election that garnered national attention (see 39th Senate District). After Killea left, a special election to fill her seat was held on the same day as the June 1990 primary.

Republican Jeff Marston won the seat, nosing out former San Diego City Councilman Mike Gotch, a personable Democrat with movie-star looks and a political ally of Killea's. In the same June election, however, Marston and Gotch won their respective party primaries, so they again faced off in November. This time, Gotch won. Thus the hapless Marston was an assemblyman for all of six months. A number of Assembly Republicans grumbled afterward that floor leader Ross Johnson did not do enough to help Marston hold the seat.

Gotch entered the Assembly as anything but a political novice. He is a veteran of numerous ups and downs in San Diego politics and at one time seemed on his way to becoming mayor. As a city councilman, he was strongly identified with environmentalists as a vocal opponent of offshore oil drilling, having served an eight-year stint on the state Coastal Commission.

Then the ride got rough for Gotch. He plunged badly on an issue of intense importance in his beachy council district: a roller coaster. At first, Gotch backed building a park at the site of the former Belmont Park amusement park and preserving its rickety old roller coaster. Then Gotch flip-flopped to support building a shopping center planned by developer friends on the site. He badly miscalculated. Gotch so infuriated Mission Beach residents that his City Council re-election was cast into doubt. Gotch, once the darling of San Diego Democrats, decided to bag it and did not seek re-election to his council seat in 1987. But he did not stray far. He backed in a big way the 1988 presidential candidacy of Gary Hart. That, too, soured.

Out of office, Gotch worked for a time for developer Doug Manchester and then got a well-paying job as an executive director of a park project. But when Killea unexpectedly moved up to the Senate, Gotch could not resist the political bug. Had it not been for the baggage he carried into the election from the Belmont Park fiasco, Gotch probably could have coasted easily into the seat against the little-known Marston. As it was, Gotch had a major fight to ultimately win the seat and roll back into politics. While he campaigned, the California Teachers Association put Gotch on its payroll.

From the Assembly, Gotch can again set his sights on what many believe has always been his true goal – running for statewide office on the model of San Diego's most successful politician, Gov. Pete Wilson.

PERSONAL: elected 1990; born Oct. 4, 1947, in San Francisco; home, San Diego; education, B.A. San Diego State University; wife, Janet; Roman Catholic.

CAREER: Local Agency Formation Commission official 1974-1979; San Diego City Council 1979-1987; state Coastal Commission 1980-1988.

COMMITTEES: Natural Resources; Local Government; Consumer Protection, Governmental Efficiency & Economic Development; Environmental Safety & Toxic Materials.

OFFICES: Capitol, (916) 445-7210, FAX (916) 324-7895; district, 1080 University Ave., H-201, San Diego 92103, (619) 232-2046.

REGISTRATION: 43.7% D, 42.3% R

1990 CAMPAIGN	Gotch – D	44.7%	$244,067
	Jeff Marston (incumbent) – R	44%	$297,039
	Ed McWilliams – L	6.1%	
	Bob Bardell – P&F	4.6%	
JUNE 5, 1990 SPECIAL ELECTION:			
	Jeff Marston – R	48.8%	$300,746
	Gotch – D	43.7%	$244,067
	Jane Evans – P&F	7.4%	

RATINGS and **KEY VOTES**: Newly elected

Peter R. Chacon (D)

79th Assembly District

The bulk of the black and Latino neighborhoods of East San Diego comprise this safely Democratic district. Meandering along the dusty mesas, the district also includes Lemon Grove, Spring Valley and the airport. A tongue of the district extends down the middle of San Diego Bay to take in a small South bay neighborhood. While the rest of San Diego has grown and gotten richer, this area has only seen more crime and poverty.

Pete Chacon

Democrat Pete Chacon has served in the Assembly for two decades, having been plucked from the obscurity of a teaching career by Democratic leaders in need of a candidate. But he has never been much of a player either in Sacramento or San Diego. He has authored housing and bilingual education legislation, matters of large concern to his district.

Chacon was chairman of the Assembly's reapportionment committee, but lost the post during the 1981 reapportionment. Once redistricting was finished, he got his chairmanship back – when it mattered little. But this time around, Assembly Speaker Willie Brown has promised to leave Chacon in charge of his committee. Whether Chacon will prove a power player on reapportionment remains an open question. Insiders expect the tough political dealing will probably occur somewhere other than in Chacon's office. In fact, the point man on reapportionment for the Assembly Democrats has turned out to be William Cavala, a shadowy staffer who is close to Speaker Brown.

Inside the Capitol, Chacon is chiefly noted for keeping his family on the campaign payroll. He skated out from under an investigation by the state attorney general's office in 1989 for accepting a $7,500 honorarium from check-cashing businesses and then killing a bill that was odious to those businesses. While prosecutors said that the timing of the transaction was "suspicious," the investigation was dropped for lack of evidence.

Moreover, Chacon has been vocally against abortion rights, putting him at odds with the prevailing attitude of his caucus and, possibly, the area he represents.

All of that might have caught up to Chacon in 1990 when he faced a strong Democratic primary challenge from Celia Ballesteros, a lawyer and former San Diego city councilwoman who was pro-choice on abortion and an ally of Democratic Sen. Lucy Killea. Ballesteros spent more than $160,000 on her campaign but won only 33.2 percent of the vote to Chacon's 53.5 percent. A third Democrat, John Warren, siphoned votes away from Ballesteros. Chacon went on to win the general election, but he should not rest easy for the next two years; Ballesteros may be back in 1992.

PERSONAL: elected 1970; born June 10, 1925, in Phoenix, Ariz.; home, San Diego; Army Air Corps 1943-1945 WWII; education, B.A. elementary education and M.A. school administration San Diego State University; wife, Jean Louise Picone; children, Chris, Paul, Ralph and Jeff; Roman Catholic.

CAREER: school administrator.

COMMITTEES: Elections, Reapportionment & Constitutional Amendments (chair); Banking, Finance & Bonded Indebtedness; Governmental Organization; Revenue & Taxation; (Joint) State's Economy.

OFFICES: Capitol, (916) 445-7610, FAX (916) 327-9696; district, 1129 G St., San Diego 92101, (619) 232-2405.

REGISTRATION: 55% D, 32.5% R

1990 CAMPAIGN:	Chacon – D	56.4%	$420,865
	Roger Covalt – R	36.4%	$556
1988 CAMPAIGN:	Chacon – D	68.5%	$221,950
	Gary Gahn – R	27.2%	$0

RATINGS:

AFL	PIRG	CLCV	NOW	CTA	CofC	CFB	NRA	FPAC
90%	100%	93%	70%	88%	18%	33%	0%	15%

KEY VOTES:

Divest S. Africa:	YES	Insurance reform:	YES	Child sick leave:	YES
Assault gun ban:	YES	Parent consent abortion:	YES	Ban AIDS discrim:	YES
Clean Air Act:	YES	Cutting old trees:	YES	Extend death penalty:	YES
Lmt product tort:	YES	Ban offshore oil:	NO	Restrict abortion funds:	–
Lower alcohol std:	YES	Basic health care:	YES	Oil spill prevent:	YES
Ethics reform:	YES	Work cancer stds:	–	Earthquake insure:	NO

J. Stephen Peace (D)
80th Assembly District

This district begins along the shoreline of San Diego Bay, where the once sleepy bedroom communities of National City and Chula Vista awakened in the 1980s. Chula Vista is building ritzy bayside hotels and home developers are paving the mesas above. The district extends eastward along the Mexican border to include all of Imperial County, a farming region that is among the poorest in the nation.

The problems of this district are those of Mexico, where the First and Third worlds crash headlong. Illegal aliens and drugs are smuggled across the border at Otay Mesa and elsewhere. Sewage from Tijuana leaks across the border into San Diego and fouls the beaches and horse farms nearby. Eastward, the New River carries highly toxic industrial and agricultural poisons – like DDT – from Mexico into the Salton Sea in Imperial County.

The Democrat who has represented this district, Steve Peace, was once known for two things: He was the producer of the cult film, "Attack of the Killer Tomatoes," and he was Willie Brown's man to see in San Diego.

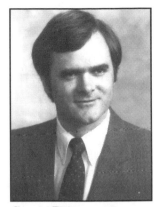

Steve Peace

Socially chummy with the speaker, Peace was considered a genius at political strategy – and that may be why the speaker tolerated Peace so long. Many of Peace's colleagues could not stand him, considering him immature and obnoxious. His floor speeches were sometimes nothing more than rants. His fabled fight with the Senate's Al Alquist (when witnesses heard Peace call Alquist a "senile old pedophile") earned him the undying hatred of the Senate, but Brown protected him.

Then in 1987 Peace and four of his colleagues turned on Brown, dubbing themselves the "Gang of Five." They pulled parliamentary maneuvers for a year, tying the Assembly up in petty intrigues. They eventually made peace in 1989.

As a legislator, Peace has paid attention to the border issues that so plague his district, working on getting a sewage treatment plant for the area. He has labored for years over a low-level nuclear waste compact with other states (which got him in trouble with Alquist), and he has kept proposed nuclear waste dumps out of Democratic districts.

At the start of the 1991-92 legislation session, the speaker fully restored Peace to his official family. Peace was made chairman of a newly created Banking, Finance and Bonded Indebtedness Committee. Peace got the "Finance" half of the old Finance and Insurance committee. Peace's new committee has the potential of becoming one of the most powerful in the Assembly, with wide-ranging authority over bonds, banks, savings and loans and financial legislation. What he does with it bears watching.

PERSONAL: elected 1982; born March 30, 1953, in San Diego; home, Rancho San Diego; education, B.A. political science UC San Diego; wife, Cheryl; children, Chad, Bret and Clint; Methodist.

CAREER: partner, Four Square Productions of National City, a film production firm; aide to Assemblymen Wadie Deddeh 1976-1980 and Larry Kapiloff 1980-1981.

COMMITTEES: Banking, Finance and Bonded Indebtedness (chair); Insurance; Utilities & Commerce; Water, Parks & Wildlife; (Joint) Prison Construction & Operations.

OFFICES: Capitol, (916) 445-7556, FAX (916) 322-2271; district, 430 Davidson St., B, Chula Vista 92010, (619) 426-1617; 1101 Airport Road B, Imperial 92251, (619) 352-3101.

REGISTRATION: 49.5% D, 38.1% R

1990 CAMPAIGN:	Peace – D	57.7%	$214,635
	Kevin Kelly – R	34.9%	$3,193
1988 CAMPAIGN:	Peace – D	58.9%	$349,406
	Steve Baldwin – R	39%	$2,984

RATINGS:

AFL	PIRG	CLCV	NOW	CTA	CofC	CFB	NRA	FPAC
81%	81%	95%	90%	77%	36%	50%	44%	8%

KEY VOTES:

Divest S. Africa:	YES	Insurance reform:	YES	Child sick leave:	YES
Assault gun ban:	NO	Parent consent abortion:	YES	Ban AIDS discrim:	YES
Clean Air Act::	–	Cutting old trees:	YES	Extend death penalty:	YES
Lmt product tort:	YES	Ban offshore oil:	YES	Restrict abortion funds:	NO
Lower alcohol std:	YES	Basic health care:	YES	Oil spill prevent:	YES
Ethics reform:	YES	Work cancer stds:	YES	Earthquake insure:	YES

7

Congress: Gulliver and the Lilliputians

Rep. Chet Holifield was built like a rhino and had the disposition to match. In 29 years in Congress, the Montebello Democrat became legendary for blistering rebukes. But on one particular day in 1972, he was in a relaxed and expansive mood as three Whittier College coeds quizzed him about Congress and his role as dean of the California delegation. One asked how often all the Californians vote the same way on a bill. Holifield wrinkled his brushy eyebrows in thought. "Well, yes," he finally replied. "There was a wine bill two or three sessions ago."

For the current dean, San Jose Democrat Don Edwards, little has changed. California has long had the most impotent of the large state delegations.

Although House Republican and Democratic caucuses try to meet weekly during sessions, the entire delegation doesn't even get together socially. It's not enough to say that the 45 members are badly divided by differences involving geography and ideology. They're scattered. The delegation has been likened to the cartoon image of a huge dust cloud rolling along the ground with feet and hands sticking out here and there.

Membership ranges from the Republican bombasts of Orange County, Robert Dornan and William Dannemeyer, to brittle liberals such as Berkeley Democrat Ron Dellums. They refuse to work together even when obvious interests of the state are at stake. Adding to the divisiveness in the delegation is the intense bitterness over the reapportionment battles in the early 1980s. The late Rep. Phil Burton of San Francisco drew lines to guarantee Democrats 28 of the 45 seats and the Democrats successfully made the gerrymander stick. With Democrats in the governor's chair and running both houses of the Legislature, there was never any question that Burton's plan would be approved. After the 1990 elections, the Democrats still held 26 seats to the Republican's 19.

Had district lines been drawn with even a pretense of fairness after the 1980 census, Republicans would hold three to five more seats. As it stands, only three

Democratic seats were taken away by Republicans in the 1980s, and in each case the defeated Democrat was under a cloud at the time. This inability to topple Democrats hardly reflects Republican registration, which crept upward throughout the '80s. The number of GOP votes cast statewide for seats in Congress matches, and sometimes surpasses, the Democratic total.

Burton's gerrymandering was in the worst tradition of the 19th century political bosses. District lines stop in the middle of city blocks, cut through backyards and snake down alleys. In San Pedro, the boundary loops across the harbor, snatches a Republican stronghold in a Democratic district, and jogs back across the water. Burton, who drew the lines personally and kept them secret from just about everyone, laconically referred to the plan as "my contribution to modern art."

But Burton's modern art was not conducive to feelings of bipartisanship within the delegation. "There's a lack of trust," said former Rep. Tony Coelho, D-Merced. "We're the nation's largest delegation and we could never pull together." That divisiveness has led to great frustration for Edwards and his senior Republican counterpart, Carlos Moorhead of Glendale, who get along well and attempt to provide some cohesion.

On a less senior level, a working alliance has been formed in recent years between two men who were the de facto leaders of their state caucuses – the GOP's Jerry Lewis of Redlands and Democrat Vic Fazio of West Sacramento. In what is a short period of time by congressional standards, Lewis became the third-ranking member of his caucus as chairman of the House Republican Conference. Fazio is vice chairman of the Democratic Caucus, the No. 5 party leadership position, and this year added the chairmanship of the Democratic Congressional Campaign Committee to his duties. That makes him the House Democrats' chief fund-raiser and recruiter, positions held at one time by former Speaker Jim Wright and President Lyndon Johnson.

SHAKE-UP IN THE DELEGATION

Lewis' influence in the California GOP caucus, however, suffered following the 1990 elections, when the addition of several conservatives shifted the balance of power in the caucus to the right. Rep. Ron Packard of Carlsbad replaced Lewis on the Committee on Committees, which makes the delegation's assignments to House committees. Newly elected Rep. John Doolittle of Rocklin replaced Rep. William Thomas of Bakersfield as the GOP point-man on state reapportionment. And both Dornan and Rep. David Dreier of Claremont got increased leadership duties.

The shake-up in the Republican caucus after the 1990 elections was calm, however, compared to what happened in the Democratic caucus. They became cannibals. Rep. Norm Mineta of San Jose led the revolt against 77-year-old Rep. Glenn Anderson of San Pedro, who chaired the Committee on Public Works and Transportation. Anderson was dumped, but Mineta lost the vote to replace him. For nearly 20 years, a Californian has chaired this important pork-barrel committee.

Now, New Jersey Rep. Robert Roe is calling the shots on mammoth federal spending projects for harbors, airports and the like.

California's delegation is the nation's largest, with 11 percent of the membership in Congress. Only New York has ever had 45 delegates and that was in the 1930s and '40s. With the 1991 reapportionment, California will get another seven seats, and the Census Bureau estimates that California is likely to continue that growth well into the 21st century, which could expand the state's congressional delegation to nearly 70 members by 2010.But that, too, can be a liability, Fazio points out. Small delegations fear California's potential dominance. "We are in some ways like the giant in (Jonathan) Swift's tale, tied down by Lilliputians. People tend to gang up on the big guy," he said.

The public works committee wasn't the only loss for the state. Alan Cranston was forced by health and scandal to give up his Majority Whip position, and he announced plans to retire in 1992. Cranston's long service and his No. 2 position in the Senate put him in a unique position to aid the state's industries and special interests. Cranston also chairs the Veterans' Affairs Committee. California also forfeited the chairmanship of the House Education and Labor Committee when Augustus Hawkins of Los Angeles retired in 1990.

Democrats, however, hold other important posts: Leon Panetta of Carmel has the Budget Committee; George Brown of Riverside chairs Science, Space and Technology; Edward Roybal of Los Angeles leads the Select Committee on Aging; and George Miller of Martinez chairs the Select Committee and Children, Youth and Families. Miller, who's been called the strongest environmentalist in the House, also took charge of the Interior Committee while Rep. Morris Udall of Arizona coped with a variety of ailments. Udall's retirement in May 1991, means Miller will likely become chairman. Miller has made good use of subcommittee posts as has Henry Waxman of Los Angeles, who's a major force on health issues. Tom Lantos of San Mateo used his housing subcommittee to pry open the HUD scandals.

Aside from Lewis, Republicans hold few important positions. Only one, Thomas, is the ranking minority member of a committee, but his House Administration panel is not a power base. Rep. Duncan Hunter of Coronado chairs the Republican Research Committee, which develops House GOP strategies on emerging issues.

Edwards and Moorhead, however, believe they've finally found the vehicle for bringing unity to the delegation. And the California Business Roundtable, an association of top business leaders, put up $200,000 to see if it will fly. In 1989, they launched the California Institute, a bipartisan research group to pursue issues important to the state. In the short term, the institute is to mobilize support for pork-barrel projects. Several major projects, such as the Superconducting Super Collider, have come along in recent years and California politicos in both Washington and Sacramento have been unable to get their acts together. The current prize is a proposed $9 billion fusion energy research facility being sought by the University of California, San Diego. Eventually, the institute is to concentrate on economic issues that would tend to unite the delegation. It plans to develop strategies for dealing with California's needs 10 to 20 years from now in areas such as trade, transportation and waste disposal.

Other areas of the country have had considerable success with such associations. There are similar institutes for Texas, 18 Northeast and Midwest states, and for 16 Sun Belt states. Partisan bickering, however, has kept California Institute from getting off the ground. It remains to be seen whether it will be a force in the 102nd Congress.

THE REAPPORTIONMENT QUESTION

Then there is the question of reapportioning the state in 1992. The election of Republican Pete Wilson as governor in 1990 was supposed to guarantee that Democrats wouldn't be able to dominate the process as they did in the early 1980s. Any deal struck in 1991 will have to be acceptable to both parties. Any standoff will leave the Supreme Court in charge of drawing the lines, which is what happened after Republican Gov. Ronald Reagan vetoed Democratic reapportionment plans in 1971.

But no one said it was going to be easy. For starters, the Democrats say there should be perhaps five new Republican seats. GOP strategists say they want 12. There's also the question of where to draw the seven new seats. The census data suggests four to six should be in Southern California. The 5-2 breakdown suggested by many would put one new seat in the Bay Area and another somewhere between Sacramento and Modesto.

The huge growth in the Southland during the past decade means that practically all Northern California districts will have to slide southward. That's going to be difficult for the liberals to swallow since they dominate the northern seats. Much of the new influx of people has been concentrated in suburban areas – traditionally GOP turf. But there is another dynamic at work in those areas.

The suburban Republican vote was soft in the in 1990 elections. GOP incumbents found their winning percentages significantly reduced. Part of that was a reflection of the recession, which brought a housing and construction slump. When Republicans can't deliver jobs, middle-of-the-road voters tend to be more enamored with the "economic fairness" doctrines espoused by Democrats. Also, thanks to Phil Burton's gerrymandering, many of the Republican congressmen are decidedly more conservative than their districts. Depending on how the 1992 lines are drawn, some of them could face divisive primaries that could weaken the winner in the runoff.

Add to the equation two wild cards. Census data is available on low-cost computer discs for the first time. Every special interest group – in fact, every nerd with a personal computer – will be in a position to analyze the data and mount challenges to redistricting plans on every elected level.

The second wild card will be the Voting Rights Act of 1982 and subsequent court decisions. They will force the creation of reapportionment plans that maximize the potential for minorities to be elected. That is the same body of law that came into play in 1991 to force the creation of the first Hispanic supervisorial district in Los Angeles County. Hispanic groups already have targeted 74 local governments in California for voting-rights challenges. They plan major involvement in congressional reapportionment. And their demands have the potential to tear the Demo-

BIOGRAPHICAL PROFILES

Following the biographical sketches of the state's two senators and members of the House of Representatives are election results from the most recent campaign. To the right of the results is the amount of money raised for the campaign. Ratings from lobbying organizations also are given. A score of 100 indicates the officeholder voted in agreement 100 percent of the time on bills of interest to that organization. Lower scores indicate fewer votes in agreement. Some organizations offer cumulative ratings for all sessions in which the person served. Others rate only the most recent session. The organizations are:

ADA - Americans for Democratic Action Inc., Suite 941, 1511 K St., N.W., Washington D.C. 20005, (202) 638-6447. Liberal. Issues include civil rights, handgun control, hate-crimes statistics, gay/lesbian discrimination, and opposition to the death penalty and defense spending. Based on 1990 votes.

ACU - American Conservative Union, 38 Ivy St., S.E., Washington, D.C. 20003, (202) 546-6555. Conservative on foreign policy, social and budget issues. Based on cumulative votes.

AFL-CIO - American Federation of Labor-Congress of Industrial Organizations, Department of Legislation, Room 309, 815 16th St., N.W., Washington, D.C. 20006. (202) 637-5000. The nation's biggest union confederation promotes labor, health and civil-rights issues. Based on 1989-90 votes.

LCV - League of Conservation Voters, Suite 804, 2000 L St., N.W., Washington, D.C. 20036. (202) 785-8683. Political arm of the environmental movement. Based on cumulative votes.

NCSC - National Council of Senior Citizens, 925-15th St., N.W., Washington, D.C. 20005, (202)347-8800. Medical, Social Security and other issues of interest to older people. Based on cumulative votes.

NTU - National Taxpayers Union, 325 Pennsylvania Ave., S.E., Washington D.C. 20003, (202) 543-1300. Conservatives devoted to reduced federal spending. Based on 1989-90 votes.

USCC - United States Chamber of Commerce, 1615 H St., N.W., Washington, D.C. 20062, (202) 659-6000. Business, trade, South Africa sanctions, welfare reform and civil-rights restrictions. Based on cumulative votes.

Congressional districts

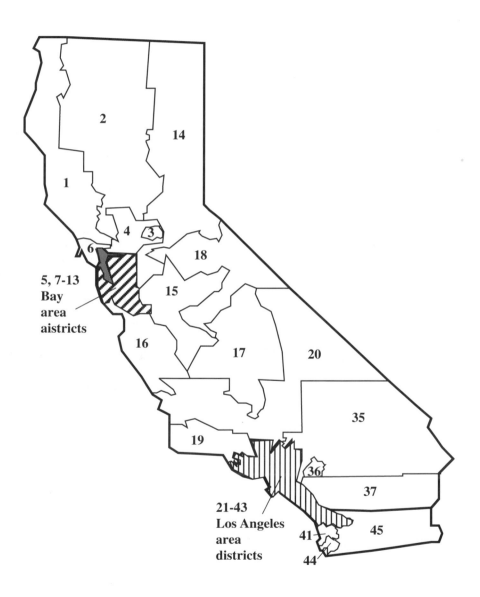

Los Angeles area congressional districts

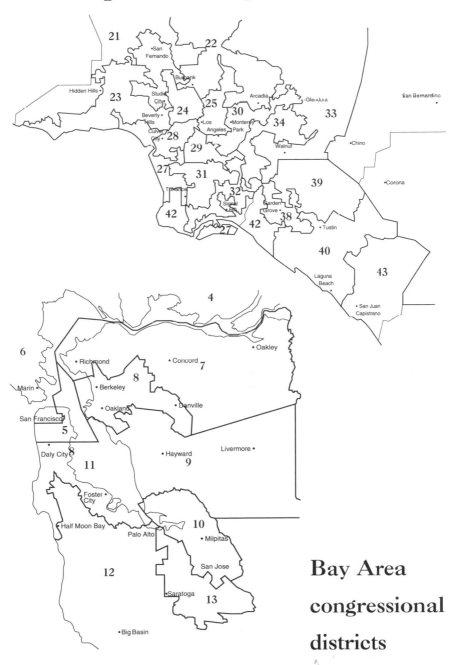

Bay Area

congressional

districts

U.S. SENATE
Alan Cranston (D)

On Jan 12, 1991, Congress took the historic vote that gave President Bush authorization to launch a war against Iraq. It had to be one of the darkest days of Alan Cranston's Senate career – if not his life. He was the only senator to miss the vote. His Senate chair had also been empty on previous days while the debate on the use of military force raged in both houses. Normally, he would have been there, a crumpled vote tally in his hands, counting noses with a degree of accuracy that had become legendary among his colleagues.

With the Senate voting 52-47 to support the president, Cranston's "no" vote wouldn't have changed the outcome. But for California's senior senator, few things are more important than to stand and be counted on

Alan Cranston

a vote against war. Since his days as a reporter in pre-World War II Europe and Africa, Cranston has had a passionate interest in promoting non-violent approaches to the settlement of international disputes.

On Jan. 12, however, he was at his sister's home in Los Altos coping with the effects of radiation treatments for cancer. The disease was winning. Nine days later he would be in Stanford Medical Center undergoing an experimental treatment that involved implanting radioactive rods directly in his prostate gland to attack the cancer more directly.

At the same time, the Senate Ethics Committee was deciding whether Cranston improperly used his influence to stifle government regulation of the nation's biggest single savings and loan debacle. Testimony suggested that Cranston was perhaps the most culpable of the five senators whose actions were being probed.

The previous November, Cranston had relinquished his job as Senate Whip, the

No. 2 leadership position among Democrats. He disclosed his cancer at that time, saying it would prevent him from running for a fifth term in 1992. Since the direct election of senators was adopted in 1914, only one other Californian, Hiram Johnson (1917-45), has served longer in the Senate than Cranston.

It seemed Cranston was simply being realistic when he announced plans to retire in 1992. Even if exonerated by the Senate Ethics Committee, revelations about his involvement in the savings and loan scandal had destroyed his career and doubtless Cranston knew it. The chances of his being re-elected again at age 78 were nil.

In 1989, it was revealed that Cranston had helped win delays in federal regulatory action against Lincoln Savings and Loan of Irvine, a subsidiary of American Continental Corp. of Phoenix, owned by Charles H. Keating Jr.

Two years earlier, files kept by the Federal Home Loan Bank Board clearly indicated that regulators knew Lincoln was essentially bankrupt and Keating had, in effect, turned it into a federally insured casino. Yet regulators, pressured by Cranston and Keating's other friends in Congress, did not close Lincoln for another two years. In the thrift's final year, regulators sat and watched as 23,000 people walked into Lincoln offices and unwittingly threw away $220 million of their savings. Lincoln eventually was declared insolvent, sticking the taxpayers with a $2.5 billion liability. But not before Keating raised $40,000 for Cranston's 1986 re-election campaign, $85,000 for the California Democratic Party and $850,000 for three voter registration groups allied with Cranston, including one for which the senator's son, Kim, was the unpaid chairman.

Cranston also wrote the Securities and Exchange Commission asking relief for junk-bond king Michael Milken, who was later convicted of securities fraud. Milken ran his operation out of Drexel Burnham Lambert's Beverly Hills office and Drexel kicked in $10,000 to one of Cranston's voter registration operations.

Cranston has maintained that the assistance he provided was no different than what he offered some 300,000 constituents over the years. And in Lincoln's case, Cranston has said he had no knowledge that the S&L was in such serious trouble. Nonetheless, the record shows he lobbied federal officials at least 12 times at critical junctures in Lincoln's regulatory fights. His chief fund-raising aide, Joy Jacobson, acted as a liaison between major contributors and Carolyn Jordan, Cranston's chief staff person on the Banking, Housing and Urban Affairs Committee.

The S&L problems took on a bipartisan hue when it was revealed that Keating may have had help from then-Vice President George Bush. California regulators also failed to investigate Lincoln's dealings in junk bonds. Los Angeles attorney Karl Samuelian, then-Gov. George Deukmejian's chief fund-raiser, represented Lincoln's parent company in dealings with the regulators. Also, Keating donated $75,000 to Deukmejian's re-election campaign.

There were no revelations that Cranston got personal investment opportunities or kickbacks – the stuff that has lead to the downfall of other politicians. Yet his actions clearly hurt all of the nation's taxpayers, including many elderly people who lost their savings. Some have suggested that Cranston was poorly served by staff people who should have warned him of the hole he was digging for himself. But in the final analysis, the blame must fall on Cranston and Cranston alone.

The irony is that Cranston got into trouble helping business. For years, critics have been painting Cranston as a foe of industry, although his record in Congress shows anything but an anti-business bias.

It's a sad end to one of the most enduring careers in California politics. Except for a two-year hiatus, Cranston held statewide elective office since 1959. When non-elected public service is counted, Cranston has been active since 1939, which is longer than either Richard Nixon or Ronald Reagan.

U.S. Senators from California

(elected by Legislature prior to 1914)

Seat A			Seat B		
John C. Fremont	D	1849	William M. Gwin	D	1849
John B. Weller	D	1852			
David C. Broderick	D	1857			
Henry P. Haun	D	1859			
Milton S. Latham	D	1860	James A. McDougall	D	1861
John Conness	Un	1863	Cornelius Cole	Un	1865
Eugene Casserly	D	1869			
John S. Hager	D	1873	Aaron A. Sargent	R	1873
Newton Booth	I–R	1875	James T. Farley	D	1879
John F. Miller	R	1881	Leland Stanford	R	1885
A.P. Williams	R	1886			
George Hearst	D	1887			
Charles N. Fenton	R	1893	George C. Perkins	R	1893
Stephen M. White	D	1893			
Thomas R. Bard	R	1899			
Frank P. Flint	R	1905			
John D. Works	R	1911	James D. Phalen	D	1915
Hiram W. Johnson	R	1917	Samuel M. Shortridge	R	1921
William F. Knowland	R	1945	William G. McAdoo	R	1932
Clair Engle	D	1959	Thomas M. Storke	D	1938
Pierre Salinger	D	1964	Sheridan Downey	D	1939
George Murphy	R	1964	Richard Nixon	R	1951
John V. Tunney	D	1971	Thomas Kuchel	R	1952
S.I. Hayakawa	R	1977	Alan Cranston	D	1969
Pete Wilson	R	1983			
John Seymour	R	1991			

Un: Union; I-R: Independent-Republican.

In all those years, Cranston's political obituary has been written many times. The pundits branded him a lightweight and confidently predicted he'd never get through the next election. Cranston simply ignored them and quietly went about building his power base in the Senate. He became majority whip in 1977, which also put him on the potent Democratic Policy and Democratic Steering committees. He chairs the Veterans' Affairs Committee and holds key positions on both the Foreign Relations and Banking Committees. He also added the Intelligence Committee to his list, which helped bolster his influence in foreign affairs.

From his first days in Congress, Cranston showed an ability to work in a bipartisan way to achieve his goals. Cranston, the New Deal and Great Society liberal, co-authored legislation with unlikely allies such as Sen. Strom Thurmond, R-S.C., and ex-Sen. Barry Goldwater, R-Ariz. "I look for an issue where I can work with them," Cranston has said, such as veterans or defense.

Cranston's ability to work with senators of all political stripes, earned him great respect. But it's also notable that none of his colleagues promoted him for the majority leader's job early in 1989, when Sen. Robert Byrd of West Virginia stepped down in favor of Sen. George Mitchell of Maine.

WINNING OVER ENEMIES

When Cranston moved to Washington in 1968, his dovish stand on the Vietnam War had made him the sworn enemy of both veterans and aerospace groups. But he soon established himself as a champion of veterans' health concerns and formed a shrewd alliance with then-Gov. Ronald Reagan's administration to bring space shuttle development home to California. Even his worst antagonists in those areas soon learned that Cranston was the man to see if they wanted something in Washington. When Lockheed's solvency depended upon a federal loan guarantee, Cranston delivered.

He worked to broker problems for the state's financial, computer electronics and agricultural industries while proving in vote after vote that he was a solid friend of labor. He championed park and environmental causes even when it cost him with loggers and conservative Democrats. Critics constantly harped that he was soft on defense and naive in foreign affairs. Cranston, though, was in office long enough to see some of those arguments come full circle. In 1973, for example, he proposed Strategic Arms Reduction Talks, or START, with the Soviet Union as the logical extension of the ongoing Strategic Arms Limitation Talks, or SALT. The criticism was withering. But by the late 1980s, START had become one of the pillars of Reagan foreign policy.

Cranston's political ambitions began to flower in the late 1940s while president of the United World Federalists, a national organization devoted to enhancing world law. From coffee klatches in Cranston's Palo Alto home, a statewide organization evolved for boosting liberal causes. The California Democratic Council, which he founded in 1952, became the dominate liberal force in the state during the 1950s and put Cranston into the state controller's office in 1958.

Cranston ran for the U.S. Senate in 1964 but was elbowed out in the primary by Pierre Salinger, who had been President John F. Kennedy's press secretary. Salinger subsequently lost to Republican actor George Murphy in the general election and left the state. Two years later, Cranston was turned out of the controller's office by Republican Assemblyman Houston Flournoy. Cranston moved to Los Angeles and went into the housing development business, but kept his campaign organization together.

In 1968, he filed for the U.S. Senate seat held by Republican Whip Thomas Kuchel. Cranston personally admired Kuchel, but he doubted the incumbent could survive the primary fight with right-wing state Superintendent of Public Instruction Max Rafferty. Cranston was right, and he went on to beat Rafferty in November. In 1974, Cranston had an easy race against former state Sen. H.L. Richardson of Glendora. Six years later, he beat Paul Gann, receiving more votes in that victory than anyone else who has been elected to Congress.

In 1984, Cranston took a fling at the presidency. Some of his staff people still don't understand why he did it. His was a disastrous campaign in which the only victory was the straw vote in Wisconsin. Eventually, he also was fined $50,000 by the Federal Elections Commission for accepting an illegal contribution of $54,000 from a Beverly Hills commodity broker.

In the midst of the presidential campaign, Cranston tried to dye the scant fringe of hair around his shiny dome. The fringe turned orange. Cranston ended the campaign with a $2 million debt and Republicans salivating for what was left of his scalp when he ran for re-election two years later. Rep. Ed Zschau of Palo Alto emerged from a crowded Republican primary and ran a tough race. Cranston's final margin was 3 percent, or 104,868 votes out of nearly 7.2 million cast. The senator credited his voter registration efforts with providing the margin. But he also was helped by conservative apathy toward Zschau, a moderate with a libertarian approach to lifestyle issues. Zschau lost to Cranston in his home turf on the San Francisco Peninsula.

Zschau's announcement in March 1991 that he would not be a candidate in 1992, still left a long list of possible Republican contenders, including Reps. Tom Campbell, David Dreier and Jerry Lewis, Attorney General Dan Lungren and several state legislators. There will be no shortage of Democrats either. Among the aspirants are Reps. Barbara Boxer, Mel Levine and Robert Matsui; Walt Disney Co. President Frank Wells; and former Gov. Jerry Brown.

PERSONAL: elected 1968; born June 19, 1914, in Palo Alto; home, Los Angeles; education, attended Pomona College and University of Mexico, B.A. Stanford University 1936; twice divorced, one living child; Protestant.

CAREER: journalist, International News Service in Europe and Africa, 1936-39; Washington lobbyist, Common Council for American Unity, 1939; language specialist, Department of War, 1942-44; U.S. Army, 1944-45; Realtor, home developer, 1947-68; state controller, 1959-67.

COMMITTEES: Veterans' Affairs (chair); Foreign Relations; Banking, Housing and Urban Affairs; (Select) Intelligence.

OFFICES: Suite 112, Hart Building, Washington, D.C. 20510, (202) 224-3553; state, Suite 980, 1390 Market St., San Francisco 94102, (415) 556-8440; Suite 515, 5757 West Century Blvd., Los Angeles 90045, (213) 215-2186; Suite 5-S-31, 880 Front St., San Diego 92188, (619) 293-5014.

1986 CAMPAIGN: Cranston - D   50% $11,037,707
                    Ed Zschau - R   47% $11,781,316

RATINGS: ADA   ACU   AFL-CIO   LCV   NCSC   NTU   USCC
              95%   0%   90%   83%   100%   7%   80%

Vote on H.J. Res. 77 authorizing war with Iraq: absent due to illness.

John F. Seymour (R)

John F. Seymour

John Seymour's political career seemed headed for oblivion when he packed up his family and headed to Mammoth Lakes for a skiing vacation during the Christmas holidays of 1990.

The slide had begun in 1987, when Seymour was bounced from his job as caucus chairman, the No. 2 Republican post in the state Senate. His party had just lost a special senate race where Assemblyman Wayne Grisham was the odds-on favorite. But Grisham, who spent much of the campaign playing golf, was ambushed by Norwalk City Councilman Cecil Green, who clinched his victory by passing out chits for more than 360,000 doughnuts on Election Day.

Seymour was state chairman for U.S. Sen. Pete Wilson's re-election campaign the following year. Then came a disastrous race for lieutenant governor in 1990. Seymour lost the primary to another obscure Orange County state senator, Marian Bergeson. Despite outspending

Bergeson, Seymour lost 44.8 percent to 55.2 percent.

But on Dec. 27, 1990, Seymour was watching the sunrise over the ancient caldera east of Mammoth when the phone rang. It was Gov.-elect Wilson offering Seymour the appointment to Wilson's U.S. Senate seat. Seymour hadn't even known he was under consideration. In fact, he was on no one's list of successors except the one that counted – Wilson's.

In picking Seymour, Wilson passed over a number of prominent Republicans whom many insiders claim would have made better candidates: Reps. Jerry Lewis of San Bernardino, David Dreier of Claremont and Tom Campbell of Palo Alto, and Orange County Supervisor Gaddi Vasquez.

None of them, however, is as close as Seymour to what Wilson has called his "compassionate conservative" philosophy. They have been friends since the 1970s, when Seymour was mayor of Anaheim and Wilson mayor of San Diego. Democrats chortled that Seymour was the logical choice since he's the only middle-aged white guy they knew who was shorter than Wilson.

The challenge for Seymour, however, is not just to get elected to the seat, but to win it twice in the next four years. He'll be on the ballot in 1992 for the last two years of Wilson's term and then again in 1994 for a full six-year term. Those two races could easily cost $40 million. And money will be especially tight in 1992, when Alan Cranston's seat also will be open.

Statistically, Seymour will be battling some long odds. Of 23 Senate appointments since 1960, only 11 have won election in their own right. The last time California had an appointed senator was July 1964, when Gov. Pat Brown appointed Democrat Pierre Salinger to replace Sen. Clair Engle, who had died in office. In November, Salinger was swamped by Republican George Murphy.

But there's more. Seymour, because of his appointment, will be 100th in Senate seniority. That will slow his move to committee assignments with visibility. He will also be 3,000 miles from his constituency. And he will be working in an atmosphere where Washington politicos are not apt to take him seriously until he wins an election on his own.

Democrat David Gambrell, appointed to the Senate from Georgia in 1971 only to lose the seat to Democrat Sam Nunn the next year, suggested Seymour's future will be closely tied to Wilson's success. If Wilson keeps his popularity despite tight budgets and a recession in the next two years, Seymour will benefit, Gambrell has said. If not, he'll suffer.

At the same time, Seymour's fate could be enmeshed in the war policies of President Bush. On Seymour's third day in office, he was forced to vote on giving Bush war powers in the Persian Gulf. Public perceptions of the correctness of Bush's course in 1992 should weigh heavily in the campaign.

Another problem for Seymour is that Republican conservatives were infuriated by his appointment. Seymour, who was a Catholic until his 1971 divorce, was strongly anti-abortion until he switched to pro-choice in 1989 as he prepared to run for lieutenant governor. "Flip-flopping on abortion has done something to his image, when on an issue of principle he was willing to make a move like that," said Brian Johnston of the National Right to Life Committee's California office. "It gives him an image of oiliness." Seymour had scarcely been in office for six weeks when conservative Rep. William Dannemeyer announced that he would oppose Seymour in the 1992 primary.

Seymour's appointment, plus the prospect of a bruising Republican primary, has made the Democrats giddy. "This is a seat the Democrats can take," said Rep. Barbara Boxer of Greenbrae, who plans to be a candidate for one of the two U.S. Senate seats in 1992. Former San Francisco Mayor Dianne Feinstein, who narrowly lost the governor's race to Wilson, was expected to run.

Yet no one should take Seymour for granted, even if he does wear a Mickey Mouse watch. Seymour made his mark on local politics when, as mayor of Anaheim, he negotiated the Los Angeles Rams football team's move from the Los Angeles Coliseum to Anaheim. And he pushed for local tax relief at the city level even before the passage of the tax-cutting Proposition 13 in 1978.

A millionaire Realtor, Seymour took his conservative, pro-business approach to the state Senate in 1982, when he won a special election. He quickly moved into the forefront of the Senate Republican leadership, teaming with Sen. Jim Nielsen in 1983 to help topple Senate Republican leader William Campbell of Hacienda Heights and Caucus Chairman Ken Maddy of Fresno.

Nielsen assumed Campbell's post as Republican leader, and Seymour moved into Maddy's No. 2 post. Together, they raised more money than any Senate GOP leadership team in history.

When first elected, Seymour was predictably conservative – an outspoken opponent of abortion and rent control, a proponent of the death penalty – and he was not always willing to negotiate. But over time, Seymour became more of a pragmatist, willing to not only listen and negotiate, but to join with Democrats in carrying legislation to benefit education, crack down on unsafe truckers and provide help to homeless people. After losing his leadership job in 1987, Seymour continued to carry many substantive bills and gradually moved toward the center politically.

He also proposed an innovative plan to help parents provide for their children's education through tax-exempt savings accounts (an idea vetoed by Gov. George Deukmejian) and has been a leader in getting legislation passed to increase penalties for drunken drivers. After the Exxon Valdez disaster in 1989, he switched his position and became an opponent of offshore oil development.

"We make mistakes," Seymour told reporters. "I'm not going to always be right. Therefore, to expect one to never change a position on an issue ... is too much to ask."

State Sen. Diane Watson, a black Democrat from Los Angeles who is as different from Seymour as are Watts and Anaheim, offered this assessment: "He's shown he's a man who can learn. He came down to Watts. He listened to our people. And he learned. I respect him for that."

Finally, there is the question of money. Seymour has personal wealth and through his real estate connections, he's a formidable fund-raiser. He was one of 50 Californians who contributed $100,000 to George Bush's 1988 presidential campaign.

PERSONAL: appointed 1991; born Dec. 3, 1937, in Mount Lebanon, Pa.; home, Anaheim; US Marine Corps 1955-1959; education, B.A. UCLA; wife Judy, six children; Protestant.

CAREER: Owner real estate brokerage and management firm; Anaheim City Council and mayor; president, California Association of Realtors, 1980; state Senate, 1982-1990.

COMMITTEES: Agriculture, Nutrition and Forestry; Energy and Natural Resources.

OFFICES: Dirksen Building, Washington, D.C. 20510, (202) 224-9652, FAX (202) 224-9612; state, 1130 O St., Fresno 93721, (209) 487-5727; Suite 915, 11111 Santa Monica Blvd., Los Angeles 90025, (213) 209-6765; 4590 MacArthur Blvd., Newport Beach 92660, (714) 756-8820; 401 B St., San Diego 92101, (619) 557-5257; 4450 Golden Gate Ave., San Francisco 94102, (415) 556-4307.

RATINGS: None as of this writing.

Vote on H.J. Res. 77 authorizing war with Iraq: Yes.

Frank Riggs (R)
1st Congressional District

California's 1st Congressional District sweeps down the north coast from the Oregon border and into the heart of the wine country north of San Francisco Bay. To the north, it's an area dependent on tourism, lumber, fishing and small farms. That gives way to the lush vineyards, mammoth poultry farms and inflated real estate values of Mendocino, Sonoma and Napa counties at the southern end.

Most of the small towns of the north coast are chronically depressed. Lumbermen are constantly at war with fishermen, although almost no one likes offshore oil development. There's a thriving counterculture that is usually held in check politically by conservative, small-town merchants and a growing

Frank Riggs

number of conservative families who've escaped from the Bay Area into the southern reaches of the district. During the 1970s, the district evolved from Republican-voting to Democratic. State officials say marijuana is the area's largest cash crop – a situation that couldn't exist without some tolerance by the establishment.

One of the surprises of the 1990 election came when upstart Republican Frank Riggs beat Rep. Douglas Bosco. A conservative Democrat, four-termer Bosco had managed to anger most traditional Democratic constituencies with a series of anti-environmental votes, lucrative land speculation deals and a closeness with savings and loan officials. The liberals voted for the spoiler in the race, Peace and Freedom candidate Darlene Comingore. She got nearly 15 percent of the vote, which enabled Riggs to squeak by Bosco with 1,500 votes in the heavily Democratic district.

The question now is, can Riggs keep the seat? He got off to a rocky start when he began waffling on a campaign promise not to accept the 25 percent pay raise Congress authorized in the previous session. Then he said he couldn't afford to sell his property holdings (another campaign promise). The campaign left him broke, Riggs pleaded, and the recession had severely eroded the value of his land.

Riggs, however, proved to be politically astute about several other things. He began conciliatory discussions with environmentalists and most were willing to say he'd probably be an improvement over Bosco. He also was one of three GOP House members nationwide to vote "no" on the resolution to authorize war with Iraq. The vote made him a hero with many Democrats, but it stunned hard-core conservatives, whose contributions he undoubtedly will need in 1992.

In early 1991 there was no shortage of Democrats waiting to challenge Riggs. Bosco said he would run again. In addition, possible candidates included the man who replaced Bosco in the Assembly, Dan Hauser of Arcata, and state Sen. Barry Keene of Benicia. If Riggs is lucky, they'll have a divisive primary, which may be the only thing that could save his seat.

PERSONAL: elected 1990; born Sept. 5, 1950, in Louisville, Ky; home, Windsor; education, B.A. Golden Gate University 1980; wife Cathy, three children.

CAREER: U.S. Army, 1972-75; peace officer for Santa Barbara and Healdsburg Police Departments and Sonoma County Sheriff, 1976-83; developer, banker, 1983-90; Windsor Union School District Board, 1984-88.

COMMITTEES: Public Works and Transportation; Banking, Finance and Urban Affairs.

OFFICES: Suite 1517, Longworth Building, Washington, D.C. 20515, (202) 225-3311; district, Suite 329, 777 Sonoma Ave., Santa Rosa 95405, (707) 525-4235.

REGISTRATION: 55% D, 33% R

1990 CAMPAIGN:	Riggs - R	43%	$257,745
	Douglas Bosco - D	42%	$408,894
	Darlene Comingore - PF	15%	$9,377
1988 CAMPAIGN:	Douglas Bosco - D	63%	$247,779
	Samuel Vanderbilt - R	28%	$6,633

RATINGS: None.

Vote on H.J. Res. 77 authorizing war with Iraq: No.

Wally Herger (R)
2nd Congressional District

The southern Cascade Range and Trinity Alps, the Sacramento Valley north of Sacramento and a small piece of the wine country in Napa County make up this increasingly conservative district. Some of the most remote parts of California are found within its boundaries, where there are clear vistas to the giant volcanoes, Mounts Lassen and Shasta.

Wally Herger

Tourism, timber and farming are the mainstays of an economy that is healthy on the valley floor and is often on the slide in wooded sections. Water is plentiful and residents expect their representatives to keep any more of their liquid gold from being siphoned off to other parts of the state. The mountains and remote villages make it an expensive area in which to campaign, a fact that favors incumbents.

Rep. Wally Herger comes from the agricultural heartland of the district, which gives him an added edge in both fund-raising and name identity. Despite the safety of the seat, Herger shows no inclination toward activism. During three terms in the Assembly, he was a conservative backbencher who consistently voted "no" on most measures. In Congress, he's shown the same posture. He initiates a few farm bills but little else.

He has vocal critics among owners of small logging companies, who claim he favors the timber giants at their expense. Fishermen are angry that he's done nothing to change the operations of federal facilities that have been killing salmon runs on the upper Sacramento River. But his inaction sits well with many of his constituents, who prize self-reliance and less government. In recessionary times, however, that could spell trouble if voters decide he's done too little to help them from his seat on the Agriculture Committee.

PERSONAL: elected 1986; born May 20, 1945, in Yuba City; home, Rio Oso; education, A.A. American River College 1968, attended CSU Sacramento; wife Pamela, eight children; Mormon.

CAREER: rancher and operator of family petroleum gas company, 1969-80; Assembly, 1980-86.

COMMITTEES: Agriculture; Merchant Marine and Fisheries; (Select) Narcotics Abuse and Control.

OFFICES: Suite 1108, Longworth Building, Washington, D.C. 20515, (202) 225-3076, FAX (202) 225-1609; district, Suite B, 20 Declaration Dr., Chico 95991, (916) 893-8363; Suite 410, 2400 Washington Ave., Redding 96001, (916) 246-5172; Suite 20, 951 Live Oak Blvd., Yuba City 95991, (916) 673-7182.

REGISTRATION: 45% D, 43% R

1990 CAMPAIGN: Herger - R	63%	$616,075
Erwin Rush - D	31%	$6,118
1988 CAMPAIGN: Herger - R	59%	$696,748
Wayne Meyer - D	39%	$193,915

RATINGS:
ADA	ACU	AFL/CIO	LCV	NCSC	NTU	USCC
6%	97%	19%	6%	8%	60%	92%

Vote on H.J. Res. 77 authorizing war with Iraq: Yes.

Robert T. Matsui (D)
3rd Congressional District

The 3rd District includes most of Sacramento and its suburbs, stretching east to the Sierra Nevada foothills. With the state Capitol and some 41,000 state workers, the area is more strongly identified with government than any other part of California.

But the government influence doesn't stop with the state. There are nearly 18,000 more federal paychecks from two Air Force bases in or adjacent to the district plus 5,000 at an Army depot and 2,400 more at regional federal offices. Such a strong civil service presence normally means friendly turf for a Democrat and Rep. Robert Matsui represents the district ably. Yet the economy is diversifying and the district is becoming more conservative along with it.

Robert   Matsui

Electronic industries and distribution centers are sprouting up in areas where rice and tomatoes once grew. Cheap land, by California standards, is feeding a boom that barely noticed recessions in the early 1980s and '90s. It's a tribute to Matsui's strength that he could advocate shutting down Mather Air Force Base (5,600 jobs) as a federal cost-cutting move and no one even mentioned the word "recall."

He's considered one of the brighter lights in the congressional delegation and has announced plans to run for the seat Sen. Alan Cranston will vacate in 1992. But it will be a long-shot campaign. Like most California House members, Matsui is virtually unknown outside his district.

As an infant, Matsui was sent to a Japanese-American internment camp during World War II. In Congress, reparations for victims of the relocation became one of his causes. His legislative interests are quite diversified, however, ranging from foster care and job training to medical care for elderly people. On the Ways and Means Committee, he has had an important role in shaping tax reform. His congressional posture has been similar to the one he established on the Sacramento City Council: a quiet and effective consensus builder. Yet those are not attributes that transfer well to a statewide campaign. In 1992, Matsui may come to that realization, too, and elect to keep his safe House seat.

PERSONAL: elected in 1978; born Sept. 17, 1941, in Sacramento; home, Sacramento; education, A.B. UC Berkeley 1963, J.D. Hastings College of Law 1966; wife Doris, one child; United Methodist.

CAREER: attorney, 1967-78; Sacramento city councilman, 1971-78.

COMMITTEE: Budget; Ways and Means.

OFFICES: Suite 2353, Rayburn Building, Washington, D.C. 20515, (202) 225-7163, FAX (202) 225-0566; district, Suite 8058, 650 Capitol Mall, Sacramento 95814, (916) 551-2846.

REGISTRATION: 53% D, 35% R

1990 CAMPAIGN: Matsui - D   60% $1,207,843

              Lowell Landowski - R   34% $4,545

1988 CAMPAIGN: Matsui - D   71% $638,688

              Lowell Landowski - R   29% $ 7,695

RATINGS:

ADA	ACU	AFL/CIO	LCV	NCSC	NTU	USCC
94%	5%	89%	81%	93%	34%	26%

Vote on H.J. Res. 77 to authorize war with Iraq: No.

Vic Fazio (D)

4th Congressional District

One of the districts clearly targeted for shrinkage in the next reapportionment is the 4th, which stretches from Sacramento and some of its nearby suburbs west to Vallejo. Growth is booming on the eastern edge around Sacramento, Davis and Dixon. From the west, Bay Area workers are spilling into the Cordelia, Fairfield and Vacaville areas in search of affordable home sites. The area's vast agricultural tracts are rapidly being paved over along the I-80 corridor.

Vic Fazio

Yet the district also includes the sleepy villages of the Sacramento-San Joaquin Delta, where life still revolves around cattle, pears, row crops and fishing. More retirees live in the area now, but that's the chief demographic change in recent years. The district is safe Democratic country, but increasingly conservative.

Nonetheless, Vic Fazio doesn't always draw a Republican opponent and he won without campaigning much against a well-financed challenger in 1990. He has flowered into one of the House's most promising members. Several publications have called him the most skillful legislator in the 45-member California delegation and a likely candidate for House speaker one day. With Rep. Tony Coelho's departure in 1989, Fazio became California's most influential House member.

He was easily elected vice chairman of the Democratic Caucus, the No. 5 position in the House's Democratic hierarchy and a frequent stepping stone to greater things. Fazio, a former assemblyman, came to Washington well schooled in the workings of legislative bodies. He caught the notice of party leaders by doing many of the thankless chores that others eschew, such as facilitating congressional pay raises and serving on the ethics committee. In 1989, he was instrumental in keeping Congress' free mailing privileges intact despite efforts by Sen. Pete Wilson to divert a chunk of newsletter funds elsewhere. He also quickly became known as a consensus builder.

As Fazio's power has increased, he's used it to solidify relationships with other congressmen. One of the keys to his strength is the chairmanship of the legislative subcommittee of Appropriations. That gives him enormous say on which programs get funded. He has a reputation for being the man to see in the delegation when there's a difficult political or legislative problem. At the same time, he has diligently worked for his district and has been a friend of the two huge Air Force bases located there, even though he publicly supports cutbacks in Pentagon spending.

He serves on another Appropriations subcommittee with jurisdiction over energy and water projects. That's an extremely important post for his district, but it also has made Fazio the chief mediator in one of the longest-running, no-win disputes in California – whether to build the Auburn Dam on the American River. But then again, no-win issues are one of his specialties. Fazio's voting in Washington tends to be more liberal than his posturing in the district, but none of his opponents has been able to use that issue effectively.

At the beginning of this session, Fazio took on added responsibilities for the Democratic Congressional Campaign Committee, the party's political arm in the House. He's the first person in the history of Congress to hold two leadership positions. He'll also play a key role in California's redistricting battle.

PERSONAL: elected 1978; born Oct. 11, 1942, in Winchester, Mass; home, West Sacramento; education, B.A. Union College in Schenectady, N.Y., 1965, attended CSU Sacramento; wife Judy; Episcopalian.

CAREER: congressional and legislative staff, 1966-75; co-founder, California Journal magazine; Assembly, 1975-78.

COMMITTEES: Appropriations; (Select) Hunger.

OFFICES: Suite 2113, Rayburn Building, Washington, D.C. 20515, (202) 225-0354, FAX (202) 225-5716; district, Suite 330, 2525 Natomas Park Dr., Sacramento 95833, (916) 978-4381; 844-B Union Ave., Fairfield 94533, (707) 426-4333.

REGISTRATION: 52% D, 37% R

1990 CAMPAIGN: Fazio - D		55%	$845,622
	Mark Baughman - R	39%	$40,439
1988 CAMPAIGN: Fazio - D		99%	$529,334

RATINGS:

ADA	ACU	AFL/CIO	LCV	NCSC	NTU	USCC
89%	6%	90%	72%	93%	30%	30%

Vote on H.J. Res. 77 to authorize war with Iraq: No.

Nancy Pelosi (D)
5th Congressional District

All but the northwest corner of San Francisco lies
within the district the late Rep. Phil Burton drew for
himself. Burton was a labor Democrat who missed
becoming House speaker by one vote in 1976. His
roots were in San Francisco's tough working-class
community, but he also was a messiah for the Sierra
Club and mingled well with the city's financial and
developer barons. His death in 1983 could have set
off a raucous fight among the new constituencies that
had been gaining political power – gays, Asians and
Hispanics. But his wife, Sala, stepped in and the
scepter was passed. She succumbed to cancer in
1987. The fight to replace her pitted straight liberals
against gays in the Democratic primary. Longtime

Nancy Pelosi

party activist Nancy Pelosi was the victor over gay Supervisor Harry Britt. But there
was no lingering bitterness. Pelosi had many gay supporters and also was an
acceptable choice for Roman Catholic, society, environmental and labor factions.

If anything, the election showed how seriously San Francisco's gay political
leadership had been ravaged by the AIDS epidemic. The gay community simply
couldn't mobilize itself as it had in previous years. Pelosi came to Congress a
wealthy housewife who long ago paid her dues licking envelopes and walking
precincts in Democratic campaigns. Her father, a congressman from 1939-47, and
a brother were mayors of Baltimore. Pelosi had been state Democratic Party
chairwoman, a member of the Democratic National Committee and chaired the
Democratic National Convention in 1984.

Although new to Congress, she has been quickly learning the ropes and has been
willing to take on the thankless chores that make friends and increase visibility.
She's Northern California Democratic whip and a member of the executive board
of the Democratic Study Group.

PERSONAL: elected 1987; born March 26, 1940, in Baltimore; home, San
Francisco; education, B.A. Trinity College, Washington, D.C., 1962; husband Paul,
five children; Roman Catholic.

CAREER: public relations executive, 1984-86.

COMMITTEE: Appropriations.

OFFICES: Suite 1005, Longworth Building, Washington, D.C. 20515, (202)
225-8259; district, Suite 13407, 450 Golden Gate Ave., San Francisco 94102, (415)
556-4862.

REGISTRATION: 64% D, 19% R

1990 CAMPAIGN:			
Pelosi - D	77%	$462,664
Alan Nichols - R	23%	$153,947

1988 CAMPAIGN: Pelosi - D   76% $616,936
                    Bruce O'Neill - R   19% $19,245
RATINGS: ADA   ACU   AFL/CIO   LCV   NCSC   NTU   USCC
              100%   1%   96%   89%   100%   35%   17%
Vote on H.J. Res. 77 authorizing war with Iraq: No.

Barbara Boxer (D)
6th Congressional District

Barbara Boxer

Some of the great mortgages of the Western world are nestled among the fir and redwood trees of Marin County, which makes up half of the 6th District electorate. The remainder of the district is scattered. To the south, it includes the northwest corner of San Francisco, once a predominantly middle-class area that is becoming increasingly affluent and Asian. Near the Presidio there are extremely expensive homes with sweeping sea views. Poor blacks inhabit the Fillmore District. To the north the district swings around the top of San Francisco Bay to the one-time socialist, blue-collar city of Vallejo. It also takes in the farms, small towns and counterculture havens that dot slices of Solano and Sonoma counties. The district lines originally were gerrymandered for John Burton, Phil Burton's brother, whose tenuous hold on his seat was complicated by drug and alcohol problems. The younger Burton decided not to run for re-election in 1982. The lines were altered somewhat and the seat came close to going Republican in that election.

Marin County Supervisor Barbara Boxer, once John Burton's aide, won the seat with only 52 percent of the vote, but has never had trouble since. It's a district of informed people who turn out to vote. Marin is still the trend-setter, a bastion of yuppie attitudes long before the term was coined. Voters tend to be environmentally aware and economically conservative. It's been a good fit for Boxer, who as a freshman exposed the Air Force purchase of the $7,622 coffee pot.

Almost overnight, Boxer became one of Congress' experts on defense procurement issues. By her third term, she was on the Armed Services Committee, which was once one of the most exclusive old-boy clubs of the House. But she's also worked her staff to exhaustion on a variety of other issues popular in her district, such as AIDS research, transportation, dial-a-porn, consumer protection, offshore oil bans, high-school dropouts, abortion rights and other women's issues. She was elected president of her freshman class and has been moving up the leadership ladder in a variety of areas ever since. She currently is whip-at-large for the Democratic Caucus.

Boxer is one of the few California congressional members who is developing a national following. In a Democratic administration, she could be considered for a Cabinet post. And if she ever found herself in a tough race, she could expect dollars to flow in from women's groups throughout the country.

For now, however, the always-outspoken congresswoman is running for the U.S. Senate in 1992. She had the brass to announce for Alan Cranston's seat before he was willing to give it up and has been all over the state meeting voters and collecting money. The likelihood of primary opposition from someone such as Rep. Mel Levine or Lt. Gov. Leo McCarthy doesn't bother her. "I'm a fighter," she says. And she dreams of the day when she can walk her 4-foot-11-inch frame into the male bastion of the Senate and yell: "Wake up, guys!"

PERSONAL: elected 1982; born Nov. 11, 1940, in Brooklyn, N.Y.; home, Greenbrae; education, B.A. Brooklyn College 1962; husband Stewart, two children; Jewish.

CAREER: stockbroker and financial researcher, 1962-65; reporter for the weekly Pacific Sun, 1972-74; aide to Rep. John Burton, 1974-76; Marin County Supervisor, 1976-82.

COMMITTEES: Armed Services; Government Operations; (Select) Children, Youth and Families.

OFFICES: Suite 307, Cannon Building, Washington, D.C. 20515, (202) 225-5161; district, Suite 300, 3301 Kerner Blvd., San Rafael 94904, (415) 457-7272; 450 Golden Gate Ave., San Francisco 94102, (415) 626-6943.

REGISTRATION: 59% D, 27% R

1990 CAMPAIGN: Boxer - D   68% $921,666

Bill Boerum - R   32% $32,788

1988 CAMPAIGN: Boxer - D   73% $351,687

William Steinmetz - R   27% $50,532

RATINGS:

ADA	ACU	AFL/CIO	LCV	NCSC	NTU	USCC
94%	3%	95%	89%	99%	34%	21%

Vote on H.J. Res. 77 to authorize war with Iraq: No.

George Miller (D)
7th Congressional District

The 7th District begins in the backwaters of San Francisco Bay and stretches inland along the south shore of the Carquinez Straight. The grubbiest of the industrial towns in the district is Richmond, which also is more than 50 percent black. To the east lie a series of roughneck refinery and factory towns – Pinole, Hercules, Rodeo, Martinez and Pittsburg.

To the south are the affluent suburbs of Concord and Pleasant Hill. Those areas of Contra Costa County traditionally have been populated by youngish couples in search of affordable starter homes. But prices there have become so outlandish in recent years that young families are fleeing to further suburbs. Some of the more adventurous are rehabilitating homes in the industrial areas. The trend in the district is toward more conservative voters, but that seems to be of little threat to George Miller, the district's longtime liberal congressman.

Miller is one of the most committed environmentalists in the House, but he's not a dogmatic one. He knows practically every civic and labor leader in the district by first name and works tirelessly on behalf of middle-class social and economic concerns. It is a grass-roots approach that he learned from his father, a longtime state senator. He also used his chairmanship of Interior's water and power resources subcommittee to become one of the more powerful members of the delegation. In January 1990, cold shivers went through California's agriculture community when

George Miller

Miller became vice chairman of Interior. Longtime Chairman Morris Udall of Arizona, who has Parkinson's disease, was injured in a fall and may never be more than titular head of the committee again. In addition, Udall plans to retire in 1992. Miller has been given all powers normally enjoyed by the chairman. Miller and Udall never saw eye-to-eye on water policy. So now, Miller has a clear hand to wage battles against water giveaways in the San Joaquin Valley, among many others.

"We're trying to get away from measuring success by how much cement we pour," Miller once said with regard to the Central Valley Project and similar federally financed water development programs. He's a determined opponent of water subsidies for irrigation of farms with more than 960 acres under cultivation. Miller also is taking the lead in developing a new national energy policy to promote conservation and research on alternative fuels. And he's part of the Democratic leadership as a majority whip-at-large.

In a Democratic administration, he'd be a contender for interior secretary.

PERSONAL: elected 1974; born May 17, 1945, in Richmond; home, Martinez; education, A.A. Diablo Valley College 1966, B.A. San Francisco State College 1968, J.D. UC Davis 1972; wife Cynthia, two children; Roman Catholic.

CAREER: legislative aide, 1969-74; attorney, 1972-74.

COMMITTEES: Education and Labor; Interior and Insular Affairs (vice chair); (Select) Children, Youth and Families (chair).

OFFICES: Suite 2228 Rayburn Building, Washington, D.C. 20515, (202) 225-2095; district, Suite 14, 367 Civic Dr., Pleasant Hill 94523, (415) 687-3260; Suite 280, 3220 Blume Dr., Richmond 94806, (415) 222-4212.

REGISTRATION:	54% D, 34% R		
1990 CAMPAIGN:	Miller - D	61%	$469,400
	Roger Payton - R	39%	$47,918
1988 CAMPAIGN:	Miller - D	68%	$269,887
	Jean Last - R	32%	$14,710

RATINGS: ADA ACU AFL/CIO LCV NCSC NTU USCC
           100% 30%   89%   89%   96%   34%   24%
Vote on H.R. Res. 77 authorizing war with Iraq: No.

Ron Dellums (D)
8th Congressional District

Ron Dellums

Few voters in the 8th District have ambivalent feelings about Rep. Ron Dellums. In election after election, a third of the voters are solidly against him and the other two-thirds are solidly in favor. And occasionally, splinter-party candidates also make a respectable showing on Election Day. Dellums, perhaps the most liberal member of the California delegation, has a polarizing effect on people. It is a posture that was effective in the quirky arena of the Berkeley City Council, where Dellums spent four years. But it has served him less well in Congress.

His favorable votes come from the flatlands and low hills near San Francisco Bay – Oakland, Berkeley, Albany, Kensington and El Cerrito. They tend to be black, blue-collar workers or underpaid professionals employed at the University of California and related enterprises. The rest of the voters tend to live in mostly-white Republican outposts high on the ramparts of the Berkeley hills or just over the crest in the wooded ravines of Lafayette, Orinda and Moraga.

Dellums' gift for oratory gave him unusual visibility when he first went to Congress, but it led to few constructive advances for him or his district. He wouldn't help boost the flow of federal money to the university, which is its lifeblood. Other parochial concerns seemed to bore him. Like-minded colleagues tended to regard him as an unreliable ally. In time, Dellums succeeded in pushing Congress to impose sanctions on South Africa – perhaps his greatest legislative victory. He also learned to work with senior leaders, but had the misfortune of backing some of the wrong horses when Wisconsin Rep. Les Aspin was shaking the mossbacks off the Armed Services Committee in 1984. In time, Dellums and Aspin seemed to bury the hatchet. In 1990, he had a key role in killing several questionable missile systems.

In the 1980s, Dellums developed a protective attitude over the huge Oakland and Alameda military bases. But that feeling doesn't extend to Hunter's Point in San Francisco with its predominantly black community. He helped kill a proposal to home-port the battleship Missouri there. Today, he chairs the District of Columbia Committee. That gives him stature in the black community, but little elsewhere.

PERSONAL: elected 1970; born Nov. 24, 1935, in Oakland; home, Berkeley; education, A.A. Oakland City College 1958, B.A. San Francisco State College 1960, M.S.W. UC Berkeley 1962; wife Leola, three children; Protestant.

CAREER: U.S. Marine Corps, 1954-56; social worker, poverty program administrator and consultant, 1962-70.
COMMITTEES: Armed Services; District of Columbia Committee (chair); Intelligence.
OFFICES: Suite 2136 Rayburn Building, Washington, D.C. 20515, (202) 225-2661, FAX (202) 225-9817; district, Suite 105, 201 13th St., Oakland 94617, (415) 763-0370; Suite 6, 1720 Oregon St., Berkeley 94703, (415) 548-7767; Suite 160, 3732 Mount Diablo Blvd., Lafayette 94549, (415) 283-8125.
REGISTRATION: 63% D, 24% R

1990 CAMPAIGN:	Dellums - D	62%	$790,386
	Barbara Galewsky - R	38%	$0
1988 CAMPAIGN:	Dellums - D	67%	$1,174,676
	John Cuddihy - R	31%	$7,071

RATINGS:	ADA	ACU	AFL/CIO	LCV	NCSC	NTU	USCC
	100%	7%	93%	89%	99%	36%	16%

Vote on H.J. Res. 77 authorizing war with Iraq: No.

Fortney H. "Pete" Stark (D)
9th Congressional District

At its western edge, the 9th District takes in some neighborhoods of Oakland, plus Alameda and the scruffier suburbs to the south such as San Leandro, San Lorenzo and Hayward. Then it sweeps across the hills through more affluent neighborhoods to Pleasanton and Livermore. It's in the latter areas that rapid growth has occurred in recent years, bringing a conservative bent to one of the more liberal districts in the state. The working-class areas also are seeing the beginning of a renaissance as the demand for housing has boosted the price of stucco bungalows beyond the reach of middle-income people.

Pete Stark

That could be an unpleasant change for a liberal such as Rep. Pete Stark. Yet his growing seniority and clout in tax and health matters provide a solid platform from which to assist the district. Stark has become a chief lieutenant of Illinois Rep. Dan Rostenkowski on the powerful Ways and Means Committee. One day he may chair it. That's made him a key player in tax reform and a factor in almost any California issue that comes before Ways and Means.

Stark also is used to swimming against the tide and winning. He started his own bank in Walnut Creek and pulled in deposits throughout the Bay Area by using peace symbols on his checks during the Vietnam era. But he sold his bank stock once he became a member of the House Banking Committee. In 1986, the political arm of the American Medical Association spent some $200,000 to bankroll an opponent. But Stark crushed him with 70 percent of the vote and continues to be a consistent "no" vote on issues that pit the AMA against consumers. He's since become chair of the Ways and Means health subcommittee in charge of Medi-Care.

In 1989, however, he shot himself in the foot when he got into a name-calling spat with Louis Sullivan, the only black in the Reagan administration Cabinet. Stark had to apologize for calling Sullivan a "disgrace to his profession and his race." Nonetheless, Stark appeared to suffer no permanent harm.

PERSONAL: elected 1972; born Nov. 11, 1931 in Milwaukee, Wis.; home, Oakland; education, B.S. Massachusetts Institute of Technology 1953, M.B.A. UC Berkeley 1960; wife Carolyn, four children; Unitarian.

CAREER: U.S. Air Force, 1955-57; 1961-72, founder and president of a bank and a savings and loan institution.

COMMITTEES: District of Columbia; Ways and Means; (Select) Narcotics Abuse and Control; Joint Economic Committee.

OFFICES: Suite 239 Cannon Building, Washington, D.C. 20515, (202) 225-5065; district, Suite 500, 22320 Foothill Blvd., Hayward, 94541, (415) 635-1092.

REGISTRATION: 58% D, 29% R

1990 CAMPAIGN:	Stark - D	59%	$525,271
	Victor Romero - R	41%	$206,798
1988 CAMPAIGN:	Stark - D	73%	$410,540
	Howard Hertz - R	27%	$0

RATINGS:	ADA	ACU	AFL/CIO	LCV	NCSC	NTU	USCC
	100%	6%	90%	88%	95%	40%	19%

Vote on H.J. Res. 77 authorizing war with Iraq: No.

Don Edwards (D)
10th Congressional District

In the early days of the Vietnam War, one of the few voices of opposition in Congress came from an eloquent member from San Jose. Rep. Don Edwards' brand of militant liberalism has shown no sign of waning during nearly three decades in Congress. Edwards, a one-time Republican and FBI agent, is the same forceful spokesman for civil liberties and social justice that he always has been.

The Fair Housing Act of 1980 is a triumph that he wears like a badge on his lapel. But that's just one of many. He was a prime mover behind the Equal Rights Amendment, the Voter Rights Act, the fight to abolish the House Un-American Activities Committee and others. He's been a stalwart against attacks on forced busing and abortion, as

Don Edwards

well. Yet Edwards also is a fair man who insists on procedural integrity in all he does. That reputation has helped him exert some leadership over the fractious California delegation, of which he is the dean. But it's a job that tries even Edwards' patience. The California delegation isn't a house divided. It's a rabbit warren.

As the district's prune orchards and dairy farms have given way to electronics plants and housing tracts, Edwards' philosophy as been less in vogue. But he rarely even draws a Republican opponent and is immensely popular among the Hispanic people who make up nearly a third of the district. His turf takes in central and east San Jose and then stretches up the east side of San Francisco Bay to Milpitas, Union City, Newark and Fremont. It's essentially a working-class district, but is being rediscovered by yuppies who've been priced out of the area's more affluent neighborhoods.

Edwards makes effective use of his seniority on the Judiciary and Veterans Affairs committees to assist the district. And despite the fact that he's in his mid-70s, he enjoys good health and shows no sign of slowing down.

PERSONAL: elected 1962; born Jan. 6, 1915, in San Jose; home, San Jose; education, B.A. Stanford University 1936, L.L.B. 1938; wife, Edith; Unitarian.

CAREER: FBI agent, 1940-41; U.S. Navy 1941-45; title company executive, 1945-62.

COMMITTEES: Judiciary; Veterans Affairs.

OFFICES: Suite 2307 Rayburn Building, Washington, D.C. 20515, (202) 225-3072, FAX (202) 225-9460; district, Suite 100, 1042 West Hedding St., San Jose 95126, (408) 247-1711; 38750 Paseo Padre Pkwy., Fremont 94536, (415) 792-5320.

REGISTRATION: 58% D, 29% R

1990 CAMPAIGN:	Edwards - D	63%	$224,999
	Mark Patrosso - R	36%	$2,702
1988 CAMPAIGN:	Edwards - D	86%	$173,537

RATINGS:	ADA	ACU	AFL/CIO	LCV	NCSC	NTU	USCC
	100%	5%	94%	83%	99%	32%	18%

Vote on H.J. Res. 77 authorizing war with Iraq: No.

Tom Lantos (D)
11th Congressional District

From the San Francisco city limits to Redwood City, the 11th District includes all of the Peninsula except for the extremely wealthy (and Republican) communities of Hillsborough, Woodside, Portola Valley and Atherton. At the northern end are the boxy, working-class homes of Daly City and San Bruno plus Colma, the graveyard for more than a million San Franciscans. South of the airport, the suburbs become ritzier and more wooded. But congestion is everywhere – on the freeways, the streets and even the bicycle paths.

Residents tend to be pro-environment, well-educated and not particularly burdened by a social conscience. But the district's lack in social conscience didn't rub off on Rep. Tom Lantos, who, as a youth, fought the Nazis in the Hungarian underground. Unlike most congressmen, he'll wade into a state issue such as the fight to restore the Cal-OSHA worker safety program. He opposes any totalitarian regime and fights tirelessly for Israeli security.

Tom Lantos

In 1989-90, he was Congress' point man on the Housing and Urban Development agency scandals. His intense questioning of HUD officials kept the pot stirring for months and gave him enviable visibility on nightly news programs. Yet he's shown considerable independence in Congress, often tending to vote his conscience rather than the party line. The former economics professor came from behind in 1980 to unseat a Republican who'd served less than a year. Once in office, he immediately amassed a large campaign war chest and has had no serious opposition since.

PERSONAL: elected 1980; born Feb. 1, 1928, in Budapest, Hungary; home, Burlingame; education, B.A. University of Washington 1949, M.A. 1950, Ph.D UC Berkeley 1953; wife Annette, two children; Jewish.

CAREER: Economics professor and administrator for San Francisco State University and the California State University system, 1950-80; part-time bank economist and television commentator.

COMMITTEES: Foreign Affairs; Government Operations; (Select) Aging.

OFFICES: Suite 1526, Longworth Building, Washington, D.C. 20515, (202) 225-3531, FAX (202) 225-3127; district, Suite 820, 400 El Camino Real, San Mateo 94402, (415) 342-0300.

REGISTRATION: 55% D, 32% R.

1990 CAMPAIGN:	Lantos - D	66%	$788,298
	Bill Quraishi - R	28%	$97,638
1988 CAMPAIGN:	Lantos - D	71%	$269,510
	Bill Quraishi - R	24%	$95,575

RATINGS:

ADA	ACU	AFL/CIO	LCV	NCSC	NTU	USCC
78%	7%	95%	78%	97%	34%	26%

Vote on H.J. Res. 77 authorizing war with Iraq: Yes.

Tom Campbell (R)
12th Congressional District

Lines for the 12th District were drawn to cram as many south Bay Area Republicans as possible into one district. It takes in some of the richest communities in the state (Hillsborough, Atherton, Woodside and Portola Valley), the heart of the

Silicon Valley in San Mateo and Santa Clara counties and then skirts San Jose and runs down Highway 101 to the garlic capital of Gilroy. Despite that, the voters show increasing independence. For years, the district was the stronghold of liberal Republican Pete McCloskey. He was replaced by Ed Zschau. But Alan Cranston, whose father made a fortune as a real estate agent there, carried the district against Zschau in the 1986 Senate race.

Rep. Ernest Konnyu, a fringe conservative, became a one-term wonder when sexual harassment of his staff became public. He was replaced in 1988 by a brilliant Stanford economist and law professor, Tom Campbell, another liberal Republican who had

Tom Campbell

the backing of both Zschau and electronics mogul David Packard. Campbell appeals to the wealthy, egghead and electronics factions in this district. And he's one of the few Republicans who is a genuine friend of environmentalists. He brings to Congress trade and tax knowledge that could be used to forge favorable trade opportunities for the district's computer electronics industries.

Campbell hopes to succeed where Zschau failed. In March 1991, he announced that he would be a candidate for Sen. Alan Cranston's seat in the 1992 primary. Campbell made his announcement a few days after Zschau said that he would be unable to run in 1992. San Mateo Supervisor Tom Huening was quick to announced that he would be a candidate to fill Campbell's seat in the House.

PERSONAL: elected 1988; born Aug. 14, 1952, in Chicago, Ill.; home, Palo Alto; education, B.A. and M.A. University of Chicago 1973, J.D. Harvard University 1976, Ph.D University of Chicago 1980; wife Susanne; no religious affiliation.

CAREER: attorney, 1978-80; White House and U.S. Justice Department positions, 1980-81; Federal Trade Commission, 1981-83; Stanford law professor, 1983-88.

COMMITTEES: Science, Space and Technology; Judiciary; Banking.

OFFICES: Suite 313 Cannon Building, Washington, D.C. 20515, (202) 225-5411. FAX (202) 225-5944; district, Suite 105, 599 North Mathilda, Sunnyvale 94086, (415) 321-9154.

REGISTRATION: 49% D, 38% R

1990 CAMPAIGN:	Campbell - R	60%	$1,286,200
	Robert Palmer - D	34%	$109,410
1988 CAMPAIGN:	Campbell - R	52%	$1,440,639
	Anna Eshoo - D	46%	$1,089,570

RATINGS:	ADA	ACU	AFL/CIO	LCV	NCSC	NTU	USCC
	44%	48%	22%	100%	21%	54%	83%

Vote on H.J. Res. 77 authorizing war with Iraq: Yes.

Norman Y. Mineta (D)

13th Congressional District

The 13th District is compact and probably will shrink more after the next reapportionment. It includes most of San Jose, which surpassed San Francisco to become the state's third largest city in 1989, and the suburbs of Campbell, Santa Clara and Los Gatos. Most of the growth has been in the more affluent suburbs, but skyrocketing housing values in San Jose are changing the economic mix of this region. The region's computer electronics industries produce an increasing number of dinks (double-income, no kids), and few lower-paid workers in those industries can afford to live near their jobs.

Norman Mineta

Despite the conservative trend, Norm Mineta consistently runs ahead of the Democratic registration in the district. The popular former San Jose mayor seems fully recovered from a heart attack in 1986 and has a solid place in the House leadership as one of 10 deputy majority whips. He also has a reputation for finding soft spots in the budget.

As a senior member of the Public Works Committee, Mineta was the Californian to see for airport development money and other aviation issues. But in late 1990, personal ambition got the best of Mineta and he launched a nasty battle to oust Chairman Glenn Anderson, D-San Pedro. Anderson was toppled, but Mineta couldn't muster the votes to succeed him. As a result, the chairmanship of one of the most important pork-barrel committees in Congress went to New Jersey. Anderson probably would have retired at the end of this term, so there was little justification for Mineta's challenge. Beyond that, a congressman is foolish to challenge a senior colleague unless he has his votes in order. Mineta probably damaged his standing permanently in both the state and national caucuses. It also remains to be seen how charitable the new chairman, Rep. Robert Roe, will be toward his one-time opponent.

Like Rep. Robert Matsui, Mineta spent part of his youth in a Japanese detention camp during World War II. He's led the fight to redress those wrongs. In another arena, however, he's been in the forefront of efforts to open up Japanese markets to Silicon Valley products. He's also pressured the Japanese to end whaling and protect arctic wildlife.

PERSONAL: elected 1974; born Nov. 12, 1931, in San Jose; home, San Jose; education, B.S. UC Berkeley 1953; wife May, two children; United Methodist.

CAREER: U.S. Army 1953-56; insurance agency owner, 1956-74; San Jose City Council, 1967-71; San Jose Mayor, 1971-74.

COMMITTEES: Public Works and Transportation; Space, Science and Technology.

OFFICES: Suite 2350, Rayburn Building, Washington, D.C. 20515, (202) 225-2631; district, Suite 310, 1245 South Winchester Blvd., San Jose 95128, (408) 984-6045.

REGISTRATION: 49% D, 38% R 1988

1990 CAMPAIGN:	Mineta - D	58%	$666,915
	David Smith - R	35%	$670
1988 CAMPAIGN:	Mineta - D	67%	$521,674
	Luke Sommer - R	30%	$25,511

RATINGS:

ADA	ACU	AFL/CIO	LCV	NCSC	NTU	USCC
94%	11%	89%	78%	91%	39%	26%

Vote on H.J. Res. 77 authorizing war with Iraq: No.

John Doolittle (R)
14th Congressional District

John Doolittle

One of the state's largest congressional districts, the 14th takes in pieces of San Joaquin County and swings north through the Sierra Nevada to the Oregon border. It contains most of the state's least-populated counties (Alpine, Plumas, Sierra, Lassen and Modoc), but also the booming foothill communities of the northern Mother Lode and the agricultural towns around Stockton. Placer County, which became Rep. John Doolittle's home base a few years ago, is one of the fastest-growing in the state.

Since the late 1960s, refugees from smog-belt counties have been streaming into the foothills in search of cleaner air, less congestion and more traditional lifestyles free of crime and drugs. The irony, however, is that the foothills have become the state's second most productive marijuana-growing region and are distinguished by a unique population of mass murderers, renegade bikers, grave robbers and cult worshipers.

Rep. Norm Shumway, who held the seat 12 years, stood for the conservative values many of the district's residents revere. When he announced he would be retiring to care for his ailing wife, most pundits thought the seat would easily pass to another Morman, then-state Sen. John Doolittle. But Doolittle's victory was anything but easy. He hadn't counted on the strong campaign by former teacher Patricia Malberg, whom Shumway easily vanquished two years before.

Doolittle, who was only 29 years old when he made his first try for public office in 1980, carried considerable baggage into the race. He presides over a tight-lipped and sometimes paranoid staff of ideological warriors directed by John Feliz, an ex-Los Angeles police detective. Doolittle doesn't flinch at being called a moral zealot. But he's sometimes more zealot than moral. He's a strident opponent of abortion, soft judges, pornography, declining social standards, gun control and free-spending liberals. Yet when it comes to his personal ambitions, Doolittle finds it easy to stoop in low places. Each of his campaigns has been marked by mudslinging and gross distortion of his opponent's record, and he and Feliz have been fined for campaign violations. Doolittle and Feliz are proteges of former ex-state Sen. Bill Richardson, for years the Senate's gun-toting conservative mastermind.

Doolittle's ability to slay opponents was not overlooked in the state Senate. Republicans made him the No. 2 Republican after a leadership shake-up in 1987. (Ironically, the man he replaced was John Seymour, whom Gov. Pete Wilson appointed as his successor in the U.S. Senate.) Doolittle surprised his Senate critics by working well with the Democratic leadership on the body's administrative chores. Many of those same critics predicted Doolittle would miss the Senate once he took up residence on the back benches of Congress. Doolittle, though, clearly has other plans. Before he was even sworn in, conservatives in the California GOP caucus succeeded in making Doolittle their lead man on reapportionment. To do so, they ran over Rep. William Thomas, a six-term moderate from Bakersfield. With the right-wing firmly in charge of the caucus, Doolittle should feel comfortable in his new home.

When the United States went to war in the Persian Gulf, Doolittle, who used student and religious deferments to stay out of the Vietnam War, joined the Dornans and Dannemeyers in calling war protesters "malcontents" and "scum."

PERSONAL: elected 1990; born Oct. 30, 1950, in Glendale, Calif.; home, Rocklin, education, B.A. UC Santa Cruz 1972, J.D. McGeorge School of Law 1978; wife Julia, one child; Mormon.

CAREER: lawyer; aide to Sen. H.L. Richardson; state Senate, 1980-90.

COMMITTEES: Interior and Insular Affairs; Merchant Marine and Fisheries.

OFFICES: Suite 1213, Longworth Building, Washington, D.C. 20510, (202) 225-2511, FAX (202) 225-5444; district, Suite 260, 1624 Santa Clara Dr., Roseville, 95661, (916) 785-5560.

REGISTRATION: 45% D, 44% R

1990 CAMPAIGN: Doolittle - R	51%	$529,813
Patricia Malberg - D	49%	$222,011
1988 CAMPAIGN: Norm Shumway - R	63%	$492,349
Patricia Malberg - D	37%	$103,678

RATINGS: None as of this writing.

Vote on H.J. Res. 77 authorizing war with Iraq: Yes.

Gary Condit (D)
15th Congressional District

The 15th district twists up the San Joaquin Valley from western Fresno County to the San Joaquin County line, taking in all of Merced, Stanislaus and Mariposa counties along the way. Fast-growing Modesto is the population center. It includes the richest agricultural region in the valley and is growing both more Hispanic and more politically diverse as Bay Area workers filter into the valley in search of cheaper housing. Nearly a quarter of the residents now have Spanish surnames.

The district has been safe turf for conservative Democrats since the 1950s. Newcomers may bring changes, but probably not dramatic ones.

From this furtile ground came Rep. Tony Coelho, who in just eight years went from freshman to majority whip, the No. 3 Democratic position in the House. But then came revelations about a questionable junk-bond purchase and personal loan. Rather than face a gauntlet like the one that felled Speaker Jim Wright of Texas, Coelho simply resigned in midterm.

Gary Condit

With help from Coelho, Assemblyman Gary Condit of Ceres easily won the post in a 1989 special election. Condit established conservative credentials during his seven years in the Assembly. Crime and drug bills occupied most of his time, and he was one of the dissident "Gang of Five" who made life unpleasant for Assembly Speaker Willie Brown. Condit's legislative record in the Assembly, however, was far from distinguished. He's also no Coelho when it comes to wheeling and dealing in party circles. On the Agriculture Committee, Condit is well positioned to serve his district. If he makes a mark anywhere, it probably will be there.

PERSONAL: special election 1989; born April 21, 1948 in Salina, Okla.; home, Ceres; education, A.A. Modesto College 1970, B.A. Stanislaus State College 1972; wife Carolyn, two children; Baptist.

CAREER: production worker, Riverbank Ammunition Depot, 1972-76; community relations, National Medical Enterprises, 1976-82; Ceres City Council, 1972-74, mayor 1974-76; Stanislaus County Board of Supervisors, 1976-82; Assembly 1982-89.

COMMITTEES: Agriculture; Government Operations.

OFFICES: Suite 1529, Longworth Building, Washington, D.C. 20515, (202) 225-6131. FAX (202) 225-0819; district, 415 West 18th St., Merced 95340, (209) 383-4455; 920 13th St., Modesto 95354, (209) 527-1914.

REGISTRATION: 55% D, 36% R 1989

1990 CAMPAIGN:	Condit - D	66%	$234,432
	Cliff Burris - R	34%	$23,939
1989 CAMPAIGN:	Condit - D	57%	$417,000
	Clare Berryhill - R	35%	$207,000

| **RATINGS**: | ADA | ACU | AFL/CIO | LCV | NCSC | NTU | USCC |
| | 56% | 33% | 76% | 60% | 56% | 37% | 40% |

Vote on H.J. Res. 77 authorizing war with Iraq: Yes.

Leon Panetta (D)

16th Congressional District

This is one of the few districts in California where there's been a noticeable shift to the left in the 1970s and '80s. The environmental fights, which always take on increased intensity in coastal areas, are in part responsible for the change as residents have become increasingly concerned about onshore land development and offshore oil drilling.

Leon Panetta

The 16th District takes in some of the most scenic land on the California coast, including Big Sur and Monterey Bay. Preservation of those resources is not a partisan issue. Republican coast dwellers value their views and clean beaches as much as anyone. Another reason for the change is the growth of the University of California, Santa Cruz, at the extreme northern end of the district. The campus is a place that hasn't left the 1960s. The Santa Cruz City Council is every bit as revisionist as Berkeley's and Santa Cruz's sharp shift to the political port (it was once a Republican city) neutralizes GOP strongholds in Monterey, San Benito and San Luis Obispo counties, which are also part of the district.

Rep. Leon Panetta is sometimes accused of not paying enough attention to politics in the sprawling district. But he hasn't needed to. His unpaid wife runs his district offices and is the more effective politician of the two. That's left the Republican-turned-Democrat free to concentrate on legislative duties and, in a relatively short time, he's become one of the most powerful Californians in Washington. In 1989, he took over chairmanship of the Budget Committee, which makes him a major player in national fiscal policy. Budget is one of the committees whose members are limited to six years. That means President Bush will have to contend with Panetta all through his first term.

Colleagues claim no one in Congress has a better grasp of budget issues. Panetta is committed to dealing with deficits, even if some sacrosanct Democratic programs must be sacrificed. If it's possible for Congress and the administration to forge new bipartisan reforms, Panetta undoubtedly will be the one who takes them there.

On the Agriculture Committee, Panetta has had to walk a fine line between the powerful growers in his district and the strident environmentalists. He's helped growers keep their cheap labor with amendments to immigration bills that preserved their guest-worker provisions. He also worked to expand childhood nutrition programs. That is an area in which Panetta has sincere conviction, but it also has the happy effect of increasing growers' markets. But he has been tough on controls of pesticides, as well. In the Reagan administration, he successfully thwarted an effort to pre-empt California's tougher pesticide laws.

PERSONAL: elected 1976; born June 28, 1938, in Monterey; home, Carmel Valley; education, B.A. University of Santa Clara 1960, J.D. 1963; wife Sylvia, three children; Roman Catholic.

CAREER: U.S. Army 1963-65; aide to U.S. Sen. Thomas Kuchel, 1966-69; director U.S. Office of Civil Rights, 1969-70; executive assistant to mayor of New York, 1970-71; attorney 1971-76.

COMMITTEES: Agriculture; Budget; House Administration; (Select) Hunger.

OFFICES: Suite 339, Cannon Building, Washington, D.C. 20515, (202) 225-2861; district, 380 Alvarado St., Monterey 93940, (408) 649-3555; 701 Ocean Ave., Santa Cruz 95060, (408) 429-1976; 200 West Alisal, Salinas 93901, (408) 424-2229; 1160 Marsh St., San Luis Obispo 93401, (805) 541-0143.

REGISTRATION: 51% D, 35% R

1990 CAMPAIGN:	Panetta - D	74%	$295,399
	Jerry Reiss - R	22%	$23,939
1988 CAMPAIGN:	Panetta - D	79%	$252,336
	Stanley Monteith - R	21%	$69,563

RATINGS:
ADA	ACU	AFL/CIO	LCV	NCSC	NTU	USCC
83%	14%	76%	83%	78%	38%	36%

Vote on H.J. Res. 77 authorizing war with Iraq: No.

Calvin Dooley (D)
17th Congressional District

This swing seat – one of the very few in the delegation – takes in a piece of Kern County north of Bakersfield plus Kings and Tulare counties and eastern Fresno County. The growers and small-town shopkeepers had a tradition of electing Democrats, but that changed in 1978, when Charles "Chip" Pashayan Jr. upset an incumbent. Pashayan became a tireless advocate for farmers and began winning re-elections with hefty numbers of Democratic votes. In time, he also won a seat on the Rules Committee. Even a messy divorce didn't seem to hurt him.

Calvin Dooley

But then came the savings and loan scandals and revelations that Pashayan had carried water for some of the worst of the S&L charlatans. Visalia farmer Cal Dooley won an easy victory after an exceedingly nasty campaign. Despite Dooley's prominence as a family cotton farmer, the California Farm Bureau Federation made no secret of its dismay at Pashayan's defeat. No other Central Valley congressman is as well-positioned as Pashayan was to push agriculture concerns.

Dooley, however, is in the majority party and he has the potential to be even more helpful to agribusiness in the long run. He represents a new generation of wealthy growers who are well educated, politically involved and astute businessmen. He is an articulate spokesman for homespun values who can be expected to work for continued water subsidies and a relaxation of trade restrictions. If he chooses to make a career of Congress, he could be chairman of the agriculture committee some day. Dooley also brings a social conscience to the Congress. In Tulare County, he was active in civic, education and senior citizen endeavors.

PERSONAL: elected 1990; born Jan. 11, 1954, in Visalia; home, Visalia; education, B.S. UC Davis 1977, M.S. Stanford University 1987; wife Linda, two children; Protestant.

CAREER: cotton farmer; aide to state Sen. Rose Ann Vuich, 1987-89.

COMMITTEES: Agriculture; Small Business.

OFFICES: Suite 1022 Longworth Building, Washington, D.C. 20515, (202) 225-3341. FAX (202) 225-9308; district, Suite E, 711 N. Court St., Visalia 93277, (209) 733-8348.

REGISTRATION: 48% D, 42% R.

1990 CAMPAIGN:	Dooley - D	55%	$547,763
	Charles Pashayan - R	45%	$557,949
1988 CAMPAIGN:	Charles Pashayan - R	71%	$206,677
	Vincent Lavery - D	29%	$5,227

RATINGS: None as of this writing.

Vote on H.J. Res. 77 authorizing war with Iraq: No.

Richard H. Lehman (D)
18th Congressional District

The 18th District is another where the late Rep. Phil Burton outdid himself to create a Democratic district. The district corkscrews through blue-collar sections of Fresno and into Sanger, where the current incumbent lives. It takes in all of Madera County, includes the sparsely populated counties of Mono, Tuolumne and Calaveras, and then sneaks into the working-class neighborhoods of Stockton. A Democrat has to commit moral turpitude to lose here.

Rep. Richard Lehman is the lucky beneficiary of Burton's handiwork. Lehman – a one-time legislative aide who won a seat in the Assembly at age 28 – had backed the losing side in an Assembly leadership struggle. As a consolation prize, district lines were

Richard Lehman

drawn to his specifications. In Congress, Lehman is known as an environmentalist, especially on the subject of mountain wilderness. But, like other Central Valley Democrats, he also is an effective supporter of agribusiness. For the working-class areas of his convoluted district, Lehman offers support for education, consumers and drug rehabilitation. That plays well in a district with one of the state's highest percentages of traditional family units. Lehman was just 34 when he entered Congress. He can look forward to a long career with ever-increasing responsibility.

PERSONAL: elected 1982; born July 20, 1948, in Sanger, Calif.; home, Sanger; education, A.A. Fresno City College 1968, attended CSU Fresno, B.A. UC Santa Cruz 1971.

CAREER: California National Guard, 1970-76; legislative aide 1970 76; Assembly, 1976-82.

COMMITTEES: Energy and Commerce; Interior and Insular Affairs.

OFFICES: Suite 1319, Longworth Building, Washington, D.C. 20515, (202) 225-4540. FAX (202) 225-4562; district, Suite 210, 2115 Kern St., Fresno 93721, (209) 487-5760; Suite 216, 401 North San Joaquin St., Stockton, (209) 946-6353; Suite 101, 424 N. Highway 49, Sonora 95370, (209) 533-1426.

REGISTRATION: 58% D, 33% R

1990 CAMPAIGN: Lehman - D	100%	$302,473
1988 CAMPAIGN: Richard Lehman - D	70%	$193,681
David Linn - R	30%	$ 89,260

RATINGS:	ADA	ACU	AFL/CIO	LCV	NCSC	NTU	USCC
	94%	3%	93%	72%	96%	38%	25%

Vote on H.J. Res. 77 authorizing war with Iraq: Yes.

Robert J. Lagomarsino (R)
19th Congressional District

Rep. Robert Lagomarsino got the scare of his political life in 1988. When the votes were counted, the veteran congressman won by slightly less than 1 percent out of 228,000 votes cast. It was the toughest race in his 30-year career as an elected official. Lagomarsino and state Sen. Gary Hart, D-Santa Barbara, had spent more than $3 million, making it the most expensive congressional race in the nation.

Hart didn't go for a rematch in 1990, when his Senate seat was up. But in 1992 he'll have another free ride and the added incentive of the Proposition 140 limits on state legislative terms. Hart will probably be in the race and perhaps that will be enough to retire Lagomarsino voluntarily. He'll be 66 then.

Robert Lagomarsino

As a ranking Republican on the Foreign Affairs Committee, Lagomarsino had been the administration's point man on Central American policy. It was bad enough that he'd been mauled by the liberals on the committee. But Hart continues to do the same thing in his district. Fortunately for Lagomarsino, he has always been a fanatic about constituent service. That could save him again if he chooses to run.

Santa Barbara has long been considered one of the jewels of the coastal counties and an ideal retirement locale. Yet there are plenty of working folks, too, and a number of them lost their jobs when the Reagan administration moth-balled much of Vandenburg Air Force Base. A portion of Ventura County, which is Lagomarsino's home base, still has major Navy installations. But its civilian employment is limited and most of the military personnel who vote mail their absentee ballots elsewhere. But if Lagomarsino decides on another term, he probably can count on fund-raising support from Ron and Nancy Reagan. Their mountain-top ranch is in the district.

PERSONAL: elected 1974; born Sept. 4, 1926, in Ventura; home, Ventura; education, B.A. University of Santa Barbara 1950, L.L.B. University of Santa Clara 1953; wife Norma Jean, three children; Roman Catholic.

CAREER: U.S. Navy, 1941-45; attorney, 1954-74; Ojai City Council, 1958, and mayor 1959-61; state Senate 1961-74.

COMMITTEES: Foreign Affairs; Interior and Insular Affairs.

OFFICES: Suite 2332 Rayburn Bldg., Washington, D.C. 20515, (202) 225-3601; district, Suite 101, 5740 Ralston St., Ventura 93003, (805) 642-2200; 314 E. Carrillo, Santa Barbara 93101, (805) 963-1708; 104-E East Boone St., Santa Maria 93454, (805) 922-2131.

REGISTRATION: 41% D, 49% R.

1990 CAMPAIGN:	Lagomarsino - R	54%	$643,444
	Anita Ferguson - D	45%	$11,404
1988 CAMPAIGN:	Lagomarsino - R	50%	$1,470,674
	Gary Hart - D	49%	$1,548,193

RATINGS:	ADA	ACU	AFL/CIO	LCV	NCSC	NTU	USCC
	11%	88%	12%	44%	14%	46%	84%

Vote on H.J. Res. 77 authorizing war with Iraq: Yes.

William M. Thomas (R)
20th Congressional District

If the late Rep. Phil Burton was the winning strategist in the redistricting battles of the 1980s, there had to be a loser. That person was Rep. Bill Thomas, who spent a lot of time trying to salvage what he could for the California Republican Party. It wasn't possible to gerrymander Thomas out of his seat, but Burton did the next best thing. He gave him a seat that stretches from the Nevada border to the Pacific Ocean.

The 20th District includes remote Inyo County in the high desert, most of Kern County's farm and oil lands in the Central Valley, the desert region of Los Angeles County and the least populated areas of San Luis Obispo County. The far-flung constituency is separated by two major mountain ranges, and the highest (Mount Whitney) and lowest (Death Valley) points in the contiguous United States. At least the district is predominantly conservative and should provide Thomas with a safe seat for as long as he wants it. Thomas' home base is Bakersfield, the right-leaning farm and oil town at the heart of the district. To the east, more conservatives are clustered around the sprawling military bases in the Mojave Desert. To the south, the district dips into Palmdale and Lancaster, booming communities with socially conservative young families.

William Thomas

William Thomas has become one of the Republican leaders in the House and is young enough to expect more advancement. He is vice chairman of the National Republican Congressional Committee and he seems to know what buttons to push to get recalcitrant Republicans aboard administration bills. But there's a coolness with Rep. Jerry Lewis, the most powerful member of the California GOP delegation. A few years ago, Lewis beat Thomas in an election for the California seat on the Republican Committee on Committees. The committee dispenses assignments and the loss hurt Thomas' standing in the delegation. At the beginning of the 102nd Congress in 1991, conservatives seized control of the state delegation and Thomas found his role diminished. Rep. John Doolittle of Rocklin succeeded him as the caucus point man on reapportionment.

Besides party work, Thomas has been active on both the Budget and Agriculture committees. He's supported increasing the retirement age for Social Security and was chief Republican sponsor of a bill to require uniform poll-closing hours so that early results from Eastern states don't influence the national outcome.

The former community college instructor has done a lot to try to bring young people into the party, using campaign funds to conduct talent searches for people to fill minor posts and holding weekend retreats for college students. He's also an inveterate tinkerer in both Kern County and the state party machinery, a fact that gave him unpleasant moments during and after the state GOP convention in February 1989. Some delegates showed up on the floor wearing anti-Thomas buttons. Thomas' behind-the-scenes power plays were denounced by some of his oldest allies: ex-Assemblyman Joe Shell of Bakersfield and state Senate Minority Leader Ken Maddy of Fresno.

In Kern County, there's a Thomas clique and then there's the rest of the GOP. "The Thomas faction and its leader believe if you're not with us 1,000 percent, you're against us," said Assemblyman Phil Wyman, R-Tehachapi. "It's the kind of mentality you expect from a warlord." Thomas, however, contends that his opponents "don't want to broaden the base of the party. Those who are in a power base don't want it dissipated."

PERSONAL: elected 1978; born Dec. 6, 1941, in Wallace, Idaho; home, Bakersfield, education, A.A. Santa Ana College 1959, B.A. San Francisco State University 1963, M.A. 1965; wife Sharon, two children; Baptist.

CAREER: instructor, Bakersfield Community College, 1965-74; California assemblyman, 1974-78.

COMMITTEES: House Administration; Ways and Means; Budget.

OFFICES: Suite 2402, Rayburn Building, Washington, D.C. 20515, (202) 225-2915, FAX (202) 225-8798; district, Suite 220, 4100 Truxton Ave., Bakersfield 93309, (805) 327-3611; Suite 115, 848 West Jackman, Lancaster, (805) 948-2634; Suite 203, 1390 Price St., Pismo Beach 93449, (805) 773-2533.

REGISTRATION: 41% D, 49% R 1988 1990

1990 CAMPAIGN:	Thomas - R	59%	$430,525
	Michael Thomas - D	36%	$695
1988 CAMPAIGN:	Thomas - R	71%	$329,354
	Lita Reid - D	27%	$15,814

RATINGS:	ADA	ACU	AFL/CIO	LCV	NCSC	NTU	USCC
	17%	77%	13%	22%	9%	41%	92%

Vote on H.J. Res. 77 authorizing war with Iraq: Yes.

Elton Gallegly (R)
21st Congressional District

Since the late 1960s, white families have been fleeing increasingly seedy sections of the San Fernando Valley. New communities have sprouted up beyond the valley's west and northerly hills. Towns such as Simi Valley, which were barely more than crossroads 20 years ago, are now flourishing communities in the 21st District.

The district still takes in some neighborhoods on the fringe of the valley, such as Northridge, Granada Hills, Chatsworth and Tujunga. But the bulk of its mostly white and upwardly mobile families live beyond the hills in Ventura County communities such as Thousand Oaks and Camarillo.

Elton Gallegly

One of the newcomers to the Ventura part of the district in the '60s was an ambitious young man with a real estate license named Elton Gallegly. In time, the boom made him wealthy, he became mayor of Simi Valley and was elected to Congress. Gallegly seems to fit the district well. He's a family man who is devoted to hard work and traditional values. And like many baby boomers, he is Republican but not doctrinaire.

In a short time, Gallegly has become identified with anti-drug legislation. He was elected to chair his freshman Republican caucus. In his second term, he won a seat on the coveted Foreign Affairs Committee. He appears to have a bright future in Congress if he chooses to stay there.

PERSONAL: elected 1986; born March 7, 1944, in Huntington Park, Calif.;

home, Simi Valley; education, attended Los Angeles State College; wife Janice, four children; Protestant.

CAREER: real estate firm owner, 1968-86; Simi Valley City Council, 1979-80, Mayor 1980-86.

COMMITTEES: Foreign Affairs; Interior and Insular Affairs.

OFFICES: Suite 107, Cannon Building, Washington, D.C. 20515, (202) 225-5811; district, Suite 110, 9301 Oakdale Ave., Chatsworth 91311, (818) 341-2121; Suite 207, 200 North Westlake Blvd., Thousand Oaks 91362, (805) 496-4700.

REGISTRATION: 37% D, 52% R

1990 CAMPAIGN:	Gallegly - R	58%	$599,454
	Richard Freiman - D	35%	$13,706
1988 CAMPAIGN:	Gallegly - R	69%	$465,310
	Donald Stevens - D	29%	$0

RATINGS:

ADA	ACU	AFL/CIO	LCV	NCSC	NTU	USCC
11%	93%	11%	33%	10%	41%	96%

Vote on H.J. Res. 77 authorizing war with Iraq: Yes.

Carlos Moorhead (R)
22nd Congressional District

This solidly Republican district is skewered by the San Gabriel Mountains. South and within long reaches of the range are the more affluent suburbs of the Los Angeles smog belt: Glendale, Pasadena, San Marino, Temple, Sierra Madre, Arcadia, Monrovia, La Canada, La Crescenta and part of Burbank. Most of the residents are white, older and well educated. Across the mountains are the newer and booming suburbs of Newhall and Saugus, where younger families are found in town houses that staircase up the hillsides.

Carlos Moorhead

The affable congressman from the area is Carlos Moorhead, the dean of the Republican delegation. Moorhead doesn't try to assert his leadership very often, perhaps because he knows it would be a waste of time. GOP members have a history of independence and some seem to regard the solidly Republican Moorhead as not ideological enough to suit their tastes.

Moorhead busies himself with legislation in a variety of important areas – but none that attract much attention – such as patent and copyright law, energy conservation, natural gas deregulation and operations of the border patrol. Almost alone, he's battled with Pacific Northwest congressmen to give California a fair share of the federal low-cost power generated in that region. He's the No. 2 minority member of the Judiciary Committee and is known for faithful constituent service. No doubt he'll retire from the seat one day. At this point, he seems unbeatable.

PERSONAL: elected 1972; born May 6, 1922, in Long Beach; home, Glendale; education, B.A. UCLA 1943, J.D. USC 1949; wife Valery, five children; Presbyterian.

CAREER: U.S. Army, 1942-45 (retired Army Reserve lieutenant general); attorney, 1949-72; Assembly, 1967-72.

COMMITTEES: Energy and Commerce; Judiciary.

OFFICES: Suite 2346, Rayburn Building, Washington, D.C. 20515, (202) 225-4176, FAX (202) 226-1279; district, 420 North Brand Blvd., Glendale 91203, (818) 247-8445; 301 East Colorado Blvd., Pasadena 91101, (818) 792-6168.

REGISTRATION: 35% D, 55% R

1990 CAMPAIGN: Moorhead - R		59%	$444,157
David Bayer - D		35%	$40,872
1988 CAMPAIGN: Moorhead - R		70%	$234,920
John Simmons - D		26%	$18,046

RATINGS:

ADA	ACU	AFL/CIO	LCV	NCSC	NTU	USCC
6%	95%	7%	17%	8%	57%	90%

Vote on H.J. Res. 77 authorizing war with Iraq: Yes.

Anthony C. Beilenson (D)
23rd Congressional District

From Beverly Hills to the shores of Malibu, the 23rd District takes in the area that many Americans imagine when "Los Angeles" is mentioned. But there are also the tidy apartments near Wilshire Boulevard, the gay enclave of West Los Angeles and the mansions of Pacific Palisades. Across the Santa Monica Mountains, the district takes in the comfortable suburbs of Van Nuys, Reseda, Canoga Park, Encino, Tarzana and Woodland Hills.

Anthony Beilenson

Although furs and Rolls Royces abound in the area, many the residents are upper middle-class professionals. Most of the southern portions of the district are peopled by older, predominantly Jewish and liberal voters. Across the mountains, neighborhoods are more homogeneous but leaning conservative. Lower-income people are disappearing as homes are snapped up by two-income couples with few children.

One might expect a glitzy liberal to represent this area in Congress. But Rep. Tony Beilenson is one of the more anonymous members of the delegation. He typifies the Jewish professional of the district. He's a solid and conscientious performer whose skills as a legislator are widely respected in the House. He seems nearly devoid of partisanship, which sometimes annoys those who would like to see him use his seat on the Rules Committee to the greater advantage of Democrats.

Those most annoyed with Beilenson are the highly partisan members of the "west side" political organization headed by Reps. Howard Berman and Henry Waxman. Beilenson has steadfastly refused to kowtow to the group, despite their similar ideological positions, and he once conducted a nasty squabble with Berman and Waxman over the changing of his district boundaries. Beilenson is known for studying issues thoroughly and voting his conscience. He's an expert on the budget and was responsible for creating the Santa Monica Mountains National Recreation area. Credible Republicans have run against him, but none has gotten very far.

PERSONAL: elected 1976; born Oct. 26, 1932, in New Rochelle, N.Y.; home, Los Angeles; education, A.B. Harvard University 1954, L.L.B. 1957; wife, Dolores, three children; Jewish.

CAREER: attorney 1957-59; counsel to Assembly Committee on Finance and Insurance, 1960; counsel to California Compensation and Insurance Fund, 1961-62; Assembly, 1963-66; state Senate, 1966-77.

COMMITTEES: Budget; Rules.

OFFICES: Suite 1025, Longworth Building, Washington, D.C. 20515, (202) 225-5911; district, Suite 14223, 11000 Wilshire Blvd., Los Angeles 90024, (213) 209-7801; Suite 222, 18401 Burbank Blvd., Tarzana 91356, (818) 345-1560.

REGISTRATION: 54% D, 36% R

1990 CAMPAIGN:	Beilenson - D	62%	$231,386
	Jim Saloman - R	34%	$358,367
1988 CAMPAIGN:	Beilenson - D	64%	$140,486
	Jim Saloman - R	33%	$100,956

RATINGS:

ADA	ACU	AFL/CIO	LCV	NCSC	NTU	USCC
83%	8%	74%	94%	90%	42%	26%

Vote on H.J. Res. 77 authorizing war with Iraq: No.

Henry A. Waxman (D)

24th Congressional District

The 24th District stretches from downtown Los Angeles to Beverly Hills, taking in all of Hollywood, Hancock Park and Los Feliz. Then it runs over the crest of the Santa Monica Mountains to include North Hollywood and Universal City. Since World War II, the neighborhoods of this entertainment industry-connected area have been solidly Jewish and liberal. At the southern and seedier end of the district, an area where the Hollywood technicians and extras once lived, the residents are increasingly Hispanic and Korean. These minorities, however, tend to vote in small numbers. There also are an increasing number of gays, who do vote.

Waxman, one of the sharpest intellects in Congress, has drawn on the extreme wealth of the district to build one of the most important power bases in the Democratic Party with ex-Assembly chum Howard Berman, and to a lesser extent Mel Levine, both of whom followed Waxman to Congress. The Berman-Waxman organization raises vast sums of money and conducts hardball political campaigns, often with extensive use of direct mail.

Most of the day-to-day operations are run by Berman's brother, Michael, and Carl D'Agostino, who own a campaign management firm known as BAD Campaigns. But the congressmen are instrumental in recruiting promising candidates and in seeing to it that their campaigns get infusions of money and workers. Their interests don't stop with the Congress. Their hands reach deeply into local and national politics as well. Gary Hart's presidential campaign was one of their causes until he crashed and burned. Waxman, in the meantime, has bucked the House seniority system to grab key subcommittees, where he advances his interests in health, clean air and geriatrics issues.

Henry Waxman

Probably no Democrat has more influence on health issues. In the Reagan administration, he was the Democrats' first line of defense against weakening health and air programs. He's also a leader on abortion rights and funding for AIDS research. Waxman's seat is secure, which allows him to carry a heavy legislative loads. He's on the verge of being in the House's top leadership now. If the right openings occur, it shouldn't take much to propel him further.

PERSONAL: elected 1974; born Sept. 12, 1939, in Los Angeles; home, Los Angeles; education, B.A. UCLA 1961, J.D. 1964; wife Janet, two children; Jewish.

CAREER: attorney, 1965-68; Assembly, 1968-74.

COMMITTEES: Energy and Commerce; Government Operations; (Select) Aging.

OFFICES: Suite 2418, Rayburn Building, Washington, D.C. 20515, (202) 225-3976, FAX (202) 225-4099; district, Suite 400, 8425 West Third St., Los Angeles 90048, (213) 651-1040.

REGISTRATION: 59% D, 28% R

1990 CAMPAIGN:	Waxman - D	69%	$500,847
	John Cowles - R	25%	$1,835
1988 CAMPAIGN:	Waxman - D	72%	$191,334
	John Cowles - R	24%	$15,449

RATINGS:	ADA	ACU	AFL/CIO	LCV	NCSC	NTU	USCC
	100%	6%	89%	89%	99%	34%	22%

Vote on H.J. Res. 77 authorizing war with Iraq: No.

Edward R. Roybal (D)
25th Congressional District

As the sun sets over Santa Monica Bay, the skyscrapers of downtown Los Angeles cast long shadows over the city's Mexican-American barrio. Yet California's most heavily Hispanic district (58 percent), is anything but a slum. It's an area of nondescript apartment houses and stucco bungalows, where the medium income is below the city's average. But it is also a community where families flourish and the attitudes are optimistic. Most households have two working parents, and extended families living under one roof are common. Lawns are neatly trimmed, vegetable gardens abound and people awake to the sound of crowing roosters.

Edward Roybal

The district takes in some tenement areas of downtown Los Angeles and then swings east and north to Boyle Heights, East Los Angeles and Highland Park. A predominantly black part of Pasadena also is included. Rep. Edward Roybal, who has represented the area on the Los Angeles City Council and then in Congress since 1949, is so safe here that Republicans usually don't bother to oppose him. In 1978, the House reprimanded him for taking a $1,000 contribution from Korean businessman Tongsun Park and converting it to his own use. But that didn't seem to cost him anything at home. Constituents claimed he was a victim of discrimination.

Roybal has important seniority but has never been one of Congress' workhorses. Still, he has been a helpful vote for California on the Appropriations Committee and has shown that he can exert influence when an immigration issue is before the House. As chairman of the Select Committee on Aging, he's been active in shoring up Social Security. His daughter, Lucille Roybal-Allard, now represents part of the district in the state Assembly. She'll be his likely successor.

PERSONAL: elected 1962; born Feb. 10, 1916, in Albuquerque, N.M.; home, Los Angeles; education, attended UCLA, and Southwestern University; wife Lucille, three children; Roman Catholic.

CAREER: U.S. Army, 1944-45; program manager, Los Angeles County Tuberculosis and Health Association, 1945-49; Los Angeles City Council 1949-62.

COMMITTEES: Appropriations; (Select) Aging (chair).

OFFICES: Suite 221, Rayburn Building, Washington, D.C. 20515, (202) 225-6235, FAX (202) 226-1251; district, Suite 1706, 300 North Los Angeles St., Los Angeles 90012, (213) 894-4870.

REGISTRATION: 67% D, 22% R

1990 CAMPAIGN: Roybal - D		71%	$144,260
Steven Renshaw - R		24%	$0
1988 CAMPAIGN: Roybal - D		86%	$67,957

RATINGS:	ADA	ACU	AFL/CIO	LCV	NCSC	NTU	USCC
	100%	8%	94%	72%	98%	31%	19%

Vote on H.J. Res. 77 authorizing war with Iraq: No.

Howard L. Berman (D)

26th Congressional District

From Rep. Howard Berman's home in the Holly-wood Hills, the Santa Monica Mountains tumble northward to the floor of the San Fernando Valley. Mansions have replaced the colorful shanties that once dominated the higher elevations. The middle-class homes on scraped-off slopes now sell for near-mansion prices. And even the bungalows in the heart of the valley are beyond the financial reach of the working-class people who are becoming fewer and fewer in the area. Many of the houses in Van Nuys and Panorama City are now being torn down to make way for the walled-in condo havens so popular with yuppies. Yet the area is still solidly Democratic with the help of carefully drawn boundaries that reach into Burbank. Jews are a potent political force in the district, but their numbers are declining. Hispanic neighborhoods straddle the Golden State Freeway. And there are black neighborhoods in Pacoima.

Howard Berman

Berman shares the strongest political machine in Southern California with Reps. Henry Waxman and Mel Levine. Together, they have legendary fund-raising capability and substantial success at the ballot box. Berman is often the most politically assertive of the three, working hand-in-hand with two ace strategists and campaign managers, Berman's brother, Michael, and Carl D'Agostino. They're often accused of creating puppets and keeping them in power with contributions raised elsewhere. That's been said about Reps. Julian Dixon, Esteban Torres and Matthew Martinez. If that was the intent, it hasn't worked in the cases of Dixon and Torres, who show substantial independence. Martinez, however, doesn't show much of anything.

Berman was a divisive force in the Assembly, fomenting a spiteful revolt against then-Speaker Leo McCarthy in 1980 that preoccupied the house for a year. McCarthy had planned to leave the Assembly and if Berman had been willing to wait two more years, he would have been the likely heir. But Berman had other plans. Willie Brown eventually emerged from the fray with Republican backing and won the speakership, beginning his long reign. Brown then got rid of his potential rival by creating a new congressional district on the west side of Los Angeles. Berman has been more of a team player in Congress and is now majority whip-at-large.

As an urban legislator, Berman has been well positioned politically to be a stalwart defender of the United Farm Workers. He has been active on border and immigration issues, anti-apartheid legislation and other civil libertarian matters that play well in his district. But he's also been an astute observer of Mideast politics. He was warning against the consequences of chemical-nuclear capability in Iraq long before the Bush administration figured out that Saddam Hussein could never be a reliable ally. On the Judiciary Committee, he also has been able to assist his show-business constituents with copyright and licensing protections.

PERSONAL: elected, 1982; born, April 15, 1941, in Los Angeles; home, Los Angeles; education, B.A. UCLA 1962, L.L.B. 1965; wife Janis, two children; Jewish.

CAREER: attorney, 1966-72; Assembly 1973-82.

COMMITTEES: Budget, Foreign Affairs, Judiciary.

OFFICES: Suite 137, Cannon Building, Washington, D.C. 20515, (202) 225-4695; district, Suite 506, 14600 Roscoe Blvd., Panorama City 91402, (818) 891-0543.

REGISTRATION: 57% D, 33% R

1990 CAMPAIGN:	Berman - D	61%	$510,538
	Roy Dahlson - R	35%	$83,775
1988 CAMPAIGN:	Berman - D	70%	$409,233
	G.C. Broderson - R	30%	$0

RATINGS:	ADA	ACU	AFL/CIO	LCV	NCSC	NTU	USCC
	100%	5%	89%	78%	100%	34%	26%

Vote on H.J. Res. 77 authorizing war with Iraq: Yes.

Mel Levine (D)
27th Congressional District

In most parts of the country, the posh waterfront precincts of a major city would be solidly Republican. But this is Los Angeles and few things fit the norm. The 27th District starts at Pacific Palisades and takes in Santa Monica, Venice, Playa Del Rey, El Segundo, Torrance, Manhattan Beach, Hermosa Beach and Redondo Beach. It's an odd mixture of stately homes, counterculture habitats and refinery towns. In the liberal bastion of Santa Monica, the median home price exceeds $550,000. Then the district reaches into solidly Democratic inland areas, some of which are black or Hispanic, including Inglewood, Lennox and Lawndale.

Mel Levine

Its perennially youthful congressman, Mel Levine, is one of the promising liberal Democrats who is likely to be a candidate in 1992 for one of the state's two U.S. Senate seats. In the interim, he labors to please a constituency so diverse that it includes leftover beatniks from the '50s, people who skateboard for a living by advertising bistros in Venice, refinery machinists, yacht salesmen and financial and oil titans. Levine got a scare in 1986 when former Los Angeles Ram Rob Scribner made a run at him. But he ended the race with a solid victory and went back to fighting against offshore oil development, for the interests of Israel and accountability in defense spending – issues that seem to please most of his constituents regardless of political philosophy. This is an area where even refinery workers belong to the Sierra Club. A Republican with celebrity status might give Levine another hard run, but Levine has done a lot to solidify his support since Scribner's attempt and would have a huge campaign war chest for the fight. He is a close ally of Reps. Howard Berman and Henry Waxman, but he doesn't seem to be as driven to manipulate Los Angeles-area politics as actively as his two mentors.

From his seat on the Interior Committee, Levine got Santa Monica Bay included in the National Estuaries Program. That was a vital step in the effort to clean up the severely polluted bay. He wrote the successful law that required President Ronald Reagan to get congressional approval before sending troops to Central America.

PERSONAL: elected 1982; born, June 7, 1943, in Los Angeles; home, Los Angeles; education, A.B. UC Berkeley 1964, M.P.A. Princeton University 1966, J.D. Harvard University 1969; wife Jan, three children; Jewish.

CAREER: attorney, 1969-71 and 1973-77; legislative assistant to U.S. Sen. John Tunney, 1971-73; California assemblyman 1977-82.

COMMITTEES: Foreign Affairs; Interior and Insular Affairs; Judiciary; (Select) Narcotics Abuse and Control.

OFFICES: Suite 2443, Rayburn Building, Washington, D.C. 20515, (202) 225-6451, FAX (202) 225-6975; district, Suite 447, 5250 Century Blvd., Los Angeles 90045, (213) 410-9415.

REGISTRATION: 54% D, 34% R

1990 CAMPAIGN: Levine - D	57%	$1,496,790
David Cohen - R	37%	$148,295
1988 CAMPAIGN: Levine - D	68%	$398,597
Dennis Galbraith - R	30%	$15,239

RATINGS:	ADA	ACU	AFL/CIO	LCV	NCSC	NTU	USCC
	100%	5%	90%	78%	97%	35%	29%

Vote on H.J. Res. 77 authorizing war with Iraq: Yes.

Julian C. Dixon (D)
28th Congressional District

Through the 1980s, Democrats controlled the House of Representatives, but not its Committee on Standards of Official Conduct, better known as the ethics committee. That was the fiefdom of Rep. Julian Dixon, and Dixon is his own man. Though a party loyalist on most issues, Dixon is aggressively non-partisan when it comes to issues of right and wrong. And that's true whether the subject of the investigation is someone as obscure as Rep. Jim Weaver of Oregon (who speculated in commodities with campaign funds) or as powerful as Speaker Jim Wright of Texas (whose tangled financial deals eventually drove him from office and whose investigation gave Dixon his first taste of national notoriety).

No sooner did the committee finish with the Wright investigation than it began its first investigation of a fellow California Democrat, Rep. Jim Bates, who was found guilty by the committee in October 1989 of sexually harassing staff members. Bates was defeated the following year just as Dixon was giving up the chairmanship. Normally, the ethics chairman rotates every six years. But Dixon established such a strong reputation for fairness that colleagues prevailed upon him to stay on for most of the decade.

He showed the same temperament when chairing the Democratic convention's platform committee in 1984. Dixon, who is black, also won't allow race to color his judgment. As a member of the District of

Julian Dixon

Columbia Committee, he's demanded accountability by the city's black leadership. He also showed no hesitation to brand Yassir Arafat a terrorist at a time when the Rev. Jesse Jackson was comparing the PLO's struggle to the battle for racial equity in this country. In all things, Dixon is a conciliator and a fact-finder. Those are qualities he's used effectively to defuse antagonisms between Jewish and black communities in the Los Angeles area.

Dixon's district, the second-most Democratic in the state, is the home of many of Los Angeles' middle-and upper-middle-class blacks. There are middle-class white and Hispanic portions, too. All seem to coexist in relative harmony. But street gang warfare in recent years is threatening the stability of the area. The 28th lies on the floor of the Los Angeles basin between downtown and the Los Angeles International Airport. The main communities are Inglewood, Culver City and Ladera Heights.

Dixon, a former state legislator, is allied with the Berman-Waxman organization in local politics and has been tabbed by the group to run for the Los Angeles County Board of Supervisors if and when the legendary Kenneth Hahn retires from his south-central Los Angeles County supervisor post.

PERSONAL: elected, 1978; born Aug. 8, 1934, in Washington, D.C.; home, Culver City; education, B.S. Los Angeles State College 1962, L.L.B. Southwestern University 1967; wife Betty, one child; Episcopalian.

CAREER: U.S. Army, 1957-60; Attorney, 1967-73; Assembly, 1972-78.

COMMITTEES: Appropriations.

OFFICES: Suite 2400, Rayburn Building, Washington, D.C. 20515, (202) 225-7084. FAX (202) 225-4091; district, Suite 208, 5100 West Goldleaf Circle, Los Angeles 90056, (213) 678-5424.

REGISTRATION: 72% D, 19% R

1990 CAMPAIGN:		
Dixon - D	73%	$161,900
George Adams - R	22%	$6,600

1988 CAMPAIGN: Dixon - D   76% $114,523
                   George Adams - R   20% $0

RATINGS:

ADA	ACU	AFL/CIO	LCV	NCSC	NTU	USCC
100%	4%	97%	78%	98%	32%	26%

Vote on H.J. Res. 77 authorizing war with Iraq: No.

Maxine Waters (D)
29th Congressional District

At the heart of California's most heavily Demo-cratic district is Watts, scene of the infamous riots of the mid-1960s. Then, as now, the issues are poverty, crime, drugs, lack of community facilities and sub-standard housing. But there's a newer element – street gangs. The area was mostly black when Watts was burning nearly a quarter century ago. Now, there are more Hispanics, and the two cultures collide nightly in vicious gang warfare. The conflict is not all racial, however. It's often black against black or brown against brown in battles where crack cocaine figures prominently as the cause – or at least as a co-conspirator.

Maxine Waters

The district also takes in working-class neighbor-hoods in Huntington Park, South Gate and Downey. From 1934 to 1990, the man who represented the area first in the Assembly and then in Congress was Augustus Hawkins. The black Claude Pepper, as he was called, worked tirelessly – although often anonymously – on behalf of low-income and disadvantaged people.

When he announced his retirement at age 83, it was a foregone conclusion that Assemblywoman Maxine Waters would replace him. She shares Hawkins fervor for the downtrodden, but her style is decidedly different. Many Assembly col-leagues of both parties made no secret of their joy to see her leave.

Waters is a brassy bundle of energy who approaches most issues with a firmly closed mind. Facts don't interest her, only preconceived notions. Around the state Capitol, she was known as "Mama Doc" for her absolutist approach to politics. Always strident, sometimes yelling, "She has a tongue that could open a wall safe," a colleague said. When Rep. Dan Lungren was trying unsuccessfully to win confirmation as state treasurer, Waters openly baited other minorities who testified in his behalf. But with Speaker Willie Brown as her mentor, Waters could get away with almost anything.

No one has ever accused Waters of shirking work, however. She grew up in poverty and began her career as a Head Start teacher and civic organizer in Watts. She was an aide to Los Angeles City Councilman David Cunningham before winning her Assembly seat in 1976. Thanks to Brown, Waters held key committee appointments that gave her the clout to wage war for "my constituency," as she calls it: the poor, the non-white and women. She had a fair number of successes. But there doubtless would have been many more if it had not been for her caustically combative style. Republicans tended to vote against almost any Waters bill simply because she was the author.

Along the way, Waters established herself as a player in national politics, one of an inner circle of advisers to Jesse Jackson and his 1984 and '88 campaigns for the presidency. She was instrumental in persuading Willie Brown to become Jackson's national campaign chairman in 1988.

But Waters' close ties to Brown backfired for both in 1986. At her behest, Brown anointed her son, Ed, as the Democratic candidate in another Assembly district in southern Los Angeles County – one not nearly as Democratic nor as black as her own. Young Waters was badly defeated in a district that the Democrats should have won, and did win, two years later with another candidate. To Maxine Waters' credit, she paid off her son's campaign debts.

Waters has no mentor of Brown's caliber in the House, but she went there already well known to members of the Black Caucus. If she antagonizes as many people in Washington as she did in Sacramento, some long knives are likely to be out for her. But Waters seems unconcerned. "I'm just me and I won't change," she has said.

PERSONAL: elected 1990; born Aug. 15, 1938, in St. Louis, Mo.; home, Los Angeles; education, B.A. CSU Los Angeles; husband Sidney Williams, three children.

CAREER: Head Start teacher; chief deputy to Los Angeles City Councilman David Cunningham, 1973-76; partner in a public relations firm; assemblywoman, 1976-90.

COMMITTEES: Banking, Finance and Urban Affairs; Veterans' Affairs.

OFFICES: Suite 1207 Longworth Building, Washington, D.C. 20515. (202) 225-2201, FAX (202) 225-7854; district, 4509 S. Broadway, Los Angeles 90037, (213) 233-0733.

REGISTRATION: 82% D, 12% R

1990 CAMPAIGN: Waters - D		80%	$740,793
Bill De Witt - R		18%	$0
1988 CAMPAIGN: Augustus Hawkins - D		83%	$65,833
Reuben Franco - R		14%	$4,629

RATINGS: None as of this writing.

Vote on H.J. Res. 77 authorizing war with Iraq: No.

Matthew G. Martinez (D)
30th Congressional District

After the 1980 census, the late Rep. Phil Burton set out to draw two Hispanic districts in Los Angeles County. As a result, the 30th and 34th districts look like something left on the floor of a pretzel bakery. At the 30th's southern tip are the factory and warehouse areas of Bell Gardens and Commerce. It twists through Monterey Park, Alhambra and San Gabriel, then northeasterly, taking in parts of El Monte, Baldwin Park and Azusa.

The district becomes more affluent the further north one travels. The neighborhoods are heavily Hispanic but there are growing numbers of Koreans, Chinese and other Asians who own many of the retail businesses along the crowded thoroughfares.

On paper, the district should be fairly safe Democratic turf. But it hasn't turned out that way. Many of the upwardly mobile Hispanics and Asians appear to have left their Democratic roots in poorer neighbor-

Matthew Martinez

hoods. They're ticket-splitters and often favor candidates who promise less government intervention in their lives. And then there's their congressmen, Matthew Martinez, who seems to have trouble relating to the constituency. He's had a series of difficult primaries and runoffs. Even against an unknown in 1986, he carried only 63 percent of the vote.

Some claim Martinez is simply a creation of Rep. Howard Berman and never would have gained public office without the Berman-Waxman organization's cash and campaign moxie. Berman plucked Martinez from obscurity to run against an incumbent assemblyman, Jack Fenton, during a nasty Assembly leadership battle in 1980, then boosted him into Congress just two years later.

Whatever his political origins, Martinez has been a less-than-impressive political figure. A California Magazine survey rated him the dimmest bulb in the delegation and one of the five worst representatives overall, someone who makes little impact even on his own district.

PERSONAL: elected 1982; born Feb. 14, 1929, in Walsenburg, Colo.; home, Monterey Park; education, attended Los Angeles Trade Technical School; divorced; Roman Catholic.

CAREER: U.S. Marine Corps, 1947-50; upholstery shop owner, 1957-82; Monterey Park City Council, 1974-76; mayor, 1976-80; Assembly, 1980-82.

COMMITTEES: Education and Labor; Government Operations; (Select) Children, Youth and Families.

OFFICES: Suite 2446, Rayburn Building, Washington, D.C. 20515, (202) 225-5464, FAX (202) 225-5467; district, 400 N. Montebello Blvd., Montebello 90640, (213) 722-7731.

REGISTRATION: 58% D, 31% R

1990 CAMPAIGN:	Martinez - D	59%	$209,495
	Reuben Franco - R	36%	$72,572
1988 CAMPAIGN:	Martinez - D	60%	$460,622
	Ralph Ramirez - R	36%	$382,111

RATINGS: ADA   ACU   AFL/CIO   LCV   NCSC   NTU   USCC
                 78%   6%   98%   72%   98%   37%   24%

Vote on H.J. Res. 77 authorizing war with Iraq: No.

Mervyn M. Dymally (D)
31st Congressional District

Mervyn Dymally

The 31st District sprawls on both sides of the Harbor Freeway south of the Los Angeles city limits. It contains the gang-infested areas of Compton and Willowbrook, and the aging suburbs of Lynwood, Paramount and Bellflower, plus a sizable chunk of Gardena. About half of its population is black or Hispanic. There has been a noticeable influx of Asians in the last decade. And there are still sizable white neighborhoods in Bellflower and Gardena.The district is solidly Democratic, so much so that Rep. Mervyn Dymally doesn't need to spend much time there. In fact, he doesn't spend much time in Congress either. Year after year, he's one of the best-traveled members of House, often mixing into Third World politics in places as far flung as Micronesia, Ivory Coast and his native Trinidad. Meanwhile, his legislative accomplishments are almost nil despite the fact that he chairs the Foreign Affairs subcommittee on Africa.

Often there's an odor to Dymally's activities. Suggestions that he was involved in corruption of the state's Medi-Cal system led to his defeat by Mike Curb after one term as lieutenant governor, but nothing was ever proven. He often accepts, some say solicits, free trips from special interests. One such trip in 1989 involved a visit to Uganda, where he tried to persuade the government to hire a friend and campaign contributor as an agent for U.S. aid sent to the country. Dymally, however, usually contends that his critics are motivated by racism and greed.

Dymally won the seat in 1980 in one of the most dramatic comebacks seen in California in recent years. He took almost half the vote in the primary despite the fact that two ex-congressmen were among his four opponents. He's won easily ever since, and it seems nothing short of a conviction could boot him out.

PERSONAL: elected 1980; born May 12, 1926, in Cedros, Trinidad; home, Compton; education, B.A. California State College, Los Angeles B.A. 1954, M.A. 1969, Ph.D. U.S. International University 1978; wife, Alice, two children; Episcopalian.

CAREER: teacher, 1955-61; manager, California Disaster Office, 1961-62; Assembly, 1962-66; state Senate, 1966-75; lieutenant governor, 1975-79.

COMMITTEES: District of Columbia; Foreign Affairs; Post Office and Civil Service.

OFFICES: Suite 1717, Longworth Building, Washington, D.C. 20515, (202) 225-5425, FAX (202) 225-6847; district, 322 West Compton Blvd., Compton 90220, (213) 632-4318.

REGISTRATION: 71% D, 20% R

1990 CAMPAIGN: Dymally - D   68% $434,143

                     Eunice Sato - R   32% $0

1988 CAMPAIGN: Dymally - D   72% $481,799

                     Arnold May - R   26% $10,169

RATINGS:

ADA	ACU	AFL/CIO	LCV	NCSC	NTU	USCC
100%	4%	94%	72%	96%	26%	23%

Vote on H.J. Res. 77 authorizing war with Iraq: Absent.

Glenn M. Anderson (D)
32nd Congressional District

Glenn Anderson

The 32nd District isn't shaped like anything tangible. It lurches from San Pedro through the Democratic areas of Long Beach and Lakewood and then reaches northward to clutch Hawaiian Gardens. The children of Yugoslav and Italian fishermen still inhabit the port areas. The Long Beach and Lakewood portions are a mixture of middle-class white and Hispanic neighborhoods. Hawaiian Gardens is also Hispanic, but Koreans may soon be dominant.

It's an ideal district for Glenn Anderson, whose long career in California politics dates back to 1940. Yet it's unlikely that he'll be back for another term. At age 77, he was ousted from the chairmanship of the Public Works and Transportation Committee in December 1990. The charge was led by a longtime colleague, Rep. Norman Mineta, D-San Jose. Mineta claimed Anderson couldn't get things done at a time when voters were angry with Congress' inaction. And it was said Anderson's memory had slipped so badly that he couldn't run a meeting without his staff writing out everything for him.

As Anderson saw it, his major failing was that he was too democratic. He was the first public works chairman to share power with the heads of his five subcommittees. That slowed things down and gave the appearance of weakness. Nonetheless, Mineta got Anderson out as chairman but he failed in his quest to replace him. The net effect is that California lost the chairmanship of one of the most important pork-barrel committees to New Jersey.

Anderson's long service on the committee had a dramatic impact on port and highway development in south Los Angeles. He also was a good friend of water development interests and mass transit. But under Anderson, it wasn't all pork. He insisted on seeing economic justifications for projects.

Consumer protection is another of his interests. His amendments created a seat-belt law for children and forced states to raise their drinking age to 21 in order to be eligible for federal highway money. Anderson might have been governor had it not been for the Watts riots. Gov. Pat Brown was out of state and Anderson, then lieutenant governor, was blamed for being too slow to send in the National Guard. The next year, both Brown and Anderson were buried by the Ronald Reagan-Ed Reinecke landslide.

Anderson went to Congress two years later.

PERSONAL: elected 1968; born Feb. 21, 1913, in Hawthorne, Calif.; home, San Pedro; education, B.A. UCLA 1936; wife Lee, three children; Episcopalian.

CAREER: mayor of Hawthorne, 1940-43; Assembly 1943 and 1945-51; U.S. Army, 1943-45; lieutenant governor, 1958-67.

COMMITTEE: Public Works and Transportation; Merchant Marine and Fisheries.

OFFICES: Suite 2329, Rayburn Building, Washington, D.C. 20515, (202) 225-6676, FAX (202) 225-1597; district, 300 Long Beach Blvd., Long Beach 90801, (213) 437-7665.

REGISTRATION: 55% D, 35% R

1990 CAMPAIGN:	Anderson - D	62%	$411,845
	Sanford Kahn - R	38%	$7,590
1988 CAMPAIGN:	Anderson - D	67%	$457,410
	Sanford Kahn - R	30%	$20,608

RATINGS:	ADA	ACU	AFL/CIO	LCV	NCSC	NTU	USCC
	94%	20%	83%	50%	89%	26%	28%

Vote on H.J. Res. 77 authorizing war with Iraq: Yes.

David Dreier (R)
33rd Congressional District

Although the lines have been redrawn many times, the 33rd District still contains large areas that Richard Nixon represented in Congress 40 years ago. It takes in Whittier, Nixon's home, then jumps the Puente Hills to include Covina, San Dimas, La Verne, Pomona and Glendora. Whittier is becoming more Hispanic, but no less conservative. Other suburbs are predominantly white, upper middle-class areas where life would be much more pleasing without the air pollution that piles up at the base of the San Gabriel Mountains.

Twenty-eight-year-old Rep. David Dreier went to Congress in 1980 from this area not to make laws, but to undo them. He was a strident foe of government regulation in most of its forms. He has worked for a balanced budget, more federal lands and services in private hands and deregulation of trucking, airlines, pipelines and banking. Some senior Republican colleagues on the Banking Committee find his ideological commitment tedious, but none can argue that he is inconsistent.

Dreier is more reminiscent of the Goldwater Republicans who demanded ideological litmus tests before full acceptance within party ranks. On that score, he's in step with a large faction of his party in California. But his influence spans beyond there. He recruits GOP candidates for congressional races in Western states.

David Dreier

Dreier first beat a complacent incumbent Democrat. Then, in 1982, he defeated Rep. Wayne Grisham when redistricting dumped them both in the new 33rd. He's had phenomenal success as a fund-raiser, but is little known outside his district. Many in conservatives circles thought Dreier would be appointed to the U.S. Senate when Pete Wilson was elected governor in 1990. They must have been bitterly disappointed.

PERSONAL: elected 1980; born July 5, 1952, in Kansas City; home, La Verne; education, B.A. Claremont McKenna College 1975, M.A. 1976; unmarried; Christian Scientist.

CAREER: public relations, Claremont McKenna College, 1975-79; public relations, Industrial Hydrocarbons Corp., 1979-80.

COMMITTEE: Rules.

OFFICES: Suite 411, Cannon Building, Washington, D.C. 20515, (202) 225-2305, FAX (202)-225-4745; district, 112 North Second Ave., Covina 91723, (818) 339-9078.

REGISTRATION: 42% D, 48% R

1990 CAMPAIGN: Dreier - R   63% $591,313

                Georgia Webb - D   32% $29,612

1988 CAMPAIGN: Dreier - R   69% $186,183

                Nelson Gentry - D   26% $0

RATINGS:

ADA	ACU	AFL/CIO	LCV	NCSC	NTU	USCC
17%	95%	1%	50%	5%	60%	92%

Vote on H.J. Res. 77 authorizing war with Iraq: Yes.

Esteban E. Torres (D)
34th Congressional District

This is another of the districts drawn by the late Rep. Phil Burton to ensure Hispanic representation in Southern California. Slightly more than half of the residents have Hispanic surnames in an area that 30 years ago was almost exclusively white suburbs. The district also has a higher concentration of families than any other in California.

The 34th District straddles the San Gabriel River southwest of Los Angeles. Pico Rivera, Baldwin Park, La Puente and the City of Industry lie in the northern section.

To the south are South Whittier, Santa Fe Springs and Norwalk. Many of the residents work in aerospace, manufacturing, refinery and government jobs, and two-income families are common. Defense cutbacks have hit hard in the area. A growing number of Asians are taking over the retail shops that clutter the main streets. Most voters are traditionally Democratic, but conservative and committed to family values. Their congressman, Esteban Torres, shares those family concerns and is strongly anti-abortion. But on most other matters, he's stridently liberal. His preoccupation with the welfare of Third World countries and encouraging large social programs from Washington doesn't play particularly well in this district.

Esteban Torres

That helps explain why he's had well-financed challengers from time to time. Torres helps compensate for his more-liberal-than-the-district views by campaigning almost non-stop from election to election. He's constantly in the district, attending community gatherings, visiting nursing homes and assisting Democratic hopefuls at other levels. One of his latest causes has been the seriously polluted water table in the San Gabriel Valley. The issue has given him a lot of visibility, but meaningful cleanup is probably impossible.

Torres' staff is considered one of the better in the delegation. And he also has another ace in hand, the fund-raising support of the Berman-Waxman machine. Like many of the residents, Torres got where he is by working hard and overcoming racial barriers. He went from assembly-line worker to union official, to poverty programs and then on to posts where he could promote his concerns in President Jimmy Carter's administration. He remains committed to government as a force in improving social interaction in society. The district seems to be moving away from that orientation, but not quickly enough to threaten Torres' tenure.

PERSONAL: elected 1982; born Jan. 30, 1930, in Miami, Ariz.; home, La Puente; education, A.A. East Los Angeles Community College 1959, B.A. CSU Los Angeles 1963, graduate work at the University of Maryland and American University; wife Arcy, five children; no religious affiliation.

CAREER: U.S. Army, 1949-53; assembly-line worker, Chrysler Corp., 1953-63; United Auto Workers representative, 1963-68; director, East Los Angeles Community Union, 1968-74; UAW representative, 1974-77; ambassador to UNESCO, 1977-79; special assistant to President Jimmy Carter, 1979-81; president, International Enterprise and Development Corp, 1981-82.

COMMITTEES: Banking, Finance and Urban Affairs; Small Business.

OFFICES: Suite 1740, Longworth Building, Washington, D.C. 20515, (202) 225-5256, FAX (202) 225-9711; district, Suite 101, 8819 Whittier Blvd., Pico Rivera 90660, (213) 695-0702, (818) 961-3978.

REGISTRATION: 61% D, 31% R

1990 CAMPAIGN:	Torres - D	61%	$241,635
	John Eastman - R	39%	$75,581
1988 CAMPAIGN:	Torres - D	63%	$227,098
	Charles House - R	35%	$149,886

RATINGS:

ADA	ACU	AFL/CIO	LCV	NCSC	NTU	USCC
89%	2%	98%	89%	98%	35%	25%

Vote on H.J. Res. 77 authorizing war with Iraq: No.

Jerry Lewis (R)
35th Congressional District

In an extremely short period of time by congressional standards, Rep. Jerry Lewis has risen to the
most important leadership role among California's
Republicans. As chairman of the House Republican
Conference, Lewis is the third-ranking member of
his party. He serves as a spokesman and strategist,
and more often than not carries his party's position on
the Appropriations Committee.

Jerry Lewis

At one time, the ex-assemblyman flirted with
statewide races. In 1989, he tried unsuccessfully to
move up to minority whip in the House. He remains
popular with his colleagues, however, and is still
young enough to win a higher leadership post one
day. Lewis is the ranking Republican on the legisla-
tive subcommittee of Appropriations chaired by fellow Californian Vic Fazio.
They've become one of the best bipartisan teams in Congress by seeing to it that
ideological concerns don't clutter their relationship. They know where they can
agree and where they can't. No breath is wasted trying to score philosophical points.

Soon after coming to Congress, Lewis established himself as an intellectual force
in his party. His work was soon noticed on the Republican Research Committee,
which turns out articulate reports on policy positions for the GOP. By 1985, he was
its chairman. He has worked to reshape U.S. contributions to the International
Monetary Fund and the World Bank so that there is more accountability in loans to
Third World countries. And he played a role in stopping the Reagan administration
from weakening the Clean Air Act, a law that is extremely important in smog-
burdened portions of his district. That and other centrist positions didn't sit well with
conservative members of the state GOP caucus. In 1991, they had gained enough
strength in the delegation to bounce Lewis as the California representative on the
Committee on Committees. Rep. Ron Packard took his place and now has the job
of deciding which committee assignments California Republicans get.

Most of Lewis' constituents are packed into the southwest corner of his district around San Bernardino, Chino, Upland, Redlands and Loma Linda. From there, the district stretches across the Mojave Desert all the way to Needles on the Arizona line. Some of the desert areas, however, are growing very fast – particularly around Victorville. Retirees are a growing force in the 35th as are young families who've been forced eastward by housing prices in Los Angeles and Orange counties. To the south, the district stretches into the Big Bear resort area. Lewis wins easily every two years and he is frequently mentioned as a potential 1992 U.S. Senate candidate.

PERSONAL: elected, 1978; born Oct. 21, 1934, in Seattle, Wash.; home, Redlands; education, B.A. UCLA 1956; wife Arlene, seven children; Presbyterian.

CAREER: insurance agent and manager, 1959-78; field representative to Rep. Jerry Pettis, 1968; San Bernardino School Board, 1965-68; Assembly, 1968-78.

COMMITTEE: Appropriations.

OFFICES: Suite 2312, Rayburn Building, Washington, D.C. 20515, (202) 225-5861, FAX (202) 225-6498; district, Suite 104, 1826 Orange Tree Lane., Redlands 92373, (714) 862-6030.

REGISTRATION: 38% D, 52% R

1990 CAMPAIGN:	Lewis - R	60%	$452,381
	Barry Norton - D	33%	$0
1988 CAMPAIGN:	Lewis - R	70%	$337,814
	Paul Sweeney - D	28%	$0

RATINGS:	ADA	ACU	AFL/CIO	LCV	NCSC	NTU	USCC
	6%	85%	14%	22%	19%	39%	79%

Vote on H.J. Res. 77 authorizing war with Iraq: Yes.

George E. Brown Jr. (D)
36th Congressional District

Districts may change, but not Rep. George Brown. One of the House's oldest peaceniks, Brown continues to champion liberal causes despite dramatic gains in his district's Republican registration and non-stop efforts by GOP candidates to unseat him. The cigar-chomping Brown comes from Quaker stock and is both a physicist and nuclear engineer. He was talking about global warming and the virtues of solar energy long before it was fashionable.

In 1991 Brown became chairman of the Science, Space and Technology Committee, where he was expected to join Rep. George Miller of Interior in refashioning national energy policy. In 1987 Brown quit the Intelligence Committee, saying he couldn't

George Brown

live with the committee's gag rules on topics that are general knowledge elsewhere.

Brown's long career in the House began in 1962. In 1970, he nearly won the

Democratic U.S. Senate primary and probably could have dumped GOP Sen. George Murphy. But that privilege went to neighboring House member John Tunney instead. Brown sat out for two years and was re-elected, but he returned to the House without those eight years of precious seniority.

He represents a district far different from the one that first sent him to Congress. It's been reshaped a half-dozen times in an effort to stave off Republican encroachment. Monterey Park, where Brown was first elected to public office in 1954, is 20 miles from the district's nearest border. Today, Brown has the industrial sections of Colton, Rialto and Fontana, the city of Ontario, and Democratic areas of Riverside and San Bernardino. Many of the people living in those smog-choked cities are there for lack of choices. They include many blue collar and older people who can't afford to move to more pleasant environs.

In other areas where there were once fields and orange groves, stucco subdivisions are peopled with young families who tend to be economic conservatives. An increasing number of them are upwardly mobile Hispanics. Many of these newcomers hope to have enough home equity in a few years to move elsewhere. Fortunately for Brown, many of the latter don't get around to voting. If they did, they'd be more likely to vote Republican.

Republicans might have more success against Brown if they'd quit throwing candidates from the far-right against him. Brown, however, is good on the stump, has an excellent staff and is a superb fund-raiser. Even with a more mainstream Republican opponent, those are hard pluses to overcome.

PERSONAL: elected in 1962 and served until 1971, re-elected in 1972; born March 6, 1920, in Holtville, Calif.; home, Riverside; education, B.A. UCLA 1946; wife Marta, four children; United Methodist.

CAREER: U.S. Army, 1942-45; Monterey Park City Council, 1954-58, mayor 1955-56; engineer and management consultant, city of Los Angeles, 1946-58; Assembly 1958-62.

COMMITTEES: Agriculture; chairman, Science, Space and Technology.

OFFICES: Suite 2188, Rayburn Building, Washington, D.C. 20515, (202) 225-6161, FAX (202) 225-8671; district, 657 La Cadena Dr., Colton 92324, (714) 825-2472; Suite 116, 3600 Lime St., Riverside 92502, (714) 686-8863.

REGISTRATION: 53% D, 38% R

1990 CAMPAIGN: Brown - D		53%	$818,181
Bob Hammock - R		47%	$538,281
1988 CAMPAIGN: Brown - D		54%	$532,897
John Stark - R		43%	$218,696

RATINGS: ADA	ACU	AFL/CIO	LCV	NCSC	NTU	USCC
89%	5%	90%	61%	95%	32%	22%

Vote on H.J. Res. 77 authorizing war with Iraq: No.

Alfred A. McCandless (R)
37th Congressional District

This fastest-growing district in California takes in all the Republican areas of Riverside County that Rep. George Brown didn't want. It stretches from the city of Riverside through Moreno Valley and Banning, and on to the lavish desert communities of Palm Springs and Palm Desert. From there, it's on to Indio and the rich farmlands of the Coachella Valley, then across the scorching desert to Blythe.

The Palm Springs area is home to many movie stars and retired captains of industry, plus former President Jerry Ford and ex-Vice President Spiro Agnew. But there are many less-well-off retirees living in condos and fading trailers. The service-sector is dominated by Hispanics, many of whom travel some distance to their low-paying jobs.

Alfred McCandless

Their congressman is a desert native, Rep. Al McCandless, who was once a General Motors dealer in Indio. McCandless is one of the most conservative members of the delegation. Outside his district, he's probably best known for the video privacy bill he authored after a keyhole reporter got hold of Judge Robert Bork's rental list during his unsuccessful Supreme Court confirmation bid. McCandless has shown interest in legislation benefiting handicapped people but devotes most of his time to mustering "no" votes on any bill with an appropriation.

McCandless got a scare in 1990 when actor Ralph Waite (TV's Papa Walton) of Rancho Mirage became the Democratic nominee. Waite is well positioned for another race in 1992. That may be enough to encourage McCandless to retire.

PERSONAL: elected 1982; born July 23, 1927, in Brawley, Calif.; home, La Quinta; B.A. UCLA 1951; wife Gail, five children; Protestant.

CAREER: U.S. Marine Corps, 1945-46 and 1950-52; auto dealer, 1953-75; Riverside County Supervisor, 1970-82.

COMMITTEES: Banking, Finance and Urban Affairs; Government Operations.

OFFICES: Suite 2422, Rayburn Building, Washington, D.C. 20515, (202) 225-5330; district, Suite 165, 6529 Riverside Ave., Riverside 92506, (714) 682-7127; Suite A-7, 75-075 El Paseo, Palm Desert 92260, (619) 340-2900.

REGISTRATION: 43% D, 48% R

1990 CAMPAIGN:	McCandless - R	50%	$551,786
	Ralph Waite - D	45%	$622,159
1988 CAMPAIGN:	McCandless - R	64%	$122,839
	Johnny Pearson - D	33%	$13,558

RATINGS: ADA   ACU   AFL/CIO   LCV   NCSC   NTU   USCC
        6%   90%   3%   11%   10%   61%   89%
Vote on H.J. Res. 77 authorizing war with Iraq: Yes.

Robert K. Dornan (R)
38th Congressional District

In Orange County, it seems appropriate that a congressional district would have freeways for boundaries. The 38th is one of the most intensely congested areas of Southern California. Rush-hour gridlocks are routine and residents have come to support the idea of building toll roads to separate the rich from the riffraff. The district begins at the Los Angeles County line and trends to the southeast between the Santa Ana and San Diego freeways. It ends at the Newport Freeway.

Robert Dornan

The area, as the name suggests, was once covered with orange groves. After World War II, it became a lily-white, conservative bedroom community. The construction of Disneyland in the 1950s the area a world destination, but few attitudes changed. In the 1950s and '60s, there were more John Birch Society memberships in Orange County than in all other California counties combined. The '70s saw an influx of Vietnamese, a few more Hispanics and the decline of some neighborhoods, especially in the Garden Grove area. Today, there are more Vietnamese in the 38th than any other district in the nation.

The congressman who carries the torch for many of the lingering Bircher attitudes is Robert "B-1 Bob" Dornan, the flamboyant, sometimes profane former fighter pilot who never saw a defense appropriation he didn't like. Many people underestimate Dornan. They argue that a man who bases his campaigns on shrillness, hate and character assassination can't go too far. Yet he shows remarkable staying power and fund-raising ability.

When Democrats couldn't defeat Dornan in an ocean-front Los Angeles County district, the late Phil Burton gerrymandered the district in 1982 so that Dornan couldn't be re-elected. (Rep. Mel Levine has the district now.) Undaunted, Dornan raised $1 million for an unsuccessful U.S. Senate primary race against Pete Wilson instead. He then moved south to the 38th, took on five-term Democrat Jerry Patterson in 1984 and won.

The 38th, nominally a Democratic district after the 1982 gerrymandering, was by 1984 one of the first congressional district in the nation where Vietnamese immigrants made an obvious difference. Dornan is their hero, the American who would restart the Vietnamese War if he could. In subsequent elections, even well-financed campaigns haven't been able to dislodge him.

Dornan introduces legislation, but little of it goes anywhere. Despite his identity with the long struggle to approve the B-1 bomber, others get most of the credit for getting it off the ground. Dornan is one of the most widely traveled members of Congress. Some of the junkets, to his credit, have helped close MIA and POW cases from the war years. He also brags that he's piloted every aircraft in the American defense arsenal plus some from Israel, England and France.

Wives of congressmen don't often make news outside their husband's districts, but Sallie Dornan became an exception in 1988 when she announced – wrongly – that her brother had AIDS. Dornan is fervently anti-gay, but he has shown compassion for AIDS victims and has voted for increased funding for medical research.

Dornan helped influence national policy in 1985 when he became the first die-hard conservative to endorse George Bush for the presidency. Before then, many conservatives had questioned whether Bush was "Republican enough." Dornan seconded Bush's nomination at the Republican National Convention, chaired Veterans for Bush and was co-chairman of Bush's California campaign. Many thought Dornan would get a prominent post in the administration. But the Bush administration had not called by 1991.

PERSONAL: elected 1976 and served until 1983, re-elected 1984; born April 3, 1933, in New York City; home, Garden Grove; education, attended Loyola University, Los Angeles; wife Sallie, five children; Roman Catholic.

CAREER: U.S. Air Force, 1953-58; broadcaster and TV talk-show host, 1965-73; president, American Space Frontier PAC, 1983-88.

COMMITTEES: Armed Services; (Select) Intelligence; Narcotics Abuse and Control.

OFFICES: Suite 301, Cannon Building, Washington, D.C. 20515, (202) 225-2965, FAX (202) 225-3694; district, Suite 360, 300 Plaza Alicante, Garden Grove 92642, (714) 971-9292.

REGISTRATION: 47% D, 43% R

1990 CAMPAIGN: Dornan - R		58%	$1,615,282
Barbara Jackson - D		42%	$0
1988 CAMPAIGN: Dornan - R		60%	$1,755,892
Jerry Yudelson - D		36%	$186,892

RATINGS:	ADA	ACU	AFL/CIO	LCV	NCSC	NTU	USCC
	6%	97%	9%	6%	7%	56%	86%

Vote on H.J. Res. 77 authorizing war with Iraq: Yes.

William E. Dannemeyer (R)
39th Congressional District

The safest Republican turf in California is unquestionably the 39th District, which takes in the center and eastern end of Orange County. This birthplace and launch pad for Richard Nixon is synonymous with conservative Republican values.

Although Democrats have made some inroads locally, the 39th turns in the highest percentage of GOP votes in each statewide election. Many of those votes come from the district's major towns, Fullerton, Anaheim and Orange.

Despite the extreme partisanship that characterizes the 39th, the district has sent some excellent legislators to Washington. But William Dannemeyer, the current congressman, isn't one of them. Though Dannemeyer calls himself a champion of free enterprise, Money Magazine gave him an F grade for his 1989-90 votes on measures important to investors.

William Dannemeyer

Even many of Dannemeyer's fellow conservatives are embarrassed by his right-wing pronouncements that resemble those of extremist Lyndon LaRouche. That's one of the reasons it took Dannemeyer a long time to win major committee assignments. There's no doubt that he gets popular support in the district for his stands against abortion and homosexuality, on prayer in the schools and to allow parents to block teaching of evolution in classrooms. But his punitive AIDS measure on the statewide ballot in 1988 lost even in his own district.

Dannemeyer says he's just trying to make the world safe from the AIDS scourge. Its victims release "spores" that spread the disease, he claims. To his credit, Dannemeyer has introduced some public health measures of value. But most of his AIDS rhetoric is intertwined with gay bashing ("God's plan for man is Adam and Eve, not Adam and Steve"), something he seems to relish. Dannemeyer loves to dwell on deviant sexual practices. At the GOP state convention in 1989, he introduced an anti-gay measure that described seamy sexual acts in detail. With Rep. Bob Dornan, he embarrassed the party leadership with unsuccessful resolutions to drive all gays out of the GOP.

Dannemeyer is one of many conservatives who were outraged when Gov. Pete Wilson chose state Sen. John Seymour as his replacement in the U.S. Senate. They've never forgiven Seymour for switching from pro-life to pro-choice. Dannemeyer has since announced that he'll challenge Seymour in 1992.

Some Democrats recall that Dannemeyer was once one of theirs. He served two Assembly terms as a Democrat, but switched parties and lost a state Senate race. Later, he came back to the Assembly as a one-term Republican before going to Congress.

PERSONAL: elected 1978; born Sept. 22, 1929, in Los Angeles; home, Fullerton; education, attended Santa Maria Junior College 1946-47, B.A. Valparaiso University 1950, J.D. UC Hastings Law School 1952; wife Evelyn, three children; Lutheran (Missouri Synod).

CAREER: U.S. Army, 1953-54; attorney, 1954-55; deputy district attorney,

1955-57; assistant city attorney, Fullerton, 1959-62; Assembly 1963-66; municipal and superior court judge, 1966-76; Assembly 1976-77.

COMMITTEES: Energy and Commerce; Budget.

OFFICES: Suite 2351, Rayburn Building, Washington, D.C. 20515, (202) 225-4111, FAX (202) 225-1755; district, Suite 100, 1235 North Harbor Blvd., Fullerton 92632, (714) 992-0141.

REGISTRATION: 33% D, 58% R

1990 CAMPAIGN: Dannemeyer – R	65%	$594,692
Francis Hoffman - D	31%	$0
1988 CAMPAIGN: Dannemeyer - R	74%	$250,737
Don Marquis - D	23%	$2,893

| **RATINGS**: | ADA | ACU | AFL/CIO | LCV | NCSC | NTU | USCC |
| | 6% | 96% | 5% | 17% | 6% | 72% | 86% |

Vote on H.J. Res. 77 authorizing war with Iraq: Yes.

Christopher Cox (R)
40th Congressional District

Packed along the northern end of the Orange County coast is an almost unbroken line of artsy villages, walled housing tracts and shimmering glass office buildings. Yachts and pleasure boats clog the shoreline for miles. As one moves south, development is less dense but equally presumptuous. Inland a bit are the Laguna Hills, where mountain lions still roam, and the vast holdings of the Irvine Co. From top to bottom, the district is wealthy Republican country and conservative as only Orange County can be.

In the 1970s and '80s, the area became almost a second downtown Los Angeles as companies established regional offices and research parks amid acres of parking lots. The district's well-traveled and lack-

Christopher Cox

luster congressman, Robert Badham, hung it up in 1988. The race to replace him was decided in the GOP primary (general elections are perfunctory exercises here) as 14 conservatives vied for attention and votes. The one who emerged by garnering 31 percent of the vote was one of the most interesting, attorney Chris Cox.

Cox, making his first try for public office, had a solid background. He was a Harvard lecturer with strong links to the corporate world, and he also had been a White House counsel. That impressed district residents, but probably not as much as personal campaign appearances on Cox's behalf by Oliver North, Robert Bork and Arthur Laffer. The GOP delegation saw to it that Cox got good committee assignments. Now it will be interesting to see what he does with them.

PERSONAL: elected 1988; born Oct. 16, 1952, in St. Paul, Minn.; home,

Newport; education, B.A. USC 1973, M.B.A., J.D. Harvard University 1977; single; Roman Catholic.

CAREER: attorney, 1978-86; lecturer, Harvard Business School, 1982-83; White House counsel, 1986-88.

COMMITTEES: Government Operations; Public Works and Transportation. OFFICES: Suite 412, Cannon Building, Washington, D.C. 20515, (202) 225-5611, FAX (202) 225-9177; district, Suite 430, 4000 MacArthur Blvd., Newport Beach 92660, (714) 644-4040.

REGISTRATION: 30% D, 59% R

1990 CAMPAIGN:	Cox - R	67%	$688,836
	Eugene Gratz - D	33%	$43,277
1988 CAMPAIGN:	Cox - R	67%	$1,110,126
	Lida Lenney - D	30%	$47,746

RATINGS:

ADA	ACU	AFL/CIO	LCV	NCSC	NTU	USCC
11%	96%	4%	61%	10%	56%	87%

Vote on H.J. Res. 77 authorizing war with Iraq: Yes.

Bill Lowery (R)
41st Congressional District

Northern San Diego and its suburbs have traditionally been a Republican stronghold. It's a favorite retirement place for Navy people and boasts some of the finest weather in the United States. In La Jolla, Pacific Beach and Mission Bay, many of the lavish homes don't have air conditioning because the nearby ocean supplies naturally cooled air. Democrats who work at the Scripps Institute or in service-sector jobs usually can't afford to live in the district. They commute from the smoggy towns up the Mission Valley or from working-class areas of central and south San Diego.

Bill Lowery

One might expect the district's congressman to be an archconservative, but Rep. Bill Lowery is a protege of Gov. Pete Wilson and a moderate in most things, except defense matters. He's also one of the most conservation-oriented Republicans in the delegation – at least on district issues. That is appreciated in an area where local environmental issues tend to be non-partisan. When it comes to national environmental issues, however, his votes are more traditionally Republican.

Like Wilson, Lowery is an opponent of offshore oil drilling. In 1989, he was instrumental in negotiating not only a one-year extension of the offshore drilling ban in California, but also for the first time got a delay on prelease activities by oil companies. Lowery worries about endangered song birds and has worked to resolve the problem of sewage coming across the border in the Tijuana River even though the most fetid impact is not in his district. He's also in a position to help the Navy from his seat on the military construction subcommittee of Appropriations.

There are some signs that Lowery may be growing restless. Whenever future San Diego mayors are discussed, he is usually high on the list of possible candidates.

PERSONAL: elected 1980; born May 2, 1947, in San Diego; home, San Diego; education, B.A. San Diego State University 1969; wife Katie, three children; Roman Catholic.

CAREER: public relations 1973-77; San Diego City Council 1977-80, deputy mayor 1979-80.

COMMITTEES: Appropriations.

OFFICES: Suite 2433, Rayburn Building, Washington, D.C. 20515, (202) 225-3201, FAX (202) 225-6176; Suite 6-S-15, 880 Front St., San Diego 92188, (619) 231-0957.

REGISTRATION: 37% D, 49% R

1990 CAMPAIGN:	Lowery - R	49%	$485,964
	Dan Kripke - D	44%	$65,546
1988 CAMPAIGN:	Lowery - R	66%	$407,025
	Dan Kripke - D	31%	$45,311

RATINGS:	ADA	ACU	AFL/CIO	LCV	NCSC	NTU	USCC
	11%	83%	9%	33%	13%	44%	89%

Vote on H.J. Res. 77 authorizing war with Iraq: Yes.

Dana Rohrabacher (R)
42nd Congressional District

One of the late Rep. Phil Burton's chief goals in redistricting Southern California was to provide a safe seat for Democratic Rep. Glenn Anderson in the 32nd District. As a result, the 42nd had to take in pockets of Republican communities that intrude on three sides of Anderson's stronghold. When Burton was through, the 42nd was unquestionably the screwiest-looking district in the state.

The district has two blobs east and west of Los Angeles Harbor connected by a five-mile peninsula across the mouth of the harbor. In some areas, that strip of land is only one-block wide. To the west are the Palos Verdes communities and Torrance, with stately homes and business centers linked to Pacific

Dana Rohrabacher

Rim trade. On the east are Republican areas of Long Beach plus the affluent communities of Seal Beach and Huntington Beach. Politics here aren't as extreme as those of the large Orange County communities, but they remain conservative.

Rep. Dan Lungren was safely spending his time here when Gov. George Deukmejian tapped him to become state treasurer in 1988. But the state Senate denied Lungren the seat, and he moved to Sacramento to mount his successful campaign for attorney general in 1990. That left an opening and, as with most Republican seats, it was all over in the primary. Dana Rohrabacher, one-time editorial writer for the conservative Orange County Register and speech writer for former President Ronald Reagan, emerged from dirty, eight-person race.

Few freshmen attract national attention, but Rohrabacher succeeded in spades. He emerged as Sen. Jesse Helms' chief House ally to prohibit National Endowment for the Arts grants from going to projects they considered to be obscene or sacrilegious. The arts supporters promised a national effort to try and unseat Rohrabacher in 1990, but that fizzled. Rohrabacher has said he will spend no more than 10 years in Congress. So, it looks as if the arts crowd will have to put up with him for four more terms.

PERSONAL: elected 1988; born June 21, 1947, in Corona, Calif.; home, Lomita; B.A. CSU Long Beach 1969; M.A. USC 1971; unmarried; Baptist.

CAREER: journalist, 1970-80; speech writer for President Reagan, 1981-88.

COMMITTEES: District of Columbia; Science, Space and Technology.

OFFICES: Suite 1039, Longworth Building, Washington, D.C. 20515, (202) 225-2415, FAX (202) 225-0145; district, Suite 100, 4332 Cerritos Ave., Los Alamitos 90720, (714)-761-0517; Suite 306, 2733 Pacific Coast Highway, Torrance 90505, (213) 325-0668.

REGISTRATION: 36% D, 53% R

1990 CAMPAIGN:	Rohrabacher - R	59%	$423,924
	Guy Kimbrough -D	37%	$29,555
1988 CAMPAIGN:	Rohrabacher - R	64%	$494,487
	Guy Kimbrough - D	33%	$11,889

RATINGS:	ADA	ACU	AFL/CIO	LCV	NCSC	NTU	USCC
	6%	96%	9%	28%	20%	60%	88%

Vote on H.J. Res. 77 authorizing war with Iraq: Yes.

Ronald C. Packard (R)

43rd Congressional District

Northern San Diego County and a slice of southern Orange County make up the 43rd District. Camp Pendleton Marine Corps Base sprawls though the center. To the north and south are the wealthy coastal towns of San Juan Capistrano, San Clemente, Oceanside and Carlsbad. Inland are pleasant retirement communities and some shabby trailer courts inhabited by GI families and civilian defense workers.

The climate is one of the most ideal in the United States. White, waspy retirees dominate most communities and crowd the golf courses. Spouses of Marines and a few Hispanics are available for the service-sector jobs. Politically, attitudes are in step with hard-core Orange County Republicans to the north. Yet San Clemente homeowners weren't so Republican that they welcomed having the Western White House in their midst during Richard Nixon's presidency. There were many complaints that property values were being hurt. Residents have high educational levels and intense interests in property and private enterprise. Most can afford insurance that liberates them from government health plans.

Ronald C. Packard

Their congressman, however, is anything but a right-wing ideologue. Rep. Ron Packard, a dentist, is a practical man with a commitment to assisting local government. He's taken on thorny problems such as Indian water rights and negotiated a settlement that pleased all sides. He's also made a mark in aircraft safety legislation. In the 101st Congress, Packard became the California representative on the GOP's Committee on Committees which decides assignments for members. That makes him one of the most powerful members of the delegation.

When first elected, Packard was only the fourth person in American history to win a congressional seat in a write-in campaign. In the primary, with 18 contenders running for an open seat, he was second by 92 votes to a businessman named Johnny Crean. Crean spent $500,000 of his own money to convince voters that he was then-President Ronald Reagan's personal choice for the job. Reagan, however, had never heard of him. Packard triumphed in November. Since then he's had easy races.

PERSONAL: elected 1982; born Jan. 19, 1931, in Meridian, Idaho; home, Oceanside; education, attended Brigham Young University and Portland State University, D.M.D. University of Oregon 1957; wife Jean, seven children; Mormon.

CAREER: U.S. Navy 1957-59; dentist, 1957-82; trustee, Carlsbad Unified School District, 1962-74; Carlsbad City Council 1976-78, mayor 1978-82.

COMMITTEES: Public Works and Transportation; Science, Space and Technology.

OFFICES: Suite 434, Cannon Building, Washington, D.C. 20515, (202) 225-3906, FAX (202) 225-0134; district, Suite 105, 2121 Palomar Airport Rd., Carlsbad 92009, (619) 438-0443; Suite 204, 629 Camino de los Mares, San Clemente 92672, (714) 496-2343.

REGISTRATION: 30% D, 56% R

1990 CAMPAIGN:	Packard - R	86%	$167,017
1988 CAMPAIGN:	Packard - R	72%	$160,267
	Howard Greenebaum - D	26%	$ 74,087

RATINGS:	ADA	ACU	AFL/CIO	LCV	NCSC	NTU	USCC
	11%	93%	7%	6%	8%	55%	90%

Vote on H.J. Res. 77 authorizing war with Iraq: Yes.

Randy "Duke" Cunningham (R)
44th Congressional District

Every sparkling city has its shabby underside.
Most of San Diego's working-class white, black and
Hispanic precincts have been packed into the 44th
District to create a Democratic haven in the midst of
one of the most Republican counties in the state.
Chula Vista and National City make up the southern
flank. From the downtown area, the district runs
eastward through Lemon Grove and laps over into
smoggy reaches of the Mission Valley.

Most paychecks in this area come from blue-
collar Navy jobs, small retail shops or the service
sector. There are also a fair number of people on
relief. Democrat Rep. Jim Bates used to have an easy

Randy Cunningham

time getting re-elected here, but his string ran out in
1990. The previous year, the House Ethics Committee concluded that Bates was
guilty of sexually harassing two women staffers and approving improper campaign
activity in his congressional office. That was enough to get him a vigorous primary
challenge from attorney Byron Georgiou, but Bates still gathered 63 percent of the
vote. It was a different story in the runoff, where Bates faced the GOP's Randy
"Duke" Cunningham, one of the most highly decorated fighter pilots of the Vietnam
War. Once the absentee ballots were counted, Cunningham had defeated the only
Democratic congressman south of the Los Angeles area by 1,659 votes.

Conventional wisdom says Cunningham should be easy pickings in 1992,
depending on how the new district lines are drawn. Yet if anyone could hold the seat
for the Republicans in this Navy town, it should be Cunningham. The first Vietnam
fighter ace, Cunningham holds the Navy Cross, two Silver Stars, 10 air medals, the
Purple Heart and several others. Some of his experiences were depicted in the movie
"Top Gun." After the war, he taught fighter pilots at the Navy Fighter Weapons
School at Miramar and retired as a commander. But he still found time to work in
community drug programs and civic organizations. On the stump, Cunningham
comes across as personable and sincere. He'll be tough to beat.

PERSONAL: elected 1990; born Dec. 8, 1941, in Los Angeles; home, San
Diego; education, B.A. University of Missouri 1964, M.Ed. 1965; wife Nancy, three
children; Christian.

CAREER: coach, Hinsdale (Ill.) High school, 1965-66; U.S. Navy fighter pilot,
1966-87.

COMMITTEES: Armed Services; Merchant Marine and Fisheries.

OFFICES: Suite 1017, Longworth Building, Washington, D.C. 20515, (202)
225-5452, FAX (202) 225-2558; district, Suite 220, 3450 College Ave., San Diego
92115, (619) 287-8851; Suite A, 430 David St., Chula Vista 92010, (619) 691-1166.

REGISTRATION: 53% D, 35% R

1990 CAMPAIGN: Cunningham - R	46%	$539,721
Jim Bates - D	45%	$773,364
1988 CAMPAIGN: Jim Bates - D	60%	$480,679
Rob Butterfield - R	37%	$218,388

RATINGS: None as of this writing.

Vote on H.J. Res. 77 authorizing war with Iraq: Yes.

Duncan Hunter (R)
45th Congressional District

The 45th District stretches across the bottom of California in an area that has seen momentous change in recent decades and is apt to see much more. At the coast, it begins in the old beach village of Coronado, runs south on the Silver Strand to Imperial Beach, and then swings east through middle-class and upper-middle-class suburbs.

Duncan Hunter

Once clear of San Diego, the district takes in the rock piles of eastern San Diego County and all of Imperial County. The San Diego portions are comfortably Republican. Imperial County is becoming solidly Hispanic, but the white grower class still controls the political scene. Immigration pressures, however, are eroding the white dominance everywhere but in the richest San Diego portions in the district.

In the Imperial Valley, friction between growers and workers continues to mount. A wide range of border issues fester here: immigration, pollution, drug trafficking and educational and social services for new arrivals. It's going to be difficult for a mere mortal congressman to juggle the issues here in future years with the disparity between haves and have-nots, the racial conflicts and the inconsistent national policies on border issues. It would take a hawkish Republican who's a former poverty lawyer to satisfy the diverse elements. Rep. Duncan Hunter is exactly that. As a bonus, he seems to have limitless energy to pursue his goals.

Hunter was a combat officer in Vietnam, went to night law school and began his practice in an old barber shop in San Diego's barrio. He went on to beat Democrat Lionel Van Deerlin, an 18-year veteran. Hunter has annoyed some colleagues by stepping over them to get what he wants. But his talents have been recognized by party leaders. He chairs the Republican Research Committee, charged with developing GOP strategies for emerging issues. Hunter is using the committee to focus on minority recruitment for the party. He also is leading the charge to put the military into the forefront of drug interdiction efforts. California's GOP delegation hasn't many stars, but Hunter is definitely one with great promise.

PERSONAL: elected 1980; born May 31, 1948, in Riverside, Calif.; home, Coronado; B.S.L. Western State University 1976, J.D. 1976; wife Lynne, two children; Baptist.

CAREER: U.S. Army, 1969-71; attorney, 1976-80.

COMMITTEES: Armed Services; (Select) Hunger.

OFFICES: Suite 133, Cannon Building, Washington, D.C. 20515, (202) 225-5672, FAX 202-225-0235; district, 366 South Pierce St., El Cajon 92020, (619) 579-3001; Suite G, 1101 Airport Road, Imperial 92251, (619) 353-5420; 825 Imperial Beach Blvd., Imperial Beach 92032, (619) 423-3011.

REGISTRATION: 36% D, 50% R

1990 CAMPAIGN: Hunter - R   73% $368,560

                  Joe Shea - D   27% $0

1988 CAMPAIGN: Hunter - R   74% $489,395

                  Pete Lepiscopo - D   24% $8,136

RATINGS:

ADA	ACU	AFL/CIO	LCV	NCSC	NTU	USCC
6%	92%	21%	6%	11%	54%	86%

Vote on H.J. Res. 77 authorizing war with Iraq: Yes.

How California's congressional delegation has grown

Census	California representatives	Total number of representatives
1840	2	232
1850	2	237
1860	3	243
1870	4	293
1880	6	332
1890	7	357
1900	8	391
1910	11	435
1930	20	435
1940	23	435
1950	30	437
1960	38	435
1970	43	435
1980	45	435

No apportionment was made following the 1920 census because of a legislative deadlock.

8

Lobbyists – a vital link in the process

When infamous lobbyist Artie Samish appeared on the cover of Collier's magazine in 1949, posed with a ventriloquist's dummy on his knee, he etched an image into the political consciousness of California: lobbyists as puppeteers standing in the shadows pulling strings while legislators danced vacuously on the public stage. Reality is much more complicated and far less sinister. Lobbyists are neither good nor evil. They have become, however, a linchpin in the legislative process.

Lobbyists are a critical link between lawmakers and industries, professional associations, consumer advocates and other combatants in California politics. They carry the intricate information about the details of an industry or the desires of a professional group to the people who make the laws. The lion's share of the bills introduced in the Legislature are proposed, and at least sketched-out, by lobbyists. They also help devise legislative strategies, manage bills, work with staff members, produce grass-roots pressure and, often, manage the media.

Legislative advocates, as they prefer to call themselves, are the professionals in the multilayered, arcane world of California politics. They deal in a bewildering system that has more twists and turns and hidden hallways than the Capitol building. It is an environment in which the unguided can easily end up running down a corridor that goes nowhere.

Influential lobbyists are successful for a host of reasons. Chief among them is the ability of their clients to make campaign contributions – or "participate in the political process," as it is euphemistically called in the trade. But that is only one tool, and few advocates remain effective for long using money alone. The vast majority trade heavily on their knowledge of the Legislature and the causes they represent, their political acumen, the grass-roots connections of their clients and, perhaps most important, their individual relationships with elected officials and staff.

One of most profound changes in the "third house," as the lobbying corps is called, is the shift to the full-service lobbying company. There are fewer and fewer major one- or two-person operations that rely on their good will in the Capitol and their overall knowledge of the political system. Instead, as in Washington, D.C., a cadre of firms have sprouted with specialists, in-house attorneys, public relations experts – all of which look and run like law firms. In fact, to explain their role, lobbyists most often compare themselves with lawyers. They say they are advocates, plain and simple. They are hired to win today and again tomorrow and to protect their clients just as lawyers do whatever is possible to protect theirs. California's massive growth has created even more demand for advocates. As the booms continue in population, business and government, as society grows more complex, as every interest in the state becomes more and more interwoven with government, the demand for lobbyists increases.

In 1977, the secretary of state's office registered 538 lobbyists and 761 clients who hired them. In 1990, there were 854 lobbyists and 1,451 clients. Ironically, the passage of anti-government, anti-tax Proposition 13 in 1978 helped fuel that growth by centralizing the financing of schools and local governments in Sacramento. Interests with a stake in those finances muscled up by hiring more lobbyists in the capital. The best measure of growth is the amount of money spent lobbying the Legislature. According to the Fair Political Practices Commission, $40 million was spent on lobbying during the 1975-76 session of the Legislature. In just the first half of the 1987-88 session, more than $75 million was spent by trade associations, corporations, utilities and others. In 1988, $82.9 million was spent. The total for the 1987-88 legislative season was nearly 295 percent greater than 12 years before.

A GROWTH INDUSTRY

Lobbyists say privately that one major reason for the increased demand is that everybody else is getting a lobbyist these days. Interests entering the legislative field feel like soldiers without rifles if they are not armed with a good lobbyist.

But it is not just mutual armament in dealing with the Legislature that has sparked the explosion. Industries and interests are coming to realize that all levels of government, including state agencies and commissions, require expert representation. The state's gigantic bureaucracy can be even more unfathomable than the Legislature. A growing number of lobbyists are former state officials who have learned the pathways and players in key state agencies. And they are finding themselves in demand from a variety of interests with huge stakes in the decisions dealt out by the regulators. The state Departments of Food and Agriculture and Health Services, for example, played key roles in defining and administering Proposition 65, the 1986 Safe Drinking Water Act. That law has had a multimillion-dollar impact on scores of businesses. As a result, chemical, pesticide, agricultural and other California companies with a stake have lobbyists working those agencies.

The labyrinthine legislative process and the ever-increasing demands on lawmakers' time and attention makes it nearly impossible for someone outside of the inner political circles to have much of an impact on the workings of the Legislature. Given the lobbyists' essential role, it would seem the door is open for them to play puppet masters in the way Artie Samish once did. But that is not the case. In fact, the same system that makes lobbyists so vital prevents any one advocate or interest from asserting control. There are so many interests and so much pressure from every quarter, that it is virtually impossible for one lobbyist, or even a handful, to indiscriminately muscle bills through.

It takes a monumental effort to push any measure burdened with controversy through the Capitol. The bill must survive at least two committees and a floor vote in each house, possibly a conference committee and other floor votes, and then it must win the governor's signature. Those are seven chances, at a minimum, to kill a bill. Passing it means winning at every step. And it is easy for many lobbyists, especially those representing single-issue interests, to confuse the issue or throw enough doubt into lawmakers' minds to get them to vote "no" or at least to be absent so there are not enough votes to pass a bill. For legislators, there is always less political damage in sticking with the status quo, whether by voting no or just by not voting. In fact, much of what lobbyists do is defensive. They spend much more energy trying to kill bills that may hurt their clients than breaking new ground or pushing proposals.

ALL SHAPES, SIZES AND SKILLS

So, with all those lobbyists wandering the halls of the Capitol, the teeming atmosphere of California politics looks at first glance as if it might fit the image of the marketplace of ideas and interests envisioned by the framers of American democracy. But only at first glance. The Capitol is not a place where decision-makers blend those ideas and choose simply on merit. And if any one set of players is responsible for that, it would be lobbyists.

For one reason, lobbyists, like anyone else, come in a variety of levels of skill, influence and experience. The better ones often win regardless of the merits of their case, because victories in the Capitol are based on politics, not virtue. The different categories of lobbyists each brings its own weapons and weaknesses. Those include:

● **Public-interest lobbyists**: Often called "white-hat lobbyists," these are the people who work for consumer groups, good-government organizations, environmentalists or any of those people who aim to represent the public at large. These lobbyists, for the most part, are the weakest in the Capitol. Their best weapon is public sentiment. Because of that, they are about the only lobbyists consistently willing to talk with reporters and to make their issues public. They often resort to calling press conferences to announce their positions or unhappiness, hoping it will generate enough public reaction to influence the votes of legislators. But with only meager financial resources they have little to offer lawmakers other than public approval. As often as not, they are fighting against moneyed interests, and unless the issue is something that will ignite the public – and there are few of those since most Californians pay scant attention to the Legislature – public-interest lobbyists spend much of their time working on damage control rather than passing legislation.

● **Association lobbyists**: These are the advocates who work for one specific organization, such as the California Association of Realtors. Some of these organizations have tremendous resources, a large grass-roots network and fat campaign war chests to dole out. And depending on their causes, they, too, sometimes feel comfortable using the press and public sentiment to help push their issues. But they also have some disadvantages. Since their legislative goals have to be agreed upon by the association's directors and membership, they often have less flexibility to adjust in midstream. In addition, they spend a good deal of their time organizing their association, and trying to keep internal politics out of state politics.

● **Contract lobbyists**: They are the hired guns, the quintessence of what the public envisions as the lobbying corps. And for the major contract lobbyists and the powerful lobbying firms handling large client loads, that image generally fits. They often are the ones who have been around the Capitol for years, who know the game from every angle and who have enough of a client list, campaign war chest, history in politics, stored up favors and political acumen to make lawmakers listen. But contract lobbyists come in many sizes and shapes. Some work for public-interest groups, which forces them to operate like those "white-hat lobbyists." Others represent cities or semi-public entities and can distribute few campaign contributions. Still others work for smaller, less powerful companies or industries and have never gathered enough clout to make the inner circles.

● **Company lobbyists**: Some of the larger companies have their own in-house advocates, who are often a cross between association and contract lobbyists. They are some of the real inside players in the Capitol, with the resources and money to be influential. And like many contract lobbyists – and legislators – they often are most comfortable functioning out of the glare of public scrutiny. Since they work for only one client, they generally have the flexibility to compromise and roll with the inevitable political punches. However, because they only represent one company, no matter how powerful, they usually need to work within coalitions or at least try to eliminate opposition from companies within their industry. If they cannot, they can find themselves with little clout.

THE IMPORTANCE OF MONEY

For lobbyists, success goes to those who understand best the nature of influence. They understand timing, organization and the value of information. They have built relationships with legislators, consultants, even a key secretary or two. And, for the big-time lobbyists, they understand the connection between politics and money.

It is an absolute axiom of modern political life, especially in a state such as California, that a politician without money is not a politician for long. In these days of computer-aided, television-oriented, high-tech campaigns, no candidate without a healthy chunk of cash can hope to win. And no group is more aware of that than the lobbyists. They have found themselves squarely in the middle of the campaign financing free-for-all.

Lobbyists have become the main conduits for contributions, as well as the pipeline to their clients for the requests for funds from politicians. But lobbyists are more the vehicle for those campaign contributions than the reason. Take lobbyists out of the picture and the interests that contribute and the legislators who raise money would still find ways to connect. In fact, many lobbyists portray themselves as victims of a system that requires nearly constant fund-raising. That view is in vivid contrast to the widely held image of lobbyists padding the halls of the Capitol hoping to corrupt legislators with bundles of bills in their briefcases.

Victims or not, those with money still win their share of Capitol battles. And the need for cash is a fact of life lobbyists frequently have to sell to clients. Without money, the lobbyists lose access to legislators.

The actual impact of campaign contributions on the drafting of laws can be small since many other lobbyists and interests are also buying access. Generally, money plays the deciding role only in turf fights that do not affect a legislator's district or do not become an issue in the media, such as when two financial interests like banks and savings and loans battle over state regulations.

While the influence of money is not necessarily direct, it is thorough. For starters, the big-money interests can afford to hire the best lobbyists, who in turn use that money to conduct public relations campaigns, to organize in the districts of targeted legislators and to hire enough staff to make sure nothing is missed.

In addition, the skills of those top lobbyists often include the judicious deployment of the client's campaign contributions. Many lobbyists make sure a client's money goes to legislators in position to help that client, but they also funnel some of that money to lawmakers who have been consistent friends. That in turn, adds clout to the lobbyist's own status independent of his or her clients.

When a lawmaker is approached by a top lobbyist such as Clayton Jackson, that legislator is not simply thinking about the one employer whose cause Jackson may be advocating, but about Jackson's long list of clients – including insurance, finance and high-tech companies – whose combined campaign contributions total more than $2 million annually. Legislators have too little time to see all the people who want to argue their cases. And when push comes to shove and there are two lobbyists waiting in the office lobby, the one who will get in is always the one who has consistently contributed to campaigns.

ALL RELATIONSHIPS ARE PERSONAL

In fact, the investment of campaign money earns more than simple access because, as in any business, when two people have dealt with and grown to trust each other over the years, a relationship develops. That brings up another primary rule of California politics: Everything that happens in the Capitol comes down to basic human relationships, rather than institutional ones. Lobbyists and legislators hold nothing more precious than their relationships with each other. If a lawmaker likes you and trusts you, he will listen. If a lobbyist thinks of you as a friend, he will make sure you receive timely information and equally useful campaign contributions.

In the storm that is Capitol politics, both legislators and lobbyists are grateful for any safe harbor. For veteran lawmakers and influential lobbyists, those symbiotic relationships often grow into genuine friendships. And those friendships, creations of convenience though they may be, can have as much influence on California's laws as any other aspect of the state's politics.

The most marked advantage of a lobbyist's friendship with a legislator is that member's willingness to listen to a friend argue for or against a bill. That becomes even more significant during the end-of-session tempests, when hundreds of bills can be dispatched in a few hours. That is when bills are changing, members are under the gun and a lobbyist doesn't have time to document arguments about a set of amendments. Members are left with no choice but to ask the lobbyists if the changes are acceptable to his or her clients. If they trust each other, the lobbyist can look the legislator in the eye and tell him the truth – with neither feeling nervous.

A study done for former Assembly Speaker Jesse Unruh during the mid-1970s asked legislators what they thought was the most corrupting influence in politics. The answer that came back the most often was "friendship." One legislator said, "I never voted for a bad bill, but I voted for a lot of bad authors."

THE INVASION OF EX-MEMBERS

Former lawmakers are one rapidly growing class of lobbyists that begin with ready-made friendships in the Capitol. These people have worked together, seen each other almost every day, experienced the same pressures and developed the same interests. They have an emotional bond like university alumni. Approximately two-dozen former legislators lobby either full- or part-time. Others are not registered, either because they do not lobby enough to qualify as official lobbyists or because their contacts and connections are less direct.

The list of some of the more prominent or active among the former legislators includes former Sens. John Briggs, Clair Burgener, Dennis Carpenter, John Foran, Bob Wilson and George Zenovich; and former Assembly members Gordon Duffy, Jean Duffy, Joe Gonsalves, John Knox, Frank Murphy Jr., Robert Naylor, Paul Priolo and John P. Quimby. Even James Garibaldi, the dean of the lobbying corps, was an assemblyman in the mid-1930s. Former Sen. William Campbell also belongs on the list. As president of the California Manufacturers Association, he is not registered to lobby. But Campbell spends a great deal of his time maintaining old Capitol ties, letting the word out on what would be good for the CMA, and showing up on the legislative floors, just coincidentally, he insists, about the time a vote is due on a critical CMA issue.

In addition, former legislative or administration staff members turn their expertise and inside relationships into influential lobbying jobs, often focusing on the Legislature and the committees and subject areas in which they had been involved. There are dozens of lobbyists who were ex-legislative staff members, but the largest group is probably the legion of former aides to Assembly Speaker Willie Brown, which includes Bill Rutland, Kathleen Snodgrass, Jackson Gualco, John Mockler and Kent Stoddard.

Ex-administration officials, of course, find themselves in great demand to lobby the agencies they once worked in. No major Wilson aides had defected to the lobbying corps by mid-1991, but the third house is full of former Deukmejian administrators, including Michael Franchetti, Deukmejian's first finance director; David Swoap, once a health and welfare secretary; David Ackerman, a former deputy business, transportation and housing undersecretary; Rodney Blonien, an ex-corrections undersecretary; and Randy Ward, who headed the state Department of Conservation. Former Deukmejian chief of staff Steven Merksamer also must be included in that list, although he is not a registered lobbyist. Merksamer's law/lobbying firm – Nielsen, Merksamer, Hodgson, Parrinello & Mueller – represents some of America's largest companies and is one of the most influential firms on the state scene. There also are top lobbyists who were state officials in earlier administrations, including Richard B. Spohn, former Gov. Jerry Brown's director of the state Department of Consumer Affairs; and George Steffes, an aide to then-Gov. Ronald Reagan in the early 1970s.

A study in 1986 by political scientists Jerry Briscoe and Charles Bell, then at the University of the Pacific and the University of California, Davis, respectively, found 36 percent of the registered lobbyists had served in government. This steady stream from the Capitol to the third house had for years inspired "anti-revolving door" bills from lawmakers or outside groups such as Common Cause. Those proposals would have prohibited state officials and lawmakers from lobbying their former houses or agencies for a year or two after leaving state service, but most were brushed aside by the people who had the most to lose, the legislators themselves.

In 1990, however, constituents and good-government groups were putting pressure on lawmakers, who were under the cloud of an FBI investigation, to clean up their ethics. Under the gun also from looming ethics and term-limit initiatives, the lawmakers passed their own half-hearted ethics reform bill and put it before voters as Proposition 112. The measure, which limited lawmakers' outside income in exchange for creating the independent Citizens Compensation Commission to set salaries, included anti-revolving door provisions that prohibited former lawmakers or top-level administrators from lobbying their old colleagues for one year after leaving office. Proposition 112 was approved by voters in June 1990. Those locks on the revolving doors were to go into effect on Jan. 1, 1991, but Deukmejian, ever-watchful for his friends, forced the effective date to be changed to Jan. 7 – the day after he left office – which made his entire staff exempt.

The fact that former lawmakers and staffers are in demand as lobbyists underscores the changes in the third house in recent years. One of the biggest changes may be the nature of the relationships between lawmakers and lobbyists. Today, those relationships most often are based on shared interests and friendships. Sometimes families of lawmakers and lobbyists play together on weekends or holidays. That is a far cry from the days of duck hunting or drunken revelry in the 1930s, '40s and '50s, when Artie Samish said he supplied his legislative friends with "a baked potato, a girl or money."

While Samish, who was imprisoned for tax-evasion in 1956, was probably the most extreme case in California, many lobbyists used a few good meals or a round of drinks to create a bridge to lawmakers. With that bridge, they could then argue the merits of their cases. Those bridges were built on an old-fashioned, good-old-boy network. Some of the more well-known lobbyists ran up tabs of $1,500-a-month wining and dining legislators. And, not infrequently, lawmakers signed a lobbyist's name to a restaurant or bar tab even when the lobbyist was not there.

There also were regular, institutionalized social affairs paid for by a number of lobbyists and open to all lawmakers and many key members of the staff. The most spectacular of those was the "Moose Milk," a lavish lunch and open bar held Thursdays in the former El Mirador Hotel across from the Capitol. There also was the lunch at the Derby Club on Tuesdays and the "Clam and Corral" at the Senator Hotel on Wednesdays. The purpose was nothing more than good times, good will and, of course, access.

Those days began to change in 1966 when Californians made their Legislature full time. That meant career politicians and full-time staff. No longer were lobbyists the only people who understood the state's industries and the fine points in bills. Lawmakers and their larger staffs had more time and more information of their own.

And with the professionalization of the Legislature, lawmakers began to develop both areas of expertise and fiefdoms to protect. Specialists, usually committee chairmen, emerged in banking, insurance, health and dozens of others fields. For lobbyists that had two implications.

THE OLD-BOY NETWORK BREAKS DOWN

First, that meant the lobbyists had to have better, more specific information. A simple, "trust me on this one," became less convincing. Lobbyists had to learn the fine points of the industries and clients they represented. And second, with power spread through the committee chairmen and their staffs, it became increasingly difficult for just a few lobbyists to handle major legislation. So lobbyists, too, became specialists. Not only did they concentrate on specific subjects, but different lobbyists became valuable to clients because of their relationships with specific lawmakers.

The biggest step in the transformation of the lobbying corps from the days of camaraderie to a law firm-like atmosphere was Proposition 9, the Political Reform

Act passed in 1974. That initiative required detailed disclosure and it limited the gifts and meals lobbyists could buy legislators to $10 a month. With that act, the Moose Milk and the free meals disappeared, eventually to be replaced by a more businesslike lobbying industry. In fact, that measure inspired a group of longtime lobbyists to form the Institute of Governmental Advocates, an association to lobby for lobbyists, which filed a successful law suit to set aside portions of the measure.

With the increasing difficulty of establishing social relationships with lawmakers, the growing complexity of society and the heightened representation of interests in recent years, many people predict the slow extinction of the one-person lobbying operation. In its place has emerged the multiservice firm with a number of lobbyists, lawyers and public-relations specialists. Some small lobbying operations have merged, others have joined with political consulting or public relations companies, and still others have grown out of law firms. Whatever their origin, lobbying firms with big staffs, big client lists and big campaign war chests are coming to dominate the political landscape.

That also has changed the outside view of lobbyists. Potential clients are wooed not by connections and understanding of the system, as the old, one-person operations used to do. Instead, the big firms advertise themselves as people with the wherewithal to handle every aspect of the legislative and political battle.

There has been a change in the relationship with lawmakers as well. Because lobbyists with large client lists have less and less time to deal with their clients, they have less ability to impress upon their employers the reality of politics. Lobbyists often need to spend much of their time convincing clients to ask for tiny changes that take place over several sessions rather than to expect major revisions in the law. But as their firms grow, they simply lose the ability to convince their clients to go slow. That means lobbyists bring more and more unfiltered demands to lawmakers, making it harder to reconcile requests for different interests. The result: legislative stalemate, or lobbylock, as it is called around the Capitol.

The lobbyists

DONALD K. BROWN

If there is one person in Sacramento who epitomizes the public's age-old notion of a lobbyist, it's Donald "Big O" BrOwn. He is a "juice" – or money – player, an insider who uses power-politics and who rarely lets legislators forget that standing behind him is a collection of clients who are among the biggest campaign contributors in the state.

BrOwn, who changed the legal spelling of his name to distinguish himself from another Donald Brown, is considered one of the most effective lobbyists in Sacramento. But unlike the other big juice players, BrOwn's clout has little to do with technical expertise. Instead, it is based on his inside connections and his ability to direct, or withhold, huge amounts of campaign cash. When Nancy Burt, the savvy former top aide to Senate President Pro Tem David Roberti, began looking for other work after the 1990 elections, it seemed only logical that she would land with BrOwn.

His client list, which has shrunk a bit in recent years, is still long and heavy with financial power. It includes the Summa Corp. and the empire of the late Howard Hughes, the Irvine Co., the California Manufacturers Association, the Pharmaceutical Manufacturers Association, the Southland Corp. and the state's mortgage brokers. Together, his clients give as much or more than the clients of any lobbyist in California. In 1990, BrOwn's firm collected nearly $2 million in lobbying fees, according to documents filed with the secretary of state.

Some lobbyists and staff members describe BrOwn as arrogant, others say he can be personable. All agree that his forte is politics, not policy. In fact, he makes it almost a point of pride that he stays in the background and out of the nitty-gritty. Lobbyists with whom BrOwn has worked say he lets associates do the lion's share of lobbying and bill analysis, leaving him free to remind lawmakers of the ample campaign contributions of his clients. Staffers say they have been corralled by BrOwn, who told them little more than, "Go see so-and-so about his bill." The other lobbyists would handle the details. BrOwn just wanted them to know he thought the bill was important.

Yet for all the power politics, BrOwn does not look the part. With his tweeds and soft shoes and thick mustache, he appears more a college professor than a hard-nosed lobbyist. And BrOwn is something of an enigma in Capitol politics because he so consistently stays out of the limelight. He tends to deal with legislative leaders. In fact there are a number of junior legislators who have never met BrOwn.

BrOwn also stays away from public appearances, rarely if ever testifying before committees and avoiding the press the way campers avoid poison oak. In fact, he even put a clause in one of his client contracts that prevented him from making press statements.

DENNIS CARPENTER

Dennis Carpenter seems never to have left the Legislature. A former FBI agent, attorney, international cattle trader and Republican state senator from Orange County, Carpenter retains the air of a senator as well as his connections to Orange County. In 1990, Carpenter's firm earned $2.1 million in lobbying fees from such powerhouse clients as RJR/Nabisco Inc. and the Association of California Insurance Companies.

Carpenter's firm has been one of the fastest growing in California, with five lobbyists, including his wife, Aleta, who was a school district advocate before they married. When he took on the insurance industry as a client, not only did he get involved in one of the highest profile fights in the Capitol, the battle over auto insurance reform, but he also added another high profile lobbyist, Kathy Snodgrass. She is a former staff member and good friend of Assembly Speaker Willie Brown's and has been doing a good chunk of the nuts-and-bolts lobbying for insurers for several years. Carpenter also represents Orange County and its transportation commission.

But the firm has changed as it has grown. Carpenter separated from the man with whom he set up his lobbying practice, former Democratic Sen. George Zenovich. The split was amicable, and Zenovich took a few clients, including Fresno County, to his own, much lower-key operation.

Carpenter's success, however, is related to more than just his connections. Like many former lawmakers, he knows the system well, and he knows who else knows the system and what they can do for him. He is a big, easy man who never seems pushed. His is the classic laid-back style, the kind where he stands casually with one shoe on the lower railing outside the Senate or Assembly as he briefs a legislator on a bill. Not only does that make him easy to like, but it makes him easy to underestimate.

MICHAEL FRANCHETTI

It has never been a secret with whom Michael Franchetti has influence. George Deukmejian helped get this firm started in 1984, when the governor gave Franchetti a strong endorsement during a fund-raiser, saying, "I always like to give a young lawyer a plug."

Franchetti was Deukmejian's first finance director, but amid partisan fighting over deep budget cuts, he was denied Senate confirmation and was forced to give up the post after a year. His partner until he split to start his own firm in 1990 was David Swoap, Deukmejian's first health and welfare secretary. They represent two trends in the lobbying business – the increasing interest in lobbying administrative departments and agencies, and the growing number of former administration officials who have set up lobbying operations.

Of those former officials, Franchetti has been one of the most successful. He focuses much of his attention on former colleagues who remain under Gov. Wilson and continues to expand lobbying efforts to other agencies and departments. He handles some legislative lobbying chores, but has few strong connections among lawmakers. Instead, he is often brought in as part of a team by other lobbyists who work the Legislature and need Franchetti's influence in the administration. After the bill becomes law, Franchetti is often retained to track its implementation by a department or agency.

But his success comes from more than just connections. He often handles the technical aspects of issues rather than the political fights, functioning more like a lawyer than a lobbyist in some cases. So much of what happens in the agencies involves debates over seemingly small points of law, but the cumulative impact of that kind of lobbying can be enormous.

Because of their success, Franchetti and Swoap were subjected to ample criticism for typifying the revolving door between government service and lobbying, but it didn't hurt their business. Clients such as drug firms and hospitals, the California Chiropractic Association, Mobil Oil Corp. and PepsiCo Inc. paid them about $1 million in 1990 before their split.

JAMES GARIBALDI

James Garibaldi, known around Sacramento as "The Judge" and to intimates as "Gary," is the closest thing to royalty in Capitol circles. He is treated with deference to his considerable influence; his age, 83; and, most important, his more than 40 years of lobbying.

Garibaldi is a throwback to the days when legislative business was done in richly paneled rooms on thickly padded leather couches. That, in fact, describes his office. He is friendly, charming and never seems out of sorts. Although slowed by age, Garibaldi retains his mental faculties and continues to be a major force in the Capitol. He does not make the walk across the street to the Capitol as often as he used to, but when he does, it is to deal with leaders. And they usually listen.

Part of the reason he is still influential is that he knows the system and its nuances. His clients have been with him for years, and he knows the details of those industries as well as anyone in the Capitol. In addition he is easy for legislators to deal with. He doesn't ask for much, and he doesn't make threats. But his words carry the weight of his own legacy of influence.

Garibaldi is nothing if not adaptable, and it shows in his lobbying strategy. He once helped defeat a bill to legalize dog racing in California – an idea feared by his horse racing clients – by teaming with lobbyists who called it cruelty to animals. And he was instrumental in enacting a tax break for the horse racing industry at a time when the state government was in a financial pinch.

Garibaldi conducts himself with an air of authority. In the world of politics, that in itself lends him authority. A visit with Garibaldi has the feel of being granted an audience. New members are flattered to meet him, it almost confers a status on them. Plus, Garibaldi plays up the image of invincibility. His client list is filled with blue-chip interests such as liquor dealers, the National Association of Securities Dealers, the California Association of Highway Patrolmen and the Leslie Salt Co. He is still among the top earning lobbyists, bringing in $520,000 in fees in 1990.

Garibaldi is a former assemblyman and Superior Court judge. He also was instrumental in creating the Institute of Governmental Advocates, the lobbyists' lobbying organization.

JOE GONSALVES

Joe Gonsalves has been called by one legislator the sweetest man in the Capitol. Unassuming, soft-spoken, unerringly polite, Gonsalves is also one of the most consistently successful lobbyists, especially considering the issues he deals with.

A former assemblyman, he makes a specialty of representing cities. His clients include nearly 20 municipalities, most of them smaller cities south and east of Los

Angeles. And most are contract cities, which means they pay either private companies or other municipalities for many of their essential services. The problems of those cities often pose a dilemma for lawmakers because what one of those cities wants can be precisely what a neighboring community opposes. Legislators have to choose whom to disappoint.

Gonsalves, more than any lobbyist in Sacramento, has been successful in pushing those interests. He does it with hard work, connections and by organizing local officials to lobby legislators, both in Sacramento and back home in their districts. As one lobbyist said of Gonsalves, "If you're on the other side of his issue, you have serious problems."

Above all else, Gonsalves is persistent. He never lets legislators forget his issue. He covers all his bases with staff members and dogs every bill from start to finish. But in that persistence, his approach is always gentlemanly and understated. Gonsalves wears neither the high-fashion nor expensive suits often worn by other lobbyists. Instead, his clothes, like his approach, are businesslike and straight forward.

Gonsalves worked alone for a number of years, but has been joined recently by his son, Anthony. Besides the cities, he also lobbies for several redevelopment agencies plus horse racing and dairy interests, a collection that earned him about $680,000 in 1988.

CLAYTON JACKSON

It is impossible to figure a formula for picking California's top lobbyist, but by any measure Clay Jackson has to be a contender. Never mind that his firm is consistently among the top earners, or that he is extremely influential, or that his clients give enormous amounts of campaign money. The man simply looks like a lobbyist. At 6-foot-6 and with his conservative gray suits and ever-present cigar, he is imposing, intimidating and impossible to ignore when standing in a back corner of a hearing room or a Capitol corridor. And he wins.

As much as any lobbyist in Sacramento in recent years, Jackson has been involved in high-profile, high-stakes battles – most notably over insurance- and tort-reform legislation. He was one of the principal lobbyists responsible for fending off repeated attacks on the state's insurance industry and was one of the driving forces behind the 1987 easing of liability laws, a hallmark of Capitol wheeling and dealing that has become known as the Frank Fat's Napkin Deal because details were drafted on a napkin from a restaurant a few blocks from the Capitol.

Besides the insurance industry – Jackson shifted clients from California companies to the large, national insurance carriers after an internal blowup over strategy – he represents a number of power-hitting interests, including the Anheuser-Busch Cos., the California Hotel & Motel Association and California's independent thrift and loan companies. His clients paid him more than $2.2 million in lobbying fees in 1990, making him the top-earning lobbyist.

The financial clout of Jackson's clients is considerable. Some lobbyists say he would be far less effective without it. But many friends and foes agree that is only a part of the reason for his success. Jackson may be as shrewd a political strategist as works the halls of the Capitol. He knows the system, the players and is a master deal-maker. One key to lobbying is knowing when little pieces of legislation might hurt or help a client, and there are times when Jackson, who understands the minutest details of the industries he represents, sees those pieces as do few others.

It is hard to argue with someone who so thoroughly does his homework. It is even harder to argue when that person has both the physical and political stature of Jackson. His personal style – he can be charming and polite, or as tough as he needs to be – lends further impact to his arguments. In a hearing room, he often stands along a wall, making eye contact with members he is trying to influence, letting his presence alone remind them of his clients' interests.

JAY D. MICHAEL

Most lobbyists would trade an arm for the resources Jay D. Michael has to throw into political wars. Michael is the chief lobbyist for the California Medical Association, one of the most influential interests in the state, and he is on top of the pyramid of association lobbyists.

The CMA is one of the state's biggest campaign contributors every year. With the proper handling, that alone would make the association influential. But the CMA is also well-organized, it has plenty of staff and it has influence with members in both parties because there are, after all, doctors in every legislator's district, and they are, for obvious reasons, influential civic leaders. Yet even that combination of money and organization does not make an interest powerful. The CMA has been a major force for years because Michael knows how to put those resources to work. Michael is an insider and a good strategist. His job is to protect the pocketbooks of doctors, and he has been extremely successful for a number of years.

In recent years, the CMA has been part of some unusual alliances that have resulted in high-profile, high-impact deals. Michael and the CMA were key players in the negotiations that brought about a major tort reform bill in 1987. Part of that bill extended protections for doctors against malpractice suits, protections that the CMA had first won in an earlier battle during the mid-1970s with the doctors' archenemies, the trial lawyers.

The CMA also was part of the coalition that pushed Proposition 99, the 1988 initiative that increased the cigarette tax by 25 cents a pack. One of the provisions of that initiative reimburses doctors for treating poor patients who have no way to pay their bills. Michael and the CMA later tried to barter CMA support for a ballot measure to increase the gas tax in exchange for even more of the Proposition 99 money, a campaign that failed but was noteworthy for an informal – and critics say infernal – alliance between the CMA and the tobacco industry.

Michael's access to political inner circles, where only the heavy-hitting lobbyists go, is a rarity for an association lobbyist, who often must rely on grass-roots organizing to wield influence. While Michael uses the CMA's grass roots well, his ability to use the system and the financial clout of doctors has put his organization among the elite interests in the state.

Michael is an affable, approachable guy. His manner is understated and belies the influence he wields. And like so many of the top lobbyists, he would have opponents forget his connections and political acumen, which he masks with a friendly, hail-fellow, well-met style.

RICHARD RATCLIFF

Richard Ratcliff has never been among California's top-earning lobbyist, but he represents something that is fading from the scene—the influential, one-person lobbying operation. Ratcliff has been lobbying in Sacramento since long before the Legislature went full time. He has rarely had much campaign money with which to pry open doors, nor does he have a long client list to lend clout to his requests. But he has always been an insider, respected for playing it straight. He is one of those rare lobbyists who is genuinely liked by almost every faction in the Capitol. He has friends among old-boy staff members, legislative leaders and young reporters.

His appearance is almost always casual. Even on days when he must put on a tie under his tweed or corduroy coats in order to testify before a committee, he still is as likely as not to wear jeans and cowboy boots. And his beard, peppered with gray, makes him look even more like he belongs on a horse herding cattle rather than in the ornate halls of the Capitol trying to corral votes.

His client list is substantive, if not overwhelming – it earned him $220,000 in 1990 – and it includes chemical companies and a coalition of international companies doing business in California. With those clients come complex issues, often involving tax law and trade. By necessity and inclination, Ratcliff deals much more with the intricacies of issues rather than politics. Although no lobbyist can be successful without understanding and using a good deal of politics, Ratcliff's best tools are his expertise and his ability to construct a compromise.

His approach is that of a man who is not certain he can answer a question. "Well, I'm not sure I'm the best guy for this," he might start, and then launch into an explanation that covers excruciating detail. His appearances before a committee are not statements that his clients oppose something – sometimes the only tack taken by some of the power-playing lobbyists. Instead, they are discourses about the issue, its background and complexities and, when his clients oppose a bill, a caution that lawmakers should move slowly.

Ratcliff is one of the leaders of the Institute of Governmental Advocates. He has spent a good deal of effort pushing a code of conduct for lobbyists that includes obligations toward clients, legislators and the public and a caution against raiding other firms for clients – a practice that pits the big firms against the smaller operations, such as his.

GEORGE STEFFES

George Steffes is something of a bridge between the old and new styles of lobbying. The old way was dominated by personal connections and camaraderie; the new uses large firms and campaign money. Steffes is good at both.

A former aide to Gov. Ronald Reagan, Steffes got his start in the older days of lobbying, and he is one of those in the elite ranks who deals with legislative leaders and other high-power lobbyists. That is evidenced by his leadership in the affairs of the Institute of Governmental Advocates, which was created by "old boy" lobbyists, and by his willingness to serve as a spokesman for the lobbying industry.

He was one of the first major lobbyists to expand into a full-service firm, and he now runs one of the state's largest lobbying operations. The firm's seven lobbyists and support staff handle nearly 40 clients. He is considered a money player, well-versed in power politics. And like other juice lobbyists, Steffes often gets other lobbyists to handle the day-to-day details while he works on strategy and politics, including the not inconsiderable job of recruiting and holding clients.

But Steffes is also around the Capitol constantly, patiently waiting outside the Assembly and Senate railings to talk with legislators. He still uses as a lobbying tool his friendships with important lawmakers as well as a generally amicable approach. While Steffes may not handle all the small details, he does his homework and he knows his issues. In playing the political game, he can be as hard-nosed as any lobbyist. In dealing with other lobbyists or staff members, he can be particularly demanding. And like many of the other lobbyists who succeed at playing hardball, Steffes gets away with it because of his understanding of politics and his powerful collection of clients.

Besides a number of horse racing interests, his clients include mining companies, hospital associations, foreign auto companies, insurers, Adolph Coors Co., American Express Co., Exxon U.S.A., Hughes Aircraft Co. and Union Pacific Corp. That brought him slightly more than $1.4 million in fees in 1990.

The lobbying firms

A-K ASSOCIATES INC.

Once the perennially top-earning lobbying firm, A-K in recent years has scaled back its operation and undergone a substantial shake-up. At its peak, it had six California lobbyists, three more in Washington, D.C, and more than 40 clients. It still remains among California's elite operations, earning about $790,000 in 1990, but it is no longer head and shoulders above the pack.

In political circles, A-K is still regarded as a powerhouse, but it is also noted for having experienced one of the most bitter rivalries over clients. The firm remains in the hands of its founders, S. Thomas Konovaloff and J. Michael Allen, but a brother of each man, Nicholai Konovaloff and Richard D. Allen, split from the firm, each to set up his own lobbying practice. When they tried to take some business with them, the real lobbying began – the lobbying of clients. Nicholai Konovaloff landed a few big names, among them the R.J. Reynolds Tobacco Co., but A-K kept most of the heavy hitters, including the industry-funded Tobacco Institute.

As an ironic result of that battle, A-K, possibly more than any other firm, became expert at wooing clients. Konovaloff and Allen went out and found businesses apparently having governmental troubles and then convinced them that those problems could be solved by experienced lobbyists who knew the system and the players. Their success begat success. As they grew and offered more and more services, they built a reputation as big-time players, which became a self-fulfilling prophesy, as is so often the case in politics. Legislators, assuming A-K had substantial clout, gave the firm access and due consideration, which gave it clout. And clients, wanting the biggest firm, signed up, making A-K the biggest of firms.

But A-K's stature also was earned through solid lobbying and consistent success. Both Konovaloff and Allen have good reputations as knowledgeable, hard-working lobbyists. They have built a number of close ties to key people in the Capitol, and they play the insider's game. They maintain those friendships, keep their issues out of the public spotlight, provide substantive information and whisper rather than shout requests.

In addition, as one of the first full-service lobbying firms, A-K manages a client's interests from start to finish, whether the needs are legislative or legal. And their size gives them the ability to handle both large and small clients, as their eclectic client list shows. Besides the tobacco industry, they also work for surety companies, dental plans, Chrysler Corp. and a reclamation district, among others.

CALIFORNIA ADVOCATES

California Advocates may be the lowest profile operation among the influential lobbying firms. It is a thoroughly professional outfit, regarded well by legislators and lobbyists alike. In fact, it operates much like its president, Loren Smith, who is a straight player, neither pushy nor flashy, thorough, effective and well-liked.

The firm's four lobbyists get their influence not from throwing out campaign money – although they admit to advising clients that it never hurts to buy a few fund-raiser tickets – but from in-depth knowledge of their subjects, of the legislative and regulatory processes and, occasionally, of legislators and regulators themselves. On that front, the firm, which represents Coca-Cola and others in the beverage industry, picked up liters of familiarity in hiring Randy Ward, who headed the state's recycling program under Gov. Deukmejian.

Lobbyists with California Advocates, particularly Smith and Ralph Simoni, are also rarities around a usually tight-lipped third house. They not only answer questions from the ever-impertinent press corps, but they are actually respected by those reporters. Much of that respect stems from the way they have played the hands of their industry clients in difficult battles such as the fight over a bottle bill and a mandatory seat-belt law. While bending little, they at least appeared to cooperate with environmental groups and consumer advocates more than do most industry lobbyists. If nothing else, that shows they are as adept at PR as lobbying.

The firm was established in 1970 and has steadily risen to the upper tier of California lobbying firms. In 1990, it earned $800,000 in fees, and besides the beverage industry, its client list includes car dealers, a number of financial institutions and the California Judges Association.

NIELSEN, MERKSAMER, HODGSON, PARRINELLO & MUELLER

Most lobbying firms try to remain non-partisan, even if their major connections are with one party. That is hardly the case of Nielsen, Merksamer, Hodgson, Parrinello and Mueller. In fact, its rather substantial lobbying business grew out of its political activities.

Nielsen is more or less the official law firm of the California Republican Party with people such as Steve Merksamer, one-time chief of staff to former Gov. Deukmejian; Bob Naylor, a former Assembly minority leader and state party chairman; Vigo "Chip" Nielsen, a longtime Republican activist; and Charles Bell, a counsel for the Republican Party. The firm handles every political chore, from raising money, to writing initiatives and ballot arguments, to handling election law. Merksamer originally derived his stature from his connections to Deukmejian, but he has evolved as a top party figure in his own right. Members of the firm were key voices helping to push Gov. Wilson into the 1990 gubernatorial campaign.

Their style is that of some old-time Washington firms – a full-service tune played to a strictly political beat. It was heavily involved in the efforts that led to Proposition 111, the 1990 gas-tax increase. But the corps of lobbyists in the firm are also involved in legislative battles. It was Naylor, who is officially registered as a lobbyist, and Merksamer, who is not but acts as a sort of high-level contact man, who were major organizers of the 1987 "Frank Fat's Napkin" tort-reform deal. They helped push almost every major economic power in the state – insurers, manufacturers, doctors, lawyers and more – into a multilevel compromise that also gave new protections to their clients, the tobacco industry. The firm's lobbyists often trade on their connections in the governor's office, although those have weakened slightly since power shifted from Deukmejian to Wilson.

Nielsen is the major California firm for the powerful tobacco lobby. It represents industry giants Philip Morris U.S.A. and R.J. Reynolds, plus the industry's public relations and political vehicle, the Tobacco Institute. Other powerful clients include the Irvine Co., the Southland Corp., General Mills, Summa Corp. and Waste Management Inc. That lineup in 1990 earned the firm $1.7 million in lobbying fees.

NOSSMAN, GUNTHER, KNOX & ELLIOT

One look at the list of clients would be enough to convince anyone that Nossman, Gunther, Knox & Elliot is a major player on the Sacramento scene. The firm has major insurance companies, some large municipal agencies, Avis Rent-A-Car, General Electric, Pearle Health Systems, the Recording Industry Association of America, lending institutions and some high-technology companies, among others. All told, Nossman earned $1.6 million in 1990, and it has been one of the fastest growing of any California lobbying firm. It is another of the full-service firms, with six lobbyists and everything from lawyers to public relations people to Washington connections.

Nossman uses its resources well. Its lobbyists are well-versed in the issues and the firm can fight battles on every front. Nossman also uses the resources of its clients well, throwing their campaign contributions into the fray. Its lobbyists have been successful on a range of issues, and its reputation is that of the firm for clients who want to do whatever it takes to win. Like many of the larger firms, Nossman is as good at recruiting and keeping clients as it is at fighting legislative battles. In a day when the big firms are gaining more and more of an advantage at persuading interests to use them as lobbyists, Nossman's John Knox, a former assemblyman, is regarded as one of the more successful people at winning over and satisfying clients, as well as one of the smartest politicians to serve in the Legislature.

But unlike some full-service firms, Nossman's lobbying efforts have become centered around one individual, John Foran. A legislator for more than two decades, Foran was the chairman of the Senate Transportation Committee and was regarded as one of the more knowledgeable men in the state on such issues. He still has more connections in the Capitol than some current lawmakers. Foran's style is Mr. Nice Guy. Unlike some of the other top lobbyists, he never seems to be really pressuring anyone. And unlike a few of the top lobbyists who make a point of standing inside the railing outside the Assembly floor – a move that is partly an effort to send a message about their clout to lawmakers and other lobbyists – unassuming Foran, with as much clout as almost anyone, usually waits patiently on the other side.

The major associations

THE CALIFORNIA CHAMBER OF COMMERCE

The representative of the state's mainstream businesses, the California Chamber of Commerce's approach can best be described as pragmatically conservative. For years, it has been most involved in bread-and-butter issues such as labor relations and workers' compensation issues. But more recently, transportation has taken on new priority, and the chamber was the mainstay of the effort in 1990 that passed Proposition 111, the fuel-tax increase. It has also helped lead the fight against some of the state's environmental initiatives, including Proposition 65, the clean-water and toxics-control measure that passed in 1986, and Proposition 128, the all-encompassing Big Green environmental initiative, which failed in 1990.

The chamber employs a dozen lobbyists, either full-time or retained by contract, including Alister McAlister, a longtime chairman of the Assembly Finance and

Insurance Committee. But its most energetic and influential mover and shaker is its president, Kirk West, an insider among state Republican leaders and a force among legislators despite the fact that he is not registered as a lobbyist.

CALIFORNIA FARM BUREAU FEDERATION

With a bent toward the state's larger farmers, the California Farm Bureau Federation is the state's most influential agriculture lobby. It has for decades fought hard for the growers on farm labor issues, and more recently has opposed increased regulation of pesticides and toxic-waste disposal. It is also a big player in the perpetual battles over water, and along with other major business lobbies, was a large part of the opposition to Proposition 65 and Big Green.

The bureau, as would be expected of a big business lobby, buys a good deal of influence with its campaign money. But it also exerts strong pressure on a core of legislators from agricultural regions such as the Central Valley, where public opinion is firmly aligned with farming interests. Those legislators, as would be expected, control the agriculture committees in both houses. The bureau has no dominant lobbyist, but its corps is hard working and thorough.

CALIFORNIA MANUFACTURERS ASSOCIATION

One of the state's major business lobbies, it speaks for many of California's biggest companies and is solidly conservative on pocketbook issues. The CMA has doggedly fought tough environmental controls, including Big Green and other ballot measures, and has been so concerned about workers' compensation issues that it formed the splinter group to focus on it, Californians for Compensation Reform. It also has lobbied the Legislature and the Public Utilities Commission for trucking deregulation (usually opposing the trucking industry) and against trucking safety requirements in attempts to bring down shipping rates.

The CMA has become one of California's bigger money players. One of its major contract lobbyists is Donald "Big O" BrOwn. It also hired away from the Legislature former Sen. William Campbell, an Orange County Republican who has a sunny disposition and who, as a legislator, had a reputation for sneaky special-interest deals. Campbell, the CMA's president, is a ubiquitous presence around the Legislature, but he is not a registered lobbyist. And since he's not officially a lobbyist, Campbell is allowed, as a former member, access to the Senate and Assembly floors, something that is denied other lobbyists. Campbell recently returned the favor of employment by hiring as a contract lobbyist E.A. "Rick" Melendez, the former head of ARCO's lobbying operation and the man who led the CMA search team that eventually hired Campbell.

CALIFORNIA TEACHERS ASSOCIATION

An organization that has grown in influence in recent years, the California Teachers Association hit pay dirt with Proposition 98, the 1988 initiative that guaranteed schools a big cut of state financing. Although active on labor issues, CTA's top priority, despite what its leaders say, is to get money for schools – which generally translates to salaries for teachers. The CTA has isolated itself from most other social welfare groups that would seem to be natural allies because it has been reluctant to let go of any purse strings. That was hammered home in 1990 when the CTA joined forces with the alcohol industry to oppose a variety of public interest groups, mental health organizations and hospitals that were pushing Proposition 134, a liquor tax hike measure. The CTA's opposition was one of precedent, not principle. None of the new tax money would have gone to schools, and CTA wants no exemptions to Proposition 98's promised share of new revenues.

The CTA gives large campaign contributions, has a savvy lobbying team with strong ties to Assembly Speaker Willie Brown and is organized in every nook and cranny in the state, a combination that makes it formidable. It is led by Political Director Alice Huffman, who was head of the state Office of Economic Opportunity under Gov. Jerry Brown, and Owen Waters, who is something of a political guru with years of lobbying experience.

CALIFORNIA TRIAL LAWYERS ASSOCIATION

Although its 5,000 members make it one of the smallest of the major players, the California Trial Lawyers Association is one of the most powerful interests on the state political scene. For decades, it has held off its mortal enemies – the state insurance industry and the California Medical Association – in a war without end. The CTLA has untiringly fought for insurance regulation and generous workers' compensation, against tort reform and no-fault insurance, always pushing the right to sue. Aligned with a variety of consumer advocates, it was a major part of the insurance initiative war in 1988, sponsoring its own failed initiative and opposing Proposition 103, the only survivor of the five ballot measures.

Along with its little brother-in-arms, the California Applicants Attorneys Association, the CTLA is a consummate inside player, dominating the Legislature's judiciary committees and giving piles of campaign cash. Its clout comes from that money, from the fact that a long list of legislators are also lawyers and from its very able battalion of lobbyists. Among them are two of California's most effective: Donald Green, an aggressive, hard-nosed, patient advocate whose firm, Green and Azevedo, works almost exclusively for the attorneys; and ex-Sen. Bob Wilson, another longtime lobbyist.

THE INSURANCE INDUSTRY

Once united, more or less, under one umbrella organization – the Association of California Insurance Companies – the state's major insurance companies have scattered to a variety of associations, and a number of companies are fighting the battle on their own. Once considered an immovable object around the Capitol, the industry has become one of the favorite whipping boys for some lawmakers. But while suffering defeats at the polls and bashings in the press, the insurance industry has lost only a little influence. It is still the No. 1 contributor to campaign coffers, and it can block legislation on almost any subject except auto insurance, which is too publicly volatile. Locked in a perpetual battle with the trial lawyers, the insurance industry fights a war against regulation and for workers'-compensation reform, lower health-care expenses and the adoption of no-fault insurance.

Its lobbyists include Clayton Jackson, one of the state's two or three most influential lobbyists, Dennis Carpenter and scores of others. In fact, insurers may have more lobbyists than any other industry in California. Jackson, who once handled ACIC, now works for the Alliance of American Insurers, a collection of larger, stock-owner-run companies. Carpenter now lobbies for ACIC, but it has lost a number of members and some clout. The Agents and Brokers Association, represented by John Norwood, is another influential group.

LEAGUE OF CALIFORNIA CITIES and COUNTY SUPERVISORS ASSOCIATION OF CALIFORNIA

Two separate operations, the League of California Cities and the County Supervisors Association of California are similar in nature and often allies in trying to wrest money away from the state for local government. Yet that alliance is uneasy, at best, because they usually end up fighting over who gets what state money, how property tax is divided and what programs are whose responsibility. Whenever they can, however, they try to present a united front to level as much influence as they can on legislators.

Because they represent local governments, they cannot play the money game, but they do use their expertise and public opinion whenever possible. They also try to join with those governments that hire their own lobbyists. Both have a phalanx of lobbyists led by their executive directors – for the league, it is Don Benninghoven; for the supervisors, it is Larry Naake. The supervisors also use respected contract lobbyist Kathy Rees.

THE STATE EMPLOYEE UNIONS

The state employee unions could be a formidable force on issues of common concern, but they almost never work together. Even on something as central as pay raises, they all go off on their own. If an issue goes to court, two or three different unions often file individual suits. All are involved in wage, safety, comparable worth, retirement and other traditional workplace issues. To varying degrees, however, they specialize in areas of unique interest. The California Correctional Peace Officers' Association, for example, gets into crime issues, while the Professional Engineers in California Government fights state efforts to contract work with private firms.

State unions have substantial clout in the Legislature, in part from their big spending on campaigns and their ability to marshal large numbers of election workers. The California State Employees' Association, the largest of the unions, has respected lobbyists in Sherrie Golden, Robert Zenz and Mike Varacalli, and spent more than $500,000 on candidates and ballot measures in 1989-90. The Correctional Peace Officers' Association is smaller but spends even more if the need arises. Gavin McHugh and Jeff Thompson carry their causes in the Legislature. Aaron Read and Associates handles legislation for some of the larger independent unions, including those managed by the politically potent Blanning & Baker Associates. Read's clients include unions for scientists, engineers, attorneys, highway patrolmen and foresters. Peter J. Jensen is the lobbyist for the California Union of Safety Employees.

Public interest groups

CALIFORNIA COMMON CAUSE

The California branch of the nation's largest good-government lobby, California Common Cause has fought losing battles for years on its major issues of concern: open meetings, voter registration, election financing reform and legislative ethics. Its top priority – in fact, its religion – is public financing of elections, but it remains a distant, ethereal dream. But the group, like many others dissatisfied with the Legislature, has had some recent success at the polls. In 1988, its Proposition 68, which would have created public financing of legislative races, received enough votes to pass but was canceled out by the more popular Proposition 73, a contribution-limits measure placed on the ballot to kill public financing.

California Common Cause has lost some of its public pizzazz since its high-profile director, Walter Zelman, resigned in 1990 to run for state insurance commissioner. But lobbyist Ruth Holton has been a constant presence in the Capitol, offsetting the political inexperience of the new executive director, Lisa Foster, a veteran public-interest lawyer. California Common Cause also spends a great deal of time fighting special-interest and anti-consumer legislation, often using its only real weapon, public exposure. It issues reports on campaign spending and special-interest contributions, and its people make sure reporters know about any back-room deals they can find.

CONSUMERS UNION

Like other public-interests groups, Consumers Union spends a good deal of its time in retreat, trying to slow rather than stop the advances of special interests. CU has a broad range of concerns, from consumer advocacy to good government. In recent years, it has been in the forefront of the fight to regulate insurance companies, and its leaders have been outspoken against the excesses of political consultants. The organization also has fought pitched battles with the state Department of Insurance over protection of consumers, insurance rates and, most recently, implementation of Proposition 103, the 1988 insurance-reform initiative.

In the Capitol, CU is led by its 15-year West Coast director, Harry Snyder, who functions sometimes as an insider, trying to cut pro-consumer deals, and sometimes as an outsider, standing before the press and screaming bloody murder about the latest special-interest move. He is backed by Judith Bell and Nettie Hoge, among others, all of whom focus on the details of legislation and pressing their cases aggressively. However, what clout there is for Consumers Union, or any other consumer group, comes mostly from its ability to get its criticism into the media.

PLANNING AND CONSERVATION LEAGUE

This is a coalition of 120 environmental groups, large and small, that covers the state and the full spectrum of issues. The major concerns tend to be water, toxics, air pollution, transit and resource use, but the PCL can be found in almost any environmental fight. In recent years, the group has gone outside the Capitol and to the ballot box for its major victories, and some have been substantial. The PCL was instrumental in 1988 in pushing Proposition 70, a $776 million bond for park, wildlife and coastal preservation, and Proposition 99, the tobacco tax increase. In 1990, it won on Proposition 116, a $1.9 billion bond for rail and other public transit, and on Proposition 117, which protects mountain lions, other wildlife and fisheries.

PCL, led by Executive Director Gerald Meral, has gained much of its clout from its ability to put together coalitions to push ballot measures and in making trade-offs to make those efforts politically feasible. But the PCL, with lobbyist Corey Brown, is also an ever-present voice in the Capitol. The group tries to team with other environmental or consumer-advocacy groups and liberal legislators, but often must settle for small concessions rather than big wins.

THE SIERRA CLUB

Much like the PCL, the Sierra Club tries to play a part in just about any environmental, natural-resource or energy-use issue in the state. The club, however, is one large organization and gets its clout from its activist, grass-roots membership and from its public image as good guys. Support from the Sierra Club name is the most convincing argument that politicians can use to certify for voters that they are genuine environmentalists. The Sierra Club has been a little less initiative-oriented than the PCL, but has joined most environmental ballot causes and was one of the major players behind the Big Green initiative that failed in 1990.

The Sierra Club, led by State Director Mike Paparian, often works in tandem with the PCL and other environmental groups in lobbying the Legislature or administrative agencies. It might be a bit more focused on land-use and hazardous wastes than its environmental cousin, but the objectives of the two organizations are almost identical.

9

California's movers and shakers

To the larger public, politics is an activity of politicians, the men and women who offer themselves for public office. But behind the candidates exists a complex network of professionals and amateurs who design, finance and manage the campaigns voters see. These are the movers and shakers of politics, who have at least as much influence as the out-front candidates for office. Their motives range from ideological conviction to greed, and, if anything, their role is increasing as campaigns become more expensive and sophisticated.

California's power brokers are especially obscure because of the state's unique political system, features of which include weak party structures, non-partisan local governments and a multitude of locally based political organizations. Other major states such as Illinois and New York have more formalized political power structures. During Richard Daley's heyday as mayor of Chicago, for instance, no one doubted that he was the boss, not only in his city, but of the entire Illinois Democratic Party. Those who aspired to office, whether it was the clerkship of the smallest court or the president of the United States, had to clear through Daley or his minions.

Behind-the-scenes political power in California is wielded more indirectly. And in a state of media and money politics, rather than street-level organizations, those with access to money form the elite. That fact becomes ever-more important as California's clout in national politics expands. The Los Angeles area has evolved into a source of national political money at least as important as the concrete canyons of New York City, and it continues to gain strength as new campaign finance laws make direct contributions more difficult.

California also has developed a cadre of professional campaign organizers – "consultants," as they prefer to be called – who have pioneered in the sophisticated techniques of mass political communications: television, computer-directed mail and, most recently, prerecorded video tapes that combine the impact of television with the selectivity of mail.

403

Every four years, a little ritual occurs. Those who aspire to the White House begin booking flights to Los Angeles International Airport, not to present themselves to voters, but to schmooze with a handful of men and women who reside within a few miles of one another on the West Side of Los Angeles. Most of those who make the pilgrimages to Los Angeles are Democrats because most of the West Side's political financiers also are Democrats with connections to the huge, Los Angeles-based entertainment industry. But not a few of them are Republicans. Prior to the 1988 presidential primary season, Republican Bob Dole raised more money out of Hollywood than did Democrat Michael Dukakis.

THE HOLLYWOOD BRANCH

Hollywood types tend to be passionate about their causes and free with their money, which is exactly what politicians want. It's been estimated that the Los Angeles region accounts for one-fifth of all the money spent on presidential primaries.

"There's an increasingly mutual attraction between political people and entertainment people," Stanley Scheinbaum, an economist and political activist, has said. "The politicians like the glitz and the entertainment people like the power." But Scheinbaum and others have qualms about the growing influence of entertainers – most of whom are naive – on politics through these in-and-out fund-raising visits.

"I don't think it's healthy," he says. "Basically, a few rich people get that opportunity (to meet the politicians), and I don't think the influence of these kind of people should be any greater than of those folks in the ghettos and barrios."

Among the Democrats, two organized groups have emerged in recent years. One is the Hollywood Women's Political Committee, founded in 1984 by singer/actress Barbra Streisand. The committee specializes in star-studded fund-raising extravaganzas on behalf of liberal candidates and causes. Streisand, for instance, staged a big fund-raiser for U.S. Sen. Alan Cranston at her Malibu ranch in 1986 and repackaged the entertainment as a television special, thus magnifying its financial impact. The second and newer organization is the Show Coalition, known as ShowCo, founded in 1988 by younger Hollywood figures, most of whom had been identified with Gary Hart's abortive presidential bid. ShowCo has not yet become a major fund-raising source but acts as an intermediary between politicians and entertainers, staging seminars and other non-financial events.

Sometimes the relationships between politicians and entertainers can backfire. State Assemblyman Tom Hayden, the former radical and ex-husband of actress Jane Fonda, took a group of "brat pack" actors to the 1988 Democratic convention in Atlanta for an immersion in politics. Among the young stars was Rob Lowe. Months later, it was revealed that Lowe had made explicit videotapes of sexual escapades with local girls during the convention.

Streisand and actor Robert Redford (who starred together in the semi-political movie "The Way We Were") are the prototypical Hollywood liberals, willing to devote time and money to their candidates and causes. While Streisand prefers to work directly for candidates, Redford takes a loftier, issue-oriented approach through a foundation that he has endowed. But they are not alone. Others who share their ideological commitment include Morgan Fairchild, who was especially close to Cranston before his career self-destructed; Sally Field; Cher; Gregory Peck; Ally Sheedy; Bette Midler; Goldie Hawn; Chevy Chase; Bruce Willis; Ted Danson and Ed Begley Jr.

Jerry Brown developed especially tight ties to the Hollywood Democrats during his eight years as governor and as a perennial candidate for president and U.S. senator. He was singer Linda Ronstadt's self-proclaimed "boyfriend" for a time, dated other Hollywood figures and made Lucy's El Adobe Cafe, a hangout for actors, his unofficial Los Angeles headquarters. Actors such as Warren Beatty and Jane Fonda and singers such as Ronstadt and Helen Reddy raised tons of money for Brown's non-stop campaigns, and director Francis Ford Coppola produced an ill-fated live television program in Wisconsin during Brown's second unsuccessful campaign for the presidency in 1980. Gary Hart was the Hollywood liberals' clear favorite for president in 1984 and again in 1988 until he was forced to withdraw. So far, none of the would-be presidents has won the heart of Hollywood Democrats for 1992, although several are trying hard.

Ronald Reagan personified the blurry line that separates politics and show business, and during his political career he solidified the ties that bind many in Hollywood to the GOP. The most outwardly political of the Hollywood conservatives these days is Charlton Heston, who makes commercials for Republican candidates. Heston has often been mentioned as a potential candidate himself, so often that he's developed a stock rejoinder: "I'd rather play a senator than be one." Heston's fellow Republican, Clint Eastwood, did pursue a brief political career as mayor of Carmel, but has since returned to full-time movie-making.

Comedian Bob Hope is a mainstay of Republican fund-raising events and, not surprisingly, most of the other Hollywood conservatives are of the older generation such as Frank Sinatra, Fred MacMurray and James Stewart. But some newer and younger stars also side with the GOP, such as Sylvester Stallone, Tony Danza, Chuck Norris, Jaclyn Smith and strongman-turned-actor Arnold Schwarzenegger, who's married to Kennedy clanswoman Maria Shriver.

Hollywood politics, however, involves more than the men and women whose names are found on theater marquees and record labels. The business side of show business also is heavily involved in politics in terms of both personal conviction and financial betterment. The most prominent of the Hollywood tycoons who dabble in politics is Lew Wasserman, head of the huge MCA entertainment conglomerate (which was sold to Japanese investors in 1990).

Wasserman plays both sides of the partisan fence. He is a Democrat but he had particularly close ties to Reagan from the latter's days as an MCA client and star of MCA-produced television programs. Republican Gov. Pete Wilson also established a close relationship with Wasserman during his U.S. Senate career, blocking aid to any would-be political rival. The entertainment industry, like any in California, has business in Washington and Sacramento, mostly involving tax treatment on those incredibly complex movie and television deals. Wilson, for instance, endeared himself to the show biz tycoons by protecting their interests during the writing of federal tax reform laws.

Jerry Weintraub is another movie mogul who dabbles in politics. He served on Republican George Bush's finance team in 1988, although he's best known as a Democratic campaign contributor. Producer Norman Lear has made liberal causes his second career and Frank Wells, head of the Walt Disney entertainment empire, has been toying with seeking a U.S. Senate seat in 1992.

During the 1990 elections, Hollywood's political activists were recruited in record numbers to both raise money and appear in commercials. The Legislature's Democratic leaders recruited actor Jack Lemmon to make a series of TV ads – widely criticized as misleading – opposing measures to overhaul legislative redistricting processes and later persuaded actress Angela Lansbury, actor James Garner and others to pitch against measures that would impose legislative term limits. The first campaign worked but the second failed.

Hollywood environmentalists, meanwhile, went all out in 1990 for Big Green, the broad protection measure that was rejected by voters, and Forests Forever, another failed measure that would have imposed severe restrictions on logging.

Much of the Hollywood hierarchy is Jewish and politicians who want its support must adhere to a strong pro-Israel line. That's why Jerry Brown, Alan Cranston, Pete Wilson, Ronald Reagan and any other California politician who aspires to the political big time in Washington can be counted in Israel's corner. In contrast, when Rep. Pete McCloskey ran for the Senate in 1982 as a critic of Israel, he bombed in Hollywood and Republican Rep. Ed Zschau suffered a similar treatment when he ran against Cranston in 1986.

ELSEWHERE IN THE SOUTHLAND

Not everybody who writes a fat check to a politician in California is an entertainment industry figure. As a prosperous and fast-growing state, California has produced more than its share of wealthy people who give to candidates from both parties or – perhaps more important – can ask others to contribute as peers rather than political beggars.

Not surprisingly, Southern California aerospace executives tilt toward the Republicans with their promises of greater military spending. When, for instance, George Bush made a quick, money-raising trip to Southern California in 1988 while seeking the Republican presidential nomination, he stopped at the TRW aerospace plant in Redondo Beach, then headed for private fund-raising events at the Bel Air home of real estate tycoon Howard Ruby and the Rancho Mirage estate of publisher Walter Annenberg.

Donald Bren, head of the big Irvine Co. land development firm in Orange County, has emerged in recent years as a Republican financial power, supplanting such older kingmakers as auto dealer Holmes Tuttle, who was part of the group that persuaded Ronald Reagan to run for governor in 1966. (Most of those prominent early Reagan backers have since died.) Pete Wilson's election as governor in 1990 may have made Bren the most influential of the new kingmakers. He and Wilson served in the Marine Corps together and Larry Thomas, Wilson's (and George Deukmejian's) one-time press secretary, serves as Bren's chief media spokesman. The Irvine connection to Wilson was underscored when Wilson chose John Seymour, a state senator from Orange County with strong ties to the Irvine executives, as his successor in the U.S. Senate.

Financier David Murdock is another Southern California business mogul with strong Republican connections, as is Lodwrick Cook, chairman of Atlantic Richfield Co. Philip Hawley, chairman of the Carter-Hawley-Hale department store chain, was once a major Republican player but with his company's shaky financial situation in recent years, his political star has dimmed.

The Southern California business types who lean toward the Democratic side include Richard O'Neill, an heir to vast landholdings in Orange County who has been known to devote weekends to precinct-walking. He once served as state Democratic chairman. Michael Milken, the junk bond whiz kid whose career crashed in scandal and who was sentenced to a long stretch in federal prison, was closely identified with several Democratic political figures, including Cranston and former Rep. Tony Coelho. In fact, Coelho was forced to resign after revelations that he had acquired a bond through Milken under suspicious circumstances.

One of the towering figures of Southern California political financing defied easy categorization. Armand Hammer, oilman, philanthropist and private diplomat, was an adviser to and fund-raiser for countless California politicians of both parties before his death.

THE FAST-FOOD MOGULS OF SAN DIEGO

San Diego, which tries to isolate itself from Los Angeles, has developed its own infrastructure of political power brokers. Newspaper publisher Helen Copley is a powerhouse, as is Joan Kroc, who inherited the McDonald's hamburger empire and a baseball team from her late husband, Ray. Banker and deal-maker Richard Silberman, who is married to San Diego County Supervisor Susan Golding, was a big political player – even serving for a time in Jerry Brown's administration in Sacramento – until he was convicted on drug-money laundering charges in 1990.

Fast-food moguls represent a particular subspecies of political financiers in California. In addition to the Krocs, Silberman once headed the Jack-in-the-Box hamburger chain in partnership with Robert Peterson, whose wife, Maureen O'Connor, is the Democratic mayor of San Diego. And Carl's Jr. chain founder Carl Karcher is a patron of Republican and right-wing causes in Orange County.

Another subspecies is the political lawyer and the prime examples are to be found in the offices of a Los Angeles law firm headed by Charles Manatt, former Democratic national chairman, and ex-U.S. Sen. John Tunney. Mickey Kantor, one of Southern California's most effective political lawyers, is a member of the firm, and a former associate is John Emerson, who periodically takes time out from his practice to run campaigns, such as that of Gary Hart.

MOVERS AND SHAKERS OF THE NORTH

Northern California's power brokers tend to operate more quietly than their southern counterparts. Among Republicans, no one is quieter or more influential than David Packard, a co-founder of the Hewlett-Packard computer firm and perhaps California's richest man, with a personal fortune exceeding $2 billion. (Bren vies for the unofficial title.) Packard tends to support moderate to liberal Republicans. He was, for instance, instrumental in helping Tom Campbell unseat a conservative Republican incumbent, Rep. Ernest Konnyu, in 1988 in his home district on the San Francisco Peninsula.

Packard is the grand old man of Silicon Valley, the center of California's computer industry. As computer entrepreneurs have matured in business terms, they also have become civic and political leaders. One, Ed Zschau, won a seat in Congress and came within a few thousand votes of unseating Sen. Alan Cranston in 1986. He had been expected to run again in 1992, but he announced in early 1991 that he wouldn't be a candidate.

To date, the computer moguls have wielded influence mostly at the local level, helping San Jose and the rest of Silicon Valley develop an infrastructure to match their population and economic growth. But some, such as Packard, have moved beyond. His influence extends to the White House, and he was a quiet prod to Gov. George Deukmejian on doing something about California's traffic problems.

Two other Northern California tycoons whose influence extends well beyond the state are the Bechtels, Stephen Sr. and Stephen Jr., who run San Francisco-based Bechtel Corp., a worldwide construction and engineering firm. At one time, it seemed as if half the Reagan administration in Washington consisted of ex-Bechtel executives, such as Secretary of Defense Caspar Weinberger and Secretary of State George Schultz.

Among Northern California Democratic financiers, none ranks higher than San Francisco real estate investor Walter Shorenstein. Shorenstein labors tirelessly on behalf of the party's coffers and is courted just as tirelessly by presidential hopefuls. In 1989, however, Shorenstein declared independence after former Gov. Jerry Brown became state party chairman. Shorenstein and Bruce Lee, a high-ranking United Auto Workers official, established a "soft-money" drive to aid Democratic presidential nominee Michael Dukakis in California in 1988 and decided to continue the separate fund despite entreaties from Brown that they fold their operation into his party apparatus.

Another San Franciscan who has wielded a big stick in Democratic financial circles is attorney Duane Garrett, although his standing fell in 1988 after he attached himself to Bruce Babbitt's ill-fated voyage into presidential waters. He suffered another setback in 1990 when ex-San Francisco Mayor Dianne Feinstein lost the governorship, a campaign in which Feinstein's husband, investment counselor Richard Blum, emerged as a willing political financier, at least when his wife was involved. And among San Francisco insiders, Henry Berman, a "consultant" to the Seagram's liquor empire, carries much clout for his political fund raising ability. He has been especially close to Assembly Speaker Willie Brown.

Shorenstein, Garrett and Berman are valued not so much for their personal wealth, which is fairly modest in the case of the latter two, but for their organizational ability. They can pull together a substantial amount of political money simply by making a few phone calls or placing their names on invitations.

Gordon Getty, who may be California's second- or third-wealthiest man, is a different kind of political financier. Getty, a San Francisco resident, is an heir to the Getty oil fortune but devotes much of his time to private endeavors, especially composing classical music. Wife Ann Getty is a political junkie who lends her husband's name and her energies to political enterprises.

The East Bay – Oakland, Alameda County and Contra Costa County – has developed its own coterie of political pooh-bahs. Jack Brooks, a part-owner of the Raiders football team, carries a lot of weight among Democrats, and developers Joe Callahan, Ron Cowan and Ken Hoffman play major roles at the local levels. Ken Behring, a developer and owner of the Seattle Seahawks football team, has also developed a reputation for political dealing at the local level with influence that stretches into the Legislature.

SACRAMENTO MOVES UP

Sacramento, another fast-growing area, has seen its developers become political heavyweights, and not just at the local level. The Northern California and Republican equivalent of the Manatt-Tunney law firm in Southern California also is found in Sacramento and includes Steve Merksamer, a one-time top aide to Deukmejian. Merksamer and his colleagues at the firm represent top-drawer corporate clients in political affairs while Merksamer functions as a Republican insider, informally advising Deukmejian and playing a seminal role in persuading Pete Wilson to give up his U.S. Senate seat for a successful run at the governorship.

Two of Sacramento's developers, Angelo Tsakopoulos and Phil Angelides, were big-money contributors and fund-raisers for fellow Greek-Americans Michael Dukakis and Art Agnos, mayor of San Francisco, in 1988. Angelides, a former Capitol aide, is considering a run for Congress in 1992. In early 1991 he became the de facto, if not actual, head of the state Democratic Party after Jerry Brown left to run for the Senate in 1992.

They exemplify another trend in political financing in California: the creation of groups that help people of similar ethnic backgrounds pursue their political careers. Frozen out of traditional sources of Republican campaign money, for instance, George Deukmejian tapped the state's large and wealthy Armenian-American community. Los Angeles lawyer Karl Samuelian organized the effort, and with Deukmejian's victory, he became a major power in Republican politics. Similar organization efforts have aided Asian politicians such as Los Angeles City Councilman Michael Woo and Sacramento Rep. Robert Matsui, while Los Angeles' large Jewish community has been a major source of campaign money for both parties, and not just for Jewish candidates.

Hispanics and blacks have yet to develop similarly powerful ethnic fund-raising networks, although black entertainers have helped such political figures as Los Angeles Mayor Tom Bradley. The most important black political financier in the state has been Sam Williams, a Los Angeles attorney who is close to Bradley.

DOWN ON THE FARM

In California's major agricultural valleys the financial and political powers are, not surprisingly, connected to agribusiness. The state's wealthiest agribusinessmen – and two of the most influential – are Modesto's Gallo wine-making brothers, Ernest and Julio. The secretive brothers have personal wealth estimated at nearly $1 billion and are powerful political figures in the Central Valley. They played major roles in organizing and financing the successful campaign in 1990 against a ballot measure that would have sharply increased taxes on liquor.

Further south, amid the cotton fields of the lower San Joaquin Valley, the powers are the Boswells and the Salyers, two agribusiness families whose holdings sweep across the now-dry expanse of Tulare Lake. The Boswells – the largest privately owned farming operation in the world with interests in other states and Australia – and the Salyers play political hardball with campaign funds and high-priced lobbyists to protect their interests in Sacramento and Washington. And their major interests lie in protecting and enhancing the public water supplies vital to their farming operations.

Norma Foster Maddy has double-barreled political clout. She's not only the heiress to the Foster Farms chicken empire, but she's married to state Sen. Ken Maddy, the Republican leader of the Senate. And Maddy's partner in the horse racing business is John Harris, head of Harris Farms. The wine-making families of the Napa and nearby valleys are major powers in local politics and the scion of one family, Don Sebastiani, briefly served in the state Legislature.

LABOR'S LOST LOVE

At last count, about 2 million California workers belonged to labor unions, a number that's holding steady even as labor's overall share of the expanding work force has slipped to under 20 percent. Despite that relative decline, California labor leaders remain powerful political figures, able to turn out bodies and distribute money at levels that are decisive in many political conflicts. A prime example occurred in 1987, when a big labor turnout helped Democrat Cecil Green capture a Los Angeles County state Senate seat that seemed destined to go Republican. Labor fired up its troops on an issue near to worker's hearts: Republican Deukmejian's unilateral closure of the state's occupational safety and health inspection agency. Later, labor obtained voter approval of Proposition 97, a measure reinstating the agency, and won approval of a major increase in California's minimum wage. So while labor's ranks may have thinned, they can be potent.

The leading labor figure in California is Jack Henning, an old-school orator and organizer who serves as secretary-treasurer of the California Labor Federation (the AFL-CIO umbrella organization) and is largely a one-man band. Henning walks the hallways of the Capitol personally to lobby legislation affecting labor's interests and battles privately and publicly with employers and politicians who don't follow his bidding. A major overhaul of the state's system of compensating injured workers in 1989 was Henning's major accomplishment of the decade and, some believe, the high note on which he will retire. But if Henning is ready to step down, labor doesn't have anyone immediately positioned to step into his shoes. Bill Robertson, the AFL-CIO's man in Los Angeles, is a secondary labor power, as is United Auto Workers official Bruce Lee.

Cesar Chavez was an enigmatic and influential figure of the 1970s as head of the United Farm Workers' Union, but in more recent years, with a hostile Republican administration in Sacramento, his clout and that of his union have dropped like a stone.

Labor's major gains in recent years have been among public employees, and the leaders of their unions have seen their visibility and power increase, especially since they are free with campaign funds. Ed Foglia, who heads the California Teachers Association, is one of labor's new power figures. His stock rose when the CTA won voter approval in 1988 of a major overhaul of school financing. The large California State Employees' Association also is a major source of campaign money, but it rotates its presidency often, which prevents any individual from becoming a figure of independent stature.

ORGANIZATIONS OF OTHER COLORS

The public employee unions exemplify another trend in California political financing: the increasing clout of large organizations with direct financial interests in political decision-making.

In the halls of government in Sacramento, big business doesn't loom very large. The groups that count – because they annually distribute hundreds of thousands of dollars to political campaigns – are the associations of professionals, such as the California Trial Lawyers Association, the California Medical Association and the California Nurses Association. They approach fund-raising as a cost of doing business and operate their distribution systems in close consultation with their lobbyists, who daily walk the hallways of the Capitol seeking to pass and kill legislation that impacts people they represent. But that workaday attitude toward political financing also is accompanied by relative anonymity. The men and women who operate these and other associations aren't political kingmakers in the usual sense of the word, although they wield considerable political power. They are narrowly focused on their issues and uninterested in the larger political picture.

California's most powerful political agenda-setters in recent years have been those most adept at writing, financing and organizing campaigns for the increasingly numerous ballot measures. But increasing voter resistance to their schemes, as evidenced in the 1990 election returns, may signal an end to their days in the political sun.

THE INITIATIVE ENTREPRENEURS

The prototypical initiative entrepreneurs were Howard Jarvis and Paul Gann, two old men (both now dead) who sponsored Proposition 13 in 1978. The financial and political impact of Proposition 13 made Jarvis and Gann, especially the former, into high-profile political figures and thus into political powerhouses in the media-heavy atmosphere of the 1980s. They were besieged with requests to lend their names to additional ballot measures and to endorse candidates for office and they engaged in both. Gann even became a candidate himself for the U.S. Senate in 1980, losing to Cranston.

In the mid-1980s, a new crop of initiative designers arose, this time on the left side of the political ledger. Initially, the most spectacularly successful was Harvey Rosenfield, a young consumer advocate and Ralph Nader disciple who founded "Voter Revolt." In 1988 his organization put together Proposition 103, a successful auto insurance reform initiative that won in the face of a $60 million-plus opposition campaign financed by the insurance industry. Rosenfeld, whose penchant for publicity has been likened to that of Jarvis, immediately launched a second initiative campaign for the 1990 ballot, aimed at modifying Proposition 13 to remove its benefits from business property. And he, too, played political kingmaker by endorsing a candidate for the state insurance commissioner's position. But after his success with Proposition 103, Rosenfield fell on hard times. His candidate for insurance commissioner, Conway Collis, lost badly and none of Rosenfield's other initiatives made it to the ballot. Rosenfield's organization, meanwhile, experienced severe money problems, and he was forced to pare staff and close offices, desperately seeking some new issue that could put him back on top.

In Sacramento, meanwhile, an informal coalition of environmentalists is establishing its own ongoing initiative factory and already has several wins under its belt. Gerald Meral, the bearded, mild-mannered administrator of the Planning and Conservation League, operates as the consortium's coordinator, and he and his colleagues have devised a unique system of promoting their measures. Groups are invited to join the consortium by supplying a quota of cash or signatures. The contribution to the consortium entitles the donor to direct a share of the proceeds. The system was used on Proposition 70, a park bond issue, and Proposition 99, a cigarette tax measure in 1988, both successfully, and in 1990 for Proposition 116, a big rail-bond issue, and Proposition 134, a liquor tax measure for 1990, with the rail bonds winning.

Assemblyman Lloyd Connelly, a liberal Democrat from Sacramento, has been closely allied with the Meral consortium and became, in his self-effacing way, a powerful figure in setting the political agenda of the late 1980s. A much better known Democratic assemblyman, Tom Hayden, also is playing the initiative game. Hayden was a force behind the anti-toxics initiative, Proposition 65, in 1986 and Proposition 128, the so-called "Big Green" environmental protection measure, in 1990, which lost in the face of the anti-initiative mood of voters.

Republicans, too, are using the initiative as a tool of partisan and ideological warfare. Ross Johnson, the Assembly's Republican leader, has been especially active. He co-sponsored a campaign finance reform measure, Proposition 73, that was approved by voters in 1988 and backed one of the unsuccessful reapportionment initiatives in 1990. But beyond Johnson, the right side of the initiative business is moribund after the deaths of Jarvis and Gann. Gann's son, Richard, and daughter, Linda Gann-Stone, stepped in to keep his organization alive, but neither can command the media attention of their father. Even as the state edges rightward in its overall political orientation, the political left has captured the momentum in the use of initiatives to further its agenda.

MERCENARIES OF THE POLITICAL WARS

Standing just behind the candidates and the front men for the initiative campaigns are legions of professionals to whom the explosion of political activity in California is a lucrative growth industry, so much so that pros who used to practice out of Washington and New York are shifting their operations to California. Professional signature-gathering firms, fund-raisers, media consultants, pollsters, campaign strategists, accountants and even attorneys who specialize in writing, attacking and defending ballot propositions have reaped tens of millions of dollars in the 1980s as the mercenaries of the initiative wars. The most obviously profitable of those campaigns was the $100 million battle over five insurance initiatives in 1988. One campaign consultant alone earned over $10 million in fees.

The consultants, however, aren't just paid soldiers in California's political wars. Whether they are helping candidates or fighting over ballot measures, they have also become major players in determining who runs or what proposal is put before voters. They, too, shape the political agenda. Some specialize in Democratic or liberal candidates and causes, while others exclusively work the Republican and conservative side. And a few plow the middle, working for whomever has the most money or the best chance of winning.

Although professional campaign strategists theoretically stand in the background while the candidate is out front, sometimes their importance is reversed. When Clint Reilly announced in 1989 that he was giving up his management of Dianne Feinstein's campaign for governor, it was a political event of the first magnitude since Reilly, a credentialed professional, had been one of the ex-San Francisco mayor's most valuable assets. Reilly's departure lowered Feinstein's political stock and forced her to engage in a damage-control operation.

Dozens of campaign management firms operate in California but only a relative handful command statewide attention. Reilly, who operates under the name of Clinton Reilly Campaigns, is based in San Francisco and specializes in Democrats such as Feinstein, but he earned his biggest fee, more than $10 million, as the major strategist for the insurance industry in the 1988 ballot battle. And he kept the money despite the industry's wipeout at the polls. Reilly managed Feinstein's mayoralty campaigns and has advised Bill Honig, who was elected as state Superintendent of Public Instruction in 1982. Reilly also has done a number of local campaigns, including Gary Condit's 1989 victory in a special congressional election in the San Joaquin Valley, and will be overseeing Rep. Robert Matsui's U.S. Senate campaign in 1992. Abrasive and opinionated, Reilly is a controversial figure who feuded publicly for years with Assembly Speaker Willie Brown.

A rising star among the Democratic-oriented consultants is Richie Ross, who was Willie Brown's chief political adviser until striking out on his own after Brown lost some Assembly races in 1986. Ross, headquartered in Sacramento, had two statewide victories in 1988: Proposition 98, a school financing measure, and Proposition 97, a labor-backed proposal to restore the state worker safety program canceled by Gov. Deukmejian. He also managed Art Agnos' come-from-behind campaign for mayor of San Francisco in 1987 and was tapped by Agnos to run the campaign for a new baseball stadium in 1989. Ross suffered a big setback in 1990, however, when his candidate for governor, John Van de Kamp, blew an early lead and lost the Democratic nomination to Dianne Feinstein.

The most prominent Democratic campaign management firm in Southern California is BAD Campaigns, operated by Michael Berman, brother of Rep. Howard Berman, and Carl D'Agostino, a former aide to Ken Cory when Cory was state controller. BAD, based in Beverly Hills, specializes in candidates endorsed by the political organization headed by Reps. Howard Berman and Henry Waxman. The Berman-Waxman organization dominates politics on Los Angeles' West Side and dabbles in campaigns throughout Southern California. BAD also advised Gray Davis, the West Side Democrat elected as state controller in 1980, and is likely to operate Rep. Mel Levine's expected campaign for the Senate in 1992.

Los Angeles-based Cerrell Associates functions mostly as a public relations company, but it also handles some Democratic campaigns. Firm owner Joe Cerrell has national influence in Democratic politics.

A newcomer to the upper ranks of Democratic consultants is Sacramento's Townsend & Co. Owned by David Townsend, the firm broke out of the local category in 1988, when his firm managed – unsuccessfully – the campaign against a statewide cigarette tax ballot measure. But Townsend is beefing up to go after other statewide candidates and issues.

Another striver is Darry Sragow, who worked on Sen. Alan Cranston's successful campaign in 1986 and Lt. Gov. Leo McCarthy's failed 1988 bid for the U.S. Senate. In 1990, he replaced Reilly on the Feinstein effort. David Doak and Robert Shrum of Los Angeles are often called to advise Democratic campaigns on media strategy and theme-setting, leaving overall management to others.

There seem to be more Republican campaign management firms than Democratic ones, perhaps because the Republicans, as the minority party, lack the campaign-staff-in-place on the legislative payroll. While legislative staffers regularly take leaves from state service to go into the field to manage Democratic campaigns for the Legislature, Republicans usually call upon professionals.

THE REPUBLICAN PROFESSIONALS

For years, the GOP professional field was dominated by Stu Spencer and Bill Roberts. But with the latter's death and the former's semiretirement (he is still an on-call adviser), a new flock of GOP-oriented consultants has arisen. The hottest of them these days is Otto Bos, a former San Diego newspaper reporter who became then-Mayor Pete Wilson's press secretary and then segued into statewide politics when Wilson ran, successfully, for the U.S. Senate in 1982. Bos ran Wilson's second-term campaign in 1988 and went into business for himself with Wilson, the Republican candidate for governor in 1990, as his chief client. Bos, George Gorton and Dick Dresner own a San Diego-based campaign consulting firm and with Wilson's two big back-to-back wins the firm is expected to rake in big bucks in future campaigns.

Until a few years ago, the splashiest Republican consulting firm was based in Sacramento and operated by two young former legislative staffers, Sal Russo and Doug Watts. They made a name for themselves as managers of Ken Maddy's spectacular, if failed, bid for the governorship in 1978, then hit the big time as operators of George Deukmejian's narrow victory for governor in 1982. They also managed the successful campaign against the Peripheral Canal in 1982 and even moved briefly into official positions in the new administration.

Russo and Watts added Ed Rollins, the former Reagan White House political director, to their firm and did much of the media work for Ronald Reagan's presidential re-election campaign in 1984. But after that spectacular rise, the firm fell on hard times and eventually broke up. Watts is now a New York-based political consultant while Russo has remained in Sacramento and has a new firm, Russo, Marsh and Associates. Before the breakup, Russo, Watts and Rollins crashed and burned on an unsuccessful 1986 campaign against a toxic waste initiative. More recently, Russo lost a special congressional election in the San Joaquin Valley to fill ex-Rep. Tony Coelho's seat. The word in political circles is that Russo and partner Tony Marsh need a winner bad.

Another GOP campaign consultant with a string of strikeouts is Los Angeles-based Ronald Smith, who specializes in moderate to liberal Republican candidates. Smith came close with then-Rep. Ed Zschau's campaign for the U.S. Senate in 1986 and has had to settle for wins at the local level, including Tom Campbell's congressional campaign in 1988 on the San Francisco Peninsula. He tried again in 1990, but suffered another loss when state Sen. Marian Bergeson failed to win the lieutenant governorship. Another consultant who concentrates on moderate GOP candidates is Joe Shumate of San Francisco. He's confined himself to local campaigns, and he scored a noteworthy win in 1988 when a pro-choice Republican, Tricia Hunter, won a hard-fought special election for the state Assembly in San Diego County.

The Dolphin Group of Los Angeles has tried to move into the big time, but so far has settled for pieces of larger campaigns and a few local efforts on its own. Allan Hoffenblum of Los Angeles eschews statewide campaigns in favor of handling many Republican legislative and congressional candidates and has run up a high batting average. Gary Huckaby and Carlos Rodriguez, partners in a Sacramento firm, are trying to emulate Hoffenblum's approach with some success, as are Wayne Johnson and Ray McNally, who also operate their own firms in Sacramento.

Ken Khachigian was a speech writer for Reagan and Deukmejian and now hires out as a media and strategy specialist.

THE MIDDLE-OF-THE-ROADERS

While most California campaign consultants have partisan identification, some purposely avoid such labeling and concentrate, instead, on the increasingly lucrative ballot measure field. The granddaddy of these operations is Woodward & McDowell of Burlingame, known for its high-budget campaigns for and against major propositions. It was W&M, for instance, that persuaded Californians to adopt a state lottery in 1982, working with money from a major lottery supply firm.

The campaign firm, operated by Richard Woodward and Jack McDowell, hit a wall in 1988. It lost a campaign to change the Gann spending limit in June and then had a mixed result on auto insurance initiatives in the fall. It successfully battled insurance industry-sponsored measures, but was unable to secure passage of its own insurance proposition, sponsored mostly by trial lawyers. The firm staged a major comeback in 1990 when it managed the campaign against the year's highest profile ballot measure, a sweeping environmental initiative dubbed "Big Green."

A winner in 1988 was Bill Zimmerman of Santa Monica and his partners, Jack Fiman and Daniel Dixon. Veterans of Gary Hart's 1984 presidential campaign and identified mostly with liberal or Democratic causes, the firm was instrumental in the success of Proposition 103, the one auto insurance measure to win. Zimmerman and Co. clearly hope to cash in on the increasing willingness of liberals to use the initiative process, something they once shunned, but the chief Zimmerman client, Harvey Rosenfield's Voter Revolt, was barely staying alive.

TESTING THE PUBLIC MOOD

The most basic tool of contemporary politics and political journalism is the poll, and California abounds with takers of the public pulse. The best known is Mervin Field of San Francisco, whose California Poll has been a staple of newspapers and television broadcasts for decades. Field's poll has itself become a major factor in handicapping politicians by determining how much attention from the media and respect from potential contributors a candidate can command.

But Field doesn't offer his services to individual politicians or campaigns. When political strategists want to know what California voters are thinking in order to tailor their campaigns, they turn to other private pollsters. Like consultants, most tend to be identified with one party or the other and some have long-standing relationships with consultants. Sacramento's Jim Moore, for instance, is known best for his efforts on behalf of candidates and causes managed by Richie Ross.

As with consultants, there seem to be more pollsters working the Republican side of the street than the Democratic. Besides Moore, the most heavily used Democratic-oriented polling firm is Fairbank, Bregman and Maullin of San Francisco. Partner Richard Maullin first achieved prominence as a strategist in the 1970s for Gov. Jerry Brown and served for years in Brown's administration before moving into consulting. Among the firm's clients have been Sen. Alan Cranston and Los Angeles Mayor Tom Bradley.

There are three Republican polling firms that handle all of the major GOP candidates. They are Arthur J. Finkelstein & Associates of Irvington, N.Y., whose California clients include state Sen. Ed Davis; Tarrance & Associates of Houston, who has handled polling for, among others, Gov. Deukmejian; and The Wirthlin Group of McLean, Va., a Republican White House favorite who has done work for Ed Zschau and former Lt. Gov. Mike Curb.

10

County government – at the crossroads

There's nothing logical about the organization of California's 58 counties. They come from a system of government suited to the 18th century, and each wave of growth in California has made that system less relevant.

Colonial Americans went back to what they knew when they set up local government. They borrowed the concept of counties from Great Britain – where those were territories administered by a count – an idea eventually adopted by every American state, except Alaska.

They also borrowed the dual nature of counties, which are at once independent local units and vassals to a larger central government. It is that dual nature that lies at the heart of the crisis in county government in California today, a problem so severe that some critics say counties should be abolished. That is not likely to happen, but as the 21st century draws near, California counties need some fundamental changes to function in a world very different from the 19th-century, post-gold rush California in which most were created.

More than half of the state residents live in seven counties in Southern California. Statewide, the counties range in population from the more than 8 million people of Los Angeles County to the 1,100 spread around Alpine County. In size, there is the 49-square mile, city-county combination of San Francisco on one end and the 20,000-square-mile San Bernardino at the other.

Nineteenth century politics and economics dictated the boundaries. The small, elongated counties of the old gold-mining region along the Sierra foothills, for example, were drawn to keep every miner within a day's horseback ride from a county seat where he could file claims. Southern California in those days was an unpopulated desert, and there was no reason to divide it.

As California's population grew in the late 19th century, local boosterism and political differences created the impetus for breaking up big counties. Mariposa County, for instance, once contained most of Southern California, the lower San

Joaquin Valley and the central coast. More than a dozen counties have been carved out of that vast territory. One is San Bernardino, still the nation's largest – and bigger than a half-dozen states.

San Francisco County once contained not only the city of San Francisco but what is now San Mateo County. When San Francisco combined its city and county governments, a group of crooked politicians lopped off San Mateo, via their friends in the Legislature, to keep control of a friendly environment. Cattle ranchers and farmers south of Los Angeles seceded to create Orange County, fearing domination by the municipal colossus then slowly forming.

The last county broke away just after World War I, when Imperial County was carved out of the arid eastern reaches of San Diego County. Since then, the number has been fixed at 58, even though the state's population has increased many times over and its economy has undergone two or three evolutions. The irony of these breakups is that today almost every large local government is trying to create new regional planning mechanisms to deal with such knotty issues as transportation and air pollution, issues that spill easily across county boundaries.

These regional governments represent one possible direction for counties. As some see it, counties should cede their land-use planning and other large-scale functions to regional entities and evolve into mere subagencies of the state. Others would have them at least merge with the cities within their boundaries so local governments could cooperate rather than compete on local planning and growth.

Either way, counties have a pack of problems to fix. From the earliest days of the state, counties have had inherent conflicts with their dual roles. On the one hand, counties are purely units of local government, providing police, fire, transportation, judicial and other services to the people living outside incorporated cities. On the other hand, counties do as they are ordered by the state, including running welfare and health-care systems for the poor.

Into the counties' treasuries come property taxes, sales taxes on transactions outside of cities and money handed down from state and federal governments and other sources. In theory, the state is supposed to pay for what it requires counties to do. In practice, state aid rarely gets close.

The system worked as long as local revenues grew and remained flexible. Originally, county supervisors could adjust property tax rates to cover whatever was needed. But the system stopped working in 1978. As state aid stagnated during the 1970s and property values soared, property tax bills went through the roof. Angry homeowners trooped to the polls to pass Proposition 13, the 1978 initiative by Howard Jarvis and Paul Gann, which staggered county governments like a blow to the head.

Proposition 13 cut and then clamped a lid on property taxes. For counties, that meant an immediate and massive loss of billions of dollars each year, and a plunge into financial peril. The state stepped in – sort of – to help the counties. But that aid continued to dwindle as demands on counties grew.

When Proposition 13 passed, the state was sitting on nearly $4 billion in reserves, built up because of the tax on inflated property values around California and because of the tight-fisted policies of then-Gov. Jerry Brown. The state started draining off that reserve to help local governments, particularly counties, in the post-Proposition 13 era. But in the early 1980s, recession and inflation hit at just about the time the reserve ran out.

George Deukmejian inherited the mess when he was sworn in as governor in 1983. Backed by a Legislature with tax-cut fever, Deukmejian preferred to tighten state belts rather than increase government's revenue, which forced more money management onto the counties.

THE THREAT OF BANKRUPTCY

Rural counties have felt the hardest pinch, since local government revenues rely on local property values and retail activity. The resource-based economies – timber, minerals, ranching and farming – of a broad swath of California, ranging from Siskiyou and Modoc counties on the state's northern border to Imperial County in the extreme south, have fallen on hard times. Their young have fled to the cities as local jobs disappeared, and their populations are stagnant in numbers and advancing in age. Tourism and recreation businesses have eased the economic crises in some areas, but those are even more seasonal and erratic than their traditional industries. They are too remote and their weather too severe to attract retirees. With high unemployment (20 percent or more in some counties), the demands of health and welfare services have gone up as revenues have become scarce. Local services such as sheriff's patrols and road maintenance have declined in those areas, but the state "mandates" continue to drain off budget resources. As a result, supervisors have become increasingly militant in their dealings with lawmakers in Sacramento.

Tehama County supervisors became national celebrities when they declared a revolt against state mandates. Neighboring Shasta County also received a flurry of publicity when it shut down its public libraries. Humboldt County supervisors allowed paved roads to revert to gravel.

In 1988, Deukmejian and the Legislature threw the counties a bone when the state assumed from counties some costs of running the court system, but that just relieved a few immediate cash-flow crises and did little to slow what some county supervisors saw an impending disaster.

Butte County was saved from becoming the first U.S. county to file for bankruptcy with a $2.8 million state bailout in 1989 and another $11 million in 1990, still leaving the county more than $3 million in the hole.

Other rural counties, including Yolo, Del Norte and Trinity, are almost in the same shape as Butte and, according to a study commissioned by the County Supervisors Association of California, possibly two dozen others are slipping into trouble. The public hospital in Alameda County, for example, turned away as many as 250 emergencies a month in 1990 and there was a 10-week wait for admission to Fresno County's juvenile hall. Mendocino County mortgaged its courthouse, and other counties have imposed hiring freezes, layoffs and service reductions.

In 1990, state budget writers sought to ease the problems of counties by granting them new authority to impose fees on cities, school districts and special districts for services rendered, such as housing jail prisoners and collecting and divvying up local taxes. The effort to tap into other local government coffers to help pay for county operations reflected the generally healthier condition of those budgets, at least on the part of cities.

20 fastest growing counties in California

County	Population on 4/1/80	Population on 4/1/90	Percent difference
Riverside	663,199	1,170,413	76.48
San Bernardino	895,016	1,418,580	58.48
Amador	19.314	30,039	55.53
Calaveras	20,710	31,998	54.51
Nevada	51,645	78,510	52.02
Placer	117,247	172,796	47.38
El Dorado	85,812	125,995	46.83
San Benito	25,005	36,697	46.76
Solano	235,203	340,421	44.75
Tuolumne	33,928	48,456	42.82
San L. Obispo	155,435	217,162	39.71
Madera	63,116	88,090	39.57
Stanislaus	265,900	370,522	39.35
Lake	36,366	50,631	39.23
San Joaquin	347,342	480,628	38.37
Kings	73,738	101,469	37.61
Kern	403,089	543,477	34.83
San Diego	1,861,846	2,498,016	34.17
Sacramento	783,381	1,041,219	32.91
Merced	134,538	178,403	32.58

Source: Bureau of the Census, 1991

Some cities, mostly free of the big-ticket health, welfare and educational responsibilities, actually found themselves in better shape after Proposition 13. Besides having major sources of revenue that are independent of the property tax, many cities have evolved into entrepreneurs of sorts, doing everything from encouraging development within their boundaries to promoting things such as shopping malls.

Before Proposition 13, property owners were required to pay separate property taxes to their county governments and to cities, if they were inside an incorporated area. That discouraged incorporation of county areas outside established cities. But the 1978 tax initiative ended that. And the loss of property tax revenue shifted local government attention to the sales tax. Under California tax law, a chunk of sales tax is returned to the local government in which the sale occurred. If a mall is inside a city, the city's coffers get the sales tax, not the county's. Suddenly cities were drawing new boundaries to include shopping centers, auto dealerships and other high-volume retail areas. More than 30 new cities have been formed since Proposition 13, most of them in suburbs and some containing huge populations.

County officials, who once encouraged the creation of new cities to relieve themselves of the cost of police or fire protection and other services, found they were losing more and more tax revenue as cities gobbled up sales-tax-producing businesses and development. And that fight over sales taxes to replace the lost property taxes has driven counties into bitter rivalries with each other and with city governments. The scramble for taxable development has become so intense that in some counties, land-use decisions are based almost entirely on competition for revenue rather than good planning.

Gov. Wilson, in his 1991-92 budget, proposed a mixed blessing that some county officials believe is at least a start. Wilson suggested handing over to counties complete responsibility for mental and community health services. (Through 1990, the state was supposed to pay for up to 90 percent of the cost of those programs, but in reality it often paid for far less.) In return, counties were offered new, potent sources of revenue. Wilson proposed increasing vehicle license fees by $769 million and turning that over to counties. Plus, he wanted counties to get $173 million of an alcohol tax increase. Wilson also proposed giving counties the power to raise more money. His plan called for allowing counties and school districts to float local bonds on a simple majority, rather than a two-thirds vote of the public. And counties would be allowed to raise their sales taxes up to a half-cent, with a majority vote of the public, to pay for drug enforcement and more police.

As California expands by more than 5 million people a decade, growth fights will become even more dominant in counties. Both large-scale policies and individual projects will face intense scrutiny, and the old cozy friendships between supervisors and developers will be strained.

For years, most boards of supervisors have been politically conservative and pro-development, since their constituents usually live in suburban or rural areas. A majority of current supervisors are Republicans. In counties such as Los Angeles, the supervisors approved the developers' projects almost without question and the developers poured millions of dollars into the incumbents' campaign treasuries, making them nearly invulnerable at the polls and keeping the cycle alive. But the rise of the anti- or slow-growth forces, even in strong Republican areas such as Orange County, has scrambled the picture. Few supervisors in fast-growing counties now admit to supporting growth, even though their voting records and lists of campaign contributors might say otherwise.

San Diego County, for example, is dealing with the growth fight by requiring major development to occur only within a city, negating much of the land-use power that has translated into political power in many counties. The city of San Diego has become the de facto regional decision-maker for the county.

A different direction for county evolution may be in copying the San Francisco model. Even though city-county consolidation plans failed at the polls in Sacramento County in 1974 and 1990, local officials there are looking at ways to combine some offices, including the planning departments, as a way to discourage incorporation efforts that could siphon off sales taxes.

Wilson's budget proposals could ease some pain for counties, but more changes are needed. Specific proposals have ranged from abolishing counties altogether to giving the counties more guaranteed revenue sharing through the sales tax. Some people argue that counties should create contractual, rather than dependent, relationships with the state to administer the big-ticket programs. And, naturally, there also has been some discussion among supervisors of writing their own initiative to improve their political and financial standing.

Alameda County

Area: 825.4 sq. mi.; Population: (1990) 1,279,182, (1980) 1,105,379; Registration: (1990) D-62.5% R-24.6%; Unemployment: (Jan. 1991) 5.4%; County supervisors: Edward Campbell, Mary King, Don Perata, Charles Santana, Warren Widener; 1221 Oak St., Room 536, Oakland 94612; (415) 272-6347.

Writer Gertrude Stein once said of Oakland, Alameda County's principal city, "There's no there there." She didn't mean it that way, but the phrase has come to stand as a declaration that Oakland and, by extension, Alameda County, lacks character.

What Alameda County, on the eastern shore of San Francisco Bay, really lacks is a spotlight. It exists in the shadow of San Francisco, its big-city cousin across the bay, despite the best efforts of the community boosters to establish a separate image.

And were it not in that shadow, Alameda County clearly would be one of

California's most notable areas. It contains a piece of almost every social group found in the state – from the funky, 1960ish ambiance of Berkeley, home of the University of California's first and most important campus, to the wealth of Piedmont, the industrial communities of Fremont and San Leandro, and the urban, problem-plagued city of Oakland itself.

Every time Oakland seems ready to take a step away from its difficulties, a new crisis pushes it back. Oakland's baseball team, the A's, rose during the 1980s as a powerhouse, but the city's efforts to re-acquire the Raiders football team left it embarrassed after revelations that the millions being offered the Raiders would be needed to bail out, among other things, a nearly-bankrupt school system. The city pushed an ambitious downtown redevelopment plan, but one of its centerpieces, a sparkling new hotel, suffered from low patronage and the city had to rescue it financially.

Even the political establishment, in one of the rare major cities dominated by blacks, has been fragmented and ineffective, especially in dealing with the crime and drug problems plaguing the city.

For years, the political leader of Oakland had been Lionel Wilson, a former judge, the mayor from 1976 to 1990. He is a black man who was militant enough to draw support from the Black Panthers but moderate enough to placate the white business establishment. But Wilson ran out of steam in 1990, losing in the primary election. Former Assemblyman Elihu Harris beat Councilman Wilson Riles Jr. in an all-black, all-Democrat runoff. Harris focused his campaign and his early efforts in office on the city's two biggest woes, its struggling schools and its immense drug problem.

While Oakland struggles to shed its crime-ridden image and claim a share of California's economic boom, the southern and eastern reaches of Alameda County seem a world away. They are part of the California Sun Belt, the fast-growing suburbs dotted with business and commercial centers that are typical of the state's growth in the 1980s.

Communities such as Livermore and Pleasanton are exploding with people and jobs and the Association of Bay Area Governments, the regional planning agency, has projected that 70 percent of Alameda County's job growth between 1985 and 2005 will be in the southern and eastern parts of the county.

Alameda's diversity produces political tension that is both geographic – urban Oakland and Berkeley vs. the suburbs – and social. Much like the state as a whole, the suburbs are growing much faster than the older urban areas. That means they are gaining political clout that may move the county's politics to the right.

At the polls, Alameda County, thanks to both Oakland and Berkeley, is as consistently left-of-center as nearby San Francisco, giving Democratic candidates for statewide office a substantial Bay Area base. Democrats outnumber Republicans by 2.5 to 1, which gives the county all-Democrat legislative and congressional delegations. And those Democratic lawmakers are on the left side of the scale, even within their own party. Assemblyman Tom Bates of Oakland is one of the most liberal members of his house, as is Oakland Sen. Nicholas Petris. And Rep. Ron Dellums of Berkeley has a national reputation for his liberal leanings, which drives military advocates crazy since, by seniority, Dellums now wields major influence over Pentagon spending.

The politics of Berkeley – known to its detractors as "Berserkeley" – are so far to the left that conventional liberals are, in relative terms, the local right-wing. Berkeley established a national trend for left-of-center cities, most of them college towns, to involve themselves in issues of international politics and the global environmental. Gus Newport, Berkeley's mayor for much of the 1980s, was a globe-trotting apostle for left-wing politics.

But while Berkeley's politics evolved out of the University of California and the "free speech," civil rights and anti-war movements of the 1960s, the politics of the campus itself are much more moderate now. Student government, in fact, is dominated by the more conservative campus parties and the fraternity and sorority systems are stronger than ever, leading to a rather odd twist of the traditional town vs. gown tensions.

University officials want to expand the campus and its support facilities, especially student housing, but city officials resist. The standoff has meant an annual scramble for housing and another of the Bay Area's miserable traffic scenes. UC officials have even explored moving their statewide administrative offices out of Berkeley altogether.

But the future Alameda County and the region hinges more on economic trends than local politics. The Port of Oakland is a highly sophisticated doorway for commerce between California and the fast-growing Pacific Rim nations.

Those rapidly growing suburbs of the southern and eastern county include many high-tech plants, an extension of the Silicon Valley across the bay. The Association of Bay Area Governments projects a growth of Alameda County jobs from about a half-million in 1980 to nearly 800,000 by 2005. That boom would far exceed population growth and make Alameda County a destination for commuters, many from the even-newer suburbs in the San Joaquin Valley to the east.

Most of those new jobs, however, will be in trade and services and will be centered in the suburban portions of the county, rather than older communities, such as Oakland, along the bay. That means continued problems for Oakland and the county as a whole, which must budget for the staggering health, welfare and law enforcement demands.

Meanwhile, county supervisors, facing a $50 million gap in their 1990-91 budget, had to cut 280 positions. Besides the obvious trims, that meant such things as letting go a new class of graduates from the sheriff's academy. In effect, the county spent the money to train deputies who would work in some other county.

Alpine County

Area: 726.6 sq. mi.; Population: (1990) 1,113, (1980) 1,097; Registration: (1990) D-39.3% R-42.3%; Unemployment: (Jan. 1991) 4.7%; County supervisors: John Brissenden, John Bennett, Donald Jardine, Eric Jung, Claudia Ann Wade; P.O. Box 158, Markleeville 96120; (916) 694-2281.

A brochure from the county's Chamber of Commerce advises visitors to "Get lost in Alpine County." It would not be hard.

This is California's smallest county in population, a tiny reminder of California's 19th century beginnings south of Lake Tahoe. There certainly is no boom here, and, if anything, it is shrinking. It grew by only 16 people for the entire decade of the 1980s and actually lost about 80 people in the last two years.

Not that local residents mind much. Most of them live there because they enjoy the solitude, which is a good thing, since winter snows close all but a few roads. Mining was the county's original reason for being, but ranching and later tourism – especially skiing during the winter – have become its economic mainstays.

Like the rest of California's mountain regions, Alpine is politically conservative. But during the early 1970s, a group of homosexual activists tried to organize a move to Alpine en masse to establish a friendly government. It never happened, but it kept the county stirred up for months.

Amador County

Area: 601.3 sq. mi.; Population: (1990) 30,3039, (1980) 19,314; Registration: (1990) D-49.7% R-41.6%; Unemployment: (Jan. 1991) 8.8%; County supervisors: Edward Bamert, John Begovich, Stephanie D'Agostini, Timothy Davenport, Steve Martin; 108 Court St., Jackson 95642; (209) 223-6470.

Like other counties in the "Mother Lode" east of Sacramento, Amador is experiencing the joys and pains of growth. Swollen by commuters and retirees, Amador is the state's third-fastest-growing county and the most rapidly developing of the foothill areas. In the 1980s, it boomed by more than 55 percent.

But the numbers are deceiving. The census counts the inmates at the new Mule Creek State Prison near Ione and they represent more than a third of the growth. But there are still many newcomers who bring money into the county, as do the tens of thousands of tourists who flock to its quaint old gold-rush towns on weekends.

There is some friction, as might be expected, between the old-timers and the steady stream of "flatlanders." The new settlers often bring with them higher incomes or big-city equity that pumps up local real estate prices beyond the reach of some longtime residents.

The county was once conservatively Democratic, but the influx of new people has moved it to the right – a fact most keenly felt by former Assemblyman Norm Waters, a conservative Democrat who survived by a whisker in 1988 and then lost to the same Republican, David Knowles, in 1990.

Butte County

Area: 1,664.8 sq. mi.; Population: (1990) 182,120, (1980) 143,851; Registration: (1990) D-43.9% R-43.8%; Unemployment: (Jan. 1991) 10.5%; County supervisors: Kevin Campbell, Jane Dolan, Leonard Fulton, Haskel McInturf, Edward McLaughlin; 25 County Center Drive, Oroville 95966; (916) 538-7224.

Just say "Butte County" and watch any county official in California cringe. It has become the watchword for the financial woes that counties continue to face. In 1989, then again in 1990, Butte County came within days of becoming the first county in the United States to file for bankruptcy. It was saved by the state with a $2.8 million bailout in 1989 and another $11 million in 1990, still leaving the county more than $3 million in the hole.

According to reports from the state legislative analyst and the California Counties Foundation, many of the reasons for Butte's troubles went beyond the control of the county supervisors. The county has been plagued by slow growth in property values, made worse because supervisors, when they had the discretion before Proposition 13, had always been reluctant to hike property tax rates. It has lost tax revenue to city incorporations and annexations, continues to attract people in need of health and welfare services, and maintenance costs continue to escalate on everything from its roads and buildings to its sheriffs' patrol cars, some of which have tracked over 300,000 miles.

Meanwhile, voters have rejected every tax hike put before them. In 1990, they turned down four tax increases or bond measures, leaving county libraries closed, animal control services abandoned, the jails overcrowded and county firefighters on the brink of being disbanded.

Butte County is in the middle of the vast, largely rural area north and east of Sacramento with neither rich natural resources nor the attributes attractive to home buyers. While growing at about the average rate for California counties, about 25 percent, most of the region has missed the statewide economic boom, partly because it was bypassed by Interstate 5, the main north-south highway through California, leaving it a little too inaccessible for major developers. Cheap housing, though much of it is substandard, has made the area especially attractive to welfare recipients who have fled higher-cost and crime areas.

The fastest growing area is not Oroville, the county seat, but Chico, home to the only branch of the state college system in the region and an attractive town of 35,000 with tree-lined streets, 19th century Victorian homes and the park where Errol Flynn and Olivia DeHaviland filmed Robin Hood.

The presence of California State University, Chico, gives the community a lively political and cultural life. In the early 1980s, adherents of Tom Hayden's economic democracy movement won control of the city government. But they were ousted a few years later by a right-wing countermovement. Of the left's brief hegemony, only Jane Dolan, Chico's liberal county supervisor, remains.

The bulwarks of the local economy are the university, an agricultural industry dominated by orchard crops and some tourism, much of it attracted by the state-owned Oroville Reservoir. But the university's Center for Economic Development and Planning is trying to foster an interest in wider economic development throughout the 12-county region centered in Butte.

The center sees the agricultural and other resource-based elements of the local economy continuing to lag and predicts the area, with its comfortable rural life and relatively low housing and other living costs, is primed for development. But if that growth spurt does come, it will be years away.

Butte County is a conservative area, Chico and the university notwithstanding, with about an equal number of Republicans and Democrats. But it votes very Republican. All local state and federal legislators are Republicans.

Calaveras County

Area: 1,036.4 sq. mi.; Population: (1990) 31,998, (1980) 20,710; Registration: (1990) D-45.9% R-44.4%; Unemployment: (Jan. 1991) 12.8%; County supervisors: Richard Gordon, Michael McRay, Michael Dell'Orto, Thomas Taylor, Thomas Tyron; 891 Mountain Road, San Andreas 95249; (209) 754-6370.

The most famous thing about Calaveras County is a fictional frog-jumping contest that became real. Writer Mark Twain described it in a whimsical tale about life during the gold rush. Now, the town of Angels Camp runs a real version every spring.

Hordes of tourists that the frog-jumping contest attracts are a big piece of the changing local economy. It has moved away from mining and agriculture and toward tourism and retirees. Highway 49, which cuts through the county, can be a slow crawl on Sunday afternoons. Another sign is the precarious future of an asbestos mine, the nation's largest, which provides 5 percent of all county jobs.

The population, as in other counties in the Sierra foothills, is growing far faster than most of California. It was up by more than 54 percent, but in sheer numbers, its growth does not approach the boom that is hitting foothill counties closer to Sacramento. But as it grows – mostly with retired refugees from the state's urban centers – it continues a slow shift to the right. Democrats are close, in fact, to becoming a minority.

Colusa County

Area: 1,155.8 sq. mi.; Population: (1990) 16,275, (1980) 12,791; Registration: (1990) D-47% R-44.7%; Unemployment: (Jan. 1991) 25.4%; County supervisors: W.D. Mills, Kay Nordyke, Patricia Scofield, William Waite, David Womble; 546 Jay St., Colusa 95932; (916) 458-2101.

Colusa County gets a lot a visitors. Of course, few of them know it. Interstate 5, California's main north-south artery, bisects the county about an hour's drive north of Sacramento. But it bypasses the county seat, Colusa, and at 65 mph, Williams, a town of fewer than 2,000 souls, is not much to notice.

There are a few highway-related businesses in Williams, but the county's chief economic underpinning is agriculture. In 1988, Williams annexed more than 2,000 acres of farmland – more than three times the size of the city then – in hopes of attracting high-tech industry or at least food processors or canneries, but so far the move has had little impact on the area's economy. The Employment Development Department estimates that farming provides nearly half of the county's direct employment. The chief crop is rice, which is subject both to the availability of water and the vagaries of international markets. And, as would be expected of rural counties in California, supervisors have been struggling every year to pass a leaner and leaner budget.

Colusa is too far from Sacramento, the closest urban area, to be much of a target for suburban home buyers, and the area has neither the mountains nor the lakes and rivers that have made other rural regions havens for retirees. The population is growing about as fast as California as a whole, but there seem to be few indications that Colusa's basic character will change soon.

Contra Costa County

Area: 797.9 sq. mi.; Population: (1990) 803,732, (1980) 656,331; Registration: (1990) D-51.5% R-37%; Unemployment: (Jan. 1991) 5.8%; County supervisors: Nancy Fahden, Sunne McPeak, Tom Powers, Robert Schroder, Thomas Torlakson; 651 Pine St., 11th floor, Martinez 94553; (415) 646-2371.

A generation ago, Contra Costa County was a typical Northern California bedroom suburb. The county's lush hills and valleys were a refuge for commuters who spent their days working in Oakland or San Francisco and were affluent enough to afford to live in the well-kept country atmosphere in communities such as Walnut Creek, Moraga, Orinda and Lafayette.

Contra Costa County

But in recent years, Contra Costa has exploded with jobs in places such as San Ramon's Bishop Ranch. The new complexes along Interstate 680 have become destinations for less affluent commuters, who have moved even further east into the new bedroom communities of the San Joaquin Valley in search of affordable housing.

Between 1985 and 1990, Contra Costa's employment increased by more than 20 percent. Acres and acres of development along I-680 have spawned a new phrase: "Contra Costapolis," and sparked a no-growth backlash among residents fed up with hours-long traffic jams. As in so many growing areas, local politics of the 1980s became defined by that single issue, and politicians caught being too cozy with developers felt the lash of angry voters. The issue came to a head in 1985, when anti-growth candidates won a series of local elections and slow-growth ballot measures were adopted.

In many ways, the county is a microcosm of California. Along the outer reaches of San Francisco Bay, communities such as Martinez, Pittsburg and Antioch remain blue-collar bastions filled with oil refineries and other industrial facilities. But even those areas are sprouting suburban housing developments. Richmond, on the east shore of San Francisco Bay, has a large and Democratic-voting black population, and many of the urban problems to match. It is a high-crime area with a school system on the verge of bankruptcy. The more affluent eastern suburbs, as would be expected, supply legions of Republican voters, leaving the county's voter registration relatively close to California's as a whole.

Also like the rest of California, Contra Costa is fighting the battle of the dwindling county budget. It has continually delayed a new jail, among other county responsibilities. Supervisors have been shopping around for years, trying to find a place to put the county's garbage or industrial sludge, and have even tried to pay other, even poorer, counties to take it.

Contra Costa's dominating political figure is not a politician, but Dean Lesher, the outspoken octogenarian who publishes the Contra Costa Times newspaper. Lesher battles ceaselessly against anti-growthers and for the establishment of a state college campus in the county, known locally as "Dean Lesher U."

Del Norte County

Area: 1,003 sq. mi.; Population: (1990) 23,460, (1980) 18,217; Registration: (1990) D-48.5% R-36.7%; Unemployment: (Jan. 1991) 15.1%; County supervisors: Helga Burns, Mark Mellett, Clarke Moore, Glenn Smedley, Ray Thompson; 450 H St., Crescent City 95531; (707) 464-7204.

Del Norte County is about as far north as you can go and still be in California. For generations, the local economy was based on cutting trees and catching fish. Both industries fell on hard times during the 1970s and '80s, and local boosters pushed hard to add a third element: keeping bad guys behind bars. That "dream" was realized when the state opened Pelican Bay State Prison, where the worst of California's inmates live in extreme isolation.

Del Norte found itself in a rare surge of commercial investment as the prison took shape near the Oregon border north of Crescent City, and the $30 million annual payroll pumped new life into the economy. Suddenly, one of the state's most chronically depressed areas was beginning the look like one of its more prosperous.

But the prison brought with it new problems. So far, commercial investment has lagged behind projections, many of the jobs went to people from outside the county, and welfare rolls have increased as families of prisoners moved into the area.

Nonetheless, the prison is still considered a political plum, one picked by the county's state senator, Barry Keene, the Senate's Democratic floor leader. Keene is one of several Democrats who have been winning regularly along the state's north coast, one of the few California regions to move to the left politically in recent years.

El Dorado County

Area: 1,804.8 sq. mi.; Population: (1990) 125,995, (1980) 85,812; Registration: (1990) D-44.3% R-45.4%; Unemployment: (Jan. 1991) 6.5%; County supervisors: Robert Dorr, William Center, Vernon Gerwer, James Sweeney, John Upton; 330 Fair Lane, Placerville 95667; (916) 626-2464.

The names of the county and its county seat, Placerville, reveal their origins as one of the centers of the 19th century gold rush. In the late 20th century, El Dorado County is at the center of another land rush.

Retirees and commuters alike are packing into El Dorado County, seeking cleaner air, friendlier communities and more reasonable living costs. But their sheer numbers threaten to destroy those very qualities. As one recent arrival put it in a newspaper interview: "Everywhere I look, I'm threatened."

Between 1980 and 1990, the county's population surged by almost 47 percent as developers converted pastures into "ranchettes" and rolling hills into subdivisions. Population growth is highest in the communities closest to Sacramento, such as Cameron Park and El Dorado Hills, and water shortages have become common.

As it grows, El Dorado is turning to the right politically. Republicans in 1990 moved ahead of Democrats in registration for the first time.

Fresno County

Area: 5,998.3 sq. mi.; Population: (1990) 667,490, (1980) 587,329; Registration: (1990) D-53.9% R-38.2%; Unemployment: (Jan. 1991) 13.7%; County supervisors: Judy Andreen, A. Vernon Conrad, Sharon Levy, Deran Koligan, Doug Vagim; 2281 Tulare St., Room 300, Fresno 93721; (209) 488-3531.

Fresno County is the middle of California geographically, culturally and politically. Its major city, Fresno, is big enough – over 300,000 – to have some big-city advantages and ills. But it remains, at heart, an overgrown farm town. Its image was captured perfectly by a satirical television movie, "Fresno," in which things of little consequence had great consequence there.

The county's location, equidistant from Los Angeles and San Francisco, and its relatively low labor and land costs, have sparked flurries of non-agricultural industrial development, but the city and the region remain dependant upon agriculture. It was in Fresno County that the term "agribusiness" was coined, and large-scale, scientific agriculture remains the heart of both its economy and its culture. Crops as varied as cotton and grapes abound in the fertile flatlands of the nation's most productive agricultural county.

But as the unofficial capital of the San Joaquin Valley, Fresno has also developed educational, medical and governmental facilities to serve the whole region. That has put pressure on county resources, as did the killing freeze at the end of 1990 and the continuing California drought.

More than a third of Fresno County's population is Hispanic, but, as in other areas of the state, Hispanics have not developed into a strong political force. Instead, voters in Fresno County and the San Joaquin Valley mirror larger political trends in the state. They are nominally Democratic but lean toward the conservative side; they often are willing to elect Republicans. That puts the valley into the swing position when it comes to close statewide races and explains why candidates for state and national offices spend disproportionately large amounts of scarce campaign time around Fresno's isolated media market. Late in George Bush's 1988 presidential campaign, he created a flap when he refused his aides' request to visit Fresno, saying he couldn't stand to see "those damn dancing raisins" again.

The exception to the conservative tilt is the more liberal leaning of the city of

Fresno, due largely to its blue-collar and farm-worker residents. George McGovern, Walter Mondale and Michael Dukakis all won in the city itself, although they did miserably in the rest of the county. Fresno's mayor, ex-television newscaster Kathy Humphrey, exemplifies the slightly more liberal trend in city politics.

But centrism is still the dominant political credo of Fresno County. Local government is the spawning ground for most legislators and congressmen, who tend toward the pragmatic. Chief among them, and typical of the breed, is state Sen. Ken Maddy, the Senate's Republican leader and a one-time gubernatorial possibility who is married to the heiress of the Foster Farms chicken empire, the perfect combination of politics and agribusiness.

Glenn County

Area: 1,319 sq. mi.; Population: (1990) 24,798, (1980) 21,350; Registration: (1990) D-45.6% R-43.9%; Unemployment: (Jan. 1991) 18.2%; County supervisors: Marilyn Baker, Ken Burbank, Dick Mudd, Jim Mann, Joanne Overton; P.O. Box 391, Willows 95988; (916) 934-3834.

The 19th century courthouse in Willows is a symbol for all of Glenn County: quiet, tradition bound, slow to change. Interstate 5, the state's main north-south freeway, bisects Willows and the county, but has had small impact. There are a few highway-related businesses, but otherwise the city and the county remain what they have been for generations – agricultural communities whose economies are tied to the value of farm products. Farming and government account for half of Glenn's employment.

Jim Mann, a dairy farmer turned county supervisor, is trying to change that. Mann works for a regional economic development center in nearby Chico and is trying to offset chronically high unemployment by promoting the area as a site for light industry, stressing the low cost of living and the easy freeway access. But so far, there have been no big takers.

Like the rest of the region, Glenn County is struggling with its budget and it is politically conservative, voting Republican most of the time.

Humboldt County

Area: 3,599.5 sq. mi.; Population: (1990) 119,118, (1980) 108,525; Registration: (1990) D-57.7% R-30.7%; Unemployment: (Jan. 1991) 10.9%; County supervisors: Stan Dixon, Julie Fulkerson, Bonnie Neely, Harry Pritchard, Anna Sparks; 825 Fifth St., Eureka 95501; (707) 445-7509.

Eureka (population 25,000) is the political, economic and cultural center of California's remote, beautiful north coast. The region was settled by loggers, who felled giant redwoods and cut them into timbers to shore up gold mines in the mid-

19th century. Cutting and processing timber, and catching and processing fish, have been Humboldt County's economic mainstays for generations, even after a substantial, if seasonal, tourist trade developed after World War II.

Both of those resource-based industries have fallen on hard times in recent years, however, and many of the area's young men and women moved away looking for more dependable jobs. As they left, they were replaced in the 1960s and '70s by urban refugees, universally dubbed hippies, and an economic and political transformation of the area began. In the **Humboldt County** 1980s, the urban refugees had sold homes in Los Angeles or the San Francisco Bay Area, and were a bit more conservative, but only a bit.

Marijuana has become a substantial cash crop. Environmentalism, once a dirty word, has become a powerful movement. And the politics of the area, once conservative, have begun moving leftward, with liberal Democrats replacing Republicans in legislative seats. There are still major political battles between the pro-lumber businesses and the environmentalists. But most often, the latter win.

Imperial County

Area: 4,597.4 sq. mi.; Population: (1990) 109,303, (1980) 92,110; Registration: (1990) D-54.2% R-34.7%; Unemployment: (Jan. 1991) 18.4%; County supervisors: James Bucher, Bill Cole, Abe Seabolt, Sam Sharp, Wayne Van De Graaff; 940 W. Main St., El Centro 92243; (619) 339-4220.

If farmers could not grow three crops a year in this region at times, it is doubtful anyone would live in the Imperial Valley.

Much of the valley, which occupies California's southeastern corner, lies below sea level and is covered with sand. Summer temperatures can reach more than 120 degrees in what little shade can be found in the almost treeless landscape.

Imperial was the last California county to be created, carved off San Diego County just after World War I. There is a lively trade in both goods and human bodies over the Mexican border south of El Centro, and Imperial County has one of California's highest concentrations of Hispanic residents, nearly 56 percent in the 1980 census. That fact is accompanied by a harsh reality: Imperial also has one of the state's highest unemployment rates and is chronically near the top in terms of poverty. The county is also chronically on the financial edge as it tries to pay for health and welfare services.

Local boosters hope that a fledgling winter vacation industry – a kind of poor man's Palm Springs – will brighten the local economy. But the only good economic news in recent years has been the decision by the state to build two new prisons in the county.

Inyo County

Area: 10,097.9 sq. mi.; Population: (1990) 18,281, (1980) 17,895; Registration: (1990) D-40.4% R-48.7%; Unemployment: (Jan. 1991) 8.4%; County supervisors: Warren Allsup, Keith Bright, Robert Campbell, Sam Dean, Paul Payne; P.O. Drawer N, Independence 93526; (619) 878-2411.

There is only one word to describe Inyo County: empty. That is only in terms of people, however. Inyo, wedged onto the eastern slope of the Sierra, next to Nevada, contains some of the state's most spectacular, if starkest, natural scenery plus an active volcanic field.

Inyo is California's second largest county in size, but it has the second slowest growth rate. The population climbed by a whopping 386 people during the 1980s.

The federal government owns more than 85 percent of the land. Extraction of minerals from Inyo's arid mountains, ranching and tourism are the county's chief economic activities; and hating Los Angeles – which locked up the area's water in back-room maneuvers a half-century ago and which supplies hordes of summer and weekend visitors – seems to be the chief local pastime. Mining has been on the wane in recent years and local leaders have been looking for something – perhaps a state prison – to replace the lost employment.

Politically, Inyo's few voters lean to the right and give Republican candidates big majorities.

Kern County

Area: 8,170.3 sq. mi.; Population: (1990) 543,477, (1980) 403,089; Registration: (1990) D-46.3% R-44.2%; Unemployment: (Jan. 1991) 12.7%; County supervisors: Roy Asburn, Ben Austin, Karl Hettinger, Pauline Larwood, Mary Shell; 1415 Truxton Ave., Bakersfield 93301; (800) 322-0722.

If California is a smaller scale model of the United States, then Kern County is its Oklahoma. There are oil wells, farms and country music recording studios. And many of the county's inhabitants trace their ancestry to the waves of migrants from Oklahoma, Texas and Arkansas before, during and after World War II.

When the oil and farming industries are down, Kern County is down. When they are up, the county rolls in money. There have been efforts to diversify the county's economy, taking advantage of its location 100 miles north of the Los Angeles megalopolis, and they have been partially successful. But for the foreseeable future, farming and oil will rule.

True to its cultural roots, Kern County is very conservative politically. It elects Republicans to its legislative and congressional seats and gives GOP candidates at the top of the ticket big margins. But it could give them more if people were inclined. In the 1990 elections, Kern had the lowest voter turnout in the state. As elsewhere, the county's large Hispanic minority is politically impotent.

Kings County

Area: 1,435.6 sq. mi.; Population: (1990) 101,469, (1980) 73,738; Registration: (1990) D-52.9% R-37.4%; Unemployment: (Jan. 1991) 15.3%; County supervisors: Les Brown, Dom Faruzzi, Joe Hammond Jr., Nick Kinney, Abel Meirelles; Government Center, Hanford 93230; (209) 582-3211.

Kings County, sliced from a corner of neighboring Tulare County in the late 19th century, has achieved a remarkable economic diversity to accompany its large-scale agricultural base.

Starting in the early 1960s, the county lured such non-agricultural projects as a tire factory, the Lemoore Naval Air Station and a carpet mill. In more recent years, the state has built two large prisons in the small farming towns of Avenal and Corcoran. The county seat, Hanford, has even developed a mild tourism industry centered on its town square, with its old-fashioned ice cream parlor and 19th century buildings redeveloped into shops. There's also a small Chinatown. That non-farm development has given it a more stable economy than many other San Joaquin Valley counties and also has fueled a relatively fast population growth. Its 37 percent increase from 1980 to 1990 is unusually big for an area in the middle of the farm belt.

Politically, Kings mirrors the valley: conservative-voting on most issues, but willing to elect Democrats who do not tilt too far to the left.

Lake County

Area: 1,326.5 sq. mi.; Population: (1990) 50,631, (1980) 36,366; Registration: (1990) D-53.4% R-36.5%; Unemployment: (Jan. 1991) 14.1%; County supervisors: Voris Brumfield, L.D. Franklin, Gary Lambert, Karan Mackey, Walter Wilcox; 255 N. Forbes St., Lakeport 95453; (707) 263-2367.

Lake County's name says it all. The county's major asset, scenically and economically, is Clear Lake, California's largest natural body of fresh water. Dotted along the lake are dozens of small communities that subsist on summer tourism, fishermen and retirees.

Lake County

There are so many retirees settling in Lake County, a three-hour drive from San Francisco, that the median age of residents is about 15 years higher than the state's average. The county's economy has other elements, such as ranching and geothermal power development, but retirees' pension checks are becoming steadily more important. The retirees tend to be of the working class variety, so the local politics remain pro-Democratic.

Retirees produce a steady increase in the demand for county services, while property values have been virtually flat. Lake County is another on the long, long list counties that had to cut services and trim jobs to balance its 1990-91 budget.

The Clear Lake basin is a favorite hunting ground for archaeologists as it has been inhabited for centuries. One stone tool fragment from the area has been dated at 10,000 years old.

Lassen County

Area: 4,690.3 sq. mi.; Population: (1990) 27,598, (1980) 21,661; Registration: (1990) D-49.1% R-37.8%; Unemployment: (Jan. 1991) 14.1%; County supervisors: James Chapman, Hughes deMartimprey, Gary Lemke, Jean Loubet, Lyle Lough; 707 Nevada St., Susanville 96130; (916) 257-8311.

The biggest employer in Lassen County, on the northern Nevada border, is the California Department of Corrections. Beyond the prison at Susanville, Lassen is mostly timber and ranching country, with a steady summer and fall tourist trade. It shares Lassen National Volcanic Park with three other counties, but the active volcano that gave the county its name, Mt. Lassen, is actually in Shasta County.

Many – perhaps most – of Lassen's residents are happy the county has missed out on the industrialization and population growth hitting much of California. Indeed, when the state proposed to expand its prison and add another 200 jobs, it was opposed by local residents, who would prefer to leave things as they are: quiet and peaceful.

Lassen's population is growing at about the rate of the California average, and many of the newcomers are retired ex-urbanites who traded in the equity on their homes for the quiet of the country. Financially and politically, the county is like the rest of northeastern California: the county's budget is in miserable shape and the people are conservative with a don't-tread-on-me attitude toward government and taxes.

Los Angeles County

Area: 4,079.3 sq. mi.; Population: (1990) 8,863,164, (1980) 7,477,517; Registration: (1990) D-54.5% R-35.3%; Unemployment: (Jan. 1991) 6.6%; County supervisors: Michael Antonovich, Deane Dana, Ed Edelman, Kenneth Hahn, Gloria Molina; 500 W. Temple St., Los Angeles 90012; (213) 974-1411.

Los Angeles County is the 800-pound gorilla of California and its politics. It contains more than 30 percent of the state's people and wields cultural, economic and political influence of global scope. It is the new American melting pot, the destination for immigrants from hundreds of other societies around the world. Those newcomers, in turn, are changing the face of the region.

Los Angeles, both the city and the county, has huge enclaves of Hispanics, Koreans, blacks, Armenians, Chinese and other ethnic groups. Each plays its own role in shaping the unique society that evolved from a dusty outpost of the Spanish colonial empire. They participate in an economy that is as diverse as the state as a whole, ranging from heavy manufacturing to Pacific Rim trade, high-tech manufacturing, entertainment, tourism and sweatshop factories in downtown tenements.

Other communities may throb, but the city of Los Angeles and the dozens of other towns that comprise Los Angeles County hum with the 24-hour-a-day freeway traffic that is its most infamous and pervasive feature. What would be considered rush-hour traffic anywhere else can be found in Los Angeles at almost any time: hundreds of thousands of vehicles in a slowly oozing stream, most of them holding no more than the driver.

That has given Los Angeles one of the nation's worst smog problems and has produced new government attempts to deal with it, including the establishment of a regional body with vast new powers to influence the way people live, work, commute and even barbecue their food. But any solution to the smog problem, if there is one, is decades away. Meanwhile, the freeways become more clogged.

It is a problem made worse by the inexorable shift of population out of the city's center and into the suburbs on the edge of the San Fernando Valley and the Mojave Desert. People seeking affordable homes pay instead with ever-longer commutes, even though job growth is spreading into the suburbs.

The influx of immigrants, many of them from Asia or Latin America, added more than 1.4 million to Los Angeles County's population in the last decade. That growth is more than twice as much as any other county, although in percentage terms it is a bit under the statewide rate. The slower-than-average population growth, coupled with the tendency of Hispanic and Asian immigrants not to vote, means Los Angeles County is losing a bit of its overall political clout. But the county is still a giant.

County politics tend to divide rather evenly down party lines. It is a bit more Democratic in registration than the state as a whole, but many of its Democrats tend to support Republicans for top offices. The strongly pro-Republican tilt in the remainder of Southern California more than offsets the Democratic edge in Los Angeles and gives the region a very dependable GOP flavor in races for U.S. senator, governor and president.

Within Los Angeles County, politics tend to run to extremes. The state's most conservative and most liberal officeholders can be found in its legislative and congressional delegations. The central and western portions of the county – downtown Los Angeles, heavily black south-central Los Angeles, Hispanic East Los Angeles and the wealthy Beverly Hills, Santa Monica and Westwood areas on the West Side – are strongly Democratic. State Senate President Pro Tem David Roberti; ex-radical Tom Hayden, now a state assemblyman; and Reps. Howard Berman and Henry Waxman, who head a powerful political organization, are among the powerful Democrats from the west side. But Long Beach – ex-Gov. George Deukmejian's home – and the Anglo suburbs on the fringes of the county vote Republican, while the San Fernando Valley is a toss-up, Democratic in the southern part, Republican in the north.

A third of the county's population is Hispanic and at least 10 percent is Asian, but neither of these fast-growing ethnic groups has become politically influential. So far, politics in the county is an Anglo and black business, as reflected in the ethnic identity of all but a few officeholders.

The county Board of Supervisors, for instance, was composed of five Anglo men until recently, despite the fact that Anglos are less than half of the county's population. Those five positions are among the most powerful in the nation, which is why their holders are called "the five little kings" by political insiders. Each supervisor has nearly 2 million constituents and a one-fifth vote on a $9 billion budget. Each also has a huge personal staff and, without an elected head of county government, together they wield vast power over land-use, transportation, health care and other matters.

The county's split political personality is revealed in the makeup of the board, three Democrats and two Republicans. Republican Deane Dana represents a coastal district and the other Republican is Mike Antonovich who has a chunk of the suburbs. The three Democrats are Ed Edelman, who represents the largely Jewish west side; Kenneth Hahn, a legendary political figure who has represented overwhelmingly black south-central Los Angeles for decades and continues to function despite debilitating health problems; and newcomer Gloria Molina, whose district includes Boyle Heights, East Los Angeles and part of the San Gabriel Valley.

Molina's ascendency to the board from the Los Angeles City Council in early

1991 marked one of the most dramatic political shifts in the county during this century. Republicans had controlled the board through the 1980s, but the U.S. Justice Department filed suit in 1985, claiming the board's GOP majority had reapportioned the county in a way that would deny Hispanic representation. The board unsuccessfully fought the suit, eventually spending nearly $10 million of the taxpayers' money on legal fees.

That forced new boundaries and a special election to replace retiring Supervisor Peter Schabarum. Molina, a farm worker's daughter who rose from grass-roots politics, beat state Sen. Art Torres to become the first Hispanic elected to the board since the 1870s. Molina, who became something of a national figure in the process, is part of a faction that had pushed the idea of expanding the board to seven to make it more representative. Now, however, Molina is seeking a nine-member board.

It has been a different story on the 15-member City Council. When the Justice Department began raising questions in the mid-'80s, district lines were redrawn to create two seats for Hispanics. With more than a third of the city's population, Hispanics could claim at least five of the 15 council seats. Blacks, at one-third of the Hispanic population, have three seats as well as the mayorship. There is one Asian councilman. Clearly, there is potential for more minority representation. But while blacks tend to vote in proportion to their numbers, Hispanics and Asians have been virtually invisible politically.

The council also was one of the first in a major city to adopt campaign contribution limits. Enlightenment of that sort is one reason Los Angeles still works as a city. That Los Angeles has a huge reservoir of civic energy is evident in such enterprises as the 1984 Olympics or its annual marathon, which is the nation's second largest.

It was the onset of World War II that propelled Los Angeles into the industrial age. As factories, warehouses, docks and other facilities were quickly built to serve the war, its population doubled and redoubled as defense workers poured in. The San Fernando Valley and other one-time ranch lands were turned into housing tracts. The naturally arid region had assured itself of a dependable water supply, thanks to some not altogether savory dealings by local landowners.

Los Angeles' boom did not slow after the war. Factories that had turned out bombers began making airliners. The automobile, a necessity in such a low-density city, sparked the development of the freeway. The state's first freeway, connecting downtown Los Angeles with Pasadena, the traditional home of moneyed families, is still carrying cars.

With so many new people coming to town, with so much money to be made and with so little sense of civic identity, Los Angeles was ripe for corruption. Three decades after the fact, the movie "Chinatown" accurately captured the ambiance of Los Angeles in the 1940s. Police were corrupt. City officials were corrupt. Newspapers were corrupt. Los Angeles was a civic joke, its downtown area a seedy slum, its once-extensive trolley system ripped out by money-grubbing bus companies, its development governed by which subdivider was most willing to grease the right palms.

Slowly, Los Angeles developed a sense of civic pride that extended beyond the latest land deal. Slowly, the city's notorious Police Department was cleaned up by William Parker, a reformist chief. The Los Angeles Times, once considered to be the nation's worst large newspaper, came under the control of Otis Chandler, a member of the family that had owned it for generations, and the new publisher turned the Times into an institution with national stature. Los Angeles developed a culture to match its fast-growing population: art museums, a symphony, charities and other amenities helped the nouveau riche – including those from the movie industry – acquire a social respectability.

While the city's upper crust began developing a social sense, the city itself continued to change. As the immigrants moved in and multiplied, the Anglos moved out to the San Fernando Valley and other suburbs, many of which are still within the city limits. The 1990 census found Los Angeles, with Anglos in the minority, to be one of the nation's most ethnically diverse cities.

But for decades, Los Angeles' politics, like the city itself, was a whites-only business. Mayors – honest or crooked – were all men who professed a conservative ideology, and none showed more than token ability to project an image outside the city. Race relations, like much of the Los Angeles lifestyle, were conducted at long distance. If anything, the 1965 riots in the overwhelmingly black Watts section of Los Angeles widened the gulf between Anglos and non-Anglos. It was a more violent replay of the "Zoot-suit riots," which had pitted Hispanics against white servicemen during World War II.

All of that seemingly changed in 1973, when Tom Bradley, a black former college athlete and one-time Los Angeles police lieutenant, won the mayorship. Bradley projected hope to minorities and pro-development moderation to the white business and political establishment. And he has survived, winning re-election four times, by continuing to walk that tightrope.

Bradley's chief mayoral accomplishment – made in close collaboration with the business community – has been the revitalization of the city's downtown. Oil companies, banks and other major corporations dumped money into the Bunker Hill project to the give downtown a skyline, even though the lower reaches of the area remain a slum. Beyond that, Bradley has delivered a city government that is reasonably efficient, reasonably honest and reasonably inclusive, especially when compared to many of the nation's other big cities.

Bradley, an intensely proud and private man, thought that his record of moderation and progress warranted a broader stage, and he ran for governor in 1982. The Democratic Party thought it had a winner in Bradley, especially following the GOP's nomination of George Deukmejian, the lackluster attorney general. Even surveys of voters leaving polling places on Election Day had Bradley winning. But when all of the votes had been counted – including several hundred thousand absentee ballots that the Republicans had semisecretly encouraged – Deukmejian eked out a paper-thin victory. Three years later, Bradley faced a tough re-election campaign himself but won. Then, driven more by pride than realism, he ran for governor again in 1986. That time, Deukmejian's victory was a landslide.

Bradley has talked about running for an unprecedented sixth term in 1993 when he will be pushing age 75. But his prospects have dimmed dramatically. The turnaround stems from a series of newspaper revelations about his personal finances, especially consulting fees he accepted from two banks that were given large deposits of city funds. The scandal continued to blossom into 1991. At the same time, the recession caught up with the city in 1990, spawning a huge deficit and leaving Bradley with tough and unpopular budget-cutting options.

One of his potential opponents, probably City Councilman Zev Yaroslavsky, will have the backing of the powerful political organization headed by Reps. Berman and Waxman, which dominates politics on Los Angeles' affluent west side, an area long a source of Bradley support. The Berman-Waxman organization is the single most powerful political force in Los Angeles, with influence that reaches to Sacramento and Washington, D.C. It even has its own professional campaign arm headed by Berman's younger brother, Michael, and his partner, Carl D'Agostino.

The organization taps into the wealthy west side professional and entertainment industry community for money, and it backs candidates for local and state offices. It has created congressmen and was instrumental in Gary Hart's 1984 presidential primary victory in California. Berman-Waxman is neo-liberal, pro-environment and a promoter of pro-Israel foreign policies. At the same time, Bradley as the incumbent will be carrying the responsibility for more than 400 gang-related murders a year. Drug abuse has become rampant in lower-income neighborhoods and upper-income mansions. Smog is worsening, traffic congestion grows exponentially and polls indicate that most Los Angeles residents think their quality of life has deteriorated. One survey found half of those polled had considered moving.

Development has re-emerged as the city's top political issue among the majority of those who turn out to vote. Environmental protection is a popular cause on the west side and in the San Fernando Valley, occasionally taking on a tone of racial exclusivity. Bradley has been in league with pro-development business and labor groups, but anti-development forces are gaining strength and the issue could dominate the 1991 City Council races. The battle over development has become, in effect, a battle over the quality of Los Angeles life. Crowding and pollution have become for many the new code words by which differing social and cultural values are measured.

Whatever happens to Bradley in the current scandals, it is likely he is Los Angeles' last black mayor as well as its first. Political power in Los Angeles in the 1990s and beyond will depend on how well organized the burgeoning Hispanic and Asian populations become, and how militant the anti-development, quality-of-life movement becomes.

Madera County

Area: 2,147.1 sq. mi.; Population: (1990) 88,090, (1980) 63,116; Registration: (1990) D-51.6% R-39.9%; Unemployment: (Jan. 1991) 13.6%; County supervisors: Harry Baker Jr., Alfred Ginsburg, Rick Jensen, Jess Lopez, Gail McIntyre; 209 W. Yosemite Ave., Madera 93637; (209) 675-7700.

Madera County is farm country, and far enough removed from the state's urban centers to avoid, at least for a while, the dubious benefits of suburbanization. Its population is growing, up 39 percent between 1980 and 1990, and much of the growth is in foothill areas popular with retirees. A portion of Yosemite National Park lies in the county, and along with many other recreational sites, such as Millerton and Bass lakes, brings a steady stream of tourists through the county.

The city of Madera and surrounding communities have had a modest amount of industrialization, most of it spilling over from the Fresno area to the south. But agriculture – especially grapes and dairy products – remains the economic linchpin, accounting for a third of the region's employment.

Despite the seemingly strong Democratic registration edge typical of San Joaquin Valley counties, Madera votes conservatively, and its growing Hispanic population – nearing a third – remains largely powerless.

Marin County

Area: 588 sq. mi.; Population: (1990) 230,096, (1980) 222,592; Registration: (1990) D-52.1% R-33.8%; Unemployment (Jan. 1991) 3.8%; County supervisors: Albert Aramburu, Brady Bevis, Harold Brown, Gary Giacomini, Bob Roumiguiere; Civic Center, Room 315, San Rafael 94903; (415) 499-7331.

They make jokes about Marin. They write books, movies and songs about Marin. It even shows up occasionally in a comic strip. It is that kind of place. The Golden Gate Bridge lands on its southern tip, whales pass close to its spectacular coastline and mountains and woods rise in all corners of the county.

It is also one of those places on which California's reputation – whether deserved or not – is built. The county is a combination of bohemianism, bourgeoisie, activism, money, exclusivity and liberal social attitudes, overlaid with an almost religious sense of environmental protection.

As the San Francisco Bay Area suburbs boomed in the early 1970s, Marin

County fought to hold the line on growth, long before such movements became popular elsewhere. And Marin residents have pretty much succeeded. Between 1980 and 1990, for example, its population grew only 3.3 percent, less than a seventh of the statewide rate and by far the slowest of any somewhat urban county.

But the success of the growth-control movement has had side effects: an incredible rise in housing costs, which has driven out the non-affluent (the median income is over 50 percent higher than neighboring Sonoma County) and major traffic problems. The traffic comes from both a boom in commuters driving northward toward Sonoma and south toward San Francisco, and from the sharp increase in jobs in Marin itself, which brings commuters into the county.

Still, much of Marin remains dedicated to keeping its natural attributes relatively undisturbed. One coastal community even refuses to have signs directing traffic to itself, so intense is the desire for isolation.

A major showdown on the growth issue occurred in 1989, when voters decided the fate of a large proposed residential and office development on the site of the former Hamilton Air Force Base. Despite the shortage and high cost of housing and support from such prominent Democrats as Lt. Gov. Leo McCarthy, the project was rejected. A corollary situation involves occasional rumblings out of Sacramento about closing San Quentin Prison and selling its exquisite site for development. Marin County residents would rather keep the prison.

Politically, Marin was once steadfastly Republican but has been moving left as environmentalism has become a more potent political force. The only Republican officeholders who survive now are those who embrace that cause.

Mariposa County

Area: 1,460.5 sq. mi.; Population: (1990) 14,302, (1980) 11,108; Registration: (1990) D-44% R-42.8%; Unemployment: (Jan. 1991) 8.5%; County supervisors: Arthur Baggett, Eric Erickson, Sally Punte, George Radanovich, Gertrude Taber; P.O. Box 784, Mariposa 95338: (209) 966-3222.

Once, in the mid-19th century, Mariposa County covered a huge swath of California, including most of the San Joaquin Valley and Southern California. But year after year, the county's boundaries were whittled down to form new counties, eventually spawning 11 in all. What's left are 1,460.5 square miles of scenic territory that include the most famous and most visited portions of Yosemite National Park.

Each year, hundreds of thousands people visit Mariposa County's rolling foothills, quaint gold-rush era towns and craggy mountains. And each year, a few more decide to stay, which is why the county's population grew by almost 30 percent between 1980 and 1990. The county's population has nearly tripled since

1960. Many of the newcomers are retirees, who bring conservative political attitudes that are turning the county into a Republican bastion.

The state projects that Mariposa's population will continue to grow rapidly, reaching 20,000 by the turn of the century as the demand for recreational opportunities continues to expand.

Mendocino County

Area: 3,510.7 sq. mi.; Population: (1990) 80,345, (1980) 66,738; Registration: (1990) D-54.6% R-31.9%; Unemployment: (Jan. 1991) 13.0%; County supervisors: Marilyn Butcher, James Eddie, Liz Henry, Nelson Redding, Norman DeVall; Courthouse, Room 113, Ukiah 95482; (707) 463-4221.

Mendocino County, like the rest of Northern California's rugged, spectacular coast, was once timber country. Cutting and processing the trees of the densely forested areas of the county remain a huge part of the economy, but within the last generation a revolution hit the county.

A wave of urban emigres flooded the area in the 1960s and '70s, creating a new economy rooted in tourism, crafts and, although illegal, the cultivation of marijuana. The extremely quaint little coastal towns such as Elk and Mendocino acquired rafts of bed-and-breakfast inns and trendy restaurants to serve weekenders from the Bay Area. And in the late 1980s, the southern part of the county started turning into suburbs as Bay Area commuters pressed ever-outward, searching for affordable housing. Politically, the change moved Mendocino County leftward, with liberal Democrats replacing conservative Democrats in elected offices.

The county's budget, however, suffers many of the same problems facing other rural counties. In fact, supervisors went so far as to take out a mortgage on their courthouse to help balance the 1990-91 budget.

Merced County

Area: 2007.7 sq. mi.; Population: (1990) 178,403, (1980) 134,558; Registration: (1990) D-54.7% R-35.1%; Unemployment: (Jan. 1991) 16.9%; County supervisors: Michael Bogna Jr., Wyatt Davenport, Ann Klinger, Jerald O'Banion, Dean Peterson; 2222 M St., Merced 95340; (209) 385-7366.

Merced County advertises itself as the gateway to Yosemite National Park, but its future appears to be tied less to the mountainous eastern end of the county than to its western flatlands, which are on the verge of a suburban explosion.

The mind may boggle at the prospect, but Los Banos, a quiet and fairly isolated farm town on the west side of the San Joaquin Valley, is laying plans to become part of the San Francisco Bay megalopolis as rising housing costs drive commuters further from the central cities. In this case, the upgrading of Highway 152 to a full freeway will give commuters a straight drive from little Los Banos into the packed Santa Clara Valley south of San Jose. Even without such suburbanization, Merced County's population is up more than 32 percent between 1980 and 1990, still faster than the state average. And its politics, which had been conservative Democrat, seem to be edging rightward with the growth.

Merced is considered as well managed a county as any in the state, according to the California Counties Foundation. But as in many other counties, budget writers have been tightening belts yearly and soon may have no room left.

Modoc County

Area: 4,340.4 sq. mi.; Population: (1990) 9,678, (1980) 8,610; Registration: (1990) D-45.4% R-43.6%; Unemployment: (Jan. 1991) 17.1%; County supervisors: Melvin Anderson, Nancy Huffman, Mick Jones, Don Polson, John Schreiber; P.O. Box 131, Alturas 96101; (916) 233-3939.

A form letter that Modoc County employment officials send to would-be job seekers says it all. The weather can be extreme, the economy is seasonal and "Modoc County (has) virtually no growth," the letter bluntly tells those who think that the isolated, rugged and beautiful county would be a paradise.

The few thousand souls who live in Modoc County, located in California's upper right-hand corner, like it just the way it is. But there are laments that a lack of jobs drives young people from the area into the cities hundreds of miles away.

Timber and cattle are the mainstays of the economy, although government – local, state and federal – is the largest employer. Increasingly, summer homes are being built by urbanites seeking isolation. There are so many summer residents, in fact, that something of a political schism has developed between them and the year-round people. Apart from that, the politics are solidly conservative.

Mono County

Area: 3,103 sq. mi.; Population: (1990) 9,956 (1980) 8,577; Registration: (1990) D-35.3% R-46.2%; Unemployment: (Jan. 1991) 7.6%; County supervisors: Michael Jarvis, Andrea Lawrence, Dan Paranick, Don Rake, William Reid; P.O. Box 715, Bridgeport 93517; (619) 932-7911.

The dominant feature of Mono County – and one focal point of its politics – is Mono Lake and its striking geologic features nearby. The lake has shrunk markedly in the last half-century, a constant reminder that the county's fate is largely in the hands of Los Angeles.

Through a series of subterfuges, Los Angeles gained control over water supplies on the eastern slope of the Sierra and pipes much of that southward. Local residents are caught in the political and legal battle over whether the diversions should continue uninterrupted or whether more water should be allowed to flow into Mono Lake and thus save the scenic and ecological wonder from shrinking further. It's been a long and expensive matter, but court decisions are going the way of saving the lake.

Mono County

Mono Lake also symbolizes the tourism industry that has gradually replaced ranching and mining as the chief source of jobs. Contributing to that economic evolution is Mammoth Lakes, a major skiing area. Incorporated during the 1980s, Mammoth Lakes is now the economic center of the county and is large enough to dictate political policy to the rest of the residents.

In the '80s, Mammoth Lakes was found to be sitting atop an active volcano. At one point, it became so restive that a state of emergency was declared. Tourism and housing values took an immediate plunge, and Mammoth politicians responded with demands that state and federal geologists suppress all future negative news of that sort. Time has brought a little more enlightenment to the political leadership, but not much.

Monterey County

Area: 3,324.1 sq. mi.; Population: (1990) 355,660 (1980) 290,444; Registration: (1990) D-49.3% R-36.6%; Unemployment: (Jan. 1991) 16.6%; County supervisors: Marc Del Piero, Sam Karas, Thomas Perkins, Barbara Shipnuck, Karin Strasser Kauffman; P.O. Box 1728, Salinas 92902; (408) 424-8611.

Even in a state that is blessed with great natural beauty, Monterey County is something special. Its abundant attractions – rugged coastline, windblown woods, quaint towns and nearly perfect weather – have become the focal point of county politics. Bluntly put, those who have already captured a piece of Monterey for themselves are increasingly active in protecting it against outsiders. Almost any development project, from a hotel to a highway, sparks controversy. Politics in Monterey, Carmel and other Monterey Peninsula communities revolve around that tension.

The mayorship of Monterey and the balance of power on the City Council shifted out of the hands of pro-development forces in the early 1980s after Monterey underwent a surge of hotel construction, including erection of a downtown hotel dubbed "Sheraton General" for its hospital-like appearance.

At the same time, however, the peninsula's economy is almost entirely dependent upon the tourist industry. The result is non-stop political churning over the future of the area, a two-hour drive south from San Francisco. The battle of Monterey achieved national publicity in 1986 when actor Clint Eastwood was elected mayor of Carmel for two years on a pro-development platform.

Outside of the Peninsula, most of Monterey County is agricultural. While the cities of Monterey and Salinas, the counties two major population centers, are only a few miles apart, economically and socially they are two different worlds. Salinas and other inland communities rely on the price of the vegetables they produce, but they also are beginning to feel suburbs creeping in as commuters spill farther and farther out of the San Jose area to the north. The politics of Salinas and environs are being altered by the new suburbs and by the slowly emerging strength of Hispanics. Although more than a third of the population in many communities, Hispanics have been politically powerless. But key court decisions have opened avenues of political activity at the local level, especially in Salinas, which shifted to a district form of city voting after a court decision ordered districts formed in nearby Watsonville.

The economic and social contrasts found within the county are mirrored in its politics – liberal-environmentalist along the coast and conservative inland. Overall voting patterns are similar to those of the state, but they are not stable. Suburban development pulls the county toward the Republicans while Hispanic political activity pushes toward the Democrats.

Napa County

Area: 796.9 sq. mi.; Population: (1990) 110,765, (1980) 99,199; Registration: (1990) D-50.3% R-39.1%; Unemployment: (Jan. 1991) 6.6%; County supervisors: Paul Battisti, Vincent Ferriole, John Mikolajcik, Fred Negri, Mel Varrelman; 1195 Third St., Napa 94559; (707) 253-4386.

Once upon a time – and not too many years ago – the Napa Valley was a little-known corner of California.

That seems like a fairly tale these days. As wine-drinking evolved into something akin to a secular religion in the 1970s and '80s, the Napa Valley became a mecca. Napa County's once quiet agricultural valley, an hour's drive northeast from San Francisco, evolved with astonishing speed into a tourist draw. New wineries sprouted like mushrooms and the valley acquired bushels of inns, hotels, restaurants and other tourist-oriented facilities.

In the early 1980s, there began a backlash among residents tired of weekend traffic jams and jacked-up prices aimed at visitors. While rising home prices, controls on new development and a lack of local jobs has kept population growth scant, the battles over tourist-oriented development remain intense. One noticed statewide is a squabble over a "wine train" that runs through the valley.

Nevada County

Area: 992.2 sq. mi.; Population: (1990) 78,510, (1980) 51,645; Registration: (1990) D-39.1% R-47.7%; Unemployment: (Jun. 1991) 8.2%; County supervisors: James Callaghan, Todd Juvinall, Bill Schultz, G.B. Tucker, Jim Weir; 950 Maidu Ave., Nevada City 95959; (916) 265-1480.

Nevada County is typical of the fast-growing Sierra foothill region of California. Between 1980 and 1990, it recorded a whopping 52 percent population growth, the fifth-largest rate in the state, as increasing numbers of retirees, Sacramento commuters and urban escapees settled there.

The county has developed a home-grown electronics industry and a burgeoning retail trade market, supplemented in some corners by marijuana cultivation. The Nevada City-Grass Valley area has become a regional commercial and cultural center, and there is a thriving arts community in North San Juan. The combination of foothill and mountain beauty and mild climate continues to draw both visitors and those looking for new roots. And the major question facing the county is whether to impose stricter curbs on development.

Nevada County, like other foothill communities, has been moving to the right politically. Republicans outnumber Democrats and voters have that "leave-me-alone" philosophy that dominates the region.

Orange County

Area: 785.1 sq. mi.; Population: (1990) 2,410,556, (1980) 1,932,921; Registration: (1990) D-33.9% R-55.6%; Unemployment: (Jan. 1991) 4.7%; County supervisors: Thomas Riley, Don Roth, Roger Stanton, Gaddi Vasquez, Harriett Wieder; 10 Civic Center, Santa Ana 92701; (714) 834-3100.

No piece of California typifies the state's development rush more than Orange County, a patch of coastline and rolling hills immediately south of Los Angeles. Prior to World War II, Orange County was cattle ranges (controlled by big, Spanish-land-grant ranchers such as the Irvines and the O'Neills), vegetable fields and citrus orchards.

After the war, and especially after 1955, the county exploded with houses and suburbs. It achieved national and international attention for two very different attributes: it is the home of Disneyland, the planet's first, and possibly most charming, theme amusement park, and it is a major hotbed of right-wing politics.

As the British Broadcasting Corp. said in a 1976 documentary on Orange County: "This is the culmination of the American dream." That dream was a home in the suburbs, two cars and maybe a ski boat, and a barbeque in the back yard. Orange County reproduced it hundreds of thousands of times in one generation.

When Walt Disney opened his amusement park in 1955, Anaheim was a city of 35,000. Over the next 30 years, along with the growth of motels, fast-food outlets and restaurants, Anaheim's population increased ninefold, matching what was happening in Orange County as a whole, which became the state's second-most populous county. But the county continues to exist in the shadow of much-larger, infinitely-more-glamorous Los Angeles to the north. Even its professional sports teams, the Los Angeles Rams football team and the California Angels baseball team, don't take their names from the county. And Orange County is the largest urban area in the country without its own network television service.

Although no one city dominates Orange County, Irvine and nearby Costa Mesa are its center. The region's dazzling new performing arts center is in Costa Mesa, and the county's growing airport, named for the late actor and county resident John Wayne, lies just outside that city. Together with the development of the UC Irvine campus and the community of Irvine, the two cities have created a cultural locus that had been lacking during the county's go-go phase of growth.

This area, sprawled on both sides of Interstate 405, epitomizes the change that occurred in the 1970s. While new suburbs sprouted further east in Riverside County, slowing the population growth in Orange County, the region became a center for the development of California's post-industrial economy rooted in trade, services and high-tech fabrication. Only downtown Los Angeles rivals the area's concentration of office space. UC Irvine has become a center for biotech research and development and the county has more than 700 high-tech companies.

The development of the Irvine-centered commercial and cultural complex also shows the shift of emphasis from the older cities of Santa Ana and Anaheim in the north to the central and southern parts of the county. The older communities, meanwhile, have found themselves with large and growing Hispanic and Southeast Asian communities. The Hispanics have not become a political force, but Vietnamese-Americans were a key factor in U.S. Rep. Robert "B-1 Bob" Dornan's election to Congress in 1984.

As Orange County developed into an employment center, the commute patterns also changed, eventually producing traffic congestion of mythic proportions. In that part of the state, traffic is a preoccupation. No one makes plans, no one gives directions, no one shops without considering traffic. Besides the local drivers, the county's mostly older freeways handle thousands and thousands of cars from suburbs in Riverside and elsewhere – suburbs created in response to the skyrocketing home prices in Orange County. Traffic, in turn, has fueled a local anti-growth movement that has drawn support from both conservatives and liberals. And it has convinced people of the need for toll roads.

As home prices went up, population growth slowed further. In the early 1980s, the county was growing slower than the state as a whole and by the mid-1980s, San Diego supplanted Orange as the state's second-most populous county. Growth in the county's southern portion in the late 1980s pushed Orange County's growth rate up to just about the state average of 25 percent for the decade.

Politics have always been conservative, even though Democrats achieved a short-lived plurality of voter registration in the mid-1970s. But one by one, the Democratic state legislators and congressmen who had won office in the 1970s bit the dust in the 1980s. The Republican grip has solidified in recent years, and the GOP now has a quarter-million voter advantage and an all-Republican delegation in Washington. In Sacramento, there's one Assembly Democrat (Tom Umberg) and Democratic Sen. Cecil Green's district includes the area around Buena Park. A big Republican turnout in Orange County is critical to statewide GOP candidates.

The odd quality of local politics was illustrated by an incident in 1988. Local Republican officials hired armed guards to stand outside polling places in a severely contested state Assembly election. The guards carried signs warning that illegal aliens and non-citizens could not vote. Democrats claimed that the action discouraged Hispanics from voting while Republicans said they were guarding against a feared invasion of illegal voters. It resulted in a lawsuit seeking to set aside the election of Republican Curt Pringle. The suit went nowhere, but Pringle lost in 1990 to Garden Grove Democrat Umberg.

The county, however, is producing some statewide political figures. One Orange County state senator, Marian Bergeson, was the GOP nominee for lieutenant governor in 1990, losing to incumbent Leo McCarthy. Bergeson beat another then-Orange County state senator, John Seymour, for that nomination, which didn't hurt Seymour a bit. He was appointed to fill Gov. Wilson's seat in the U.S. Senate, and Seymour will be facing U.S. Rep William Dannemeyer of Fullerton for the 1992 Republican nomination for that post. In addition, Supervisor Gaddi Vasquez is being groomed by GOP leaders to become a major Hispanic political figure.

Placer County

Area: 1,506.5 sq. mi.; Population: (1990) 172,796, (1980) 117,247; Registration: (1990) D-43.2% R-46.4%; Unemployment: (Jan. 1991) 7.4%; County supervisors: George Beland, Alex Ferreira, Mike Fluty, Susan Hogg, Phil Ozenick; 175 Fulweiler Ave., Auburn, 95603; (916) 823-4641.

Fast-growing Placer County represents three distinct pieces of the variegated California landscape.

The western portion, centered in and around Roseville, has evolved in recent

years into a booming residential and industrial suburb of Sacramento County, with an expanding connection to the Silicon Valley computer complex. The
middle part of the county around Auburn, the quaint,
gold rush era foothill county seat, is growing rapidly
too, with commuters, retirees and urban expatriates.
And the eastern part of the county is high-mountain
country that includes the northern shore of Lake
Tahoe, which also is feeling development pressure.

The common denominator – and a major reason
for the county's growth – is Interstate 80, the major
east-west highway that connects San Francisco and

Placer County

Sacramento with the rest of the continent. The county's population has grown by
nearly 50 percent in the 1980s, and it will continue to expand at that rapid clip – an
expansion that is moving the area's politics ever rightward.

Plumas County

*Area: 2,618.4 sq. mi.; Population: (1990) 19,739,
(1980) 17,340; Registration: (1990) D-49.7% R-
38.4%; Unemployment: (Jan. 1991) 19.8%; County
supervisors: Bill Coates, John Schramel, Joyce
Scroggs, Jim Smith, Donald Woodhall; P.O. Box
207, Quincy 95971; (916) 283-0280.*

Plumas County folks often feel more cultural and
economic affinity with Nevada than with expansive,
fast-changing California. Reno, 80 miles to the
southeast, is the nearest big town, and much of the
county's economic activity crosses the state border.

Seventy percent of the county's land is owned by the federal government, mostly
by the Forest Service, and the troubled lumber industry is the mainstay of the
economy, which gets a little supplement from tourism. It shares with other rural
counties a chronically high unemployment rate and major budget problems.
Plumas' population is growing at about half the rate of the rest of the state, and most
of those newcomers are retirees and others seeking quiet refuge in the area's heavily
forested lands.

Overall, the county's politics are predictably conservative, although there has
been a years-long battle for control of the Board of Supervisors that has included
charges of election-rigging.

Riverside County

*Area: 7,243 sq. mi.; Population: (1990) 1,170,413, (1980) 663,199; Registra-
tion: (1990) D-44% R-46.7%; Unemployment: (Jan. 1991) 10.1%; County super-*

visors: Walt Abraham, Kay Ceniceros, Melba Dunlap, Patricia Larson, A. Norton Younglove; 4080 Lemon St., Riverside 92501; (714) 787-2010.

Riverside County is Southern California's newest boom area and the state's fastest growing county by far. It and neighboring San Bernardino County are developing at a breakneck rate reminiscent of the San Fernando Valley and Orange County development following World War II. The cause of the growth is the same: young families searching for affordable suburban homes.

Riverside County

While home prices soared to the quarter-million-dollar mark in Los Angeles and Orange counties, developers subdivided large tracts of arid Riverside County and sold houses for less than half that amount. The desire for that typically American value – the house in the suburbs – is so strong that newly minted Riverside residents are willing to commute as long as two hours each way to the job centers closer to the coast.

The county, which began the decade with 663,199 people, exploded by 76 percent by 1990. The impacts of that dizzying growth have been many. They range from suddenly crowded freeways to the worsening of the county's chronic smog problems. Untold acres of orange groves – which had been the county's chief economic support until the real estate boom – were uprooted to make room for the new subdivisions and that, in turn, sparked an anti-growth backlash in the mid-1980s.

While growth issues remain the county's major political battles, the suburban-style expansion is moving Riverside sharply to the right in the same way growth affected Orange County after World War II. Not too many years ago, Riverside was solidly Democratic, but by 1988 Republicans had pulled ahead in registration and the remaining Democratic officeholders, especially Assemblyman Steve Clute, face perilous times.

Riverside County's growing conservatism is getting a shove from Palm Springs, the high-desert community where retired captains of industry live. Given its new large and conservative population, Riverside is likely to benefit from post-1990 census reapportionment, and that will mean more opportunities for Republicans. The problem for the GOP, however, is that many newcomers don't vote. So much of their time is gobbled up by long commutes each day, anything out of their routine such as a trip to the polling place is apt to be viewed as a burden.

Sacramento County

Area: 1,015.3 sq. mi.; Population: (1990) 1,041,219, (1980) 783,381; Registration: (1990) D-54.3% R-36.4%; Unemployment: (Jan. 1991) 6.6%; County supervisors: Illa Collin, Grantland Johnson, Toby Johnson, Sandra Smoley, Jim

Streng, 700 H St., Suite 2450, Sacramento 95814; (916) 440-5451.

For decades, the Sacramento area slept while other urban areas boomed. It was known as a terminally dull government community, filled with civil servants who labored not only for the state government agencies but for dozens of federal offices as well.

At one point, more than 40 percent of the Sacramento County's work force collected public paychecks, and the metropolitan area, which included most of the county as well as chunks of neighboring

Sacramento County

counties, seemed to be nothing but a collection of endless suburban tracts and shopping centers — including one built shortly after World War II that was California's first.

In the late 1970s, however, the Sacramento region began to awaken. Soaring housing costs and clogged roads in the Bay Area began pushing development outward, and Sacramento, with its cheaper housing and relatively easy lifestyle, became an attractive spot for employers looking to relocate. Today, government continues to be the economic backbone of the area, but the hottest growth is in the private sector. Public employment has declined to less than a third of the total payroll.

Downtown Sacramento began sprouting skyscrapers, fields were converted to high-tech job centers and dozens of subdivisions sprang up. By 1989, Sacramento had been featured on the cover of a national news magazine as one of the country's best places to live. It had become the fastest growing region in the state and one of the nation's fastest growing metropolitan areas. New sports and cultural amenities put Sacramento on the brink of becoming a major metropolitan area, on a par with such second-tier cities as Denver, Kansas City and Atlanta.

But there are downsides to Sacramento's heady growth, such as traffic congestion and worsening air quality. And the area is beset by perhaps the worst mish-mash of governmental authority in the state. The city of Sacramento is only a fifth of the metropolitan area, and the county has the highest proportion of unincorporated, urbanized area of any in the state. Attempts at city-county consolidation failed in 1974 and again in 1990.

That left the city and county to squabble over development, sales taxes and political influence. Although the supervisors represent much more of the county, it is the City Council that reaps most of the publicity, for better or worse. And Sacramento is the largest city in the state with a part-time council. Two-term Democratic Mayor Anne Rudin, who seems to relish that amateur status, must decide in 1991 whether to run for a third term or let power flow to another.

Because the area had for so long been a governmental center, it has not reaped the private sector, corporate leadership vital to developing the social and cultural structures of most major communities. In more recent years some of the land developers who have profited from Sacramento's growth have tried to fill that role, but it is yet to be realized, and the major emphasis has been on professional sports.

As with most government enclaves, Sacramento County has been dependably Democratic in its voting patterns. But with suburbanization and private-sector job development, that, too, is changing. Democrats still dominate in the city, but the fast-growing suburbs are voting more and more Republican.

San Benito County

Area: 1,397.1 sq. mi.; Population: (1990) 36,697, (1980) 25,005; Registration: (1990) D-51.1% R-38.1%; Unemployment: (Jan. 1991) 20.9%; County supervisors: Rita Bowling, Curtis Graves, Mike Graves, Ruth Kesler, Richard Scagliotti; 440 Fifth St., Hollister 95023; (408) 637-4641.

San Benito County lies in a little recess of public consciousness, overshadowed by its larger and/or more glamorous neighbors, Santa Clara and Monterey counties. But that may be changing.

As the extended Bay Area continues to march southward, San Benito County is growing at a healthy rate and seems poised for a boom. From 1980 to 1990, the county population spurted up by 46 percent, and as Highway 152, the major east-west route through the county, is turned into a full freeway, more commuter-oriented development appears certain.

The question is whether this growth will overwhelm the slow-paced, rural lifestyle that has been San Benito's hallmark. Another question is whether the county's very large Hispanic population – San Juan Bautista is the headquarters of El Teatro Campesino, the farm worker's theater – will assume political power in keeping with its numbers or continue to play a secondary role.

San Bernardino County

Area: 20,164 sq. mi.; Population: (1990) 1,418,380, (1980) 895,016; Registration: (1990) D-44.4% R-46.2%; Unemployment: (Jan. 1991) 7.9%; County supervisors: Robert Hammock, Jon Mikels, Barbara Crum Riordan, Marsha Turoci, Larry Walker, 385 N. Arrowhead Ave., San Bernardino 92415; (714) 387-4811.

San Bernardino County – or San Berdoo, as it is almost universally called – is huge. The county covers more land than any other in the United States, and its 20,000-plus square miles constitute more than an eighth of California. But most of those square miles are unpopulated desert, and more than three-fourths of them are owned by the federal government.

Politically, culturally and economically, most of what counts in San Bernardino lies in the western portion nearest Los Angeles, and that's a sore point with residents in the rest of the county. There was a failed effort in 1988 to split San Bernardino County and create a new county in the desert called Mojave.

The western slab of San Berdoo, along with neighboring Riverside County, is what boosters call the "Inland Empire," and that once-fanciful name is taking on new weight as commuters in search of affordable homes convert the once-grimy industrial towns of western San Bernardino County, such as Rialto and Fontana, into bedroom communities. San Bernandino was second only to Riverside County in population growth, expanding by about 58 percent between 1980 and 1990.

Along with the growth have come all the usual problems: environmental damage, smog, and social dislocation. There is some growth in jobs in the area, especially around Ontario International Airport, but the job-people mix is a continuing headache for local leaders.

The heavy industries that had been San Bernardino's economic foundation, typified by the now-cold steel works at Fontana, have given way to shopping centers, freight handling and other post-industrial economic activities. Dairy farmers around Chino, who used to supply much of the Los Angeles area's milk, are finding that the scent of cows is not compatible with the dreams of new suburbanites. On the plus side, the growth in land values has given San Bernardino one of the healthiest county budgets in the state.

Politically, San Berdoo has historically been blue-collar Democrat, tending to vote conservatively: Republican at the top of the ticket and Democratic for local and state offices. But the suburbs brought partisan change. In 1988, Democrats dropped below Republicans in registration, and local Democratic officeholders are feeling the pinch while Republicans see a bright future.

San Diego County

Area: 4,280.6 sq. mi.; Population: (1990) 2,498,016, (1980) 1,861,846; Registration: (1990) D-38.1% R-48.6%; Unemployment: (Jan. 1991) 6.3%; County supervisors: George Bailey, Brian Bilbray, Susan Golding, John MacDonald, Leon Williams; 1600 Pacific Highway, San Diego 92101; (619) 531-5198.

San Diego is the California of popular legend: sunny days, sparkling beaches, sail-bedecked harbors, red-tiled roofs, palm trees and laid-back people everywhere. A lot of folks want a piece of that legend, which makes San Diego County a popular destination for everyone from young professionals to retirees. In a state of diverse geography, San Diego might have the most variation in one county. Within a few miles, there are ocean beaches, rolling hills, snowy mountains and stark desert. That diversity means people looking for just about any environment have wandered into the county. In fact, it has become the second-most populous county in the state. By 2010, nearly 1 in 10 Californians will be a San Diegan.

But the rocketing growth in San Diego over the past generation, more than doubling in population since 1960, also raises the question: If everyone comes for the San Diego lifestyle, will there be any of that lifestyle left? For many, the answer is No. That's why growth and its control have become the overriding political issue in the county.

Two recent events crystallized San Diego's uncertainty about its future and its collective fear about becoming another Los Angeles. Voters rejected a couple of growth restriction ballot measures in 1988, but when San Diego Gas and Electric Co. proposed to merge with Los Angeles-based Southern California Edison, there was a fear bordering on panic among residents and politicians of both parties.

San Diego also has a tense relationship with its neighbor to the south – Tijuana. The contrast between Tijuana, with its 1.5 million mostly poor residents, and San Diego could not be more striking. It is where the Third World bumps into the First World. And like matter meeting anti-matter, the collision is often explosive. Drugs and illegal aliens steadily flow across the border, and Mexican and American police have exchanged gunfire along the border, mistaking each other for bandits. A routine sight every evening are the campfires of Mexican nationals lining up along the border to dash into San Diego after dark.

San Diego also is downhill from Tijuana, which means Mexican sewage regularly pollutes San Diego beaches. The problem has become so severe that San Diegans are pressuring Gov. Pete Wilson, a former mayor of San Diego, to declare a state of emergency. More than any city in the state, San Diego is one city that needs a foreign policy.

For most of the 20th century, San Diego had been known mostly as a Navy town and as a center for aircraft production. But in the mid-1960s, San Diego County began diversifying economically and its population started to grow. With growth controls in the city of San Diego, the fastest-growing part of the county is the north. The San Diego Association of Governments estimates that between 1980 and 2000, central San Diego County will grow by only 12 percent while outlying suburbs will more than double in population.

Politically, San Diego always has been a paradox. A tolerant attitude toward lifestyles and a strong blue-collar manufacturing base have not prevented San Diego from being largely Republican territory. But local GOP leaders, including Wilson, tend to be from the moderate wing of the party. In addition, a core of Democratic activists keeps the party fairly well represented in legislative seats.

Centrist and conservative Republicans clashed in northern San Diego County in August 1989 after Assemblyman Bill Bradley died of cancer. The special election to fill Bradley's seat was called just after the Supreme Court reopened the abortion issue, and it quickly became the nexus of the battle between two Republicans in the mostly Republican district. When the dust settled, a pro-choice Republican nurse, Tricia Hunter, bested an anti-abortion conservative endorsed by many Republican leaders in the Assembly. It was a symbolic setback for conservatives and a renewal of the moderate bent in local GOP politics.

Recent mayors such as Wilson and Roger Hedgecock – a Republican who lost his office after being involved in a financial ponzi scheme – and current Mayor Maureen O'Connor, a Democrat, all fit that centrist mold. In 1991, The mayor's race could be wide open since O'Connor has said she will not run for re-election. The rumor mill has Hedgecock, now a popular radio talk show host, as a possible candidate, but the two top early contenders appear to be Republican Supervisor Susan Golding, and Republican Councilman Ron Roberts. Democratic state Sen. Lucy Killea also may be a contender.

Politicians long referred to San Diego as a cul-de-sac – too far from the spotlight to be anything but a political dead end – until the election of Wilson to the U.S. Senate and then to the governor's post. Because San Diego County is growing so much faster than the state, it will grow in influence as well. And because it is continuing to edge toward the Republicans politically, San Diego will become more important to the GOP in statewide races. If Republicans are to become the dominant party in California, many pundits believe it will be the San Diego-style moderates who will make it happen – not the right-wing ideologues.

Yet there's another trend in San Diego that many Republicans find disturbing. The centrists in the party don't vote as faithfully as more conservative Republicans. A low turnout in San Diego in 1986, for example, spelled defeat for then-Rep. Ed Zschau in a very tight race against Democratic U.S. Sen. Alan Cranston. In November 1990, the statewide voter turnout was 54.2 percent. But in San Diego County, it was only 51.5 percent despite the fact that hometown candidate Pete Wilson was locked in a tight race for governor.

San Francisco County

Population: (1990) 731,700, (1980) 678,974; Registration: (1990) D- 64.7% R-18.6%; Unemployment: (Jan. 1991) 5.1; Mayor: Art Agnos; City/county supervisors: Roberta Achtenberg, Angela Alioto, Harry Britt, Jim Gonzalez, Terence Hallinan, Tom Hsieh, Willie Kennedy, Bill Maher, Carol Migden, Kevin Shelley, Doris Ward; 400 Van Ness Ave., San Francisco 94102; (415) 554-5184; Incorporated: 1850.

San Franciscans scarcely acknowledged the 1989 event that was front-page news elsewhere. The state Department of Finance, in its periodic updating of population data, calculated that San Jose, 50 miles to the south, had passed San Francisco to become the state's third most populous city behind Los Angeles and San Diego.

So what, San Franciscans shrugged. They have the cable cars, the hills, the tall buildings, the banks, the bay, the opera, the theater, the Giants, the 49ers and the tourist business. San Jose just had the people, they seemed to say, and not very interesting people at that.

Smugness aside, San Francisco, the only consolidated city-county, is in transition and not all the trends are positive. It has lost its maritime trade to more modern ports such as nearby Oakland. Its industrial base, including the famous fishing industry, has shrunk. It has lost its position as the West's financial capital to much-hated Los Angeles. It is continuing to lose office jobs to suburban centers in places such as Contra Costa and San Mateo counties. It is losing middle-class whites to the suburbs and gentrification has driven many blacks out as well. The economic slide has weakened and scattered the labor strength, which once made San Francisco the most heavily unionized city west of Chicago. And after the 1989 Loma Prieta earthquake, San Francisco even lost some of its allure for tourists and convention-eers.

The danger of those trends is that San Francisco is becoming a caricature of itself, a place where only the wealthy and the poor live, a city dependent on the fickle tourist trade. But it is still a dazzling city with cosmopolitan attitudes found in few places on the West Coast. It has become, in effect, the capital of Asian California. And the gay rights movement is just the latest manifestation of San Francisco's well-known tolerance for unconventional lifestyles, a tradition rooted in the city's founding as a port of entry for gold rush fortune seekers and continued through decades of boom and bust, crooked mayors, quakes and fires.

San Francisco is a city of intense politics resembling those of New York or Chicago more than Los Angeles or San Diego. Every San Franciscan, or so it can seem, belongs to some political pressure group. They range from lifestyle- and ethnic-oriented groups to neighborhood and environmental associations. And they exist to oppose – strenuously – anything envisioned as a threat to their value systems. Republicans are an endangered species in a city that a couple of generations ago was a GOP stronghold, so most of the political plotting pits Democrat against Democrat.

Political generalizations are dangerous amid such diversity, but there is a broad issue at the core of the city's recent political history: development. Although San Francisco's population is stable and much of its employment base has fled, there is a continuing pressure to develop hotels and other tourist-related and retail facilities. San Francisco's business community bases its hopes on the city's continued attractiveness to out-of-towners, either shoppers from the suburbs or tourists and conventioneers. But development, in the minds of many, threatens the "real San

Francisco," however that may be defined.

City politics swerve back and forth as first one group then the other dominates. That's why San Francisco has freeways that stop in mid-air, dropping streams of cars onto city streets at the most inopportune places, and why every proposal for change creates a volcanic reaction.

The pro-development mayorship of Joseph Alioto was followed by the liberal reign of George Moscone. But Moscone was shot and killed in his office, bringing in another pro-development mayor, Dianne Feinstein. When Feinstein's second full term ended in 1987, it was time for another great debate over the future of San Francisco.

It featured John Molinari, a one-time Republican allied with the business community, against Art Agnos, one of the city's two state Assembly members (the other is Assembly Speaker Willie Brown). Molinari was the candidate of the status quo. Agnos galvanized groups united by their distaste for business as usual: gays, environmental activists, ethnic minorities and others.

Agnos, a first-generation Greek-American, came to San Francisco from Massachusetts as a social worker and wound up as Leo McCarthy's aide. McCarthy is one of San Francisco's longest-lasting political figures, serving as a city supervisor, a state assemblyman (he was Brown's predecessor as speaker) and, since 1983, as California's lieutenant governor. Agnos won his own Assembly seat in 1976 and achieved a reputation in Sacramento as a hard-nosed but pragmatic legislative technician. His biggest accomplishment was building a bipartisan coalition, that included Republican Gov. Deukmejian, to enact a "workfare" program for welfare recipients. His biggest setback was Deukmejian's veto of his bill to outlaw job discrimination against homosexuals.

Along the way, Agnos became a wealthy man, thanks to dealings with Sacramento developer Angelo Tsakopoulos. Agnos said Tsakopoulos had promised to make him rich, freeing him to practice politics without worry about his family's finances. That connection haunted Agnos, however, when he was fined by the Fair Political Practices Commission for failing to reveal all his financial dealings with Tsakopoulos.

Agnos' battle with Molinari, a conventional Italian-American politician and perennial mayoral hopeful, was an attempt to revive a liberal organization that had dominated San Francisco's politics for a generation until two of its leaders died.

With labor backing, Willie Brown, George Moscone and the Burton brothers, Phillip and John, created that organization in the halcyon days of the 1960s. Both Burtons went to Congress after stints in the Assembly, Brown climbed the Assembly ladder and Moscone became a state senator and later mayor.

Phil Burton was a dominating presence in Congress and nearly became speaker before his death in 1982. Brother John struggled in his older brother's shadow and began to abuse drugs and alcohol before he left Congress after Phil's death. In 1988, he won a special election for Agnos' seat in the Assembly.

Moscone's 1975 mayoral campaign was the Brown-Burton-Moscone organization's crowning achievement in city politics. They had wrested power from the old-line establishment, and gays, ethnic minorities and other "outs" became "ins." But when political rival Dan White assassinated Moscone and gay rights leader Harvey Milk in 1978, the flow of power reversed as Feinstein succeeded Moscone and then won two terms on her own.

For the 1987 race, Agnos and his campaign manager, Richie Ross, a longtime aide to Speaker Brown, devised a novel campaign that stressed neighborhood organization. They used a widely distributed paperback book that laid out Agnos' ambitious agenda of social and political change.

But Agnos' administration has spent much of its efforts handling a stream of problems, most of them caused by events far beyond Agnos' control. The first year was dominated by a whopping budget deficit Feinstein left behind. His second year was overshadowed by a police brutality scandal; a threat from Giants baseball team owner Bob Lurie to leave the city if a new stadium wasn't built to replace windy Candlestick Park; the continuing presence of thousands of homeless men and women camped in front of City Hall; and a killer earthquake. His third year in office saw a quake-induced recession as visitors stayed away in droves as well as the defeat of Agnos' plan to build a downtown stadium for the Giants.

In tone, his reign has remained left-of-center, as exemplified by an Agnos-sponsored law giving spousal benefits to the long-term partners of homosexual city employees. But experience has made Agnos more conciliatory. He no longer goes out of his way to antagonize business leaders. He dons a tuxedo to hobnob with the rich at civic events. And he pleased the old guard by backing a downtown ballpark, a set of waterfront hotels, and a massive 315-acre business/residential complex south of the Bay Bridge.

But he has also lost some support from his traditional anti-growth constituency, and he has angered police and firefighters, divided labor, and offended Chinese merchants by supporting efforts to tear down the quake-damaged Embarcadero Freeway. A poll in early 1991 showed Agnos' popularity had dropped to its lowest point, producing a parade of potential challengers against his November 1991 re-election bid. Among them are Supervisor Tom Hsieh, former police chief Frank Jordan, and former sheriff, supervisor and now assessor, Richard Hongisto.

The longer-term questions about San Francisco center on its diversity. It is the nation's most ethnically mixed city, and the most noticeable element of that diversity are the Asians, who have moved beyond Chinatown and Japantown, to become an important economic factor in virtually every neighborhood. But, so far, that personal and economic clout has not translated into political power, mostly because they do not vote in great numbers. Only one of San Francisco's supervisors is Asian.

Blacks are declining in numbers as soaring housing costs drive them out of the city, but they continue to enjoy political power disproportionate to their number.

Hispanics from a dozen nations continue to settle in San Francisco, but, as in other California cities, they have yet to become a political bloc. Only one supervisor is Hispanic.

Beyond ethnic lines, San Francisco's people are spread across a rainbow of ideologies and lifestyles. The most visible are lesbians and gays, whose political leadership, like the rest of that community, has been decimated by AIDS. There is even a residue of conservatism to be found in middle-class neighborhoods, personified by state Sen. Quentin Kopp, a Democrat-turned-independent.

If the old power structure seems to be breaking down, no single political group is rising to replace it. Instead, dozens of interest groups battle constantly among themselves for power and influence at City Hall, and the alliances are as solid as the fog that flows in and out of the Golden Gate. Any high-profile issue – the new Giants stadium, for example – brings forth legions of activists. Agnos is trying to maintain a governing coalition. But it is a constant struggle. Any wrong move, sometimes any move at all, brings out the knives of rivals and media critics.

But in San Francisco's fast-changing political climate, nothing lasts forever. Gays are demanding more power to accompany their rising economic clout, and the city is likely to produce the state's first openly gay state legislator. Asians are the city's latent political powerhouse, but, at least to date, lack a charismatic leader.

The city, meanwhile, continues to become less like a mini-New York, dominated by banks and big business, and to resemble more a collection of identifiable communities with employment concentrated in smaller businesses. A 1988 study by Bank of America concluded that San Francisco's future depends on the expansion of small business, and it is in those neighborhood-based businesses that much of the city's economic vitality and political activism is found. Gays have been especially successful in translating neighborhood businesses into economic and political clout. Asians seem to be following that model as well, but blacks and Hispanics have not moved into those channels.

San Joaquin County

Area: 1,436.2 sq. mi.; Population: (1990) 480,628, (1980) 347,342; Registration: (1990) D-53.6% R-38%; Unemployment: (Jan. 1991) 13.9%; County supervisors: George Barber, Evelyn Costa, Ed Simas, William Sousa, Douglass Wilhoit; 222 E. Weber St., Stockton 95202; (209) 944-3113.

It wasn't too many years ago that San Joaquin County in California's vast Central Valley was farm country. But the crop thriving in many of those fields these days is housing for San Francisco Bay Area refugees. San Joaquin County's population is up more than 38 percent since 1980, and it is a change most noticeable in the once-quiet farm towns such as Tracy and Manteca in the county's southern and western corners,

The change is less dramatic in San Joaquin County's biggest city, Stockton, but even that town is changing from an agricultural center with a few non-farm industries into a regional retail and service hub that includes two colleges, most notably the University of the Pacific.

San Joaquin voters mirror those in the Central Valley in registering Democrat but often voting conservatively. Stockton, however, with its ethnic diversity and industrial base, is a dependable Democratic area.

San Luis Obispo County

Area: 3,326.2 sq. mi.; Population: (1990) 217,162, (1980) 155,435; Registration: (1990) D-39.7% R-47.3%; Unemployment: (Jan. 1991) 6.1%; County supervisors: David Blakely, Ruth Brackett, Evelyn Delany, Laurence Laurent, Harry Ovitt; County Government Center, San Luis Obispo 93408; (805) 549-5450.

Midway between San Francisco and Los Angeles, blessed with a beautiful blend of coastline, beaches, mountains and near-perfect weather, San Luis Obispo, both city and county, represents another version of California heaven. The county's soaring population is up by about 40 percent since 1980.

Folks fleeing the pains of urban life have cashed in their inflated home equities and headed either north or south along Highway 101. But, as in so many other places around the state, the newcomers are pumping up local housing costs and threatening, at least in the minds of many, to damage the qualities that make "SLO-town," as local college students call it, so pleasant.

For the moment, San Luis Obispo County seems to be weathering the assault, mostly because it has a well-balanced economy rooted in agriculture, tourism and the civil service payrolls of a state college, a maximum security prison and a state hospital.

Politically, despite the presence of the college and so many public employees, San Luis Obispo is Republican and unlikely to change.

San Mateo County

Area: 530.8 sq. mi.; Population: (1990) 649,623, (1980) 587,329; Registration: (1990) D-52.4% R-34.2%; Unemployment: (Jan, 1991) 3.8%; County supervisors: Anna Eshoo, Mary Griffin, Tom Huening, Tom Nolan, William Schumacher; 401 Marshall St., Redwood City 94063; (415) 363-4000.

San Mateo County, the swath of the San Francisco Peninsula directly south of San Francisco itself, isn't very large, but it contains all the enormous social and economic extremes of California.

Portions of the hilly county such as Hillsborough and Atherton are as wealthy as California gets. The business executives and professionals — many with prime offices in San Francisco — who live in those communities of gently winding, tree-shaded streets earn an average of almost $100,000 a year.

Northern San Mateo County, the area nearest to San Francisco and containing San Francisco International Airport, is blue collar and middle class, with incomes a third of those found in the wealthier areas. Along the coast there is everything from middle-class suburbs to the ramshackle houses of the 1960s

San Mateo County

and '70s runaways. And at the southern edge of the county along the bay there is East Palo Alto, a mostly black community where people struggle to survive against drugs, crime and poverty.

San Mateo is typical of California's closer-in suburban areas: there is scant population growth (just 10 percent between 1980 and 1990), soaring home prices and expansive employment growth mostly in white-collar and service jobs. As a recipient of commuters as well as a supplier, the county suffers changing and confusing traffic problems.

The Association of Bay Area Governments estimates that between 1985 and 2005, San Mateo will employ 90,000 more people, with the majority of jobs in finance, insurance and real estate accounting. Hard evidence of that trend includes the new office complexes along the Bayshore Freeway or in Foster City, which was created 30 years ago on San Francisco Bay landfill.

San Mateo has the political diversity to match its social differences. The blue-collar and poorer areas are rock-solid Democratic, while the affluent middle of the county tends to be Republican, albeit of the moderate, pro-environment, libertarian-lifestyle variety personified by ex-Rep. Pete McCloskey, one of the area's best known political figures.

Santa Barbara County

Area: 2,744.7 sq. mi.; Population: (1990) 369,608, (1980) 298,694; Registration: (1990) D-42.9% R-43.4%; Unemployment: (Jan. 1991) 6.8%; County supervisors: Gloria Ochoa, Dianne Owens, Tom Rogers, Michael Stoker, William Wallace; 105 E. Acapamu St., Santa Barbara 93101; (805) 681-4200.

Santa Barbarans live, or think they live, in the sights of a perpetually hungry animal. The animal is Los Angeles, the pulsating powerhouse to the south. Santa Barbarans fear that it threatens to swallow up their pleasant lifestyle and convert their region into just another suburb. "Quality-of life," however defined, is the dominant political and social issue of the area. To some, it means a never-ending anger at the presence of oil-drilling platforms off the Santa Barbara coast, with the latent danger of another serious spill. That's why "GOO," standing for "Get Oil Out," adorns the bumpers of many local cars. And to others, it means resisting new subdivisions in the hills or more hotels along the waterfront.

Santa Barbara County is growing, though slower than the state average. But overall, local activists have managed to block most major development. The price for that is soaring real estate prices that preclude all but the affluent, which has helped create a somewhat exclusive social atmosphere that is reinforced by the trendy shops in Santa Barbara's ranch-style downtown business district.

Outside of the city, Santa Barbara is self-consciously rural. Ex-President Ronald Reagan's ranch typifies life in the hills and horse country above the coast, and there are several small communities that serve these affluent rustics. There also is Vandenberg Air Force Base space center on the northern edge of the county, near Santa Maria, from which many satellite-carrying rockets are launched.

Politically, Santa Barbara County has a near tie between Democrats and Republicans, with Republicans outnumbering Democrats by about 2,000 people. That translates into something of a split political personality. Santa Barbara tends to vote Republican at the top of the ticket and the local congressman, Robert Lagomarsino, is a Republican. But both state legislators from the area are liberal Democrats who have withstood Republican challenges.

Santa Clara County

Area: 1,315.9 sq. mi.; Population: (1990) 1,497,577, (1980) 1,295,071; Registration: (1990) D-50.1% R-36.6%; Unemployment: (Jan. 1991) 5.6%; County supervisors: Rod Diridon, Ron Gonzales, Michael Honda, Zoe Lofgren, Dianne McKenna; 70 W. Hedding St., 10th floor, San Jose 95110; (408) 299-2323.

Santa Clara County is one of the engines that drives the economy of the San Francisco Bay Area, and its fuel is the computer industry. Between 1980 and 1985, nearly half of all new jobs in the nine-county region were created in Santa Clara County, and most were connected to "Silicon Valley," which used to be a geographic term but now is a generic description for the computer-oriented, electronic industries found in and around Santa Clara County.

The Association of Bay Area Governments estimates that between 1985 and 2005, Santa Clara will add nearly 400,000 new jobs, more than half of them in manufacturing and wholesale trade. While the high-tech companies have had their peaks and valleys, the direction over the long term has been consistently upward. But economic success has had its price, including toxic contamination of groundwater from chemicals used in the high-tech plants.

San Jose, the county's largest city, is a nationwide joke on how not to deal with growth. Homes, shopping centers and business complexes sprang up everywhere with little thought to transportation or other infrastructure. San Jose and other Santa Clara County cities competed, rather than co-operated, and developers played political leaders against each other.

For years the downtown looked like a victim of aerial bombing as stores fled for suburban shopping centers. But in recent years, led by former Mayor Tom McEnery, the city has been reborn. San Jose has completed the first phase of a trolley system; begun a downtown redevelopment project that includes a convention center, a Fairmont hotel and a high-tech museum; improved its airport; and started planning for a major sports complex in the hope of luring the San Francisco Giants 40 miles south.

San Jose still has a long way to go. Its school system filed for bankruptcy protection in the mid-1980s. Like other big cities, it has poverty, drug and crime problems. Mayor Susan Hammer, a liberal Democrat like McEnery, continues to push in the aggressive direction set by her predecessor.

While Santa Clara, the fourth most populous county in the state, is still growing, high home prices (the median is about $250,000) and traffic jams worse than anywhere in the state except Orange County have removed much of the bloom from the rose. A partial saving grace has been that Santa Clara's business and political leaders saw the king-size traffic headache relatively early and moved to deal with it. In 1985 Santa Clara was the first county to enact a local sales tax increase to pay for transportation improvements, a step that other congested areas continue to struggle with. The sales tax override campaign was approved by voters because local industry put its financial muscle behind it, and the victory marked the maturation of the high-tech industry and its executives into a civic force. Some executives – David Packard most prominently – have become compelling political and civic figures, and the industry is providing the financial and political muscle for San Jose's redevelopment.

Santa Clara's transportation and other infrastructure improvements also are made easier because Santa Clara representatives virtually control the state budget process. A San Jose senator, Alfred Alquist, chairs the Senate's budget committee, and the Assembly's committee is chaired by San Jose Assemblyman John Vasconcellos.

Despite the county's effort, however, the mismatch of job development and population will continue to cause strains. The county budget is feeling the strain of growth and social change. It assumes one of the largest social welfare budgets of all

California counties, partly because of the growing number of Asian immigrants and other poor people. The county coffers have been saved in the past by high property values, but property values are almost flat and damage from the 1989 Loma Prieta earthquake is another budget drain.

Besides San Jose, which recently surpassed San Francisco to become the state's third-largest city, there are other communities of importance. Palo Alto, on the county's northern edge, is the home of Stanford University. It was the presence of Stanford that initially gave rise to the high-tech industry.

Along Highway 101 south of San Jose, the one-time farm towns of Morgan Hill and Gilroy (which bills itself as the garlic capital of the world) are growing rapidly as they fill up with spill over from Silicon Valley. Fields and orchards are turning into subdivisions and industrial parks.

With its population and economic clout, Santa Clara County has become an area of great political importance. Generally, it has been faithfully Democratic, a reflection of its working-class history. But as home prices soar and affluent people steadily move in, Santa Clara's politics seem to be edging toward the center.

Santa Cruz County

Area: 439.6 sq. mi.; Population: (1990) 229,734, (1980) 188,141; Registration: (1990) D-57% R-29%; Unemployment: (Jan. 1991) 10.4%; County supervisors: Janet Beautz, Ray Belgard, Fred Keeley, Robley Levy, Gary Patton; 701 Ocean St., Santa Cruz 95060; (408) 425-2201.

Three decades ago, Santa Cruz was a quiet, conservative, seaside community. But the combination of an unconventional University of California campus, which opened in 1965, the coming of the hippie era and Santa Cruz's scenic beauty has turned the region—particularly the city of Santa Cruz—into one of the bohemian capitals of California.

The county's politics have turned sharply to the left and become hostile to new development – especially after Santa Cruz began attracting commuters from the nearby Silicon Valley. For the foreseeable future, the development wars will continue to be a huge piece of local politics.

Santa Cruz has had some new dilemmas recently. Its liberal attitudes, lush mountains and pleasant weather have attracted a large number of homeless people and just plain wanderers, placing another burden on an already strained county budget and creating more fights over whether to be harsh or helpful. The county's budget was almost pushed over the brink by the 1989 Loma Prieta earthquake, which destroyed bridges, roads and buildings, including the Pacific Garden Mall in downtown Santa Cruz. Although the county has used a number of revenue hikes recently permitted by the state, its budget remains in woeful shape.

Shasta County

Area: 3,850.2 sq. mi.; Population: (1990) 147,036, (1980) 115,715; Registration: (1990) D-45% R-43.3%; Unemployment: (Jan. 1991) 13.1%; County supervisors: Bob Bosworth, Patricia Clarke, Maurice Johannessen, Francie Sullivan, Molly Wilson, 1500 Court St., Room 207, Redding 96001; (916) 225-5556.

After Butte and Yolo Counties, Shasta may be next on the list of counties in horrible fiscal shape. It already has taken some drastic steps. The public library system was closed in 1988, and voters defeated two tax hikes that would have re-opened some or all of the branches. In 1987, the county's general hospital was shut down, bankrupted, according to a County Supervisors Association of California study, by slow or inadequate state reimbursement for services to its patients, a vast majority of whom are indigent.

The county has been helped — a bit — by recent climbs in property values and by tight money management, but its budget remains on the critical list. The property value increase has come from strong growth, particularly in Redding, the county's only city of any size. The area's hot summers and mild winters, the beauty of nearby mountains and Lake Shasta, and great outdoor recreation are drawing "urban-equity refugees," the empty-nesters and retirees seeking less hectic lifestyles.

Shasta County's population has been expanding faster than average, although official unemployment remains high. The major employers in the county continue to be resource-oriented manufacturing, principally lumber and mineral products, but those businesses are slowly shrinking. Local boosters hope to attract one of the three new University of California campuses now in the planning stages. Politically, Shasta is conservative and becoming more so.

Sierra County

Area: 958.6 sq. mi.; Population: (1990) 3,318, (1980) 3,073; Registration: (1990) D-48.1% R-37.5%; Unemployment: (Jan. 1991) 16.4%; County supervisors: Donald Bowling, Lenny Gallegos, Nevada Lewis, Jerry McCaffrey, Donald McIntosh; P.O. Drawer D, Downieville 95936; (916) 289-3295.

Sierra County, the second least populous California county, has a chronically high unemployment rate that is usually more than double the state average. But local politics do not hinge on such mundane matters as economic growth and population change. Few though they may be, Sierra

County's residents fight old-fashioned political turf battles mixed in with some-times wild moves and countermoves.

The division is mostly geographic, the eastern side of the county against the west. Sierrans fight over such things as whether the county seat should remain in Downieville, in the west, or be moved to Loyalton, in the east. At one point, a male county supervisor was sued for sexual discrimination by a female supervisor. All of that makes the twice-monthly board meetings the best show in the county.

When not fighting with each other, Sierrans usually vote conservatively, although there's a vociferous liberal, environmental contingent.

Siskiyou County

Area: 6,318.3 sq. mi.; Population: (1990) 43,531, (1980) 39,732; Registration: (1990) D-50.2% R-37.7%; Unemployment: (Jan. 1991) 18.4%; County supervisors: Norma Lee Frey, Patti Mattingly, George Thackeray, Ivan Young, Roger Zwanziger; P.O. Box 338, Yreka 96097; (916) 842-8081.

A half-century ago, there was a semi-serious political drive mounted in the northernmost Califor-nia counties and the southernmost Oregon counties to break away and create a new state, called "Jefferson." Residents of the area felt they were being dominated and ignored by the urban centers far from them. Secessionist fever cooled, but there remains a residual feeling – one very evident in scenic and sparsely populated Siskiyou County – of colonial status. The fate of Siskiyou's timber industry, which accounts for at least one of every 10 jobs, is dependent on the outcome of battles in Sacramento or Washington, D.C., over preservation or use of federally owned timber in the county. There's an equally emotional battle over proposals for a major ski resort on Mount Shasta, the dormant volcano that is Siskiyou's most dominant landmark.

Siskiyou County does have one part of its make-up that is unusual for a rural California county: a substantial black population that grew out of workers imported from the South by lumber mills. In 1986, Charles Byrd became California's only elected black sheriff.

Solano County

Area: 872.2 sq. mi.; Population: (1990) 340,421, (1980) 235,203; Registration: (1989) D-55% R-32.7%; Unemployment: (Jan. 1991) 7.7%; County supervisors: Sam Caddle, William Carroll, Osby Davis, Lee Simmons, Jan Stewart; 580 W. Texas St., Fairfield 94533; (707) 429-6218.

Solano County used to be a predictable part of California. Vallejo was an industrial city, the site of a major Navy shipyard and water-oriented industries. Fairfield was the county seat but otherwise a farm town on the edge of the Central

Valley. Benicia was a sleepy little bit of history, the site of a former military arsenal and, briefly, a 19th century California capital. And Vacaville was another farm town that also had a state prison. But the relentless expansion has changed Solano County in ways no one would have imagined a few years ago.

Vallejo has become a tourist center with the relocation of Marine World Africa USA on a former golf course. Industry – most prominently a big Anheuser-Busch brewery – has come to Fairfield. And throughout Solano County, the sounds of hammers and saws at work have become part of the

Solano County

background noise as field after field has been transformed into subdivisions and shopping malls. Solano's population shot up by more than 44 percent between 1980 and 1990, and there is no sign that it will slow.

Solano County is being loaded from two directions. While the western portion is transformed into a suburb of the Bay Area, the eastern side, including the once-sleepy farm town of Dixon, falls within the orbit of fast-growing Sacramento. The county's location between the two major Northern California urban complexes also makes it attractive to industrial developers. The Association of Bay Area Governments predicts that Solano will add 58,000 jobs and about 150,000 residents between 1985 and 2005. Not unexpectedly, the county is experiencing growing pains: traffic jams, overburdened water and sewage treatment facilities and other services. The county's budget is feeling the strain as most of the revenue benefits from growth are going into the coffers of its incorporated cities, while the county continues to foot the bill for more and more services.

As would be expected, the growth also has fueled a backlash among residents worried that their rural, relatively quiet lifestyles are being destroyed. The county has been Democratic territory – especially blue-collar Vallejo. But with suburbanization comes a noticeable shift to the right, with Republicans looking for future gains.

Sonoma County

Area: 1,597.6 sq. mi.; Population: (1990) 388,222, (1980) 299,681; Registration: (1990) D-55.4% R-33.3%; Unemployment: (Jan. 1991) 6.1%; County supervisors: Ernest Carpenter, Nick Esposti, James Haberson, Janet Nicholas, Tim Smith; 575 Administration Drive, Santa Rosa 95403; (707) 527-2241.

In 1986, the Sonoma County Planning Department told county supervisors that the county was growing so fast that it had already as many people as had been predicted for the turn of the century. And there is no end in sight.

When Marin County virtually shut down development in the 1970s, pressure shifted directly to the north, rapidly changing Petaluma — the one-time "Chicken

Capital of the World" — and Santa Rosa, the county seat, into big suburbs. Those cities are changing even more as Santa Rosa develops a significant employment base of its own and becomes a destination point for commuters from housing developments even further up Highway 101, the main north-south artery.

Sonoma County

The Association of Bay Area Governments notes that Sonoma County's population tripled between 1950 and 1980, with half of that growth coming in the last decade. It is expected to increase by another 44 percent between 1985 and 2005.

Jobs are growing more slowly, so Sonoma is expected to continue in its role as a bedroom community, at least until after the turn of the century. But as in so many other areas, the qualities that have made Sonoma County so attractive – the rural lifestyle, the soft natural beauty – may be threatened by the immensity of the growth.

An anti-growth backlash has risen, with environmentalists and chicken farmers forming unusual political alliances to fight the conversion of agriculture land into houses and shopping centers. Petaluma was the site of an early development battle when local officials, trying to curtail the damage to the agricultural community in the 1970s, passed a law limiting housing development to 500 units a year. The ensuing lawsuit reached the U.S. Supreme Court, which ruled in Petaluma's favor and thus validated local growth-control laws. A poll of residents listed traffic as the most important issue, followed by education and development.

Politically, Sonoma County has a split personality. The western portion, home to a large gay community and environmental activism, is Democratic and liberal, while the rapidly suburbanizing eastern portion is conservative and Republican. For years, politicians divided the county more or less along north-south Highway 101 while drawing congressional and legislative districts. Republicans represented the wine country in the eastern portion of the county, while Democrats won in the west. That changed a bit in 1990 when longtime state Sen. Jim Nielsen, a Republican, lost to Democrat Mike Thompson.

Stanislaus County

Area: 1,521.2 sq. mi.; Population: (1990) 370,522, (1980) 265,900; Registration: (1990) D-54.4% R-37.1%; Unemployment: (Jan. 1991) 15.6%; County supervisors: Nick Blom, Paul Caruso, Pat Paul, Raymond Clark Simon, Rolland Starn; 1100 H St., Modesto 95354; (209) 525-6414.

Nowhere in California are the changes that come with suburbanization more starkly evident than in Stanislaus County. For decades, this San Joaquin Valley county was purely agricultural, home of some of the nation's best-known farm products, such as Gallo wine and Foster Farms chicken. But its relative proximity to the San Francisco Bay Area meant it was destined to explode with houses and shopping centers as commuters, especially young ones without big pay-checks, searched for affordable homes. Stanislaus' population swelled by over 39 percent between 1980 and 1990.

As the character of the area changes, so does its politics, away from agriculture and toward issues more identified with suburban life, some of which conflict with farming. Stanislaus and its major city, Modesto, sit in the middle of a long-term fight over how suburban or agricultural the region will become.

Stanislaus County

Sutter County

Area: 607 sq. mi.; Population: (1990) 64,415, (1980) 52,246; Registration: (1990) D-40.1% R-50.2%; Unemployment: (Jan. 1991) 20.8%; County supervisors: Joseph Benatar, Barbara LeVake, Pete Licari, Larry Montna, Ron Southard; 463 Second St., Yuba City 95991; (916) 741-7106.

Yuba City and its sister city just across the river, Marysville, found themselves in the national spot-light in 1986 when Rand McNally listed the area as the worst place to live in the United States. The ranking was based on a mish-mash of statistics better suited to large cities than to relatively rural towns. The area was dragged down by such things as its lack of rapid transit and cultural amenities, as well as one very legitimate factor: its high unemployment rate. Unemployment is a sticky problem in agricultural Sutter County, but the region may be on the verge of an economic boom.

Highway 99, which links Yuba City-Marysville with Sacramento, 40 miles away, will be a four-lane freeway within a few years, and there are indications that the population boom in the Sacramento area will zoom up that freeway. A county-commissioned study predicts the first area to become suburbanized will likely be the southern reaches of the county, which will be a shorter commute time from downtown Sacramento than the crowded areas of eastern Sacramento County. Developers have been quietly acquiring tracts of farmland for years in anticipation.

Politically, Sutter County is very conservative, with a Republican registration majority, and is likely to remain so.

Tehama County

Area: 2,976 sq. mi.; Population: (1990) 49,620, (1980) 38,888; Registration: (1990) D-48.6% R-39.1%; Unemployment: (Jan. 1991) 16.9%; County supervi-

sors: Burton Bundy, Phil Gunsauls, Floyd Hicks, Jo Ann Landingham, Vance Wood; P.O. Box 250, Red Bluff 96080; (916) 527-4655.

A 1988 article in a California magazine described them as "The Revolutionary Junta of Tehama County." Time magazine told the same story, albeit more briefly, in an article entitled "Going Broke in California." Tehama County supervisors put themselves in the spotlight when they threatened to shut down county government because Proposition 13 and a stingy state government had left them without enough money to take care of legal mandates. They backed down and the state took over partial funding of trial courts.

Tehama County

Tehama County subsists on agriculture – mostly cattle ranching – and timber production, but much of the potential commercial activity is siphoned away by the larger and more vigorous out-of-county communities of Redding and Chico. That leaves the county with relatively low sales-tax revenues, and the county's woeful budget hinges on help from the state.

Tehama County sits in the middle of the upper Central Valley near few landmarks of note and attracting relatively few tourists or retirees. Its most notable feature may be that Red Bluff, its chief city, sometimes makes the weather charts as the hottest place in the state.

Trinity County

Area: 4,844.9 sq. mi.; Population: (1990) 13,063, (1980) 11,858; Registration: (1990) D-47.5% R-37.2%; Unemployment: (Jan. 1991) 21.3%; County supervisors: Matthew Leffler, Patricia Mortensen, Stan Plowman, Dee Potter, Arnold Whitridge; P.O. Drawer 1258, Weaverville 96093; (916) 623-1217.

Nothing is more pervasive in Trinity County than a sense of disconnection to late 20th century California. Weaverville, the county seat and only town of consequence, still contains 19th century storefronts built during the gold rush. And much of the county's scant population is scattered in homesteads and tiny crossroads communities.

Most of Trinity County's residents are happy in their isolation. They cut timber, raise cattle, and occasionally pan for gold — or grow marijuana — to support themselves and wish the rest of the world would leave them alone.

As legend has it, Weaverville was the inspiration for the fictional kingdom of Shangri-la, and there is something mystical about the Trinity Alps, the magnificent and sometimes impenetrable range of mountains occupying much of the county. It is unlikely Trinity will share in any of the changes sweeping the state since it is a long and difficult drive from any population center.

Like other rural counties, the budget coffers are getting pretty bare. Voters turned down a 1988 sales-tax hike and state bailout measures have not helped much. For example, a plan to let the counties keep traffic fines has mattered little in a county where there is not one stoplight.

Tulare County

Area: 4,844.9 sq. mi.; Population: (1990) 311,921, (1980) 245,738; Registration: (1990) D-48.3% R-41.8%; Unemployment: (Jan. 1991) 19.7%; County supervisors: Bill Buckley, John Conway, Clyde Gould, Charles Harness, Lorie Mangine; 2800 W. Burrel, Visalia 93291; (209) 733-6271.

Although in the middle of San Joaquin Valley farm country, Tulare County is not just another valley farming community. The county and its principal city, Visalia, have worked for economic diversification with uncommon vigor, and it has paid off with dozens of industrial facilities.

Tulare County's location in the middle of the valley and near to recreation spots in the Sierra has helped economic development. So has an almost entrepreneurial approach to government. But despite the new industry and accompanying services, unemployment still runs at twice the state average, a reflection of the seasonal nature of agriculture, the top industry. Tulare's biggest development efforts now are directed at winning one of the proposed new University of California campuses.

And despite the development, the demand on the county for health and welfare services are far outgrowing the new revenue as the growth also brings more poor people to the area. The county is one of six in the state that spends more than half of its budget on those services.

Politically, Tulare is medium-conservative, voting for Democrats only when they avoid the liberal label.

Tuolumne County

Area: 2,292.7 sq. mi.; Population: (1990) 48,456, (1980) 33,928; Registration: (1990) D-49.6% R-40.4%; Unemployment: (Jan. 1991) 10.1%; County supervisors: Kathleen Campana, Ken Marks, Larry Rotelli, Norman Tergeson, Charles Walter; 2 S. Green St., Sonora 95370; (209) 533-5521.

Tuolumne County was born in the California gold rush and 130 years later finds itself in the midst of a new one. A huge new gold mine, working the spoils of generations of mining operations in the area, opened in 1986 and gave the county a much-needed steady payroll.

But overall, an even bigger rush is being made to develop around some of Tuolumne's scenic wonders. Its population is growing fast – almost 43 percent between 1980 and 1990 – and most of that growth comes from retirees and other people escaping cities. Drawn by the county's mild climate, slow-pace and recreational opportunities, the newcomers are fueling the economy with pensions and the investment of equity from the sale of urban homes. The construction of homes and new retail services have become new foundations of the economy.

Tuolumne County

The growth is taking its toll on county services, too. As crime increased with population, Tuolumne County poured funds into a money-wasting hodgepodge of four courtrooms spread among four buildings. Still awaiting funds are a solid waste problem, an aging county hospital, road improvements and fire equipment that is starting to break down.

Politically, Tuolumne County is conservative and likely to become more so as it grows.

Ventura County

Area: 1,863.6 sq. mi.; Population: (1990), 669,016, (1980) 529,174; Registration: (1990) D-40.5% R-47.4%; Unemployment: (Jan. 1991) 7.5%; County supervisors: Maggie Erickson Kildee, John Flynn, Vicky Howard, Susan Lacey, Maria Vanderkolk; 800 S. Victoria Ave., Ventura 93009; (805) 654-2929.

Not too many years ago, one could have accurately described Ventura County as rural. Its dominant industries were citrus, other forms of agriculture and oil. The pace of life was slow. Los Angeles was a long hour's drive away.

But in an astonishingly short time, Ventura County has been overrun by the ever-expanding Southern California megalopolis.

As freeway routes were punched through the coastal hills from the San Fernando Valley and into the cities of Oxnard, Santa Paula and Ventura, developers began turning agricultural tracts into subdivisions, shopping centers, office complexes and industrial parks.

One area of the county has been dubbed "Gallium Gulch," a takeoff on Silicon Valley, because it has become a center for developing gallium arsenide into a commercial product. The new technology has drawn some of the largest names in American industry. Meanwhile, as the farm economy continues to stumble along, more and more farmers sell their land to developers.

Ventura County also has begun to exploit its coastal resources, seeking some of the recreational and vacation activity that the rest of Southern California has long enjoyed. The city of Ventura, long accustomed to having tourists pass through en route to Santa Barbara to the north, is now developing marinas, hotels and other facilities of its own. Like Santa Barbara, it is also starting to make a big deal out of its historic roots as a mission town (the official name of the city is San Buenaventura, after the local mission).

As Ventura County evolves economically, it is changing socially. The agricultural and blue-collar workers now face soaring home prices. And the county is feeling all the other common growing pains, including heavy traffic, especially on Highway 101, the major route connecting it with Los Angeles.

The change may be especially evident in Oxnard, a one-time farm town with a large Hispanic population. Its proximity to the Pacific and to freeways leading to the San Fernando Valley and Los Angeles is converting Oxnard into a somewhat expensive, white-collar bedroom town. The county has long managed one of the state's most stable budgets, but even Ventura may soon be feeling the money crunch hitting most other counties, according to a 1990 report from the California Counties Foundation.

As Ventura County suburbanizes and grows, its politics are becoming more conservative. It has a Republican voter majority, and Democratic candidates are finding that an ever-steeper hill to climb.

Yolo County

Area: 1,034 sq. mi.; Population: (1990) 141,092, (1980) 113,374; Registration: (1990) D-54.1% R-32.7%; Unemployment: (Jan. 1991) 9.6%; County supervisors: Clark Cameron, George DeMars, Betsy Marchard, Cowles Mast, Helen Thomson; 625 Court St., Woodland 95695; (916) 666-8195.

Many observers expected Yolo County to be the state's first to declare bankruptcy, and only continual belt-tightening has kept it from fiscal disaster. It has huge health and welfare expenses, a low tax base and it lost a big chunk of revenue when West Sacramento incorporated.

West Sacramento, just across the river from downtown Sacramento, had been ignored by the bigger city's boom and had an image of being a low-income, run-down, quasi-red light district. It is counting on a huge, upscale marina-commercial-residential project along the Sacramento River to upgrade its image and its fortunes.

West Sacramento is one end of the vividly contrasting county. Away to the west and north are rolling hills, farms and a few sparse towns that seem to belong to a different time. In between are two very different cities: Woodland, the conservative county seat that is a farm town on the verge of becoming a suburb, and Davis – or the People's Republic of Davis, as its detractors call it. Davis is the university town, with political activism that extends down to the street-light level. It has been trying to resist developer pressure to become yet another Sacramento bedroom, but even that progressive city is slowly failing.

Yuba County

Area: 639.1 sq. mi.; Population: (1990) 58,228, (1980) 49,733; Registration: (1990) D-47.3% R-40.3%; Unemployment: (Jan. 1991) 16.7%; County supervisors: Thomas Belza, Bill Harper, Michelle Mathews, Joan Saunders, Leah Stocker; 215 Fifth St., Marysville, 95901; (916) 741-6461.

Yuba County is next door to Sutter County. The county seats, Yuba's Marysville and Sutter's Yuba City, are just one river apart. But the two counties are developing along different lines.

Much of Sutter lies next to Sacramento County. It is likely to become more and more suburban. But most of Yuba County lies well to the north of Sacramento County and it is likely to remain rural for the foreseeable future. Marysville itself, however, may be destined for semisuburban status as the highways connecting it and Yuba City to both Sacramento and the burgeoning high-tech industrial areas in nearby Placer County are widened into freeways.

In addition, the area can count on a steady payroll from Beale Air Force Base, which not only escaped the recent round of base closures but will probably grow as units shift from other bases, particularly Mather Air Force Base in Sacramento County.

Yuba County, with a less than 50 percent Democratic registration, votes conservatively.

11

Press vs. politicians–never-ending war

An aide to Assembly Speaker Willie Brown once put out a 15-page guide with detailed advice for legislators on how to deal with the news media. On the cover of the guide was a cartoon with a farmer, sitting on a tractor, telling a reporter that the two of them are in the same business.

"We are?" the reporter asks.

"This here's a manure spreader," the farmer responds.

That about sums up the mutual feelings of California's politicians and the people who cover them for print and broadcast media around the state. As often as not, each thinks the other is spreading manure.

It has become a given in American politics that a certain tension and wariness exists in the dealings between reporters and politicians. That is certainly the case in California. Gone are the days when the Capitol press corps and the state's political media were part of the inside establishment. Then, reporters and politicians ate and drank together, and neither group judged the other too harshly.

Much of that has changed over the years. The creation of a full-time Legislature in the mid-1960s brought a change in the Capitol press corps, too. There came a new generation of reporters, more serious and more critical, in the wake of the Vietnam War and Watergate. Despite occasional chumminess between some reporters and politicians today, the press continues to move toward much harder reporting about campaign spending, conflicts of interest and ethical problems, not to mention a continuing FBI investigation that apparently began after prosecutors read newspaper articles about Capitol influence peddling.

A number of reasons account for the battles between reporters and politicians. For starters, politicians have an almost single-minded concern about their images, as might be expected of people whose careers depend upon public approval. To project any image, they need the media, but often the publicity they get is not exactly what they wanted. For example, when politicians stage events to score a few points with the public, political reporters, striving for the journalistic Grail of objectivity, feel compelled to throw in other views and counterarguments.

In this constant war over image, Willie Brown has waged an ongoing battle. In early 1991, he said in a series of interviews that opponents and the press had created a completely inaccurate image of him. He insisted that voters had not heard that he really is a consummate political negotiator, an achiever of big public policy steps and an "extraordinarily sensitive human being." He said reporters have been too happy to carry stories criticizing him as well as the Legislature. Reporters rolled their eyes at Brown's comments. Most Capitol news people feel they fall far short of revealing all the ways Brown manipulates the legislative process for purely political ends. But despite their distaste, most went back and dutifully reported Brown's complaints, substantive or not, and then tried to find critics to give their stories balance.

Many legislators in the Capitol have a list of complaints about the press. They say both privately and publicly that stories about recent FBI investigations, campaign contributions and political shenanigans stain the Legislature with a few broad strokes, obscuring the hard work and good intentions of many lawmakers.

Reporters don't buy that argument. If anything, they feel their stories often make legislators look too statesmanlike. They say most stories deal with the substance and progress of bills and budgets, and that too few reports cover the wheeling and dealing that goes into most legislation or the enormous influence that powerful interests exert in the Capitol.

INHERENT DIFFERENCES

But the differences between political reporters and the people they cover run much deeper than simply the nature of the stories. Politicians and news people often have very different expectations.

In a sense, news people see it as their job to be the loyal opposition, always asking critical questions, always making elected representatives justify to voters why they should remain in office. When politicians try to tell only part of a story, news people feel it is their obligation to bring the other side to the public.

Such independence does not sit well with many career politicians, who have spent much of their lives surrounded by partisan advocates. They do not easily accept the idea that reporters or editors can function without grinding personal or political axes. Instead, they assume, as they would of anyone who causes problems, that news people oppose them for ideological or political reasons.

In addition, legislators, administration officials and even the governor get angry when reporters do not show that most valued of political attributes – loyalty. Loyalty is everything to a politician. Reporters, instead, are loyal to their stories. Some politicians are left feeling betrayed when they joke with reporters, talk about movies or restaurants or their children's baby teeth, and then find a critical story the next day. Their frustration is deepened by their inability to control news people.

Everyone else in the system is willing to negotiate or compromise, except the media. (Although reporters do haggle with sources, it is over anonymity or details, not story slants.) Politicians know they need the press, but it is the one major piece of the political picture outside their grasp.

Reporters, on the other hand, often feel they are being manipulated too much. If a politician understands the news media's universally accepted rules of engagement – for example, that every side gets to have a say, that the opinions of major figures such as the governor or the Assembly speaker usually are newsworthy, that reporters cannot simply say somebody is lying or distorting information – they can color the reporting of events. It is just such manipulation that has given rise to "spin doctors." While still less prevalent in Sacramento than in Washington D.C., political consultants, realizing reporters need quotes to flesh out a story and give each side's arguments, have created a new art form of interpreting events – attempting to put "spin" on a story – to make their candidates look good.

Efforts to control media coverage have heightened the tension in Sacramento in recent years as more and more politicians have taken to bashing the press as a means of discrediting stories. Former state Sen. Larry Stirling, now a San Diego Municipal Court judge, was one of the most consistent practitioners. Almost every story about ethical problems in the Legislature or the influence of campaign spending generated a response from Stirling, who would say that newspapers were either trying to boost circulation or crying wolf.

Former Gov. George Deukmejian had become especially adept at deflecting criticism by blaming the messenger. For instance, Deukmejian, who made fiscal frugality a cornerstone of his political image, ran into problems when a series of state fiscal agencies reported the state had a deficit for the 1987-88 fiscal year. Deukmejian, whose state Department of Finance predicted a year-end finish narrowly in the black, complained at length about the coverage of the story, and that complaint became part of the story.

It is hard to assess the impact that complaints such as Deukmejian's or Brown's have on the public's perception of a story, but it is clear they have done little to cool the media's intense scrutiny of the Legislature and political campaigns.

A HARDER EDGE TO COVERAGE

While only the major papers – such as the Los Angeles Times, The Sacramento Bee, the San Francisco Chronicle and the San Jose Mercury – spend large chunks of news space and resources on long, investigative pieces on the Legislature and other Capitol stories, almost every one of the two dozen papers and news services that cover the Capitol regularly has added a harder edge to its coverage and focused more and more attention on ethics and political reform.

At the same time, many of the papers, including the Orange County Register, the Riverside Press Enterprise and the Los Angeles Daily News, are focusing their coverage on issues that affect their circulation areas and leaving broad, statewide topics to the wire services and papers such as the Times and The Bee, which offer their own news services. In part, this emphasis on legislators and issues particular to a circulation area comes in response to newspaper marketing surveys that show readers are more concerned with local issues and events and have limited interest in state politics.

While newspapers have added more and more reporters in Sacramento, television news has moved away from Capitol coverage in any form. During the 1960s and 1970s, most large stations in San Francisco, Los Angeles and San Diego maintained Sacramento bureaus, lured there by the glamour of Govs. Ronald Reagan and Jerry Brown and by the desire of many local stations to follow the networks' lead in covering hard news. The San Diego stations were the first to pull out, leaving a decade ago, and the last Los Angeles station left in 1983. KRON-TV in San Francisco, the last out-of-town holdout, closed its Capitol bureau in 1988.

Television news has not entirely given up on California political coverage. The Sacramento stations still cover the Capitol, and most major stations spend a good deal of resources covering statewide races and important ballot measures. But a University of Southern California study found stations outside Sacramento averaged barely one minute per news hour of coverage of the Legislature during a period of intense activity during the 1988 session.

Television is shying away from politics for a number of reasons, and money is at the top of the list. Television stations used to make money almost faster than they could count it, and the local news operations were their biggest earners. But now, television stations face increased competition from cable networks, superstations and video recorders, as well as from talk and game shows on competing stations.

In response, station managers are listening more and more to their consultants, who produce surveys that say viewers are not particularly interested in politics. In addition, as smaller profits have lessened resources, expensive out-of-town bureaus have become expendable. Thus, with the exception of the major news stories such as the inauguration of Pete Wilson as governor, state politics are covered almost exclusively with short mentions of legislative action or a local visit by a politician.

NEW FORMS OF TV COVERAGE

There have been a few developments running counter to that trend. One has been the growth of Northern California News Satellite, which sells Capitol coverage regularly to about two dozen stations. However, much of that coverage is often used as brief stories rather than the more in-depth reports that bureaus might have supplied, and the ready pictures with a sound bite can be a too-easy substitute for real reporting.

The other change was the start of live broadcasts of Assembly proceedings and the development Cal-SPAN, the cable channel modeled after C-SPAN, which covers Congress.

Speaker Brown was the force behind the $1 million effort to televise the lower house. The Assembly bought robotic cameras, a full control room and the rest of the equipment needed to cover floor sessions and some committees. The coverage is broadcast by the Assembly only internally. From there Cal-SPAN steps in.

Cal-SPAN sells to California cable systems the coverage supplied by the Assembly. Plans call for it eventually to carry gavel-to-gavel coverage of both houses – Senate President Pro Tem David Roberti has been less enthusiastic than Brown about live TV coverage – plus news conferences and programs with commentary and analysis of state politics. In addition, commercial stations who patch in or buy Cal–SPAN can use the broadcasts on their news shows. The consensus among those involved with the live TV so far has been that Cal–SPAN's impact on the Legislature is about the same as was C-SPAN's effect on Congress: Lawmakers dress up, try to slim down and occasionally they arrive on time.

While Cal-SPAN's pictures opened up the Assembly for television viewers, the speaker closed off access for reporters, banishing them from the edges of the Assembly floor, where they had roamed for years, chatting with members and filling in their stories without formal press conferences. Reporters were given desks off the floor in the back of the chamber with the staff. Brown's spokesman said the move was made to improve decorum, and it was done at the request of members and news people. The Capitol press corps was livid, as were a number of Assembly members who liked having reporters nearby – the easier to get their names in the news.

Brown's corralling of reporters and the interest in televising the Legislature are more signs that California politicians have become media savvy, or at least media conscious. They certainly continue to try to control the media coverage they receive. This is most visible in those campaigns where candidates and consultants have mastered the "bite of the day" technique of presenting splashy, often vague statements designed to boost their images rather than explain campaign issues. Campaign consultants also have become more adept at whispering in reporters' ears, attempting to plant story ideas that help them or hurt their opponents, or to put spin on everything involved in the campaigns, from polling to money-raising to issues.

At the same time, reporters are trying to do more than carry campaign statements to their readers and viewers. Most major papers are trying to examine candidates more carefully, over a longer period and on more issues than ever before. They are looking not only at voting records but consistency, ethics, financial holdings, spouses' activities and, occasionally, sexual behavior. As a result, there is an increased wariness developing. Where once reporters and candidates would relax after a campaign swing with dinner or drinks, both groups now keep their distance. And where once consultants would answer questions about their polling or money-raising honestly, now every utterance has the best face painted on it. So candidates are careful with what they say around reporters, and reporters believe only half of what they hear from candidates.

Media coverage is crucial to the success of political campaigns, especially statewide contests. There are thousands of miles to cover and dramatically varied constituencies to reach. In fact, just about the only effective way to reach the state's 13.5 million registered voters is through television. Candidates and initiative sponsors are eager to get on the local news, especially in Southern California, and local news stations are eager to cover big-name candidates and major ballot campaigns. Television news, despite all but abandoning the dull and gray day-to-day political coverage in the off season, is more interested in campaign coverage in California than ever before.

Politicians and political consultants are thrilled by this turn. Local TV news reaches many more people than do newspaper stories, and because it is the magic of television, it has more impact. Plus, campaigns can occasionally get messages out without a balancing point of view by playing to TV's fascination with live technology. A live interview or live coverage of an event can give viewers a much less filtered theme or message than even a 15-second sound bite.

Outside of campaigns, consultants and politicians are working harder than ever to attract and control press coverage. While they want their names in the news, they ask a lot more from their publicity than just spelling their name correctly. Politicians and consultants are using more and more devices to gain favorable coverage.

Stunts – disguised as news conferences – often are used to call attention to issues. Recent examples include using an ambulance to deliver petitions to the Capitol from people supporting more money for emergency rooms, and lining up about 1,000 hospital administrators like a marching band spelling out H-E-L-P to ask for aid to hospital budgets. Another of the more common moves is the press conference to announce the introduction of a bill. That gives one or more legislators a chance to be identified with a newsworthy issue. Sometimes a serious effort to move the bill follows, and sometimes the bills are abandoned, having served their purpose by letting the lawmakers take a tough stand without angering any of the interests opposed to the measure.

Another ploy is the ever-popular "spontaneous" statement during a legislative debate. It sounds like an heartfelt line coming from that lawmaker's deep well of conviction. As often as not, these are suggested by aides, practiced beforehand and timed to fit a TV sound bite.

PROFESSIONAL MEDIA MANAGERS

The increased sophistication in the interplay with the media has moved politicians to seek professional help in hunting for press coverage. Even legislators who are rarely quoted in hometown media are employing aides whose sole responsibility is to deal with the press or sometimes chase down reporters to get their boss' name in the paper. But on-staff press aides are only so effective. In greater and greater numbers, even unspectacular legislators who are not running for higher office – at least for now – are hiring the services of a growing number of political public relations firms. Those firms also are being used by special interests pushing or resisting particular bills in the Capitol. In fact, it is not uncommon to have every side represented by PR people.

One big job for these firms is to put their clients, either politicians or special interests with a stake in legislation, in touch with the media. The major firms that engage in political PR around Sacramento – among them PBN Company; Stoorza, Ziegaus and Metzger; and Townsend and Company – all employ people who either were former members of the Capitol press corps or who dealt with the press at length in legislative offices. They know what reporters are interested in and how to get their client's views into a story. And they realize that competition for reporters' time and interest is intense, so they can help their clients by making it easier and faster for reporters to get information.

Many PR people also try to call attention to their clients by putting them in touch with news people through casual breakfasts or lunches or even backyard barbecues. No immediate stories are expected from these events, but it makes the reporters and politicians feel more comfortable with each other and, as often as not, the politicians may find their names appearing in stories a little more readily. In effect, this new breed of political PR consultant is a lobbyist of the media, working in conjunction with those who lobby the officeholders.

The attention being focused on California's political press is beginning to be matched by the media's own introspection. When a few legislators introduced bills to reduce press access to public records or to give public figures more power to sue for libel, a debate among the members of the Capitol press corps began over the role of journalists in fighting for access to information. Although none of the proposed measures made it through the Legislature, the debate within the press is likely to continue between people who believe reporters should actively lobby lawmakers to keep information public and those who argue that journalists have a responsibility to their readers and viewers, and that by lobbying for anything, journalists compromise themselves.

This self-examination has intensified since a Sacramento television reporter, who covered the Capitol and state government, was found in 1989 to have had a consulting contract with the California Highway Patrol for five years to teach them how to deal with the media. That reporter was removed from the Capitol beat by his station and reprimanded by the Capitol Correspondents Association, but Capitol reporters have continued to wrestle with the ethics of outside income – such as speeches to trade associations and free-lance writing for professional or industry publications – or possible conflicts of interest created by the jobs held by spouses.

Newspapers and news services

ASSOCIATED PRESS

Sacramento bureau: 925 L St., Suite 320, Sacramento, 95814; (916) 448-9555.
Doug Willis, correspondent and political writer; John Howard, news editor;

reporters: Rodney Angove, Steve Geissinger, Kathleen Grubb, Jennifer Kerr, Steve Lawrence; photographers Walter Zeboski and Rich Pedroncelli.

The Associated Press is a news cooperative with approximately 100 member newspapers and 400 broadcasters in California who receive AP reports.

The Sacramento office is an all-purpose news bureau covering breaking stories from Fairfield east to the Nevada border and from Stockton north to the Oregon border. Roughly two-thirds of the bureau's time is spent reporting on California politics and state government.

Willis has been in AP's Sacramento bureau since 1969 and has directed the bureau since 1974. Howard came to the bureau as news editor in 1980 from AP's San Francisco office.

The AP staff is a veteran one: Angove, who joined AP in 1959, has spent 19 years in Sacramento; Geissinger moved to the bureau in 1984 from the Salinas Californian; Grubb joined AP in 1987 from the Vacaville Reporter; Kerr joined AP in 1973 and has been in Sacramento since 1978; Lawrence came to Sacramento in 1973 from AP's Los Angeles office; Zeboski has been with AP since 1949, the last 27 years in Sacramento; Pedroncelli, a former Sacramento Union photographer and long-time AP stringer, joined the staff in 1990.

BAKERSFIELD CALIFORNIAN

Capitol bureau: 925 L St., Suite 1190, Sacramento, 95814; (916) 324-4585.

Michael Otten, bureau chief.

The bureau primarily covers news of interest to the Californian's Kern County circulation base. Otten joined the paper in 1989 after more than 30 years with the Sacramento Union, the last five of those years as Capitol bureau chief. Otten writes a political column for the Californian, and writes another that appears in the Union.

CAPITOL NEWS SERVICE

1113 H St., Sacramento, 95814; (916) 445-6336; Los Angeles office (213) 462-6371.

Fred Kline, editor; Eric Bjune and Paul Gary, reporters.

A small, independent news service serving small dailies and weeklies. The news service was founded in 1939 and was taken over by Kline, a veteran newsman, in 1971.

CHICO ENTERPRISE-RECORD

Capitol bureau: 520 P St., No. 19, Sacramento 95814; (916) 444-6747.

Mike Gardner, reporter.

The opening of this bureau in 1990 was prompted by the paper's need to report on attempts to obtain state aid for fiscally strapped Butte County. Gardner, who has been with the paper since 1986, concentrates on stories of interest to Chico-area readers.

CONTRA COSTA TIMES/LESHER NEWSPAPERS

Capitol bureau: 925 L St., Suite 348, Sacramento, 95814; (916) 441-2101.
Virgil Meibert, bureau chief.

The bureau covers local legislators, the effect of state government decisions on local communities and regional issues for six Lesher newspapers in the San Francisco Bay Area: the Contra Costa Times, Antioch Daily Ledger, Pittsburg Post-Dispatch, San Ramon Valley Times, Valley Times in Pleasanton and West County Times covering the Richmond-Pinole area.

Prior to becoming Lesher's Sacramento bureau chief in 1988, Meibert spent 24 years with the Oakland Tribune, the last 14 years as its Sacramento bureau chief.

COPLEY NEWS SERVICE

Capitol bureau: 925 L St., Suite 1190, Sacramento, 95814; (916) 445-2934.
Robert P. Studer, bureau chief; James P. Sweeney, political writer.

The bureau covers stories of particular interest to a group of Copley newspapers in the Los Angeles area: the Torrance Daily Breeze, the San Pedro News and the Santa Monica Evening Outlook. It occasionally helps two other Copley newspapers, the San Diego Union and the San Diego Tribune, which also have Sacramento bureaus. In addition, the bureau serves roughly 100 California clients, including daily and weekly newspapers and broadcasters who subscribe to the Copley News Service.

Studer, who also writes analyses on statewide issues, has been with the Copley chain for more than 50 years and has been Sacramento bureau chief since 1974. Sweeney joined the bureau in 1985 from the Torrance Daily Breeze, where he had been an assistant city editor.

DAILY RECORDER

1115 H St., Sacramento, 95814; (916) 444-2355.
Anne Ternus, reporter.

This Sacramento-based legal-profession newspaper is one of several owned by the Daily Journal Corp. of Los Angeles. It concentrates on news of interest to the legal community, lobbyists and Capitol staffers.

Ternus has been the Daily Recorder's Capitol correspondent since 1990.

GANNETT NEWS SERVICE

Capitol bureau: 925 L St., Suite 110, Sacramento, 95814; (916) 446-1036.
Jake Henshaw, bureau chief; Ray Sotero, reporter.

The bureau has two permanent writers and a rotating temporary reporter on loan from a Gannett newspaper. They cover stories of local and statewide interest to the chain's California newspapers: the Indio Daily News, Marin Independent Journal, the Palm Springs Desert Sun, the Salinas Californian, the San Bernardino Sun, the Stockton Record and the Visalia Times-Delta. The bureau also occasionally covers stories for the Reno Gazette Journal and USA Today.

Henshaw came to Sacramento in 1987 from the GNS Washington bureau, where he had worked since 1978. He became bureau chief in Sacramento in 1990. Sotero moved to GNS in 1990 from The Sacramento Bee's Capitol Bureau, where he had covered issues for the Fresno Bee and Modesto Bee since 1988. He had previously worked for five years in Modesto.

LONG BEACH PRESS-TELEGRAM

Capitol bureau: 925 L St., Suite 315, Sacramento, 95814; (916) 448-1893.

Lawrence L. Lynch, reporter.

This is one of two Knight-Ridder newspapers with bureaus in Sacramento, the other being the San Jose Mercury-News. The one-person bureau's main focus is stories of local interest to Long Beach readers, including coverage of local legislators and major statewide issues.

Lynch has been with the paper since 1970 in various positions, including political writer and editorial writer. He took over the Capitol bureau in 1989.

LOS ANGELES DAILY JOURNAL

Capitol bureau: 925 L St., Suite 325, Sacramento, 95814; (916) 445-8063.

Thomas L. Dresslar, bureau chief; Hallye Jordan, reporter.

The bureau covers news of interest to the legal community ranging from the death penalty to probate law. In addition to the Daily Journal, the bureau's work appears in the San Francisco Banner Journal and other Daily Journal Corp. publications.

Dresslar came to the bureau from the Daily Recorder in Sacramento in 1987. Jordan joined the bureau in 1987 from the Orange County Register.

LOS ANGELES DAILY NEWS

Capitol bureau: 925 L St., Suite 335, Sacramento, 95814; (916) 446-6723.

James W. Sweeney, bureau chief; Sandy Harrison, reporter.

Los Angeles office: Rick Orlov, (213) 485-3720.

The bureau's primary focus is on state government, political news of interest to its San Fernando Valley readers and major statewide stories.

Sweeney transferred to Sacramento in 1988 from the Daily News city room, where he had covered local government and politics since 1984. Harrison joined the bureau in 1989 and had covered local government for the Daily News.

Orlov covers City Hall and state and local politics from the Los Angeles office. He has been with the paper since 1977 and previously worked for Copley News Service.

LOS ANGELES TIMES

Capitol bureau: 1125 L St., Suite 200, Sacramento, 95814; (916) 445-8860.

George Skelton, bureau chief; staff writers: Virginia Ellis, Ralph Frammolino (Orange and San Diego editions), Jerry Gillam,Mark Gladstone (Los Angeles

County zone sections and San Fernando Valley edition), Carl Ingram, Paul Jacobs, Richard C. Paddock, Douglas Shuit, William Trombley, Max Vanzi (news editor), Daniel Weintraub.

Los Angeles office: Cathleen Decker, (213) 237-4652, and Bill Stall, (213) 237-4550, political writers.

The Los Angeles Times Sacramento bureau primarily takes a statewide approach to its coverage of Capitol issues. It does in-depth political analyses, personality profiles and investigative stories involving the state bureaucracy as well as daily coverage of the Legislature, the governor and other state agencies.

The Times also provides stories of local and regional interest to its primary audience of Los Angeles area readers. Two reporters within the bureau focus on news of local interest to Times editions in San Diego, Orange County, the San Fernando Valley and Los Angeles area zones. Times stories also appear in newspapers that subscribe to the Times-Mirror wire service.

Skelton, a former Capitol correspondent for UPI who moved to the Times in 1974, is in his second tour of duty as the Times' Capitol bureau chief. He has also worked as Times politics editor in Los Angeles and as White House correspondent.

The Times bureau includes Ellis, who came to Sacramento in 1988 from the Dallas Times Herald, where she was chief of its Capitol bureau in Austin; Frammolino, who moved to Sacramento in 1989 from the Times' San Diego edition; Gillam, the president of the Capitol Correspondents Association and a member of the bureau since 1961; Gladstone, who joined the bureau in 1984 and has been with the Times since 1981; Jacobs, who has been with the Times since 1978 and who moved to Sacramento in 1983; Paddock, who has been with the Times since 1977 and in Sacramento since 1982; Ingram, a former UPI Capitol correspondent who joined the Times in 1978; Shuit, who has been with the Times since 1967 and in the bureau since 1980; Trombley, who has been with the Times since 1964 and in Sacramento since 1989; Vanzi, who moved to the bureau in 1990 from the Times main office, where he had worked since 1984 as an assistant city editor; and Weintraub, who arrived in 1987 after four years in other Times assignments.

Decker and Stall are based in Los Angeles and cover statewide and national political stories. Decker joined the Times in 1978 after having worked as a Times intern. She worked primarily covering local and national politics since 1985 before being designated a political writer in 1990. Stall, a veteran Times writer, was an editorial writer for the Times when he returned to political writing in 1990.

OAKLAND TRIBUNE

Capitol bureau: 925 L St., Suite 385, Sacramento, 95814; (916) 445-5424.

Kathy Zimmerman McKenna, bureau chief.

The bureau focuses on issues of interest to the East Bay and statewide stories.

Zimmerman McKenna transferred to Sacramento in 1988 from Oakland, where she had been covering City Hall for the Tribune.

ORANGE COUNTY REGISTER

Capitol bureau: 925 L St., Suite 305, Sacramento, 95814; (916) 445-9841.

Marc S. Lifsher and Chris Knap, correspondents.

Santa Ana office: Larry Peterson, political writer, (714) 953-2223.

The bureau's main mission is to cover political and government stories of statewide and local interest for the rapidly growing Orange County daily. Lifsher joined the bureau in 1983 from the Dallas Times Herald. Knap came to the bureau in 1989 from the Register's city room, where he was the county government reporter. Peterson covers state and national politics from the main office.

RIVERSIDE PRESS-ENTERPRISE

Capitol bureau: 925 L St., Suite 312, Sacramento, 95814; (916) 445-9973.

Dan Smith, bureau chief.

Riverside: Joan Radovich, political writer, (714) 782-7567.

The bureau's main charge is to cover Riverside County legislators and issues of local interest as well as major breaking political and government stories. Smith became the Press-Enterprise's Capitol correspondent in 1988. He has worked for the paper since 1984 and had previously covered local politics and government. Radovich, the paper's former City Hall reporter, became its political writer in 1989.

SACRAMENTO BEE / McCLATCHY NEWSPAPERS

Capitol bureau: 925 L St., Suite 1404, Sacramento, 95814; (916) 321-1199.

William Endicott, bureau chief; Rick Rodriguez, deputy bureau chief; Dan Walters, political columnist; staff writers: Amy Chance, Thorne Gray, Stephen Green, Rick Kushman, Jon Matthews, James Richardson, Joe Rosato (Fresno Bee coverage), Herbert A. Sample, Kathie Smith (Modesto Bee coverage).

McClatchy Newspapers: Martin Smith, political editor, P.O. Box 15779, Sacramento, 95852; (916) 321-1914.

Fresno Bee: Jim Boren, political writer, (209) 441-6307.

The Sacramento Bee's Capitol bureau primarily takes a statewide view in its coverage of issues and politics. It regularly offers political analyses, features and daily coverage of state government and political issues. In addition, bureau members work on in-depth special projects ranging from investigative reports on the Legislature to examination of emerging political trends. In election years, bureau reporters cover both state and national campaigns. The impact of The Bee's political, legislative and state government coverage has increased in recent years with the growth of the McClatchy News Service. About 60 California newspapers subscribe to MNS, with many using stories covered by The Bee's Capitol bureau.

Bureau Chief Endicott took over The Bee's Capitol bureau in 1985, coming to the paper from the Los Angeles Times, where he had worked for 17 years in various positions, including San Francisco bureau chief, political writer and the last two years as the Times' Capitol bureau chief.

Rodriguez became deputy bureau chief in 1987 after a stint as an editorial writer. He came to Sacramento from the Fresno Bee as a Capitol bureau reporter in 1982.

Walters' column appears six days a week in The Bee and is distributed statewide by McClatchy News Service. He joined the paper as a political columnist in 1984 after 11 years with the Sacramento Union, the last nine in its Capitol bureau.

Martin Smith has been political editor of McClatchy Newspapers since 1977 and has been covering politics since 1965. He writes a political column three times a week that is distributed statewide by McClatchy News Service. He is a member of The Sacramento Bee's editorial board.

The Bee's Capitol staff includes: Chance, who joined the paper in 1984 from the Fort Worth Star-Telegram to cover Sacramento City Hall and moved to the Capitol bureau in 1986; Gray, who moved to Sacramento from the Modesto Bee in 1983; Green, who moved to The Bee in 1978 from the Seattle Post-Intelligencer and to the Capitol bureau in 1985; Kushman, a former Sacramento Union reporter and television assignment editor who joined the bureau in 1987; Matthews, who joined the bureau in 1986 from the Anchorage Daily News; Richardson, who became the Riverside Press Enterprise's Capitol bureau chief in 1985 and moved to The Bee in 1988; Rosato, a Fresno Bee reporter since 1969 who moved to the Capitol Bureau in 1990 to provide Fresno coverage; Sample, a former Los Angeles Times reporter who joined the bureau in 1986; and Smith, who had worked at The Modesto Bee since 1978 before joining the Capitol Bureau as the Modesto correspondent in 1991.

Boren covers politics for the Fresno Bee. He joined the paper in 1972 and has been the political writer since 1980.

SACRAMENTO UNION

Capitol bureau: 925 L St., Suite 1190, Sacramento, 95814; (916) 440-0545.

Trinda Pasquet and J.P. Tremblay, reporters.

The main charge of this bureau is to cover news of local interest to Sacramento area readers. The Union generally relies on wire stories for its major breaking news reports on state government and political issues.

Pasquet, the Union's former courthouse reporter, joined the bureau from the Union's city room in 1989. Tremblay joined the bureau in 1990 from the Union's editorial department, where he had been a copy editor since 1989.

SAN DIEGO TRIBUNE

Sacramento bureau: 925 L St., Suite 1190, Sacramento, 95814; (916) 445-6510.

Ron Roach, Sacramento bureau chief.

San Diego: Ray Huard and Sharon Spivak, political writers.

The bureau's main mission is to cover news of interest to San Diego area readers and major statewide stories. Roach also occasionally writes commentaries and analyses. This is one of three Copley Newspapers bureaus in Sacramento.

Roach has been the Tribune's Capitol correspondent since 1978, coming to the newspaper after several years with the Associated Press, the last three as news editor of its Sacramento bureau.

Huard and Spivak cover local, state and national politics from the main office. Spivak also occasionally assists Roach in Sacramento.

SAN DIEGO UNION

Sacramento bureau: 925 L St., Suite 1190, Sacramento 95814; (916) 448-2066.

Daniel C. Carson, bureau chief; Ed Mendel, staff writer.

San Diego office: Gerard Braun, (619) 293-1230; John Marelius, (619) 293-1231, reporters.

This Copley newspaper's Sacramento bureau splits its time covering stories of local interest, including the San Diego area's 11-member legislative delegation, and statewide political and government stories. The two writers also regularly contribute to a political column and stories are distributed by the Copley News Service.

Carson has been with the Union since 1977 and in Sacramento since 1982, the last two years as bureau chief. Mendel, a former Sacramento Union reporter, worked as editor of the now-defunct Golden State Report prior to joining the Union in 1990.

Braun and Marelius cover statewide political issues and are based in the main office in San Diego.

SAN FRANCISCO CHRONICLE

Sacramento bureau: 1121 L St., Suite 408, Sacramento 95814; (916) 445-5658.

Vlae Kershner, bureau chief; Rob Gunnison, Greg Lucas, staff writers.

San Francisco office: Jerry Roberts, political editor, (415) 777-7124; Susan Yoachum, political writer, (415) 777-7123.

The Sacramento bureau's primary emphasis is on statewide government and political news. Chronicle Capitol bureau stories also move over the New York Times wire and are picked up by other subscribing California newspapers.

Kershner, who joined the bureau in 1989, was economics editor for the Chronicle prior to becoming bureau chief in 1990.

Gunnison moved to the Chronicle in 1985 from United Press International's Sacramento bureau, where he had worked for 11 years. Lucas joined the bureau in 1988 from the Los Angeles Daily Journal's Sacramento staff.

Roberts, a longtime Chronicle staffer, has been the paper's political editor since 1987. He and Yoachum, a former San Jose Mercury-News reporter who joined the Chronicle in 1990, do much of the local, state and national political reporting from the home office in San Francisco.

SAN FRANCISCO EXAMINER

Sacramento bureau: 925 L St., Suite 320A, Sacramento 95814; (916) 445-4310.

Steven A. Capps, bureau chief; Tupper Hall, reporter.

San Francisco office: John Jacobs, chief political writer, (415) 777-7868; George Raine, political writer (415) 777-7866.

This Hearst paper's Sacramento bureau covers major statewide stories and stories of interest to San Francisco Bay Area readers. Capps joined the bureau in 1980 after spending three years with United Press International in San Francisco and Los Angeles. Hall joined the bureau in late 1989 after serving as the Los Angeles Herald Examiner's Sacramento bureau chief since 1985.

Jacobs has been the paper's chief political writer since 1987. He joined the paper in 1978 from the Washington Post. He is on leave in 1991 but is expected to return for the 1992 election year. Raine is a former Newsweek reporter who joined the Examiner in 1987 and became a political writer in 1990.

SAN FRANCISCO RECORDER

Sacramento bureau: 925 L St., Suite 315, Sacramento, 95814; (916)448-2935.
Bill Ainsworth, reporter.

This paper covers state government, politics and lobbying from a legal perspective. Ainsworth, a former Sacramento Union reporter for $2^{1}/2$ years, opened the bureau in 1990.

SAN JOSE MERCURY-NEWS

Sacramento bureau: 925 L St., Suite 345, Sacramento, 95814; (916) 441-4601.
Gary Webb, bureau chief; Tom Farragher and Mitchel Benson, staff writers.
San Jose office: Phil Trounstine, political editor, (408) 920-5657.

The Sacramento bureau relies on wire services to cover the bulk of daily Capitol stories and concentrates more on off-agenda and investigative stories of statewide and local interest. Stories also move over the Knight-Ridder wire and are picked up by other newspapers.

Webb came to Sacramento in 1989 from the Cleveland Plain Dealer, where he had been an investigative reporter in the statehouse bureau in Columbus. Farragher, who has been with the Mercury News since 1987, was the City Hall reporter in San Jose when he moved to Sacramento in late 1990. Benson, who has been with the paper for five years and formerly covered environmental issues, joined the bureau in 1991.

Trounstine is responsible for national, statewide and local political coverage from the home office. He joined the paper in 1978 from the Indianapolis Star and has been political editor since 1986.

UNITED PRESS INTERNATIONAL

Sacramento bureau: 925 L St., Suite 1185, Sacramento, 95814; (916) 445-7755.
Chris Crystal, bureau manager; reporters: Robert Crabbe, Ken Hoover, Clark McKinley, Ted Appel.

UPI's Sacramento bureau is responsible for covering breaking news in the northeastern quadrant of California, although the bureau's emphasis is on government news. It also offers political analyses and campaign coverage for its clients.

Chris Crystal took over as bureau manager in July 1989, moving from San Francisco. She has been with UPI for 11 years and was a Washington correspondent from 1983 to 1987.

Staff writers: Crabbe, who has been with UPI for 27 years, much of it in Asia, and in the bureau since 1980; Hoover, who joined the bureau in 1987 from the Los Angeles Daily News; McKinley, who has been with UPI for 18 years and in Sacramento since 1978; and Appel, who transferred from Los Angeles in 1989.

Magazines

CALIFORNIA JOURNAL

1714 Capitol Ave., Sacramento, 95814; (916) 444-2840.

Richard Zeiger, editor; A.G. Block, managing editor.

The California Journal, founded by a group of Capitol staffers as a non-profit institution, celebrated its 20th anniversary in 1989. The monthly magazine, which relies primarily on free-lance writers, takes an analytical view of California politics and government. It has a circulation of about 19,000. The California Journal also publishes various books about California government and politics. It became a for-profit organization in 1986 with Tom Hoeber, one of the founders, as publisher.

Zeiger took over as the magazine's editor in 1984. Prior to that, he had been with the Riverside Press-Enterprise for 16 years, the last seven as its Sacramento bureau chief. Block was a free-lance writer when he joined the magazine in 1983.

CALIFORNIA REPUBLIC

1390 Market St., suite 910; San Francisco, 94102; (415) 558-9888.

Dirk Olin, executive editor.

This tabloid began publishing in 1991. It is a bipartisan monthly that attempts to put statewide issues in a national perspective and local issues in a statewide perspective. Olin is a former Sacramento correspondent for the California Lawyer magazine. He has worked as a Washington correspondent for the St. Petersburg (Fla.) Times and has written for The New Republic.

Newsletters

CALIFORNIA EYE / THE POLITICAL ANIMAL

P.O. Box 3249, Torrance, 90510; (213) 515-1511.

Joe Scott, editor.

Scott publishes two biweekly political newsletters. The California Eye, begun in 1980, is aimed at analyzing and forecasting trends in state politics, while The Political Animal, started in 1973, takes a nationwide approach with some California news included. Scott also writes a twice-weekly column that appears in the Sacramento Union, the San Diego Union and other papers.

CALIFORNIA POLITICAL WEEK

P.O. Box 1468, Beverly Hills, 90213; (213) 659-0205.

Dick Rosengarten, editor and publisher.

This newsletter takes a look at trends in politics and local government throughout the state. It was established in 1979. Rosengarten is a former print and broadcast journalist who has also worked in public relations and as a campaign manager.

POLITICAL PULSE

926 J St., Room 1218, Sacramento 95814; (916) 446-2048.

Bud Lembke, editor and publisher.

This newsletter, which looks at political news, trends and personalities, was started in 1985. Lembke was a Los Angeles Times reporter for 21 years and a former press secretary to Senate President Pro Tem David Roberti. Subscribers receive 23 issues a year.

NEW WEST NOTES

P.O. Box 221364, Sacramento 95822; (916) 395-0709.

Bill Bradley, editor and publisher.

Formerly called the Larkspur Report, this monthly newsletter aims to give a California perspective to political and economic affairs through Bradley's analysis. Bradley was a senior consultant to former U.S. Sen. Gary Hart in his presidential bids. He also writes columns for the Sacramento News and Review and California Business Magazine.

Radio

CALNET / AP RADIO

926 J St., Suite 1014, Sacramento 95814; (916) 446-2234.

Steve Scott, correspondent.

Calnet produces a daily, half-hour program of news and commentary focusing on state government and political news. It is carried by public radio stations in 12 California markets. Scott has covered the Capitol as a stringer for several radio stations since 1986. He joined Calnet in 1988 and also strings for Associated Press radio.

KCBS-San Francisco

925 L St., Suite A, Sacramento 95814; (916) 445-7372.

Jim Hamblin, correspondent.

Hamblin covers the Legislature and government stories as well as other breaking news for this San Francisco-based news radio station. Hamblin has covered state government and politics for 20 years and has been based in Sacramento since 1987.

KXPR/FM

3416 American River Drive, Suite B, Sacramento, 95864; (916) 485-5977.

Mike Montgomery, reporter.

This member station of the National Public Radio network is one of the few that regularly covers the state Capitol and government. Montgomery has been covering political and Capitol stories since December 1983.

Television

Los Angeles
KABC-TV

4151 Prospect Ave., Los Angeles 90027; (213) 668-?880.

Mark Coogan, John North, correspondents. Bill Press, Bruce Herschensohn, political commentators.

Coogan and North cover major local and state political stories and collaborate on events such as conventions or elections. Coogan, who started at KABC in 1976, spent 1979 and 1980 as the southern Africa bureau chief for ABC News, then came back to KABC as a political reporter in 1980. North, who started covering California politics in 1979 for KABC, also spent some time at the network until he came back to KABC in 1982.

The station also offers political commentary from Press, a liberal former aide to Gov. Jerry Brown who ran unsuccessfully for insurance commissioner in 1990, and conservative Herschensohn, an unsuccessful candidate for the Republican nomination for U.S. Senate in 1986 who is contemplating another try in 1992.

KCBS-TV

6121 Sunset Blvd., Los Angeles 90028; (213) 460-3553.

Ruth Ashton Taylor, political editor; Terry Anzur, political reporter.

Ashton Taylor, the political editor, began her television career in 1949 as a producer on Edward R. Murrow's original show. She moved from CBS to the network-owned station in 1966 in the capacity of political reporter. Anzur joined the station in 1990 from WCBS-TV in New York where she covered local and state politics.

KNBC-TV

3000 West Alameda, Burbank 91523; (818) 840-3425.

Linda Douglass, political editor.

This Los Angeles station covers national, state and local political stories. Douglass, the political editor, started at KNBC in 1985 after jumping across town from KCBS-TV, where she was a longtime political reporter.

Sacramento
KCRA-TV

3 Television Circle, Sacramento 95814; (916) 444-7316.

Steve Swatt, Capitol correspondent.

Swatt has covered the Capitol, state government and politics full-time since 1979 for this NBC-affiliate. He also covers national politics during election years. Swatt has been with the station since 1969, joining it from United Press International's Los Angeles bureau. KCRA's Capitol reports are often picked up by other stations.

KOVR-TV

2713 KOVR Drive, West Sacramento 95605; (916) 374-1313.

Jack Kavanagh, reporter.

This ABC-affiliate covers the Capitol as news stories occur. Kavanagh, a veteran KOVR reporter, took over the Capitol beat in 1990.

KTXL-TV

4655 Fruitridge Rd., Sacramento 95820; (916) 454-4548.

Lonnie Wong, reporter.

Wong has been covering the Capitol and state government for radio and television since 1973. He has been with KTXL, an independent station that covers politics on a spot-news basis, since 1980.

KXTV

400 Broadway, Sacramento 95818; (916) 321-3300.

Deborah Pacyna, Capitol correspondent.

Pacyna has covered state politics and government for this CBS-affiliate since 1984 and also covers national politics during election years. She came to the station from WPXI-TV in Pittsburgh, Pa.

NORTHERN CALIFORNIA NEWS SATELLITE

1121 L St., Suite 109, Sacramento 95814; (916) 446-7890.

Steve Mallory, president.

NCNS is a video wire service that covers the Capitol, state government and other major breaking news for 16 subscribing television stations stretching from San Diego to Medford, Ore. It offers voice-overs, live interviews, election coverage as well as daily reports, all transmitted by satellite. In addition, its facilities are often used by out-of-town stations that travel to Sacramento to cover news. NCNS made its first news transmission in July 1987 and has filled a void created by the closure of all out-of-town television news bureaus.

This is Mallory's second stint in Sacramento. He served as KNBC's Sacramento bureau chief for three years before moving to Beirut as an NBC correspondent in 1978. Subsequent assignments for NBC took him to London, Moscow and Tokyo before he returned to set up his company.

San Francisco
KGO-TV

900 Front St.; San Francisco 94111; (415) 954-7936.

Lisa Stark, correspondent.

This ABC-affiliate formerly had a bureau in Sacramento but has been covering the Capitol and other statewide stories out of the main office.

Stark is a general assignment reporter who does the bulk of the station's political reporting. She came to the station in 1984 from Portland, Ore., where she also did political reporting.

KRON-TV

1001 Van Ness Ave., San Francisco 94109; (415) 441-4444.

Rollin Post, political correspondent.

Post covers state and local politics and offers political analysis for this NBC-affiliate. Post has been with the station since 1989 and has covered politics for San Francisco area stations since 1965. KRON had the distinction for several years of being the only station outside Sacramento to maintain a full-time Capitol bureau,

Index

A

A-K Associates Inc. **394-395**

abortion 18, 43, 123, 145, 152, 172, 176, 192, 201, 215, 227, 230, 237–238, 243, 263, 294, 296, 297, 298–299, 302, 318–319, 350, 363

abortion, fund restriction (key vote) 102

abortion, parental consent (key vote) 100

Abraham, Walt 453

Achtenberg, Roberta 205, 458

Ackerman, David 385

ACU *See* American Conservative Union

ADA *See* Americans for Democratic Action Inc.

Adams, George 355

Adler, Howard 289

Adolph Coors Co. 394

AFL-CIO 411 *See also* American Federation of Labor-Congress of Industrial Organizations

Agents and Brokers Association 400

Aging, Dept. of 68

Agliano, Nat A. 90

Agnos, Art 136, 205, 409, 414, 460–461

Agonia, Henry 74

Agricultural Workers, Commission on 66

Aguirre, Ron 275

Aid to Families with Dependent Children 23

AIDS 111, 136, 202, 232, 257, 350, 369, 370, 462

AIDS, ban discrimination (key vote) 100

Ailes, Roger 46

Ainsworth, Bill 492

air quality 438

Air Resources Board 70–71

Alameda County 423–425

Alarcon, Evelina 269

Alatorre, Richard 267

Alcohol and Drug Programs, Dept. of 68

alcohol standards (key vote) 102

Alcoholic Beverage Control, Dept. of 64

Alioto, Angela 458

Alioto, Joseph 460

Allen, Anna 235

Allen, Doris J. 169, **290–291**

Allen, J. Michael 394–395

Allen, Richard D. 394–395

Allenby, Cliff 82

Allert, Irene 243

Alliance of American Insurers 400

Allred, Gloria 144–145

Allsup, Warren 435

Alpert, Deirdre W. "Dede" **295–296**

Alpine County 426

Alquist, Alfred E. 28, **126–128**, 466

Alquist, Mai 127

Amador County 426–427

American Express Co. 394

American Conservative Union 309

American Federation of Labor-Congress of Industrial Organizations 98, 309

American Medical Association 332

Americans for Democratic Action Inc. 309

Amundson, Dennis 69

Anaheim 450

Andal, Dean 226

Anderson, Bruce 185

Anderson, Carl West 89

Anderson, Glenn M. 306–307, **360–361**, 373

Anderson, Melvin 446
Andreen, Judy 432
Angelides, Phil 409
Angove, Rodney 485
Anheuser-Busch Cos. 391
animal rights 239
Annenberg, Walter 406
Antioch Daily Ledger 486
Antonovich, Michael 438, 439
Anzur, Terry 495
AP radio 494
Aparicio, Frank 80
Appel, Ted 492–493
appellate court justices 88–90
Applied Materials Inc. See Morgan,
   James C.
Arabian, Armand 83, **87–88**
Arafat, Yassir 355
Aramburu, Albert 443
Archie-Hudson, Marguerite **258–259**
Arciniega, Tomas 79
Ardaiz, James A. 90
Areias, John Rusty **224–226**
Arguelles, John 83, 87
Arnall, Roland 79
Arnold, Chris 68
Arthur J. Finkelstein & Associates 417
Asburn, Roy 435
Ashby, Herbert L. 89
Ashton Taylor, Ruth 495
assault weapon ban 123, 133, 134,
   138, 147, 159–160, 190, 192, 219,
   227, 237–238, 239, 266, 278
assault weapon ban (key vote) 99–100
Associated Press 484–485
Association of Bay Area Governments
   424, 425, 464, 465, 470, 471
Association of Calif. Insurance Cos.
   388, 399–400
Atkinson, Richard 79
Atlantic Richfield Co 398 See also
   Cook, Lowrick

Aubry, Lloyd 67
Auburn Dam 325
Augustine, Curt 212
Austin, Ben 435
auto insurance reform See Proposition
   103
Avis Rent-A-Car 397
Ayala, Ruben S. 118, **168–169**, 281

B

Babbitt, Bruce 409
Baca, Joe 283
BAD Campaigns 414 See also
   Berman, Michael; D'Agostino, Carl
Bader, Charles 168, 281
Badham, Robert 371
Bagdasarian, Marian 79
Baggett, Arthur 444
Bailey, George 456
Baird, Borgny 79–80
Baird, Janice 81
Baker Jr., Harry 443
Baker, Marilyn 433
Baker, Warren 79
Baker, William P. 193, **203-204**, 215
Bakersfield Californian 485
Bakhous, Robert 239
Baldwin, Steven 304
Ball, David 271
Ballesteros, Celia 302
Bamattre-Manoukian, P. 90
Bamert, Edward 426
Bane, Marlene 246–247
Bane, Thomas J. 139, **245–247**
Barber, George 462
Bardell, Bob 301
Bardos, Phillip 79–80
bargaining units 62, 63
Batchelder, Roger 180
Bates, Jim 355, 376, 377
Bates, Tom H. **199-200**, 253
Battisti, Paul 448

Baughman, Mike 325
Baxter, Marvin Ray 83, **88–90**
Bayer, David 348
Beautz, Janet 467
Becerra, Xavier **273**
Bechtel Corp. 408
Bechtel Jr., Stephen 408
Bechtel Sr., Stephen 408
Becktell, Evelyn 166
Beers, Charles 294
Begley Jr., Ed 405
Begovich, John 426
Behring, Ken 409
Beilenson, Anthony **348–349**
Beland, George 451
Belgard, Ray 467
Bell, Charles 385, 396
Bell, Judith 402
Belli, Lia 109
Belza, Thomas 477
Benatar, Joseph 472
Bender, Christine 64
Benke, Patricia D. 90
Bennett, John 426
Bennett, William **55–56**
Benninghoven, Don 400
Benson, David 79
Benson, John E. 88
Benson, Mitchel 492
Bentley, Carol J. 176, **298–299**
Berg, Clifford 148–149
Bergeson, Marian C. **172-173**, 317–318, 416
Bergondy, Bruce 122
Berkeley 424, 425
Berman, Henry 409
Berman, Howard L. 209, 246, 349, 349–350, **352–353**
Berman, Michael 350, 352, 414
Berman-Waxman organization 142, 251, 255, 260, 349–350, 352, 355, 358, 414, 442

Berryhill, Clare 339
Bertolet, Daniel 128
Best, Hollis G. 90
Best, Robert 65
Beteta, Fred 254
Beverly, Robert G. **159–160**
Bevis, Brady 443
"Big Green" *See* Proposition 128
Bilas, Richard A. 81
Bilbray, Brian 71, 456
Bird, Rose Elizabeth 31, 40, 44, 83–84, 213
Bjune, Eric 485
Black, Shirley Temple 123
Blakely, David 463
Blanning & Baker Associates 401
Blease, Coleman A. 90
Block, A.G. 493
Blom, Nick 471
Blonien, Rodney 385
Blum, Richard 17, 409
Boating and Waterways, Dept. of 74
Boatwright, Daniel **115–117**, 171
Boerum, Bill 328
Boggs, Diane 278
Bogna Jr., Michael 445
Boland, Paula L. **243**
Bontadelli Jr., Peter 74
Bookhammer, Charles 266
Boren, Jim 489–490
Boren, Roger W. 89
Bos, Otto 60, 415
Bosco, Douglas 321
Boston, Dr. Eugene 71
Bosworth, Bob 468
Bowler, Larry 197
Bowling, Donald 468
Bowling, Rita 455
Boxer, Barbara 316, 319, **327–328**
Boyle, Richard 250
Brackett, Ruth 463
Bradley, Bill 494

Bradley, Tom 32, 44, 119, 137, 410, 417, 441, 441–442
Bradley, William 458
Brann, Richard 108
Braun, Gerard 491
Bren, Donald 407, 408
Briggs, John 384
Bright, Bill 195
Bright, Keith 435
Brinigar, Paul 81
Briscoe, Jerry 385
"Brispec" 93, 139, 163
Brissenden, John 426
Britt, Harry 326, 458
Broder, David 46
Broderson, G.C. 353
Brokaw, Barry 116, 149
Bronshvag, Vivien 195
Bronzan, Bruce C. **232–233**
Brooks, Jack 409
Brophy, Roy 78
Broussard, Allen Edgar **85–86**
Brown, Art 291
Brown, Corey 402
Brown, Dennis 272
BrOwn, Donald K. **387–388**, 398
Brown, George 171
Brown, Harold 443
Brown Jr., Edmund G. "Jerry" 7–10, 14–15, 16, 18, 26, 30, 31, 35, 41, 44, 49, 83, 85–86, 107, 206, 227, 244, 316, 405, 406, 407, 408, 409, 417, 420
Brown Jr., George E. **365–366**
Brown Jr., Willie L. 78, 79, 101, 118, 144, 147, 160, 187, 192, 196, **207-212**, 213, 214, 218, 220, 222, 223, 224, 231, 232, 234, 238, 240, 242, 244, 244–245, 246, 247, 248, 257, 258, 261, 266, 268, 278, 280, 283, 286, 301, 303, 352, 356, 399, 409, 414, 460, 479, 481–482

Brown, Kathleen **45–47**
Brown, Les 436
Brown Sr., Edmund G. "Pat" 4–6, 30–31, 85, 109, 361
Brown-Burton organization 205, 461
Browning-Ferris Industries 215
Brulte, Jim **281–282**
Brumfield, Voris 436
Bucher, James 434
Buckley, Bill 474
Buckley, Tim S. 90
budget **21-29,** 95, 203, 227
    automatic cuts 23
    county fees 421
    deficit 33
    general fund 28
Bundy, Burton 473
Buonaiuto, Joe 189
Burbank, Ken 433
Burg, Carl 223
Burgener, Clair 76, 78, 384
Burke, Yvonne Brathwaite 78
Burns, Helga 431
Burris, Cliff 339
Burt, Nancy **387–388**
Burton, John L. **205-206**, 327, 460
Burton, Phil 16, 109, 305–306, 326, 344, 368, 460
Burton, Sala 326
Burton, Susanne 60
Bush, George 38, 281, 312, 313, 318, 320, 369, 406, 432
Butcher, Marilyn 445
Butte County 427–428
Butterfield, Rob 377
Byouk, John 189
Byrd, Charles 469

C

Caddle, Sam 469
Caffrey, John 71
Cal-OSHA *See* Proposition 97

Cal-SPAN 481–483
Calaveras County 428–429
Calderon, Charles M. 140, **153–155**, 273, 274
California Poll 11, 13
Calif. Abortion Rights Action League 297
California Advocates **395–396**
Calif. Applicants Attorneys Association 399
Calif. Association of Highway Patrolmen 390
Calif. Business Roundtable 27, 307–308
Calif. Chamber of Commerce 98, 397–398
Calif. Chiropractic Association 390
Calif. Coastal Commission 73, 82, 300
Calif. Coastal Zone Commission 82
Calif. Community Colleges Board of Governors 79–80
Calif. Conservation Corps 73, 189
Calif. Correctional Peace Officers' Association 400
Calif. Counties Foundation 427, 446, 476
Calif. Democratic Council 3, 315
Calif. Dept. of Corrections 437
Calif. Energy Resources Conservation and Development 81
"California Environmental Protection Agency" 66, 70, 218, 274
California Eye 493
Calif. Farm Bureau Federation 66, 98, 341, 398
Calif. Highway Patrol 65, 484
Calif. Hotel & Motel Association 391
California Institute 307–308
Calif. Integrated Waste Management Board 71
California Journal 493
Calif. Judges Association 396

Calif. Labor Federation 411
Calif. League of Conservation Voters 98
Calif. Manufacturers Association 384, 388, 398
Calif. Medical Association 392–393, 411–412
Calif. Nurses Association 297, 411–412
California Poll 417
California Political Week 494
California Republic 493
Calif. State Employees' Association 401, 411
Calif. State University presidents 79
Calif. State University trustees 79
Calif. Teachers Association 14, 27, 98, 300, 398–399, 411
Calif. Tire Recycling Act of 1989 71
Calif. Trial Lawyers Association 399, 411–412
Calif. Union of Safety Employees 401
Californians for Compensation Reform 398
Callaghan, James 449
Callahan, Joe 409
Calnan, Selma 277
Calnet 494
Caltrans See Transportation, Dept. of
Cameron, Clark 476
campaign
    funding 38, 53, 91, 92–93, 227, 409–410, 423
    See also Hollywood money
    management 413–415
    reform 279–280, 413, 440
Campaign California 253
Campaign for Economic Democracy 253
Campana, Kathleen 474
Campbell, Edward 423
Campbell, Bill 263

Campbell, Kevin 427
Campbell, Robert J. **198-199**, 435
Campbell, Tom 123, 316, 318, **334–335**, 408, 416
Campbell, W. Glenn 78
Campbell, William 79, 129, 163, 319, 384, 398
cancer, work standards (key vote) 103
Cannella, Salvatorre **226-228**
Cannon, Aleta 201
Capaccioli, Walter P. 90
capital punishment 30, 33, 40, 83, 84
Capitol Correspondents Association 11, 484
Capitol News Service 485
Capps, Steven A. 491–492
Carpenter, Aleta 388–389
Carpenter, Dennis 384, **388–389**
Carpenter, Ernest 470
Carpenter, Paul 55, 93, 166
Carpenter, Richard 76
Carr, Frances N. 90
Carrabino, Joseph 78
Carroll, Brian 287
Carroll, William 469
Carson, Daniel C. 491
Carter-Hawley-Hale *See* Hawley, Philip
Caruso, Paul 471
Casmalia Resources 136
Catellus Inc. 211
Caudle, Arlie 184
Cavala, William 301
Ceniceros, Kay 453
Center for Economic Development and Planning 428, 433
Center, William 431
Ceravolo, Sam 245
Cerrell Associates *See* Cerrell, Joe
Cerrell, Joe 414
Chacon, Peter R. **301–302**
Chance, Amy 489–490

Chandler, Christopher R. **185-186**
Chapman, James 437
Chase, Chevy 405
Chavez, Cesar 411
Chavez, Richard 76
Cher 405
Chesbro, Wesley 71
Chico 428
Chico Enterprise-Record 485
child care 136
Child Development, Education, secretary of 77
child sick leave (key vote) 99
Chin, Ming W. 88
Christo 236
Chrysler Corp. 395
cigarette tax *See* Proposition 99 and Major Risk Medical Insurance Program
Citizens Compensation Commission 81, 94, 385
city-county consolidation 454, 459
Clark Jr., Frank 78
Clarke, Patricia 468
Clean Air Act 218, 364
Clean Air Act (key vote) 100
clean-water and toxics-control *See* Proposition 65
Cleary, James 79
Clinton Reilly Campaigns *See* Reilly, Clint
Clute, Pam 286
Clute, Steve W. 170, **285–287**
Coastal Conservancy 72
coastal protection 38
Coastal Protection Act 289
Coates, Bill 452
Coca-Cola 395
Coelho, Tony 224, 306, 324, 339, 407
Cohen, David 354
Cole, Bill 434
Collin, Illa 453

Collins, B.T. 72
Collis, Conway 56, 412
Colorado River Board of Calif. 72
Colusa County 429
Comingore, Darlene 321
Commerce, Dept. of 64
Committee on Committees 345
Common Cause 56–57, 80, 186, 246, 249, 250, 280, 385, 401
Condit, Gary 226, 254, **338–339**, 414
Conklin, Bruce 186
Connell, Ginny 241
Connelly, Lloyd G. **190-191**, 413
Connolly, Thomas 299
Conrad, A. Vernon 432
Conran, James 75
Conservation, Dept. of 73
Conservation Foundation 72–73
Considine, R. James 79
Consumer Affairs, Dept. of 75
Consumer Services Agency, State and 74–77
Consumers Union 401–402
Contra Costa County 429–430
Contra Costa Times 486
Control, Board of 94
Conway, John 474
Coogan, Mark 495
Cook, Lowrick 407
Cook, Terry 189
Copley, Helen 407
Copley News Service 486, 491
Copley Newspapers 490, 491
Coppola, Francis Ford 405
Corporations, Dept. of 64
Corrections, Board of 71
Corrections, Dept. of 71, 72, 148
Correia, Jeannine 297
Corrigan, Robert 79
Cortese, Dominic L. **222-224**
Cory, Kenneth 44, 414
Costa, Evelyn 462

Costa, James M. **230–232**
Costa Mesa 450
Cottle, Christopher C. 90
County Supervisors Association of Calif. 400, 420, 468
Covalt, Roger 302
Covitz, Carl D. **63–64**
Cowan, Ron 211, 409
Cowles, John 350
Cox, Christopher **371–372**
Coyle, Tim 64
Crabbe, Robert 492–493
Cranston, Alan 3, **312–317**, 328, 404, 406, 407, 415, 417, 458
Cranston, Kim 313
Craven, William A. 145, **174-175**, 284
credit cards 224–225
credit rating, state See Standard & Poor's
crime victims groups 83
Crosby Jr., Thomas F. 90
Croskey, H. Walter 89
"cross-filing" 3–4
Crowley, Barbara 81
Crown, Robert 121
Crystal, Chris 492–493
Cuddihy, John 331
Cunningham, Randy "Duke" **376–377**
Curb, Mike 17, 359, 417
Curry, Tom 214
cutting old trees (key vote) 100

D

Dabney, Howard M. 90
D'Agostini, Stephanie 426
D'Agostino, Carl 350, 352, 414
Dahl, Bruce 247
Dahlson, Roy 353
Daily Journal Corp 486, 487
Daily Recorder 486
Damkar, Harry 135
Dana Jr., Deane 262

Dana Sr., Deane 262, 438, 439
Danielson, George E. 89
Dannemeyer, William E. 165, 305, 319, **370–371**
Danson, Ted 405
Danza, Tony 405
Davenport, Timothy 426
Davenport, Wyatt 445
Davidiank, Ben 80
Davies, John 36
Davis, Ed M. **137–139**, 240, 417
Davis, Gray **43–45**, 58, 76, 82, 202, 251, 414
Davis, Kevin 266
Davis, Lynn 141
Davis, Osby 469
Davis, Rodney 90
Davis, William 65
Day, Thomas 79
De Witt, Bill 357
"deadwood" 11
Dean, Sam 435
death penalty *See* capital punishment
death penalty, expansion (key vote) 101
Decker, Cathleen 488
Deddeh, Wadie P. **178–180**
Del Norte County 431
Del Piero, Marc 447
Delany, Evelyn 463
Dell'Orto, Michael 428
Dellums, Ronald 305, **330–331**
DeMars, George 476
deMartimprey, Hughes 437
Democratic Congressional Campaign Committee 325
Democratic Study Group 326
Detweiler, Robert 79
Deukmejian, George 14, 17, 21–22, 23, 27, 30, 31–33, 39, 40, 41, 45, 49, 50, 59–60, 60–61, 78, 81, 82, 83–84, 94, 118, 121, 125, 131, 147–148, 160, 161, 163, 172, 204, 213, 215, 218, 227, 231, 232, 236, 237–238, 249, 259–260, 265, 270, 274, 280, 293, 313, 385, 389, 396, 407, 408, 410, 411, 415, 416, 417, 420, 441–442, 460, 480
DeVall, Norman 445
development 222, 228, 422–423, 442, 459, 472
    anti-growth 443–444, 447–448, 448–449, 451, 453, 457, 461, 465, 471
Developmental Services, Dept. of 69
Devich, Robert A. 89
Dibiaso, Nicholas J. 90
Dills Brothers 161
Dills, Clayton 161
Dills, Ralph C. 96, 152, **161–162**, 265
DiMarco, Maureen 60, **77**
Dimes Against Crimes 48
"diploma mills" *See* education: standards
Diridon, Rod 465
disabled & mentally ill 232
Dixon, Daniel 416
Dixon, Julian C. 352, **354–356**
Dixon, Stan 433
Doak, David 415
Dolan, Jane 427, 428
Dole, Robert 39, 404
Dolphin Group 416
Dominelli, J. David 295
Dooley, Calvin **341–342**
Doolittle, John 114, 306, **337–338**, 345
Doonesbury 221
Dornan, Robert K. 305, **368–369**
Dornan, Sallie 369
Dorr, Robert 106, 431
Dossee, Robert L. 88
Douglas, Helen Gahagan 3
Douglas, Peter 82

Douglass, Linda 495
Dowell, Soap 82
Dreier, David 306, 316, 318, **361–362**
Dresner, Dick 415
Dresslar, Thomas L. 487
Drexel Burnham Lambert 313
Dronenburg Jr., Ernest J. **57–58**
Dronenburg, Kathryn 78
Drought Center 72
Duffel, Joseph 81
Duffy, Gordon 384
Duffy, Jean 188, 384 *See also*
    Moorehead
Dugan, Jack 189
Dukakis, Michael 11, 289, 404, 408,
    409, 433
Dunlap, Melba 453
Duplissea, Bill 216, 248
Dymally, Mervyn M. 266, **359–360**

E

Eagleson, David 83, 88
Earth Conservation Corps 75
Earth First! 107–108
earthquake
    Loma Prieta 40, 459, 467
    preparedness 225
earthquake insurance (key vote) 103
Eastin, Delaine **213–214**, 257
Eastman, John 364
Eastwood, Clint 405, 448
Eaton, Elliot 203
Eaves, Gerald R. **282–283**
Eckert, Patricia 81–82
economy 1–2, 7, 12, 21, 28, 420–423
Eddie, James 445
Edelman, Ed 438, 439
Edmand, Ray 213
education 257, 319
    funding 23, 26–27, 50, 160, 198,
        213, 249, 422
    standards 26–27, 50, 123

Education, Dept. of 78
Education, State Board of 50, 77–78
Edwards, Don 305, **332–333**
Egigian, Sam 71
Eisenhower, Dwight 4
El Dorado County 431–432
Elder, Dave A. **270–271**
Elia, Franklin D. 90
Ellis, Jim 177, 298
Ellis, Virginia 487–488
Emerson, John 408
Employment Development Dept. 69
Endicott, William 489–490
Energy Commission 126–127
Engle, Clair 5, 6
environment 125, 132, 161, 190, 194,
    198, 213, 217, 228, 272, 274, 290,
    293, 300, 315
Environmental Protection Agency 136
    See also "Calif. Environmental
    Protection Agency"
Eowan, Anne 82
Epple, Robert D. **277–279**
Epstein, Norman L. 89
Equalization, Board of 53–55, 160
Erickson, Eric 444
Erwin, Robert 282
Eshoo, Anna 335, 463
Esposti, Nick 470
ethics 44, 47–48, 55, 158, 198, 215,
    221–222, 231, 233, 276, 301, 312–
    315, 338, 354–355, 376, 385–386,
    460
    gifts and honorariums 39, 223
    reform 19, 56, 216 *See also*
        Proposition 112
ethics reform (key vote) 103
Eu, Henry 48
Eu, March Fong 12, **47–49**, 58
Evans, Anthony 79
Evans, Jane 175, 301
Exxon U.S.A. 394

F

Fahden, Nancy 429

Fair Employment and Housing Act 252

Fair Employment and Housing, Dept. of 75

Fair Housing Act of 1980 332–333

Fair Political Practices Commission 48, 80, 156, 158, 233, 295, 380, 460

Fairbank, Bregman and Maullin 417

Fairchild Camera 123

Fairchild, Morgan 405

Falgatter, Martha 79

Farr, Samuel S. **228-229**

Farragher, Tom 492

Farrell, Robert 258

Faruzzi, Dom 436

fast-food politics 407–408

Faulkner, Terence 212

Fazio, Vic 306, **324-325**

FBI 93–94, 131, 140, 187, 211, 220, 248, 260, 279 *See also* "Brispec"

Federal Communications Commission 38

Federal Election Commission 165, 316

Federal Home Loan Bank Board 313

Federation of Tax Administrators 57

Feinstein, Dianne 11, 15, 16, 18, 36, 39, 56, 84, 118, 213, 215, 221, 319, 409, 414, 415, 460, 461

Felando, Gerald 159, **262–263**, 290

Feliz, John 337–338

Fenimore, George 80

Fennell, Marie 288

Ferguson, Anita 344

Ferguson, Gilbert W. 163, 238, 242, 253, **289–290**

Ferreira, Alex 451

Ferriole, Vincent 448

Fessler, Daniel 81, 82

Fiedler, Bobbi 138

Field, Mervin 11, 417

Field, Sally 405

Fierro, Evelyn 250

Filante, William J. **194-195**

Fiman, Jack 416

Finance, Dept. of 66–67

Fink, Bruce 285

Finkelstein, Arthur J. 417

Finster, E.H. 71

Fish and Game, Dept. of 73–74

Fitzgerald, Patrick 119

Flanigan, Terrance 79

Flores, Joan Milke 47

Flournoy, Houston 9, 316

Floyd, Richard E. **264–266**

Fluty, Mike 451

Flynn, John 475

Foglia, Ed 411

Fonda, Jane 253, 404, 405

Fondse, Adrian 112

Fong, Matthew K. **58**, 160

Food and Agriculture, Dept. of 65–66, 380

Foran, John 117, 179, 384, 397

Ford, Gerald 39

Ford, John 188

Ford, Wesley 276

Forestry and Fire Prevention, Dept. of 73

"Forests Forever" *See* Proposition 130

Foster Farms *See* Maddy, Norma Foster

Foster, Lisa 401

Frammolino, Ralph 487–488

Franchetti, Michael 147, 385, **389–390**

Franchise Tax Board 76

Franco, Reuben 357, 358

Francois, Terry 211

"Frank Fat's napkin deal" 121, 391, 396. *See also* tort reform

Frankel, David 255

Franklin, Gerald 295

Franklin, L.D. 436
Franklin, Tom 252
Frazee, Robert C. **294–295**
Free Market Political Action Committee 99
Freeman, Elaine 81
"FREEPAC" *See* Free Market Political Action Committee
Freiman, Richard 347
Fresno, city of 432
Fresno County 389, 432–433
Frey, Norma Lee 469
Friedman, Terry B. **251–252**
Frizzelle, Nolan 169, 272, **287–288**
Froehlich Jr., Charles W. 90
Fronteras de las Californias 177
Frost, Michael 71, 218
Fukuto, Morio L. 89
Fulkerson, Julie 433
Fullerton, Gail 79
Fulton, Leonard 427

G

Gabriel, Helen 247
Gahn, Gary 302
GAIN 94, 157–158, 460
Galbraith, Dennis 354
Galewsky, Barbara 331
Gallegly, Elton **346–347**
Gallegos, Lenny 468
Gallo, Ernest and Julio 410
Gallups, Michael 290
Gambrell, David 318
"Gang of Five" 154, 211, 224, 254, 283, 303, 339
Gann limit *See* Proposition 4
Gann, Paul 10, 96, 316, 412
Gann, Richard 413
Gann-Stone, Linda 413
Gannett News Service 486–487
Garamendi, John **51–53**, 112, 226

Garamendi, Patti 51, 52, 112, 226
Garcia, Alex 145
Gardner, David 78, 79
Gardner, Kevin 281
Gardner, Mike 485
Garibaldi, James 384, **390**
Garner, James 143, 406
Garrett, Duane 409
Garris, Eric 219
Gary, Paul 485
gas-tax increase *See* Proposition 111
Gates, Donald N. 89
Gates, Mike 191
gay rights 138, 192, 205, 251–252, 459, 460, 461, 462
Gear, Jonathan 200
Geissinger, Steve 485
Gelber, Louise 142
General Electric 397
General Mills 396
General Services, Dept. of 76
Gentry, Nelson 362
George, Ronald M. 89
Georgiou, Byron 376
Gerth, Donald 79
Gerwer, Vernon 431
Getty, Ann 409
Getty, Gordon 409
Giacomini, Gary 443
Gianturco, Adriana 31
Gilbert, Arthur 89
gill net ban *See* Proposition 132
Gillam, Jerry 487–488
Gillespie, Roxani 53
Gilmore, Ben 225
Ginsburg, Alfred 443
Givens, Eric 260
Gladstone, Mark 487–488
Glass Packaging Institute 218
Glenn County 433
Goertzen, Jack E. 89
Goldberg, Gerald 76

Golden, Sherrie 401
Golding, Susan 407, 456, 458
Gomez, James H. 72
Gonsalves, Anthony 391
Gonsalves, Joe 384, **390–391**
Gonzales, Ray 133
Gonzales, Ron 465
Gonzalez, Jim 458
Goodwyn, Bob 219
Gordon, Milton 79
Gordon, Richard 428
Gordon, Rita 82
Gorton, George 415
Gotch, Michael J. **299–301**
Gould, Clyde 474
Gould, Russell 60, 67
Graham, Janice 163, 164
Granada, Ron 223
Gratz, Eugene 372
Graves, Curtis 455
Graves, Mike 455
Gray, Anthony 162
Gray, James 79
Gray, Russell 119
Gray, Thorne 489–490
Green and Azevedo 399
Green, Cecil **166–167**, 317, 411
Green, Donald 399
Green, Stephen 489–490
Greene, Bill **155–157**
Greene, Leroy F. 114–115
Greenebaum, Howard 376
Gregory, Bion 163
Griffin, Mary 463
Griffin, Tom 196
Grignon, Margaret M. 89
Grigsby, Calvin 211
Grimes, Frank 81
Grisham, Wayne 163, 167, 248, 278, 317, 362
"Grizzly Bears" 199–200, 215, 218, 221, 251, 255, 269

Grodin, Joseph 83, 84
Grosz, Karen 79–80
Grubb, Kathleen 485
Grundmann, Don 203
Gualco, Jackson 385
Guarneri, Rodney 271
Guiton, Bonnie **74–75**
Gunnison, Rob 491
Gunsauls, Phil 473

H

Haak, Harold 79
Haaland, Doug 233
Haberson, James 470
Hachmeister, Jack 160
Hage, Clay 286
Hahn, Kenneth 355, 438, 439
Haidinger, Timothy 79–80
Haleva, Jerry 149
Hall, Steven 283
Hall, Tupper 491–492
Hallett, Carol 279
Hallinan, Terence 458
Hallisey, Jeremiah 78
Hamblin, Jim 494
Hammer, Armand 407
Hammer, Susan 466
Hammock, Robert 366, 455
Hammond Jr., Joe 436
Hampton, Claudia 79
Hancock, Loni 199
Handley, Margie 108
Haning III, Zerne P. 89
Hannigan, M.J. 65
Hannigan, Thomas M. **187-188**
Hansberger, David 275
Hansen, Beverly K. **193-194**
Hanson, Dale 76
Hardeman, Dale 167
Harman, Willis 78
Harmon, Gloria 76

Harness, Charles 474
Harper, Bill 477
Harris, Elihu 200, 424
Harris Farms *See* Harris, John
Harris, John 410
Harris, Robert Alton 84
Harris, Thomas A. 90
Harrison, Sandy 487
Hart, Gary 300, 405, 408, 416
Hart, Gary K. 26, **135–137**, 239, 343, 344, 350
Hart-Holifield, Emily 267
Harvey, Trice J. **235–237**
Hatamiya, Lon 186
Hauck, Bill 60
Hauser, Daniel E. **184-185**, 321
Hawkins, Augustus 307, 356
Hawley, Philip 407
Hawn, Goldie 405
Hawthorne, J. Thomas 81
Hayakawa, S.I. 163, 253, 281
Hayden, Thomas E. 251–252, **252–254**, 289, 404, 413, 428
Hayes, Thomas 45–46, 60, **66–67**, 76, 82
Haynes, Raymond 171
Hayward, Steven 81
Health and Welfare Agency 67–70
health care 129, 190, 194, 199, 215, 350, 420, 422
health insurance 196–197
health insurance (key vote) 102
Health Services, Dept. of 68–69, 380
Hecker, Siegfried 79
Hedgecock, Roger 177, 458
Heidig, Ed 73
Heine, Lyman 79
Helms, Jesse 374
Henderson, Dorinda 76
Hendricks, Jim 111
Henning, Jack 411
Henry, Liz 445

Henshaw, Jake 486–487
Henson, Greg 120
Herger, Wally 165, 185, **322–323**
Herschensohn, Bruce 495
Hertz, Howard 122, 332
Hester, Sandra 153
Heston, Charlton 405
Hettinger, Karl 236, 435
Heuer, Donald 281
Hewlett-Packard *See* Packard, David
Hicks, Floyd 473
Hill, Elizabeth 22 *See also* legislative analyst
Hill, Frank 93, **162-163,** 263
Hinkel, Warren 118
Hinz Jr., Edward A. 89
Hoeber, Tom 493
Hoffenblum, Alan 416
Hoffman, Francis Frank166, 170, 284, 371
Hoffman, Ken 409
Hoge, Nettie 402
Hogg, Susan 451
Holifield, Chet 305
Hollenhorst, Thomas E. 90
Hollywood money 404–406
Hollywood Women's Political Committee 404
Holmdahl, DeWayne 137
Holton, Ruth 250, 401
Hom, Gloria 79
Honda, Michael 465
Hongisto, Richard 461
Honig Jr., Louis William "Bill" 27, **49–51**, 78, 79, 138, 414
Honig, Nancy 50
Hoover, Ken 492–493
Hoover, William 180
Hope, Bob 405
Horcher, Paul V. **263-264**
Hornreich, Sam 299
House, Charles 364

Housing and Community Development, Dept. of 64
Housing and Urban Development Agency *See* HUD scandals
Howard, John 484–485
Howard, Vicky 475
Hsieh, Tom 458, 461
Huard, Ray 490–491
Huckaby, Gary 416
HUD scandals 307, 334
Huening, Tom 335, 463
Huerta, Dolores 205
Huff, Jesse 71
Huffman, Alice 399
Huffman, Nancy 446
Huffman, Richard D. 90
Hughan, Roberta 71
Hughes Aircraft Co. 394
Hughes, Howard 388
Hughes, Teresa P. 26, **256–258**
Hullar, Theodore 79
Humboldt County 420, 433–434
Humphrey, Kathy 433
Hunter, Duncan 307, **377–378**
Hunter, Patricia Rae **296–298**, 416
Hurt, Gerald 231
Huynh, Vi Phuong 296

I

Ichikawa, Betty 71
immigration 2, 12, 26, 50, 438 *See also* minorities
Imperial County 434–435
Indio Daily News 486
Industrial Relations, Dept. of 67
infrastructure 7, 30, 33
Ingalls, Walter 285–286
Ingram, Carl 488
initiatives 19–20, 95, 190
"Inland Empire" 456
"Inland Empire Caucus" 282, 283

Institute of Governmental Advocates 387, 390, 393, 394
insurance
  commissioner 96 *See also* Garamendi, John
  industry 399-400
  reform 20, 113 *See also* Proposition 103
insurance, ban donations (key vote) 100
insurance reform (key vote) 99
Inyo County 435
Irvine 450
Irvine Co. 388, 396, 407
Isenberg, Phillip L. **196-197**, 289
Israel 352, 354, 406
Ivers, William 74
Izumi, Ricky 81

J

Jackson, Barbara 369
Jackson, Clayton **391–392**
Jackson, Jesse 201, 207, 355, 357
Jacobs, John 491–492
Jacobs, Paul 488
Jacobson, Joy 313
Jadiker, Mary 193
Japanese-Americans, reparations 238, 242, 289, 323, 336
Jardine, Donald 426
Jarvis, Howard 10, 96, 412
Jarvis, Michael 446
Jarvis-Gann *See* Proposition 13
Jeffe, Sherry Bebitch 210
Jensen, Peter J. 401
Jensen, Rick 443
Johannessen, Maurice 468
Johnson, Grantland 453
Johnson, Hiram 3, 313
Johnson, J. Ross 80, 94, 154, 163, 193, 227, 234, 240, 248, **279–281**, 293, 297, 300, 413

Johnson Jr., Earl 89
Johnson, Raynolds 276
Johnson, Toby 453
Johnson, Wayne 416
Johnston, Brian 319
Johnston, Patrick W. **112–113**, 226
Jones, Mick 446
Jones, William L. **234–235**
Jordan, Carolyn 313
Jordan, Frank 461
Jordan, Hallye 487
Josephson, Michael 145
judicial appointments 33, 88
Junco, Tirso del 78
Jung, Eric 426
Juvinall, Todd 449

K

KABC-TV 495
Kahn, Sanford 361
Kaldor, Ron 82
Kantor, Mickey 408
Karas, Sam 447
Karcher, Carl 407
Karlton, Lawrence 80
Kashiwabara, John 79
Katz, Richard D. 81, **244-245**
Kauffman, Karen Strasser 447
Kaufman, Marcus 83, 87
Kavanagh, Jack 496
Kaye, Loren 60
KCBS-San Francisco 494
KCBS-TV 495
KCRA-TV 495–496
Keating Jr., Charles H. 246, 313
Keeley, Fred 467
Keene, Barry D. 51–52, **106–108**, 321, 431
Kelley, David G. 170, **292–294**
Kelly, Kevin 304
Kennard, Joyce Luther 83, **86–87**
Kennedy, David 74

Kennedy, Lori 125, 126
Kennedy, Willie 458
Kern County 435–436
Kerr, Jennifer 485
Kershner, Vlae 491
Kesler, Ruth 455
Ketron, Bruce 194
Kevorkian, Art S. 81
Kevorkian, Kenneth 81
key votes 99
KGO-TV 496–497
Khachigian, Ken 416
Khachigian, Meredith 78
Kildee, Maggie Erickson 475
Killea, Lucy L. 145, **175-178**, 299, 302, 458
Kimbrough, Guy 374
King, Donald B. 89
King, Mary 423
King, Rita 185
Kings County 436
Kinney, Nick 436
Kizer, Kenneth 69
Klehs, Johan M. **202-203**
Klein, Joan Dempsey 89
Kline, Fred 485
Kline, J. Anthony 88
Klinger, Ann 445
Knabe, Don 167
Knap, Chris 489
Knapp, Lynn 222
KNBC-TV 495
Knight, Goodwin 4
Knight-Ridder 487, 492
Knowland, William 3, 4
Knowles, David C. H. **191-193**
Knox, John 384, 397
Kolender, William 80
Koligan, Deran 432
Koll, Donald 134–135
Kolligian, Leo 78
Konnyu, Ernest 219, 335, 408

Konovaloff, Nicholai 394–395
Konovaloff, S. Thomas 394–395
Koop, C. Everett 136
Kopp, Quentin 80, 81, **117–119**
KOVR-TV 496
Kremer, Daniel J. 90
Krevans, Julius 79
Kripke, Dan 373
Kroc, Joan 407
Kroc, Ray 407
KRON-TV 481, 497
KTXL-TV 496
Kuchel, Thomas 316
Kushman, Rick 489–490
KXPR/FM 494–495
KXTV 496

L

La Bounty, Hugh 79
labor unions 227, 410–411
Lacey, Susan 475
LaFollette, Marian 243, 289
Lagomarsino, Robert J. 136, **343–344**
Lake County 436–437
Lambert, Gary 436
Lancaster, Chris 277
Lancaster, William H. **276–277**
Landau, Marilyn 263
Landingham, Jo Ann 473
Landmark Communities Inc. See
  Covitz, Carl D.
Landowski, Lowell 324
Lang, Richard 227
Lansbury, Angela 406
Lansdale, Marianthi 79
Lanterman Developmental Disabilities
  Services Act 69
Lanterman-Petris-Short Act 69, 120
Lantos, Tom 307, **333–334**
Larkin, Tom 149
Larkspur Report 494
LaRouche, Lyndon 370

Larson, Patricia 453
Larwood, Pauline 435
Lassen County 437–438
Last, Jean 329
Laurent, Laurence 463
Lavery, Vincent 342
Lawrence, Andrea 446
Lawrence, Steve 485
LCV See League of Conservation
  Voters
League of Calif. Cities 400
League of Conservation Voters 309
Lear, Norman 406
Lee, Barbara **200–233**
Lee, Bruce 408, 411
Lee, David 79–80
Lee, Dorothy 78
Leffler, Matthew 473
Legan, Tom 125, 126
legislative analyst 22, 27, 28, 61, 427
  See also Hill, Elizabeth
Lehman, Richard H. **342–343**
Lembke, Bud 494
Lemke, Gary 437
Lemmon, Jack 406
Lempert, Edward T. **216-217**
Lempert, Ted 107
Lenney, Lida 372
Leonard, Bill 275
Leonard Jr., William R. 96, **151–153**
Leonard Sr., William 81, 152
Lepiscopo, Pete 378
LeSage, Michael 130
Lesher, Dean 79, 115, 430
Lesher Newspapers 486
Leslie, Robert Timothy 106, **188-189**
Leslie Salt Co. 390
LeVake, Barbara 472
Levi, David 289
Levine, Mel 316, 349–350, 352, **353–354**, 368, 414
Levy, Bob 220

Levy, Joseph 81
Levy, Robley 467
Levy, Sharon 432
Lewis, Jerry 306, 316, 318, 345, **364–365**
Lewis, John R. 169, 174, 248, **284–285**
Lewis, Nevada 468
liability limitation. *See* tort reform
Liberator, John 64–65
Licari, Pete 472
Lieberg, Leland 273
Lifsher, Marc S. 489
Lillie, Mildred L. 89
Lincoln Savings and Loan 125, 246, 313
Linn, David 343
Lipp, Jerome 81
liquor tax *See* Proposition 134
Lockwood, John 76
Lockyer, William **120–122**
Lofgren, Zoe 465
logging 108, 125, 184, 469
Long Beach Press-Telegram 487
Long, Michael 261
Longshore, Richard 291–292
Lopez, Jess 443
Los Angeles City Council 440
Los Angeles, city of 438, 440–442
Los Angeles County 438–442
Los Angeles County Board of Supervisors 150, 154, 268
Los Angeles Daily Journal 487
Los Angeles Daily News 480, 487
Los Angeles Times 441, 480, 487–488
lottery 416
Loubet, Jean 437
Lough, Lyle 437
Low, Harry W. 89
Lowe, Rob 404
Lowery, Bill **372-373**
Lucas, Greg 491

Lucas, Malcolm Millar 83, **84–85**
Lungren, Brian 42
Lungren, Dan **41–43**, 118, 131, 147–148, 167, 316, 356, 374
Lurie, Bob 461
Luz International Corp. 124
Lybarger, John Jay 230
Lyles, Dick 297
Lynch, Lawrence L. 487
Lynn, Norman 267

M

MacDonald, John 456
Mackey, Karan 436
MacMurray, Fred 405
Maddy, Kenneth L. 127, **128–130**, 142, 319, 345, 410, 415
Maddy, Norma Foster 128–129, 410
Madera County 443–444
Madigan, Mike 36
Maestas, Marta 273
magazines 493
"Magnificent Seven" 183, 193, 234
Maher, Bill 458
Maher, Bishop Leo T. 176, 298–299
Major Risk Medical Insurance Program 82
Malberg, Patricia 337, 338
Malkasian, William 78
Mallory, Steve 496
Mammoth Lakes 447
Manatt, Charles 408
Manchester, Doug 300
Mangine, Lorie 474
Mann, Jeanette 249
Mann, Jim 433
Manning, Kenneth 263
Marchard, Betsy 476
Marcus, Jeffrey 242
Marelius, John 491
Margolin, Burt M. 156, 251, **254–256**, 265

Margosian, Arthur 79–80
marijuana 434, 473
Marin County 443–444
Marin Independent Journal 486
Mariposa County 444–445
Marks, Ken 474
Marks, Milton **108–110**
Marler Jr., Fred W. 90
Marquis, Don 371
Marsh, George 191
Marsh, Keith F. 151
Marsh, Tony 415
Marshall, Carol 110
Marston, Jeff 300
Martin, Andrew 138
Martin, Robert L. 90
Martin, Steve 426
Martinez, Diane 273
Martinez, Matthew G. 273, 352, **357–359**
Martinez, Vilma 78
mass transit 31, 38, 187, 213, 466
Mast, Cowles 476
Masters, David 283
Mathews, Michelle 477
Mathews, Peter 291
Matsui, Robert T. 191, 316, 323–324, 410, 414
Matthews, Jon 489–490
Mattingly, Patti 106, 189, 469
Maughan, W. Don 71
Maullin, Richard 417
Mavrogeorge, Brian 206
May, Arnold 360
Mays, Thomas J. **272**
MCA 405
McAllister, Alister 213, 397–398
McCabe, Pat 173
McCaffrey, Jerry 468
McCandless, Alfred A. **367–368**
McCarthy, Leo 39, **39–41**, 78, 79, 82, 209, 245, 246, 352, 415, 444, 460

McClatchy News Service 489
McClatchy Newspapers 489–490
McClintock, Thomas M. **240–241**, 280
McCloskey, Pete 123, 335, 406, 464
McClure, Martin 193
McColl, Gloria 298
McCorquodale, Daniel A. **124–126**
McCrae, Curtis 79
McCrone, Alistair 79
McDowell, Jack 416
McDowell, Marion 78
McEnery, Tom 466
McGoldrick, Bernie 235
McGovern, George 209
McHugh, Gavin 401
McIntosh, Donald 468
McInturf, Haskell 427
McIntyre, Gail 443
McKenna, Dianne 465
McKinley, Clark 492–493
McKinster, Art W. 90
McLaughlin, Edward 427
McMullen, James 76
McNally, Ray 416
McPeak, Sunne 116, 429
McRay, Michael 428
McWilliams, Ed 301
Mecca, Andrew 68
Medi-Cal 204
media managers 483–484
Mediterranean fruit fly 66
Meeks, Larry 68
Mehas, Peter 78
Meibert, Virgil 486
Meirelles, Abel 436
Melendez, E.A. "Rick" 398
Mellett, Mark 431
Mello, Henry J. **134–135**
Melville, James 295
Mendel, Ed 491
Mendocino County 445

Meral, Gerald 190, 402, 412–413
Merced County 445–446
Merksamer, Steven 385, 409
Merrill, Robert W. 88
Mertes, David 80
Meyer, Wayne 323
Michael, Elizabeth 255
Michael, Jay D. **392–393**
Midler, Bette 405
Migden, Carol 458
Mikels, Jon 455
Mikolajcik, John 448
Milk, Harvey 461
Milken, Michael 313, 407
Mill, Betsy 175
Miller, George 307, **328–330**
Mills, Jim 145
Mills, W.D. 429
Mineta, Norman Y. 306–307, **336–337**
minorities 1, 13, 14, 48, 58, 92, 198,
    432, 434, 439–440, 442, 443, 448,
    450 *See also* immigration
    affirmative action 31, 61–63
    Asian 368, 459, 461, 467
    black 461, 469
    Hispanic 150, 154, 455, 457, 462
Mobil Oil Corp. 390
Mobley, Ernest 79–80, 130
Mockler, John 385
Modoc County 446
Mojonnier, Sunny 295
Molina, Gloria 150, 269, 438, 439–
    440
Molinari, John 460
"Monday Morning Group" 170
Mono County 446–447
Monteith, Stanley 341
Monterey County 447–448
Montgomery, Mike 494–495
Montna, Larry 472
Montoya, Joseph 80, 93, 116, 118,
    140, 153–154, 274

Moore, Clarke 431
Moore, Gwen A. 93, **259–260**, 261
Moore, Jim 417
Moore, John 79
Moore, Joseph 78
Moore Jr., Henry T. 90
Moorhead, Carlos 306, **347-348**
Moorhead, Jean 188 *See also* Duffy
Moose Milk 386
Moretti, Robert 7, 9, 209
Morgan, James C. 123
Morgan, Rebecca Q. **122–124**
Moriarty, W. Patrick 93
Mortensen, Patricia 473
Moscone, George 207, 460
Mosk, Stanley **85**
Mosman, James 77
Motor Vehicles, Dept. of 65
mountain lions *See* Proposition 117
Mountjoy, Richard L. 237–238, **250–
    251**
Mudd, Dick 433
Mule Creek State Prison 426
Munitz, Barry 79
Murdock, David 407
Murphy, George 6, 316, 366
Murphy, John 296
Murphy Jr., Frank 384
Murray Jr., Willard H. **266–267**

N

Naake, Larry 400
Nader, Ralph 412
Nagle, Thomas 69
Naiman, Jack 140
Napa County 448–449
Nares, Gilbert 90
Nathanson, Mark 140
National Association of Securities
    Dealers 390
National Council of Senior Citizens
    309

National Endowment for the Arts 374
National Estuaries Program 354
National Organization for Women 213, 297
National Organization for Women, Inc., Calif. 98
National Public Radio 495
National Republican Congressional Committee 345
National Rifle Association 99, 134, 138, 195, 225, 266
National Right to Life Committee 319
National Tax Association 57
National Taxpayers Union 309
Naylor, Robert 248, 279, 384, 396
NCSC *See* National Council of Senior Citizens
Neal, Kathy 71
Neely, Bonnie 433
Neely, Gary 263–264
Neely, Johnnie 156
Negri, Fred 448
Nestande, Bruce 81
Nesterczuk, George 81
Nevada County 449
Nevin, Mike 214
New West Notes 494
New York Times News Service 491
Newport, Gus 425
news services 484–493
newsletters 493–494
Newsom, William A. 88
newspapers 484–493
Nicholas, Janet 470
Nichols, Alan 326
Nicholson, George 90
"nickel-a-drink" *See* Proposition 134
Nielsen, Jim 110–111, 166, 319
Nielsen, Merksamer, Hodgson, Parrinello & Mueller 385, **396**
Nielsen, Vigo "Chip" 396
Nixon, Richard 3, 5, 31, 38, 42

Nolan, Patrick J. 93, 211, 219, 235, **247–249**, 265, 279, 280, 293
Nolan, Tom 124, 463
Norcal Solid Waste Systems Inc. 187, 211
Nordyke, Kay 429
Norred, Buck 223
Norris, Chuck 405
North, John 495
Northern Calif. News Satellite 481, 496
Norton, Barry 365
Norwood, John 400
Nossman, Gunther, Knox & Elliot **396–397**
Nott, Michael G. 89
NTU *See* National Taxpayers Union
Nuckolls, John 79
Nymeyer, Mark 282

O

Oakland 423–425
Oakland Tribune 488
O'Banion, Jerald 445
Occupational Safety and Health Standards, state 103
Ochoa, Gloria 464
O'Connell, Jack **238–240**
O'Connor, Maureen 407, 458
offshore oil ban (key vote) 101
offshore oil drilling 38, 45, 125, 184, 319, 354, 372–373, 465
Ohanesian, John 81
Ohanian, John D. 82
oil spill cleanup 107, 217, 236
oil spill cleanup (key vote) 102
O'Keefe, Dan 125
Olin, Dirk 493
Olivier, Arthur 267
Olmsted, Scott 175
Olsen, Steve 60

Olvera, Dale 268
O'Melveny and Myers 46
O'Neill, Bruce 327
O'Neill, Richard 407
Operating Industries Inc. 153
Orange County 389, 449–451
Orange County Register 374, 480
Orlov, Rick 487
Oroville Reservoir 428
Ortega, Reuben A. 89
O'Shaughnessy, Connie 239
ostrich breeding 236
Otten, Michael 485
Overton, Joanne 433
Ovitt, Harry 463
Owens, Dianne 464
Ozenick, Phil 451

P

Pacific Rim 425
Packard, David 335, 408, 466
Packard, Ronald C. 306, **374–375**
Pacyna, Deborah 496
Paddock, Richard C. 488
Painting and Decorating Contractors
   of Calif. 223
Palm Springs Desert Sun 486
Palmer, Robert 335
Panelli, Edward A. **86**
Panetta, Leon **340–341**
Papan, Louis J. 56, 111, 117, 119,
   214, 274
Paparian, Mike 402
Paranick, Dan 446
park, wildlife and coastal preservation
   bonds See Propositions 70 and 149
Parker, Erlinda 294
Parkhurst, John 79–80
Parks and Recreation, Dept. of 74
parks and wildlife 45
Parnell, Francis 195

Pashayan Jr., Charles "Chip" 341, 342
Pasquet, Trinda 490
Passi, Gary 252
Patrosso, Mark 333
Patterson, Jerry 368
Patton, Gary 467
Paul, Pat 471
Payne, Paul 435
Payton, Roger 329
PBN Company 484
Peace, J. Stephen 127, 283, **302–304**
Pearle Health Systems 397
Pearson, Johnny 368
Peck, Gregory 405
Pedroncelli, Rich 485
Pelican Bay State Prison 431
Pelosi, Nancy **326–327**
Peltason, J.W. 79
PepsiCo Inc. 390
Perata, Don 423
Perino, Carmen 112, 226
Peripheral Canal 415
Perkins, Thomas 447
Perley, James F. 89
Persian Gulf War 179, 286, 292, 312,
   318, 352–353
Persily, Coleman 195
"personnel-years" 60
Pesqueira, Ralph 79
Peters, Kenneth 78
Peterson, Dean 445
Peterson, J. Clinton 88
Peterson, Larry 489
Peterson, Robert 407
Petrie, Dennis 242
Petris, Nicholas C. **119–120**, 200
Pharmaceutical Manufacturers
   Association 388
Philip Morris U.S.A. 396
Pittsburg Post-Dispatch 486
Placer County 451–452
Planned Parenthood 145

Planning and Conservation League 190, 402, 412–413
Plants, Lovie 183
Plowman, Stan 473
Plumas County 452
Poche, Marcel 89
Podegracz, David 141
Polanco, Richard G. **267–269**
Poling, Timothy 162
Political Animal 493
Political Pulse 494
Political Reform Act of 1974 76, 80, 386–387
Pollacek, William 117
polling place guards 109, 292
Polson, Don 446
Port of Oakland 425, 459
Potter, Dee 473
Powers, Tom 429
Premo, Eugene M. 90
Prentiss, Lee 151
presidential primary 231
Presley, Robert B. 139–140, 145, **170–172**, 173, 286, 293
Press, Bill 495
Pringle, Curt 291–292
Priolo, Paul 279, 384
prison construction 33, 71, 131, 148, 171, 268, 431
Prison Terms, Board of 71
Pritchard, Harry 433
Proaps, Linda 271
Professional Engineers in Calif. Government 400
Proposition 4 13–14, 14, 22, 33–35, 165, 187, 416
Proposition 9 386–387
Proposition 13 10, 13–14, 22, 23, 26, 35, 187, 222, 239, 380, 412, 419–420, 422
"Proposition 13 babies" 11, 18, 35, 152, 248, 250, 262, 272, 279

Proposition 65 190, 253, 380, 397, 398, 413, 415
Proposition 68 80, 279–280, 401
Proposition 70 402, 413
Proposition 73 80, 118, 176–177, 279–280, 401, 413
Proposition 97 167, 411, 414
Proposition 98 22, 23, 50, 249, 398–399, 414
Proposition 99 190, 197, 392, 402, 413
Proposition 102 370
Proposition 103 52, 113, 140, 141, 399, 401, 412, 416
Proposition 105 95
Proposition 111 14, 23, 33, 244, 396, 397
Proposition 112 80, 81, 93, 129, 147, **216**, 250, 385 *See also* ethics
Proposition 116 231, 402, 413
Proposition 117 402
Proposition 126 138, 223
Proposition 128 111, 227, 253, 397, 398, 402, 406, 413, 416
Proposition 130 406
Proposition 131 190
Proposition 132 290
Proposition 134 190, 399, 413, 422
Proposition 140 91, 95, 96, 145, 148, 190, 193, 210, 220, 265
Proposition 149 135
Pryor, Luanne 272
Public Employees' Retirement System 76
Public Interest Research Group, Calif. 98
public opinion surveys 14, 417 *See also* California Poll
public relations 483
public spending limit *See* Proposition 4
public transit *See* mass transit

Public Utilities Commission 81
Puglia, Robert K. 90
Punte, Sally 444

Q

Quackenbush, Charles W. **219-220**
Quality Education Project 50
Quimby, John P. 384
Quraishi, Bill 334

R

R.J. Reynolds Tobacco Co. 395, 396
Racanelli, John T. 88
Radanovich, George 444
radio 494–495
Radovich, Joan 489
Rafferty, Max 316
Raiders *See* Brooks, Jack
rail and transit bonds *See* Prop. 116
Raine, George 491–492
Rake, Don 446
Rakow, Sally 81
Ralph C. Dills Act of 1977 63
Ralston, Shirley 80
Ramachandran, Raga 78
Ramirez, Manuel A. 90
Ramirez, Ralph 358
Rancho Seco nuclear power plant 253
Ratcliff, Richard **393**
ratings, by special interest groups 98–
   99
Rattigan, Joseph 80
Raye, Vance W. 90
Read, Aaron and Associates 401
Reagan, Ronald 5–7, 13, 30, 31, 38,
   39, 109, 136, 137, 248, 308, 315,
   354, 361, 374, 405–406, 407, 415
   faked signature 248, 264–265, 284
Real Estate, Dept. of 64
reapportionment 5, 11, 15–20, 39, 92,
   97, 109, 249, 280, 301, 305, 308,
   325, 338

Reardon, Timothy A. 89
Recording Industry Association of
   America 397
recycling 213, 218
Redding, Nelson 445
Reddy, Helen 405
Redford, Robert 404–405
"Redwood Summer" 107–108
Rees, Kathy 400
Rees, Norma 79
Rehabilitation, Dept. of 70
Reid, Lita 346
Reid, William 446
Reilly, Clint 414
Reinecke, Ed 361
Reiner, Ira 42, 138, 251
Reiss, Jerry 341
Rendleman, Jim 245
Reno Gazette Journal 487
Renshaw, Steven 351
reparations to Japanese-Americans *See*
   Japanese-Americans, reparations
Republican Research Committee 364,
   377
Resources Agency 72–74
revenue refund 22, 50
Reynoso, Cruz 83
Richardson, Anne 171
Richardson, H.L. 109, 120, 151, 316,
   338
Richardson, James 489–490
Riggs, Frank **320–321**
Riles Jr., Wilson 49-50, 424
Riley, Bryan 257
Riley, Thomas 449
Rinehart, James 217
Riordan, Barbara Crum 71, 455
Riverside County 452–453
Riverside Press-Enterprise 480–481,
   489
Rivinius, Robert 80
RJR/Nabisco Inc. 388

Roach, Ron 490–491
Robbins, Alan E. 93, **139–141**
Roberti, David A. 51–52, 107, 109, 116, 120, 127, 129, **144–149**, 157, 167, 170–171, 172–173, 174, 177, 222, 482
Roberti, June 146
Roberts, Bill 415
Roberts, Eric 194
Roberts, Jerry 491
Roberts, Ron 458
Robinson, Richard 291–292
Rodda, Al 114
Rodriguez, Carlos 416
Rodriguez, Guillermo 78
Rodriguez, Rick 489–490
Rogers, Carey 137
Rogers, Donald A. **132-133**, 235–236
Rogers, Tom 464
Rohrabacher, Dana **373–374**
Rollins, Ed 415
Romero, David 78
Romero, Victor 332
Ronstadt, Linda 405
Roos, Michael 239, 244–245, 256
Rosato, Joe 489–490
Rosenfield, Harvey 20, 412, 416
Rosengarten, Dick 494
Rosenthal, Alan 92
Rosenthal, Herschel **142–144**
Ross, Richie 414, 417, 461
Rosser, James 79
Rotelli, Larry 474
Roth, Don 449
Roth, Lester William 89
Roumiguiere, Bob 443
Roybal, Edward R. 269, **350–351**
Roybal-Allard, Lucille **269–270**
Royce, Edward R. **164–166**
Ruby, Howard 406
Rudin, Anne 454
Rush, Erwin 323

Russell, Newton R. **141–142**
Russo, Marsh and Associates *See* Marsh, Tony; Russo, Sal
Russo, Sal 415
Rutland, Bill 385
Ryan, Leo 214

S

Sacramento Bee 480, 489–490
Sacramento, city of 454
Sacramento County 453–455
Sacramento Union 189, 490
Saenger, Ted 79
Safe Drinking Water Act 380 *See also* Proposition 65
Salazar, Gloria 259
Salinas Californian 486
Salinger, Pierre 6, 316
Saloman, Jim 349
SALT *See* Strategic Arms Limitation Talks
Samaniego, Eliseo 71
Samish, Artie 379, 386
Sample, Herbert A. 489–490
Samuelian, Karl 313, 410
San Benito County 455
San Bernardino County 455–456
San Bernardino Sun 486
San Diego Association of Governments 457
San Diego, city of 457–458
San Diego County 456–458
San Diego Tribune 486, 490–491
San Diego Union 486, 491
San Francisco 458–462
San Francisco Banner Journal 487
San Francisco Bay Conservation and Development Committee 72
San Francisco Chronicle 147, 215, 480, 491
San Francisco Examiner 491–492

San Francisco Recorder 492
San Joaquin County 462–463
San Jose 466-467
San Jose Jammers 223
San Jose Mercury-News 480, 487, 492
San Luis Obispo County 463
San Mateo County 463–464
San Pedro News 486
San Ramon Valley Times 486
Sandoval, Joe **72-72**
Santa Barbara County 464–465
Santa Clara County 465–467
Santa Cruz County 467
Santa Fe-Southern Pacific Realty 211
Santa Monica Evening Outlook 486
Santa Monica Mountains Conservancy 72
Santana, Charles 423
Sato, Eunice 360
Saunders, Joan 477
Sauter, Van Gordon 46
Savings and Loan, Dept. of 65
savings and loan industry 57, 113, 131, 140, 246, 249, 313–314
Sayles, Thomas 80
Scagliotti, Richard 455
Scenic Rivers Act 217
Schabarum, Peter 96, 440
Schaffarzick, Dr. Ralph 82
Scheinbaum, Stanley 404
Schraer, Rosemary 79
Schrager, Michael 143
Schramel, John 452
Schreiber, John 446
Schroder, Robert 429
Schultz, Bill 449
Schultz, George 408
Schumacher, William 463
Schwarzenegger, Arnold 405
Scofield, Patricia 429
Scotland, Arthur G. 90
Scott, Joe 493

Scott, Steve 494
Scribner, Rob 353–354
Scroggs, Joyce 452
Seabolt, Abe 434
Seagram *See* Berman, Henry
Seapointe Savings & Loan 57
Seastrand, Andrea **229–230**
Seastrand, Eric 229
Seattle Seahawks *See* Behring, Ken
Sebastiani, Don 193, 410
secretary of environmental affairs 70
Seismic Safety Commission 82, 126–127
self-esteem commission 221, 265
senior citizens 213
Senior Legislature 134
sentencing reform 121
Seymour, John F. 18, 91, 123, 166, 169, 284, 317–320, 338, 407
Shank, Charles 79
Shansby, J. Gary 79
Sharp, Sam 434
Sharpless, Jananne 71
Shasta County 468
Shea, Joe 378
Sheble, Bud 73
Sheedy, Ally 405
Sheehan, Anne 64
Sheingold, Larry 135, 167, 168, 176
Sheldon, Stephen 270
Shell, Joe 345
Shell, Mary 435
Shelley, Kevin 458
Sher, Byron **217-219**, 234
Sherman, Brad **56–57**, 76
Shipnuck, Barbara 447
Shorenstein, Walter 408
Short-Doyle Act 69
Show Coalition 404
Shrum, Robert 415
Shuit, Douglas 488
Shumate, Joe 416

Shumway, Norman 82, 337
Sias, Daniel 143
Sierra Club 184, 402
Sierra County 468–469
"Silicon Valley" 465
Silicon Valley Toxics Coalition 123
Sills, David G. 90
Silvestri, Robert 119, 216
Simas, Ed 462
Simmons, John 348
Simmons, Lee 469
Simon, Raymond Clark 471
Simoni, Ralph 395–396
Sims III, Richard M. 90
Sinatra, Frank 405
Siskiyou County 469
Skelton, George 487–488
Skillicorn, Jack 229
Small Schools Association 213
Smedley, Glenn 431
Smith, Arlo 41–42
Smith, Dan 489
Smith, David 337
Smith, Jaclyn 405
Smith, Jerome A. 88
Smith, Jim 452
Smith, Kathie 489–490
Smith, Loren 395
Smith, Martin 489–490
Smith, Ronald 416
Smith, Tim 470
Smith, William French 78
Smoley, Sandra 114, 115, 453
Smoller, Fred 285
Snodgrass, Kathleen 385, 388–389
Snyder, Harry 402
Social Services, Dept. of 70
Solano County 469–470
Sommer, Luke 337
Sonenshine, Sheila Prell 90
Sonoma County 470–471
Sonoma County Planning Dept. 470

Sotero, Ray 486
Sousa, William 462
South Africa, divestiture (key vote) 99
South Coast Air Quality Management
  District 171, 172–173
Southard, Ron 472
Southland Corp. 388, 396
Sparks, Anna 433
Sparks, Keith F. 90
Speier, K. Jacqueline 111, **214-216**
Spencer, Stu 415
Spencer, Vaino H. 89
"spin doctors" 3
Spivak, Sharon 490–491
Spohn, Richard B. 385
Sragow, Darry 415
Stacy, Bill 79
Stall, Bill 488
Stallone, Sylvester 405
Standard & Poor's 23
Stanislaus County 471–472
Stanton, Roger 449
Stark, Fortney H. "Pete" **331–332**
Stark, John 367
Stark, Lisa 496–497
Starn, Rolland 471
START See Strategic Arms Reduction
  Talks
State Banking Dept. 64
State Fire Marshal, Office of 76
State Lands Commission 82
State Personnel Board 61–62, 76
State Teachers Retirement System 77
Statewide Health Planning and
  Development, Office of 68
Statham, R. Stan **183-184**
Steffes, George 385, **394**
Stein, Joseph 78
Stein, William D. 88
Steinmetz, William 328
Stennis, Willie 79
Stevens, Donald 347

Stevens, Robert 79
Stewart, James 405
Stewart, Jan 469
Stiern, Walter 132
Stirling, Larry 176, 298, 480
Stocker, Leah 477
Stockton Record 486
Stoddard, Kent 385
Stoker, Michael 464
Stone, Steven J. 89
Stone, William A. 90
Stoner, Alice 76
Stoorza, Ziegaus and Metzger 484
Stout, Gloria 254
Strait, Ray 293
Strankman, Gary E. 88
Strategic Arms Limitation Talks 315
Strategic Arms Reduction Talks 315
Streisand, Barbra 404–405
Streng, Jim 454
Strock, James **70**
Stroh, Jay R. 64
Studer, Robert P. 486
Sullivan, Francie 468
Sullivan, Joe 115
Summa Corp. 388, 396
Superfund 123, 274
Supreme Court justices 84–88
Supreme Court, state 97
Sutley, Irv 111
Sutter County 472
Swatt, Steve 495–496
Sweeney, James 431
Sweeney, James P. 486
Sweeney, James W. 487
Sweeney, Paul 365
Swoap, David 385, 389

T

Taber, Gertrude 444
Tahoe Regional Planning Agency 72

Tainter, Bill 70
Tanner, Sally M. 154, **274–275**
Tarrance & Associates 417
taxes 22, 33–35, 36, 187, 202, 203–204, 230
county 422, 427
Taylor, Thomas 428
Tehama County 472–473
television campaigns 5–6
television news 481, 483
Tergeson, Norman 474
term limitation See Proposition 131
Ternus, Anne 486
Thackeray, George 469
Thaxter, James F. 90
Thierbach, Christian F. 292
Thomas, Barbara 201
Thomas, Bill 235
Thomas, Gerti 78
Thomas, Larry 407
Thomas, Michael 346
Thomas, William M. 306, 338, **344-346**
Thompson, Duane 80
Thompson, Jeff 401
Thompson, Michael **110–111**
Thompson, Ray 431
Thomson, Helen 476
Thorne, Steve 297
Tian, Chang-Linn 79
Tijuana 457
timber See logging
Times-Mirror wire service 488
Timlin, Robert J. 90
Tisbert, Ronald 238
Tobacco Institute 395, 396
tobacco tax See Propositon 99
Tobin, L. Thomas 82
Todd Jr., William L. 90
Toledano, Jim 288
toll roads 368
Torlakson, Thomas 429

Torrance Daily Breeze 486
Torres, Art 145, 148, **150–151**, 269, 273
Torres, Esteban E. 352, **362–364**
tort limitation (key vote) 101
tort reform 119, 121, 391, 392, 396
  See also "Frank Fat's napkin deal"
Tower, John 38
Townsend & Co. 484 *See also*
  Townsend, David
Townsend, David 414 415
toxics 136, 150, 186, 232, 244
Toy, Larry 80
Transportation Commission 81
Transportation, Dept. of 23, 65
Tremblay, J.P. 490
Trinity County 473–474
Trombley, William 488
Trounstine, Phil 492
TRW 406
Tsakopoulos, Angelo 409, 460
Tucker, G.B. 449
Tucker Jr., Curtis R. **261–262**
Tucker Sr., Curtis R. 232, 261
Tulare County 474
Tunney, John 6, 253, 366, 408
Tuolumne County 474–475
Turner, Paul A. 89
Turner, Steve 169
Turoci, Marsha 455
Tuttle, Holmes 407
Tyron, Thomas 428

U

Udall, Morris 307
Udinsky, Jerald 200
Uehling, Barbara 79
Ugalde, Jesse 77
Umberg, Robin 292
Umberg, Thomas J. **291–292**
Union Pacific Corp. 394

United Auto Workers 411 *See also*
  Lee, Bruce
United Farm Workers 205, 352–353, 411
United Press International 492–493
United States Chamber of Commerce 309
United World Federalists 315
University of Calif. Board of Regents 78–79
University of Calif. Chancellors 79
University of Calif. Student Association. 198
Unruh, Jesse 4, 5, 19, 44, 147–148, 207, 210, 245–246, 384
Upton, John 431
Urquidi, Joe 154
USA Today 487
USCC *See* United States Chamber of Commerce

V

Vagim, Doug 432
Valasco, Henry 275
Valladares, Monica 222
"Valley Boys" 148–149
Valley Times, Pleasanton 486
Van De Graaff, Wayne 434
Van de Kamp, John 16, 41, 44, 202, 284, 414
Van Deerlin, Lionel 377
Van Vleck, Gordon 73
Vanderbilt, Samuel 321
Vanderkolk, Marcia 475
Vanzi, Max 488
Vaquer, Armand 159
Varacalli, Mike 401
Varrelman, Mel 448
Vartabedian, Steven M. 90
Vasconcellos, John 28, 127, **220-222**, 265, 276, 466

Vasquez, Gaddi 318, 449, 451
Ventura, Brent 219
Ventura County 475–476
Veterans Affairs, Dept. of 77
Vial, Donald 80
Vick, Scott 79
Vietnam Memorial 187
Visalia Times-Delta 486
Vitti, Anthony 79
Vogel, Miriam A. 89
Vollbrecht, John 249
Voss, Henry **66**
voter
    registration 11–15, 35–36, 48, 256, 258, 259, 269, 299
    turnout 436, 458
"Voter Revolt" 412, 416
Voting Rights Act 97
Vuich, Rose Ann **130–132**, 234

W

Wada, Yori 78
Wade, Claudia Ann 426
Waite, Ralph 368
Waite, William 429
Walker, Larry 455
Walker, West 229
Wallace, Philip 112, 113
Wallace, William 464
Wallin, Edward J. 90
Walt Disney Co. 406 *See also* Wells, Frank
Walt, Harold 73
Walter, Charles 474
Walters, Dan 489–490
Ward, Doris 458
Ward, Lorrie 76
Ward, Randy 385, 395
Warren, Charles 82
Warren, Earl 3, 30, 33
Warren, John 302

Wasserman, Lew 38, 405–406
Waste Management Inc. 396
water 168, 360–361
    quality 186, 190, 363
    rights 186, 190, 197, 223, 231, 375, 447
Water Resources Control Board, State 71
Water Resources, Dept. of 74–75
Waters, Ed 357
Waters, Maxine 258, **356–357**
Waters, Norman 191–192, 280
Waters, Owen 399
Watkins, Dean 78
Watson, Diane E. 121, **157-159**, 319
Watson, Muriel 180
Watts, Doug 415
Watts riots 361
Waxman, Henry A. 307, 349, **349–350**, 352
Webb, Gary 492
Webb, George 241
Webb, Georgia 362
Weinberger, Caspar 408
Weintraub, Daniel 488
Weintraub, Jerry 406
Weir, Jim 449
welfare 420, 431, 434, 466, 474 *See also* GAIN
Wells, Frank 316, 406
Wendt, Wayne 277
West County Times, Richmond 486
West, Kirk 60, 398
Wheeler, Douglas P. **72–74**
White, Bob 36, 60, 177
White, Clinton W. 88
White, Dan 461
White House 16
White, Steve 158
Whitridge, Arnold 473
Widener, Warren 423
Wieder, Harriett 71, 449

Wiener, Howard B. 90
Wiggins, Charles 277
Wilcox, Walter 436
Wildlife Conservation Board 72
Wilhoit, Douglass 462
Wilk, G. Michel 82
Williams, David 198
Williams, Harold 78
Williams, Leon 456
Williams, Sam 410
Williams, Wendell 204
Williamson Act 187
Willis, Bruce 405
Willis, Doug 484–485
Willis, Tim 185
Wilson, Betty 37
Wilson, Bob 121, 384, 399
Wilson, Earl 238
Wilson, Gayle Graham 37, 39
Wilson, James 37
Wilson, Lionel 201, 424
Wilson, Molly 468
Wilson, Pete 11, 16, 17, 18, 21–22,
  23, 27, 33, **36–39**, 41, 58, 59–60, 66,
  72, 78, 79, 84, 111, 120, 121, 123,
  129, 138, 144, 148, 152, 158, 160,
  177, 189, 218, 221, 239, 249, 255,
  260, 265, 274, 308, 317–318, 325,
  368, 372, 396, 405–406, 407, 415,
  422, 457, 458
Wilson, Robin 79
Wilson, William 269
Windham, Aden 235
Wirth, Mark 263
Wirthlin Group 417
Womble, David 429
Wong, Lonnie 496
Woo, Michael 410
Wood, Vance 473
Woodhall, Donald 452
Woodruff, Paul A. **275–276**
Woods, Arleigh 89

Woods, Fred 89
Woodward & McDowell *See*
  McDowell, Jack; Woodward,
  Richard
Woodward, Richard 416
Work, Don R. 90
"workfare" *See* GAIN
World Wildlife Fund 72 73
Wortman, Dr. Andrew 71
Wray, Chester 290
Wright, Cathie M. **241-242**, 243, 289
Wright, Victoria 242
Wylie, Scott 80
Wyman, Phillip D. **237–238**, 289, 345

Y

Yaroslavsky, Zev 442
Yeager, Jacques 78
Yeamans, Robin 220
Yegan, Kenneth R. 89
Yoachum, Susan 491
Yolo County 476–477
Yosemite National Park 444
Young, Bruce 93, 278
Young, Charles 79
Young, Ivan 469
Young, Jim 133
Younger, Evelle 10
Younglove, A. Norton 453
Youth and Adult Correctional Agency
  71–72
Youth Authority 71, 72
Youthful Offender Parole Board 71
Yuba City 472
Yuba County 477
Yudelson, Jerry 369–370

Z

Zanelli, Jerry 148–149
Zeboski, Walter 485

Zeiger, Richard 493
Zelman, Walter 401
Zeltner, Paul 248, 266
Zenovich, George 128, 384, 389
Zenz, Robert 401
Zimmerman and Co. *See* Zimmerman,
  Bill
Zimmerman, Bill 416
Zimmerman McKenna, Kathy 488
Zolin, Frank 65
Zschau, Ed 123, 138, 316, 335, 406,
  408, 416, 417, 458
Zwanziger, Roger 469

California Political Almanac staff

Amy Chance joined The Sacramento Bee in 1984 as a city government reporter and moved to the newspaper's Capitol Bureau two years later. Formerly a reporter for the Fort Worth Star-Telegram, Chance now covers California's governor and other state politicians. Born in Wilmington, Del., she is a graduate of San Diego State University. She began her career as an intern at the Los Angeles Times in San Diego County.

Thorne Gray joined The Sacramento Bee's Capitol bureau in 1983 after 17 years with The Modesto Bee, where he covered government, environment, water and energy issues. Gray was raised in Los Angeles. He was graduated from Cornell University and holds a master's degree in journalism from Northwestern University. At the Capitol bureau, he has covered health issues and the state budget.

Stephen Green has worked for The Sacramento Bee since 1978 as both a writer and editor. Since 1985, he's covered state government and politics from the Capitol bureau. Previously, he worked for the Portland (Ore.) Journal, the Seattle Post-Intelligencer, the Associated Press in Philadelphia and the National Observer in Washington, D.C. The Spokane native holds bachelor's and master's degrees in journalism from the University of Oregon.

John L. Hughes worked for three years as The Sacramento Bee's Capitol bureau news editor before taking his current position as the paper's letters editor. Born in Champaign, Ill., and raised in Los Angeles, he served in the Navy during the Vietnam War, after which he attended Los Angeles Valley College and USC. He worked for newspapers in Burbank and Lodi, Calif., before coming to The Bee in 1980.

Rick Kushman joined The Sacramento Bee's Capitol Bureau in 1987. He has worked as assignment editor at KXTV-TV, the CBS affiliate in Sacramento, as city hall reporter for the Sacramento Union and at the San Luis Obispo Telegram-Tribune. Born in San Francisco, he holds a bachelor's degree from the University of California, Davis, and a master's degree from Stanford University.

James Richardson, a native of Berkeley, was graduated from UCLA and has studied government at Cambridge University, England. He has been covering the state Capitol since 1985, first as correspondent for the Riverside Press-Enterprise and then with The Sacramento Bee. Previously, he was a local political reporter for The San Diego Union. Richardson has been active with Investigative Reporters and Editors Inc.

Lori Korleski Richardson is metro news editor of The Sacramento Bee. Prior to joining the paper in 1987, the University of Houston graduate and Houston native worked as an assistant news editor at The Orange County (Calif.) Register. She also has worked at the Dallas Morning News, the St. Petersburg (Fla.) Times, The Beaumont (Texas) Enterprise, and The Dallas Times Herald.

Rick Rodriguez became deputy Capitol bureau chief of The Sacramento Bee in 1987 after a stint as an editorial writer. He joined the Capitol bureau as a reporter in 1982 from The Fresno Bee and began his career at his hometown paper, the Salinas Californian. A graduate of Stanford University, Rodriguez also has studied in Guadalajara.

Dan Walters has been a journalist for 30 years, half of which have been spent covering the Capitol, first for the Sacramento Union and since 1984 for the Sacramento Bee. He writes the only daily newspaper column about California politics, which appears in some 45 papers, and is the author of *The New California: Facing the 21st Century.*